Evaluation Guide for Merrill Algebra Two with Trigonometry

Merrill Algebra Two with Trigonometry provides a comprehensive course in algebra.

Merrill Algebra Two was high school teacher developed and written and classroom tested. This contemporary text provides every opportunity for student success.

To further strengthen the presentation of the text material, many special features have been included in the text.

To examine selected examples of the features of *Merrill Algebra Two*, please turn to the following pages.

Student Annotations explain steps in problem solving.

Highlighting in color helps students identify important concepts as they study.

Review and Test material provided in the Vocabulary, Chapter Summary, Chapter Review, and Chapter Test enable students to review and evaluate their progress.

(pp. 515–536) The **BASIC Appendix** at the back of the text provides a short course in BASIC programming.

Excursions in Algebra provide interesting extra topics in the history, development, and uses of algebra.

(pp. 55, 171) **Using Computers** helps students understand the uses and limitations of computers.

Special feature pages provide extra topics in four areas.

(pp. 153, 293) **Reading Algebra:** reading and interpreting algebraic symbols

(pp. 115, 363) **Using Money:** consumer-related topics

(pp. 242, 442–443) **Using Algebra:** applications of algebra

(pp. 17, 501) **Careers:** careers of real people

Annotations in the Teacher's Annotated Edition give an objective for each lesson, teaching suggestions, answers to problems, and suggested daily assignment of problems.

Teacher's Guide and Tests for Merrill Algebra Two with Trigonometry

Authors
Foster • Rath • Winters

Charles E. Merrill Publishing Co.
A Bell & Howell Company
Columbus, Ohio

Toronto London Sydney

ISBN 0-675-0391-4
Published by
CHARLES E. MERRILL PUBLISHING CO.
A Bell & Howell Company
Columbus, Ohio 43216

Printed in the United States of America

Teacher's Guide and Tests for Merrill Algebra Two with Trigonometry

Contents

Teacher's Guide Preface for Merrill Algebra Two with Trigonometry

Merrill Algebra Two with Trigonometry provides a comprehensive course in algebra. The approach is based upon the experience of highly successful algebra teachers. Prior to publication their manuscript was edited and field tested in other classrooms across the nation.

Merrill Algebra Two with Trigonometry is separated into seventeen chapters to provide study sections of appropriate length to facilitate learning. Each chapter contains the following.

Student Annotations help students to identify important concepts as they study.

Selected Answers allow students to check their progress as they work. These are provided at the back of the text.

Vocabulary sections enable students to focus on increasing their mathematical vocabulary.

Chapter Summaries provide students a compact listing of major concepts presented within each chapter.

Chapter Reviews enable students to review each chapter by working sample problems from each section.

Chapter Tests enable students to check their own progress. An independent test for each chapter is provided in the teacher's guide.

The following special features appear periodically throughout the text.

Careers depict real-life people who utilize mathematics. The careers are exciting and rewarding. They are typical of careers that may be aspired to by students of this text.

Using Money provide insights into how mathematics can be utilized in making consumer decisions.

Using Algebra illustrate how algebra can be and is used in everyday life.

Reading Algebra provide students with the instruction needed to read and interpret mathematical symbolism.

Excursions in Algebra enliven and help maintain student interest by providing interesting side trips. Topics are varied and include history, glimpses into the development and uses of algebra as well as puzzles and games.

Using Computers instruct students in writing programs using the BASIC computer language as well as provide insights into how computers are used.

Student Features

7-3 Graphing $y = a(x - h)^2$

You have studied parabolas with equations of the form $y = ax^2$. No matter what the value of a, each parabola has axis of symmetry $x = 0$ and vertex (0, 0).

Below, the graphs of $y = x^2$, $y = (x - 3)^2$, and $y = (x + 3)^2$ are drawn on the same set of axes.

Notice that each graph has the same shape. The only difference is their horizontal position.

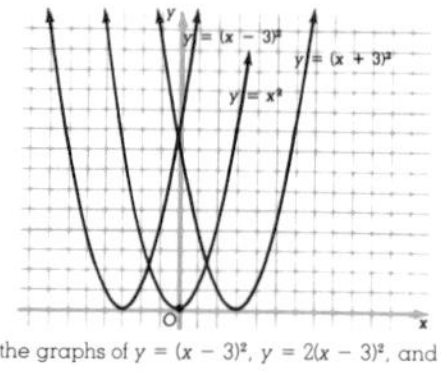

Below, the graphs of $y = (x - 3)^2$, $y = 2(x - 3)^2$, and $y = \frac{1}{2}(x - 3)^2$ are drawn on the same set of axes.

Notice that each graph has the same vertex and axis of symmetry. The only difference is their shape. Their widths vary.

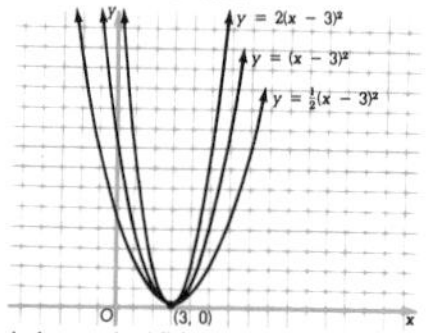

In general, the graph of $f(x) = a(x - h)^2$ has the same shape and direction of opening as the graph of $f(x) = ax^2$. But its position is shifted h units to the right or left.

$y = a(x - h)^2$	a is positive	a is negative
Vertex	$(h, 0)$	$(h, 0)$
Axis of symmetry	$x = h$	$x = h$
Direction of opening	upward	downward
As the value of $\lvert a \rvert$ increases, the graphs of $y = a(x - h)^2$ narrow.		

196 QUADRATIC RELATIONS AND FUNCTIONS

examples

1 **Graph $f(x) = {}^{-}3(x - 5)^2$.**

Since h is 5, the vertex is (5, 0) and the axis of symmetry is $x = 5$.

Since a is ${}^{-}3$, the graph opens downward and is narrower than the graph of $f(x) = x^2$.

It is helpful to find several points on the graph other than the vertex.

$f(4) = {}^{-}3(4 - 5)^2$ or ${}^{-}3$
$f(6) = {}^{-}3(6 - 5)^2$ or ${}^{-}3$
$f(3) = {}^{-}3(3 - 5)^2$ or ${}^{-}12$
$f(7) = {}^{-}3(7 - 5)^2$ or ${}^{-}12$

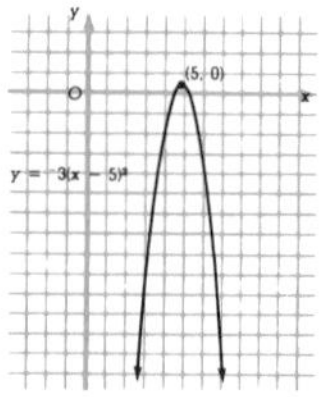

2 **Graph $f(x) = 3x^2 + 12x + 12$.**

First, write the equation in the form $f(x) = a(x - h)^2$, if possible.

$f(x) = 3x^2 + 12x + 12$
$= 3(x^2 + 4x + 4)$
$= 3(x + 2)^2$
$= 3(x - {}^{-}2)^2$

Therefore, a is 3 and h is ${}^{-}2$.
The vertex is $({}^{-}2, 0)$.
The axis of symmetry is $x = {}^{-}2$.
The graph opens upward and is narrower than the graph of $f(x) = x^2$.

$f({}^{-}1) = 3({}^{-}1 - {}^{-}2)^2$ or 3
$f({}^{-}3) = 3({}^{-}3 - {}^{-}2)^2$ or 3
$f(0) = 3(0 - {}^{-}2)^2$ or 12
$f({}^{-}4) = 3({}^{-}4 - {}^{-}2)^2$ or 12

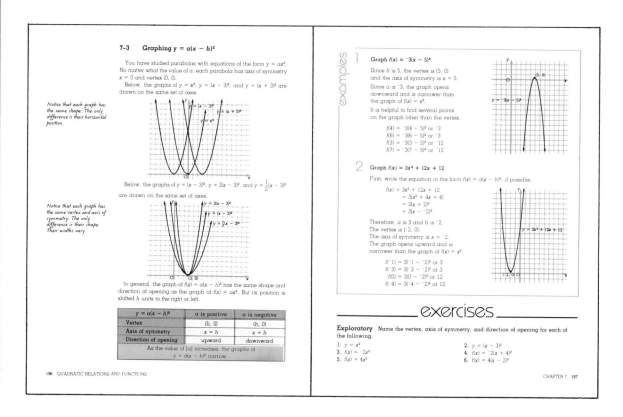

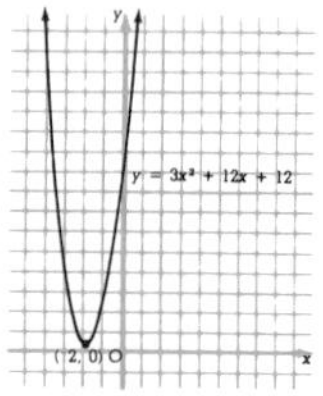

exercises

Exploratory Name the vertex, axis of symmetry, and direction of opening for each of the following.

1. $y = x^2$
2. $y = (x - 3)^2$
3. $f(x) = {}^{-}2x^2$
4. $f(x) = {}^{-}2(x + 4)^2$
5. $f(x) = 4x^2$
6. $f(x) = 4(x - 2)^2$

CHAPTER 7 197

Lesson Features

The text is divided into 17 chapters. Each chapter contains from 6 to 10 easily managed lessons. Each lesson is composed of a short explanation, completely worked examples, and Exploratory and Written Exercises.

The text is very readable with color and graphics used to enhance the learnability of the material.

Student annotations provide explanations and steps for problem solving. Highlighting and color boxes emphasize important concepts.

Completely worked examples provide students with ample models for problem-solving techniques. Examples are clearly marked and explanations of steps provided where necessary.

exercises

Exploratory Use division to simplify each expression.

1. $\frac{7^4}{7^5}$ 2. $\frac{12^6}{12^4}$ 3. $\frac{g^6}{g^3}$
4. $\frac{h^{16}}{h^2}$ 5. $\frac{a^{10}}{a^{10}}$ 6. $\frac{14r^{11}}{2r^{10}}$
7. $\frac{8a^2b^4}{2b}$ 8. $\frac{3^3r^3s^3}{9r^2}$ 9. $\frac{36x^3y^5}{12x^2y^2}$
10. $\frac{6xy^2 - 3xy + 2x^2y}{xy}$ 11. $\frac{a^3b^2 - a^2b + 2a}{^{-}ab}$ 12. $\frac{6r^2s^2 + 3rs^2 - 9r^2s}{3rs}$

Written Find each solution.

1. $(x^2 - 12x - 45) \div (x + 3)$
2. $(a^2 + 7a - 60) \div (a + 12)$
3. $(6y^2 + 7y - 3) \div (2y + 3)$
4. $(15b^2 + 14b - 8) \div (5b - 2)$
5. $(8a^2 + 34a + 19) \div (2a + 7)$
6. $(20b^2 - 17b - 61) \div (5b + 7)$
7. $(28y^2 + 23y - 12) \div (7y - 3)$
8. $(80x^2 + 6x - 4) \div (10x - 3)$
9. $(a^2 - 5a - 84) \div (a + 7)$
10. $x^2 + 20x + 91) \div (x + 7)$
11. $(y^2 + 15y + 36) \div (y + 3)$
12. $(b^2 + 17b + 52) \div (b + 4)$
13. $(6x^2 + 11x - 35) \div (3x - 5)$
14. $(15m^2 - m - 6) \div (5m + 3)$
15. $(a^2 - 5ab + 6b^2) \div (a - 3b)$
16. $(12x^2 - 4xy - y^2) \div (2x - y)$
17. $(6z^2 - 2z - 28) \div (3z + 7)$
18. $(3b^2 - 7ba - 20a^2) \div (3b + 5a)$
19. $(a^2 + 4a - 16) \div (a - 6)$
20. $(y^2 + y - 8) \div (y - 3)$
21. $(8x^2 - 4x + 11) \div (x + 5)$
22. $(x^2 + 5x + 4) \div (x + 2)$
23. $(6a^2 + 23a + 25) \div (2a + 3)$
24. $(126k^2 + 113k - 26) \div (14k - 3)$
25. $(56m^2 - 113m + 59) \div (8m - 7)$
26. $(20r^2 + 7r - 10) \div (5r - 2)$
27. $(6y^3 + 11y^2 - 4y - 4) \div (3y - 2)$
28. $(8x^3 - 22x^2 - 5x + 12) \div (4x + 3)$
29. $(6a^3 + 5a^2 + 9) \div (2a + 3)$
30. $(8b^2 - 4b + 1) \div (2b - 1)$
31. $(m^3 - 1) \div (m - 1)$
32. $(a^3 - 8) \div (a - 2)$
33. $(y^3 - 9y^2 + 27y - 28) \div (y - 3)$
34. $(x^3 + 6x^2 + 12x + 12) \div (x + 2)$
35. $(6a^3 + 5a^2 - 13a - 17) \div (3a + 2)$
36. $(2p^3 + 7p^2 - 29p + 29) \div (2p - 3)$
37. $(m^3 - 7m + 3m^2 - 21) \div (m^2 - 7)$
38. $(48p^3 - 15 + 6p^2 - 40p) \div (6p^2 - 5)$
39. $(x^3 + 4x - 4) \div (x + 2)$
40. $(2t^3 - 2t - 3) \div (t - 1)$
41. $(x^4 + 4) \div (x^2 - 2x + 2)$
42. $(y^4 + 4y^3 + 10y^2 + 12y + 9) \div (y^2 + 2y + 3)$
43. $(a^4 - 3a^2 + 1) \div (a^2 + a - 1)$
44. $(x^4 - 4x^2 + 12x - 9) \div (x^2 + 2x - 3)$

45. Is $3y - 2$ a factor of $6y^3 - y^2 - 5y + 2$? Write yes or no.
46. Is $4x + 5$ a factor of $4x^3 + x^2 + 10$? Write yes or no.
47. One factor of $a^3 - 2a^2 - a + 2$ is $a - 2$. Find the other factors.
48. One factor of $2m^3 - 11m^2 + 18m - 9$ is $m - 3$. Find the other factors.
49. Find the remainder for $(x^2 + 3x + 5) \div (x - 2)$.
50. Let $f(x) = x^2 + 3x + 5$. Find $f(2)$.
51. How do the answers to problems **49** and **50** compare?

124 POLYNOMIALS

Vocabulary

monomial (102)
coefficient (102)
degree of monomial (102)
like terms (102)
polynomial (106)
binomial (106)
trinomial (106)
degree of polynomial (106)
FOIL (108)
synthetic division (125)

Chapter Summary

1. Properties of Exponents: For any numbers a and b, and non-negative integers m and n, the following hold.
   1. $a^m \cdot a^n = a^{m+n}$
   2. $(a^m)^n = a^{m \cdot n}$
   3. $(ab)^m = a^m b^m$
   4. $\frac{a^m}{a^n} = a^{m-n}$ as long as $a \neq 0$ and $m > n$ (103)

Chapter Review

4-1 Simplify each expression.

1. $y^9 \cdot y^2$ 2. $(xy^4)(^{-}5x^2y^3)$ 3. $(x^3)^2$
4. $(4a^2)^3$ 5. $\frac{a^6}{a^2}$ 6. $\frac{14a^4b^3}{(7ab)^2}$
7. $(5a)(6a^2b)(3ab^3) + (4a^2)(3b^3)(2a^2b)$ 8. $(3a)(a^2b)^3 + (2a)^2(^{-}a^5b^3)$

4-2 Simplify each expression by performing the indicated operations.

9. $(4b^3 + 7b^2 - 3b + 5) + (^{-}3b^3 + 8b^2 - 7)$
10. $(p^4 + 5p^2 - 3p + 7) - (p^3 + p^2 - 3p + 5)$
11. $(4a - 5)(a + 7)$ 12. $(3m - 7)^2$

Chapter Test

Simplify each expression.

1. $(m^2)^5$ 2. $\frac{16b^7}{2b^5}$ 3. $(4a^2b^2)(5ab^3)$
4. $(5x)(6x^2y^3) + (2xy)^3$ 5. $3x^2y + 4 - 3x^2y$
6. $(3y^4 + 5y^3 + y - 7) + (4y^4 - 3y^3 + 7y^2 - 3y + 8)$
7. $(4b^3 + 7b^2 - 3b + 5) - (2b^3 - 5b^2 + 2b + 7)$
8. $(2y + 7)(y - 3)$ 9. $(3m + 5)^2$
10. $(y - 4)(3y^2 - 5y + 4)$ 11. $(x + 3)(2x - 5)(3x + 4)$

Exercises

Exploratory Exercises can be used in classes to clarify concepts. The ample number of Written Exercises can be used to solidify student understanding. All exercises progress in difficulty level from the beginning to the end of the exercise set.

Review and Test

Material at the end of each chapter provides students with an opportunity to evaluate their progress. The Vocabulary, Chapter Summary, and Chapter Review summarize the concepts and problems presented in each chapter. The Chapter Test permits students to test their understanding.

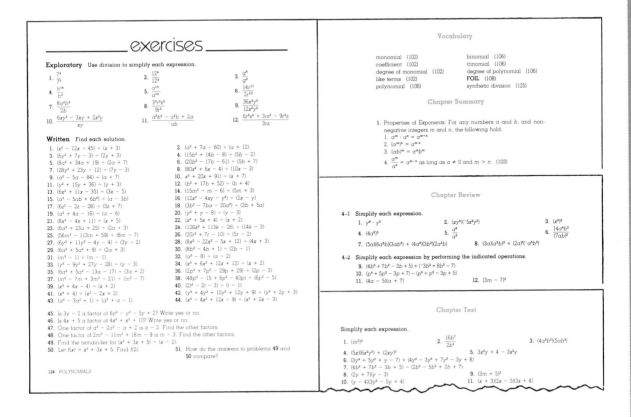

Teacher Features

The Teacher's Annotated Edition includes the Teacher's Guide and annotated pages from the student text.

Annotated Pages

10-1 Multiplying Rational Expressions

All polynomials, including constants are rational expressions. But not all rational expressions are polynomials.

Objective: To multiply rational polynomial expressions.

Rational numbers and **rational algebraic expressions** are similar.

A rational number can be expressed as the quotient of two integers.

$$\frac{2}{3} \qquad \frac{415}{100}$$

There are often values of the variable for which a rational algebraic expression is not defined. The first expression is not defined for $x = 5$. The second expression is not defined for $^-2 \pm \sqrt{3}$.

A rational algebraic expression can be expressed as the quotient of two polynomials.

$$\frac{2x}{x-5} \qquad \frac{p^2-25}{p^2+4p+1}$$

To simplify a rational algebraic expression, divide both numerator and denominator by their greatest common factor (GCF).

examples

1 Simplify $\frac{2x(x-5)}{(x-5)(x^2-1)}$.

$$\frac{2x(x-5)}{(x-5)(x^2-1)} = \frac{2x}{x^2-1}$$

The GCF is $(x-5)$.

2 Simplify $\frac{x^2-x^2y}{x^3-x^3y}$.

$$\frac{x^2-x^2y}{x^3-x^3y} = \frac{x^2(1-y)}{x^3(1-y)} = \frac{1 \cdot x^2(1-y)}{x \cdot x^2(1-y)} = \frac{1}{x}$$

The GCF is $x^2(1-y)$.

Both rational numbers and rational expressions are multiplied the same way. Multiply numerators and multiply denominators.

$$\frac{2}{3} \cdot \frac{4}{5} = \frac{2 \cdot 4}{3 \cdot 5} \text{ or } \frac{8}{15}$$

$$\frac{(x+1)}{(x-4)} \cdot \frac{(2x+3)}{(3x-1)} = \frac{(x+1)(2x+3)}{(x-4)(3x-1)} \text{ or } \frac{2x^2+5x+3}{3x^2-13x+4}$$

278 RATIONAL POLYNOMIAL EXPRESSIONS

examples

3 Find $\frac{4a}{5b} \cdot \frac{15b}{16a}$.

$$\frac{4a}{5b} \cdot \frac{15b}{16a} = \frac{60ab}{80ab} = \frac{3 \cdot 20ab}{4 \cdot 20ab} = \frac{3}{4}$$

The GCF is 20ab.

4 Find $\frac{x^2-9}{x^2+x-12} \cdot \frac{x+2}{x+3}$.

$$\frac{x^2-9}{x^2+x-12} \cdot \frac{x+2}{x+3} = \frac{(x^2-9)(x+2)}{(x^2+x-12)(x+3)}$$

$$= \frac{(x-3)(x+3)(x+2)}{(x-3)(x+4)(x+3)} \quad \textit{Factor.}$$

$$= \frac{x+2}{x+4}$$

The GCF is $(x-3)(x+3)$.

exercises

Max: 1-28, 1-42; **Avg:** 1-28, 1-41 odds; **Min:** 1-41 odds

Exploratory For each expression, find the greatest common factor (GCF) of the numerator and denominator.

1. $\frac{24}{72}$ 24; $\frac{1}{3}$
2. $\frac{99}{132}$ 33; $\frac{3}{4}$
3. $\frac{13x}{39x^2}$ 13x; $\frac{1}{3x}$
4. $\frac{42y}{18xy}$ 6y; $\frac{7}{3x}$
5. $\frac{38a^2}{42ab}$ 2a; $\frac{19a}{21b}$
6. $\frac{79a^2b}{158a^3bc}$ $79a^2b$; $\frac{1}{2ac}$
7. $\frac{42y^2}{56y}$ 14y; $\frac{3y}{4}$
8. $\frac{8x^2-x^3}{16-2x}$ $(8-x)$; $\frac{x^2}{2}$
9. $\frac{y^2-9}{y^2+6y+9}$ $y+3$; $\frac{y-3}{y+3}$
10. $\frac{y^2+8y-20}{y^2-4}$ $(y-2)$; $\frac{y+10}{y+2}$
11. $\frac{x^2-x-20}{x^2+7x+12}$ $(x+4)$; $\frac{x-5}{x+3}$
12. $\frac{y^2+4y+4}{3y^2+5y-2}$ $(y+2)$; $\frac{y+2}{3y-1}$
13. $\frac{a^2+2a+1}{2a^2+3a+1}$ $(a+1)$; $\frac{a+1}{2a+1}$
14. $\frac{2b^2-9b+9}{b^2-6b+9}$ $(b-3)$; $\frac{2b-3}{b-3}$

15-28. Simplify each expression in problems 1-14. See second part of answers above.

CHAPTER 10 279

Annotations

Annotated pages give an objective for each lesson and teaching suggestions and hints for that lesson.

Answers

For teacher convenience, the daily assignment is annotated on the page as well as all answers that would fit on the page. A calculator symbol is used to denote those exercises that are appropriate for calculator use. This symbol appears *only* in the Teacher's Annotated Edition so that the use of a calculator is left to the discretion of the teacher.

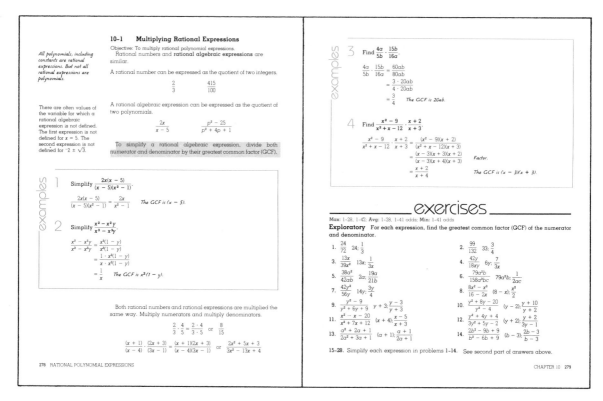

Teacher's Guide

Teacher Notes

The Teacher's Guide has Teacher Notes for each chapter including a chapter overview and notes for each lesson.

Teacher's Notes

Chapter 1 Equations and Inequalities

Chapter Overview This chapter is predominantly a review of the concepts, terminology, and symbolism of *Algebra One*. It eases the student back into mathematical routines and introduces some new material as well.

Lesson Notes

1-1 This section reminds the student of the meaning of terms such as constant, variable, value, and exponent. The rules for the order of operation are presented. Even though the students should already know these, be sure they can use them correctly and consistently. The students will have much better success if they can use these rules properly. In example 4, the relationship between Celsius and ...

... set up equations from word problems. Following the problem-solving procedure outlined in the examples will help the students to learn how to attack a problem. Answers should be checked by re-reading the problem to see if they satisfy all the conditions of the problem.

1-5 The definition of absolute value is often difficult for students to understand when applied to a variable which stands for a negative number. It may help to read the definition as follows. For any number a, if a is positive or zero, then the absolute value of a equals a; if a is negative, then the absolute value of a equals the opposite of a. It is important for students to write out a sentence using or in solving an equation which contains an absolute value. For example, $|x + 2| = 5$ yields the ...

Tests

An independent test for each chapter and two semester tests are included in the testing portion.

Independent Test for Chapter 1 (answers in italics)

1. Find the value of $6 + 8^2 \div 4 - 2$. *20*
2. Find the value of $3 + 6 \cdot 3 \div 2 - 5$. *7*
3. Evaluate $\frac{3a^2 + 2b}{c^2}$ if $a = 1$, $b = 2$, and $c = 3$. $\frac{7}{9}$
4. State the property shown by $3x + {}^-3x = 0$. *additive inverse*
5. State the property shown by $5\left(\frac{1}{5}\right) = \left(\frac{1}{5}\right)5$. *commutative of* $\times$
6. State the property shown by $4x + 8 = 4(x + 2)$. *distributive*
7. Solve $4x = 18$. $x = 4.5$
8. Solve $5x + 2 = 3x + 24$. $x = 11$
9. Solve $m - 5 = 16$. $m = 21$
10. The width of a rectangle is 3 meters more than $\frac{1}{4}$ its length. The perimeter is 26 meters. Find the length and width. *8, 5*
11. Jill Rhodes paid \$36,000 for her home several years ago. She sells it for \$50,400. What percent is the selling price of the original price? *140%*
12. Solve $|2x + 3| = 7$. $x = 2, {}^-5$
13. Solve $|x + 5| + 4 = 3$. *no solutions*
14. Solve $4|x - 2| = 24$. $x = 8, {}^-4$

Teacher's Answer Key

The Teacher's Answer Key provides answers that do not appear on the annotated pages.

23. $y = -\frac{5}{2}x + 16$ **24.** $y = 13x - 58$ **25.** $y = \frac{2}{11}x + \frac{6}{11}$ **26.** $y = \frac{2}{5}x - \frac{3}{5}$ **27.** $y = \frac{5}{2}x + 18$ **28.** $x = 6$; no slope-intercept form **29.** $y = 3$ **30.** $y = \frac{3}{2}x$ **31.** $y = \frac{1}{2}x + 1$ **32.** $y = \frac{3}{4}x - 7$ **33.** $y = \frac{2}{3}x - 6$ **34.** $y = -\frac{4}{5}x - \frac{7}{5}$ **35.** $y = 4x - 11$ **36.** $y = 5x$ **37.** $y = -\frac{3}{2}x + 10$ **38.** $y = -\frac{8}{3}x + 6$ **39.** $2x + 3y = 12$ **40.** $2x - y = {}^-6$ **41.** $6x + 5y = 30$ **42.** $4x + 3y = 24$ **43.** $3x - 4y = 1$ **44.** $10x + y = 6$ **45.** $5x + 2y = 32$ **46.** $13x - y = 58$ **47.** $2x - 11y = {}^-6$ **48.** $2x - 5y = 3$ **49.** $5x - 2y = {}^-36$ **50.** $x = 6$ **51.** $y = 3$ **52.** $3x - 2y = 0$ **53.** $x - 2y = {}^-2$ **54.** $3x - 4y = 28$ **55.** $2x - 3y = 18$ **56.** $4x + 5y = {}^-7$ **57.** $4x - y = 11$ **58.** $5x - y = 0$ **59.** $3x + 2y = 20$ **60.** $8x + 3y = 18$

Page 58 Written

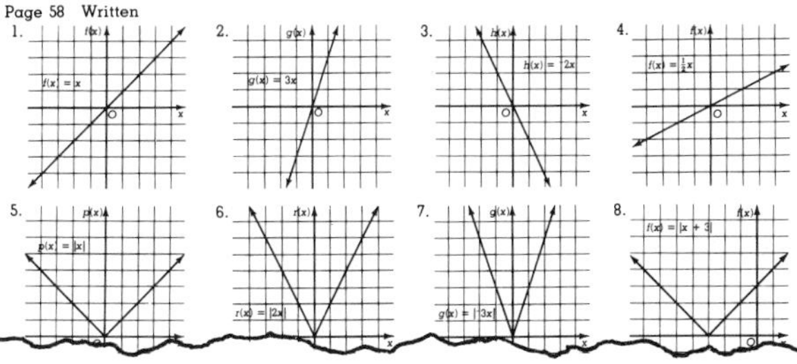

Special Features

The following special feature pages in the student text provide interesting and useful extra topics.

Reading Algebra

Reading Algebra pages discuss the special problems of reading mathematics.

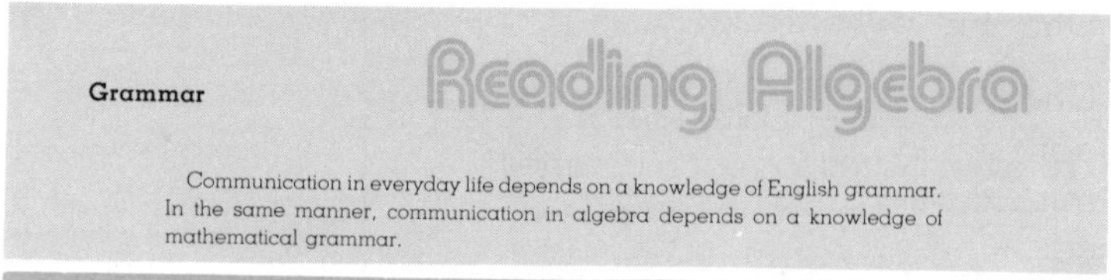
Grammar

Reading Algebra

Communication in everyday life depends on a knowledge of English grammar. In the same manner, communication in algebra depends on a knowledge of mathematical grammar.

Using Money

Using Money pages present various consumer topics.

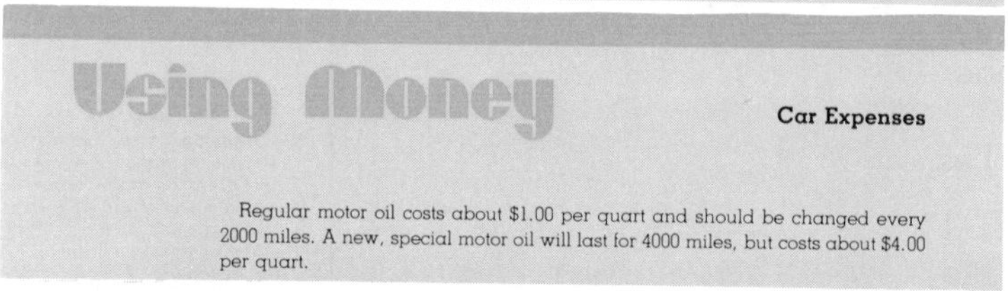
Using Money

Car Expenses

Regular motor oil costs about $1.00 per quart and should be changed every 2000 miles. A new, special motor oil will last for 4000 miles, but costs about $4.00 per quart.

Using Algebra

Using Algebra pages present applications of algebra and show how algebra is used in the real world.

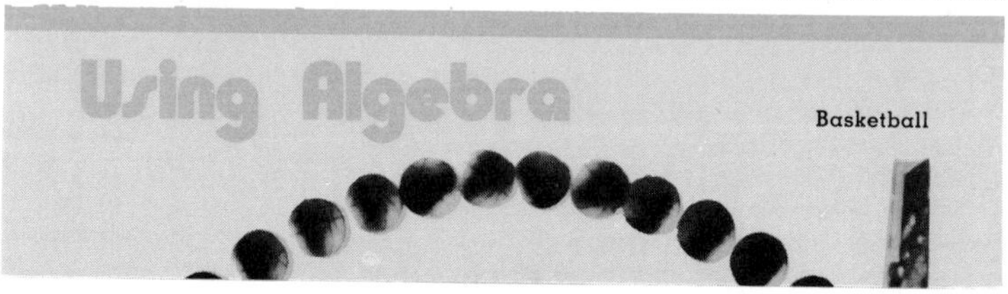

Careers

Careers pages present relevant, interesting careers and show how algebra is used in the work world.

Using Computers

Using Computers provides insights into how computers are used and introduces students to programs in BASIC.

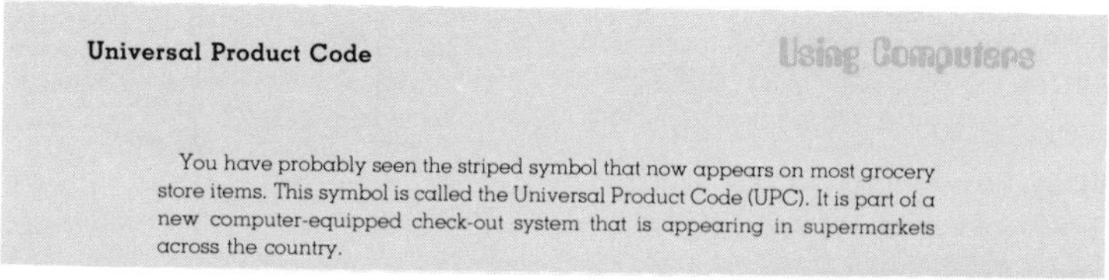
Universal Product Code

Using Computers

You have probably seen the striped symbol that now appears on most grocery store items. This symbol is called the Universal Product Code (UPC). It is part of a new computer-equipped check-out system that is appearing in supermarkets across the country.

Appendix: BASIC

The BASIC Appendix provides a short course in the BASIC programming language.

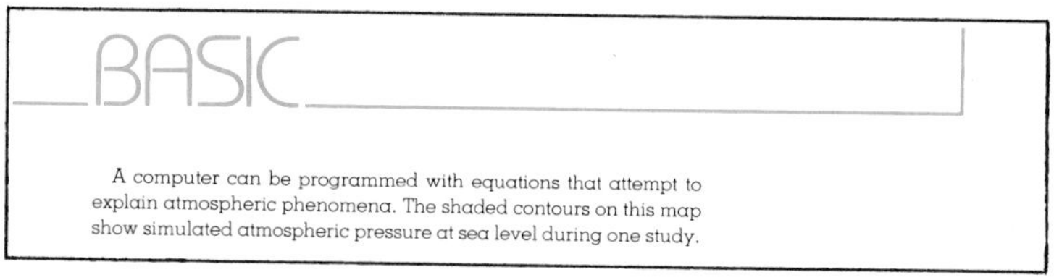
BASIC

A computer can be programmed with equations that attempt to explain atmospheric phenomena. The shaded contours on this map show simulated atmospheric pressure at sea level during one study.

Excursions in Algebra

Excursions in Algebra provide short topics in the history, development, and uses of algebra. These topics can be used for enrichment or as a break from day-to-day routine.

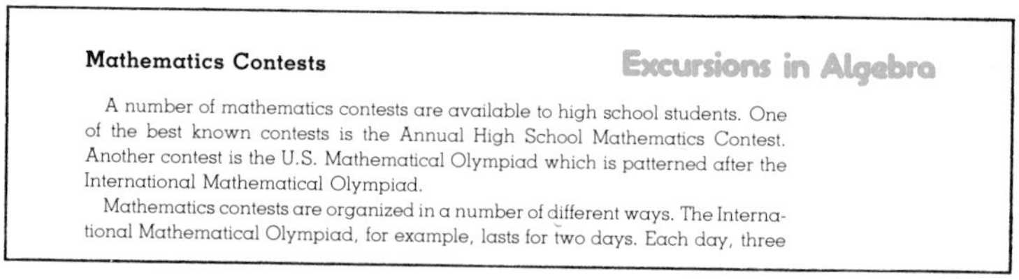
Mathematics Contests

Excursions in Algebra

A number of mathematics contests are available to high school students. One of the best known contests is the Annual High School Mathematics Contest. Another contest is the U.S. Mathematical Olympiad which is patterned after the International Mathematical Olympiad.

Mathematics contests are organized in a number of different ways. The International Mathematical Olympiad, for example, lasts for two days. Each day, three

Teacher's Notes

Chapter 1 Equations and Inequalities

Chapter Overview This chapter is predominantly a review of the concepts, terminology, and symbolism of *Algebra One*. It eases the student back into mathematical routines and introduces some new material as well.

Lesson Notes

1-1 This section reminds the student of the meaning of terms such as constant, variable, value, and exponent. The rules for the order of operation are presented. Even though the students should already know these, be sure they can use them correctly and consistently. The students will have much better success if they can use these rules properly. In example **4**, the relationship between Celsius and Fahrenheit temperatures is given. It is based on these two facts: $1°F = \frac{5}{9}°C$ and $0°C = 32°F$. Often throughout the book there is important material in the examples, in the form of annotations, which is not repeated in the text of the lesson.

1-2 The properties in this section help the student to understand the structure and development of the real number system. The distributive property for multiplication over addition is necessary to understand common monomial factoring later.

1-3 Students have used the substitution property of equality many times before, often without naming it. The properties of equality used in solving equations are review for most students in *Algebra Two*. Students need to realize that the application of the properties of equality to an equation results in an equivalent equation—that is, an equation with the same solution set. Review with students why division by zero is not possible.

1-4 Students must be helped to understand that it takes both time and practice to learn to set up equations from word problems. Following the problem-solving procedure outlined in the examples will help the students to learn how to attack a problem. Answers should be checked by re-reading the problem to see if they satisfy all the conditions of the problem.

1-5 The definition of absolute value is often difficult for students to understand when applied to a variable which stands for a negative number. It may help to read the definition as follows. For any number a, if a is positive or zero, then the absolute value of a equals a; if a is negative, then the absolute value of a equals the opposite of a. It is important for students to write out a sentence using *or* in solving an equation which contains an absolute value. For example, $|x + 2| = 5$ yields the sentence $x + 2 = 5$ *or* $x + 2 = {}^{-}5$.

1-6 This section uses the set notation $\{x|x < 5\}$ to represent the set of all numbers x such that x is less than 5. Students need plenty of practice in multiplying inequalities by a negative number. They may forget to reverse the order of the inequality when multiplying or dividing by a negative number.

1-7 Compound sentences containing *and* and *or* are introduced. Discussion of examples of these sentences and the conditions necessary for them to be true should prove helpful. Encourage students to use the procedures outlined to use inequalities in problem solving.

1-8 The material on absolute value inequalities may be new to many students. The use of the number line is helpful in showing the solutions to problems which have *and* or *or*. The absolute value inequality $|x| < 5$ yields the compound sentence $x > {}^{-}5$ *and* $x < 5$. This can be abbreviated ${}^{-}5 < x < 5$. The absolute value inequality $|x| > 5$ yields the compound sentence $x < {}^{-}5$ *or* $x > 5$.

This cannot be abbreviated since no number is both less than $^{-}5$ and greater than 5.

Chapter 2 Linear Relations and Functions

Chapter Overview This chapter teaches the concepts of relations and functions. The student learns to graph linear equations and inequalities on the coordinate plane.

Lesson Notes

2-1 This section teaches the basics of the coordinate plane and graphing. Much of this material is not new to the student, but it is important that it is well understood.

2-2 When discussing relations and functions, the use of mappings helps students to visualize domain and range. Be sure students understand that if a single element of the domain is paired with more than one element of the range, then the set of ordered pairs is not a function. The vertical line test is an easy way to apply the definition of a function.

2-3 This section introduces the standard form of a linear equation: $ax + by = c$ where not both a and b are zero. Students should use three points to graph a linear equation. It is easier to find three ordered pairs if the equation is solved for x. If $ax + by = c$, then $ax = {}^{-}by + c$ and $x = -\frac{b}{a}y + \frac{c}{a}$. Then assign a value to y, and calculate the value of x for each of the three points.

2-4 This section discusses alternate ways of finding points to draw the graph of a linear equation. If one ordered pair of the graph has been found, slope can be used to find another. The use of the x-intercept and the y-intercept is another way to find two ordered pairs of the graph.

2-5 An equation of the form $y = mx + b$ is in slope-intercept form. This section explains how to find the equation of a line in several ways. The student learns to find the equation of a line if the slope and y-intercept are given, or if two points are given.

2-6 The graphing of the absolute value function and the greatest integer function will require some time to understand. The greatest integer function is a step function. Examples which yield real-life step functions are postage rates and parking garage fees. It may be helpful to graph the amounts charged at a parking garage which charges 30 cents for each half-hour, or part thereof. Help students to see why $[^{-}3.2]$ is $^{-}2$ and not $^{-}3$.

2-7 In this section, the student again has the opportunity to set up linear equations from word problems. Many service industries use linear functions in their rate structures.

2-8 The student can use the knowledge gained in graphing lines to graph inequalities. The student needs to clearly understand that a solid line boundary is part of the graph while a broken line boundary is not.

Chapter 3 Systems of Equations and Inequalities

Chapter Overview This chapter deals with systems of linear equations and inequalities. It introduces topics such as matrices and determinants, Cramer's rule, solution of systems of three equations in three variables, and linear programming. Solution by augmented matrices is included.

Lesson Notes

3-1 Parallel and perpendicular lines are defined in terms of slope. The student has the opportunity to use graphing and computational skills to solve problems involving sets of parallel, perpendicular, or intersecting lines.

3-2 The student can relate the work with parallel and intersecting lines to analyzing systems of equations. Nonparallel lines indicate that the system is consistent, independent, and has one common solution. Parallel lines mean that the system is inconsistent and has no common solution, or it is consistent and dependent and has more than one solution.

3-3 Students may have better success with the elimination method. This method is helpful in understanding matrix row operations later.

3-4 This section deals with the use of matrices and determinants to solve systems of equations. It also gives an example of finding the determinant of a 3×3 matrix using expansion by minors. In the example, the top row is used to expand it by minors. The row and column containing the 2 are deleted, giving the term $2\begin{vmatrix} 6 & 7 \\ 9 & 10 \end{vmatrix}$. Similarly, deleting the row and column containing the 3 yields the term $^{-}3\begin{vmatrix} 5 & 7 \\ 8 & 10 \end{vmatrix}$, and deleting the row and column containing the 4 yields $4\begin{vmatrix} 5 & 6 \\ 8 & 9 \end{vmatrix}$.

3-5 The students may be interested to know that the method of solving systems of equations by Cramer's rule is a method often used to solve systems using a computer.

3-6 This section deals with solving a system of three equations in three variables. It is important that the student understands the method of elimination, in order to understand the solution of a system using augmented matrices.

3-7 This may be the first time the student has seen matrix row operations. If so, the student will need to see a lot of examples. With augmented matrices, it may be helpful to draw a vertical line between the last two columns. The line indicates where the equals signs occur in the system of equations.

3-8 This section reviews graphing skills and the concept of intersection of sets as solutions of systems of inequalities. It is a good preparation for the next section which deals with linear programming.

3-9 Linear programming is probably new to the students. It is one of the topics which is actually used in business to make decisions about production and marketing.

Chapter 4 Polynomials

Chapter Overview This chapter extends student capabilities both in multiplying polynomials and in factoring. The chapter includes both long division and synthetic division as well as the binomial expansion, sum and difference of cubes, and factoring four terms by grouping.

Lesson Notes

4-1 This section is primarily a review of fundamentals prior to studying polynomials in depth. It reviews the basic laws of exponents when the exponents are positive integers. Exponents which are negative integers, zero, or rational numbers are taught in Chapter 11.

4-2 The distributive property is essential to the multiplication of polynomials. Remind students often to write polynomials so that the powers of a variable are in ascending or descending order. This will be helpful in factoring. Students should memorize the FOIL rule.

4-3 This section deals with powers of binomials. This is a good time to discuss Pascal's Triangle. There is an Excursion in Algebra dealing with Pascal's Triangle on page 114. An application of Pascal's Triangle is predicting coin tosses in experiments. Here three coins are tossed. The green row indicates the following results.

1		
1 1		
1 2 1		
1 3 3 1	1 way	HHH
	3 ways	HHT, HTH, THH
	3 ways	TTH, THT, HTT
1 4 6 4 1	1 way	TTT

4-4 Remind students to look for a greatest common factor when factoring any polynomial. The factors for the sum of two cubes may be developed as follows.

$$\begin{aligned} a^3 + b^3 &= a^3 + a^2b - a^2b + b^3 \\ &= a^2(a + b) - b(a^2 - b^2) \\ &= a^2(a + b) - b((a + b)(a - b)) \\ &= (a + b)(a^2 - b(a - b)) \\ &= (a + b)(a^2 - ab + b^2) \end{aligned}$$

A similar development can be done for their difference.

4-5 In this section, trinomials are factored by testing for perfect squares and by using the reverse of FOIL.

4-6 Factoring by grouping may not be easily understood by the students. They will need both patience and practice.

4-7 This section on dividing polynomials begins with dividing one monomial by another. Next, a polynomial is divided by a monomial. It is important that the student keeps like terms in the appropriate columns. It may be helpful to write $x^3 + x + 1$ as $x^3 + 0 \cdot x^2 + x + 1$.

4-8 Synthetic division is introduced as a shortcut for dividing one polynomial by another. It is a tool which the student needs to learn to use well.

Chapter 5 Roots

Chapter Overview This chapter reviews the concept of the radical and extends it to include *n*th roots. The student learns to use radicals to solve equations. The fact that equations such as $x^2 + 5 = 0$ cannot be solved using radicals provides a motivation for and transition to the development of the complex numbers.

Lesson Notes

5-1 The definition of an *n*th root needs to be reviewed and reinforced often, as does the concept of principal root. Emphasis needs to be placed on the fact that $\sqrt{a^2} = |a|$. The divide-and-average method is an excellent computer application.

5-2 When using the product property of radicals, students must learn to find the largest factor which is a perfect square, a perfect cube, and so on. Students will find it very helpful to know the squares and cubes of the first few positive integers.

5-3 Students may need a review of the concept of combining like terms before they can compute with radicals very efficiently. They may have difficulty seeing that $4\sqrt{5} + 6\sqrt{5}$ is $10\sqrt{5}$. Factoring may help. $4\sqrt{5} + 6\sqrt{5} = (4 + 6)\sqrt{5} = 10\sqrt{5}$. Emphasize that $\sqrt{2}$ and $\sqrt[3]{2}$ are not like radicals and cannot be combined. The FOIL method is used to multiply binomials such as $(6 + \sqrt{3})(7 - \sqrt{41})$. The multiplication of conjugates should be stressed. It might be well to do this in general as follows.

$$\begin{aligned} (a + b\sqrt{c})(a - b\sqrt{c}) &= a^2 - ab\sqrt{c} + ab\sqrt{c} - b^2(\sqrt{c})^2 \\ &= a^2 - b^2c \end{aligned}$$

5-4 The quotient property of radicals should not be very difficult if the student understood Sections 5-2 and 5-3. Rationalizing the denominator where the index of the radical is greater than 2 may provide a challenge to many students.

5-5 Techniques for solving equations which have radical coefficients or variables in the radicand are illustrated in the examples. When solving equations with a variable in the radicand, both sides of the equation must be raised to a power. This procedure yields an equation which may not have the same solution set as the original equation. Therefore, every solution must be checked by substitution in the original equation.

5-6 This section deals with imaginary numbers and the operations of addition and multiplication using imaginary numbers. Explain how to simplify powers of i.

For example,

$$i^{77} = (i^2)^{38}i = (^-1)^{38}i = 1 \cdot i = i$$
$$i^{79} = (i^2)^{39}i = (^-1)^{39}i = {}^-1 \cdot i = {}^-i$$

5-7 This section extends the number system to include the complex numbers. It defines addition and multiplication of complex numbers and identifies complex conjugates. Some exercises use the methods of solving a system of equations, so some review may be in order.

5-8 This section uses conjugates as a tool to divide complex numbers and to rationalize them when necessary.

5-9 This section is fairly abstract. It identifies the properties of a field and applies them to the complex number system.

Chapter 6 Quadratic Equations

Chapter Overview The solution of quadratic equations is the theme of this chapter. Methods used include factoring, completing the square, and using the quadratic formula.

Lesson Notes

6-1 Quadratic equations are solved by factoring, using the zero product property. Stress that no other constant can be substituted for zero in this property.

6-2 The method of completing the square is introduced here. It will be necessary for the development of the quadratic formula later.

6-3 Students need to memorize the formula and get a great deal of practice using it. Wherever possible, the student should be able to derive the quadratic formula by completing the square.

6-4 The discriminant is defined. The discriminant is very useful in solving quadratic equations. If the value of the discriminant is positive, the equation has two real solutions. If it is zero, there is exactly one real solution. If it is negative, there are two imaginary solutions.

6-5 The relationship between roots and coefficients is identified. This relationship is used to form quadratic equations.

6-6 Quadratic equations are needed to solve word problems. Encourage students to draw a diagram whenever possible.

6-7 Methods used to solve quadratic equations are applied to equations of higher degree which are in quadratic form.

Chapter 7 Quadratic Relations and Functions

Chapter Overview This chapter builds on the knowledge of quadratic equations to define a quadratic function. Graphs of quadratic functions are investigated. They include parabolas which have the line $x = 0$ as the axis of symmetry as well as parabolas which have other axes of symmetry. Quadratic inequalities are also studied.

7-1 The student identifies the various terms of a quadratic function. The quadratic functions are used to solve word problems.

7-2 The vertex and axis of symmetry are most important in helping the student to draw the graph of a parabola. Note that so far all equations are of the form $y = ax^2$. If a is positive, the parabola opens upward; otherwise it opens downward. Using the axis of symmetry to find the reflection of a known point yields another point of the graph.

7-3 The equations of the form $y = a(x - h)^2$ are studied next. The graph of $y = a(x - h)^2$ has the same shape as the graph of $y = ax^2$. The graph shifts to the right if h is positive and to the left if h is negative. For example, the graph of $y = 2(x - 3)^2$ is shifted 3 units to the right of $y = 2x^2$ and has the same shape. Its axis of symmetry is $x = 3$. The graph of $y = 2(x + 3)^2$ or $y = 2(x - (^-3))^2$ shifts to the left.

7-4 The graph of the quadratic equation of the form $y = a(x - h)^2 + k$ has a vertex at the point (h, k) and the axis of symmetry is $x = h$. Changing the value of k shifts the graph vertically. Review completing the square to help students transform an equation into the form $y = a(x - h)^2 + k$.

7-5 Encourage the students to follow the procedures outlined for solving problems involving a maximum or minimum using parabolas.

7-6 The student has an opportunity to graph quadratic inequalities. If the parabola which is the boundary of the resulting region is not part of the graph, it should be drawn as a broken curve. Encourage students to test several ordered pairs to check their answers.

7-7 Review the mathematical meaning of the word *and* and the word *or* before using the algebraic procedures suggested in this section.

Chapter 8 Conics

Chapter Overview In this chapter the distance formula for points in the coordinate plane is reviewed. The distance formula is applied in the definitions of the various conic sections. Each conic section is treated in the same way. It is defined, it is illustrated by an example, the generalized formula is given, its graph and equation are studied. The chapter also deals with the solution of systems of quadratic equations and inequalities.

Lesson Notes

8-1 This section develops the concept of distance between two points on the number line before developing the distance formula for the distance between two points on the coordinate plane. The formula for determining the coordinates of the midpoint of a segment if the coordinates are known is developed in the exercises.

8-2 This section gives a formal definition of a parabola. This section has been condensed quite a bit. Therefore, the teacher may want to expand on the ideas included in the section.

8-3 Students learn that the equation for a circle is quadratic in both variables. Also, the coefficients of the two variables are the same. More practice in completing the square is provided.

8-4 This section introduces the student to ellipses through definition, example, and formula. The teacher may wish to expand on this material as well as the material in Section 8-3.

8-5 By the time the student can use the concepts related to the parabola, circle, and ellipse, the concepts related to the hyperbola may be learned quickly. Encourage students to check the domain and range of each hyperbola, and to use the asymptotes when sketching the graph. Hyperbolas with equations of the form $xy = k$ are found in the exercises. They represent hyperbolas having the x-axis and the y-axis as asymptotes.

8-6 This section ties together all the lessons of Sections 8-2 through 8-5. It is helpful to students to recognize how each conic section can be formed by slicing a hollow cone.

8-7 Students solve systems of quadratic equations by graphing. They will find that estimation is necessary in some cases.

8-8 It is possible to estimate solutions to quadratic systems by graphing. However, for most systems, it is necessary to use algebra to obtain exact solutions.

8-9 The same methods used to solve systems of linear inequalities may be used to solve systems of quadratic inequalities.

Chapter 9 Polynomial Functions

Chapter Overview This chapter defines and investigates polynomial functions. The Remainder Theorem and the Factor Theorem are presented and used to help the student find the zeros of a function $f(x)$, which are solutions to the equation $f(x) = 0$. The student learns to recognize the nature of the solutions by using the Fundamental Theorem of Algebra and the Complex Conjugates Theorem. The chapter also includes material on approximating zeros, graphing polynomials, composition of functions, and inverse functions.

Lesson Notes

9-1 Students need to practice evaluating many polynomials in one variable. Explain that the degree of a polynomial in more than one variable is the largest sum of exponents in any one term, including the understood ones in a term such as $6x^2y$.

9-2 It may be necessary to review division of polynomials using long division or using synthetic division before presenting the main ideas in the section. Students should learn these theorems very well as they will be very helpful in later sections of the chapter. The teacher may want to prove one or both of these important theorems in class.

9-3 Students should be able to use the rational zero theorem to find one or more zeros of a polynomial and then find the remaining ones by factoring.

9-4 In this section, methods are presented to help the student determine if a polynomial has real or imaginary solutions, and the number of each kind. It also helps in determining whether the real solutions are negative or positive. This is useful in applying the rational zero theorem.

9-5 The location principle is very helpful in estimating zeros of a polynomial. The student needs to have a good intuitive grasp of this principle as well as to be able to state it from memory. The teacher may want to use the computer in applications of the location principle.

9-6 Be sure students work through each example in graphing. Help them to see the general method employed, of factoring and finding the values of the zeros, determining where the values of the function are positive and where they are negative, plot a number of points and join them with a smooth curve. The computer is useful in finding many ordered pairs which satisfy the polynomial and drawing an accurate graph.

9-7 Mappings can be used to show composition of functions. In order to find the composite function $f \circ g$, the range of g must be a subset of the domain of f. Examples where composition is not commutative should be discussed.

9-8 The idea of inverse functions comes up often in mathematics. The teacher may want to show that the inverse of a function can be found by reversing the order of each pair in the given function. If this is shown on a graph, the teacher could explain that this procedure is equivalent to reflecting the graph of the function about the line $y = x$.

Chapter 10 Rational Polynomial Expressions

Chapter Overview Rational expressions are defined. Operations such as multiplying and dividing rational expressions are reviewed, using the greatest common factor. Students have an opportunity to work with complex fractions as well. Addition and subtraction of rational expressions are reviewed using the least common denominator. Rational equations are solved in one section and are used to solve word problems in the next. The chapter also deals with direct and inverse variation.

Lesson Notes

10-1 Encourage students to factor numerators and denominators in order to find the greatest common factor and to simplify the resulting expression. Remind students that a fraction is not defined when the value of the denominator is zero.

10-2 Dividing one rational algebraic expression by another is the same as multiplying the first one by the inverse of the second. The example $\frac{4x^2y}{15a^3b^3} \div \frac{2xy^2}{5ab^3}$ is solved by multiplying $\frac{4x^2y}{15a^3b^3} \cdot \frac{5ab^3}{2xy^2}$. Be sure to point out that neither $15a^3b^3$ nor $2xy^2$ can be zero. Students should realize that it is the numerator of the divisor which cannot be zero. In the example above, none of a, b, x, or y can be zero.

10-3 Review the concepts of prime numbers, prime factors, and least common denominator by discussing examples in class.

10-4 Encourage students to use the method of multiplying both sides of a rational equation by the least common denominator to clear fractions. This method may save many computational errors on the part of the students. Be sure students check every solution for each equation. If the solution to the equation obtained by multiplying to clear fractions makes any denominator in the original equation zero, it is *not* a solution to the original equation.

10-5 The most important skill here is to be able to set up a correct equation. Students should check the answer to see if it satisfies all the conditions of the word problem.

10-6 Direct and inverse variation are concepts which have many practical applications. Some of them are found in this section. Another example of direct variation is found in Hooke's law which states that the stretching of a spring varies directly with the force acting on the spring. The behavior of a gas under varying pressures shows inverse variation.

Chapter 11 Exponents

Chapter Overview This chapter builds on the knowledge of exponents which the student has already gained. The chapter deals primarily with three topics: various levels of exponents, simplification of expressions containing exponents, and solution of equations involving exponents.

Lesson Notes

11-1 This section defines the zero exponent and negative integer exponents. It assumes the laws for positive integer exponents. The teacher may want to review these laws before beginning this lesson. Be sure the student understands that the patterns leading to the definitions of zero and negative integer exponents are based on successive division.

11-2 The material learned in the first section is immediately applied in this section which deals with scientific notation. Time spent on this section is valuable since these concepts will be seen again in the chapter dealing with logarithms.

11-3 The equivalence of the forms $a^{\frac{1}{2}}$, $\sqrt{a}$ is established for specific numbers, as is the equivalence of the forms $b^{\frac{1}{3}}$ and $\sqrt[3]{b}$. The laws of exponents previously learned are applied. The definition of rational numbers as exponents holds for n even, and can be extended to include $b < 0$ if n is odd. In the definition of rational exponents, $\sqrt[n]{b}$ is not a real number when n is even and b is less than zero.

11-4 This section builds on the knowledge and experience the student has already gained with simplifying expressions containing radicals and complex fractions. The problems in this section include the more difficult expressions having fractional exponents. A set of conditions for simplified expressions is also included. Help students to understand how an appropriate rationalizing factor is chosen.

11-5 Students have the opportunity to solve extremely simple equations having fractional exponents. They learn to raise each side of the equation to a power so that the power of the variable is one. This method is extended to equations in quadratic form.

11-6 The solution of radical equations is reviewed and extended to equations containing more than one radical. Solving radical equations in a chapter on exponents emphasizes the equivalence of radicals and fractional exponents.

Chapter 12 Exponential and Logarithmic Functions

Chapter Overview This chapter teaches the meaning of logarithms and the basic properties of logarithms. The students learn to find common logarithms and antilogarithms and to use common logarithms to solve problems.

Lesson Notes

12-1 Logarithms are introduced as the inverse relation of exponents. In order to continue the study of logarithms, the students should have a genuine understanding of this relationship between logarithms and exponents.

12-2 This section presents $y = b^x$ and $y = \log_b x$ as inverse *functions.* The property of equality for exponential and logarithmic functions, as well as two applications of the property of inverse functions ($b^{\log_b x} = x$ and $\log_b b^x = x$), are discussed. These concepts are needed throughout the chapter.

12-3 The properties of logarithms are derived from intuitive arguments using exponents. The students should learn to apply these properties. The concepts presented in Section 12-2 are used to show that the product property is true. The students may use similar methods to show the quotient property and the power property are also true.

12-4 Common logarithms are introduced in this section. An emphasis on scientific notation helps to simplify the tasks of finding logarithms and antilogarithms. The use of calculators to find logarithms and antilogarithms is not recommended until the students fully grasp the underlying concepts. Using calculators to find logarithms of numbers less than 1 poses a special problem. Unlike traditional procedure, calculators exhibit such logarithms as negative numbers. Scientific notation helps to clearly separate the mantissa and the characteristic and to provide an understanding of what happens when a calculator is used to find logarithms of numbers less than 1.

12-5 Interpolation is the important concept of this section. For this reason calculators should not be used to find logarithms and antilogarithms directly. However, they may be used as a computational tool in applying the concept of interpolation. Letting students use calculators for menial arithmetic tasks allows them to appreciate the broader concept. The work becomes more enjoyable when the drudgery is gone.

12-6 The presumption of this section is that most students will have access to a 4-function calculator rather than the more sophisticated models. For this reason, logarithms are still useful to compute roots and powers. For problems requiring internal multiplication and division before finding roots and powers, the use of calculators is recommended. Logarithms were devised to be a labor-saving device. Teachers should not cling to logarithms when a better labor-saving device is available. The traditional approach is demonstrated, however, in order that all approaches are discussed.

12-7 The solutions of exponential equations rely on the equality property of logarithms in Section 12-2 and the power property in Section 12-3 as well as the general rules for solving algebraic equations. The students learn to find the logarithms for any base by using exponential equations. Calculators can free the students from doing dull calculations and allow them to spend their time in constructive thinking.

12-8 In this section, the general formula for growth and decay, $y = n\,e^{kt}$, is presented. The students learn to use the techniques developed in Section 12-7 to solve problems.

Chapter 13 Sequences and Series

Chapter Overview This chapter provides an introduction to the topics of sequences and series, which may be new to some students. Topics which are developed include arithmetic sequences and series, geometric sequences and series, special sequences in mathematics, the general term of a sequence or a series, factorial notation, and the binomial expansion.

Lesson Notes

13-1 This section begins with an informal numerical illustration of a sequence. Out of this illustration the concept and terminology of sequences are drawn. The section includes definitions of an arithmetic sequence, and a discussion of arithmetic means.

13-2 This section introduces sigma notation and provides practice in using it, prior to developing the concept of a series. Stress the convenience of sigma notation. Some students may be intimidated by it because "it looks hard."

13-3 Here the concept of an arithmetic series is introduced in an informal way, as well as the use of the symbol S_n. Both are then defined formally. The exercises provide practice in using these ideas. Encourage students to practice using sigma notation.

13-4 This section develops the concept of a geometric sequence informally, and then defines a geometric sequence and its nth term. Geometric means are also investigated.

13-5 Geometric series are introduced informally in an example. The concept of a partial sum is carefully developed by an example which leads to the definition of the sum of a geometric series.

13-6 This section deals with infinite geometric series from an investigative viewpoint. A calculator was used to find the partial sums which are included. The formula for an infinite geometric series is given. It can be used directly by the students without requiring the use of a calculator. The text carefully avoids defining the sum of an infinite geometric series in terms of limits.

13-7 This section opens with the Fibonacci sequence. It includes Leibniz's series for π. The section also discusses finding patterns in other sequences.

13-8 This section shows various methods which can be used to find the general term of sequences and series. Both recursive forms and nth term forms are used.

13-9 The Binomial Theorem is used to expand binomials. Patterns which are helpful in writing the expansion are pointed out to the student. Factorial notation is introduced here, as is the equivalent form of the Binomial Theorem which uses both sigma notation and factorial notation. The examples show how to find a particular term of an expansion.

Chapter 14 Probability

Chapter Overview This chapter introduces combinations and permutations. The students learn to find the probability and the odds of success and failure.

Lesson Notes

14-1 This section presents the basic counting principle. Stress that the basic counting principle is valid for *independent* events.

14-2 In permutations, the order of the objects is important. This text uses the notation $P(n, r)$ to represent the number of permutations of n objects taken r at a time. Point out that other texts may use other notations ($P_{n,r}$ or ${}_nP_r$). Review the meaning of $n!$ and discuss the fact that $(n - n)! = 1$. The students should understand the difference between an ordinary linear permutation and a permutation with repetitions.

14-3 Students should understand that circular permutations do not exist every time a group of items is arranged in a circle. If one position on the circle is distinguished from the other positions on the circle, the permutation is linear. Students may have difficulty visualizing reflections. They may wish to experiment with the arrangement of keys on a circular key chain. Example **4** presents a case that is a linear permutation which is also reflective. The Exploratory Exercises give the students an opportunity to identify permutations as circular or linear and as reflective or not reflective.

14-4 The students should understand that in permutations order is important and in combinations order is not important. The Exploratory Exercises provide practice in identifying permutations and combinations. This text uses the notation $C(n, r)$ to mean the number of combinations of n items taken r at a time. Point out to the students that Examples **2**, **3**, and **4** are applications of the basic counting principle in Section 14-1. In each of these examples, the number of combinations of 2 or more independent events is calculated and then the basic counting principle is used to find the total number of possibilities.

14-5 In probability, an event can either succeed or fail. Point out that the probability of an event is never less than 0 or greater than 1. The students should understand that as the probability becomes greater, the more likely the event will occur. In odds, the number of ways to succeed and the number of ways to fail are used to form a different ratio. The students should notice that the odds may be greater than 1 and that the greater the number, the more likely the event will occur.

14-6 The probability of two dependent events and the probability of two independent events are discussed in this section. The students must be able to identify independent and dependent events before they can apply the rules. Therefore, the Exploratory Exercises provide practice in such identification.

14-7 This section discusses the probability of mutually exclusive events and the probability of inclusive events. By doing the Exploratory Exercises, the students gain practice in identifying which events are mutually exclusive and which are inclusive. At the end of this section, there is a page on binomial expansions. Students should study this page before continuing to Section 14-8.

14-8 If the preceding page on binomial expansions has not been discussed, review binomial expansions before starting this section. Be certain that the students understand the two conditions needed for a binomial trial to exist.

Chapter 15 Statistics

Chapter Overview This chapter introduces the basic concepts of statistics. The students learn how tables and graphs are used to present data. They learn to calculate median, mode, mean, range, standard deviation, and prediction equations.

Lesson Notes

15-1 In this section, the students learn to organize data by using tables and to read tables to find specific information. Various materials can be used to enrich this lesson. The students can practice reading tables in their textbooks from other subject areas, in newspapers, or in magazines. They can also gather data from the school or community and use the data to form tables.

15-2 Discuss the different purposes of bar graphs, pictographs, line graphs, and circle graphs. The bar graphs, pictographs, and line graphs show specific quantities, while circle graphs show how the parts are related to the whole. Line graphs indicate trends or changes more clearly than bar graphs or pictographs. As in Section 15-1, there is a wealth of material available in the school and community which can be used to enrich this lesson.

15-3 The students should understand the definitions of median, mode, and mean. Point out that the mean is affected by an extremely high or low number in the set of data. When an extreme value is included in a set, the median and mode are more representative of the set than the mean.

15-4 Since the range is affected by extremely high or low values in the set, the standard deviation is an important measure of dispersion. Review the sigma notation and then make certain that the students understand the equation

$$\text{standard deviation} = \sqrt{\frac{\sum_{i=1}^{n} (x_i - \overline{x})^2}{n}}.$$

Remind the students that the significance of the standard deviation can only be evaluated when both the standard deviation and the mean are considered.

15-5 Not all distributions are normal. Show the students some distribution graphs that are not normal. The graphs may have two or more modes or be skewed to the left or right. However, explain that when a very large sample is used, the graph is frequently a normal distribution curve. The students should study the characteristics of a normal distribution before starting the exercises.

15-6 This section introduces scatter diagrams and prediction equations. Each student must draw a line which seems to be suggested by the dots on the scatter diagram. Since these lines will vary slightly, the prediction equations will also vary. Ask the students to compare their answers and discuss which answers are reasonable.

Chapter 16 Trigonometric Functions and Identities

Chapter Overview This chapter introduces the study of trigonometry. The students learn the definitions of the trigonometric functions and study basic identities.

Lesson Notes

16-1 This section lays the groundwork for the rest of the chapter. The students learn the meaning of standard position of an angle, initial side, terminal side, coterminal angles, and radian. They also learn that the measure of an angle may be positive or negative depending on the direction of rotation.

16-2 The first two trigonometric functions, sine and cosine, are defined in terms of an ordered pair on the unit circle. The study of sine and cosine leads to the definition of periodic function. The Greek letter theta (θ) is used to indicate the angle measure. The students may wish to learn and use other letters from the Greek alphabet.

16-3 The students should draw the graphs of several functions involving sine and cosine. They should plot a number of points for each of these graphs. The amplitude and period of these functions are easily determined from the equation. Be certain that the students carefully study the domain and range and observe the relationship between the amplitude and the range.

16-4 Tangent, cotangent, secant, and cosecant are defined in terms of sine and cosine. Study the graphs in this section and discuss the values of θ for which the functions are undefined. Every student should graph each of the four functions presented in this section.

16-5 Several basic trigonometric identities are defined and developed in this section. The students should memorize them. Point out that some identities are undefined for certain values of θ.

16-6 In order to be successful in verifying identities, the students should memorize the basic trigonometric identities and have good algebra skills. Many students will require teacher assistance.

16-7 This section introduces two new letters from the Greek alphabet, alpha (α) and beta (β). Be certain the students understand the meaning of $\pm$ and $\mp$ and the sum and difference formulas. The formula $\tan(\alpha - \beta) = \frac{\tan\alpha - \tan\beta}{1 + \tan\alpha\tan\beta}$ is presented in the exercises.

16-8 When using the double angle and half angle formulas, the students must determine in which quadrant the angle is located. Using this information, the students will be able to determine whether their answer should be positive or negative.

16-9 Factoring, squaring each side, and substituting basic identities are the usual techniques for solving trigonometric equations. Some of these methods may introduce solutions which are not solutions of the original equation. Therefore, all solutions to the trigonometric equation should be checked.

16-10 When studying this lesson, point out the difference between $\cos x$ and $\mathrm{Cos}\ x$. The students should understand that $\mathrm{Arccos}\ y$ and $\mathrm{Cos}^{-1}\ y$ are the same. Continue the discussion with Arcsine and Arctangent.

Chapter 17 Right Triangle Trigonometry

Chapter Overview This chapter continues the study of trigonometry. The students learn to apply trigonometry to triangles.

Lesson Notes

17-1 This section redefines the trigonometric functions in terms of right triangles. Review the Pythagorean Theorem. A good understanding of the new definitions and the Pythagorean Theorem will lay the groundwork for success throughout this chapter.

17-2 The students learn to use the trigonometric table in the back of the book. Interpolation similar to that used when studying logarithms is presented. If calculators which contain the trigonometric functions are available, the students should learn to use the calculators after they have mastered the use of the table. When using the calculators to find sin 23°47′, they should change 47′ to hundredths of a degree and then find sin 23.78°.

17-3 The students learn to use trigonometric functions to solve right triangles. Discuss angle of elevation and angle of depression and review alternate interior angles. Encourage the students to draw diagrams before solving the word problems. If calculators are available, they should be used to solve the problems at the end of this section.

17-4 In this section, the students solve more right triangles. Again, encourage students to draw diagrams and use calculators if they are available.

17-5 The students learn that the trigonometric functions may be used to solve triangles that are not right triangles. In this section, the students learn to use the Law of Sines. Point out that the Law of Sines deals with two sides of a triangle and the angles opposite those sides.

17-6 The Law of Cosines is necessary to find an angle of a triangle if three sides are given or to find the third side if two sides and the included angle are given. The use of a hand calculator will speed up the calculations.

17-7 When two sides and the angle opposite one of them is given, the triangle may have two solutions, one solution, or no solution. The students should be able to recognize when the number of solutions of a triangle is in question and then to determine how many solutions there will be. When two triangles exist, the students should find a complete solution for each of the triangles.

Appendix BASIC

Appendix Overview One of the goals in this appendix is to let the students have direct experience in writing and running programs as soon as possible. Students begin doing very simple programs in the first section. After this, the material begins to build and expand in terms of complexity. The main topics included are assignment of variables, FOR-NEXT loops, IF-THEN statements, flow charts, subscripted variables, and internal functions, in that order. Computer systems may vary in several ways such as sign-on, sign-off procedures, panic stop, spacing used in printouts, and so on. The teacher will need to guide the students carefully where their system varies.

Lesson Notes

The Language of BASIC The variables and operational symbols used in BASIC are introduced to the student. Variables may have one letter followed by a single digit. They are similar to those used in Algebra. PRINT and END statements and line numbers are used immediately to do two-line programs where computations are done within the PRINT statement. When variables replace the numbers, the same program can be used for any selected numbers by incorporating READ and DATA statements into the program. The use of READ and DATA statements is illustrated.

Assignment of Variables Help students to understand that the concepts of assignment of a value to a variable and equality are two different uses of the same symbol, namely the equals sign. The meaning of assignment is demonstrated in the process of incrementing a variable. Help students to realize that there may be more than one valid program to accomplish a given task.

FOR-NEXT Loops The first program in this section illustrates a program which does repeated operations without the convenience of a loop. It may help students to understand how convenient it is to be able to use a loop in a computer program. Techniques of summation within a loop are demonstrated.

IF-THEN Statements An IF-THEN statement can tell the computer to make a comparison. It also instructs the computer what to do next based on the results of the comparison. When the programmer does not know beforehand where a loop will end, an IF-THEN statement lets the computer do the work of finding where the loop ends. The section includes a counting technique to be used with these statements. Note that a counter K may begin at zero or one, depending on the individual program.

Flow Charts Many simple programs can be written without the use of a flow chart. Flow charts are necessary in complicated programs and are useful in visualizing the steps in solving a problem by writing a computer program. They are also useful in debugging a program which is not working as planned. Flow charts are not introduced until the student can do enough programming to find them helpful. Note that some texts use a circle for beginning and ending rather than an oval.

Subscripted Variables These variables are introduced to expand the input possibilities of programs. They help to simplify input and output within programs when large amounts of data are involved. Systems may vary concerning when a DIM statement is required, or the maximum allowable size for a subscript.

Internal Functions Students should realize that many procedures occur so often in programming that they are "built-in" to the computer. A few of these are illustrated in this section. Systems may vary in the way an internal function is stated in a program. For example, many compilers use RND(X) with X a dummy variable as is done in this section. Others may use RND only. The teacher may have to make changes in the material taught to conform to the school's particular system.

Assignment Guide

The Assignment Guide is provided to help in planning the year's work. Three courses are outlined in order to allow flexibility in response to your curriculum requirements and the abilities of your students.

1. An algebra course
2. An algebra course with BASIC
3. An algebra course with trigonometry

The Assignment Guide gives a suggested time schedule. Adjust it to the needs of your students.

Each lesson in the text includes more exercises than an average class normally could complete. To help you meet the needs of your students, three daily assignments are annotated on the exercise pages— a maximum assignment, an average assignment, and a minimum assignment.

Suggested Time Schedule
(number of teaching days)

Chapter	BASIC	1	2	3	4	5	6	7	8
Algebra Course	0	10	10	15	10	13	10	10	16
Algebra with BASIC	10	10	10	13	10	10	10	10	14
Algebra with Trigonometry	0	9	9	13	9	10	10	10	12

Chapter	9	10	11	12	13	14	15	16	17
Algebra Course	15	10	8	10	13	10 days optional		0	0
Algebra with BASIC	13	10	8	10	12	10 days optional		0	0
Algebra with Trigonometry	11	8	7	9	10	0	0	15	8

Independent Test for Chapter 1 (answers in italics)

1. Find the value of $6 + 8^2 \div 4 - 2$. *20*
2. Find the value of $3 + 6 \cdot 3 \div 2 - 5$. *7*
3. Evaluate $\frac{3a^2 + 2b}{c^2}$ if $a = 1$, $b = 2$, and $c = 3$. $\frac{7}{9}$
4. State the property shown by $3x + {}^{-}3x = 0$. *additive inverse*
5. State the property shown by $5\left(\frac{1}{5}\right) = \left(\frac{1}{5}\right)5$. *commutative of x*
6. State the property shown by $4x + 8 = 4(x + 2)$. *distributive*
7. Solve $4x = 18$. $x = 4.5$
8. Solve $5x + 2 = 3x + 24$. $x = 11$
9. Solve $m - 5 = 16$. $m = 21$
10. The width of a rectangle is 3 meters more than $\frac{1}{4}$ its length. The perimeter is 26 meters. Find the length and width. *8, 5*
11. Jill Rhodes paid $36,000 for her home several years ago. She sells it for $50,400. What percent is the selling price of the original price? *140%*
12. Solve $|2x + 3| = 7$. $x = 2, {}^{-}5$
13. Solve $|x + 5| + 4 = 3$. *no solutions*
14. Solve $4|x - 2| = 24$. $x = 8, {}^{-}4$
15. Solve $3|x - 5| - 2 = 34$. $x = 17, {}^{-}7$
16. Solve $3t - 5 > 31$. $\{t \mid t > 12\}$
17. Solve $2(x + 3) \leq 54$. $\{x \mid x \leq 24\}$
18. Solve $42 \leq {}^{-}3(s + 2)$. $\{s \mid s \leq {}^{-}16\}$
19. Solve $4x + 3 < 39$. $\{x \mid x < 9\}$
20. James' club is having a fund-raising contest. The leader in the contest has raised $78.64 and James has raised $24.30. How much must James raise to win the contest? *at least $54.34*
21. How many 30¢ candy bars can be bought with $10? *at most 33*
22. Solve $|x + 3| < 5$. $\{x \mid {}^{-}8 < x < 2\}$
23. Solve $3|x + 4| \geq 15$. $\{x \mid x \geq 1 \text{ or } x \leq {}^{-}9\}$
24. Solve $4|x - 5| + 3 \leq 35$. ${}^{-}3 \leq x \leq 13$
25. Solve $7|x - 9| - 2 > 47$. $\{x \mid x < 2 \text{ or } x > 16\}$

Independent Test for Chapter 2 (answers in italics)

1. Graph $\frac{3s}{5} = 3$ on the real number line.

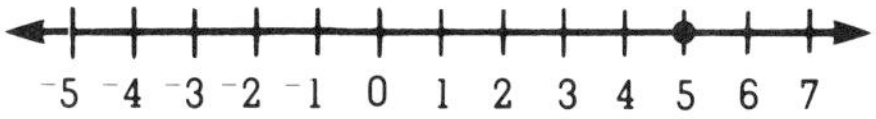

2. Graph $|x + 3| > 1$ on the real number line.

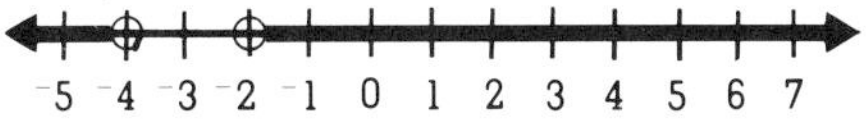

3. Graph $y - 4 \geq 2(y - 3)$ on the real number line.

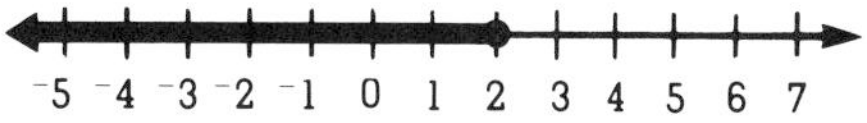

4. Is the relation $\{(^-3, 2), (^-2, 1), (^-1, 0), (^-1, 1), (0, 1)\}$ a function? *no*
5. Find $f(3)$ if $f(x) = 10x + 3x^2$. *$f(3) = 57$*
6. Find $g(^-2)$ if $g(x) = 5x^2 - 8x$. *$g(^-2) = 36$*
7. Graph $y = 3x + 2$.

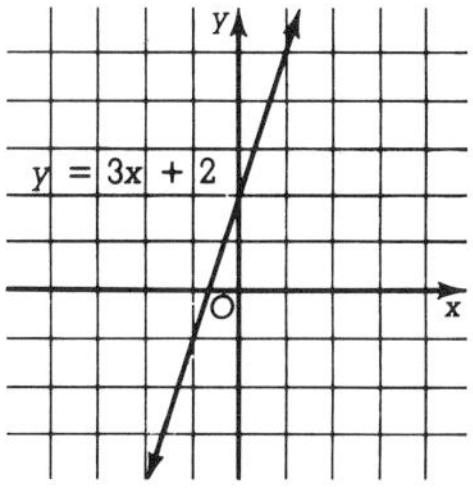

8. Graph $y = {^-x} + 5$.

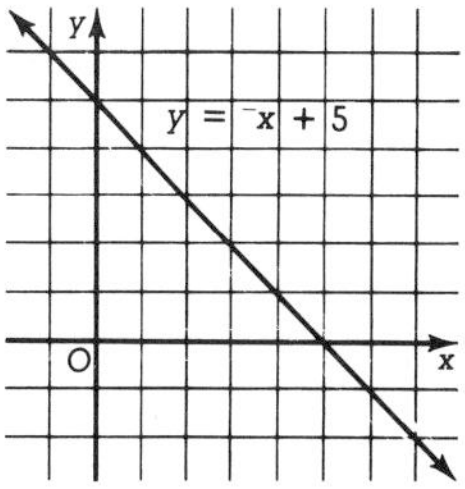

9. State the slope of $y = {^-3x} + 7$. *⁻3*
10. State the y-intercept of $y = 2x - 5$. *⁻5*
11. Determine the slope of a line that passes through (5, 9) and (3, 1). *4*
12. Find the slope and y-intercept of $2y - 6x = 18$. *3, 9*
13. Find the slope and y-intercept of $5y + 10x = 35$. *⁻2, 7*
14. Find the slope and y-intercept of $4y - 9x = 24$. *$\frac{9}{4}$, 6*
15. Graph the function $g(x) = [2x + 4]$.

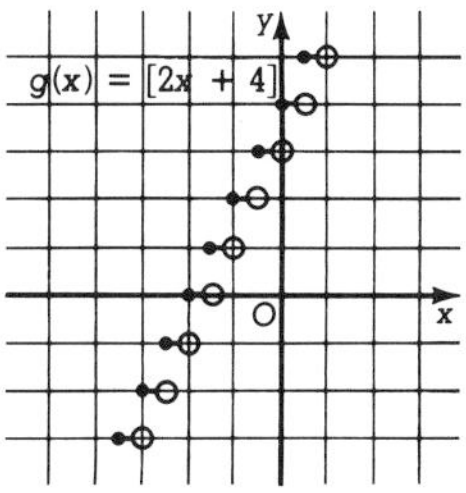

16. Graph the function $f(x) = {^-|x|} + 3$.

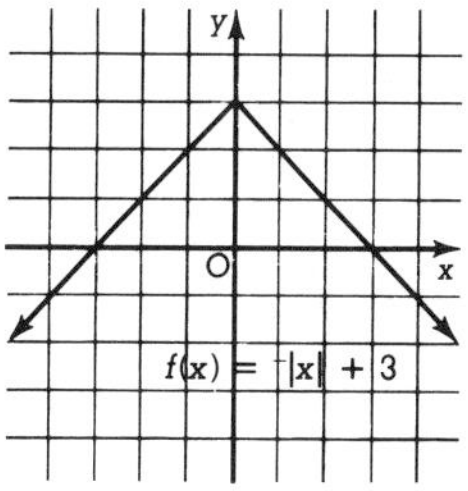

17. The number of German marks to be exchanged varies with the number of dollars. Recently, the rate was 2 marks for 1 dollar. Write an equation to describe the relationship between number of marks and number of dollars. *$m = 2d$*
18. If Bill has \$25 to be changed to marks, determine how many marks he should receive. *50*
19. Graph $y > |3x|$.

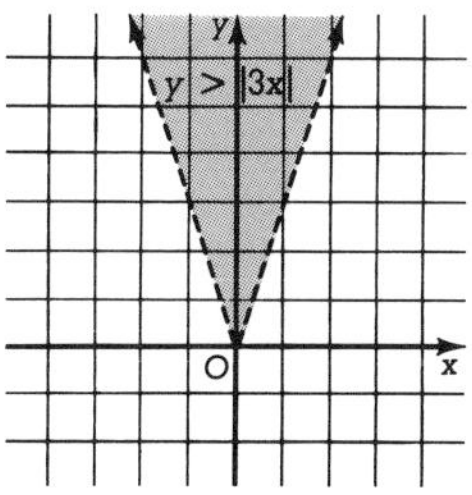

20. Graph $^-2x + 7 \geq y$.

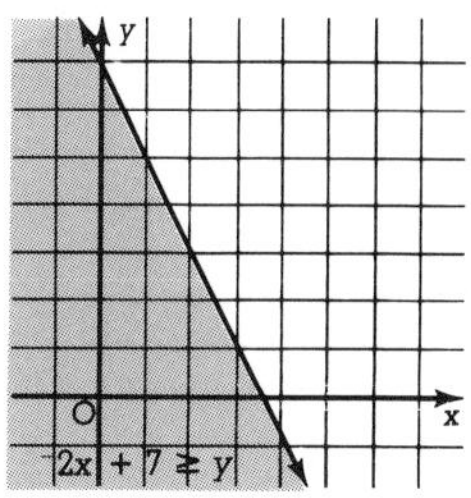

Independent Test for Chapter 3 (answers in italics)

1. State whether the graphs of $y = 3x + 7$ and $y = 3x - 4$ are parallel, perpendicular, or neither. *parallel*
2. Find the equation of a line that passes through (3, 2) and is parallel to a line whose equation is $y = 7x - 3$. $y = 7x - 19$
3. Find the equation of a line that passes through (4, 7) and is perpendicular to a line whose equation is $y = 2x - 5$. $y = -\frac{1}{2}x + 9$
4. Graph the equations $y = 7x - 8$ and $y = 3x - 12$. State the solution to the system of equations. *(−1, −15)*
5. Graph the equations $y = 3x + 5$ and $y = 3x - 9$. State the solution to the system of equations. *no solutions*
6. Graph the equations $x + y = 13$ and $x - y = 3$. State the solution to the system of equations. *(8, 5)*
7. Solve the system $x + y = 17$ and $x - y = 7$. *(12, 5)*
8. Solve the system $6x + 7y = 19$ and $x + y = 5$. $(16, {}^-11)$
9. Find $\begin{vmatrix} 6 & 3 \\ 4 & 5 \end{vmatrix}$. *18*
10. Find $\begin{vmatrix} 8 & 4 & 7 \\ 2 & {}^-3 & 2 \\ {}^-4 & 6 & 5 \end{vmatrix}$. ${}^-288$
11. Solve the system of equations $4x - 2y = 15$ and $5x + 3y = 7$ using Cramer's rule. $\left(\frac{59}{22}, -\frac{47}{22}\right)$
12. Solve the system of equations $x + 4y = 3$ and $4x + 3y = 7$ using Cramer's rule. $\left(\frac{19}{13}, \frac{5}{13}\right)$
13. Solve the system of equations $x + 2y - 3z = 5$, $x - y + 2z = {}^-3$, and $x + y - z = 2$. $(0, 1, {}^-1)$
14. Solve the system of equations $3x - 2y + z = 5$, $x + y + z = 2$, and $x + 3y - 2z = 4$. $\left(\frac{39}{19}, \frac{7}{19}, -\frac{8}{19}\right)$
15. Solve the system $2x - y + z = 5$, $3x + 2y - z = 4$, and $x + y - 3z = 2$ using augmented matrices. $\left(\frac{35}{17}, -\frac{22}{17}, -\frac{7}{17}\right)$
16. Solve the system $x - 2y + 3z = 4$, $3x + 5y - z = 2$, and $2x - 4y + z = 1$ using augmented matrices. $\left(\frac{29}{55}, \frac{4}{11}, \frac{7}{5}\right)$
17. Solve the system $y \le 5$ and $x > 4$ by graphing.
18. Solve the system $2x + 3y > 4$ and $5x - 3y < 10$ by graphing.
19. Graph the system of inequalities $y \le 3, 5 \le x \le 9$, and $y \ge 0$. Label the vertices of the polygon formed.
20. For problem 19, find the maximum and minimum values of $4x + 3y$. *(9, 3) max; (5, 0) min.*

17.
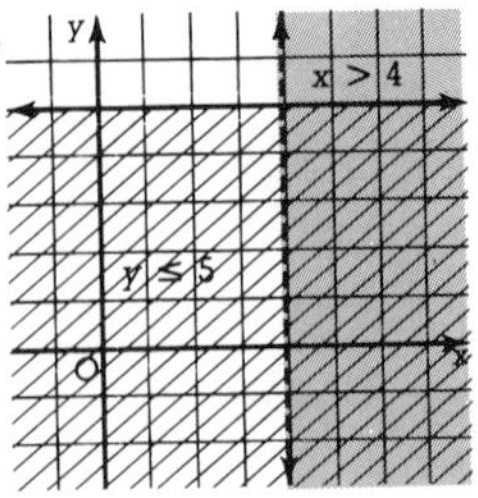

18.
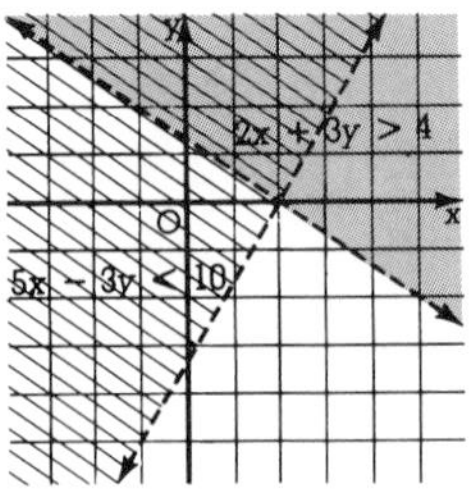

19.
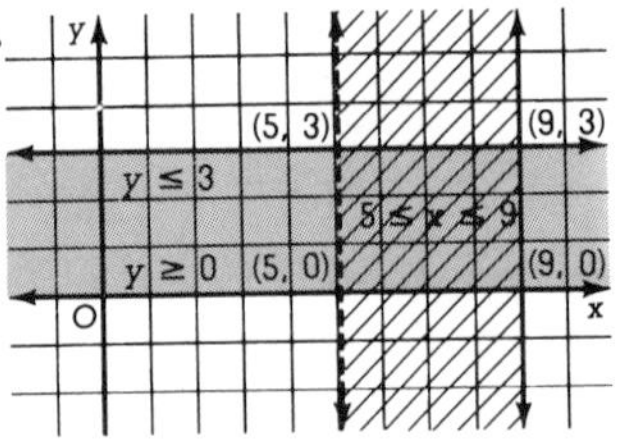

Independent Test for Chapter 4 (answers in italics)

1. Simplify $5c^2 + 2c^2 - 3c^2 + 4c^2$. $8c^2$
2. Simplify $\frac{15m^3}{5m}$. $3m^2$
3. Simplify $(3x)(2x^2y)(2y) + (4x^2y)(3xy)$. $24x^3y^2$
4. Simplify $(4x^2)^3$. $64x^6$
5. Simplify $(5m^6 + 3m^3 + 9m + 5) + (9m^6 - 2m^4 + 3m - 7)$. $14m^6 - 2m^4 + 3m^3 + 12m - 2$
6. Simplify $(3x^2 + 2x - 7) - (2x^2 - 3x - 5)$. $x^2 + 5x - 2$
7. Simplify $(s + 2)(s^2 + 3s + 6)$. $s^3 + 5s^2 + 12s + 12$
8. Simplify $(n + 2)(3n - 5)$. $3n^2 + n - 10$
9. Expand $(m - n)^3$. $m^3 - 3m^2n + 3mn^2 - n^3$
10. Expand $(2a + b)^4$. $16a^4 + 32a^3b + 24a^2b^2 + 8ab^3 + b^4$
11. Factor $n^2 - 144$. $(n + 12)(n - 12)$
12. Factor $m^3 - 64$. $(m - 4)(m^2 + 4m + 16)$
13. Factor $8x^3 + 27y^3$. $(2x + 3y)(4x^2 - 6xy + 9y^2)$
14. Factor $25x^2 - 30xy + 9y^2$. $(5x - 3y)^2$
15. Factor $x^2 - 4x - 45$. $(x + 5)(x - 9)$
16. Factor $6m^2 + 11m - 35$. $(2m + 7)(3m - 5)$
17. Factor $7x^2 - 19x - 6$. $(7x + 2)(x - 3)$
18. Factor $x^3 + 6x^2 + 12x + 8$. $(x + 2)^3$
19. Factor $m^2 + 2mn + n^2 - 4x^2$. $(m + n - 2x)(m + n + 2x)$
20. Factor $x^3 + 3x^2 - 4x - 12$. $(x + 2)(x - 2)(x + 3)$
21. Simplify $\frac{30m^3n^2 - 18m^4n^3}{6m^3n^2}$. $5 - 3mn$
22. Divide $a^3 + 10a^2 + 31a + 30$ by $a + 2$. $a^2 + 8a + 15$
23. Divide $x^3 + 4x^2 + 3x + 9$ by $x^2 + 5$. $x + 4 - \frac{2x + 11}{x^2 + 5}$
24. Use synthetic division to find $(x^3 + 4x^2 - 17x - 60) \div (x + 3)$. $x^2 + x - 20$
25. Use synthetic division to find $(m^3 - 3m^2 - 18m + 40) \div (m + 4)$. $m^2 - 7m + 10$

Independent Test for Chapter 5 (answers in italics)

1. Find $\sqrt{121}$. *11*
2. Find $\sqrt[3]{^-125}$. $^-5$
3. Find $\sqrt{x^2 + 2xy + y^2}$. $|x + y|$
4. Simplify $\sqrt[3]{24a^6b^5}$. $2a^2b\sqrt[3]{3b^2}$
5. Simplify $\sqrt{3}(\sqrt{6} + \sqrt{3})$. $3\sqrt{2} + \sqrt{3}$
6. Simplify $\sqrt{3ab^3} \cdot \sqrt{27a^3b^5}$. $9a^2b^4$
7. Simplify $(5 + \sqrt{6})(4 - \sqrt{6})$. $14 - \sqrt{6}$
8. Simplify $5\sqrt{72} + 12\sqrt{2}$. $42\sqrt{2}$
9. Simplify $(3 + \sqrt{2})(3 - \sqrt{2})$. *7*
10. Simplify $\frac{6}{5 + \sqrt{3}}$. $\frac{15 - 3\sqrt{3}}{11}$
11. Simplify $\frac{\sqrt[3]{81}}{\sqrt[3]{3}}$. *3*
12. Simplify $\sqrt[3]{\frac{2}{5}}$. $\frac{\sqrt[3]{50}}{5}$
13. Solve $\sqrt{x} - 9 = 0$. $x = 81$
14. Solve $\sqrt{x + 7} = 13$. $x = 162$
15. Solve $\sqrt[3]{y + 7} = 4$. $y = 57$
16. Simplify $3i + 7i - 4i$. $6i$
17. Simplify $(5\sqrt{^-3})(4\sqrt{^-12})$. $^-120$
18. Simplify $\sqrt{^-64} + \sqrt{^-121}$. $19i$
19. Simplify $(7 - 12i) + (15 - 7i)$. $22 - 19i$
20. Simplify $(12 - 7i) - (15 + 3i)$. $^-3 - 10i$
21. Simplify $(5 + 2i)(5 - 2i)$. *29*
22. Simplify $\frac{32}{\sqrt{7} + 3i}$. $2\sqrt{7} - 6i$
23. Simplify $\frac{3}{4 + 7i}$. $\frac{12 - 21i}{65}$
24. Find the additive inverse of $3 - 4i$. $^-3 + 4i$
25. Find the additive inverse of $^-5 - 7i$. $5 + 7i$

Independent Test for Chapter 6 (answers in italics)

1. Solve $2x^2 - 7x - 15 = 0$. *$5, -\frac{3}{2}$*
2. Solve $x^2 + 6x + 9 = 0$. *$^-3$*
3. Solve $6x^2 + 11x - 35 = 0$. *$\frac{5}{3}, -\frac{7}{2}$*
4. Solve $x^2 = 6x$. *$0, 6$*
5. Solve $x^2 - 14x + 46 = 0$ by completing the square. *$x = 7 \pm \sqrt{3}$*
6. Solve $x^2 + 6x - 7 = 0$ by completing the square. *$x = {}^-7, 1$*
7. Solve $m^2 + 12m + 5 = 0$ by completing the square. *$m = {}^-6 \pm \sqrt{31}$*
8. Solve $3t^2 - 5t + 7 = 0$ using the quadratic formula. *$\dfrac{5 \pm i\sqrt{59}}{6}$*
9. Solve $7x^2 + 3x + 9 = 0$ using the quadratic formula. *$\dfrac{^-3 \pm 9i\sqrt{3}}{14}$*
10. Solve $6m^2 - m - 35 = 0$ using the quadratic formula. *$\frac{5}{2}, -\frac{7}{3}$*
11. Solve $3x^2 + 8x + 5 = 0$. *$-\frac{5}{3}, {}^-1$*
12. Solve $t^2 + 6t + 9 = 0$. *$^-3$*
13. Solve $5x^2 - 7x + 2 = 0$. *$1, \frac{2}{5}$*
14. Find the quadratic equation for which the sum of the solutions is $^-7$ and their product is 12. *$x^2 + 7x + 12 = 0$*
15. Find the quadratic equation for which the sum of the solutions is $\dfrac{5}{2}$ and their product is $\dfrac{9}{2}$. *$2x^2 - 5x + 9 = 0$*
16. Find the quadratic equation that has solutions $3 + 2i$ and $3 - 2i$. *$x^2 - 6x + 13 = 0$*
17. Find two consecutive integers whose product is 506. *22, 23 or $^-22, {}^-23$*
18. Four times the square of a number equals 28 times the number. Find the number. *0, 7*
19. Solve $x^4 - 34x^2 + 225 = 0$. *$5, {}^-5, 3, {}^-3$*
20. Solve $x^4 - 68x^2 + 256 = 0$. *$8, {}^-8, 2, {}^-2$*

Independent Test for Chapter 7 (answers in italics)

1. Write $f(x) = (x - 5)^2$ in quadratic form. *$f(x) = x^2 - 10x + 25$*
2. Write $f(x) = 4(x + 2)^2$ in quadratic form. *$f(x) = 4x^2 + 16x + 16$*
3. Write $f(x) = \frac{1}{3}(3x - 9)^2$ in quadratic form. *$f(x) = 3x^2 - 18x + 27$*
4. Write a quadratic equation to describe the product of two numbers whose difference is 23. *$P = n^2 + 23n$*
5. Graph $y = x^2$, $y = 2x^2$, and $y = 4x^2$ on the same set of axes.
6. State the vertex, axis of symmetry, and direction of opening for the graph of $f(x) = 5x^2$. *(0, 0); $x = 0$; up*
7. For (3, 27) determine a value of a such that the point is on the graph of $f(x) = ax^2$. *$a = 3$*
8. Write $f(x) = 4x^2 + 24x + 36$ in the form $f(x) = a(x - h)^2$. *$f(x) = 4(x - {}^-3)^2$*
9. Graph $f(x) = 5x^2$ and $g(x) = 5(x + 2)^2$ on the same set of axes.
10. Name the vertex, axis of symmetry, and direction of opening for the graph of $f(x) = {}^-3(x + 2)^2$. *($^-2$, 0); $x = {}^-2$; down*
11. Graph $f(x) = 5(x - 3)^2 + 1$. **12.** Graph $f(x) = 2x^2 + 4x - 6$. **13.** Graph $f(x) = \frac{1}{2}(x + 2)^2 - 4$.
14. Find two numbers whose difference is 6 and whose product is a minimum. *3, $^-3$*
15. Find two numbers whose sum is 36 and whose product is a maximum. *18, 18*
16. Graph $y < x^2 + 10x + 25$. **17.** Graph $y > x^2 - 6x + 11$. **18.** Graph $y \le x^2 - 8x + 4$.
19. Solve $x^2 + 3x - 10 \le 0$. *$\{x \mid {}^-5 \le x \le 2\}$* **20.** Solve $x^2 - x \ge 12$. *$\{x \mid x \ge 4 \text{ or } x \le {}^-3\}$*

5.
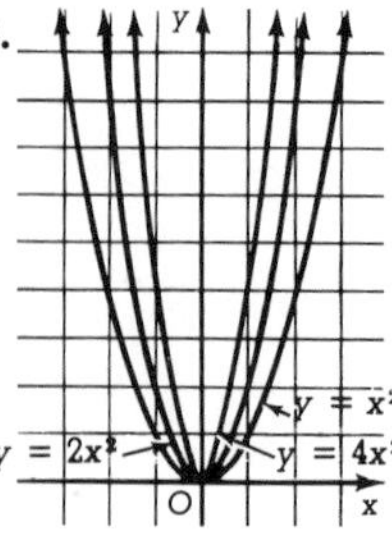

9.
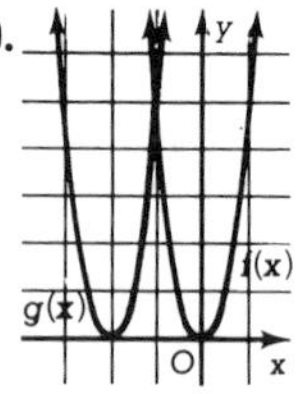

11.
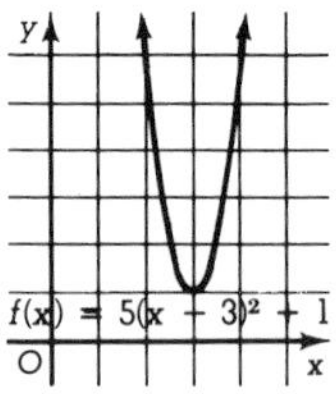

12.
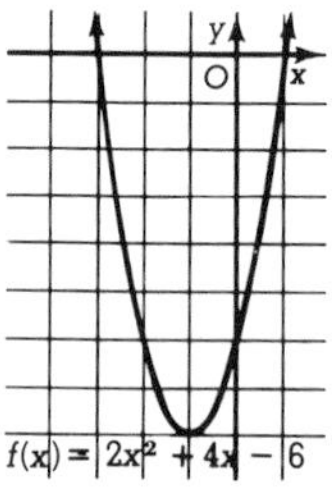

13.
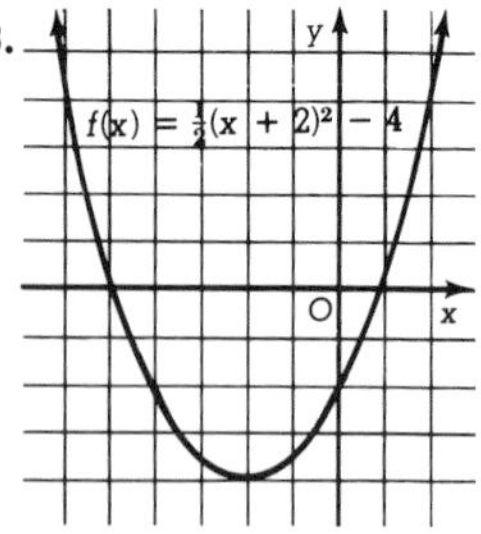

16.
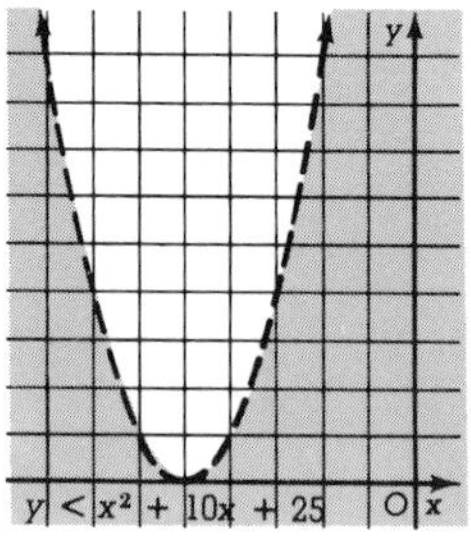

17.
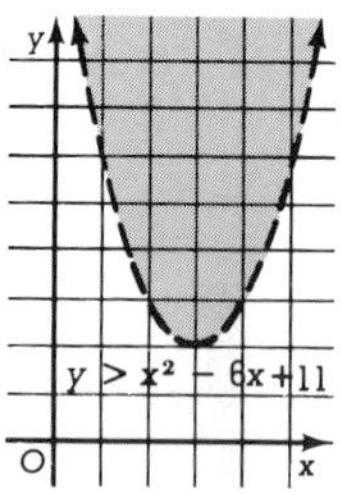

18.
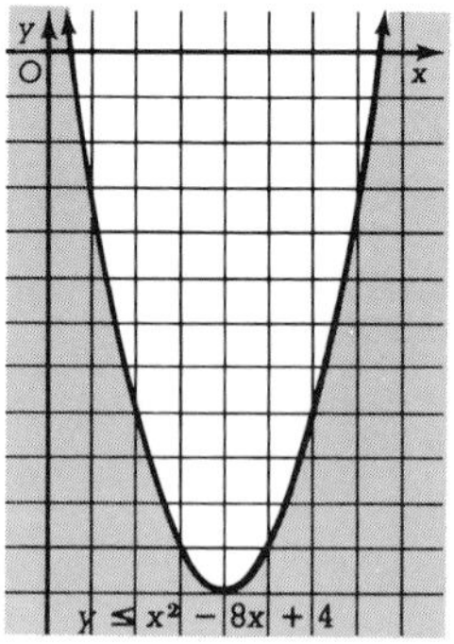

Independent Test for Chapter 8 (answers in italics)

1. Use the distance formula to find the distance between (4, 6) and (2, 10). *$2\sqrt{5}$*
2. Use the distance formula to find the distance between ($^-2$, 5) and (6, 11). *10*
3. Name the vertex for the parabola with equation $y = 3x^2 - 12x + 6$. *(2, $^-6$)*
4. Name the axis of symmetry for the parabola with equation $y = 3x^2 - 12x + 16$. *$x = 2$*
5. Name the focus and direction of opening for the parabola with equation $y = 2x^2 + 28x + 90$. *($^-7$, $^-7\frac{7}{8}$); up*
6. State the center of the circle with equation $x^2 + y^2 - 10x + 6y = 47$. *(5, $^-3$)*
7. State the radius of the circle with equation $x^2 + y^2 - 10x + 6y = 47$. *9*
8. State the center and foci for the ellipse with equation $\frac{x^2}{16} + \frac{y^2}{25} = 1$. *(0, 0); (0, $^\pm3$)*
9. State the intercepts for the ellipse with equation $\frac{x^2}{81} + \frac{y^2}{36} = 1$. *($^\pm9$, 0), (0, $^\pm6$)*
10. State the center and foci for the ellipse with equation $\frac{(x-3)^2}{25} + \frac{(y-2)^2}{16} = 1$.

    (3, 2); (6, 2), (0, 2)
11. State the intercepts of the hyperbola with equation $\frac{x^2}{25} - \frac{y^2}{9} = 1$. *(5, 0), ($^-5$, 0)*
12. State the foci of the hyperbola with equation $\frac{y^2}{144} - \frac{x^2}{100} = 1$. *(0, $2\sqrt{61}$), (0, $^-2\sqrt{61}$)*
13. State the equations of the asymptotes of the hyperbola with equation $\frac{x^2}{64} - \frac{y^2}{36} = 1$. *$y = \pm\frac{3}{4}x$*
14. Which conic section is represented by $\frac{x^2}{15} + \frac{y^2}{12} = 1$? *ellipse*
15. Which conic section is represented by $x^2 + y^2 = 81$? *circle*
16. Which conic section is represented by $y^2 - y + 9 = x$? *parabola*
17. Graph the system $y = {}^-x^2$, $y = x$. State the solution. *(0, 0), ($^-1$, $^-1$)*
18. State the solutions of the system $2x^2 + y^2 = 36$ and $y = 2x$. *($\sqrt{6}$, $2\sqrt{6}$), ($^-\sqrt{6}$, $^-2\sqrt{6}$)*
19. State the solutions of the system $x^2 + y^2 = 9$ and $x^2 + y^2 = 4$. *no solutions*
20. Graph the solutions of $x^2 + y^2 \le 9$ and $y = x$.

17.
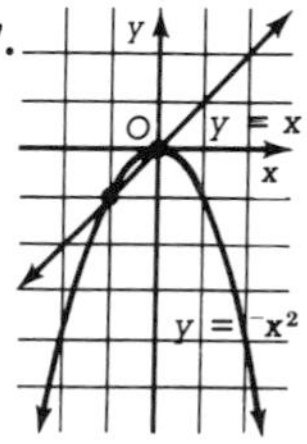

20.
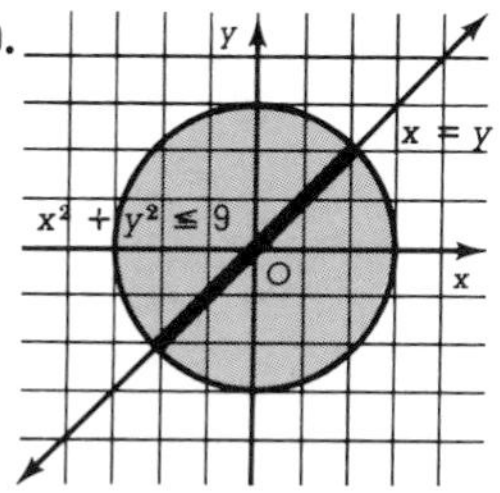

Independent Semester Test for Chapters 1–8 (answers in italics)

1. Evaluate $\dfrac{4a^2 - 3b}{2c^2}$ if $a = 2$, $b = 3$, $c = 1$. *$\frac{7}{2}$*
2. State the property shown by $3(x - 6) = 3x - 18$. *distributive*
3. Solve $6x + 3 = 3x + 21$. *$x = 6$*
4. Solve $5|x - 2| = 45$. *$x = 11, {}^-7$*
5. Solve $4t - 7 > 33$. *$t > 10$*
6. Solve $4|x - 3| \leq 16$. *${}^-1 \leq x \leq 7$*
7. Graph $|x - 5| < 8$ on the real number line.

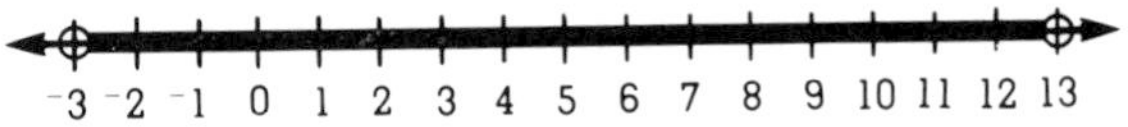

8. Find $f({}^-1)$ if $f(x) = 6x^2 + x - 5$. *0*
9. Graph $y = 7x + 3$.
10. Determine the slope of a line that passes through (13, 7) and (8, 2). *1*
11. Find the slope and the y-intercept of $3y - 9x = 24$. *3; 8*
12. Graph the function $g(x) = {}^-3|x| + 5$.
13. State whether the graphs of $y = 5x - 4$ and $y = 5x + 7$ are parallel, perpendicular, or neither. *parallel*
14. Graph the equations $x + y = {}^-5$ and $x - y = 5$. State the solution to the system of equations. *$(0, {}^-5)$*
15. Solve the system $2x + 3y = 14$ and $4x - 3y = 4$. *$(3, \frac{8}{3})$*
16. Find the determinant $\begin{vmatrix} 7 & 5 \\ 3 & 4 \end{vmatrix}$. *13*
17. Solve the system of equations $5x + 2y = 8$ and $3x - y = 4$ using Cramer's rule. *$(\frac{16}{11}, \frac{4}{11})$*
18. Solve the system $x + y - z = 5$, $2x + 3y - z = 7$, and $x - 2y + 3z = 2$ using Cramer's rule. *$(\frac{32}{7}, -\frac{9}{7}, -\frac{12}{7})$*
19. Solve the system $x + y < 4$ and $x > 3$ by graphing.
20. Simplify $(2x^4)^4$. *$16x^{16}$*
21. Simplify $(3x^4 + 5x^3 - 2x^2 - x + 7) + (5x^4 - 7x^3 - 3x^2 + x - 9)$. *$8x^4 - 2x^3 - 5x^2 - 2$*
22. Expand $(x + y)^3$. *$x^3 + 3x^2y + 3xy^2 + y^3$*
23. Factor $m^3 - 8$. *$(m - 2)(m^2 + 2m + 4)$*
24. Factor $x^2 - 3x - 54$. *$(x + 6)(x - 9)$*
25. Factor $x^3 + 9x^2 + 27x + 27$. *$(x + 3)^3$*

9.
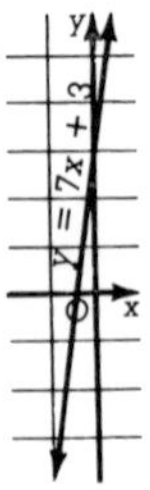

12.
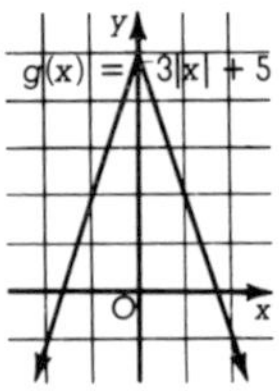

14.
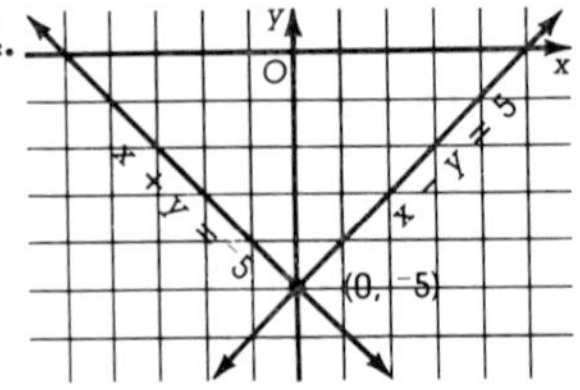

19.
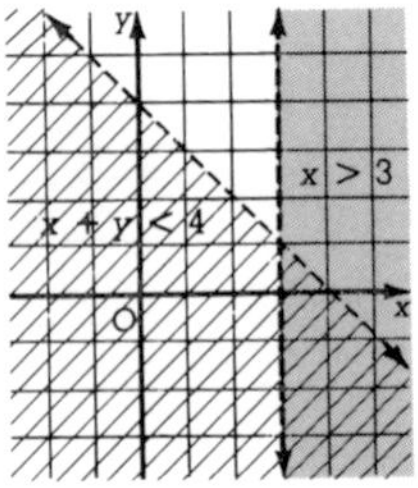

26. Simplify $\dfrac{24a^4b^5 - 36a^3b^2}{6a^2b^2}$. $4a^2b^3 - 6a$

27. Find $\sqrt[3]{^{-}64}$. $^{-}4$

28. Simplify $\sqrt{48a^5b^3}$. $4a^2b\sqrt{3ab}$

29. Simplify $4\sqrt{50} + 6\sqrt{2}$. $26\sqrt{2}$

30. Solve $\sqrt{x} - 3 = 0$. 9

31. Simplify $(3\sqrt{^{-}8})(4\sqrt{^{-}2})$. $^{-}48$

32. Simplify $(4 + 3i)(4 - 3i)$. 25

33. Solve $x^2 + 8x + 15 = 0$. $x = {}^{-}5, {}^{-}3$

34. Solve $x^2 - 4x - 45 = 0$. $x = 9, {}^{-}5$

35. Solve $x^2 - 3x + 5 = 0$ using the quadratic formula. $x = \dfrac{3 \pm i\sqrt{11}}{2}$

36. Solve $6m^2 - m - 35 = 0$. $m = \frac{5}{2}, -\frac{7}{3}$

37. Find the quadratic equation for which the sum of the solutions is 7 and the product is 12. $x^2 - 7x + 12 = 0$

38. Solve $x^4 - 40x^2 + 144 = 0$. $x = 6, {}^{-}6, {}^{-}2, 2$

39. Write $f(x) = 3(x + 4)^2$ in quadratic form. $f(x) = 3x^2 + 24x + 48$

40. For (4, 80) determine a value of a such that the point is on the graph of $f(x) = ax^2$. $a = 5$

41. Write $f(x) = 2x^2 + 20x + 50$ in the form $f(x) = a(x - h)^2$. $f(x) = 2[x - ({}^{-}5)]^2$

42. Graph $y = x^2 + 2x - 3$.

43. Use the distance formula to find the distance between (9, 9) and (3, 1). *10*

44. Name the vertex and axis of symmetry for the parabola with equation $y = 3x^2 - 12x + 17$. $(2, 5);\ x = 2$

45. Name the focus and direction of opening for the parabola with equation $y = 3x^2 - 12x + 17$. $(2, \frac{61}{12})$; *up*

46. State the center and radius of the circle with equation $x^2 - 4x + y^2 - 6y = 23$. $(2, 3); 6$

47. State the center of the hyperbola with equation $\dfrac{x^2}{4} - \dfrac{y^2}{1} = 1$. $(0, 0)$

48. State the foci of the hyperbola with equation $\dfrac{x^2}{4} - \dfrac{y^2}{1} = 1$. $(\pm\sqrt{5}, 0)$

49. Which conic section is represented by $x^2 + y^2 = 64$? *circle*

50. Graph the solutions of $x^2 + y^2 > 16$ and $y = x + 1$.

42.

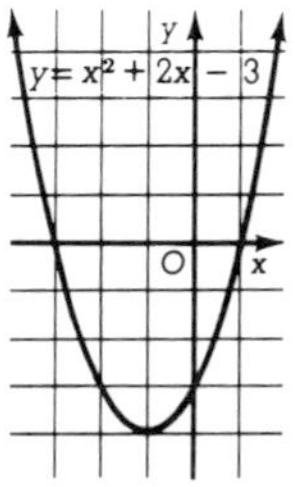

50.

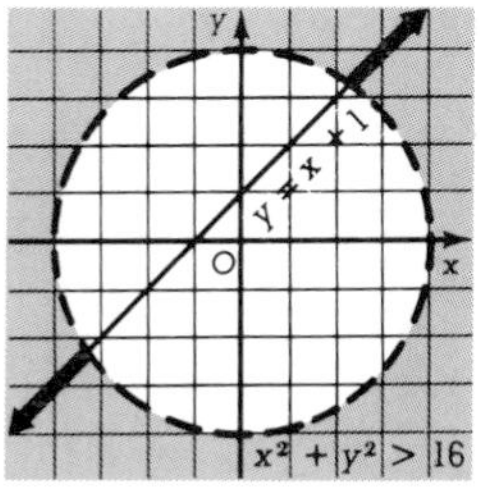

Independent Test for Chapter 9 (answers in italics)

1. Is $x^2 + 3x + 5$ a polynomial in one variable? *yes*
2. Is $3x^2 + 6xy + 5y$ a polynomial in one variable? *no*
3. Find $p(3)$ for $p(x) = {}^-3x^2 + 8$. *$^-19$*
4. Find $p(^-1)$ for $p(x) = 4x^4 + 5x^2 + 3x - 9$. *$^-3$*
5. Divide $4x^3 + 3x^2 + 6x - 7$ by $x - 5$. *$(4x^2 + 23x + 121) + \frac{598}{5}$*
6. Find the remainder for $(x^3 + 3x^2 - 6x + 5) \div (x - 2)$. *13*
7. Find the remainder for $(3x^4 + 2x^2 + 6) \div (x - 1)$. *11*
8. Factor $x^3 - 2x^2 - 5x + 6$. *$(x - 1)(x + 2)(x - 3)$*
9. Find all rational zeros for $f(x) = (x - 5)(x + 6)(3x + 7)$. *$5, {}^-6, -\frac{7}{3}$*
10. Find all rational zeros for $f(x) = 6x^3 - 29x^2 + 23x + 30$. *$-\frac{2}{3}, \frac{5}{2}, 3$*
11. Find all rational zeros for $f(x) = 2x^3 + 7x^2 - 42x - 72$. *$-\frac{3}{2}, 4, {}^-6$*
12. State the number of positive real zeros for $f(x) = 3x^2 - x + 2$. *2 or 0*
13. State the number of negative real zeros for $f(x) = 4x^4 + 3x^3 - 6x^2 + 6x - 9$. *1*
14. State the number of positive real zeros, negative real zeros, imaginary zeros for $f(x) = 16x^3 + 6x^2 - 7x + 3$. *2 or 0; 1; 0 or 2*
15. Approximate to the nearest tenth the real zeros of $f(x) = x^2 + x - 8$. *$2.4, {}^-3.4$*
16. Approximate to the nearest tenth the real zeros of $f(x) = 2x^2 - 10x + 11$. *3.4, 1.6*
17. Graph $f(x) = \frac{1}{2}x^3$.
18. Graph $f(x) = {}^-x^3 + x$.
19. Graph $f(x) = (x + 1)^2(x - 3)$.
20. If $f(x) = 3x + 5$ and $g(x) = x - 1$, find $[f \circ g](2)$. *8*
21. If $f(x) = 5x + 7$ and $g(x) = 2x^2 - 3$, find $[f \circ g](x)$. *$10x^2 - 8$*
22. If $f(x) = 2x^2 + 3$ and $g(x) = 3x + 5$, find $[f \circ g](x)$. *$18x^2 + 60x + 53$*
23. Is the inverse of $g(x) = \frac{x + 6}{5}$ a function? *yes*
24. Write the equation for the inverse of $f(x) = \frac{x + 2}{7}$. *$g(x) = 7x - 2$*
25. Write the equation for the inverse of $f(x) = x^2 - 5$. *$g(x) = \pm\sqrt{x + 5}$*

17.
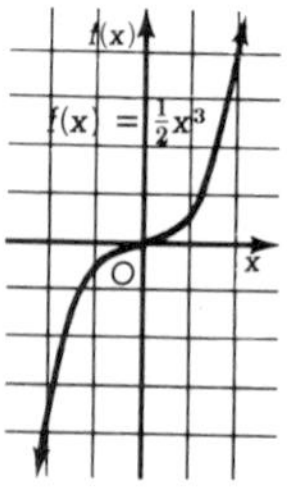

18.
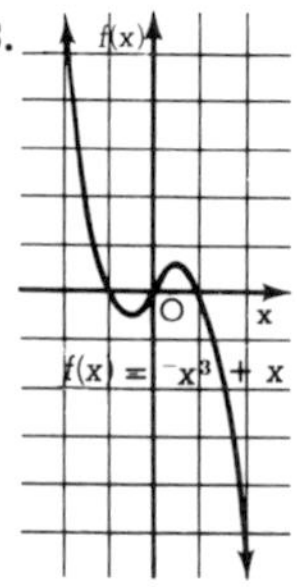

19.
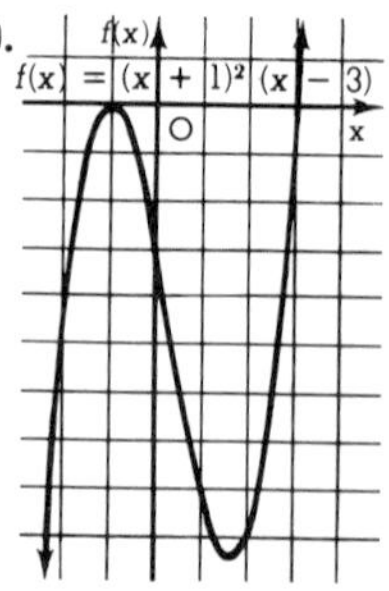

Independent Test for Chapter 10 (answers in italics)

For problems 1–18 write your answers in simplest form.

1. Find the product of $\frac{4}{10} \cdot \frac{5}{2}$. *1*
2. Find the product of $\frac{2}{3} \cdot \frac{15}{16}$. $\frac{5}{8}$
3. Find the product of $\frac{7xy}{3x} \cdot \frac{15x^2y}{21x^2y^3}$. $\frac{5}{3y}$
4. Find the product of $\frac{x^2 + 9x + 20}{x^2 + 6x + 9} \cdot \frac{x + 3}{x + 4}$. $\frac{x + 5}{x + 3}$
5. Find the product of $\frac{5n^2 - n}{n + 1} \cdot \frac{n + 1}{3n}$. $\frac{5n - 1}{3}$
6. Find the quotient of $\frac{x + 3}{12} \div \frac{x + 3}{3}$. $\frac{1}{4}$
7. Find the quotient of $\frac{14a}{17b^2} \div \frac{42a}{34b}$. $\frac{2}{3b}$
8. Find the quotient of $\frac{24xy}{15ab} \div \frac{4x^2y}{3a^2b}$. $\frac{6a}{5x}$
9. Find the quotient of $\frac{x^3}{x^2 - 64} \div \frac{x^2}{x + 8}$. $\frac{x}{x - 8}$
10. Find the sum of $\frac{3}{5} + \frac{4}{7x}$. $\frac{21x + 20}{35x}$
11. Find the sum of $\frac{4}{3x} + \frac{5}{2x}$. $\frac{23}{6x}$
12. Find the sum of $\frac{6}{x^2 - 4} + \frac{2}{x - 2}$. $\frac{2x + 10}{x^2 - 4}$
13. Find the difference of $\frac{5x}{x^2 - 25} - \frac{2}{x - 5}$. $\frac{3x - 10}{x^2 - 25}$
14. Solve and check $\frac{11}{x - 5} = \frac{x + 3}{x - 5}$. $x = 8$
15. Solve and check $x + 4 = \frac{21}{x}$. $x = {}^{-}7, 3$
16. Solve and check $\frac{x - 5}{3x} = \frac{x + 4}{3x + 1}$. $x = -\frac{5}{26}$
17. Solve and check $\frac{7}{x + 4} = \frac{3}{x - 5}$. $x = \frac{47}{4}$
18. Solve and check $\frac{3}{x - 3} = \frac{x + 2}{x - 3}$. $x = 1$
19. A plane travels at a rate of 400 mph in calm air. It travels 700 miles against a headwind in the same time it could have traveled 900 miles with the wind. What is the rate of the wind? *50 mph*
20. The ratio of 5 less than a number to 4 more than a number is 1 to 4. What is the number? *8*
21. If y varies directly with x and $y = 2$ when $x = 3$, find y when $x = 12$. *8*
22. If y varies directly with x and $y = 5$ when $x = 7$, find y when $x = 35$. *25*
23. If y varies inversely with x and $y = 1$ when $x = 5$, find y when $x = 10$. $\frac{1}{2}$
24. If y varies inversely with x and $y = 3$ when $x = 2$, find y when $x = 1$. *6*
25. If it costs \$3.50 to have 36 photographic slides developed, how much will it cost to have 180 slides developed? *\$17.50*

Independent Test for Chapter 11 (answers in italics)

1. Simplify $\left(\frac{t}{2}\right)^{-3}$. $\mathit{\frac{8}{t^3}}$
2. Simplify $\frac{x^3}{x^5}$. $\mathit{\frac{1}{x^2}}$
3. Simplify $\frac{y^3}{y^{-2}}$. $\mathit{y^5}$
4. Evaluate $\frac{9^0}{4^2}$. $\mathit{\frac{1}{16}}$
5. Evaluate $\left(\frac{5}{2}\right)^{-4}$. $\mathit{\frac{16}{625}}$
6. Express 862,000 in scientific notation. *8.62* $\times$ *10*^{5}
7. Express 0.00012 in scientific notation. *1.2* $\times$ *10*$^{-4}$
8. Express 4.1×10^{-6} in decimal notation. *0.0000041*
9. Evaluate $(1.8 \times 10^6)(4 \times 10^9)$. Express the answer in scientific notation. *7.2* $\times$ *10*^{15}
10. Evaluate $\frac{7.8 \times 10^{-3}}{2.3 \times 10^{-5}}$. Express the answer in scientific notation. *3.4* $\times$ *10*^{2}
11. Express $\sqrt[4]{x^3}$ using exponents. $\mathit{x^{\frac{3}{4}}}$
12. Express $\sqrt[5]{32st^3}$ using exponents. $\mathit{2s^{\frac{1}{5}}t^{\frac{3}{5}}}$
13. Express $a^{\frac{2}{5}}b^{\frac{3}{5}}$ using radicals. $\mathit{\sqrt[5]{a^2b^3}}$
14. Evaluate $\left(\frac{9}{16}\right)^{\frac{1}{2}}$. $\mathit{\frac{3}{4}}$
15. Evaluate $(27)^{\frac{2}{3}}$. *9*
16. Simplify $t^{-\frac{3}{4}}$. $\mathit{\frac{t^{\frac{1}{4}}}{t}}$
17. Simplify $\frac{ab}{b^{\frac{1}{3}}}$. $\mathit{ab^{\frac{2}{3}}}$
18. Simplify $\frac{1 - x}{x^{\frac{1}{3}}}$. $\mathit{\frac{x^{\frac{2}{3}} - x^{\frac{5}{3}}}{x}}$
19. Simplify $\frac{x - y}{x^{\frac{1}{2}} + y^{\frac{1}{2}}}$. $\mathit{x^{\frac{1}{2}} - y^{\frac{1}{2}}}$
20. Evaluate $\left(\frac{1}{64}\right)^{-\frac{2}{3}}$. *16*
21. Solve $y^{\frac{4}{3}} = 16$. *8*
22. Solve $x^{-2} - 4 = 0$. $\pm\frac{1}{2}$
23. Solve $x^{\frac{1}{2}} - 5x^{\frac{1}{4}} + 6 = 0$. *16, 81*
24. Solve $\sqrt[3]{x - 2} = 4$. *66*
25. Solve $x + \sqrt{10 - 2x} = 5$. *3, 5*

Independent Test for Chapter 12 (answers in italics)

For this test, students will need access to a table of common logarithms of numbers.

1. Rewrite $7^3 = 343$ in logarithmic form. *$\log_7 343 = 3$*
2. Rewrite $\log_8 4096 = 4$ in exponential form. *$8^4 = 4096$*
3. Evaluate $\log_{16} 4$. *$\frac{1}{2}$*
4. Solve $\log_x 9 = 1$. *9*
5. Solve $\log_8 y = 3$. *512*
6. Evaluate $5^{\log_5 3}$. *3*
7. Evaluate $\log_7 7^6$. *6*
8. Solve $\log_6 (5 - 3a) = \log_6 (a^2 - 5)$. *$^-5$, 2*
9. If $\log_5 6 = 1.1133$ and $\log_5 2 = 0.4306$, evaluate $\log_5 12$. *1.5439*
10. If $\log_5 6 = 1.1133$ and $\log_5 2 = 0.4306$, evaluate $\log_5 3$. *0.6827*
11. If $\log_5 2 = 0.4306$, evaluate $\log_5 8$. *1.2918*
12. Solve $\log_3 (x + 3) + \log_3 (x - 2) = \log_3 14$. *$^-5$, 4*
13. Solve $\log_2 (2x + 6) - \log_2 x = 3$. *1*
14. Use a table to find log 3060. *3.4857*
15. Use a table to find antilog (0.4713 − 5). *0.0000296*
16. Interpolate to find log 0.05986. *0.7771 − 2*
17. Interpolate to find antilog 2.8940. *783.4*
18. Use logarithms to evaluate $(23.6)^6$. *172,800,000*
19. Use logarithms to evaluate $\sqrt[4]{111}$. *3.246*
20. Use logarithms to evaluate $\sqrt[5]{45(2.03)^{10}}$. *8.822*
21. Evalute $\log_7 44$. *1.9447*
22. Solve $4^x = 28$. *2.4036*
23. Solve $2^y = 5^{y-2}$. *3.5129*
24. Assume $150 is deposited in a saving account. The interest rate is 6.5% compounded continuously. When will the money be triple the original amount? ($A = Pe^{rt}$, $e = 2.718$, and $\log e = 0.4343$) *16.9 years*
25. In 5 years, radioactivity reduces the mass of a 100-gram sample of an element to 80 grams. Find the constant k for this element. ($y = Ne^{kt}$, $e = 2.718$, and $\log e = 0.4343$) *$^-0.0446$*

Independent Test for Chapter 13 (answers in italics)

1. Find the first five terms of the arithmetic sequence where $a_1 = 11$ and $d = 3.5$. *11, 14.5, 18, 21.5, 25*
2. Find the 31st term of the arithmetic sequence where $a = 6$ and $d = 7$. *216*
3. Find a_{25} for the arithmetic sequence $^-2$, 4, 10, ... *142*
4. Find the missing terms for the arithmetic sequence $^-8$, ___, ___, ___, 12. *$^-3$, 2, 7*
5. Evaluate $\sum_{k=1}^{4} (3k^2 + 1)$. *94*
6. Evaluate $\sum_{x=3}^{7} (2x - 4)$ 30
7. Find the sum of the arithmetic series where $a_1 = 5$, $a_n = 104$, and $n = 34$. *1853*
8. Find the sum of the arithmetic series where $a_1 = 7$, $d = 11$, and $n = 20$. *2230*
9. Find the sum of the arithmetic series $11 + 15 + 19 + \cdots + 103$. *1368*
10. Find the common ratio of the geometric sequence $\frac{2}{5}, \frac{6}{5}, \frac{18}{5}, \frac{54}{5}, \ldots$. *3*
11. Find the first four terms of the geometric sequence where $a_1 = 3$ and $r = {}^-3$. *3, $^-9$, 27, $^-81$*
12. Find the fifth term of the geometric sequence where $a_1 = 40$ and $r = \frac{1}{2}$. $\frac{5}{2}$
13. Find the geometric means of 4, ___, ___, 108. *12, 36*
14. Find the sum of the geometric series where $a_1 = 7$, $r = 2$, and $n = 5$. *217*
15. Find the sum of the geometric series where $a_1 = 256$, $a_n = 81$, and $r = \frac{3}{4}$. *781*
16. Find the sum of the geometric series $16 + 8 + 4 + \cdots$ to 6 terms. $31\frac{1}{2}$
17. Find the sum of the infinite geometric series where $a_1 = 9$ and $r = \frac{2}{3}$. *27*
18. Find a common fraction equivalent to the repeating decimal $0.\overline{41}$. $\frac{41}{99}$
19. Complete the sequence 4, 4, 8, 12, 20, 32, ___, ___, ___. *52, 84, 136*
20. Find the first four terms of the sequence where $a_1 = 3$, $a_2 = 10$, and $a_{n+2} = a_{n+1} + 2a_n$. *3, 10, 16, 36*
21. Describe the sequence 3, 12, 48, 192, . . . recursively. $a_{n+1} = 4a_n$, $a_1 = 3$
22. Describe the sequence 4, 8, 12, 16, . . . in terms of n. $a_n = 4n$
23. Write $\frac{1}{2} + \frac{2}{3} + \frac{3}{4} + \frac{4}{5} + \cdots + \frac{19}{20}$ in summation notation. $\sum_{k=1}^{19} \frac{k}{k+1}$
24. Evaluate $\frac{7!}{4!}$ 210
25. Write $\frac{(k+5)!}{(k+3)!}$ in expanded form and simplify. $(k + 5)(k + 4)$

Independent Test for Chapter 14 (answers in italics)

1. A company manufactures bicycles in 8 different styles. Each style comes in 7 different colors. How many different bicycles does the company make? *56*
2. Evaluate $P(9, 4)$). *3025*
3. Evaluate $P(7, 7)$. *5040*
4. How many ways can 6 children form a line to use the drinking fountain? *720*
5. How many ways can 4 people be seated in a row of 6 chairs? *360*
6. How many ways can the letters from SIEVE be arranged? *60*
7. How many ways can 5 children form a circle? *24*
8. How many ways can 7 people be seated at a circular table? *720*
9. How many ways can 6 keys be placed on a keyring? *60*
10. How many ways can 7 charms be placed on a bracelet with a clasp? *2520*
11. Evaluate C(12, 4). *495*
12. Evaluate C(6, 5). *6*
13. How many different groups of 3 people can be formed from a group of 8 people? C(8, 3) or 56
14. Five cheerleaders will be chosen from a group of 15 students. How many different cheerleading squads can be formed? *3003*
15. There are 6 men and 7 women in a group. How many ways can 5 people be selected so that 2 are men and 3 are women? C(6, 2) · C(7, 3) or 525
16. The odds of an event occurring are 4 to 7. What is the probability that the event will occur? $\frac{4}{11}$
17. The probability of an event occurring is $\frac{2}{25}$. What are the odds that it will occur? *2 to 23*
18. There are 6 blue marbles and 5 red marbles in a bag. One marble is chosen at random. What is the probability that it is red? $\frac{5}{11}$
19. From a standard deck of 52 cards, 2 cards are picked at random. What is the probability that both are face cards (king, queen, or jack) if no replacement occurs? $\frac{11}{221}$
20. A red die and a blue die are tossed. What is the probability that the red die will show a 6 and the blue die will show an even number: $\frac{1}{12}$

Independent Test for Chapter 15 (answers in italics)

1. Thirty students took a test with 25 questions. The following list gives the number of questions each student answered correctly.

23	19	25	21	19	20
18	13	19	18	17	23
23	20	21	20	19	16
19	22	25	18	19	20
16	20	21	23	22	18

Use the data to make a table with headings ***Number of Correct Answers*** and ***Frequency.***

1\.

Number of Correct Answers	12	13	14	15	16	17	18	19	20	21	22	23	24	25
Frequency	1	1	0	0	2	1	4	6	5	3	4	5	0	2

2. How many students in problem 1 answered exactly 20 questions correctly? *5*
3. How many students in problem 1 answered at least 18 questions correctly? *25*
4. Draw a bar graph to show the frequency distribution of the number of correct answers in problem 1.

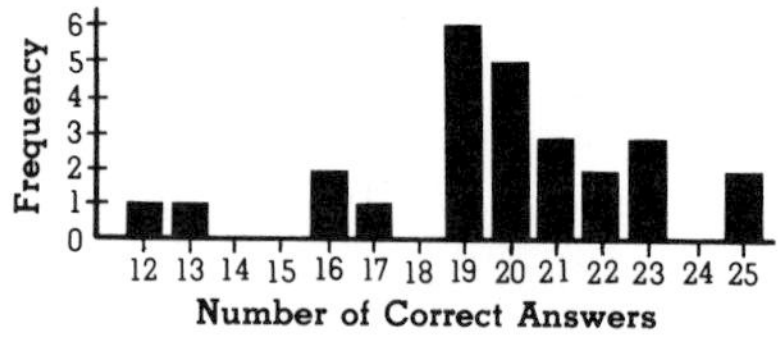

5. Find the median of the distribution in problem 1. *19.5*
6. Find the mode of the distribution in problem 1. *19*
7. Find the mean of the distribution in problem 1. *19.53*
8. Find the range of the distribution in problem 1. *13*
9. Find the standard deviation of {5, 3, 3, 2, 2}. about 1.1
10. The yearly incomes of 12,000 workers are distributed normally. Suppose the mean yearly income is $12,000 and the standard deviation is $2500. What percent of the incomes are above $14,500? *16%*
11. How many of the workers in problem 10 make between $7000 and $17,000? *11,400*
12. According to a certain prediction equation, the average baby who is 3 months old weighs 11 pounds. The average baby who is 8 months old weighs 17 pounds. Let x stand for the age in months and y stand for the weight in pounds. Find the slope of the prediction equation. *1.2*
13. Find the y-intercept of the prediction equation discussed in problem 12. *7.4*
14. Find the prediction equation discussed in problem 12. $y = 1.2x + 7.4$
15. Use the equation in problem 14 to predict the weight of the average baby who is 5 months old. *13.4*

Independent Test for Chapter 16 (answers in italics)

1. Change 120° to radian measure. $(2\pi)/3$
2. Change $^{-}15°$ to radian measure. $^{-}\pi/12$
3. Change $-\frac{1}{8}\pi$ to degree measure. $^{-}22\frac{1}{2}°$
4. Find the smallest positive angle that is coterminal with 960°. *240°*
5. Find the smallest positive angle that is coterminal with $^{-}555°$. *165°*
6. Evaluate cos 315°. $\sqrt{2}/2$
7. Evaluate $\sin\frac{5}{3}\pi$. $^{-}\sqrt{3}/2$
8. What is the amplitude of $5\cos 2\theta$? *5*
9. What is the period of $2\sin\frac{1}{3}\theta$? 6π
10. Evaluate tan 330°. $^{-}\sqrt{3}/3$
11. Evaluate csc $^{-}135°$. $^{-}\sqrt{2}$
12. Evaluate $\sec\frac{3}{2}\pi$. *undefined*
13. If $\cos\theta = -\frac{2}{5}$, find $\sin\theta$ for values of θ between 90° and 180°. $\sqrt{21}/5$
14. If $\tan\theta = \frac{2}{3}$, find $\sec\theta$ for values of θ between 180° and 270°. $^{-}\sqrt{13}/3$
15. Verify the identity $\frac{1-\cos^2 x}{\sin x \cos x} = \tan x$. see below
16. Verify the identity $\sec^4\theta - \tan^4\theta = 1 + 2\tan^2\theta$. see below
17. Evaluate cos 105°. $(\sqrt{2}-\sqrt{6})/4$
18. Evaluate sin 285°. $(^{-}\sqrt{6}-\sqrt{2})/4$
19. If $\sin x = \frac{1}{6}$, find $\cos 2x$. $\frac{17}{18}$
20. If $\sin x = -\frac{4}{5}$ and x is in the third quadrant, find $\sin 2x$. $\frac{24}{25}$
21. If $\cos x = -\frac{1}{4}$ and x is in the second quadrant, find $\sin\frac{x}{2}$. $\sqrt{10}/4$
22. If $0° \le x \le 360°$, solve $2\sin x\cos x = \cos x$. *30°, 90°, 150°, 270°*
23. If $0° \le x \le 360°$, solve $6\sin x\cos x = 3$. *45°*
24. Evaluate $\text{Tan}^{-1}\,1$. *45°*
25. Evaluate $\text{Sin}^{-1}\left(-\frac{\sqrt{2}}{2}\right)$. *$^{-}45°$*

15.

$$\frac{1-\cos^2 x}{\sin x\cos x} \stackrel{?}{=} \tan x$$
$$\frac{\sin^2 x + \cos^2 x - \cos^2 x}{\sin x\cos x} \stackrel{?}{=} \tan x$$
$$\frac{\sin^2 x}{\sin x\cos x} \stackrel{?}{=} \tan x$$
$$\frac{\sin x}{\cos x} \stackrel{?}{=} \tan x$$
$$\tan x = \tan x$$

16.

$$\sec^4\theta - \tan^4\theta \stackrel{?}{=} 1 + 2\tan^2\theta$$
$$(\sec^2\theta + \tan^2\theta)(\sec^2\theta - \tan^2\theta) \stackrel{?}{=} 1 + 2\tan^2\theta$$
$$[(1+\tan^2\theta) + \tan^2\theta][(1+\tan^2\theta) - \tan^2\theta] \stackrel{?}{=} 1 + 2\tan^2\theta$$
$$(1 + 2\tan^2\theta)\cdot 1 \stackrel{?}{=} 1 + 2\tan^2\theta$$
$$1 + 2\tan^2\theta = 1 + 2\tan^2\theta$$

Independent Test for Chapter 17 (answers in italics)

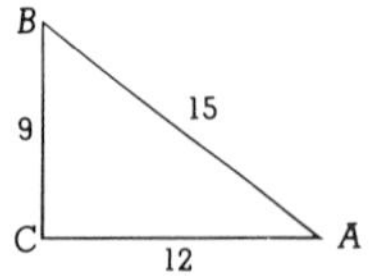

1. Find the value of sin A to the nearest 4 decimal places. *0.6000*
2. Find the value of cos A to the nearest 4 decimal places. *0.8000*
3. Find the value of tan B to the nearest 4 decimal places. *1.3333*
4. Find the value of tan 30°. Write the answer in fraction form. $\sqrt{3}/3$
5. Use a table to find cos 73°. *0.2924*
6. Use a table to find tan 28°40′. *0.5467*
7. Interpolate to find sin 62°27′. *0.8866*
8. If tan x = 2.414, find x to the nearest minute. *67°30′*
9. If sin x = 0.2315, find x to the nearest minute. *13°23′*
10. Solve the right triangle where A = 15° and b = 10. *a = 2.68, c = 10.35, B = 75°*
11. Solve the right triangle where B = 42° and b = 12. *a = 13.33, c = 17.93, A = 48°*
12. Solve the right triangle where A = 68° and c = 8. *a = 7.42, b = 3.00, B = 22°*
13. The top of a lighthouse is 52 feet above sea level. A man sailing a boat at sea observes the measure of the angle of elevation of the top of the lighthouse to be 39°. How far is the boat from the foot of the lighthouse? *64.2 ft*
14. A ramp is 10 feet long. The bottom of the ramp rests on the ground and the top of the ramp is 3 feet above the ground. What is the measure of the angle formed by the ramp with the ground? *17°28′*
15. If possible, solve the triangle where A = 71°, B = 42°, and a = 7. *b = 4.95, c = 6.81, C = 67°*
16. If possible, solve the triangle where A = 135°, a = 9, and b = 15. *none*
17. If possible, solve the triangle where A = 47°, a = 20, and b = 16. *c = 27.13, B = 35°49′, C = 97°11′*
18. If possible solve the triangle where A = 73°, a = 5, and b = 17. *none*
19. If possible, solve the triangle where A = 35°, a = 15, and b = 18. *c = 25.63, B = 43°30′, C = 101°30′; c = 3.87, B = 136°30′, C = 8°30′*
20. If possible, solve the triangle where A = 95°, B = 25°, and c = 20. *a = 23.01, b = 9.76, C = 60°*

Independent Semester Test for Chapters 9-17 (answers in italics)

1. Find $p(4)$ for $p(x) = 2x^2 + 6x - 5$. *51*
2. Find the remainder for $(x^3 + 2x^2 - 7x - 5) \div (x - 2)$. *$^-3$*
3. Find all rational zeros for $f(x) = x^3 + x^2 - 58x - 112$. *$^-7, 8, ^-2$*
4. State the number of positive real zeros for $f(x) = 3x^2 - 5x + 2$. *2 or 0*
5. If $f(x) = 3x + 2$ and $g(x) = x + 5$ find $[f \circ g](x)$. *$3x + 17$*
6. Find the product of $\frac{x^2 + 4x - 21}{x^2 + 7x + 10} \cdot \frac{x + 2}{x + 7}$. *$\frac{x - 3}{x + 5}$*
7. Find the quotient of $\frac{6x^2}{5ab} \div \frac{36xy}{20a^2b}$. *$\frac{2ax}{3y}$*
8. Find the sum and check $\frac{15}{x^2 - 9} + \frac{5}{x - 3}$. *$\frac{5x + 30}{x^2 - 9}$*
9. Solve and check $\frac{3}{x - 5} = \frac{8}{x + 2}$. *$x = \frac{46}{5}$*
10. Suppose y varies directly with x and $y = 3$ when $x = 4$. Find y when $x = 20$. *$y = 15$*
11. Simplify $\frac{x^6}{x}$, $x \neq 0$. *x^5*
12. Simplify $\left(\frac{y}{y^4}\right)^{-3}$, $y \neq 0$. *y^9*
13. Express 82,510,000 in scientific notation. *8.251×10^7*
14. Express $\sqrt[3]{8x^{12}y^2}$ using exponents. *$2x^4y^{\frac{2}{3}}$*
15. Simplify $\frac{x^{\frac{1}{2}}}{x^{\frac{1}{2}} - x^{\frac{5}{2}}}$. *$\frac{1}{1 - x^2}$*
16. Solve. $\sqrt{3x + 4} = 4$ *4*
17. Rewrite $11^4 = 14641$ in logarithmic form. *$\log_{11} 14641 = 4$*
18. Evaluate $\log_5 5^6$. *6*
19. Solve $\log_3 12 + \log_3 m = \log_3 16$. *$\frac{4}{3}$*
20. If $\log 295 = 2.4698$ find $\log 2950$. *3.4698*
21. Interpolate to find the logarithm of 531.2. *2.7253*
22. State x in terms of common logarithms. $4^x = \sqrt{13}$. *$\frac{\log 13}{2 \log 4}$*
23. Write $\sum_{x=3}^{7} (2x + 3)$ in expanded form and find the sum. *$9 + 11 + 13 + 15 + 17 = 65$*
24. Find the sum of the arithmetic series where $a_1 = 3$, $d = 7$, and $n = 10$. *345*
25. Find the fifth term of a geometric sequence in which $a_1 = 9$ and $r = 2$. *144*
26. Find the sum of the geometric series where $a_1 = 3$, $r = 2$, and $n = 4$. *45*

27. Find the sum of the infinite geometric series where $a_1 = 12$ and $r = \frac{2}{5}$. *20*
28. Find the fifth term of the sequence for which $a_{n+1} = a_n + 3$ and $a_1 = 5$. *17*
29. How many ways can five children slide down a slide? *120*
30. How many ways can the letters from PIZZAS be arranged? *360*
31. How many ways can 6 people be seated at a circular table? *120*
32. How many ways can 3 dancers be selected from 10 who audition? *120*
33. A bag contains 4 red marbles, 2 white marbles, and 6 green marbles. One marble is chosen at random. What is the probability that it is red? $\frac{1}{3}$
34. Suppose in problem 33 two marbles were selected without replacement. What is the probability that both are red? $\frac{1}{11}$
35. Suppose you are to draw a circle graph of how a family spends its annual income of $12,300. They spend $2080 a year for food. How many degrees should be used to show food expenditures in the graph? *60.9°*

The following number of free throws were made by players on the basketball team: 26, 69, 38, 36, 20, 23, 21, 8, 9, 10, 3, 7, 0, 0, 0.

36. What is the median? *10*
37. What is the mean? *18*
38. What is the range? *69*

39. Is the standard deviation of the numbers 8, 5, 1, 1, and 0 closest to 1.8, 2.5, 2.8, or 3.1? *3.1*
40. Suppose 300 items are normally distributed. How many items are within one standard deviation of the mean? *204*
41. Find the value of sin 225°. $-\frac{\sqrt{2}}{2}$
42. Evaluate tan 315°. $^{-}1$
43. Find a value for $\sin\theta$ between 90° and 180° if $\cos = -\frac{5}{13}$. $\frac{12}{13}$
44. Evaluate sin 15°. $\frac{\sqrt{6}-\sqrt{2}}{4}$
45. Find $\arccos\left(\frac{\sqrt{3}}{2}\right)$. *30°*
46. Approximate the value of cos 36°42′. *0.8018*
47. Approximate the value of sec 27°15′. *1.125*
48. Solve the right triangle with one acute side $b = 8$ and angle $A = 48°24'$. $B = 41°36'$, $c = 12.04$, $a = 9$
49. Solve the right triangle where $a = 5$, $c = 9.4$ and C is right. $b = 7.96$, $A = 32°08'$, $B = 57°52'$
50. Solve the triangle where $A = 35°$, $B = 79°30'$ and $a = 7$. $b = 12$, $c = 11.1$, $C = 65°30'$

Teacher's Answer Key

CHAPTER 2 LINEAR RELATIONS AND FUNCTIONS

Page 40 Exploratory

1. 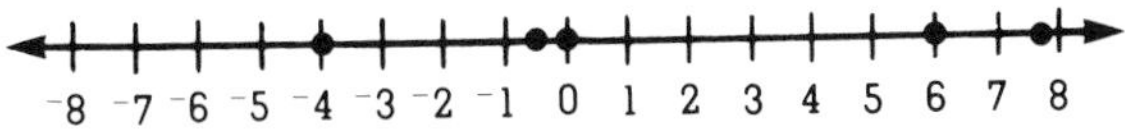

2. 

3. 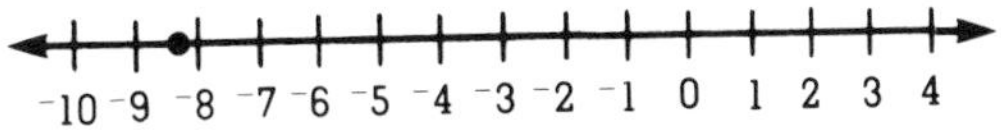

4. 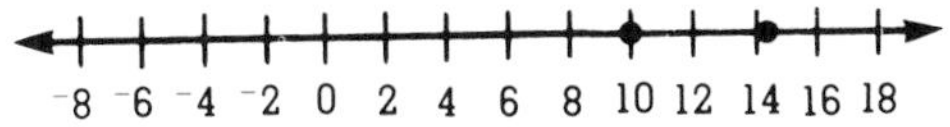

5. 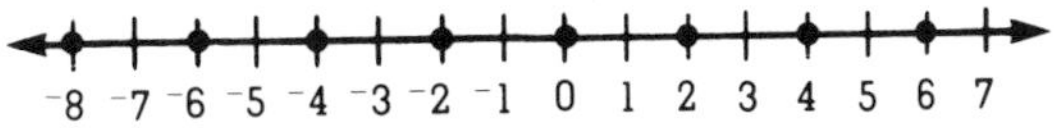

6. 

7. 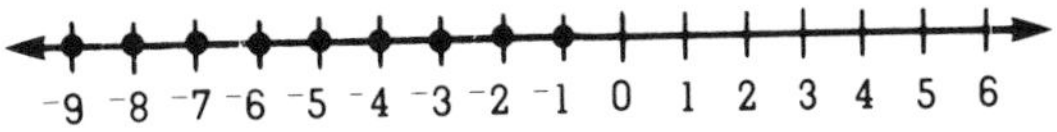

8. 

9. 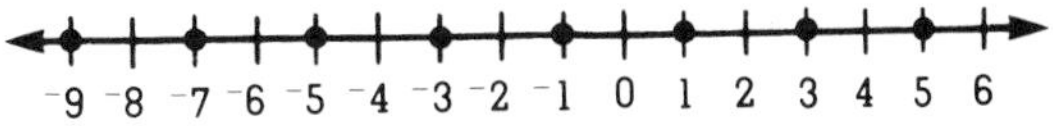

15–22. 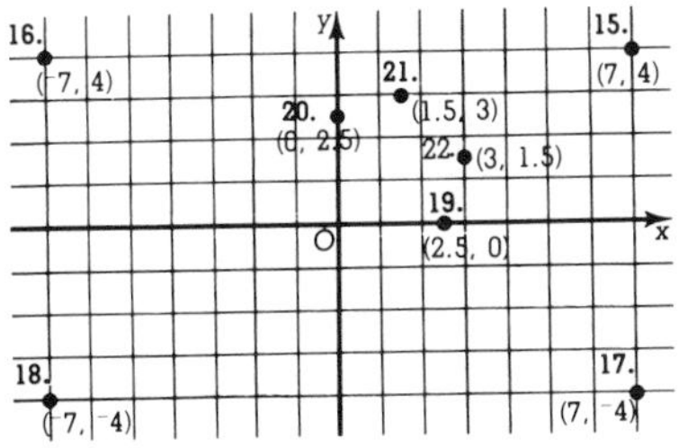

Page 40 Written

1. 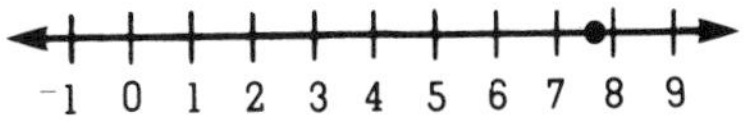

2. 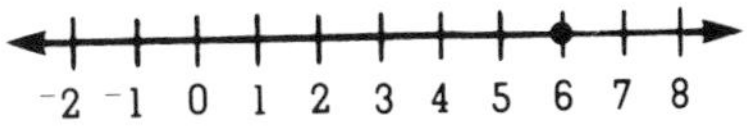

3. 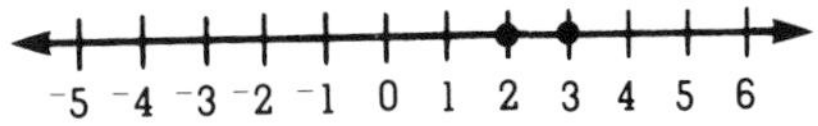

4. 

5. 

6. 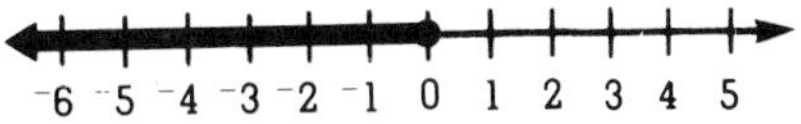

7. 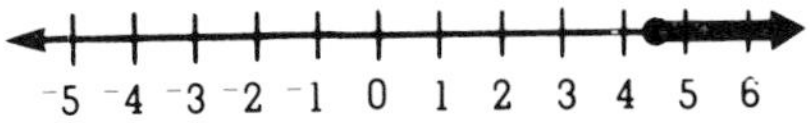

8. 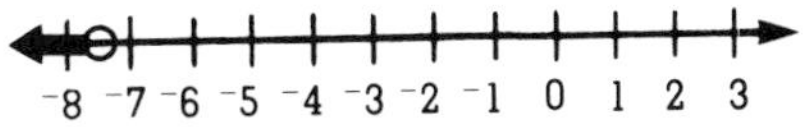

9. 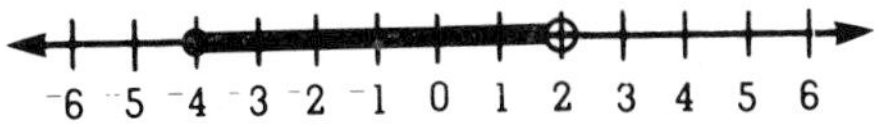

10. 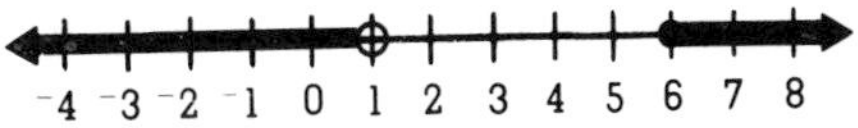

11. 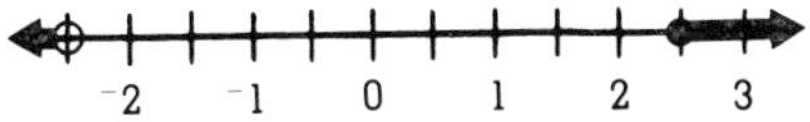

12. 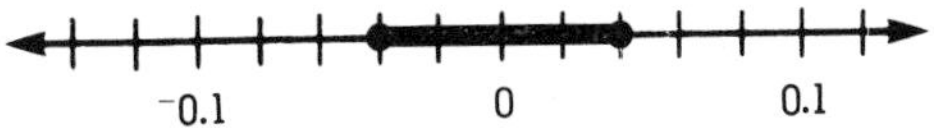

13. 

14. 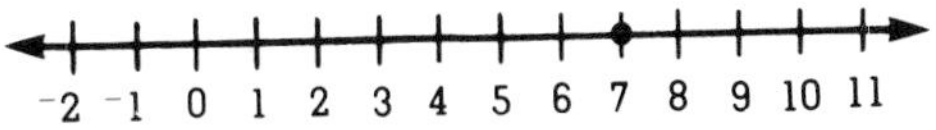

15. 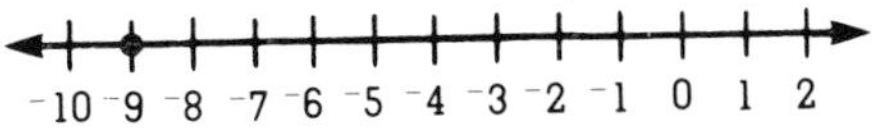

16. 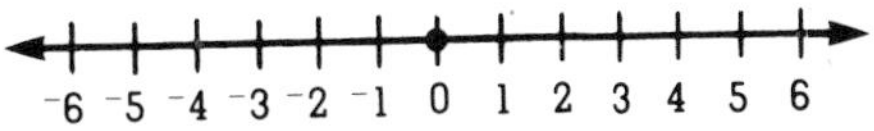

17. 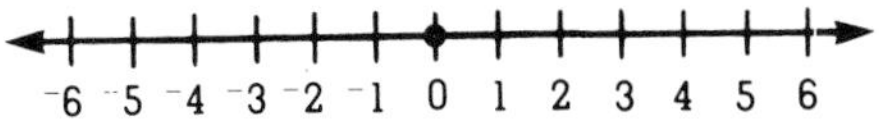

18. 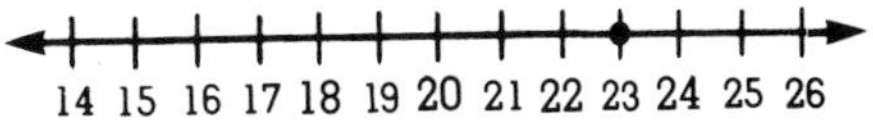

19. 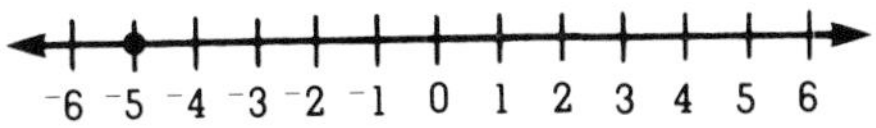

20. 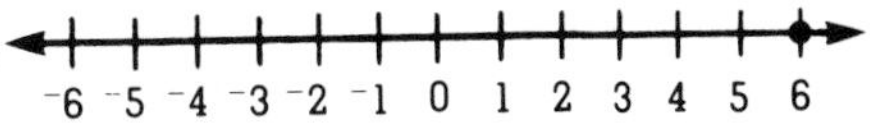

21. 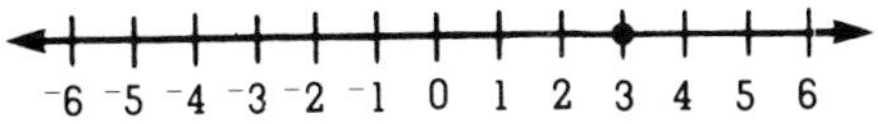

22. 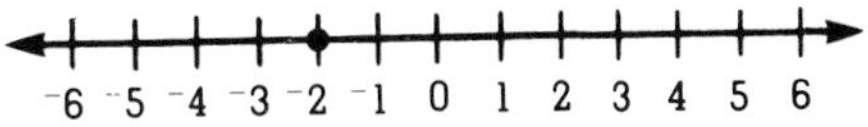

23. 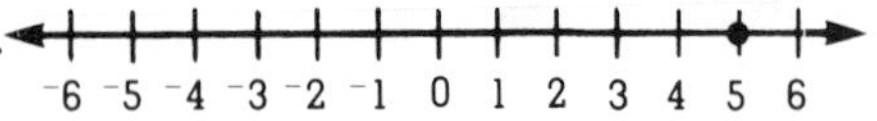

24. 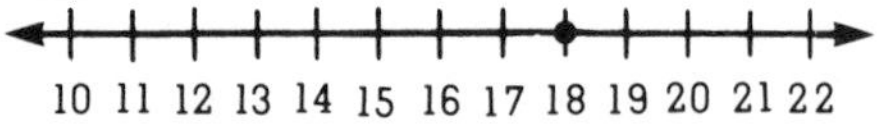

25. 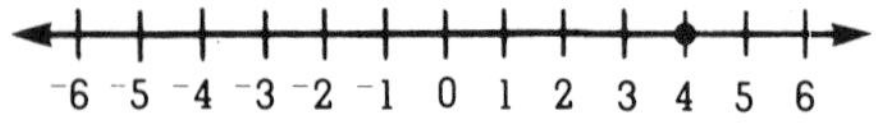

26. 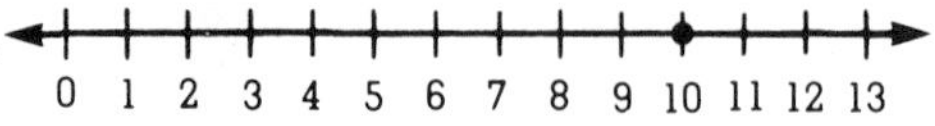

27. 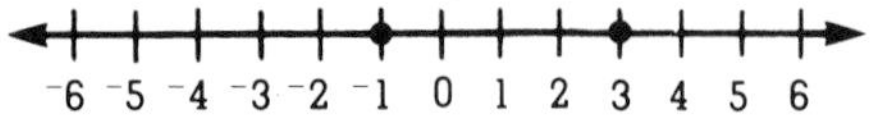

28. 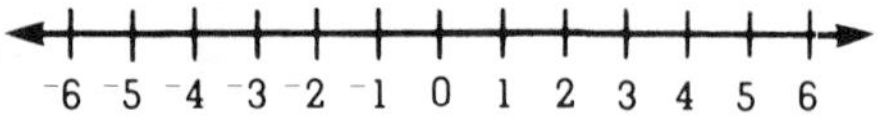

29. 

30. 

31. 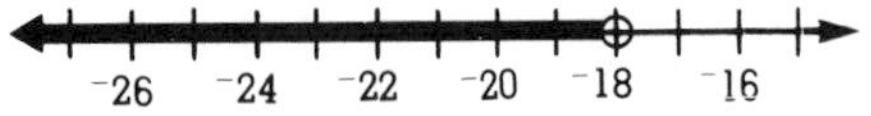

32. 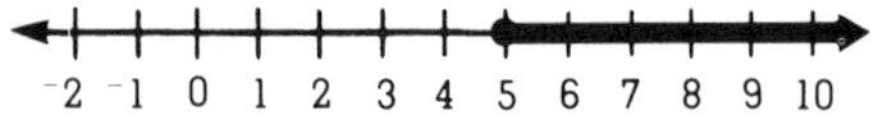

33. 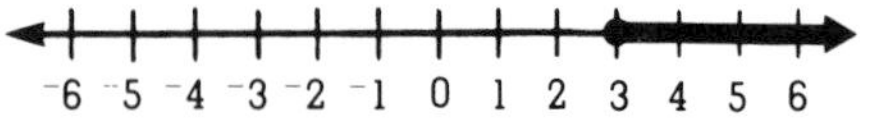

34. 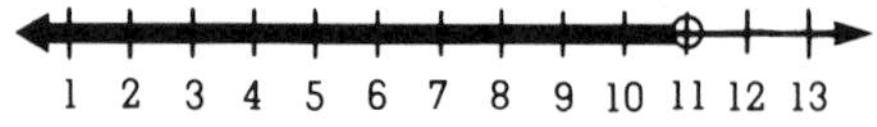

35. 

36. 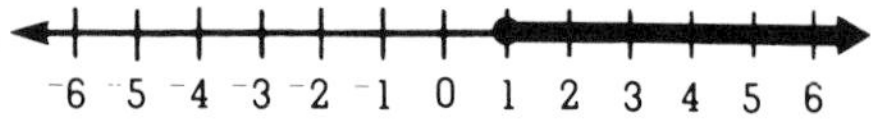

37. 

38. 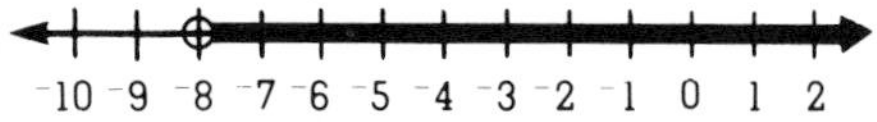

39. 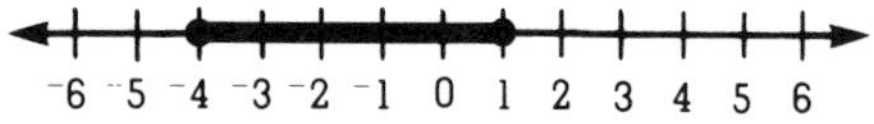

40. 

Pages 43-44 Exploratory **1.** domain = {0, 2, 5}, range = {1, 4} **2.** domain = {-3, 3, 8}, range = {2, 3} **3.** domain = {1, 3, 4}, range = {1, 3, 4} **4.** domain = {6}, range = {4} **5.** domain = {2}, range = {1, 3, 4, 7} **6.** domain = {1, 3, 5}, range = {3} **7.** domain = {-17, 4, 8}, range = {-2, 3, 4, 8} **8.** domain = {1, 5}, range = {1, 5} **9.** domain = {2, 8}, range = {2, 8} **10.** domain = {-3, 0, 1, 2}, range = {4} **11.** domain = {-3, -2, 2, 4}, range = {-3, -2, 2, 4} **12.** domain = {-3, -2, 2, 4}, range = {-4, -2, 2, 3} **13.** domain = {8}, range = {6} **14.** domain = {-3}, range = {-4, -2, 2, 3} **15.** domain = {-3, 5}, range = {-3, 5} **16.** domain = {-3, -2, 2, 4}, range = {3} **17.** domain = {0}, range = {0} **18.** domain = $\{\frac{3}{4}, 3, 6, 8\}$, range = $\{-2, \frac{2}{3}, 4\}$

Pages 44-45 Written **1.** {(-3, 3), (-2, 2), (-1, 1), (0, 0), (1, 1), (2, 2), (3, 3)}, domain = {-3, -2, -1, 0, 1, 2, 3}, range = {3, 2, 1, 0} **2.** {(-2, 0), (-1, 2), (-1, -2), (1, 3), (1, -3), (2, 5), (2, -5), (3, 6), (3, -7)}, domain = {-2, -1, 1, 2, 3}, range = {6, 5, 3, 2, 0, -2, -3, -5, -7}

Page 48 Written

1. 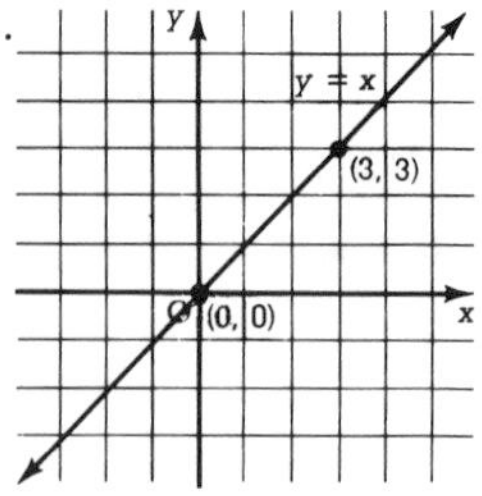

2. 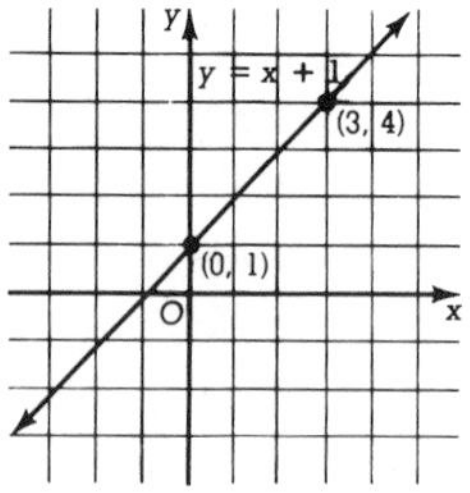

3. 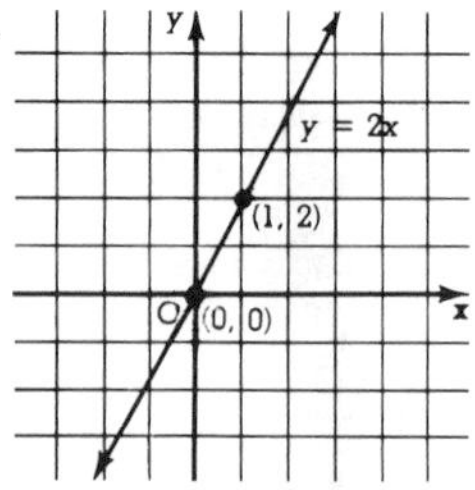

4. 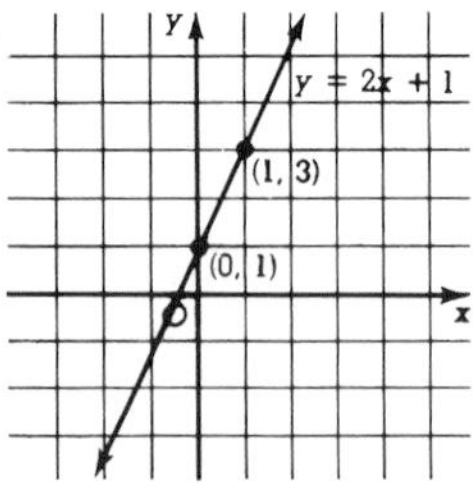

5.
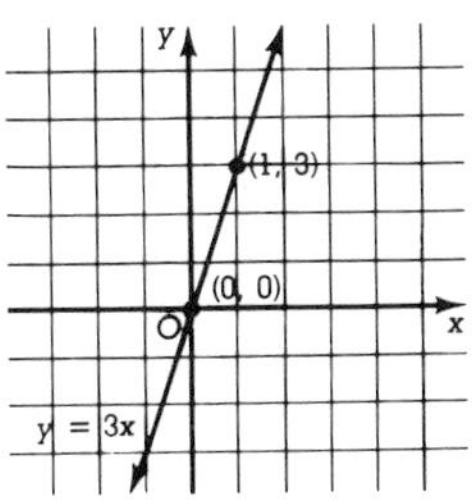

6.
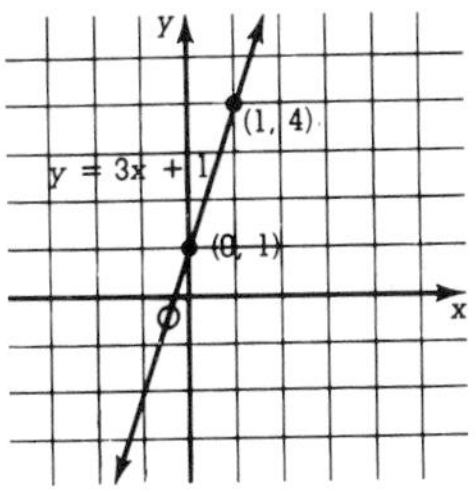

7.
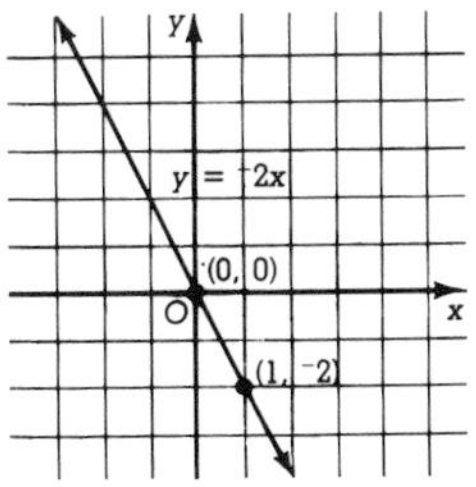

8.
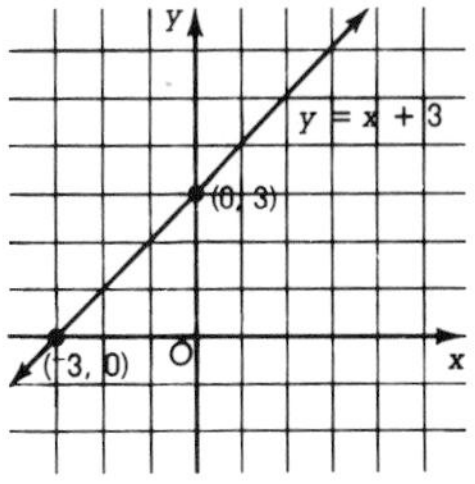

9.
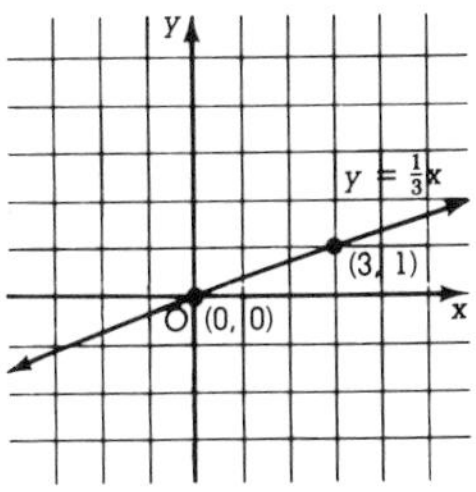

10.
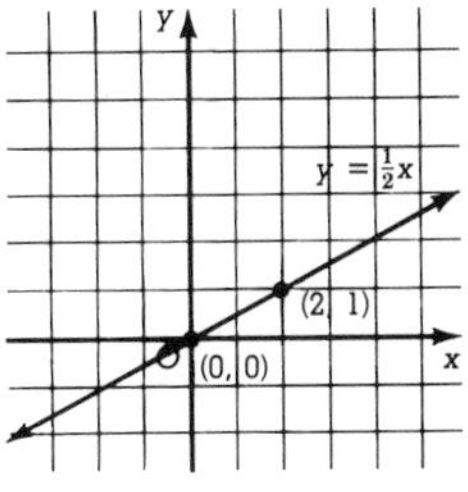

11.
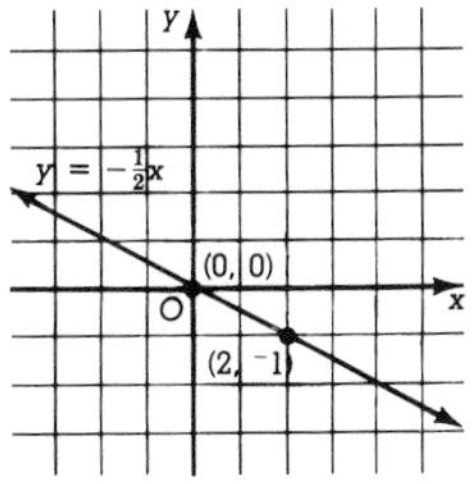

12.
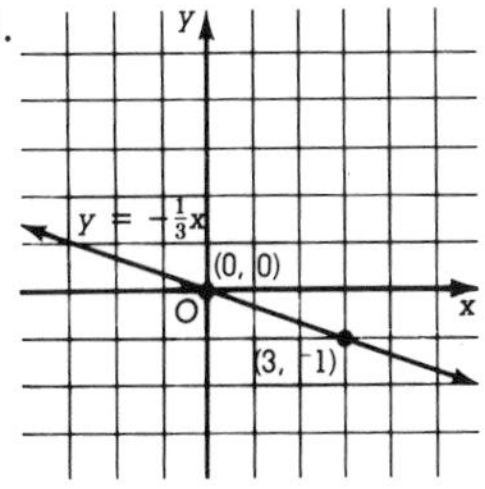

13.
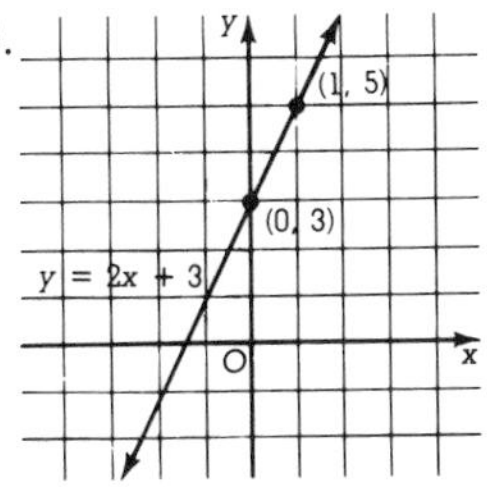

14.
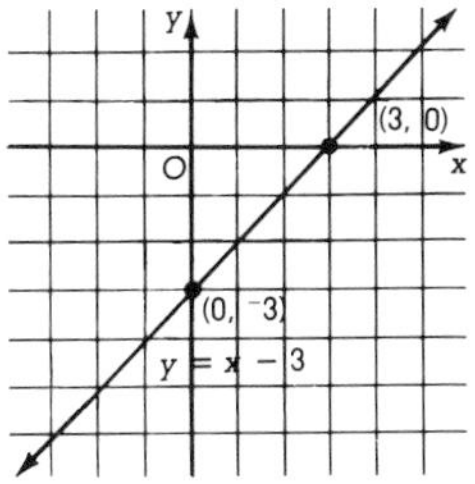

15.
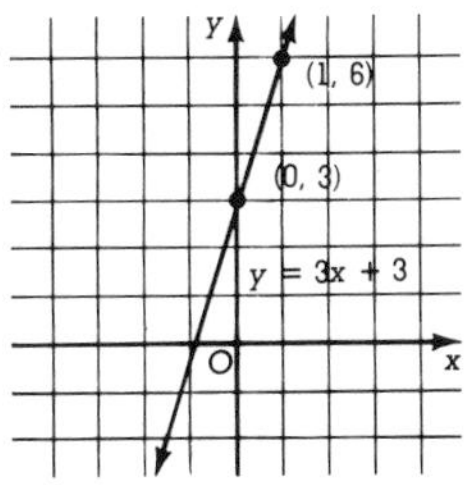

16.
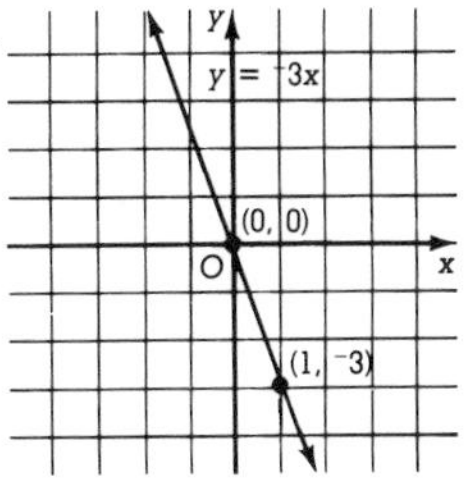

17.
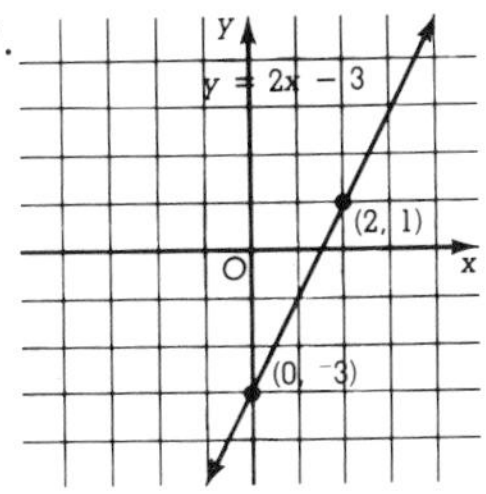

18.
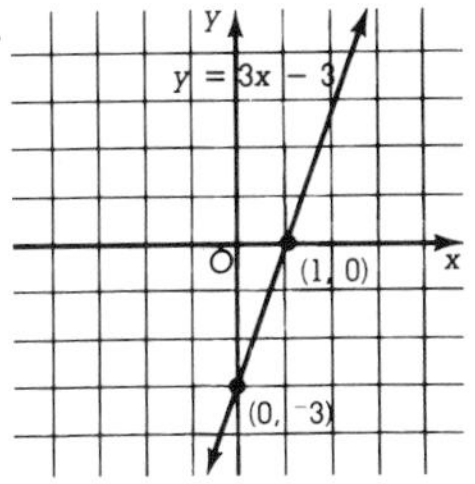

19.
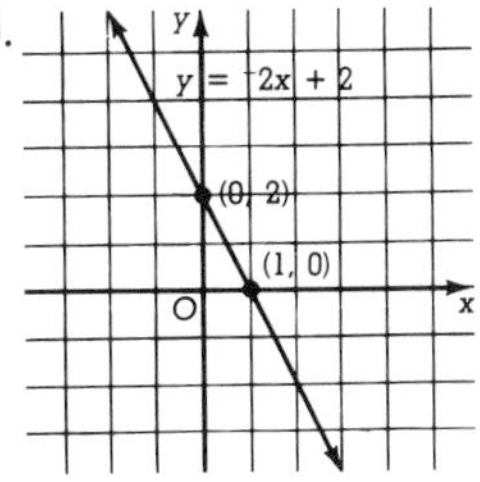

20.
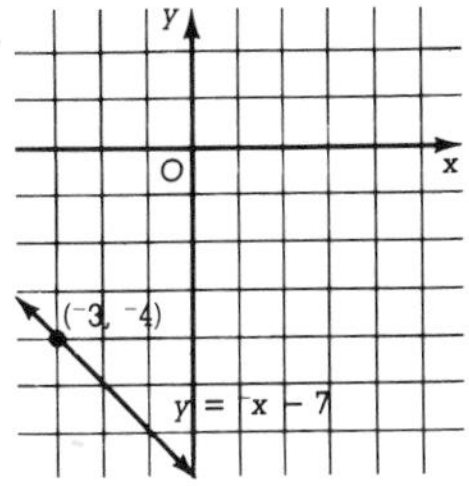

Page 54 Exploratory 1. $y = -\frac{2}{5}x + 2$ 2. $y = 3x - 6$ 3. $y = -\frac{2}{3}x + \frac{4}{3}$ 4. $y = -\frac{1}{2}x + \frac{11}{8}$ 5. $y = 4$ 6. $y = x - 2$ 7. $y = \frac{3}{2}x - 2$ 8. no slope-intercept form 9. $2x - y = 6$ 10. $4x + y = 1$ 11. $x - y = 9$ 12. $4x - y = {}^{-}5$ 13. $5x - 8y = {}^{-}8$ 14. $x - 3y = 0$ 15. $3x - y = 0$ 16. $3x - 3y = 2$

Page 54 Written 1. slope = $-\frac{3}{2}$; y-intercept = 3; x-intercept = 2 2. slope = $-\frac{1}{6}$; y-intercept = 2; x-intercept = 12 3. slope = ${}^{-}2$; y-intercept = 4; x-intercept = 2 4. slope = 5; y-intercept = ${}^{-}5$; x-intercept = 1 5. slope = 1; y-intercept = ${}^{-}3$; x-intercept = 3 6. slope = $\frac{2}{5}$; y-intercept = 4; x-intercept = ${}^{-}10$ 7. slope = $\frac{2}{3}$; y-intercept = $-\frac{4}{3}$; x-intercept = 2 8. slope = $\frac{1}{4}$; y-intercept = $\frac{5}{2}$; x-intercept = ${}^{-}10$ 9. slope = $-\frac{3}{5}$; y-intercept = $\frac{12}{5}$; x-intercept = 4 10. slope = 3; y-intercept = $-\frac{9}{2}$; x-intercept = $\frac{3}{2}$ 11. slope = ${}^{-}11$; y-intercept = 4; x-intercept = $\frac{4}{11}$ 12. slope = $\frac{3}{8}$; y-intercept = $-\frac{3}{2}$; x-intercept = 4 13. slope = $-\frac{2}{9}$; y-intercept = 2; x-intercept = 9 14. slope = $\frac{3}{2}$; y-intercept = $-\frac{5}{4}$; x-intercept = $\frac{5}{6}$ 15. no slope; no y-intercept; x-intercept = $\frac{11}{4}$ 16. slope = $\frac{4}{3}$; y-intercept = ${}^{-}4$; x-intercept = 3 17. $y = -\frac{2}{3}x + 4$ 18. $y = 2x + 6$ 19. $y = -\frac{6}{5}x + 6$ 20. $y = -\frac{4}{3}x + 8$ 21. $y = \frac{3}{4}x - \frac{1}{4}$ 22. $y = {}^{-}10x + 6$

23. $y = -\frac{5}{2}x + 16$ **24.** $y = 13x - 58$ **25.** $y = \frac{2}{11}x + \frac{6}{11}$ **26.** $y = \frac{2}{5}x - \frac{3}{5}$ **27.** $y = \frac{5}{2}x + 18$ **28.** $x = 6$; no slope-intercept form **29.** $y = 3$ **30.** $y = \frac{3}{2}x$ **31.** $y = \frac{1}{2}x + 1$ **32.** $y = \frac{3}{4}x - 7$ **33.** $y = \frac{2}{3}x - 6$ **34.** $y = -\frac{4}{5}x - \frac{7}{5}$ **35.** $y = 4x - 11$ **36.** $y = 5x$ **37.** $y = -\frac{3}{2}x + 10$ **38.** $y = -\frac{8}{3}x + 6$ **39.** $2x + 3y = 12$ **40.** $2x - y = {}^-6$ **41.** $6x + 5y = 30$ **42.** $4x + 3y = 24$ **43.** $3x - 4y = 1$ **44.** $10x + y = 6$ **45.** $5x + 2y = 32$ **46.** $13x - y = 58$ **47.** $2x - 11y = {}^-6$ **48.** $2x - 5y = 3$ **49.** $5x - 2y = {}^-36$ **50.** $x = 6$ **51.** $y = 3$ **52.** $3x - 2y = 0$ **53.** $x - 2y = {}^-2$ **54.** $3x - 4y = 28$ **55.** $2x - 3y = 18$ **56.** $4x + 5y = {}^-7$ **57.** $4x - y = 11$ **58.** $5x - y = 0$ **59.** $3x + 2y = 20$ **60.** $8x + 3y = 18$

Page 58 Written

1.
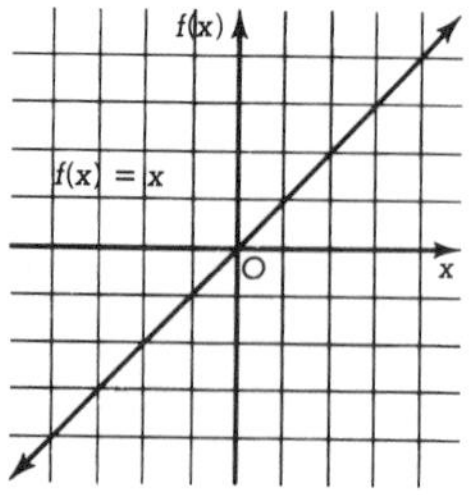

2.
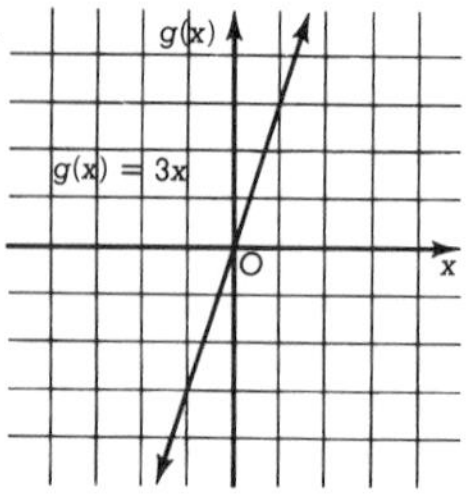

3.
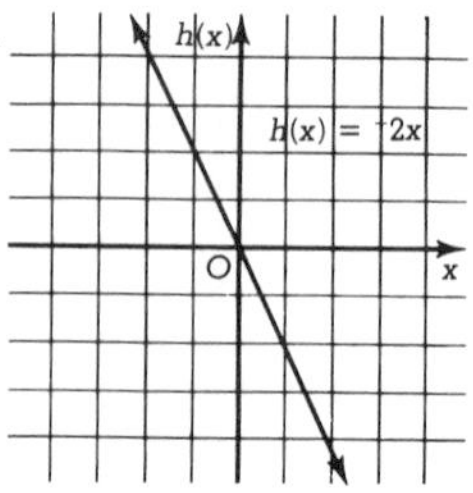

4.
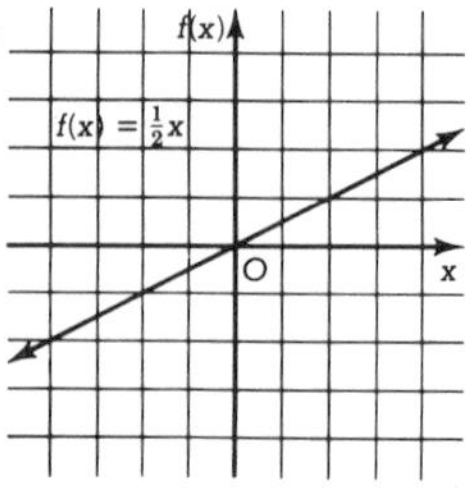

5.
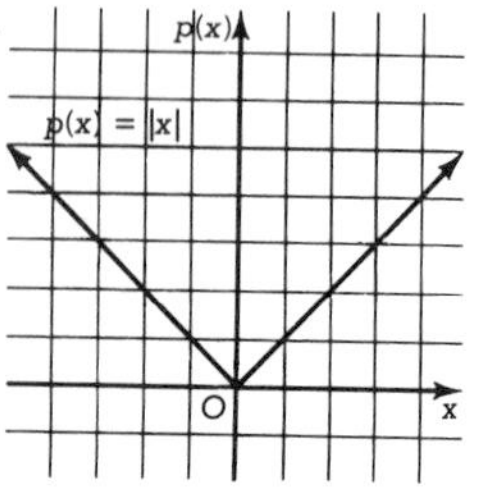

6.
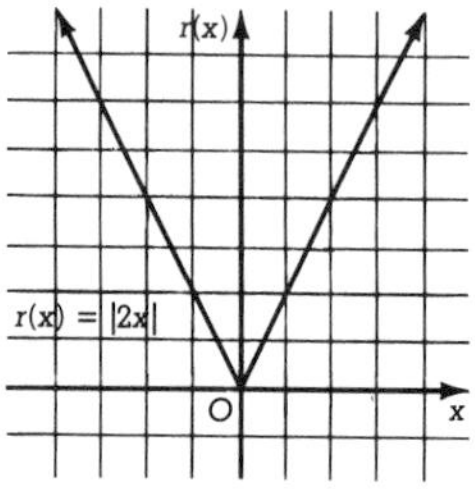

7.
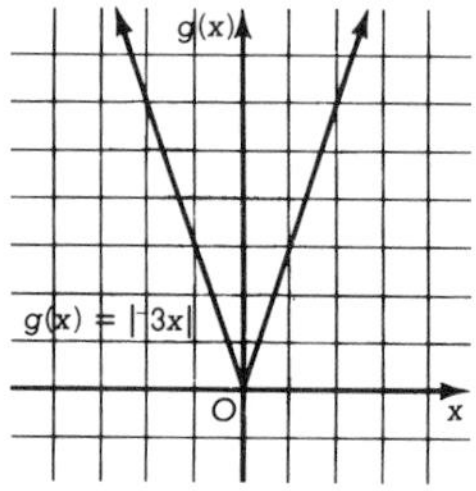

8.
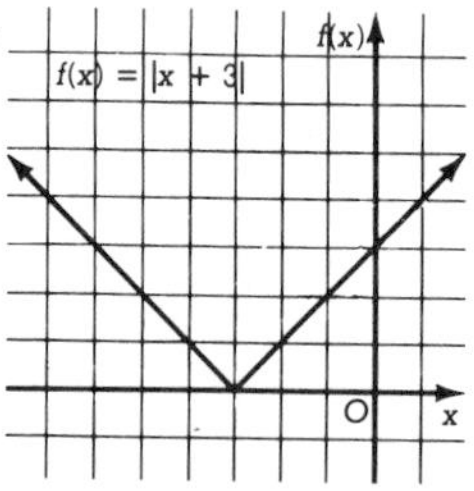

9.
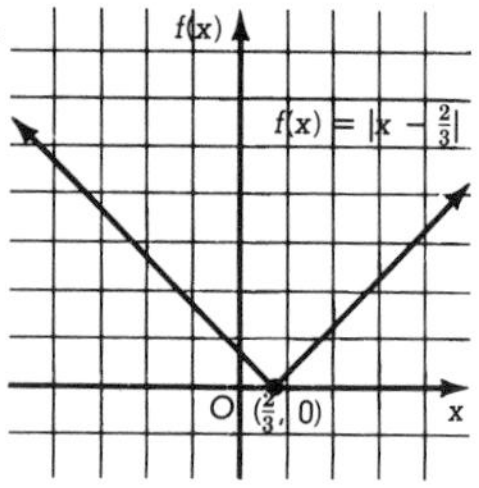

10.
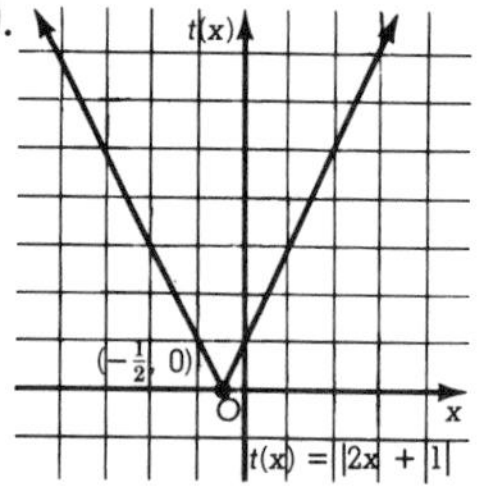

11.
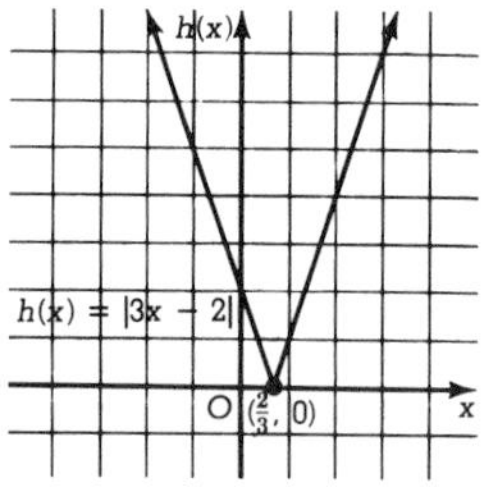

12.
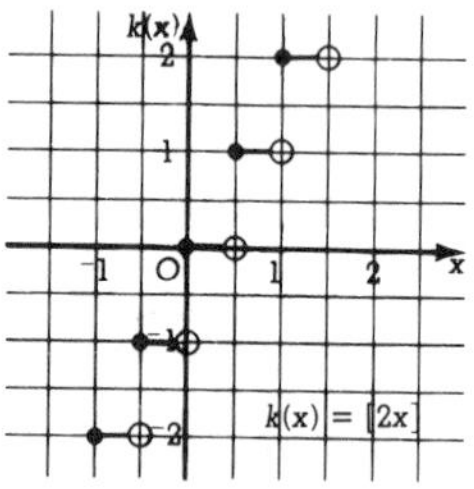

13.
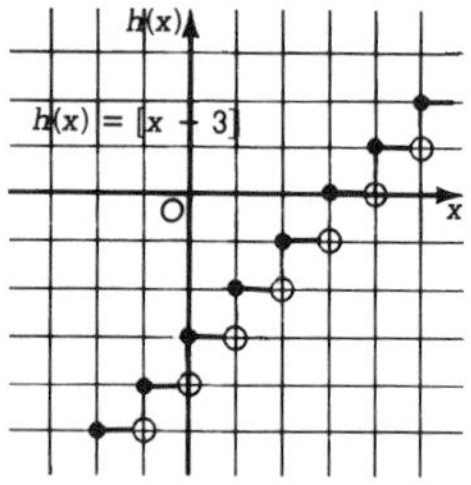

14.
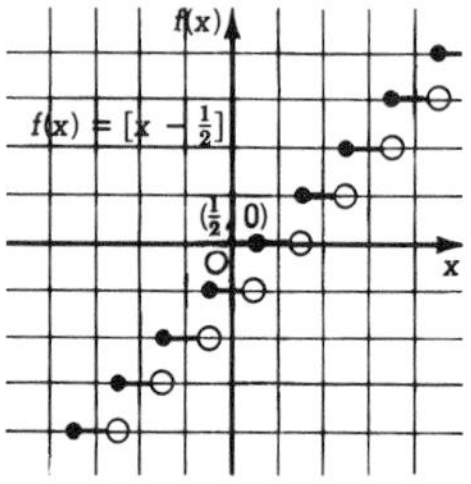

15.
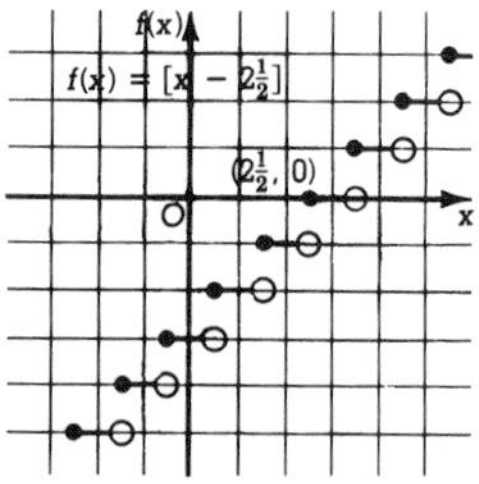

16.
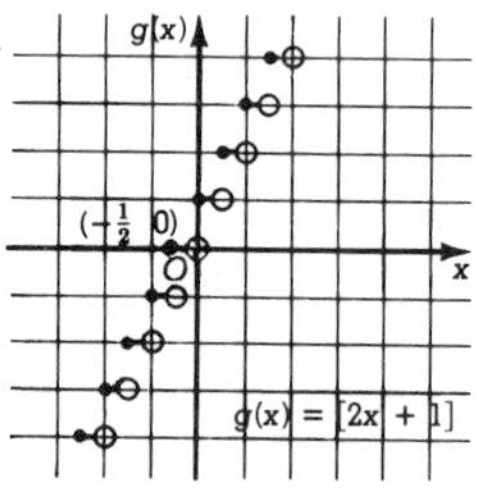

17.
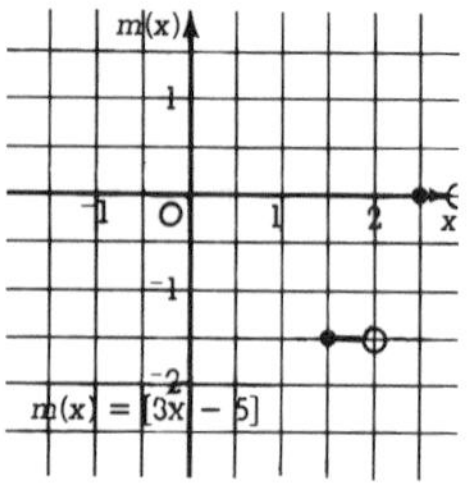

18.
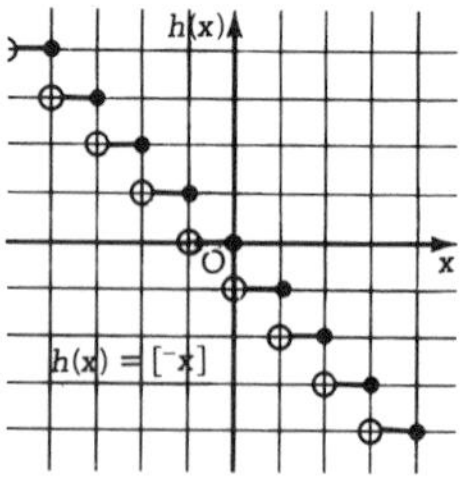

19.
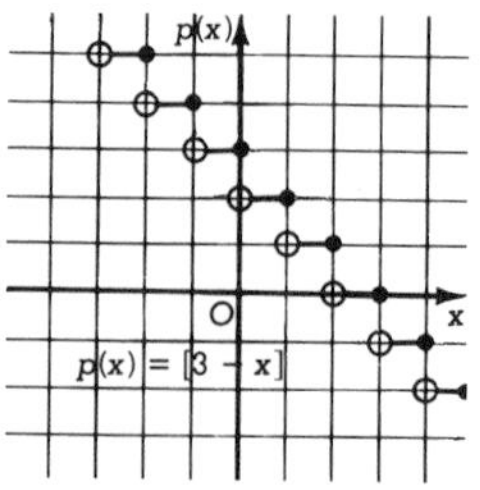

20.
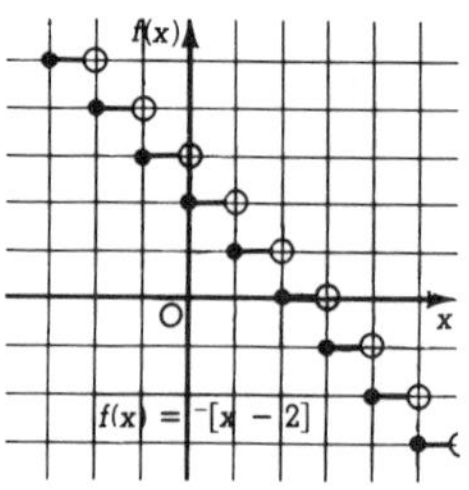

21.
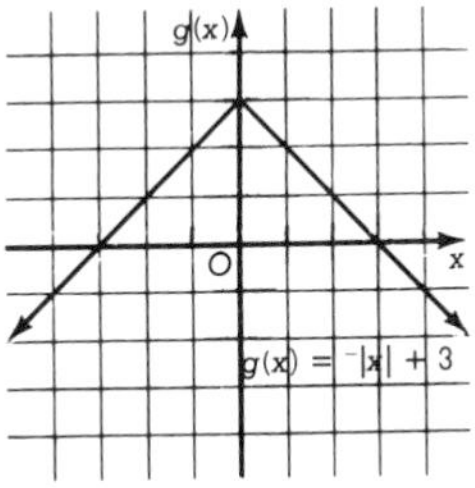

22.
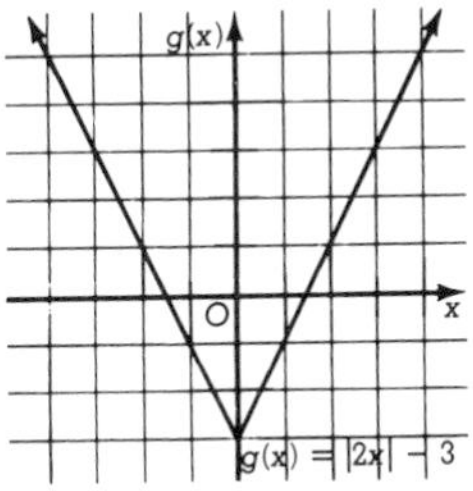

23.
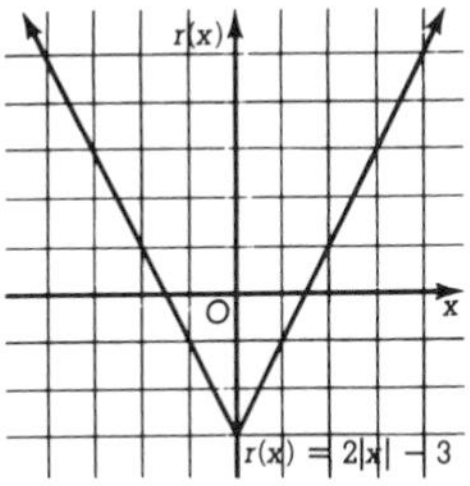

24.
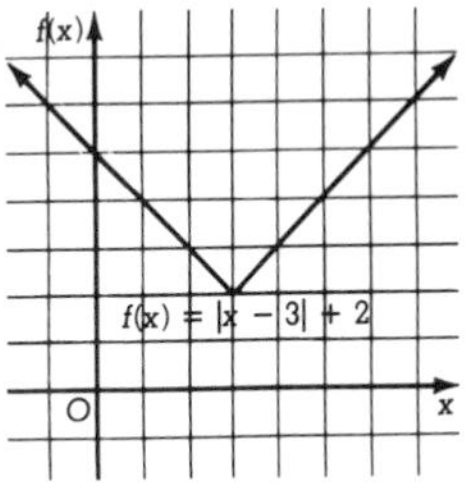

25. The graph of $y = 2[x]$ jumps by twos at integer values of x. The graph of $y = [2x]$ jumps by ones at intervals of $\frac{1}{2}$ unit. 26. identical 27. The graph of $y = |x - 3|$ is like $y = |x|$ moved 3 units *to the right*. The graph of $y = |x| - 3$ is like $y = |x|$ moved 3 units down. 28. identical 29. The graph of $y = |2x + 5|$ is like $y = |2x|$ moved 2.5 units to the *left*. The graph of $y = |2x| + 5$ is like $y = |2x|$ moved 5 units *up*. 30. identical 31. The graphs of $y = |ax|$ and $y = a|x|$ are identical if $a \geq 0$. The graph of $y = a|x|$ opens down if $a < 0$. 32. The graph of $y = |x + b|$ is like $y = |x|$ moved b units right or left. The graph of $y = |x| + b$ is like $y = |x|$ moved b units up or down. 33. The graph of $y = {}^{-}3[x]$ jumps by three at intervals of one unit. The graph of $y = [{}^{-}3x]$ jumps by ones at intervals of $\frac{1}{3}$ unit.
34. The two graphs have the same shape but $y = {}^{-}2|x|$ opens *down* and $y = |{}^{-}2x|$ opens up.

Page 63 Written

1.
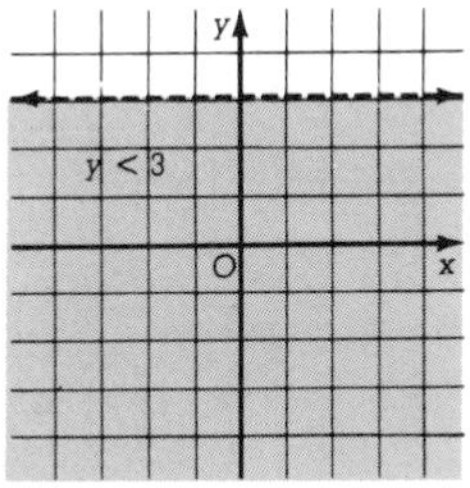

2.
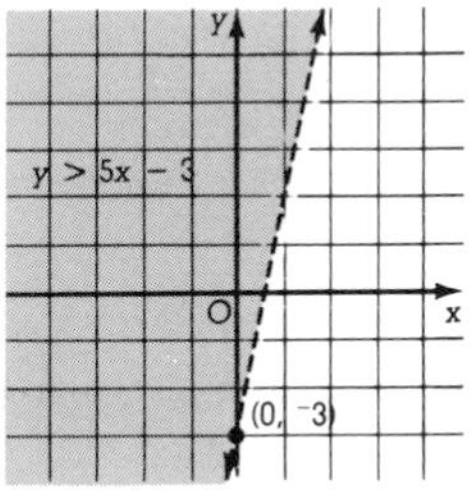

3.
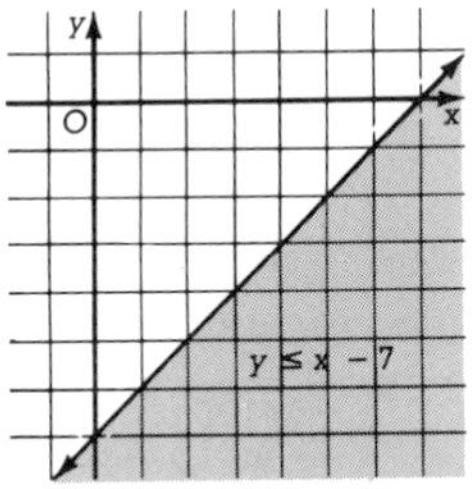

4.
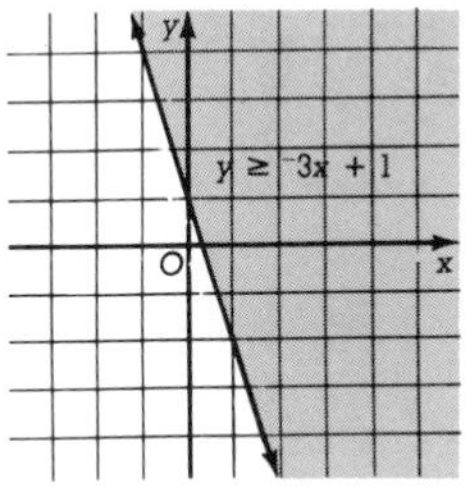

5.
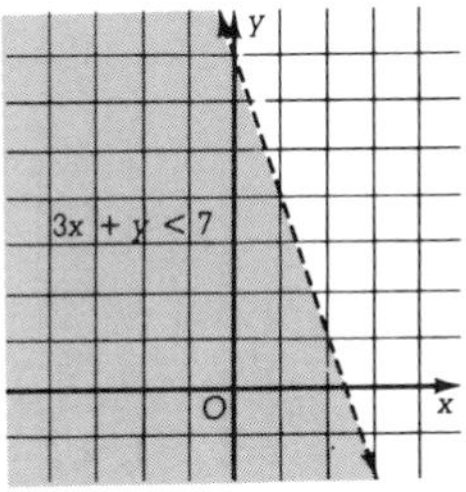

6.
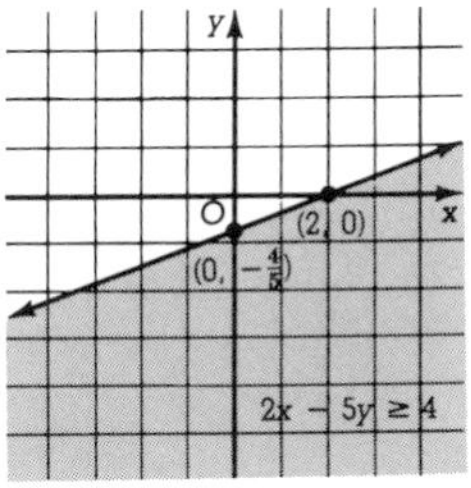

7.
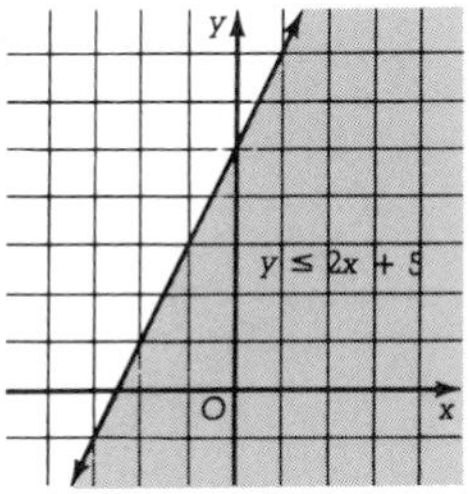

8.
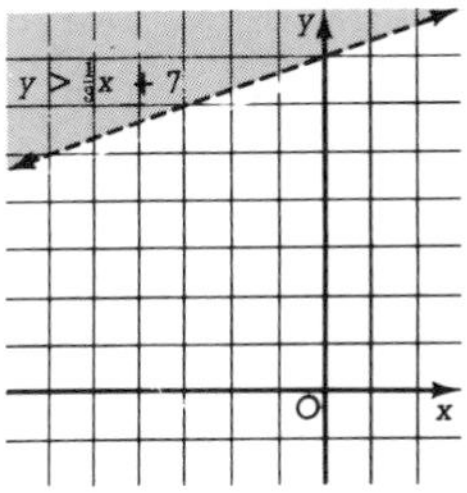

9.
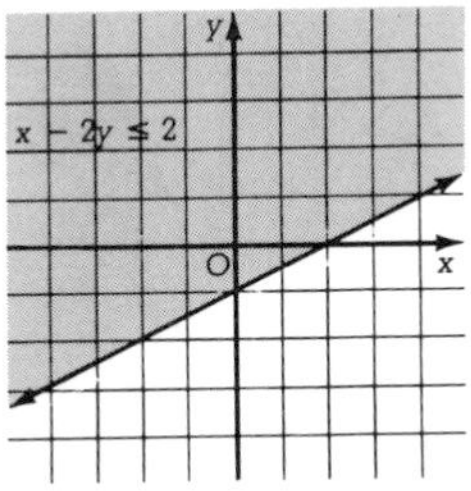

10.
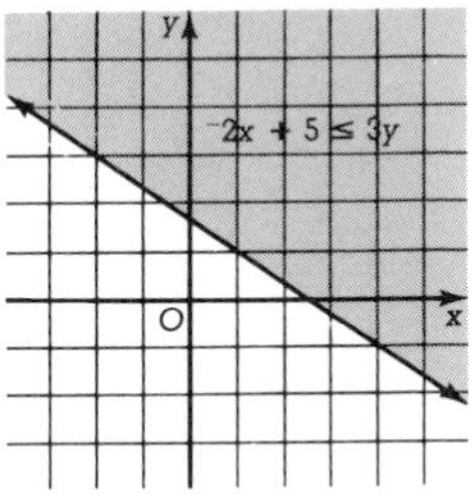

11.
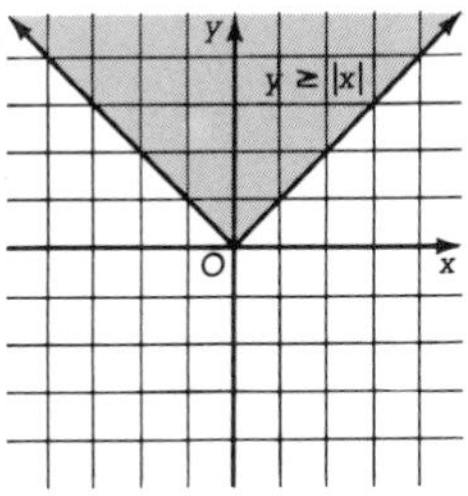

12.
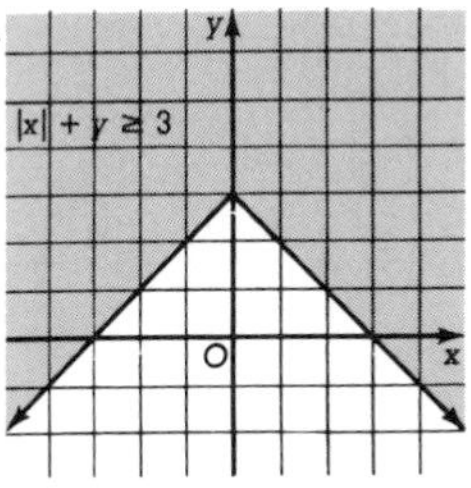

13. 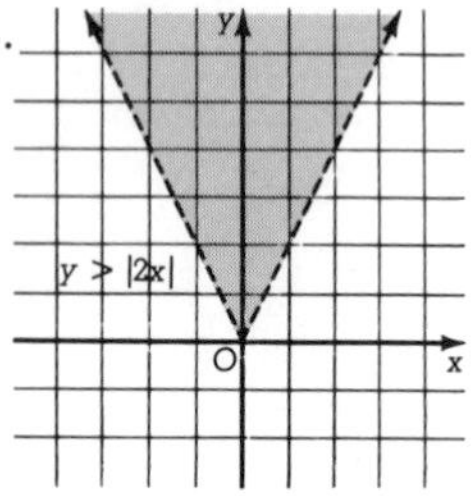

14. 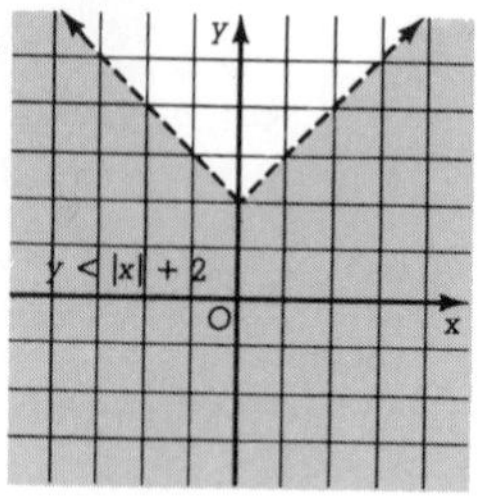

15. 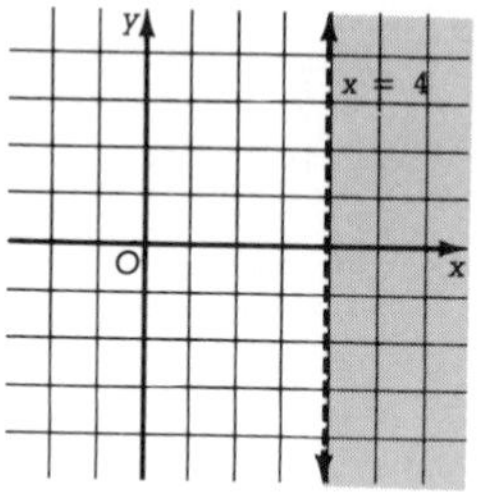

16. 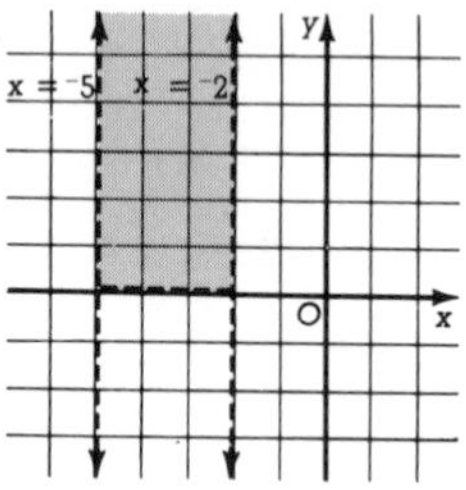

17. 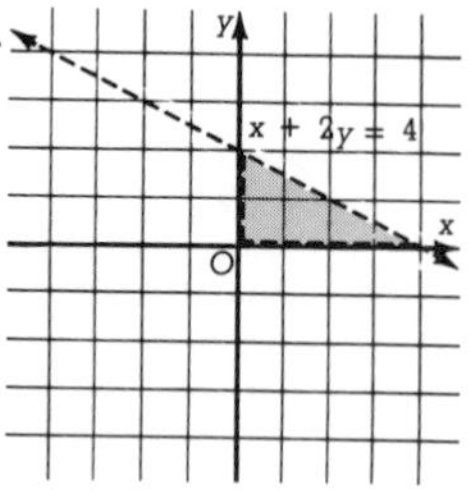

18. 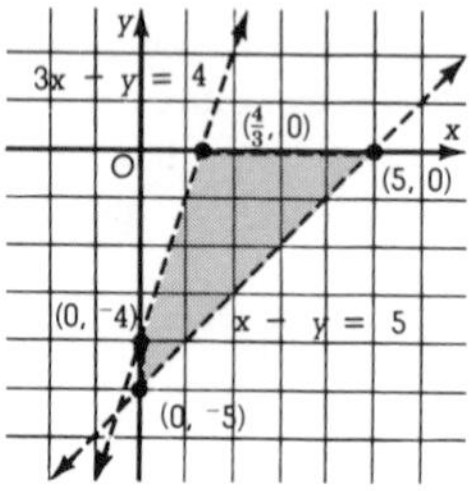

Pages 66–67 Chapter Review

1. 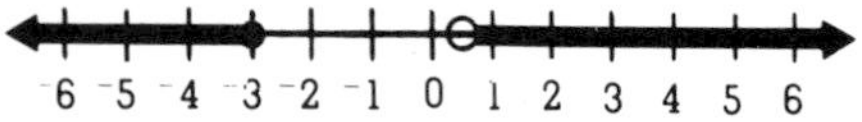

2. 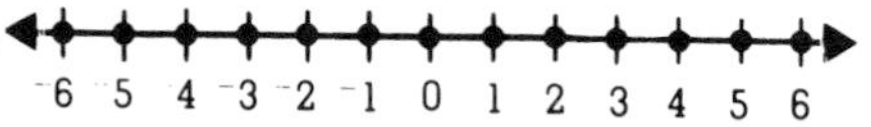

3. 

4. 

5. 

6. 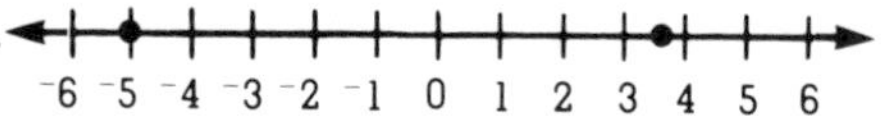

7. 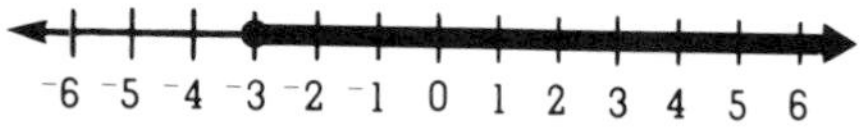

8. 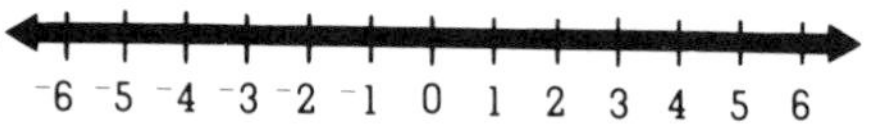

9. domain = {⁻4.5, ⁻3.5, 4.5}; range = {1, 2, 3, 4} **10.** domain = {1, 2, 3, 4, 5}; range = {⁻4.5, ⁻3.5, 4.5} **11.** domain = {$x|x$ is real}; range = {4} **12.** domain = {4}; range = {$y|y$ is real}

28. 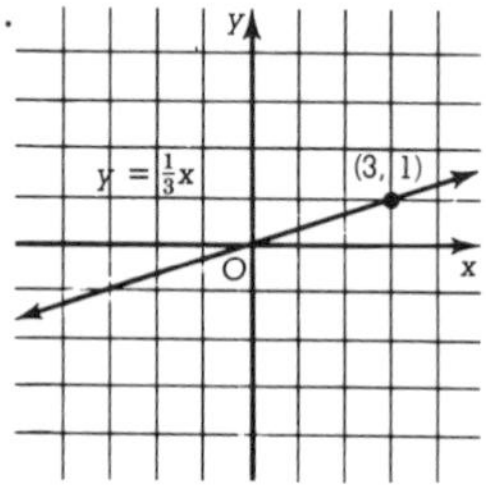

29. 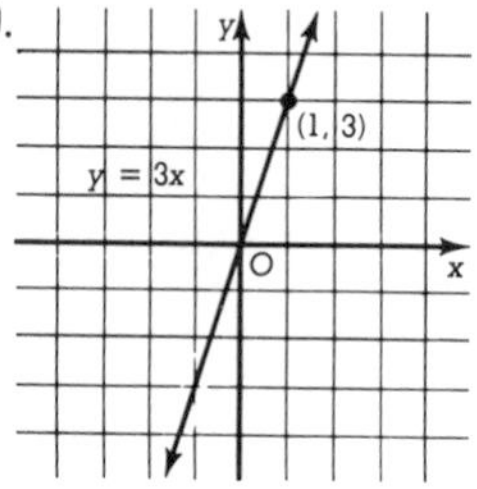

30. 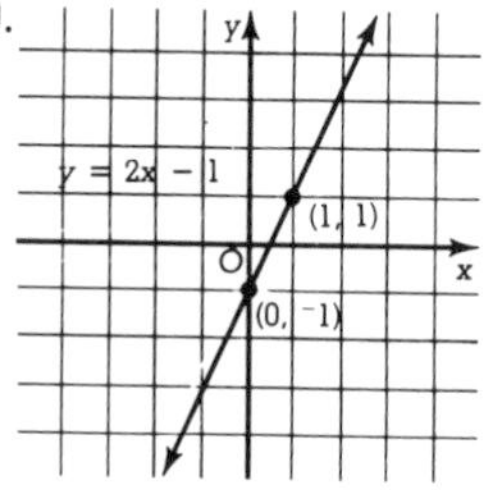

31. 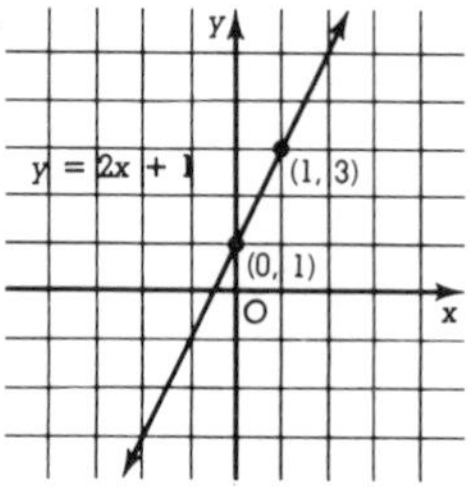

40. $y = \frac{5}{2}x + 5$ **41.** $y = -\frac{6}{7}x - \frac{18}{7}$ **42.** $y = 5x - 7$ **43.** $y = \frac{2}{3}x - \frac{14}{3}$ **44.** $5x - 2y = {}^{-}10$ **45.** $6x + 7y = {}^{-}18$ **46.** $5x - y = 7$ **47.** $2x - 3y = 14$

48. 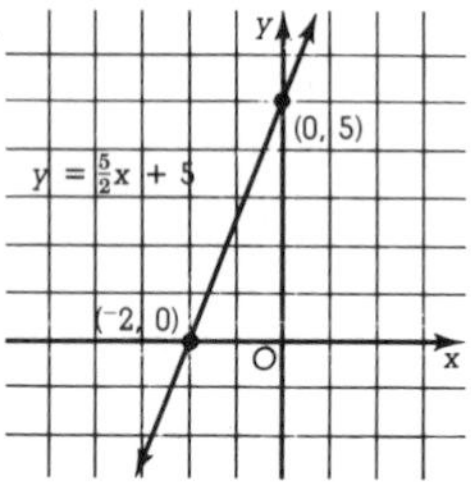

49. 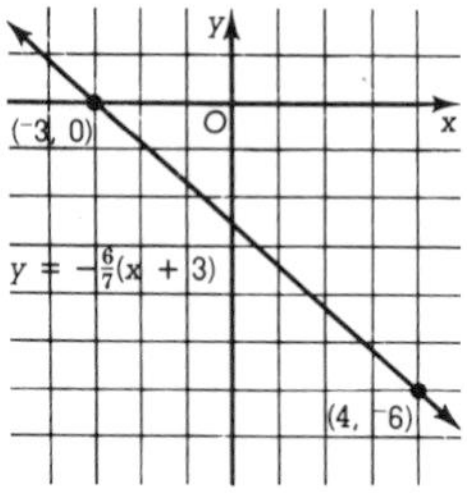

50. 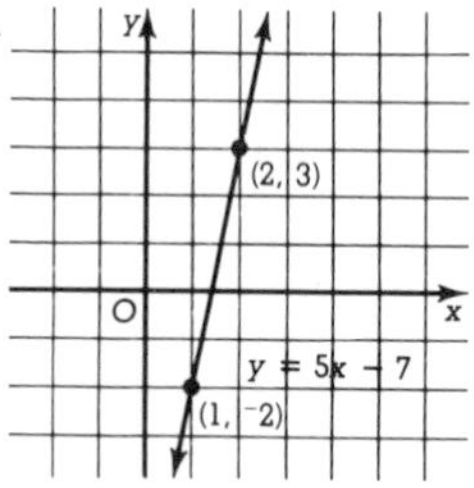

51. 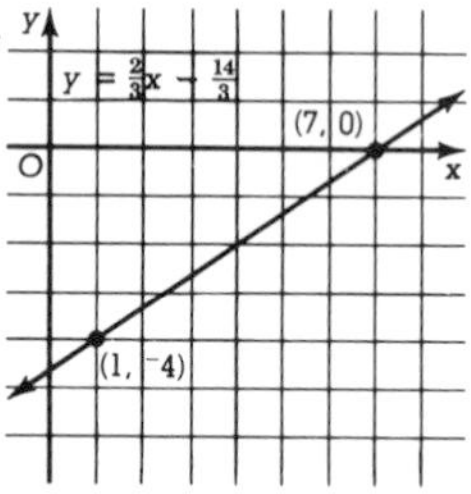

52.
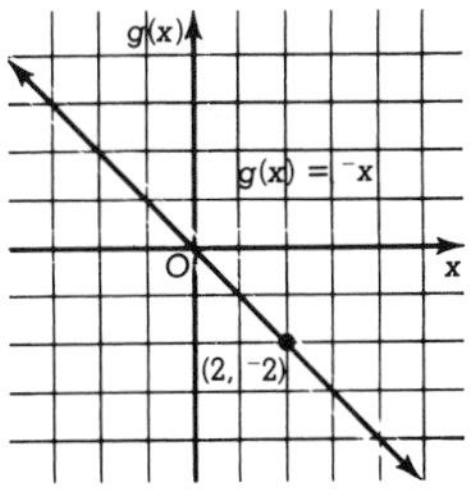

53.
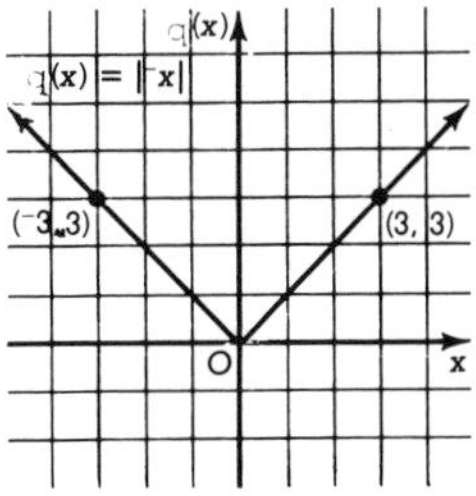

54.
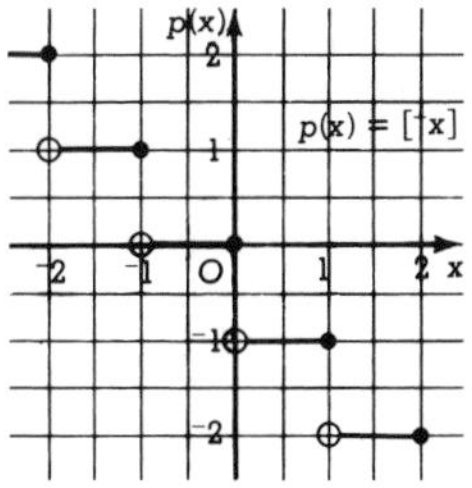

55.
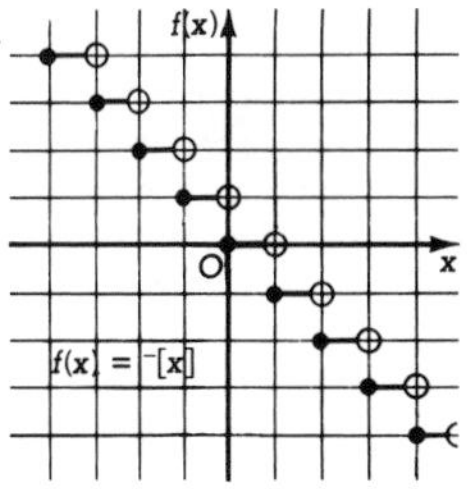

57.
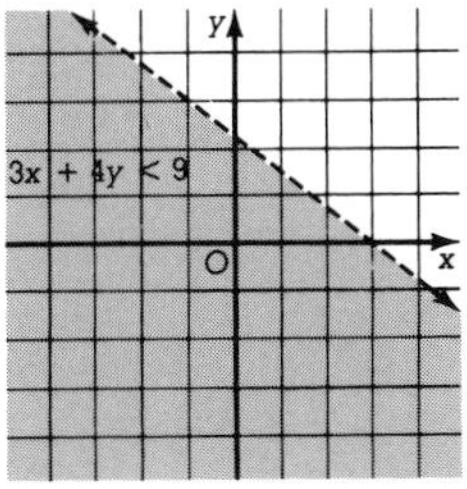

58.
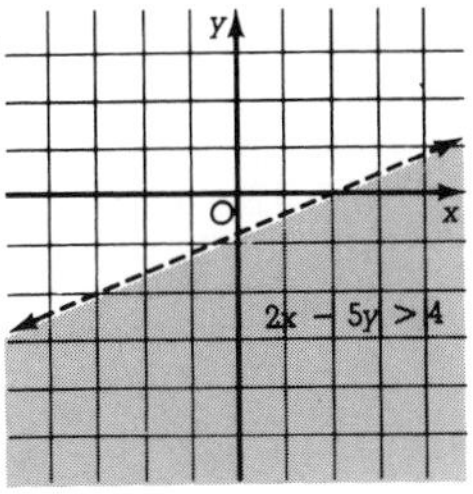

59.
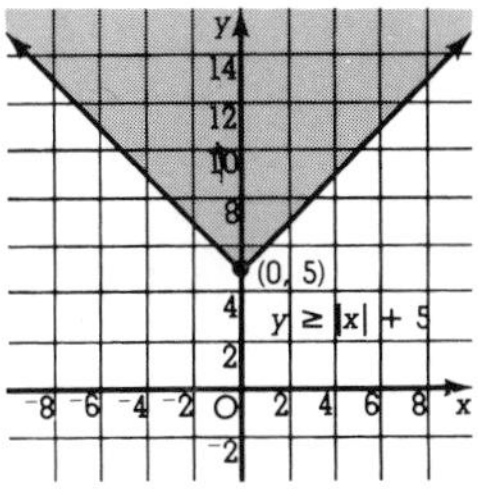

60.
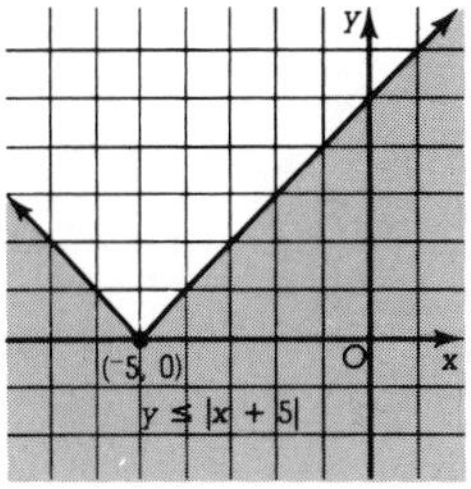

Page 68 Chapter Test

1.
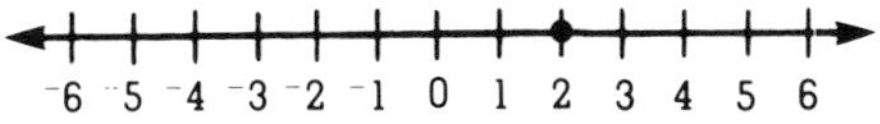

2.
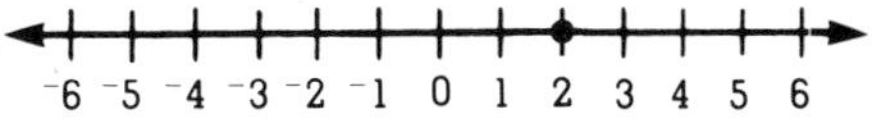

3.
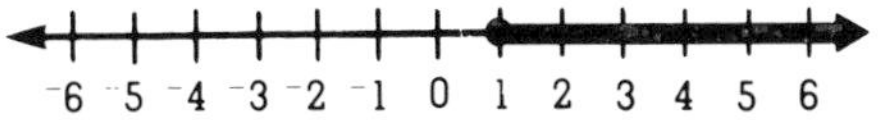

4.

5.
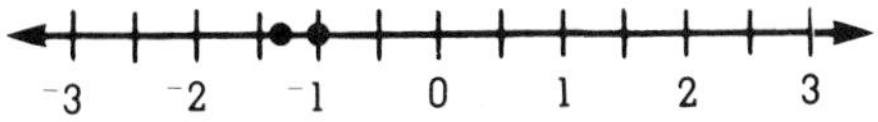

6.
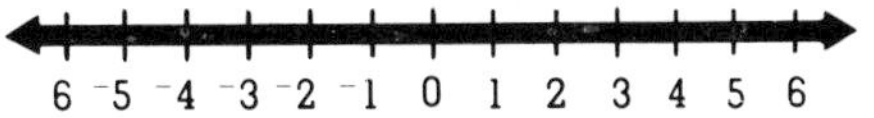

7. domain = {1, 7, 9, 2}; range = {2, ⁻3, 7} **8.** domain = {1.4}; range = {1.4, 1.5}

9. domain = {$x|x$ is real}; range = {$y|y$ is real} **10.** domain = {5}; range = {$y|y$ is real}

22.
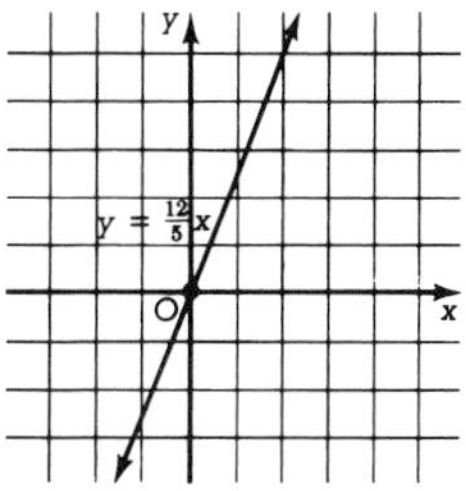

23.
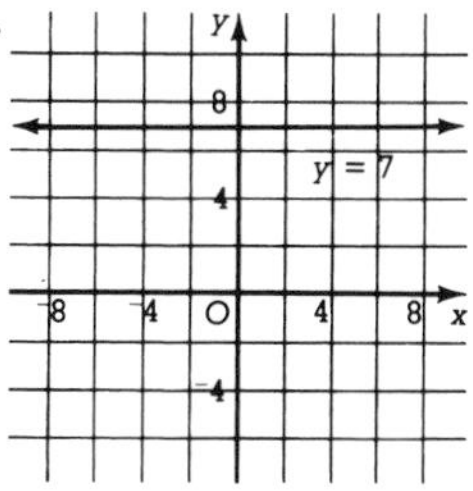

24.
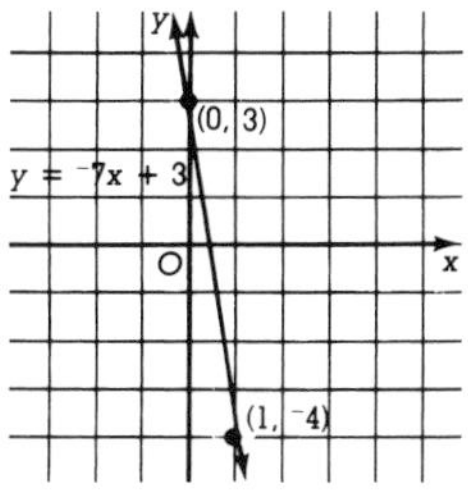

25.
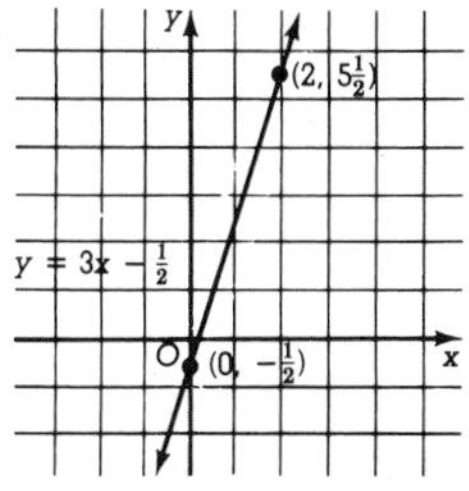

26.
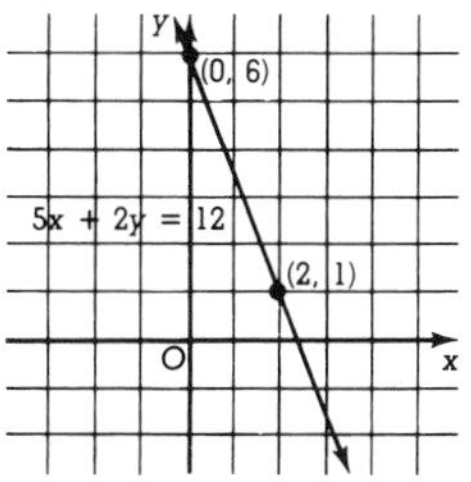

27.
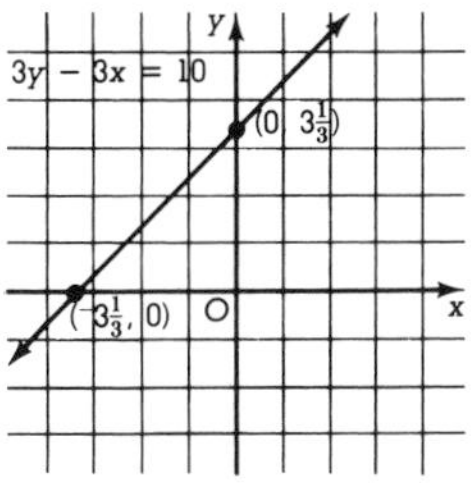

28.
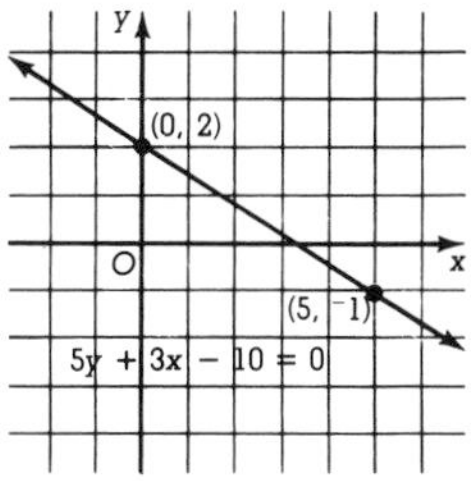

29.
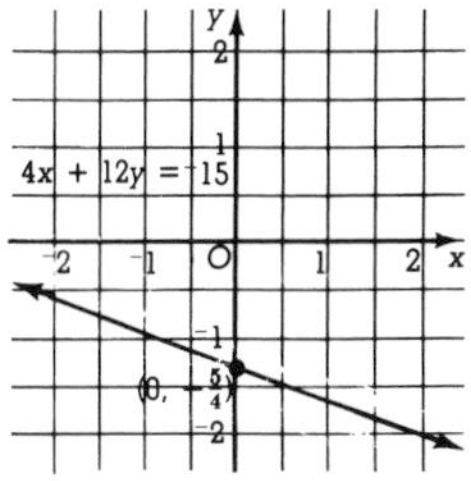

30. 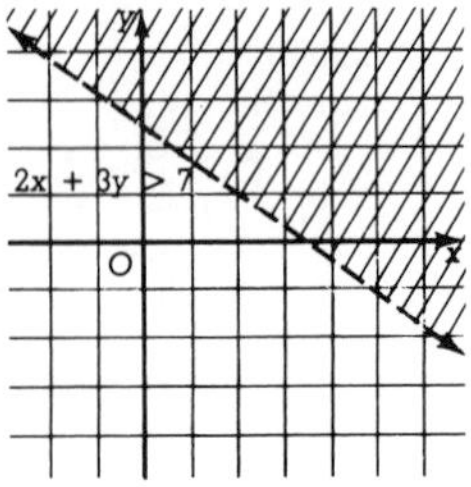

31. 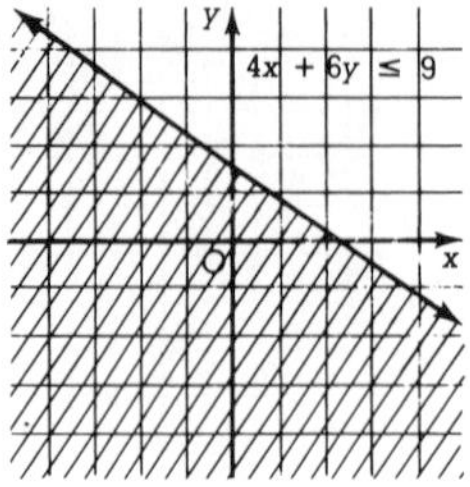

32. 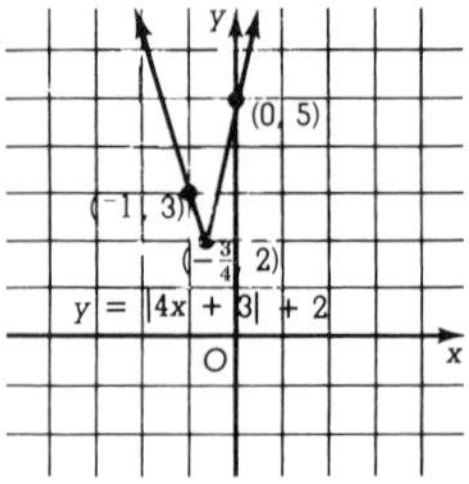

33. 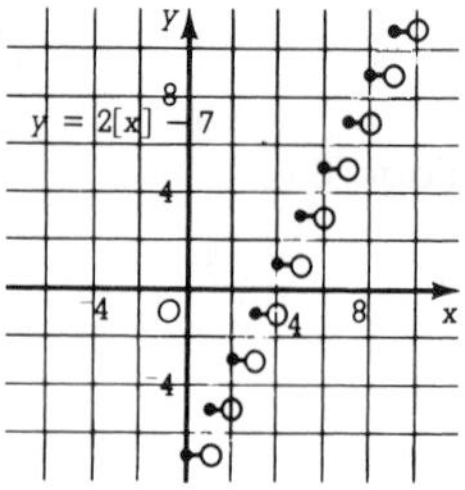

34. 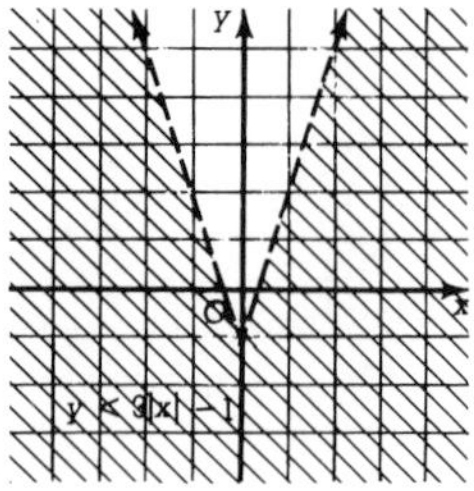

35. 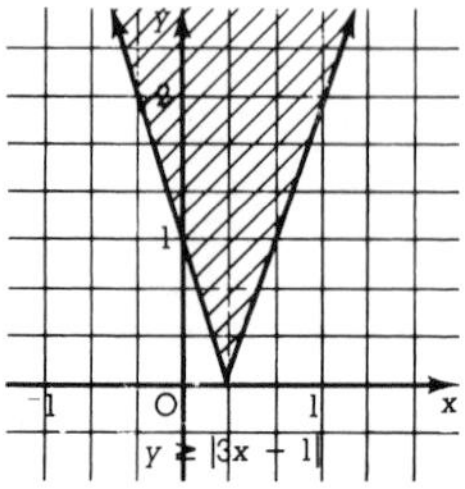

36. $y = \frac{4}{5}x - 4$ 37. $y = {}^-x + 7$
38. $y = 4x - 2$ 39. $y = \frac{1}{5}x + 7$
40. $y = 4x + 10$ 41. $y = {}^-x - 6$
42. $4x - 5y = 20$ 43. $x + y = 7$
44. $4x - y = {}^-2$ 45. $4x - y = {}^-10$
46. $x - 5y = {}^-35$ 47. $x + y = {}^-6$

CHAPTER 3 SYSTEMS OF EQUATIONS AND INEQUALITIES

Page 72 Written 23. A line connecting (1, 3) and (5, 9) has slope $\frac{3}{2}$. A line connecting (1, 3) and (4, 1) has slope $-\frac{2}{3}$. These two lines are perpendicular since $(-\frac{2}{3})(\frac{3}{2}) = {}^-1$. 24. A line connecting ($^-6$, 5) and ($^-2$, 7) has slope $\frac{1}{2}$. A line connecting (5, 3) and (1, 1) has slope $\frac{1}{2}$. These two lines are parallel since their slopes are the same. A line connecting ($^-6$, 5) and (1, 1) has slope $-\frac{4}{7}$. A line connecting ($^-2$, 7) and (5, 3) has slope $-\frac{4}{7}$. These two lines are parallel since their slopes are the same.

25.
```
10 INPUT A,B,C,P,Q
20 PRINT "Y="-(A/B)"X+"(Q+(A/B)*P)
30 GO TO 10
40 END
```
26.
```
10 INPUT A,B,C,P,Q
20 PRINT "Y="B/A"X+"(Q-(B/A)*P)
30 GO TO 10
40 END
```

Page 76 Written 17. consistent and independent 18. consistent and independent 19. inconsistent 20. inconsistent 21. consistent and dependent 22. consistent and dependent 23. consistent and independent 24. consistent and independent 25. consistent and independent 26. consistent and independent 27. inconsistent 28. inconsistent 29. consistent and independent 30. consistent and independent 31. consistent and dependent 32. consistent and dependent

Page 79 Written 31.
```
10 INPUT A,B,C,D,E,F
20 PRINT A"X+"B"Y="C
30 PRINT D"X+"E"Y="F
40 IF A*E-B*D=0 THEN 90
50 X = (C*E-B*F)/(A*E-B*D)
60 Y = (A*F-C*D)/(A*E-B*D)
70 PRINT "THE SOLUTION IS "("X","Y")"
80 GO TO 10
90 PRINT "NO UNIQUE SOLUTION"
100 GO TO 10
110 END
```

Page 85 Exploratory 1. $\frac{\begin{vmatrix} 5 & 2 \\ 11 & -6 \end{vmatrix}}{\begin{vmatrix} 3 & 2 \\ 5 & -6 \end{vmatrix}}, \frac{\begin{vmatrix} 3 & 5 \\ 5 & 11 \end{vmatrix}}{\begin{vmatrix} 3 & 2 \\ 5 & -6 \end{vmatrix}}$ 2. $\frac{\begin{vmatrix} 11 & -8 \\ 3 & -2 \end{vmatrix}}{\begin{vmatrix} 7 & -8 \\ 9 & -2 \end{vmatrix}}, \frac{\begin{vmatrix} 7 & 11 \\ 9 & 3 \end{vmatrix}}{\begin{vmatrix} 7 & -8 \\ 9 & -2 \end{vmatrix}}$ 3. $\frac{\begin{vmatrix} -11 & -8 \\ 3 & -8 \end{vmatrix}}{\begin{vmatrix} 1 & -8 \\ 8 & -8 \end{vmatrix}}, \frac{\begin{vmatrix} 1 & -11 \\ 8 & 3 \end{vmatrix}}{\begin{vmatrix} 1 & -8 \\ 8 & -8 \end{vmatrix}}$

4. $\frac{\begin{vmatrix} 2 & -1 \\ 5 & 1 \end{vmatrix}}{\begin{vmatrix} 3 & -1 \\ 1 & 1 \end{vmatrix}}, \frac{\begin{vmatrix} 3 & 2 \\ 1 & 5 \end{vmatrix}}{\begin{vmatrix} 3 & -1 \\ 1 & 1 \end{vmatrix}}$ 5. $\frac{\begin{vmatrix} 11 & 2 \\ 5 & -1 \end{vmatrix}}{\begin{vmatrix} 4 & 2 \\ 3 & -1 \end{vmatrix}}, \frac{\begin{vmatrix} 4 & 11 \\ 3 & 5 \end{vmatrix}}{\begin{vmatrix} 4 & 2 \\ 3 & -1 \end{vmatrix}}$ 6. $\frac{\begin{vmatrix} 11 & 6 \\ 6 & 1 \end{vmatrix}}{\begin{vmatrix} 2 & 6 \\ 5 & 1 \end{vmatrix}}, \frac{\begin{vmatrix} 2 & 11 \\ 5 & 6 \end{vmatrix}}{\begin{vmatrix} 2 & 6 \\ 5 & 1 \end{vmatrix}}$ 7. $\frac{\begin{vmatrix} \frac{1}{2} & 6 \\ \frac{1}{4} & -8 \end{vmatrix}}{\begin{vmatrix} \frac{1}{3} & 6 \\ 1 & -8 \end{vmatrix}}, \frac{\begin{vmatrix} \frac{1}{3} & \frac{1}{2} \\ 1 & \frac{1}{4} \end{vmatrix}}{\begin{vmatrix} \frac{1}{3} & 6 \\ 1 & -8 \end{vmatrix}}$

8. $\frac{\begin{vmatrix} \frac{1}{6} & \frac{1}{5} \\ \frac{1}{9} & \frac{1}{8} \end{vmatrix}}{\begin{vmatrix} \frac{1}{4} & \frac{1}{5} \\ \frac{1}{7} & \frac{1}{8} \end{vmatrix}}, \frac{\begin{vmatrix} \frac{1}{4} & \frac{1}{6} \\ \frac{1}{7} & \frac{1}{9} \end{vmatrix}}{\begin{vmatrix} \frac{1}{4} & \frac{1}{5} \\ \frac{1}{7} & \frac{1}{8} \end{vmatrix}}$ 9. $\frac{\begin{vmatrix} 0.56 & 0.41 \\ 0.77 & -0.41 \end{vmatrix}}{\begin{vmatrix} 0.30 & 0.41 \\ 0.23 & -0.41 \end{vmatrix}}, \frac{\begin{vmatrix} 0.30 & 0.56 \\ 0.23 & 0.77 \end{vmatrix}}{\begin{vmatrix} 0.30 & 0.41 \\ 0.23 & -0.41 \end{vmatrix}}$ 10. $\frac{\begin{vmatrix} 61 & 0.63 \\ 0.6 & -0.77 \end{vmatrix}}{\begin{vmatrix} 0.61 & 0.63 \\ 0.63 & -0.77 \end{vmatrix}}, \frac{\begin{vmatrix} 0.61 & 61 \\ 0.63 & 0.6 \end{vmatrix}}{\begin{vmatrix} 0.61 & 0.63 \\ 0.63 & -0.77 \end{vmatrix}}$

Page 85 Written 1. $(\frac{13}{7}, -\frac{2}{7})$ 2. $(\frac{1}{29}, -\frac{39}{29})$ 3. $(2, \frac{13}{8})$ 4. $(\frac{7}{4}, \frac{13}{4})$ 5. $(2.1, 1.3)$ 6. $(\frac{25}{28}, \frac{43}{28})$ 7. $(\frac{33}{52}, -\frac{5}{104})$ 8. $\left(-\frac{14}{27}, \frac{40}{27}\right)$ 9. $\left(\frac{0.5453}{0.2173}, \frac{0.1022}{0.2173}\right)$ 10. $\left(\frac{-47.348}{-0.8666}, \frac{-38.064}{-0.8666}\right)$

Page 92 Written

1.
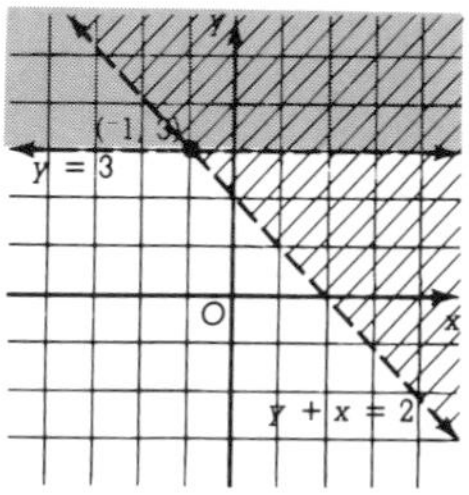

2.
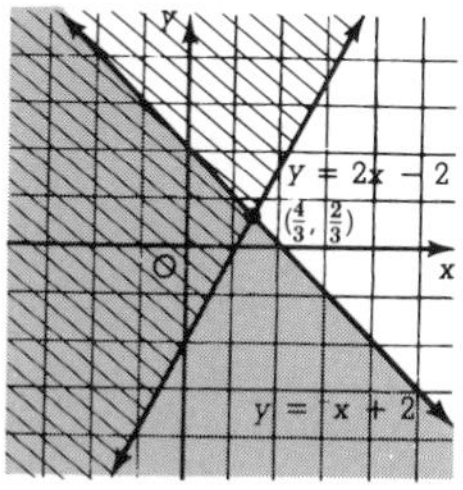

3.
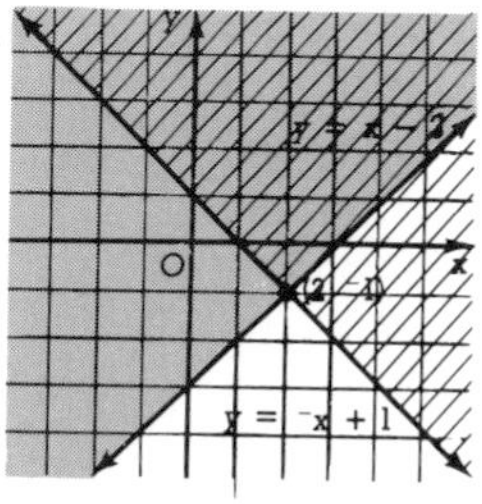

4.
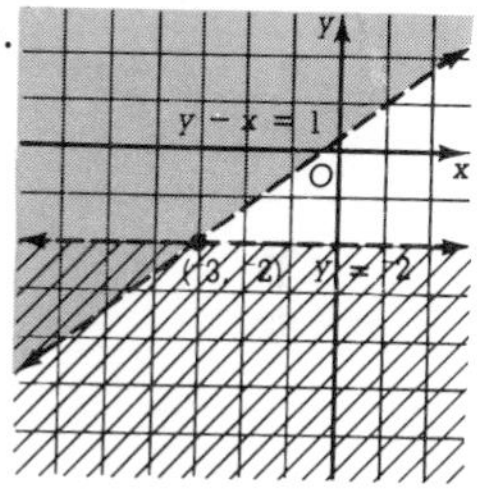

5.
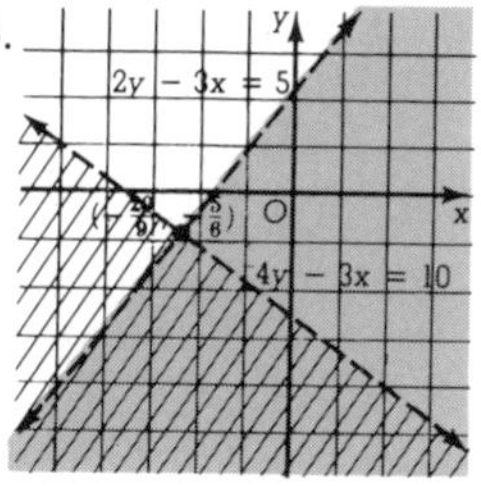

6.
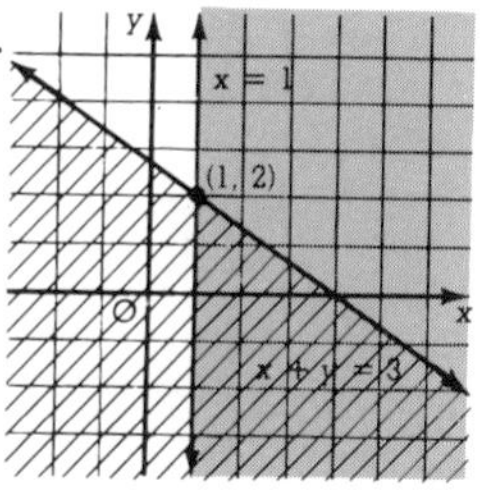

7.
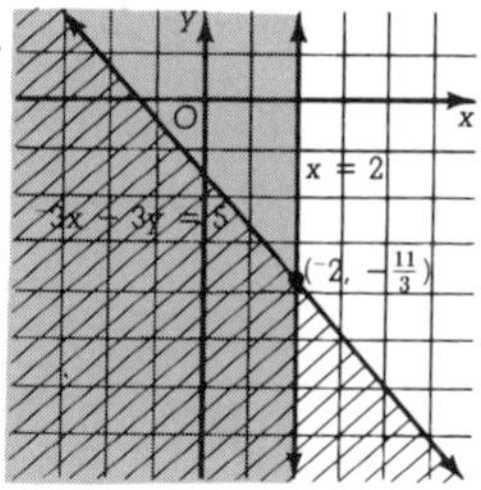

8.
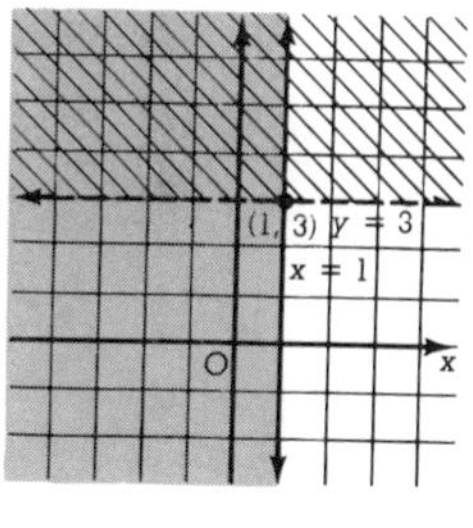

9.
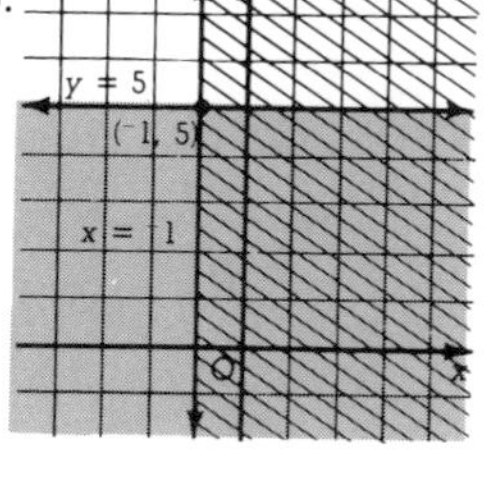

10.
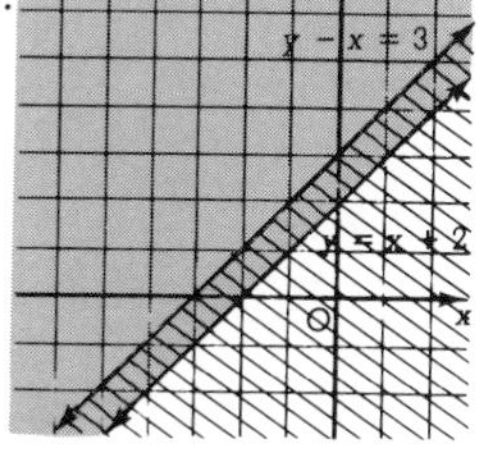

11.
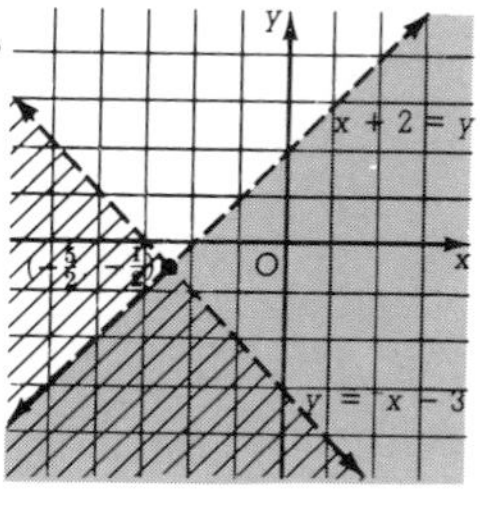

12.
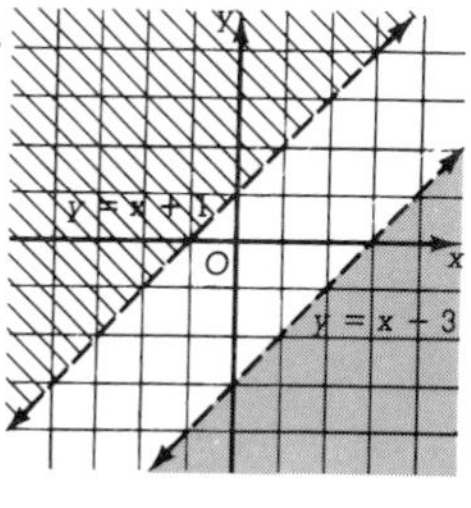

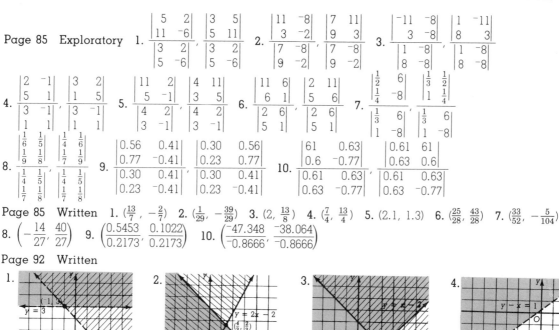

Page 96 Written 1. vertices: (1, 2), (1, 4), (5, 8), (5, 2); max. 11; min. -5 2. vertices: (1, 5), (3, 7), (5, 7), (5, 1); max. 7; min. -15 3. vertices: (0, 2), (4, 3), $(\frac{7}{3}, -\frac{1}{3})$; max. 25; min. 6 4. vertices: $(-3, -3)$, $(-3, 2)$, (0, 5), $(\frac{5}{3}, \frac{5}{3})$; max. 3; min. -10 5. vertices: (2, 2), (2, 8), (6, 12), $(6, -6)$; max. 30; min. 8 6. vertices: (0, 2), (4, 3), (2, 0); max. 13; min. 2 7. vertices: (0, 0), (0, 2), (2, 4), (5, 1), (5, 0); max. 25; min. -6 8. vertices: (0, 0), (0, 1), (2, 2), (4, 1), (5, 0); max. 15; min. -5

Pages 98–99 Chapter Review

33. 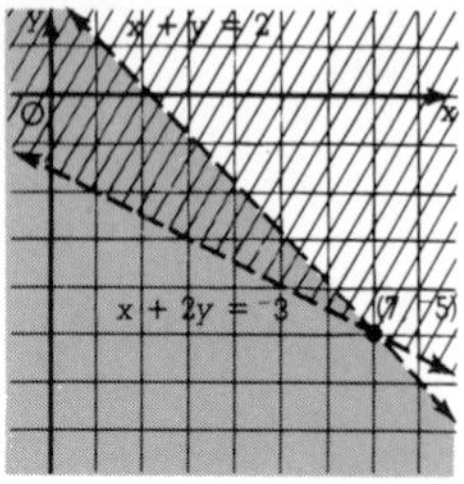

34. 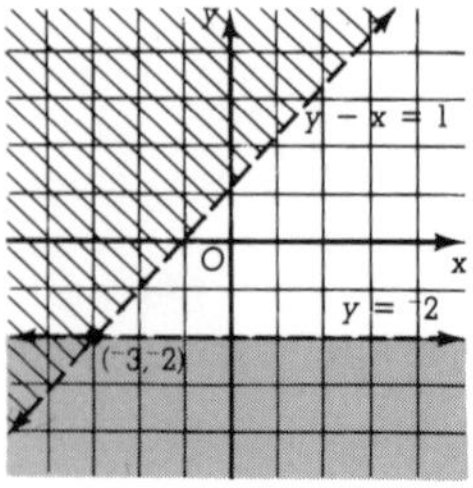

35. 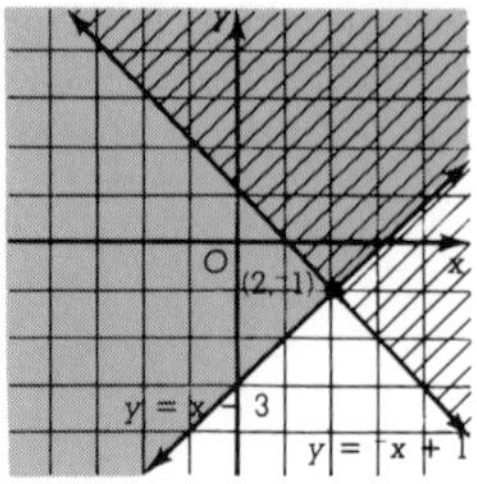

36. 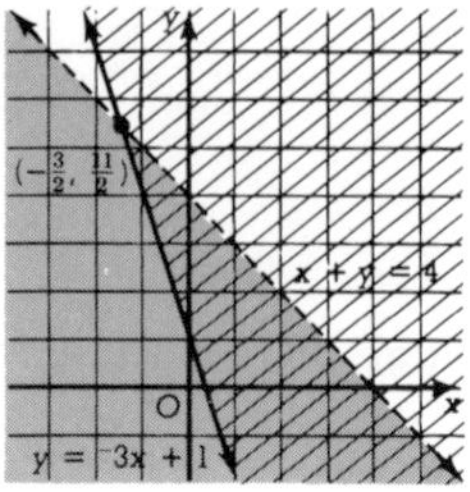

37. vertices: (0, 0), (0, 3), $(\frac{3}{2}, \frac{3}{2})$, (2, 0); max. 12; min. 0

38. vertices: (0, 0), (0, 6), (3, 6), (5, 4), (5, 0); max. 24; min. 0

Page 100 Chapter Test

17. 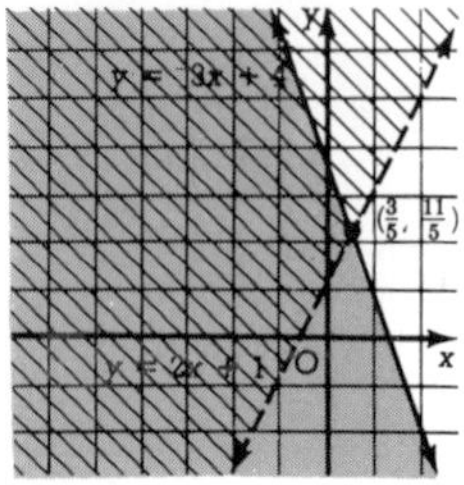

18. 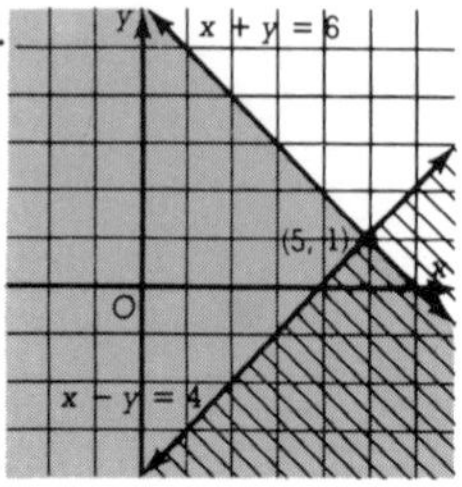

19. vertices: (0, 0), (0, 2), (2, 2), (4, 0); max. 8; min. 0

20. vertices: (0, 0), (0, 6), (4, 2), (4, 0); max. 12; min. $^-12$

CHAPTER 4 POLYNOMIALS

Pages 108–109 Written 1. $5x^2 + 1$ 2. $5y^2 - 2y + 3$ 3. $4p^2 + 10p + 2$ 4. $4m^2 + m + 1$ 5. $r^2 - r + 6$ 6. $k^2 + 3k - 9$ 13. $6x^2 + 31x + 35$ 14. $y^4 + 12y^2 + 35$ 15. $m^4 + m^2 - 20$ 16. $6y^2 + 5y - 56$ 17. $x^6 + 6x^3 + 9$ 18. $y^8 - 14y^4 + 49$ 19. $m^4 - 49$ 20. $2r^4 - 7r^2 - 15$ 21. $b^4 + 16b^2 + 64$ 22. $4a^2 + 12ab + 9b^2$ 23. $9a^2 - 12ab + 4b^2$ 24. $16a^2 - 25b^2$ 39. $m^2 + 8m + 16$ 40. $x^2 - 16x + 64$ 41. $y^2 - 4y + 4$ 42. $k^2 + 12k + 36$ 43. $y^2 - 25$ 44. $x^2 - 9$ 45. $4p^2 + 4pq^3 + q^6$ 46. $x^2 - 6xy + 9y^2$ 47. $a^2 - 36b^2$ 48. $1 + 14y + 49y^2$ 49. $1 - 14y + 49y^2$ 50. $1 - 49y^2$ 51. $16m^2 - 24mn + 9n^2$ 52. $25r^2 - 20r + 4$ 53. $4 - 12y + 9y^2$ 54. $4s^2 + 28st + 49t^2$ 55. $1 + 8r + 16r^2$ 56. $36a^2 + 24a + 4$ 57. $16a^2 - 4b^2$ 58. $25x^2 - 144$ 59. $x^6 - y^2$

Page 111 Written 1. $x^4 + 4x^3m + 6x^2m^2 + 4xm^3 + m^4$ 2. $r^6 + 6r^5s + 15r^4s^2 + 20r^3s^3 + 15r^2s^4 + 6rs^5 + s^6$ 3. $y^7 + 7y^6p + 21y^5p^2 + 35y^4p^3 + 35y^3p^4 + 21y^2p^5 + 7yp^6 + p^7$ 4. $x^3 - 3x^2y + 3xy^2 - y^3$ 5. $b^5 - 5b^4z + 10b^3z^2 - 10b^2z^3 + 5bz^4 - z^5$ 6. $r^6 - 6r^5m + 15r^4m^2 - 20r^3m^3 + 15r^2m^4 - 6rm^5 + m^6$ 7. $32m^5 + 80m^4y + 80m^3y^2 + 40m^2y^3 + 10my^4 + y^5$ 8. $81r^4 + 108r^3y + 54r^2y^2 + 12ry^3 + y^4$ 9. $64b^6 + 192b^5x + 240b^4x^2 + 160b^3x^3 + 60b^2x^4 + 12bx^5 + x^6$ 10. $16x^4 + 96x^3y + 216x^2y^2 + 216xy^3 + 81y^4$ 11. $243x^5 - 810x^4y + 1080x^3y^2 - 720x^2y^3 + 240xy^4 - 32y^5$ 12. $64m^6 - 576m^5 + 2160m^4 - 4320m^3 + 4860m^2 - 2916m + 729$ 13. $32y^5 + 80y^4 + 80y^3 + 40y^2 + 10y + 1$ 14. $64 + 96x + 60x^2 + 20x^3 + \frac{15}{4}x^4 + \frac{3}{8}x^5 + \frac{1}{64}x^6$ 15. $\frac{1}{729}y^6 + \frac{2}{27}y^5 + \frac{5}{3}y^4 + 20y^3 + 135y^2 + 486y + 729$

Page 114 Exploratory 1. $(r - 3)(r + 3)$ 2. $2(x^2 + 3y + 4b)$ 3. $x(x + y + 3)$ 4. $3(a^2 + 2a + 3y)$ 5. $(4y - 5)(4y + 5)$ 6. $(2m - 7)(2m + 7)$ 7. $2(a - 3)(a + 3)$ 8. $3(d - 4)(d + 4)$ 9. $r^2(r^2 + rs + s^2)$ 10. $3q(p^2 - pq + q^2)$ 11. $(x - 2)(x^2 + 2x + 4)$ 12. $(3 + x)(9 - 3x + x^2)$

Page 114 Written 1. $4m(2m + a + 4y)$ 2. $(b - 12)(b + 12)$ 3. $(y - 1)(y^2 + y + 1)$ 4. $7p(m + 3p - 2x)$ 5. $(m - 11)(m + 11)$ 6. $(b - 2a)(b^2 + 2ab + 4a^2)$ 7. $3r(r - 3)(r + 3)$ 8. $(2a + 1)(4a^2 - 2a + 1)$ 9. $(1 + r)(1 - r + r^2)$ 10. $2y(y - 7)(y + 7)$ 11. $(2 + x)(4 - 2x + x^2)$ 12. $(ab - 3)(a^2b^2 + 3ab + 9)$ 13. $(2a - 3)(2a + 3)$ 14. $2(r - 2s)(r^2 + 2rs + 4s^2)$ 15. $(3y - 8)(3y + 8)$ 16. $3(m + 2p)(m^2 - 2pm + 4p^2)$ 17. $(2b - 3x)(4b^2 - 6bx + 9x^2)$ 18. $(3p - 2q)(3p + 2q)$ 19. $ab(1 - a)(1 + a + a^2)$ 20. $(4s - 9r)(4s + 9r)$ 21. $(r - s)(r + s)(r^2 + s^2)$ 22. $s^3(r - 2)(r^2 + 2r + 4)$ 23. $(4y - 1)(16y^2 + 4y + 1)$ 24. $(m^2 - 3)(m^4 + 3m^2 + 9)$ 25. $(y^2 + 5)(y^4 - 5y^2 + 25)$ 26. $(2y - k)(2y + k)(4y^2 + k^2)$ 27. $(1 - 2m^2)(1 - 2m^2 + 4m^4)$

Page 114 Excursion **1.** 1, 4, 6, 4, 1 **2.** 1, 5, 10, 10, 5, 1 **3.** 1, 6, 15, 20, 15, 6, 1 **4.** 1, 7, 21, 35, 35, 21, 7, 1 **5.** $a^4 + 4a^3b + 6a^2b^2 + 4ab^3 + b^4$ **6.** $a^6 + 6a^5b + 15a^4b^2 + 20a^3b^3 + 15a^2b^4 + 6ab^5 + b^6$ **7.** $a^8 + 8a^7b + 28a^6b^2 + 56a^5b^3 + 70a^4b^4 + 56a^3b^5 + 28a^2b^6 + 8ab^7 + b^8$ **8.** $a^9 + 9a^8b + 36a^7b^2 + 84a^6b^3 + 126a^5b^4 + 126a^4b^5 + 84a^3b^6 + 36a^2b^7 + 9ab^8 + b^9$ **9.** $x^6 + 6x^5y + 15x^4y^2 + 20x^3y^3 + 15x^2y^4 + 6xy^5 + y^6$ **10.** $x^6 - 6x^5y + 15x^4y^2 - 20x^3y^3 + 15x^2y^4 - 6xy^5 + y^6$ **11.** $16a^4 + 32a^3b + 24a^2b^2 + 8ab^3 + b^4$ **12.** $x^6 - 18x^5y + 135x^4y^2 - 540x^3y^3 + 1215x^2y^4 - 1458xy^5 + 729y^6$

Page 124 Written **1.** $x - 15$ **2.** $a - 5$ **3.** $3y - 1$ **4.** $3b + 4$ **5.** $4a + 3 - \frac{2}{2a + 7}$ **6.** $4b - 9 + \frac{2}{5b + 7}$ **7.** $4y + 5 + \frac{3}{7y - 3}$ **8.** $8x + 3 + \frac{5}{10x - 3}$ **9.** $a - 12$ **10.** $x + 13$ **11.** $y + 12$ **12.** $b + 13$ **13.** $2x + 7$ **14.** $3m - 2$ **15.** $a - 2b$ **16.** $6x + y$ **17.** $2z - \frac{16}{3} + \frac{28}{3(3z + 7)}$ **18.** $b - 4a$ **19.** $a + 10 + \frac{44}{a - 6}$ **20.** $y + 4 + \frac{4}{y - 3}$ **21.** $8x - 44 + \frac{231}{x + 5}$ **22.** $x + 3 - \frac{2}{x + 2}$ **23.** $3a + 7 + \frac{4}{2a + 3}$ **24.** $9k + 10 + \frac{4}{14k - 3}$ **25.** $7m - 8 + \frac{3}{8m - 7}$ **26.** $4r + 3 - \frac{4}{5r - 2}$ **27.** $2y^2 + 5y + 2$ **28.** $2x^2 - 7x + 4$ **29.** $3a^2 - 2a + 3$ **30.** $4b + \frac{1}{2b - 1}$ **31.** $m^2 + m + 1$ **32.** $a^2 + 2a + 4$ **33.** $y^2 - 6y + 9 - \frac{1}{y - 3}$ **34.** $x^2 + 4x + 4 + \frac{4}{x + 2}$ **35.** $2a^2 + \frac{1}{3}a - \frac{41}{9} - \frac{71}{9(3a + 2)}$ **36.** $p^2 + 5p - 7 + \frac{8}{2p - 3}$ **37.** $m + 3$ **38.** $8p + 1 - \frac{10}{6p^2 - 5}$ **39.** $x^2 - 2x + 8 - \frac{20}{x + 2}$ **40.** $2t^2 + 2t - \frac{3}{t - 1}$ **41.** $x^2 + 2x + 2$ **42.** $y^2 + 2y + 3$ **43.** $a^2 - a - 1$ **44.** $x^2 - 2x + 3$

Page 128 Written **1.** $2x^2 + x + 5 + \frac{6}{x - 2}$ **2.** $3y^2 + 11y + 1 + \frac{5}{y - 3}$ **3.** $2a^2 - a - 1 + \frac{4}{a + 1}$ **4.** $3m^2 + m + 3 + \frac{2}{m - 1}$ **5.** $x^3 + x - 1$ **6.** $3y^3 - 9y^2 + 7y - 6$ **7.** $6k^2 - k - 2$ **8.** $z^3 + z^2 + 3z + 1$ **9.** $2b^2 - 5b - 3$ **10.** $x^2 + 4x + 3$ **11.** $y^3 - 11y^2 + 31y - 21$ **12.** $a^3 - 6a^2 - 7a + 60$ **13.** $2x^3 + x^2 + 3x - 1 + \frac{5}{x - 3}$ **14.** $2a^3 - 3a^2 - 3a - 1 - \frac{4}{a - 1}$ **15.** $y^3 + 3y^2 - 16y + 55 - \frac{166}{y + 3}$ **16.** $h^4 + 2h^3 - 2h^2 - \frac{3}{h - 2}$ **17.** $2x^3 + x^2 - 2x + \frac{3}{2x - 1}$ **18.** $b^2 - 2b - 3 + \frac{7}{2b + 1}$ **19.** $2x^2 - 8x + 1 + \frac{5}{3x - 2}$ **20.** $2y^3 + 3y^2 + y - 1 - \frac{13}{2y - 3}$ **21.** $x^4 - 2x^3 + 4x^2 - 8x + 16$ **22.** $x^4 + 2x^3 + 4x^2 + 5x + 10$

Page 132 Chapter Test **12.** $m^5 + 5m^4k + 10m^3k^2 + 10m^2k^3 + 5mk^4 + k^5$ **13.** $y^4 + 8y^3 + 24y^2 + 32y + 16$ **14.** $64x^6 - 960x^5 + 6000x^4 - 20{,}000x^3 + 37{,}500x^2 - 37{,}500x + 15{,}625$ **15.** $y^6 - 18y^5 + 135y^4 - 540y^3 + 1215y^2 - 1458y + 729$

CHAPTER 5 ROOTS

Page 139 Written **19.** 14 **20.** 22 **21.** $140\sqrt[3]{5}$ **22.** $12\sqrt[3]{3} + 6\sqrt[3]{2}$ **23.** $^-2$ **24.** $3\sqrt[4]{5}$ **25.** $\sqrt[4]{90}$ **26.** $4m^2\sqrt{2r}$ **27.** $2ab^2\sqrt[3]{ab}$ **28.** $xy\sqrt[3]{3xy}$ **29.** $4|xy|\sqrt{x}$ **30.** $3x^2z^2\sqrt{5}$ **31.** $2ab^2\sqrt[3]{9b}$ **32.** $5mb^2\sqrt[4]{m}$ **33.** $3b^2r^2\sqrt[4]{3r}$

Page 142 Written **1.** $8\sqrt{2} - 8$ **2.** $6\sqrt{2} + 6$ **3.** $5\sqrt{5} - 10\sqrt{2}$ **4.** $^-7\sqrt{7}$ **5.** $4 - 7\sqrt{3}$ **6.** $4\sqrt{5} + 23\sqrt{6}$ **7.** $11\sqrt[3]{5}$ **8.** $\sqrt[3]{6}$ **9.** $^-\sqrt[3]{2}$ **10.** $12\sqrt{2}$ **11.** $2\sqrt[3]{2} - 4\sqrt{2}$ **12.** $\sqrt[3]{2} + \sqrt{3}$ **13.** $14\sqrt{6} + 2\sqrt[3]{3}$ **14.** $5\sqrt{2}$ **15.** $2\sqrt{3} + 3$ **16.** $3\sqrt[3]{m}$ **17.** $3\sqrt[3]{5} - 3\sqrt[3]{3}$ **18.** $5\sqrt[4]{5}$ **19.** $|x|y^2\sqrt{2}$ **20.** $(|x| + 1)\sqrt[4]{x^2}$ **21.** $3|yz|\sqrt[4]{z^2}$ **22.** $9\sqrt{6}$ **23.** $|z| + z^2 + z^4$ **24.** $(x^2y^3 - 2x^2y^2)\sqrt[3]{3}$ **25.** $17 + 8\sqrt{2}$ **26.** $12 + 3\sqrt{3} + 4\sqrt{6} + 3\sqrt{2}$ **27.** $25 + 5\sqrt{6} - 5\sqrt{2} - 2\sqrt{3}$ **28.** $45 + 2\sqrt{3}$ **29.** $3 - 5\sqrt{11}$ **30.** $3\sqrt{5} + \sqrt{30} - \sqrt{6} - 3$ **31.** $1 + \sqrt{15}$ **32.** $^-7$ **33.** $21 + 8\sqrt{5}$ **34.** 1.1×10^2 **35.** 9×10^4 **36.** 1.2×10^4 **37.** $9\sqrt[3]{2} - 6$ **38.** $16\sqrt[3]{3} - 12$ **39.** $y^3 + 4$ **40.** $x^3 - 3$ **41.** $(x - \sqrt{5})(x + \sqrt{5})$ **42.** $(m - \sqrt{11})(m + \sqrt{11})$ **43.** $(y - \sqrt{6})(y + \sqrt{6})$ **44.** $(a + 2\sqrt{5})^2$ **45.** $(b - 5\sqrt{2})^2$ **46.** $r(r - \sqrt{2})(r + \sqrt{2})$

Page 149 Written 23. $\pm\sqrt{y^2 - r^2}$ if $y \geq r$ 24. $\frac{2mM}{r^3}$ if $r \neq 0$ 25. $\frac{u}{4T^2}$ if $T \neq 0$ 26. $\frac{T}{4v^2 - 1}$ if $4v^2 - 1 \neq 0$ 27. $\frac{m^6g^2}{r}$ if $r \neq 0$

Page 156 Written 27. $1 - i$, $^-1 + 5i$, $6 + 2i$ 28. $4 + 3i$, $^-2 + 5i$, $7 + 11i$ 29. 14, $4i$, 53 30. 8, $6i$, 25 31. 2, $2i$, 2 32. 0, $2 + 2i$, ^-2i 33. $x = 2$, $y = 3$ 34. $x = 6$, $y = \frac{7}{2}$ 35. $x = {}^-1$, $y = {}^-3$ 36. $x = 2$, $y = 3$ 37. $x = 3$, $y = 1$ 38. $x = \frac{67}{11}$, $y = \frac{19}{11}$

Page 158 Written 20. $\frac{7\sqrt{2} + 21i}{11}$ 21. $\frac{1 + 4i\sqrt{3}}{7}$ 22. $\frac{^-1 + 2i\sqrt{2}}{3}$ 23. $\frac{2 - 3i\sqrt{5}}{7}$ 24. $\frac{^-3 - 4i\sqrt{7}}{11}$ 25. $\frac{16 + 63i}{50}$ 26. 9 27. $\frac{^-1 - i}{2}$ 28. $\frac{^-44 + 117i}{50}$ 33. $1^3 = 1 \cdot 1 \cdot 1 = 1$ 34. $(-\frac{1}{2} + \frac{1}{2}i\sqrt{3})^3 = (-\frac{1}{2} - \frac{1}{2}i\sqrt{3})(-\frac{1}{2} + \frac{1}{2}i\sqrt{3}) = \frac{1}{4} + \frac{3}{4} + \frac{1}{4}i\sqrt{3} - \frac{1}{4}i\sqrt{3} = 1$ 35. $(-\frac{1}{2} - \frac{1}{2}i\sqrt{3})^3 = (-\frac{1}{2} + \frac{1}{2}i\sqrt{3})(-\frac{1}{2} - \frac{1}{2}i\sqrt{3}) = \frac{1}{4} + \frac{3}{4} + \frac{1}{4}i\sqrt{3} - \frac{1}{4}i\sqrt{3} = 1$

Page 161 Exploratory 1. no additive identity, no inverses 2. no multiplication inverse 3. not closed under addition or multiplication, no identities 4. not closed under addition or multiplication, no identities 5. not closed under addition or multiplication, no identities

Page 161 Written 18. $\frac{1 - 4i}{17}$ 19. $\frac{^-i\sqrt{3}}{3}$ 20. $\frac{3 + 2i}{13}$ 21. $\frac{11 - i}{122}$ 22. $\frac{2 + 5i}{29}$ 23. $\frac{3 + 4i}{25}$ 24. $\frac{^-1 + 4i}{34}$ 25. $\frac{^-3 + 2i}{13}$ 26. $\frac{2 + i}{5}$ 27. $\frac{5 - 4i}{41}$ 28. $\frac{^-i}{6}$ 29. $-\frac{1}{3}$

Let $a + bi$ and $c + di$ be two complex numbers.

30. $(a + bi) + (c + di) = (a + c) + (b + d)i$ definition of complex addition
a and c are real numbers definition of complex numbers
$a + c$ is a real number reals are closed under addition
b and d are real numbers definition of complex numbers
$b + d$ is a real number reals are closed under addition
$(a + c) + (b + d)i$ is a complex number definition of complex numbers

31. $(a + bi)(c + di) = (ac - bd) + (ad + bc)i$ definition of complex multiplication
a, b, c, and d are real numbers definition of complex numbers
ac, bd, ad, and bc are real numbers reals are closed under multiplication
$ac - bd$ and $ad + bc$ are real numbers reals are closed under addition
$(ac - bd) + (ad + bc))i$ is a complex number definition of complex numbers

Let $a + bi$, $c + di$, and $e + fi$ be complex numbers.

32. $[(a + bi) + (c + di)] + (e + fi) = [(a + c) + (b + d)i] + (e + fi)$ definition of complex addition
$= [(a + c) + e] + [(b + d) + f]i$ definition of complex addition
$= [a + (c + e)] + [b + (d + f)]i$ associativity for addition of reals
$= (a + bi) + [(c + e) + (d + f)i]$ definition of complex addition
$= (a + bi) + [(c + di) + (e + fi)]$ definition of complex addition

33. $[(a + bi)(c + di)](e + fi) = [(ac - bd) + (ad + bc)i](e + fi)$ definition of complex multiplication
$= [(ac - bd)e - (ad + bc)f] + [(ac - bd)f + (ad + bc)e]i$
definition of complex multiplication
$= [(ac)e - (bd)e - (ad)f - (bc)f] + [(ac)f - (bd)f + (ad)e + (bc)e]i$
distributivity for reals
$= [a(ce) - b(de) - a(df) - b(cf)] + [a(cf) - b(df) + a(de) + b(ce)]i$
associativity for multiplication of reals
$= [a(ce) - a(df) - b(cf) - b(de)] + [a(cf) + a(de) + b(cd) - b(df)]i$
commutivity for addition of reals
$= [a(ce - df) - b(cf + de)] + [a(cf + de) + b(ce - df)]i$
distributivity for reals
$= (a + bi)[(ce - df) + (cf + de)i]$ definition of complex multiplication
$= (a + bi)[(c + di)(e + fi)]$ definition of complex multiplication

CHAPTER 6 QUADRATIC EQUATIONS

Page 174 Written **43.**

```
10 INPUT A, B, C
20 IF B↑2−4*A*C<0 THEN 60
30 PRINT (−B+SQR(B↑2−4*A*C))/(2*A)
40 PRINT (−B−SQR(B↑2−4*A*C))/(2*A)
50 GO TO 70
60 PRINT "NO REAL ROOTS"
70 END
```

Page 174 Excursion **1.** 1 + 2 + 4 + 7 + 14 **2.** 1 + 2 + 4 + 8 + 16 + 31 + 62 + 124 + 248 **3.** 1 + 2 + 4 + 8 + 16 + 32 + 64 + 127 + 254 + 508 + 1016 + 2032 + 4064

Page 177 Written **1.** 144, two real **2.** 16, two real **3.** 0, one real **4.** 484, two real **5.** $^-16$, two imaginary **6.** $^-16$, two imaginary **7.** 1, two real **8.** 16, two real **9.** 81, two real **10.** 100, two real **11.** 169, two real **12.** 0, one real **13.** $^-144$, two imaginary **14.** $^-196$, two imaginary **15.** 25, two real **16.** 225, two real **17.** 144, two real **18.** $^-276$, two imaginary **19.** 196, two real **20.** 225, two real **21.** 289, two real **22.** 144, two real **23.** $^-36$, two imaginary **24.** $^-1$, two imaginary **25.** 1, two real **26.** 1, two real **27.** 81, two real **28.** 400, two real **29.** 0, one real **30.** 140, two real **31.** $^-3$, two imaginary **32.** $^-100$, two imaginary **33.** 16, two real **34.** 289, two real **35.** 36, two real **36.** 0, one real **37.** $\frac{9}{16}$, two real **38.** $\frac{11}{15}$, two real

39.

```
10 INPUT A,B,C
15 LET X=B↑2−4*A*C
20 PRINT "DISCRIMINANT =" X
30 IF X=0 THEN 70
40 IF X<0 THEN 80
50 PRINT "TWO REAL SOLUTIONS"
60 GO TO 90
70 PRINT "ONE REAL SOLUTION"
75 GO TO 90
80 PRINT "TWO IMAGINARY SOLUTIONS"
90 END
```

40.

```
10 INPUT A, B, C
20 LET X=B↑2−4*A*C
30 IF X<0 THEN 80
40 IF X=0 THEN 60
50 PRINT (−B+SQR(X))/(2*A);
60 PRINT (−B−SQR(X))/(2*A)
70 GO TO 110
80 X=ABS(X)
90 PRINT −B/(2*A)"+"SQR(X)/(2*A)"i"
100 PRINT −B/(2*A)"−"SQR(X)/(2*A)"i"
110 END
```

CHAPTER 7 QUADRATIC RELATIONS AND FUNCTIONS

Page 191 Written **9.** x = one of the numbers; product = $40x - x^2$ **10.** x = one of the numbers; product = $36x - x^2$ **11.** x = lesser number; product = $64x + x^2$ **12.** x = lesser number; product = $25x + x^2$ **13.** x = number of \$1 increases; income = $2400 + 140x - 20x^2$ **14.** area = $120x - 2x^2$

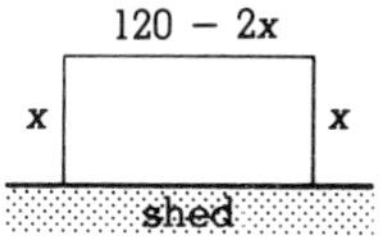

Page 194 Written 1.

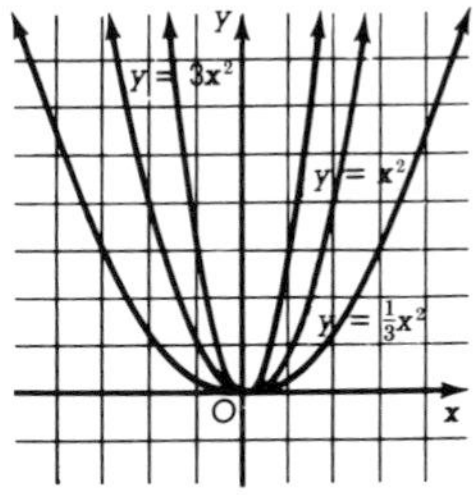

2.

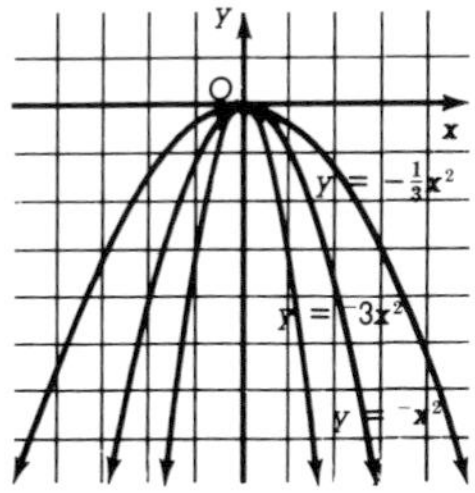

3. 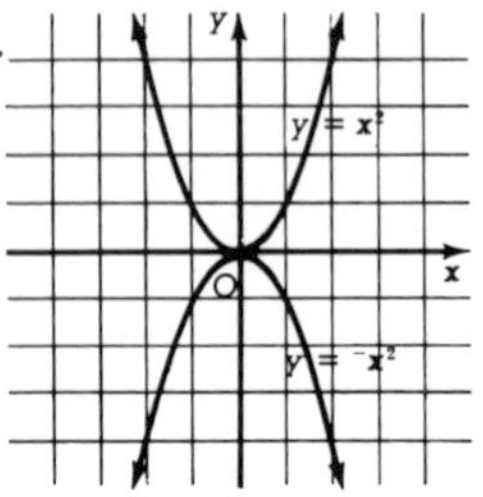

4. 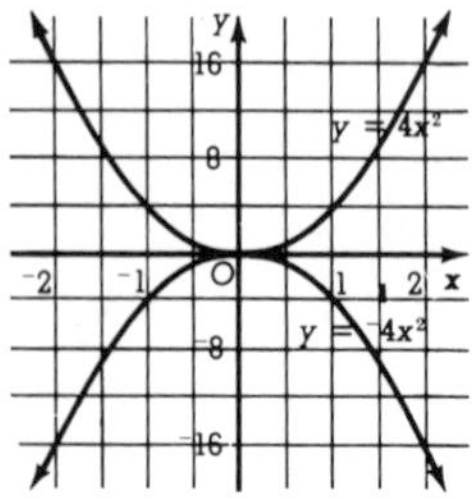

5. 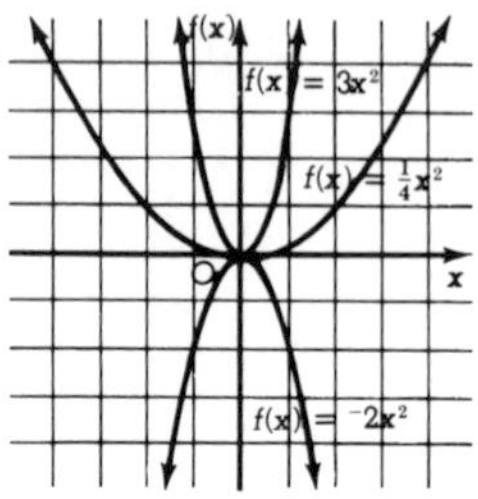

6. 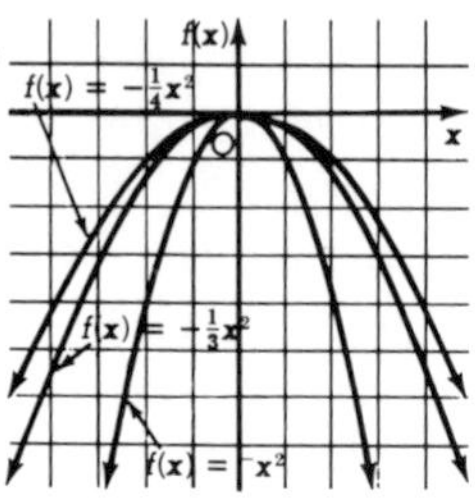

Page 198 Written 11. (1, 0); $x = 1$; up 12. ($^-4$, 0); $x = {}^-4$; up 13. ($^-2$, 0); $x = {}^-2$; up 14. ($^-3$, 0); $x = {}^-3$; down 15. ($^-5$, 0); $x = {}^-5$; up 16. (1, 0); $x = 1$; up 17. (1, 0); $x = 1$; down 18. (4, 0); $x = 4$; up 19. ($\frac{11}{2}$, 0); $x = \frac{11}{2}$; up 20. ($-\frac{15}{2}$, 0); $x = -\frac{15}{2}$; up

21. 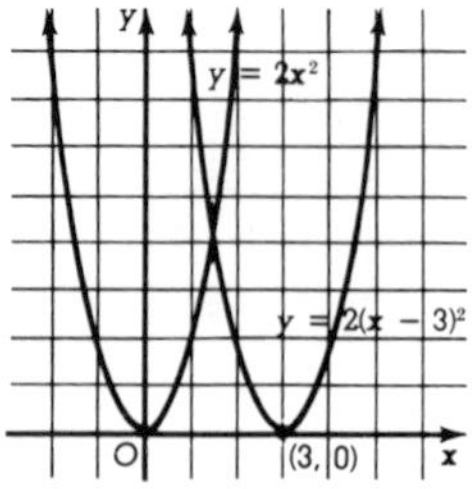

22. 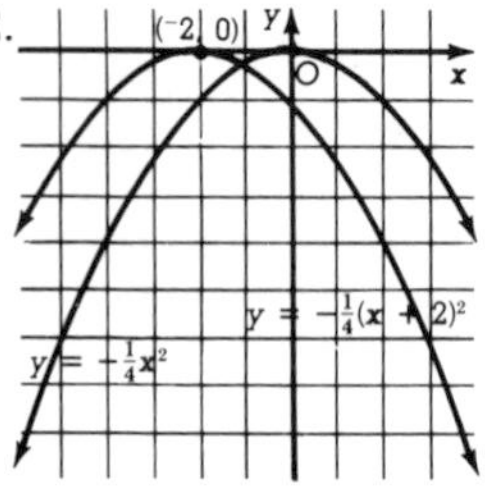

23. 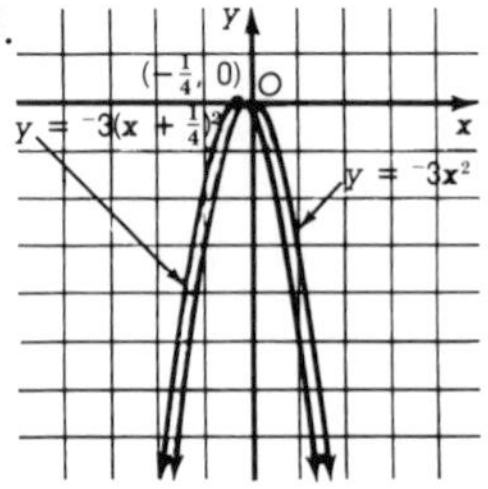

24. 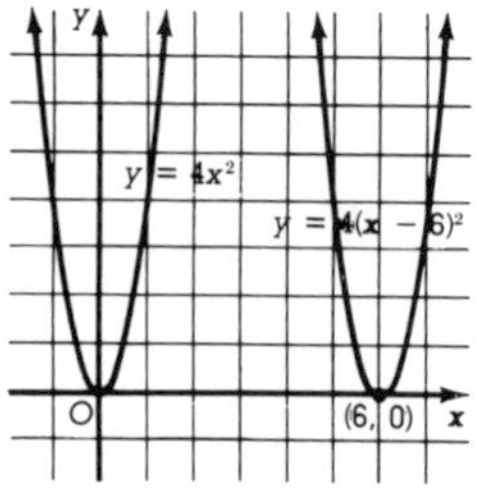

25. 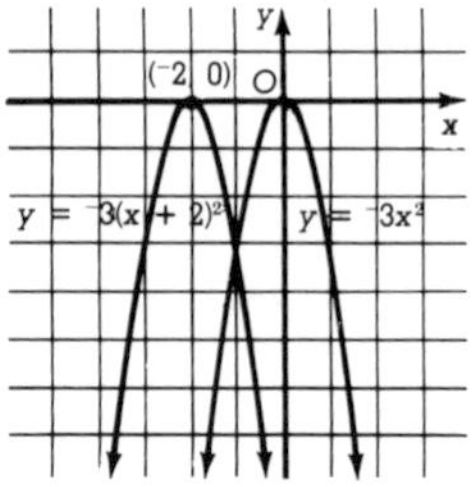

26. 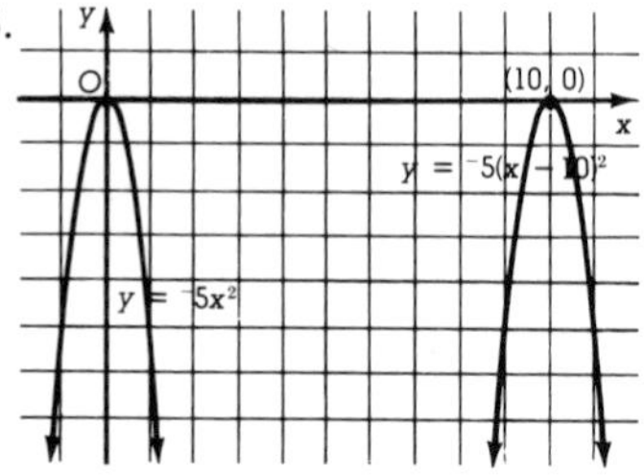

Page 201 Written 1. 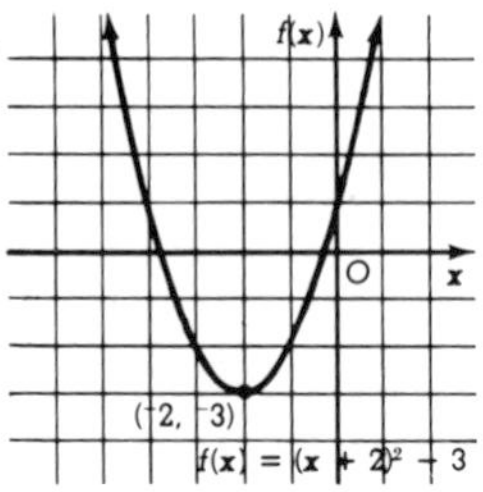

2. 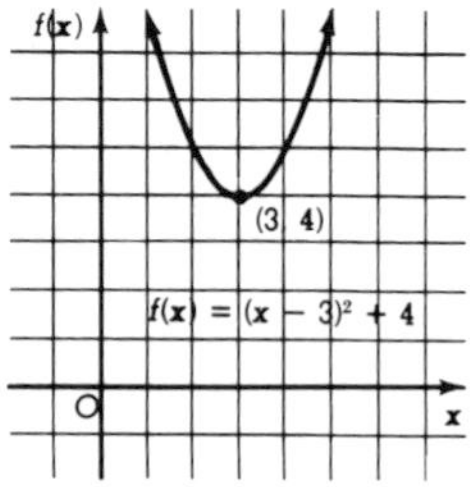

3. 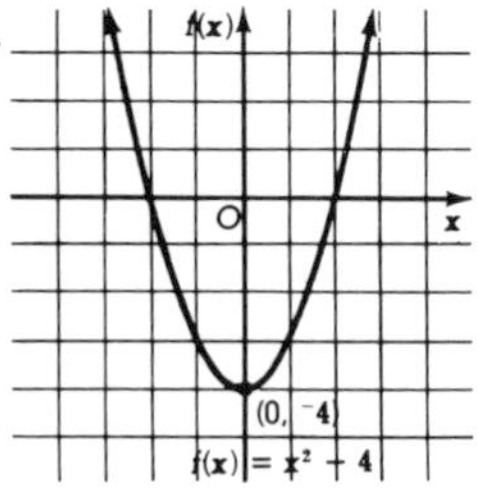

4. 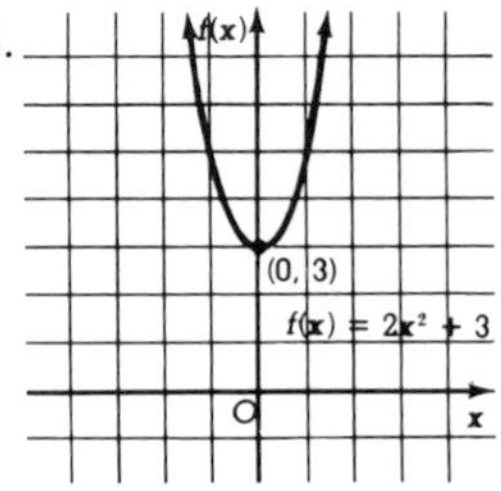

5. 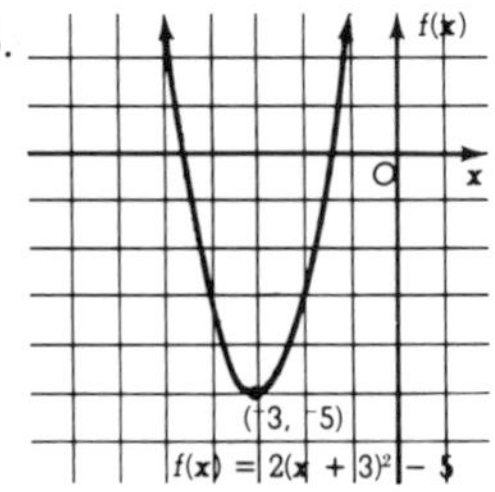

6. 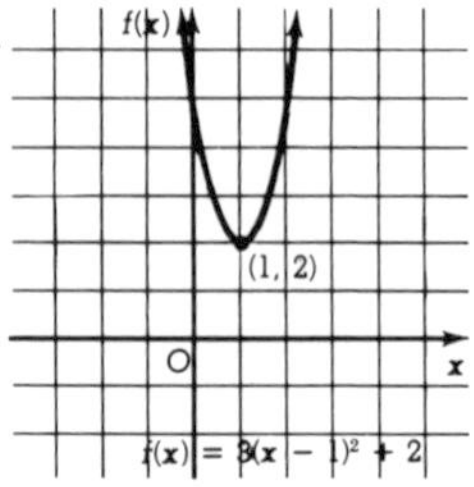

7. 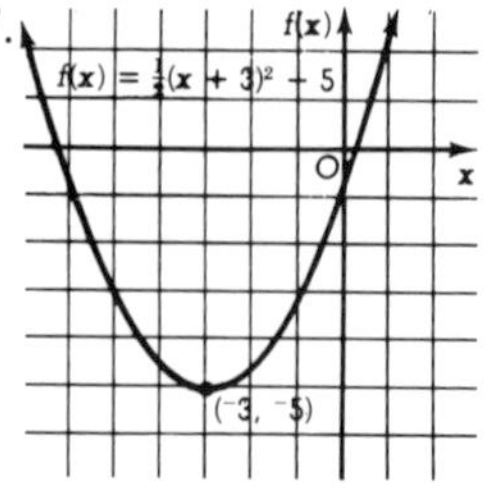

8. 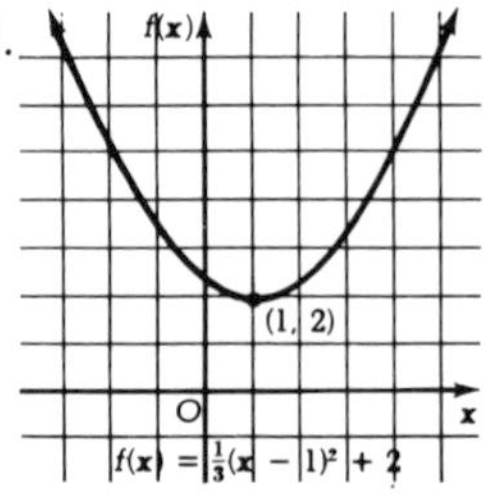

9. 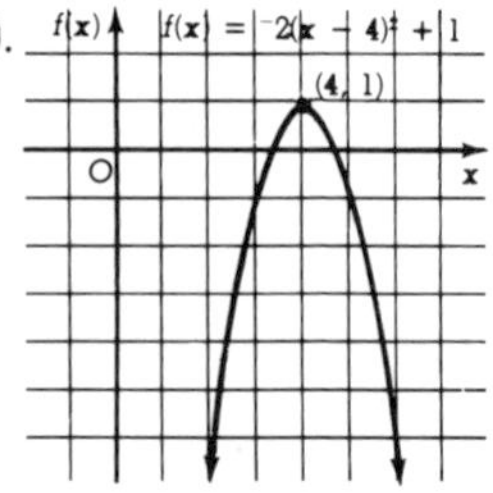

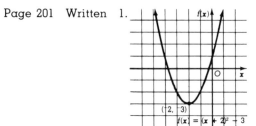

10. 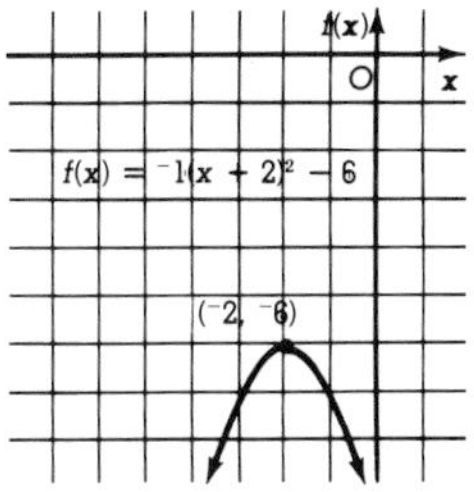

11. 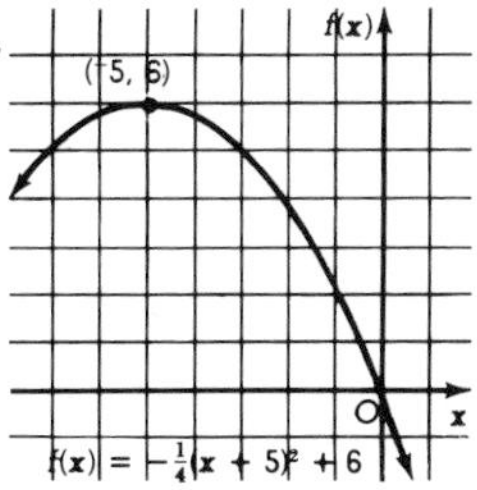

12. 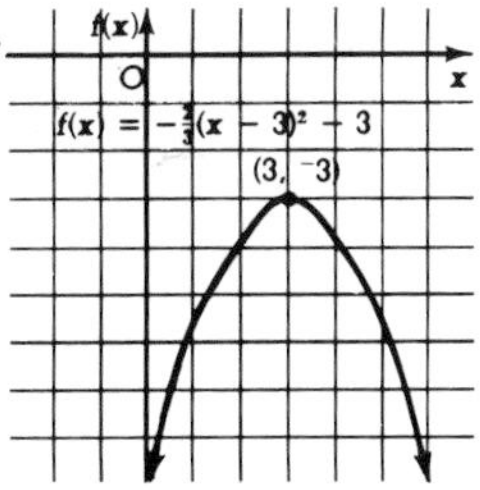

13. $h = -\dfrac{b}{2a}$; $k = \dfrac{4ac - b^2}{4a}$

14.
```
5  DATA . . .
10 READ A,B,C
15 LET H=−B/(2*A)
20 LET K=(4*A*C−B↑2)/(4*A)
25 PRINT "AXIS OF SYMMETRY: X="H
30 PRINT "VERTEX AT (" H","K")"
35 IF A<0 THEN 50
40 PRINT "GRAPH OPENS UPWARD"
45 GO TO 55
50 PRINT "GRAPH OPENS DOWNWARD"
55 END
```

Page 205 Written

12. 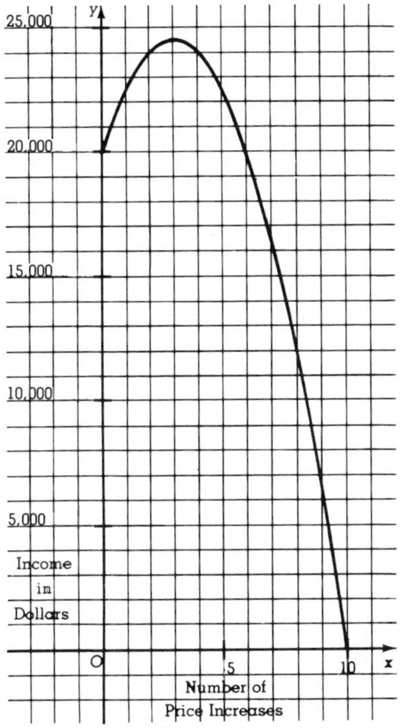

17. 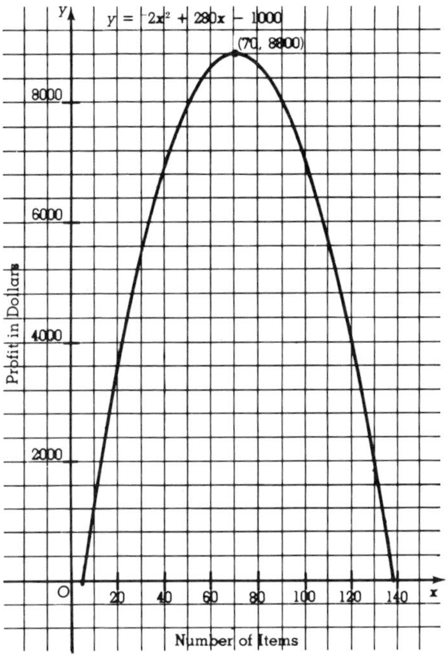

Page 207 Written

1.
$y \leq x^2 - 13x + 36$
or $y \leq (x - 6\frac{1}{2})^2 - 6\frac{1}{4}$
$(6\frac{1}{2}, 6\frac{1}{4})$

2.$y > x^2 + x - 30$
or $y > (x + \frac{1}{2})^2 - 30\frac{1}{4}$
$(\frac{1}{2}, -30\frac{1}{4})$

3.$y \geq x^2 + 3x - 18$
or $y \geq (x + \frac{3}{2})^2 - 20\frac{1}{4}$
$(-\frac{3}{2}, -20\frac{1}{4})$

4.$y < x^2 - x - 20$
or $y < (x - \frac{1}{2})^2 - 20\frac{1}{4}$
$(\frac{1}{2}, -20\frac{1}{4})$

5.$y \leq x^2 - 16$
$(0, -16)$

6.
$y > x^2 + 3x - 4$
or $y > (x + \frac{3}{2})^2 - 6\frac{1}{4}$
$(-\frac{3}{2}, -6\frac{1}{4})$

7.
$y < x^2 + 4x + 3$
or $y < (x + 2)^2 - 1$
$(-2, -1)$

8.
$y > 4x^2 - 8x + 3$
or $y > 4(x - 1)^2 + 1$
$(1, -1)$

9.
$y \leq 2x^2 + x - 3$ or
$y \leq 2(x + \frac{1}{4})^2 - 3\frac{1}{8}$
$(-\frac{1}{4}, -3\frac{1}{8})$

10.
$y > x^2 + 2x + 1$ or
$y > (x + 1)^2$
$(-1, 0)$

11.$y \leq x^2 + 6x + 9$ or
$y \leq (x + 3)^2$
$(-3, 0)$

12.$y \geq x^2 + 8x + 16$ or
$y \geq (x + 4)^2$
$(-4, 0)$

13.
$y > x^2 - 6x + 8$ or
$y > (x - 3)^2 - 1$
$(3, -1)$

14.
$y \leq x^2 - 7x + 10$ or
$y \leq (x - 3\frac{1}{2})^2 - 2\frac{1}{4}$
$(3\frac{1}{2}, -2\frac{1}{4})$

15.
$y < 3x^2 + 5x + 2$ or
$y < 3(x + \frac{5}{6})^2 - \frac{1}{12}$
$(-\frac{5}{6}, -\frac{1}{12})$

Page 211 Chapter Review

7.
$y = 2x^2$

8.
$y = -\frac{1}{3}x^2$

11.$y = (x - 3)^2$
$(3, 0)$

12.$y = x^2 + 4x + 4$

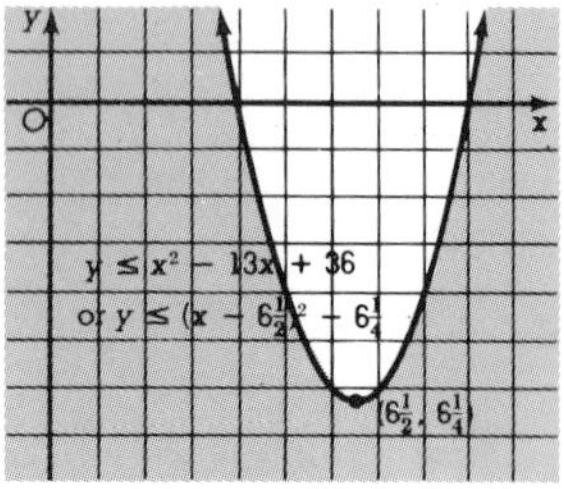

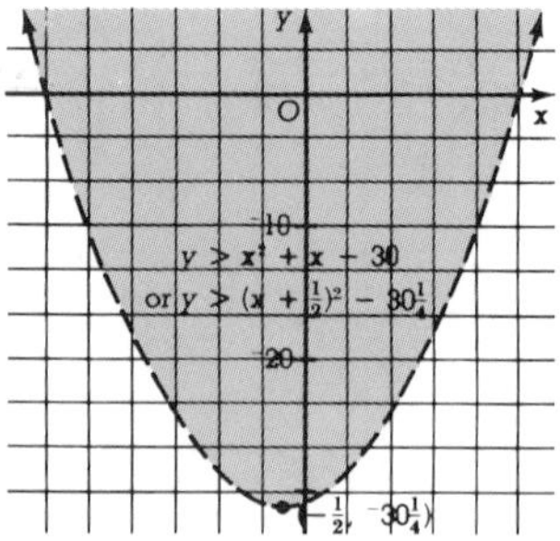

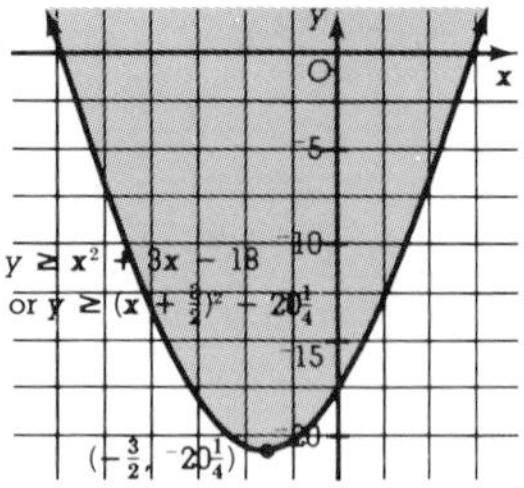

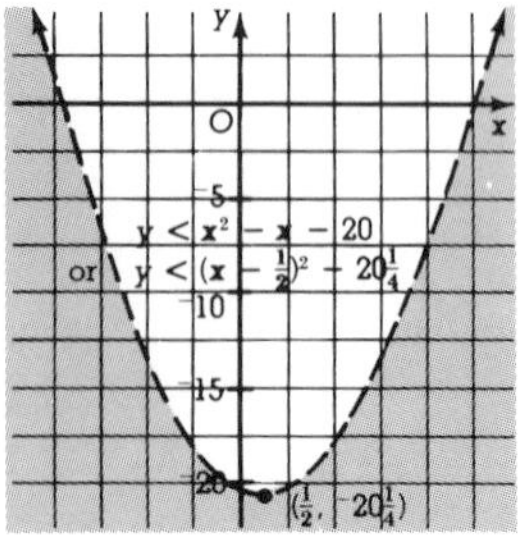

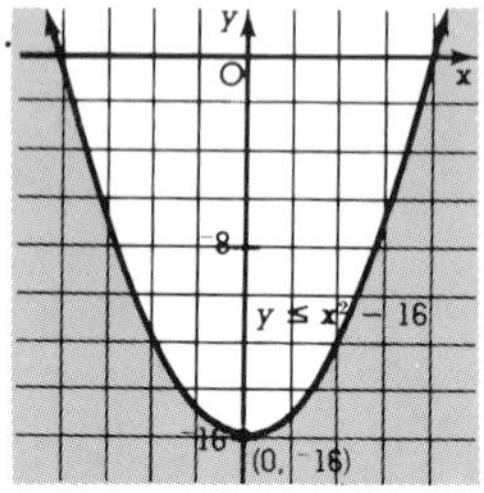

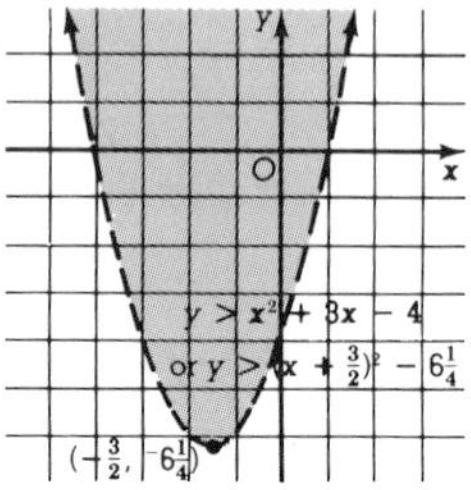

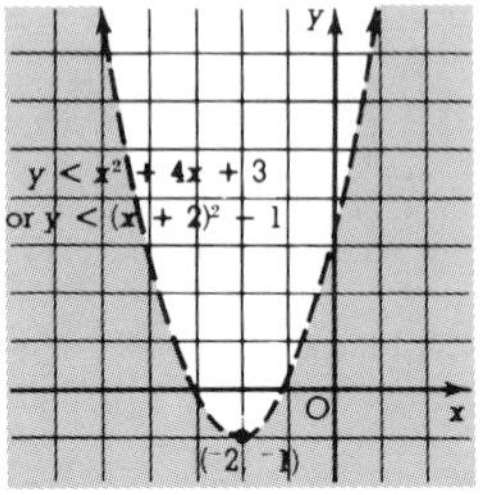

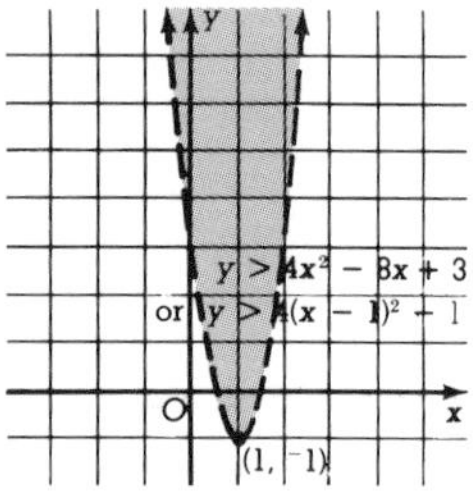

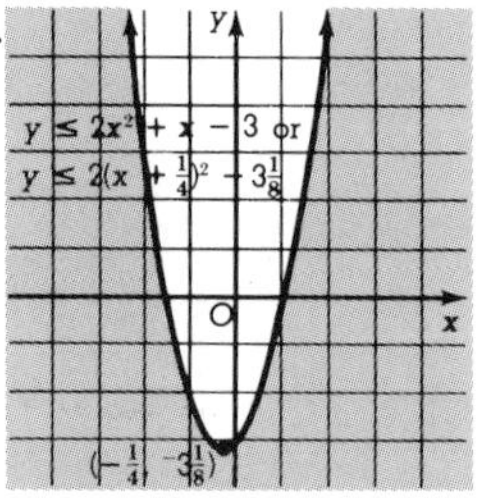

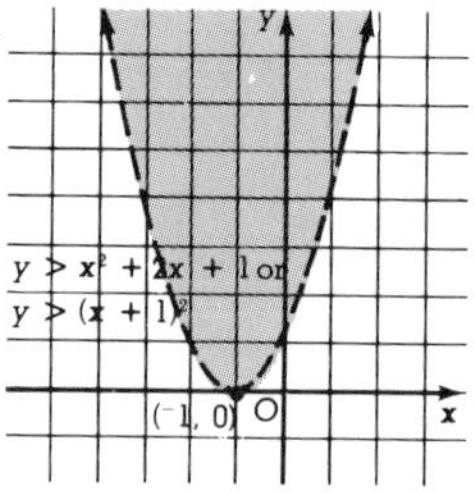

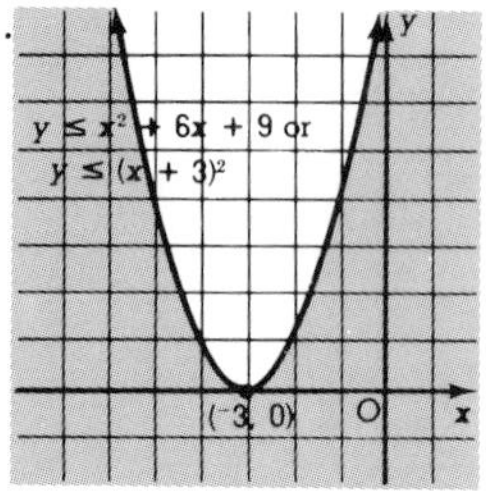

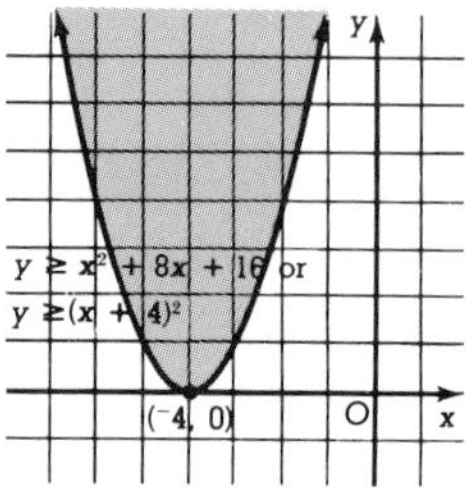

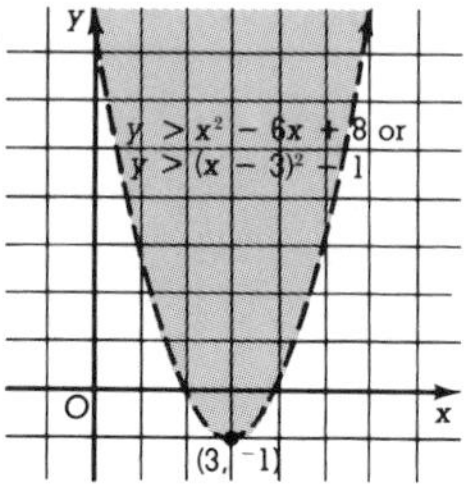

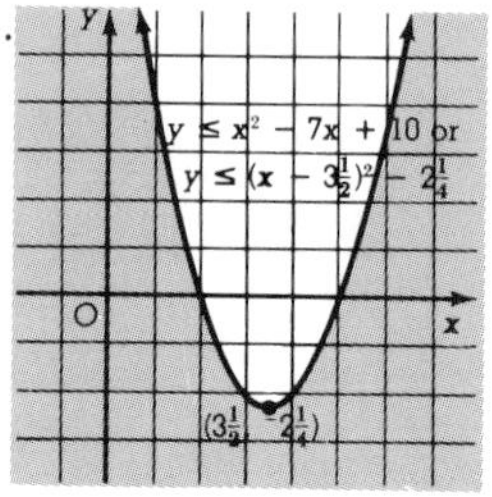

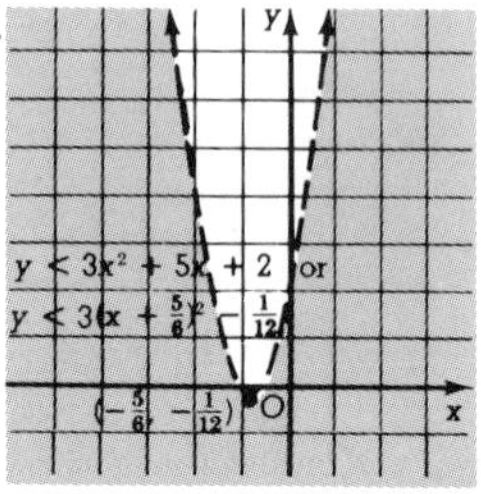

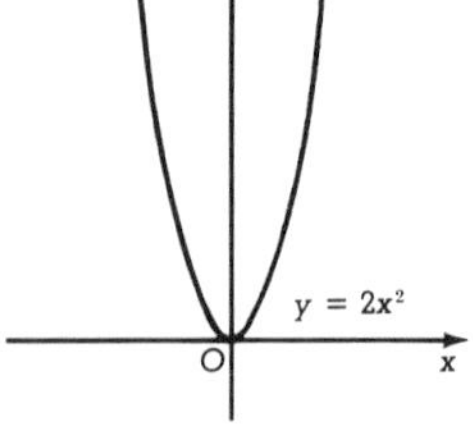

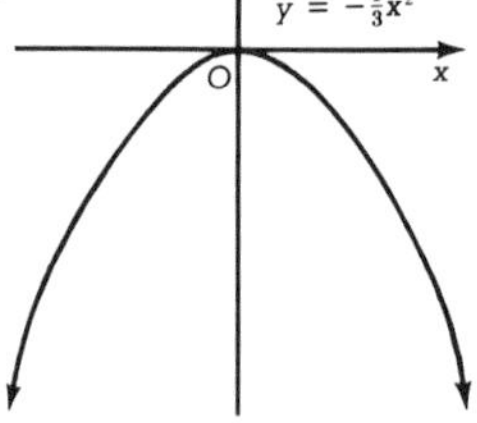

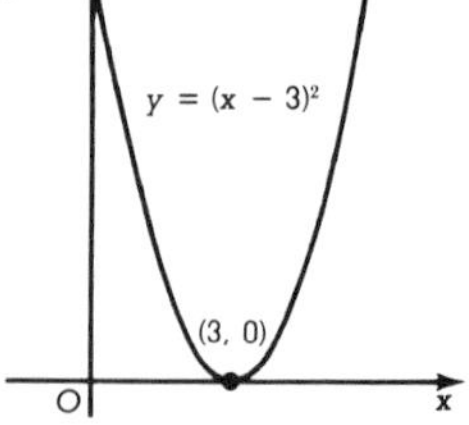

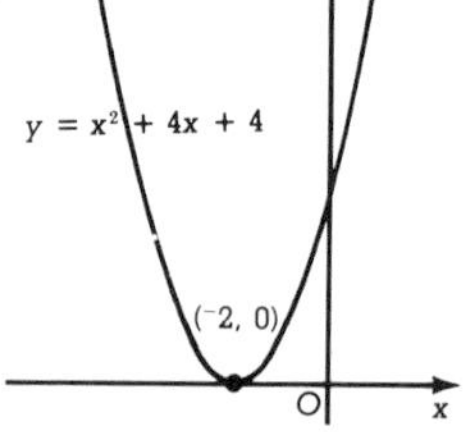

13.
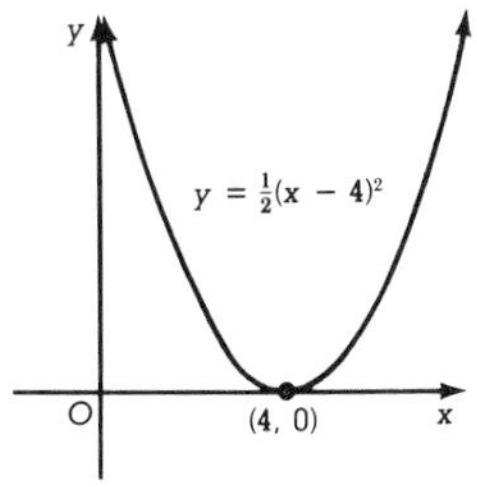

14.
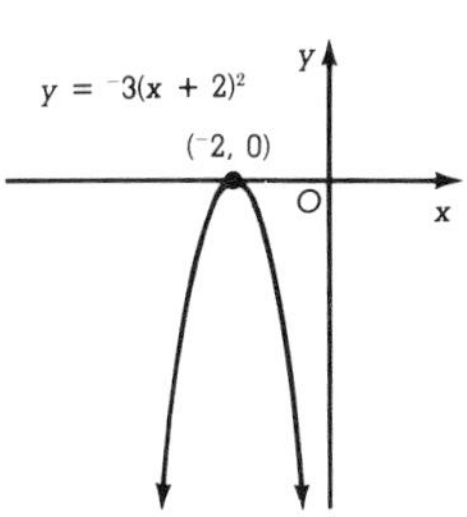

15.
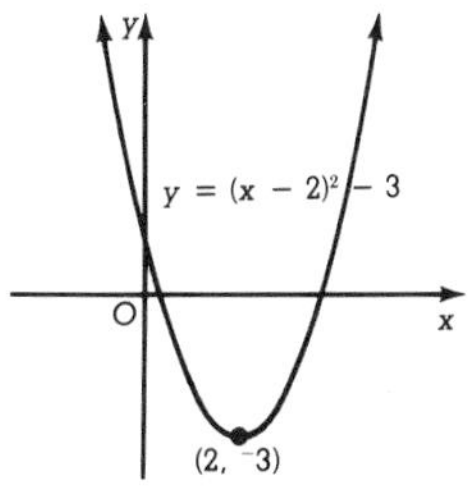

16.
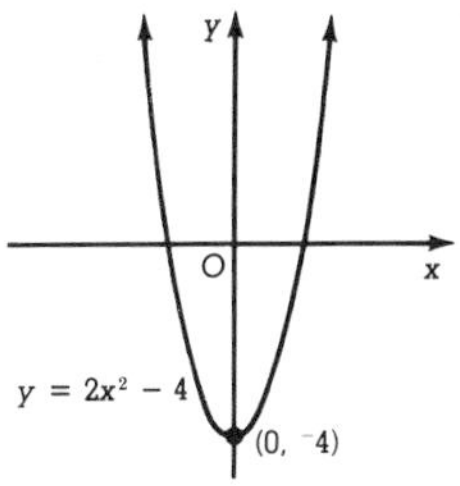

17.
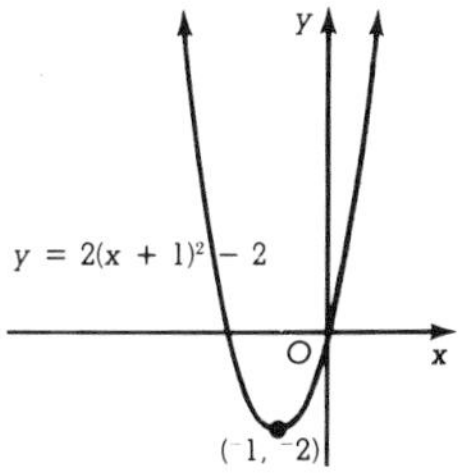

18.
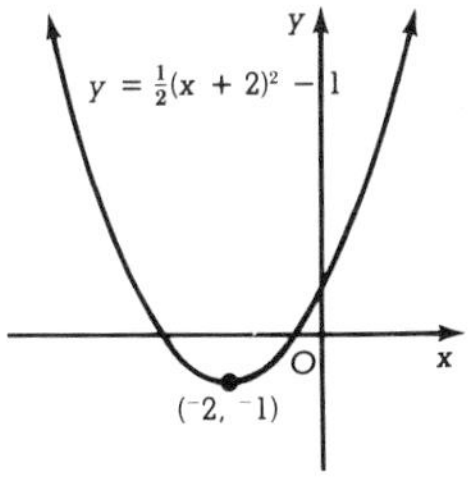

21.
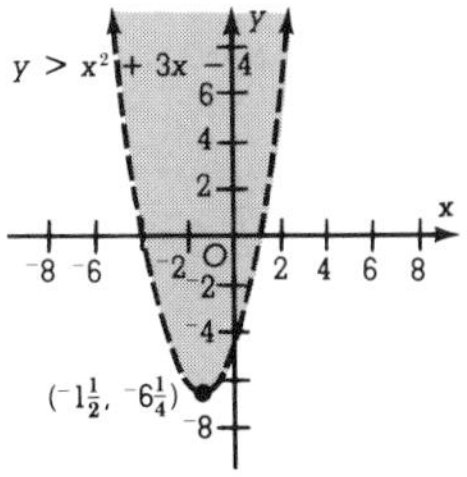

22.
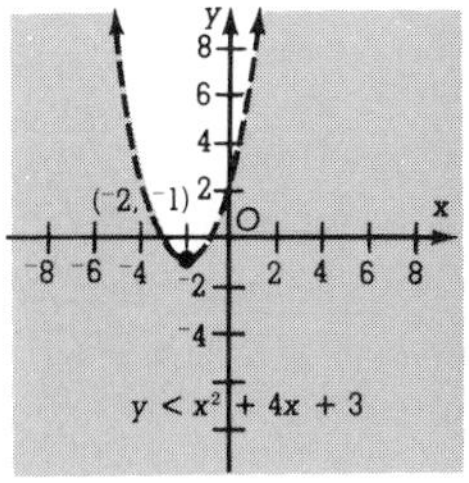

Page 212 Chapter Test

5.
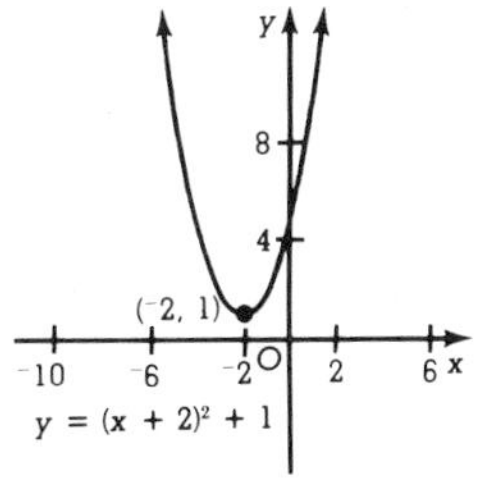

6.
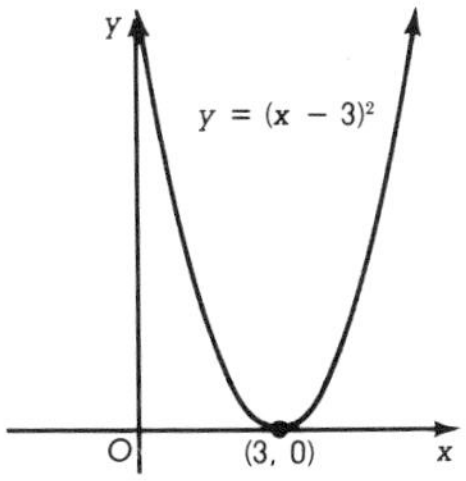

7.
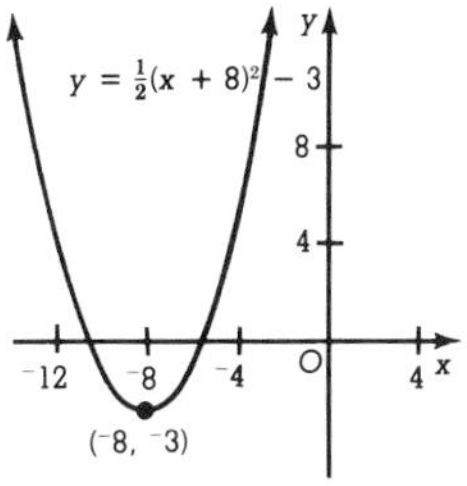

8.
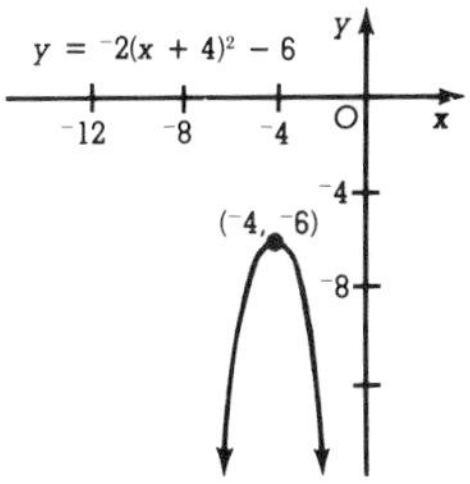

9.
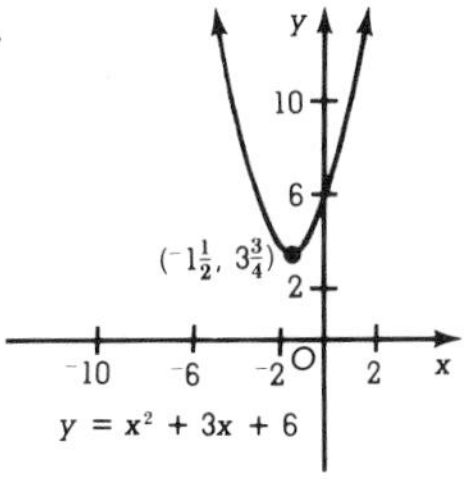

10.
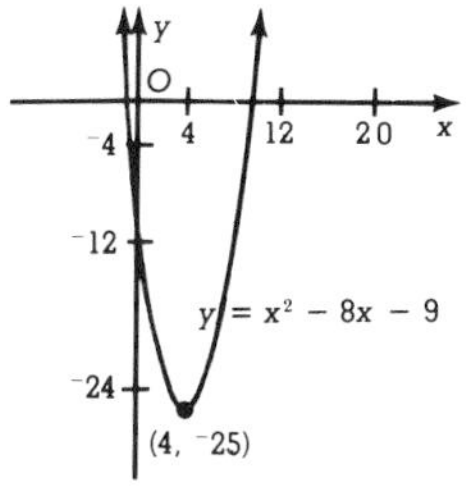

13.
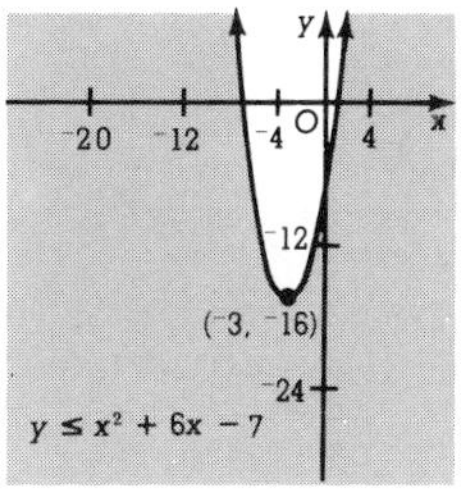

14.
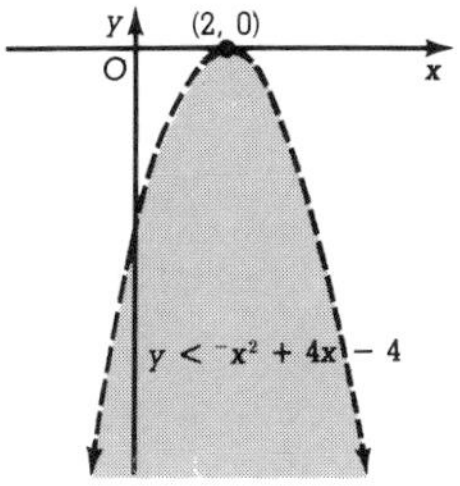

CHAPTER 8 CONICS

Page 219 Written Graphs for problems **1-18** are all parabolas. **1.** $(0, 0)$; $x = 0$; $(0, \frac{3}{2})$; $y = -\frac{3}{2}$; up **2.** $(0, 0)$; $y = 0$; $(-2, 0)$; $x = 2$; left **3.** $(-2, 3)$; $x = -2$; $(-2, 3\frac{1}{4})$; $y = 2\frac{3}{4}$; up **4.** $(4, -2)$; $x = 4$; $(4, -1)$; $y = -3$; up **5.** $(8, -1)$; $x = 8$; $(8, -\frac{7}{8})$; $y = -\frac{9}{8}$ **6.** $(-3, 2)$; $x = -3$; $(-3, 2\frac{1}{16})$; $y = 1\frac{15}{16}$; up **7.** $(0, 1)$; $x = 0$; $(0, \frac{5}{4})$; $y = \frac{3}{4}$; up **8.** $(-2, 0)$; $x = -2$; $(-2, \frac{3}{2})$; $y = -\frac{3}{2}$; up **9.** $(2, -3)$; $y = -3$; $(3, -3)$; $x = 1$; right **10.** $(4, 8)$; $y = 8$; $(3, 8)$; $x = 5$; left **11.** $(3, 24)$; $x = 3$; $(3, 24\frac{1}{4})$; $y = 23\frac{3}{4}$; up **12.** $(4, -4)$; $y = -4$; $(\frac{17}{4}, -4)$; $x = \frac{15}{4}$; right **13.** $(-24, 7)$; $y = 7$; $(-23\frac{3}{4}, 7)$; $x = -24\frac{1}{4}$; right **14.** $(-2, -3)$; $x = -2$; $(-2, -\frac{11}{4})$; $y = -\frac{13}{4}$; up **15.** $(-\frac{13}{4}, 1)$; $y = 1$; $(-\frac{9}{4}, 1)$; $y = -\frac{17}{4}$; right **16.** $(3, 5)$; $x = 3$; $(3, 5\frac{1}{2})$; $y = 4\frac{1}{2}$; up **17.** $(4, 2)$; $x = 4$; $(4, 2\frac{1}{12})$; $y = 1\frac{11}{12}$; up **18.** $(\frac{115}{4}, \frac{5}{2})$; $y = \frac{5}{2}$; $(\frac{116}{4}, \frac{5}{2})$; $x = \frac{114}{4}$; right

Graphs for problems **29-38** are all parabolas. The vertex and direction of opening are given. **29.** $(2, 5)$; down **30.** $(3, 3)$; up **31.** $(8, 2)$; down **32.** $(0, 1)$; up **33.** $(5, 1)$; up **34.** $(5, 2)$; right **35.** $(\frac{1}{2}, -1)$; right **36.** $(4, \frac{3}{2})$; down **37.** $(\frac{1}{2}, 4)$; left **38.** $(-\frac{1}{2}, 3)$; right

Page 231 Written Graphs for problems **19–24** are all rectangular hyperbolas. Intercepts are given. **19.** $(^-3, 0)$, $(3, 0)$ **20.** $(^-4, 0)$, $(4, 0)$ **21.** $(^-6, 0)$, $(6, 0)$ **22.** $(0, \sqrt{6})$, $(0, ^-\sqrt{6})$ **23.** $(0, 9)$, $(0, ^-9)$ **24.** $(0, 3\sqrt{2})$, $(0, ^-3\sqrt{2})$ **28.** The x-axis and y-axis are asymptotes. The center is $(0, 0)$. There are no intercepts. **34.** Rectangular hyperbolas opening up and down with vertices $(^-2, 7)$ and $(^-2, ^-1)$.

Page 234 Written **41.** parabola opening up with vertex $(0, 0)$ **42.** circle with center $(0, 0)$ and radius 3 **43.** ellipse with center $(0, 0)$ and intercepts $(0, 2)$, $(0, ^-2)$, $(\sqrt{2}, 0)$, $(^-\sqrt{2}, 0)$ **44.** circle with center $(0, 0)$ and radius $3\sqrt{3}$ **45.** hyperbola with center $(0, 0)$ and x-axis and y-axis as asymptotes **46.** parabola opening up with vertex $(-\frac{3}{2}, -\frac{5}{4})$ **47.** hyperbola opening left and right, with intercepts $(2\sqrt{2}, 0)$ and $(^-2\sqrt{2}, 0)$ **48.** ellipse with center $(0, 0)$ and intercepts $(2, 0)$, $(^-2, 0)$, $(0, \sqrt{6})$, $(0, ^-\sqrt{6})$ **49.** parabola opening down with vertex $(\frac{1}{2}, \frac{9}{4})$ **50.** hyperbola with center $(0, 0)$ and x-axis and y-axis as asymptotes **51.** hyperbola opening left and right, with intercepts $(3, 0)$ and $(^-3, 0)$ **52.** circle with center $(0, 0)$ and radius 2 **53.** ellipse with center $(0, ^-1)$ and intercepts $(0, ^-1 + \sqrt{3})$, $(0, ^-1 - \sqrt{3})$ **54.** hyperbolas opening left and right, with intercepts $(\frac{2}{3}, 0)$ and $(-\frac{2}{3}, 0)$ **55.** hyperbola with center $(0, 0)$ and x-axis and y-axis as asymptotes **56.** parabola opening right with vertex $(4, 4)$ **57.** ellipse with center $(3, ^-2)$ and vertices $(0, ^-2)$, $(6, ^-2)$, $(3, 3)$, $(3, ^-7)$ **58.** hyperbola opening up and down with intercepts $(0, 4)$ and $(0, ^-4)$ **59.** circle with center $(0, 0)$ and radius $\frac{7\sqrt{13}}{13}$ **60.** hyperbola with center $(0, 0)$ and x-axis and y-axis as asymptotes

Page 241 Written

1.
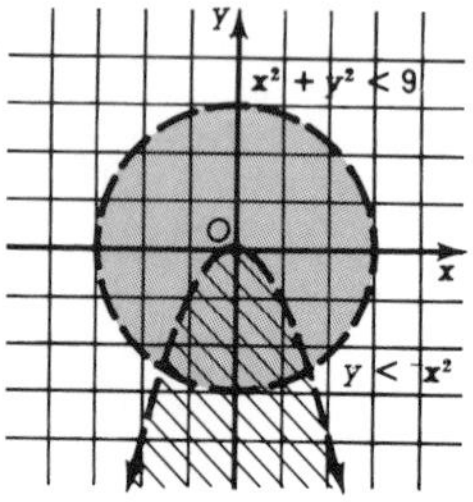

2.
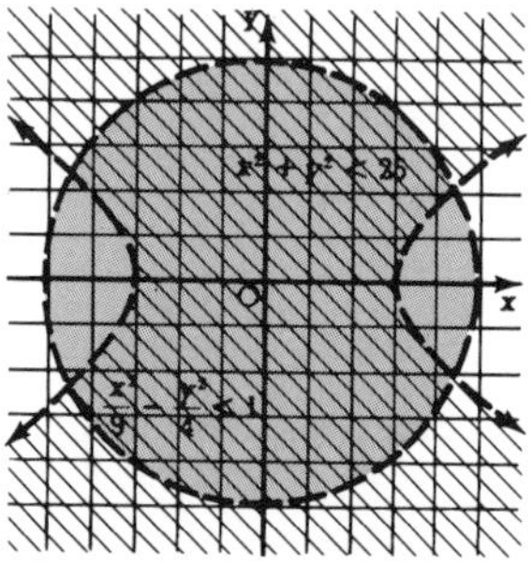

3.
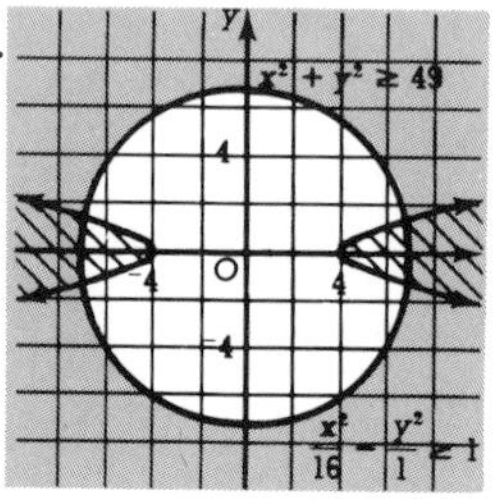

4.
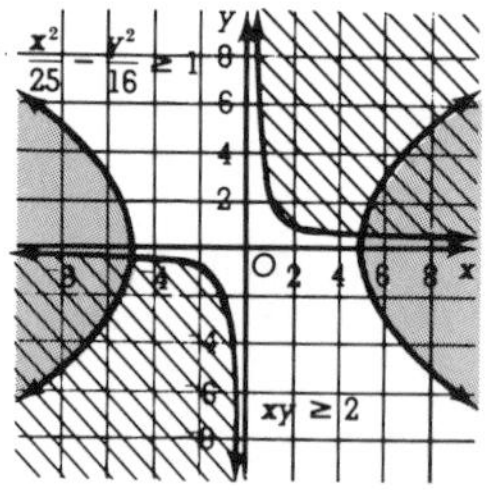

5.
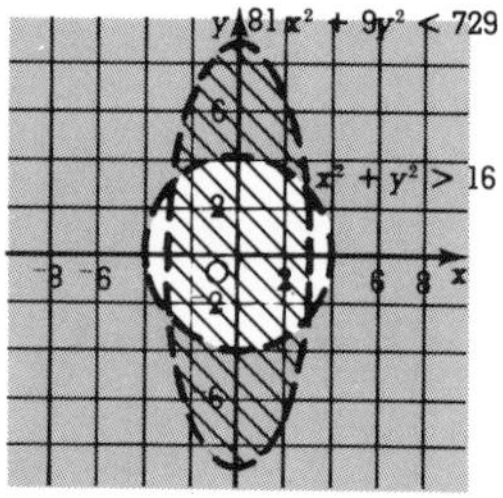

6.
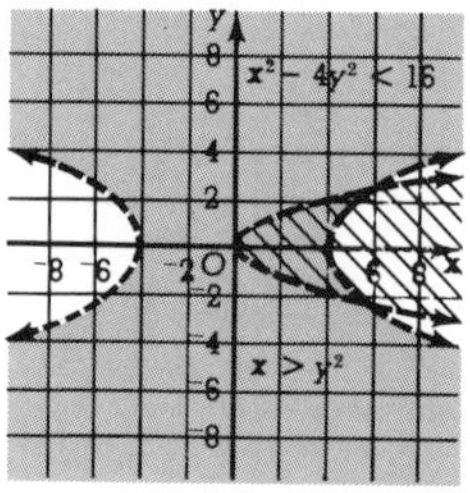

7.
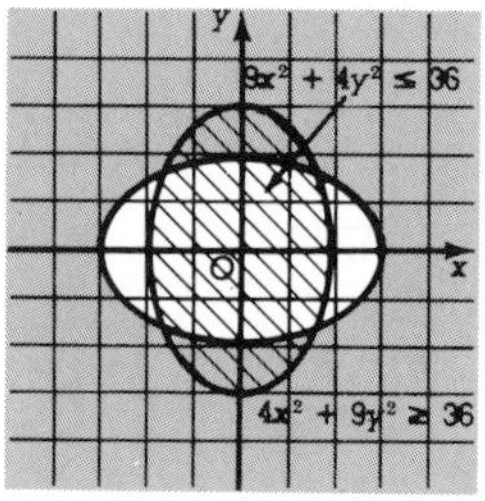

8.
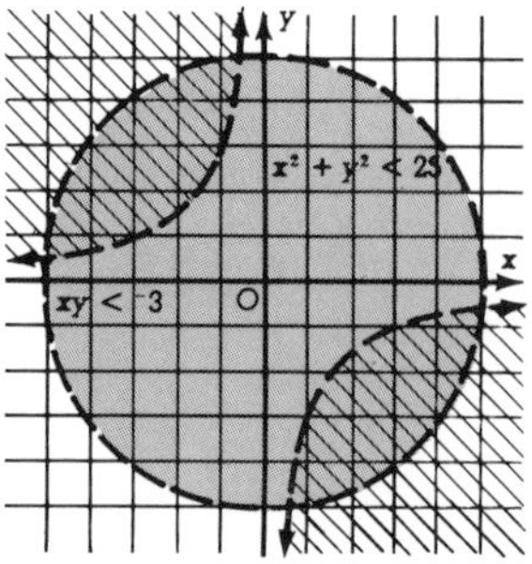

9.
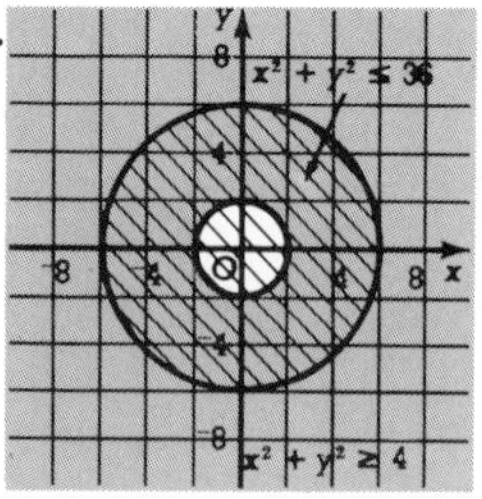

10.
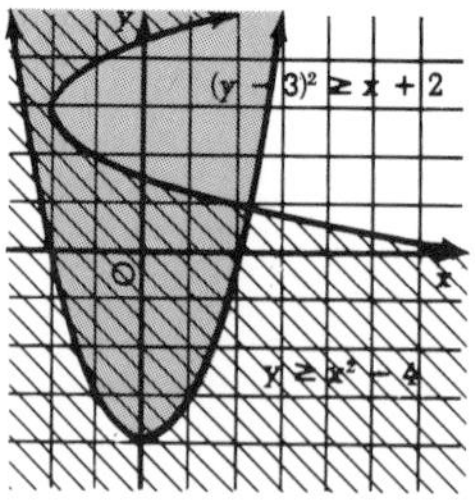

11.
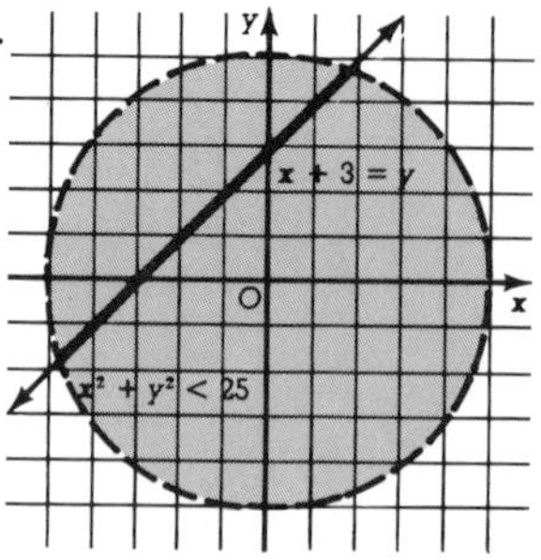

12.
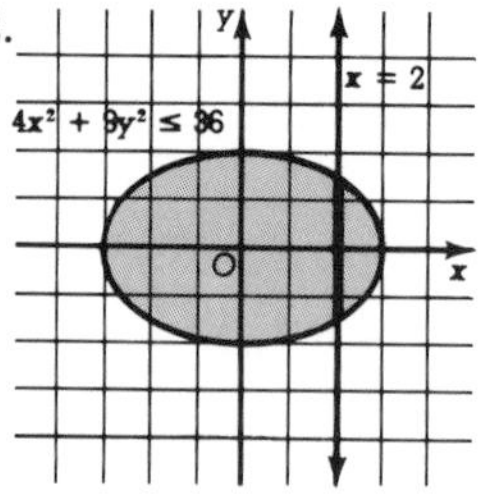

13. 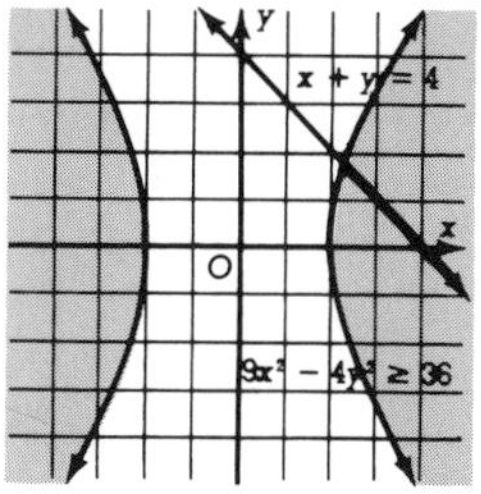

14. 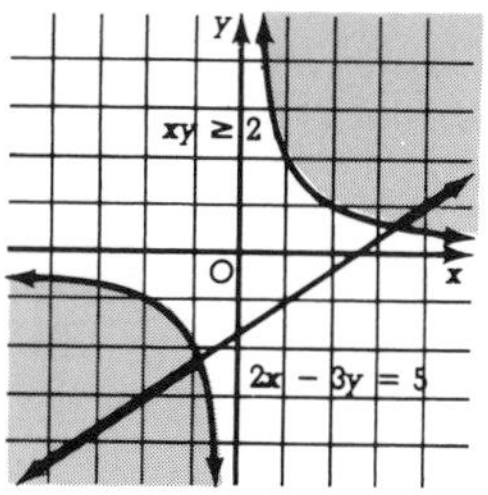

15. 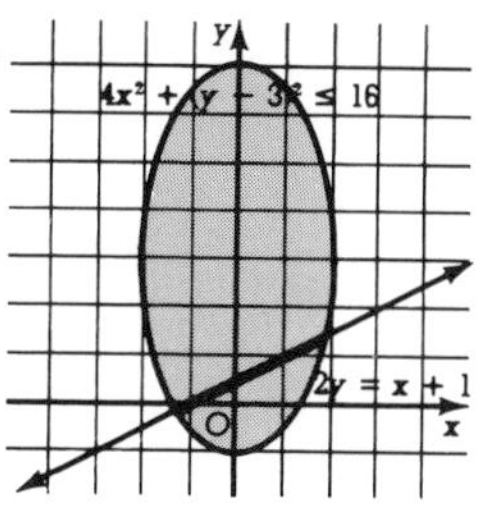

16. 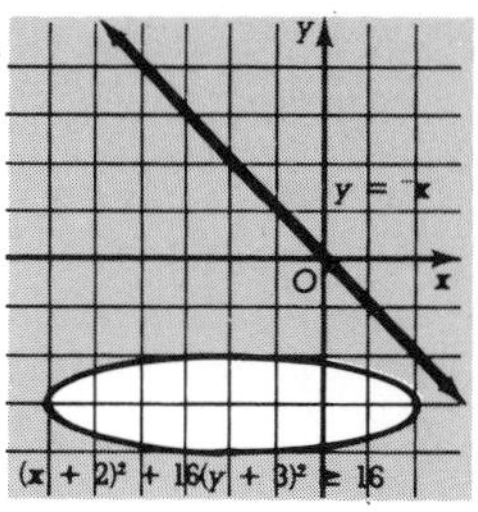

17. 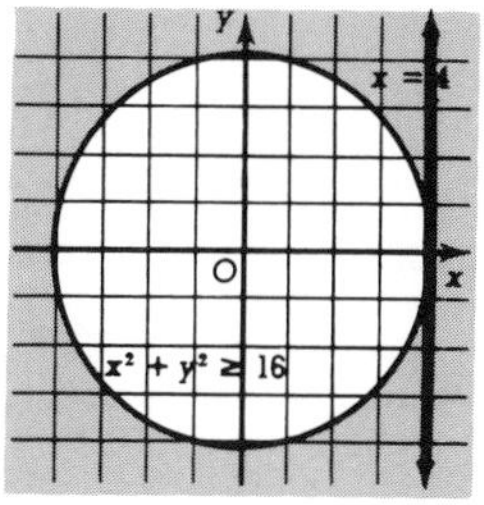

18. 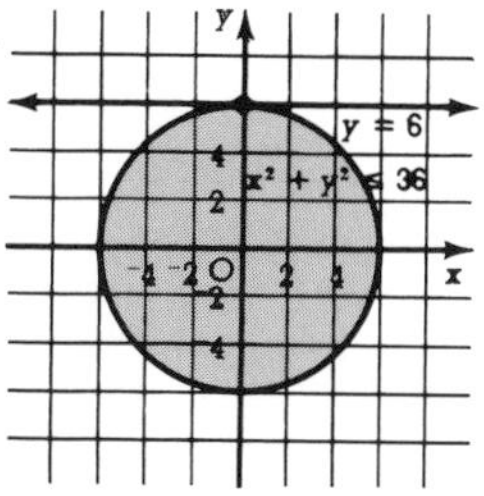

Page 245 Chapter Review

29. 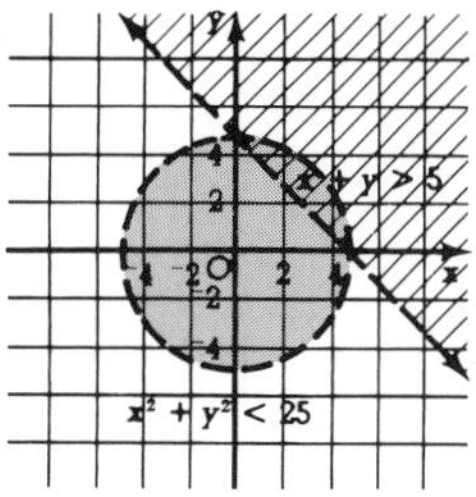

30. 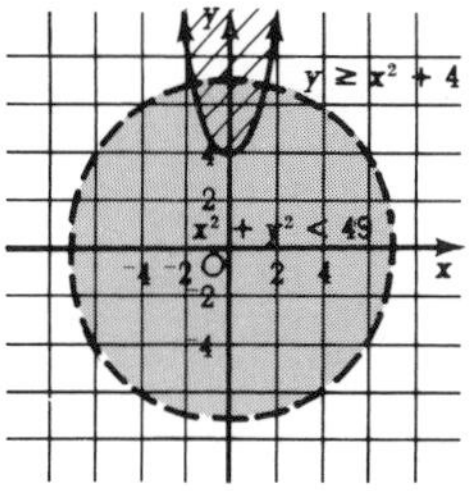

Page 246 Chapter Test

19. 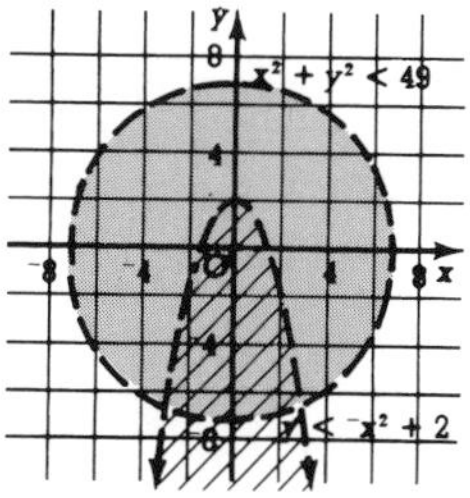

20. 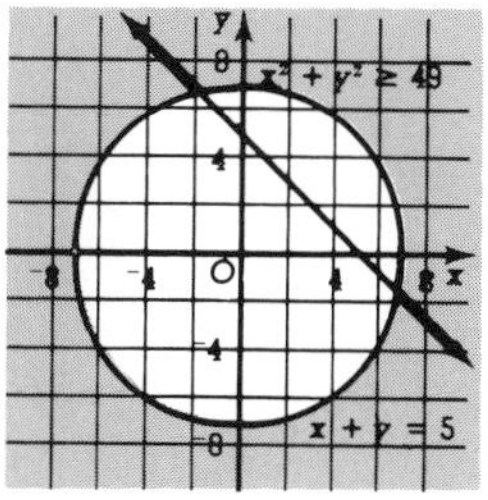

CHAPTER 9 POLYNOMIAL FUNCTIONS

Page 250 Written **11.** 7 **12.** 19 **13.** $\frac{16}{3} + 2\sqrt{2}$ **14.** $^-22$ **15.** $^-9$ **16.** 16 **17.** $^-18$ **18.** 16 **19.** 12 **20.** $61\frac{2}{3}$ **21.** $^-8$ **22.** 24 **23.** $7 - 3\sqrt{2}$ **24.** 83 **25.** 41 **26.** 621 **27.** $^-108$ **28.** 251 **29.** $-\frac{151}{2}$ **30.** $^-195$
31. $3x + 3h + 1$ **32.** $4(x + h)^2 + 3(x + h) - 3$ **33.** $\frac{(x + h)^2}{3} + (x + h)\sqrt{2} + 4$ **34.** $^-3(x + h)^3 + 2$
35. $^-2(x + h)^3 + 4(x + h) - 1$ **36.** $5(x + h)^4 - 8(x + h)^3$ **37.** $3(x + h) - 8(x + h)^2 + (x + h)^3$
38. $2(x + h)^4 - 3(x + h)^3 + 8$ **39.** $\frac{5}{2}(x + h)^3 - 8$ **40.** $7(x + h)^3 + \frac{7}{3}(x + h) + 1$ **41.** $^-3x - 10$
42. $^-4x^2 - 27x - 18$ **43.** $-\frac{x^2}{3} - x\sqrt{2} - 2x - 5 - 3\sqrt{2}$ **44.** $3x^3 + 27x^2 + 27x + 7$ **45.** $2x^3 + 18x^2 + 14x - 5$
46. $^-5x^4 - 52x^3 - 18x^2 + 12x + 9$ **47.** $^-x^3 - x^2 + 36x + 12$ **48.** $^-2x^4 - 21x^3 - 9x^2 + 3x - 5$
49. $-\frac{5}{2}x^3 - \frac{45}{2}x^2 - \frac{45}{2}x + \frac{1}{2}$ **50.** $^-7x^3 - 63x^2 - \frac{196}{3}x - 29$
51.

```
 5 FOR X=-6 OR 6
10 LET Y  X↑4-X↑3+X↑2-X+1     20 NEXT X
15 PRINT X;Y                  25 END
```

Page 253 Exploratory **1.** $x - 1$ R. $^-1$ **2.** $x^2 + 2$ R. 2 **3.** $x^2 - 9x + 11$ R. $^-12$ **4.** $x + 5$ R. $^-16$ **5.** $x^4 + 3x^3 + 6x^2 + 12x + 26$ R. 51 **6.** $2x^3 - 2x^2 + x - 1$ R. 2 **7.** $x^4 - 2x^3 + 4x^2 - 8x + 16$ **8.** $x^4 + 2x^3 + 4x^2 + 5x + 10$

Page 253 Written **1.** $2x^3 + 8x^2 - 3x - 1 = (2x^2 + 12x + 21)(x - 2) + 41$ **2.** $x^3 - 64 = (x^2 + 4x + 16)(x - 4) + 0$ **3.** $x^4 - 16 = (x^3 + 2x^2 + 4x + 8)(x - 2) + 0$ **4.** $x^3 + 27 = (x^2 - 3x + 9)(x + 3) + 0$
5. $4x^4 + 3x^3 - 2x^2 + x + 1 = (4x^3 + 7x^2 + 5x + 6)(x - 1) + 7$ **6.** $6x^3 + 9x^2 - 6x + 2 = (6x^2 - 3x)(x + 2) + 2$
7. $3x^5 - 2x^3 + 2x + 2 = (3x^4 - 3x^3 + x^2 - x + 3)(x + 1) - 1$ **8.** $^-2x^2 - 3x - 1 = (^-2x + 1)(x + 2) - 3$
9. $3x^3 + 2x^2 - 4x - 1 = (3x^2 + \frac{1}{2}x - \frac{17}{4})(x + \frac{1}{2}) + \frac{9}{8}$ **10.** $x^4 - 2x^3 + 4x^2 + 6x - 8 = (x^3 - \frac{3}{2}x^2 + \frac{13}{4}x + \frac{61}{8})(x - \frac{1}{2}) - \frac{67}{16}$

31.
```
 10 DATA . . . (DEGREE, C, COEFFICIENTS)
 20 READ N,C
 30 FOR X=0 TO N
 40 READ A(X)
 50 NEXT X
 60 PRINT A(0);
 70 FOR X=1 TO N
 80 LET A(X)=A(X)-A(X-1)*C
 90 PRINT A(X);
100 NEXT X
110 END
```

Page 256 Exploratory **1.** $\pm1, \pm2$ **2.** $\pm1, \pm5$ **3.** $\pm1, \pm2, \pm3, \pm6$ **4.** $\pm1, \pm3$ **5.** $\pm1, \pm2, \pm4, \pm8$ **6.** $\pm1, \pm2, \pm5, \pm10$ **7.** ±1 **8.** $\pm1, \pm3, \pm9$ **9.** $\pm1, \pm2, \pm4, \pm5, \pm10, \pm20$ **10.** $\pm1, \pm3, \pm5, \pm15$ **11.** $\pm1, \pm\frac{1}{2}, \pm\frac{1}{3}, \pm\frac{1}{6}$ **12.** ±1 $\pm2, \pm\frac{1}{2}, \pm\frac{1}{3}, \pm\frac{1}{6}, \pm\frac{2}{3}$ **13.** $\pm1, \pm2, \pm4, \pm\frac{1}{3}, \pm\frac{2}{3}, \pm\frac{4}{3}$ **14.** $\pm1, \pm3, \pm\frac{1}{2}, \pm\frac{3}{2}$ **15.** $\pm1, \pm3, \pm5, \pm15, \pm\frac{1}{2}, \pm\frac{3}{2}, \pm\frac{5}{2}, \pm\frac{15}{2}$ **16.** $\pm1, \pm3, \pm6, \pm2, \pm9, \pm18, \pm\frac{1}{3}, \pm\frac{2}{3}$ **17.** $\pm1, \pm3, \pm5, \pm15, \pm\frac{1}{2}, \pm\frac{3}{2}, \pm\frac{5}{2}, \pm\frac{15}{2}, \pm\frac{1}{6}, \pm\frac{5}{6} \pm\frac{15}{6}, \pm\frac{1}{3}, \pm\frac{5}{3}$

Page 266 Written

1.
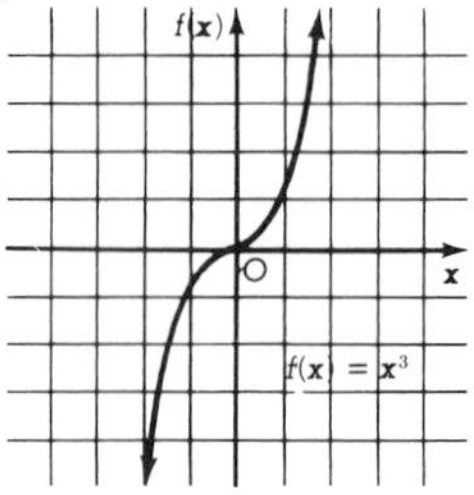

2.
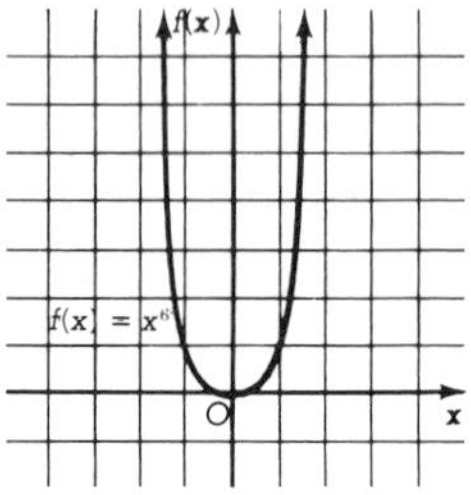

3.
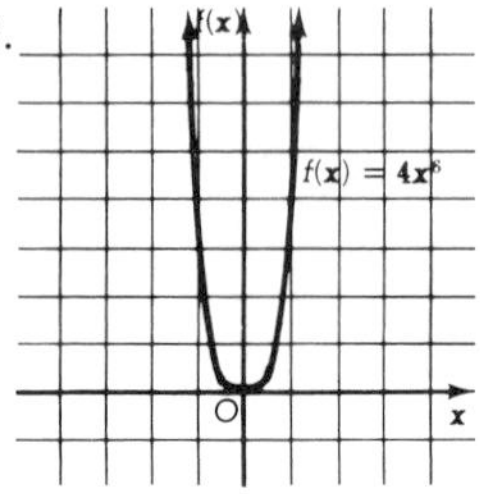

4.
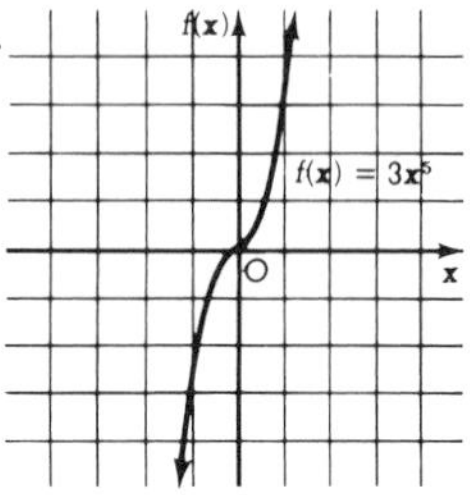

5.
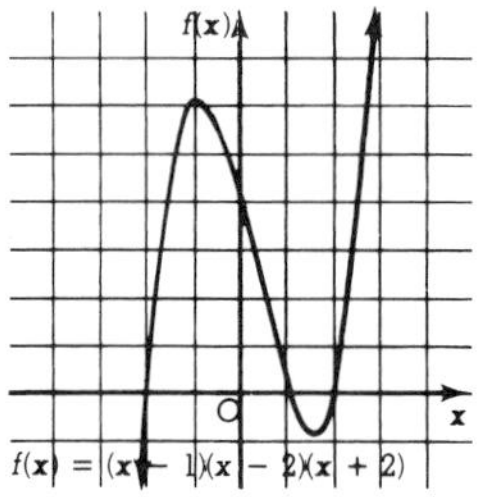

6.
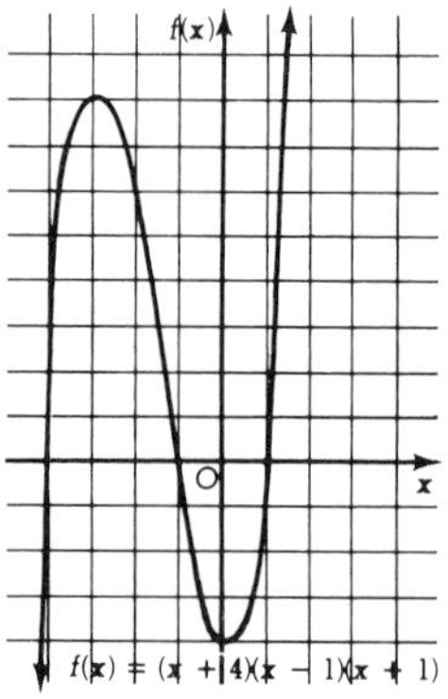

7.
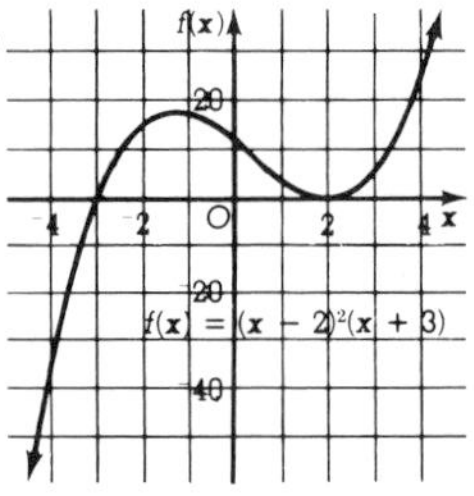

8.
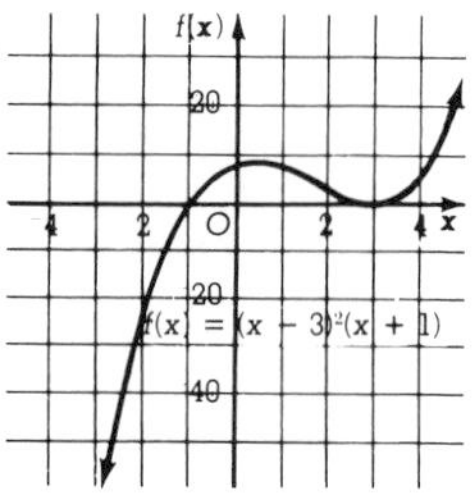

9.
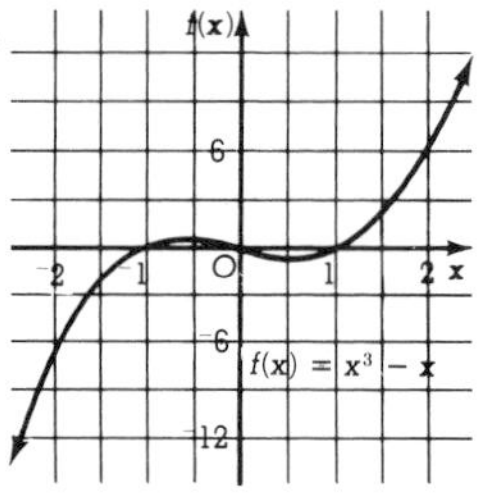

10.
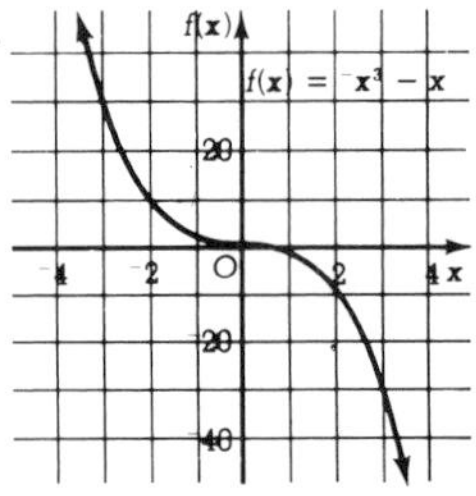

11.
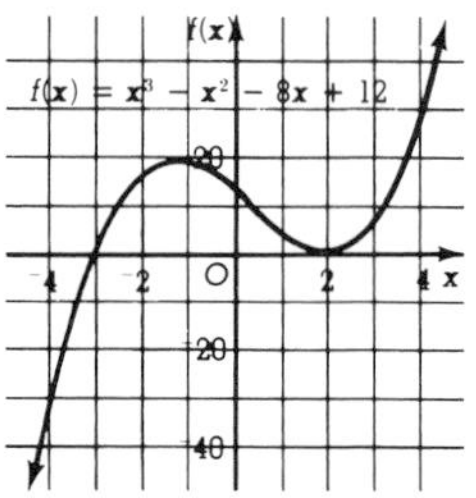

12.
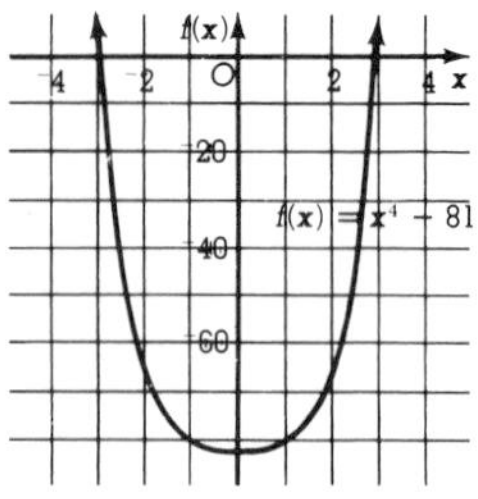

13.
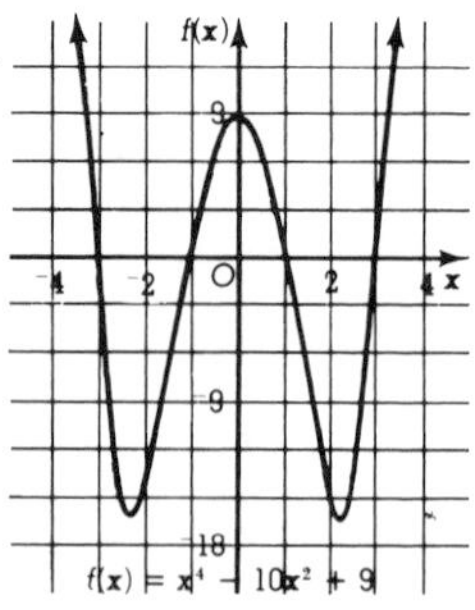

14.
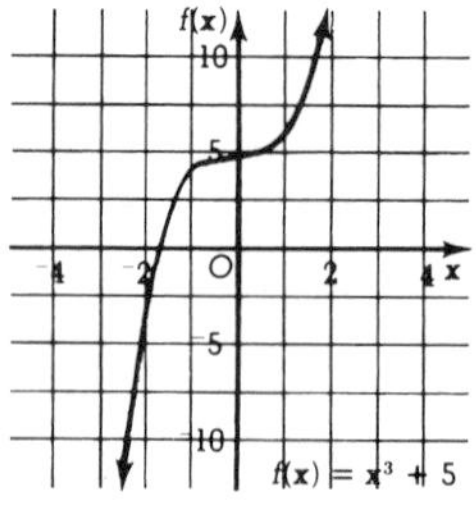

15.
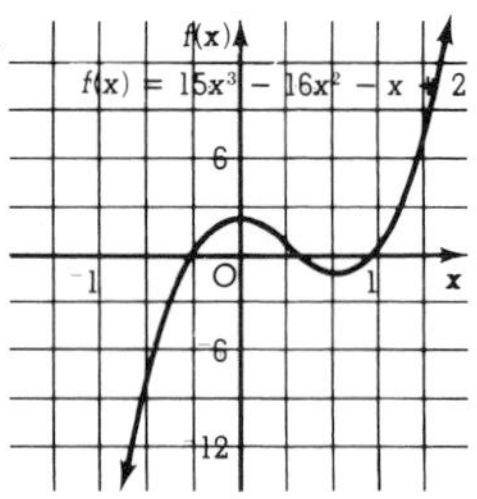

16. 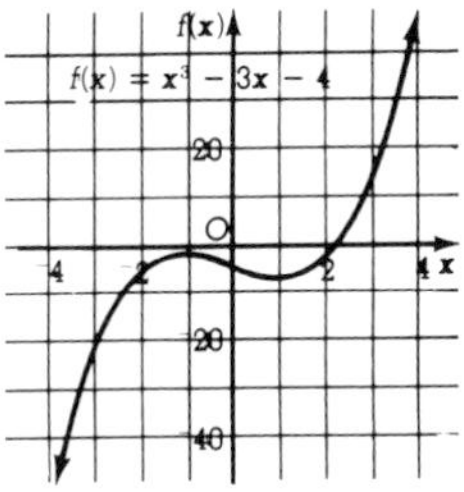

17. 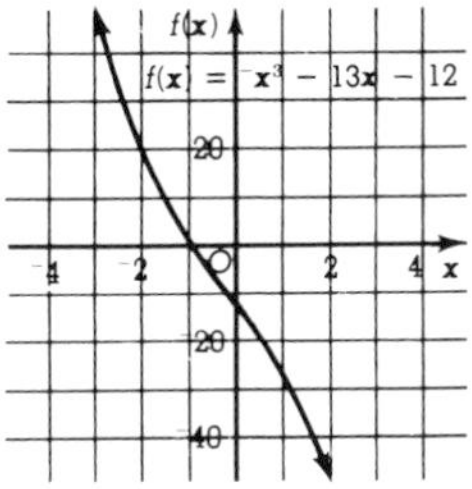

18. 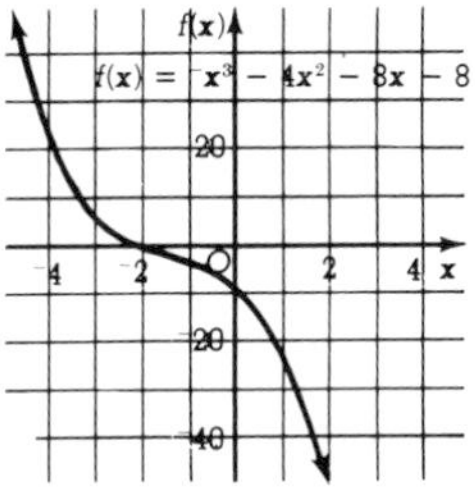

Page 269 Written

21.
```
10 FOR X=-6 TO 6
20 LET G=X↑2+2
30 LET F=G↑2+8*G-1
40 PRINT X;F
50 NEXT X
60 END
```

Page 272 Written

11. 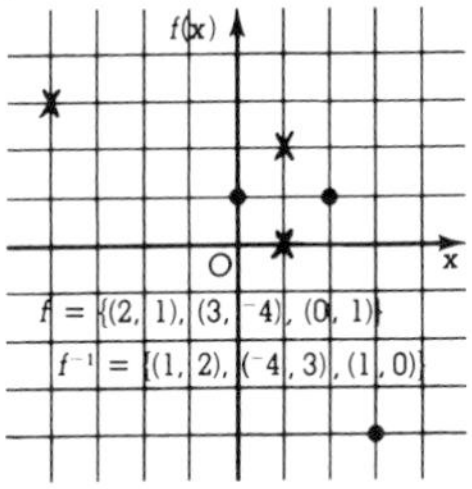

12. 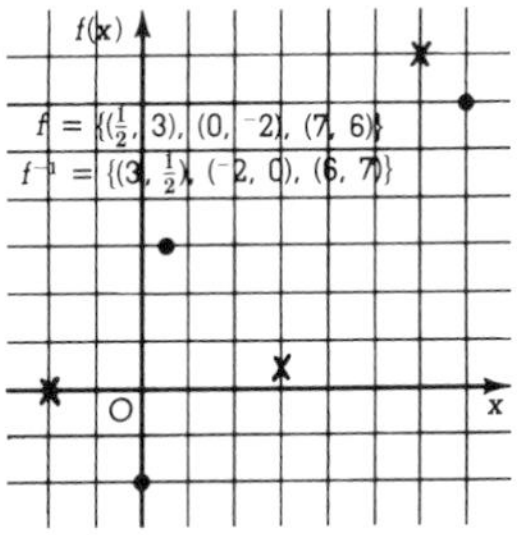

13. 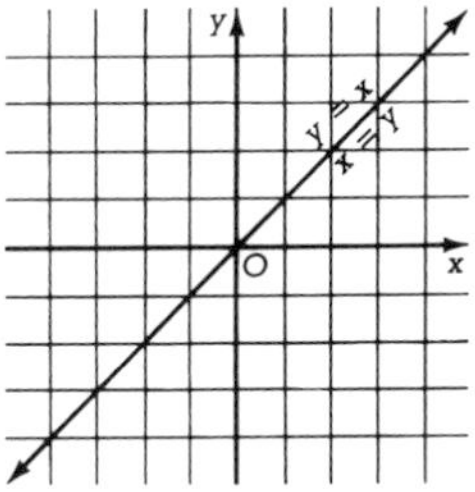

14. 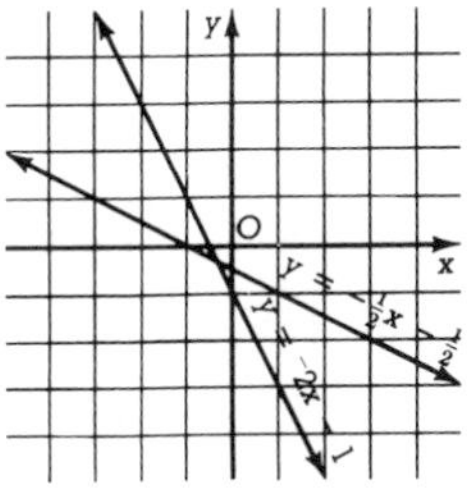

15. 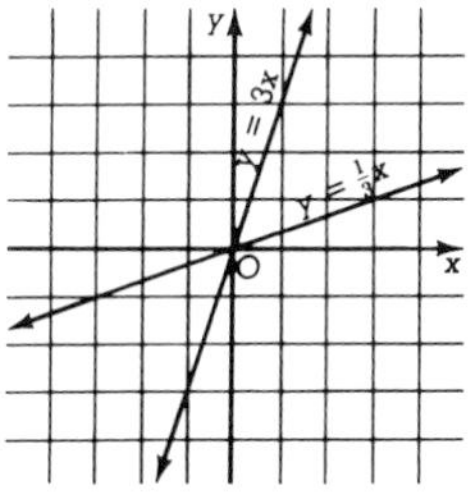

16. 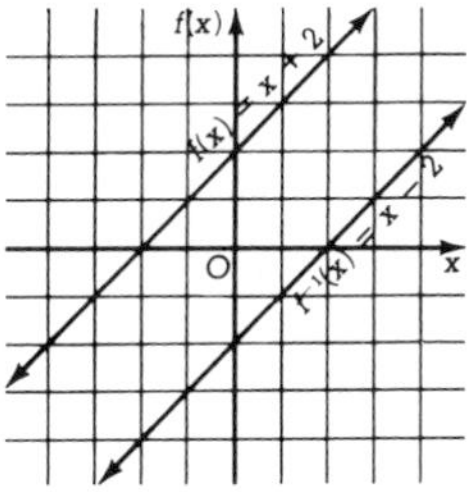

17. 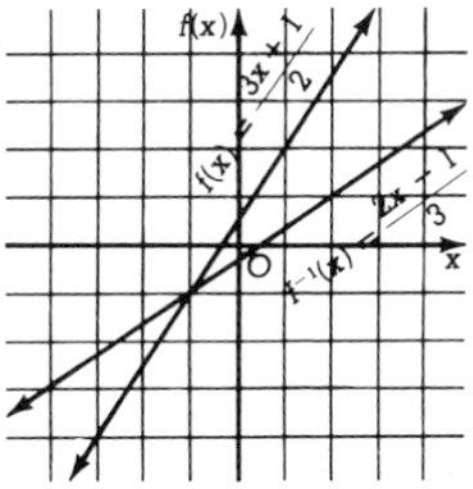

18. 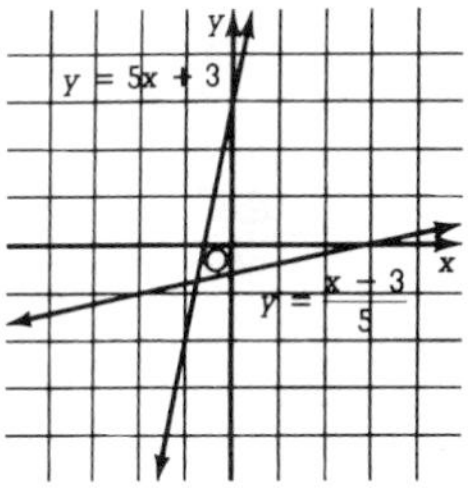

19. 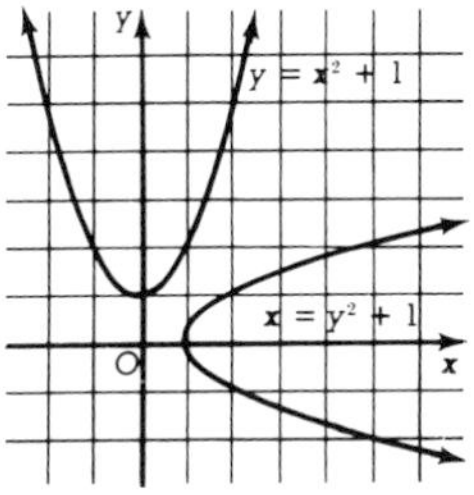

20. 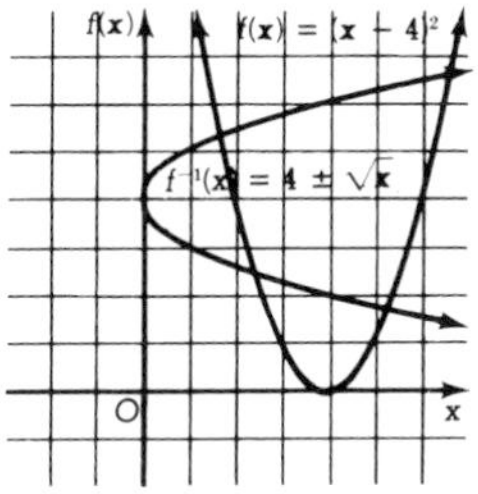

Page 275 Chapter Review

24. 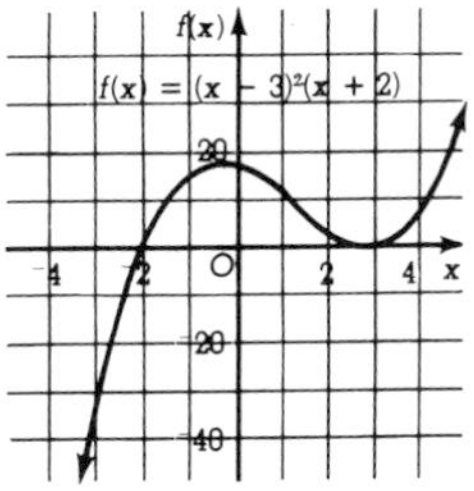

25. 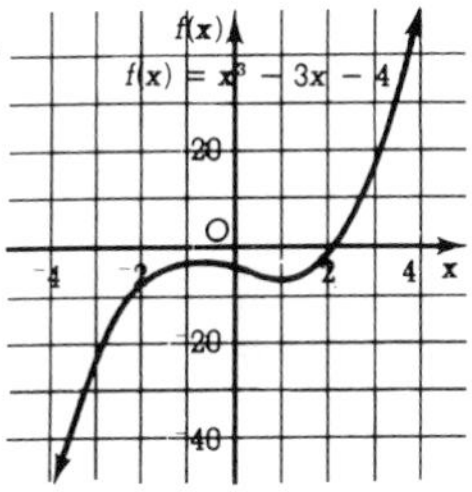

30. 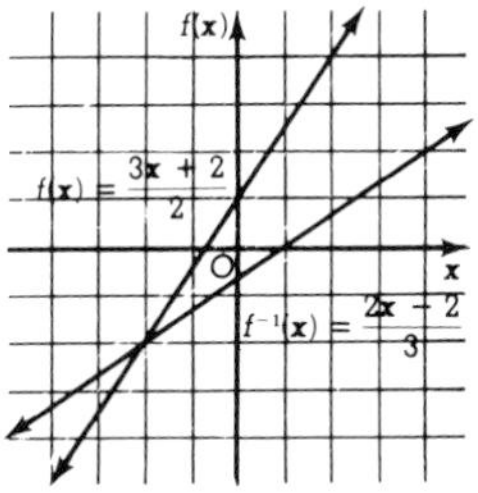

31. 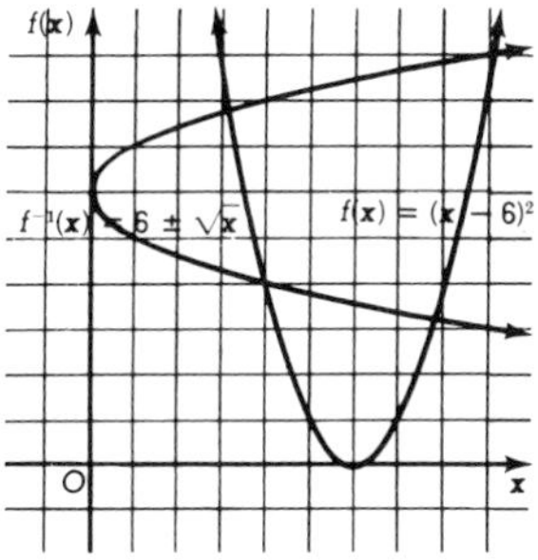

Page 276 Chapter Test

19. 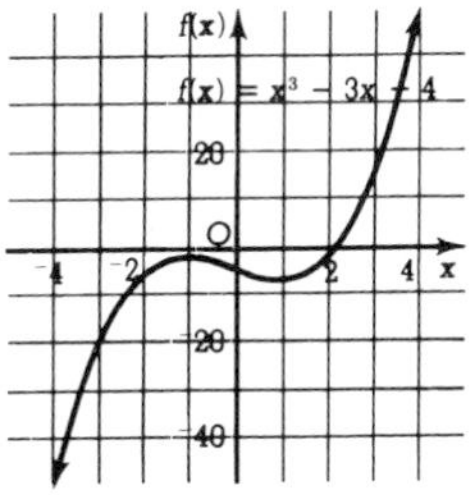

CHAPTER 10 RATIONAL POLYNOMIAL EXPRESSIONS

Page 284 Written 33.

```
10  DATA . . .
20  READ P,Q
30  PRINT Q"/"P
40  PRINT Q/P
50  END
```

Page 296 Written 14.

```
10  FOR H=1 TO 11
20  LET X=60/11*H
30  PRINT H "HOURS"X"MINUTES"
40  NEXT H
50  END
```

CHAPTER 12 EXPONENTIAL AND LOGARITHMIC FUNCTIONS

Page 333 Written

17.
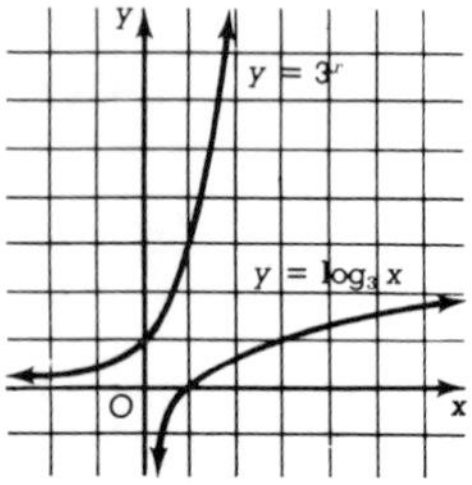

18.
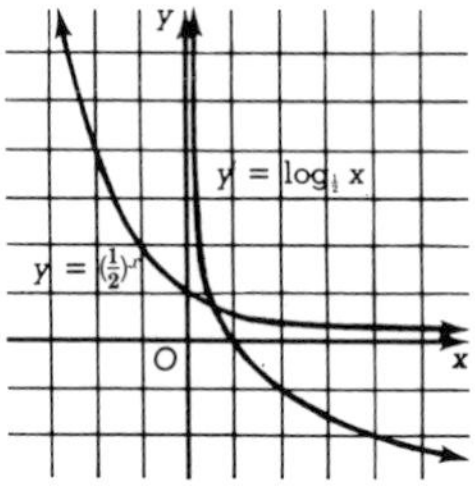

19.
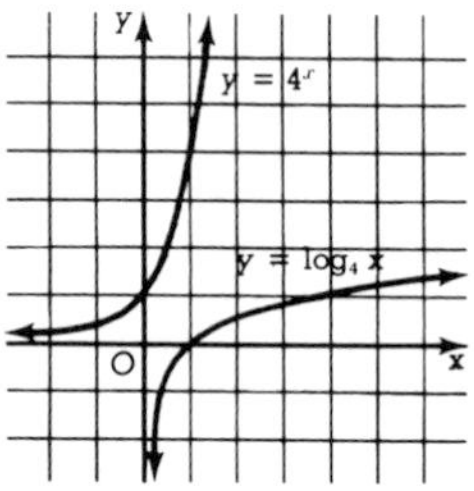

20.
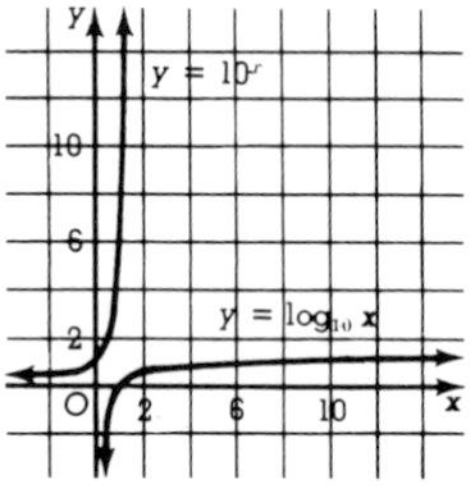

21. $\log_4 4 + \log_4 16 \stackrel{?}{=} \log_4 64$
$1 + 2 = 3$

22. $\log_3 27 + \log_3 3 \stackrel{?}{=} \log_3 81$
$3 + 1 = 4$

23. $\log_2 32 - \log_2 4 \stackrel{?}{=} \log_2 8$
$5 - 2 = 3$

24. $\log_6 36 - \log_6 6 \stackrel{?}{=} \log_6 6$
$2 - 1 = 1$

25. $\log_3 27 \stackrel{?}{=} 3 \log_3 3$
$3 \stackrel{?}{=} 3(1)$
$3 = 3$

26. $\log_4 16 \stackrel{?}{=} 2 \log_4 4$
$2 \stackrel{?}{=} 2(1)$
$2 = 2$

27. $\frac{1}{2} \log_3 81 \stackrel{?}{=} \log_3 9$
$\frac{1}{2}(4) \stackrel{?}{=} 2$
$2 = 2$

28. $\frac{1}{3} \log_5 25 \stackrel{?}{=} 2 \log_5 \sqrt[3]{5}$
$\frac{1}{3}(2) \stackrel{?}{=} 2 \log_5 5^{\frac{1}{3}}$
$\frac{2}{3} \stackrel{?}{=} \frac{2}{3} \log_5 5$
$\frac{2}{3} = \frac{2}{3}$

29. $\log_2 8 \cdot \log_8 2 \stackrel{?}{=} 1$
$3 \cdot \frac{1}{3} \stackrel{?}{=} 1$
$1 = 1$

30. $\log_5 25 \cdot \log_{25} 5 \stackrel{?}{=} 1$
$2 \cdot \frac{1}{2} \stackrel{?}{=} 1$
$1 = 1$

31. $\log_{10} [\log_3 (\log_4 64)] \stackrel{?}{=} 0$
$\log_{10} [\log_3 3] \stackrel{?}{=} 0$
$\log_{10} 1 \stackrel{?}{=} 0$
$0 = 0$

32. $\log_2 64 \stackrel{?}{=} 3 \log_8 64$
$6 \stackrel{?}{=} 3(2)$
$6 = 6$

33. $\log_3 81 \stackrel{?}{=} \frac{4}{3} \log_2 8$
$4 \stackrel{?}{=} \frac{4}{3}(3)$
$4 = 4$

34. $\log_4 [\log_2 (\log_3 81)] \stackrel{?}{=} \frac{1}{2}$
$\log_4 [\log_2 4] \stackrel{?}{=} \frac{1}{2}$
$\log_4 2 \stackrel{?}{=} \frac{1}{2}$
$\frac{1}{2} = \frac{1}{2}$

35. 6, $^{-}5$ 36. $\frac{1}{3}$ 37. 9 38. 49

Page 347 Written 1. 260,900 2. 5.861×10^6 3. 0.3039 4. 1.803×10^{-4} 5. 7.267×10^{10} 6. 1.849×10^{16} 7. 4.937 8. 12.76 9. 1.770 10. 1.522 11. 12.84 12. 14.07 13. 0.1194 14. 0.5495 15. 0.05185 16. 0.01686 17. 0.1495 18. 0.2339 19. $^-0.6649$ 20. $^-0.7312$

Page 351 Written 1. 3.6479 2. 2.5542 3. 1.1059 4. 0.7603 5. 2.7737 6. 2.7304 7. 2.2619 8. 2.1133 9. $^-3.3219$ 10. $^-2.465$ 11. 1.1673 12. 2.085

36.
$$\begin{aligned} a^x &= a^{\log_a n} \\ a^x &= n \\ \log_b a^x &= \log_b n \\ x \log_b a &= \log_b n \\ x &= \frac{\log_b n}{\log_b a} \end{aligned}$$

CHAPTER 13 SEQUENCES AND SERIES

Pages 377–378 Exploratory 7. $\frac{7}{10} + \frac{7}{100} + \frac{7}{1000} + \cdots = \frac{7}{9}$ 8. $\frac{3}{10} + \frac{3}{100} + \frac{3}{1000} + \cdots = \frac{1}{3}$

9. $\frac{73}{100} + \frac{73}{10{,}000} + \frac{73}{10{,}000{,}000} + \cdots = \frac{73}{99}$ 10. $\frac{8}{10} + \frac{8}{100} + \frac{8}{1000} + \cdots = \frac{8}{9}$

11. $\frac{152}{1000} + \frac{152}{1{,}000{,}000} + \cdots = \frac{152}{999}$ 12. $\frac{746}{1000} + \frac{746}{1{,}000{,}000} + \cdots = \frac{746}{999}$

13. $\frac{93}{100} + \frac{93}{10{,}000} + \frac{93}{1{,}000{,}000} + \cdots = \frac{31}{33}$ 14. $\frac{75}{100} + \frac{75}{10{,}000} + \frac{75}{1{,}000{,}000} + \cdots = \frac{25}{33}$

Page 381 Written 1. 1, 1, 2, 3, 5, 8, 13, 21, 34, 55, 89, 144, 233, 377, 610, 987, 1597, 2584, 4181, 6765 2. 0.6928 3. 1, 2, 1.5, $1.\overline{66}$, 1.6, 1.625, 1.61538, 1.61905, 1.61765, 1.61818, 1.61798, 1.61806, 1.61803, 1.61804, 1.61803 4. $L_m = F_{m+1} + F_{m-1}$ for $m \geq 2$

Page 384 Written 10. 2, 6, 18, 54, 162, 486 11. 7, 12, 17, 22, 27, 32 12. 3, 5, 8, 13, 21, 34 13. 1, 2, 2, 4, 8, 32 14. 2, 3, 7, 13, 27, 53 15. 5, 11, 6, $^-5$, $^-11$ 16. $a_{n+1} = a_n + 4$, $a_1 = 3$; $a_n = 4n - 1$ 17. $a_{n+1} = a_n + 5$, $a_1 = 4$; $a_n = 5n - 1$ 18. $a_{n+1} = 5a_n$; $a_1 = 3$; $a_n = 3 \times 5^{n-1}$

19. $a_{n+1} = \frac{1}{2}an$, $a_1 = \frac{3}{2}$; $a_n = \frac{3}{2^n}$ 20. $a_{n+1} = a_n + 5$, $a_1 = 5$; $a_n = 5n$ 21. $a_{n+1} = \frac{1}{5}a_n$, $a_1 = \frac{7}{2}$; $a_n = \frac{7}{2 \times 5^{n-1}}$

22. $\sum_{n=1}^{5} 7n - 4$ 23. $\sum_{n=1}^{5} \frac{3n+1}{5}$ 24. $\sum_{n=1}^{5} \frac{3n}{n+2}$ 25. $\sum_{n=1}^{5} 6(-\frac{1}{3})^{n-1}$ 26. $\sum_{n=1}^{6} (\frac{3}{4}) \times n$ 27. $\sum_{n=1}^{6} \frac{n^2+1}{n}$

28. $\sum_{n=1}^{5} 2n(2n+3)$ 29. $\sum_{n=1}^{6} \frac{(^-1)^{n+1}}{2n-1}$

Page 387 Written 5. $a^7 + 7a^6b + 21a^5b^2 + 35a^4b^3 + 35a^3b^4 + 21a^2b^5 + 7ab^6 + b^7$

6. $32x^5 + 80x^4y + 80x^3y^2 + 40x^2y^3 + 10xy^4 + y^5$ 7. $x^6 - 6x^5y + 15x^4y^2 - 20x^3y^3 + 15x^2y^4 - 6xy^5 + y^6$ 8. $x^8 - 4x^7y + 7x^6y^2 - 7x^5y^3 + \frac{35}{8}x^4y^4 - \frac{7}{4}x^3y^5 + \frac{7}{16}x^2y^6 - \frac{1}{16}xy^7 + \frac{1}{256}y^8$

CHAPTER 14 PROBABILITY

Page 410 Excursion 1.

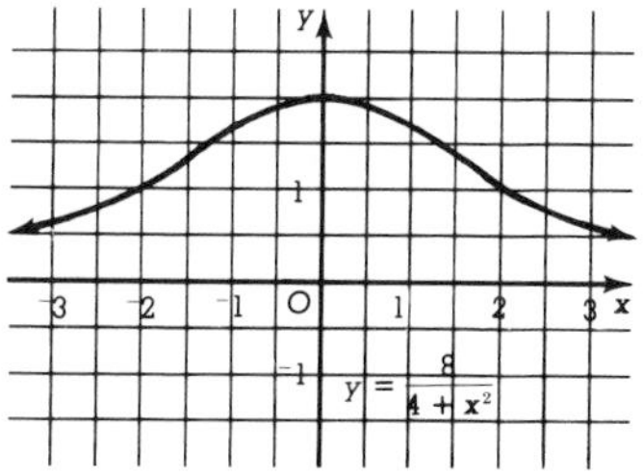

2.

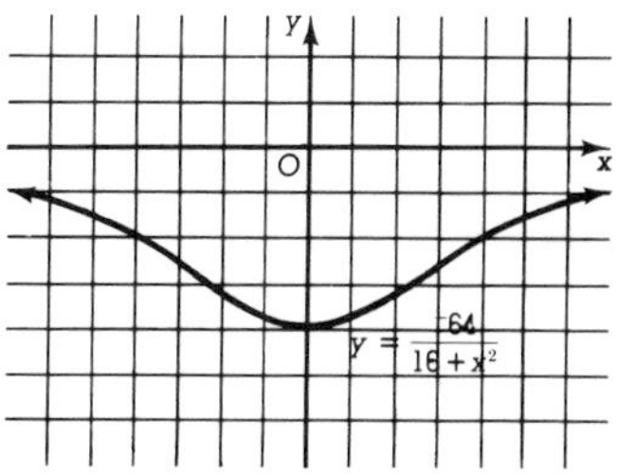

CHAPTER 15 STATISTICS

Pages 424-425 Written 1.

Number of Dots	2	3	4	5	6	7	8	9	10	11	12
Frequency	4	4	5	9	4	9	8	5	7	7	2

4.

Precipitation (inches)	17	18	19	20	21	22	23	24	25	26	27	28	29	30	31
Number of Cities	2	0	3	5	2	7	3	3	10	7	11	2	0	10	6

Precipitation (inches)	32	33	34	35	36	37	38	39	40	41	42	43	44	45	46
Number of Cities	0	7	0	4	3	1	4	0	2	4	0	0	0	3	1

9.

Precipitation (inches)	17-19	20-22	23-25	26-28	29-31
Number of Cities	5	14	16	20	16

Precipitation (inches)	32-34	35-37	38-40	41-43	44-46
Number of Cities	7	8	6	4	4

Pages 428-429 Written

1.

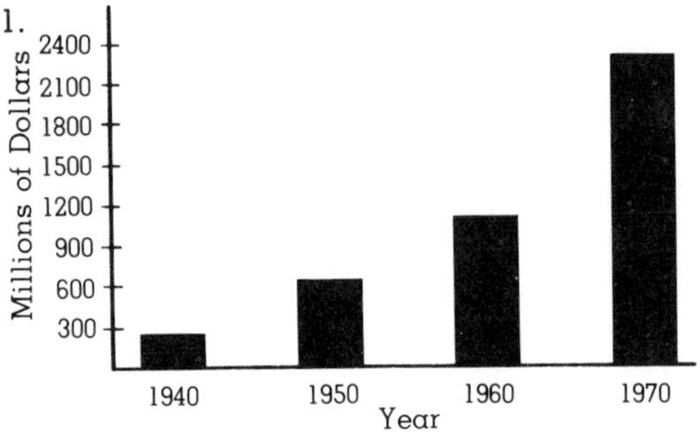

2.

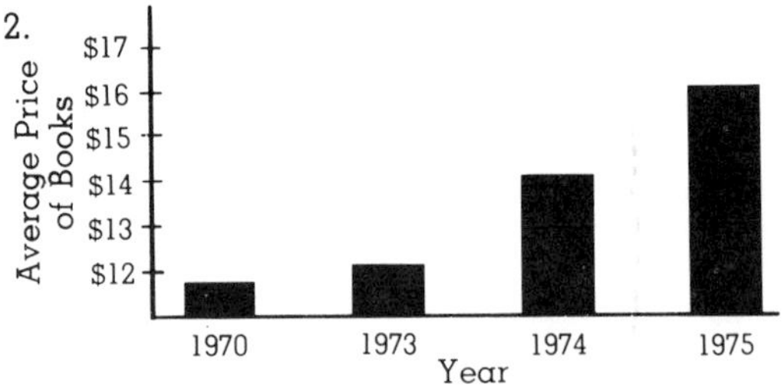

3.

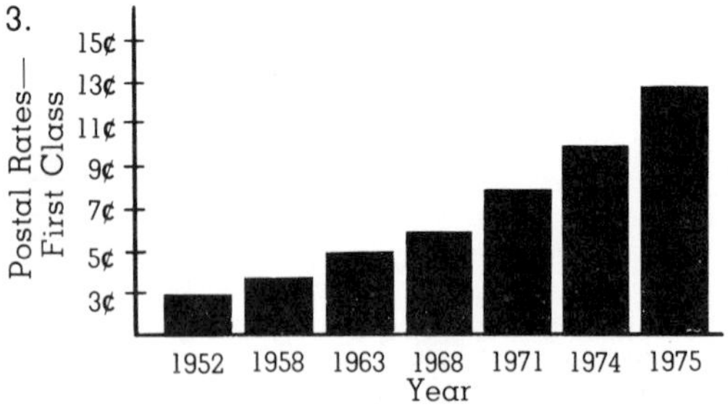

4.

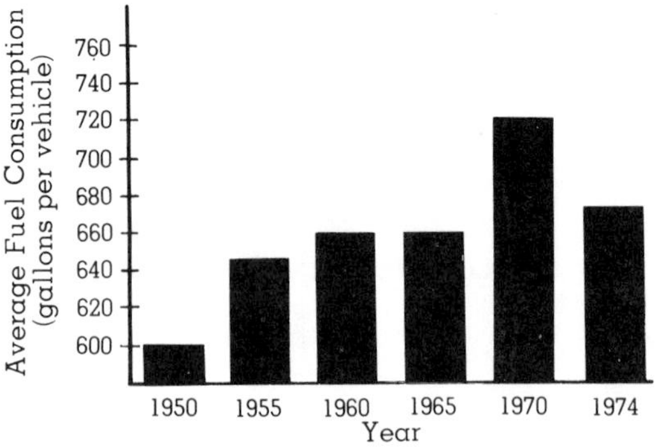

5.

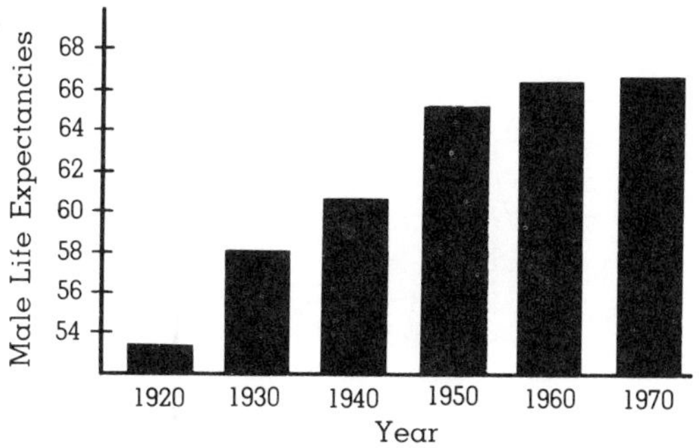
Male Life Expectancies
68
66
64
62
60
58
56
54
1920
1930
1940
1950
1960
1970
Year

6.

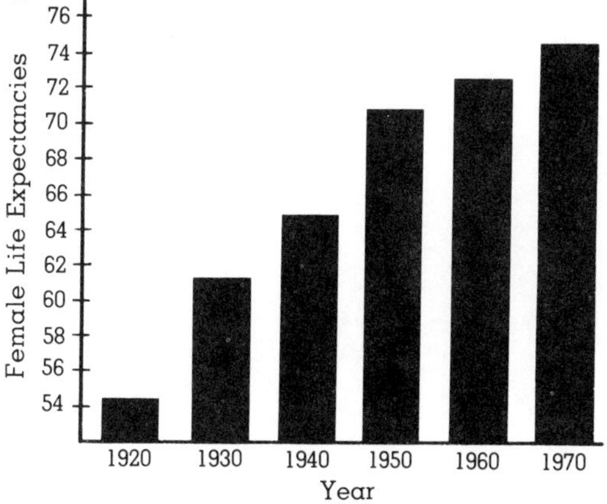
Female Life Expectancies
76
74
72
70
68
66
64
62
60
58
56
54
1920
1930
1940
1950
1960
1970
Year

7.

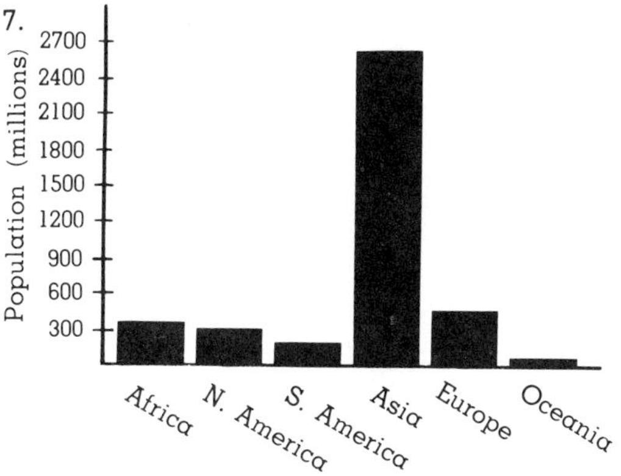
Population (millions)
2700
2400
2100
1800
1500
1200
900
600
300
Africa
N. America
S. America
Asia
Europe
Oceania

8.

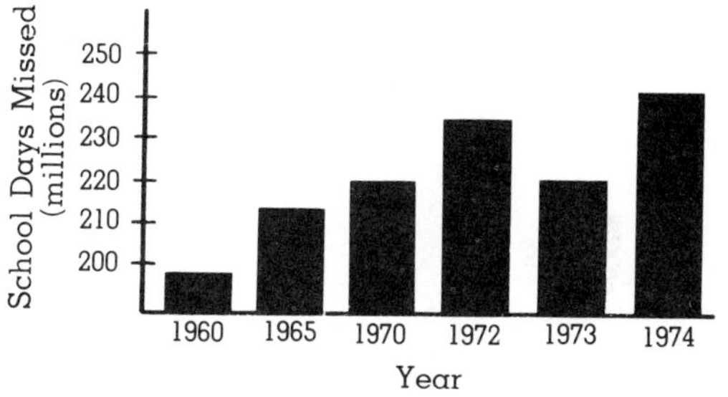
School Days Missed (millions)
250
240
230
220
210
200
1960
1965
1970
1972
1973
1974
Year

9.

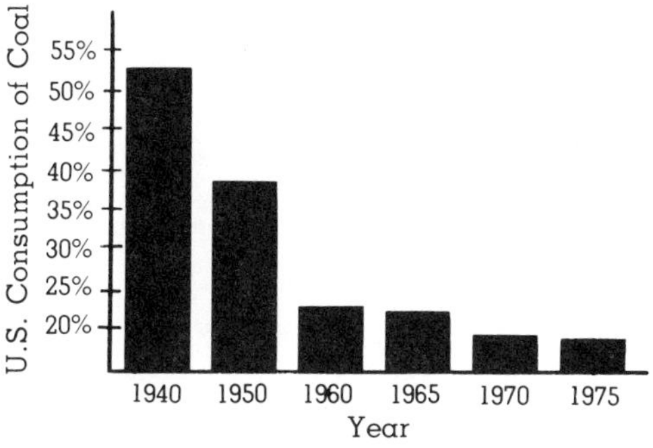
U.S. Consumption of Coal
55%
50%
45%
40%
35%
30%
25%
20%
1940
1950
1960
1965
1970
1975
Year

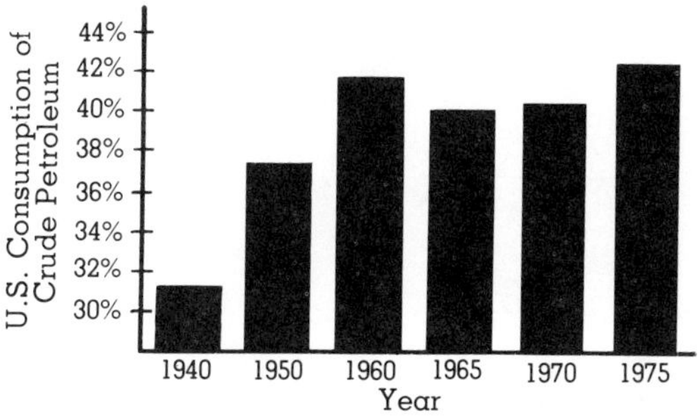
U.S. Consumption of Crude Petroleum
44%
42%
40%
38%
36%
34%
32%
30%
1940
1950
1960
1965
1970
1975
Year

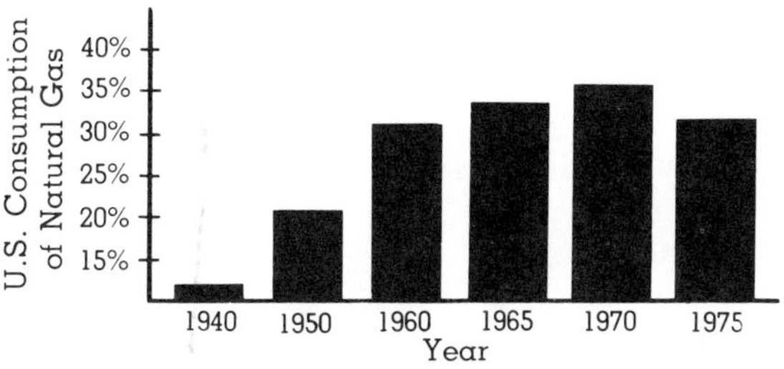
U.S. Consumption of Natural Gas
40%
35%
30%
25%
20%
15%
1940
1950
1960
1965
1970
1975
Year

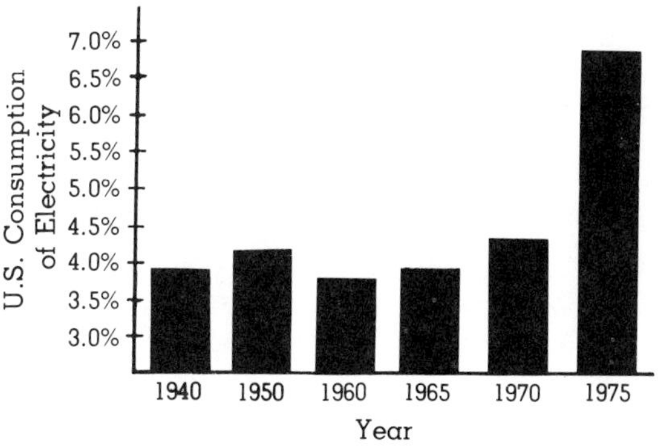
U.S. Consumption of Electricity
7.0%
6.5%
6.0%
5.5%
5.0%
4.5%
4.0%
3.5%
3.0%
1940
1950
1960
1965
1970
1975
Year

10.

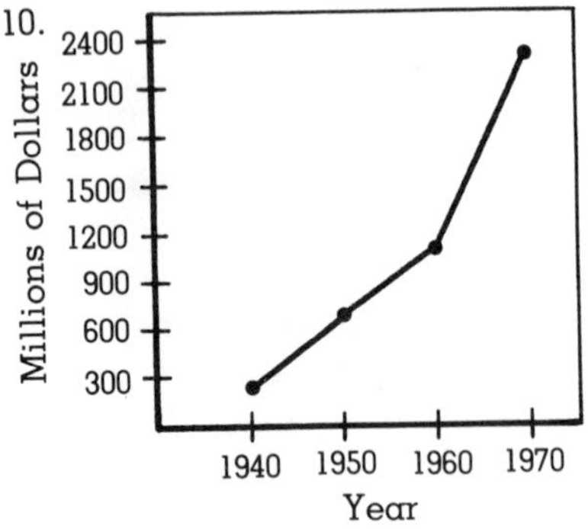

11.

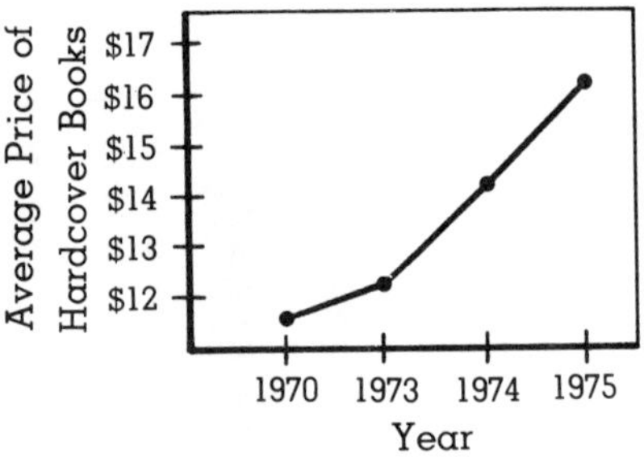

12.

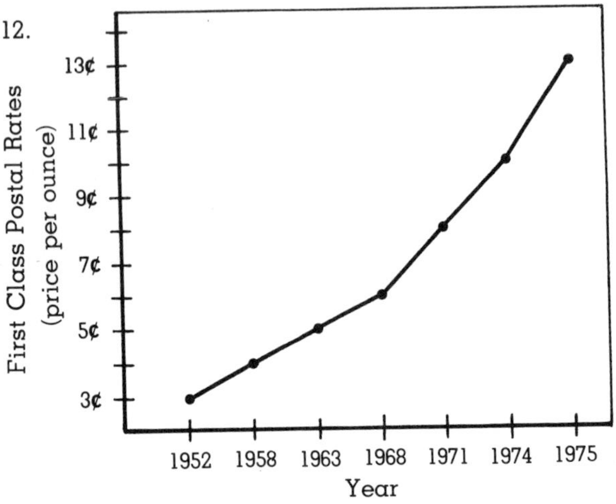

13.

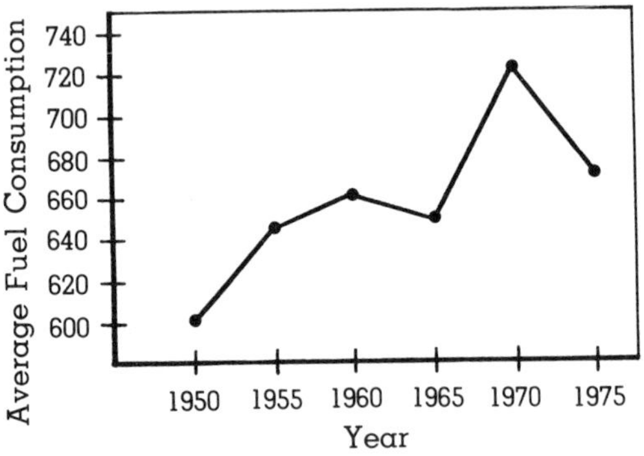

14.

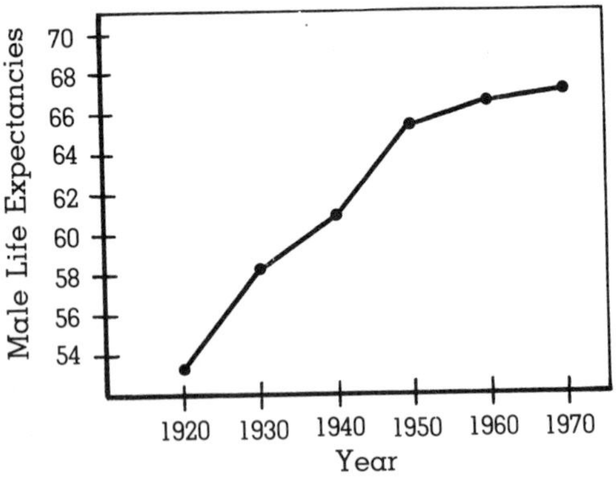

15.

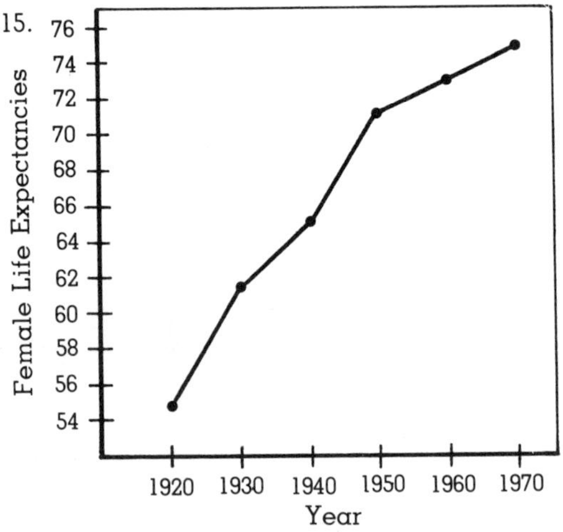

16.

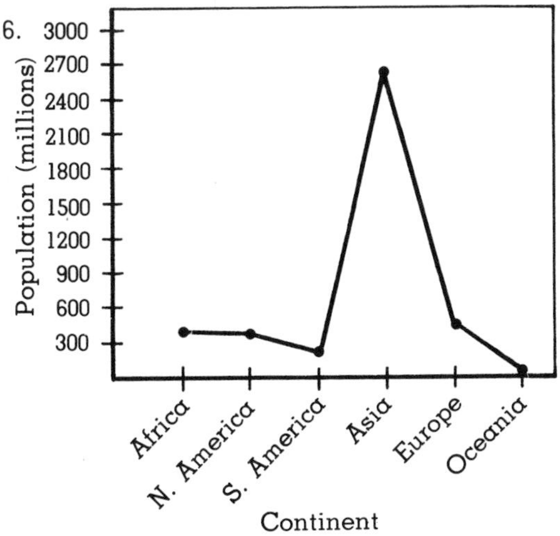
Population (millions)
3000
2700
2400
2100
1800
1500
1200
900
600
300
Africa
N. America
S. America
Asia
Europe
Oceania
Continent

17.

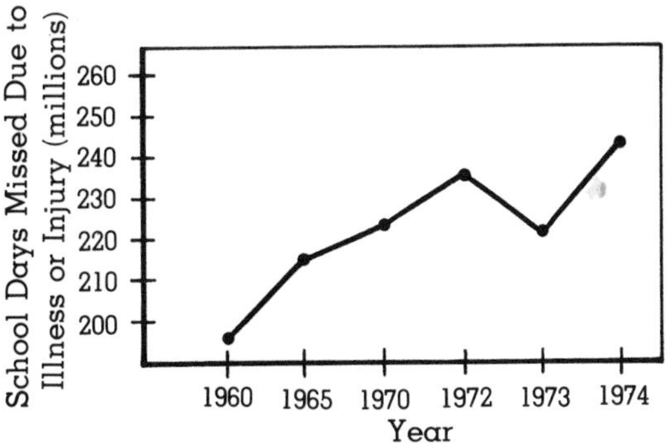
School Days Missed Due to Illness or Injury (millions)
260
250
240
230
220
210
200
1960
1965
1970
1972
1973
1974
Year

18.

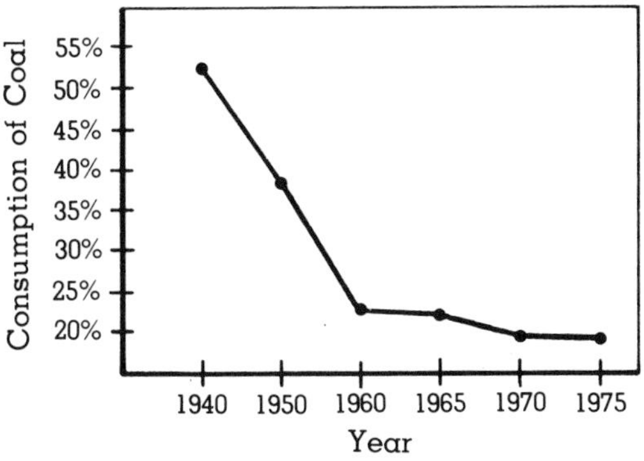
Consumption of Coal
55%
50%
45%
40%
35%
30%
25%
20%
1940
1950
1960
1965
1970
1975
Year

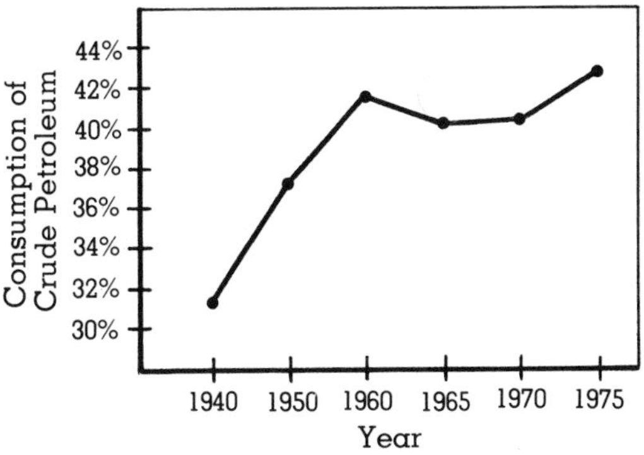
Consumption of Crude Petroleum
44%
42%
40%
38%
36%
34%
32%
30%
1940
1950
1960
1965
1970
1975
Year

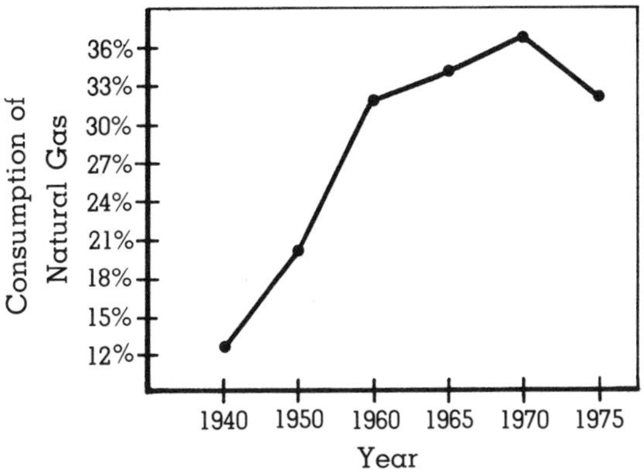
Consumption of Natural Gas
36%
33%
30%
27%
24%
21%
18%
15%
12%
1940
1950
1960
1965
1970
1975
Year

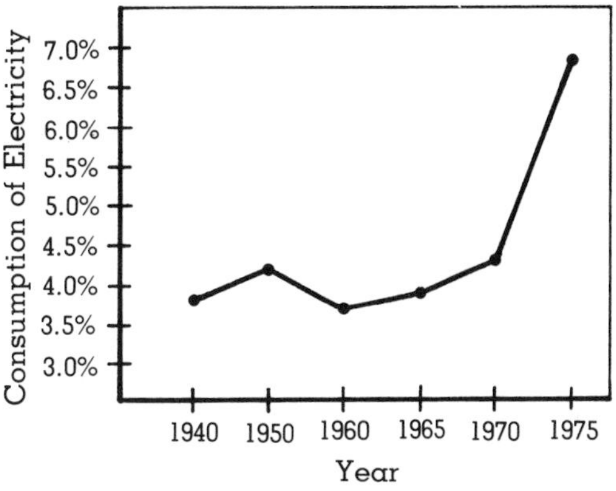
Consumption of Electricity
7.0%
6.5%
6.0%
5.5%
5.0%
4.5%
4.0%
3.5%
3.0%
1940
1950
1960
1965
1970
1975
Year

19.

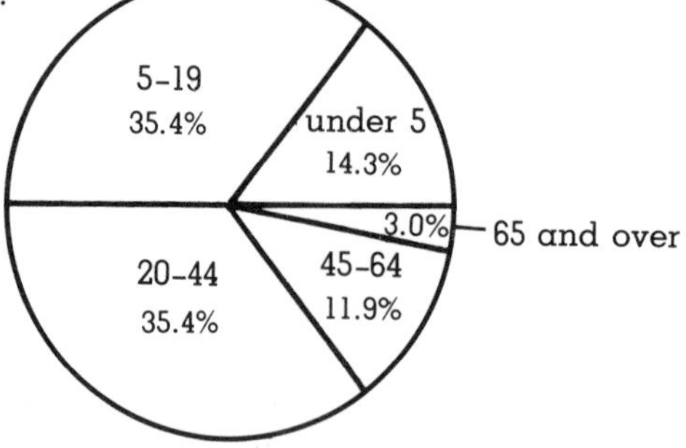

Population Distribution by Age, 1870

20.

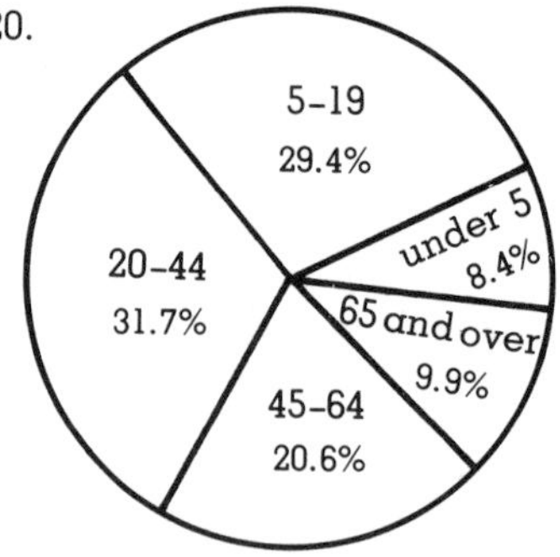

Population Distribution by Age, 1970

21.

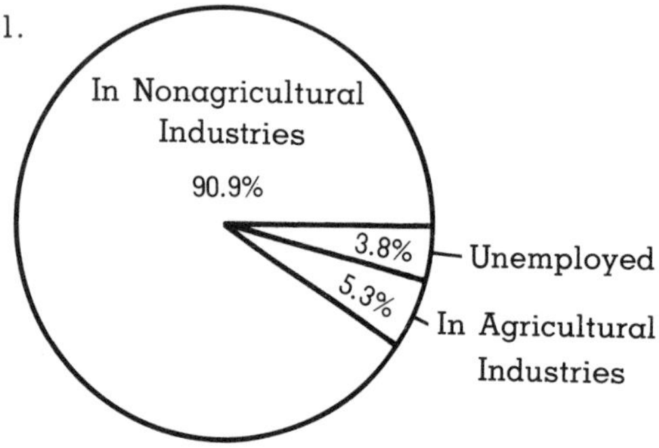

Civilian Labor Force, 1966

22.

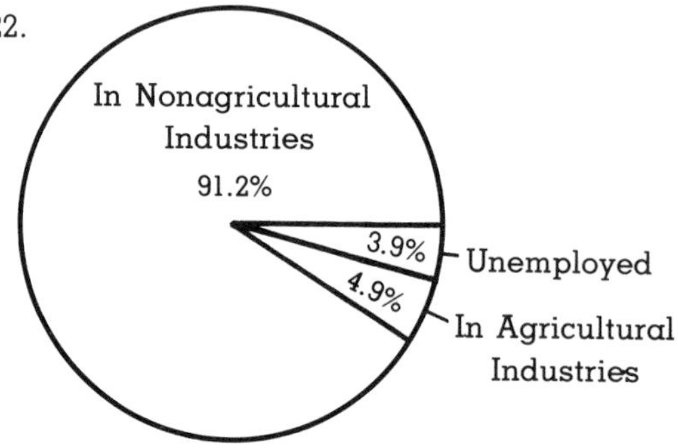

Civilian Labor Force, 1967

23.

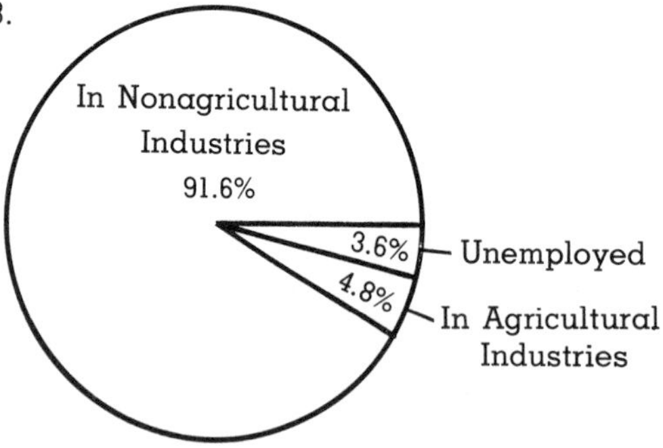

Civilian Labor Force, 1968

24.

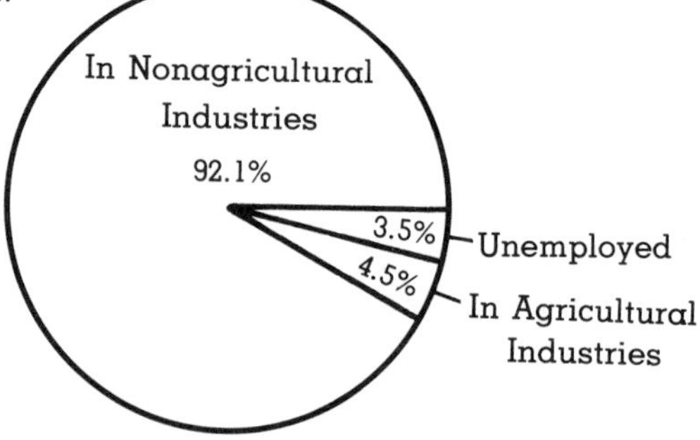

Civilian Labor Force, 1969

25.

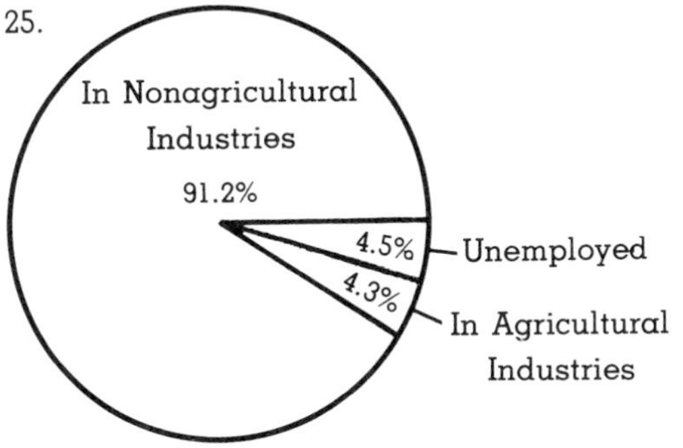

Civilian Labor Force, 1970

Page 441 Written

13.

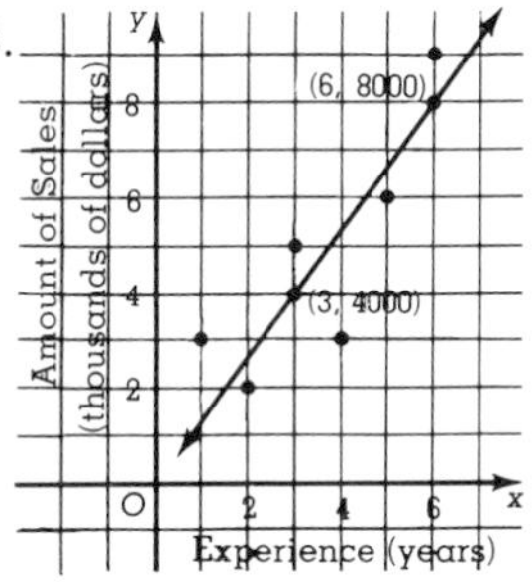

17.

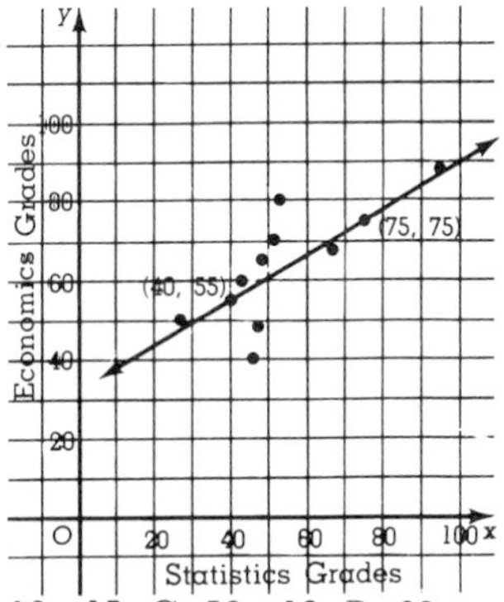

Page 432 Written Answers may vary for problems **13–24.** **13.** A, 1 **14.** B, 13 **15.** C, 50 **16.** D, 60 **17.** E, 74 **18.** F, 53 **19.** G, 39 **20.** H, 11 **21.** I, 1 **22.** median 39 **23.** mode 1 **24.** mean 33.6

Page 435 Written 20.

```
10  DATA
12  L=100: REM MAX NO. OF ITEMS
15  DIM A(L)
20  S=0
25  READ N
30  FOR X=1 TO N
40  READ A(X)
50  S = STA(X)
60  NEXT X
70  M=S/N
80  S=0
90  FOR X=1 TO N
100  D = A(X)-M
110  S=S+D↑2
120  NEXT X
130  V=SQR(S/N)
140  PRINT "STAN. DEV. IS", V
150  END
```

Page 445 Chapter Review

9.

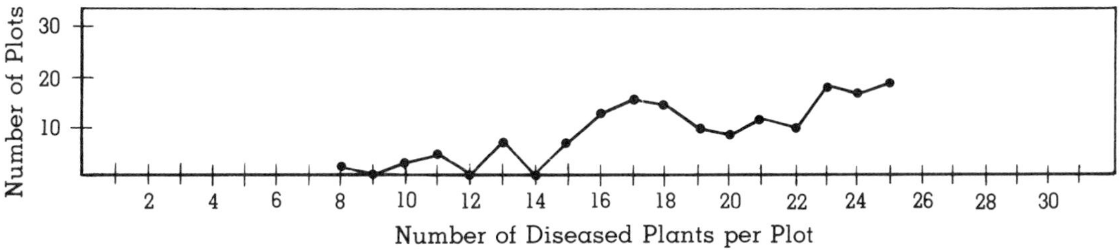

Page 446 Chapter Test

1.

Temperature (degrees Fahrenheit)	31	30	29	28	27	26	25	24	23	22	21	20	19	18	17	16	15	14	13
Frequency	3	2	3	0	3	2	2	2	1	2	0	1	1	2	2	3	1	0	2

Temperature (degrees Fahrenheit)	12	11	10	9	8	7	6	5	4	3	2	1	0	−1	−2	−3	−4	−5	−6	−7
Frequency	3	0	0	0	1	1	1	3	1	0	0	0	0	0	0	0	0	0	0	1

CHAPTER 16 TRIGONOMETRIC FUNCTIONS AND IDENTITIES

Page 459 Written

1.

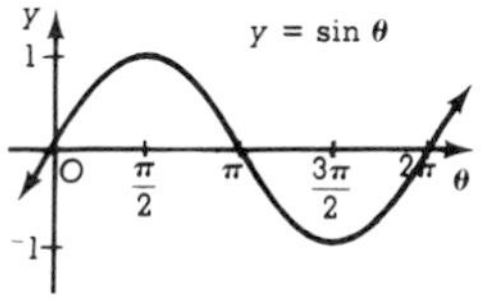

2.

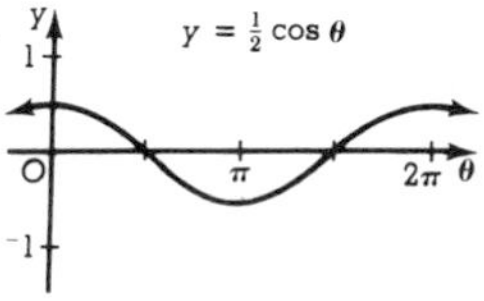

3.

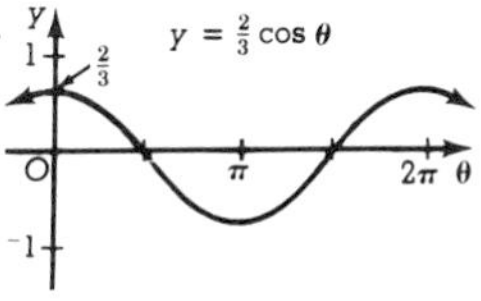

4.

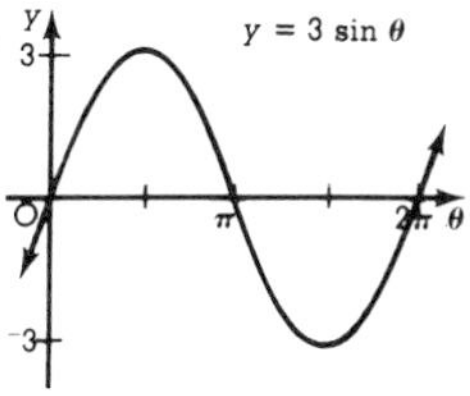

5.
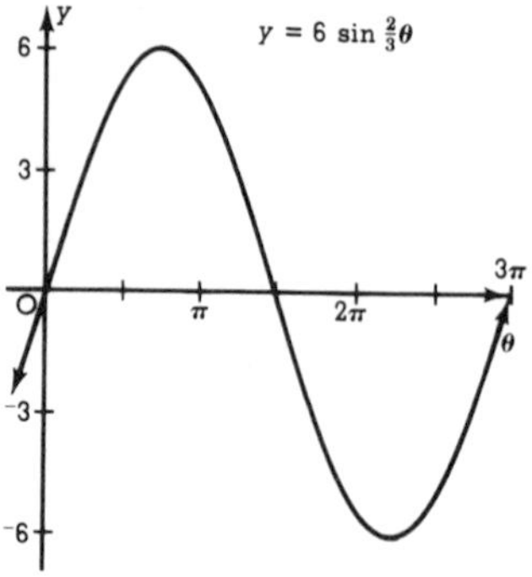

6.
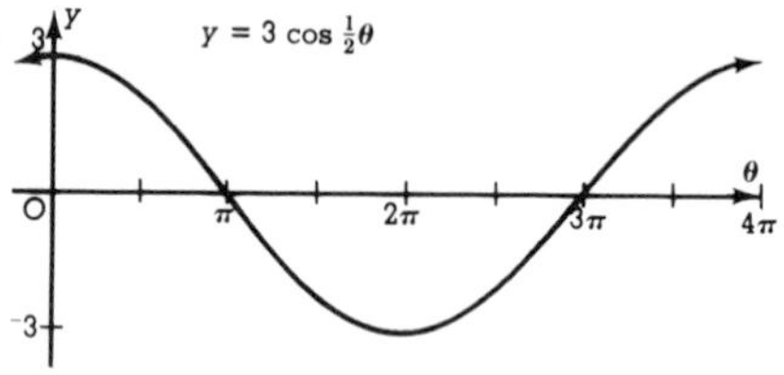

7.
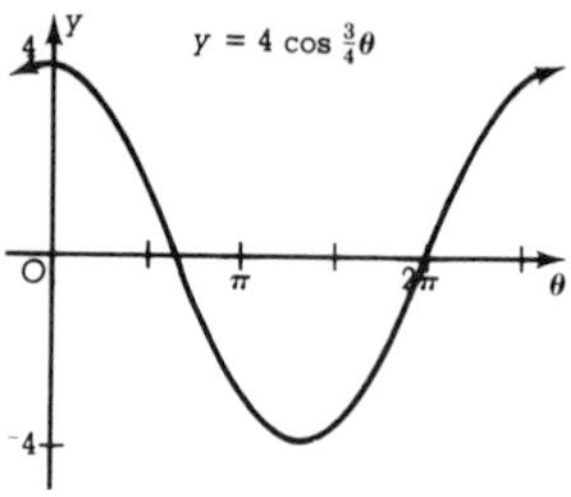

8.
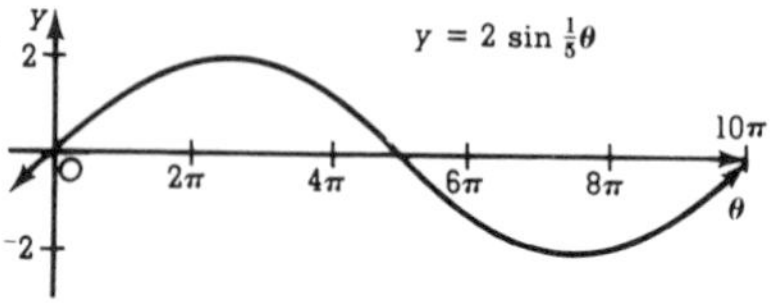

9.
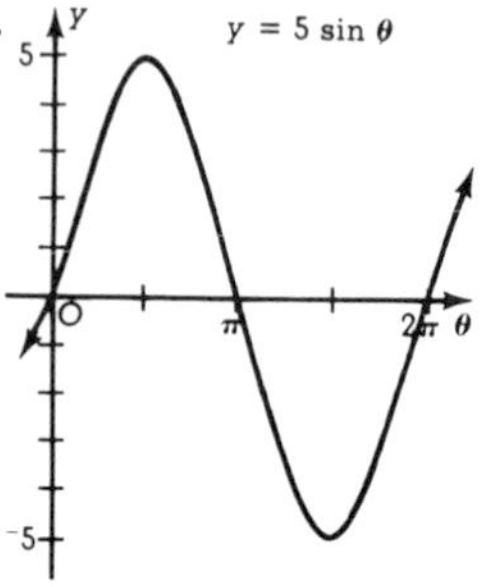

10.
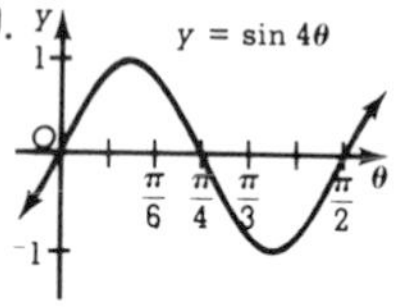

11.
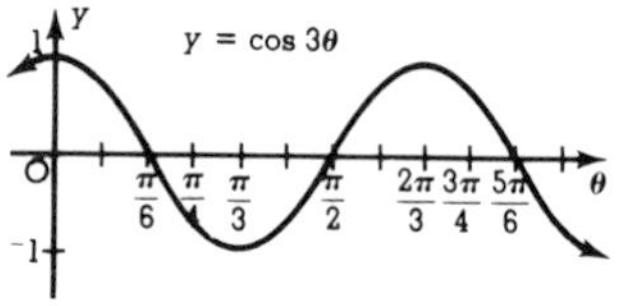

12.
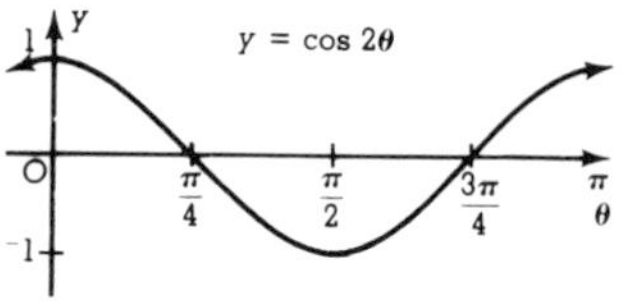

13.
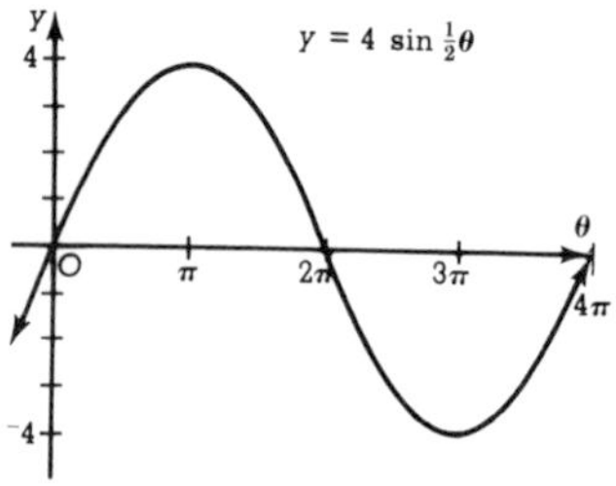

14.
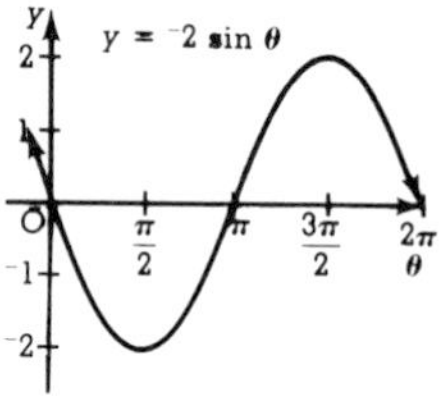

15.
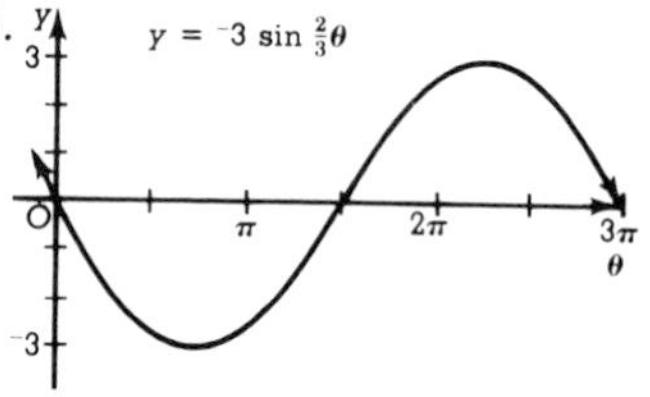

16.
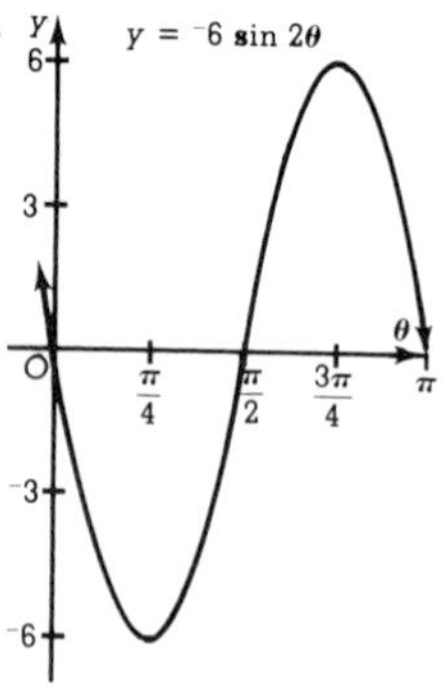

17.
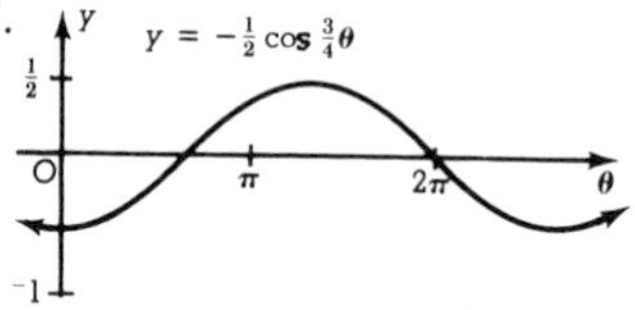

18.
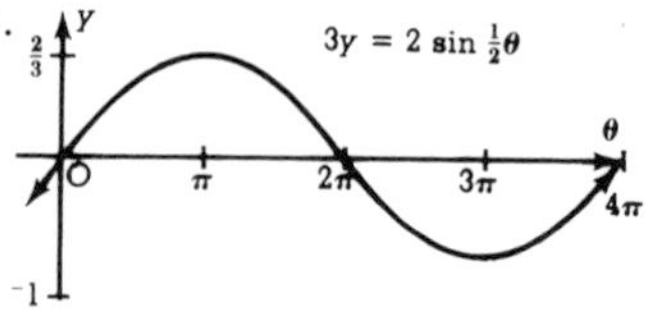

19.

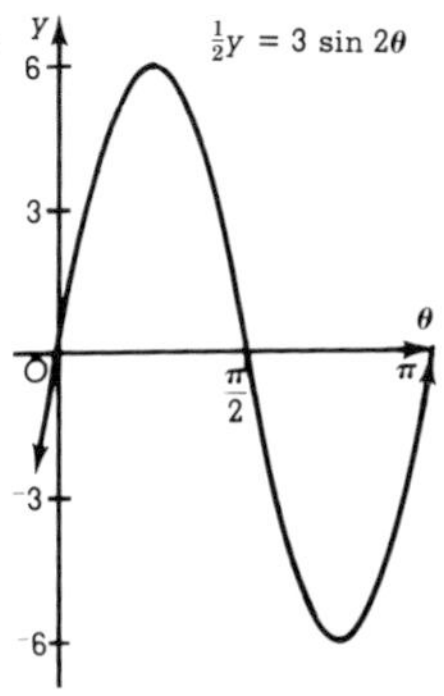

20.

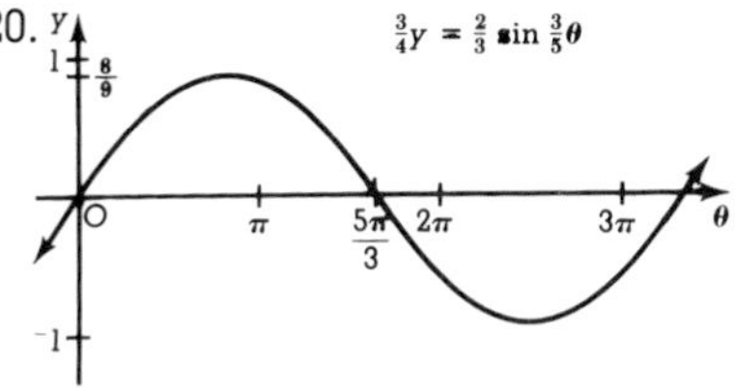

Pages 461–462 Exploratory 13. $\{y \mid {}^{-}1 \leq y \leq 1\}$ 14. $\{y \mid {}^{-}1 \leq y \leq 1\}$ 15. all reals 16. all reals 17. $\{y \mid y \geq 1 \text{ or } y \leq {}^{-}1\}$ 18. $\{y \mid y \geq 1 \text{ or } y \leq {}^{-}1\}$

Page 462 Written 7. decreasing 8. decreasing 9. increasing 10. decreasing 11. increasing 12. increasing 13. decreasing 14. increasing 15. increasing 16. decreasing 17. decreasing 18. increasing 19. increasing 20. increasing 21. increasing 22. decreasing 23. decreasing 24. decreasing

53.

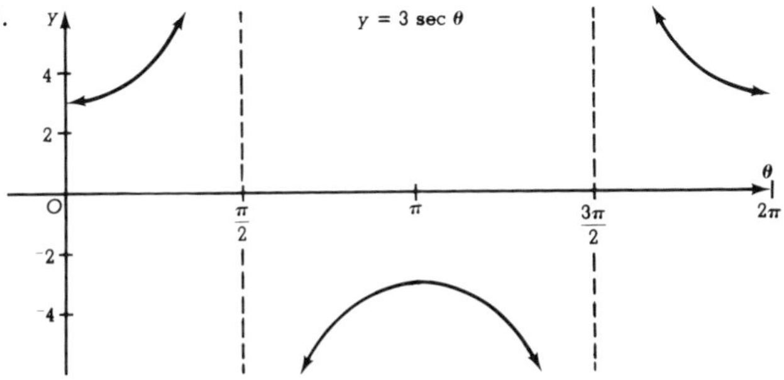

54.

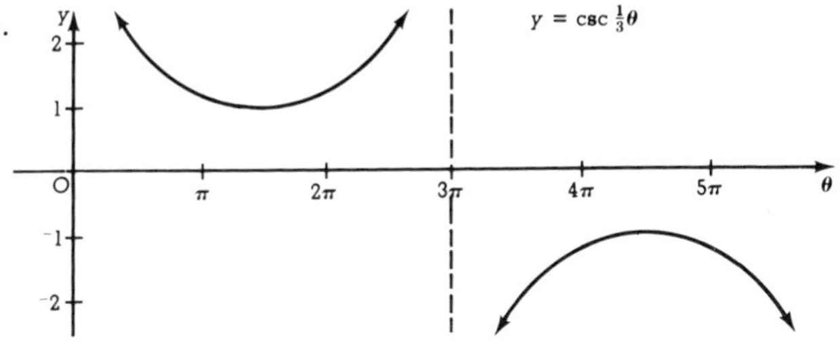

55.

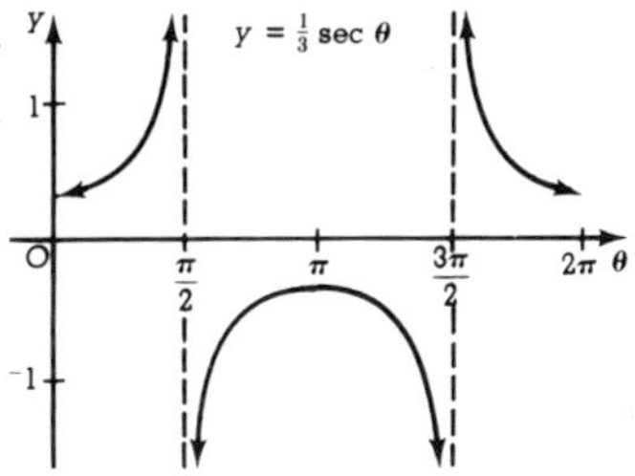

56.

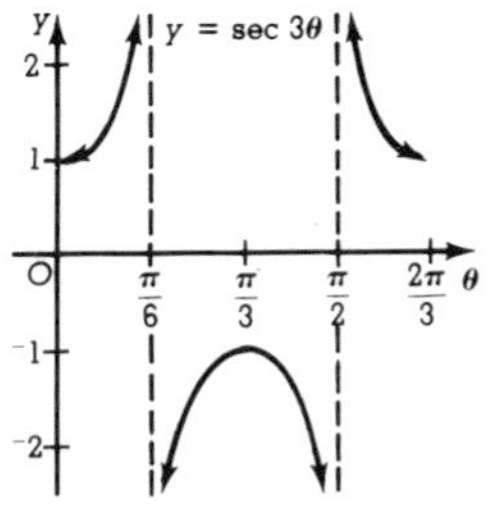

57.

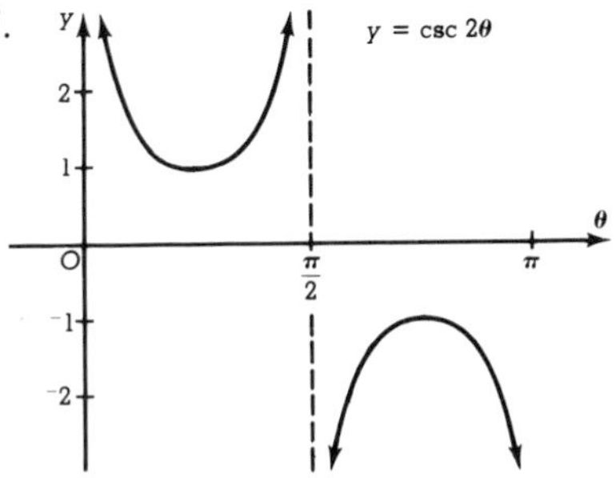

58.

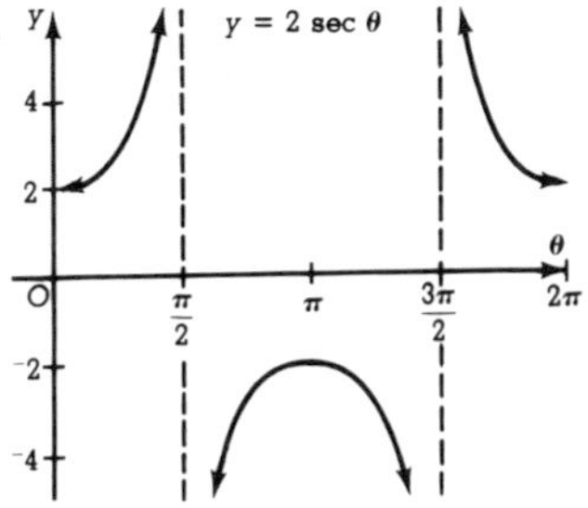

59.

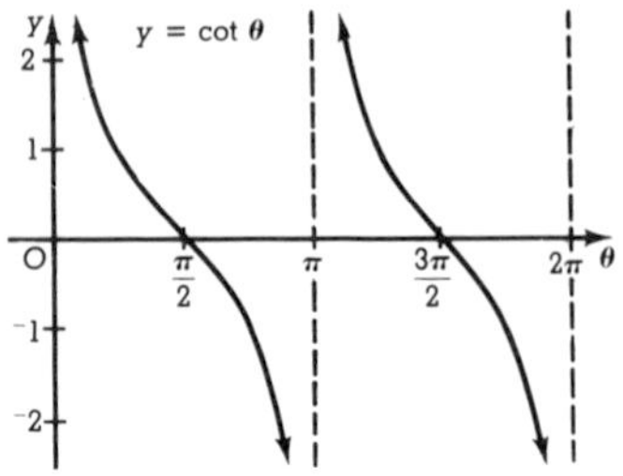

60.

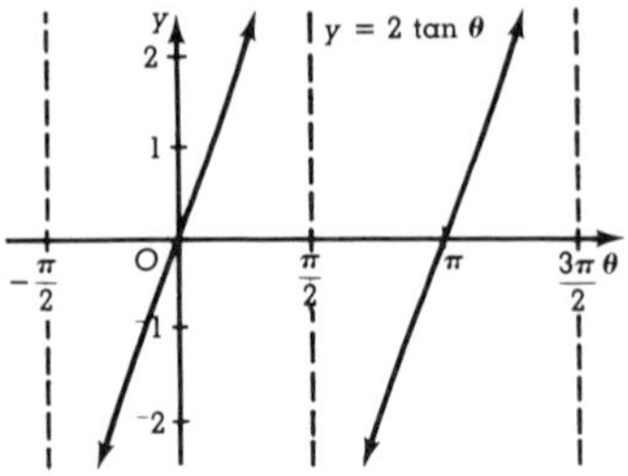

61.

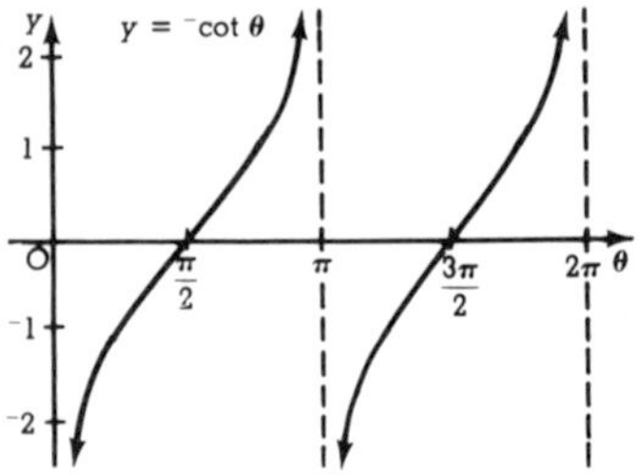

62.

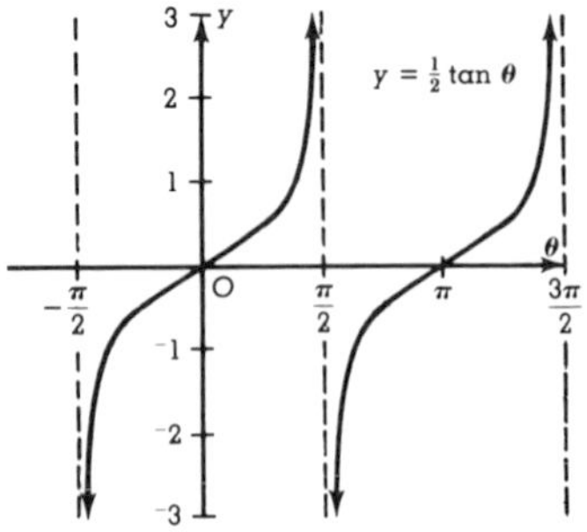

63.

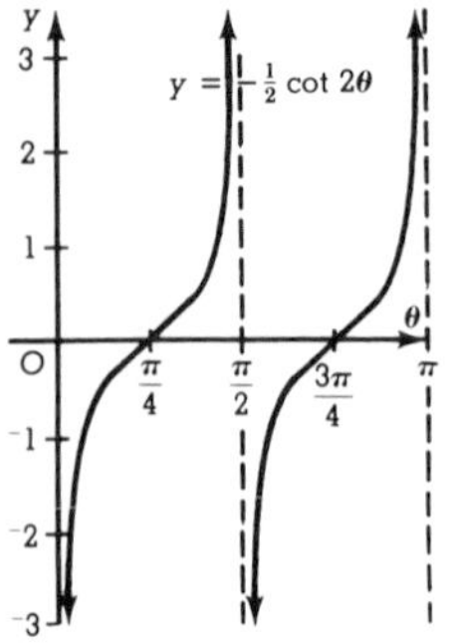

64.

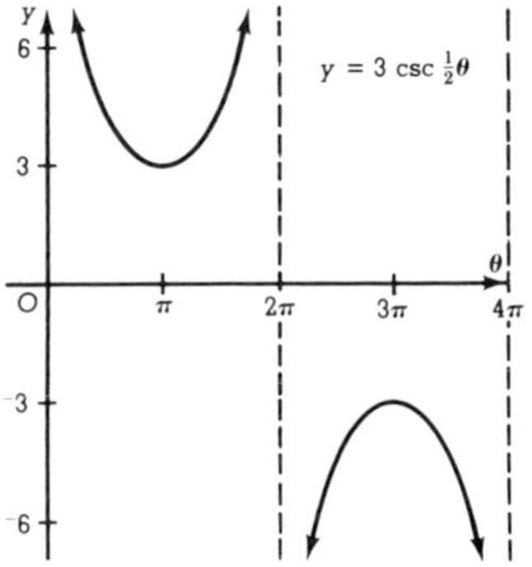

Page 465 Written

27.
$$1 + \cot^2 \theta \stackrel{?}{=} \csc^2 \theta$$
$$\frac{\sin^2 \theta + \cos^2 \theta}{\sin^2 \theta} \stackrel{?}{=} \csc^2 \theta$$
$$\frac{1}{\sin^2 \theta} \stackrel{?}{=} \csc^2 \theta$$
$$\csc^2 \theta = \csc^2 \theta$$

28.
$$\frac{\sec \theta}{\csc \theta} \stackrel{?}{=} \tan \theta$$
$$\frac{\frac{1}{\cos \theta}}{\frac{1}{\sin \theta}} \stackrel{?}{=} \tan \theta$$
$$\frac{1}{\cos \theta} \cdot \frac{\sin \theta}{1} \stackrel{?}{=} \tan \theta$$
$$\frac{\sin \theta}{\cos \theta} \stackrel{?}{=} \tan \theta$$
$$\tan \theta = \tan \theta$$

29.
$$\sin x \sec x \stackrel{?}{=} \tan x$$
$$\sin x \cdot \frac{1}{\cos x} \stackrel{?}{=} \tan x$$
$$\frac{\sin x}{\cos x} \stackrel{?}{=} \tan x$$
$$\tan x = \tan x$$

30.
$$\sec \alpha - \cos \alpha \stackrel{?}{=} \sin \alpha \tan \alpha$$
$$\frac{1}{\cos \alpha} - \cos \alpha \stackrel{?}{=} \sin \alpha \tan \alpha$$
$$\frac{1 - \cos^2 \alpha}{\cos \alpha} \stackrel{?}{=} \sin \alpha \tan \alpha$$
$$\frac{\sin^2 \alpha}{\cos \alpha} \stackrel{?}{=} \sin \alpha \tan \alpha$$
$$\frac{\sin \alpha \sin \alpha}{\cos \alpha} \stackrel{?}{=} \sin \alpha \tan \alpha$$
$$\sin \alpha \tan \alpha = \sin \alpha \tan \alpha$$

Page 468 Exploratory

1.
$$\csc^2 \theta - \cot^2 \theta \stackrel{?}{=} 1$$
$$\frac{1}{\sin^2 \theta} - \cot^2 \theta \stackrel{?}{=} 1$$
$$\frac{1}{\sin^2 \theta} - \frac{\cos^2 \theta}{\sin^2 \theta} \stackrel{?}{=} 1$$
$$\frac{1 - \cos^2 \theta}{\sin^2 \theta} \stackrel{?}{=} 1$$
$$\frac{\sin^2 \theta}{\sin^2 \theta} \stackrel{?}{=} 1$$
$$1 = 1$$

2.
$$\tan \theta \cot \theta \stackrel{?}{=} 1$$
$$\tan \theta \cdot \frac{1}{\tan \theta} \stackrel{?}{=} 1$$
$$\frac{\tan \theta}{\tan \theta} \stackrel{?}{=} 1$$
$$1 = 1$$

3.
$$\frac{\sin^2 \theta + \cos^2 \theta}{\sin^2 \theta} \stackrel{?}{=} \csc^2 \theta$$
$$\frac{1}{\sin^2 \theta} \stackrel{?}{=} \csc^2 \theta$$
$$\csc^2 \theta = \csc^2 \theta$$

4.
$$\frac{\tan x}{\sin x} \stackrel{?}{=} \sec x$$
$$\frac{\frac{\sin x}{\cos x}}{\sin x} \stackrel{?}{=} \sec x$$
$$\frac{\sin x}{\cos x} \cdot \frac{1}{\sin x} \stackrel{?}{=} \sec x$$
$$\frac{1}{\cos x} \stackrel{?}{=} \sec x$$
$$\sec x = \sec x$$

5. $\csc^2 r - \cot^2 r \stackrel{?}{=} 1$
$$\csc^2 r - (\csc^2 r - 1) \stackrel{?}{=} 1$$
$$\csc^2 r - \csc^2 r + 1 \stackrel{?}{=} 1$$
$$1 = 1$$

6. $\cos\alpha \csc\alpha \stackrel{?}{=} \cot\alpha$
$$\cos\alpha \frac{1}{\sin\alpha} \stackrel{?}{=} \cot\alpha$$
$$\frac{\cos\alpha}{\sin\alpha} \stackrel{?}{=} \cot\alpha$$
$$\cot\alpha = \cot\alpha$$

7. $\sin\theta \cot\theta \stackrel{?}{=} \cos\theta$
$$\sin\theta \cdot \frac{\cos\theta}{\sin\theta} \stackrel{?}{=} \cos\theta$$
$$\cos\theta = \cos\theta$$

8. $\tan x \csc x \stackrel{?}{=} \sec x$
$$\frac{\sin x}{\cos x} \cdot \frac{1}{\sin x} \stackrel{?}{=} \sec x$$
$$\frac{1}{\cos x} \stackrel{?}{=} \sec x$$
$$\sec x = \sec x$$

Page 468 Written

1. $\tan\beta(\cot\beta + \tan\beta) \stackrel{?}{=} \sec^2\beta$
$$\tan\beta\left(\frac{1}{\tan\beta} + \tan\beta\right) \stackrel{?}{=} \sec^2\beta$$
$$1 + \tan^2\beta \stackrel{?}{=} \sec^2\beta$$
$$\sec^2\beta = \sec^2\beta$$

2. $\cos^2\theta + \tan^2\theta\cos^2\theta \stackrel{?}{=} 1$
$$\cos^2\theta + \frac{\sin^2\theta}{\cos^2\theta} \cdot \cos^2\theta \stackrel{?}{=} 1$$
$$\cos^2\theta + \sin^2\theta \stackrel{?}{=} 1$$
$$1 = 1$$

3. $\csc x \sec x \stackrel{?}{=} \cot x + \tan x$
$$\frac{1}{\sin x} \cdot \frac{1}{\cos x} \stackrel{?}{=} \frac{\cos x}{\sin x} + \frac{\sin x}{\cos x}$$
$$\frac{1}{\sin x} \cdot \frac{1}{\cos x} \stackrel{?}{=} \frac{\cos^2 x + \sin^2 x}{\sin x \cos x}$$
$$\frac{1}{\sin x \cos x} = \frac{1}{\sin x \cos x}$$

4. $\sec^2 x - \tan^2 x \stackrel{?}{=} \tan x \cot x$
$$1 \stackrel{?}{=} \tan x \cdot \frac{1}{\tan x}$$
$$1 \stackrel{?}{=} \frac{\tan x}{\tan x}$$
$$1 = 1$$

5. $\frac{\sec\theta}{\sin\theta} - \frac{\sin\theta}{\cos\theta} \stackrel{?}{=} \cot\theta$
$$\frac{1}{\cos\theta\sin\theta} - \frac{\sin\theta}{\cos\theta} \stackrel{?}{=} \cot\theta$$
$$\frac{1 - \sin^2\theta}{\cos\theta\sin\theta} \stackrel{?}{=} \cot\theta$$
$$\frac{\cos^2\theta}{\cos\theta\sin\theta} \stackrel{?}{=} \cot\theta$$
$$\frac{\cos\theta}{\sin\theta} \stackrel{?}{=} \cot\theta$$
$$\cot\theta = \cot\theta$$

6. $\frac{1}{\sec^2\theta} + \frac{1}{\csc^2\theta} \stackrel{?}{=} 1$
$$\frac{1}{\frac{1}{\cos^2\theta}} + \frac{1}{\frac{1}{\sin^2\theta}} \stackrel{?}{=} 1$$
$$\cos^2\theta + \sin^2\theta \stackrel{?}{=} 1$$
$$1 = 1$$

7. $\frac{\sin\alpha}{1 - \cos\alpha} + \frac{1 - \cos\alpha}{\sin\alpha} \stackrel{?}{=} 2\csc\alpha$
$$\frac{\sin^2\alpha + (1 - \cos\alpha)}{(1 - \cos\alpha)(\sin\alpha)} \stackrel{?}{=} \frac{2}{\sin\alpha}$$
$$\frac{\sin^2\alpha + 1 - 2\cos\alpha + \cos^2\alpha}{(1 - \cos\alpha)\sin\alpha} \stackrel{?}{=} \frac{2}{\sin\alpha}$$
$$\frac{2 - 2\cos\alpha}{(1 - \cos\alpha)\sin\alpha} \stackrel{?}{=} \frac{2}{\sin\alpha}$$
$$\frac{2(1 - \cos\alpha)}{(1 - \cos\alpha)\sin\alpha} \stackrel{?}{=} \frac{2}{\sin\alpha}$$
$$\frac{2}{\sin\alpha} = \frac{2}{\sin\alpha}$$

8. $\frac{\sec\alpha + \csc\alpha}{1 + \tan\alpha} \stackrel{?}{=} \csc\alpha$
$$\frac{\frac{1}{\cos\alpha} + \frac{1}{\sin\alpha}}{1 + \frac{\sin\alpha}{\cos\alpha}} \stackrel{?}{=} \frac{1}{\sin\alpha}$$
$$\frac{\frac{\sin\alpha + \cos\alpha}{\cos\alpha + \sin\alpha}}{\frac{\cos\alpha + \sin\alpha}{\cos\alpha}} \stackrel{?}{=} \frac{1}{\sin\alpha}$$
$$\frac{\sin\alpha + \cos\alpha}{\cos\alpha \cdot \sin\alpha} \cdot \frac{\cos\alpha}{\cos\alpha + \sin\alpha} \stackrel{?}{=} \frac{1}{\sin\alpha}$$
$$\frac{1}{\sin\alpha} = \frac{1}{\sin\alpha}$$

9. $\frac{\cos^2 x}{1 - \sin x} \stackrel{?}{=} 1 + \sin x$
$$\frac{\cos^2 x}{1 - \sin x} \cdot \frac{1 + \sin x}{1 + \sin x} \stackrel{?}{=} 1 + \sin x$$
$$\frac{\cos^2 x(1 + \sin x)}{1 - \sin^2 x} \stackrel{?}{=} 1 + \sin x$$
$$\frac{\cos^2 x(1 + \sin x)}{\cos^2 x} \stackrel{?}{=} 1 + \sin x$$
$$1 + \sin x = 1 + \sin x$$

10. $$\frac{1-\cos\theta}{1+\cos\theta} \stackrel{?}{=} (\csc\theta - \cot\theta)^2$$
$$\frac{1-\cos\theta}{1+\cos\theta} \stackrel{?}{=} \left(\frac{1}{\sin\theta} - \frac{\cos\theta}{\sin\theta}\right)^2$$
$$\frac{1-\cos\theta}{1+\cos\theta} \stackrel{?}{=} \left(\frac{1-\cos\theta}{\sin\theta}\right)^2$$
$$\frac{1-\cos\theta}{1+\cos\theta} \stackrel{?}{=} \frac{(1-\cos\theta)^2}{\sin^2\theta}$$
$$\frac{1-\cos\theta}{1+\cos\theta} \stackrel{?}{=} \frac{(1-\cos\theta)^2}{1-\cos^2\theta}$$
$$\frac{1-\cos\theta}{1+\cos\theta} \stackrel{?}{=} \frac{(1-\cos\theta)(1-\cos\theta)}{(1-\cos\theta)(1+\cos\theta)}$$
$$\frac{1-\cos\theta}{1+\cos\theta} = \frac{1-\cos\theta}{1+\cos\theta}$$

11. $$\frac{\sin\theta}{\sec\theta} \stackrel{?}{=} \frac{1}{\tan\theta + \cot\theta}$$
$$\frac{\sin\theta}{\frac{1}{\cos\theta}} \stackrel{?}{=} \frac{1}{\frac{\sin\theta}{\cos\theta} + \frac{\cos\theta}{\sin\theta}}$$
$$\sin\theta \cdot \cos\theta \stackrel{?}{=} \frac{1}{\frac{\sin^2\theta + \cos^2\theta}{\cos\theta \cdot \sin\theta}}$$
$$\sin\theta \cdot \cos\theta \stackrel{?}{=} \frac{1}{\frac{1}{\cos\theta \cdot \sin\theta}}$$
$$\sin\theta \cdot \cos\theta = \cos\theta \cdot \sin\theta$$

12. $$\frac{\sec\theta + 1}{\tan\theta} \stackrel{?}{=} \frac{\tan\theta}{\sec\theta - 1}$$
$$\frac{\frac{1}{\cos\theta} + 1}{\frac{\sin\theta}{\cos\theta}} \stackrel{?}{=} \frac{\frac{\sin\theta}{\cos\theta}}{\frac{1}{\cos\theta} - 1}$$
$$\frac{1+\cos\theta}{\cos\theta} \cdot \frac{\cos\theta}{\sin\theta} \stackrel{?}{=} \frac{\frac{\sin\theta}{\cos\theta}}{\frac{1-\cos\theta}{\cos\theta}}$$
$$\frac{1+\cos\theta}{\sin\theta} \stackrel{?}{=} \frac{\sin\theta}{\cos\theta} \cdot \frac{\cos\theta}{1-\cos\theta}$$
$$\frac{1+\cos\theta}{\sin\theta} \stackrel{?}{=} \frac{\sin\theta}{(1-\cos\theta)} \frac{(1+\cos\theta)}{(1+\cos\theta)}$$
$$\frac{1+\cos\theta}{\sin\theta} \stackrel{?}{=} \frac{\sin\theta\,(1+\cos\theta)}{1-\cos^2\theta}$$
$$\frac{1+\cos\theta}{\sin\theta} \stackrel{?}{=} \frac{\sin\theta\,(1+\cos\theta)}{\sin^2\theta}$$
$$\frac{1+\cos\theta}{\sin\theta} = \frac{1+\cos\theta}{\sin\theta}$$

13. $$\frac{\cot x + \csc x}{\sin x + \tan x} \stackrel{?}{=} \cot x \cdot \csc x$$
$$\frac{\frac{\cos x}{\sin x} + \frac{1}{\sin x}}{\sin x + \frac{\sin x}{\cos x}} \stackrel{?}{=} \frac{\cos x}{\sin x} \cdot \frac{1}{\sin x}$$
$$\frac{\frac{\cos x + 1}{\sin x}}{\sin x\left(1 + \frac{1}{\cos x}\right)} \stackrel{?}{=} \frac{\cos x}{\sin x} \cdot \frac{1}{\sin x}$$
$$\frac{\frac{\cos x + 1}{\sin x}}{\sin x\left(\frac{\cos x + 1}{\cos x}\right)} \stackrel{?}{=} \frac{\cos x}{\sin x} \cdot \frac{1}{\sin x}$$
$$\left(\frac{\cos x + 1}{\sin x}\right)\left(\frac{1}{\sin x}\right)\left(\frac{\cos x}{\cos x + 1}\right) \stackrel{?}{=} \frac{\cos x}{\sin^2 x}$$
$$\frac{\cos x}{\sin^2 x} = \frac{\cos x}{\sin^2 x}$$

14. $$\frac{1 - 2\cos^2\theta}{\sin\theta\cos\theta} \stackrel{?}{=} \tan\theta - \cot\theta$$
$$\frac{1 - 2\cos^2\theta}{\sin\theta\cos\theta} \stackrel{?}{=} \frac{\sin\theta}{\cos\theta} - \frac{\cos\theta}{\sin\theta}$$
$$\frac{1 - 2\cos^2\theta}{\sin\theta\cos\theta} \stackrel{?}{=} \frac{\sin^2\theta - \cos^2\theta}{\cos\theta\sin\theta}$$
$$\frac{1 - 2\cos^2\theta}{\sin\theta\cos\theta} \stackrel{?}{=} \frac{1 - \cos^2\theta - \cos^2\theta}{\cos\theta\sin\theta}$$
$$\frac{1 - 2\cos^2\theta}{\sin\theta\cos\theta} = \frac{1 - 2\cos^2\theta}{\sin\theta\cos\theta}$$

15. $$\cos^2 x + \tan^2 x \cos^2 x \stackrel{?}{=} 1$$
$$\cos^2 x + \frac{\sin^2 x}{\cos^2 x} \cdot \cos^2 x \stackrel{?}{=} 1$$
$$\cos^2 x + \sin^2 x \stackrel{?}{=} 1$$
$$1 = 1$$

16. $$\frac{\cos x}{1 + \sin x} + \frac{\cos x}{1 - \sin x} \stackrel{?}{=} 2\sec x$$
$$\frac{\cos x\,(1 - \sin x) + \cos x\,(1 + \sin x)}{(1 + \sin x)(1 - \sin x)} \stackrel{?}{=} \frac{2}{\cos x}$$
$$\frac{\cos x - \cos x \sin x + \cos x + \cos x \sin x}{1 - \sin^2 x} \stackrel{?}{=} \frac{2}{\cos x}$$
$$\frac{2\cos x}{\cos^2 x} \stackrel{?}{=} \frac{2}{\cos x}$$
$$\frac{2}{\cos x} = \frac{2}{\cos x}$$

17.
$$\frac{1+\tan^2\theta}{\csc^2\theta} \stackrel{?}{=} \tan^2\theta$$
$$\frac{\sec^2\theta}{\csc^2\theta} \stackrel{?}{=} \tan^2\theta$$
$$\frac{\frac{1}{\cos^2\theta}}{\frac{1}{\sin^2\theta}} \stackrel{?}{=} \tan^2\theta$$
$$\frac{1}{\cos^2\theta}\cdot\frac{\sin^2\theta}{1} \stackrel{?}{=} \tan^2\theta$$
$$\frac{\sin^2\theta}{\cos^2\theta} \stackrel{?}{=} \tan^2\theta$$
$$\tan^2\theta = \tan^2\theta$$

18.
$$\tan x\,(\cot x + \tan x) \stackrel{?}{=} \sec^2 x$$
$$\tan x\left(\frac{1}{\tan x} + \tan x\right) \stackrel{?}{=} \sec^2 x$$
$$1 + \tan^2 x \stackrel{?}{=} \sec^2 x$$
$$\sec^2 x = \sec^2 x$$

19.
$$\frac{\sec x}{\sin x} - \frac{\sin x}{\cos x} \stackrel{?}{=} \cot x$$
$$\frac{\frac{1}{\cos x}}{\sin x} - \frac{\sin x}{\cos x} \stackrel{?}{=} \frac{\cos x}{\sin x}$$
$$\frac{1}{\cos x \sin x} - \frac{\sin x}{\cos x} \stackrel{?}{=} \frac{\cos x}{\sin x}$$
$$\frac{1}{\sin x \cos x} - \frac{\sin^2 x}{\sin x \cos x} \stackrel{?}{=} \frac{\cos x}{\sin x}$$
$$\frac{1-\sin^2 x}{\sin x \cos x} \stackrel{?}{=} \frac{\cos x}{\sin x}$$
$$\frac{\cos^2 x}{\sin x \cos x} \stackrel{?}{=} \frac{\cos x}{\sin x}$$
$$\frac{\cos x}{\sin x} = \frac{\cos x}{\sin x}$$

20.
$$\frac{1+\tan r}{1+\cot r} \stackrel{?}{=} \frac{\sin r}{\cos r}$$
$$\frac{1+\frac{\sin r}{\cos r}}{1+\frac{\cos r}{\sin r}} \stackrel{?}{=} \frac{\sin r}{\cos r}$$
$$\frac{\frac{\cos r + \sin r}{\cos r}}{\frac{\sin r + \cos r}{\sin r}} \stackrel{?}{=} \frac{\sin r}{\cos r}$$
$$\frac{\cos r + \sin r}{\cos r}\cdot\frac{\sin r}{\cos r + \sin r} \stackrel{?}{=} \frac{\sin r}{\cos r}$$
$$\frac{\sin r}{\cos r} = \frac{\sin r}{\cos r}$$

Page 47] Written

11. $\sin(270° - \theta) = \sin 270° \cos\theta - \cos 270° \sin\theta$
$= {}^{-}1 \cdot \cos\theta - 0 \cdot \sin\theta$
$= {}^{-}\cos\theta$

12. $\cos(270° - \theta) = \cos 270° \cdot \cos\theta + \sin 270° \cdot \sin\theta$
$= 0 - 1 \cdot \sin\theta$
$= {}^{-}\sin\theta$

13. $\sin(180° + \theta) = \sin 180° \cos\theta + \cos 180° \sin\theta$
$= 0 - 1 \cdot \sin\theta$
$= {}^{-}\sin\theta$

14. $\cos(180° + \theta) = \cos 180° \cos\theta - \sin 180° \sin\theta$
$= {}^{-}1 \cdot \cos\theta - 0$
$= {}^{-}\cos\theta$

15. $\sin(90° + \theta) = \sin 90° \cos\theta + \cos 90° \sin\theta$
$= 1 \cdot \cos\theta + 0$
$= \cos\theta$

16. $\cos(90° + \theta) = \cos 90° \cos\theta - \sin 90° \sin\theta$
$= 0 - 1 \cdot \sin\theta$
$= {}^{-}\sin\theta$

21.
$$\sin(x+y)\cdot\sin(x-y) \stackrel{?}{=} \sin^2 x - \sin^2 y$$
$$(\sin x \cos y + \cos x \sin y)(\sin x \cos y - \cos x \sin y) \stackrel{?}{=} \sin^2 x - \sin^2 y$$
$$\sin^2 x \cos^2 y - \cos^2 x \sin^2 y \stackrel{?}{=} \sin^2 x - \sin^2 y$$
$$\sin^2 x\,(1 - \sin^2 y) - (1 - \sin^2 x)\sin^2 y \stackrel{?}{=} \sin^2 x - \sin^2 y$$
$$\sin^2 x - \sin^2 x \sin^2 y - \sin^2 y + \sin^2 x \sin^2 y \stackrel{?}{=} \sin^2 x - \sin^2 y$$
$$\sin^2 x - \sin^2 y = \sin^2 x - \sin^2 y$$

22.
$$\sin\left(\theta + \frac{\pi}{3}\right) - \cos\left(\theta + \frac{\pi}{6}\right) \stackrel{?}{=} \sin\theta$$
$$\left(\sin\theta\cos\frac{\pi}{3} + \cos\theta\sin\frac{\pi}{3}\right) - \left(\cos\theta\cos\frac{\pi}{6} - \sin\theta\sin\frac{\pi}{6}\right) \stackrel{?}{=} \sin\theta$$
$$\frac{1}{2}\sin\theta + \frac{\sqrt{3}}{2}\cos\theta - \frac{\sqrt{3}}{2}\cos\theta + \frac{1}{2}\sin\theta \stackrel{?}{=} \sin\theta$$
$$\sin\theta = \sin\theta$$

23.
$$\sin(60° + \theta) + \sin(60° - \theta) \stackrel{?}{=} \sqrt{3}\cos\theta$$
$$[\sin 60° \cos\theta + \cos 60° \sin\theta] + [\sin 60° \cos\theta - \cos 60° \sin\theta] \stackrel{?}{=} \sqrt{3}\cos\theta$$
$$\frac{\sqrt{3}\cos\theta}{2} + \frac{\sin\theta}{2} + \frac{\sqrt{3}\cos\theta}{2} - \frac{\sin\theta}{2} \stackrel{?}{=} \sqrt{3}\cos\theta$$
$$\sqrt{3}\cos\theta = \sqrt{3}\cos\theta$$

24.
$$(\sin x + \cos y)^2 + (\sin y + \cos x)^2 \stackrel{?}{=} 2 + 2\sin(x + y)$$
$$\sin^2 x + 2\sin x \cos y + \cos^2 y + \sin^2 y + 2\sin y \cos x + \cos^2 x \stackrel{?}{=} 2 + 2\sin(x + y)$$
$$\sin^2 x + \cos^2 x + \sin^2 y + \cos^2 y + 2\sin x \cos y + 2\sin y \cos x \stackrel{?}{=} 2 + 2\sin(x + y)$$
$$1 + 1 + 2(\sin x \cos y + \sin y \cos x) \stackrel{?}{=} 2 + 2\sin(x + y)$$
$$2 + 2\sin(x + y) = 2 + 2\sin(x + y)$$

25.
$$\cos(x + y)\cos(x - y) \stackrel{?}{=} \cos^2 y - \sin^2 x$$
$$(\cos x \cos y - \sin x \sin y)(\cos x \cos y + \sin x \sin y) \stackrel{?}{=} \cos^2 y - \sin^2 x$$
$$\cos^2 x \cos^2 y - \sin^2 x \sin^2 y \stackrel{?}{=} \cos^2 y - \sin^2 x$$
$$(1 - \sin^2 x)\cos^2 y - \sin^2 x(1 - \cos^2 y) \stackrel{?}{=} \cos^2 y - \sin^2 x$$
$$\cos^2 y - \sin^2 x \cos^2 y - \sin^2 x + \sin^2 x \cos^2 y \stackrel{?}{=} \cos^2 y - \sin^2 x$$
$$\cos^2 y - \sin^2 x = \cos^2 y - \sin^2 x$$

26.
$$\sin(x + 30°) + \cos(x + 60°) \stackrel{?}{=} \cos x$$
$$\sin x \cos 30° + \cos x \sin 30° + \cos x \cos 60° - \sin x \sin 60° \stackrel{?}{=} \cos x$$
$$\frac{\sqrt{3}}{2}\sin x + \frac{1}{2}\cos x + \frac{1}{2}\cos x - \frac{\sqrt{3}}{2}\sin x \stackrel{?}{=} \cos x$$
$$\cos x = \cos x$$

27.
$$\cos(30° + x) - \cos(30° - x) \stackrel{?}{=} {}^-\sin x$$
$$[\cos 30° \cos x - \sin 30° \sin x] - [\cos 30° \cos x + \sin 30° \sin x] \stackrel{?}{=} {}^-\sin x$$
$$\frac{\sqrt{3}\cos x}{2} - \frac{\sin x}{2} - \frac{\sqrt{3}\cos x}{2} - \frac{\sin x}{2} \stackrel{?}{=} {}^-\sin x$$
$${}^-\sin x = {}^-\sin x$$

28.
$$\sin\left(x + \frac{\pi}{4}\right) + \cos\left(x + \frac{\pi}{4}\right) \stackrel{?}{=} \sqrt{2}\cos x$$
$$\sin x \cos\frac{\pi}{4} + \cos x \sin\frac{\pi}{4} + \cos x \cos\frac{\pi}{4} - \sin x \sin\frac{\pi}{4} \stackrel{?}{=} \sqrt{2}\cos x$$
$$\frac{\sqrt{2}}{2}\sin x + \frac{\sqrt{2}}{2}\cos x + \frac{\sqrt{2}}{2}\cos x - \frac{\sqrt{2}}{2}\sin x \stackrel{?}{=} \sqrt{2}\cos x$$
$$2\left(\frac{\sqrt{2}}{2}\cos x\right) \stackrel{?}{=} \sqrt{2}\cos x$$
$$\sqrt{2}\cos x = \sqrt{2}\cos x$$

Challenge **Page 471**
$$\tan(\alpha - \beta) = \frac{\sin(\alpha - \beta)}{\cos(\alpha - \beta)}$$
$$= \frac{\sin\alpha\cos\beta - \cos\alpha\sin\beta}{\cos\alpha\cos\beta + \sin\alpha\sin\beta}$$
$$= \frac{\dfrac{\sin\alpha\cos\beta}{\cos\alpha\cos\beta} - \dfrac{\cos\alpha\sin\beta}{\cos\alpha\cos\beta}}{\dfrac{\cos\alpha\cos\beta}{\cos\alpha\cos\beta} + \dfrac{\sin\alpha\sin\beta}{\cos\alpha\cos\beta}}$$
$$= \frac{\tan\alpha - \tan\beta}{1 + \tan\alpha\tan\beta}$$

Page 474 **Written** 9. $\frac{\sqrt{2 + \sqrt{3}}}{2}$ 10. $\frac{2\sqrt{5}}{5}$ 11. $-\frac{\sqrt{6}}{6}$ 12. $\frac{\sqrt{5}}{5}$ 13. $\frac{\sqrt{26}}{26}$ 14. $-\frac{\sqrt{15}}{5}$ 15. $-\frac{1}{4}\sqrt{8 + 2\sqrt{7}}$ 16. $-\frac{\sqrt{3}}{3}$ 17. $\frac{\sqrt{2 - \sqrt{3}}}{2}$ 18. $\frac{\sqrt{5}}{5}$ 19. $\frac{\sqrt{30}}{6}$ 20. $\frac{2\sqrt{5}}{5}$ 21. $\frac{5\sqrt{26}}{26}$ 22. $-\frac{\sqrt{10}}{5}$ 23. $\frac{1}{4}\sqrt{8 - 2\sqrt{7}}$ 24. $\frac{\sqrt{6}}{3}$ 25. $\frac{1}{2}$ 26. $-\frac{7}{25}$ 27. $-\frac{1}{9}$ 28. $-\frac{7}{25}$ 29. $-\frac{119}{169}$ 30. $-\frac{23}{25}$ 31. $-\frac{1}{8}$ 32. $-\frac{7}{9}$

33. $\cos^2 2x + 4\sin^2 \cos^2 x \stackrel{?}{=} 1$
$\cos^2 2x + \sin^2 2x \stackrel{?}{=} 1$
$1 = 1$

34. $(\sin x + \cos x)^2 \stackrel{?}{=} 1 + \sin 2x$
$\sin^2 x + 2\sin x \cos x + \cos^2 x \stackrel{?}{=} 1 + \sin 2x$
$\sin^2 x + \cos^2 x + 2\sin x \cos x \stackrel{?}{=} 1 + \sin 2x$
$1 + 2\sin x \cos x \stackrel{?}{=} 1 + \sin 2x$
$1 + \sin 2x = 1 + \sin 2x$

35. $\sin^4 x - \cos^4 x \stackrel{?}{=} 2\sin^2 x - 1$
$(\sin^2 x - \cos^2 x)(\sin^2 x + \cos^2 x) \stackrel{?}{=} 2\sin^2 x - 1$
$(\sin^2 x - \cos^2 x) \cdot 1 \stackrel{?}{=} 2\sin^2 x - 1$
$[\sin^2 x - (1 - \sin^2 x)] \cdot 1 \stackrel{?}{=} 2\sin^2 x - 1$
$\sin^2 x - 1 + \sin^2 x \stackrel{?}{=} 2\sin^2 x - 1$
$2\sin^2 x - 1 = 2\sin^2 x - 1$

36. $\sin 2x \stackrel{?}{=} 2\cot x \sin^2 x$
$2\sin x \cos x \stackrel{?}{=} 2\,\dfrac{\cos x}{\sin x} \cdot \sin^2 x$
$2\sin x \cos x = 2\cos x \sin x$

37. $\sin^2 \theta \stackrel{?}{=} \frac{1}{2}(1 - \cos 2\theta)$
$\sin^2 \theta \stackrel{?}{=} \frac{1}{2}[1 - (1 - 2\sin^2 \theta)]$
$\sin^2 \theta \stackrel{?}{=} \frac{1}{2}[2\sin^2 \theta)]$
$\sin^2 \theta = \sin^2 \theta$

38. $\dfrac{1}{\sin x \cos x} - \dfrac{\cos x}{\sin x} \stackrel{?}{=} \tan x$
$\dfrac{1 - \cos^2 x}{\sin x \cos x} \stackrel{?}{=} \tan x$
$\dfrac{\sin^2 x}{\sin x \cos x} \stackrel{?}{=} \tan x$
$\tan x = \tan x$

Pages 484–485 Chapter Review

27. 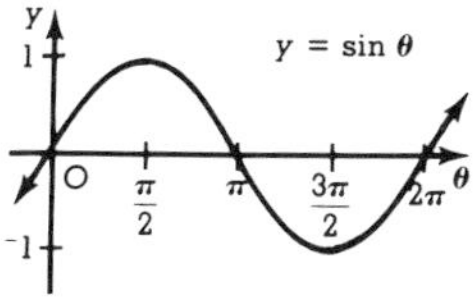

28. 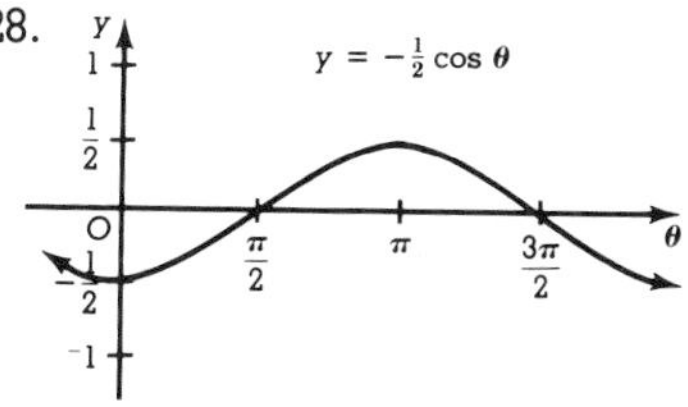

29. 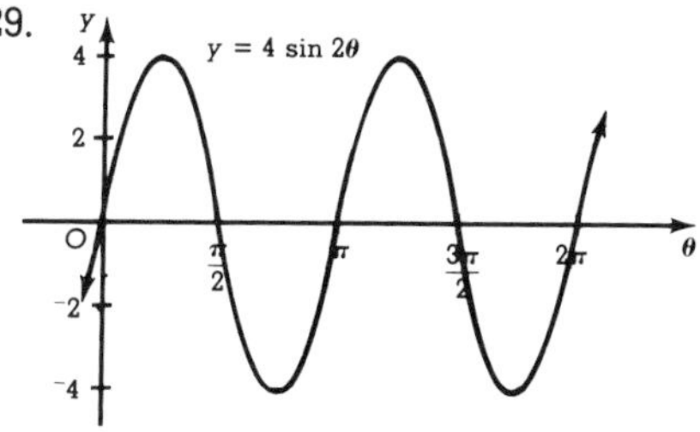

46. $\sin^4 x - \cos^4 x \stackrel{?}{=} \sin^2 x - \cos^2 x$
$(\sin^2 x - \cos^2 x)(\sin^2 x + \cos^2 x) \stackrel{?}{=} \sin^2 x - \cos^2 x$
$(\sin^2 x - \cos^2 x) \cdot 1 \stackrel{?}{=} \sin^2 x - \cos^2 x$
$\sin^2 x - \cos^2 x = \sin^2 x - \cos^2 x$

47. $\dfrac{\sin \theta}{\tan \theta} + \dfrac{\cos \theta}{\cot \theta} \stackrel{?}{=} \cos \theta + \sin \theta$
$\dfrac{\sin \theta}{\frac{\sin \theta}{\cos \theta}} + \dfrac{\cos \theta}{\frac{\cos \theta}{\sin \theta}} \stackrel{?}{=} \cos \theta + \sin \theta$
$\cos \theta + \sin \theta = \cos \theta + \sin \theta$

48. $\dfrac{\sin \theta}{1 - \cos \theta} \stackrel{?}{=} \csc \theta + \cot \theta$
$\dfrac{\sin \theta}{1 - \cos \theta} \stackrel{?}{=} \dfrac{1}{\sin \theta} + \dfrac{\cos \theta}{\sin \theta}$
$\dfrac{\sin \theta}{1 - \cos \theta} \stackrel{?}{=} \dfrac{1 + \cos \theta}{\sin \theta}$
$\dfrac{\sin \theta}{1 - \cos \theta} \stackrel{?}{=} \dfrac{(1 + \cos \theta)(1 - \cos \theta)}{\sin \theta(1 - \cos \theta)}$
$\dfrac{\sin \theta}{1 - \cos \theta} \stackrel{?}{=} \dfrac{1 - \cos^2 \theta}{\sin \theta\,(1 - \cos \theta)}$
$\dfrac{\sin \theta}{1 - \cos \theta} \stackrel{?}{=} \dfrac{\sin^2 \theta}{\sin \theta\,(1 - \cos \theta)}$
$\dfrac{\sin \theta}{1 - \cos \theta} \stackrel{?}{=} \dfrac{\sin \theta}{1 - \cos \theta}$

49. $\tan x + \cot x \stackrel{?}{=} \sec x \csc x$
$\dfrac{\sin x}{\cos x} + \dfrac{\cos x}{\sin x} \stackrel{?}{=} \sec x \csc x$
$\dfrac{\sin^2 x + \cos^2 x}{\cos x \sin x} \stackrel{?}{=} \sec x \csc x$
$\dfrac{1}{\cos x \sin x} \stackrel{?}{=} \sec x \csc x$
$\sec x \csc x = \sec x \csc x$

Page 486 Chapter Test

17. 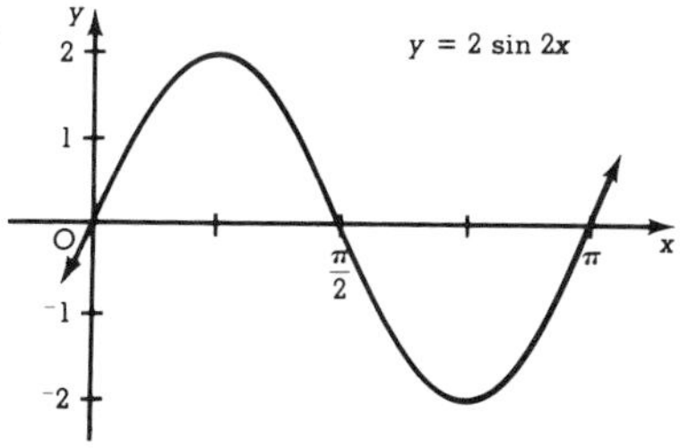

18. 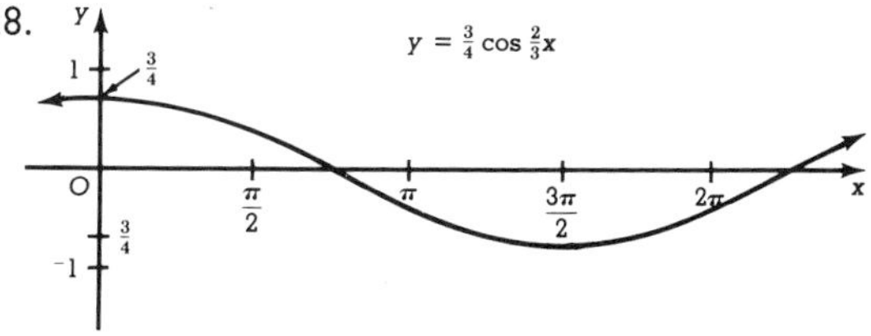

25. $\dfrac{\cos x}{1 - \sin^2 x} \stackrel{?}{=} \sec x$

$\dfrac{\cos x}{\cos^2 x} \stackrel{?}{=} \sec x$

$\dfrac{1}{\cos x} \stackrel{?}{=} \sec x$

$\sec x = \sec x$

26. $\dfrac{\sec x}{\sin x} - \dfrac{\sin x}{\cos x} \stackrel{?}{=} \cot x$

$\dfrac{\frac{1}{\cos x}}{\sin x} - \dfrac{\sin x}{\cos x} \stackrel{?}{=} \cot x$

$\dfrac{1}{\sin x \cos x} - \dfrac{\sin x}{\cos x} \stackrel{?}{=} \cot x$

$\dfrac{1}{\sin x \cos x} - \dfrac{\sin^2 x}{\sin x \cos x} \stackrel{?}{=} \cot x$

$\dfrac{1 - \sin^2 x}{\sin x \cos x} \stackrel{?}{=} \cot x$

$\dfrac{\cos^2 x}{\sin x \cos x} \stackrel{?}{=} \cot x$

$\dfrac{\cos x}{\sin x} \stackrel{?}{=} \cot x$

$\cot x = \cot x$

27. $\dfrac{1 + \tan^2 \theta}{\cos^2 \theta} \stackrel{?}{=} \sec^4 \theta$

$\dfrac{\sec^2 \theta}{\cos^2 \theta} \stackrel{?}{=} \sec^4 \theta$

$\sec^2 \theta \cdot \dfrac{1}{\cos^2 \theta} \stackrel{?}{=} \sec^4 \theta$

$\sec^2 \theta \sec^2 \theta \stackrel{?}{=} \sec^4 \theta$

$\sec^4 \theta = \sec^4 \theta$

CHAPTER 17 RIGHT ANGLE TRIGONOMETRY

Page 490 Exploratory 1. $\sin A = \frac{5}{13}$, $\cos A = \frac{12}{13}$, $\tan A = \frac{5}{12}$, $\sin B = \frac{12}{13}$, $\cos B = \frac{5}{13}$, $\tan B = \frac{12}{5}$
2. $\sin A = \dfrac{2\sqrt{5}}{5}$, $\cos A = \dfrac{\sqrt{5}}{5}$, $\tan A = 2$, $\sin B = \dfrac{\sqrt{5}}{5}$, $\cos B = \dfrac{2\sqrt{5}}{5}$, $\tan B = \dfrac{1}{2}$
3. $\sin A = \dfrac{3\sqrt{13}}{13}$, $\cos A = \dfrac{2\sqrt{13}}{13}$, $\tan A = \dfrac{3}{2}$, $\sin B = \dfrac{2\sqrt{13}}{13}$, $\cos B = \dfrac{3\sqrt{13}}{13}$, $\tan B = \dfrac{2}{3}$

Page 497 Written 1. $a = 3.86$, $b = 13.46$, $B = 74°$ 2. $b = 4.94$, $c = 10.88$, $B = 27°$ 3. $c = 13.82$, $a = 8.36$, $B = 52°45'$ 4. $b = 17.26$, $a = 8.42$, $A = 26°$ 5. $c = 12.14$, $b = 8.15$, $A = 47°50'$ 6. $c = 5.61$, $a = 0.68$, $A = 7°$ 7. $b = 1.35$, $a = 5.85$, $A = 77°$ 8. $b = 10.35$, $c = 13.72$, $A = 41°$ 9. $c = 186.71$, $a = 181.82$, $B = 13°$ 10. $a = 9.06$, $c = 23.79$, $B = 67°38'$ 11. $c = 39.35$, $b = 21.43$, $A = 57°$ 12. $c = 61.94$, $b = 43.59$, $A = 45°15'$ 13. $a = 13.26$, $b = 8.97$, $B = 34°5'$ 14. $b = 1.26$, $c = 4.07$, $A = 72°$ 15. $a = 7$, $b = 7$, $B = 45°$

Page 504 Written

15. $\dfrac{\sin A}{a} = \dfrac{\sin C}{c}$

$\dfrac{\sin A}{\sin C} = \dfrac{a}{c}$

$\dfrac{\sin A}{\sin C} - 1 = \dfrac{a}{c} - 1$

$\dfrac{\sin A - \sin C}{\sin C} = \dfrac{a - c}{c}$

16. Use the method shown in problem 15 to show the following.

$\dfrac{\sin B}{\sin C} + 1 = \dfrac{b}{c} + 1$

$\dfrac{\sin B + \sin C}{\sin C} = \dfrac{b + c}{c}$

$\dfrac{\sin B + \sin C}{b + c} = \dfrac{\sin C}{c}$

and $\dfrac{\sin B - \sin C}{b - c} = \dfrac{\sin C}{c}$

By the Law of Sines conclude the following.

$\dfrac{\sin B + \sin C}{b + c} = \dfrac{\sin B - \sin C}{b - c}$

$\dfrac{b + c}{b - c} = \dfrac{\sin B + \sin C}{\sin B - \sin C}$

17. $\dfrac{\sin A}{a} = \dfrac{\sin B}{b}$

$\dfrac{a}{\sin A} = \dfrac{b}{\sin B}$

$\dfrac{a}{b} = \dfrac{\sin A}{\sin B}$

18. $\dfrac{\sin B}{b} = \dfrac{\sin A}{a}$

$\dfrac{a}{b} = \dfrac{\sin A}{\sin B}$

$\dfrac{a}{b} + 1 = \dfrac{\sin A}{\sin B} + 1$

$\dfrac{a + b}{b} = \dfrac{\sin A + \sin B}{\sin B}$

$\dfrac{b}{a + b} = \dfrac{\sin B}{\sin A + \sin B}$

Page 507 Written Use the diagram on page 505

17. $a^2 + b^2 - 2ab\cos C = [(b - x)^2 + h^2] + b^2 - 2ab\left(\frac{b - x}{a}\right)$
$= b^2 - 2bx + x^2 + h^2 + b^2 - 2b^2 + 2bx$
$= x^2 + h^2$
$= c^2$

18. $a^2 + c^2 - 2ac\cos B = [h^2 + (b - x)^2] + [x^2 + h^2] - 2ac\cos[180° - (A + C)]$
$= [h^2 + b^2 - 2bx + x^2] + [x^2 + h^2] - 2ac\left[\frac{x^2 - bx + h^2}{ac}\right]$
$= 2h^2 + 2x^2 - 2bx + b^2 - 2x^2 + 2bx - 2h^2$
$= b^2$

19.
$a^2 = b^2 + c^2 - 2bc\cos A$
${}^-2bx\cos A = a^2 - b^2 - c^2$
$2bc - 2bc\cos A = a^2 - b^2 - c^2 + 2bc$
$2bc - 2bc\cos A = (a - b + c)(a + b - c)$
$1 - \cos A = \frac{(a - b + c)(a + b - c)}{2bc}$

20.
$a^2 = b^2 + c^2 - 2bc\cos A$
${}^-a^2 + b^2 + c^2 = 2bc\cos A$
$\frac{{}^-a^2 + b^2 + c^2}{2bc} = \cos A$
$\frac{{}^-a^2 + b^2 + c^2}{2bc} + \frac{2bc}{2bc} = 1 + \cos A$
$\frac{(a + b + c)(b + c - a)}{2bc} = 1 + \cos A$

Page 513 Chapter Review **37.** $B = 65°$, $a = 2.54$, $b = 5.44$ **38.** $B = 40°$, $b = 9.23$, $c = 14.36$ **39.** $A = 5°$, $b = 70.98$, $c = 71.25$ **40.** $A = 59°$, $a = 10.29$, $b = 6.14$ **41.** $B = 73°50'$, $c = 17.96$, $b = 17.25$ **42.** $A = 28°40'$, $a = 10.93$, $c = 22.79$ **43.** $A = 74°45'$, $a = 30.87$, $b = 8.42$ **44.** $B = 42°38'$, $a = 26.07$, $c = 35.42$ **45.** 55.53 meters **46.** 4483.43 feet **47.** $c = 3.16$, $A = 18°26'$, $B = 71°34'$ **48.** $b = 13.23$, $A = 48°35'$, $B = 41°25'$ **49.** $a = 7.14$, $A = 45°34'$, $B = 44°26'$ **50.** $c = 26$, $A = 22°37'$, $B = 67°23'$ **51.** $c = 14.53$, $A = 63°26'$, $B = 26°34'$ **52.** $b = 17.44$, $A = 40°42'$, $B = 49°18'$ **53.** $a = 22.36$, $A = 48°11'$, $B = 41°49'$ **54.** $a = 4.39$, $A = 59°21'$, $B = 30°39'$ **55.** 38°39′ **56.** 43.69 meters **57.** $B = 66°49'$, $C = 63°11'$, $c = 11.65$ **58.** $B = 60°19'$, $C = 36°31'$, $c = 47.9$ **59.** $c = 89.69$, $A = 51°$, $a = 70.22$ **60.** $a = 28.28$, $c = 38.63$, $C = 105°$ **61.** $B = 80°$, $a = 8.85$, $a = 14.96$ **62.** $b = 85.33$, $c = 90.04$, $C = 73°$ **63.** $A = 41°27'$, $C = 65°32'$, $c = 12.37$ **64.** $C = 65°$, $a = 4.84$, $b = 6.43$ **65.** $a = 4.36$, $B = 23°24'$, $C = 96°35'$ **66.** $c = 6.43$, $A = 34°19'$, $B = 80°41'$ **67.** $c = 4.54$, $A = 58°02'$, $B = 81°58'$ **68.** $b = 36.16$, $C = 4°12'$, $A = 151°48'$ **69.** $b = 11.21$, $A = 92°01'$, $C = 34°49'$ **70.** $B = 77°22'$, $A = 51°19'$, $C = 51°19'$ **71.** $C = 112°37'$, $A = 30°30'$, $B = 36°53'$ **72.** $C = 103°34'$, $A = 38°13'$, $B = 38°13'$ **73.** 0 **74.** 2, $B = 53°28'$, $C = 86°32'$, $c = 12.42$; $B = 126.32$, $C = 13°28'$, $c = 2.9$ **75.** 1, $B = 35°8'$, $C = 98°52'$, $c = 13.74$ **76.** 1, $c = 11.5$, $C = 20°39'$, $B = 29°21'$ **77.** 0 **78.** 1, $B = 90°$, $C = 60°$, $c = 10.39$ **79.** 2, $B = 70°42'$, $C = 55°18'$, $c = 12.19$; $B = 109°18'$, $C = 16°42'$, $c = 4.26$ **80.** 1, $c = 7.6$, $B = 43°55'$, $C = 74°05'$

APPENDIX BASIC

Page 524 Written 6.

```
10 PRINT "LENGTH","WIDTH","PERIMETER","AREA"
20 FOR Y=1 TO 3
30 READ A,B
40 PRINT A,B,2*A+2*B,A*B
50 NEXT Y
60 DATA 8,5,9,6,13,17
70 END
```

Page 527 Written

16.

```
10 LET K=0
20 LET P=3
30 LET K=K+1
40 PRINT P
50 LET P=P*3
60 IF P<900000 THEN 30
70 PRINT P/3, 3↑K
80 END
```

17.

```
10 LET P=1
20 PRINT "N"; "N FACTORIAL"
30 FOR X=1 TO 9
40 LET P=P*X
50 PRINT X; P
60 NEXT X
70 END
```

Page 530 Written

1.

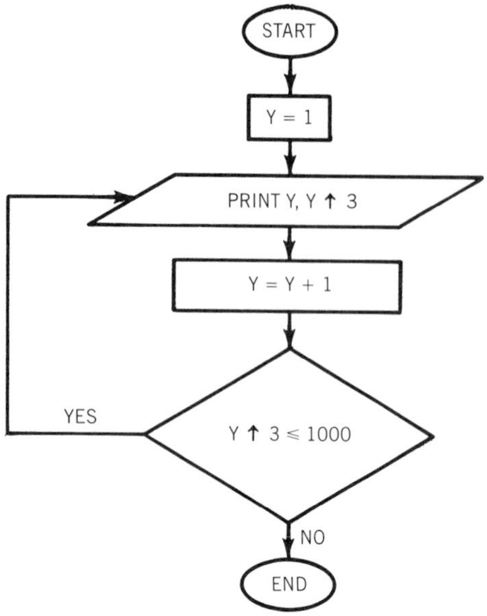

2.

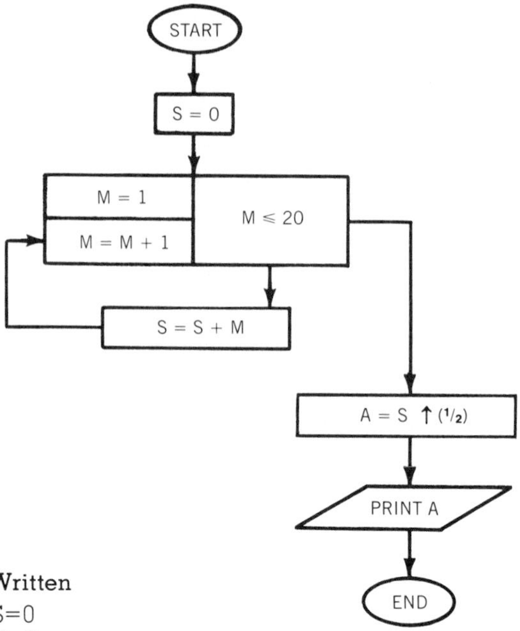

5.

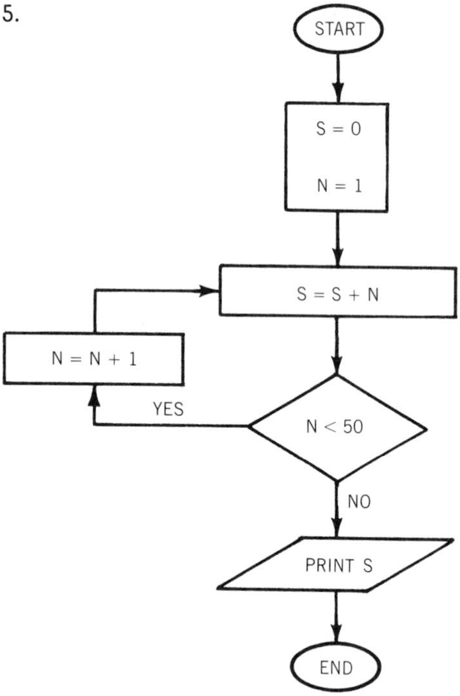

Page 530 Written

5.
```
10 LET S=0
20 LET N=0
30 LET N=N+1
40 LET S=S+N
50 IF N<50 THEN 30
60 PRINT S
70 END
```

6.
```
10  READ A,B,C
20  IF A<B THEN 50
30  IF A<C THEN 110
40  GO TO 80
50  IF B<C THEN 100
60  IF A<C THEN 120
70  GO TO 130
80  IF B<C THEN 140
90  GO TO 150
100 PRINT A,B,C
105 GO TO 160
110 PRINT B,A,C
115 GO TO 160
120 PRINT A,C,B
125 GO TO 160
130 PRINT C,A,B
135 GO TO 160
140 PRINT B,C,A
145 GO TO 160
150 PRINT C,B,A
155 DATA . . . . .
160 END
```

7.
```
10  READ X,Y
20  IF X=0 THEN 70
30  IF Y=0 THEN 150
40  IF X>0 THEN 90
50  IF Y>0 THEN 190
60  GO TO 210
70  IF Y=0 THEN 110
80  GO TO 130
90  IF Y>0 THEN 170
100 GO TO 230
110 PRINT "ORIGIN"
120 GO TO 240
130 PRINT "ON Y-AXIS"
140 GO TO 240
150 PRINT "ON X-AXIS"
160 GO TO 240
170 PRINT "QUAD I"
180 GO TO 240
190 PRINT "QUAD II"
200 GO TO 240
210 PRINT "QUAD III"
220 GO TO 240
230 PRINT "QUAD IV"
235 DATA . . . . . . .
240 END
```

6.

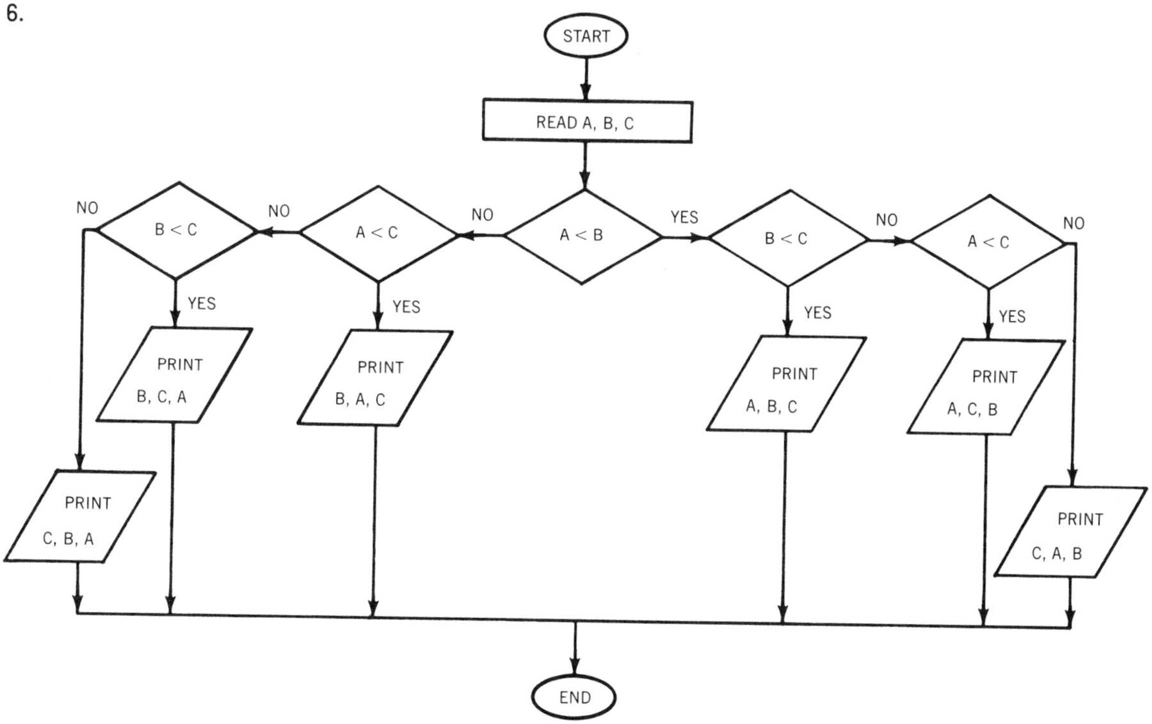
START
READ A, B, C
A < B
YES
NO
B < C
A < C
NO
YES
PRINT
A, B, C
A, C, B
C, A, B
B, A, C
B, C, A
C, B, A
END

7.

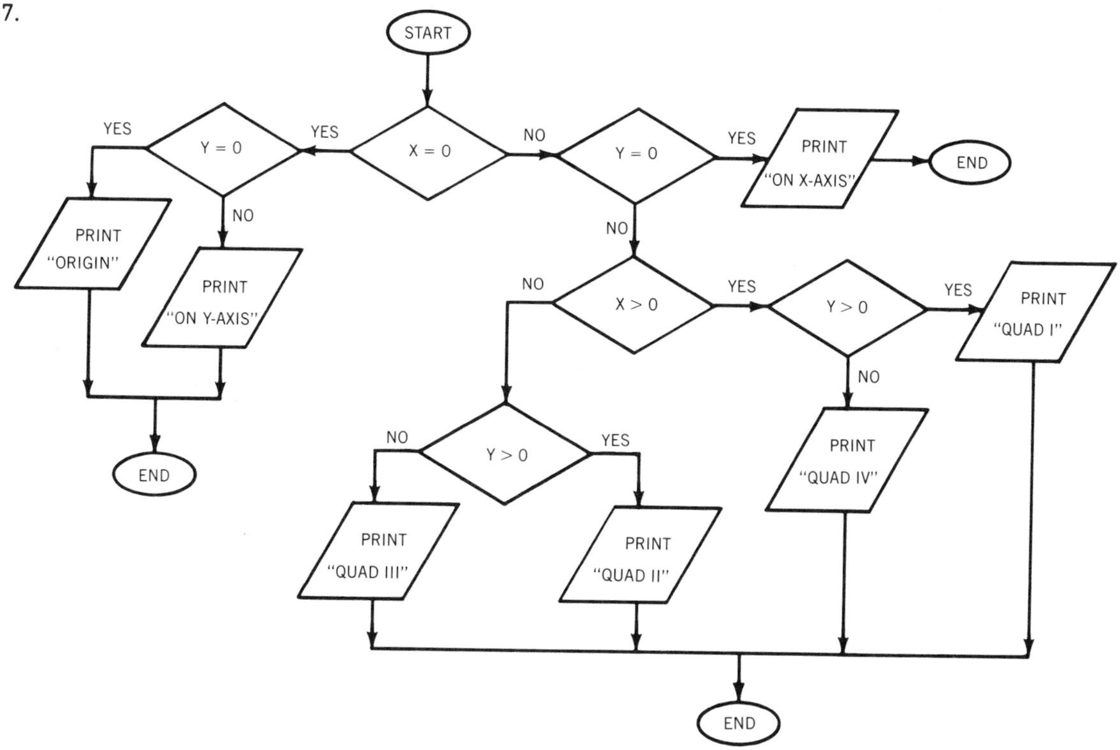
START
X = 0
YES
NO
Y = 0
PRINT
"ORIGIN"
"ON Y-AXIS"
"ON X-AXIS"
END
X > 0
Y > 0
"QUAD I"
"QUAD IV"
"QUAD III"
"QUAD II"

Page 533 Written

31.
```
  5 LET S=0
 10 FOR K=1 TO 5
 20 READ A(K)
 30 LET S=S+A(K)
 40 NEXT K
 50 PRINT S/5
 55 LET S=0
 60 FOR A=1 TO 5
 70 READ B(A)
 80 LET S=S+B(A)
 90 NEXT A
100 PRINT S/5
110 DATA 67,72,74,63,81
111 DATA 91,87,81,83,89
120 END
```

32.
```
10 FOR X=1 TO 10
20 READ A(X)
30 IF A(X)>=0 THEN 60
40 PRINT -A(X);
50 GO TO 70
60 PRINT A(X);
70 NEXT X
80 DATA 5,3,7,0,-1,15,-11,-12,-6,-22
90 END
```

Page 536 Written

12.
```
 10 READ A,B,C
 20 IF B↑2-4*A*C<0 THEN 90
 30 IF B↑2-4*A*C>0 THEN 60
 40 LET X=-B/(2*A)
 45 PRINT "ONE ROOT"; X
 50 GO TO 100
 60 LET X=(-B-SQR(B↑2-4*A*C))/(2*A)
 65 LET Y=(-B+SQR(B↑2-4*A*C))/(2*A)
 70 PRINT "TWO ROOTS"; X,Y
 80 GO TO 100
 90 PRINT "NO REAL ROOTS"
 95 DATA, 1,5,6
100 END
```

3 4 5 6 7 8 9 10 11 12 13 14 15 — 85 84 83 82 81

TEACHER'S
ANNOTATED EDITION

Merrill ALGEBRA TWO with Trigonometry

FOSTER • RATH • WINTERS

CHARLES E. MERRILL PUBLISHING CO.
A Bell & Howell Company
Columbus, Ohio

Toronto • London • Sydney

The cover photograph shows the Federal Reserve Bank in Minneapolis, Minnesota. It provides a dramatic illustration of how algebra is used in everyday life. To build the bank, cables were suspended from two towers forming catenary curves. Catenaries have equations of the form $y = \frac{e^x + e^{-x}}{2}$.

ISBN 0-675-03491-4
ISBN 0-675-03490-6
Published by
CHARLES E. MERRILL PUBLISHING CO.
A Bell & Howell Company
Columbus, Ohio 43216

Printed in the United States of America

Merrill ALGEBRA TWO with Trigonometry

AUTHORS

Alan G. Foster is head of the Mathematics Department at Addison Trail High School, Addison, Illinois. He has taught mathematics courses at every level of the high school curriculum. Mr. Foster obtained his B.S. from Illinois State University and his M.A. in mathematics from the University of Illinois, with additional work at University of Colorado, University of Wyoming, Northern Illinois University, Purdue, Northwestern, Princeton, Illinois Institute of Technology, and National College of Education. Mr. Foster is active in professional organizations at local, state, and national levels, frequently speaking or conducting workshops. He is a past president of the Illinois Council of Teachers of Mathematics.

James N. Rath is former chairperson of the Mathematics Department at Darien High School, Darien, Connecticut. He has taught mathematics at every level of the high school curriculum in both public and parochial schools. Mr. Rath did his undergraduate work at Catholic University of America. He obtained his M.Ed. and M.A. in mathematics from Boston College. Mr. Rath developed a minicourse in BASIC for the Darien Public Schools and is a member of several local, state, and national professional organizations.

Leslie J. Winters is chairperson of the Mathematics Department at John F. Kennedy High School, Granada Hills, California. He has taught mathematics at every level from junior high to college. He holds the following degrees: B.A., mathematics, Pepperdine University; B.S., secondary education, University of Dayton; M.S., secondary education, University of Southern California; M.A., mathematics, Boston College. Mr. Winters co-authored "Flow Chart Mathematics" for Victor Corporation and is a frequent speaker at local, state, and national conferences.

CONSULTANTS

Dr. M. M. Ohmer
Dean, College of Sciences
Nicholls State University
Thibodaux, Louisiana

Dr. Jack Price
Superintendent of Schools
Vista, California

REVIEWERS

Finis Brown
Mathematics, Physics, and Chemistry Teacher
Claude High School
Claude, Texas

Doris Gruntfest
Head, Mathematics Department
Kennedy High School
Paterson, New Jersey

Richard Hanson
Mathematics Teacher
Rio Americano High School
Sacramento, California

Harriet Keisling
Chairman, Mathematics Department
Pioneer High School
Ann Arbor, Michigan

Vincent O'Connor
Mathematics Supervisor
Milwaukee Public Schools
Milwaukee, Wisconsin

Frank Propp
Mathematics Department Chairman
Arlington High School
Arlington, Massachusetts

Eloise Rudy
Mathematics Consultant
The School District of Greenville County
Greenville, South Carolina

Louise Watkins
Supervisor of Mathematics
Howard County Board of Education
Columbia, Maryland

Grateful acknowledgement is made to the following individuals for their significant contributions to the development of MERRILL ALGEBRA TWO WITH TRIGONOMETRY: Richard Forst, James Southwell, Lee Yunker.

STAFF

Editorial
Project Editor: Elaine C. Murphy
Managing Editor: Donald W. Collins
Editors: Betty Tenney, Bonnie Johnston, Arthur L. Block, Renee Keown, Lynn E. Straley

Photo Editor: Wendy Rector

Art
Project Artist: Lewis H. Bolen
Art Director: Lester Shumaker
Book Designer: Lester Shumaker
Artists: Walter F. Kazmerzak, William L. Bolen, Ann Diehl

PHOTO CREDITS

Cover Photo: Hedrich Blessing, courtesy of P.P.G. Industries
1, Ohio State University Department of Photography; **17,** © 1978 Betty Medsger; **21,** Keenland Association; **24,** The Scottish National Portrait Gallery; **28,** Larry Hamill; **37** top left, John H. Gerard; **37** top right, Hal H. Harrison; **37** bottom left, U.S.D.A.; **37** bottom right, Ohio Dept. of Natural Resources; **48,** Brown Brothers; **59,** William Maddox; **69, 73,** © 1978 Betty Medsger; **93,** International Harvester; **95,** Hickson-Bender Photography/The Power Mfg. Company; **100, 129,** Hickson-Bender Photography; **133,** U.S. Weather Bureau; **165,** Battelle Memorial Institute; **183,** Larry Hamill; **189,** Hickson-Bender Photography/General Telephone Company; **203,** H. E. Edgerton/M.I.T.; **213,** NASA; **220,** Hickson-Bender Photography; **224,** Larry Hamill; **234,** American Airlines; **242,** Goodyear Aircraft Corp.; The Columbus Dispatch; **273,** Historical Pictures Service, Inc.; **277,** Hickson-Bender Photography; **281,** © 1978 Betty Medsger; **285,** Hickson-Bender Photography; **294,** The Ohio Farmer Magazine; **303,** M. E. I. Charlton, Inc.; **307,** Standard Oil Company, New Jersey; **310,** Battelle Memorial Institute; **320,** Hickson-Bender Photography; **327,** George D. Olsen; **334,** U.S. Forest Service Photo; **359,** Carolina Biological Supply Company; **360,** Indianapolis Motor Speedway; **364, 379,** Larry Hamill; **391,** Grant Heilman; **392,** Hickson-Bender Photography; **421,** Peter Gridley for Photo Researchers; **432, 447,** Hickson-Bender Photography; **452,** The Granger Collection; **482,** Ben Rose for Sports Illustrated © Time, Inc.; **501,** Hickson-Bender Photography; **515,** General Research Laboratory/U.S. Weather Bureau.

PREFACE

Merrill Algebra Two with Trigonometry is unique in that it was developed in the classroom by experienced high school teachers. Their manuscript then was edited and field tested in other classrooms across the nation. The authors' goals were to reverse such trends as declining student scores on standardized tests and a content erosion in the high school mathematics curriculum. To achieve these goals, the following strategies were used.

Build upon a Solid Foundation. Review is provided for those topics generally presented in first year algebra. In this way, students' understanding is strengthened before more difficult concepts are introduced.

Utilize Sound Pedagogy. Merrill Algebra Two covers all topics generally presented at this level in logical sequence. Each concept presented is used within that lesson and in other sections of the text.

Gear Presentation for Learning. The reading level has been carefully controlled throughout the text. Furthermore, many photographs, illustrations, charts, graphs, and tables provide help for students in visualizing the ideas presented. Hence, students are able to read with increased understanding.

Use Relevant Real-Life Applications. Applications are provided not just for practice, but also for help in understanding how concepts are used and how this course prepares students for the future.

The text offers a variety of special features to aid the student in learning algebra.

Student Annotations	Help students to identify important concepts as they study.
Selected Answers	Allow students to check their progress as they work. These answers are provided at the back of the text.
Vocabulary	Enables students to focus on increasing their mathematical vocabulary.
Chapter Summary	Provides students with a compact listing of major concepts presented within each chapter.
Chapter Review	Enables students to review each chapter by working sample problems from each section.
Chapter Test	Enables students to check their own progress.

The following special features appear periodically throughout the text.

Careers	Depict real-life people who use mathematics. These careers are exciting and rewarding. They are typical of careers that may be aspired to by students of this text.
Using Money	Provides insights into how mathematics can be used in making consumer decisions.
Using Algebra	Illustrates how algebra can be and is used in everyday life.
Reading Algebra	Provides students with the instruction needed to read and interpret mathematical symbolism.
Excursions in Algebra	Enliven and help maintain student interest by providing interesting side trips. Topics are varied and include history, glimpses into development and uses of algebra, puzzles and games.
Using Computers	Instructs students in writing programs using the BASIC computer language as well as provides insights into how computers are used.
BASIC	A unit instructing students in writing programs using the BASIC computer language is provided at the back of the text. This can be taught as a unit or interspersed throughout the year.

CONTENTS

Right Triangle Trigonometry 487

17

Appendix: BASIC 515

Chapter 1

Equations and Inequalities

When people play games, they agree on certain rules. To solve equations and inequalities, you use agreed upon properties of a number system.

1-1 Expressions and Formulas

Objective: To use the order of operations and evaluate expressions.

We often use mathematical expressions like $4(x + 2y) - 5x^3$. This expression contains the following kinds of symbols.

constants:	4 2 5 3	
variables:	x y	stand for unknown quantities
operation symbols:	$+$ $-$	tell which operations are involved
grouping symbols:	( )	tell order for doing operations

The following numerical expressions all stand for sixteen. Sixteen is called the **value** of each one.

$$4^2 \qquad 9 + 7 \qquad (12 \div 2) + 10$$

The expression 4^2 has a small numeral to the upper right. This numeral is called an **exponent**. An exponent tells how many times a number is used as a factor.

4^2 means $4 \cdot 4$ $\qquad$ 10^1 means 10 $\qquad$ x^5 means $x \cdot x \cdot x \cdot x \cdot x$

Each numerical expression should have only one value. To find this value you must know the order for doing the operations. For example, you must know whether to add or to multiply first. The following rules tell you the order.

Order of Operations

1. **Evaluate all powers.**
2. **Then do all multiplications and divisions from left to right.**
3. **Then do all additions and subtractions from left to right.**

example 1

Find the value of $4 + 8^2 \div 4 \cdot 2$.

$4 + 8^2 \div 4 \cdot 2 = 4 + 64 \div 4 \cdot 2$	*Evaluate all powers.*
$= 4 + 16 \cdot 2$	*Do all multiplications*
$= 4 + 32$	*and divisions left to right.*
$= 36$	*Do all additions and subtractions left to right.*

The value is 36.

Grouping symbols change the order of operations. Start with the operations inside the innermost grouping symbols.

Be sure students understand the difference between expressions like $6x^2$ and $(6x)^2$.

example 2

Find the value of $[(4 + 8)^2 \div 4] \cdot 2$.

$[(4+8)^2 \div 4] \cdot 2 = [(12)^2 \div 4] \cdot 2$ *First add 4 and 8.*

$= [144 \div 4] \cdot 2$ *Then find 12^2.*

$= [36] \cdot 2$ *Now divide 144 by 4.*

$= 72$ The value is 72.

Mathematical expressions with at least one variable are called **algebraic expressions.** Substitute a value for each variable to evaluate an algebraic expression.

example 3

Evaluate $5x^2 + 3xy$ if $x = {}^-5$ and $y = 3$.

Students may need much practice here.

$5x^2 + 3xy = 5(^-5)^2 + 3(^-5)(3)$ *Replace x by $^-5$ and y by 3.*

$= 5(25) + 3(^-5)(3)$ *Find $(^-5)^2$.*

$= 125 + {}^-45$ *Multiply left to right.*

$= 80$ The value is 80.

In a formula, if you know replacements for every variable, except one, you can find a replacement for that variable.

A **formula** is a mathematical sentence about the relationships among certain quantities. For example, $A = l \cdot w$ relates the area of a rectangle to its length and width.

example 4

The relationship between Celsius temperature (C) and Fahrenheit temperature (F) is given by $C = \frac{5(F - 32)}{9}$. Find C if $F = 68$.

$C = \frac{5(F - 32)}{9}$ *Write the formula.*

$C = \frac{5(68 - 32)}{9}$ *Replace F by 68.*

$C = \frac{180}{9}$ *Subtract 32 from 68. Multiply 5 by 36.*

$C = 20$ *Divide 180 by 9.*

The Celsius temperature is 20°.

exercises

Max: 1–15, 1–32, Challenge; Avg: 1–15, 1–31 odds; Min: 1–31 odds

Exploratory Find the value of each expression.

1. $2 + 8 - 3$ 7
2. $5 - 3 \cdot 2$ $^-1$
3. $5 - (4 + 3)^2$ $^-44$
4. $2(6 + 1)$ 14
5. $2 \cdot 6 + 1$ 13
6. $3^3 - 2^3$ 19
7. $3(2^2 + 3)$ 21
8. $5^2 \div 2^5$ $\frac{25}{32}$
9. $2 + 5^2$ 27
10. $(5 - 7)^2$ 4
11. $2(3 + 8) - 1$ 21
12. $2(8) - 8 \div 4$ 14
13. $5^2 - (3 + 2)^2$ 0
14. $3 + (3 - 3)^3 - 3$ 0
15. $3 \times 2 - 2$ 4

Written Find the value of each expression.

1. $(6 + 5) \cdot 4 - 3$ 41
2. $(6 + 5)(4 - 3)$ 11
3. $12 + 8 \div 4$ 14
4. $12 + (8 \div 4)$ 14
5. $12 \div 8 \cdot 4$ 6
6. $12 \div (8 \cdot 4)$ $\frac{3}{8}$
7. $(5 + 3)^2 - 16 \div 4$ 60
8. $5 + 3^2 - 16 \div 4$ 10
9. $2 \cdot 9 \div 6 + 7$ 10
10. $8 - 2 \cdot 3 - 3$ $^-1$
11. $12 + 18 \div 6 + 7$ 22
12. $4 + 8 \cdot 4 \div 2 - 10$ 10

Evaluate if $a = 3$, $b = 7$, $c = {}^-2$, and $d = \frac{1}{2}$.

13. $6a^3 - 2b$ 148
14. $3ad + bc$ $-\frac{19}{2}$
15. $3ab - 6bc$ 147
16. $(a + c)^3 + d^2$ $\frac{5}{4}$
17. $c^2 - 5d$ $\frac{3}{2}$
18. $(a + b - c)^2$ 144
19. $12a^2 + bc$ 94
20. $4a - 12cd$ 24
21. $\frac{6ac}{d}$ $^-72$
22. $\frac{3ab}{cd}$ $^-63$
23. $\frac{5a + 3c}{3b}$ $\frac{3}{7}$
24. $\frac{3ab^2 - d^3}{a}$ $146\frac{23}{24}$

Simple interest (I) is calculated using $I = prt$. The letter p stands for principal, r stands for rate, and t stands for time in years. Find I given the following values.

25. $p = 1000$, $r = 0.06$, and $t = 3$ 180
26. $p = 2500$, $r = 0.09$, and $t = 2\frac{1}{2}$ 562.5
27. $p = 5000$, $r = 0.08$, and $t = 5$ 2000
28. $p = 2000$, $r = 0.12$, and $t = 3\frac{1}{2}$ 840

The formula for the area of a trapezoid is $A = \frac{h}{2}(b + B)$. A stands for the area, h stands for the altitude, and b and B stand for the bases. Calculate the area of the trapezoid given the following values.

29. $b = 12$, $B = 20$, and $h = 8$ 128
30. $b = 4$, $B = 11$, and $h = 7$ 52.5
31. $h = 10$, $b = 6$, and $B = 14$ 100
32. $h = 8$, $B = 16$, and $b = 12$ 112

$4 + [(8^2 \div 4) \cdot 2] = 36$ $[(4 + 8^2) \div 4] \cdot 2 = 34$ $(4 + 8^2) \div (4 \cdot 2) = 8.5$

Challenge Show that you can find three different answers to $4 + 8^2 \div 4 \cdot 2$ depending on how you group. Should this be allowed? If not, why not?

Without order of operations agreements $4 + 8^2 \div 4 \cdot 2$ could mean something different to different people. Order of operations prevents ambiguous meanings. Grouping symbols allow us to change the meaning.

Reading Algebra

Understanding Symbols

Understanding algebra depends largely on understanding the symbols used in algebra. The symbols of language are the letters of the alphabet. In English, there are just 26 letters, and most letters have one or two sounds. On the other hand, there are many symbols used in mathematics, and the meaning of these symbols frequently depends on how they are used. Notice how the symbol **4** is used in each expression.

Expression	Translation
4	four
40	forty
0.04	four hundredths
4^2	four squared
2^4	two to the fourth power
$\frac{1}{4}$	one-fourth

In like manner, the symbol — may be used in several ways.

Expression	Translation
$9 - 4$	nine minus four
$^{-}4$	negative four
$\frac{3}{4}$	three-fourths
$\begin{array}{r} 5 \\ \times\ 4 \\ \hline 20 \end{array}$	five times four equals twenty

Exercises Match each expression with the correct translation.

1. $3a$ b
2. a^3 e
3. $3a^2 + 1$ a
4. $(3a + 1)^2$ c
5. $(3a)^2 + 1$ f
6. $\frac{a}{3}$ d

a. three times a squared plus one
b. three times a
c. three times a plus one, quantity squared
d. a divided by three
e. a to the third power
f. three times a, quantity squared, plus one

Write each algebraic expression in words. Answers vary.

7. $3ad + bc$
8. $6a^3 - 2b$
9. $(a + b - c)^2$
10. $(a + c)^3 + d^2$
11. $\frac{6ac}{d}$
12. $\frac{5a + 3c}{3b}$

1–2 Properties of Addition and Multiplication

Objective: To use properties of addition and multiplication and simplify expressions.

One basic idea of mathematics is commutativity. For example, the sum of two numbers is the same regardless of the order in which they are written. This idea also holds for the product of two numbers.

$$8 + 3 = 3 + 8 \qquad 24.6 + 19.3 = 19.3 + 24.6$$
$$5 \cdot 9 = 9 \cdot 5 \qquad 13.7 \cdot 2.5 = 2.5 \cdot 13.7$$

Commutative Properties

For all numbers a and b,
$$a + b = b + a \text{ and,}$$
$$a \cdot b = b \cdot a.$$

Another basic idea of mathematics is associativity. To add three numbers, you add two numbers at a time. To find $8 + 6 + 4$, for example, you could add the sum of 8 and 6 to 4. Or you could add 8 to the sum of 6 and 4. Either way, the sum is 18.

$$(8 + 6) + 4 = 14 + 4 = 18 \qquad 8 + (6 + 4) = 8 + 10 = 18$$

The way you group, or associate, three or more numbers does not change their sum. A similar property holds for multiplication. The way you group, or associate, three or more numbers does not change their product.

Associative Properties

For all numbers a, b, and c,
$$(a + b) + c = a + (b + c) \text{ and,}$$
$$(a \cdot b) \cdot c = a \cdot (b \cdot c).$$

Associativity is needed because addition and multiplication are *binary operations*.

The commutative and associative properties used together make addition and multiplication easier.

example 1

Find $1 + 2 + 3 + 4 + 5 + 6 + 7 + 8 + 9$.

$$\begin{aligned}
&1 + 2 + 3 + 4 + 5 + 6 + 7 + 8 + 9\\
&= (1 + 9) + (2 + 8) + (3 + 7) + (4 + 6) + 5\\
&= 10 + 10 + 10 + 10 + 5\\
&= 45
\end{aligned}$$

The sum is 45.

example 2

Simplify $6 \cdot 2 \cdot 12 \cdot 5$.

$$\begin{aligned} 6 \cdot 2 \cdot 12 \cdot 5 &= (6 \cdot 12) \cdot (2 \cdot 5) \\ &= 72 \cdot 10 \\ &= 720 \end{aligned}$$

The product is 720.

The sum of any number and zero is identical to the number you start with.

$2 + 0 = 2$ $\qquad$ $0 + {}^{-}8 = {}^{-}8$ $\qquad$ $7.7 + 0 = 7.7$

Zero is the **additive identity.**

The product of any number and one is identical to the number you start with.

$6 \cdot 1 = 6$ $\qquad$ $1 \cdot {}^{-}9 = {}^{-}9$ $\qquad$ $1 \cdot 18.3 = 18.3$

One is the **multiplicative identity.**

For any number a,

$$a + 0 = a = 0 + a \text{ and,}$$
$$a \cdot 1 = a = 1 \cdot a.$$

Identity Properties

If the sum of two numbers is zero, they are called **additive inverses.**

$2 + {}^{-}2 = 0$ $\qquad$ ${}^{-}85.2 + 85.2 = 0$

If the product of two numbers is one, they are usually called **multiplicative inverses.**

$2 \cdot \frac{1}{2} = 1$ $\qquad$ $\frac{1}{19} \cdot 19 = 1$

For any number a,

$$a + {}^{-}a = 0 = {}^{-}a + a \text{ and,}$$
$$\text{if } a \text{ is } \textit{not} \text{ zero, } a \cdot \frac{1}{a} = 1 = \frac{1}{a} \cdot a.$$

Inverse Properties

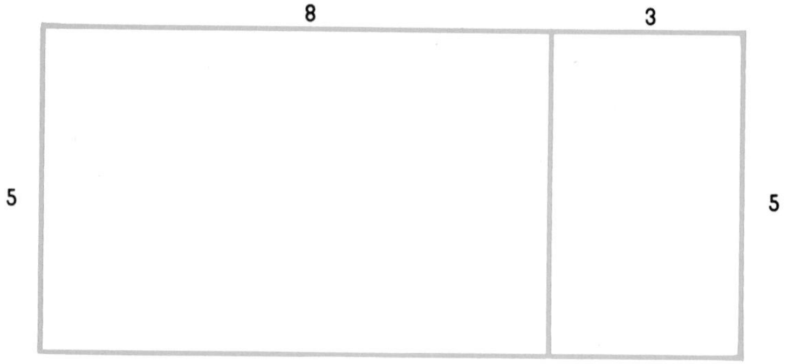

You can find the area of this rectangle in two different ways.

METHOD 1: multiply the length by the width
$A = (5)(8 + 3)$
$A = (5)(11)$
$A = 55$

METHOD 2: add the areas of the smaller rectangles
$A = 5(8) + 5(3)$
$A = 40 + 15$
$A = 55$

This example shows that (5)(8 + 3) and (5)(8) + (5)(3) have the same value, 55. Other similar examples lead to the following generalization.

Distributive Property

For all numbers a, b, and c,
$$a(b + c) = ab + ac \text{ and,}$$
$$(b + c)a = ba + ca.$$

Test to see if other distributive properties exist, such as addition with respect to division.

We say that multiplication is distributive with respect to addition. The distributive property can be used to simplify expressions containing *like terms*. In $5y + 7y$, for example, $5y$ and $7y$ are like terms.

examples

3 **Simplify $5y + 7y$.**

$$5y + 7y = (5 + 7)y$$
$$= 12y$$

4 **Simplify $13a + 6b - 8a + 3b$.**

$$13a + 6b - 8a + 3b = 13a - 8a + 6b + 3b \quad \text{Use the commutative property.}$$
$$= (13 - 8)a + (6 + 3)b \quad \text{Use the distributive property.}$$
$$= 5a + 9b$$

exercises

Max: 1–14, 1–30, Challenge; **Avg:** 1–14, 1–29 odds; **Min:** 1–25 odds

Exploratory **State the property shown in each of the following.**

1. $8 + (6 + 4) = (8 + 6) + 4$ associative
2. $7(5) = 5(7)$ commutative
3. $(a + b)c = ac + bc$ distributive
4. $a(3 - 2) = a \cdot 3 - a \cdot 2$ distributive
5. $8 + (1 + 6) = 8 + (6 + 1)$ commutative
6. $3 + {}^-3 = 0$ additive inverse
7. $2(3 + 6) = 2(3) + 2(6)$ distributive
8. $9 - (3 + 4) = 9 - (4 + 3)$ commutative
9. $3 + 6 = 6 + 3$ commutative
10. $8(6 - 7) = (6 - 7)8$ commutative
11. $11 + (6 + 4) = (6 + 4) + 11$ commutative
12. $8\left(\frac{1}{8}\right) = 1$ multiplicative inverse
13. ${}^-9 + 9 = 9 + {}^-9$ commutative
14. $3(47) = 3(40) + 3(7)$ distributive

Written **State the property shown in each of the following.**

1. $3(9) = 9(3)$ commutative
2. $(5 + 6) + 3 = 5 + (6 + 3)$ associative
3. $(4 + 11) \cdot 6 = 4(6) + 11(6)$ distributive
4. $(a + b) + {}^-(a + b) = 0$ additive inverse
5. $11 + a = a + 11$ commutative
6. $(3 + 9) + 14 = 14 + (3 + 9)$ commutative
7. $3 + (a + b) = (a + b) + 3$ commutative
8. $7 \cdot 1 = 7$ multiplicative identity
9. $8(5 + 3) = 40 + 24$ distributive
10. $3a + 6 = 3(a + 2)$ distributive
11. $(11a + 3b) + 0 = 11a + 3b$ additive identity
12. $8(4) = 4(8)$ commutative
13. $3\left(\frac{1}{3}\right) = 1$ multiplicative inverse
14. $(4 + 9a)2b = 2b(4 + 9a)$ commutative
15. $a + b + 0 = a + b$ additive identity
16. $\left(\frac{1}{m}\right)m = 1$ multiplicative inverse
17. $11(3a + 2b) = 11(2b + 3a)$ commutative
18. $5a + {}^-5a = 0$ additive inverse
19. $1 = ax^2 \cdot \frac{1}{ax^2}$ multiplicative inverse
20. $0 + 7 = 7$ additive identity

Simplify.

21. $8 + 15 - 3$ 20
22. $5(13 + 25)$ 190
23. $3(5a + 6b) + 8(2a - b)$ $31a + 10b$
24. $3a + 5b + 7a - 3b$ $10a + 2b$
25. $\frac{1}{4}(12 + 20a) + \frac{3}{4}(12 + 20a)$ $12 + 20a$
26. $a^2(a^2 + 2a - 3) + a(a^2 - 2a) + (a^2 - 3)$ $a^4 + 3a^3 - 4a^2 - 3$
27. If $a + b = a$, what is the value of b? What is b called? 0, additive identity
28. If $ab = 1$, what is the value of a? What is a called? $1/b$, multiplicative inverse
29. If $ab = a$, what is the value of b? What is b called? 1, multiplicative identity
30. If $a + b = 0$, what is the value of a? What is a called? ${}^-b$, additive inverse

Challenge **Explain what is wrong with the following sentence.**

$$\text{If } a\left(\frac{1}{a}\right) = 1, \text{ then } 0\left(\frac{1}{0}\right) = 1.$$

The expression $\frac{1}{0}$ is *not* defined. The Multiplicative Inverse Property holds only if a is *not zero.*

1–3 Equations

Objective: To solve equations using properties of equality.

Some relations have three very important properties. In your arithmetic, you have assumed these properties for equality.

Reflexive Property of Equality	**For any number a, $a = a$.**
Symmetric Property of Equality	**For all numbers a and b, if $a = b$, then $b = a$.**
Transitive Property of Equality	**For all numbers a, b, and c, if $a = b$ and $b = c$, then $a = c$.**

example 1

State the property shown in each of the following.

1. $21.4 = 21.4$ — 1. reflexive property
2. If $36 \cdot 2 = 72$, then $72 = 36 \cdot 2$. — 2. symmetric property
3. If $8 = 6 + 2$ and $6 + 2 = 5 + 3$ then $8 = 5 + 3$. — 3. transitive property

An important property of equality is the substitution property.

Substitution Property of Equality	**For all numbers a and b, if $a = b$, then a may be replaced by b.**

The solution set of an open sentence is the set of all replacements for variables that make the sentence true.

Solving an equation means finding replacements for variables in the equation so that a true sentence results. Sometimes an equation can be solved by performing the indicated operations and using substitution. Sentences with variables to be replaced are called open sentences.

example 2

Solve $y = 3(4) + 7$.

$y = 3(4) + 7$

$y = 12 + 7$ *Substitute 12 for 3(4).*

$y = 19$ *Substitute 19 for 12 + 7.*

The solution is 19. The solution set is {19}.

Sometimes an equation can be solved by adding or subtracting the same number to both sides of the equation.

example 3

Solve $x + 28.3 = 56.0$.

$$x + 28.3 = 56.0$$
$$x + 28.3 + {}^{-}28.3 = 56.0 + {}^{-}28.3 \quad \textit{Add } {}^{-}28.3 \textit{ to both sides.}$$
$$x = 27.7 \quad \textit{Substitution.}$$

The solution is 27.7. The solution set is {27.7}.

For any numbers a, b, and c, if $a = b$, then $a + c = b + c$ and $a - c = b - c$.

Addition and Subtraction Properties of Equality

Sometimes an equation can be solved by multiplying or dividing both sides by the same number.

examples 4

Solve $7x = 42$.

$$7x = 42$$
$$\frac{1}{7} \cdot 7x = \frac{1}{7} \cdot 42 \quad \textit{Multiply both sides by } \frac{1}{7}.$$
$$x = 6 \quad \textit{Substitution.}$$

The solution is 6. The solution set is {6}.

5

Solve $7x = 42$.

$$7x = 42$$
$$\frac{7x}{7} = \frac{42}{7} \quad \textit{Divide both sides by 7.}$$
$$x = 6 \quad \textit{Substitution.}$$

The solution is 6. The solution set is {6}.

For any numbers a, b, and c,
if $a = b$, then $a \cdot c = b \cdot c$ and,
if c is *not* zero, $\frac{a}{c} = \frac{b}{c}$.

Multiplication and Division Properties of Equality

Many equations can be solved by using the properties of equality along with the other properties you have studied.

example 6

Solve $5x - 7 = 23$.

$5x - 7 = 23$	
$5x - 7 + 7 = 23 + 7$	*Addition property*
$5x = 30$	*Substitution*
$\frac{5x}{5} = \frac{30}{5}$	*Division property*
$x = 6$	*Substitution*

The solution is 6. The solution set is {6}.

You may combine steps when solving equations.

example 7

Solve $6(a + 5) + 10a = {}^-2$.

$6(a + 5) + 10a = {}^-2$	
$6a + 30 + 10a = {}^-2$	*Distributive and substitution properties*
$16a + 30 = {}^-2$	*Commutative, distributive, and substitution properties*
$16a = {}^-32$	*Addition and substitution properties*
$a = {}^-2$	*Division and substitution properties*

The solution is $^-2$. The solution set is $\{^-2\}$.

exercises

Max: 1–10, 1–55; **Avg:** 1–10, 1–55 odds; **Min:** 1–45 odds

Exploratory **State the property shown in each of the following.** 4. symmetric

1. $3 + (2 + 3) = 3 + (2 + 3)$ reflexive
2. $3 + (2 + 3) = 3 + 5$ substitution
3. If $3 = 2 + 1$, then $2 + 1 = 3$. symmetric
4. If $5 + 7 = 12$, then $12 = 7 + 5$.
5. If $7 = 2 + 5$, and $2 + 5 = \sqrt{49}$, then $7 = \sqrt{49}$. transitive
6. If $8 + 1 = 9$ and $9 = 3 + 6$, then $8 + 1 = 3 + 6$. transitive
7. $81 = 81$ reflexive
8. $9 + 5 = (6 + 3) + 5$ substitution
9. If $2 + 1 = 3$, then $6 + (2 + 1) = 6 + 3$. substitution
10. If $8 = 6 + 2$ and $6 + 2 = 5 + 3$, then $8 = 5 + 3$. transitive

Written State the property shown in each of the following.

1. If $8 + 1 = 9$, then $9 = 8 + 1$. symmetric
2. If $6 + 9 = 5 + 10$ and $5 + 10 = 15$, then $6 + 9 = 15$. transitive
3. If $7 + 4 = 7 + 3 + 1$ and $7 + 3 + 1 = 10 + 1$, then $7 + 4 = 10 + 1$. transitive
4. $9 + (2 + 10) = 9 + 12$ substitution
5. $6 + 8 = 6 + 8$ reflexive
6. If $11 - 5 = 4 + 2$, then $4 + 2 = 11 - 5$. symmetric
7. $4 + 7 + 9 = 11 + 9$ substitution
8. $4 + 7 + 9 = 4 + 7 + 9$ reflexive

Find the value of each expression.

9. $(21 + 18) \div 3 \cdot 4^2$ 208
10. $(72 \div 9) \div 2 + 5^3$ 129
11. $[25(6 \cdot 3) - 14] \div 2$ 218
12. $20(3 + 7) - 4(3 + 7)$ 160
13. $6(6 + 38) - 3(17 \div 3)$ 247
14. $(4 \cdot 3) + 2 \div 5$ 12.4
15. $[(2 \cdot 12) - (6 \div 3)] \div 2$ 11
16. $[2(12 - 3) \div 3] \div 2$ 3
17. $\frac{4(3 + 22)}{5^2} + \frac{(9 - 5)7}{2^2}$ 11
18. $\frac{(11 \cdot 15) + (2 \cdot 5)}{3^2 + 4^2}$ 7

Solve each equation.

19. $4x = 30$ 7.5
20. $a + 17 = 31$ 14
21. $3x + 8 = 29$ 7
22. $4 - 7x = 25$ $^{-}3$
23. $\frac{3}{4}r + 1 = 10$ 12
24. $1 + \frac{2}{3}y = 27$ 39
25. $5t + 7 = 2t + 13$ 2
26. $3x - 4 = 7x + 11$ $^{-}3.75$
27. $\frac{3}{4}x = \frac{1}{3}$ $\frac{4}{9}$
28. $\frac{2}{3}m = 12$ 18
29. $3 - 0.2x = 18$ $^{-}75$
30. $5 + 7b = 1\frac{2}{3}$ $-\frac{10}{21}$
31. $c - 4 = 29$ 33
32. $9x + 4 = 2\frac{1}{2}$ $-\frac{1}{6}$
33. $\frac{8e}{9} + \frac{1}{3} = \frac{3}{5}$ $\frac{3}{10}$
34. $4x + \frac{3}{5} = 1\frac{7}{10}$ $\frac{11}{40}$
35. $8 - x = 5x + 32$ $^{-}4$
36. $4 + 3p = p - 12$ $^{-}8$
37. $5q = \frac{2}{5}$ $\frac{2}{25}$
38. $\frac{3}{8} - \frac{1}{4}x = \frac{1}{16}$ $\frac{5}{4}$
39. $\frac{3}{4}s - \frac{1}{2} = \frac{1}{4}s + 5$ 11
40. $\frac{2}{3} - \frac{3}{5}x = \frac{2}{5}x + \frac{4}{3}$ $-\frac{2}{3}$
41. $1.2x + 3.7 = 13.3$ 8
42. $4.5 - 3.9m = 20.1$ $^{-}4$
43. $5(3x + 5) = 2x - 8$ $-\frac{33}{13}$
44. $2(6 - 7k) = 2k - 4$ 1
45. $\frac{1}{5}z + \frac{1}{5} = \frac{2}{5}$ 1
46. $\frac{3}{4}x = \frac{5}{7}$ $\frac{20}{21}$
47. $285 - 38x = 2033$ 46
48. $0.8v - 12 = 21.6$ 42
49. $^{-}3 + x = {}^{-}42$ $^{-}39$
50. $1.1x - 0.09 = 2.22$ 2.1

51. $1.3 - 0.003x = 0.67$ 210
52. $\frac{3}{7}x = 4\frac{1}{2}$ $\frac{21}{2}$
53. $2467 - 897s = 10091.5$ $^{-}8.5$
54. $8061 = 295x - 1084$ 31
55. $847.6b - 3269.5 = 610.1b + 2406.75$ 23.9

1-4 Using Equations

Objective: To use equations to solve problems.

You can use equations to solve verbal problems. First you should read the problem carefully and define a variable.

You can buy some 3¢ stamps and the same number of 10¢ stamps for a total of 52¢. How many of each kind of stamp will you buy?

Define a variable. The problem asks for how many stamps of each kind. Let n stand for the number of each kind of stamp.

After defining a variable you should write an equation that describes the relationships in the problem.

Write an equation. cost of 3¢ stamps + cost of 10¢ stamps = 52¢

$$3n + 10n = 52$$

Next you should solve the equation and check the solution.

Solve the equation.

$$3n + 10n = 52$$
$$13n = 52$$
$$n = 4$$

Students should read the problem carefully to be sure they understand the question. In some cases a picture or diagram is helpful.

Check the solution.

$$3n + 10n = 52$$
$$3(4) + 10(4) \stackrel{?}{=} 52$$
$$12 + 40 \stackrel{?}{=} 52$$
$$52 = 52$$

Answer the problem. You will buy *four* 3¢ and *four* 10¢ stamps.

Problem Solving Procedure

1. **Define a variable.**
2. **Write an equation.**
3. **Solve the equation.**
4. **Check the solution.**
5. **Answer the problem.**

examples

1

Minna Walker wants to pay about \$6300 for a new car. The dealer says the car costs \$7200. Minna's price is what percent of the dealer's price?

Define a variable. The problem asks for a percent of the dealer's price. Let x stand for the percent of the dealer's price.

Write an equation.

$$\frac{\text{percent of dealer's price}}{100} = \frac{\text{Minna's price}}{\text{Dealer's price}}$$

$$\frac{x}{100} = \frac{6300}{7200}$$

Solve the equation.

$$\frac{x}{100} = \frac{6300}{7200}$$

$$\frac{x}{100} \cdot 100 = \frac{6300}{7200} \cdot 100$$

$$x = 87.5$$

Check the solution.

$$\frac{x}{100} = \frac{6300}{7200}$$

$$\frac{87.5}{100} \stackrel{?}{=} \frac{6300}{7200}$$

$$0.875 = 0.875$$

Answer the problem. Minna's price is 87.5% of the dealer's price.

2

Henry Takahashi drove for 3 hours at 40 miles per hour. He drove 50 miles per hour for the rest of the trip. If Henry drove a total of 240 miles, how long did he drive at 50 miles per hour?

Define a variable. The problem asks for the length of time Henry drove at 50 miles per hour. Let t stand for the length of time Henry drove at 50 miles per hour.

Write an equation.

$$\text{total distance} = \text{distance at 40 mph} + \text{distance at 50 mph}$$

$$240 = 40 \cdot 3 + 50 \cdot t$$

Solve the equation.

$$240 = 40 \cdot 3 + 50 \cdot t$$

$$240 = 120 + 50t$$

$$120 = 50t$$

$$2.4 = t$$

Check the solution.

$$240 = 40 \cdot 3 + 50 \cdot t$$

$$240 \stackrel{?}{=} 40 \cdot 3 + 50(2.4)$$

$$240 \stackrel{?}{=} 120 + 120$$

$$240 = 240$$

Answer the problem. Henry drove 2.4 hours at 50 miles per hour.

exercises

Max: 1–4, 1–10; Avg: 1–4, 1–9 odds; Min: 1–4, 1–7 odds

Exploratory **Solve each problem.**

1. One kilowatt of electricity costs the consumer about $0.06. The cost of running a refrigerator for one month is $4.98. How many kilowatts of electricity does a refrigerator use in one month? 83
2. Anton paid $21.00 to run his air conditioner last month. His air conditioner uses about 300 kilowatts per month. How much is Anton paying for 1 kilowatt of electricity? $0.07
3. A color T.V. uses twice as much electricity as a black and white T.V. It costs about $5.50 to use a color T.V. for one month. How much would it cost to run a black and white T.V. instead? $2.75
4. A sound travels 4.93 kilometers in 14.5 seconds. How fast does sound travel? 0.34 kilometers per second

Written **Solve each problem.**

1. Bonnie Mankiewicz wants to pay about $4900 for a new car. The dealer says the car costs $5600. Bonnie's price is what percent of the dealer's price? 87.5%
2. Junior Walker got $1500 trade-in on his car. The dealer is selling Junior's car for $1800. The dealer's selling price is what percent of the trade-in value? 120%
3. Alicea Paloma got $2000 trade-in on her car. The dealer is selling her car for $2400. The dealer's selling price is what percent of the trade-in value? 120%
4. You can buy some $0.03 stamps and the same number of $0.10 stamps for a total of $1.04. How many of each kind of stamp will you buy? 8
5. A rectangle has a perimeter of 102 centimeters. The length of the rectangle is 13 centimeters greater than the width. How wide is the rectangle? 19 centimeters
6. The width of a rectangle is 5 meters more than one-half its length. The perimeter is 286 meters. Find the length and width. length is 92 m, width is 51 m
7. The width of a rectangle is 12 units less than its length. If you add 30 units to both the length and width, you double the perimeter. Find the length and width of the original rectangle. 36 units, 24 units
8. Alice is on her way to San Diego, 270 miles away. She drives 40 miles per hour for 3 hours. She drives 50 miles per hour for the rest of her trip. How long does Alice drive at 50 miles per hour? 3 hours
9. San Francisco and Los Angeles are 470 miles apart by train. An express train leaves Los Angeles at the same time a passenger train leaves San Francisco. The express train travels 10 miles per hour faster than the passenger train. The two trains pass each other in 2.5 hours. How fast is each train traveling? passenger train 89 mph express train 99 mph
10. To estimate when to harvest her early pea crop, an Indiana farmer counts heat units. As of June 1 she has counted 865 heat units. There are usually 30 heat units per day in June. Early peas require 1165 heat units to mature. The farmer can plan to harvest her crop in how many more days? 10 days

CAREERS

Engineer

Edwina Lewis is a professional engineer. Her particular field is designing submarines.

There are many things that she must consider. One of these is to make sure that a submarine's structure can withstand the pressure at various depths. The pressure can be found by using the following formula.

$P = hd$ *h stands for depth and d stands for density of water*

Example Find the pressure at a depth of 300 meters.

The density of water is 1 gram per cubic centimeter. So, first convert 300 meters to centimeters.

300 meters = (300 · 100) centimeters *1 meter is 100 centimeters*
= 30,000 centimeters

Then, use the formula for pressure.

$P = hd$
= 30,000 centimeters · 1 gram per cubic centimeter $cm \cdot \frac{g}{cm^3} = \frac{g}{cm^2}$
= 30,000 grams per square centimeter

Since there are 1000 grams in 1 kilogram, the pressure is 30 kilograms per square centimeter.

To allow for error and deterioration of materials, a safety factor of 2 is used. Thus, the submarine would be designed to withstand a pressure of 30 · 2 or 60 kilograms per square centimeter.

Exercises Find the pressure at the following depths. Use the safety factor to allow for error and deterioration of materials.

1. 250 meters 50 **2.** 400 meters 80 **3.** 500 meters 100 **4.** 600 meters 120

5–8. For each depth in problems **1–4,** find the design pressure if a safety factor of 2.25 is used. **5.** 56.25 **6.** 90 **7.** 112.5 **8.** 135

1–5 Absolute Value

Objective: To solve absolute value equations.

Certainly $^{-}5$ and 5 are quite different, but they do have something in common. They are the same distance from 0 on the number line.

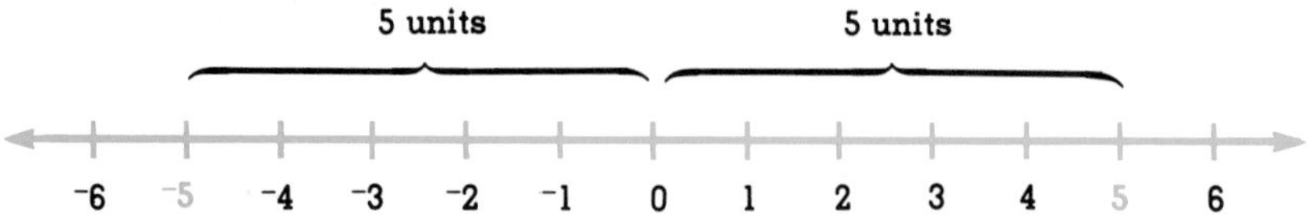

We say that $^{-}5$ and 5 have the same **absolute value.** The absolute value of a number is the number of units it is from 0 on the number line. Students need a careful explanation of absolute value.

The absolute value of $^{-}5$ is 5.
$|^{-}5| = 5$

The absolute value of 5 is 5.
$|5| = 5$

We can also define absolute value in the following way.

Definition of Absolute Value

For any number a,
if a is positive or zero, then $|a| = a$,
if a is negative, then $|a| = {}^{-}a$.

examples

1 **Find the absolute value of 3 and of $^{-}7$.**

$|3| = 3$
$|^{-}7| = {}^{-}(^{-}7)$ or 7

2 **Find the absolute value of x − 5.**

If x is 5 or greater, then $|x - 5| = x - 5$.
If x is less than 5, then $|x - 5| = {}^{-}(x - 5)$.
Be sure students understand this example.

3 **Find $|3x - 2| + 7.2$ if $x = {}^{-}3$.**

$$\begin{aligned} |3x - 2| + 7.2 &= |3(^{-}3) - 2| + 7.2 \\ &= |^{-}9 - 2| + 7.2 \\ &= |^{-}11| + 7.2 \\ &= 11 + 7.2 \\ &= 18.2 \end{aligned}$$

The value is 18.2.

Some equations contain absolute value expressions. You can use the definition of absolute value to solve the equations.

examples

4 **Solve $|x - 7| = 12$.**

$$|x - 7| = 12$$

If $x - 7$ is positive or zero $\quad x - 7 = 12$ or $^-(x - 7) = 12$ *If $x - 7$ is negative*

$$x = 19 \qquad x - 7 = {}^-12$$

$$x = {}^-5$$

Check: $|x - 7| = 12$

$|19 - 7| \stackrel{?}{=} 12$ or $|{}^-5 - 7| \stackrel{?}{=} 12$

$|12| \stackrel{?}{=} 12 \qquad |{}^-12| \stackrel{?}{=} 12$

$12 = 12 \qquad 12 = 12$

The solutions are 19 and $^-5$. The solution set is $\{19, {}^-5\}$.

5 **Solve $5|2x + 3| = 30$.**

When solving equations of the form $a|x + b| = c$, *first* divide both sides by a.

$$5|2x + 3| = 30$$

$$|2x + 3| = 6$$

If $2x + 3$ is positive or zero $\quad 2x + 3 = 6$ or $^-(2x + 3) = 6$ *If $2x + 3$ is negative*

$$2x = 3 \qquad 2x + 3 = {}^-6$$

$$x = \frac{3}{2} \qquad 2x = {}^-9$$

$$x = -\frac{9}{2}$$

Check: $5|2x + 3| = 30$

$5\left|2\left(\frac{3}{2}\right) + 3\right| \stackrel{?}{=} 30$ or $5\left|2\left(-\frac{9}{2}\right) + 3\right| \stackrel{?}{=} 30$

$5|3 + 3| \stackrel{?}{=} 30 \qquad 5|{}^-9 + 3| \stackrel{?}{=} 30$

$5|6| \stackrel{?}{=} 30 \qquad 5|{}^-6| \stackrel{?}{=} 30$

$30 = 30 \qquad 5(6) \stackrel{?}{=} 30$

$30 = 30$

The solutions are $\frac{3}{2}$ and $-\frac{9}{2}$. The solution set is $\left\{\frac{3}{2}, -\frac{9}{2}\right\}$.

Some absolute value equations have *no solutions.* For example, $|x| = {}^-3$ is *never* true. Since the absolute value of a number is always positive or zero, there is no replacement for x that will make the sentence true. The equation $|x| = {}^-3$ has no solutions. The solution set has no members at all. It is called the empty set, $\emptyset$.

example 6

Solve $|3x + 7| + 4 = 0$.

$$|3x + 7| + 4 = 0$$
$$|3x + 7| = {}^{-}4$$

This sentence is *never* true. The equation has *no solution*.
The solution set is $\emptyset$.

exercises

Max: 1–15, 1–36; Avg: 1–10, 1–35 odds; Min: 1–21 odds

Exploratory Evaluate if $x = {}^{-}5$.

1. $|x|$ 5
2. $|4x|$ 20
3. $|{}^{-}2x|$ 10
4. $|x + 6|$ 1
5. $|7x - 1|$ 36
6. $|{}^{-}x|$ 5
7. $|2x + 5|$ 5
8. $|{}^{-}2x + 5|$ 15
9. $5 - |x|$ 0
10. $5 - |{}^{-}x|$ 0
11. $|x| + x$ 0
12. $|x - 7| - 8$ 4
13. $|3x + 10| - 7$ $^{-}2$
14. $7 - |3x + 10|$ 2
15. $|x + 4| + |2x|$ 11

Written Solve each open sentence.

1. $|x + 11| = 42$ 31, $^{-}53$
2. $|x + 6| = 19$ 13, $^{-}25$
3. $|x - 5| = 11$ $^{-}6$, 16
4. $|x - 3| = 17$ $^{-}14$, 20
5. $3|x + 7| = 36$ 5, $^{-}19$
6. $5|x + 4| = 45$ 5, $^{-}13$
7. $8|x - 3| = 88$ $^{-}8$, 14
8. $11|x - 9| = 121$ $^{-}2$, 20
9. $|2x + 7| = 19$ $^{-}13$, 6
10. $|3x + 12| = 48$ $^{-}20$, 12
11. $|3x - 7| = 18$ $8\frac{1}{3}$, $^{-}3\frac{2}{3}$
12. $|5x + 30| = 65$ $^{-}19$, 7
13. $|2x + 5| = 16$ $^{-}10.5$, 5.5
14. $|2x + 9| = 30$ 10.5, $^{-}19.5$
15. $|2x - 37| = 15$ 26, 11
16. $|4x - 3| = {}^{-}27$ no solutions
17. $|6x + 5| = 21$ $^{-}4\frac{1}{3}$, $2\frac{2}{3}$
18. $|2x + 7| = 0$ $-\frac{7}{2}$
19. $3|5x + 2| = 51$ $^{-}3.8$, 3
20. $8|4x - 3| = 64$ $\frac{11}{4}$, $-\frac{5}{4}$
21. $^{-}6|2x - 14| = {}^{-}42$ 3.5, 10.5
22. $5|3x - 4| = 30$ $-\frac{2}{3}$, $3\frac{1}{3}$
23. $7|3x + 5| = 25$ $-\frac{10}{21}$, $-\frac{20}{7}$
24. $4|6x - 1| = 29$ $-\frac{25}{24}$, $\frac{11}{8}$
25. $3|5x - 29| = {}^{-}3$ no solutions
26. $2|6 - 5x| = 26$ $^{-}1.4$, 3.8
27. $9|3 - 2x| = 15$ $\frac{2}{3}$, $\frac{7}{3}$
28. $2|7 - 3x| = 3$ $\frac{11}{6}$, $\frac{17}{6}$
29. $|2a + 7| = a - 4$ no solutions
30. $|7 + 3a| = 11 - a$ 1, $^{-}9$
31. $|3t - 5| = 2t$ 1, 5
32. $5|3x - 4| = x + 1$ $\frac{3}{2}$, $\frac{19}{16}$
33. $|x - 3| + 7 = 2$ no solutions
34. $3|2x - 5| = {}^{-}1$ no solutions
35. $9|x + 4| - 3 = {}^{-}8$ no solutions
36. $21 + |6x + 5| = 0$ no solutions

1-6 Inequalities

Objective: To solve inequalities using properties of inequality.

Think about two jockeys, Willie and Robyn. When you compare their weights, you can make only one of the following statements.

Willie weighs *less than* Robyn weighs	Willie weighs *the same as* Robyn weighs	Willie weighs *more than* Robyn weighs

Let w stand for Willie's weight and r stand for Robyn's weight. Then you can use inequalities and equations to show how their weights compare.

$w < r$ $\qquad$ $w = r$ $\qquad$ $w > r$

For any two numbers a and b, exactly one of the following statements is true.

$$a < b \qquad a = b \qquad a > b$$

Trichotomy Property

Suppose Willie weighs 108 pounds and Robyn weighs 113 pounds. Then Willie weighs less than Robyn weighs. They each have saddles that weigh 3 pounds. How do their weights plus saddle weights compare?

WILLIE		ROBYN
108	<	113
108 + 3	<	113 + 3
111	<	116

Willie's weight plus saddle weight is less than Robyn's. Notice that adding the same number to both sides of an inequality does *not* change the truth of the inequality.

For any numbers a, b, and c,

1. If $a > b$, then $a + c > b + c$ and $a - c > b - c$.

2. If $a < b$, then $a + c < b + c$ and $a - c < b - c$.

Addition and Subtraction Properties for Inequalities

You can use this property to solve inequalities.

example 1

Solve $9x + 7 < 8x - 2$.

$$9x + 7 < 8x - 2$$
$$^-8x + 9x + 7 < {}^-8x + 8x - 2 \qquad \textit{Add } {}^-8x \textit{ to both sides.}$$
$$x + 7 < {}^-2$$
$$x + 7 + {}^-7 < {}^-2 + {}^-7 \qquad \textit{Add } {}^-7 \textit{ to both sides.}$$
$$x < {}^-9$$

Check: To check, choose several numbers less than $^-9$. Substitute those numbers, in turn, into the inequality.

The solutions are any numbers less than $^-9$.

You know that $18 > {}^-11$ is a true inequality. If you multiply both sides of this inequality by a positive number, the result is a true inequality.

$$18 > {}^-11 \qquad \textit{A true inequality}$$
$$18(3) > {}^-11(3) \qquad \textit{Multiply both sides by 3.}$$
$$54 > {}^-33 \qquad \textit{Another true inequality}$$

Suppose you multiply both sides of a true inequality by a negative number. Try $^-2$.

$$18 > {}^-11 \qquad \textit{A true inequality}$$
$$18({}^-2) > {}^-11({}^-2) \qquad \textit{Multiply both sides by } {}^-2.$$
$$^-36 > 22 \qquad \textit{False!!!}$$

But, *reverse the inequality sign*, and the result is true.
Be sure students understand when to reverse the inequality sign.

Multiplication and Division Properties for Inequalities

For any numbers a, b, and c,

1. If $c > 0$ and $a < b$, then $ac < bc$ and $\frac{a}{c} < \frac{b}{c}$.
2. If $c > 0$ and $a > b$, then $ac > bc$ and $\frac{a}{c} > \frac{b}{c}$.
3. If $c < 0$ and $a < b$, then $ac > bc$ and $\frac{a}{c} > \frac{b}{c}$.
4. If $c < 0$ and $a > b$, then $ac < bc$ and $\frac{a}{c} < \frac{b}{c}$.

The following examples show how this property is used to solve inequalities.

examples

2 Solve $-\frac{y}{3} < 4$.

$$-\frac{y}{3} < 4$$

$$(^-3)\left(-\frac{y}{3}\right) > (^-3)(4)$$ *Change the order of the inequality since $^-3$ is negative.*

$$y > {}^-12$$

The solutions are any numbers greater than $^-12$.
The solution set can be written $\{y|y > {}^-12\}$. It is read *the set of all numbers* y *such that* y *is greater than* $^-12$.

3 Solve $9x + 4 < 13x - 7$.

$$9x + 4 < 13x - 7$$

$$^-13x + 9x + 4 < {}^-13x + 13x - 7$$ *Add ^-13x to both sides.*

$$^-4x + 4 < {}^-7$$

$$^-4x + 4 + {}^-4 < {}^-7 + {}^-4$$ *Add $^-4$ to both sides.*

$$^-4x < {}^-11$$

$$\left(-\frac{1}{4}\right)(^-4x) > \left(-\frac{1}{4}\right)(^-11)$$ *Multiply both sides by $-\frac{1}{4}$ and change the order.*

$$x > \frac{11}{4}$$

The solutions are any numbers greater than $\frac{11}{4}$. The solution set is $\left\{x|x > \frac{11}{4}\right\}$.

exercises

Max: 1–15, 1–32, 1–4; Avg: 1–15, 1–31 odds; Min: 1–15 odds, 1–25 odds

Exploratory Replace each ▒ with <, >, or = to make each sentence true.

1. $^-7$ ▒ $^-(6 + 2)$ >
2. $^-5$ ▒ $^-3$ <
3. $^-5\frac{1}{3}$ ▒ $^-5$ <
4. $^-6$ ▒ $^-7 + {}^-4$ >
5. $(6 + 4) - 4$ ▒ $20 \div 5 + 1$ >
6. $^-15 - {}^-27$ ▒ 12 =
7. 0.12 ▒ 0.012 >
8. $1\frac{7}{8}$ ▒ $1\frac{3}{4}$ >
9. $2\frac{1}{4} + 3$ ▒ $2\frac{1}{4}$ >
10. $2\frac{1}{4} - 3$ ▒ $2\frac{1}{4}$ <
11. $2\frac{1}{4} - 3$ ▒ 3 <
12. $\frac{1}{3}$ ▒ $\frac{3}{9}$ =
13. $(4 + 6)^3$ ▒ $(5 + 5)^3$ =
14. $10^3 + 1$ ▒ 10^3 >
15. 2^4 ▒ 4^2 =

Written Solve each inequality. $\geq$ *means greater than or equal to* $\leq$ *means less than or equal to*

1. $3x + 7 > 43$ $\{x|x > 12\}$
2. $2t - 9 < 21$ $\{t|t < 15\}$
3. $7n - 5 \geq 44$ $\{n|n \geq 7\}$
4. $5x + 4 \geq 34$ $\{x|x \geq 6\}$
5. $5r + 8 > 24$ $\{r|r > 3.2\}$
6. $6s - 7 < 29$ $\{s|s < 6\}$
7. $8 - 3x < 44$ $\{x|x > {}^{-}12\}$
8. $15 - 2t \geq 55$ $\{t|t \leq {}^{-}20\}$
9. $11 - 5y < {}^{-}77$ $\{y|y > 17.6\}$
10. $29 - 7y < 24$ $\{y|y > \frac{5}{7}\}$
11. $5(x - 3) \geq 15$ $\{x|x \geq 6\}$
12. $9(x + 2) < 72$ $\{x|x < 6\}$
13. $5(2x - 7) > 10$ $\{x|x > 4.5\}$
14. $3(4x + 7) < 21$ $\{x|x < 0\}$
15. $3(3w + 1) \geq 48$ $\{w|w \geq 5\}$
16. $25 \leq {}^{-}5(4 - p)$ $\{p|p \geq 9\}$
17. $5(5z - 3) \leq 60$ $\{z|z \leq 3\}$
18. ${}^{-}42 > 7(2x + 3)$ $\{x|x < {}^{-}4.5\}$
19. ${}^{-}4(13 - 6t) < 26$ $\{t|t < 3.25\}$
20. $40 \leq {}^{-}6(5r - 7)$ $\{r|r \leq \frac{1}{15}\}$
21. $7x - 5 > 3x + 4$ $\{x|x > 2.25\}$
22. $3x + 1 < x + 5$ $\{x|x < 2\}$
23. $1 - 2x \leq 5x - 2$ $\{x|x \geq \frac{3}{7}\}$
24. $3 - 2x \geq 0$ $\{x|x \leq \frac{3}{2}\}$
25. $\frac{3x}{4} - \frac{1}{2} < 0$ $\{x|x < \frac{2}{3}\}$
26. $\frac{3x - 5}{2} \leq 0$ $\{x|x \leq \frac{5}{3}\}$
27. $0.01x - 2.32 \geq 0$ $\{x|x \geq 232\}$
28. $x - 5 < 0.1$ $\{x|x < 5.1\}$
29. $\frac{2x + 3}{5} \leq 0.03$ $\{x|x \leq {}^{-}1.425\}$
30. $\frac{2x + 3}{5} \geq {}^{-}0.03$ $\{x|x \geq {}^{-}1.575\}$
31. $\frac{5 - 2x}{4} \geq {}^{-}0.001$ $\{x|x \leq 2.502\}$
32. $\frac{5 - 2x}{4} \leq 0.001$ $\{x|x \geq 2.498\}$

Challenge Find the set of all numbers x satisfying the given conditions.

1. $x + 1 > 0$ and $x - 3 < 0$
2. $x - 1 < 0$ and $x + 2 > 0$
3. $3x - 2 \geq 0$ and $5x - 1 \leq 0$
4. $2x + 1 > 0$ and $x - 1 > 0$

1. $\{x|{}^{-}1 < x < 3\}$ 2. $\{x|{}^{-}2 < x < 1\}$ 3. $\emptyset$ 4. $\{x|x > 1\}$
Students will learn compound inequalities in the next section.

Excursions in Algebra

History

Mary Fairfax Somerville (1780–1872) wrote several books aimed at popularizing current scientific theories. As did many others, she began studying mathematics with Euclid's *Geometry*. She later taught herself subjects such as conic sections, trigonometry, and calculus.

1-7 Using Inequalities

Objective: To use inequalities to solve problems.

The following table is for state income tax. Corinna figured her tax to be \$47.38. According to the table, this means her taxable income is at least \$7225, but less than \$7250.

If Ohio taxable income (Line 5) is:

At Least	But less than	The tax liability is:
7,100	7,125	46.13
7,125	7,150	46.38
7,150	7,175	46.63
7,175	7,200	46.88
7,200	7,225	47.13
7,225	7,250	47.38
7,250	7,275	47.63
7,275	7,300	47.88
7,300	7,325	48.13
7,325	7,350	48.38
7,350	7,375	48.63

Let c stand for Corinna's taxable income. Then two inequalities, $c \geq 7225$ and $c < 7250$, describe her taxable income. The sentence, $c \geq 7225$ and $c < 7250$, is called a **compound sentence.** A compound sentence containing **and** is true only if both parts of it are true. A compound sentence containing **or** is true if at least one part of it is true.

≥ can mean at least.

≤ can mean at most.

Another way of writing $c \geq 7225$ and $c < 7250$ is as follows.

$$7225 \leq c < 7250$$

The sentence is read, "c is greater than or equal to 7225 *and* less than 7250." (Inequality sentences containing **or** *cannot* be combined in this way.)

example 1

Fred is paying \$48.38 in taxes. Write an inequality to describe his taxable income.

According to the table, Fred's taxable income is at least \$7325, but less than \$7350.

Let f stand for Fred's taxable income. Then Fred's taxable income can be described as follows.

$$7325 \leq f < 7350$$

Inequalities can be used to solve practical problems. You use the following procedure.

Problem Solving Procedure

1. Define a variable.
2. Write an inequality.
3. Solve the inequality.
4. Check the solution.
5. Answer the problem.

examples

2 **Cory has \$10 to spend on gasoline. Gasoline costs between 64¢ and 75¢ per gallon. How many gallons of gasoline can Cory buy?**

Define a variable. The problem asks for how many gallons of gasoline Cory can buy.
Let g stand for the number of gallons Cory can buy.

Write an inequality. \$10 = 1000¢

Least possible cost ≤ Cory's cost ≤ greatest possible cost.

$$64g \leq 1000 \leq 75g$$

The cost of gasoline equals the cost per gallon times the number of gallons.

Solve the inequality.

$64g \leq 1000$ AND $1000 \leq 75g$

$g \leq 15\frac{5}{8}$ AND $13\frac{1}{3} \leq g$

Check the solution. To check, choose several numbers between $13\frac{1}{3}$ and $15\frac{5}{8}$. Substitute those numbers, in turn, into the inequality.

Answer the problem. Cory can buy from $13\frac{1}{3}$ gallons to $15\frac{5}{8}$ gallons of gas. This can be written $13\frac{1}{3} \leq g \leq 15\frac{5}{8}$.

3 **The Clippers have won 24 baseball games and have lost 40 games. They have 60 more games to play. To win at least 50% of *all* their games, how many more games must they win?**

Define a variable. The problem asks for how many additional games the Clippers must win to win at least 50% of their games.
Let w stand for the number of additional games they must win.

Write an inequality.

$$\text{\% of games won} \geq 50\%$$

$$\frac{\text{number of games won}}{\text{number of games played}} \geq 50\%$$

$$\frac{24 + w}{24 + 40 + 60} \geq 0.50$$

Solve the inequality.	$\frac{24 + w}{24 + 40 + 60} \geq 0.50$
	$\frac{24 + w}{124} \geq 0.50$
	$24 + w \geq 62$
	$w \geq 38$
Check the solution.	To check, choose several numbers greater than 38. Substitute those numbers, in turn, into the inequality.
Answer the problem.	The Clippers must win at least 38 more games.

exercises

Max: 1–9, 1–13; **Avg:** 1–9, 1–9; **Min:** 1–9

Exploratory For each kind of plant, there is a combination of maximum and minimum temperatures beyond which the plant will *not* grow. Between these limits is a temperature at which growth is best. This is called the optimum temperature. The chart gives these temperatures for some crops.

GROWTH TEMPERATURES FOR TYPICAL CROPS (°F)

Crops	Maximum	Best	Minimum
Oats	88–99	77–88	32–41
Melons	111–122	88–99	59–64
Lettuce	85–100	50–85	34–40

1. $88 \leq$ max oat temp ≤ 99
2. $77 \leq$ best oat temp ≤ 88
3. $32 \leq$ min oat temp ≤ 41
4. $111 \leq x \leq 122$ 5. $88 \leq b \leq 99$
6. $59 \leq n \leq 64$ 7. $85 \leq x \leq 100$
8. $50 \leq b \leq 85$ 9. $34 \leq n \leq 40$

1–3. Write inequalities to describe the growth temperatures for oats.
4–6. Write inequalities to describe the growth temperatures for melons.
7–9. Write inequalities to describe the growth temperatures for lettuce.

Students should choose the variables.

Written Solve each problem.

1. A skating meet has 6 judges' scores which count. If a skater needs 33 points to win a medal, how many points on the average are needed from each judge?
   at least 5.5 points per judge
2. You have \$25 to buy tickets to a rock concert. The tickets cost \$6.00 apiece. What is the greatest number of tickets you can buy? 4
3. Edd owes Elaine \$525. How much money must he earn to have at least \$50 after paying Elaine? \$575
4. The 1970 census gives the population of Phoenix at 581,000 people. It was estimated that at least 1 million people live in the metropolitan area. How many people live in the metropolitan area, but *not* in Phoenix? at least 419,000 people

5. Eleanor has \$110.37 in her checking account. The bank does not charge for checks if \$50 or more is in the account. For how much can she make a check and not be charged? \$60.37 or less

6. How many 13¢ stamps can you buy for \$10? at most 76

7. Anna is running second in a gymnastics meet. The front runner has completed her routines and has collected 75.0 points. Anna now has 58.6 points. How many points must Anna score on her last routine, the free exercise, to exceed the front runner's score? more than 16.4 points

8. Karin has 56.2 points. How many points must Karin score to exceed the front runner's score? more than 18.8 points

9. There are 3 judges for each event. Karin's first two scores are 6.1 and 6.4. What does Karin need on her last score to exceed the front runner's total score? more than 6.3 points

10. One number is twice another number. Twice the lesser number increased by the greater number is at least 85. What is the *least* possible value for the lesser number? 21.25

11. Alan has \$11 to spend on gasoline. Where Alan lives, gasoline costs between 80¢ and 88¢ per gallon. How many gallons of gasoline can Alan buy? $12.5 \leq g \leq 13.75$

12. Joanne's softball team has won 11 games and has lost 8 games. They have 11 more games to play. To win at least 50% of *all* games, how many more games must they win? at least 4 games

13. Renata has 8 gallons of a 40% anti-freeze solution. How much 100% anti-freeze must be added to make a solution that is at least 60% anti-freeze? at least 4 gallons

1-8 Absolute Value Inequalities

Objective: To solve absolute value inequalities.

The absolute value of a number represents its distance from zero on the number line. You can use this idea to help solve absolute value inequalities.

examples

1 **Solve $|x| < 3$.**

You can translate $|x| < 3$ in the following way.

The distance between x and 0 is less than 3.

$$|x| \qquad < \qquad 3$$

To make $|x| < 3$ true, you must substitute values for x that are less than 3 units from 0.

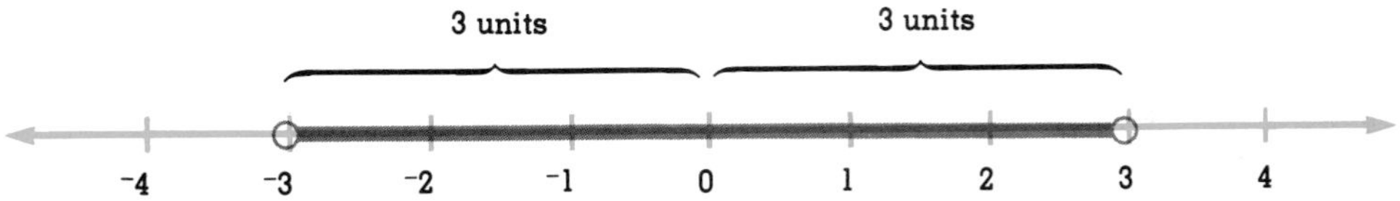

All the numbers between ${}^-3$ and 3 are less than three units from zero. The solution set is $\{x|{}^-3 < x < 3\}$.

2 **Solve $|2x - 5| > 9$.**

The inequality $|2x - 5| > 9$ says that $2x - 5$ is more than 9 units from 0.

If 2x − 5 is negative.	$2x - 5 < {}^-9$	or	$2x - 5 > 9$	*If 2x − 5 is positive or zero.*
	$2x < {}^-4$		$2x > 14$	
	$x < {}^-2$		$x > 7$	

Any number less than ${}^-2$ or any number greater than 7 will make the sentence true. The solution set is $\{x|x < {}^-2 \quad \text{or} \quad x > 7\}$.

Some absolute value inequalities have *no solutions*. For example, $|x| < {}^-7$ is *never* true. Since the absolute value of a number is always positive or zero, there is no replacement for x that will make the sentence true. The inequality $|x| < {}^-7$ has no solutions.

example 3

Solve $|4x - 9| + 6 < 2$.

$|4x - 9| + 6 < 2$
$|4x - 9| < {}^{-}4$

This sentence is *never true.*
The inequality has *no solutions.*
The solution set is $\emptyset$.

Some absolute value inequalities are *always true.* For example, $|x| > {}^{-}5$ is *always* true. Since the absolute value of a number is always positive or zero, any replacement for x will make the sentence true.

example 4

Solve $|10x + 3| + 5 > 0$.

$|10x + 3| + 5 > 0$
$|10x + 3| > {}^{-}5$

This sentence is always true.
The solutions are any real number. The solution set is the set of reals.

exercises

Max: 1–12, 1–32, 1, 2; **Avg:** 1–12, 1–31 odds; **Min:** 1–31 odds

Exploratory **Write an absolute value inequality for each sentence.**

1. All numbers between $^{-}3$ and 3. $|x| < 3$
2. All numbers less than 8 and greater than $^{-}8$. $|x| < 8$
3. All numbers greater than 6 or less than $^{-}6$. $|x| > 6$
4. All numbers less than or equal to 5, and greater than or equal to $^{-}5$. $|x| \leq 5$
5. $x > 3$ or $x < {}^{-}3$ $|x| > 3$
6. $x < 6$ and $x > {}^{-}6$ $|x| < 6$
7. $x \leq 4$ and $x \geq {}^{-}4$ $|x| \leq 4$
8. $x \geq 7$ or $x \leq {}^{-}7$ $|x| \geq 7$
9. ${}^{-}6 < x < 6$ $|x| < 6$
10. ${}^{-}3 < x < 3$ $|x| < 3$
11. $x > {}^{-}2$ and $x < 2$ $|x| < 2$
12. $x < 10$ and $x > {}^{-}10$ $|x| < 10$

Written **Solve each inequality.**

1. $|x| < 9$ $\{x|{}^{-}9 < x < 9\}$
2. $|x| \geq 2$ $\{x|x \geq 2 \text{ or } x \leq {}^{-}2\}$
3. $|x + 1| > 3$ $\{x|x > 2 \text{ or } x < {}^{-}4\}$
4. $|x + 1| \leq 3$ $\{x|{}^{-}4 \leq x \leq 2\}$

5. $|x - 4| \le 8$ $\{x|^{-}4 \le x \le 12\}$
6. $|3x| < 6$ $\{x|^{-}2 < x < 2\}$
7. $|7x| \ge 21$ $\{x|x \le {}^{-}3 \text{ or } x \ge 3\}$
8. $|x - 9| > 5$ $\{x|x < 4 \text{ or } x > 14\}$
9. $|x| > 7$ $\{x|x > 7 \text{ or } x < {}^{-}7\}$
10. $|5x| < 35$ $\{x|^{-}7 < x < 7\}$
11. $|2x| \le 26$ $\{x|^{-}13 \le x \le 13\}$
12. $|2x| \ge {}^{-}64$ all reals
13. $|3x| < {}^{-}15$ $\emptyset$
14. $|5x| < 15$ $\{x|^{-}3 < x < 3\}$
15. $|x + 3| > 17$ $\{x|x < {}^{-}20 \text{ or } x > 14\}$
16. $|x - 4| \le {}^{-}12$ $\emptyset$
17. $|x - 12| < 42$ $\{x|^{-}30 < x < 54\}$
18. $|x + 9| \ge 17$ $\{x|x \le {}^{-}26 \text{ or } x \ge 8\}$
19. $|2x - 9| \le 27$ $\{x|^{-}9 \le x \le 18\}$
20. $|3x + 11| > 1$ $\{x|x > -\frac{10}{3} \text{ or } x < {}^{-}4\}$
21. $|4x - 3| \ge 12$ $\{x|x \ge \frac{15}{4} \text{ or } x \le -\frac{9}{4}\}$
22. $|3x + 7| \le 26$ $\{x|^{-}11 \le x \le \frac{19}{3}\}$
23. $|5x + 7| < 81$ $\{x|^{-}17.6 < x < 14.8\}$
24. $|3x + 11| > 42$ $\{x|x > 10\frac{1}{3} \text{ or } x < {}^{-}17\frac{2}{3}\}$
25. $|6x + 25| + 14 < 6$ $\emptyset$
26. $6 + |3x| > 0$ all reals
27. $|2x - 5| \le 7$ $\{x|^{-}1 \le x \le 6\}$
28. $|4x| + 3 \le 0$ $\emptyset$
29. $|x| \le x$ $\{x|x \ge 0\}$
30. $|x| > x$ $\{x|x < 0\}$
31. $|x + 2| - x \ge 0$ all reals
32. $2 + |3 - 2x| > 0$ all reals

Challenge Solve each inequality.

1. $|x + 1| + |x - 1| \le 2$
   $\{x|^{-}1 \le x \le 1\}$
2. $|x + 3| + |x - 3| > 8$
   $\{x|x < {}^{-}4 \text{ or } x > 4\}$

Mathematics Contests

Excursions in Algebra

A number of mathematics contests are available to high school students. One of the best known contests is the Annual High School Mathematics Contest. Another contest is the U.S. Mathematical Olympiad which is patterned after the International Mathematical Olympiad.

Mathematics contests are organized in a number of different ways. The International Mathematical Olympiad, for example, lasts for two days. Each day, three problems are presented with four and one-half hours allowed to solve them. The problems are assigned points according to difficulty. Some contests provide short-answer questions with time limits like six minutes.

In one contest the following question appeared. The time limit for this question and another paired with it was 11 minutes. Eighty-six percent of the contestants answered the question correctly. Time yourself as you work the problem.

> A club found that it could achieve a membership ratio of 2 adults for each minor either by inducting 24 adults or by expelling x minors. Find x.

Answer: $x = 12$

Vocabulary

value (2)
exponent (2)
order of operations (2)
algebraic expressions (3)
formula (3)
commutative properties (6)
associative properties (6)
identity properties (7)
inverse properties (7)
distributive property (8)
properties of equality:
- reflexive (10)
- symmetric (10)
- transitive (10)
- substitution (10)
- addition and subtraction (11)
- multiplication and division (11)

absolute value (18)
trichotomy (21)
properties of inequalities:
- addition and subtraction (21)
- multiplication and division (22)

compound sentence (25)

Chapter Summary

1. Order of Operations: 1. Evaluate all powers. 2. Then do all multiplications and divisions from left to right. 3. Then do all additions and subtractions from left to right. (2)
2. Evaluate algebraic expressions by substituting a value for each variable (3)
3. In a formula, if you know replacements for every variable, except one, you can find a replacement for that variable. (3)
4. Properties of operations: (8)

For any numbers a, b, and c		
	Addition	Multiplication
Commutative	$a + b = b + a$	$a \cdot b = b \cdot a$
Associative	$(a + b) + c = a + (b + c)$	$(a \cdot b) \cdot c = a \cdot (b \cdot c)$
Identity	$a + 0 = a = 0 + a$	$a \cdot 1 = a = 1 \cdot a$
Inverse	$a + {}^{-}a = 0 = {}^{-}a + a$	If a is *not* zero, then $a \cdot \frac{1}{a} = 1 = \frac{1}{a} \cdot a$.
Distributive of multiplication over addition: $a(b + c) = ab + ac$ and $(b + c)a = ba + ca$		

5. Solving an equation means finding replacements for variables in the equation so that a true sentence results. Sentences with variables to be replaced are called open sentences. (10)

6. Properties of equality and inequality: (22)

For any numbers a, b, and c	
trichotomy:	$a < b$, or $a = b$, or $a > b$
Equality	
reflexive:	$a = a$
symmetric:	If $a = b$, then $b = a$.
transitive:	If $a = b$ and $b = c$, then $a = c$.
substitution:	If $a = b$, then a may be replaced by b.
addition and subtraction:	If $a = b$, then $a + c = b + c$, and $a - c = b - c$.
multiplication and division:	If $a = b$, then $a \cdot c = b \cdot c$, and if c is *not* zero, $\frac{a}{c} = \frac{b}{c}$.
Inequality	
addition and subtraction:	1. If $a > b$, then $a + c > b + c$ and $a - c > b - c$. 2. If $a < b$, then $a + c < b + c$ and $a - c < b - c$.
multiplication and division:	1. If $c > 0$ and $a < b$, then $ac < bc$ and $\frac{a}{c} < \frac{b}{c}$. 2. If $c > 0$ and $a > b$, then $ac > bc$ and $\frac{a}{c} > \frac{b}{c}$. 3. If $c < 0$ and $a < b$, then $ac > bc$ and $\frac{a}{c} > \frac{b}{c}$. 4. If $c < 0$ and $a > b$, then $ac < bc$ and $\frac{a}{c} < \frac{b}{c}$.

7. The absolute value of a number is the number of units it is from zero on the number line. For any number a, if a is positive or zero, then $|a| = a$. If a is negative, then $|a| = {}^{-}a$. (18)

8. Problem Solving Procedure for Equations and Inequalities:
   1. Define a variable. 2. Write an equation or inequality.
   3. Solve the equation or inequality. 4. Answer the problem.
   5. Check the solution. (26)

Chapter Review

1-1 Find the value of each expression.

1. $(4 + 6)^2 - 24 \div 3$ 92
2. $4 + 6^2 - 24 \div 3$ 32
3. $3 + 9^2 \times 3 \div 6 - 10$ 33.5
4. $(3 + 9)^2 \times 3 \div 6 - 10$ 62

Evaluate if $a = -\frac{1}{2}$, $b = 4$, $c = 5$, and $d = {}^-3$.

5. $\frac{6ac}{d}$ 5
6. $\frac{3ab}{cd}$ $\frac{2}{5}$
7. $\frac{4a + 3c}{3b}$ $\frac{13}{12}$
8. $\frac{3ab^2 - d^3}{a}$ $^-6$

1-2 State the property shown in each of the following.

9. $3 + (a + b) = (a + b) + 3$ commutative
10. $(3 + a) + b = 3 + (a + b)$ associative
11. $(a + b) + 0 = (a + b)$ additive identity
12. $(a + b) + {}^-(a + b) = 0$ additive inverse

Simplify.

13. $(9 + 48)7 + 3$ 402
14. $(27 - 24)8 - 9$ 15
15. $7p + 9q - 10p + 4q$ $13q - 3p$
16. $15r + 18s + 16r - 8s$ $31r + 10s$
17. $\frac{1}{3}(27 + 9x) + \frac{2}{3}(27 + 9x)$ $27 + 9x$
18. $(14y + 7z)\frac{1}{7} - (7z + 14y)\frac{2}{7}$ $^-z - 2y$

1-3 State the property shown in each of the following.

19. If $12 - 7 = 3 + 2$, then $3 + 2 = 12 - 7$ symmetric
20. $5x + 3y = 5x + 3y$ reflexive
21. $3r + (7 - 1)s = 3r + 6s$ substitution
22. If $12 - 7 = 10 - 5$ and $10 - 5 = 5$, then $12 - 7 = 5$. transitive

Find the value of each expression.

23. $(50 + 75) \div 25$ 5
24. $169 \div (28 - 15)$ 13
25. $[5(19 - 4) \div 3] - 4$ 21
26. $[(3^2 - 2^2)3 + 5] \div 4$ 5

Solve each equation.

27. $15x + 25 = 2(x - 4)$ $-\frac{33}{13}$
28. $3(6 - 4x) = 4x + 2$ 1
29. $\frac{3}{4}y + \frac{3}{4} = \frac{5}{2}$ $\frac{7}{3}$
30. $\frac{2}{7}a = \frac{16}{5}$ $\frac{56}{5}$

1-4 Solve each problem.

31. The width of a rectangle is 4 meters more than one-third its length. The perimeter is 64 meters. Find the length and width. width 11 m, length 21 m
32. A rectangle has a perimeter of 78 centimeters. The length of the rectangle is 13 centimeters greater than the width. How wide is the rectangle? 13 cm

33. To estimate when to harvest his snap bean crop, a South Carolina farmer counts heat units. As of May 1, he has counted 1022 heat units. There are usually 19 heat units per day in May. Snap beans require 1250 heat units to mature. The farmer can plan to harvest his crop in how many more days? 12 more days

34. Rockford and Chicago are 126 miles apart by train. An express train leaves Chicago at the same time a passenger train leaves Rockford. The express train travels 15 miles per hour faster than the passenger train. The two trains pass each other in 0.7 hours. How fast is each train traveling? passenger 82.5 mph
express 97.5 mph

1-5 Solve each open sentence.

35. $|2x - 37| = 15$ 11, 26

36. $|4x - 3| = {}^{-}27$ no solutions

37. $|p - 3| + 7 = 2$ no solutions

38. $8|2a - 3| = 64$ $^{-}2.5, 5.5$

1-6 Solve each inequality.

39. $8(2x - 1) > 11x + 31$ $\{x|x > \frac{39}{5}\}$

40. $5(8 - 2x) > 24 + 2x$ $\{x|x < \frac{4}{3}\}$

41. $3 - 4x \leq 6x + 5$ $\{x|x \geq -\frac{1}{5}\}$

42. $4(3x + 2) + 6 \geq 7x - 9$ $\{x|x \geq -\frac{23}{5}\}$

1-7 Solve each problem.

43. You have \$50 to buy tickets to a concert. The tickets cost \$8.00 apiece. What is the greatest number of tickets you can buy?
6 tickets

44. Jeremiah has \$256.98 in his checking account. The bank does not charge for checks if \$100 or more is in the account. For how much can he write a check and not be charged? no more than \$156.98

45. Tania has 10 gallons of a 50% anti-freeze solution. How much 100% anti-freeze must she add to make a solution that is at least 80% anti-freeze?
15 gallons

46. Roxie has \$4.80 to spend on gasoline. Where Roxie lives gasoline costs between \$0.96 and \$1.20 per gallon. How many gallons of gasoline can Roxie buy? from 4 to 5 gallons

1-8 Solve each inequality.

47. $7 + |9 - 2x| > 4$ all reals

48. $|6 + 7x| + 11 \leq 2$ $\emptyset$

49. $|2x + 5| \leq 4$ $\{x|-\frac{9}{2} \leq x \leq -\frac{1}{2}\}$

50. $|3x + 7| \geq 26$ $\{x|x \geq 6\frac{1}{3} \text{ or } x \leq {}^{-}11\}$

Chapter Test

State the property shown in each of the following.

1. $(5 \cdot r) \cdot s = 5 \cdot (r \cdot s)$ associative
2. $(5 \cdot r) \cdot s = s \cdot (5 \cdot r)$ commutative
3. $\left(4 \cdot \frac{1}{4}\right) \cdot 3 = \left(4 \cdot \frac{1}{4}\right) \cdot 3$ reflexive
4. $(6 - 2)a - 3b = 4a - 3b$ substitution
5. If $2(7) + 3 = 14 + 3$ and $14 + 3 = 17$, then $2(7) + 3 = 17$. transitive
6. If $(a + b)c = ac + bc$, then $ac + bc = (a + b)c$. symmetric

Find the value of each expression.

7. $(2 + 3)^3 - 4 \div 2$ 123
8. $[2 + 3^3 - 4] \div 2$ 12.5
9. $(2^5 - 2^3) + 2^3$ 32
10. $[5(19 - 4) \div 3] - 4^2$ 9

Evaluate if $a = {}^-9$, $b = \frac{2}{3}$, $c = 8$, and $d = {}^-6$.

11. $\frac{a}{b^2} + c$ $^-12.25$
12. $\frac{db + 4c}{a}$ $-\frac{28}{9}$
13. $2b(4a + d^2)$ 0
14. $\frac{4a + 3c}{3b}$ $^-6$

Solve each open sentence.

15. $2x - 7 - (x - 5) = 0$ 2
16. $5y - 3 = {}^-2y + 10$ $\frac{13}{7}$
17. $\frac{a}{4} + 3 = \frac{5}{2}$ $^-2$
18. $2 + 9x - 105 = {}^-x - 3$ 10
19. $5t + 7 = 5t + 3$ no solutions
20. $5r - (5 + 4r) = (3 + r) - 8$ all reals
21. $|5x + 10| - 3 = 0$ $-\frac{7}{5}, -\frac{13}{5}$
22. $|5x + 10| + 3 = 0$ no solutions
23. $|4x - 8| + x = 12$ $-\frac{4}{3}, 4$
24. $|4x - 5| + 4 = 7x + 8$ $\frac{1}{11}, {}^-3$
25. $4 > m + 1$ $\{m \mid m < 3\}$
26. $4p + 8 \geq 12$ $\{p \mid p \geq 1\}$
27. $3(2 + 3r) + r < 2(9 - r)$ $\{r \mid r < 1\}$
28. $7x - 9 < 3(4x + 2)$ $\{x \mid x > {}^-3\}$
29. $|5 + t| \leq 8$ $\{t \mid {}^-13 \leq t \leq 3\}$
30. $|9x - 4| + 8 > 4$ all reals

31. San Francisco and Los Angeles are 470 miles apart by train. An express train leaves San Francisco at the same time a passenger train leaves Los Angeles. The express train travels 10 miles per hour faster than the passenger train. If the passenger train travels 89 miles per hours, in how many hours will the trains pass each other? 2.5 hours

32. Gloria's softball team has won 13 games and lost 7 games. They have 12 more games to play. To win at least 50% of *all* games, how many more games must they win? 3 more games

Chapter

2

Linear Relations and Functions

Plants and animals can be classified according to various characteristics. Similarly, relations and functions can be classified according to their characteristics.

2-1 The Coordinate Plane

Objective: To graph on the number line and coordinate plane.

Unless stated otherwise, the word numbers means real numbers.

The graph of all real numbers is the entire number line.

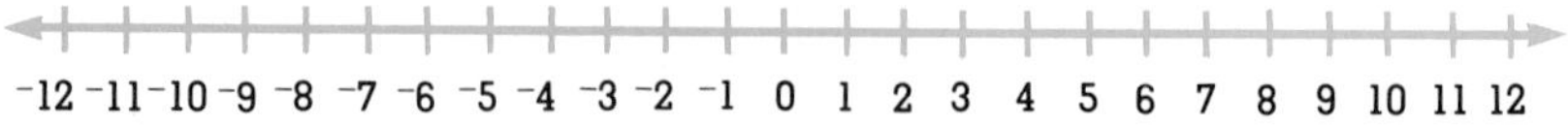

Points on the Number Line

Each real number corresponds to exactly one point on a number line. Each point on a number line corresponds to exactly one real number.

examples

1 Graph {⁻1, ⁻0.3, 0.5, 3, 5}.

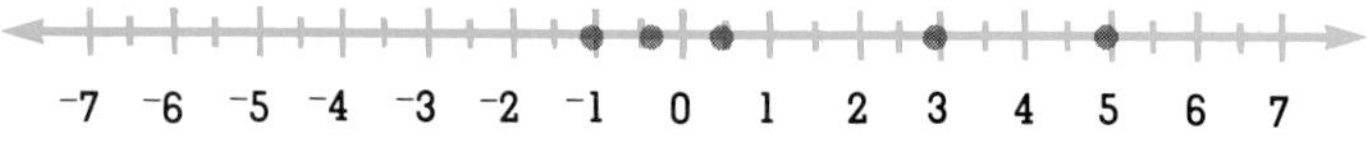

2 Graph the integers.

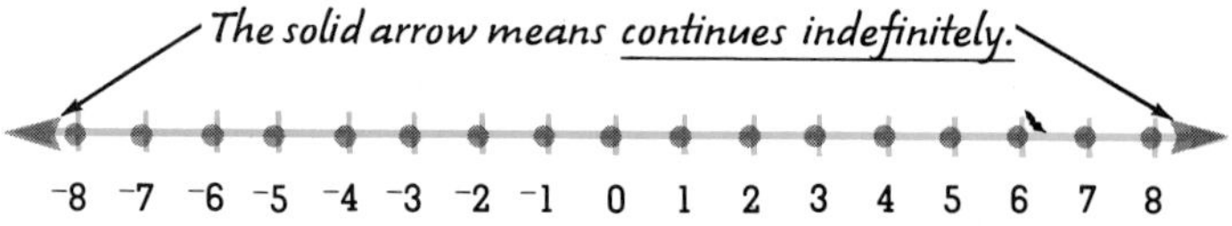

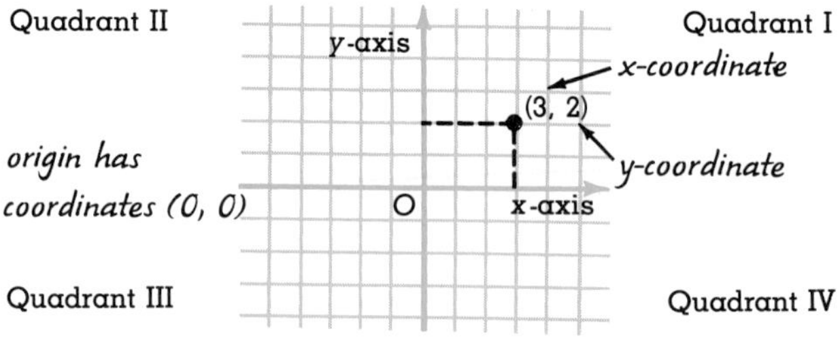

The graph of all **ordered pairs** of real numbers is the entire plane.

Two perpendicular number lines separate the plane into four parts, called **quadrants.** The horizontal number line usually is called the **x-axis.** The vertical number line usually is called the ***y*-axis.**

When a system of axes is set up on a plane, the plane is called a coordinate plane.

The numbers assigned to a point in a coordinate plane are called the coordinates of the point.

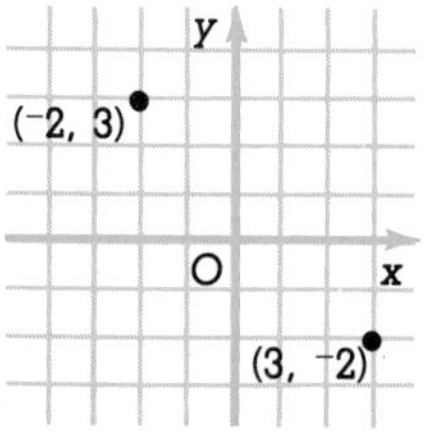

You represent a point in a plane by an ordered pair. This means the coordinates are in a particular order. For example, (⁻2, 3) and (3, ⁻2) do *not* represent the same point.

Points in the Plane

Each point in a coordinate plane corresponds to exactly one ordered pair of numbers. Each ordered pair of numbers corresponds to exactly one point in a coordinate plane.

The graph of an open sentence is the graph of the solution of that open sentence.

You can use the number line to graph the solutions of open sentences in one variable.

examples

3 **Graph 7x = 42.**

$7x = 42$
$x = 6$

4 **Graph 2*t* − 9 < 21.**

$2t - 9 < 21$
$2t < 30$
$t < 15$

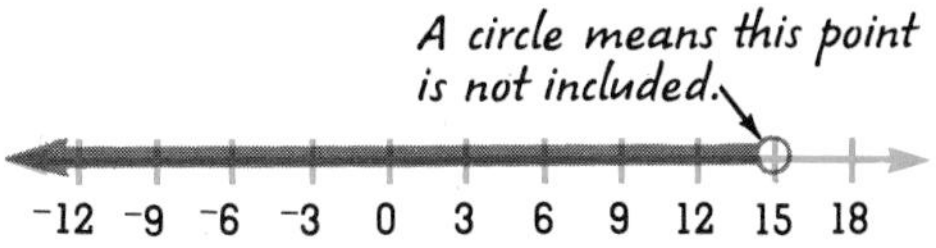

5 **Graph ⁻3 ≤ x < 7.**

$^-3 \le x$ or $x < 7$

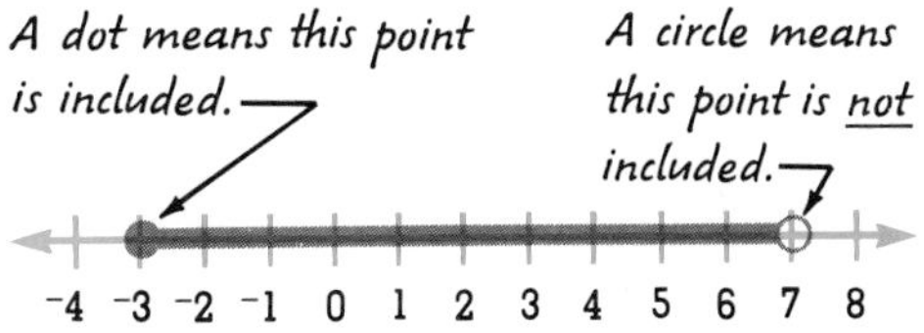

You can write the solutions to open sentences in two variables as sets of ordered pairs. These solutions can be graphed in the coordinate plane. The following graph represents the solution to $y = 3x$.

An infinite number of ordered pairs will satisfy $y = 3x$. The graph of these ordered pairs is a straight line.

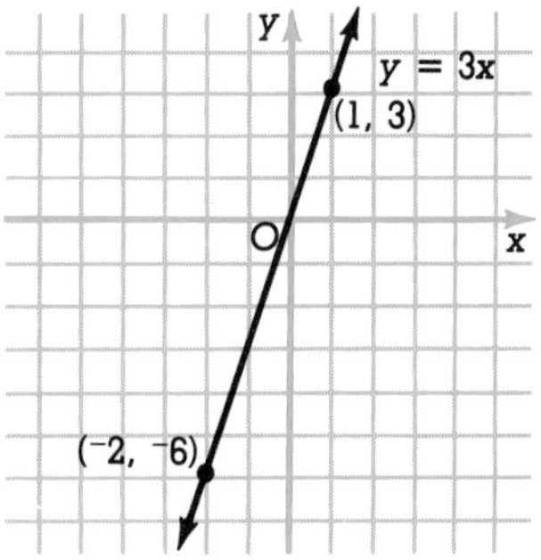

When variables other than x and y are used, assume that the letter coming first in the alphabet represents the horizontal coordinate.

exercises

Max: 1–22, 1–40; **Avg:** 1–22, 1–39 odds; **Min:** 1–39 odds

Exploratory **Graph each set on the real number line.**

1. $\{^-4, -\frac{1}{2}, 0, 6, 7\frac{2}{3}\}$
2. $\{^-3, 0, 3\}$
3. $\{^-8.2\}$
4. $\{14.1, 10\}$
5. {all even numbers}
6. $\{3, 6, 9, 12, 15, \ldots\}$
7. $\{^-1, ^-2, ^-3, ^-4, \ldots\}$
8. {all real numbers}
9. {all odd numbers}

For answers to problems **1–9** and **15–22**, see the Teacher's Guide.

In which quadrant will (x, y) lie given the following conditions?

10. x is positive and y is positive I
11. x is positive and y is negative IV
12. x is negative and y is negative III
13. x is negative and y is positive II
14. x is negative and y is 0 none

Graph each ordered pair.

15. (7, 4)
16. ($^-7$, 4)
17. (7, $^-4$)
18. ($^-7$, $^-4$)
19. (2.5, 0)
20. (0, 2.5)
21. (1.5, 3)
22. (3, 1.5)

For answers to problems **1–12**, see the Teacher's Guide.

Written **Graph each set on the number line.**

1. $\{7.7\}$
2. $\{6\}$
3. $\{2, 3\}$
4. $\left\{-\frac{3}{5}\right\}$
5. $\{x|x > {}^-3\}$
6. $\{a|a \leq 0\}$
7. $\{p|p \geq 4\frac{1}{2}\}$
8. $\{x|x < {}^-7.5\}$
9. $\{s|{}^-4 \leq s < 2\}$
10. $\{r|r > 6 \text{ or } r < 1\}$
11. $\{q|q < {}^-2.5 \text{ or } q \geq 2.5\}$
12. $\{t|{}^-0.04 \leq t \leq 0.04\}$

Graph each open sentence on the number line. For graphs to problems **13–40**, see the Teacher's Guide.

13. $\frac{2}{3}m = 26$ 39
14. $\frac{1}{4}s - 1 = \frac{3}{4}$ 7
15. $4t = t - 27$ $^-9$
16. $2k + 7 = k + 7$ 0
17. $3x - 2 = 2x - 2$ 0
18. $12q - 24 = 45 + 9q$ 23
19. $a + 5 = 5(a + 5)$ $^-5$
20. $3(u - 2) + 1 = u + 7$ 6
21. $2(x + 1) - 3 = 8 - x$ 3
22. $2(3p - 4) + 5 = 2p - 11$ $^-2$
23. $\frac{1}{2}(y + 1) = 3$ 5
24. $\frac{1}{3}(x - 3) = 5$ 18
25. $3w - (10 - w) = w + 2$ 4
26. $3(n - 3) - n = n + 1$ 10
27. $|v - 1| + 2 = 4$ 3, $^-1$
28. $|3e + 7| + 6 = 1$ no solutions
29. $|x| = x$ $\{x|x \geq 0\}$
30. $\left|\frac{x}{3} + 2\right| = 3$ 3, $^-15$
31. $2(x - 6) > 3(x + 2)$ $\{x|x < {}^-18\}$
32. $50(c - 3) \geq 25 + 15c$ $\{c|c \geq 5\}$
33. $5(r - 3) \leq 6(r - 3)$ $\{r|r \geq 3\}$
34. $y - 5 > 3(y - 9)$ $\{y|y < 11\}$
35. $2(1 + 2b) > 5b - (3 - 2b)$ $\{b|b < \frac{5}{3}\}$
36. $(x + 1) + 2(3 - 2x) \leq 3(2 + x) - 5$ $\{x|x \geq 1\}$
37. $6(1 - x) - 4(2 - x) \leq x + 7$ $\{x|x \geq {}^-3\}$
38. $5(w - 1) - (2w + 1) < 5(w + 2)$ $\{w|w > {}^-8\}$
39. $5 \geq |2r + 3|$ $\{r|{}^-4 \leq r \leq 1\}$
40. $1 - |h + 3| < 5$ all reals

2-2 Relations and Functions

Objective: To learn about relations and functions.

Year	Kilowatt Hours
1950	330
1955	550
1960	750
1965	1050
1970	1500
1972	1750
1974	1820

The amount of electricity used in recent years in the U.S. can be written as a set of ordered pairs. The first coordinate represents year and the second coordinate represents billion kilowatt hours.

{1950, 330), (1955, 550), (1960, 750), (1965, 1050), (1970, 1500), (1972, 1750), (1974, 1820)}

A set of ordered pairs is called a **relation.** The set of first coordinates, in this case years, is called the **domain** of the relation. The set of second coordinates, billion kilowatt hours, is called the **range** of the relation.

The use of mappings helps students visualize domain and range.

A relation is a set of ordered pairs. The domain is the set of all first coordinates of the ordered pairs. The range is the set of all second coordinates of the ordered pairs.

Definition of Relation, Domain, and Range

example 1

State a relation shown by the graph. Then state the domain and range of the relation.

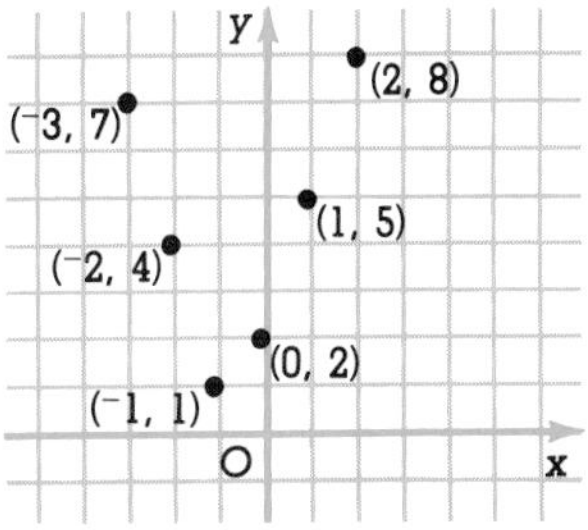

The relation is
{(⁻3, 7), (⁻2, 4), (⁻1, 1), (0, 2), (1, 5), (2, 8)}.

The domain is {⁻3, ⁻2, ⁻1, 0, 1, 2}.

The range is {7, 4, 1, 2, 5, 8}.

The graph on the left shows how the cost of operating an appliance is related to the amount of electricity it uses. The graph on the right shows the amount of electricity various appliances use.

COST OF ELECTRICITY

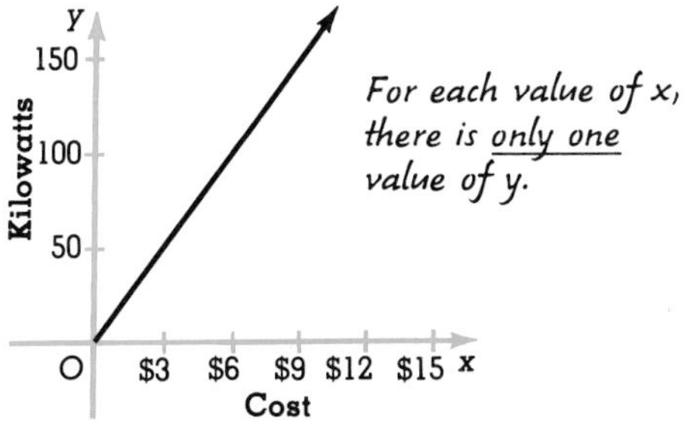

CONSUMPTION OF ELECTRICITY

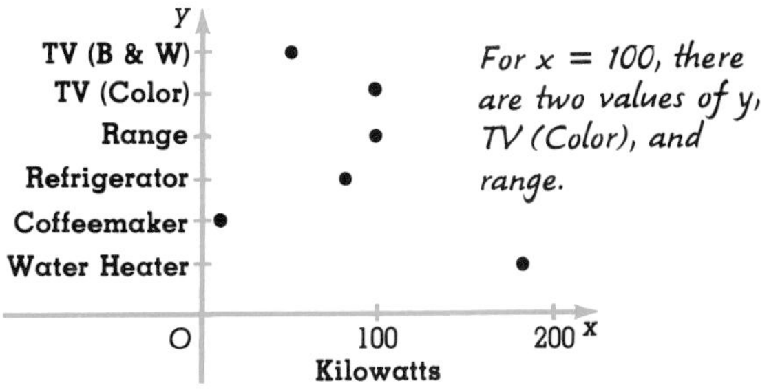

The first graph shows a special type of relation called a **function.**

Definition of Function

A function is a relation in which each element of the domain is paired with exactly one element of the range.

examples

2 **Is {(2, 3), (3, $^-4$), (4, 1), (1, 3)} a function?**

This relation is a function since each element of the domain is paired with exactly one element of the range.

3 **Is {(4, 4), ($^-2$, 3), (4, 2), (3, 4), (1, 1)} a function?**

This relation is *not* a function. The element 4 of the domain is paired with two different elements of the range, 4 and 2.

4 **Does $y = 4x$ represent a function?**

You could make a table of values. But suppose you try just one value of x. Substitute 3 for x. What is the corresponding value of y? Is there more than one value for y? When x is 3, y is 12. There is only one value for y. If you try other values of x you will see that they are always paired with exactly one value of y. The equation $y = 4x$ does represent a function.

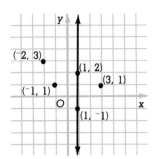

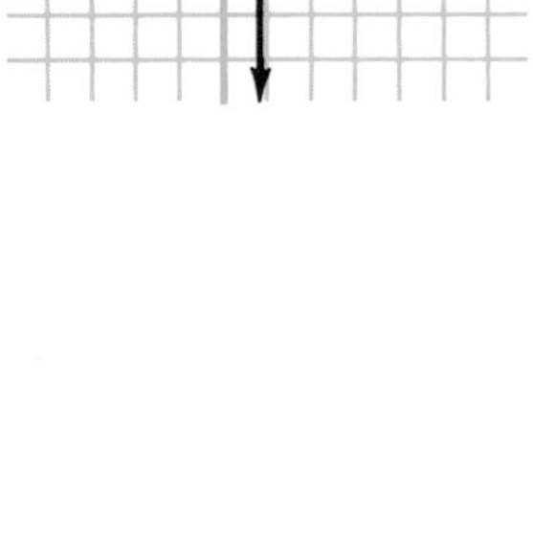

The graph on the left represents the following relation.

{($^-2$, 3), ($^-1$, 1), (1, 2), (1, $^-1$), (3, 1)}

Emphasize that all functions are relations, but *not* all relations are functions.

Suppose you drew a vertical line through each point on the graph. The vertical line through (1, 2) would also pass through (1, $^-1$). This shows that the relation is *not* a function. There are two elements of the range, 2 and $^-1$, that pair with the domain element 1.

Vertical Line Test for a Function

If any vertical line drawn on the graph of a relation passes through no more than one point of that graph, then the relation is a function.

example 5

Use the vertical line test to determine if the relation graphed is a function.

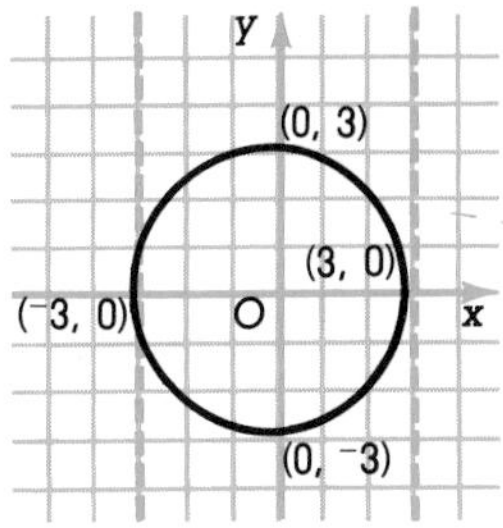

A vertical line will pass through two points of the graph except at (3, 0) and $(^-3, 0)$. Therefore, the graph does *not* represent a function.

Equations that represent functions often are written in a special way. The equation $y = 2x + 1$ can be written $f(x) = 2x + 1$. If 3 is an element of the domain of the function, then $f(3)$ is the corresponding element of the range. To show that the value of $f(3)$ is 7, you write $f(3) = 7$.

You can use letters other than f to represent a function. For example, the equation $y = 4x + 3$ can be written $g(x) = 4x + 3$.

example 6

Find $f(15)$ if $f(x) = 100x - 5x^2$.

$$
\begin{aligned}
f(x) &= 100x - 5x^2 \\
f(15) &= 100(15) - 5(15)^2 \quad \textit{Substitute 15 for x.} \\
&= 1500 - 5(225) \\
&= 1500 - 1125 \\
&= 375
\end{aligned}
$$

Often we give only the equation for a function without naming the domain. In this book, we mean the domain is all real numbers for which the corresponding range values are also real numbers.

For answers to problems 1–18, see the Teacher's Guide.

exercises

Max: 1–36, 1–33; **Avg:** 1–36, 1–33 odd; **Min:** 1–33 odds

Exploratory State the domain and range of each relation.

1. {(5, 1), (0, 4), (2, 1)}
2. $\{(8, 2), (^-3, 3), (8, 3), (3, 3)\}$
3. {(4, 4), (1, 1), (3, 3)}
4. {(6, 4)}
5. {(2, 1), (2, 3), (2, 7), (2, 4)}
6. {(1, 3), (5, 3), (3, 3)}
7. $\{(4, 3), (8, ^-2), (^-17, 4), (^-17, 8)\}$
8. {(1, 5), (5, 1)}
9. {(8, 8), (2, 2)}
10. $\{(0, 4), (2, 4), (1, 4), (^-3, 4)\}$
11. $\{(^-3, ^-3), (^-2, ^-2), (2, 2), (4, 4)\}$
12. $\{(^-3, 3), (^-2, 2), (2, ^-2), (4, ^-4)\}$

13. $\{(8, 6)\}$

14. $\{(^-3, 3), (^-3, 2), (^-3, ^-2), (^-3, ^-4)\}$

15. $\{(5, ^-3), (^-3, 5)\}$

16. $\{(^-3, 3), (^-2, 3), (2, 3), (4, 3)\}$

17. $\{(0, 0)\}$

18. $\left\{\left(3, \frac{2}{3}\right), \left(\frac{3}{4}, ^-2\right), (8, 4), (6, ^-2)\right\}$

19–36. State whether or not each relation in problems **1–18** is a function. Write *yes* or *no*. 20, 23, 25, 32 no; all others are yes

Written **State a relation shown by the graph. Then state the domain and range of the relation.** See Teacher's Guide for answers to problems 1 and 2.

1.

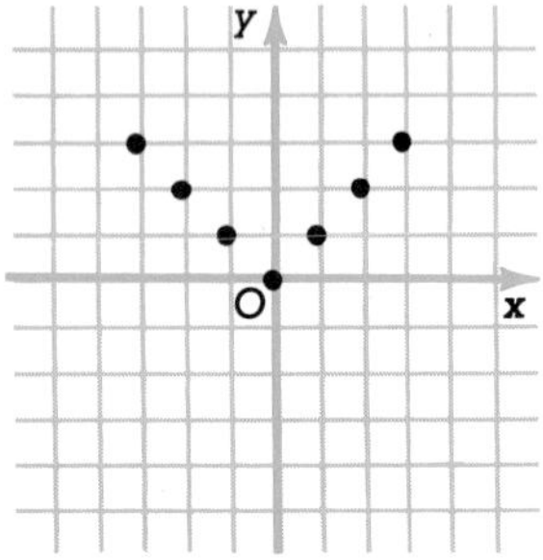

2.

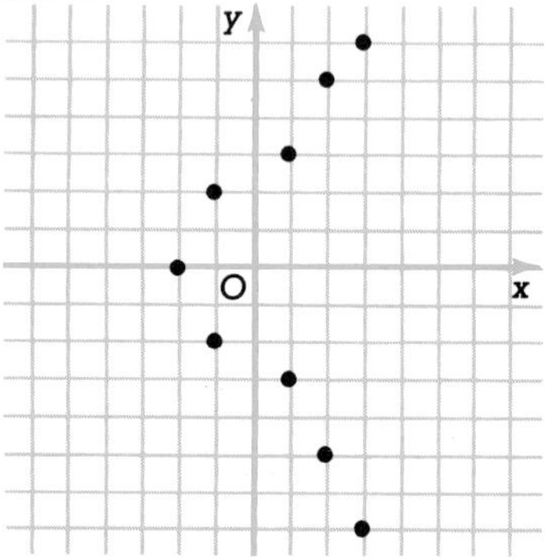

3–4. State whether the relations in problems **1** and **2** are functions. Write *yes* or *no*.
3. yes **4.** no

Use the vertical line test to determine if each relation is a function. Write *yes* or *no*.

5. yes

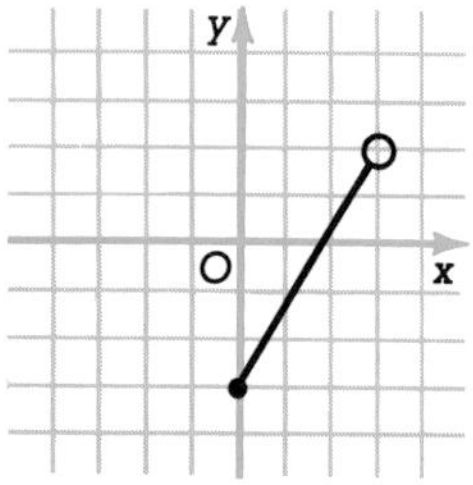

6. yes

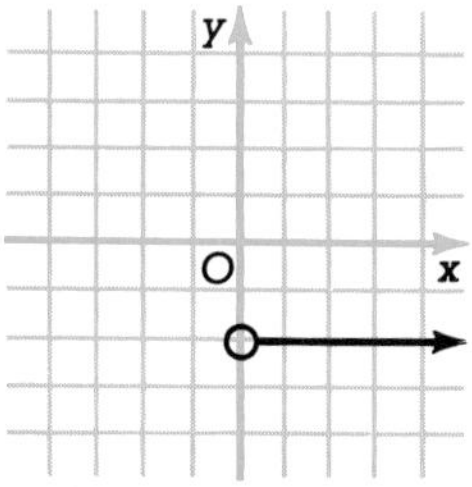

7. no

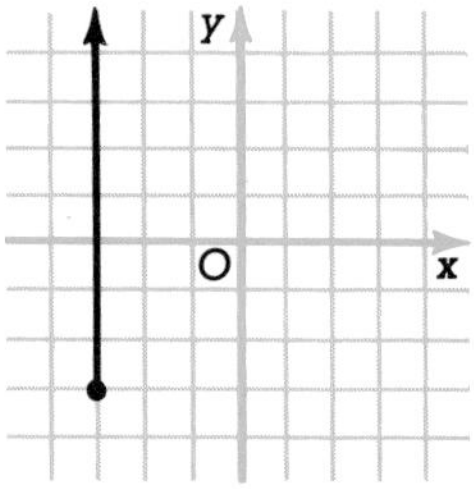

8. no

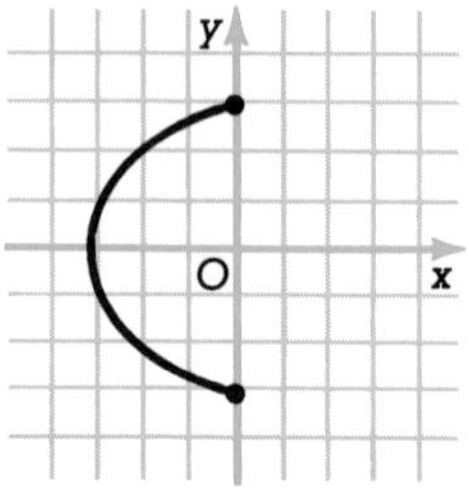

9. no

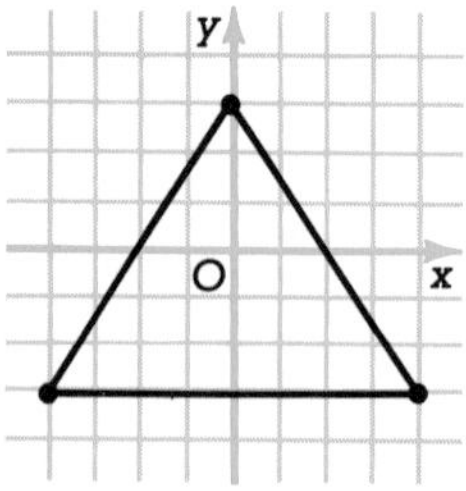

10. yes

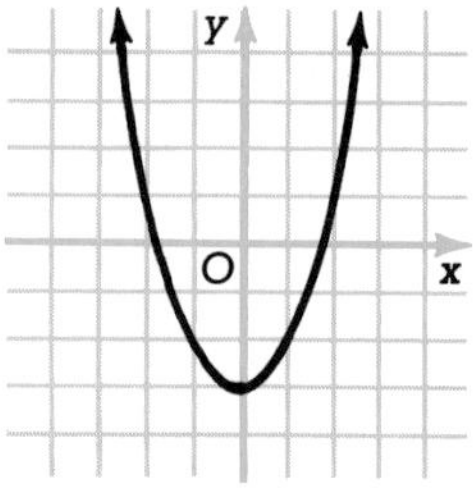

11. no

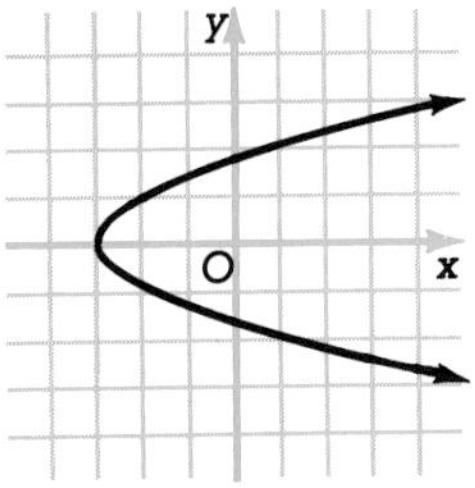

12. yes

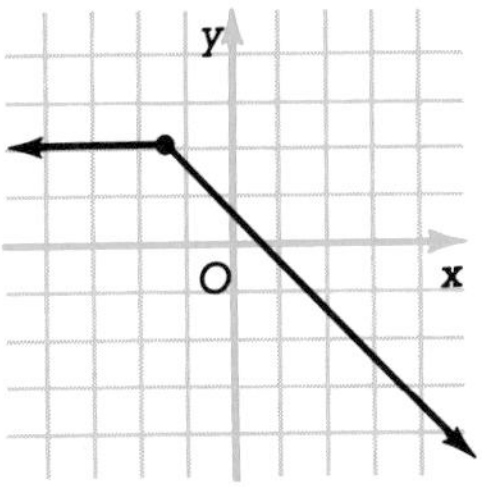

13. yes

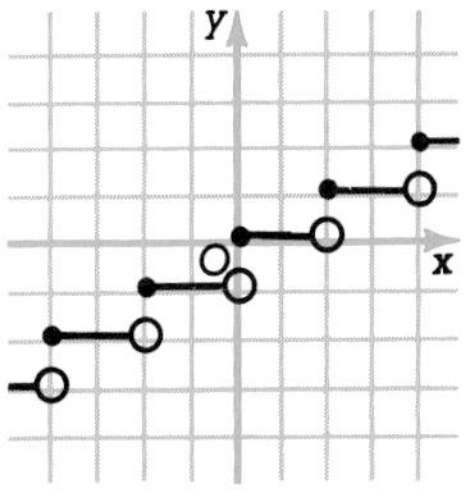

Given $f(x) = \dfrac{7}{x - 2}$, find each value.

14. $f(12)$ $\frac{7}{10}$

15. $f(3)$ 7

16. $f(^{-}1)$ $-\frac{7}{3}$

17. $f(5.5)$ 2

18. $f\left(\frac{1}{2}\right)$ $-\frac{14}{3}$

19. $f\left(\frac{2}{3}\right)$ $-\frac{21}{4}$

20. $f(^{-}5)$ $^{-}1$

21. $f(4)$ $\frac{7}{2}$

22. $f(a)$ $7/(a - z)$

23. $f(u + 2)$ $7/u$

Given $g(x) = 4x^3 + 2x^2 + x - 7$, find each value.

24. $g(0)$ $^{-}7$

25. $g(1)$ 0

26. $g(2)$ 35

27. $g(^{-}4)$ $^{-}235$

28. $g(5)$ 548

29. $g(^{-}2)$ $^{-}33$

30. $g\left(-\frac{1}{2}\right)$ $^{-}7.5$

31. $g\left(\frac{1}{2}\right)$ $^{-}5\frac{1}{2}$

32. $g(t)$ $4t^3 + 2t^2 + t - 7$

33. $g(s)$ $4s^3 + 2s^2 + s - 7$

Sets of Numbers

Excursions in Algebra

Some important sets of numbers are listed below.

The set of natural or counting numbers, **N**
N = {1, 2, 3, 4, 5, . . .}

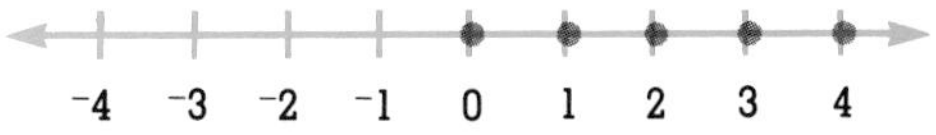

The set of integers, **Z**
Z = {. . . , $^{-}2$, $^{-}1$, 0, 1, 2, . . .}

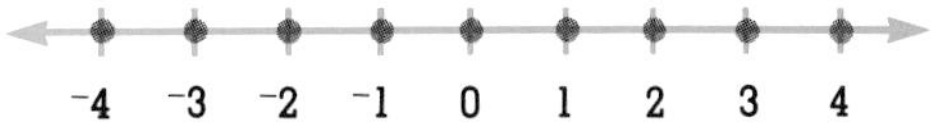

The set of rational numbers, **Q**

$$\mathbf{Q} = \left\{\frac{m}{n},\ m \text{ and } n \text{ are integers and } n \text{ is } \textit{not} \text{ zero}\right\}$$

= {all terminating and repeating decimals}

Numbers like $-\frac{2}{3}$, 1.1, 2, and 0 are rational.

Suggest that students try to make a number line graph of the rational numbers.

The set of irrational numbers, **I**
I = {all nonterminating, nonrepeating decimals}

Numbers like $\sqrt{2}$ and π are irrational.

The set of all real numbers, **R**
R = {all decimals}

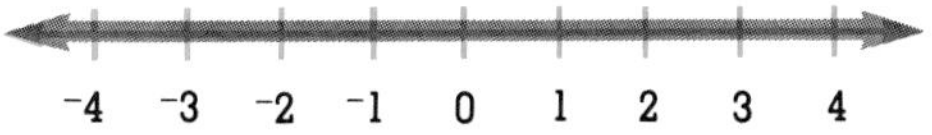

Taken together, the sets of rational and irrational numbers make up the real numbers.

2-3 Linear Functions

Objective: To graph linear equations in two variables.

An equation whose graph is a straight line is called a **linear equation** in two variables.

Definition of Linear Equation in Two Variables

A linear equation in two variables is an equation in two variables that may be written in the form $ax + by = c$ where a, b, and c are real numbers, and a and b are *not both* zero.

The form $ax + by = c$ is called the standard form of a linear equation in two variables.

In a linear equation in two variables each term is a constant, like 7, or a constant times a variable, like $7x$. Thus, $4x + 3y = 7$, $2x = 8 + y$, $5m - n = 1$, and $y = 7$ are linear equations in two variables. But $3x + y^2 = 7$ and $\frac{1}{x} + y = 4$ are *not*. Note that $0x + 1y = 7$.

Since two points determine a line, you need only two points to graph a linear equation in two variables. In checking your work it is helpful to use a third point.

example 1

Graph $2a = 3b - 4$.

First, rewrite the equation in standard form.

$$2a - 3b = {}^-4$$

Since the equation can be written in standard form, it is a linear equation in two variables and has a straight line graph.

Transform the equation so a is on one side.

$$a = \frac{3}{2}b - 2$$

Next find three ordered pairs that satisfy the equation. Use a table of values for a and b.

Then, plot the ordered pairs and connect them with a line.

b	a	(a, b)
0	$^-2$	$(^-2, 0)$
2	1	(1, 2)
4	4	(4, 4)

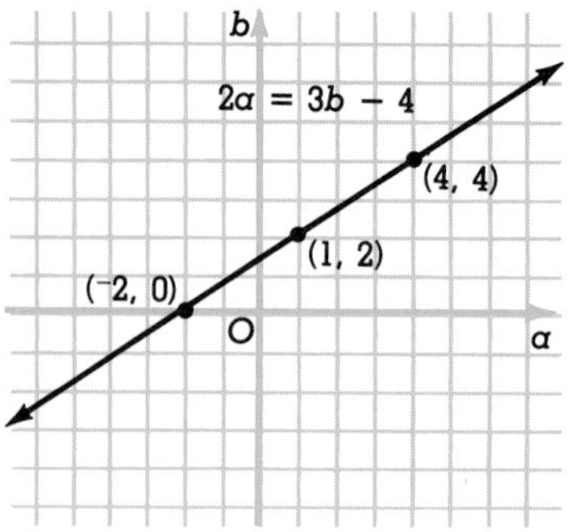

Not all linear equations in two variables represent functions.

example 2

Graph $x = 3$ and use the vertical line test to determine if it represents a function.

No matter what value of y you choose, the value of x paired with it is 3. Thus, (3, 0), (3, 2), and (3, 6) are all points on the line.

The graph is a vertical line. Any vertical line drawn on the graph of the equation passes through every point of that graph. The relation is *not* a function.

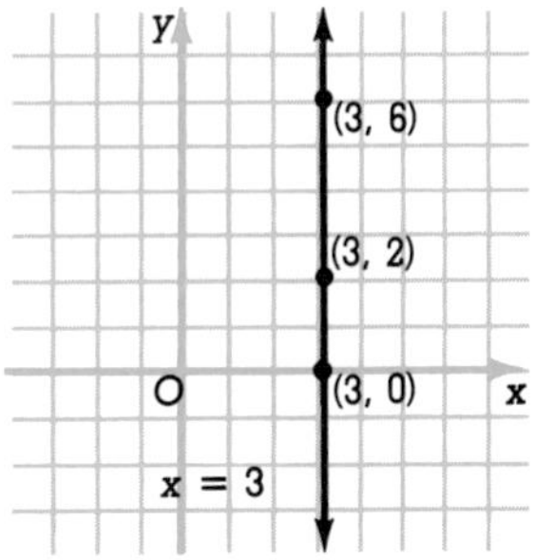

Any function whose ordered pairs satisfy a linear equation in two variables is called a **linear function.**

Definition of Linear Function

A linear function can be defined by $f(x) = mx + b$ where m and b are real numbers.

In the definition of a linear function, m and b may be zero.

If $m = 0$, then $f(x) = b$. The graph is a horizontal line. This function is also called a **constant function.**

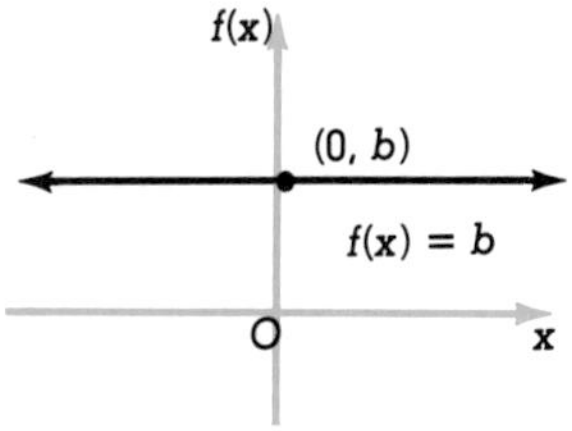

If $b = 0$, then $f(x) = mx$. The graph passes through the origin.

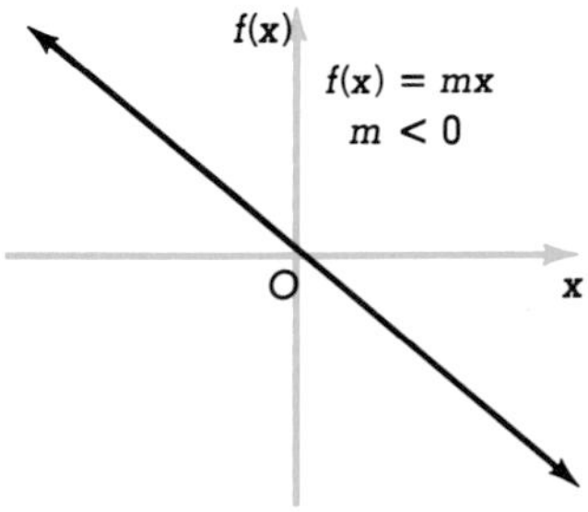

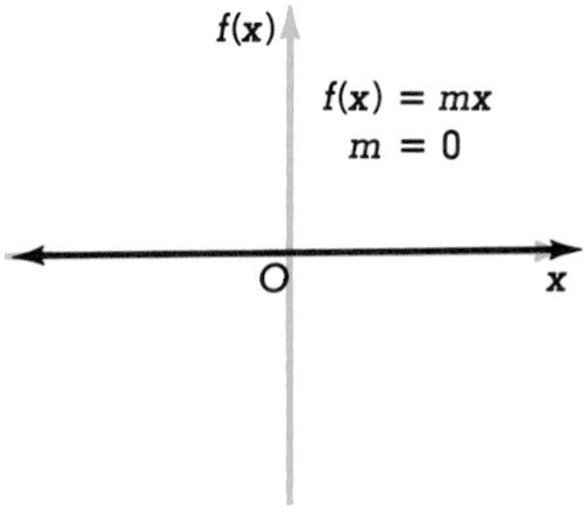

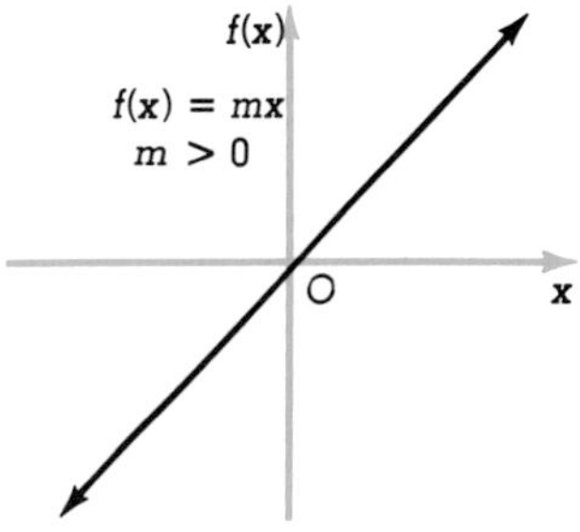

exercises

Max: 1–12, 1–20; Avg: 1–12, 1–19 odds; Min: 1–19 odds

Exploratory State whether or not each equation is a linear equation. Write *yes* or *no*.

1. $x^2 + y^2 = 7$ no
2. $x + y = 4$ yes
3. $x - 3 = 8$ yes
4. $x^2 = 9$ no
5. $x - 2y = 5$ yes
6. $a + 3b = 7$ yes
7. $5m^2 = n^2$ no
8. $y = {}^-4x$ yes
9. $7 = 2y$ yes
10. $5x - y^2 = 3$ no
11. $x + 5 = 2y$ yes
12. $7 - 6y = 24$ yes

For answers to problems 1–20, see the Teacher's Guide.

Written Graph each equation.

1. $y = x$
2. $y = x + 1$
3. $y = 2x$
4. $y = 2x + 1$
5. $y = 3x$
6. $y = 3x + 1$
7. $y = {}^-2x$
8. $y = x + 3$
9. $y = \frac{1}{3}x$
10. $y = \frac{1}{2}x$
11. $y = -\frac{1}{2}x$
12. $y = -\frac{1}{3}x$
13. $y = 2x + 3$
14. $y = x - 3$
15. $y = 3x + 3$
16. $y = {}^-3x$
17. $y = 2x - 3$
18. $y = 3x - 3$
19. $y = {}^-2x + 2$
20. $y = {}^-x - 7$

Excursions in Algebra

History

René Descartes (1596–1650) was a French mathematician and philosopher. He is credited with the invention of a branch of mathematics called analytic geometry. Analytic geometry is a combination of ideas from algebra and geometry. Analytic geometry uses the following.

1. The coordinate plane
2. Each point in a coordinate plane corresponds to exactly one ordered pair of numbers, and vice versa.
3. Graphs of expressions like $f(x) = 2x + 1$

Descartes, in 1637, became the first mathematician to put the three steps together.

Sometimes, ordered pairs are referred to as Cartesian coordinates. The word Cartesian is taken from the name Descartes.

2-4 Slopes and Intercepts

Objective: To determine the slope and intercepts of a line.

The following graph shows the line described by $f(x) = 4x$.

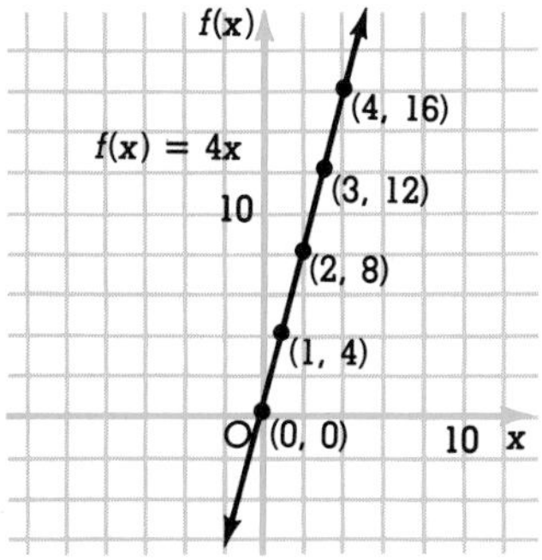

x	4x
0	0
1	4
2	8
3	12
4	16

+1 +1 +1 +1 (x); +4 +4 +4 +4 (4x)

Notice that the y-coordinates increase 4 units for each 1 unit increase in the corresponding x-coordinates. You can use a ratio to show how the change in y-coordinates compares to the change in corresponding x-coordinates.

$$\frac{\text{change in } y\text{-coordinates}}{\text{change in corresponding } x\text{-coordinates}} = \frac{4}{1} \text{ or } 4$$

This ratio is called the *slope* of the line. The slope of a line is a measure of its steepness. Notice that the slope of the line described by $f(x) = 4x$ is given by the coefficient of x.

The slope of a line described by $f(x) = mx + b$ is m. Slope is also given by the following equation.

$$\text{slope} = \frac{\text{change in } y\text{-coordinates}}{\text{change in corresponding } x\text{-coordinates}}$$

Definition of Slope

example 1

Determine the slope of the line that passes through $(0, {}^-5)$ and $(1, {}^-3)$.

$$\text{slope} = \frac{\text{change in } y\text{-coordinates}}{\text{change in corresponding } x\text{-coordinates}}$$

$$= \frac{{}^-5 - {}^-3}{0 - 1}$$

$$= \frac{{}^-2}{{}^-1}$$

$= 2$ The slope of the line is 2.

The slope of the line that passes through (a, b) and (c, d) is given by the following equation.

$$\text{slope} = \frac{b - d}{a - c}$$

Think of a line as running from left to right.

If the line rises to the right, then the slope is positive.

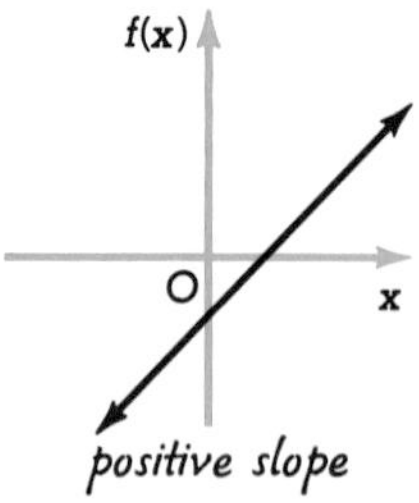

If the line is horizontal, then the slope is zero.

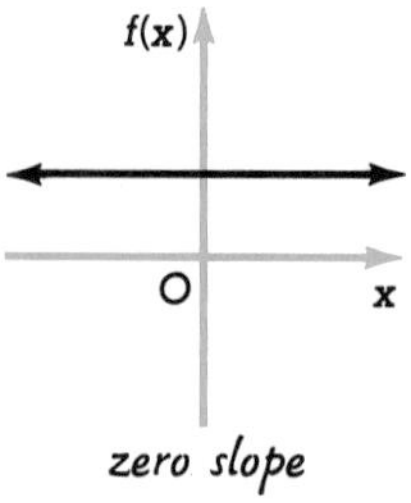

If the line falls to the right, then the slope is negative.

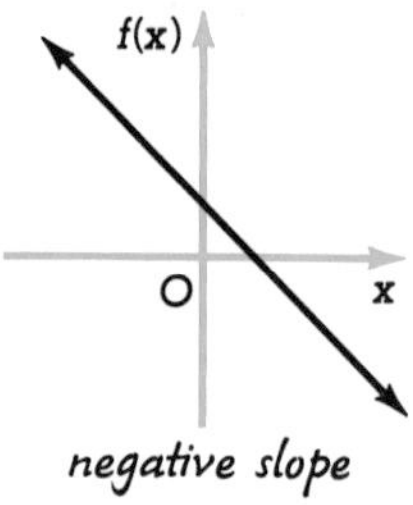

If the line is vertical, then the slope is *undefined*.

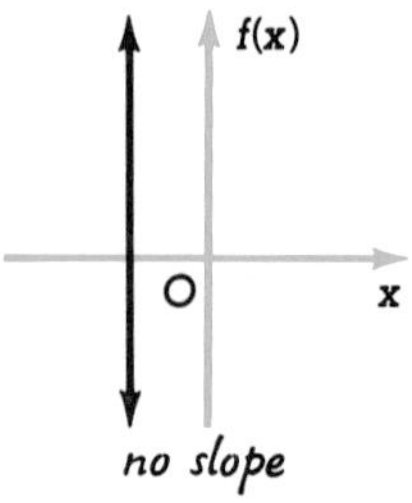

The graphs of $f(x) = 3x + 2$, $g(x) = 3x$, and $h(x) = 3x - 5$ are lines with the same slope. But, these lines do *not* pass through the same points.

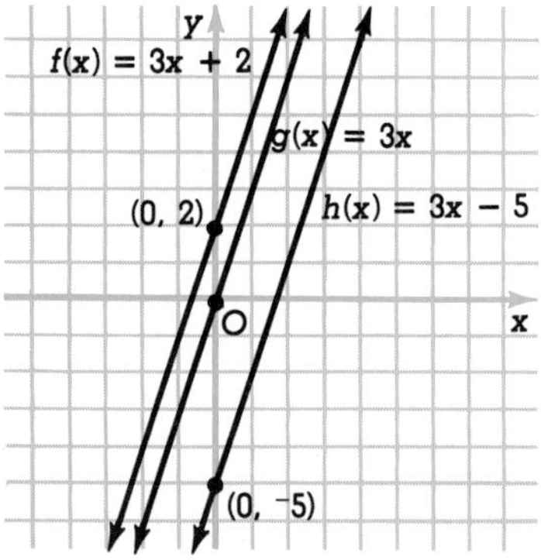

The slope of each line is 3.

Consider the points where each line crosses the y-axis.

The x-coordinate of each point is 0.

$f(x) = 3x + 2$	crosses at (0, 2)
$g(x) = 3x$	crosses at (0, 0)
$h(x) = 3x - 5$	crosses at (0, $^-5$)

The values of the functions at these points are called the **y-intercepts** of the lines. The y-intercept is the value of the function when x is 0.

$f(x) = 3x + 2$	has y-intercept 2
$g(x) = 3x$	has y-intercept 0
$h(x) = 3x - 5$	has y-intercept $^-5$

The **x-intercept** of a line is the value of x when y is zero. What are the x-intercepts of the lines described above? $f(x)$, $-\frac{2}{3}$; $g(x)$, 0; $h(x)$, $\frac{5}{3}$

exercises

Max: 1–13, 1–28; Avg: 1–13, 1–27 odds; Min: 1–27 odds

Exploratory State the slope, y-intercept, and x-intercept for each graph.

1. 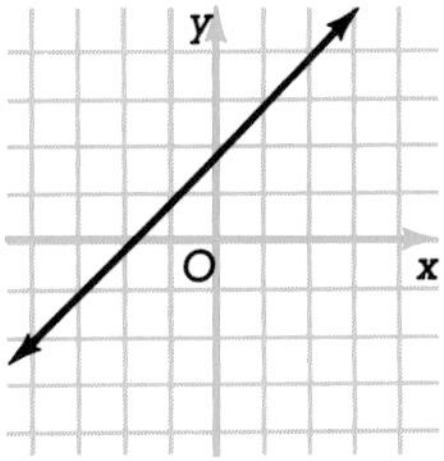

1, 2, $^-2$

2. 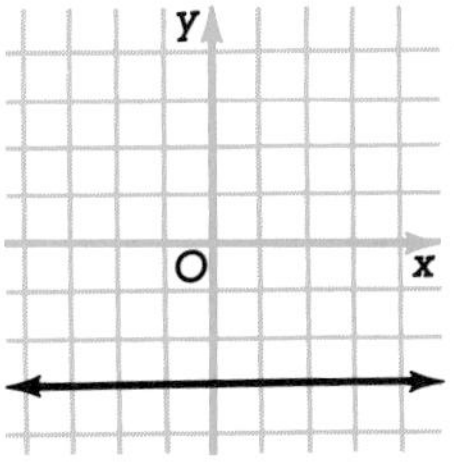

0, $^-3$, none

3. 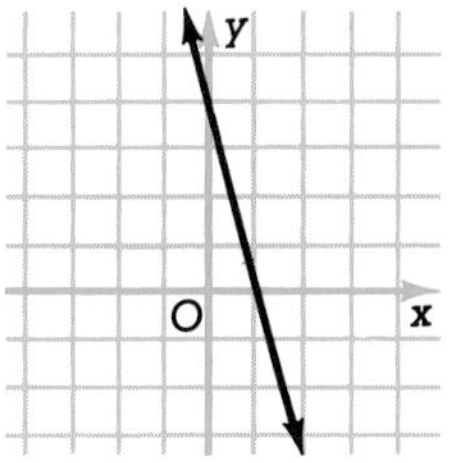

$^-4$, 4, 1

4. 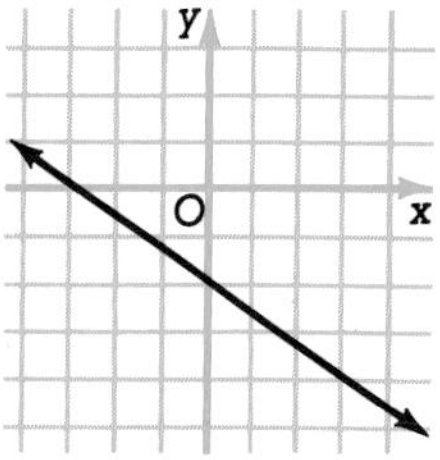

$-\frac{2}{3}$, $^-2$, $^-3$

State the slope and y-intercept of each equation.

5. $y = {^-4}x + 8$ $^-4$, 8
6. $y = 2x + 6$ 2, 6
7. $y = 3x + 12$ 3, 12
8. $y = \frac{3}{5}x - 3$ $\frac{3}{5}$, $^-3$
9. $y = \frac{2}{3}x - \frac{1}{2}$ $\frac{2}{3}$, $-\frac{1}{2}$
10. $y = -\frac{2}{3}x + \frac{1}{2}$ $-\frac{2}{3}$, $\frac{1}{2}$
11. $y = {^-x} + 5$ $^-1$, 5
12. $y = x - 7$ 1, $^-7$
13. $y = x - 1$ 1, $^-1$

Written State the slope, y-intercept, and x-intercept for each graph.

1. 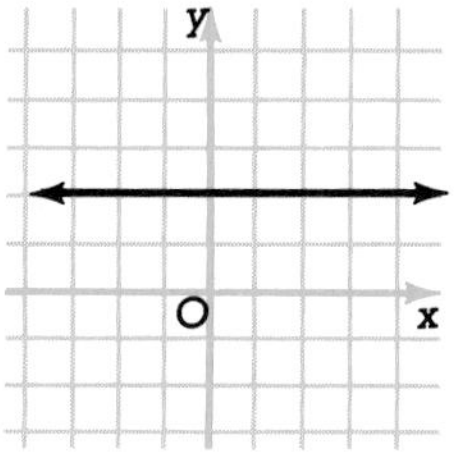

0, 2, none

2. 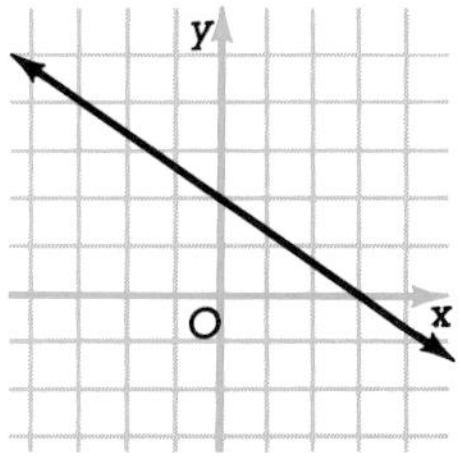

$-\frac{2}{3}$, 2, 3

3. 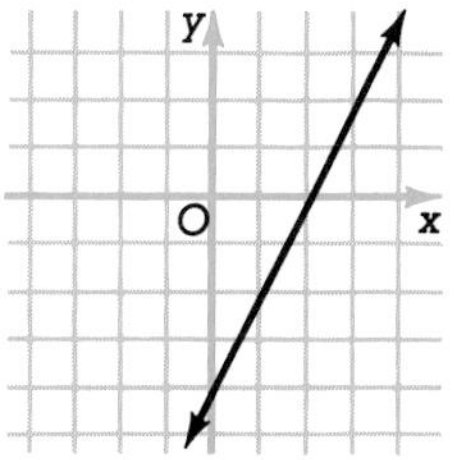

2, $^-4$, 2

4. 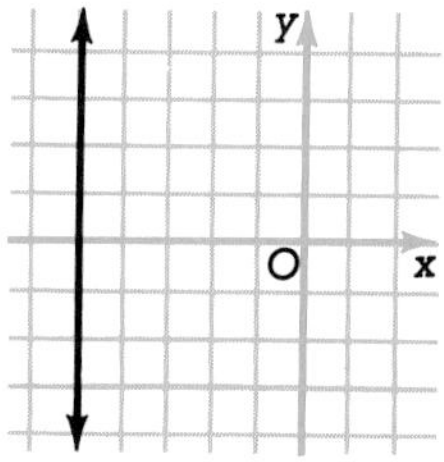

none, none, $^-5$

State the slope and y-intercept of each equation.

5. $y = 3x - 9$ 3, $^-9$
6. $y = {^-2}x + 5$ $^-2$, 5
7. $y = 7x + 1$ 7, 1
8. $y = -\frac{2}{3}x - 5$ $-\frac{2}{3}$, $^-5$
9. $y = \frac{1}{3}x + \frac{4}{3}$ $\frac{1}{3}$, $\frac{4}{3}$
10. $y = 2x + \frac{1}{3}$ 2, $\frac{1}{3}$
11. $y = 0.4x + 1.2$ 0.4, 1.2
12. $y = 1.75x - 2.3$ 1.75, $^-2.3$
13. $y = 0.75x$ 0.75, 0
14. $y = 7x$ 7, 0
15. $y = {^-2}$ 0, $^-2$
16. $x = 4$ undefined, none

Determine the slopes of lines passing through each pair of points.

17. (6, 1) and (8, $^-4$) $-\frac{5}{2}$
18. (5, 7) and (4, $^-6$) 13
19. ($^-3$, 0) and (8, 2) $\frac{2}{11}$
20. ($^-6$, $^-3$) and (4, 1) $\frac{2}{5}$
21. ($^-8$, $^-2$) and ($^-4$, 8) $\frac{5}{2}$
22. (6, 1) and (6, 7) undefined
23. (2.5, 3) and (1, $^-9$) 8
24. (0, 0) and $\left(\frac{3}{2}, \frac{1}{4}\right)$ $\frac{1}{6}$
25. $\left(1\frac{3}{4}, \frac{1}{3}\right)$ and $\left(2, \frac{1}{3}\right)$ 0

A line has slope 7. For each pair of points on the line, find the missing coordinate.

26. (x, 8) and (4, 1) 5
27. (6, y) and (2, $^-13$) 15
28. (3, $^-6$) and (7, y) 22

2-5 Forms of Linear Equations in Two Variables

Objective: To learn the slope-intercept and standard forms of linear equations in two variables.

The graph of $y = 4x + 3$ has slope 4 and y-intercept 3. When the equation is written in this form the slope and y-intercept are easy to find. The equation is said to be in **slope-intercept form.**

Definition of Slope-Intercept Form

The slope-intercept form of the equation of a line is $y = mx + b$. The slope is m and the y-intercept is b.

examples

1 **Find the slope and y-intercept of the graph of $5x - 3y = 12$. Then draw the graph.**

$$5x - 3y = 12$$
$$^-3y = {}^-5x + 12$$
$$y = \frac{5}{3}x - 4$$

The slope is $\frac{5}{3}$ and the y-intercept is $^-4$.

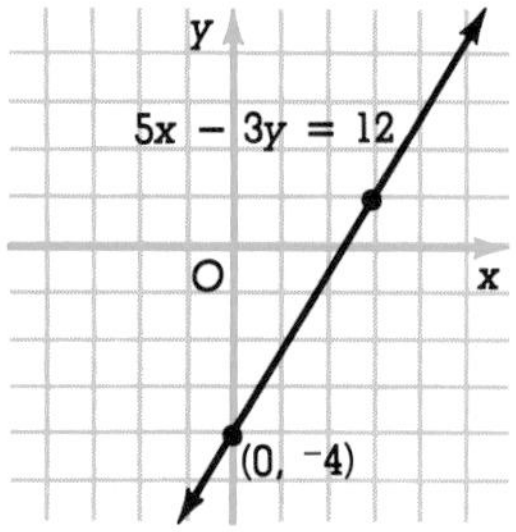

2 **Find the slope-intercept form of a line passing through $(^-2, 5)$ and $(3, 0)$.**

First find the slope.

$$\text{slope} = \frac{\text{change in } y\text{-coordinates}}{\text{change in corresponding } x\text{-coordinates}}$$
$$= \frac{5 - 0}{^-2 - 3}$$
$$= \frac{5}{^-5}$$
$$= {}^-1$$

Next, substitute the slope and coordinates of one point in the general slope-intercept form and solve for b.

$y = mx + b$
$5 = (^-1)(^-2) + b$ *Substitute 5 for y, ⁻1 for m, and ⁻2 for x.*
$5 = 2 + b$
$3 = b$

The slope-intercept form of the line is $y = {}^-x + 3$.

A linear equation in two variables may be written in the form $ax + by = c$ where a, b, and c are real numbers, and a and b are *not both* zero. This is called the **standard form** of the equation of a line.

Usually a, b, and c are given as integers that have greatest common factor 1.

examples

3 **Find the standard form of a line with slope $\frac{2}{3}$ passing through (4, 7).**

First, substitute the slope and coordinates of the point into the general slope-intercept form and solve for **b**.

$y = mx + b$

$7 = \left(\frac{2}{3}\right)(4) + b$ *Substitute 7 for y, $\frac{2}{3}$ for m, and 4 for x.*

$7 = \frac{8}{3} + b$

$\frac{13}{3} = b$

Write the equation in slope-intercept form and change it to standard form.

$y = \frac{2}{3}x + \frac{13}{3}$ *Substitute $\frac{2}{3}$ for m and $\frac{13}{3}$ for b.*

$3y = 2x + 13$

$^{-}13 = 2x - 3y$ The standard form of the line is $2x - 3y = {}^{-}13$.

4 **Find the slope and y-intercept of a line with equation in standard form.**

If b is not zero, the slope and y-intercept are found by solving the equation for y.

$ax + by = c$

$by = {}^{-}ax + c$

$y = -\frac{a}{b}x + \frac{c}{b}$ The slope is $-\frac{a}{b}$ and the y-intercept is $\frac{c}{b}$.

Consider the line with equation $y = {}^{-}2x + 4$. The standard form of this equation is $2x + y = 4$. The following calculations use the information from Example **4** to find the slope and y-intercept.

$\text{slope} = -\frac{a}{b}$ $\quad$ $y\text{-intercept} = \frac{c}{b}$

$= -\frac{2}{1}$ or $^{-}2$ $\quad$ $= \frac{4}{1}$ or 4

Notice that these values are the same as the values you would obtain from the slope-intercept form of the equation.

For answers to problems 1–16 and 1–60, see the Teacher's Guide.

exercises

Max: 1–16, 1–60; **Avg:** 1–16, 1–59 odds; **Min:** 1–59 odds

Exploratory Find the slope-intercept form of each equation.

1. $2x + 5y = 10$
2. $3x - y = 6$
3. $2x + 3y = 4$
4. $4x + 8y = 11$
5. $y = 4$
6. $2x - 2y = 4$
7. $3x - 2y = 4$
8. $2x = 11$

Find the standard form of each equation.

9. $y = 2x - 6$
10. $y = {}^{-}4x + 1$
11. $y = x - 9$
12. $y = 4x + 5$
13. $y = \frac{5}{8}x + 1$
14. $y = \frac{1}{3}x$
15. $y = 3x$
16. $y = x - \frac{2}{3}$

Written Find the slope, y-intercept, and x-intercept of the graphs of each equation.

1. $3x + 2y = 6$
2. $x + 6y = 12$
3. $2x + y = 4$
4. $5x - y = 5$
5. $x - y = 3$
6. $2x - 5y = {}^{-}20$
7. $2x - 3y = 4$
8. $4y - x = 10$
9. $3x + 5y = 12$
10. $6x - 2y = 9$
11. $11x + y = 4$
12. $3x - 8y = 12$
13. $\frac{2}{3}x + 3y = 6$
14. $\frac{3}{4}x - \frac{1}{2}y = \frac{5}{8}$
15. $4x = 11$
16. $\frac{3}{4}y - x = {}^{-}3$

Find the slope-intercept form of lines satisfying the following conditions.

17. x-intercept = 6, y-intercept = 4
18. x-intercept = $^{-}3$, y-intercept = 6
19. x-intercept = 5, y-intercept = 6
20. x-intercept = 6, y-intercept = 8
21. x-intercept = $\frac{1}{3}$, y-intercept = $-\frac{1}{4}$
22. x-intercept = $\frac{3}{5}$, y-intercept = 6
23. passes through (6, 1) and (8, $^{-}4$)
24. passes through (5, 7) and (4, $^{-}6$)
25. passes through ($^{-}3$, 0) and (8, 2)
26. passes through ($^{-}6$, $^{-}3$) and (4, 1)
27. passes through ($^{-}8$, $^{-}2$) and ($^{-}4$, 8)
28. passes through (6, 1) and (6, 7)
29. passes through (4, 3) and (6, 3)
30. passes through (4, 6) and (0, 0)
31. slope = $\frac{1}{2}$ and passes through (6, 4)
32. slope = $\frac{3}{4}$ and passes through (8, $^{-}1$)
33. slope = $\frac{2}{3}$ and passes through (6, $^{-}2$)
34. slope = $-\frac{4}{5}$ and passes through (2, $^{-}3$)
35. slope = 4 and passes through (2, $^{-}3$)
36. slope = 5 and passes through the origin
37. slope = $-\frac{3}{2}$ and passes through (6, 1)
38. slope = $-\frac{8}{3}$ and passes through (0, 6)

39–60. Find the standard form of the equation of each line satisfying the conditions of problems **17–38**.

Life

Simulation games are games that resemble real life processes. The game called LIFE, created by John Horton Conway, is one example. It shows, in a simple way, the evolution of a society of *living* organisms as it ages with time.

You can play LIFE using a grid of squares and counters in two different colors, say black and green. The counters are placed on the grid, one to a square. Then you change the positions of the counters according to the following *genetic laws*, or rules, for births, deaths, and survivals.

SURVIVALS Every counter with 2 or 3 neighboring counters survives for the next generation.

DEATHS Every counter with 4 or more neighbors dies from overpopulation. Every counter with only one neighbor or none dies from isolation.

BIRTHS Every empty cell with exactly three neighbors is a birth cell. A counter is placed on the cell for the next generation.

To help eliminate mistakes in play, the following procedure is suggested.

1. Start with a pattern of black counters.
2. Put a green counter where each birth cell will occur.
3. Put a second black counter on top of each death cell. Ignore the green counters when determining death cells.
4. Check the new pattern. Then, remove all dead counters, and replace the newborn green counters with black counters.

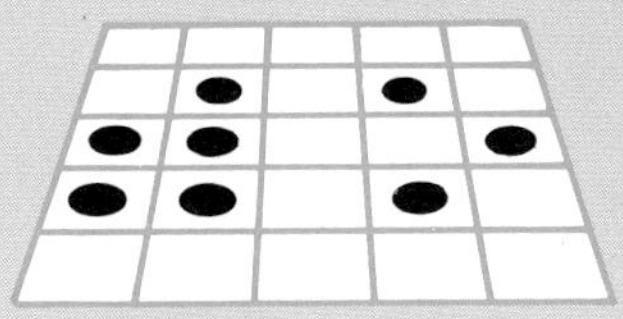

first generation

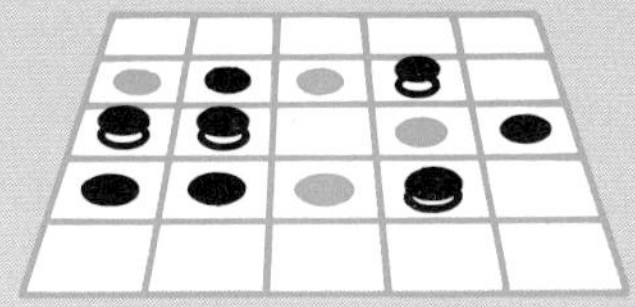

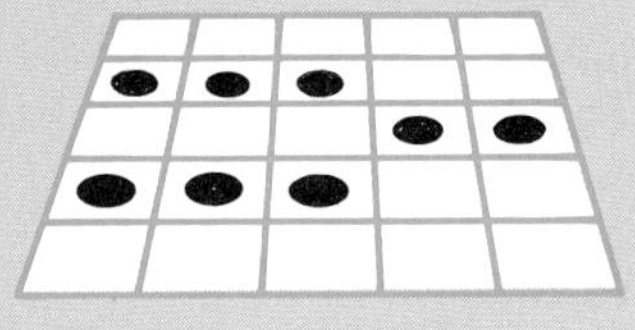

second generation

Notice that births and deaths occur simultaneously. Together, they are a move to the next generation.

When you play this game, you will find that many patterns either die, reach a stable repeating pattern or become blinkers, alternating between two patterns. The pattern on the right stabilizes.

Computers are very helpful in simulations because they can display the changes, and a number of patterns can be observed in a short period of time.

Exercises Find the next six generations for each of the following.

1. 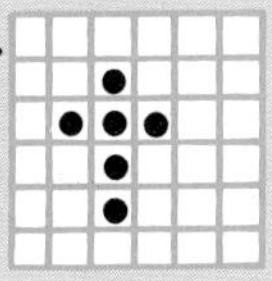
2. 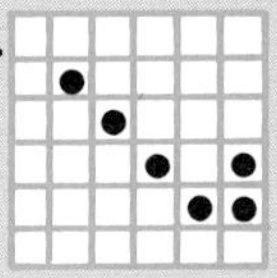
3. 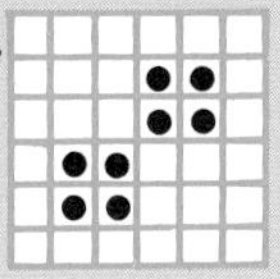
4. 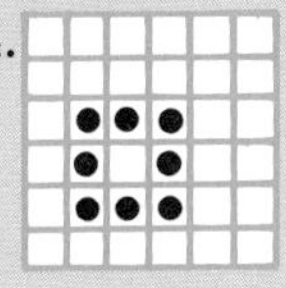
5. 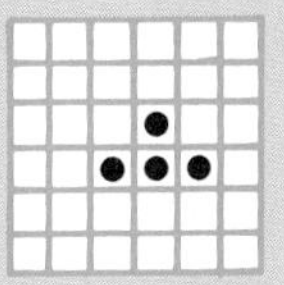

See student work.

2–6 Special Functions

Objective: To graph special nonlinear functions.

Recall that a linear function can be described by $y = mx + b$ or $f(x) = mx + b$ where m and b are real numbers. There are some kinds of linear functions which have special names.

If $m = 0$, the function is called a **constant function.** Its graph is a horizontal line.

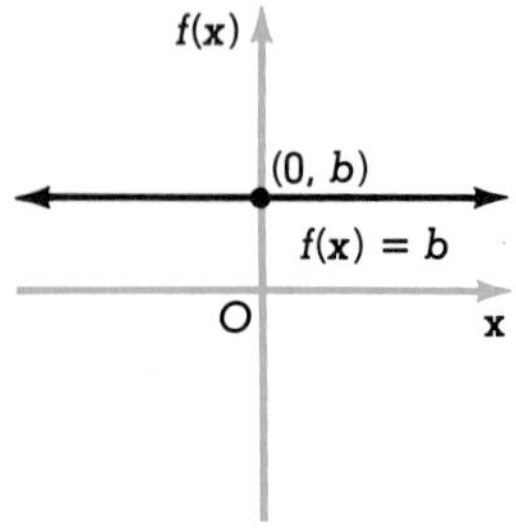

If $b = 0$ and $m = 1$, the function is called the **identity function.** Its graph passes through the origin and forms congruent angles with the axes.

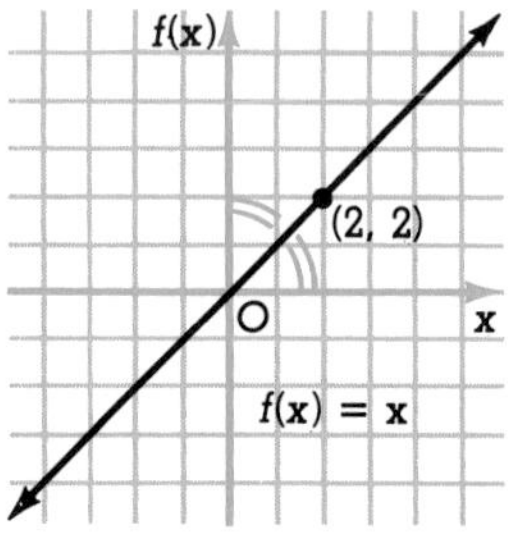

If $b = 0$ and $m \neq 0$, the function is called a **direction variation.** Its graph passes through the origin.

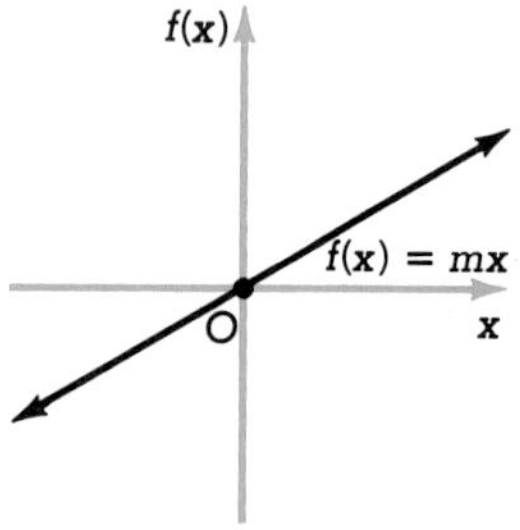

Definition of Constant Function

A linear function described by $y = b$ or $f(x) = b$ is called a constant function.

Definition of Identity Function

A linear function described by $y = x$ or $f(x) = x$ is called the identity function.

Definition of Direct Variation

A linear function described by $y = mx$ or $f(x) = mx$ where $m \neq 0$ is called a direct variation. The constant m is called the constant of variation or constant of proportionality.

A special language often is used with direct variation. The cost of electricity (c) *varies directly with* the amount of electricity (k) used means $c = mk$. You could also say the cost of electricity *is directly proportional* to the amount of electricity used.

Several other functions are closely related to linear functions. Absolute value functions are one example.

Consider $f(x) = |x|$ or $y = |x|$. When x is positive or zero the function is like $y = x$. When x is negative the function is like $y = {}^{-}x$. The graph of $f(x) = |x|$ is shown on the left.

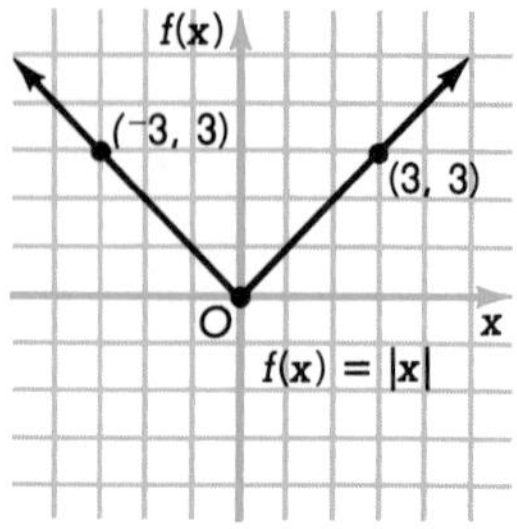

All of the following graphs represent absolute value functions.

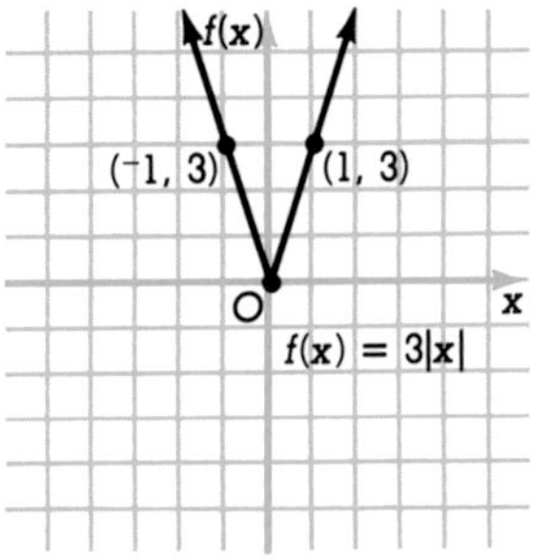

The domain is {x|x is real}.
The range is {y|y ≥ 0}.

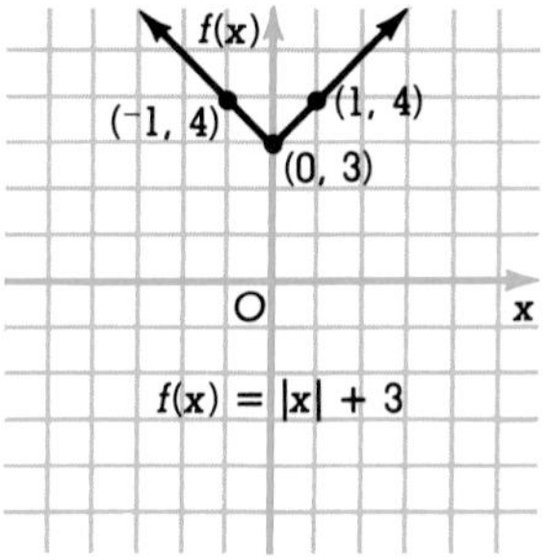

The domain is {x|x is real}.
The range is {y|y ≥ 3}.

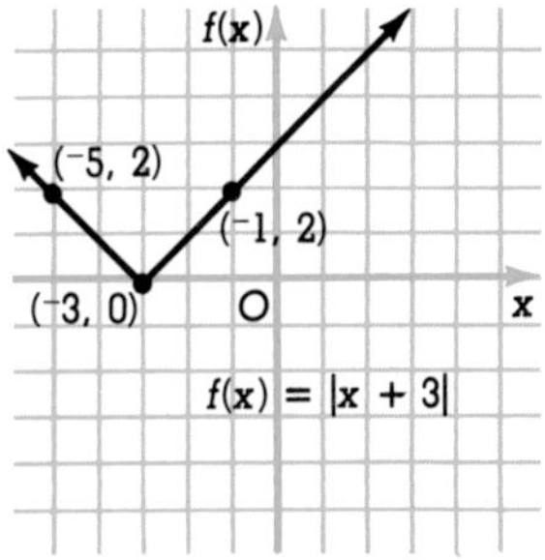

The domain is {x|x is real}.
The range is {y|y ≥ 0}.

Step functions like the ones graphed below are also related to linear functions.

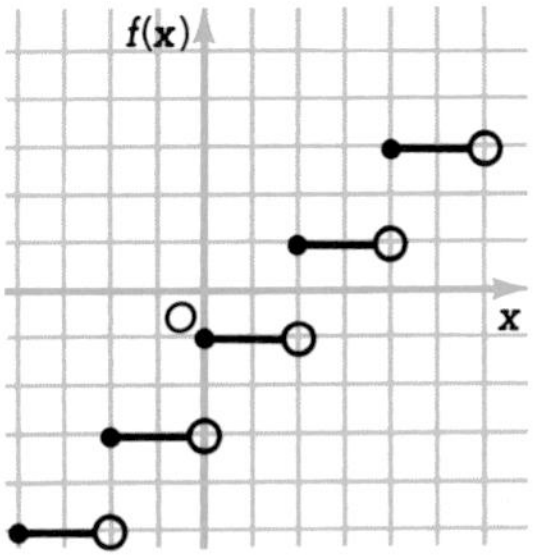

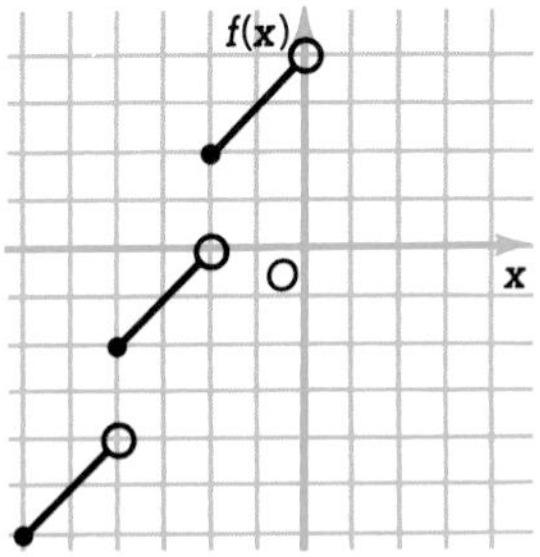

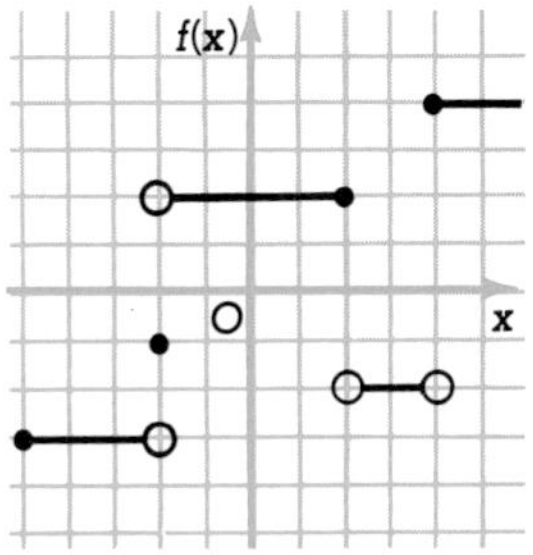

One type of step functions is called **greatest integer functions.** *The greatest integer of* x is written $[x]$ and means the greatest integer *not* greater than x. For example, $[6.2]$ is 6 and $[^-1.8]$ is $^-2$.

example 1

Graph $f(x) = [x]$.

x	[x]
0	0
0.2	0
0.6	0
1.0	1
1.5	1
2.0	2
2.5	2

The domain is all real numbers.

The range is all integers.

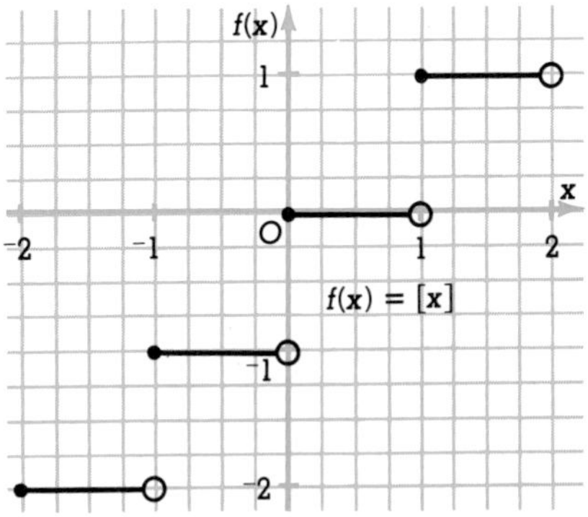

exercises

Max: 1–24, 1–34; Avg: 1–24, 1–33 odds; Min: 1–33 odds

Exploratory Identify each function as C for *constant*, as I for *identity*, as D for *direct variation*, as A for *absolute value*, or as G for *greatest integer functions*.

1. $f(x) = |3x - 2|$ A
2. $f(x) = [^-x]$ G
3. $g(x) = 3x$ D
4. $g(x) = [2x]$ G
5. $y = |2x|$ A
6. $f(x) = |2x + 1|$ A
7. $f(x) = \left|x - \frac{2}{3}\right|$ A
8. $g(x) = 19$ C
9. $g(x) = [2x + 1]$ G
10. $h(x) = {}^-2x$ D
11. $f(x) = \frac{1}{2}x$ D
12. $p(x) = x$ I or D
13. $h(x) = [x - 3]$ G
14. $f(x) = {}^-3x$ D
15. $g(x) = |x + 3|$ A
16. $h(x) = {}^-7$ C
17. $m(x) = |^-3x|$ A
18. $f(x) = \left[x - \frac{1}{2}\right]$ G
19. $f(x) = [x - 2\frac{1}{2}]$ G
20. $f(x) = [3x - 5]$ G
21. $m(x) = \frac{2}{3}$ C
22. $g(x) = {}^-x$ D
23. $k(x) = |x - 8|$ A
24. $f(x) = 0$ C

For answers to problems 1–34, see the Teacher's Guide.

Written Graph each function.

1. $f(x) = x$
2. $g(x) = 3x$
3. $h(x) = {}^-2x$
4. $f(x) = \frac{1}{2}x$
5. $p(x) = |x|$
6. $r(x) = |2x|$
7. $g(x) = |^-3x|$
8. $f(x) = |x + 3|$
9. $f(x) = \left|x - \frac{2}{3}\right|$
10. $t(x) = |2x + 1|$
11. $h(x) = |3x - 2|$
12. $k(x) = [2x]$
13. $h(x) = [x - 3]$
14. $f(x) = \left[x - \frac{1}{2}\right]$
15. $f(x) = [x - 2\frac{1}{2}]$
16. $g(x) = [2x + 1]$
17. $m(x) = [3x - 5]$
18. $h(x) = [^-x]$
19. $p(x) = [3 - x]$
20. $f(x) = {}^-[x - 2]$
21. $g(x) = {}^-|x| + 3$
22. $g(x) = |2x| - 3$
23. $r(x) = 2|x| - 3$
24. $f(x) = |x - 3| + 2$

Explain how the graphs of each pair of equations differ.

25. $y = 2[x]$ and $y = [2x]$
26. $y = [x + 5]$ and $y = [x] + 5$
27. $y = |x - 3|$ and $y = |x| - 3$
28. $y = |3x|$ and $y = 3|x|$
29. $y = |2x + 5|$ and $y = |2x| + 5$
30. $y = [2x + 5]$ and $y = [2x] + 5$
31. $y = |ax|$ and $y = a|x|$
32. $y = |x + b|$ and $y = |x| + b$
33. $y = {}^-3[x]$ and $y = [^-3x]$
34. $y = {}^-2|x|$ and $y = |^-2x|$

2-7 Using Linear Functions

Objective: To use linear functions in solving problems.

During the metric changeover, many measurements will be given in both systems. Road signs are one example.

Number of kilometers varies directly with number of miles. The information on the road sign can be used to find an equation for the relationship.

Let k stand for number of kilometers.
Let m stand for number of miles.
Let c stand for the constant of variation.

$$k = cm$$
$$161 = c(100)$$
$$1.61 = c$$

Thus, the relationship between kilometers and miles can be described as follows.

$$k = 1.61m$$

example 1

It is 111 miles from Toledo to Cleveland. How many kilometers is this?

$k = 1.61m$
$k = 1.61(111)$
$k = 178.71$

It is 178.71 kilometers from Toledo to Cleveland. This figure would probably be rounded to 179 for a road sign.

example 2

Sales tax is directly proportional to the amount of purchase. Write an equation to describe the relationship if sales tax is 5¢ for each dollar. Also, complete the chart for store clerks to use. (Round up to the nearest cent.)

Amount	0.05	0.10	0.15	0.20	0.25	0.50	0.75	1.00
Tax								
Amount	2.00	3.00	4.00	5.00	10.00	15.00	20.00	25.00
Tax								

Let a stand for amount of purchase.
Let t stand for tax.
Let c stand for the constant of proportionality.

$$t = ca$$
$$0.05 = c\,(1.00)$$
$$0.05 = c$$ The equation is $t = 0.05a$.

To complete the chart, substitute values for the amount in the equation and solve for t.

Amount	0.05	0.10	0.15	0.20	0.25	0.50	0.75	1.00
Tax	0.01	0.01	0.01	0.01	0.02	0.03	0.04	0.05
Amount	2.00	3.00	4.00	5.00	10.00	15.00	20.00	25.00
Tax	0.10	0.15	0.20	0.25	0.50	0.75	1.00	1.25

Linear functions other than direct variation can also be used to solve verbal problems.

Ace Mechanics have a standard $15 shop charge for every job. In addition, the mechanic charges $8 per hour. The relationship between total charge and the time a mechanic spends on the job can be described with a linear equation in two variables.

Let c stand for total charge for job.
Let t stand for time spent on job.

total charge = *mechanic charge* + *shop charge*

$$c = 8t + 15$$

Sandy Howard spent 3 hours on Jane's car. How much will Ace Mechanics charge?

$$c = 8t + 15$$
$$= 8(3) + 15$$
$$= 24 + 15$$
$$= 39$$ Ace Mechanics will charge Jane $39.

exercises

Max: 1–24, 1–10; **Avg:** 1–24, 1–9 odds; **Min:** 1–9 odds

Exploratory Solve each problem.

1. A distance of 100 yards is the same as a distance of 91.44 meters. Write an equation to describe the relationship between yards and meters. $m = 0.9144y$
2. An area of 25.9 square kilometers is about the same as an area of 10 square miles. Write an equation to describe the relationship. $k = 2.59m$

3–15. Light travels faster than sound. If you count the number of seconds between when you see lightning and when you hear it, you can estimate how far away it is. The distance d in kilometers between you and the lightning is estimated by $d = 0.32s - 0.4$ where s is the number of seconds. Complete the chart for estimating the distance.

Time (seconds)	1	2	3	4	5	10	15	20	25	30	40	50	60
Distance (kilometers)	−0.08	0.24	0.56	0.88	1.20	2.80	4.40	6.00	7.60	9.20	12.40	15.60	18.80

16–24. Crickets vary their number of chirps with the temperature. If you count the number of chirps in a minute, you can tell the temperature. The temperature t in degrees Celsius is estimated by $t = 0.2(n + 32)$ where n is the number of chirps in one minute. Complete the chart for estimating the temperature.

Chirps	50	60	70	80	90	100	110	120	130
Temperature (Celsius)	16.4°	18.4°	20.4°	22.4°	24.4°	26.4°	28.4°	30.4°	32.4°

Written Solve each problem.

1. Frontier Mechanics have a standard $12 shop charge for every job they take. In addition, the mechanic working on the job charges $10 per hour. Write an equation to describe the relationship between time spent on a job and total charge for the job. $c = 12 + 10t$
2. Cindy Baker spent 4 hours on a car. How much will Frontier Mechanics charge? $52
3. Joshua Levy spent 2.5 hours on a car. How much will Frontier Mechanics charge? $37
4. Frontier Mechanics charged $47 for a job. How much time did the mechanic work? 3.5 hours
5. Frontier Mechanics charged $100 for a job. How much time did the mechanic work? 8.8 hours
6. Inches of snowfall is directly proportional to inches of rainfall. Thirty-five inches of snow is about the same as 3.5 inches of rain. Write an equation to describe the relationship between inches of snowfall and inches of rainfall. $s = 10r$
7. Twelve inches of snowfall is equivalent to how much rainfall? 1.2 inches
8. Forty-eight inches of snowfall is equivalent to how much rainfall? 4.8 inches
9. Eleven inches of rainfall is equivalent to how much snowfall? 110 inches
10. Four and one-half inches of rainfall is equivalent to how much snowfall? 45 inches

2-8 Graphing Linear Inequalities in Two Variables

Objective: To graph linear inequalities in two variables.

The graph of $y = -\frac{2}{3}x + \frac{5}{3}$ is a line which separates the coordinate plane into two regions.

The graph of $y > -\frac{2}{3}x + \frac{5}{3}$ is the region *above* the line. In that region the value of y is greater than $-\frac{2}{3}x + \frac{5}{3}$.

The graph of $y < -\frac{2}{3}x + \frac{5}{3}$ is the region *below* the line. In that region the value of y is less than $-\frac{2}{3}x + \frac{5}{3}$.

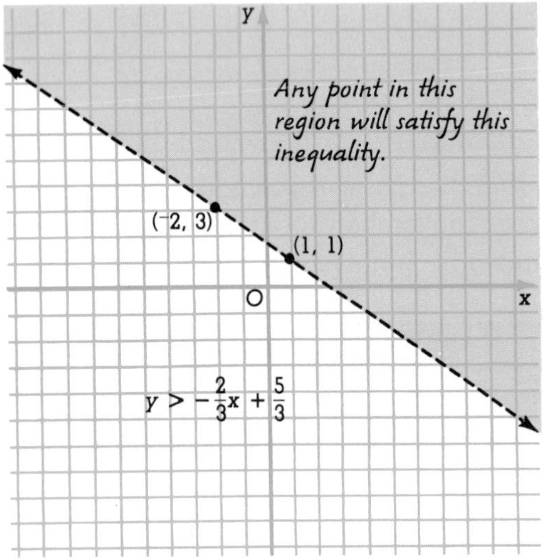

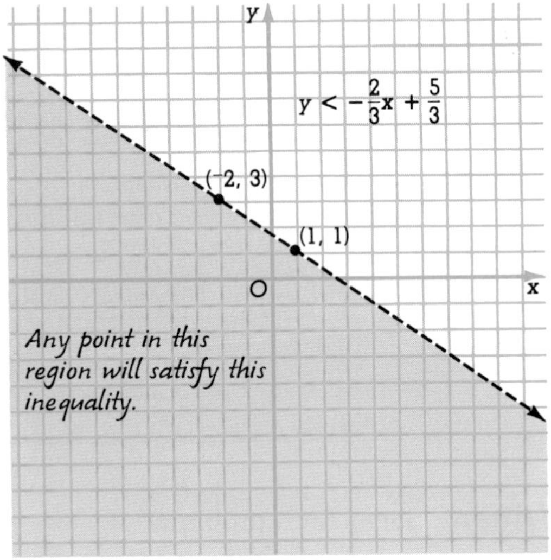

The line described by $y = -\frac{2}{3}x + \frac{5}{3}$ is called the *boundary* of each region. If the boundary is part of a graph it is drawn as a solid line. If the boundary is *not* part of a graph it is drawn as a broken line.

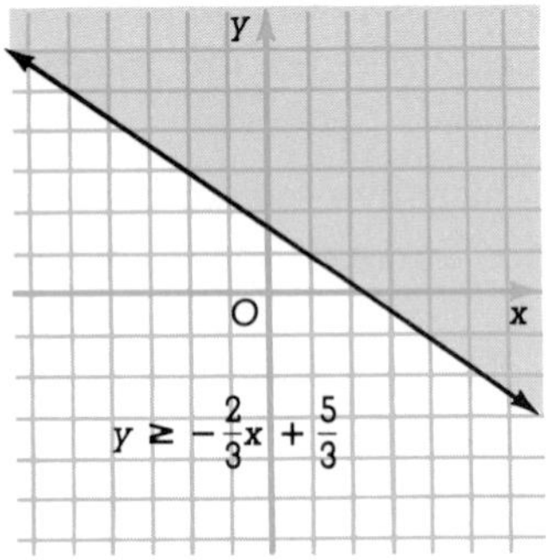

Note that ≥ tells you the boundary is included.

Note that > tells you the boundary is not included.

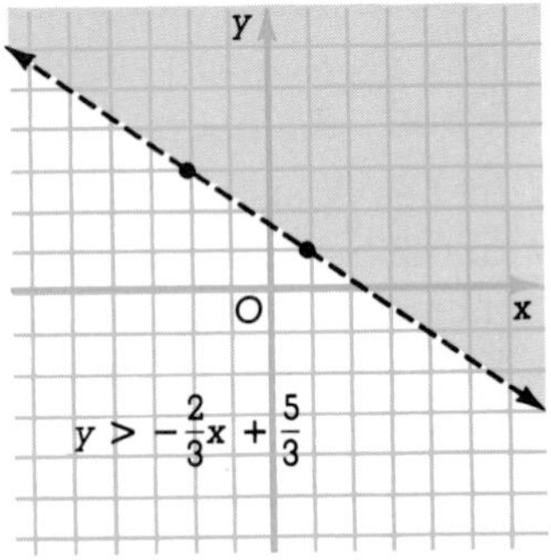

examples

1 **Graph $2y - 5x \le 1$.**

$$2y - 5x \le 1$$
$$2y \le 5x + 1$$
$$y \le \frac{5}{2}x + \frac{1}{2}$$

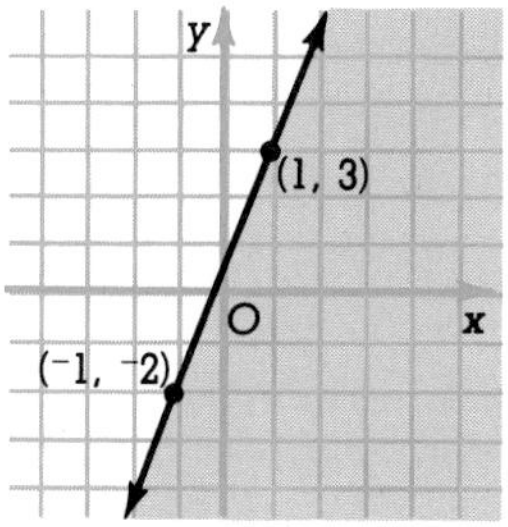

Note that the boundary is included.

2 **Graph $y \ge |x| - 1$.**

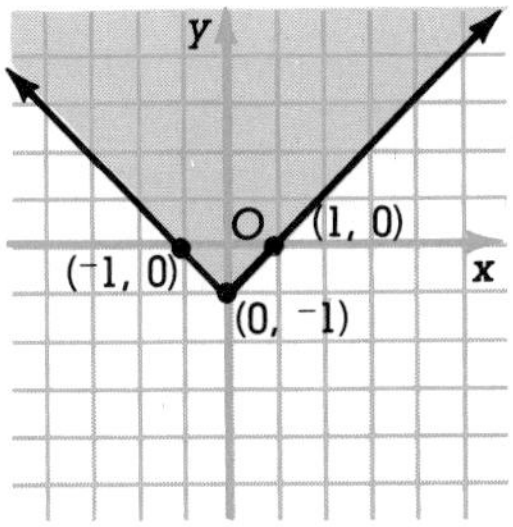

Note that the boundary is included.

exercises

Max: 1–8, 1–18, Challenge; **Avg:** 1–8, 1–17 odds; **Min:** 1–17 odds

Exploratory Name which points, (0, 0), (2, ⁻3), or (⁻1, 2) lie on the graph of each inequality.

1. $x + 2y < 7$ all three
2. $3x - y \ge 2$ (2, ⁻3)
3. $3x + 2y \le 0$
4. $x + y \ge 7$ none
5. $4x + 2y \ge 7$ none
6. $5x - y > 2$
7. $y < 0$ (2, ⁻3)
8. $4x \ge {}^-12$ all three

3. (0, 0), (2, ⁻3)
6. (2, ⁻3)

For answers to problems 1–18, see the Teacher's Guide.

Written Draw the graph of each inequality.

1. $y < 3$
2. $y > 5x - 3$
3. $y \le x - 7$
4. $y \ge {}^-3x + 1$
5. $3x + y < 7$
6. $2x - 5y \ge 4$
7. $y \le 2x + 5$
8. $y > \frac{1}{3}x + 7$
9. $x - 2y \le 2$
10. ${}^-2x + 5 \le 3y$
11. $y \ge |x|$
12. $|x| + y \ge 3$
13. $y > |2x|$
14. $y < |x| + 2$
15. Graph all points to the right of $x = 4$.
16. Graph all points in the second quadrant between $x = {}^-2$ and $x = {}^-5$.
17. Graph all points in the first quadrant bounded by the two axes and $x + 2y = 4$.
18. Graph all points in the fourth quadrant bounded by the two axes and the lines $3x - y = 4$ and $x - y = 5$.

Using Money

Car Expenses

Regular motor oil costs about \$1.00 per quart and should be changed every 2000 miles. A new, special motor oil will last for 4000 miles, but costs about \$4.00 per quart.

Suppose a car holds 5 quarts of oil. Which of the motor oils is more economical for oil changes?

Regular Oil	Special Oil
at 2000 miles replace 5 quarts	
at 4000 miles replace 5 quarts	at 4000 miles replace 5 quarts
10 quarts at \$1.00 per quart	*5 quarts at \$4.00 per quart*
$10 \cdot \$1.00 = \$10.00$	$5 \cdot \$4.00 = \$20.00$

The regular oil is more economical for oil changes.

The manufacturers of the special oil claim that by using their oil, a car can travel up to 23 more miles per tankful of gasoline. Does this make up for the extra cost of the oil?

Example Suppose a car's gasoline tank holds 16 gallons, and the car's mileage is 20 miles per gallon of gasoline. And suppose gasoline costs \$0.60 per gallon. If special oil is used, would the gasoline savings make up for the extra cost of the oil?

$20 \cdot 16 = 320$	*Find the number of miles per tank.*
$4000 \div 320 = 12.5$	*Find the number of tanks for 4000 miles.*
$12.5 \cdot 23 = 287.5$	*Find the extra miles for 12.5 tanks.*
$287.5 \div 20 \approx 14.4$	*Find the gallons of gas saved.*
$14.4 \cdot \$0.60 = \$8.64$	*Find the cost of the gas saved.*

The information above shows that the extra cost of special oil is \$10.00. Since the gasoline savings is only \$8.64, it does *not* make up for the extra cost of the oil.

Exercises Will gasoline savings make up for the extra cost of special oil if the following information changes are made?

1. Gasoline costs \$0.68 per gallon. no

2. Mileage is 25 miles per gallon. no

3. Regular oil is changed every 1000 miles. yes

4. The car gets 30 extra miles per tank. yes

5. The car holds 4 quarts of oil. yes

6. Mileage is 15 miles per gallon. yes

7. The regular oil lasts 1000 miles. yes

8. Special oil lasts 2000 miles. no

Vocabulary

coordinate plane (38)
ordered pairs (38)
quadrants (38)
x-axis (38)
y-axis (38)
origin (38)
relation (41)
domain (41)
range (41)
function (41)
vertical line test (42)
linear equation (46)
linear function (47)
slope (49)
y-intercept (50)
slope-intercept form (52)
standard form (53)
constant function (56)
identity function (56)
direct variation (56)
greatest integer function (57)
linear inequalities (62)

Chapter Summary

1. Points on the Number Line: Each real number corresponds to exactly one point on a number line. Each point on a number line corresponds to exactly one real number. (38)
2. Points in the Plane: Each point in a coordinate plane corresponds to exactly one ordered pair of numbers. Each ordered pair of numbers corresponds to exactly one point in a coordinate plane. (38)
3. The graph of an open sentence is the graph of the solution of that open sentence. (39)
4. Definition of Relation, Domain, and Range: A relation is a set of ordered pairs. The domain is the set of all first coordinates of the ordered pairs. The range is the set of all second coordinates of the ordered pairs. (41)
5. Definition of Function: A function is a relation in which each element of the domain is paired with exactly one element of the range. (42)
6. Vertical Line Test for a Function: If any vertical line drawn on the graph of a relation passes through no more than one point of that graph, then the relation is a function. (42)
7. Definition of Linear Equation in Two Variables: A linear equation in two variables is an equation in two variables that may be written in the form $ax + by = c$ where a, b, and c are real numbers, and a and b are *not both* zero. (46)
8. Definition of Linear Function: A linear function can be defined by $f(x) = mx + b$ where m and b are real numbers. (47)
9. Definition of Slope: The slope of a line described by $f(x) = mx + b$ is m. Slope is also given by the following equation.

$$\text{slope} = \frac{\text{change in } y\text{-coordinates}}{\text{change in corresponding } x\text{-coordinates}} \quad (49)$$

10. The y-intercept is the value of a function when x is 0. (50)
11. Definition of Slope-Intercept Form: The slope-intercept form of the equation of a line is $y = mx + b$. The slope is m and the y-intercept is b. (52)
12. A linear equation in two variables may be written in the form $ax + by = c$ where a, b, and c are real numbers, and a and b are *not both* zero. This is called the standard form of the equation of a line. (53)
13. Definition of Constant Function: A linear function described by $y = b$ or $f(x) = b$ is called a constant function. (56)
14. Definition of Identity Function: A linear function described by $y = x$ or $f(x) = x$ is called the identity function. (56)
15. Definition of Direct Variation: A linear function described by $y = mx$ or $f(x) = mx$ where $m \neq 0$ is called a direct variation. The constant m is called the constant of variation or constant of proportionality. (56)
16. *The greatest integer of* x is written $[x]$ and means the greatest integer *not* greater than x. (57)

Chapter Review

For answers to problems 1–8, 9–12, 28–31, 40–55, and 57–60, see the Teacher's Guide.

2-1 Graph each set on the number line.

1. $\{n | n > \frac{1}{2} \text{ or } n \leq {}^-3\}$
2. all integers
3. all odd numbers
4. $\{x | {}^-5 \leq x < 0\}$

Graph each equation or inequality on the number line.

5. $7r - 5 = 3r - 5$ $\{0\}$
6. $|3p + 2| - 6 = 7$ $\{\frac{11}{3}, {}^-5\}$
7. $6(1 - x) - 4(2 - x) \leq x + 7$ $\{x | x \geq {}^-3\}$
8. $1 - |q + 7| < 5$ $\{q | q \text{ is real}\}$

2-2 State the domain and range of each relation.

9. $\{(4.5, 1), ({}^-4.5, 2), (4.5, 3), ({}^-3.5, 4)\}$
10. $\{(1, 4.5), (2, {}^-4.5), (3, 4.5), (4, {}^-3.5), (5, {}^-3.5)\}$
11. $\{(x, y) | y = 4\}$
12. $\{(x, y) | x = 4\}$

13–16. State whether or not each relation in problems **9–12** is a function. functions circled

Use the vertical line test to determine if each relation is a function. functions circled

17.
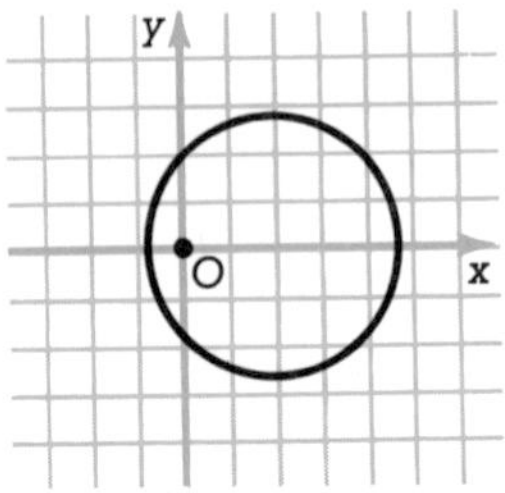

18.
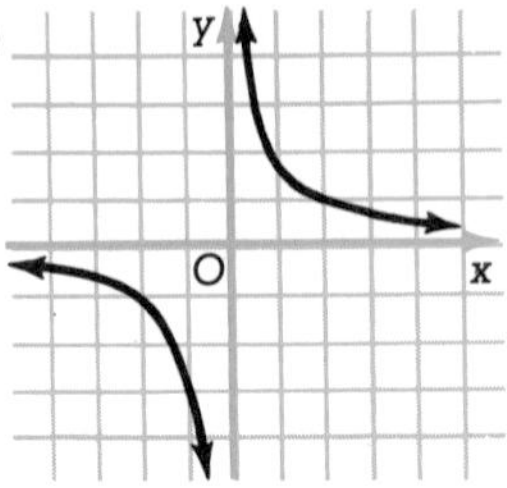

19.
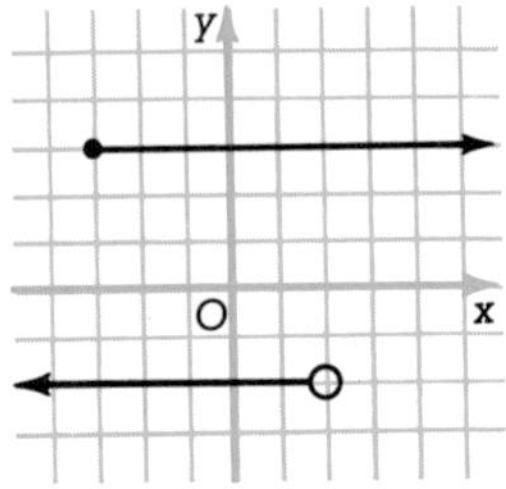

Given $f(x) = 2x^3 + 4x^2 + 4x + 1$, find each value.

20. $f(0)$ 1
21. $f(^-3)$ $^-29$
22. $f(a)$
23. $f(a + b)$

22. $2a^3 + 4a^2 + 4a + 1$ 23. $2(a + b)^3 + 4(a + b)^2 + 4(a + b) + 1$

2-3 **State whether or not each equation is a linear equation in two variables. Write *yes* or *no*.**

24. $x^2 + y^2 = 4$ no
25. $xy = 12$ no
26. $y = 5$ yes
27. $x + y = 9$ yes

Graph each equation.

28. $y = \frac{1}{3}x$
29. $y = 3x$
30. $y = 2x - 1$
31. $y = 2x + 1$

2-4 **32–35.** State the slope and y-intercept of each equation in problems **28–31.**

32. $\frac{1}{3}$, 0 33. 3, 0 34. 2, $^-1$ 35. 2, 1

A line has slope $\frac{2}{3}$. For each pair of points on the line, find the missing coordinate.

36. $(0, 6)$ and $(^-6, y)$ 2
37. $(^-9, 0)$ and $(x, 10)$ 6
38. $(x, 7)$ and $(^-3, 4)$ $\frac{3}{2}$
39. $(^-7, y)$ and $(3, 8)$ $\frac{4}{3}$

2-5 **Find the slope-intercept form of lines satisfying the following conditions.**

40. x-intercept $^-2$ and y-intercept 5
41. passes through $(^-3, 0)$ and $(4, ^-6)$
42. slope 5 and y-intercept $^-7$
43. slope $\frac{2}{3}$ and passes through $(1, ^-4)$

44–47. Find the standard form of lines satisfying the conditions of problems **40–43.**

48–51. Draw the graphs of lines satisfying the conditions of problems **40–43.**

2-6 **Graph each function.**

52. $g(x) = {}^-x$
53. $q(x) = |{}^-x|$
54. $p(x) = [{}^-x]$
55. $f(x) = {}^-[x]$

2-7 56. A temperature of 32°F is the same as 0°C. A temperature of 212°F is the same as 100°C. Write a linear equation in two variables to describe the relationship between degrees Fahrenheit and degrees Celsius. $F = \frac{9}{5}C + 32$

2-8 **Graph each inequality.**

57. $3x + 4y < 9$
58. $2x - 5y > 4$
59. $y \geq |x| + 5$
60. $y \leq |x + 5|$

Chapter Test

For answers to problems 7–10 and 22–47, see the Teacher's Guide.

Graph each equation or inequality on the number line.

1. $^-2r - 3(r - 2) = r - 6$ $\{2\}$
2. $2(m - 4) + 3(m + 2) = 8$ $\{2\}$
3. $1 + 3(x - 2) \geq {}^-2(2x - 1)$ $\{x|x \geq 1\}$
4. $5(3t + 2) < 4(3t + 4)$ $\{t|t < 2\}$
5. $|5p + 6| - p = 2$ $\{^-1, {}^-1\frac{1}{3}\}$
6. $|4a + 2| + 5 > 5$ $\{a|a \text{ is real}\}$

State the domain and range of each relation.

7. $\{(1, 2), (7, 2), (9, {}^-3), (2, 7)\}$
8. $\{(1.4, 1.4), (1.4, 1.5)\}$
9. $\{(x, y)|x + y = 3\}$
10. $\{(x, y)|x = 5\}$

11–14. State whether or not each relation in problems **7–10** is a function. functions circled

Use the vertical line test to determine if each relation is a function. functions circled

15.

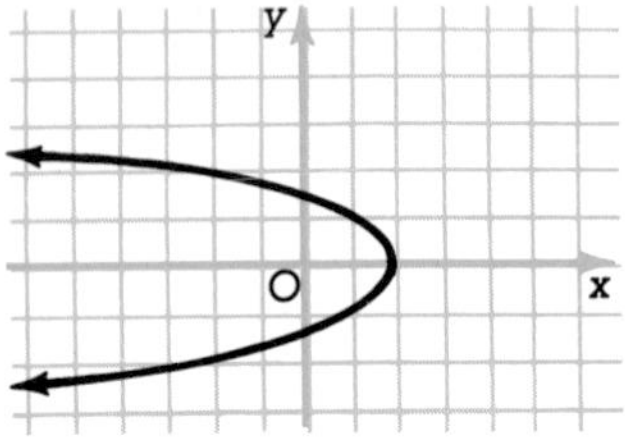

16.

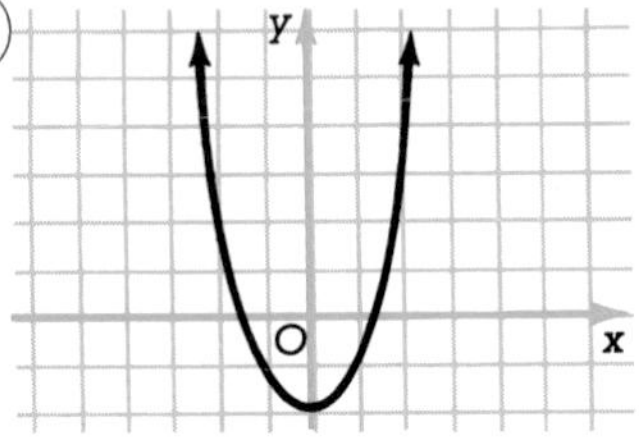

17.

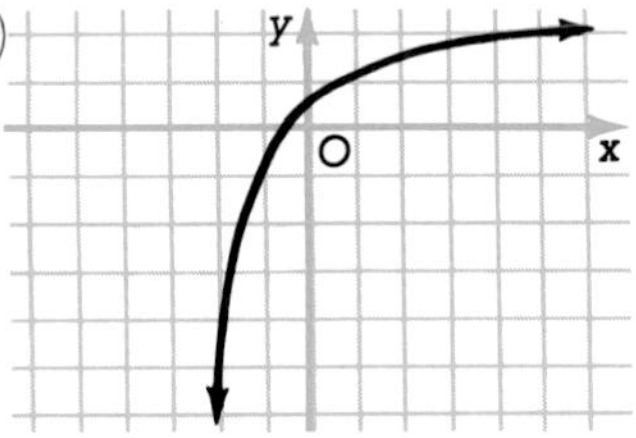

Given $f(x) = 2x^3 + 3x^2 - 5x - 4$, find each value.

18. $f(^-3)$ $^-16$
19. $f(1)$ $^-4$
20. $f(c)$ $2c^3 + 3c^2 - 5c - 4$
21. $f(x - c)$ $2(x - c)^3 + 3(x - c)^2 - 5(x - c) - 4$

Graph each equation or inequality.

22. $y = \frac{12}{5}x$
23. $y = 7$
24. $y = {}^-7x + 3$
25. $y = 3x - \frac{1}{2}$
26. $5x + 2y = 12$
27. $3y - 3x = 10$
28. $5y + 3x - 10 = 0$
29. $4x + 12y = {}^-15$
30. $2x + 3y > 7$
31. $4x + 6y \leq 9$
32. $y = |4x + 3| + 2$
33. $y = 2[x] - 7$
34. $y < 3|x| - 1$
35. $y \geq |3x - 1|$

Find the slope-intercept form of lines satisfying the following conditions.

36. x-intercept 5 and y-intercept $^-4$
37. passes through (0, 7) and (5, 2)
38. slope 4 and passes through $\left(\frac{2}{3}, \frac{2}{3}\right)$
39. slope $\frac{1}{5}$ and passes through (0, 7)
40. passes through ($^-1$, 6) and ($^-3$, $^-2$)
41. x-intercept $^-6$ and y-intercept $^-6$

42–47. Find the standard form of lines satisfying the conditions of problems **36–41.**

A line has a slope $-\frac{2}{5}$. For each pair of points on the line, find the missing coordinate.

48. (5, 1) and (15, y) $^-3$
49. (x, 2) and ($^-5$, 5) $\frac{5}{2}$

50. The average person who is 172 cm tall weighs 68.4 kg. The average person who is 190 cm tall weighs 85.5 kg. Write a linear equation to approximate the relationship between the height and weight of an average person. $17.1h = 18w + 1710$

Chapter 3

How should production be scheduled to meet a given sales order at minimum cost to the company?

Systems of Equations and Inequalities

One of the most practical applications of mathematics to business and biology is the branch of mathematics called linear programming. Linear programming depends on the graphs of linear equations and inequalities.

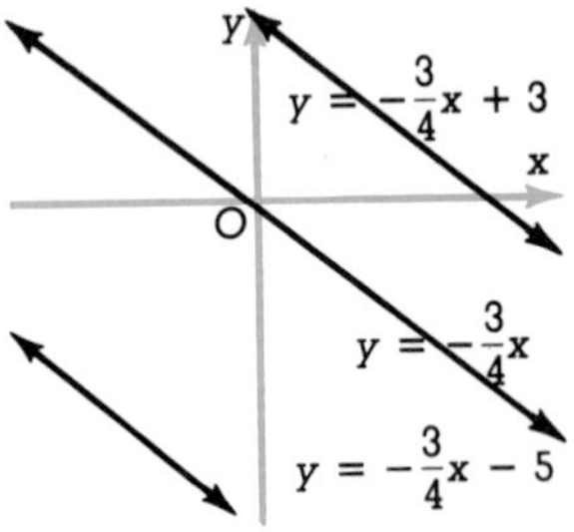

Definition of Parallel Lines

3–1 Parallel and Perpendicular Lines

Objective: To learn about the slopes of parallel and perpendicular lines.

The graphs of $y = -\frac{3}{4}x - 5$, $y = -\frac{3}{4}x$, and $y = -\frac{3}{4}x + 3$ are straight lines that have the same slope. They are called **parallel lines.**

In a plane, lines with the same slope are called parallel lines. Also, vertical lines are parallel.

examples

1 **Find the slope of a line *parallel* to a line whose equation is $3y - 6x = 15$.**

Parallel lines have the same slope.
Find the slope of the line whose equation is $3y - 6x = 15$. To do so, write the equation in slope-intercept form. *$y = mx + b$*

$3y - 6x = 15$
$y = 2x + 5$

The slope of any line parallel to the given line is 2.

2 **Find the equation of a line that passes through (4, 6) and is *parallel* to a line whose equation is $y = \frac{2}{3}x + 5$.**

First, find the slope.

$y = \frac{2}{3}x + 5$ is in slope-intercept form.

The slope is $\frac{2}{3}$.

Next use (4, 6) and the slope $\frac{2}{3}$ to find the y-intercept.

$y = mx + b$

$6 = \left(\frac{2}{3}\right)(4) + b$ *Substitution.*

$6 = \frac{8}{3} + b$

$\frac{10}{3} = b$ *The y-intercept is $\frac{10}{3}$.*

The equation of the line is $y = \frac{2}{3}x + \frac{10}{3}$.

The graphs of $y = \frac{5}{3}x + 2$ and $y = -\frac{3}{5}x + 6$ are straight lines that are perpendicular. Notice how their slopes are related.

$$\left(\frac{5}{3}\right)\left(-\frac{3}{5}\right) = {}^{-}1$$

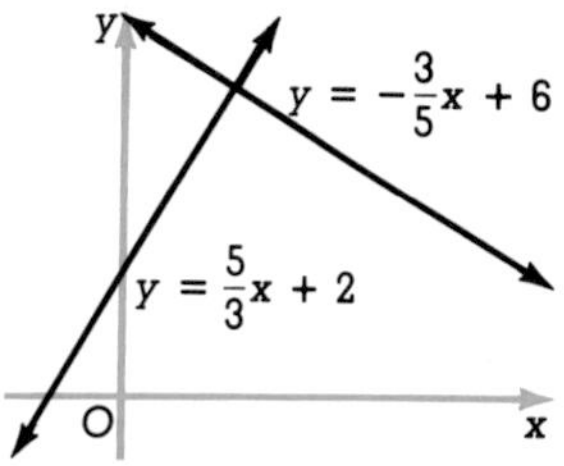

Definition of Perpendicular Lines

Two nonvertical lines are perpendicular if and only if the product of their slopes is $^{-}1$. Any vertical line is perpendicular to any horizontal line.

examples

3 **Find the slope of a line perpendicular to a line whose equation is $3y - x = 2$.**

$3y - x = 2$

$3y = x + 2$

$y = \frac{1}{3}x + \frac{2}{3}$ *This equation is in slope-intercept form.*

The slope of the given line is $\frac{1}{3}$.

$\frac{1}{3} \cdot m = {}^{-}1$ *Let m stand for the slope of the perpendicular line.*

$m = {}^{-}3$ The slope of any line perpendicular to the given line is $^{-}3$.

4 **Find the equation of a line that passes through (4, 6) and is perpendicular to a line whose equation is $y = \frac{2}{3}x + 5$.**

The slope of the given line is $\frac{2}{3}$. *$y = \frac{2}{3}x + 5$ is in slope-intercept form.*

$\frac{2}{3} \cdot m = {}^{-}1$ *Let m stand for the slope of the perpendicular line.*

$m = -\frac{3}{2}$

The slope of the perpendicular line is $-\frac{3}{2}$,

$y = mx + b$ *Let b stand for the y-intercept of the perpendicular line.*

$6 = \left(-\frac{3}{2}\right)(4) + b$ *The line passes through (4, 6) and has slope $-\frac{3}{2}$.*

$12 = b$ *The y-intercept is 12.*

The equation of the line is $y = -\frac{3}{2}x + 12$. *This could be written $3x + 2y = 24$.*

exercises

Max: 1–12, 1–26; Avg: 1–12, 1–25 odds; Min: 1–12, 1–21 odds

Exploratory Find the slope of each line parallel to lines with the following equations.

1. $y = 4x + 2$ 4 7. $-\frac{1}{4}$
2. $y = 2x + 5$ 2 8. $-\frac{1}{2}$
3. $y = -\frac{1}{3}x + 6$ $-\frac{1}{3}$ 9. 3
4. $2y = 3x - 8$ $\frac{3}{2}$ 10. $-\frac{2}{3}$
5. $6y - 6x = 0$ 1 11. $^{-}1$
6. $3x - 8y = 11$ $\frac{3}{8}$ 12. $-\frac{8}{3}$

7–12. Find the slope of each line perpendicular to the lines whose equations are given in problems **1–6.**

Written State whether the graphs of the following equations are parallel, perpendicular, or neither.

1. $x + y = 5$, $x + y = {}^{-}10$ parallel
2. $x + y = 5$, $x - y = 5$ perpendicular
3. $2y + 3x = 5$, $3y - 2x = 5$ perpendicular
4. $2y + 3x = 5$, $3y + 3x = 5$ neither
5. $3x - 8y = 11$, $3x - 6y = 10$ neither
6. $y = 2x$, $y = 2x - 4$ parallel

Find the equation of a line that passes through each given point and is parallel to a line with the given equation.

7. $(4, 2)$; $y = 2x - 4$ $y = 2x - 6$
8. $(0, 0)$; $3x - y = 4$ $y = 3x$
9. $(3, 1)$; $y = \frac{1}{3}x + 6$ $y = \frac{1}{3}x$
10. $\left(\frac{1}{2}, \frac{1}{3}\right)$; $x + y = 4$ $y = {}^{-}x + \frac{5}{6}$
11. $({}^{-}3, {}^{-}1)$; $y + x = 6$ $y = {}^{-}x - 4$
12. $(7, {}^{-}1)$; $2y - 3x = 1$ $y = \frac{3}{2}x - \frac{23}{2}$

13–18. Find the equation of a line that passes through each given point and is perpendicular to a line with the given equation in problems **7–12.** 13. $y = -\frac{1}{2}x + 4$ 14. $y = -\frac{1}{3}x$
15. $y = {}^{-}3x + 10$ 16. $y = x - \frac{1}{6}$ 17. $y = x + 2$ 18. $y = -\frac{2}{3}x + \frac{11}{3}$

Find the value of a for which the graph of the first equation is perpendicular to the graph of the second equation.

19. $y = ax - 5$; $2y = 3x$ $-\frac{2}{3}$
20. $y = ax + 2$; $3y - 4x = 7$ $-\frac{3}{4}$
21. $y = \frac{a}{3}x - 6$; $4x + 2y = 6$ $\frac{3}{2}$
22. $3y + ax = 8$; $y = \frac{3}{4}x + 2$ 4

23. Show that (1, 3), (4, 1), and (5, 9) are vertices of a right triangle.
24. Show that $({}^{-}6, 5)$, $({}^{-}2, 7)$, $(5, 3)$, and $(1, 1)$ are vertices of a parallelogram.
25. Write a computer program to find the equation of a line passing through (p, q) and parallel to a line whose equation is $ax + by = c$.
26. Write a computer program to find the equation of a line passing through (p, q) and perpendicular to a line whose equation is $ax + by = c$.

For answers to problems **23–26,** see the Teacher's Guide.

CAREERS

Archeologist

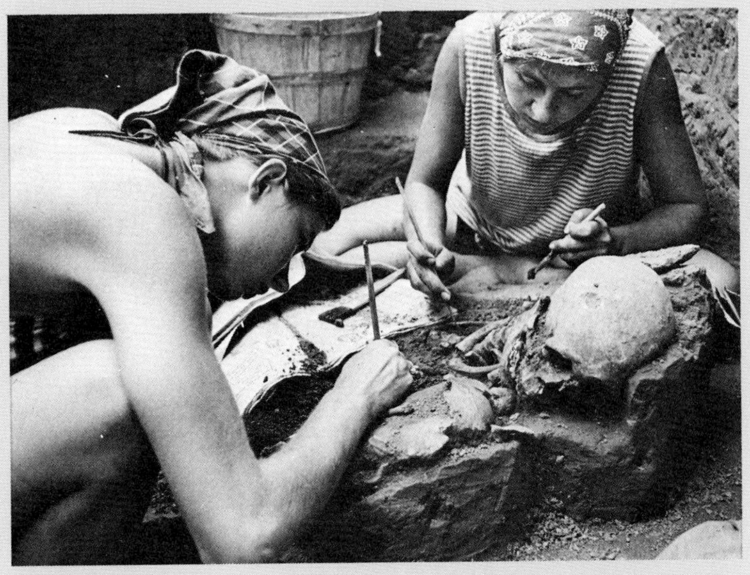

Jeanne Cezanne is an archeologist. Her specific job is identifying ancient documents, paintings, and art. Often, she must translate writings from a language that has not been used for several centuries. In this work she not only must understand the language, but the numeration system as well.

One ancient Greek system used the symbols shown below for powers of ten.

symbol	I	Δ	H	X	M
word	ena	deka	heka	chilioi	mynioi
meaning	1	10	100	1000	10,000

The system also had a unique way of showing five times each of the powers.

𐅃 meant 5

𐅄 meant 5 × 10 or 50

𐅅 meant 5 × 100 or 500

This pattern was probably one of the first attempts to express numbers concisely. Follow the same pattern to find Greek numerals for 5000 and 50,000.

Exercises Find the meaning for each of the following numerals.

1. 𐅃II
2. 𐅄II
3. 𐅅𐅄III
4. X𐅄II
5. 𐅆𐅄𐅃
6. XXΔ
7. MXHΔII
8. XX𐅄Δ

1. 7 **2.** 52 **3.** 553 **4.** 1052 **5.** 5055 **6.** 2010 **7.** 11,112 **8.** 2060

3-2 Systems of Equations

Objective: To learn about systems of equations.

The cost of renting a car from ACE is \$7 per day plus 10¢ per mile driven. The cost of renting a similar car from QUALITY is \$8 per day plus 8¢ per mile driven. Crystal needs to rent a car for one day. Should she rent from ACE or QUALITY?

Let r stand for the cost of renting a car for one day.
Let d stand for the number of miles driven in one day.

You can write the following equations.

$r = 7 + 0.10d$ *Cost of renting car from ACE for one day*

$r = 8 + 0.08d$ *Cost of renting car from QUALITY for one day*

Graphing these two equations shows how the costs compare. The graphs show that the QUALITY car costs more if less than 50 miles are driven. The QUALITY and ACE car cost the same if 50 miles are driven. The ACE car costs more if more than 50 miles are driven.

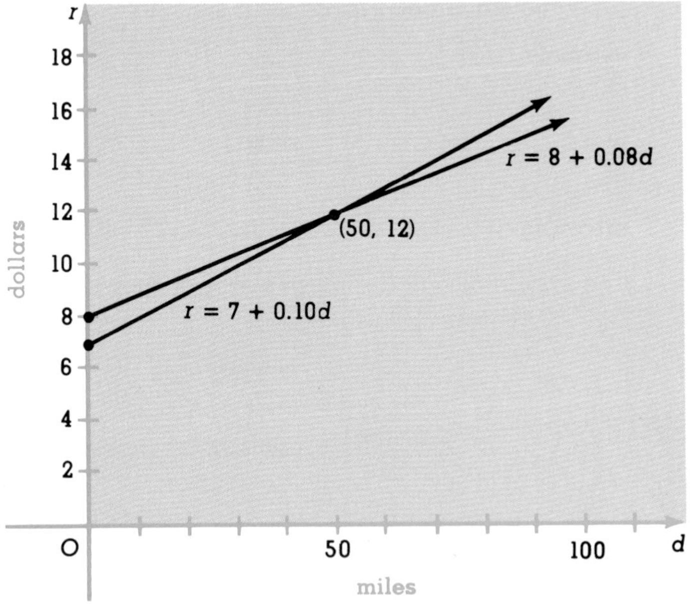

Each point on a line satisfies the equation of the line. Since (50, 12) is on both lines graphed above, it satisfies both equations.

Together the equations $r = 7 + 0.10d$ and $r = 8 + 0.08d$ are called a **system of equations.** The solution of the system is (50, 12).

example 1

Solve the system of equations.

$3x - y = 1$
$2x + y = 4$

The slope-intercept form of $3x - y = 1$ is $y = 3x - 1$. The slope-intercept form of $2x + y = 4$ is $y = {}^{-}2x + 4$. The two lines have different slopes. The graphs of the equations are intersecting lines. The solution of the system is (1, 2).

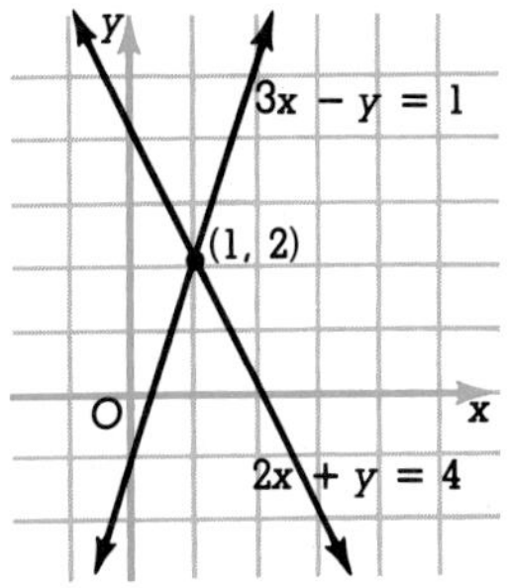

A system of equations that has *one* ordered pair as its solution is said to be **consistent** and **independent.** However, not all systems have one ordered pair as the solution.

examples 2

Solve the system of equations.

$y = {}^{-}3x - 2$
$y = {}^{-}3x + 3$

Both lines have the same slope but different y-intercepts. The graph of the equations are parallel lines. Since they do not intersect, there is *no solution* to the system of equations. Such a system is said to be **inconsistent.**

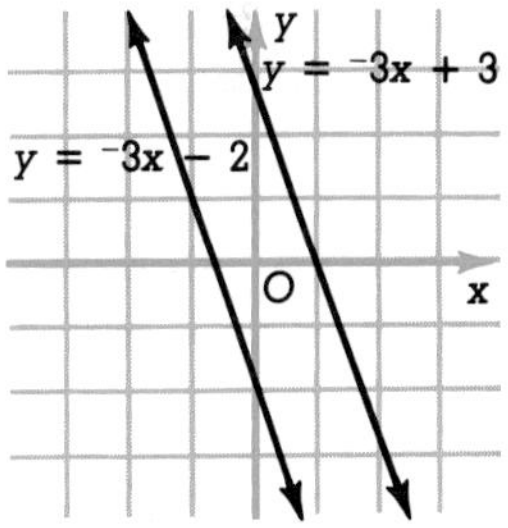

3

Solve the system of equations.

$2y + 3x = 6$
$4y + 6x = 12$

The slope-intercept form of $2y + 3x = 6$ is $y = -\frac{3}{2}x + 3$.

The slope-intercept form of $4y + 6x = 12$ is $y = -\frac{3}{2}x + 3$.

Both lines have the same slope and the same y-intercept. The graphs of the equations are the same line. Any ordered pair on the graph satisfies both equations. So, there is an *infinite number* of solutions to this system of equations. Such a system is said to be **consistent** and **dependent.**

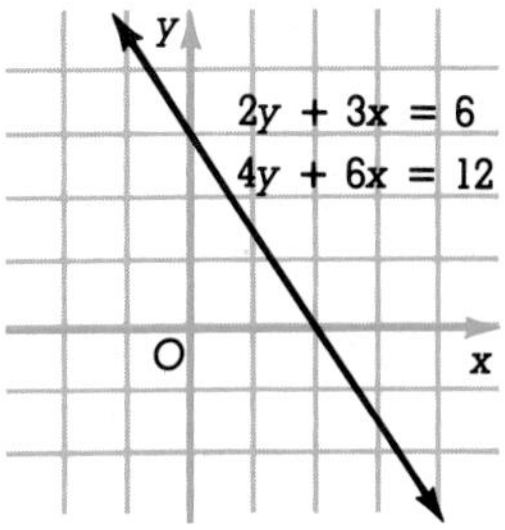

The solution set is $\{(x, y) | 2x + 3y = 6\}$.

exercises

Max: 1–6, 1–32; Avg: 1–6, 1–31 odds; Min: 1–6, 1–31 odds

Exploratory State the ordered pair which is the intersection of each pair of lines.

1. a, b $(^-3, 6)$
2. a, e $(3, 3)$
3. a, d $(5, 2)$
4. b, c $(^-5, 1)$
5. c, d $(2, ^-4)$
6. e, d $(4, 0)$

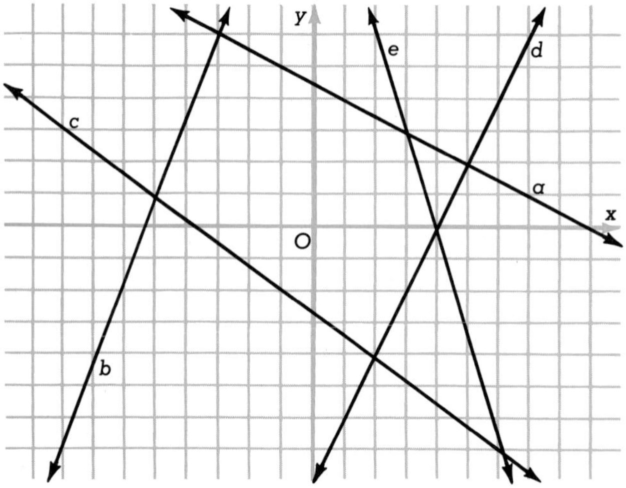

Written Graph the equations. Then state the solution to the system of equations.

1. $x + y = 4$, $2x + 3y = 9$ $(3, 1)$
2. $x + y = 6$, $x - y = 2$ $(4, 2)$
3. $x + y = 6$, $3x + 3y = 3$ no solutions
4. $x + 1 = y$, $2x - 2y = 8$ no solutions
5. $x + 2y = 5$, $3x - 15 = {}^-6y$ $\{(x, y) | x + 2y = 5\}$
6. $2x + 4y = 8$, $x + 2y = 4$ $\{(x, y) | x + 2y = 4\}$
7. $y = {}^-3x$, $6y - x = {}^-38$ $(2, ^-6)$
8. $x + y = 1$, $3x + 5y = 7$ $(^-1, 2)$
9. $x + y = {}^-6$, $2x - y = 2$ $\left(-\frac{4}{3}, -\frac{14}{3}\right)$
10. $3x + 6 = 7y$, $x + 2y = 11$ $(5, 3)$
11. $x + 5y = 10$, $x + 5y = 15$ no solutions
12. $3x - 8y = 4$, $6x - 42 = 16y$ no solutions
13. $2x + 3y = {}^-4$, ${}^-3x + y = {}^-5$ $(1, ^-2)$
14. ${}^-2x + 5y = {}^-14$, $x - y = 1$ $(^-3, ^-4)$
15. $2x + 3y = 5$, ${}^-6x - 9y = {}^-15$ $\{(x, y) | 2x + 3y = 5\}$
16. $9x - 5 = 7y$, $4\frac{1}{2}x - 3\frac{1}{2}y = 2\frac{1}{2}$ $\{(x, y) | 9x - 5 = 7y\}$

17–32. Tell whether each system in problems **1–16** is consistent and independent, consistent and dependent, or inconsistent.

For answers to problems **17–32**, see the Teacher's Guide.

3-3 Solving Systems of Equations

Objective: To learn to solve systems of equations.

Usually a system of equations is easier to solve by algebraic methods rather than by graphing. Two such methods are the **substitution method** and the **elimination method.**

From their work in Algebra One, some students may prefer either the substitution method or the elimination method. Use this preference to aid the teaching process, but require all students to try both methods.

examples

1 **Use the substitution method to solve the system of equations.**

$$y = 3x - 1$$
$$3x + 2y = 16$$

The first equation says that y is equal to $3x - 1$. Therefore, $3x - 1$ can be *substituted* for y in the second equation.

$$3x + 2y = 16$$
$$3x + 2(3x - 1) = 16 \quad \textit{Substitute } 3x - 1 \textit{ for } y.$$
$$3x + 6x - 2 = 16 \quad \textit{The resulting equation has only one variable now, } x.$$
$$9x - 2 = 16$$
$$9x = 18$$
$$x = 2$$

Now find y by substituting 2 for x in the equation $y = 3x - 1$.

$$y = 3x - 1$$
$$y = 3(2) - 1 \quad \textit{Substitute 2 for } x.$$
$$y = 5$$

The solution is (2, 5).

2 **Use the elimination method to solve the system of equations.**

$$4x + 2y = {}^-8$$
$$x - 2y = {}^-7$$

Add the second equation to the first equation.

$$4x + 2y = {}^-8$$
$$x - 2y = {}^-7 \quad \textit{Add.}$$
$$5x = {}^-15 \quad \textit{The variable } y \textit{ is eliminated.}$$
$$x = {}^-3 \quad \textit{Solve for } x.$$

Now substitute $^-3$ for x in $x - 2y = {}^-7$ to find y.

$$x - 2y = {}^-7$$
$$({}^-3) - 2y = {}^-7 \quad \textit{Substitute } {}^-3 \textit{ for } x.$$
$${}^-2y = {}^-4$$
$$y = 2$$

The solution is ($^-3$, 2).

example 3

Use the elimination method to solve the system of equations.

$$2x + 3y = 2$$
$$3x - 4y = {}^-14$$

Adding the two equations does *not* eliminate a variable. However, if the first equation is multiplied by 4 and the second equation is multiplied by 3, the system *can* be solved by adding.

$2x + 3y = 2$	**Multiply by 4.** →	$8x + 12y = 8$
$3x - 4y = {}^-14$	**Multiply by 3.** →	$9x - 12y = {}^-42$

Now add to eliminate y. Then solve for x.

$$\begin{aligned} 8x + 12y &= 8 \\ 9x - 12y &= {}^-42 \end{aligned} \quad \textit{Add.}$$
$$17x = {}^-34 \quad \textit{The variable y is eliminated.}$$
$$x = {}^-2 \quad \textit{Solve for x.}$$

Point out to the students that there is more than one way to solve a system of equations. This system could be solved by multiplying the first equation by $^-3$ and the second equation by 2.

Finally, substitute $^-2$ for x and solve for y. Use the original first equation.

$$\begin{aligned} 2x + 3y &= 2 \\ 2({}^-2) + 3y &= 2 \\ {}^-4 + 3y &= 2 \\ 3y &= 6 \\ y &= 2 \end{aligned}$$

The solution is $({}^-2, 2)$.

exercises

Max: 1–10, 1–32; **Avg:** 1–10, 1–29 odds, 31, 32; **Min:** 1–10, 1–29 odds

Exploratory **For each system, state the multipliers you would use to eliminate one variable by addition.**

1. $2x + 3y = 7$ 3; $3x - 7y = 2$ $^-2$ — to eliminate x
2. $x - y = 1$ $^-1$; $3x - y = 4$ — to eliminate y
3. $6x - 4y = 11$; $4x + y = 6$ 4 — to eliminate y
4. $x + 2y = 3$ $^-5$; $5x - 3y = 2$ — to eliminate x
5. $3x + 4y = 7$ 2; $2x + 5y = 11$ $^-3$ — to eliminate x
6. $x + 8y = 11$ 3; $^-3x + 7y = 6$ — to eliminate x
7. $3x + 4y = 7$ 3; $4x - 3y = 1$ 4 — to eliminate y
8. $2x - 3y = 0$ 2; $6x + 6y = 7$ — to eliminate y
9. $x + y = 6$; $^-2x + y = {}^-3$ $^-1$ — to eliminate y
10. $3x - 5y = {}^-13$ 4; $4x + 3y = 2$ $^-3$ — to eliminate x

Written **Solve each system of equations by the substitution method.**

1. $2x + 2y = 4$, $x - 2y = 0$ $\left(\frac{4}{3}, \frac{2}{3}\right)$
2. $6x - 4y = {}^{-}6$, $3x + y = 3$ $\left(\frac{1}{3}, 2\right)$
3. $y = 3x$, $x + 2y = {}^{-}21$ $({}^{-}3, {}^{-}9)$
4. $2m + n = 1$, $m - n = 8$ $(3, {}^{-}5)$
5. $x - 2y = 5$, $3x - 5y = 8$ $({}^{-}9, {}^{-}7)$
6. $3x + 4y = {}^{-}7$, $2x + y = {}^{-}3$ $({}^{-}1, {}^{-}1)$

7–12. Solve each system of equations in problems **1–6** by the elimination method. See answers above.

Solve each system of equations.

13. $3x + 2y = 40$, $x - 7y = {}^{-}2$ $(12, 2)$
14. $3x - 5y = {}^{-}13$, $4x + 3y = 2$ $({}^{-}1, 2)$
15. $\frac{1}{4}x + y = \frac{7}{2}$, $\frac{1}{2}x - \frac{1}{4}y = 1$ $\left(\frac{10}{3}, \frac{8}{3}\right)$
16. $3y - 2x = 4$, $\frac{1}{6}(3y - 4x) = 1$ $\left({}^{-}1, \frac{2}{3}\right)$
17. ${}^{-}9x - 6y = {}^{-}15$, $13x + 7y = \frac{55}{3}$ $\left(\frac{1}{3}, 2\right)$
18. $2x - y = 36$, $3x + \frac{1}{2}y = 26$ $(11, {}^{-}14)$
19. $2x + 3y = 8$, $x - y = 2$ $(2.8, 0.8)$
20. $5m + 2n = {}^{-}8$, $4m + 3n = 2$ $({}^{-}4, 6)$
21. $x + y = 6$, $x - y = 4.5$ $(5.25, 0.75)$
22. $3x + \frac{1}{3}y = 10$, $2x - 5 = \frac{1}{3}y$ $(3, 3)$
23. $2y - 3x = 0$, $x - y + 2 = 0$ $(4, 6)$
24. $2x + 3y - 8 = 0$, $3x + 2y - 17 = 0$ $(7, {}^{-}2)$
25. $\frac{1}{3}x + 5 = \frac{2}{3}y$, $\frac{1}{2}x + \frac{1}{3}y = \frac{1}{2}$ $({}^{-}3, 6)$
26. $\frac{2x + y}{3} = 5$, $\frac{3x - y}{5} = 1$ $(4, 7)$
27. $ax + by = c$, $dx + ey = f$ $\left(\frac{ce - bf}{ae - bd}, \frac{af - cd}{ae - bd}\right)$
28. $\frac{1}{3}x + \frac{1}{3}y = 5$, $\frac{1}{6}x - \frac{1}{9}y = 0$ $(6, 9)$

29. $34x - 63y = {}^{-}1063$, $14x + 43y = 2251$ $(41, 39)$
30. $108x + 537y = {}^{-}1395$, ${}^{-}214x - 321y = 535$ $(2, {}^{-}3)$
31. Write a computer program to solve the system $ax + by = c$ and $dx + ey = f$. Input the value of a, b, c, d, e, and f. Print out the system and its solution, if it exists. See Teacher's Guide.
32. The sum of two numbers is 42. Their difference is 12. What are the numbers? 27 and 15

Computer Languages

Every location in a computer's memory contains some arrangement of magnetic or electronic indicators. The original computers were programmed by setting thousands of switches. It often took as long as an entire day to prepare the computer ENIAC for a problem. *ENIAC was one of the first electronic computers.*

Every modern computer has its own **machine language.** Machine languages are numerical codes which represent basic machine operations. For example, suppose *26* is the code in the circuitry for *addition*. Then, *26, 78, 354* could mean *add the value in the 78th memory location to the value in the 354th memory location*. The memory locations for *78* and *354* are in the data part of the memory.

Machine languages make it possible to store the steps of a problem in a computer. Thus, a single program can be used for any set of figures that are placed in the data part of a computer's memory.

Programs in **assembly language** are much easier to read than are programs in machine language. Assembly languages use symbolic words to represent the numerical codes of machine languages. For example, an assembly language might use *add* rather than *26*. A special computer program called an **assembler** is used to translate programs from assembly language into numerical machine language that can be "understood" by the circuitry of the computer.

Most computer users never use assembly or machine languages, nor consider how a computer functions inside. They use programs written in **problem-oriented languages** such as BASIC (**B**eginner's **A**ll-purpose **S**ymbolic **I**nstruction **C**ode), FORTRAN (**For**mula **Tran**slator), and COBOL (**Co**mmon **B**usiness-**O**riented **L**anguage). The codes and rules of grammar for these languages are closer to standard speaking languages than either assembly or machine languages. Problem-oriented languages are designed to meet the needs of particular types of problems, rather than particular kinds of computers. By making a few small changes, the same problem-oriented language can be used with different computers.

Computer programs called **compilers** are used to translate problem-oriented languages into machine language. A FORTRAN compiler, for example, translates a FORTRAN program into machine language for later use. The first compiler was developed in 1952 by Dr. Grace M. Hopper for the UNIVAC computer.

A program that actually carries out the steps specified in a program written in a problem-oriented language is called an **interpreter.** Compiler and interpreter programs for a problem-oriented language are *specific* to a given computer system. The problem-oriented language itself is not.

3-4 Determinants

Objective: To learn how to calculate determinants.

An arrangement of numerals in rows and columns like the one below is called a **matrix.** The following matrix has two rows and four columns.

$$\begin{bmatrix} 1 & 9 & 5 & 7 \\ 6 & 4 & 12 & 2 \end{bmatrix} \text{ is a 2 by 4 matrix.}$$

A square matrix has the same number of rows as columns.

$$\begin{bmatrix} 2 & 1 \\ 3 & 4 \end{bmatrix} \text{ is a 2 by 2 square matrix.}$$

$$\begin{bmatrix} 4 & 1 & 2 \\ ^{-}3 & 0 & 1 \\ 5 & 2 & 6 \end{bmatrix} \text{ is a 3 by 3 square matrix.}$$

Each square matrix has a value called the **determinant** of the matrix.

The determinant of $\begin{bmatrix} 2 & 1 \\ 3 & 4 \end{bmatrix}$ is 5.

The determinant of $\begin{bmatrix} 2 & 1 \\ 3 & 4 \end{bmatrix}$ is denoted by $\det\begin{bmatrix} 2 & 1 \\ 3 & 4 \end{bmatrix}$ or $\begin{vmatrix} 2 & 1 \\ 3 & 4 \end{vmatrix}$.

If $M = \begin{bmatrix} a & b \\ c & d \end{bmatrix}$, then $\det M = ad - cb$.

Definition of 2 by 2 Determinant

example 1

Find the determinant of $\begin{bmatrix} 2 & 1 \\ 3 & 4 \end{bmatrix}$.

$$\det\begin{bmatrix} 2 & 1 \\ 3 & 4 \end{bmatrix} = 2 \cdot 4 - 3 \cdot 1$$
$$= 5$$

The determinant is 5.

If $N = \begin{bmatrix} a & b & c \\ d & e & f \\ g & h & i \end{bmatrix}$, then
$\det N = aei + bfg + cdh - gec - hfa - idb$.

Definition of 3 by 3 Determinant

example 2

Find the determinant of $\begin{bmatrix} 1 & 2 & 3 \\ 4 & 5 & 6 \\ 7 & 8 & 9 \end{bmatrix}$.

$$\begin{matrix} 1 & 2 \\ 4 & 5 \\ 7 & 8 \end{matrix}$$

$$\det\begin{bmatrix} 1 & 2 & 3 \\ 4 & 5 & 6 \\ 7 & 8 & 9 \end{bmatrix} = 1 \cdot 5 \cdot 9 + 2 \cdot 6 \cdot 7 + 3 \cdot 4 \cdot 8 - 7 \cdot 5 \cdot 3 - 8 \cdot 6 \cdot 1 - 9 \cdot 4 \cdot 2$$
$$= 0$$

The determinant is 0.

exercises

Max: 1–12, 1–29; **Avg:** 1–12, 1–29 odds; **Min:** 1–12, 1–29 odds

Exploratory Find each determinant.

1. $\begin{vmatrix} 3 & 1 \\ 4 & 6 \end{vmatrix}$ 14
2. $\begin{vmatrix} 7 & -3 \\ 0 & 1 \end{vmatrix}$ 7
3. $\begin{vmatrix} 0 & 1 \\ 0 & 1 \end{vmatrix}$ 0
4. $\begin{vmatrix} 11 & -2 \\ -3 & -5 \end{vmatrix}$ -61
5. $\begin{vmatrix} 1 & 0 \\ 0 & 1 \end{vmatrix}$ 1
6. $\begin{vmatrix} -8 & -7 \\ -4 & -6 \end{vmatrix}$ 20
7. $\begin{vmatrix} 2 & 4 \\ -3 & 1 \end{vmatrix}$ 14
8. $\begin{vmatrix} -5 & 3 \\ 1 & 2 \end{vmatrix}$ -13
9. $\begin{vmatrix} 7 & 8 \\ -9 & 0 \end{vmatrix}$ 72
10. $\begin{vmatrix} 5 & 5 \\ 5 & 5 \end{vmatrix}$ 0
11. $\begin{vmatrix} -6 & -2 \\ 2 & 6 \end{vmatrix}$ -32
12. $\begin{vmatrix} 8 & -1 \\ 13 & 0 \end{vmatrix}$ 13

Written Find each determinant.

1. $\begin{vmatrix} 24 & 6 \\ -13 & -4 \end{vmatrix}$ -18
2. $\begin{vmatrix} 18 & -5 \\ -9 & 11 \end{vmatrix}$ 153
3. $\begin{vmatrix} -13 & -11 \\ 17 & -12 \end{vmatrix}$ 343
4. $\begin{vmatrix} 4 & 2 & -3 \\ 5 & 1 & 0 \\ -2 & 1 & 1 \end{vmatrix}$ -27
5. $\begin{vmatrix} 3 & 0 & 2 \\ 0 & -1 & 5 \\ 6 & 7 & 0 \end{vmatrix}$ -93
6. $\begin{vmatrix} 2 & 4 & 6 \\ 1 & 2 & 3 \\ 3 & -1 & 4 \end{vmatrix}$ 0
7. $\begin{vmatrix} 6 & 7 & 4 \\ -2 & -4 & 3 \\ 1 & 1 & 1 \end{vmatrix}$ 1
8. $\begin{vmatrix} 1 & 0 & 0 \\ 0 & 1 & 0 \\ 0 & 0 & 1 \end{vmatrix}$ 1
9. $\begin{vmatrix} 1 & 0 & 0 \\ 2 & 4 & 0 \\ 5 & -1 & -3 \end{vmatrix}$ -12
10. $\begin{vmatrix} 76 & 31 & -3 \\ 22 & 49 & 60 \\ 14 & 98 & 31 \end{vmatrix}$ $-330{,}948$
11. $\begin{vmatrix} 471 & 318 & 219 \\ 21 & 37 & -4 \\ 66 & 77 & 88 \end{vmatrix}$ 826,353
12. $\begin{vmatrix} 44 & 41 & 46 \\ 32 & -59 & 36 \\ 72 & -61 & 84 \end{vmatrix}$ $-19{,}760$

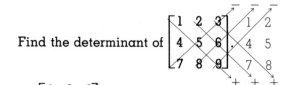

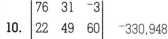

Find the value of each determinant using expansion by minors.

Sample: The following calculation shows how to find the determinant of a 3 by 3 matrix using a method called **expansion by minors.**

$$\begin{vmatrix} 2 & 3 & 4 \\ 5 & 6 & 7 \\ 8 & 9 & 10 \end{vmatrix} = 2\begin{vmatrix} 6 & 7 \\ 9 & 10 \end{vmatrix} - 3\begin{vmatrix} 5 & 7 \\ 8 & 10 \end{vmatrix} + 4\begin{vmatrix} 5 & 6 \\ 8 & 9 \end{vmatrix}$$

$$= 2(60 - 63) - 3(50 - 56) + 4(45 - 48)$$

$$= 2 \cdot {}^{-}3 - 3 \cdot {}^{-}6 + 4 \cdot {}^{-}3$$

$$= 0$$

13. $\begin{vmatrix} 2 & 0 & 2 \\ 0 & 3 & {}^{-}3 \\ {}^{-}3 & {}^{-}2 & 0 \end{vmatrix}$ 6

14. $\begin{vmatrix} 2 & 3 & 4 \\ 3 & 2 & {}^{-}1 \\ 4 & 3 & 7 \end{vmatrix}$ ${}^{-}37$

15. $\begin{vmatrix} 1 & 3 & {}^{-}2 \\ 2 & {}^{-}1 & 1 \\ {}^{-}2 & 2 & 3 \end{vmatrix}$ ${}^{-}33$

16. $\begin{vmatrix} {}^{-}1 & 1 & 2 \\ 2 & 1 & 0 \\ 3 & 6 & {}^{-}2 \end{vmatrix}$ 24

17. $\begin{vmatrix} 1 & {}^{-}1 & 1 \\ 4 & 3 & 1 \\ 0 & 5 & 2 \end{vmatrix}$ 29

18. $\begin{vmatrix} 3 & {}^{-}1 & 2 \\ 0 & 4 & 1 \\ 5 & {}^{-}2 & {}^{-}3 \end{vmatrix}$ ${}^{-}75$

19. $\begin{vmatrix} 1 & 2 & {}^{-}3 \\ 3 & {}^{-}5 & {}^{-}1 \\ 4 & 4 & 1 \end{vmatrix}$ ${}^{-}111$

20. $\begin{vmatrix} 3 & 2 & 5 \\ {}^{-}1 & 1 & 1 \\ 4 & 3 & 3 \end{vmatrix}$ ${}^{-}21$

21. $\begin{vmatrix} 4 & 0 & 1 \\ 2 & {}^{-}3 & 3 \\ 5 & 4 & {}^{-}6 \end{vmatrix}$ 47

22–25. Find the determinant of each 3 by 3 matrix in the calculation below.

Sample: The following calculation shows how to expand a 4 by 4 matrix by minors.

$$\begin{vmatrix} 2 & 3 & 4 & 5 \\ 6 & 7 & 8 & 9 \\ 10 & 11 & 12 & 13 \\ 14 & 15 & 16 & 17 \end{vmatrix} = 2\begin{vmatrix} 7 & 8 & 9 \\ 11 & 12 & 13 \\ 15 & 16 & 17 \end{vmatrix} - 3\begin{vmatrix} 6 & 8 & 9 \\ 10 & 12 & 13 \\ 14 & 16 & 17 \end{vmatrix} + 4\begin{vmatrix} 6 & 7 & 9 \\ 10 & 11 & 13 \\ 14 & 15 & 17 \end{vmatrix} - 5\begin{vmatrix} 6 & 7 & 8 \\ 10 & 11 & 12 \\ 14 & 15 & 16 \end{vmatrix}$$

22. 0 **23.** 0 **24.** 0 **25.** 0

26. Find the determinant of the 4 by 4 matrix in the above calculation. 0

Find the value of each determinant using expansion by minors.

27. $\begin{vmatrix} 1 & 2 & 3 & 1 \\ 4 & 3 & {}^{-}1 & 0 \\ 2 & {}^{-}5 & 4 & 4 \\ 1 & {}^{-}2 & 0 & 2 \end{vmatrix}$ ${}^{-}109$

28. $\begin{vmatrix} 3 & 3 & 3 & 3 \\ 2 & 1 & 2 & 1 \\ 4 & 3 & {}^{-}1 & 5 \\ 2 & 5 & 0 & 1 \end{vmatrix}$ ${}^{-}72$

29. $\begin{vmatrix} 1 & 4 & 3 & 0 \\ {}^{-}2 & {}^{-}3 & 6 & 4 \\ 5 & 1 & 1 & 2 \\ 4 & 2 & 5 & {}^{-}1 \end{vmatrix}$ ${}^{-}676$

3–5 Cramer's Rule

Objective: To learn to solve systems of equations using Cramer's Rule.

The solution to $\begin{aligned} 3x + 4y &= 7 \\ 2x + 5y &= 11 \end{aligned}$ is $\left(-\frac{9}{7}, \frac{19}{7}\right)$.

The following matrix is made using the coefficients from the equations.

$$\begin{bmatrix} 3 & 4 \\ 2 & 5 \end{bmatrix}$$

The determinant of this matrix is 7.

$3x + 4y = 7$
$2x + 5y = 11$

Other matrices can also be made using the same system of equations.

$3x + 4y = 7$
$2x + 5y = 11$

$$\begin{bmatrix} 7 & 4 \\ 11 & 5 \end{bmatrix}$$

The determinant is $^-9$.

$$\begin{bmatrix} 3 & 7 \\ 2 & 11 \end{bmatrix}$$

The determinant is 19.

$3x + 4y = 7$
$2x + 5y = 11$

Compare the determinants of the matrices to the solution of the system. They are related in the following way.

The value of x in the solution is $\dfrac{\begin{vmatrix} 7 & 4 \\ 11 & 5 \end{vmatrix}}{\begin{vmatrix} 3 & 4 \\ 2 & 5 \end{vmatrix}}$ or $-\frac{9}{7}$.

Notice that $\begin{matrix} 7 \\ 11 \end{matrix}$ is in the "x column."

The value of y in the solution is $\dfrac{\begin{vmatrix} 3 & 7 \\ 2 & 11 \end{vmatrix}}{\begin{vmatrix} 3 & 4 \\ 2 & 5 \end{vmatrix}}$ or $\frac{19}{7}$.

Notice that $\begin{matrix} 7 \\ 11 \end{matrix}$ is in the "y column."

Cramer's Rule

The solution to $\begin{aligned} ax + by &= c \\ dx + ey &= f \end{aligned}$ is (x, y) where

$$x = \frac{\begin{vmatrix} c & b \\ f & e \end{vmatrix}}{\begin{vmatrix} a & b \\ d & e \end{vmatrix}} \text{ and } y = \frac{\begin{vmatrix} a & c \\ d & f \end{vmatrix}}{\begin{vmatrix} a & b \\ d & e \end{vmatrix}} \text{ and } \begin{vmatrix} a & b \\ d & e \end{vmatrix} \neq 0.$$

In order to use Cramer's Rule, equations must be in standard form.

example 1

Use Cramer's rule to solve the following system of equations.

$$3x - 5y = {}^-7$$
$$x + 2y = 16$$

$$x = \frac{\begin{vmatrix} {}^-7 & {}^-5 \\ 16 & 2 \end{vmatrix}}{\begin{vmatrix} 3 & {}^-5 \\ 1 & 2 \end{vmatrix}} = \frac{{}^-7 \cdot 2 - 16 \cdot {}^-5}{3 \cdot 2 - 1 \cdot {}^-5} = \frac{66}{11} = 6$$

$$y = \frac{\begin{vmatrix} 3 & {}^-7 \\ 1 & 16 \end{vmatrix}}{\begin{vmatrix} 3 & {}^-5 \\ 1 & 2 \end{vmatrix}} = \frac{3 \cdot 16 - 1 \cdot {}^-7}{3 \cdot 2 - 1 \cdot {}^-5} = \frac{55}{11} = 5$$

The solution is (6, 5).

exercises

Max: 1–10, 1–11; **Avg:** 1–10, 1–11 odds; **Min:** 1–10, 1–9 odds

Exploratory **Name the matrices you would use to solve each system by Cramer's rule.**

1. $3x + 2y = 5$
   $5x - 6y = 11$
2. $7x - 8y = 11$
   $9x - 2y = 3$
3. $x + 11 = 8y$
   $8(x - y) = 3$
4. $3x - y = 2$
   $x + y = 5$
5. $4x + 2y = 11$
   $3x - y = 5$
6. $2x + 6y = 11$
   $5x + y = 6$
7. $\frac{1}{3}x + 6y = \frac{1}{2}$
   $x - 8y = \frac{1}{4}$
8. $\frac{1}{4}x + \frac{1}{5}y = \frac{1}{6}$
   $\frac{1}{7}x + \frac{1}{8}y = \frac{1}{9}$
9. $0.30x + 0.41y = 0.56$
   $0.23x - 0.41y = 0.77$
10. $0.61x + 0.63y = 61$
    $0.63x - 0.77y = 0.6$

For answers to problems **1–10**, see the Teacher's Guide.

Written

1–10. Solve each system of equations in the exploratory exercises using Cramer's rule. For answers to problems **1–10**, see the Teacher's Guide.

11. Explain why Cramer's rule will not work if a system of equations is dependent or inconsistent. The determinant of the denominator would be zero.

3-6 Systems of Three Equations

Objective: To learn to solve systems of three equations.

The system below has three equations and three variables.

$$\begin{aligned} 2x + 3y + z &= 13 \\ 4x + 2y - z &= 15 \\ x + y + z &= 6 \end{aligned}$$

Each equation is satisfied when x is 3, y is 2, and z is 1. So, a solution to this system is (3, 2, 1).

$$\begin{aligned} 2(3) + 3(2) + (1) &= 6 + 6 + 1 = 13 \\ 4(3) + 2(2) - (1) &= 12 + 4 - 1 = 15 \\ (3) + (2) + (1) &= 3 + 2 + 1 = 6 \end{aligned}$$

Algebra can be used to find the solutions to a system of three equations in three variables. First, use substitution or elimination to make a system of two equations in two variables.

Add the first and second equations.

$$\begin{array}{r} 2x + 3y + z = 13 \\ \underline{4x + 2y - z = 15} \\ 6x + 5y \phantom{{}- z} = 28 \end{array}$$

Add the second and third equations.

$$\begin{array}{r} 4x + 2y - z = 15 \\ \underline{x + y + z = 6} \\ 5x + 3y \phantom{{}+ z} = 21 \end{array}$$

The result is two equations with the same two variables.

$$\begin{aligned} 6x + 5y &= 28 \\ 5x + 3y &= 21 \end{aligned}$$

Solve this system for x and y.

$6x + 5y = 28$	Multiply by $^-3$.	$^-18x + {}^-15y = {}^-84$
$5x + 3y = 21$	Multiply by 5.	$25x + 15y = 105$
		$7x + 0 = 21$
		$x = 3$

Now substitute 3 for x in $6x + 5y = 28$ to find y.

$$\begin{aligned} 6(3) + 5y &= 28 \quad \textit{Substitute 3 for x.} \\ 18 + 5y &= 28 \\ 5y &= 10 \\ y &= 2 \end{aligned}$$

Then substitute the values for x and y in one of the original equations. Solve the equation for z.

$$\begin{aligned} x + y + z &= 6 \\ (3) + (2) + z &= 6 \\ z &= 1 \end{aligned}$$

exercises

Max: 1–6, 1–14, Challenge; Avg: 1–6, 1–13 odds; Min: 1–6, 1–13 odds

Exploratory A possible solution for each system of equations is given in green. Check to see if it is the correct solution.

1. $x + y + z = 6$ (2, 2, 2)
   $x - 3y + 2z = 1$ no
   $2x - y + 2z = 0$
2. $2x + 3y - z = 0$ (0, 0, 0)
   $x + 2y + z = 0$ yes
   $x - y + z = 0$
3. $4x + y - 2z = 0$ (3, 0, 6)
   $^-2x + y + z = 0$ no
   $x - 2y = 0$
4. $3x + 2y + z = 5$ (8, $^-11$, 3)
   $2x + y - z = 2$ yes
   $x + y + z = 0$
5. $x + y + z = 3$ (3, $^-2$, 2)
   $x - z = 1$ yes
   $y - z = {^-4}$
6. $x + y = {^-6}$ ($^-4$, $^-2$, 2)
   $x + z = {^-2}$ no
   $y + z = 2$

Written Solve each system of equations.

1. $x + 2y + z = 8$
   $2x - y - z = {^-3}$ (1, 2, 3)
   $3x - 2y + 2z = 5$
2. $x + y - z = {^-1}$
   $x + y + z = 3$ (0, 1, 2)
   $3x - 2y - z = {^-4}$
3. $x + y + z = 0$
   $2x + y - z = 2$ (8, $^-11$, 3)
   $3x + 2y + z = 5$
4. $x + y + z = 15$
   $x + z = 12$ (5, 3, 7)
   $y + z = 10$
5. $x - 2y + z = 3$
   $2x + y - 2z = 31$ (10, 1, $^-5$)
   $^-x + 2y + 3z = {^-23}$
6. $x + y + z = 2$
   $2x - 3y + 2z = {^-1}$ (3, 1, $^-2$)
   $4x + 2y - z = 16$
7. $x + y + z = 4$
   $x - y + z = 0$ (1, 2, 1)
   $x - y - z = {^-2}$
8. $a + b - 2c = 4$
   $2a + b + 2c = 0$ (0, 2, $^-1$)
   $a - 3b - 4c = {^-2}$
9. $x + y + z = 2$
   $x - y - z = 0$ (1, $^-1$, 2)
   $2x - y + 3z = 9$
10. $2x + 3y + z = 7$
    $x + y - z = 4$ $(15, -\frac{17}{2}, \frac{5}{2})$
    $3x + 4y - 2z = 6$
11. $x + y + z = {^-1}$
    $2x - y + z = 19$ (4, $^-8$, 3)
    $3x - 2y - 4z = 16$
12. $2x - y + 4z = 7$
    $x - 3y + z = {^-2}$ ($^-2$, 1, 3)
    $3x - 2y + 2z = {^-2}$
13. $x + 2y - 3z = 10$
    $^-4x + y - z = {^-10}$ $(\frac{43}{14}, -\frac{1}{14}, -\frac{33}{14})$
    $3x - 7y + 2z = 5$
14. $x + 8y + 2z = {^-24}$
    $3x + y + 7z = {^-3}$ (0, $^-3$, 0)
    $4x - 3y + 6z = 9$

Challenge Solve the system of equations.

$$w + x + y + z = 2 \quad w = 1$$
$$2w - x - y + 2z = 7 \quad x = 0$$
$$2w + 3x + 2y - z = {^-2} \quad y = {^-1}$$
$$3w - 2x - y - 3z = {^-2} \quad z = 2$$

3-7 Augmented Matrix Solutions

Objective: To learn to solve a system of equations by using an augmented matrix.

A matrix can be written for a system of equations.

System of Equations

$$\begin{aligned} 3x + 4y - 2z &= 5 \\ 2x + y - z &= 1 \\ {}^{-}x - y - 2z &= {}^{-}9 \end{aligned}$$

Matrix

$$\begin{bmatrix} 3 & 4 & {}^{-}2 & 5 \\ 2 & 1 & {}^{-}1 & 1 \\ {}^{-}1 & {}^{-}1 & {}^{-}2 & {}^{-}9 \end{bmatrix}$$

This type of matrix is called an **augmented matrix.** The system of equations can be solved by using the matrix rather than the equations themselves. Each change of the matrix represents a corresponding change of the system.

$$\begin{bmatrix} 3 & 4 & {}^{-}2 & 5 \\ {}^{-}4 & {}^{-}2 & 2 & {}^{-}2 \\ {}^{-}1 & {}^{-}1 & {}^{-}2 & {}^{-}9 \end{bmatrix}$$

Multiply by ⁻2. (Multiply second equation by ⁻2.)

$$\begin{bmatrix} {}^{-}1 & 2 & 0 & 3 \\ {}^{-}5 & {}^{-}3 & 0 & {}^{-}11 \\ {}^{-}1 & {}^{-}1 & {}^{-}2 & {}^{-}9 \end{bmatrix}$$

Replace Row 1 by sum of Row 1 and Row 2.
Replace Row 2 by sum of Row 2 and Row 3.
What do these changes represent?

$$\begin{bmatrix} {}^{-}3 & 6 & 0 & 9 \\ {}^{-}10 & {}^{-}6 & 0 & {}^{-}22 \\ {}^{-}1 & {}^{-}1 & {}^{-}2 & {}^{-}9 \end{bmatrix}$$

Multiply by 3.
Multiply by 2.

$$\begin{bmatrix} {}^{-}13 & 0 & 0 & {}^{-}13 \\ {}^{-}10 & {}^{-}6 & 0 & {}^{-}22 \\ {}^{-}1 & {}^{-}1 & {}^{-}2 & {}^{-}9 \end{bmatrix}$$

Replace by sum of Row 1 and Row 2.

The last matrix represents the following system.

$$\begin{aligned} {}^{-}13x \phantom{{}-6y-2z} &= {}^{-}13 \\ {}^{-}10x - 6y \phantom{{}-2z} &= {}^{-}22 \\ {}^{-}x - y - 2z &= {}^{-}9 \end{aligned}$$

This system has the same solution as the original system. Use algebra to solve the system.

$$\begin{aligned} {}^{-}13x &= {}^{-}13 \\ x &= 1 \end{aligned}$$ *Solve for x.*

$$\begin{aligned} {}^{-}10x - 6y &= {}^{-}22 \\ {}^{-}10(1) - 6y &= {}^{-}22 \\ {}^{-}6y &= {}^{-}12 \\ y &= 2 \end{aligned}$$

Substitute value for x. (second line)
Solve for y. (last line)

$$
\begin{aligned}
{}^-x - y - 2z &= {}^-9 \\
{}^-(1) - (2) - 2z &= {}^-9 \quad \textit{Substitute values for x and y.} \\
{}^-3 - 2z &= {}^-9 \\
{}^-2z &= {}^-6 \\
z &= 3 \quad \text{The solution is (1, 2, 3).}
\end{aligned}
$$

In general, you may use any of the following **row operations** on an augmented matrix.

Row Operations on Matrices

> **1.** Interchange any two rows.
> **2.** Replace any row with a nonzero multiple of that row.
> **3.** Replace any row with the sum of that row and another row.

exercises

Max: 1–4, 1–10; Avg: 1–4, 1–9 odds; Min: 1–4, 1–9 odds

Exploratory **State the row operations you would use to locate a zero in the second column of row one.** Answers will vary.

1. $\begin{bmatrix} 2 & 1 & 3 \\ 4 & 2 & 6 \end{bmatrix}$ Notice the matrix in problem 1 represents dependent equations.
2. $\begin{bmatrix} {}^-3 & {}^-2 & 1 \\ 4 & {}^-2 & 6 \end{bmatrix}$
3. $\begin{bmatrix} 2 & 4 & 3 \\ {}^-2 & {}^-3 & 1 \end{bmatrix}$
4. $\begin{bmatrix} {}^-6 & {}^-2 & {}^-3 \\ 4 & 3 & 1 \end{bmatrix}$

Written **Solve each system of equations using augmented matrices.**

1. $3x + 2y = 5$, $4x - 3y = 1$ (1, 1)
2. $6x + y = 9$, $3x + 2y = 0$ (2, $^-3$)
3. ${}^-2x - 3y = {}^-11$, $3x + y = {}^-1$ ($^-2$, 5)
4. $3x + 3y = {}^-9$, ${}^-2x + y = {}^-4$ $(\frac{1}{3}, -\frac{10}{3})$
5. $x + y + z = {}^-2$, $2x - 3y + z = {}^-11$, ${}^-x + 2y - z = 8$ ($^-1$, 2, $^-3$)
6. $2x + 6y + 8z = 5$, ${}^-2x + 9y - 12z = {}^-1$, $4x + 6y - 4z = 3$ $(\frac{1}{2}, \frac{1}{3}, \frac{1}{4})$
7. $4x + 2y + 3z = 6$, $2x + 7y - 3z = 0$, ${}^-3x - 9y + 2z = {}^-13$ $(-\frac{91}{11}, \frac{68}{11}, \frac{98}{11})$
8. $x + y + z = 6$, $2x - 3y + 4z = 3$, $4x - 8y + 4z = 12$ (7, 1, $^-2$)
9. $4x + 3y + z = {}^-10$, $x - 12y + 2z = {}^-5$, $x + 18y + z = 4$ $({}^-3, \frac{1}{3}, 1)$
10. $x + 2y + z = 24$, $2x - 3y + z = {}^-1$, $x - 2y + 2z = 7$ (5, 6, 7)

Reading Algebra

Shortening Computations

In mathematics, you find ways to shorten computations. For example, multiplying 46 times 3 involves finding the sum of two products, 40 times 3 and 6 times 3. However, most people eventually learn to combine the two steps.

$$\begin{array}{r} 40 + 6 \\ \times \quad\;\; 3 \\ \hline 120 + 18 \text{ or } 130 \end{array} \qquad\qquad \begin{array}{r} 46 \\ \times\ 3 \\ \hline 138 \end{array}$$

The method on the left shows how the computation works. The method on the right is faster and uses less space.

Often, when a computation is shortened, it is more difficult to see how it works. Compare the elimination method and the augmented matrix method for solving a system of equations.

$$\begin{aligned} 3x + 4y - 2z &= 5 \\ 2x + y - z &= 1 \\ {}^-x - y - 2z &= {}^-9 \end{aligned} \qquad \begin{bmatrix} 3 & 4 & {}^-2 & 5 \\ 2 & 1 & {}^-1 & 1 \\ {}^-1 & {}^-1 & {}^-2 & {}^-9 \end{bmatrix}$$

$$\begin{aligned} 3x + 4y - 2z &= 5 \\ {}^-4x - 2y + 2z &= {}^-2 \\ {}^-x - y - 2z &= {}^-9 \end{aligned} \qquad \begin{bmatrix} 3 & 4 & {}^-2 & 5 \\ {}^-4 & {}^-2 & 2 & {}^-2 \\ {}^-1 & {}^-1 & {}^-2 & {}^-9 \end{bmatrix}$$

$$\begin{array}{r} 3x + 4y - 2z = 5 \\ {}^-4x - 2y + 2z = {}^-2 \\ \hline {}^-x + 2y \qquad = 3 \end{array} \qquad \begin{array}{r} {}^-4x - 2y + 2z = {}^-2 \\ {}^-x - \;\; y - 2z = {}^-9 \\ \hline {}^-5x - 3y \qquad = {}^-11 \end{array} \qquad \begin{bmatrix} {}^-1 & 2 & 0 & 3 \\ {}^-5 & {}^-3 & 0 & {}^-11 \\ {}^-1 & {}^-1 & {}^-2 & {}^-9 \end{bmatrix}$$

$$\begin{aligned} {}^-3x + 6y &= 9 \\ {}^-10x - 6y &= {}^-22 \\ {}^-x - y - 2z &= {}^-9 \end{aligned} \qquad \begin{bmatrix} {}^-3 & 6 & 0 & 9 \\ {}^-10 & {}^-6 & 0 & {}^-22 \\ {}^-1 & {}^-1 & {}^-2 & {}^-9 \end{bmatrix}$$

$$\begin{array}{r} {}^-3x + 6y = 9 \\ {}^-10x - 6y = {}^-22 \\ \hline {}^-13x \qquad = {}^-13 \end{array} \qquad \begin{bmatrix} {}^-13 & 0 & 0 & {}^-1 \\ {}^-10 & {}^-6 & 0 & {}^-2 \\ {}^-1 & {}^-1 & {}^-2 & {}^-9 \end{bmatrix}$$

$$\begin{aligned} {}^-10x - 6y &= {}^-22 \\ {}^-x - y - 22 &= {}^-9 \end{aligned}$$

The computations may be completed as shown on page 89.

Exercises Solve each odd problem in the written exercises on page 89 using the elimination method. Compare the steps of the elimination method to the steps of the augmented matrix method. Answers may vary.

3-8 Graphing Systems of Inequalities

Objective: To learn to solve systems of inequalities by graphing.

Consider the following system of inequalities.

$$y \geq 2x - 1$$
$$y \leq {}^{-}2x - 2$$

To solve this system, find the ordered pairs that satisfy *both* inequalities. One way is to graph each inequality and find the intersection of the two graphs.

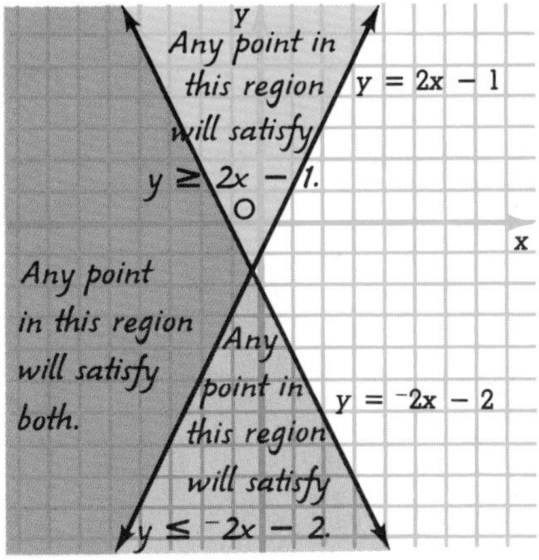

Some systems of inequalities have *no* solutions.

example 1

Solve the following system by graphing.

$y > x + 1$
$y < x - 4$

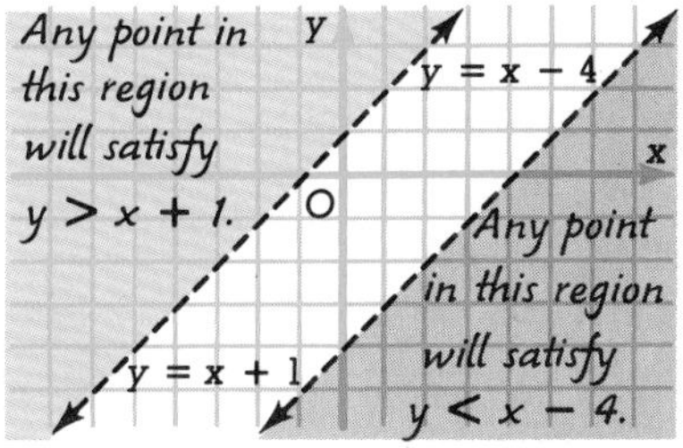

The graphs of the two inequalities have *no* points in common. So *no* ordered pair will satisfy both inequalities.

Systems of more than two inequalities can also be graphed.

example 2

Solve the following system by graphing.

$$y \le 3$$
$$x \ge {}^{-}2$$
$$y > x$$

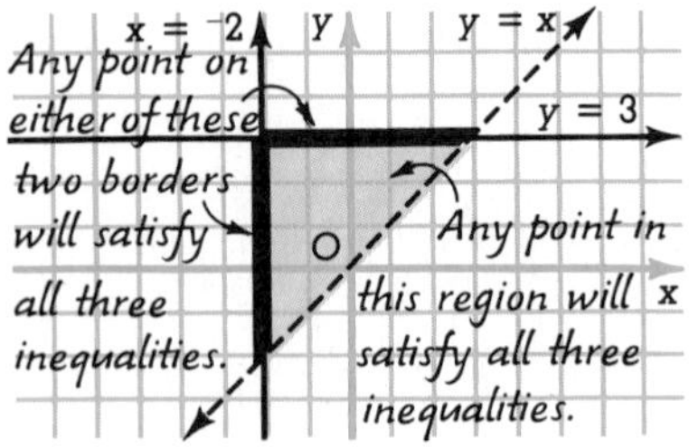

exercises

Max: 1–8, 1–12; Avg: 1–8, 1–11 odds; Min: 1–8, 1–11 odds

Exploratory Does the point given in green satisfy the system of inequalities?

1. $y < \frac{1}{2}x + 2$ (0, 0)
   $y > 3x - 2$ yes
2. $y < x - 2$ (1, 2)
   $y > {}^{-}x$ no
3. $y > {}^{-}2$ (1, 1)
   $x \le 1$ yes
4. $y < 3$ (4, 4)
   $x \ge {}^{-}1$ no
5. $y + 2x > 6$ (4, 0)
   $x < 5$ yes
6. $3y - x < 3$ (9, 3)
   $y > 2$ yes
7. $y > x + 3$ (3, 2)
   $y < {}^{-}x$ no
8. $y > x + 3$ (2, ⁻3)
   $y < {}^{-}x$ no

Written Solve each system of inequalities by graphing.

1. $y > 3$
   $y + x > 2$
2. $y \ge 2x - 2$
   $y \le {}^{-}x + 2$
3. $y \ge x - 3$
   $y \ge {}^{-}x + 1$
4. $y < {}^{-}2$
   $y - x > 1$
5. ${}^{-}4y - 3x > 10$
   $2y - 3x < 5$
6. $x \ge 1$
   $x + y \le 3$
7. $x \le 2$
   ${}^{-}3x - 3y \ge 5$
8. $y > 3$
   $x \le 1$
9. $y \le 5$
   $x \ge {}^{-}1$
10. $y - x \le 3$
    $y \ge x + 2$
11. $x + 2 > y$
    $y < {}^{-}x - 3$
12. $y > x + 1$
    $y < x - 3$

For answers to problems **1–12**, see the Teacher's Guide.

3–9 Linear Programming

Objective: To learn to solve problems using linear programming.

The Exuma Company builds two brands of lawn mowers. The Jaw is built in Ohio and the Ripper is built in Kansas. The Ohio plant can build at most 450 Jaws in one month. The Kansas plant can build at most 200 Rippers in one month.

The following chart shows the cost of building each brand of lawn mower and the profit.

Mower	Cost per Unit	Profit per Unit
Jaw	\$600	\$125
Ripper	\$900	\$200

During the month of March, the company can spend \$360,000 to build these mowers. To make the greatest profit, how many Jaws and Rippers should be built in March?

First, write a system of inequalities and graph them to show the *possible* solutions to this problem.

Let j stand for the number of Jaws built.

Let r stand for the number of Rippers built.

$0 \le j \le 450$	*The number of Jaws built is between 0 and 450 inclusive.*
$0 \le r \le 200$	*The number of Rippers built is between 0 and 200 inclusive.*
$600j + 900r \le 360{,}000$	*The cost of Jaws plus the cost of Rippers does not exceed \$360,000.*

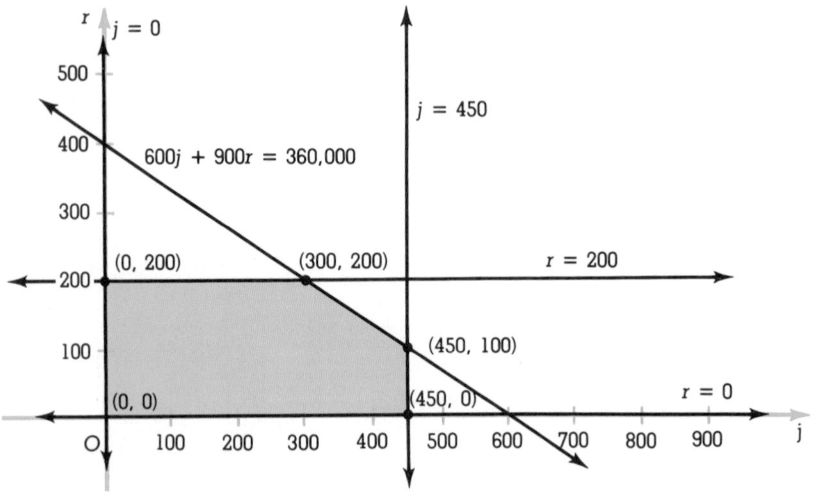

Any point in the region shown will satisfy the conditions.

Now, write an expression for profit.

Profit = Profit on Jaws + Profit on Rippers

Profit = $125j$ + $200r$

To solve the problem, find which ordered pair on the graph yields the greatest profit.

Mathematicians have shown that a maximum or minimum value is always at one of the vertices of the polygon. In this case there are five points to try.

(j, r)	(0, 0)	(0, 200)	(300, 200)	(450, 100)	(450,0)
$125j + 200r$	\$0	\$40,000	\$77,500	\$76,250	\$56,250

The Exuma Company will make the greatest profit by building 300 Jaws and 200 Rippers.

Finding a maximum or minimum value with given conditions is called **linear programming.** Use the following method to solve linear programming problems.

Linear Programming Procedure

1. Define variables.
2. Write a system of inequalities.
3. Graph the system. Find vertices of the polygon formed.
4. Write an expression to be maximized or minimized.
5. Substitute values from vertices into the expression.

example 1

Raw materials **A** and **B** are used to make one of the Target Company's products. The product must contain no more than 10 units of **A** and at least 28 units of **B.** It must cost no more than \$500. The following chart shows how much each unit of raw material costs and weighs.

Material	Cost per Unit	Weight per Unit
A	\$4	10 pounds
B	\$16	20 pounds

How much of each raw material should be used to maximize the weight?

Define variables. Let a stand for amount of material **A** used.
Let b stand for amount of material **B** used.

Write inequalities.

$0 \leq a \leq 10$ *The product contains no more than 10 units of A.*

$b \geq 28$ *The product contains at least 28 units of B.*

$4a + 16b \leq 500$

Graph the system.

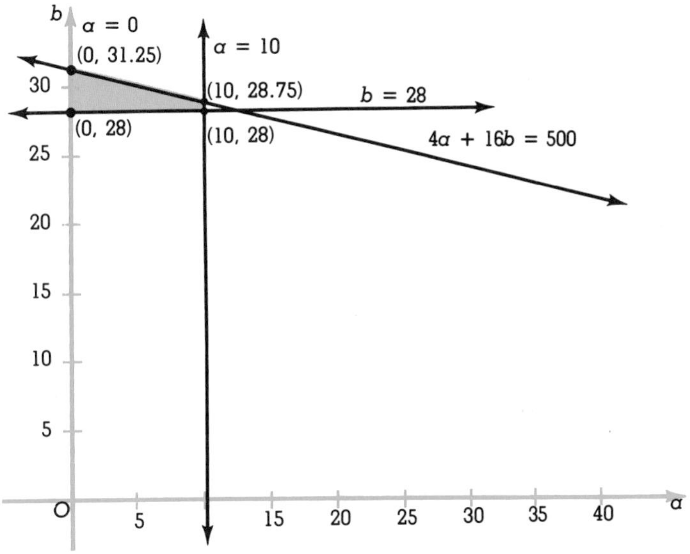

Write expression to be maximized.

Weight = Weight material **A** + Weight material **B**

Weight = $10a$ + $20b$

Substitute values into weight expression.

(a, b)	(0, 28)	(10, 28)	(0, 31.25)	(10, 28.75)
$10a + 20b$	560	660	625	675

Answer the problem. The Target Company should use 10 units of material **A** and 28.75 units of material **B** for each unit of product.

exercises

Max: 1–4, 1–9; Avg: 1–4, 1–9 odds; Min: 1–4, 1–9 odds

Exploratory Graph each system of inequalities. Name the vertices of the polygon formed.

1. $1 \leq y \leq 3$, $y \leq 2x + 1$, $y \leq -\frac{1}{2}x + 6$ (0, 1), (1, 3), (6, 3), (10, 1)
2. $x \geq 0$, $y \geq 3$, $y \geq 2x + 1$, $y \leq -\frac{1}{2}x + 6$ (0, 3), (0, 6), (2, 5), (1, 3)
3. $y \geq 1$, $y \leq 2x + 1$, $x \leq 6$ (0, 1), (6, 13), (6, 1)
4. $0 \leq x \leq 50$, $0 \leq y \leq 70$, $60 \leq x + y \leq 80$ (0, 60), (0, 70), (10, 70), (50, 30), (50, 10)

Written Graph each system of inequalities. Name the vertices of the polygon formed. Find the maximum and minimum values of the expression given in green.

1. $y \geq 2$, $1 \leq x \leq 5$, $y \leq x + 3$ $3x - 2y$
2. $y \leq 7$, $y \leq x + 4$, $y \geq {}^{-}x + 6$, $x \leq 5$ $2x - 3y$
3. $x + y \geq 2$, $4y \leq x + 8$, $y \geq 2x - 5$ $4x + 3y$
4. $y \leq x + 5$, $y \geq x$, $x \geq {}^{-}3$, $y + 2x \leq 5$ $x - 2y$
5. $y \leq x + 6$, $y + 2x \geq 6$, $2 \leq x \leq 6$ $3x + y$
6. $x + y \geq 2$, $4y \leq x + 8$, $2y \geq 3x - 6$ $3y + x$
7. $y \geq 0$, $0 \leq x \leq 5$, ${}^{-}x + y \leq 2$, $x + y \leq 6$ $5x - 3y$
8. $x \geq 0$, $y \geq 0$, $x + 2y \leq 6$, $2y - x \leq 2$, $x + y \leq 5$ $3x - 5y$

For answers to problems 1–8, see the Teacher's Guide.

9. Fashion Furniture makes two kinds of chairs, Rockers and Swivels. Two operations, **A** and **B**, are used. Operation **A** is limited to 20 hours a day. Operation **B** is limited to 15 hours per day. The following chart shows the amount of time each operation takes for one chair. It also shows the profit made on each chair.

Chair	Operation A	Operation B	Profit
Rocker	2 hr	3 hr	\$12
Swivel	4 hr	1 hr	\$10

How many chairs of each kind should Fashion Furniture make each day to maximize profit? 4 Rockers and 3 Swivels

Vocabulary

parallel lines (70)
perpendicular lines (71)
system of equations (74)
consistent system (75)
independent system (75)
inconsistent system (75)
dependent system (75)
substitution method (77)
elimination method (77)
matrix (81)
determinant (81)
expansion by minors (83)
Cramer's Rule (84)
augmented matrix (88)
row operations (89)
linear programming (94)

Chapter Summary

1. Definition of Parallel Lines: In a plane, lines with the same slope are called parallel lines. Also, vertical lines are parallel. (70)
2. Definition of Perpendicular Lines: Two nonvertical lines are perpendicular if and only if the product of their slopes is $^{-}1$. Any vertical line is perpendicular to any horizontal line. (71)
3. A system of equations that has one ordered pair as a solution is said to be consistent and independent. (75)
4. A system of equations that has no solutions is said to be inconsistent. (75)
5. A system of equations that has an infinite number of solutions is said to be consistent and dependent. (75)
6. The substitution method and the elimination method can be used to solve systems of equations. (78)
7. An arrangement of numerals in rows and columns is called a matrix. A square matrix has the same number of rows as columns. (81)
8. Definition of 2 by 2 and 3 by 3 Determinants: Each square matrix has a value called the determinant.

   If $M = \begin{bmatrix} a & b \\ c & d \end{bmatrix}$, then $\det M = ad - cb$.

   If $N = \begin{bmatrix} a & b & c \\ d & e & f \\ g & h & i \end{bmatrix}$, then $\det N = aei + bfg + cdh - gec - hfa - idb$ (81)

9. Cramer's Rule: The solution to the system $\begin{matrix} ax + by = c \\ dx + ey = f \end{matrix}$ is (x, y)

   where $x = \dfrac{\begin{vmatrix} c & b \\ f & e \end{vmatrix}}{\begin{vmatrix} a & b \\ d & e \end{vmatrix}}$ and $y = \dfrac{\begin{vmatrix} a & c \\ d & f \end{vmatrix}}{\begin{vmatrix} a & b \\ d & e \end{vmatrix}}$ and $\begin{vmatrix} a & b \\ d & e \end{vmatrix} \neq 0$. (84)

10. Row Operations on Matrices:
    1. Interchange any two rows.
    2. Replace any row with a nonzero multiple of that row.
    3. Replace any row with the sum of that row and another row. (89)
11. To solve a system of inequalities, find the ordered pairs that satisfy both inequalities. (91)
12. Linear Programming Procedure:
    1. Define variables.
    2. Write a system of inequalities.
    3. Graph the system. Find vertices of the polygon formed.
    4. Write an expression to be maximized or minimized.
    5. Substitute values from vertices into the expression. (94)

Chapter Review

3-1 Find the equation of a line that passes through each given point and is parallel to a line with the given equation.

1. (4, 6); $y = 3x - 2$ $y = 3x - 6$
2. (1, 1); $y = {}^{-}3x - 1$ $y = {}^{-}3x + 4$
3. $({}^{-}1, {}^{-}1)$; $y = 6x - 8$ $y = 6x + 5$
4. (7, 7); $2x + 3y = 6$ $y = -\frac{2}{3}x + \frac{35}{3}$

Find the equation of a line that passes through each given point and is perpendicular to a line with the given equation.

5. (3, 5); $y = 2x - 5$ $y = -\frac{1}{2}x + \frac{13}{2}$
6. (1, 4); $y = 3x - 1$ $y = -\frac{1}{3}x + \frac{13}{3}$
7. $({}^{-}1, {}^{-}1)$; $2y + 3x = 10$ $y = \frac{2}{3}x - \frac{1}{3}$
8. (0, 10); $y = 4x$ $y = -\frac{1}{4}x + 10$

3-2 Graph the equations. Then state the solution to the system of equations.

9. $x + y = {}^{-}8$, $2x - y = 2$ $({}^{-}2, {}^{-}6)$
10. $x + y = 6$, $x - y = 2$ (4, 2)
11. $x + y = 11$, $3x - 3y = 3$ (6, 5)
12. $x + y = 6$, $2x + 2y = 12$ $\{(x, y) | x + y = 6\}$

13–16. Tell whether each system in problems **9–12** is consistent and independent, consistent and dependent, or inconsistent.

13–15. consistent and independent   16. consistent and dependent

3-3 Solve each system of equations.

17. $x + y = 6$, $x - y = 4\frac{1}{2}$ $(5\frac{1}{4}, \frac{3}{4})$
18. $3x - 5y = {}^{-}13$, $4x + 3y = 2$ $({}^{-}1, 2)$

19. $2x + 3y = 8$
$x - y = 2$ $\left(\frac{14}{5}, \frac{4}{5}\right)$

20. $\frac{1}{3}x + \frac{1}{3}y = 5$
$\frac{1}{6}x - \frac{1}{9}y = 0$ (6, 9)

3-4 **Find each determinant.**

21. $\begin{vmatrix} 2 & 3 \\ 4 & 5 \end{vmatrix}$ -2

22. $\begin{vmatrix} 6 & -1 \\ 3 & -2 \end{vmatrix}$ -9

23. $\begin{vmatrix} 2 & 1 & 0 \\ 3 & 2 & 6 \\ -1 & -3 & -4 \end{vmatrix}$ 26

24. $\begin{vmatrix} 4 & 8 & 2 \\ 3 & 0 & 6 \\ -1 & -2 & -3 \end{vmatrix}$ 60

3-5 **Solve each system of equations using Cramer's rule.**

25. $7x - 8y = 11$
$9x - 2y = 3$ $\left(\frac{1}{29}, -\frac{39}{29}\right)$

26. $x + 2y = 5$
$x - y = 6$ $\left(\frac{17}{3}, -\frac{1}{3}\right)$

27. $3x + 2y = 5$
$4x - y = 3$ (1, 1)

28. $6x + 2y = 8$
$3x + 4y = -2$ (2, -2)

3-6 **Solve each system of equations.**

29. $x + y + z = 6$
$2x - y + z = 3$ (1, 2, 3)
$3x - y - 2z = -5$

30. $x + y - z = 4$
$2x - 3y + z = 1$ (3, 2, 1)
$4x - y + 2z = 12$

3-7 **Solve each system of equations using augmented matrices.**

31. $2x + y = 5$
$3x - 2y = 4$ (2, 1)

32. $x + y + z = 2$
$4x + 2y + 3z = 9$ $\left(\frac{9}{5}, -\frac{6}{5}, \frac{7}{5}\right)$
$-2x + y - 3z = -9$

3-8 **Solve each system of inequalities by graphing.**

33. $x + y < 2$
$x + 2y > -3$

34. $y < -2$
$y - x > 1$

35. $y \geq x - 3$
$y \geq -x + 1$

36. $x + y < 4$
$y \geq -3x + 1$

3-9 **Graph each system of inequalities. Name the vertices of the polygon formed. Find the maximum and minimum values of the expression given in green.**

37. $x \geq 0$ $2x + 4y$
$y \geq 0$
$x + y \leq 3$
$3x + y \leq 6$

38. $0 \leq x \leq 5$ $2x + 3y$
$0 \leq y \leq 6$
$x + y \leq 9$

For answers to problems **33–38**, see the Teacher's Guide.

Chapter Test

Find the equation of a line that passes through each given point and is parallel to a line with the given equation.

1. $(2, 4); y = 3x - 5$ $y = 3x - 2$
2. $(7, ^-4); y = ^-x + 6$ $y = ^-x + 3$

Find the equation of a line that passes through each given point and is perpendicular to a line with the given equation.

3. $(3, 4); y = 2x + 1$ $y = -\frac{1}{2}x + \frac{11}{2}$
4. $(6, ^-1); y + 2x = 5$ $y = \frac{1}{2}x - 4$

Graph each system of equations. Then state the solution to the system.

5. $x + y = 7$
   $x - y = 1$ $(4, 3)$
6. $2x + 3y = 5$
   $^-3x + 6y = 12$ $(-\frac{2}{7}, \frac{13}{7})$

Solve each system of equations.

7. $3x + 8y = ^-6$
   $4x - 2y = 11$ $(2, -\frac{3}{2})$
8. $7x + 2y = 11$
   $3x + 16 = ^-8y$ $(\frac{12}{5}, -\frac{29}{10})$

Find each determinant.

9. $\begin{vmatrix} 3 & 1 \\ ^-2 & 4 \end{vmatrix}$ 14
10. $\begin{vmatrix} 7 & 1 & 6 \\ 3 & ^-1 & 4 \\ ^-2 & 3 & 0 \end{vmatrix}$ $^-50$

Solve each system of equations using Cramer's rule.

11. $^-2x + 3y = 5$
    $x + 4y = 14$ $(2, 3)$
12. $2x - 3y = 6$
    $^-3x + 4y = 8$ $(^-48, ^-34)$

Solve each system of equations.

13. $x + y + z = ^-1$
    $2x + 4y + z = 1$ $(^-4, 2, 1)$
    $3x - y - z = ^-15$
14. $x + y + z = 7$
    $3x - 7y + 2z = 11$ $(6, 1, 0)$
    $^-4x + 21y + 3z = ^-3$

Solve each system of equations using augmented matrices.

15. $4x + y = 9$
    $^-3x + 2y = ^-4$ $(2, 1)$
16. $x + 2y + z = 4$
    $3x - 2y + z = 2$ $(1, 1, 1)$
    $4x + 2y - 3z = 3$

Solve each system of inequalities by graphing.

17. $y > 2x + 1$
    $y \leq ^-3x + 4$
18. $x + y \leq 6$
    $x - y \geq 4$

Graph each system of inequalities. Name the vertices of the polygon formed. Find the maximum and minimum values of the expression given in green.

19. $0 \leq x \leq 6$ $2x + y$
    $0 \leq y \leq 2$
    $x + y \leq 4$
20. $0 \leq x \leq 4$ $3x - 2y$
    $y + x \leq 6$

For answers to problems **17–20**, see the Teacher's Guide.

Chapter

4

Polynomials

When practicing a new song, a band may break the song into parts and then work on each part. Often in algebra, expressions are broken into parts and each part is studied.

4-1 Monomials

Objective: To learn the rules of exponents.

Expressions like $^{-}3$, y, m^7, $4x^2$, and $^{-}24ab^3$ are called **monomials.** Each expression is a constant, a variable, or a product. The numerical factor of a monomial is called the **coefficient.** For example, the coefficient of $^{-}24ab^3$ is $^{-}24$. The **degree** of a monomial is the sum of the exponents of its variables.

Monomial	Coefficient	Variables	Exponents	Degree
$^{-}3$	$^{-}3$	none	none	0
$4x^2$	4	x	2	2
m^7	1	m	7	7
$^{-}24ab^3$	$^{-}24$	a and b	1 and 3	4

Two monomials are called **like terms** if they have the same variable factors.

Like $6x^3y$ and $17x^3y$ Unlike $3a^2b$ and $4ab^2$

examples

1 **Simplify $6x^3y - 17x^3y$.**

$$6x^3y - 17x^3y = (6 - 17)x^3y \quad \textit{Distributive property}$$
$$= {}^{-}11x^3y$$

2 **Simplify $3n^4p^5 - 7n^4p^5 + 8n^4p^5$.**

$$3n^4p^5 - 7n^4p^5 + 8n^4p^5 = (3 - 7 + 8)n^4p^5 \quad \textit{Distributive property}$$
$$= 4n^4p^5$$

Exponents that are positive integers tell how many times the base is used as a factor.

x^6 ← *exponent*, x ← *base*

$$x^6 = x \cdot x \cdot x \cdot x \cdot x \cdot x$$
$$5^3z^4 = 5 \cdot 5 \cdot 5 \cdot z \cdot z \cdot z \cdot z$$

You can use the meaning of exponents to discover how to multiply powers.

example

3 **Simplify $(s^2t^3)(s^4t^5)$.**

$$(s^2t^3)(s^4t^5) = (s \cdot s \cdot t \cdot t \cdot t)(s \cdot s \cdot s \cdot s \cdot t \cdot t \cdot t \cdot t \cdot t)$$
$$= s \cdot s \cdot s \cdot s \cdot s \cdot s \cdot t \cdot t \cdot t \cdot t \cdot t \cdot t \cdot t \cdot t$$
$$= s^6t^8$$

Notice that $2 + 4 = 6$ and $3 + 5 = 8$. Also, $s^2 \cdot s^4 = s^6$ and $t^3 \cdot t^5 = t^8$.

For all numbers a, and nonnegative integers m and n,
$$a^m \cdot a^n = a^{m+n}$$

Multiplying Powers

examples

4 **Simplify $(4^2)^3$.**

$$\begin{aligned}(4^2)^3 &= 4^2 \cdot 4^2 \cdot 4^2 \\ &= 4^{2+2+2} \\ &= 4^6\end{aligned}$$

5 **Simplify $(h^4)^5$.**

$$\begin{aligned}(h^4)^5 &= h^4 \cdot h^4 \cdot h^4 \cdot h^4 \cdot h^4 \\ &= h^{4+4+4+4+4} \\ &= h^{20}\end{aligned}$$

Examples **4** and **5** suggest the following property.

For all numbers a, and nonnegative integers m and n,
$$(a^m)^n = a^{m \cdot n}.$$

Raising a Power to a Power

Example **6** shows how to raise a power to a power. Example **7** shows one way to find the power of a product.

examples

6 **Simplify $(r^5)^6$.**

$$\begin{aligned}(r^5)^6 &= r^{5 \cdot 6} \\ &= r^{30}\end{aligned}$$

7 **Simplify $(ab)^4$.**

$$\begin{aligned}(ab)^4 &= a \cdot b \cdot a \cdot b \cdot a \cdot b \cdot a \cdot b \\ &= a \cdot a \cdot a \cdot a \cdot b \cdot b \cdot b \cdot b \\ &= a^4b^4\end{aligned}$$

The power of a product is the product of the powers.

For all numbers a, b, and nonnegative integer m,
$$(ab)^m = a^mb^m.$$

Finding a Power of a Product

You can simplify many kinds of expressions using the properties of exponents along with the commutative and associative properties.

examples

8 **Simplify $(4x^2y)(^-3x^3y^4)$.**

$$\begin{aligned}(4x^2y)(^-3x^3y^4) &= 4 \cdot {}^-3 \cdot x^2 \cdot x^3 \cdot y \cdot y^4\\ &= {}^-12 \cdot x^{2+3} \cdot y^{1+4}\\ &= {}^-12x^5y^5\end{aligned}$$

9 **Simplify $(^-2r^2s^3)^3$.**

$$\begin{aligned}(^-2r^2s^3)^3 &= (^-2)^3(r^2)^3(s^3)^3\\ &= {}^-8 \cdot r^{(2\cdot 3)} \cdot s^{(3\cdot 3)}\\ &= {}^-8r^6s^9\end{aligned}$$

You can also divide powers.

example

10 **Simplify $\frac{p^9}{p^4}$.**

$$\begin{aligned}\frac{p^9}{p^4} &= \frac{p \cdot p \cdot p \cdot p \cdot p \cdot p \cdot p \cdot p \cdot p}{p \cdot p \cdot p \cdot p}\\ &= p \cdot p \cdot p \cdot p \cdot p\\ &= p^5\end{aligned}$$

Dividing Powers

For all numbers a, and nonnegative integers m and n, $\frac{a^m}{a^n} = a^{m-n}$ if $a \neq 0$ and $m > n$.

example

11 **Simplify $\frac{(2xy)^4}{(x^2y)^2}$.**

$$\begin{aligned}\frac{(2xy)^4}{(x^2y)^2} &= \frac{(2)^4(x)^4(y)^4}{(x^2)^2(y)^2}\\ &= \frac{16x^4y^4}{x^4y^2}\\ &= 16x^{(4-4)}y^{(4-2)} \qquad x^{(4-4)} = x^0 = 1\\ &= 16y^2\end{aligned}$$

example 12

Simplify $\frac{(4j^5k^2)^2}{^-(2j^2k)^3}$.

$$\frac{(4j^5k^2)^2}{^-(2j^2k)^3} = \frac{(4)^2(j^5)^2(k^2)^2}{^-(2)^3(j^2)^3(k)^3}$$
$$= \frac{16j^{10}k^4}{^-8j^6k^3}$$
$$= {}^-2j^{(10-6)}k^{(4-3)}$$
$$= {}^-2j^4k$$

exercises

Max: 1–15, 1–32; Avg: 1–15, 1–31 odds; Min: 1–31 odds

Exploratory Find the degree of each monomial.

1. $5x^3$ 3
2. $5x^3y^2z^4$ 9
3. y^5 5
4. $^-3x^2$ 2
5. $7x^4y^4$ 8
6. a^3b^4 7
7. 14rs 2
8. $24p^3q$ 4
9. $15x^3yz$ 5
10. $2x^4$ 4
11. $2^2x^3y^2z$ 6
12. a^2bc^3 6
13. 0 none
14. 5 0
15. 3z 1

Written Simplify each expression.

1. $4m + 7m + {}^-3m$ $8m$
2. $2x^3 + 3x^3 + {}^-6x^3$ $^-x^3$
3. $4d^3 - d^3 + 2d^3$ $5d^3$
4. $4ab^2 - 3ab^2$ ab^2
5. $27x^2 - 3y^2 + 12x^2$ $39x^2 - 3y^2$
6. $3x^2y + 4 - 3x^2y$ 4
7. $y^5 \cdot y^7$ y^{12}
8. $n^4 \cdot n^3 \cdot n^2$ n^9
9. $\frac{m^{10}}{m^4}$ m^6
10. $\frac{s^{12}}{s^{11}}$ s
11. $2^3 \cdot 2^4$ 2^7
12. $t^{13} \cdot t^{15} \cdot t^{18}$ t^{46}
13. $8^6 \cdot 8^4 \cdot (8^2)^2$ 8^{14}
14. $(m^3)^2$ m^6
15. $(y^5)^2$ y^{10}
16. $(2a)^3$ $8a^3$ or 2^3a^3
17. $(3a)^4$ 3^4a^4 or $81a^4$
18. $(rs^3)(^-5r^2s^3)$ $^-5r^3s^6$
19. $\frac{4a^2b^3}{2ab^3}$ $2a$
20. $\frac{12n^8}{4n^3}$ $3n^5$
21. $(5m^2k^2)(4mk^3)$ $20m^3k^5$
22. $(x^2y^2)^2x^3y^3$ x^7y^7
23. $\frac{^-66m^{10}p^{13}}{33m^2p^2}$ $^-2m^8p^{11}$
24. $\frac{48w^{14}z^{10}}{^-16w^{10}z^{10}}$ $^-3w^4$
25. $\frac{60s^{10}t^{12}}{^-12s^9t^{11}}$ ^-5st
26. $\frac{^-39c^3d^4}{13c^2d^4}$ ^-3c
27. $(^-4a)(a^2)(^-a^3) + 3a^2a^4$ $7a^6$
28. $^-2r(rk^2)(^-5rm^2) + (^-r^2)(2rk)(4km^2)$ $2r^3k^2m^2$
29. $(5a)(6a^2b)(3ab^3) + (4a^2)(3b^3)(2a^2b)$ $114a^4b^4$
30. $(5mn^2)(m^3n)(^-3p^2) + (8np)(3mp)(m^3n^2)$ $9m^4n^3p^2$
31. $(2xy^2)^3 + (2xy^2)^2(6xy^2)$ $32x^3y^6$
32. $(3a)(a^2b)^3 + (2a)^2(^-a^5b^3)$ $^-a^7b^3$

4-2 Polynomials

Objective: To find sums, differences, and products of polynomials.

Expressions like $8x + y$, $3x^2 + 2x + 4$, and $5 - 3y + 5xy^2$ are made up of monomials. Such expressions are called **polynomials.** When there are two terms a polynomial often is called a **binomial.** For example, $8x + y$ is a binomial. A **trinomial** contains three terms.

The degree of a polynomial is the degree of the monomial of greatest degree.

example 1

Find the degree of $5x^3 + 3x^2y^2 + 4xy^2 + 3x - 2$.

$5x^3$ has degree 3
$3x^2y^2$ has degree 4
$4xy^2$ has degree 3
$3x$ has degree 1
$^-2$ has degree 0

The degree of the polynomial is 4.

The terms of polynomials are usually arranged so that the powers of a variable are in ascending or descending order.

You can simplify polynomials by adding like terms as in Example 2. Examples 3 and 4 show how to add or subtract polynomials by adding or subtracting like terms.

examples 2

Simplify $6x^2y + 3xy^4 + 7y + 5xy^4 - 9x^2y + 8y$.

$$\begin{aligned} 6x^2y + 3xy^4 + 7y + 5xy^4 - 9x^2y + 8y &= (6x^2y - 9x^2y) + (3xy^4 + 5xy^4) + (7y + 8y) \\ &= (6 - 9)x^2y + (3 + 5)xy^4 + (7 + 8)y \\ &= {}^-3x^2y + 8xy^4 + 15y \end{aligned}$$

3

Add $7m^2k - 8mk^2 + 19k$ and $18mk^2 - 3k$.

$$\begin{aligned} (7m^2k - 8mk^2 + 19k) + (18mk^2 - 3k) &= \underbrace{7m^2k} - \underbrace{8mk^2 + 18mk^2} + \underbrace{19k - 3k} \\ &= 7m^2k + 10mk^2 + 16k \end{aligned}$$

4

Find $(2x^2 - 3xy + 5y^2) - (4x^2 - 3xy - 2y^2)$.

$$\begin{aligned} (2x^2 - 3xy + 5y^2) - (4x^2 - 3xy - 2y^2) &= \underbrace{2x^2 - 4x^2} - \underbrace{3xy + 3xy} + \underbrace{5y^2 + 2y^2} \\ &= {}^-2x^2 + 0xy + 7y^2 \\ &= {}^-2x^2 + 7y^2 \end{aligned}$$

You know how to multiply monomials. Examples **5** and **6** use this and the distributive property to find the product of a polynomial and a monomial. In Examples **7** and **8** the distributive property is used to multiply polynomials.

examples

5 **Find $^-2x(x^2 - 9)$.**

$$^-2x(x^2 - 9) = {^-2x} \cdot x^2 + {^-2x}(^-9)$$
$$= {^-2x^3} + 18x$$

6 **Find $3x(4xy^3 - 7x^2y - 3y)$.**

$$3x(4xy^3 - 7x^2y - 3y) = 3x \cdot 4xy^3 - 3x \cdot 7x^2y - 3x \cdot 3y$$
$$= 12x^2y^3 - 21x^3y - 9xy$$

7 **Find $(x + 4)(x + 11)$.**

$$(x + 4)(x + 11) = (x + 4) \cdot x + (x + 4) \cdot 11$$
$$= (x \cdot x) + (4 \cdot x) + (x \cdot 11) + (4 \cdot 11)$$
$$= x^2 + 4x + 11x + 44$$
$$= x^2 + 15x + 44$$

8 **Find $(3a + 2ab + b)(2a - 3b)$.**

$$(3a + 2ab + b)(2a - 3b)$$
$$= (3a + 2ab + b) \cdot 2a - (3a + 2ab + b) \cdot 3b$$
$$= (3a \cdot 2a) + (2ab \cdot 2a) + (b \cdot 2a) - (3a \cdot 3b) - (2ab \cdot 3b) - (b \cdot 3b)$$
$$= 6a^2 + 4a^2b + 2ab - 9ab - 6ab^2 - 3b^2$$
$$= 6a^2 + 4a^2b - 7ab - 6ab^2 - 3b^2$$

The following shortcut can be used to multiply binomials.

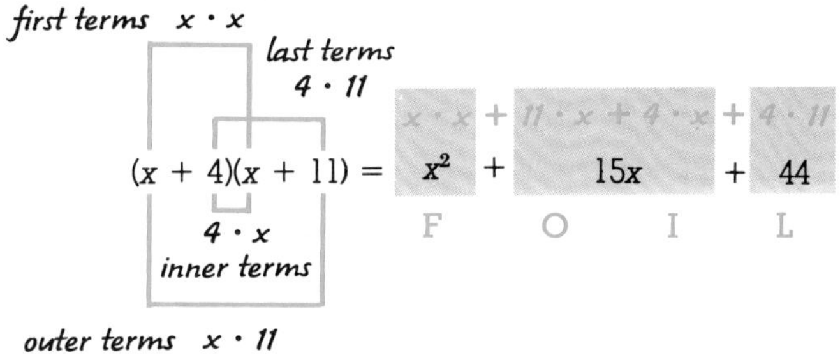

This shortcut is called the **FOIL** rule.

FOIL Rule for Multiplying Binomials

The product of two binomials is the sum of the products of

F the *first* terms,
O the *outer* terms,
I the *inner* terms, and
L the *last* terms.

examples

9 Find (2x + 3)(x − 5).

$$(2x+3)(x-5) = \overset{F}{2x \cdot x} + \overset{O}{2x \cdot {}^-5} + \overset{I}{3 \cdot x} + \overset{L}{3 \cdot {}^-5}$$
$$= 2x^2 - 10x + 3x - 15$$
$$= 2x^2 - 7x - 15$$

10 Find (5x − 3)(2x − 7).

$$(5x-3)(2x-7) = \overset{F}{5x \cdot 2x} + \overset{O}{5x \cdot {}^-7} + \overset{I}{{}^-3 \cdot 2x} + \overset{L}{{}^-3 \cdot {}^-7}$$
$$= 10x^2 - 35x - 6x + 21$$
$$= 10x^2 - 41x + 21$$

exercises

Max: 1–10, 1–59; Avg: 1–9, 1–59 odds; Min: 1–59 odds

Exploratory Find the degree of each polynomial.

1. $3x^2 + 27xy$ 2
2. $x^2 + 2x + 3$ 2
3. $a^8 + a^7b + a^6b^2 - a^2b^6 - ab^7 - b^8$ 8
4. $3x^4y^2 - 5x^2y + 3$ 6
5. $3r^5 - 3r^4 - 7r - 5$ 5
6. $z^5 + 5z^4 + 9z^3 + 9z^2$ 5
7. $m^3 + 2mn^2 + 4n^3$ 3
8. $5xy - 2x^2 - 3y^2$ 2
9. $13xy^7 + 36x^3y^5 - 2x^4y^5 - xy$ 9
10. $16x^4yz + 12x^2y^3z - 24x^3y^2z - 18xy^4z$ 6

For answers to problems 1–6, 13–24, and 39–59, see the Teacher's Guide.

Written Simplify each expression by performing the indicated operations.

1. $(2x^2 + x + 5) + (3x^2 - x - 4)$
2. $(3y^2 + 5y - 7) + (2y^2 - 7y + 10)$
3. $(p^2 + 7p - 5) + (3p^2 + 3p + 7)$
4. $(7m^2 + 9m + 3) - (3m^2 + 8m + 2)$
5. $(8r^2 + 5r + 14) - (7r^2 + 6r + 8)$
6. $(4k^2 + 10k - 14) - (3k^2 + 7k - 5)$
7. $(4x^4 + 3x^3 + x - 7) + (3x^4 - 5x^3 + 7x^2 - 3x + 8)$ $7x^4 - 2x^3 + 7x^2 - 2x + 1$
8. $(8b^5 + 4b^3 + 7b^2 - 15) + (3b^5 + 7b^3 - b + 14)$ $11b^5 + 11b^3 + 7b^2 - b - 1$
9. $(3r^6 + 4r^4 + 3r^3 + r - 8) - (4r^6 + 2r^3 + 3r + 5)$ ${}^-r^6 + 4r^4 + r^3 - 2r - 13$
10. $(2m^7 + 3m^5 + 2m^3 - 18) - (m^7 + 3m^4 + m^3 + 2m^2)$ $m^7 + 3m^5 - 3m^4 + m^3 - 2m^2 - 18$
11. $(p^4 + 6p^2 - 4p + 1) - (p^3 + p^2 + 2p + 1)$ $p^4 - p^3 + 5p^2 - 6p$
12. $(a^2 - 7a^3 - a - 3) - (10a^3 + a + 2 - a^2)$ ${}^-17a^3 + 2a^2 - 2a - 5$

13. $(2x + 7)(3x + 5)$
14. $(y^2 + 7)(y^2 + 5)$
15. $(m^2 + 5)(m^2 - 4)$
16. $(3y - 8)(2y + 7)$
17. $(x^3 + 3)^2$
18. $(y^4 - 7)^2$
19. $(m^2 - 7)(m^2 + 7)$
20. $(2r^2 + 3)(r^2 - 5)$
21. $(b^2 + 8)^2$
22. $(2a + 3b)^2$
23. $(3a - 2b)^2$
24. $(4a - 5b)(4a + 5b)$
25. $(a - 1)(a^2 - 2a - 1)$ $a^3 - 3a^2 + a + 1$
26. $(2x - 3)(x^2 - 3x - 8)$ $2x^3 - 9x^2 - 7x + 24$
27. $(x - y)(x^2 + xy + y^3)$ $x^3 + xy^3 - xy^2 - y^4$
28. $(a + b)(a^2 - ab + b^2)$ $a^3 + b^3$
29. $(m - 4)(3m^2 + 5m - 4)$ $3m^3 - 7m^2 - 24m + 16$
30. $(2t - 5)(t^2 + 7t + 8)$ $2t^3 + 9t^2 - 19t - 40$
31. $r(r - 2)(r - 3)$ $r^3 - 5r^2 + 6r$
32. $p(p + 5)(p - 1)$ $p^3 + 4p^2 - 5p$
33. $(b + 1)(b - 2)(b + 3)$ $b^3 + 2b^2 - 5b - 6$
34. $(2x - 3)(x + 1)(3x - 2)$ $6x^3 - 7x^2 - 7x + 6$
35. $(2a + 1)(a - 2)^2$ $2a^3 - 7a^2 + 4a + 4$
36. $(a - 2b)^2(2a + 3b)$ $2a^3 - 5a^2b - 4ab^2 + 12b^3$
37. $2y^4\left(\frac{3}{y} + \frac{8}{y^2} - \frac{1}{y^3}\right)$ $6y^3 + 16y^2 - 2y$
38. $8x^2\left(3x^2 + \frac{1}{4} - \frac{1}{2x} + \frac{1}{x^2}\right)$ $24x^4 + 2x^2 - 4x + 8$

You can use the **FOIL** method to find the following products.

$(a + b)^2 = a^2 + 2ab + b^2$ $(a - b)^2 = a^2 - 2ab + b^2$ $(a + b)(a - b) = a^2 - b^2$

Use the patterns shown above to find each product.

39. $(m + 4)^2$
40. $(x - 8)^2$
41. $(y - 2)^2$
42. $(k + 6)^2$
43. $(y - 5)(y + 5)$
44. $(x - 3)(x + 3)$
45. $(2p + q^3)^2$
46. $(x - 3y)^2$
47. $(a + 6b)(a - 6b)$
48. $(1 + 7y)^2$
49. $(1 - 7y)^2$
50. $(1 + 7y)(1 - 7y)$
51. $(4m - 3n)^2$
52. $(5r - 2)^2$
53. $(2 - 3y)^2$
54. $(2s + 7t)^2$
55. $(1 + 4r)^2$
56. $(6a + 2)^2$
57. $(4a - 2b)(4a + 2b)$
58. $(5x + 12)(5x - 12)$
59. $(x^3 - y)(x^3 + y)$

Scientific Notation

Excursions in Algebra

Scientists, engineers, and accountants often work with very large or very small numbers. These numbers are easier to compute with when expressed using **scientific notation.**

Example Express 300,000,000, the speed of light in meters per second, using scientific notation.

300,000,000

8

The number expressed in scientific notation is 3×10^8.

Students will learn the definition of scientific notation in Chapter **11.** In Chapter **11**, negative exponents will be introduced.

Exercises Express each of the following using scientific notation.

1. 50 5.0×10^1
2. 500 5.0×10^2
3. 5000 5.0×10^3
4. 50,000 5.0×10^4
5. 20,691 2.0691×10^4
6. 2069.1 2.0691×10^3
7. 206.91 2.0691×10^2
8. 20.691 2.0691×10^1
9. 23.4 2.34×10^1
10. 60.5 6.05×10^1
11. 7,500,000 7.5×10^6
12. 84.986 8.4986×10^1
13. 98,420 9.842×10^4
14. 11,506,000 1.1506×10^7
15. 20,006 2.0006×10^4
16. 19.0004 1.90004×10^1

4-3 Powers of Binomials

Objective: To find powers of binomials.

Look for a pattern of coefficients and exponents in the following expansions.

$$(a+b)^1 = a + b$$
$$(a+b)^2 = a^2 + 2ab + b^2$$
$$(a+b)^3 = a^3 + 3a^2b + 3ab^2 + b^3$$
$$(a+b)^4 = a^4 + 4a^3b + 6a^2b^2 + 4ab^3 + b^4$$
$$(a+b)^5 = a^5 + 5a^4b + 10a^3b^2 + 10a^2b^3 + 5ab^4 + b^5$$

You may have made the following observations.

1. In the first term, the exponent of a is the same as the exponent of the binomial.
2. In successive terms, the exponent of a decreases by 1.
3. In successive terms, the exponent of b increases by 1.
4. The degree of each term is the same as the exponent of the binomial.

Each coefficient in the expansion of $(a + b)^5$ can be found in the following way.

$$1 \;\;\; \frac{5}{1} \;\;\; \frac{5\cdot 4}{2\cdot 1} \;\;\; \frac{5\cdot 4\cdot 3}{3\cdot 2\cdot 1} \;\;\; \frac{5\cdot 4\cdot 3\cdot 2}{4\cdot 3\cdot 2\cdot 1} \;\;\; \frac{5\cdot 4\cdot 3\cdot 2\cdot 1}{5\cdot 4\cdot 3\cdot 2\cdot 1}$$
$$\downarrow \;\;\; \downarrow \;\;\; \downarrow \;\;\; \downarrow \;\;\; \downarrow \;\;\; \downarrow$$
$$1 \;\;\; 5 \;\;\; 10 \;\;\; 10 \;\;\; 5 \;\;\; 1$$

Can you write the coefficients for the expansion of $(a + b)^6$?

You can use the information above to expand binomials and solve problems.

examples

1 **Expand $(2x + 3y)^4$.**

$$\begin{aligned}(2x+3y)^4 &= 1(2x)^4 + 4(2x)^3(3y)^1 + 6(2x)^2(3y)^2 + 4(2x)^1(3y)^3 + 1(3y)^4\\ &= 16x^4 + 4(8x^3)(3y) + 6(4x^2)(9y^2) + 4(2x)(27y^3) + 81y^4\\ &= 16x^4 + 96x^3y + 216x^2y^2 + 216xy^3 + 81y^4\end{aligned}$$

a is $2x$ and b is $3y$.

2 **Expand $(5x - y)^3$.**

$$\begin{aligned}(5x-y)^3 &= 1(5x)^3 + 3(5x)^2(^-y) + 3(5x)(^-y)^2 + 1(^-y)^3\\ &= 125x^3 + 3(25x^2)(^-y) + 3(5x)(y^2) - y^3\\ &= 125x^3 - 75x^2y + 15xy^2 - y^3\end{aligned}$$

examples

3

Find the fourth term of the expansion for $(2 + x)^5$.

$\frac{5 \cdot 4 \cdot 3}{3 \cdot 2 \cdot 1}(2)^2(x)^3 = 10(2)^2(x)^3$ *a is 2 and b is x.*

The fourth term is $10(2)^2(x)^3$ or $40x^3$.

How can you find the third term without writing the complete expansion?

4

The population of Newcity increases by about 10% each year. The population is now 8000 people. What will be the population 6 years from now? Use $P = 8000(1 + 0.10)^6$.

$P = 8000(1 + 0.10)^6$

$= 8000[1^6 + 6(1)^5(0.10) + 15(1)^4(0.10)^2 + 20(1)^3(0.10)^3 + 15(1)^2(0.10)^4 + 6(1)(0.10)^5 + (0.10)^6]$

$= 8000(1 + 0.60 + 0.15 + 0.020 + 0.0015 + 0.00006 + 0.000001)$

$= 14{,}172.488$ The population will be about 14,000 people.

exercises

Max: 1–24, 1–17; Avg: 1–23, 1–17 odds; Min: 1–17 odds

Exploratory How many terms are in each expansion?

1. $(r + s)^4$ 5, $4rs^3$
2. $(a + b)^5$ 6, $10a^2b^3$
3. $(k - m)^7$ 8, $^-35k^4m^3$
4. $(m + p)^6$ 7, $20m^3p^3$
5. $(z + a)^6$ 7, $20z^3a^3$
6. $(b - z)^5$ 6, $^-10b^2z^3$
7. $(a - 3)^4$ 5, ^-108a
8. $(x - 2)^5$ 6, $^-80x^2$
9. $(y + 2)^4$ 5, $32y$
10. $(x - y)^3$ 4, $^-y^3$
11. $(p + 3)^3$ 4, 27
12. $(4 + y)^4$ 5, $16y^3$

13–24. Find the fourth term for each expansion in problems 1–12. See above.

For answers to problems 1–15, see the Teacher's Guide.

Written Expand each binomial.

1. $(x + m)^4$
2. $(r + s)^6$
3. $(y + p)^7$
4. $(x - y)^3$
5. $(b - z)^5$
6. $(r - m)^6$
7. $(2m + y)^5$
8. $(3r + y)^4$
9. $(2b + x)^6$
10. $(2x + 3y)^4$
11. $(3x - 2y)^5$
12. $(2m - 3)^6$
13. $(2y + 1)^5$
14. $\left(2 + \frac{x}{2}\right)^6$
15. $\left(\frac{y}{3} + 3\right)^6$

Solve each problem.

16. Jorma Johnson invested \$5000 at 8% annual interest for 3 years. The interest is compounded semiannually. Find the value of Jorma's investment after 3 years. Use $A = 5000(1 + 0.04)^6$. \$6326.60

17. Joanne Mauch owns a tree plantation. The value of her trees increases about 10% each year. The trees are now worth \$10,000. What will be their value 6 years from now? Use $V = 10{,}000(1 + 0.10)^6$. \$17,715.61

4-4 Factoring

Objective: To factor polynomials.

GCF is the greatest factor that a set of terms has in common.

Suppose you wish to write $10x^2 + 6x$ in factored form. First find the greatest common factor (GCF) of $10x^2$ and $6x$.

$$10x^2 = 2 \cdot 5 \cdot x \cdot x$$
$$\updownarrow \qquad \updownarrow$$
$$6x = 2 \cdot 3 \cdot x$$

The greatest common factor (GCF) of $10x^2$ and $6x$ is $2x$.

Now use the distributive property to factor the expression.

$$\begin{aligned} 10x^2 + 6x &= (2x \cdot 5x) + (2x \cdot 3) \\ &= 2x(5x + 3) \end{aligned}$$

$10x^2 + 6x$ written in factored form is $2x(5x + 3)$.

examples

1 **Factor $12xy^2 - 8x^2y$.**

$$\begin{aligned} 12xy^2 - 8x^2y &= (2 \cdot 2 \cdot 3 \cdot x \cdot y \cdot y) - (2 \cdot 2 \cdot 2 \cdot x \cdot x \cdot y) \\ &= (4xy \cdot 3y) - (4xy \cdot 2x) \qquad \textit{4xy is the GCF.} \\ &= 4xy(3y - 2x) \end{aligned}$$

2 **Factor $2m^2y + 3my^2 - 5m^2y^2 + 7my^3$.**

$$\begin{aligned} &2m^2y + 3my^2 - 5m^2y^2 + 7my^3 \\ &= (2 \cdot m \cdot m \cdot y) + (3m \cdot y \cdot y) - (5 \cdot m \cdot m \cdot y \cdot y) + (7m \cdot y \cdot y \cdot y) \\ &= (my \cdot 2m) + (my \cdot 3y) - (my \cdot 5my) + (my \cdot 7y^2) \qquad \textit{my is the GCF.} \\ &= my(2m + 3y - 5my + 7y^2) \end{aligned}$$

You have found products like $(x - 7)(x + 7)$.

$$\begin{aligned} (x - 7)(x + 7) &= x \cdot x + 7 \cdot x - 7 \cdot x - 7 \cdot 7 \\ &= x^2 \qquad\qquad\qquad\qquad - 7^2 \\ &= x^2 - 49 \end{aligned}$$

To factor $x^2 - 49$, reverse the steps.

$$\begin{aligned} x^2 - 49 &= x^2 - 7^2 \\ &= x^2 + 7x - 7x - 7^2 \\ &= (x - 7)(x + 7) \end{aligned}$$

Factoring $x^2 - 49$ shows the following pattern.

Factoring Difference of Two Squares

For any numbers a and b, $a^2 - b^2 = (a - b)(a + b)$.

examples

3

Factor $16a^2 - 4$.

$$16a^2 - 4 = 4(4a^2 - 1) \quad \textit{4 is the GCF.}$$
$$= 4[(2a)^2 - (1)^2]$$
$$= 4(2a - 1)(2a + 1)$$

4

Factor $4x^2 - \frac{1}{9}$.

$$4x^2 - \frac{1}{9} = (2x)^2 - \left(\frac{1}{3}\right)^2$$
$$= \left(2x - \frac{1}{3}\right)\left(2x + \frac{1}{3}\right)$$

Consider the following multiplications.

$$(x + y)(x^2 - xy + y^2) = x(x^2 - xy + y^2) + y(x^2 - xy + y^2)$$
$$= x^3 - x^2y + xy^2 + x^2y - xy^2 + y^3$$
$$= x^3 + y^3$$
$$(x - y)(x^2 + xy + y^2) = x(x^2 + xy + y^2) - y(x^2 + xy + y^2)$$
$$= x^3 + x^2y + xy^2 - x^2y - xy^2 - y^3$$
$$= x^3 - y^3$$

Note that if a and b are nonzero, $a^3 + b^3 \neq (a + b)^3$ and $a^3 - b^3 \neq (a - b)^3$

These multiplications show the following pattern.

For any numbers a and b,
$a^3 + b^3 = (a + b)(a^2 - ab + b^2)$ and,
$a^3 - b^3 = (a - b)(a^2 + ab + b^2)$.

Factoring Sum or Difference of Cubes

examples

5

Factor $m^3 + 27$.

$$m^3 + 27 = m^3 + 3^3$$
$$= (m + 3)(m^2 - m \cdot 3 + 3^2)$$
$$= (m + 3)(m^2 - 3m + 9)$$

6

Factor $27y^3 - 8x^3$.

$$27y^3 - 8x^3 = (3y)^3 - (2x)^3$$
$$= (3y - 2x)[(3y)^2 + 3y \cdot 2x + (2x)^2]$$
$$= (3y - 2x)(9y^2 + 6xy + 4x^2)$$

exercises

Max: 1–12, 1–27; Avg: 1–11, 1–27 odds; Min: 1–27 odds

Exploratory Factor.

1. $r^2 - 9$
2. $2x^2 + 6y + 8b$
3. $x^2 + xy + 3x$
4. $3a^2 + 6a + 9y$
5. $16y^2 - 25$
6. $4m^2 - 49$
7. $2a^2 - 18$
8. $3d^2 - 48$
9. $r^4 + r^3s + r^2s^2$
10. $3p^2q - 3pq^2 + 3q^3$
11. $x^3 - 8$
12. $27 + x^3$

For answers to problems **1-12** and **1-27**, see the Teacher's Guide.

Written Factor.

1. $8m^2 + 4am + 16my$
2. $b^2 - 144$
3. $y^3 - 1$
4. $7pm + 21p^2 - 14px$
5. $m^2 - 121$
6. $b^3 - 8a^3$
7. $3r^3 - 27r$
8. $8a^3 + 1$
9. $1 + r^3$
10. $2y^3 - 98y$
11. $8 + x^3$
12. $a^3b^3 - 27$
13. $4a^2 - 9$
14. $2r^3 - 16s^3$
15. $9y^2 - 64$
16. $3m^3 + 24p^3$
17. $8b^3 - 27x^3$
18. $9p^2 - 4q^2$
19. $ab - a^4b$
20. $16s^2 - 81r^2$
21. $r^4 - s^4$
22. $r^3s^3 - 8s^3$
23. $64y^3 - 1$
24. $m^6 - 27$
25. $y^6 + 125$
26. $16y^4 - k^4$
27. $1 - 8m^6$

Some of these problems can be factored further by using radicals. Students will review radicals in Chapter **5**.

Excursions in Algebra

Pascal's Triangle

Blaise Pascal (1623–1662) was a French mathematician. At age nineteen he invented a computing machine, a forerunner of today's computers and calculators. He also devised a quick method for finding the coefficients of the expansion for $(a + b)^n$.

You can make the following observations in the triangle of coefficients.
1. Each row begins and ends with 1.
2. Each coefficient is the sum of the two coefficients to the left and right in the row directly above.

Power	Coefficients of the Expansion
$(a + b)^0$	1
$(a + b)^1$	1 1
$(a + b)^2$	1 2 1
$(a + b)^3$	1 3 3 1
$(a + b)^4$	1 4 6 4 1
$(a + b)^5$	1 5 10 10 5 1

1 + 1 = 2

6 + 4 = 10

For answers to problems **1-12**, see the Teacher's Guide.

Exercises Use Pascal's triangle to find the coefficients of the expansion of each expression.

1. $(a + b)^4$
2. $(a + b)^5$
3. $(a + b)^6$
4. $(a + b)^7$

Use Pascal's triangle to expand each of the following.

5. $(a + b)^4$
6. $(a + b)^6$
7. $(a + b)^8$
8. $(a + b)^9$
9. $(x + y)^6$
10. $(x - y)^6$
11. $(2a + b)^4$
12. $(x - 3y)^6$

Using Money

Comparing Interest

Miki Merlin wants to take out a loan to buy a car. The bank loans Miki \$600 at 10% interest for 1 year.

$$\begin{aligned} \textit{interest} &= \textit{principal} \cdot \textit{rate} \cdot \textit{time} \\ i &= p \cdot r \cdot t \\ &= 600 \cdot 0.10 \cdot 1 \\ &= 60 \end{aligned}$$

The interest for 1 year is \$60.

Miki's credit union also makes auto loans. They charge 1% interest on the *unpaid* balance each month. The interest is \$600 · 1% or \$6 the first month.

At first glance, Miki thought this would be more than the bank charges since \$6 · 12 is \$72.

But the interest is to be on the unpaid balance each month. Since the loan would be for 1 year, \$600 ÷ 12 or \$50 principal would be repaid the first month. The interest the second month is found as follows.

$$\begin{aligned} (\$600 - 50) \cdot 1\% &= \$550 \cdot 0.01 \\ &= \$5.50 \end{aligned}$$

The interest for the second month is \$5.50.

To find the total interest, continue to find each month's interest. Then find the sum. However, there is an easier way to find the total interest.

$$\begin{aligned} \textit{total interest} &= \textit{average principal} \cdot \textit{rate per month} \cdot \textit{number of months} \\ &= \frac{600 + 50}{2} \cdot 1\% \cdot 12 \\ &= 325 \cdot 0.01 \cdot 12 \\ &= 39 \end{aligned}$$

The average principal is $\dfrac{\left(\textit{first month's principal} + \textit{last month's principal}\right)}{2}$.

How can you find the last month's principal quickly?

The interest at the credit union would be \$39.

Exercises Find the total interest at the credit union for the following loans.

1. \$900 for 1 year \$58.50

2. \$1200 for 2 years \$150

3. \$1800 for $1\frac{1}{2}$ years \$171

4. \$600 for $2\frac{1}{2}$ years \$93

4-5 Factoring Trinomials

Objective: To factor trinomials.

When factoring trinomials, first look for common monomial factors.

$$18x^3 - 48x^2y + 32xy^2 = 2x \cdot 9x^2 - 2x \cdot 24xy + 2x \cdot 16y^2$$
$$= 2x(9x^2 - 24xy + 16y^2)$$

The trinomial $9x^2 - 24xy + 16y^2$ can be factored further. Use one of the following patterns.

Factoring Perfect Squares

For any numbers a and b,
$$a^2 + 2ab + b^2 = (a + b)^2 \text{ and,}$$
$$a^2 - 2ab + b^2 = (a - b)^2.$$

example 1

Factor $9x^2 - 24xy + 16y^2$.

$$9x^2 - 24xy + 16y^2 = (3x)^2 - 2(12xy) + (4y)^2$$
$$= (3x)^2 - 2(3x)(4y) + (4y)^2$$
$$= (3x - 4y)^2$$

Use the pattern $a^2 - 2ab + b^2 = (a - b)^2$.

Thus, $9x^2 - 24xy + 16y^2$ in factored form is $2x(3x - 4y)^2$.

Many trinomials like $x^2 - 5x + 6$ are *not* perfect squares. They can be factored by reversing the following pattern.

$$(x + r)(x + s) = \underbrace{x \cdot x} + \underbrace{x \cdot s + r \cdot x} + \underbrace{r \cdot s}$$
$$= x^2 + (r + s)x + rs$$

For $x^2 - 5x + 6$, the middle coefficient $^-5$ corresponds to $r + s$. The 6 corresponds to rs. You must find two numbers, r and s, whose sum is $^-5$ and whose product is 6.

Factors of 6	Sum of Factors
1, 6	7
$^-1$, $^-6$	$^-7$
2, 3	5
$^-2$, $^-3$	$^-5$

The two numbers are $^-2$ and $^-3$.

$$x^2 - 5x + 6 = (x - 2)(x - 3)$$

example 2

Factor $x^2 - 3x - 18$.

Factors of $^{-}18$	Sum of Factors
$^{-}1$, 18	17
1, $^{-}18$	$^{-}17$
$^{-}3$, 6	3
3, $^{-}6$	$^{-}3$
$^{-}2$, 9	7
2, $^{-}9$	$^{-}7$

The two numbers are 3 and $^{-}6$. The product of 3 and $^{-}6$ is 18 and the sum of 3 and $^{-}6$ is 18.

$$x^2 - 3x - 18 = (x + 3)(x - 6)$$

To factor $x^2 - 3x - 18$ you must find factors of $^{-}18$. To factor a trinomial like $2y^2 + 7y + 6$ you must consider factors of both 2 and 6.

Factors of 2	Factors of 6
1, 2	1, 6
	2, 3

Why are only positive factors considered?

The factors of $2y^2 + 7y + 6$ will have the following form.

factors of 2

$(\square y + \square)(\square y + \square)$

factors of 6

The possible factors are as follows.

Possible Factors	Inner + Outer Terms
$(2y + 6), (y + 1)$	$6y + 2y = 8y$
$(2y + 3), (y + 2)$	$3y + 4y = 7y$
$(2y + 1), (y + 6)$	$y + 12y = 13y$
$(2y + 2), (y + 3)$	$2y + 6y = 8y$

Test each pair of factors to find the pair that give the middle term 7y.

When the factors are $(2y + 3)$ and $(y + 2)$, the sum of the inner and outer terms is $7y$. Therefore, $2y^2 + 7y + 6 = (2y + 3)(y + 2)$.

example 3

Factor $6m^2 + 19m + 10$.

Negative factors will not be considered since the trinomial has no negative terms.

Factors of 6	Factors of 10
1, 6	1, 10
2, 3	2, 5

Possible Factors	Outer + Inner Terms
$(m + 1), (6m + 10)$	$10m + 6m = 16m$
$(m + 2), (6m + 5)$	$5m + 12m = 17m$
$(m + 10), (6m + 1)$	$m + 60m = 61m$
$(m + 5), (6m + 2)$	$2m + 30m = 32m$
$(2m + 1), (3m + 10)$	$20m + 3m = 23m$
$(2m + 2), (3m + 5)$	$10m + 6m = 16m$
$(2m + 10), (3m + 1)$	$2m + 30m = 32m$
$(2m + 5), (3m + 2)$	$4m + 15m = 19m$

Find the factors that give the middle term 19m.

Therefore, $6m^2 + 19m + 10 = (2m + 5)(3m + 2)$.

exercises

Max: 1–10, 1–22; **Avg:** 1–9, 1–21 odds; **Min:** 1–21 odds

Exploratory Factor each expression.

1. $y^2 + 6y + 9$ $(y + 3)^2$
2. $r^2 + 16r + 64$ $(r + 8)^2$
3. $k^2 - 8k + 16$ $(k - 4)^2$
4. $n^2 - 10n + 25$ $(n - 5)^2$
5. $a^2 + 5a + 6$ $(a + 2)(a + 3)$
6. $b^2 + 7b + 6$ $(b + 6)(b + 1)$
7. $p^2 - 5p + 4$ $(p - 4)(p - 1)$
8. $s^2 - 6s + 8$ $(s - 2)(s - 4)$
9. $m^2 - 7m + 10$ $(m - 5)(m - 2)$
10. $2y^2 + 7y + 3$ $(2y + 1)(y + 3)$

Written Factor each expression.

1. $a^2 + 12a + 35$ $(a + 7)(a + 5)$
2. $d^2 + 4d - 21$ $(d + 7)(d - 3)$
3. $f^2 - 18f + 81$ $(f - 9)^2$
4. $r^2 - 6r + 9$ $(r - 3)^2$
5. $k^2 + 12k + 36$ $(k + 6)^2$
6. $p^2 + 14p + 49$ $(p + 7)^2$
7. $3y^2 + 5y + 2$ $(3y + 2)(y + 1)$
8. $4x^2 + 11x + 6$ $(4x + 3)(x + 2)$
9. $4z^2 - 20z + 21$ $(2z - 7)(2z - 3)$
10. $3t^2 + 13t + 12$ $(3t + 4)(t + 3)$
11. $a^2 + 4ab + 4b^2$ $(a + 2b)^2$
12. $m^2 - 6mk + 9k^2$ $(m - 3k)^2$
13. $p^2 - 4bp + 4b^2$ $(p - 2b)^2$
14. $9a^2 - 12ab + 4b^2$ $(3a - 2b)^2$
15. $4r^2 - 20rs + 25s^2$ $(2r - 5s)^2$
16. $x^3 + 2x^2 - 35x$ $x(x + 7)(x - 5)$
17. $4k^2 + 26k + 30$ $2(2k + 3)(k + 5)$
18. $6d^2 + 33d - 63$ $3(2d - 3)(d + 7)$
19. $4h^2 + 8h - 96$ $4(h + 6)(h - 4)$
20. $2a^3 - 7a^2 - 15a$ $a(2a + 3)(a - 5)$
21. $2y^3 - 8y^2 - 42y$ $2y(y - 7)(y + 3)$
22. $3m^3 + 21m^2 + 36m$ $3m(m + 3)(m + 4)$

4–6 More Factoring

Objective: To apply several kinds of factoring techniques.

Sometimes several kinds of factoring may be used to completely factor a polynomial. Rearranging and grouping terms may be helpful.

example 1

Factor $a^2 - 2ab + a - 2b$.

$$\begin{aligned} a^2 - 2ab + a - 2b &= a(a - 2b) + 1(a - 2b) && \textit{(a - 2b) is the GCF.} \\ &= (a + 1)(a - 2b) \end{aligned}$$

These factors could be found another way.

$$\begin{aligned} a^2 - 2ab + a - 2b &= a^2 + a - 2ab - 2b && \textit{Commutative property} \\ &= a(a + 1) - 2b(a + 1) && \textit{(a + 1) is the GCF.} \\ &= (a - 2b)(a + 1) \end{aligned}$$

Example **2** groups and factors the difference of two squares.

example 2

Factor $x^3 + 2x^2 - x - 2$.

$$\begin{aligned} x^3 + 2x^2 - x - 2 &= x^2(x + 2) - 1(x + 2) && \textit{(x + 2) is the GCF.} \\ &= (x^2 - 1)(x + 2) && \textit{Group } x^2 \textit{ and } {}^-1. \\ &= (x - 1)(x + 1)(x + 2) && \textit{Factor } x^2 - 1. \end{aligned}$$

These factors could be found another way.

$$\begin{aligned} x^3 + 2x^2 - x - 2 &= x^3 - x + 2x^2 - 2 && \textit{Commutative property} \\ &= x(x^2 - 1) + 2(x^2 - 1) && \textit{(}x^2 - 1\textit{) is the GCF.} \\ &= (x^2 - 1)(x + 2) && \textit{Group x and 2.} \\ &= (x - 1)(x + 1)(x + 2) && \textit{Factor } x^2 - 1. \end{aligned}$$

The next example groups, finds a perfect square trinomial, and then factors the difference of two squares.

example 3

Factor $a^2 + 4ab - 9x^2 + 4b^2$.

$$\begin{aligned} a^2 + 4ab - 9x^2 + 4b^2 &= (a^2 + 4ab + 4b^2) - 9x^2 \\ &= (a)^2 + 2(a \cdot 2b) + (2b)^2 - (3x)^2 \\ &= (a + 2b)^2 - (3x)^2 \\ &= [(a + 2b) - 3x][(a + 2b) + 3x] \\ &= (a + 2b - 3x)(a + 2b + 3x) \end{aligned}$$

The following checklist can be used to help you factor a given polynomial.

1. Check for the greatest common monomial factor.
2. Check for special products.
   a. If there are *two terms*, look for difference of squares, sum of cubes, difference of cubes.
   b. If there are *three terms*, look for perfect squares.
3. Try other factoring methods.
   a. If there are *three terms*, try the trinomial pattern.
   b. If there are *four or more terms*, try grouping.

examples

4 **Factor $14aby + 14amy + 7b^2y - 7m^2y$.**

$$\begin{aligned} 14aby + 14amy + 7b^2y - 7m^2y &= 7y[2ab + 2am + b^2 - m^2] \quad \textit{7y is the GCF.} \\ &= 7y[2a(b + m) + (b - m)(b + m)] \\ &= 7y(2a + b - m)(b + m) \end{aligned}$$

5 **Factor $m^3 - 3m^2a + 3ma^2 - a^3$.**

$$\begin{aligned} m^3 - 3m^2a + 3ma^2 - a^3 &= (m^3 - a^3) - (3m^2a - 3ma^2) \\ &= (m^2 + ma + a^2)(m - a) - 3ma(m - a) \\ &= (m^2 + ma + a^2 - 3ma)(m - a) \\ &= (m^2 - 2ma + a^2)(m - a) \\ &= (m - a)^2(m - a) \\ &= (m - a)^3 \end{aligned}$$

6 **Factor $r^3 - r^2 - 30r$.**

Factors of $^-30$	Sum of Factors
$^-1$, 30	29
$^-2$, 15	13
$^-3$, 10	7
$^-5$, 6	1
1, $^-30$	$^-29$
2, $^-15$	$^-13$
3, $^-10$	$^-7$
5, $^-6$	$^-1$

The product of 5 and $^-6$ is $^-30$ and the sum of 5 and $^-6$ is $^-1$.

$$\begin{aligned} r^3 - r^2 - 30r &= r(r^2 - r - 30) \quad \textit{r is the GCF.} \\ &= r(r - 6)(r + 5) \end{aligned}$$

exercises

Max: 1–16, 1–42, Challenge; Avg: 1–15, 1–41 odds; Min: 1–41 odds

Exploratory Complete each factorization.

1. $y(3y-2)+4k(3y-2)$ $(y+4k)(3y-2)$
2. $3x(a-2b)-4(a-2b)$ $(3x-4)(a-2b)$
3. $a(y-b)-c(y-b)$ $(a-c)(y-b)$
4. $3m(m-7)+k(m-7)$ $3m+k)(m-7)$
5. $a(a+b)-2(a+b)$ $(a-2)(a+b)$
6. $r(r-4)-p(r-4)$ $(r-p)(r-4)$
7. $2x^2(x-3)+(x-3)$ $(2x^2+1)(x-3)$
8. $b(3b-2y)-(3b-2y)$ $(b-1)(3b-2y)$
9. $(x+y)^2-\frac{1}{4}$ $\left(x+y-\frac{1}{2}\right)\left(x+y+\frac{1}{2}\right)$
10. $(2a+b)^2-\frac{1}{16}$ $\left(2a+b-\frac{1}{4}\right)\left(2a+b+\frac{1}{4}\right)$
11. $m^2-(k-3)^2$ $(m-k+3)(m+k-3)$
12. $4a^2-(3b+1)^2$ $(2a-3b-1)(2b+3b+1)$
13. $k^2(k+4)-9(k+4)$ $(k-3)(k+3)(k+4)$
14. $a^2(x+y)-b^2(x+y)$ $(a-b)(a+b)(x+y)$
15. $(x+y)(x-y)-4(x-y)$ $(x+y-4)(x-y)$
16. $(a+b)+3(a-b)(a+b)$ $(1+3a-3b)(a+b)$

10. $(2a+b-y)(2a+b+y)$
12. $(2a-3b-1)(2a+3b+1)$

Written Factor.

1. $3y^2+12yk-2y-8k$ $(y+4k)(3y-2)$
2. $3ax-6bx-4a+8b$ $(3x-4)(a-2b)$
3. $ay-ab-cy+cb$ $(a-c)(y-b)$
4. $3m^2-21m+mk-7k$ $(3m+k)(m-7)$
5. $a^2+ab-2a-2b$ $(a-2)(a+b)$
6. $r^2-4r-rp+4p$ $(r-p)(r-4)$
7. $2x^3-6x^2+x-3$ $(2x^2+1)(x-3)$
8. $3b^2-2by-3b+2y$ $(b-1)(3b-2y)$
9. $x^2+2xy+y^2-r^2$ $(x+y-r)(x+y+r)$
10. $4a^2+4ab-y^2+b^2$
11. m^2-k^2+6k-9 $(m-k+3)(m+k-3)$
12. $4a^2-6b-9b^2-1$
13. $k^3+4k^2-9k-36$ $(k-3)(k+3)(k+4)$
14. $a^2x-b^2x+a^2y-b^2y$ $(x+y)(a-b)(a+b)$
15. $x^2-y^2+4y-4x$ $(x-y)(x+y-4)$
16. $a+b+3a^2-3b^2$ $(a+b)(1+3a-3b)$
17. $a^2-b^2+8b-16$ $(a-b+4)(a+b-4)$
18. $a^2-4a+4-25x^2$ $(a-2-5x)(a-2+5x)$
19. $2ab+2am-b-m$ $(2a-1)(b+m)$
20. y^3+y^2-y-1 $(y-1)(y+1)^2$
21. $x^2+6x+9-a^2$ $(x+3-a)(x+3+a)$
22. $n^2+2nx-1+x^2$ $(n+x-1)(n+x+1)$
23. $a^2-a+\frac{1}{4}-y^2$ $\left(a-\frac{1}{2}-y\right)\left(a-\frac{1}{2}+y\right)$
24. $\frac{1}{16}-9x^2+12xy-4y^2$
25. $x^3+x^2y-xyz-x^2z$ $x(x+y)(x-z)$
26. $p^2-q^2-2p-2q$ $(p-q-2)(p+q)$
27. $18x^2-21x-9$ $3(2x-3)(3x+1)$
28. $2y^3-10y^2-72y$ $2y(y-9)(y+4)$
29. $b^2-y^2-2yp-p^2$ $(b-y-p)(b+y+p)$
30. $a^2+2ab+b^2-9$ $(a+b-3)(a+b+3)$
31. $2ab+2am+b^2-m^2$ $(2a+b-m)(b+m)$
32. $3pq+3ps+q^2-s^2$ $(3p+q-s)(q+s)$
33. $8a^3+27$ $(2a+3)(4a^2-6a+9)$
34. $16m^3-2$ $2(2m-1)(4m^2+2m+1)$
35. $3r-81r^4$ $3r(1-3r)(1+3r+9r^2)$
36. $7p^3+56s^3$ $7(p+2s)(p^2-2ps+4s^2)$
37. $x^3+y^3-x^2y-xy^2$ $(x+y)(x-y)^2$
38. $t^3+125+5t^2+25t$ $(t+5)(t^2+25)$
39. x^4-13x^2+36 $(x-3)(x+3)(x-2)(x+2)$
40. y^4-14y^2+45 $(y-3)(y+3)(y^2-5)$
41. $(r-p)^3+4rp(r-p)$ $(r-p)(r+p)^2$
42. $a(a+1)(a+2)-3a(a+1)$ $a(a-1)(a+1)$

24. $\left(\frac{1}{4}-3x+2y\right)\left(\frac{1}{4}+3x-2y\right)$

Challenge Factor.

1. $a^4-12a^3b+24a^2b^2-8ab^3$
2. $a^4-16a^2+3a^3-48a$
3. $x^3y-3x^2y-6xy+8y$ $y(x+2)(x-4)(x-1)$
4. $m^3n+m^2n-mn^3-mn^2$

1. $a(a-2b)(a^2-10ab+4b^2)$ 2. $a(a+3)(a-4)(a+4)$ 4. $mn(m-n)(m+n+1)$

4–7 Dividing Polynomials

Objective: To divide polynomials.

You can use the properties of exponents to divide a monomial by a monomial. You also use these properties to divide a polynomial by a monomial.

examples

1 **Divide $16x^4$ by $8x^3$.**

$$16x^4 \div 8x^3 = \frac{16x^4}{8x^3}$$
$$= \frac{16}{8} \cdot x^{4-3}$$
$$= 2x$$

2 **Find $\frac{{}^-49r^3s^5}{7rs^2}$.**

$$\frac{{}^-49r^3s^5}{7rs^2} = \frac{{}^-49}{7} \cdot r^{3-1}s^{5-2}$$
$$= {}^-7r^2s^3$$

3 **Find $\frac{36m^4y^4 - 18m^3y}{6m^2y}$.**

$$\frac{36m^4y^4 - 18m^3y}{6m^2y} = \frac{36m^4y^4}{6m^2y} - \frac{18m^3y}{6m^2y}$$
$$= \frac{36}{6} \cdot m^{4-2}y^{4-1} - \frac{18}{6} \cdot m^{3-2}y^{1-1}$$
$$= 6m^2y^3 - 3m$$

$y^{1-1} = y^0$ or 1.

Dividing a polynomial by a polynomial is like long division. The following example reviews long division with numbers.

example

4 **Divide 883 by 21.**

```
     42
21)883
   840     Subtract 40 · 21.
    43
    42     Subtract 2 · 21.
     1     Stop when remainder is less than 21.
```

$$\frac{883}{21} = 42\tfrac{1}{21}$$

You use a similar process to divide polynomials. Remember, you can only add or subtract like terms.

examples

5 **Divide $8y^2 + 8y + 3$ by $2y + 1$.**

Before dividing one polynomial by another, it is helpful to arrange the terms in descending powers of the variable.

$$\begin{array}{r} 4y + 2 \\ 2y + 1\overline{)8y^2 + 8y + 3} \\ \underline{8y^2 + 4y} \\ 4y + 3 \\ \underline{4y + 2} \\ 1 \end{array}$$

Subtract $4y(2y + 1)$.

Subtract $2(2y + 1)$.

Stop when degree of remainder is less than degree of $2y + 1$.

$$\frac{8y^2 + 8y + 3}{2y + 1} = 4y + 2 + \frac{1}{2y + 1}$$

6 **Divide $x^3 + 5x^2 + 5x + 16$ by $x^2 + 3$.**

$$\begin{array}{r} x + 5 \\ x^2 + 3\overline{)x^3 + 5x^2 + 5x + 16} \\ \underline{x^3 \qquad\quad + 3x} \\ 5x^2 + 2x + 16 \\ \underline{5x^2 \qquad\quad + 15} \\ 2x + 1 \end{array}$$

$$\frac{x^3 + 5x^2 + 5x + 16}{x^2 + 3} = x + 5 + \frac{2x + 1}{x^2 + 3}$$

If the divisor is a factor of a polynomial, the remainder upon division is zero.

example

7 **Show that $a + 2$ is a factor of $a^3 + 3a^2 - 2a - 8$.**

$$\begin{array}{r} a^2 + a - 4 \\ a + 2\overline{)a^3 + 3a^2 - 2a - 8} \\ \underline{a^3 + 2a^2} \\ a^2 - 2a \\ \underline{a^2 + 2a} \\ {}^{-}4a - 8 \\ \underline{{}^{-}4a - 8} \\ 0 \end{array}$$

Thus, $a^3 + 3a^2 - 2a - 8 = (a + 2)(a^2 + a - 4)$.

exercises

Max: 1–12, 1–51; Avg: 1–11, 1–49 odds; Min: 1–43 odds

Exploratory Use division to simplify each expression.

1. $\frac{7^4}{7^5}$ $\frac{1}{7}$
2. $\frac{12^6}{12^4}$ 12^2 or 144
3. $\frac{g^6}{g^3}$ g^3
4. $\frac{h^{16}}{h^2}$ h^{14}
5. $\frac{a^{10}}{a^{10}}$ 1
6. $\frac{14r^{11}}{2r^{10}}$ $7r$
7. $\frac{8a^2b^4}{2b}$ $4a^2b^3$
8. $\frac{3^3r^3s^3}{9r^2}$ $3rs^3$
9. $\frac{36x^3y^5}{12x^2y^2}$ $3xy^3$
10. $\frac{6xy^2 - 3xy + 2x^2y}{xy}$ $6y - 3 + 2x$
11. $\frac{a^3b^2 - a^2b + 2a}{^-ab}$ $^-a^2b + a - \frac{2}{b}$
12. $\frac{6r^2s^2 + 3rs^2 - 9r^2s}{3rs}$ $2rs + s - 3r$

For answers to problems 1–44, see the Teacher's Guide.

Written Find each solution.

1. $(x^2 - 12x - 45) \div (x + 3)$
2. $(a^2 + 7a - 60) \div (a + 12)$
3. $(6y^2 + 7y - 3) \div (2y + 3)$
4. $(15b^2 + 14b - 8) \div (5b - 2)$
5. $(8a^2 + 34a + 19) \div (2a + 7)$
6. $(20b^2 - 17b - 61) \div (5b + 7)$
7. $(28y^2 + 23y - 12) \div (7y - 3)$
8. $(80x^2 + 6x - 4) \div (10x - 3)$
9. $(a^2 - 5a - 84) \div (a + 7)$
10. $x^2 + 20x + 91) \div (x + 7)$
11. $(y^2 + 15y + 36) \div (y + 3)$
12. $(b^2 + 17b + 52) \div (b + 4)$
13. $(6x^2 + 11x - 35) \div (3x - 5)$
14. $(15m^2 - m - 6) \div (5m + 3)$
15. $(a^2 - 5ab + 6b^2) \div (a - 3b)$
16. $(12x^2 - 4xy - y^2) \div (2x - y)$
17. $(6z^2 - 2z - 28) \div (3z + 7)$
18. $(3b^2 - 7ba - 20a^2) \div (3b + 5a)$
19. $(a^2 + 4a - 16) \div (a - 6)$
20. $(y^2 + y - 8) \div (y - 3)$
21. $(8x^2 - 4x + 11) \div (x + 5)$
22. $(x^2 + 5x + 4) \div (x + 2)$
23. $(6a^2 + 23a + 25) \div (2a + 3)$
24. $(126k^2 + 113k - 26) \div (14k - 3)$
25. $(56m^2 - 113m + 59) \div (8m - 7)$
26. $(20r^2 + 7r - 10) \div (5r - 2)$
27. $(6y^3 + 11y^2 - 4y - 4) \div (3y - 2)$
28. $(8x^3 - 22x^2 - 5x + 12) \div (4x + 3)$
29. $(6a^3 + 5a^2 + 9) \div (2a + 3)$
30. $(8b^2 - 4b + 1) \div (2b - 1)$
31. $(m^3 - 1) \div (m - 1)$
32. $(a^3 - 8) \div (a - 2)$
33. $(y^3 - 9y^2 + 27y - 28) \div (y - 3)$
34. $(x^3 + 6x^2 + 12x + 12) \div (x + 2)$
35. $(6a^3 + 5a^2 - 13a - 17) \div (3a + 2)$
36. $(2p^3 + 7p^2 - 29p + 29) \div (2p - 3)$
37. $(m^3 - 7m + 3m^2 - 21) \div (m^2 - 7)$
38. $(48p^3 - 15 + 6p^2 - 40p) \div (6p^2 - 5)$
39. $(x^3 + 4x - 4) \div (x + 2)$
40. $(2t^3 - 2t - 3) \div (t - 1)$
41. $(x^4 + 4) \div (x^2 - 2x + 2)$
42. $(y^4 + 4y^3 + 10y^2 + 12y + 9) \div (y^2 + 2y + 3)$
43. $(a^4 - 3a^2 + 1) \div (a^2 + a - 1)$
44. $(x^4 - 4x^2 + 12x - 9) \div (x^2 + 2x - 3)$

45. Is $3y - 2$ a factor of $6y^3 - y^2 - 5y + 2$? Write yes or no. yes
46. Is $4x + 5$ a factor of $4x^3 + x^2 + 10$? Write yes or no. no
47. One factor of $a^3 - 2a^2 - a + 2$ is $a - 2$. Find the other factors. $a - 1, a + 1$
48. One factor of $2m^3 - 11m^2 + 18m - 9$ is $m - 3$. Find the other factors. $2m - 3, m - 1$
49. Find the remainder for $(x^2 + 3x + 5) \div (x - 2)$. 15
50. Let $f(x) = x^2 + 3x + 5$. Find $f(2)$. 15
51. How do the answers to problems **49** and **50** compare? They are the same.

4-8 Synthetic Division

Objective: To divide polynomials using synthetic division.

There is a shortcut for finding $3x^3 - 4x^2 - 3x - 2$ divided by $x - 3$ called **synthetic division.** These steps show how to use the shortcut.

Step 1 Write the terms of the polynomial in descending order. Then write the coefficients as shown.

$$\begin{array}{cccc} 3 & {}^{-}4 & {}^{-}3 & {}^{-}2 \end{array}$$

Step 2 The divisor is $x - 3$. Since 3 is being subtracted, write 3 to the left.

$$\begin{array}{c|cccc} 3 & 3 & {}^{-}4 & {}^{-}3 & {}^{-}2 \end{array}$$

Step 3 Bring down the first coefficient.

$$\begin{array}{c|cccc} 3 & 3 & {}^{-}4 & {}^{-}3 & {}^{-}2 \\ & & & & \\ \hline & 3 & & & \end{array}$$

Step 4 $3 \cdot 3 = 9$

$$\begin{array}{c|cccc} 3 & 3 & {}^{-}4 & {}^{-}3 & {}^{-}2 \\ & & 9 & & \\ \hline & 3 & & & \end{array}$$

Step 5 ${}^{-}4 + 9 = 5$

$$\begin{array}{c|cccc} 3 & 3 & {}^{-}4 & {}^{-}3 & {}^{-}2 \\ & & 9 & & \\ \hline & 3 & 5 & & \end{array}$$

Step 6 $3 \cdot 5 = 15$

$$\begin{array}{c|cccc} 3 & 3 & {}^{-}4 & {}^{-}3 & {}^{-}2 \\ & & 9 & 15 & \\ \hline & 3 & 5 & & \end{array}$$

Step 7 ${}^{-}3 + 15 = 12$

$$\begin{array}{c|cccc} 3 & 3 & {}^{-}4 & {}^{-}3 & {}^{-}2 \\ & & 9 & 15 & \\ \hline & 3 & 5 & 12 & \end{array}$$

Step 8 $3 \cdot 12 = 36$

$$\begin{array}{c|cccc} 3 & 3 & {}^{-}4 & {}^{-}3 & {}^{-}2 \\ & & 9 & 15 & 36 \\ \hline & 3 & 5 & 12 & \end{array}$$

Step 9 ${}^{-}2 + 36 = 34$

$$\begin{array}{c|cccc} 3 & 3 & {}^{-}4 & {}^{-}3 & {}^{-}2 \\ & & 9 & 15 & 36 \\ \hline & 3 & 5 & 12 & 34 \end{array}$$

Step 10 Write the solution.

$$3x^2 + 5x + 12 + \frac{34}{x - 3}$$

Compare the shortcut to the long method.

$$\begin{array}{r} 3x^2 + 5x + 12 \\ x - 3 \overline{)3x^3 - 4x^2 - 3x - 2} \\ \underline{3x^3 - 9x^2} \\ 5x^2 - 3x \\ \underline{5x^2 - 15x} \\ 12x - 2 \\ \underline{12x - 36} \\ 34 \end{array}$$

$$\begin{array}{c|cccc} 3 & 3 & {}^{-}4 & {}^{-}3 & {}^{-}2 \\ & & 9 & 15 & 36 \\ \hline & 3 & 5 & 12 & 34 \end{array}$$

examples

1

Find $(y^2 + 6y - 7) \div (y - 2)$.

$$\begin{array}{r|rrr} 2 & 1 & 6 & ^-7 \\ & & 2 & 16 \\ \hline & 1 & 8 & 9 \end{array}$$

The solution is $y + 8 + \frac{9}{y - 2}$.

2

Find $(2y^3 - 3y^2 - 8y + 4) \div (y + 2)$.

$$\begin{array}{r|rrrr} ^-2 & 2 & ^-3 & ^-8 & 4 \\ & & ^-4 & 14 & ^-12 \\ \hline & 2 & ^-7 & 6 & ^-8 \end{array}$$

The solution is $2y^2 - 7y + 6 - \frac{8}{y + 2}$

$y + 2$ is the same as $y - {}^-2$.

The coefficient of a is zero in $2a^3 + a^2 + 12$. Zero coefficients must be included when you do synthetic division.

examples

3

Find $(2a^3 + a^2 + 12) \div (a + 2)$.

$$\begin{array}{r|rrrr} ^-2 & 2 & 1 & 0 & 12 \\ & & ^-4 & 6 & ^-12 \\ \hline & 2 & ^-3 & 6 & 0 \end{array}$$

The solution is $2a^2 - 3a + 6$.

Check:

$$(a + 2)(2a^2 - 3a + 6) \stackrel{?}{=} 2a^3 + a^2 + 12$$
$$2a^3 - 3a^2 + 6a + 4a^2 - 6a + 12 \stackrel{?}{=} 2a^3 + a^2 + 12$$
$$2a^3 + a^2 + 12 = 2a^3 + a^2 + 12$$

4

Find $(2t^5 - 3t^4 - 50t^3 - 24t^2) \div (t - 6)$.

$$\begin{array}{r|rrrrrr} 6 & 2 & ^-3 & ^-50 & ^-24 & 0 & 0 \\ & & 12 & 54 & 24 & 0 & 0 \\ \hline & 2 & 9 & 4 & 0 & 0 & 0 \end{array}$$

The solution is $2t^4 + 9t^3 + 4t^2$.

Check:

$$(t - 6)(2t^4 + 9t^3 + 4t^2) \stackrel{?}{=} 2t^5 - 3t^4 - 50t^3 - 24t^2$$
$$2t^5 + 9t^4 + 4t^3 - 12t^4 - 54t^3 - 24t^2 \stackrel{?}{=} 2t^5 - 3t^4 - 50t^3 - 24t^2$$
$$2t^5 - 3t^4 - 50t^3 - 24t^2 = 2t^5 - 3t^4 - 50t^3 - 24t^2$$

Some divisors like $2x - 1$ have leading coefficients other than one. For example, suppose you want to divide $4x^3 + x - 1$ by $2x - 1$. You must factor these divisors and dividends *before* you can use synthetic division.

$$2x - 1 = \left(x - \frac{1}{2}\right) \cdot 2$$

$$4x^3 + x - 1 = \left(2x^3 + \frac{1}{2}x - \frac{1}{2}\right) \cdot 2$$

Factor the leading coefficient of the divisor from the divisor and dividend.

Now, use synthetic division to divide $2x^3 + \frac{1}{2}x - \frac{1}{2}$ by $x - \frac{1}{2}$.

examples

5 **Divide $4x^3 + x - 1$ by $2x - 1$.**

$$2x - 1 = \left(x - \frac{1}{2}\right) \cdot 2$$

$$4x^3 + x - 1 = \left(2x^3 + \frac{1}{2}x - \frac{1}{2}\right) \cdot 2$$

Some students may try to factor out 4. Remind students to always factor out the leading coefficient of the divisor.

$$\begin{array}{r|rrrr} \frac{1}{2} & 2 & 0 & \frac{1}{2} & -\frac{1}{2} \\ & & 1 & \frac{1}{2} & \frac{1}{2} \\ \hline & 2 & 1 & 1 & 0 \end{array}$$

The solution is $2x^2 + x + 1$.

Check the solution. Does $(2x - 1)(2x^2 + x + 1) = 4x^3 + x - 1$?

6 **Divide $3a^4 - 2a^3 + 5a^2 - 4a - 2$ by $3a + 1$.**

$$3a + 1 = \left(a + \frac{1}{3}\right) \cdot 3$$

$$3a^4 - 2a^3 + 5a^2 - 4a - 2 = \left(a^4 - \frac{2}{3}a^3 + \frac{5}{3}a^2 - \frac{4}{3}a - \frac{2}{3}\right) \cdot 3$$

$$\begin{array}{r|rrrrr} -\frac{1}{3} & 1 & -\frac{2}{3} & \frac{5}{3} & -\frac{4}{3} & -\frac{2}{3} \\ & & -\frac{1}{3} & \frac{1}{3} & -\frac{2}{3} & \frac{2}{3} \\ \hline & 1 & -1 & 2 & -2 & 0 \end{array}$$

The solution is $a^3 - a^2 + 2a - 2$.

exercises

Max: 1–7, 1–22; Avg: 1–7, 1–21 odds; Min: 1–21 odds

Exploratory Match the division problem with the correct synthetic division.

1. $(a^3 + 6a^2 + 3a + 1) \div (a - 2) = a^2 + 8a + 19 + \dfrac{39}{a - 2}$ d

2. $(z^3 + 2z^2 - 3z + 4) \div (z - 5) = z^2 + 7z + 32 + \dfrac{164}{z - 5}$ g

3. $(2y^3 - 5y + 1) \div (y + 1) = 2y^2 - 2y - 3 + \dfrac{4}{y + 1}$ e

4. $(x^3 - 11x + 10) \div (x + 3) = x^2 - 3x - 2 + \dfrac{16}{x + 3}$ c

5. $(3y^3 - 5y + 10) \div (y - 2) = 3y^2 + 6y + 7 + \dfrac{24}{y - 2}$ a

6. $(b^3 + 3b^2 - 4b + 1) \div (b + 3) = b^2 - 4 + \dfrac{13}{b + 3}$ b

7. $(5y^3 - 3y^2 + 2y - 5) \div (y + 1) = 5y^2 - 8y + 10 - \dfrac{15}{y + 1}$ f

a. $\begin{array}{r|rrr|r} 2 & 3 & 0 & -5 & 10 \\ & & 6 & 12 & 14 \\ \hline & 3 & 6 & 7 & 24 \end{array}$

b. $\begin{array}{r|rrr|r} -3 & 1 & 3 & -4 & 1 \\ & & -3 & 0 & 12 \\ \hline & 1 & 0 & -4 & 13 \end{array}$

c. $\begin{array}{r|rrr|r} -3 & 1 & 0 & -11 & 10 \\ & & -3 & 9 & 6 \\ \hline & 1 & -3 & -2 & 16 \end{array}$

d. $\begin{array}{r|rrr|r} 2 & 1 & 6 & 3 & 1 \\ & & 2 & 16 & 38 \\ \hline & 1 & 8 & 19 & 39 \end{array}$

e. $\begin{array}{r|rrr|r} -1 & 2 & 0 & -5 & 1 \\ & & -2 & 2 & 3 \\ \hline & 2 & -2 & -3 & 4 \end{array}$

f. $\begin{array}{r|rrr|r} -1 & 5 & -3 & 2 & -5 \\ & & -5 & 8 & -10 \\ \hline & 5 & -8 & 10 & -15 \end{array}$

g. $\begin{array}{r|rrr|r} 5 & 1 & 2 & -3 & 4 \\ & & 5 & 35 & 160 \\ \hline & 1 & 7 & 32 & 164 \end{array}$

For answers to problems 1–22, see the Teacher's Guide.

Written Use synthetic division to find each solution.

1. $(2x^3 - 3x^2 + 3x - 4) \div (x - 2)$
2. $(3y^3 + 2y^2 - 32y + 2) \div (y - 3)$
3. $(2a^3 + a^2 - 2a + 3) \div (a + 1)$
4. $(3m^3 - 2m^2 + 2m - 1) \div (m - 1)$
5. $(x^4 - 2x^3 + x^2 - 3x + 2) \div (x - 2)$
6. $(3y^4 - 6y^3 - 2y^2 + y - 6) \div (y + 1)$
7. $(6k^3 - 19k^2 + k + 6) \div (k - 3)$
8. $(z^4 - 3z^3 - z^2 - 11z - 4) \div (z - 4)$
9. $(2b^3 - 11b^2 + 12b + 9) \div (b - 3)$
10. $(x^3 + 2x^2 - 5x - 6) \div (x - 2)$
11. $(y^4 - 16y^3 + 86y^2 - 176y + 105) \div (y - 5)$
12. $a^4 - 5a^3 - 13a^2 + 53a + 60) \div (a + 1)$
13. $(2x^4 - 5x^3 - 10x + 8) \div (x - 3)$
14. $(2a^4 - 5a^3 + 2a - 3) \div (a - 1)$
15. $(y^4 + 6y^3 - 7y^2 + 7y - 1) \div (y + 3)$
16. $(h^5 - 6h^3 + 4h^2 - 3) \div (h - 2)$
17. $(4x^4 - 5x^2 + 2x + 3) \div (2x - 1)$
18. $(2b^3 - 3b^2 - 8b + 4) \div (2b + 1)$
19. $(6x^3 - 28x^2 + 19x + 3) \div (3x - 2)$
20. $(4y^4 - 5y^2 - 8y - 10) \div (2y - 3)$
21. $(x^5 + 32) \div (x + 2)$
22. $(x^5 - 3x^2 - 20) \div (x - 2)$

CAREERS

Heating Analyst

Beth Merritt is a heating analyst. She examines heating systems and recommends how they can be made more efficient. These recommendations may range from more or better insulation to a change in fuel.

A small hotel has a hot water system which is heated by fuel oil. Assume that the heating is 70% efficient. The following shows how to find the amount of oil needed to heat 1000 pounds of water from 52°F to 212°F.

heat required = weight · specific heat · temperature change
= 1000 lb · 1 Btu/lb°F · (212 − 52)°F
= 1000 · 1 · 160 Btu
= 160,000 Btu

Btu stands for British thermal unit. It is the amount of heat required to raise the temperature of water 1°F.

But the heating is only 70% efficient.

160,000 ÷ 70% or 228,571 Btu are needed. *Divide by the efficiency of the heating.*

Assume the oil provides 19,000 Btu per pound and weighs about 7 pounds per gallon.

228,571 ÷ 19,000 or 12 pounds of oil are needed.

12 ÷ 7 or 1.71 gallons of oil are needed.

Exercises Find the amount of fuel oil needed if one of the conditions described above is changed as follows. Water weighs 8.34 pounds per gallon.

1. 1000 gallons of water are heated. 14.3

2. The water temperature is 42°F. 1.8

3. The heating is 75% efficient. 1.6

4. The oil provides 18,500 Btu per pound. 1.8

5. The oil weighs 7.2 pounds per gallon. 1.7

Answers are given to the nearest tenth of a gallon of oil.

Vocabulary

monomial (102)
coefficient (102)
degree of monomial (102)
like terms (102)
polynomial (106)
binomial (106)
trinomial (106)
degree of polynomial (106)
FOIL (108)
synthetic division (125)

Chapter Summary

1. Properties of Exponents: For any numbers a and b, and non-negative integers m and n, the following hold.
   1. $a^m \cdot a^n = a^{m+n}$
   2. $(a^m)^n = a^{m \cdot n}$
   3. $(ab)^m = a^m b^m$
   4. $\frac{a^m}{a^n} = a^{m-n}$ as long as $a \neq 0$ and $m > n$ (103)
2. The degree of a polynomial is the degree of the monomial of greatest degree. The degree of a monomial is the sum of the exponents of its variables. (106)
3. The product of two binomials is the sum of the product of

   F the first terms,
   O the outer terms,
   I the inner terms, and
   L the last terms. (108)
4. Factoring Difference of Two Squares: For any numbers a and b, $a^2 - b^2 = (a - b)(a + b)$. (112)
5. Factoring Sum or Difference of Cubes: For any numbers a and b, $a^3 + b^3 = (a + b)(a^2 - ab + b^2)$ and, $a^3 - b^3 = (a - b)(a^2 + ab + b^2)$. (113)
6. Factoring Perfect Squares: For any numbers a and b, $a^2 + 2ab + b^2 = (a + b)^2$ and, $a^2 - 2ab + b^2 = (a - b)^2$. (116)
7. Checklist for factoring polynomials.
   1. Check for the greatest common monomial factor.
   2. Check for special products.
      a. If there are *two terms*, look for difference of squares, sum of cubes, difference of cubes.
      b. If there are *three terms*, look for perfect squares.
   3. Try other factoring methods.
      a. If there are *three terms*, try the trinomial pattern.
      b. If there are four or more terms, try grouping. (120)

Chapter Review

4-1 Simplify each expression.

1. $y^9 \cdot y^2$ y^{11}
2. $(xy^4)(^-5x^2y^3)$ $^-5x^3y^7$
3. $(x^3)^2$ x^6
4. $(4a^2)^3$ $64a^6$
5. $\frac{a^6}{a^2}$ a^4
6. $\frac{14a^4b^3}{(7ab)^2}$ $\frac{2}{7}a^2b$
7. $(5a)(6a^2b)(3ab^3) + (4a^2)(3b^3)(2a^2b)$ $114a^4b^4$
8. $(3a)(a^2b)^3 + (2a)^2(^-a^5b^3)$ $^-a^7b^3$

4-2 Simplify each expression by performing the indicated operations.

9. $(4b^3 + 7b^2 - 3b + 5) + (^-3b^3 + 8b^2 - 7)$ $b^3 + 15b^2 - 3b - 2$
10. $(p^4 + 5p^2 - 3p + 7) - (p^3 + p^2 - 3p + 5)$ $p^4 - p^3 + 4p^2 + 2$
11. $(4a - 5)(a + 7)$ $4a^2 + 23a - 35$
12. $(3m - 7)^2$ $9m^2 - 42m + 49$
13. $(y + 7)(y^2 - 3y + 5)$ $y^3 + 4y^2 - 16y + 35$
14. $(2x - 5)(x^2 + 8x - 7)$ $2x^3 + 11x^2 - 54x + 35$
15. $(m + 1)(2m + 7)(m + 3)$ $2m^3 + 15m^2 + 34m + 21$
16. $(2z - 5)(2z + 5)(z - 6)$ $4z^3 - 24z^2 - 25z + 150$

4-3 Expand each binomial.

17. $(r + s)^5$
18. $(x + y)^6$ $x^6 + 6x^5y + 15x^4y^2 + 20x^3y^3 + 15x^2y^4 + 6xy^5 + y^6$
19. $(2a + m)^4$
20. $(3x + 2y)^4$
21. Andrew Lee invested \$3000 at 8% annual interest for 4 years. The interest is compounded annually. Find the value of Andrew's investment after 4 years. Use $A = 3000(1 + 0.08)^4$. About \$4081.47.

20. $81x^4 + 216x^3y + 216x^2y^2 + 96xy^3 + 16y^4$
17. $r^5 + 5r^4s + 10r^3s^2 + 10r^2s^3 + 5rs^4 + s^5$
19. $16a^4 + 32a^3m + 24a^2m^2 + 8am^3 + m^4$

4-4 Factor.

22. $y^2 - 25$ $(y - 5)(y + 5)$
23. $3r^2s - 3rs^2 + 3s^3$ $3s(r^2 - rs + s^2)$
24. $x^4 - y^4$ $(x - y)(x + y)(x^2 + y^2)$
25. $p^3q^3 - 27q^3$ $q^3(p - 3)(p^2 + 3p + 9)$

4-5 Factor.

26. $x^2 - 7x + 10$ $(x - 2)(x - 5)$
27. $2x^2 + 7xy + 3y^2$ $(2x + y)(x + 3y)$
28. $9p^2 - 30pt + 25t^2$ $(3p - 5t)^2$
29. $r^3 + 6r^2s + 8rs^2$ $r(r + 4s)(r + 2s)$

4-6 Factor.

30. $x^2 - 2xy + x - 2y$ $(x + 1)(x - 2y)$
31. $3a^2 + 12ab - 2a - 8b$ $(3a - 2)(a + 4b)$
32. $^-b^2 + 8b + a^2 - 16$ $(a - b + 4)(a + b - 4)$
33. $4a^2 + 4ab - a^2 + b^2$ $(3a + b)(a + b)$

4-7 Find each solution using long division. Show your work.

34. $(8y^3 - 22y^2 - 5y + 15) \div (4y + 3)$ $2y^2 - 7y + 4 + 3/(4y + 3)$
35. $(2r^3 + 11r^2 - 9r - 18) \div (2r + 3)$ $r^2 + 4r - 21/2 + 27/2(2r + 3)$
36. Show that $x + 1$ is *not* a factor of $2x^3 + x^2 - 11x - 30$. Remainder isn't zero. $(2x^3 + x^2 - 11x - 30) \div (x + 1) = 2x^2 - x - 10 - 20/(x + 1)$

4-8 Use synthetic division to find each solution. Show your work.

37. $(2m^3 - 3m^2 - 8m + 1) \div (m - 4)$ $2m^2 + 5m + 12 + 49/(m - 4)$
38. $(2r^3 + r^2 - 13r + 6) \div (2r - 1)$ $r^2 + r - 6$
39. Show that $2x + 1$ is a factor of $2x^3 - 11x^2 + 12x + 9$.
40. Show that $x - 3$ is a factor of $2x^3 - 11x^2 + 12x + 9$.

39-40. $2x^3 - 11x^2 + 12x + 9 = (2x + 1)(x - 3)^2$
The remainder upon division is zero in both cases.

Chapter Test

Simplify each expression.

1. $(m^2)^5$ m^{10}
2. $\frac{16b^7}{2b^5}$ $8b^2$
3. $(4a^2b^2)(5ab^3)$ $20a^3b^5$
4. $(5x)(6x^2y^3) + (2xy)^3$ $38x^3y^3$
5. $3x^2y + 4 - 3x^2y$ 4
6. $(3y^4 + 5y^3 + y - 7) + (4y^4 - 3y^3 + 7y^2 - 3y + 8)$ $7y^4 + 2y^3 + 7y^2 - 2y + 1$
7. $(4b^3 + 7b^2 - 3b + 5) - (2b^3 - 5b^2 + 2b + 7)$ $2b^3 + 12b^2 - 5b - 2$
8. $(2y + 7)(y - 3)$ $2y^2 + y - 21$
9. $(3m + 5)^2$ $9m^2 + 30m + 25$
10. $(y - 4)(3y^2 - 5y + 4)$
    $3y^3 - 17y^2 + 24y - 16$
11. $(x + 3)(2x - 5)(3x + 4)$
    $6x^3 + 11x^2 - 41x - 60$

Expand each binomial. For answers to problems 12–15, see the Teacher's Guide.

12. $(m + k)^5$
13. $(y + 2)^4$
14. $(2x - 5)^6$
15. $(y - 3)^6$

Solve the problem.

16. Anna Cohen invested \$6000 at 7.5% annual interest for 3 years. The interest is compounded semiannually. Find the value of Anna's investment after 3 years.
    Use $A = 6000\ (1 + 0.0375)^6$. About \$7483.07.

Factor 17. $(a - 11)(a + 11)$ 18. $(k + 8)(k - 5)$ 19. $(a + 3m)^2$

17. $a^2 - 121$
18. $k^2 + 3k - 40$
19. $a^2 + 6am + 9m^2$
20. $y^3 + 125$
21. $3y^2 + 15y + 18$
22. $64a^3 - 1$
23. $8a^3 - 12a^2b + 6ab^2 - b^3$ $(2a - b)^3$ 20. $(y + 5)(y^2 - 5y + 25)$
24. $2m^3 - 6m^2 + m - 3$ $(m - 3)(2m^2 + 1)$ 21. $3(y + 3)(y + 2)$
25. $r^2 + 4rs + 4s^2 - 9y^2$ $(r + 2s - 3y)(r + 2s + 3y)$ 22. $(4a - 1)(16a^2 + 4a + 1)$

26. Use long division to find $(6y^3 - 5y^2 - 12y - 17) \div (3y + 2)$. Show your work. $2y^2 - 3y - 2 - 13/(3y + 2)$
27. Use synthetic division to find $(5m^3 - 3m^2 + 2m - 5) \div (m + 2)$. Show your work.
28. Show that $a - 3$ is a factor of $a^4 - a^3 + a^2 - 25a + 12$. $5m^2 - 13m + 28 - 61/(m + 2)$
29. One factor of $2y^3 + y^2 - 13y + 6$ is $y + 3$. Find the other factors. $(2y - 1)(y - 2)$
30. One factor of $4b^3 + 6b^2 + 40b - 22$ is $2b - 1$. Find the other factors. 2, $b^2 + 2b + 11$

28. $a^4 - a^3 + a^2 - 25a + 12 = (a - 3)(a^3 + 2a^2 + 7a - 4)$

Chapter

5

Roots

The laws of physics describe how the basic components of our universe interact. Similarly, mathematical properties describe the various operations on many types of numbers.

5–1 Roots

Objective: To learn the definition and use of the *n*th root of a number.

Squaring a number means using that number as a factor two times. Cubing a number means using that number as a factor three times.

$6^2 = 6 \cdot 6$ or 36	6 is used as a factor two times
$6^3 = 6 \cdot 6 \cdot 6$ or 216	6 is used as a factor three times

Raising a number to the *n*th power means using that number as a factor *n* times.

$5^4 = 5 \cdot 5 \cdot 5 \cdot 5$ or 625 — *5 is used as a factor four times. n is 4*

$2^8 = 2 \cdot 2 \cdot 2 \cdot 2 \cdot 2 \cdot 2 \cdot 2 \cdot 2$ or 256 — *2 is used as a factor eight times. n is 8*

The inverse of raising a number to the *n*th power is finding the ***n*th root** of that number. For example, the inverse of squaring is finding the **square root.**

To find the square root of 36, you must find two equal factors whose product is 36.

$$x^2 = 36 \qquad x \cdot x = 36$$

Since 6 times 6 is 36, one square root of 36 is 6. Since $^-6$ times $^-6$ is 36, another square root of 36 is $^-6$.

Definition of Square Root

For any numbers *a* and *b*, if $a^2 = b$, then *a* is a square root of *b*.

To find the cube root of 125, you must find three equal factors whose product is 125.

$$x^3 = 125 \qquad 5^3 = 5 \cdot 5 \cdot 5 \text{ or } 125$$

5 is a cube root of 125

Definition of *n*th Root

For any numbers *a* and *b*, and any positive integer *n*, if $a^n = b$, then *a* is an *n*th root of *b*.

The symbol $\sqrt[n]{}$ indicates an *n*th root.

index ⟶ $\sqrt[n]{256}$ ⟵ *radicand* (*radical sign* marked above the symbol)

When *no* index appears, the **radical** sign $\sqrt{}$ indicates a square root.

Some numbers have more than one real root. For example, 36 has two real square roots, 6 and $^{-}6$. The chart indicates the real nth roots of a number b.

The Real nth Roots of b

	$b > 0$	$b < 0$	$b = 0$
n even	one positve root one negative root	no real roots	one real root, 0
n odd	one positive root no negative roots	no positive roots one negative root	one real root, 0

The symbol $\sqrt[n]{b}$ indicates the principal nth root of b. The principal nth root of b is a positive number *unless* n is odd and b is negative.

$\sqrt{36} = 6$ — $\sqrt{36}$ indicates the principal square root of 36.

$^{-}\sqrt{36} = {}^{-}6$ — $^{-}\sqrt{36}$ indicates the negative of the square root of 36.

$\pm\sqrt{36} = {}^{\pm}6$ — $\pm\sqrt{36}$ indicates both square roots of 36. *$\pm$ means positive or negative*

$\sqrt[3]{^{-}27} = {}^{-}3$ — $\sqrt[3]{^{-}27}$ indicates the principal cube root of $^{-}27$.

examples

1 **Find $\pm\sqrt{64b^2}$.**

$$\pm\sqrt{64b^2} = \pm\sqrt{(8b)^2}$$
$$= {}^{\pm}8b$$

The square roots of $64b^2$ are $^{\pm}8b$.

2 **Find $^{-}\sqrt{(x + 3)^4}$.**

$$^{-}\sqrt{(x + 3)^4} = {}^{-}\sqrt{[(x + 3)^2]^2}$$
$$= {}^{-}(x + 3)^2$$

The principal square root of $(x + 3)^4$ is $(x + 3)^2$.

3 **Find $\sqrt[3]{27x^6}$.**

$$\sqrt[3]{27x^6} = \sqrt[3]{(3x^2)^3}$$
$$= 3x^2$$

The principal cube root of $27x^6$ is $3x^2$.

4 **Find $\sqrt[6]{c^6}$.**

Since $(c)^6 = c^6$, c is a sixth root of c^6.
Thus, $\sqrt[6]{c^6} = |c|$.

6 is an even number, so the principal sixth root of c^6 is a positive number.

From similar examples, you can make this generalization.

For any number a, and any integer n greater than one,
1. if n is even, then $\sqrt[n]{a^n} = |a|$.
2. if n is odd, then $\sqrt[n]{a^n} = a$.

Property of nth Roots

Values of expressions such as $\sqrt{64}$ and $\sqrt[3]{-\frac{1}{8}}$ can be represented by rational numbers.

$$\sqrt{64} = 8 \qquad \sqrt[3]{-\frac{1}{8}} = -\frac{1}{2}$$

Radical expressions such as $\sqrt{2}$ have values that are irrational. Irrational numbers cannot be written as terminating or repeating decimals. To compute with irrational numbers, you often use decimal approximations. Tables of roots and powers give approximations.

example 5

Find a decimal approximation for $\sqrt[3]{28}$.

Cubes and Cube Roots

n	n^3	$\sqrt[3]{n}$	$\sqrt[3]{10n}$	$\sqrt[3]{100n}$
1.0	1.000	1.000	2.154	4.642
1.1	1.331	1.032	2.224	4.791
1.2	1.728	1.063	2.289	4.932
1.3	2.197	1.091	2.351	5.066
2.5	15.625	1.357	2.924	6.300
2.6	17.576	1.375	2.962	6.383
2.7	19.683	1.392	3.000	6.463
2.8	21.952	1.409	3.037	6.542
2.9	24.389	1.426	3.072	6.619

Let $n = 2.8$.
Then $10n = 10(2.8)$ or 28.
So $\sqrt[3]{28} = \sqrt[3]{10(2.8)}$
$= 3.037$

Check: $(3.037)^3 = 28.01137165$

You can approximate roots by using an estimate-and-average method. We assume that if $a < b < c$, then $\sqrt{a} < \sqrt{b} < \sqrt{c}$.

example 6

Find a decimal approximation for $\sqrt{8}$.

Make an estimate. $\sqrt{4} < \sqrt{8} < \sqrt{9}$, $2 < \sqrt{8} < 3$ *Locate $\sqrt{8}$ between consecutive perfect squares.*

Average the estimates. $\frac{2 + 3}{2} = 2.5$ $\sqrt{8}$ is approximately 2.5.

Repeat these steps in order to improve your approximations.

example 7

Find a decimal approximation for $\sqrt{8}$ to three places.

Make a new estimate. $2.5 < \sqrt{8} < 3$ since $(2.5)^2 = 6.25$

Average the estimates. $\frac{2.5 + 3}{2} = 2.75$

Make a new estimate. $2.75 < \sqrt{8} < 3$ since $(2.75)^2 = 7.5625$

Average the estimates. $\frac{2.75 + 3}{2} = 2.875$ $\sqrt{8}$ is approximately 2.875.

If you continue this process to six places, your answer should be 2.828427.

exercises

Max: 1–24, 1–40; **Avg:** 1–24, 1–39 odds; **Min:** 1–39 odds

Exploratory Find the value of each expression.

1. 7^2 49 **2.** 11^2 121 **3.** 3^3 27 **4.** 4^3 64
5. 2^4 16 **6.** 3^4 81 **7.** 13^2 169 **8.** 5^3 125

Find the value of each expression.

9. $\sqrt{121}$ 11 **10.** $-\sqrt{144}$ -12 **11.** $\sqrt[3]{8}$ 2 **12.** $\sqrt[4]{16}$ 2
13. $\sqrt[3]{y^3}$ y **14.** $-\sqrt[4]{y^4}$ $-|y|$ **15.** $\sqrt[4]{y^8}$ y^2 **16.** $\sqrt[5]{32m^5}$ $2m$
17. $\sqrt[3]{-64}$ -4 **18.** $\sqrt{(x-2)^2}$ $|x-2|$ **19.** $\sqrt{x^2+6x+9}$ $|x+3|$ **20.** $\sqrt{16a^2b^4}$ $4|a|b^2$

Use your table of powers and roots to find each value.

21. $\sqrt{47}$ 6.856 **22.** 51^2 2601 **23.** $\sqrt[3]{18}$ 2.621 **24.** 19^3 6859

Written Find the value of each expression.

1. $-\sqrt{81}$ -9 **2.** $\sqrt{169}$ 13 **3.** $\sqrt{225}$ 15 **4.** $-\sqrt[3]{27}$ -3 **5.** $\sqrt[4]{81}$ 3
6. $\sqrt[3]{64}$ 4 **7.** $\sqrt[5]{-1}$ -1 **8.** $\sqrt[10]{0}$ 0 **9.** $\sqrt[3]{-1000}$ -10 **10.** $\sqrt{0.49}$ 0.7
11. $\sqrt[3]{0.125}$ 0.5 **12.** $\sqrt{121n^2}$ $11|n|$ **13.** $\sqrt{(3s)^4}$ $9s^2$ **14.** $\sqrt{(5b)^4}$ $25b^2$ **15.** $\sqrt{576}$ 24
16. $\sqrt{676}$ 26 **17.** $-\sqrt{1024}$ -32 **18.** $\sqrt{64a^2b^4}$ $8|a|b^2$ **19.** $-\sqrt{121b^2g^6}$
20. $\sqrt[3]{-8b^3m^3}$ $-2bm$ **21.** $\sqrt[3]{-27r^3s^3}$ $-3rs$ **22.** $\sqrt{(x+y)^2}$ $|x+y|$ **23.** $\sqrt{(3p+q)^2}$
24. $\sqrt[3]{(2m+n)^3}$ $2m+n$ **25.** $\sqrt[3]{(z+a)^3}$ $z+a$ **26.** $\sqrt{x^2+10x+25}$ $|x+5|$
27. $\sqrt{y^2+6y+9}$ $|y+3|$ **28.** $\sqrt{4r^2+12r+9}$ $|2r+3|$ **29.** $\sqrt{9x^2+6x+1}$ $|3x+1|$
30. $\sqrt{x^2-6xy+9y^2}$ $|x-3y|$ **31.** $\sqrt{m^2-8m+16}$ $|m-4|$ **32.** $\sqrt{4x^2+12xy+9y^2}$

19. $-11|bg^3|$ 23. $|3p+q|$ 32. $|2x+3y|$

Find a decimal approximation to three places for each of the following.

33. $\sqrt{7}$ 2.625 **34.** $\sqrt{11}$ 3.375 **35.** $\sqrt{21}$ 4.625

36–38. Find a decimal approximation to six places for the numbers in problems **33–35**.

36. 2.640625 **37.** 3.328125 **38.** 4.578125

5–2 Multiplying Radicals

Objective: To multiply radicals.

The following examples show an important property of radicals.

$\sqrt{4} \cdot \sqrt{9} = 2 \cdot 3$ or 6 $\qquad \sqrt[3]{^-8} \cdot \sqrt[3]{27} = {^-2} \cdot 3$ or $^-6$

$\sqrt{4 \cdot 9} = \sqrt{36}$ or 6 $\qquad \sqrt[3]{^-8 \cdot 27} = \sqrt[3]{^-216}$ or $^-6$

Product Property of Radicals

For any numbers a and b, and any integer n greater than one,
1. if n is even, then $\sqrt[n]{ab} = \sqrt[n]{a} \cdot \sqrt[n]{b}$ as long as a and b are positive or zero.
2. if n is odd, then $\sqrt[n]{ab} = \sqrt[n]{a} \cdot \sqrt[n]{b}$.

Any number which is the square of an integer is called a perfect square.

To simplify a square root, find any factors of the radicand that are perfect squares. Use prime factorization and the product property of radicals.

examples

1 **Simplify $\sqrt{63}$.**

$\sqrt{63} = \sqrt{3^2 \cdot 7}$ *The prime factorization of 63 is $3^2 \cdot 7$.*

$= \sqrt{3^2} \cdot \sqrt{7}$ *Product property of radicals.*

$= 3\sqrt{7}$

2 **Simplify $\sqrt{45x^2y^2}$.**

$\sqrt{45x^2y^2} = \sqrt{3^2 \cdot 5 \cdot x^2 \cdot y^2}$

$= \sqrt{3^2} \cdot \sqrt{5} \cdot \sqrt{x^2} \cdot \sqrt{y^2}$

$= 3|xy|\sqrt{5}$

To simplify nth roots, find the factors that are nth powers and use the product property.

example

3 **Simplify $\sqrt[4]{2m} \cdot \sqrt[4]{5m^3}$.**

$\sqrt[4]{2m} \cdot \sqrt[4]{5m^3} = \sqrt[4]{2m \cdot 5m^3}$ *Product property of radicals.*

$= \sqrt[4]{10m^4}$

$= \sqrt[4]{10} \cdot \sqrt[4]{m^4}$ *Product property of radicals.*

$= m\sqrt[4]{10}$

The solution is $m\sqrt[4]{10}$.

example 4

Simplify $\sqrt[3]{54x^3y^5}$.

$$\begin{aligned}\sqrt[3]{54x^3y^5} &= \sqrt[3]{3^3 \cdot 2 \cdot x^3 \cdot y^3 \cdot y^2}\\ &= \sqrt[3]{3^3} \cdot \sqrt[3]{2} \cdot \sqrt[3]{x^3} \cdot \sqrt[3]{y^3} \cdot \sqrt[3]{y^2}\\ &= 3 \cdot \sqrt[3]{2} \cdot x \cdot y \cdot \sqrt[3]{y^2}\\ &= 3xy\sqrt[3]{2y^2}\end{aligned}$$

The solution is $3xy\sqrt[3]{2y^2}$.

You can use the distributive property to help simplify radicals.

example 5

Simplify $\sqrt{6}(\sqrt{3} + 2\sqrt{15})$.

$$\begin{aligned}\sqrt{6}(\sqrt{3} + 2\sqrt{15}) &= \sqrt{6} \cdot \sqrt{3} + \sqrt{6} \cdot 2\sqrt{15}\\ &= \sqrt{18} + 2\sqrt{90}\\ &= \sqrt{3^2 \cdot 2} + 2\sqrt{3^2 \cdot 2 \cdot 5}\\ &= 3\sqrt{2} + 2 \cdot 3\sqrt{10}\\ &= 3\sqrt{2} + 6\sqrt{10}\end{aligned}$$

exercises

Max: 1–20, 1–33; Avg: 1–20, 1–33 odds; Min: 1–33 odds

Exploratory Simplify.

1. $\sqrt{8}$ $2\sqrt{2}$
2. $\sqrt{32}$ $4\sqrt{2}$
3. $\sqrt{50x^2}$ $5|x|\sqrt{2}$
4. $\sqrt{98y^4}$ $7y^2\sqrt{2}$
5. $\sqrt[3]{16}$ $2\sqrt[3]{2}$
6. $\sqrt[3]{54}$ $3\sqrt[3]{2}$
7. $\sqrt[3]{128}$ $4\sqrt[3]{2}$
8. $\sqrt[4]{32}$ $2\sqrt[4]{2}$
9. $\sqrt[4]{48}$ $2\sqrt[4]{3}$
10. $\sqrt{y^5}$ $y^2\sqrt{y}$
11. $\sqrt[3]{m^4}$ $m\sqrt[3]{m}$
12. $\sqrt[5]{r^7}$ $r\sqrt[5]{r^2}$
13. $\sqrt{3}\sqrt{15}$ $3\sqrt{5}$
14. $\sqrt{6}\sqrt{3}$ $3\sqrt{2}$
15. $\sqrt{3}\sqrt{12}$ 6
16. $\sqrt[3]{4}\sqrt[3]{4}$ $2\sqrt[3]{2}$
17. $\sqrt[3]{9}\sqrt[3]{6}$ $3\sqrt[3]{2}$
18. $\sqrt[4]{2}\sqrt[4]{24}$ $2\sqrt[4]{3}$
19. $\sqrt{5}(\sqrt{5} - \sqrt{3})$ $5 - \sqrt{15}$
20. $\sqrt{5}(\sqrt{7} + \sqrt{5})$ $\sqrt{35} + 5$

Written Simplify. For answers to problems 19–36, see the Teacher's Guide.

1. $5\sqrt{54}$ $15\sqrt{6}$
2. $4\sqrt{50}$ $20\sqrt{2}$
3. $\sqrt[3]{24}$ $2\sqrt[3]{3}$
4. $\sqrt[3]{56}$ $2\sqrt[3]{7}$
5. $\sqrt{162}$ $9\sqrt{2}$
6. $5\sqrt{18}$ $15\sqrt{2}$
7. $\sqrt[3]{-125}$ -5
8. $\sqrt[3]{88}$ $2\sqrt[3]{11}$
9. $3\sqrt{242}$ $33\sqrt{2}$
10. $\sqrt[3]{108}$ $3\sqrt[3]{4}$
11. $\sqrt[3]{192}$ $4\sqrt[3]{3}$
12. $(4\sqrt{18}) \cdot (2\sqrt{14})$ $48\sqrt{7}$
13. $(-3\sqrt{24})(5\sqrt{20})$ $-60\sqrt{30}$
14. $\sqrt{3}(\sqrt{6} - 2)$ $3\sqrt{2} - 2\sqrt{3}$
15. $\sqrt{7}(3 + \sqrt{7})$ $3\sqrt{7} + 7$
16. $\sqrt{7}(\sqrt{14} + \sqrt{21})$ $7\sqrt{2} + 7\sqrt{3}$
17. $-\sqrt{2}(\sqrt{3} + \sqrt{2})$ $-\sqrt{6} - 2$
18. $\sqrt{5}(4 + \sqrt{5})$ $4\sqrt{5} + 5$
19. $\sqrt[3]{2}(3\sqrt[3]{4} + 2\sqrt[3]{32})$
20. $\sqrt[3]{121}\sqrt[3]{88}$
21. $(7\sqrt[3]{16})(5\sqrt[3]{20})$
22. $\sqrt[3]{9}(4\sqrt[3]{9} + 2\sqrt[3]{6})$
23. $\sqrt[3]{2}(3\sqrt[3]{4} - 2\sqrt[3]{32})$
24. $\sqrt[4]{405}$
25. $\sqrt[4]{90}$
26. $\sqrt{32m^4r}$
27. $\sqrt[3]{8a^4b^7}$
28. $\sqrt[3]{3x^4y^4}$
29. $\sqrt{8x^2y} \cdot \sqrt{2xy}$
30. $\sqrt{3x^2z^3} \cdot \sqrt{15x^2z}$
31. $\sqrt[3]{3ab^5} \cdot \sqrt[3]{24a^2b^2}$
32. $\sqrt[4]{5m^3b^5} \cdot \sqrt[4]{125m^2b^3}$
33. $\sqrt[4]{3b^6r^7} \cdot \sqrt[4]{81b^2r^2}$
34. $\sqrt{1.21 \cdot 10^4}$
35. $\sqrt{0.81 \cdot 10^6}$
36. $\sqrt{1.44 \cdot 10^8}$

5-3 Computing with Radicals

Objective: To compute with radicals.

Two radical expressions are called **like radical expressions** if the indexes are alike and the radicands are alike.

$7\sqrt[3]{2}$ and $6\sqrt[3]{2}$ are like expressions.	*Both the indexes and radicands are alike.*
$\sqrt[4]{9}$ and $\sqrt[5]{9}$ are *not* like expressions.	*The indexes are not alike.*
$5\sqrt{3x}$ and $^{-}5\sqrt{3y}$ are *not* like expressions.	*The radicands are not alike.*
$\sqrt[3]{2a}$ and $\sqrt[4]{2b}$ are *not* like expressions.	*Neither the indexes nor the radicands are alike.*

You can add or subtract radicals the same way you add or subtract monomials.

Combine like terms.

$$\begin{aligned} 3x + 2x + 4y &= (3 + 2)x + 4y \\ &= 5x + 4y \end{aligned}$$

Combine like radicals.

$$\begin{aligned} 3\sqrt{6} + 2\sqrt{6} + 4\sqrt{7} &= (3 + 2)\sqrt{6} + 4\sqrt{7} \\ &= 5\sqrt{6} + 4\sqrt{7} \end{aligned}$$

example

1 **Simplify $3 + 4\sqrt{7} - 2\sqrt[3]{7} + 5 + 6\sqrt{7} + 10\sqrt[3]{7}$.**

$$\begin{aligned} 3 + 4\sqrt{7} - 2\sqrt[3]{7} + 5 + 6\sqrt{7} + 10\sqrt[3]{7} &= 3 + 5 + 4\sqrt{7} + 6\sqrt{7} - 2\sqrt[3]{7} + 10\sqrt[3]{7} \\ &= (8) + (4 + 6)\sqrt{7} + (^{-}2 + 10)\sqrt[3]{7} \\ &= 8 + 10\sqrt{7} + 8\sqrt[3]{7} \end{aligned}$$

The solution is $8 + 10\sqrt{7} + 8\sqrt[3]{7}$.

Sometimes radicals can be simplified and then added or subtracted.

examples

2 **Simplify $5\sqrt{27} + 2\sqrt{3} - 7\sqrt{48}$.**

$$\begin{aligned} 5\sqrt{27} + 2\sqrt{3} - 7\sqrt{48} &= 5\sqrt{3^2 \cdot 3} + 2\sqrt{3} - 7\sqrt{4^2 \cdot 3} \\ &= 5\sqrt{3^2}\sqrt{3} + 2\sqrt{3} - 7\sqrt{4^2}\sqrt{3} \\ &= 5 \cdot 3\sqrt{3} + 2\sqrt{3} - 7 \cdot 4\sqrt{3} \\ &= {}^{-}11\sqrt{3} \end{aligned}$$

3 **Simplify $\sqrt[3]{40} + \sqrt[3]{135}$.**

$$\begin{aligned} \sqrt[3]{40} + \sqrt[3]{135} &= \sqrt[3]{2^3 \cdot 5} + \sqrt[3]{3^3 \cdot 5} \\ &= \sqrt[3]{2^3} \cdot \sqrt[3]{5} + \sqrt[3]{3^3} \cdot \sqrt[3]{5} \\ &= 5\sqrt[3]{5} \end{aligned}$$

Expressions such as $(6 + \sqrt{2})(\sqrt{10} + \sqrt{5})$ can be simplified using the FOIL method.

$$\begin{aligned}
(6 + \sqrt{2})(\sqrt{10} + \sqrt{5}) &= \overset{F}{6\sqrt{10}} + \overset{O}{6\sqrt{5}} + \overset{I}{\sqrt{2}\sqrt{10}} + \overset{L}{\sqrt{2}\sqrt{5}} \\
&= 6\sqrt{10} + 6\sqrt{5} + \sqrt{2}\sqrt{2}\sqrt{5} + \sqrt{10} \\
&= 6\sqrt{10} + 6\sqrt{5} + 2\sqrt{5} + \sqrt{10} \\
&= 6\sqrt{10} + \sqrt{10} + 6\sqrt{5} + 2\sqrt{5} \\
&= 7\sqrt{10} + 8\sqrt{5}
\end{aligned}$$

Binomials that are of the form $a + b\sqrt{c}$ and $a - b\sqrt{c}$ are called **conjugates** of each other. Notice that the product of conjugates is a rational number.

examples

4 **Simplify $(7 + \sqrt{2})(7 - \sqrt{2})$.**

$$\begin{aligned}
(7 + \sqrt{2})(7 - \sqrt{2}) &= \overset{F}{7 \cdot 7} - \overset{O}{7\sqrt{2}} + \overset{I}{7\sqrt{2}} - \overset{L}{\sqrt{2} \cdot \sqrt{2}} \\
&= 49 - \sqrt{2^2} \\
&= 49 - 2 \\
&= 47
\end{aligned}$$

5 **Simplify $(18 - 7\sqrt{3})(18 + 7\sqrt{3})$.**

$$\begin{aligned}
(18 - 7\sqrt{3})(18 + 7\sqrt{3}) &= \overset{F}{18^2} + \overset{O}{126\sqrt{3}} - \overset{I}{126\sqrt{3}} - \overset{L}{49(\sqrt{3})^2} \\
&= 18^2 - 49 \cdot 3 \\
&= 177
\end{aligned}$$

exercises

Max: 1–17, 1–46; Avg: 1–17, 1–45 odds; Min: 1–45 odds

Exploratory Simplify.

1. $3\sqrt{7} - 4\sqrt{7}$ $-\sqrt{7}$
2. $8\sqrt[3]{6} + 3\sqrt[3]{6}$ $11\sqrt[3]{6}$
3. $3\sqrt[4]{5} - 10\sqrt[4]{5}$ $-7\sqrt[4]{5}$
4. $7\sqrt{y} + 4\sqrt{y}$ $11\sqrt{y}$
5. $5\sqrt[3]{x} + 4\sqrt[3]{x} - 6\sqrt[3]{x}$ $3\sqrt[3]{x}$
6. $7\sqrt{2} - 3\sqrt[3]{2}$
7. $\sqrt[5]{3} + 4\sqrt[5]{3}$ $5\sqrt[5]{3}$
8. $\sqrt[3]{40} - 2\sqrt[3]{5}$ 0
9. $7\sqrt[3]{3} - \sqrt[3]{24}$ $5\sqrt[3]{3}$

6. $7\sqrt{2} - 3\sqrt[3]{2}$

Multiply.

10. $(3 + \sqrt{5})(4 + \sqrt{5})$ $17 + 7\sqrt{5}$
11. $(5 + \sqrt{3})(3 - \sqrt{3})$ $12 - 2\sqrt{3}$
12. $(7 - \sqrt{2})(5 - \sqrt{2})$ $37 - 12\sqrt{2}$
13. $(3 + \sqrt{5})(3 + \sqrt{5})$ $14 + 6\sqrt{5}$
14. $(6 + \sqrt{2})(6 - \sqrt{2})$ 34
15. $(4 + \sqrt{3})^2$ $19 + 8\sqrt{3}$
16. $(2 + \sqrt{7})(3 - \sqrt{7})$ $-1 + \sqrt{7}$
17. $(1 - \sqrt{5})^2$ $6 - 2\sqrt{5}$

Written **Simplify.** For answers to problems **1–46**, see the Teacher's Guide.

1. $5\sqrt{2} + 3\sqrt{2} - 8$
2. $^{-}\sqrt{32} + 6 + \sqrt{200}$
3. $^{-}3\sqrt{5} + 5\sqrt{2} + 4\sqrt{20} - 3\sqrt{50}$
4. $3\sqrt{7} - 5\sqrt{28}$
5. $4\sqrt{12} - 3\sqrt{75} + 4$
6. $5\sqrt{20} + \sqrt{24} - \sqrt{180} + 7\sqrt{54}$
7. $7\sqrt[3]{5} + 4\sqrt[3]{5}$
8. $\sqrt[3]{48} - \sqrt[3]{6}$
9. $\sqrt[3]{54} - \sqrt[3]{128}$
10. $7\sqrt{2} + \sqrt{50}$
11. $\sqrt[3]{16} - \sqrt{32}$
12. $\sqrt[3]{2} + \sqrt{3}$
13. $7\sqrt{24} + \sqrt[3]{24}$
14. $\sqrt{98} - \sqrt{72} + \sqrt{32}$
15. $\sqrt{108} - \sqrt{48} + (\sqrt{3})^2$
16. $8\sqrt[3]{m} + 3\sqrt[3]{m} - 8\sqrt[3]{m}$
17. $\sqrt[3]{135} - \sqrt[3]{81}$
18. $\sqrt[4]{5} + 6\sqrt[4]{5} - 2\sqrt[4]{5}$
19. $^{-}\sqrt{2x^2y^4} + \sqrt{8x^2y^4}$
20. $\sqrt[4]{x^2} + \sqrt[4]{x^6}$
21. $\sqrt[4]{y^4z^6} + \sqrt[4]{16y^4z^6}$
22. $\sqrt{216} + 4\sqrt{24} - \sqrt{150}$
23. $\sqrt[4]{z^4} + \sqrt[3]{z^6} + \sqrt{z^8}$
24. $\sqrt[3]{3x^6y^9} - \sqrt[3]{24x^6y^6}$
25. $(5 + \sqrt{2})(3 + \sqrt{2})$
26. $(4 + \sqrt{3})(3 + \sqrt{6})$
27. $(5 + \sqrt{6})(5 - \sqrt{2})$
28. $(8 - \sqrt{3})(6 + \sqrt{3})$
29. $(7 + \sqrt{11})(2 - \sqrt{11})$
30. $(\sqrt{3} + \sqrt{2})(\sqrt{15} - \sqrt{3})$
31. $(\sqrt{3} + \sqrt{5})(\sqrt{12} - \sqrt{5})$
32. $(\sqrt{2} - 3)(\sqrt{2} + 3)$
33. $(4 + \sqrt{5})^2$
34. $(5 - 3\sqrt{5})(3 + \sqrt{5})$
35. $(4\sqrt{5} - 3\sqrt{2})(2\sqrt{5} + 2\sqrt{2})$
36. $(1 + \sqrt{3})^2$
37. $(3 - \sqrt[3]{4})(\sqrt[3]{2} + \sqrt[3]{16})$
38. $(4 - \sqrt[3]{9})(\sqrt[3]{3} + \sqrt[3]{81})$
39. $(y + \sqrt[3]{4})(y^2 - y\sqrt[3]{4} + \sqrt[3]{16})$
40. $(x - \sqrt[3]{3})(x^2 + x\sqrt[3]{3} + \sqrt[3]{9})$

Factor over the real numbers.

Sample: $x^2 - 3 = x^2 - (\sqrt{3})^2$
$= (x - \sqrt{3})(x + \sqrt{3})$

41. $x^2 - 5$
42. $m^2 - 11$
43. $y^2 - 6$
44. $a^2 + 4a\sqrt{5} + 20$
45. $b^2 - 10b\sqrt{2} + 50$
46. $r^3 - 2r$

Using Computers

Finding Square Roots

The following computer program approximates square roots.

```
10  INPUT N        Input values of N to find √N
20  PRINT "MAKE A GOOD ESTIMATE OF THE SQUARE ROOT OF "N"."
30  INPUT X        Input your estimate, X.
40  FOR I=1 TO 5
50  Y=N/X          Y is a new estimate.
60  X=(X+Y)/2
70  PRINT "AFTER "I" STEPS, THE SQUARE ROOT OF "N" IS";
75  PRINT "APPROXIMATELY "X"."
80  NEXT I
90  PRINT "IF YOU WISH TO TRY AGAIN, INPUT 1; OTHERWISE INPUT 0."
100 INPUT T        T is 1 or T is 0.
110 IF T=1 THEN 10
120 END
```

Exercises **Use the above program to approximate the following square roots.**

1. $\sqrt{68}$ 8.246
2. $\sqrt{947}$ 30.773
3. $\sqrt{2050}$ 45.277
4. $\sqrt{695}$ 26.363

5-4 Dividing Radicals

Objective: To divide radicals.

The following examples show an important property of radicals.

$$\frac{\sqrt{100}}{\sqrt{4}} = \frac{10}{2} \text{ or } 5 \qquad \frac{\sqrt[3]{216}}{\sqrt[3]{-27}} = \frac{6}{-3} \text{ or } {}^{-}2$$

$$\sqrt{\frac{100}{4}} = \sqrt{25} \text{ or } 5 \qquad \sqrt[3]{\frac{216}{-27}} = \sqrt[3]{-8} \text{ or } {}^{-}2$$

For any numbers a and b, except $b = 0$, and any integer n greater than one,

$$\sqrt[n]{\frac{a}{b}} = \frac{\sqrt[n]{a}}{\sqrt[n]{b}}$$ **as long as all roots are defined.**

Quotient Property of Radicals

Relate this information to the examples above.

You can use the quotient property of radicals to simplify radicals.

examples

1 **Simplify $\sqrt{\frac{3}{4}}$.**

$$\sqrt{\frac{3}{4}} = \frac{\sqrt{3}}{\sqrt{4}}$$ *Quotient property of radicals.*

$$= \frac{\sqrt{3}}{2}$$

2 **Simplify $\frac{6\sqrt[3]{80}}{5\sqrt[3]{2}}$.**

$$\frac{6\sqrt[3]{80}}{5\sqrt[3]{2}} = \frac{6}{5}\sqrt[3]{\frac{80}{2}}$$ *Quotient property of radicals.*

$$= \frac{6}{5}\sqrt[3]{40}$$

$$= \frac{6}{5}\sqrt[3]{2^3 \cdot 5}$$

$$= \frac{12}{5}\sqrt[3]{5}$$

Fractions are usually written without radicals in the denominator. The process of eliminating radicals from the denominator is called **rationalizing the denominator.**

examples

3 Simplify $\frac{3}{2\sqrt{5}}$.

$$\frac{3}{2\sqrt{5}} = \frac{3}{2\sqrt{5}} \cdot \frac{\sqrt{5}}{\sqrt{5}}$$ *Why is $\frac{\sqrt{5}}{\sqrt{5}}$ used?*

$$= \frac{3\sqrt{5}}{2\sqrt{5 \cdot 5}}$$

$$= \frac{3\sqrt{5}}{10}$$

4 Simplify $\sqrt[3]{\frac{5}{3}}$.

$$\sqrt[3]{\frac{5}{3}} = \frac{\sqrt[3]{5}}{\sqrt[3]{3}} \cdot \frac{\sqrt[3]{3^2}}{\sqrt[3]{3^2}}$$ *Why is $\frac{\sqrt[3]{3^2}}{\sqrt[3]{3^2}}$ used?*

$$= \frac{\sqrt[3]{5 \cdot 3^2}}{\sqrt[3]{3^3}}$$

$$= \frac{\sqrt[3]{45}}{3}$$

5 Simplify $\frac{1 - \sqrt{3}}{5 + 2\sqrt{3}}$.

$$\frac{1 - \sqrt{3}}{5 + 2\sqrt{3}} = \frac{1 - \sqrt{3}}{5 + 2\sqrt{3}} \cdot \frac{5 - 2\sqrt{3}}{5 - 2\sqrt{3}}$$ *Conjugates can be used to rationalize the denominator.*

$$= \frac{5 - 2\sqrt{3} - 5\sqrt{3} + 2\sqrt{3^2}}{25 - 10\sqrt{3} + 10\sqrt{3} - 4\sqrt{3^2}}$$

$$= \frac{5 - 2\sqrt{3} - 5\sqrt{3} + 6}{25 - 10\sqrt{3} + 10\sqrt{3} - 12}$$

$$= \frac{11 - 7\sqrt{3}}{13}$$

In general, a radical expression is simplified when the following conditions are met.

Conditions for Simplified Radicals

1. **The index n is as small as possible.**
2. **The radicand contains no factor (other than one) which is the nth power of an integer or polynomial.**
3. **The radicand contains no fractions.**
4. **No radicals appear in the denominator.**

Simplifying radicals makes it easier to approximate the value of an expression.

example 6

Approximate the value of $\dfrac{\sqrt[3]{45}}{\sqrt[3]{2}}$ to three decimal places.

$$\frac{\sqrt[3]{45}}{\sqrt[3]{2}} = \frac{\sqrt[3]{45}}{\sqrt[3]{2}} \cdot \frac{\sqrt[3]{2^2}}{\sqrt[3]{2^2}}$$

$$= \frac{\sqrt[3]{45 \cdot 4}}{\sqrt[3]{2^3}}$$

$$= \frac{\sqrt[3]{180}}{2} \qquad \textit{This expression is simplified.}$$

$$= \frac{5.646}{2} \qquad \textit{In the table on page 539 look under } \sqrt[3]{100N} \textit{ where N is 1.8.}$$

$$= 2.823$$

exercises

Max: 1–28, 1–54; Avg: 1–28, 1–53 odds; Min: 1–53 odds

Exploratory Simplify.

1. $\dfrac{\sqrt{6}}{\sqrt{3}}$ $\sqrt{2}$
2. $\dfrac{\sqrt{10}}{\sqrt{2}}$ $\sqrt{5}$
3. $\dfrac{\sqrt[3]{18y}}{\sqrt[3]{6}}$ $\sqrt[3]{3y}$
4. $\dfrac{\sqrt[4]{35x^5}}{\sqrt[4]{7}}$ 4. $x\sqrt[4]{5x}$
5. $\sqrt{\dfrac{5}{4}}$ $\dfrac{\sqrt{5}}{2}$
6. $\sqrt{\dfrac{7}{9}}$ $\dfrac{\sqrt{7}}{3}$
7. $\sqrt[3]{\dfrac{3}{8}}$ $\dfrac{\sqrt[3]{3}}{2}$
8. $\sqrt[3]{\dfrac{4}{27}}$ $\dfrac{\sqrt[3]{4}}{3}$
9. $\dfrac{2}{\sqrt{3}}$ $\dfrac{2\sqrt{3}}{3}$
10. $\dfrac{4}{\sqrt{2}}$ $2\sqrt{2}$
11. $\dfrac{1}{\sqrt{5}}$ $\dfrac{\sqrt{5}}{5}$
12. $\dfrac{3}{\sqrt{7}}$ $\dfrac{3\sqrt{7}}{7}$
13. $\dfrac{3}{\sqrt[3]{4}}$ $\dfrac{3\sqrt[3]{2}}{2}$
14. $\dfrac{4}{\sqrt[3]{2}}$ $2\sqrt[3]{4}$
15. $\dfrac{7}{\sqrt[3]{9}}$ $\dfrac{7\sqrt[3]{3}}{3}$
16. $\dfrac{4}{\sqrt[3]{16}}$ $\sqrt[3]{4}$

Name the conjugate for each expression.

17. $1 + \sqrt{3}$ $1 - \sqrt{3}$
18. $4 - \sqrt{5}$ $4 + \sqrt{5}$
19. $1 - \sqrt{2}$ $1 + \sqrt{2}$
20. $4 + \sqrt{3}$ $4 - \sqrt{3}$
21. $3 + \sqrt{5}$ $3 - \sqrt{5}$
22. $5 - \sqrt{2}$ $5 + \sqrt{2}$
23. $5 + 3\sqrt{3}$ $5 - 3\sqrt{3}$
24. $5 + 2\sqrt{5}$ $5 - 2\sqrt{5}$
25. $2\sqrt{2} - 3$
26. $2\sqrt{7} - 5$ $^-2\sqrt{7} - 5$
27. $\sqrt{2} - 5\sqrt{3}$ $\sqrt{2} + 5\sqrt{3}$
28. $\sqrt{7} + \sqrt{2}$

25. $^-2\sqrt{2} - 3$ 28. $\sqrt{7} - \sqrt{2}$

Written Simplify.

1. $\frac{\sqrt{10}}{\sqrt{2}}$ $\sqrt{5}$
2. $\frac{\sqrt{12}}{\sqrt{3}}$ 2
3. $\frac{\sqrt{14}}{\sqrt{2}}$ $\sqrt{7}$
4. $\frac{\sqrt{21}}{\sqrt{7}}$ $\sqrt{3}$
5. $\frac{\sqrt[3]{81}}{\sqrt[3]{9}}$ $\sqrt[3]{9}$
6. $\frac{\sqrt[3]{54}}{\sqrt[3]{6}}$ $\sqrt[3]{9}$
7. $\sqrt{\frac{5}{4}}$ $\frac{\sqrt{5}}{2}$
8. $\sqrt{\frac{7}{16}}$ $\frac{\sqrt{7}}{4}$
9. $\sqrt{\frac{8}{9}}$ $\frac{2\sqrt{2}}{3}$
10. $\sqrt{\frac{21}{12}}$ $\frac{\sqrt{7}}{2}$
11. $\sqrt[3]{\frac{5}{8}}$ $\frac{\sqrt[3]{5}}{2}$
12. $\sqrt[3]{\frac{2}{27}}$ $\frac{\sqrt[3]{2}}{3}$
13. $\sqrt[3]{\frac{54}{125}}$ $\frac{3\sqrt[3]{2}}{5}$
14. $\sqrt[3]{\frac{16}{27}}$ $\frac{2\sqrt[3]{2}}{3}$
15. $\sqrt[4]{\frac{5}{16}}$ $\frac{\sqrt[4]{5}}{2}$
16. $\sqrt[4]{\frac{7}{81}}$ $\frac{\sqrt[4]{7}}{3}$
17. $\sqrt{\frac{1}{3}}$ $\frac{\sqrt{3}}{3}$
18. $\sqrt{\frac{1}{5}}$ $\frac{\sqrt{5}}{5}$
19. $\sqrt{\frac{2}{3}}$ $\frac{\sqrt{6}}{3}$
20. $\sqrt{\frac{3}{5}}$ $\frac{\sqrt{15}}{5}$
21. $\sqrt{\frac{5}{12}}$ $\frac{\sqrt{15}}{6}$
22. $\sqrt{\frac{5}{32}}$ $\frac{\sqrt{10}}{8}$
23. $\sqrt[3]{\frac{5}{9}}$ $\frac{\sqrt[3]{15}}{3}$
24. $\sqrt[3]{\frac{9}{4}}$ $\frac{\sqrt[3]{18}}{2}$
25. $\sqrt[4]{\frac{2}{3}}$ $\frac{\sqrt[4]{54}}{3}$
26. $\sqrt[4]{\frac{3}{2}}$ $\frac{\sqrt[4]{24}}{2}$
27. $\frac{1}{3+\sqrt{5}}$ $\frac{3-\sqrt{5}}{4}$
28. $\frac{3}{5-\sqrt{2}}$ $\frac{15+3\sqrt{2}}{23}$
29. $\frac{2}{3-\sqrt{5}}$ $\frac{3+\sqrt{5}}{2}$
30. $\frac{7}{4-\sqrt{3}}$ $\frac{28+7\sqrt{3}}{13}$
31. $\frac{1+\sqrt{2}}{3-\sqrt{2}}$ $\frac{5+4\sqrt{2}}{7}$
32. $\frac{2+\sqrt{6}}{2-\sqrt{6}}$
33. $\frac{2-\sqrt{3}}{5+3\sqrt{3}}$ $\frac{19-11\sqrt{3}}{-2}$
34. $\frac{3+4\sqrt{5}}{5+2\sqrt{5}}$ $\frac{-25+14\sqrt{5}}{5}$
35. $\frac{1+3\sqrt{2}}{2\sqrt{2}-3}$ $-15-11\sqrt{2}$
36. $\frac{2+\sqrt{7}}{2\sqrt{7}-5}$
37. $\sqrt{\frac{2}{5}}+\sqrt{40}+\sqrt{10}$ $\frac{16\sqrt{10}}{5}$
38. $\sqrt{\frac{1}{5}}+\sqrt{24}+\sqrt{20}-\sqrt{\frac{2}{3}}$ $\frac{33\sqrt{5}+25\sqrt{6}}{15}$
39. $\sqrt[3]{\frac{1}{4}}+\sqrt[3]{54}-\sqrt[3]{16}$ $(3/2)\sqrt[3]{2}$
40. $\sqrt[3]{32}+\sqrt[3]{4}-\sqrt[3]{\frac{1}{2}}$ $\frac{5\sqrt[3]{4}}{2}$

32. $-5-2\sqrt{6}$ 36. $8+3\sqrt{7}$

Approximate the values of each expression to three decimal places.

41. $\sqrt{\frac{5}{4}}$ 1.118
42. $\sqrt{\frac{7}{16}}$ 0.661
43. $\sqrt{\frac{8}{9}}$ 0.943
44. $\sqrt{\frac{21}{12}}$ 1.323
45. $\sqrt[3]{\frac{5}{8}}$ 0.855
46. $\sqrt[3]{\frac{2}{27}}$ 0.420
47. $\sqrt[3]{\frac{54}{125}}$ 0.756
48. $\sqrt[3]{\frac{16}{27}}$ 0.840

Solve each problem. Round all answers to the nearest hundredth.

49. Find the time, T, in seconds for a complete swing (back and forth) of a pendulum whose length is 6 feet. Let $T = 2\pi\sqrt{\frac{L}{32}}$, where $\pi \approx 3.14$. 2.72 seconds
50. Find the time, T, in seconds for a complete swing of a pendulum whose length is 98 centimeters. Let $T = 2\pi\sqrt{\frac{L}{980}}$, where $\pi \approx 3.14$. 1.99 secon[d]
51. Find the radius, r, of a sphere whose surface area S is 616 square inches. Let $r = \frac{1}{2}\sqrt{\frac{S}{\pi}}$, where $\pi \approx \frac{22}{7}$. 7
52. Find the time, t, in seconds required for a freely falling body to fall a distance s of 150 feet. Let $t = \frac{1}{4}\sqrt{s}$. 3.06 seconds

5-5 Equations with Radicals

Objective: To solve equations containing radicals.

You can use the properties of radicals to solve equations.

examples

1 **Solve $x + 2 = x\sqrt{3}$.**

$$x + 2 = x\sqrt{3}$$
$$x - x\sqrt{3} = {}^-2$$
$$x(1 - \sqrt{3}) = {}^-2 \quad \textit{Distributive property}$$
$$x = \frac{{}^-2}{1 - \sqrt{3}}$$
$$x = \frac{{}^-2}{1 - \sqrt{3}} \cdot \frac{1 + \sqrt{3}}{1 + \sqrt{3}} \quad \textit{The conjugate of } 1 - \sqrt{3} \textit{ is } 1 + \sqrt{3}.$$
$$x = \frac{{}^-2(1 + \sqrt{3})}{1 + \sqrt{3} - \sqrt{3} - 3}$$
$$x = \frac{{}^-2(1 + \sqrt{3})}{{}^-2}$$
$$x = 1 + \sqrt{3}$$

Check: $x + 2 = x\sqrt{3}$

$$(1 + \sqrt{3}) + 2 \stackrel{?}{=} (1 + \sqrt{3})\sqrt{3}$$
$$\sqrt{3} + 3 = \sqrt{3} + 3$$

The solution is $1 + \sqrt{3}$.

2 **Solve $(3 + \sqrt{2})x - 2 + 6\sqrt{2} = 4 + 7\sqrt{2}$.**

$$(3 + \sqrt{2})x - 2 + 6\sqrt{2} = 4 + 7\sqrt{2}$$
$$(3 + \sqrt{2})x = 6 + \sqrt{2}$$
$$x = \frac{6 + \sqrt{2}}{3 + \sqrt{2}}$$
$$x = \frac{6 + \sqrt{2}}{3 + \sqrt{2}} \cdot \frac{3 - \sqrt{2}}{3 - \sqrt{2}}$$
$$x = \frac{18 - 6\sqrt{2} + 3\sqrt{2} - 2}{9 - 3\sqrt{2} + 3\sqrt{2} - 2}$$
$$x = \frac{16 - 3\sqrt{2}}{7}$$

Variables may appear in the radicand of a radical. Equations containing such radicals are called **radical equations.**

example 3

Solve $3 - \sqrt{x - 2} = 0$.

$$
\begin{aligned}
3 - \sqrt{x - 2} &= 0 \\
3 &= \sqrt{x - 2} \\
3^2 &= (\sqrt{x - 2})^2 \quad \textit{Square both sides.} \\
9 &= x - 2 \\
11 &= x
\end{aligned}
$$

Check:

$$
\begin{aligned}
3 - \sqrt{x - 2} &= 0 \\
3 - \sqrt{11 - 2} &\stackrel{?}{=} 0 \\
3 - \sqrt{9} &\stackrel{?}{=} 0 \\
3 - 3 &\stackrel{?}{=} 0 \\
0 &= 0
\end{aligned}
$$

The solution is 11.

Squaring both sides of an equation *may* produce results that do not satisfy the equation.

$x = 2$	This equation has *one* solution, 2.
$(x)^2 = (2)^2$	Square both sides.
$x^2 = 4$	This equation has *two* solutions, 2 and $^-2$.

example 4

Solve $7 + \sqrt{a - 3} = 1$.

$$
\begin{aligned}
7 + \sqrt{a - 3} &= 1 \\
\sqrt{a - 3} &= {}^-6 \\
(\sqrt{a - 3})^2 &= ({}^-6)^2 \\
a - 3 &= 36 \\
a &= 39
\end{aligned}
$$

Check:

$$
\begin{aligned}
7 + \sqrt{a - 3} &= 1 \\
7 + \sqrt{39 - 3} &\stackrel{?}{=} 1 \\
7 + \sqrt{36} &\stackrel{?}{=} 1 \\
13 &\neq 1
\end{aligned}
$$

The answer does *not* check.
The equation has *no* solutions.

example 5

Solve $\sqrt[3]{3y-1} - 2 = 0$.

$$\sqrt[3]{3y-1} - 2 = 0$$
$$\sqrt[3]{3y-1} = 2$$
$$(\sqrt[3]{3y-1})^3 = 2^3$$
$$3y - 1 = 8$$
$$3y = 9$$
$$y = 3$$

Check: $\sqrt[3]{3y-1} - 2 = 0$

$$\sqrt[3]{3(3)-1} - 2 \stackrel{?}{=} 0$$
$$\sqrt[3]{8} - 2 \stackrel{?}{=} 0$$
$$2 - 2 \stackrel{?}{=} 0$$
$$0 = 0$$

The solution is 3.

exercises

Max: 1–12, 1–27; Avg: 1–12, 1–27 odds; Min: 1–27 odds

Exploratory Solve each equation.

1. $\sqrt{x} = 2$ 4
2. $\sqrt{y} = 3$ 9
3. $m + 2\sqrt{5} = 7$ $7 - 2\sqrt{5}$
4. $2 + m = {}^-5\sqrt{3}$ ${}^-2 - 5\sqrt{3}$
5. $\sqrt{2x+7} = 3$ 1
6. $\sqrt{3x+7} = 7$ 14
7. $\sqrt[3]{x-2} = 3$ 29
8. $\sqrt[4]{2x+7} = 2$ $\frac{9}{2}$
9. $x\sqrt{3} - 5 = 7$ $4\sqrt{3}$
10. $x\sqrt{5} + 6 = 3$ $-\frac{3}{5}\sqrt{5}$
11. $x\sqrt{3} + 4 = 7 + \sqrt{3}$ $1 + \sqrt{3}$
12. $2z\sqrt{7} + 3 = 5 + 6\sqrt{7}$ $(21 + \sqrt{7})/7$

Written Solve each equation.

1. $6 + 2x\sqrt{3} = 0$ ${}^-\sqrt{3}$
2. $2 + 5n\sqrt{10} = 0$ ${}^-\sqrt{10}/25$
3. $x\sqrt{2} + 3x = 4$ $(12 - 4\sqrt{2})/7$
4. $x - x\sqrt{5} = 2$ $(1 + \sqrt{5})/{}^-2$
5. $3x + 5 = x\sqrt{3}$ $({}^-15 - 5\sqrt{3})/6$
6. $2x + 7 = {}^-x\sqrt{2}$ $(7\sqrt{2} - 14)/2$
7. $2x - x\sqrt{11} = 13$ $(26 + 13\sqrt{11})/{}^-7$
8. $13 - 3x = x\sqrt{5}$ $(39 - 13\sqrt{5})/4$
9. $\sqrt{m} - 8 = 0$ 64
10. $\sqrt{t} - 4 = 0$ 16
11. $\sqrt{y-5} = 7$ 54
12. $\sqrt{x-4} = 3$ 13
13. $\sqrt[3]{y+1} = 2$ 7
14. $\sqrt[3]{m-1} = 3$ 28
15. $\sqrt[3]{y+2} = 4$ 62
16. $\sqrt[3]{r+1} = 5$ 124
17. $\sqrt[4]{2a} = 3$ $40\frac{1}{2}$
18. $\sqrt[4]{3p} = 2$ $5\frac{1}{3}$
19. $\sqrt{2x+3} = 7$ 23
20. $\sqrt{3y-5} = 4$ 7
21. $\sqrt{5y+1} + 6 = 10$ 3
22. $\sqrt{1+2r} - 4 = {}^-1$ 4

For answers to problems **23–27**, see the Teacher's Guide.

Solve each equation for the variable indicated.

23. $y = \sqrt{r^2 + s^2}$ for s
24. $r = \sqrt[3]{\dfrac{2mM}{c}}$ for c
25. $T = \dfrac{1}{2}\sqrt{\dfrac{u}{g}}$ for g
26. $v = \dfrac{1}{2}\sqrt{1 + \dfrac{T}{\ell}}$ for ℓ
27. $m^2 = \sqrt[3]{\dfrac{rp}{g^2}}$ for p

5–6 Imaginary Numbers

Objective: To learn about imaginary numbers.

Numbers like $\sqrt{2}$ and π are irrational.

Some equations have irrational solutions.

examples

1 **Solve $5x^3 + 6 = 126$.**

$$5x^3 + 6 = 126$$
$$5x^3 = 120$$
$$x^3 = 24$$
$$x = \sqrt[3]{24}$$
$$x = 2\sqrt[3]{3}$$

The solution is $2\sqrt[3]{3}$.

2 **Solve $x^2 - 5 = 0$.**

$$x^2 - 5 = 0$$
$$x^2 = 5$$
$$\sqrt{x^2} = \sqrt{5}$$
$$|x| = \sqrt{5}$$
$$x = \pm\sqrt{5}$$

The solutions are $\sqrt{5}$ and $^-\sqrt{5}$.

The equation $x^2 = {}^-1$ has *no* solution among the real numbers. This is because the square of a real number is positive.

We define a new number i to be a solution to $x^2 = {}^-1$. This number is called the **imaginary unit.** The imaginary unit i is *not* a real number.

Using i as you would any constant, you can define square roots of negative numbers.

Both i and ^-i are square roots of $^-1$. There is, in fact, no way of telling which of the two roots is i and which is ^-i. We assign the letter i to one of the roots and then stick to the notation.

$$i^2 = {}^-1 \quad \text{so} \quad \sqrt{^-1} = i$$
$$(2i)^2 = 2^2i^2 \text{ or } {}^-4 \quad \text{so} \quad \sqrt{^-4} = 2i$$
$$(i\sqrt{3})^2 = i^2(\sqrt{3})^2 \text{ or } {}^-3 \quad \text{so} \quad \sqrt{^-3} = i\sqrt{3}$$

Definition of Imaginary Number

For any positive real number b,

$$\sqrt{^-(b)^2} = bi,$$

where i is a number whose square is $^-1$.

The number i is called the imaginary unit, and bi is called a pure imaginary number.

Imaginary numbers are simplified by rewriting them as the product of i and a real number.

examples

3 **Simplify $\sqrt{^-24}$.**

$$\sqrt{^-24} = i\sqrt{24} = i\sqrt{4 \cdot 6} = 2i\sqrt{6}$$

4 **Simplify $\sqrt{^-16} + \sqrt{^-25}$.**

$$\sqrt{^-16} + \sqrt{^-25} = i\sqrt{16} + i\sqrt{25} = 4i + 5i = 9i$$

5 **Simplify $\sqrt{^-3} \cdot \sqrt{^-12}$.**

$$\sqrt{^-3} \cdot \sqrt{^-12} = i\sqrt{3} \cdot i\sqrt{12} = i^2\sqrt{36} = {^-1} \cdot 6 = {^-6}$$

Simplifying powers of i reveals a curious pattern.

$i^1 = i$

$i^2 = {^-1}$

$i^3 = i^2 \cdot i = {^-1} \cdot i = {^-i}$

$i^4 = i^2 \cdot i^2 = {^-1} \cdot {^-1} = 1$

$i^5 = i^4 \cdot i = 1 \cdot i = i$

$i^6 = i^5 \cdot i = i^2 = {^-1}$

$i^7 = i^6 \cdot i = {^-1} \cdot i = {^-i}$

$i^8 = i^4 \cdot i^4 = 1 \cdot 1 = 1$

The values i, $^-1$, ^-i, and 1 repeat in cycles of four.

examples

6 **Simplify i^{15}.**

$$i^{15} = i^4 \cdot i^4 \cdot i^4 \cdot i^3 = 1 \cdot 1 \cdot 1 \cdot {^-i} = {^-i}$$

7 **Simplify i^{86}.**

$i^{86} = (i^2)^{43}$ *$i^2 = {^-1}$*

$= ({^-1})^{43}$ *$^-1$ raised to an odd power is $^-1$.*

$= {^-1}$

examples

8 **Solve $x^2 + 4 = 0$.**

$$\begin{aligned} x^2 + 4 &= 0 \\ x^2 &= {}^{-}4 \\ x^2 &= 4 \cdot {}^{-}1 \\ x &= {}^{\pm}2i \end{aligned}$$

The solutions, both imaginary, are $2i$ and ${}^{-}2i$.

9 **Solve $3x^2 + 15 = 0$.**

$$\begin{aligned} 3x^2 + 15 &= 0 \\ 3x^2 &= {}^{-}15 \\ x^2 &= {}^{-}5 \\ x^2 &= {}^{-}1 \cdot 5 \\ x &= {}^{\pm}i\sqrt{5} \end{aligned}$$

The solutions are $i\sqrt{5}$ and ${}^{-}i\sqrt{5}$.

exercises

Max: 1–16, 1–40; **Avg:** 1–16, 1–39 odds; **Min:** 1–39 odds

Exploratory Simplify.

1. $\sqrt{{}^{-}36}$ $6i$
2. $\sqrt{{}^{-}64}$ $8i$
3. $4\sqrt{{}^{-}2}$ $4i\sqrt{2}$
4. $6\sqrt{{}^{-}4}$ $12i$
5. $\sqrt{{}^{-}3}\sqrt{{}^{-}3}$ ${}^{-}3$
6. $\sqrt{{}^{-}2}\sqrt{{}^{-}2}$ ${}^{-}2$
7. $\sqrt{{}^{-}5}\sqrt{5}$ $5i$
8. $\sqrt{{}^{-}7}\sqrt{7}$ $7i$
9. $3 \cdot 2i$ $6i$
10. $5 \cdot 7i$ $35i$
11. $4i + 7i$ $11i$
12. $12i - 3i$ $9i$
13. $5i - 8i$ ${}^{-}3i$
14. i^3 ${}^{-}i$
15. i^6 ${}^{-}1$
16. i^{91} ${}^{-}i$

Written Simplify.

1. $\sqrt{{}^{-}81}$ $9i$
2. $\sqrt{{}^{-}121}$ $11i$
3. $\sqrt{{}^{-}50}$ $5i\sqrt{2}$
4. $\sqrt{{}^{-}98}$ $7i\sqrt{2}$
5. $\sqrt{\frac{{}^{-}4}{9}}$ $\frac{2}{3}i$
6. $\sqrt{\frac{{}^{-}9}{16}}$ $\frac{3}{4}i$
7. $\sqrt{\frac{{}^{-}1}{3}}$ $\frac{i\sqrt{3}}{3}$
8. $\sqrt{\frac{{}^{-}1}{2}}$ $\frac{i\sqrt{2}}{2}$
9. i^5 i
10. i^{10} ${}^{-}1$
11. i^{11} ${}^{-}i$
12. i^{43} ${}^{-}i$
13. $\sqrt{{}^{-}4} + \sqrt{{}^{-}1}$ $3i$
14. $\sqrt{{}^{-}9} + \sqrt{{}^{-}16}$ $7i$
15. $\sqrt{{}^{-}25} + \sqrt{{}^{-}36}$ $11i$
16. $\sqrt{{}^{-}49} + \sqrt{{}^{-}100}$ $17i$
17. $3i + 2i$ $5i$
18. $7i - 5i$ $2i$
19. $2i + 12i$ $14i$
20. $13i - 14i$ ${}^{-}i$
21. $\sqrt{{}^{-}8}\sqrt{{}^{-}2}$ ${}^{-}4$
22. $\sqrt{{}^{-}15}\sqrt{{}^{-}5}$ ${}^{-}5\sqrt{3}$
23. $\sqrt{{}^{-}14}\sqrt{{}^{-}7}$ ${}^{-}7\sqrt{2}$
24. $\sqrt{{}^{-}3}\sqrt{{}^{-}18}$ ${}^{-}3\sqrt{6}$
25. $(\sqrt{{}^{-}3})^2$ ${}^{-}3$
26. $(\sqrt{{}^{-}12})^2$ ${}^{-}12$
27. $(\sqrt{{}^{-}3})^3$ ${}^{-}3i\sqrt{3}$
28. $(\sqrt{{}^{-}4})^3$ ${}^{-}8i$
29. $({}^{-}2\sqrt{{}^{-}8})(3\sqrt{{}^{-}2})$ 24
30. $(4\sqrt{{}^{-}12})({}^{-}2\sqrt{{}^{-}3})$ 48
31. $(6\sqrt{{}^{-}24})({}^{-}3\sqrt{6})$ ${}^{-}216i$
32. $(2\sqrt{15})({}^{-}3\sqrt{{}^{-}15})$ ${}^{-}90i$
33. $(2i)(3i)^2$ ${}^{-}18i$
34. $5i({}^{-}2i^2)$ $10i$

Solve each equation.

35. $x^2 + 16 = 0$ ${}^{\pm}4i$
36. $x^2 + 49 = 0$ ${}^{\pm}7i$
37. $x^2 + 169 = 0$ ${}^{\pm}13i$
38. $x^2 + 144 = 0$ ${}^{\pm}12i$
39. $x^2 + 3 = 0$ ${}^{\pm}i\sqrt{3}$
40. $x^2 + 12 = 0$ ${}^{\pm}2i\sqrt{3}$

Reading Algebra

Double Meaning

In mathematics, many words have specific definitions. However, when these words are used in everyday language, they frequently have a different meaning. Study each pair of sentences. How does the meaning of the word in boldface differ?

A. Plants receive nourishment and water from their **roots.**
B. The square **roots** of 36 are 6 and $^-6$.

A. The United States is a major world **power.**
B. Raising a number to the nth **power** means using that number as a factor n times.

A. I am **positive** I left my homework in my locker.
B. For any numbers a and b, and any **positive** integer n, if $a^n = b$, then a is an nth root of b.

A. The **principal** will speak at the school assembly.
B. The symbol $\sqrt[n]{b}$ indicates the **principal** nth root of b.

A. The soup tastes a little **odd.**
B. For any number a and any integer n greater than one, if n is **odd,** then $\sqrt[n]{a^n} = a$.

Read the following. Which words are mathematical words? Which words are ordinary words? Which mathematical words have another meaning in everyday language?

Product Property of Radicals — **For any nonnegative number a and b and any integer n greater than one, $\sqrt[n]{ab} = \sqrt[n]{a} \cdot \sqrt[n]{b}$.**

Simplifying a square root means finding the square root of the greatest perfect square factor of the radicand. You use the product property of radicals to simplify square roots.

Exercises Write two sentences for each word. First, use the word in everyday language. Then use the word in a mathematical context. Answers may vary.

1. index
2. negative
3. even
4. rational
5. irrational
6. like
7. rationalize
8. imaginary
9. real
10. degree
11. absolute
12. identity

5-7 Complex Numbers

Objective: To learn about and compute with complex numbers.

Numbers such as $3 + 5i$, $6 + i$, and $27 + 2i$ are called **complex numbers.** Notice they each represent the sum of a real number and an imaginary number.

Definition of Complex Number

A complex number is any number that can be written in the form $a + bi$ where a and b are real numbers and i is the imaginary unit.

a is called the real part. *b is called the imaginary part.*

As long as $b \neq 0$, a complex number $a + bi$ is also called an imaginary number.

Any real number is also a complex number. For example, $\sqrt{2}$ can be written as $\sqrt{2} + 0i$. Its imaginary part is 0. A complex number is also a real number *only if its imaginary part is 0.*

Two complex numbers have the same value if and only if their real parts are equivalent and their imaginary parts are equivalent.

example 1

Find values for r and s such that $2r + 3si = 6 + 2i$.

$$2r + 3si = 6 + 2i$$
$$2r = 6 \quad \text{and} \quad 3s = 2$$
$$r = 3 \qquad s = \frac{2}{3}$$

Check: $2(3) + 3\left(\frac{2}{3}\right)i \stackrel{?}{=} 6 + 2i$

$$6 + 2i = 6 + 2i$$

To add or subtract complex numbers, you combine their real parts and combine their imaginary parts.

examples

2 **Find $(3 + 6i) + (7 - 2i)$.**

$$(3 + 6i) + (7 - 2i) = (3 + 7) + (6i - 2i)$$
$$= 10 + 4i$$

3 **Find $(6 - 5i) - (3 - 2i)$.**

$$(6 - 5i) - (3 - 2i) = (6 - 3) + (^-5i - {^-2i})$$
$$= 3 - 3i$$

You can multiply complex numbers using the **FOIL** method.

examples

4 **Find $(6 - 7i)(4 + 3i)$.**

$$\begin{aligned} & \quad\ \text{F} \qquad\quad \text{O} \qquad\qquad \text{I} \qquad\qquad \text{L} \\ (6 - 7i)(4 + 3i) &= 6 \cdot 4 + 6 \cdot 3i + {}^-7i \cdot 4 + {}^-7i \cdot 3i \\ &= 24 + 18i - 28i - 21i^2 \\ &= (24 + 21) + (18i - 28i) \qquad \pmb{{}^-21i^2 = 21} \\ &= 45 - 10i \end{aligned}$$

5 **Find $(3 + 5i)(3 - 5i)$.**

$$\begin{aligned} & \quad\ \text{F} \qquad\quad \text{O} \qquad\qquad \text{I} \qquad\qquad \text{L} \\ (3 + 5i)(3 - 5i) &= 3 \cdot 3 + 3 \cdot {}^-5i + 5i \cdot 3 + 5i \cdot {}^-5i \\ &= 9 - 15i + 15i - 25i^2 \\ &= (9 + 25) + ({}^-15i + 15i) \qquad \pmb{{}^-25i^2 = 25} \\ &= 34 \end{aligned}$$

Complex numbers of the form $a + bi$ and $a - bi$ are called **conjugates** of each other. Notice that the product of complex conjugates is always a real number.

example

6 **Find $(a + bi)(a - bi)$.**

$$\begin{aligned} & \quad\ \text{F} \qquad\quad \text{O} \qquad\qquad \text{I} \qquad\qquad \text{L} \\ (a + bi)(a - bi) &= a \cdot a + a \cdot {}^-bi + bi \cdot a + bi \cdot {}^-bi \\ &= a^2 - abi + abi - b^2i^2 \\ &= (a^2 + b^2) + ({}^-abi + abi) \qquad \pmb{b^2i^2 = {}^-b^2} \\ &= a^2 + b^2 \end{aligned}$$

The following chart summarizes the basic operations with complex numbers.

For any complex numbers $a + bi$ and $c + di$,
$a + bi = c + di$ if and only if $a = c$ and $b = d$
$(a + bi) + (c + di) = (a + c) + (b + d)i$
$(a + bi) - (c + di) = (a - c) + (b - d)i$
$(a + bi)(c + di) = (ac - bd) + (ad + bc)i$

exercises

Max: 1–20, 1–38; **Avg:** 1–20, 1–37 odds; **Min:** 1–37 odds

Exploratory Simplify.

1. $(6 + 3i) + (2 + 8i)$ $8 + 11i$
2. $(4 - i) + (3 + 3i)$ $7 + 2i$
3. $(5 + 2i) - (2 + 2i)$ 3
4. $(7 - 6i) - (5 - 6i)$ 2
5. $(7 + 3i) + (3 - 3i)$ 10
6. $(2 + 4i) - (2 - 4i)$ $8i$
7. $4(5 + 3i)$ $20 + 12i$
8. $^-6(2 - 3i)$ $^-12 + 18i$
9. $(4 + \sqrt{^-2}) + (3 + \sqrt{^-3})$ $7 + (\sqrt{2} + \sqrt{3})i$
10. $(13 + \sqrt{^-3}) - (20 - \sqrt{^-2})$ $^-7 + (\sqrt{2} + \sqrt{3})i$

Find values of x and y for which each equation is true.

11. $x + yi = 5 + 6i$ $x = 5, y = 6$
12. $x + yi = 2 - 3i$ $x = 2, y = {}^-3$
13. $x - yi = 7 - 2i$ $x = 7, y = 2$
14. $x - yi = 4 + 5i$ $x = 4, y = {}^-5$
15. $x + 2yi = 3$ $x = 3, y = 0$
16. $2x + yi = 5i$ $x = 0, y = 5$

Find each product.

17. $(1 + 3i)(2 + 4i)$ $^-10 + 10i$
18. $(2 - 3i)(1 + 4i)$ $14 + 5i$
19. $(2 - 3i)(1 - 4i)$ $^-10 - 11i$
20. $(3 + 2i)(4 - i)$ $14 + 5i$

Written Simplify.

1. $(3 + 2i) + (4 + 5i)$ $7 + 7i$
2. $(2 + 6i) + (4 + 3i)$ $6 + 9i$
3. $(9 + 6i) - (3 + 2i)$ $6 + 4i$
4. $(11 - 3i) - (^-4 + 5i)$ $15 - 8i$
5. $(5 + 7i) + (^-3 + 2i)$ $2 + 9i$
6. $(8 - 7i) + (^-5 - i)$ $3 - 8i$
7. $(3 - 11i) - (^-5 + 4i)$ $8 - 15i$
8. $(^-6 - 2i) - (^-8 - 3i)$ $2 + i$
9. $(4 + 2i\sqrt{3}) + (1 - 5i\sqrt{3})$ $5 - 3i\sqrt{3}$
10. $(8 - 3i\sqrt{5}) + (^-3 + 2i\sqrt{5})$ $5 - i\sqrt{5}$
11. $2(^-3 + 2i) + 3(^-5 - 2i)$ $^-21 - 2i$
12. $^-6(2 - i) + 3(4 - 5i)$ ^-9i
13. $(2 - 3i)(5 + i)$ $13 - 13i$
14. $(5 + 3i)(6 - i)$ $33 + 13i$
15. $(6 - 2i)^2$ $32 - 24i$
16. $(2 + i\sqrt{3})^2$ $1 + 4i\sqrt{3}$
17. $(7 - i\sqrt{2})(5 + i\sqrt{2})$ $37 + 2i\sqrt{2}$
18. $(4 - 3i)(7 - 2i)$ $22 - 29i$
19. $(3 + 2i)^2$ $5 + 12i$
20. $(3 + 4i)^2$ $^-7 + 24i$
21. $(\sqrt{2} + i)(\sqrt{2} - i)$ 3
22. $(2 - \sqrt{^-3})(2 + \sqrt{^-3})$ 7
23. $(2 + i)(3 - 4i)(1 + 2i)$ $20 + 15i$
24. $(6 - i)(5 + 2i)(3 + 3i)$ $75 + 117i$
25. $(7 - 5i)(2 - 3i)(7 + 5i)$ $148 - 222i$
26. $(9 + 2i)(5 + i)(9 - 2i)$ $425 + 85i$

For answers to problems **27–38**, see the Teacher's Guide.

Find the sum, difference, and product for each pair of complex numbers.

27. $2i$, $1 - 3i$
28. $1 + 4i$, $3 - i$
29. $7 + 2i$, $7 - 2i$
30. $4 + 3i$, $4 - 3i$
31. $1 + i$, $i^3 + i^4$
32. $1 + i$, $i^2 + i^3$

Find values of x and y for which each sentence is true.

33. $2x + 5yi = 4 + 15i$
34. $3x + 2yi = 18 + 7i$
35. $(x - y) + (x + y)i = 2 - 4i$
36. $(2x + y) + (x - y)i = 7 - i$
37. $(x + 2y) + (2x - y)i = 5 + 5i$
38. $(x + 4y) + (2x - 3y)i = 13 + 7i$

5-8 Dividing Complex Numbers

Objective: To divide complex numbers.

Fractions are usually written without imaginary numbers in the denominators. As with radicals, you often **rationalize the denominator.**

examples

1 **Simplify** $\frac{3 + 7i}{2i}$.

$$\frac{3 + 7i}{2i} = \frac{3 + 7i}{2i} \cdot \frac{2i}{2i}$$ *Why is $\frac{2i}{2i}$ used?*

$$= \frac{6i + 14i^2}{4i^2}$$

$$= \frac{^-14 + 6i}{^-4}$$

$$= \frac{^-2(7 - 3i)}{^-2 \cdot 2}$$

$$= \frac{7 - 3i}{2}$$

2 **Simplify** $\frac{4 + 3i}{1 - 2i}$.

$$\frac{4 + 3i}{1 - 2i} = \frac{4 + 3i}{1 - 2i} \cdot \frac{1 + 2i}{1 + 2i}$$ *Conjugates can be used in rationalizing the denominator.*

$$= \frac{4 \cdot 1 + 4 \cdot 2i + 3i \cdot 1 + 3i \cdot 2i}{1 \cdot 1 + 1 \cdot 2i + {^-2i} \cdot 1 + {^-2i} \cdot 2i}$$

$$= \frac{4 + 8i + 3i - 6}{1 + 2i - 2i + 4}$$

$$= \frac{^-2 + 11i}{5}$$

exercises

Max: 1–39, 1–35; **Avg:** 1–39, 1–35 odds; **Min:** 1–35 odds

Exploratory Find the conjugate of each complex number.

1. $2 + i$ $2 - i$ **2.** $2 - i$ $2 + i$ **3.** $1 + 3i$ $1 - 3i$ **4.** $3 - 2i$ $3 + 2i$

5. $4i$ ^-4i **6.** $7i$ ^-7i **7.** ^-5i $5i$ **8.** ^-3i $3i$

9. 6 6 **10.** 8 8 **11.** $5 - 6i$ $5 + 6i$ **12.** $12 + i$ $12 - i$

13–24. Find the product of each number and its conjugate in problems **1-12.**

13. 5 **14.** 5 **15.** 10 **16.** 13 **17.** 16 **18.** 49 **19.** 25 **20.** 9 **21.** 36 **22.** 64 **23.** 61 **24.** 145

Show that each of the following is a fourth root of 16.

36. 2 $2^4 = 16$ **37.** $^-2$ $(^-2)^4 = 16$ **38.** $2i$ **39.** ^-2i

38. $(2i)^4 = 2^4 i^4 = 16 \cdot 1 = 16$ **39.** $(^-2i)^4 = (^-2)^4 i^4 = 16 \cdot 1 = 16$

Written Find the product of each complex number and its conjugate.

1. $3 - 7i$ 58
2. $6 + 5i$ 61
3. $2 - 9i$ 85
4. $17 - i$ 290
5. $2 - 3i$ 13
6. $3i$ 9
7. ^-2i 4
8. ^-10i 100

Simplify. For answers to problems **20-28** and **33-35**, see the Teacher's Guide.

9. $\frac{3 - 2i}{1 - i}$ $\frac{5 + i}{2}$
10. $\frac{4 + 5i}{1 + i}$ $\frac{9 + i}{2}$
11. $\frac{1 + i}{3 + 2i}$ $\frac{5 + i}{13}$
12. $\frac{1 - i}{4 - 5i}$ $\frac{9 + i}{41}$
13. $\frac{3 + 5i}{2i}$ $\frac{5 - 3i}{2}$
14. $\frac{4 - 7i}{^-3i}$ $\frac{7 + 4i}{3}$
15. $\frac{5 - 6i}{^-3i}$ $\frac{6 + 5i}{3}$
16. $\frac{2 + i}{5i}$ $\frac{1 - 2i}{5}$
17. $\frac{3}{4 - i}$ $\frac{12 + 3i}{17}$
18. $\frac{2}{6 + 5i}$ $\frac{12 - 10i}{61}$
19. $\frac{4}{\sqrt{3} + 2i}$ $\frac{4\sqrt{3} - 8i}{7}$
20. $\frac{7}{\sqrt{2} - 3i}$
21. $\frac{2 + i\sqrt{3}}{2 - i\sqrt{3}}$
22. $\frac{1 + i\sqrt{2}}{1 - i\sqrt{2}}$
23. $\frac{3 - i\sqrt{5}}{3 + i\sqrt{5}}$
24. $\frac{2 - i\sqrt{7}}{2 + i\sqrt{7}}$
25. $\frac{(2 + 3i)^2}{(3 + i)^2}$
26. $\frac{(3 + 3i)^2}{(1 + i)^2}$
27. $\frac{1 - i}{(1 + i)^2}$
28. $\frac{(4 + 3i)^2}{(3 - i)^2}$

Find the multiplicative inverse of each complex number.

29. $3 + i$ $(3 - i)/10$
30. $2 - 5i$ $(2 + 5i)/29$
31. $7 - 3i$ $(7 + 3i)/58$
32. $3 + 7i$ $(3 - 7i)/58$

Show that each of the following is a cube root of 1.

33. 1
34. $-\frac{1}{2} + \frac{1}{2}i\sqrt{3}$
35. $-\frac{1}{2} - \frac{1}{2}i\sqrt{3}$

Excursions in Algebra

Complex Puzzle

Evaluate each of the following expressions.

R: $8i(1 - i) - 2(4 + 3i)$ $2i$

U: $(4i)(^-2i)$ 8

L: $(5 + 4i)^2$ $9 + 40i$

E: $i(2 + i)(3 - 4i)$ $5 + 10i$

Use your solutions to answer the following question.

In 1777, what Swiss mathematician was the first to use i for the imaginary unit?

E	U	L	E	R
$5 + 10i$	8	$9 + 40i$	$5 + 10i$	$2i$

This section is optional.

5–9 Properties of Complex Numbers

Objective: To learn the properties of complex numbers.

The following chart summarizes the properties for addition and multiplication of real numbers.

	For any real numbers a, b, and c	
	Addition	Multiplication
commutative	$a + b = b + a$	$a \cdot b = b \cdot a$
associative	$(a + b) + c = a + (b + c)$	$(a \cdot b) \cdot c = a \cdot (b \cdot c)$
identity	$a + 0 = 0 + a$	$a \cdot 1 = 1 \cdot a$
inverse	$a + {}^-a = 0 = {}^-a + a$	$a \cdot \frac{1}{a} = 1 = \frac{1}{a} \cdot a$ if $a \neq 0$
distributive of multiplication over addition	$a(b + c) = ab + ac$ and $(b + c)a = ba + ca$	

Also, the real numbers are said to be closed under addition and multiplication. This means that the sum or product of any two real numbers is also a real number.

A mathematical system that has the properties stated above is called a **field.** The real number system forms a field. The rational number system forms a field. The complex number system also forms a field.

The real number system consists of the real numbers along with the operations of addition and multiplication.

examples

1 **Show that addition of complex numbers is commutative.**

Let $a + bi$ and $c + di$ be two complex numbers.

$(a + bi) + (c + di) = (a + c) + (b + d)i$ — *Definition of complex addition*

$= (c + a) + (d + b)i$ — *Commutativity of addition for reals*

$= (c + di) + (a + bi)$ — *Definition of complex addition*

2 **Show that multiplication of complex numbers is commutative.**

Let $a + bi$ and $c + di$ be two complex numbers.

$(a + bi)(c + di) = (ac - bd) + (ad + bc)i$ — *Definition of complex multiplication*

$= (ca - db) + (da + cb)i$ — *Commutativity of multiplication for reals*

$= (ca - db) + (cb + da)i$ — *Commutativity of addition for reals*

$= (c + di)(a + bi)$ — *Definition of complex multiplication*

It is left as an exercise to show that addition and multiplication of complex numbers are associative.

examples

3 **Show that 0 is the additive identity for complex numbers.**

Let $a + bi$ be a complex number.

$$\begin{aligned}(a + bi) + 0 &= (a + bi) + (0 + 0i)\\ &= (a + 0) + (b + 0)i\\ &= a + bi\end{aligned}$$

4 **Show that 1 is the multiplicative identity for complex numbers.**

Let $a + bi$ be a complex number.

$$\begin{aligned}(a + bi)(1) &= (a + bi)(1 + 0i)\\ &= (a \cdot 1 - b \cdot 0) + (a \cdot 0 + b \cdot 1)i\\ &= a + bi\end{aligned}$$

If $a + bi$ is a complex number, then $^{-}a - bi$ is its additive inverse.

$$\begin{aligned}(a + bi) + (^{-}a - bi) &= (a - a) + (b - b)i\\ &= 0 + 0i\\ &= 0\end{aligned}$$

The multiplicative inverse of $a + bi$ is $\dfrac{a - bi}{a^2 + b^2}$.

$$\begin{aligned}(a + bi)\left(\frac{a - bi}{a^2 + b^2}\right) &= \frac{(a + bi)(a - bi)}{a^2 + b^2}\\ &= \frac{a^2 + b^2}{a^2 + b^2}\\ &= 1\end{aligned}$$

example

5 **Show that multiplication is distributive over addition for complex numbers.**

Let $a + bi$, $c + di$, and $e + fi$ be complex numbers.

$$\begin{aligned}(a + bi)[(c + di) + (e + fi)] &= (a + bi)[(c + e) + (d + f)i]\\ &= [a(c + e) - b(d + f)] + [a(d + f) + b(c + e)]i\\ &= [ac + ae - bd - bf] + [ad + af + bc + be]i\\ &= [(ac - bd) + (ae - bf)] + [(ad + bc) + (af + be)]i\\ &= [(ac - bd) + (ad + bc)i] + [(ae - bf) + (af + be)i]\\ &= (a + bi)(c + di) + (a + bi)(e + fi)\end{aligned}$$

$$\begin{aligned}[(c + di) + (e + fi)](a + bi) &= (a + bi)[(c + di) + (e + fi)]\\ &= (a + bi)(c + di) + (a + bi)(e + fi)\\ &= (c + di)(a + bi) + (e + fi)(a + bi)\end{aligned}$$

exercises

Max: 1-5, 1-33; Avg: 1-5, 1-33 odds; Min: 1-33 odds

Exploratory Which field properties are *not* satisfied by each set of numbers?

1. natural numbers
2. integers
3. pure imaginary numbers
4. irrational numbers
5. imaginary numbers For answers to problems **1-5**, see the Teacher's Guide.

Written Choose several complex numbers and perform the necessary operation to show each of the following properties. Answers will vary.

1. commutative property of addition
2. commutative property of multiplication
3. associative property of addition
4. associative property of multiplication
5. distributive property of multiplication over addition

Find the additive inverse for each complex number.

6. $1 + 4i$ $^-1 - 4i$
7. $i\sqrt{3}$ $^-i\sqrt{3}$
8. $3 - 2i$ $^-3 + 2i$
9. $11 + i$ $^-11 - i$
10. $2 - 5i$ $^-2 + 5i$
11. $3 - 4i$ $^-3 + 4i$
12. $^-2 - 8i$ $2 + 8i$
13. $^-3 - 2i$ $3 + 2i$
14. $2 - i$ $^-2 + i$
15. $5 + 4i$ $^-5 - 4i$
16. $6i$ ^-6i
17. $^-3$ 3

18-29. Find the multiplicative inverse for each complex number in problem **6-17**.
For answers to problems **18-33**, see the Teacher's Guide.

Show each of the following.

30. Show that the complex numbers are closed under addition.
31. Show that the complex numbers are closed under multiplication.
32. Show that addition of complex numbers is associative.
33. Show that multiplication of complex numbers is associative.

Groups

Excursions in Algebra

A **group** is a mathematical system that has one operation. This operation must be associative. In addition, there is an identity and all elements of a group have inverses.

The real numbers form a group under addition.

1. For any real numbers a, b, and c, $(a + b) + c = a + (b + c)$. *Addition is associative.*
2. For any real number a, $a + 0 = a = 0 + a$. *0 is the additive identity.*
3. For any real number a, $a + {}^-a = 0 = {}^-a + a$. *$^-a$ is the additive inverse of a.*

Exercises **Are the following systems groups? Write *yes* or *no*.**

1. rationals, under addition yes
2. integers, under multiplication no
3. whole numbers, under addition no
4. integers, under addition yes
5. 0 and 1, under addition no
6. rationals, under multiplication yes

A group is not necessarily commutative. A commutative group is Abelian, named after Niels Abel (1802-1829), a Norwegian mathematician.

Vocabulary

nth root (134)
square root (134)
radical sign (134)
index (134)
radicand (134)
conjugates (141)
radical equations (147)
imaginary unit (150)
pure imaginary number (150)
complex number (154)
real part (154)
imaginary part (154)
complex conjugates (155)
field (159)

Chapter Summary

1. Definition of Square Root: For any numbers a and b, if $a^2 = b$, then a is a square root of b. (134)
2. Definition of nth Root: For any numbers a and b, and any positive integer n, if $a^n = b$, then a is an nth root of b. (134)
3. The Real nth Roots of b (135)

	$b > 0$	$b < 0$	$b = 0$
n even	one positive root one negative root	no real roots	one real root, 0
n odd	one positive root no negative roots	no positive roots one negative root	one real root, 0

4. Property of nth Roots: For any number a, and any integer n greater than one,
   1. if n is even, then $\sqrt[n]{a^n} = |a|$.
   2. if n is odd, then $\sqrt[n]{a^n} = a$. (135)
5. Product and Quotient Properties of Radicals: For any numbers a and b, and any integer n greater than one,
   1. if n is even, then $\sqrt[n]{ab} = \sqrt[n]{a} \cdot \sqrt[n]{b}$ and $\sqrt[n]{\frac{a}{b}} = \frac{\sqrt[n]{a}}{\sqrt[n]{b}}$ as long as $a \geq 0$ and $b > 0$. (138)
   2. if n is odd, then $\sqrt[n]{ab} = \sqrt[n]{a} \cdot \sqrt[n]{b}$ and $\sqrt[n]{\frac{a}{b}} = \frac{\sqrt[n]{a}}{\sqrt[n]{b}}$ as long as $b \neq 0$. (143)
6. Conditions for Simplified Radicals: 1. The index n is as small as possible. 2. The radicand contains no factor (other than one) which is the nth power of an integer or polynomial. 3. The radicand contains no fractions. 4. No radicals appear in the denominator. (144)
7. Definition of Imaginary Number: For any positive real number, b, $\sqrt{^-(b)^2} = bi$ where i is a number whose square is $^-1$. (150)
8. Definition of a Complex Number: A complex number is any

number that can be written in the form $a + bi$ where a and b are real numbers and i is the imaginary unit. (154)

9. For any complex numbers $a + bi$ and $c + di$,
   1. $a + bi = c + di$ if and only if $a = c$ and $b = d$.
   2. $(a + bi) + (c + di) = (a + c) + (b + d)i$.
   3. $(a + bi) - (c + di) = (a - c) + (b - d)i$.
   4. $(a + bi)(c + di) = (ac - bd) + (ad + bc)i$. (155)

Chapter Review

5-1 Find the principal root of each expression.

1. $\sqrt{49a^2}$ $7|a|$ 2. $\sqrt[3]{-27}$ -3 3. $\sqrt[4]{16}$ 2 4. $\sqrt[3]{8x^3y^6}$ $2xy^2$

Use a table of powers and roots to find each value.

5. $\sqrt[3]{39}$ 3.391 6. $\sqrt[3]{290}$ 6.619 7. $(9.8)^3$ 941.192 8. $\sqrt{300}$ 17.321

5-2 Simplify.

9. $\sqrt[3]{48a^2}$ $2\sqrt[3]{6a^2}$ 10. $\sqrt[3]{48a^4}$ $2a\sqrt[3]{6a}$ 11. $\sqrt[4]{32m^5}$ $2m\sqrt[4]{2m}$

12. $-3\sqrt{18} \cdot 5\sqrt{15}$ $-45\sqrt{30}$ 13. $\sqrt{5}(\sqrt{10} + 2)$ $5\sqrt{2} + 2\sqrt{5}$ 14. $\sqrt{3}(\sqrt{6} + \sqrt{12})$ $3\sqrt{2} + 6$

15. $\sqrt[3]{3}(\sqrt[3]{16} + \sqrt[3]{9})$ $2\sqrt[3]{6} + 3$ 16. $(3 + \sqrt{5})(3 - \sqrt{5})$ 4 17. $\sqrt[3]{2xy^4}\sqrt[3]{36x^2y^2}$ $2xy^2\sqrt[3]{9}$

5-3 Simplify.

18. $3\sqrt{12} - 4\sqrt{75} + 4$ $-14\sqrt{3} + 4$ 19. $\sqrt[3]{40} + \sqrt[3]{135} - \sqrt[3]{5}$ $4\sqrt[3]{5}$

20. $(6 + \sqrt{2})(10 + \sqrt{5})$ $60 + 10\sqrt{2} + 6\sqrt{5} + \sqrt{10}$ 21. $(m + \sqrt[3]{2})(m^2 - m\sqrt[3]{2} + \sqrt[3]{4})$ $m^3 + 2$

5-4 Simplify.

24. $\dfrac{4\sqrt{3} + 4\sqrt{2} - \sqrt{6} - 3}{13}$

22. $\sqrt{\dfrac{10}{2}}$ $\sqrt{5}$ 23. $\dfrac{\sqrt[3]{80}}{\sqrt[3]{2}}$ $2\sqrt[3]{5}$ 24. $\dfrac{\sqrt{3} + \sqrt{2}}{4 + \sqrt{3}}$ 25. $\dfrac{4}{\sqrt[3]{16}}$ $\sqrt[3]{4}$

5-5 Solve each equation.

26. $\sqrt{2x + 7} = 3$ 1 27. $\sqrt[3]{y + 2} = 4$ 62 28. $\sqrt{5y + 1} + 6 = 10$ 3

5-6 Simplify.

29. $\sqrt{-8}$ $2i\sqrt{2}$ 30. $\sqrt{-24}$ $2i\sqrt{6}$ 31. i^7 $-i$

32. $3i + 2i$ $5i$ 33. $\sqrt{-3} \cdot \sqrt{-3}$ -3 34. $(2\sqrt{5})(-3\sqrt{-5})$ $-30i$

5-7 Find the sum, difference, and product for each pair of complex numbers.

35. $(7 + 2i)$, $(5 - 3i)$ $12 - i$, $2 + 5i$, $41 - 11i$ 36. $(3 + 8i)$, $(3 - 8i)$ 6, $16i$, 73

37. Find values of x and y for which $2x + 5yi = 4 + 15i$ is true. $x = 2$, $y = 3$

5-8 Simplify.

38. $\dfrac{4 + 3i}{1 - 2i}$ $\dfrac{-2 + 11i}{5}$ 39. $\dfrac{7 - 3i}{2i}$ $\dfrac{-3 - 7i}{2}$ 40. $\dfrac{(4 - 3i)^2}{(3 + i)^2}$ $\dfrac{-44 - 117i}{50}$

5-9 41. Which property of the complex number field is shown by $(2 + 7i) + (3 - 5i) = (3 - 5i) + (2 + 7i)$? Commutative property of addition.

Chapter Test

Find the principal root of each expression.

1. $\sqrt{81x^2}$ $9|x|$
2. $\sqrt[3]{-27y^3}$ $-3y$
3. $\sqrt{x^2 - 8xy + 16y^2}$ $|x - 4y|$

Simplify.

4. $\sqrt[3]{108m^4}$ $3m\sqrt[3]{4m}$
5. $\sqrt{-50}$ $5i\sqrt{2}$
6. $(4 - \sqrt{3})(4 + \sqrt{3})$ 13
7. $2\sqrt{27} + 2\sqrt{3} - 7\sqrt{48}$ $-20\sqrt{3}$
8. $7\sqrt[3]{16} \cdot 5\sqrt[3]{20}$ $140\sqrt[3]{5}$
9. $(\sqrt{3} - \sqrt{5})(\sqrt{15} + 3)$ $-2\sqrt{3}$
10. $\dfrac{3}{\sqrt[3]{4}}$ $\dfrac{3\sqrt[3]{2}}{2}$
11. $\dfrac{3}{\sqrt[4]{8}}$ $\dfrac{3\sqrt[4]{2}}{2}$
12. $\dfrac{2 + \sqrt{3}}{1 - \sqrt{2}}$ $-2 - \sqrt{3} - 2\sqrt{2} - \sqrt{6}$
13. $\sqrt[3]{2}(\sqrt[3]{24} - \sqrt[3]{4})$ $2\sqrt[3]{6} - 2$
14. $\sqrt[3]{16x^3} + 5\sqrt[3]{54x^3} - 3\sqrt[3]{128x^3}$ $5x\sqrt[3]{2}$
15. $\sqrt{\dfrac{5}{32}} + \sqrt{90} + \dfrac{\sqrt{30}}{\sqrt{3}} - \sqrt{\dfrac{2}{5}}$ $\dfrac{157\sqrt{10}}{40}$
16. $3i + \sqrt{-4}$ $5i$
17. $\sqrt{-3} \cdot \sqrt{-24}$ $-6\sqrt{2}$

Find the sum, difference, and product for each pair of complex numbers.

18. $7 - 3i,\ 4 + 5i$ $11 + 2i,\ 3 - 8i,\ 43 + 23i$
19. $4 - 6i,\ 4 + 6i$ $8,\ -12i,\ 52$

Simplify.

20. $\dfrac{4 - 5i}{3 + 7i}$ $\dfrac{-23 - 43i}{58}$
21. $\dfrac{4 - 7i}{2i}$ $\dfrac{-7 - 4i}{2}$
22. $\dfrac{(2 + 3i)^2}{(1 - i)^2}$ $\dfrac{-12 - 5i}{2}$

Solve each equation.

23. $\sqrt{2x - 5} = 9$ 43
24. $(3 + i)x + 6 - i = -8i$ $\dfrac{-5 - 3i}{2}$

25. Which property of the complex number field is shown by $[(3 + 4i) + (4 + 2i)] + (6 - 5i) = (3 + 4i) + [(4 + 2i) + (6 - 5i)]$? Associativity of addition.

Chapter 6

Quadratic Equations

Certain compounds can only be obtained if various substances are combined in sufficient quantities and under the specific conditions indicated by a chemical formula. In mathematics, formulas are derived for use in obtaining solutions to various types of equations.

6-1 Quadratic Equations

Objective: To solve quadratic equations using factoring.

Any quadratic equation can be written in the form $ax^2 + bx + c = 0$ when a, b, and c are real numbers, and $a \neq 0$.

Equations like $x^2 - 8 = 0$, $x^2 - 2x - 15 = 0$, and $ax^2 + bx + c = 0$ are called **quadratic equations.** You have learned how to solve some types of quadratic equations as shown below.

example 1

Solve $x^2 - 8 = 0$.

$$x^2 - 8 = 0$$
$$x^2 = 8$$
$$x = \pm\sqrt{8} \text{ or } \pm 2\sqrt{2}$$

Other quadratic equations can be solved using factoring. This method depends on the following property.

Zero Product Property

For any numbers a and b, if $ab = 0$, then $a = 0$ or $b = 0$.

Both a and b can be zero.

examples 2

Solve $x^2 - 2x - 15 = 0$.

$x^2 - 2x - 15 = 0$

$(x - 5)(x + 3) = 0$ *Factor.*

$x - 5 = 0$ or $x + 3 = 0$ *Zero product property*

$x = 5$ or $x = {}^-3$

Check: $x^2 - 2x - 15 = 0$

$(5)^2 - 2(5) - 15 \stackrel{?}{=} 0$ or $({}^-3)^2 - 2({}^-3) - 15 \stackrel{?}{=} 0$

$0 = 0$ $\quad$ $0 = 0$

The solutions are 5 and $^-3$.

3

Solve $9x^2 - 24x = {}^-16$.

$9x^2 - 24x = {}^-16$

$9x^2 - 24x + 16 = 0$

$(3x - 4)(3x - 4) = 0$

$3x - 4 = 0$ or $3x - 4 = 0$

$3x = 4$ $\quad$ $3x = 4$

$x = \frac{4}{3}$ $\quad$ $x = \frac{4}{3}$

Check: $9x^2 - 24x = {}^-16$

$$9\left(\frac{4}{3}\right)^2 - 24\left(\frac{4}{3}\right) \stackrel{?}{=} {}^-16$$
$$16 - 32 \stackrel{?}{=} {}^-16$$
$${}^-16 = {}^-16$$

The solution is $\frac{4}{3}$.

exercises

Max: 1–20, 1–36, 1–6; Avg: 1–20, 1–35 odds; Min: 1–35 odds

Exploratory Identify which of the following equations are quadratic equations.

(1.) $4x^2 + 7x - 3 = 0$

(2.) $4x^2 - 2x + 11 = 0$

(3.) $2x^2 + 7x = 0$

4. $5x^4 - 7x^2 = 0$

5. $3x^3 + 4 = 0$

(6.) $9x^2 - x + 4 = 0$

(7.) $\frac{1}{2}x^2 + \frac{3}{4} = 0$

8. $\frac{2}{3}x^3 - 3x^2 + 2x = 0$

9. $x^2 + 7x - 3 = x^3$

(10.) $3x^2 - 9 = x$

Quadratic equations are circled.

Solve each equation.

11. $(x - 4)(x + 5) = 0$ $4, {}^-5$
12. $(x - 3)(x - 7) = 0$ $3, 7$
13. $(x + 6)(x + 2) = 0$ ${}^-6, {}^-2$
14. $(x + 8)(x + 1) = 0$ ${}^-8, {}^-1$
15. $x(x - 7) = 0$ $0, 7$
16. $x(x + 4) = 0$ $0, {}^-4$
17. $(2x + 3)(3x - 1) = 0$ $-\frac{3}{2}, \frac{1}{3}$
18. $(2x + 5)(x - 1) = 0$ $-\frac{5}{2}, 1$
19. $(3x + 7)(x + 5) = 0$ $-\frac{7}{3}, {}^-5$
20. $(x + 4)(5x - 1) = 0$ ${}^-4, \frac{1}{5}$

Written Solve each equation.

1. $x^2 + 6x + 8 = 0$ ${}^-2, {}^-4$
2. $x^2 + 4x + 3 = 0$ ${}^-3, {}^-1$
3. $x^2 - 9x + 20 = 0$ $4, 5$
4. $x^2 - 8x + 12 = 0$ $2, 6$
5. $x^2 + 3x - 10 = 0$ ${}^-5, 2$
6. $x^2 - 4x - 21 = 0$ $7, {}^-3$
7. $x^2 - 3x = 4$ $4, {}^-1$
8. $x^2 + 6x = 27$ ${}^-9, 3$
9. $x^2 + 3x = 0$ $0, {}^-3$
10. $x^2 - x = 12$ $4, {}^-3$
11. $x^2 + x - 30 = 0$ ${}^-6, 5$
12. $x^2 - 5x = 0$ $0, 5$
13. $2x^2 + 5x + 3 = 0$ $-\frac{3}{2}, {}^-1$
14. $2x^2 + 9x + 4 = 0$ $-\frac{1}{2}, {}^-4$
15. $2x^2 - 3x = 9$ $-\frac{3}{2}, 3$
16. $3x^2 + 13x - 10 = 0$ $\frac{2}{3}, {}^-5$
17. $3x^2 = 5x$ $0, \frac{5}{3}$
18. $10x^2 - x = 3$ $-\frac{1}{2}, \frac{3}{5}$
19. $6x^2 + 13x + 6 = 0$ $-\frac{3}{2}, -\frac{2}{3}$
20. $10x^2 + 33x = 7$ $-\frac{7}{2}, \frac{1}{5}$
21. $12x^2 + 25x + 12 = 0$ $-\frac{4}{3}, -\frac{3}{4}$
22. $6x^2 - 5x = 25$ $-\frac{5}{3}, \frac{5}{2}$
23. $24x^2 - 22x + 3 = 0$ $\frac{1}{6}, \frac{3}{4}$
24. $2x^2 - 5x = 0$ $0, \frac{5}{2}$
25. $4x^2 - 11x - 3 = 0$ $-\frac{1}{4}, 3$
26. $4x^2 - 17x + 4 = 0$ $\frac{1}{4}, 4$
27. $x^2 + 3x = 40$ $5, {}^-8$
28. $6m^2 + 7m - 3 = 0$ $\frac{1}{3}, -\frac{3}{2}$
29. $3x^2 - 14x + 8 = 0$ $\frac{2}{3}, 4$
30. $2y^2 + 11y - 21 = 0$ ${}^-7, \frac{3}{2}$
31. $12x^2 - 17x - 5 = 0$ $-\frac{1}{4}, \frac{5}{3}$
32. $3t^2 + 4t = 15$ ${}^-3, \frac{5}{3}$
33. $12x^2 + 8x - 15 = 0$ $\frac{5}{6}, -\frac{3}{2}$
34. $18x^2 + 3x - 1 = 0$ $\frac{1}{6}, -\frac{1}{3}$
35. $x^2 + 4x + 4 = 0$ ${}^-2$
36. $18x^2 - 3x = 15$ $-\frac{15}{18}, 1$

Challenge Solve each equation.

1. $n^3 = 9n$ $0, 3, {}^-3$
2. $4t^2 = 25$ $\frac{5}{2}, -\frac{5}{2}$
3. $121 = 16b^2$ $\frac{11}{4}, -\frac{11}{4}$
4. $a^3 = 81a$ $0, 9, {}^-9$
5. $35x^3 + 16x^2 = 12x$ $0, -\frac{6}{7}, \frac{2}{5}$
6. $18x^3 + 16x = 34x^2$ $\frac{8}{9}, 1, 0$

6–2 Completing the Square

Objective: To solve quadratic equations by completing the square.

Completing the square is used not only to solve quadratic equations, but also to change the form of an equation so that its graph is more easily recognized.

An equation like $(x - 4)^2 = 5$ can be solved by taking the square root of both sides.

$$(x - 4)^2 = 5$$
$$\sqrt{(x-4)^2} = \sqrt{5}$$
$$|x - 4| = \sqrt{5}$$
$$x - 4 = \pm\sqrt{5}$$
$$x = 4 \pm \sqrt{5}$$

The solutions are $4 + \sqrt{5}$ and $4 - \sqrt{5}$.

The equation $x^2 - 6x + 9 = 2$ can be solved in a similar way.

$$x^2 - 6x + 9 = 2$$
$$(x - 3)^2 = 2$$
$$x - 3 = \pm\sqrt{2}$$
$$x = 3 \pm \sqrt{2}$$

The solutions are $3 + \sqrt{2}$ and $3 - \sqrt{2}$.

To solve a quadratic equation by taking square roots you must have a perfect square equal to a constant. A method called **completing the square** is based on this concept.

Consider the following perfect squares.

$$(x + 7)^2 = x^2 + 14x + 49 \qquad (14 \div 2)^2 = 7^2 \text{ or } 49$$

$$(x + b)^2 = x^2 + 2bx + b^2 \qquad (2b \div 2)^2 = b^2$$

The pattern shown above can be used to complete the square when two terms are known. Complete the square for $x^2 - 8x$.

$$x^2 - 8x + \underline{\quad} \qquad (^-8 \div 2)^2 = (^-4)^2 \text{ or } 16$$

The answer is $x^2 - 8x + 16$.

This example shows how to solve a quadratic equation by completing the square.

example 1

Solve $x^2 - 8x + 11 = 0$.

$x^2 - 8x + 11 = 0$	*Not a perfect square.*
$x^2 - 8x = {}^-11$	*Subtract 11 from each side.*
$x^2 - 8x + 16 = {}^-11 + 16$	*Add* $\left(\frac{^-8}{2}\right)^2$ *or 16 to each side.*
$(x - 4)^2 = 5$	*Factor.*
$x - 4 = \pm\sqrt{5}$	*Take the square root of each side.*
$x = 4 \pm \sqrt{5}$	*Solve for x.*

When the coefficient of the squared term is *not* 1, another step is required.

examples

2 **Solve $2m^2 - 8m + 3 = 0$.**

$$2m^2 - 8m + 3 = 0$$

$$m^2 - 4m + \frac{3}{2} = 0 \qquad \textit{Divide each side by 2.}$$

$$m^2 - 4m = -\frac{3}{2}$$

$$m^2 - 4m + 4 = -\frac{3}{2} + 4 \qquad \textit{Add } ({}^-4 \div 2)^2 \textit{ or 4 to each side.}$$

$$(m - 2)^2 = \frac{5}{2} \qquad \textit{Factor.}$$

$$m - 2 = \pm\sqrt{\frac{5}{2}} \qquad \textit{Take the square root of each side.}$$

$$m - 2 = \pm\frac{\sqrt{10}}{2} \qquad \textit{Rationalize the denominator.}$$

$$m = 2 \pm \frac{\sqrt{10}}{2} \qquad \textit{Solve for m.}$$

The solutions are $2 + \frac{\sqrt{10}}{2}$ and $2 - \frac{\sqrt{10}}{2}$.

3 **Solve $3x^2 - 11x - 4 = 0$.**

$$3x^2 - 11x - 4 = 0$$

$$x^2 - \frac{11}{3}x - \frac{4}{3} = 0 \qquad \textit{Divide each side by 3.}$$

$$x^2 - \frac{11}{3}x = \frac{4}{3}$$

$$x^2 - \frac{11}{3}x + \frac{121}{36} = \frac{4}{3} + \frac{121}{36} \qquad \textit{Add } \left(-\frac{11}{3} \div 2\right)^2 \textit{ or } \frac{121}{36} \textit{ to each side.}$$

$$\left(x - \frac{11}{6}\right)^2 = \frac{169}{36} \qquad \textit{Factor.}$$

$$x - \frac{11}{6} = \pm\frac{13}{6} \qquad \textit{Take square root of each side.}$$

$$x = 4 \text{ or } x = -\frac{1}{3}$$

The solutions are 4 and $-\frac{1}{3}$.

exercises

Max: 1–21, 1–44; **Avg:** 1–21, 1–43 odds; **Min:** 1–43 odds

Exploratory State whether or not each trinomial is a perfect square.

1. $x^2 + 4x + 4$ yes
2. $a^2 + 14a + 28$ no
3. $b^2 - 6b - 9$ no
4. $x^2 - x + \frac{1}{4}$ yes
5. $m^2 - 10m + 25$ yes
6. $a^2 - 3a + \frac{9}{2}$ no
7. $x^2 + 5x + \frac{25}{4}$ yes
8. $t^2 - 12t - 36$ no
9. $c^2 + 14c + 49$ yes

Find the value of c that makes each trinomial a perfect square.

10. $y^2 - 6y + c$ 9
11. $x^2 + 2x + c$ 1
12. $m^2 - 20m + c$ 100
13. $t^2 + 40t + c$ 400
14. $n^2 + 12n + c$ 36
15. $x^2 + 18x + c$ 81
16. $y^2 + 3y + c$ $\frac{9}{4}$
17. $r^2 - 9r + c$ $\frac{81}{4}$
18. $s^2 + 11s + c$ $\frac{121}{4}$
19. $a^2 - 100a + c$ 2500
20. $n^2 - n + c$ $\frac{1}{4}$
21. $x^2 + 15x + c$ $\frac{225}{4}$

Written Find the value of c that makes each trinomial a perfect square.

1. $x^2 + 6x + c$ 9
2. $x^2 - 10x + c$ 25
3. $y^2 + \frac{1}{2}y + c$ $\frac{1}{16}$
4. $a^2 + 9a + c$ $\frac{81}{4}$
5. $r^2 + r + c$ $\frac{1}{4}$
6. $x^2 - 16x + c$ 64
7. $y^2 - 3y + c$ $\frac{9}{4}$
8. $m^2 - \frac{2}{3}m + c$ $\frac{1}{9}$
9. $b^2 + 7b + c$ $\frac{49}{4}$
10. $a^2 - \frac{4}{5}a + c$ $\frac{4}{25}$
11. $r^2 + 50r + c$ 625
12. $n^2 - 30n + c$ 225

Solve by completing the square.

13. $x^2 - 7x + 12 = 0$ 3, 4
14. $r^2 - 6r + 8 = 0$ 2, 4
15. $x^2 - 8x + 15 = 0$ 3, 5
16. $y^2 - 3y = 88$ $^-8$, 11
17. $x^2 + 8x - 20 = 0$ $^-10$, 2
18. $r^2 - 3r = 28$ 7, $^-4$
19. $x^2 + 2x - 48 = 0$ 6, $^-8$
20. $z^2 - 2z = 24$ 6, $^-4$
21. $m^2 + 3m - 180 = 0$ $^-15$, 12
22. $x^2 + 12x + 4 = 0$ $^-6 \pm 4\sqrt{2}$
23. $x^2 + 8x - 84 = 0$ 6, $^-14$
24. $r^2 + 5r - 8 = 0$ $(-5 \pm \sqrt{57})/2$
25. $x^2 - 3x - 7 = 0$ $(3 \pm \sqrt{37})/2$
26. $t^2 + 4t = 96$ $^-12$, 8
27. $m^2 - 8m + 16 = 0$ 4
28. $s^2 - 10s + 21 = 0$ 7, 3
29. $x^2 - 7x + 5 = 0$ $(7 \pm \sqrt{29})/2$
30. $x^2 - \frac{3}{4}x + \frac{1}{8} = 0$ $\frac{1}{2}, \frac{1}{4}$
31. $3x^2 + 7x + 2 = 0$ $^-2, -\frac{1}{3}$
32. $4x^2 + 19x - 5 = 0$ $\frac{1}{4}, {}^-5$
33. $x^2 + 3x - 40 = 0$ $^-8$, 5
34. $6m^2 + 7m - 3 = 0$ $-\frac{3}{2}, \frac{1}{3}$
35. $3x^2 - 14x + 8 = 0$ $4, \frac{2}{3}$
36. $2y^2 + 11y - 21 = 0$ $\frac{3}{2}, {}^-7$
37. $12x^2 - 17x - 5 = 0$ $\frac{5}{3}, -\frac{1}{4}$
38. $2x^2 - 3x + 4 = 0$
39. $t^2 + 3t + 8 = 0$
40. $x^2 - 6x + 10 = 0$
41. $4a^2 - a + 3 = 0$
42. $6s^2 + 2s - 3 = 0$ $(-1 \pm \sqrt{19})/6$
43. $3x^2 - 12x + 4 = 0$ $2 \pm \frac{2}{3}\sqrt{6}$
44. $3t^2 + 4t - 15 = 0$ $\frac{5}{3}, {}^-3$

38–41. No real solutions.

Finding Cube and Fourth Roots

The following computer program approximates cube roots. The program requires a radicand and an initial guess for each set of data.

```
10  READ A, X(0)      A is the radicand. X(0) is the initial guess.
20  LET N=0
30  LET X(N+1)=(1/3)*(2*X(N)+A/(X(N)↑2)
40  IF ABS(X(N+1)-X(N))<=0.001 THEN 70
50  LET N=N+1
60  GO TO 30
70  PRINT X(N+1) "IS THE CUBE ROOT OF" A
80  PRINT "CHECK" A↑(1/3)
85  DATA 6,2
90  END
```

The results of running this program follow.

```
RUN
1.81712 IS THE CUBE ROOT OF 6
CHECK 1.81712
```

A few simple changes yield a program for finding fourth roots and showing each approximately as it is found by the computer. The following lines can be substituted in the program above. In this case, the data in line 85 has also been changed.

```
30  LET X(N+1)=(1/4)*(3*X(N)+A/(X(N)↑3)
35  PRINT X(N+1)
70  PRINT X(N+1) "IS THE FOURTH ROOT OF" A
80  PRINT "CHECK" A↑(1/4)
85  DATA 75,4
```

The results of running the new program follow.

```
RUN
3.29297    2.99482    2.94417    2.94283    2.94283
2.94283 IS THE FOURTH ROOT OF 75
CHECK 2.94283
```

Exercises Find the cube and fourth roots for each of the following.

1. 12 2.28943, 1.86121 **2.** 31 3.14138, 2.35961 **3.** 47 3.60883, 2.61833 **4.** 98 4.61044, 3.14635

6-3 The Quadratic Formula

Objective: To develop the quadratic formula and use it to solve quadratic equations.

Completing the square can be used to develop a general formula for solving quadratic equations.

Note that the quadratic formula is derived for $a > 0$. Now, $ax^2 + bx + c = 0$ implies that $^-ax^2 - bx - c = 0$. Also, if $a < 0$, then $^-a > 0$. Thus, you can use the quadratic formula to solve $^-ax^2 - bx - c = 0$.

Start with the general form of a quadratic equation. $ax^2 + bx + c = 0$

Divide by a so the coefficient of x^2 becomes 1. $x^2 + \frac{b}{a}x + \frac{c}{a} = 0$

Subtract $\frac{c}{a}$ from each side. $x^2 + \frac{b}{a} = -\frac{c}{a}$

Complete the square. $x^2 + \frac{b}{a}x + \left(\frac{b}{2a}\right)^2 = -\frac{c}{a} + \left(\frac{b}{2a}\right)^2$

Factor. $\left(x + \frac{b}{2a}\right)^2 = -\frac{c}{a} + \frac{b^2}{4a^2}$

Add. $\left(x + \frac{b}{2a}\right)^2 = \frac{b^2 - 4ac}{4a^2}$

Take the square root of each side. $\left|x + \frac{b}{2a}\right| = \pm\sqrt{\frac{b^2 - 4ac}{4a^2}}$

Assume a is positive and simplify. *What happens if a is negative?* $x + \frac{b}{2a} = \pm\frac{\sqrt{b^2 - 4ac}}{2a}$

Solve for x. $x = \frac{^-b \pm \sqrt{b^2 - 4ac}}{2a}$

This formula is called the **quadratic formula** and can be used to solve *any* quadratic equation.

Quadratic Formula

The solutions of a quadratic equation of the form $ax^2 + bx + c = 0$ with $a \neq 0$ are given by this formula.

$$x = \frac{^-b \pm \sqrt{b^2 - 4ac}}{2a}$$

example 1

Solve $x^2 - 3x - 28 = 0$ using the quadratic formula.

$x = \frac{^-b \pm \sqrt{b^2 - 4ac}}{2a}$ *$ax^2 + bx + c = 0$*, *$x^2 - 3x - 28 = 0$*

$= \frac{^-(^-3) \pm \sqrt{(^-3)^2 - 4(1)(^-28)}}{2(1)}$ *$a = 1, b = {}^-3, c = {}^-28$*

$= \frac{3 \pm \sqrt{121}}{2}$ Solving by factoring, when possible, is often faster than solving by the quadratic formula.

$= \frac{3 \pm 11}{2}$ The solutions are $\frac{3 + 11}{2}$ and $\frac{3 - 11}{2}$ or 7 and $^-4$.

The quadratic formula yields *both* solutions to a quadratic equation, even if those solutions are imaginary.

examples

2 **Solve $x^2 + 4 = 0$.**

$$x = \frac{^-b \pm \sqrt{b^2 - 4ac}}{2a} \qquad ax^2 + bx + c = 0$$
$$\qquad x^2 \quad + 4 = 0$$

$$= \frac{^-0 \pm \sqrt{0^2 - 4(1)(4)}}{2(1)} \qquad a = 1, b = 0, c = 4$$

$$= \frac{\pm\sqrt{^-16}}{2}$$

$$= \frac{^\pm 4i}{2}$$

$= {}^\pm 2i$ The solutions are $2i$ and ^-2i.

3 **Solve $3x^2 - 5x + 9 = 0$.**

$$x = \frac{^-b \pm \sqrt{b^2 - 4ac}}{2a} \qquad ax^2 + bx + c = 0$$
$$\qquad 3x^2 - 5x + 9 = 0$$

$$= \frac{^-(^-5) \pm \sqrt{(^-5)^2 - 4(3)(9)}}{2(3)} \qquad a = 3, b = {}^-5, c = 9$$

$$= \frac{5 \pm \sqrt{25 - 108}}{6}$$

$$= \frac{5 \pm \sqrt{^-83}}{6}$$

$$= \frac{5 + i\sqrt{83}}{6} \quad \text{or} \quad x = \frac{5 - i\sqrt{83}}{6}$$

exercises

Max: 1–12, 1–43; **Avg:** 1–12, 1–43 odds; **Min:** 1–43 odds

Exploratory **State the values of a, b, and c for each quadratic equation.**

1. $5x^2 - 3x + 7 = 0$ 5, $^-3$, 7
2. $2x^2 + x - 3 = 0$ 2, 1, $^-3$
3. $z^2 + 2z - 1 = 0$ 1, 2, $^-1$
4. $m^2 + m = 0$ 1, 1, 0
5. $5x^2 - 3 = 0$ 5, 0, $^-3$
6. $3z^2 - \frac{1}{2}z + 7 = 0$ 3, $-\frac{1}{2}$, 7
7. $4x^2 = 7$ 4, 0, $^-7$
8. $7y^2 - 2y = 4$ 7, $^-2$, $^-4$
9. $5x^2 + 7 = 0$ 5, 0, 7
10. $3r^2 = 2r - 1$ 3, $^-2$, 1
11. $4x^2 - 6x - 1 = 0$ 4, $^-6$, $^-1$
12. $x^2 = 1 - x$ 1, 1, $^-1$

Written Solve each equation using the quadratic formula.

1. $x^2 - x - 30 = 0$ $6, -5$
2. $x^2 + 10x + 16 = 0$ $-2, -8$
3. $y^2 + 2y - 15 = 0$ $-5, 3$
4. $r^2 + 13r + 42 = 0$ $-7, -6$
5. $t^2 - 10t + 24 = 0$ $6, 4$
6. $s^2 + 5s - 24 = 0$ $3, -8$
7. $3x^2 - 7x - 20 = 0$ $4, -\frac{5}{3}$
8. $6m^2 - m - 15 = 0$ $\frac{5}{3}, -\frac{3}{2}$
9. $4x^2 - 11x - 3 = 0$ $3, -\frac{1}{4}$
10. $24x^2 - 14x - 5 = 0$ $\frac{5}{6}, -\frac{1}{4}$
11. $14r^2 + 33r - 5 = 0$ $\frac{1}{7}, -\frac{5}{2}$
12. $6y^2 + 19y + 15 = 0$ $-\frac{5}{3}, -\frac{3}{2}$
13. $20a^2 + 3a - 2 = 0$ $\frac{1}{4}, -\frac{2}{5}$
14. $15x^2 + 34x + 15 = 0$ $-\frac{3}{5}, -\frac{5}{3}$
15. $24y^2 - 2y - 15 = 0$ $\frac{5}{6}, -\frac{3}{4}$
16. $3x^2 + 5x = 28$ $-4, \frac{7}{3}$
17. $x^2 - 5x + 4 = 0$ $4, 1$
18. $2x^2 + 3x + 3 = 0$ $(-3 \pm i\sqrt{15})/4$
19. $2x^2 - x - 15 = 0$ $3, -\frac{5}{2}$
20. $4x^2 - 9x + 5 = 0$ $1, \frac{5}{4}$
21. $6y^2 + 8y + 5 = 0$ $(-4 \pm i\sqrt{14})/6$
22. $14r^2 - 45r - 14 = 0$ $\frac{7}{2}, -\frac{2}{7}$
23. $2x^2 - 5x + 3 = 0$ $1, \frac{3}{2}$
24. $5m^2 + 7m + 3 = 0$ $(-7 \pm i\sqrt{11})/10$
25. $12x^2 - 7x - 12 = 0$ $\frac{4}{3}, -\frac{3}{4}$
26. $3t^2 - 12t = 0$ $0, 4$
27. $21x^2 + 20x - 1 = 0$ $-1, \frac{1}{21}$
28. $6x^2 + x - 12 = 0$ $\frac{4}{3}, -\frac{3}{2}$
29. $2x^2 - 5x + 4 = 0$ $(5 \pm i\sqrt{7})/4$
30. $8r^2 = 60$ $\sqrt{30}/2, -\sqrt{30}/2$
31. $6y^2 - 5y - 6 = 0$ $\frac{3}{2}, -\frac{2}{3}$
32. $12x^2 - 11x = 3$ $(11 \pm \sqrt{265})/24$
33. $x^2 - 9x + 21 = 0$ $(9 \pm i\sqrt{3})/2$
34. $7n^2 + 20n - 32 = 0$ $\frac{8}{7}, -4$
35. $t^2 = 13t$ $0, 13$
36. $2z^2 + 2z + 3 = 0$ $(-1 \pm i\sqrt{5})/2$
37. $6t^2 - 2t + 1 = 0$ $(1 \pm i\sqrt{5})/6$
38. $7y^2 = y + 2$ $(1 \pm \sqrt{57})/14$
39. $5x^2 - x - 4 = 0$ $1, -\frac{4}{5}$
40. $24t = 7t^2$ $0, \frac{24}{7}$
41. $8r^2 + 6r + 1 = 0$ $-\frac{1}{2}, -\frac{1}{4}$
42. $3x^2 - 6x + 8 = 0$ $(3 \pm i\sqrt{15})/3$
43. Write a computer program to find the *real* roots only of quadratic equations.
    See Teacher's Guide for answer.

Excursions in Algebra

Perfect Numbers

Hrotsvitha (932–1002) was a nun who lived in a Benedictine Abbey in Saxony. She was one of the first persons to write about **perfect numbers.** A perfect number is one that is equal to the sum of its *aliquot* parts. That is, it is equal to the sum of all its factors including 1, but *not* including itself. Consider this example.

$$6 = \underbrace{1 + 2 + 3}_{\text{factors of 6, but not including 6}}$$

Hrotsvitha wrote about three perfect numbers other than 6, namely 28, 496, and 8128.

For answers to problems **2**, and **3**, see the Teacher's Guide.

Exercises **Show that each of the following are perfect numbers.**

1. $28 = 1 + 2 + 4 + 7 + 14$
2. 496
3. 8128

6-4 The Discriminant

Objective: To use the discriminant to describe the solutions of quadratic equations.

In the quadratic formula, the expression $b^2 - 4ac$ is called the **discriminant.** It can give information about the solutions of a quadratic equation.

Recall that all coefficients of quadratic equations discussed are real numbers.

example 1

Solve $x^2 - 14x + 49 = 0$ using the quadratic formula.

$$x = \frac{^-b \pm \sqrt{b^2 - 4ac}}{2a}$$

$$= \frac{^-(^-14) \pm \sqrt{(^-14)^2 - 4(1)(49)}}{2(1)} \qquad a = 1,\ b = {}^-14,\ c = 49$$

$$= \frac{14 \pm \sqrt{196 - 196}}{2}$$

$$= \frac{14 \pm \sqrt{0}}{2} \qquad \text{The value of the discriminant is 0.}$$

$$= 7$$

The equation $x^2 - 14x + 49 = 0$ has *only one solution*, 7. When the value of the discriminant is 0, the equation has only one solution.

example 2

Solve $2x^2 - 5x + 3 = 0$ using the quadratic formula.

$$x = \frac{^-b \pm \sqrt{b^2 - 4ac}}{2a}$$

$$= \frac{^-(^-5) \pm \sqrt{(^-5)^2 - 4(2)(3)}}{2(2)} \qquad a = 2,\ b = {}^-5,\ c = 3$$

$$= \frac{5 \pm \sqrt{25 - 24}}{4}$$

$$= \frac{5 \pm \sqrt{1}}{4} \qquad \text{The value of the discriminant is positive.}$$

$$= \frac{3}{2} \text{ or } 1$$

The equation $2x^2 - 5x + 3 = 0$ has *two real solutions*, $\frac{3}{2}$ and 1. When the value of the discriminant is positive, the equation has two real solutions.

example 3

Solve $3x^2 + 4x + 5 = 0$ using the quadratic formula.

$$x = \frac{^-b \pm \sqrt{b^2 - 4ac}}{2a}$$

$$= \frac{^-(4) \pm \sqrt{(4)^2 - 4(3)(5)}}{2(3)} \qquad a = 3,\ b = 4,\ c = 5$$

$$= \frac{^-4 \pm \sqrt{^-44}}{6} \qquad \text{The value of the discriminant is negative.}$$

$$= \frac{^-4 \pm 2i\sqrt{11}}{6}$$

$$= \frac{^-2 \pm i\sqrt{11}}{3}$$

The equation $3x^2 + 4x + 5 = 0$ has *two imaginary solutions*, $\frac{^-2 + i\sqrt{11}}{3}$ and $\frac{^-2 - i\sqrt{11}}{3}$. When the value of the discriminant is negative, the equation has two imaginary solutions.

The chart summarizes the information from the discriminant.

Discriminant	Solutions
positive	two real solutions
zero	one real solution
negative	two imaginary solutions

examples 4

Describe the nature of the solutions to $2x^2 - 11x + 13 = 0$.

$$\begin{aligned} b^2 - 4ac &= (^-11)^2 - 4(2)(13) \qquad a = 2,\ b = {}^-11,\ c = 13 \\ &= 121 - 104 \\ &= 17 \end{aligned}$$

The value of the discriminant is positive, so $2x^2 - 11x + 13 = 0$ has two real solutions.

5

Describe the nature of the solutions to $x^2 + 6x + 10 = 0$.

$$\begin{aligned} b^2 - 4ac &= (6)^2 - 4(1)(10) \qquad a = 1,\ b = 6,\ c = 10 \\ &= 36 - 40 \\ &= {}^-4 \end{aligned}$$

The value of the discriminant is negative, so $x^2 + 6x + 10 = 0$ has two imaginary solutions.

exercises

Max: 1–14, 1–40; Avg: 1–14, 1–39 odds; Min: 1–39 odds

Exploratory State the sign of the discriminant for each quadratic equation, then describe the nature of its solutions.

1. $x^2 + 5x - 2 = 0$ +, 2 real
2. $y^2 + 6y + 9 = 0$ 0, 1 real
3. $2x^2 - 5x + 3 = 0$ +, 2 real
4. $a^2 = 16$ +, 2 real
5. $t^2 - 8t + 16 = 0$ 0, 1 real
6. $5x^2 + 16x + 3 = 0$ +, 2 real
7. $2y^2 + y - 10 = 0$ +, 2 real
8. $6a^2 + 2a + 1 = 0$ −, 2 imaginary
9. $12a^2 - 7a + 1 = 0$ +, 2 real
10. $^-3x^2 + x - 2 = 0$ −, 2 imaginary
11. $x^2 + 4 = 0$ −, 2 imaginary
12. $3a^2 - a + 3 = 0$ −, 2 imaginary
13. $m^2 - 9 = 0$ +, 2 real
14. $3c^2 - 5c + 3 = 0$ −, 2 imaginary

Solutions are given. See Teacher's Guide for other answers.

Written State the value of the discriminant for each quadratic equation. Describe the nature of the solutions. Then solve each equation.

1. $x^2 - 2x - 35 = 0$ $7, ^-5$
2. $4x^2 + 8x + 3 = 0$ $-\frac{3}{2}, -\frac{1}{2}$
3. $x^2 - 4x + 4 = 0$ 2
4. $3t^2 + 20t = 7$ $^-7, \frac{1}{3}$
5. $x^2 - 2x + 5 = 0$ $1 \pm 2i$
6. $x^2 - 6x + 13 = 0$ $3 \pm 2i$
7. $2x^2 - 3x + 1 = 0$ $1, \frac{1}{2}$
8. $x^2 + 12x + 32 = 0$ $^-8, ^-4$
9. $2x^2 + 11x + 5 = 0$ $^-5, -\frac{1}{2}$
10. $x^2 + 4x - 21 = 0$ $^-7, 3$
11. $3y^2 + 11y - 4 = 0$ $^-4, \frac{1}{3}$
12. $x^2 - 10x + 25 = 0$ 5
13. $4x^2 - 8x + 13 = 0$ $(2 \pm 3i)/2$
14. $x^2 + 4x + 53 = 0$ $^-2 \pm 7i$
15. $y^2 + 11y + 24 = 0$ $^-8, ^-3$
16. $2a^2 - 13a = 7$ $7, -\frac{1}{2}$
17. $4y^2 - 9 = 0$ $\frac{3}{2}, -\frac{3}{2}$
18. $13x^2 - 20x + 13 = 0$ $(10 \pm i\sqrt{69})/13$
19. $3x^2 - 10x - 8 = 0$ $4, -\frac{2}{3}$
20. $a^2 + a - 56 = 0$ $^-8, 7$
21. $3x^2 - 19x + 6 = 0$ $6, \frac{1}{3}$
22. $x^2 - 12x = 0$ $0, 12$
23. $x^2 - 8x + 25 = 0$ $4 \pm 3i$
24. $x^2 - 3x + \frac{5}{2} = 0$ $(3 \pm i)/2$
25. $c^2 - 13c + 42 = 0$ $7, 6$
26. $3a^2 + 7a + 4 = 0$ $^-1, -\frac{4}{3}$
27. $2x^2 + 7x - 4 = 0$ $^-4, \frac{1}{2}$
28. $3a^2 + 22a + 7 = 0$ $^-7, -\frac{1}{3}$
29. $x^2 + x + \frac{1}{4} = 0$ $-\frac{1}{2}$
30. $x^2 - 35 = 0$ $\pm\sqrt{35}$
31. $x^2 - x + 1 = 0$ $(1 \pm i\sqrt{3})/2$
32. $x^2 + 4x + 29 = 0$ $^-2 \pm 5i$
33. $4a^2 + 16a + 15 = 0$ $-\frac{3}{2}, -\frac{5}{2}$
34. $2x^2 + 15x = 8$ $\frac{1}{2}, ^-8$
35. $y^2 = 6y$ $0, 6$
36. $16n^2 + 8n = ^-1$ $-\frac{1}{4}$
37. $y^2 - \frac{1}{4}y = \frac{1}{8}$ $\frac{1}{2}, -\frac{1}{4}$
38. $c^2 + \frac{1}{15}c - \frac{2}{15} = 0$ $\frac{1}{3}, -\frac{2}{5}$
39. Write a computer program to find the value of the discriminant for given quadratic equations. The program should print the value of the discriminant and describe the nature of the solutions for each equation. See Teacher's Guide.
40. Write a computer program that will solve any quadratic equation using the quadratic formula. Be sure to print out complex solutions if they exist. See Teacher's Guide.

6-5 Sum and Product of Solutions

Objective: To use the sum and product of solutions to quadratic equations.

Sometimes an equation must be found to fit certain conditions. For example, suppose you know that the solutions of a quadratic equation are 5 and $^-7$. Find the quadratic equation.

Let x stand for a solution to the equation. Then $x = 5$ or $x = {}^-7$. If $x = 5$, then $x - 5 = 0$. If $x = {}^-7$, then $x + 7 = 0$.

$$(x - 5)(x + 7) = 0 \qquad \textit{Why?}$$
$$x^2 + 2x - 35 = 0$$

The quadratic equation $x^2 + 2x - 35 = 0$ has solutions 5 and $^-7$. Solve that equation as a check.

Consider the sum and product of 5 and $^-7$.

$$\text{sum} = 5 + {}^-7 = {}^-2 \qquad \text{product} = 5 \cdot {}^-7 = {}^-35$$

How are the sum and product related to $x^2 + 2x - 35 = 0$?

Suppose you know that the solutions of a quadratic equation are r and s. Find the quadratic equation.

Let x stand for a solution to the equation. Then $x = r$ or $x = s$. If $x = r$, then $x - r = 0$. If $x = s$, then $x - s = 0$.

$$(x - r)(x - s) = 0 \qquad \textit{Why?}$$
$$x^2 - xs - xr + rs = 0$$
$$x^2 - (s + r)x + rs = 0$$

The quadratic equation $x^2 - (s + r)x + rs = 0$ has solutions r and s. How are the sum and product of r and s related to this equation?

The general quadratic equation is usually written as $ax^2 + bx + c = 0$, $a \neq 0$. Since a is not zero, you can divide both sides of the equation by a.

$$ax^2 + bx + c = 0$$
$$(ax^2 + bx + c) \div a = 0 \div a \qquad \textit{Divide both sides by } a.$$
$$x^2 + \frac{b}{a}x + \frac{c}{a} = 0$$

By comparing $x^2 + \frac{b}{a}x + \frac{c}{a} = 0$ and $x^2 - (s + r)x + rs = 0$, you can draw the following conclusion.

Sum and Product of Solutions

The solutions to $ax^2 + bx + c = 0$ with $a \neq 0$ are r and s if and only if the following is true.

$$r + s = -\frac{b}{a} \text{ and } rs = \frac{c}{a}$$

examples

1 **Find a quadratic equation that has solutions $5 + 2i$ and $5 - 2i$.**

$$\text{sum} = (5 + 2i) + (5 - 2i)$$
$$= 10 \qquad -\frac{b}{a} \text{ is } 10$$
$$\text{product} = (5 + 2i)(5 - 2i)$$
$$= 25 - 10i + 10i - 4i^2$$
$$= 29 \qquad \frac{c}{a} \text{ is } 29$$

The equation is $x^2 - 10x + 29 = 0$.

2 **Are 2 and 7 solutions of $y^2 + 9y + 14 = 0$?**

$$\text{sum} = 2 + 7 \qquad a = 1, b = 9, c = 14$$
$$= 9 \qquad -\frac{b}{a} = -\frac{9}{1} = {}^-9$$
$$\text{product} = 2 \cdot 7 \qquad \frac{c}{a} = \frac{14}{1} = 14$$
$$= 14$$

The sum does *not* equal the value of $-\frac{b}{a}$. Thus, 2 and 7 are not *both* solutions.

exercises

Max: 1–15, 1–52, Challenge; **Avg:** 1–15, 1–51 odds; **Min:** 1–51 odds

Exploratory State the sum and the product of the solutions of each quadratic equation.

1. $x^2 + 7x - 4 = 0$ $^-7, {}^-4$
2. $x^2 + 8x + 7 = 0$ $^-8, 7$
3. $x^2 - 3x + 5 = 0$ $3, 5$
4. $2x^2 + 8x - 3 = 0$ $^-4, -\frac{3}{2}$
5. $3x^2 + 7x - 9 = 0$ $-\frac{7}{3}, {}^-3$
6. $2x^2 + 7 = 0$ $0, \frac{7}{2}$
7. $5x^2 - 3x = 0$ $\frac{3}{5}, 0$
8. $4x^2 + 3x - 12 = 0$ $-\frac{3}{4}, {}^-3$
9. $5x^2 = 3$ $0, -\frac{3}{5}$
10. $2x^2 + 9x = 0$ $-\frac{9}{2}, 0$
11. $3x^2 - 2x + 11 = 0$ $\frac{2}{3}, \frac{11}{3}$
12. $7x^2 = 0$ $0, 0$
13. $2x^2 - \frac{1}{2}x + \frac{2}{3} = 0$ $\frac{1}{4}, \frac{1}{3}$
14. $x^2 + 4x - \frac{5}{3} = 0$ $^-4, -\frac{5}{3}$
15. In $ax^2 + bx + c = 0$, if $b = 0$, what do you know about the solutions? They are additive inverses. If $c = 0$, what do you know about the solutions? One solution is zero.

Written Find the sum and the product of the solutions of each quadratic equation. Then solve each equation.

1. $x^2 + 6x - 7 = 0$ $^-6; {}^-7; {}^-7, 1$
2. $2x^2 - 5x - 3 = 0$ $\frac{5}{2}; -\frac{3}{2}; 3, -\frac{1}{2}$
3. $y^2 + 5y + 6 = 0$ $^-5; 6; {}^-3, {}^-2$
4. $6m^2 - 17m + 6 = 0$ $\frac{17}{6}; 1; (17 \pm \sqrt{145})/12$

5. $x^2 - 3x + 1 = 0$ $3; 1; (3 \pm \sqrt{5})/2$

6. $2x^2 - 5x + 1 = 0$ $\frac{5}{2}; \frac{1}{2}; (5 \pm \sqrt{17})/4$

7. $3c^2 - 8c - 35 = 0$ $\frac{8}{3}; -\frac{35}{3}; 5, -\frac{7}{3}$

8. $4a^2 + 21a = 18$ $-\frac{21}{4}; -\frac{9}{2}; \frac{3}{4}, {}^-6$

9. $2x^2 - 6x + 5 = 0$ $3; \frac{5}{2}; (3 \pm i)/2$

10. $a^2 - a - 30 = 0$ $1; {}^-30; 6, {}^-5$

11. $9x^2 + 9x = 10$ ${}^-1; -\frac{10}{9}; \frac{2}{3}, -\frac{5}{3}$

12. $x^2 - 16 = 0$ $0; {}^-16; 4, {}^-4$

13. $2x^2 - 7x = 15$ $\frac{7}{2}; -\frac{15}{2}; 5, -\frac{3}{2}$

14. $8x^2 + 6x + 1 = 0$ $-\frac{3}{4}; \frac{1}{8}; -\frac{1}{2}, -\frac{1}{4}$

15. $15c^2 - 2c - 8 = 0$ $\frac{2}{15}; -\frac{8}{15}; \frac{4}{5}, -\frac{2}{3}$

16. $x^2 + 9x + 25 = 0$ ${}^-9; 25; ({}^-9 \pm i\sqrt{19})/2$

17. $a^2 + 2a - 24 = 0$ ${}^-2; {}^-24; {}^-6, 4$

18. $3x^2 - 5x + 2 = 0$ $\frac{5}{3}; \frac{2}{3}; 1, \frac{2}{3}$

19. $5x^2 - 2x + 6 = 0$ $\frac{2}{5}; \frac{6}{5}; (1 \pm i\sqrt{29})/5$

20. $x^2 + 4x - 77 = 0$ ${}^-4; {}^-77; 7, {}^-11$

21. $6t^2 + 28t - 10 = 0$ $-\frac{14}{3}; -\frac{5}{3}; {}^-5, \frac{1}{3}$

22. $3x^2 - 7x + 3 = 0$ $\frac{7}{3}; 1; (7 \pm \sqrt{13})/6$

23. $y^2 + 25y + 156 = 0$ ${}^-25; 156; {}^-13, {}^-12$

24. $7s^2 + 5s - 1 = 0$ $-\frac{5}{7}; -\frac{1}{7}; ({}^-5 \pm \sqrt{53})/14$

25. $12x^2 + 19x + 4 = 0$ $-\frac{19}{12}; \frac{1}{3}; -\frac{1}{4}, -\frac{4}{3}$

26. $8x^2 + 9 = 18x$ $\frac{9}{4}; \frac{9}{8}; \frac{3}{2}, \frac{3}{4}$

27. $3x^2 - 7x + 5 = 0$ $\frac{7}{3}; \frac{5}{3}; (7 \pm i\sqrt{11})/6$

28. $4k^2 + 27k - 7 = 0$ $-\frac{27}{4}; -\frac{7}{4}; \frac{1}{4}, {}^-7$

Find quadratic equations with the following solutions.

29. $8, {}^-2$ $x^2 - 6x - 16 = 0$

30. $5, {}^-2$ $x^2 - 3x - 10 = 0$

31. $6, 4$ $x^2 - 10x + 24 = 0$

32. ${}^-2, 3$ $x^2 - x - 6 = 0$

33. $6, {}^-6$ $x^2 - 36 = 0$

34. ${}^-9, {}^-4$ $x^2 + 13x + 36 = 0$

35. $3, \frac{1}{2}$ $2x^2 - 7x + 3 = 0$

36. $5, \frac{2}{3}$ $3x^2 - 17x + 10 = 0$

37. $-\frac{3}{4}, 12$ $4x^2 - 45x - 36 = 0$

38. $-\frac{1}{2}, \frac{1}{2}$ $4x^2 - 1 = 0$

39. $\frac{1}{3}, \frac{1}{2}$ $6x^2 - 5x + 1 = 0$

40. $\frac{3}{4}, {}^-4$ $4x^2 + 13x - 12 = 0$

41. $\frac{5}{8}, \frac{1}{4}$ $32x^2 - 28x + 5 = 0$

42. $-\frac{2}{5}, \frac{2}{5}$ $25x^2 - 4 = 0$

43. $\frac{7}{8}, -\frac{7}{8}$ $64x^2 - 49 = 0$

44. $\sqrt{3}, 2\sqrt{3}$

45. $2 + \sqrt{3}, 2 - \sqrt{3}$

46. $3i, {}^-3i$

47. $2 + 5i, 2 - 5i$

48. $3 + 7i, 3 - 7i$

49. $5 + 2i\sqrt{3}, 5 - 2i\sqrt{3}$

50. $8 - \sqrt{5}, \sqrt{5}$

51. $\frac{1 + \sqrt{7}}{2}, \frac{1 - \sqrt{7}}{2}$

52. $\frac{5 - 3i}{4}, \frac{5 + 3i}{4}$

For answers to problems **44–52**, see Teacher's Guide.

Challenge Solve each of the following.

1. Find k such that ${}^-1$ is a solution to $x^2 + kx - 7 = 0$. $k = {}^-6$
2. Find k such that the solutions to $x^2 + kx + 24 = 0$ are in the ratio of 2 to 3. $k = 10$ or $k = {}^-10$

Excursions in Algebra

Contest Problem

The following problem appeared in a high school contest of the Mathematical Association of America.

Suppose r and s are solutions to the equation $ax^2 + bx + c = 0$. Find the value of $\frac{r^2 + s^2}{r^2s^2}$ in terms of a, b, and c. (Hint: $r^2 + s^2 = (r + s)^2 - 2rs$) $\frac{b^2 - 2ac}{c^2}$

Free Checking Accounts

Some banks offer free checking accounts if you maintain a minimum balance. Dick Gallegez wondered if this is really a "gimmick." He might do better to use a regular account, put the minimum amount in savings, and collect interest.

Example Dick's bank offers free checking if a minimum of $200 is kept on deposit. If not, the bank charges $1.50 plus a service charge of 5¢ per check. Would he do better with free checking or with savings at 5% interest?

First, he finds the bank charges on a regular checking account. Dick writes about 20 checks a month.

$$\begin{array}{r} 20 \\ \times\ \$0.05 \\ \hline \$1.00 \end{array} \quad \textit{number of checks} \qquad\qquad \begin{array}{r} \$1.00 \\ +\ \$1.50 \\ \hline \$2.50 \end{array} \quad \begin{array}{l} \textit{charge for checks} \\ \textit{fixed charge} \\ \textit{total charges} \end{array}$$

The free checking would save about $2.50 each month.

Now, compare this with what the minimum balance of $200 would earn at 5% interest.

$$\begin{aligned} i &= p \cdot r \cdot t \\ &= 200 \cdot 0.05 \cdot \frac{1}{12} \qquad \textit{One month} = \frac{1}{12}\textit{ year.} \\ &\approx 0.83 \end{aligned}$$

He could earn about $0.83 a month interest. In this example, free checking would be better.

Exercises Find out if free checking would be better in each of the following situations.

1. The bank charges a flat rate of $2.00 on all accounts with minimum balances less than $300. You could earn 6% interest if the minimum balance were in savings. yes
2. The bank charges a minimum of $2.50 or 5¢ a check, whichever is greater. The minimum for free checking is $250. You write about 30 checks a month and could earn $5\frac{1}{2}$% interest on money in savings. yes
3. The bank charges $1.00 per month or 10¢ a check, whichever is greater, if the minimum balance is less than $250. You could earn 6% interest if the minimum balance were in savings and write about 15 checks per month. yes
4. The bank charges $3.00 per month on all accounts in which the minimum balance is less than $300. You could earn 7% interest on a long-term savings deposit. yes

6-6 Using Quadratic Equations

Objective: To use quadratic equations to solve problems.

Sometimes a drawing will help you write an equation to solve a problem. Consider the following problem.

> The Pinetown Recreation Bureau planned to build an ice-skating rink with dimensions 30 meters by 60 meters. Their budget has been cut, so they must reduce the area of the rink to 1000 square meters. A strip will be removed from one end, and a strip of the same width will be removed from one side. Find the width of the strips.

Define a variable. The problem asks for the width of the strips. Let w stand for the width of the strips.

Make a drawing.

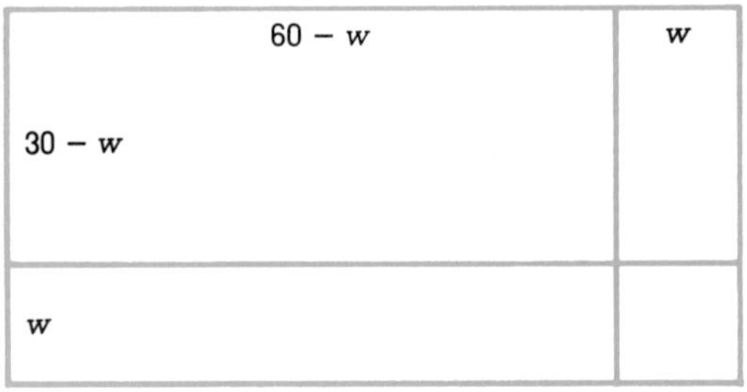

Write an equation.

$$\textit{length} \cdot \textit{width} = \textit{area}$$

$$(30 - w)(60 - w) = 1000$$

Solve the equation.

$$\begin{aligned}(30 - w)(60 - w) &= 1000\\ 1800 - 30w - 60w + w^2 &= 1000\\ 1800 - 90w + w^2 &= 1000\\ 800 - 90w + w^2 &= 0\\ (10 - w)(80 - w) &= 0\end{aligned}$$

$$10 - w = 0 \quad \text{or} \quad 80 - w = 0$$
$$10 = w \quad \text{or} \quad 80 = w$$

Answer the problem. Each strip will be 10 meters wide.

Always check all solutions to a problem!

There are two solutions to the equation, 10 and 80. But only one, 10, can be used in answering the problem. The other solution, 80, is not a reasonable answer. Why? Both dimensions of the rink are less than 80 m at the start.

exercises

Max: 1–12; Avg: 1–11 odds; Min: 1–11 odds

Written Solve each problem.

1. Find two consecutive integers whose product is 702. 26, 27 or $^-26$, $^-27$
2. Find two consecutive even integers whose product is 288. 16, 18 or $^-18$, $^-16$
3. Find two consecutive odd integers whose product is 1443. 37, 39 or $^-39$, $^-37$
4. Find two consecutive integers whose product is 552. 23, 24 or $^-24$, $^-23$
5. If the product of two consecutive odd integers is decreased by one-third the smaller integer, the result is 250. 15, 17
6. If the product of two consecutive integers is decreased by 20 times the larger integer, the result is 442. 33, 34 or $^-14$, $^-13$
7. Find two consecutive even integers whose sum of their squares is 244. 10, 12 or $^-12$, $^-10$
8. Three times the square of a number equals 24 times the number. Find the number. 8 or 0
9. A local park is 30 meters long by 20 meters wide. Plans are being made to double the area by adding a strip at one end and another of the same width on one side. Find the width of the strips. 10 meters
10. Jackie Ruben is building a children's playhouse. She wants each window to have an area of 315 square inches for adequate air. For eye appeal, she wants each window to be six inches higher than wide. What are the dimensions of each window? 15 inches by 21 inches
11. The length of Hillcrest Park is 6 feet more than its width. A walkway 3 feet wide surrounds the outside of the park. The total area of the walkway is 288 square feet. Find the dimensions of the park. 18 feet by 24 feet
12. A rectangular picture is 12 by 16 inches. If a frame of uniform width contains an area of 165 square inches, what is the width of the frame? 2.5 inches

Excursions in Algebra

Handshakes

At the conclusion of a committee meeting, a total of 28 handshakes were exchanged. Assuming each person was equally polite toward all the others, how many people were present? (Hint: Assume n persons were at the meeting. With how many persons did each person shake hands? Use a quadratic equation.)
$n(n - 1)/2 = 28$; 8

6–7 Quadratic Form

Objective: To solve higher degree equations which are in quadratic form.

The equation $x^4 - 20x^2 + 64 = 0$ is not a quadratic equation. But it looks very much like a quadratic equation. It is in **quadratic form.**

Definition of Quadratic Form

For any numbers a, b, and c, except $a = 0$, an equation that may be written as $a[f(x)]^2 + b[f(x)] + c = 0$, where $f(x)$ is some expression in x, is in quadratic form.

In an equation such as $x^2 + 2x + 1 = 0$, $f(x)$ is just x.

An equation in quadratic form can be solved by the same methods used for solving quadratic equations.

examples

1 **Solve $x^4 - 13x^2 + 36 = 0$.**

$$x^4 - 13x^2 + 36 = 0$$
$$(x^2 - 9)(x^2 - 4) = 0$$
$$(x + 3)(x - 3)(x + 2)(x - 2) = 0$$
$$x + 3 = 0 \quad \text{or} \quad x - 3 = 0 \quad \text{or} \quad x + 2 = 0 \quad \text{or} \quad x - 2 = 0$$
$$x = {}^-3 \quad \text{or} \quad x = 3 \quad \text{or} \quad x = {}^-2 \quad \text{or} \quad x = 2$$

The solutions are $^-3$, 3, $^-2$, and 2.

2 **Solve $x^4 - 20x^2 + 64 = 0$.**

$$x^4 - 20x^2 + 64 = 0$$
$$(x^2)^2 - 20x^2 + 64 = 0$$ *The equation is in quadratic form.*

$$x^2 = \frac{{}^-b \pm \sqrt{b^2 - 4ac}}{2a}$$ *The equation is quadratic in x^2.*

$$= \frac{{}^-({}^-20) \pm \sqrt{({}^-20)^2 - 4(1)(64)}}{2(1)}$$ *$a = 1$, $b = {}^-20$, $c = 64$*

$$= \frac{20 \pm \sqrt{400 - 256}}{2}$$
$$= \frac{20 \pm \sqrt{144}}{2}$$
$$= \frac{20 \pm 12}{2}$$
$$x^2 = 16 \quad \text{or} \quad x^2 = 4$$
$$x = {}^\pm 4 \quad \text{or} \quad x = {}^\pm 2$$

The solutions are 4, $^-4$, 2 and $^-2$.

example 3

Solve $x - 7\sqrt{x} - 8 = 0$.

$$x - 7\sqrt{x} - 8 = 0$$

$$(\sqrt{x})^2 - 7(\sqrt{x}) - 8 = 0 \qquad f(x) = \sqrt{x}$$

$$\sqrt{x} = \frac{^-b \pm \sqrt{b^2 - 4ac}}{2a}$$

$$= \frac{^-(^-7) \pm \sqrt{(^-7)^2 - 4(1)(^-8)}}{2(1)} \qquad a = 1, b = {^-7}, c = {^-8}$$

$$= \frac{7 \pm \sqrt{81}}{2}$$

$$= \frac{7 \pm 9}{2}$$

$$\sqrt{x} = 8 \quad \text{or} \quad \sqrt{x} = {^-1}$$

$$x = 64 \quad \text{or} \quad x = 1$$

Check:

$$x - 7\sqrt{x} - 8 = 0$$
$$64 - 7\sqrt{64} - 8 \stackrel{?}{=} 0$$
$$64 - 7 \cdot 8 - 8 \stackrel{?}{=} 0$$
$$64 - 56 - 8 \stackrel{?}{=} 0$$
$$0 = 0$$

$$x - 7\sqrt{x} - 8 = 0$$
$$1 - 7\sqrt{1} - 8 \stackrel{?}{=} 0$$
$$1 - 7 - 8 \stackrel{?}{=} 0$$
$$^-14 \neq 0$$

The solution is 64.

exercises

Max: 1–16, 1–20; Avg: 1–16, 1–19 odds; Min: 1–19 odds

Exploratory State whether or not each equation is in quadratic form.

1. $x^4 + 5x^2 + 3 = 0$
2. $4y^4 - 3y^2 + 2 = 0$
3. $6x^4 + 7x - 8 = 0$
4. $6x^4 + 8x^2 = 0$
5. $6x + 5\sqrt{x} - 2 = 0$
6. $2p + 5\sqrt{p} = 9$
7. $5r^4 - 3r^3 + 2r = 0$
8. $x^4 + 5x - 4 = 0$
9. $x\sqrt{x} + 6x = 7\sqrt{x}$
10. $5x^4 = 2x^2 + 1$
11. $9q^4 = 4$
12. $3p = \sqrt{p}$
13. $m^4 + 9m^2 + 18 = 0$
14. $t^5 - 2t^3 - t = 0$
15. $3x^4 = x^2$
16. $x^4 - 11x^2 + 24 = 0$

Written Solve each equation.

1. $x^4 - 5x^2 + 4 = 0$ $\quad {^\pm 2}, {^\pm 1}$
2. $x^4 - 3x^2 + 2 = 0$ $\quad {^\pm 1}, \pm\sqrt{2}$
3. $x^4 - 25x^2 + 144 = 0$ $\quad {^\pm 4}, {^\pm 3}$
4. $x^4 - 40x^2 + 144 = 0$ $\quad {^\pm 6}, {^\pm 2}$
5. $x^4 - 26x^2 + 25 = 0$ $\quad {^\pm 5}, {^\pm 1}$
6. $x^4 - 16 = 0$ $\quad 2, {^-2}, 2i, {^-2i}$
7. $x^4 + 9x^2 + 18 = 0$ $\quad {^\pm i\sqrt{3}}, {^\pm i\sqrt{6}}$
8. $x^4 - 25 = 0$ $\quad \pm\sqrt{5}, {^\pm i\sqrt{5}}$
9. $x^4 - 9 = 0$ $\quad \pm\sqrt{3}, {^\pm i\sqrt{3}}$
10. $x^4 - 2x^2 - 8 = 0$ $\quad {^\pm 2}, {^\pm i\sqrt{2}}$
11. $x^4 - 6x^2 + 8 = 0$ $\quad {^\pm 2}, \pm\sqrt{2}$
12. $x^4 - 11x^2 + 24 = 0$ $\quad {^\pm 2\sqrt{2}}, \pm\sqrt{3}$
13. $x^4 - 9x^2 = 0$ $\quad 0, 3, {^-3}$
14. $x^4 - 36 = 0$ $\quad \pm\sqrt{6}, {^\pm i\sqrt{6}}$
15. $x - 9\sqrt{x} + 8 = 0$ $\quad 64, 1$
16. $x - 13\sqrt{x} + 36 = 0$ $\quad 81, 16$
17. $x - 2\sqrt{x} + 1 = 0$ $\quad 1$
18. $x - 16\sqrt{x} + 64 = 0$ $\quad 64$
19. $x - 64\sqrt{x} = 0$ $\quad 0, 4096$
20. $x^4 = 64$ $\quad {^\pm 2\sqrt{2}}, {^\pm 2i\sqrt{2}}$

Vocabulary

quadratic equation (166)
zero product property (166)
completing the square (168)
quadratic formula (172)
discriminant (175)
quadratic form (184)

Chapter Summary

1. Zero Product Property: For any numbers a and b, if $ab = 0$, then $a = 0$ or $b = 0$. (166)
2. Completing the square can be used to solve quadratic equations. (168)
3. Quadratic Formula: The solutions of a quadratic equation of the form $ax^2 + bx + c = 0$ with $a \neq 0$ are given by the following formula.

$$x = \frac{^{-}b \pm \sqrt{b^2 - 4ac}}{2a} \quad (172)$$

4. The discriminant, $b^2 - 4ac$, gives information about the solutions of a quadratic equation. (176)

Discriminant	Solutions
positive	two real solutions
zero	one real solution
negative	two imaginary solutions

5. The solutions to $ax^2 + bx + c = 0$, with $a \neq 0$, are r and s if and only if the following is true.

$$r + s = -\frac{b}{a} \text{ and } rs = \frac{c}{a} \quad (178)$$

6. Definition of Quadratic Form: For any numbers a, b, and c, except $a = 0$, an equation that may be written as $a[f(x)]^2 + b[f(x)] + c = 0$, where $f(x)$ is some expression in x, is in quadratic form. (184)
7. An equation in quadratic form can be solved by the same methods used for solving quadratic equations. (184)

Chapter Review

6-1 Solve each equation.

1. $(2x + 3)(3x - 1) = 0$ $-\frac{3}{2}, \frac{1}{3}$
2. $(x + 7)(4x - 5) = 0$ $^-7, \frac{5}{4}$
3. $2x^2 + 5x + 3 = 0$ $-\frac{3}{2}, ^-1$
4. $2x^2 + 9x + 4 = 0$ $-\frac{1}{2}, ^-4$
5. $15a^2 + 13a = 6$ $-\frac{6}{5}, \frac{1}{3}$
6. $8b^2 + 10b = 3$ $\frac{1}{4}, -\frac{3}{2}$

6-2 Find the value of c that makes each trinomial a perfect square.

7. $x^2 + 14x + c$ 49
8. $a^2 - 7a + c$ $\frac{49}{4}$

Solve by completing the square.

9. $x^2 - 20x + 75 = 0$ 15, 5
10. $x^2 - 5x - 24 = 0$ 8, $^-3$
11. $2t^2 + t - 21 = 0$ $-\frac{7}{2}$, 3
12. $r^2 + 4r = 96$ $^-12$, 8

6-3 Solve each equation using the quadratic formula.

13. $3x^2 - 11x + 10 = 0$ 2, $\frac{5}{3}$
14. $4x^2 - 12x = 0$ 0, 3
15. $2p^2 - 7p - 9 = 0$ $\frac{9}{2}, ^-1$
16. $2q^2 - 5q + 4 = 0$ $(5 \pm i\sqrt{7})/4$

6-4 State the value of the discriminant for each quadratic equation. Describe the nature of the solutions.

17. $4x^2 - 40x + 25 = 0$ 1200, 2 real
18. $2y^2 + 6y + 5 = 0$ $^-4$, 2 imaginary
19. $n^2 = 8n - 16$ 0, 1 real
20. $7b^2 = 4b$ 16, 2 real

6-5 Find the sum and the product of the solutions for each quadratic equation.

21. $x^2 - 12x - 45 = 0$ 12, $^-45$
22. $2m^2 - 10m + 9 = 0$ 5, $\frac{9}{2}$
23. $3s^2 - 11 = 0$ $\pm\sqrt{33}/3$
24. $2x^2 = 3 - 5x$ $-\frac{5}{2}, -\frac{3}{2}$

Find quadratic equations with the following solutions.

25. 4, $^-6$ $x^2 + 2x - 24 = 0$
26. $\frac{3}{4}, \frac{1}{3}$ $12x^2 - 13x + 3 = 0$
27. $5 - 3i, 5 + 3i$ $x^2 - 10x + 34 = 0$
28. $2 - \sqrt{3}, 2 + \sqrt{3}$ $x^2 - 4x + 1 = 0$

6-6 Solve each problem.

29. The square of a number decreased by twenty times that number is 384. Find the number. 32 or $^-12$
30. Find five consecutive integers such that the sum of the squares of the smallest and largest is 208. See below.
31. A rectangular lawn has dimensions 24 feet by 32 feet. A sidewalk will be constructed along the inside edges of all four sides. The remaining lawn will have an area of 425 square feet. The walk will be how wide? 3.5 feet (24.5 is *not* a reasonable answer.)

6-7 Solve each equation.

32. $x^4 - 8x^2 + 16 = 0$ $^\pm2$
33. $x^4 - 12x^2 + 27 = 0$ $^\pm3, \pm\sqrt{3}$
34. $p - 4\sqrt{p} - 45 = 0$ 81
35. $r + 9\sqrt{r} = ^-8$ no solutions

30. 8, 9, 10, 11, 12 or $^-12, ^-11, ^-10, ^-9, ^-8$

Chapter Test

Solve each equation.

1. $x^2 + 8x - 33 = 0$ $^-11, 3$
2. $6y^2 - y - 15 = 0$ $-\frac{3}{2}, \frac{5}{3}$
3. $x^2 - 6x + 8 = 0$ $4, 2$
4. $y^2 + 7y - 18 = 0$ $^-9, 2$
5. $3x^2 + x - 14 = 0$ $2, -\frac{7}{3}$
6. $12x^2 - 5x = 3$ $-\frac{1}{3}, \frac{3}{4}$
7. $5x^2 - 125 = 0$ $^{\pm}5$
8. $4x^2 = 324$ $^{\pm}9$
9. $x^2 + 6x - 216 = 0$ $^-18, 12$
10. $3x^2 + 4x + 2 = 0$ $(^-2 \pm i\sqrt{2})/3$
11. $x^4 - 9x^2 + 20 = 0$ $^{\pm}2, \pm\sqrt{5}$
12. $x - 9\sqrt{x} + 8 = 0$ $64, 1$
13. $2x + 3\sqrt{x} = 9$ $\frac{9}{4}$
14. $x^4 - 11x^2 - 80 = 0$ $^{\pm}4, ^{\pm}i\sqrt{5}$

Find the value of c that makes each trinomial a perfect square.

15. $n^2 + 6n + c$ 9
16. $x^2 - 5x + c$ $\frac{25}{4}$

State the value of the discriminant for each quadratic equation. Describe the nature of the solutions.

17. $6x^2 + 7x - 5 = 0$ 169, 2 real
18. $2y^2 - 9y + 11 = 0$ $^-7$, 2 imaginary
19. $9a^2 - 30a + 25 = 0$ 0, 1 real
20. $7m^2 = 4m$ 16, 2 real

Find the sum and the product of the solutions for each quadratic equation.

21. $x^2 - 15x + 56 = 0$ $15, 56$
22. $2x^2 - 3x - 12 = 0$ $\frac{3}{2}, ^-6$
23. $x + 7 = 4x^2$ $\frac{1}{4}, -\frac{7}{4}$
24. $2x^2 = 3 - 5x$ $-\frac{5}{2}, -\frac{3}{2}$

Find quadratic equations with the following solutions.

25. $0, ^-3$ $x^2 + 3x = 0$
26. $8, ^-3$ $x^2 - 5x - 24 = 0$
27. $\frac{4}{3}, \frac{2}{3}$ $9x^2 - 18x + 8 = 0$
28. $5 + 2i, 5 - 2i$ $x^2 - 10x + 29 = 0$

29. The sum of the squares of two consecutive odd integers is 1154. Find the integers. 23, 25 or $^-25, ^-23$
30. The Dolphin Pool Company will build a pool for Sally Wadman having 600 square feet of surface. Ms. Wadman's pool, with a deck of uniform width, has dimensions 30 feet by 40 feet. What will be the width of the decking around the pool?
    5 feet (30 is *not* a reasonable answer.)

Chapter 7

Quadratic Relations and Functions

Many architectural designs have the shape of mathematical curves. In this chapter, you will study the equations and graphs for some of these curves.

7-1 Quadratic Functions

Objective: To identify quadratic functions

$f(x) = bx + c$ describes a linear function.

A rocket is launched with an initial velocity of 50 meters per second. The height, h, of the rocket t seconds after blast-off is given by the equation $h(t) = 50t - 5t^2$. This equation is an example of a quadratic equation. Quadratic equations are used to describe **quadratic functions.**

Definition of Quadratic Function

A quadratic function is a function described by an equation of the form $f(x) = ax^2 + bx + c$ where $a \neq 0$.

$f(x) = c$ describes a constant function.

The term ax^2 is called the *quadratic term.* The term bx is the *linear term.* The term c is the *constant term.*

examples

1 **Write $f(x) = (x + 3)^2 + 5$ in quadratic form. Identify the quadratic term, the linear term, and the constant term.**

$$\begin{aligned} f(x) &= (x + 3)^2 + 5 \\ &= x^2 + 6x + 9 + 5 \\ &= x^2 + 6x + 14 \end{aligned}$$

The quadratic term is x^2.
The linear term is $6x$.
The constant term is 14.

2 **A theater has seats for 500 people. It is filled to capacity for each show and tickets cost \$3.00 per show. The owner wants to increase ticket prices. She estimates that for each \$0.20 increase in price, 25 fewer people will attend. Write a quadratic equation to describe the owner's income after she increases her prices.**

Let p = number of \$0.20 price increases.
Then $3.00 + 0.20p$ = ticket price.
And $500 - 25p$ = number tickets sold.

Income = (number of tickets sold) · (ticket price)

$$\begin{aligned} I &= (500 - 25p) \cdot (3.00 + 0.20p) \\ &= 1500 + 100p - 75p - 5p^2 \\ &= 1500 + 25p - 5p^2 \end{aligned}$$

exercises

Max: 1–20, 1–14; Avg: 1–20, 1–13 odds; Min: 1–13 odds

Exploratory State whether each of the following equations is quadratic or not.

1. $f(x) = x^2 + 3x + 5$
2. $f(x) = {}^-3x^2 - 8x - 7$
3. $f(x) = 2x - 6$
4. $f(x) = (x - 4)^2$
5. $g(x) = {}^-3(x - 4)^2 - 6$
6. $p(x) = x + 1$
7. $m(x) = 3x^2$
8. $r(s) = s^2 + 2s$
9. $f(x) = \frac{1}{x^2} + \frac{1}{x} + 1$
10. $g(x) = -\frac{1}{3}x + \frac{4}{5}$

For each equation identify the quadratic term, the linear term, and the constant term.

11. $f(x) = x^2 + 3x - \frac{1}{4}$ x^2; $3x$; $-\frac{1}{4}$
12. $f(x) = 4x^2 - 8x - 2$ $4x^2$; ${}^-8x$; ${}^-2$
13. $m(x) = x^2 - 3x - \frac{1}{4}$ x^2; ${}^-3x$; $-\frac{1}{4}$
14. $g(p) = \frac{1}{3}p^2 + 4$ $\frac{1}{3}p^2$; 0; 4
15. $g(a) = 3a^2 - 2$ $3a^2$; 0; ${}^-2$
16. $n(x) = {}^-4x^2 - 8x - 9$ ${}^-4x^2$; ${}^-8x$; ${}^-9$
17. $z = x^2 + 3x$ x^2; $3x$; 0
18. $q = {}^-4x^2 - 2x$ ${}^-4x^2$; ${}^-2x$; 0
19. $h(x) = (x + 3)^2$ x^2; $6x$; 9
20. $h(x) = (2x - 5)^2$ $4x^2$; ${}^-20x$; 25

Written Write each equation in quadratic form.

1. $f(x) = (x - 2)^2$ $f(x) = x^2 - 4x + 4$
2. $f(x) = 3(x + 4)^2$ $f(x) = 3x^2 + 24x + 48$
3. $f(x) = {}^-4(2x - 4)^2$ $f(x) = {}^-16x^2 + 64x - 64$
4. $f(x) = (x + 2)^2 + 8$ $f(x) = x^2 + 4x + 12$
5. $f(x) = {}^-3(x - 4)^2 - 6$ $f(x) = {}^-3x^2 + 24x - 54$
6. $f(x) = \frac{1}{5}(10x - 5)^2$ $f(x) = 20x^2 - 20x + 5$
7. Write a quadratic equation to describe the area of a square in terms of its sides. $A = s^2$
8. Write a quadratic equation to describe the area of a circle in terms of its radius. $A = \pi r^2$

Define a variable and write a quadratic equation to describe each of the following.

9. The product of two numbers whose sum is 40
10. The product of two numbers whose sum is 36
11. The product of two numbers whose difference is 64
12. The product of two numbers whose difference is 25
13. A taxi service transports 300 passengers a day between two airports. The charge is \$8.00. The owner estimates that for each \$1 increase in fare, he will lose 20 passengers. Write a quadratic equation to describe the owner's income after he increases his prices.
14. Ms. Mauch has 120 meters of fence to make a rectangular pen for her ducks. She will use the side of a shed for one side of the pen. Write a quadratic equation to describe the area of the pen.

For answers to problems **9–14**, see Teacher's Guide.

7-2 Parabolas

Objective: To identify parabolas and their properties.

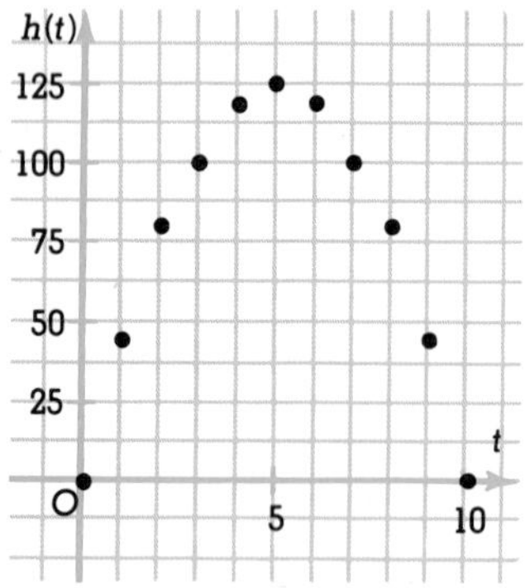

Graphs of quadratic functions have a general shape called a **parabola.** Consider the following situation.

> A rocket is launched with an initial velocity of 50 meters per second. The height, h, of the rocket t seconds after blast-off is given by $h(t) = 50t - 5t^2$.

You can draw a graph by making a table of values, plotting points, and connecting the points with a smooth curve. The resulting graph is a parabola.

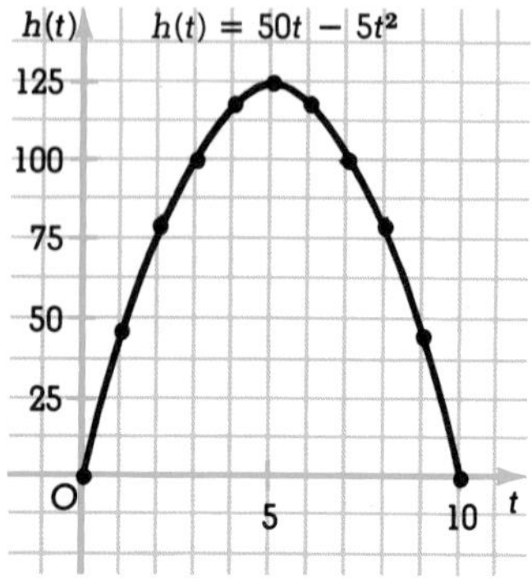

t	$50t - 5t^2$	$h(t)$
0	$50(0) - 5(0)^2$	0
1	$50(1) - 5(1)^2$	45
2	$50(2) - 5(2)^2$	80
3	$50(3) - 5(3)^2$	105
4	$50(4) - 5(4)^2$	120
5	$50(5) - 5(5)^2$	125
6	$50(6) - 5(6)^2$	120
7	$50(7) - 5(7)^2$	105
8	$50(8) - 5(8)^2$	80
9	$50(9) - 5(9)^2$	45
10	$50(10) - 5(10)^2$	0

Test values of t like 4.9 and 5.1 to determine if the maximum height is reached at 5 seconds.

Notice that 10 seconds after blast-off, the height of the rocket is zero. This means that it has returned to earth. It appears to have reached its maximum height of 125 meters at 5 seconds after blast-off. Test some other values of t between 4 and 6 to check.

Parabolas have certain common characteristics. They all have a **vertex** and an **axis of symmetry.**

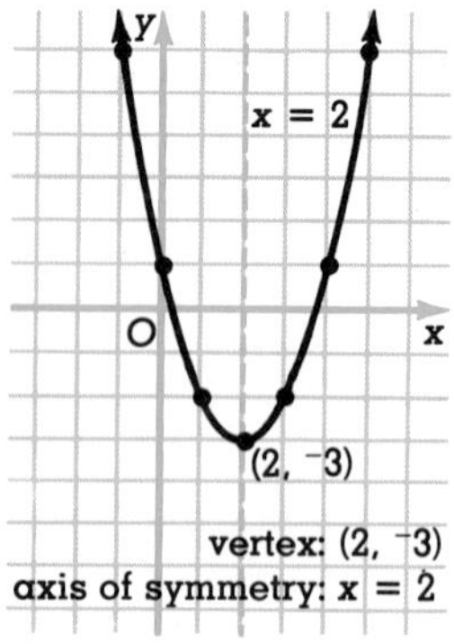

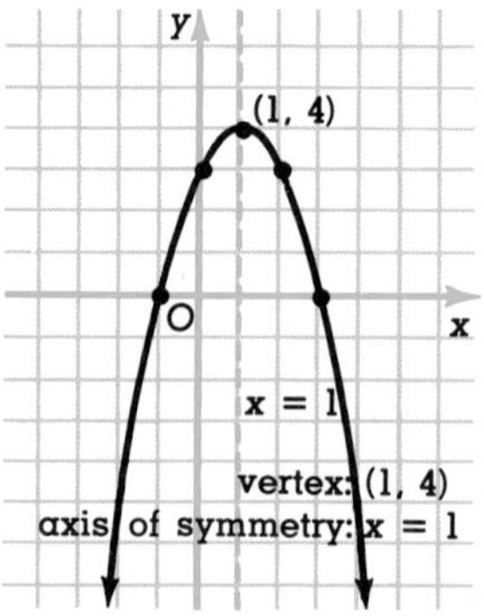

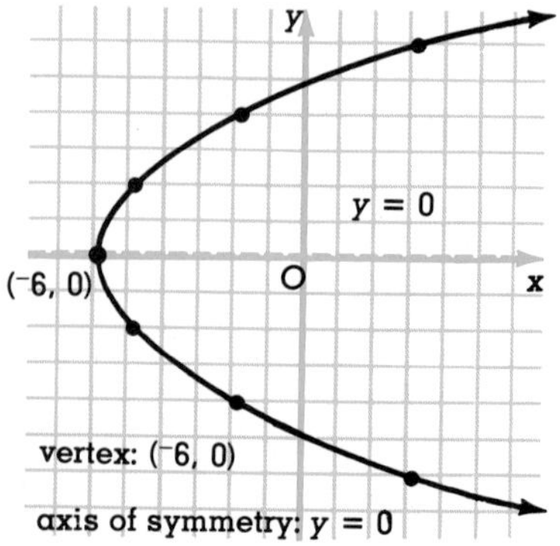

If the sketches are folded along the axis of symmetry, the two halves of the parabolas coincide.

The graphs of $y = x^2$, $y = 2x^2$, $y = 3x^2$, and $y = \frac{1}{2}x^2$ are drawn on the same set of axes.

Each graph has vertex (0, 0).
Each graph has axis of symmetry $x = 0$.

Each graph opens upward.
The greater the coefficient of x^2, the narrower the graph.

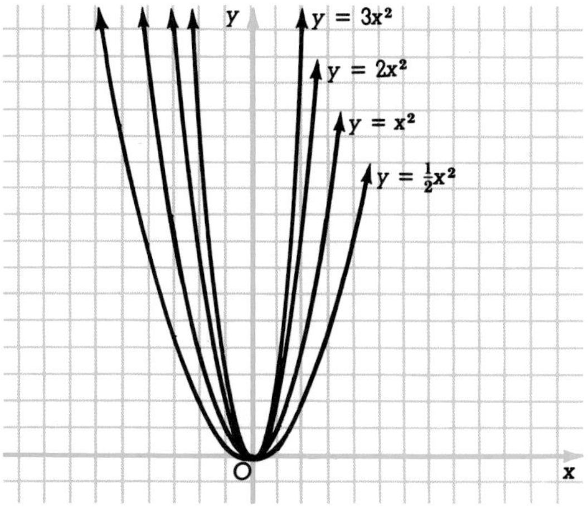

The graphs of $y = {}^{-}x^2$, $y = {}^{-}2x^2$, $y = {}^{-}3x^2$, and $y = -\frac{1}{2}x^2$ are drawn on the same set of axes.

Each graph has vertex (0, 0).
Each graph has axis of symmetry $x = 0$.

Each graph opens downward.
The lesser the coefficient of x^2, the narrower the graph.

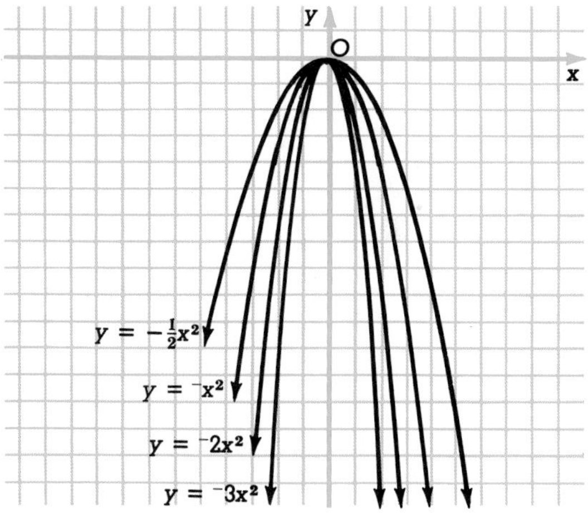

By studying these graphs, and many like them, the following conclusions can be made about the graph of $y = ax^2$.

$y = ax^2$	a is positive	a is negative
Vertex	(0, 0)	(0, 0)
Axis of symmetry	$x = 0$	$x = 0$
Direction of opening	upward	downward
As the value of $\lvert a\rvert$ increases, the graphs of $y = ax^2$ narrow.		

exercises

Max: 1–12, 1–28; Avg: 1–12, 1–27 odds; Min: 1–27 odds

Exploratory Complete each table of values.

1–3.

x	$^-3$	$\frac{1}{3}$	2
x^2	9	$\frac{1}{9}$	4

4–6.

x	6	$^-4$	$\frac{1}{2}$
$^-2x^2$	$^-72$	$^-32$	$-\frac{1}{2}$

7–9.

x	3	9	$\frac{1}{3}$
$\frac{1}{3}x^2$	3	27	$\frac{1}{27}$

10–12.

x	4	6	$^-9$
$-\frac{1}{2}x^2$	$^-8$	$^-18$	$^-40\frac{1}{2}$

For answers to problems 1–6, see Teacher's Guide.

Written For each problem, sketch the graphs of the equations on the same set of axes.

1. $y = x^2$, $y = 3x^2$, $y = \frac{1}{3}x^2$
2. $y = {}^-x^2$, $y = {}^-3x^2$, $y = -\frac{1}{3}x^2$
3. $y = x^2$, $y = {}^-x^2$
4. $y = 4x^2$, $y = {}^-4x^2$
5. $f(x) = 3x^2$, $f(x) = {}^-2x^2$, $f(x) = \frac{1}{4}x^2$
6. $f(x) = -\frac{1}{4}x^2$, $f(x) = -\frac{1}{3}x^2$, $f(x) = {}^-x^2$

For each equation, state the vertex, axis of symmetry, and direction of opening.

7. $f(x) = 2x^2$ (0, 0); $x = 0$; up
8. $f(x) = -\frac{1}{3}x^2$ (0, 0); $x = 0$; down
9. $y = {}^-x^2$ (0, 0); $x = 0$; down
10. $y = 4x^2$ (0, 0); $x = 0$; up
11. $f(x) = \frac{1}{3}x^2$ (0, 0); $x = 0$; up
12. $f(x) = 4x^2$ (0, 0); $x = 0$; up
13. $y = \frac{3}{4}x^2$ (0, 0); $x = 0$; up
14. $y = \frac{7}{9}x^2$ (0, 0); $x = 0$; up
15. $f(x) = -\frac{4}{3}x^2$ (0, 0); $x = 0$; down
16. $f(x) = 49x^2$ (0, 0); $x = 0$; up

Determine a value of a so that each point described is on the graph of $f(x) = ax^2$.

17. (2, 2) $\frac{1}{2}$
18. (4, $^-4$) $-\frac{1}{4}$
19. (1, 1) 1
20. (6, 6) $\frac{1}{6}$
21. (3, $^-18$) $^-2$
22. ($^-2$, 5) $\frac{5}{4}$
23. $\left(\frac{1}{2}, {}^-1\right)$ $^-4$
24. ($^-3$, 3) $\frac{1}{3}$
25. ($^-1$, 3) 3
26. ($^-1$, 1) 1
27. If the coordinates (4, 4) satisfy the equation $f(x) = \frac{1}{4}x^2$, then what equation does (4, $^-4$) satisfy? $f(x) = -\frac{1}{4}x^2$
28. How does the graph of $f(x) = 4x^2$ compare to the graph of $f(x) = {}^-3x^2$? It opens upward rather than downward. It is narrower.

Reading Algebra

Grammar

Communication in everyday life depends on a knowledge of English grammar. In the same manner, communication in algebra depends on a knowledge of mathematical grammar.

Arrangement of symbols is an important part of grammar. Examples in music, English, and mathematics are given below. In each case, the statement on the left communicates a thought. The statement on the right is nonsense.

	Grammatical	Ungrammatical
Music		
English	I took a walk in the woods.	Walk took woods in I
Mathematics	$3 + 4 \neq 12$	$+ \neq 3\ 12\ 4$

Punctuation also plays an important role in grammar. Study the two sentences.

Mother, sister Carol, Andrew, and I went to the theater.

Mother, sister, Carol, Andrew, and I went to the theater.

In the first sentence, four people, namely my mother, my sister Carol, Andrew, and I, went to the theater. In the second sentence, five people, namely my mother, my sister, Carol, Andrew, and I, went to the theater.

Now study the following mathematical sentences.

$$g(a) = 3a^2 - 2 \qquad G(a) = (3a)^2 - 2$$

In the first sentence, g of a equals three times a squared, minus two. In the second sentence, G of a equals three times a, quantity squared, minus two. In other words, in the first sentence, square a and then multiply by three. In the second sentence, multiply three times a and then square the product.

Exercises For each pair of equations, explain how the first and second equation differ.

1. $f(x) = (x - 2)^2$ $\quad F(x) = x^2 - 2$

2. $f(x) = 3(x + 4)^2$ $\quad F(x) = (3x + 4)^2$

3. $f(x) = x^2 + 3x + 5$ $\quad F(x) = x^2 + 3(x + 5)$

4. $f(x) = (x - 4)^2$ $\quad F(x) = (4 - x)^2$

5. $h(x) = (2x - 5)^2$ $\quad H(x) = (2x)^2 - 5^2$

6. $m(x) = (^-2x)^2 + 3$ $\quad M(x) = {}^-(2x)^2 + 3$

7. $g(x) = 4x^2 - 2$ $\quad G(x) = 4(x^2 - 2)$

8. $n(x) = (x + 2)^2 + 8$ $\quad N(x) = x^2 + 4 + 8$

Wording of answers may vary.

7-3 Graphing $y = a(x - h)^2$

Objective: To graph parabolas of the form $y = a(x - h)^2$.

You have studied parabolas with equations of the form $y = ax^2$. No matter what the value of a, each parabola has axis of symmetry $x = 0$ and vertex (0, 0).

Below, the graphs of $y = x^2$, $y = (x - 3)^2$, and $y = (x + 3)^2$ are drawn on the same set of axes.

Notice that each graph has the same shape. The only difference is their horizontal position.

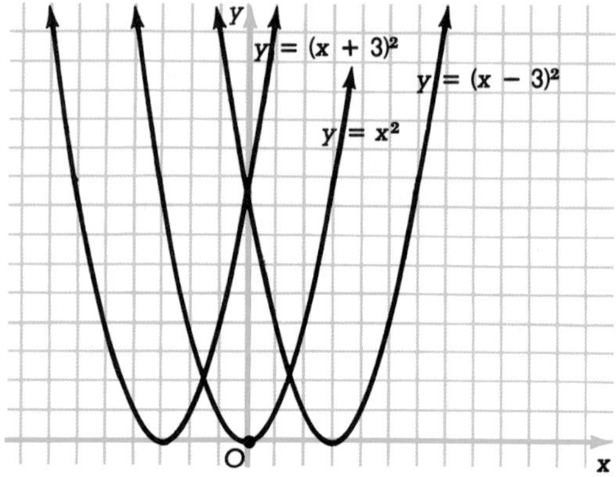

Below, the graphs of $y = (x - 3)^2$, $y = 2(x - 3)^2$, and $y = \frac{1}{2}(x - 3)^2$ are drawn on the same set of axes.

Notice that each graph has the same vertex and axis of symmetry. The only difference is their shape. Their widths vary.

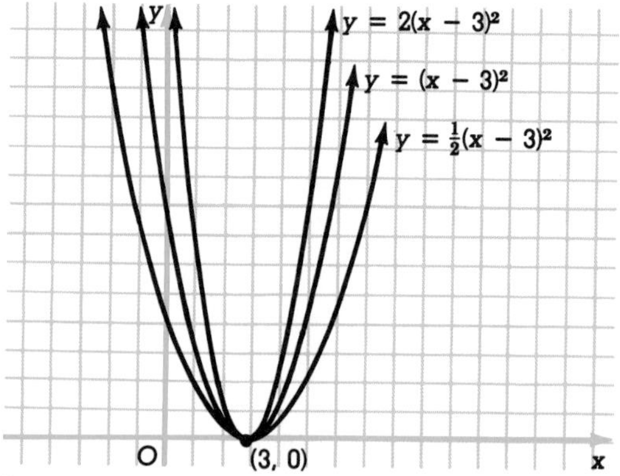

In general, the graph of $f(x) = a(x - h)^2$ has the same shape and direction of opening as the graph of $f(x) = ax^2$. But its position is shifted h units to the right or left.

$y = a(x - h)^2$	a is positive	a is negative
Vertex	$(h, 0)$	$(h, 0)$
Axis of symmetry	$x = h$	$x = h$
Direction of opening	upward	downward
As the value of $\lvert a \rvert$ increases, the graphs of $y = a(x - h)^2$ narrow.		

examples

1

Graph $f(x) = {}^-3(x - 5)^2$.

Since h is 5, the vertex is (5, 0) and the axis of symmetry is $x = 5$.

Since a is $^-3$, the graph opens downward and is narrower than the graph of $f(x) = x^2$.

It is helpful to find several points on the graph other than the vertex.

$f(4) = {}^-3(4 - 5)^2$ or $^-3$
$f(6) = {}^-3(6 - 5)^2$ or $^-3$
$f(3) = {}^-3(3 - 5)^2$ or $^-12$
$f(7) = {}^-3(7 - 5)^2$ or $^-12$

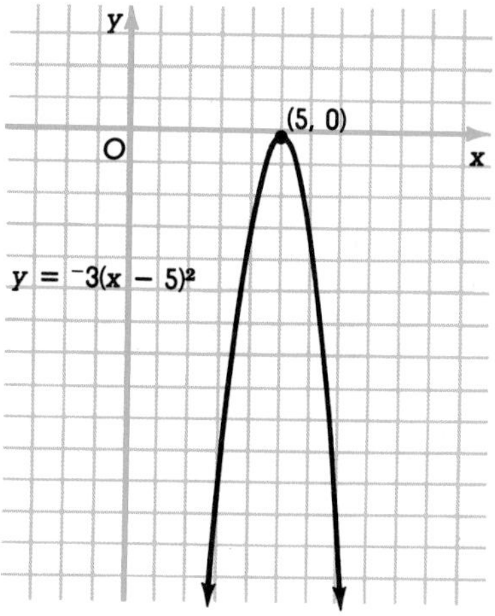

2

Graph $f(x) = 3x^2 + 12x + 12$.

First, write the equation in the form $f(x) = a(x - h)^2$, if possible.

$$\begin{aligned} f(x) &= 3x^2 + 12x + 12 \\ &= 3(x^2 + 4x + 4) \\ &= 3(x + 2)^2 \\ &= 3(x - {}^-2)^2 \end{aligned}$$

Therefore, a is 3 and h is $^-2$.
The vertex is $(^-2, 0)$.
The axis of symmetry is $x = {}^-2$.
The graph opens upward and is narrower than the graph of $f(x) = x^2$.

$f(^-1) = 3(^-1 - {}^-2)^2$ or 3
$f(^-3) = 3(^-3 - {}^-2)^2$ or 3
$f(0) = 3(0 - {}^-2)^2$ or 12
$f(^-4) = 3(^-4 - {}^-2)^2$ or 12

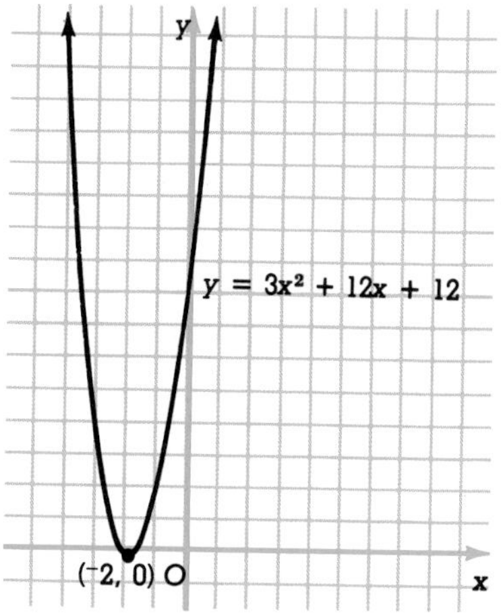

exercises

Max: 1–10, 1–30; **Avg:** 1–10, 1–29 odds; **Min:** 1–29 odds

Exploratory Name the vertex, axis of symmetry, and direction of opening for each of the following.

1. $y = x^2$ (0, 0); $x = 0$; up
2. $y = (x - 3)^2$ (3, 0); $x = 3$; up
3. $f(x) = {}^-2x^2$ (0, 0); $x = 0$; down
4. $f(x) = {}^-2(x + 4)^2$ $(^-4, 0)$; $x = {}^-4$; down
5. $f(x) = 4x^2$ (0, 0); $x = 0$; up
6. $f(x) = 4(x - 2)^2$ (2, 0); $x = 2$; up

7. $y = \frac{1}{3}(x + 2)^2$ $(^-2, 0); x = {}^-2$; up

8. $y = (x - 4)^2$ $(4, 0); x = 4$; up

9. $f(x) = \frac{1}{4}(x - 2)^2$ $(2, 0); x = 2$; up

10. $f(x) = \frac{2}{3}\left(x - \frac{3}{4}\right)^2$ $(\frac{3}{4}, 0); x = \frac{3}{4}$; up

Written Write each equation in the form $f(x) = a(x - h)^2$.

1. $f(x) = x^2 - 2x + 1$ $f(x) = (x - 1)^2$

2. $f(x) = x^2 + 8x + 16$ $f(x) = (x + 4)^2$

3. $f(x) = \frac{2}{5}x^2 + \frac{8}{5}x + \frac{8}{5}$ $f(x) = \frac{2}{5}(x + 2)^2$

4. $f(x) = {}^-3x^2 - 18x - 27$ $f(x) = {}^-3(x + 3)^2$

5. $f(x) = 6x^2 + 60x + 150$ $f(x) = 6(x + 5)^2$

6. $f(x) = 4x^2 - 8x + 4$ $f(x) = 4(x - 1)^2$

7. $f(x) = {}^-9x^2 + 18x - 9$ $f(x) = {}^-9(x - 1)^2$

8. $f(x) = \frac{3}{4}x^2 - 6x + 12$ $f(x) = \frac{3}{4}(x - 4)^2$

9. $f(x) = 4x^2 - 44x + 121$ $f(x) = 4(x - \frac{11}{2})^2$

10. $f(x) = 4x^2 + 60x + 225$ $f(x) = 4(x + \frac{15}{2})^2$

11–20. Name the vertex, axis of symmetry and direction of opening for the equations in problems 1–10. For answers to problems 11–26, see Teacher's Guide.

Draw the graphs for each pair of equations on the same set of axes.

21. $y = 2x^2$ and $y = 2(x - 3)^2$

22. $f(x) = -\frac{1}{4}(x + 2)^2$ and $f(x) = -\frac{1}{4}x^2$

23. $f(x) = {}^-3x^2$ and $g(x) = {}^-3\left(x + \frac{1}{4}\right)^2$

24. $f(x) = 4x^2$ and $h(x) = 4(x - 6)^2$

25. $y = {}^-3x^2$ and $y = {}^-3(x + 2)^2$

26. $f(x) = {}^-5x^2$ and $g(x) = {}^-5(x - 10)^2$

27. Write the equation of a parabola with position 3 units to the right of the parabola with equation $f(x) = x^2$. $f(x) = (x - 3)^2$

28. Write the equation of a parabola with position 4 units to the left of the parabola with equation $f(x) = {}^-2x^2$. $f(x) = {}^-2(x + 4)^2$

29. Write the equation of a parabola with position $\frac{3}{4}$ unit to the left of the parabola with equation $f(x) = -\frac{1}{4}x^2$. $f(x) = -\frac{1}{4}(x + \frac{3}{4})^2$

30. Write the equation of a parabola with position 6 units to the right of the parabola with equation $f(x) = 5x^2$. $f(x) = 5(x - 6)^2$

Excursions in Algebra

Age of Diophantus

The solution to this riddle is the age of the ancient Greek mathematician, Diophantus.

His youth lasted one-sixth of his life. He grew a beard after one-twelfth more. He married after one-seventh more. He had a son 5 years later. His son lived half as long as his father. Diophantus died 4 years after his son died. 84

7-4 Graphing $y = a(x - h)^2 + k$

Objective: To graph parabolas of the form $a(x - h)^2 + k$.

Below, the graphs of $y = x^2$, $y = x^2 + 3$, and $y = x^2 - 3$ are drawn on the same set of axes.

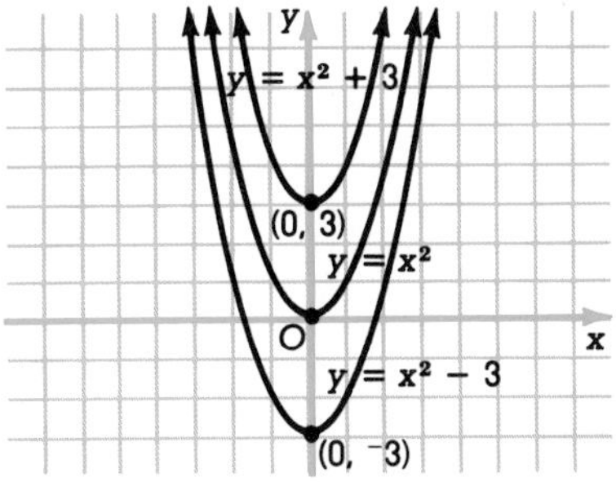

Notice that each graph has the same shape. The only difference is their vertical position.

Study the graphs of $y = x^2 - 3$, $y = (x - 2)^2 - 3$, and $y = (x + 2)^2 - 3$.

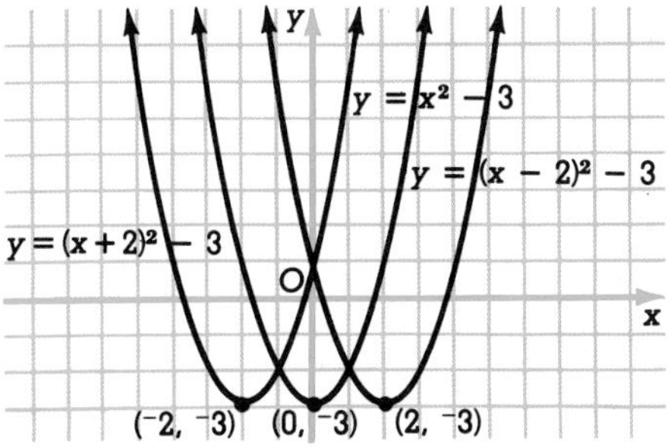

How do these graphs compare?

How do you think the graphs of $y = (x + 2)^2 - 3$, $y = 4(x + 2)^2 - 3$, and $y = \frac{1}{4}(x + 2)^2 - 3$ compare?

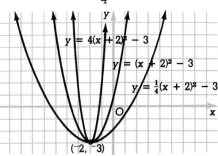

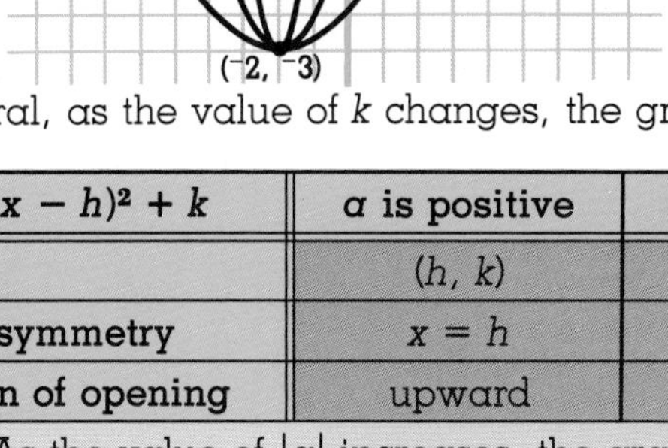

In general, as the value of k changes, the graph of $f(x) = a(x - h)^2 + k$ is shifted vertically.

$y = a(x - h)^2 + k$	a is positive	a is negative
Vertex	(h, k)	(h, k)
Axis of symmetry	$x = h$	$x = h$
Direction of opening	upward	downward
As the value of $\lvert a \rvert$ increases, the graphs of $y = a(x - h)^2 + k$ narrow.		

examples

1 **Graph $f(x) = \frac{1}{2}(x - 2)^2 - 5$.**

The value of a is $\frac{1}{2}$, h is 2, and k is $^-5$.

The vertex is $(2, {}^-5)$.
The axis of symmetry is $x = 2$.
The graph opens upward and is wider than the graph of $f(x) = x^2$.

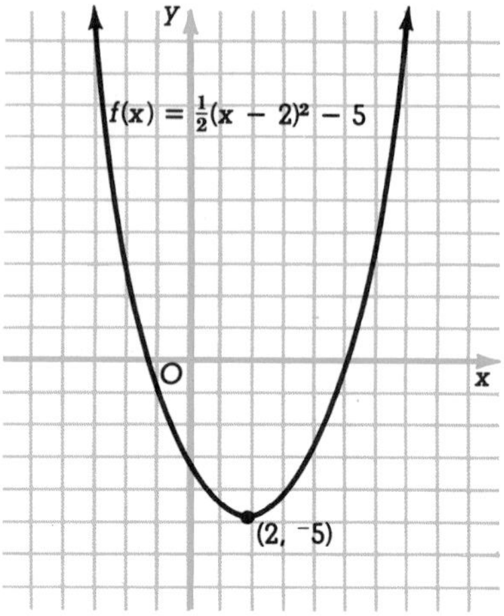

x	$\frac{1}{2}(x - 2)^2 - 5$	$f(x)$
4	$\frac{1}{2}(4 - 2)^2 - 5$	$^-3$
0	$\frac{1}{2}(0 - 2)^2 - 5$	$^-3$
6	$\frac{1}{2}(6 - 2)^2 - 5$	3
$^-2$	$\frac{1}{2}(^-2 - 2)^2 - 5$	3

2 **Graph $f(x) = 2x^2 - 12x + 19$.**

First, write the equation in the form $f(x) = a(x - h)^2 + k$.
To do this, you must complete the square.

$$\begin{aligned} f(x) &= 2x^2 - 12x + 19 \\ &= 2(x^2 - 6x) + 19 \\ &= 2(x^2 - 6x + 9) + 19 - 2(9) \\ &= 2(x - 3)^2 + 1 \end{aligned}$$

Therefore, a is 2, h is 3, and k is 1.
The vertex is (3, 1).
The axis of symmetry is $x = 3$.
The graph opens upward and is narrower than the graph of $f(x) = x^2$.

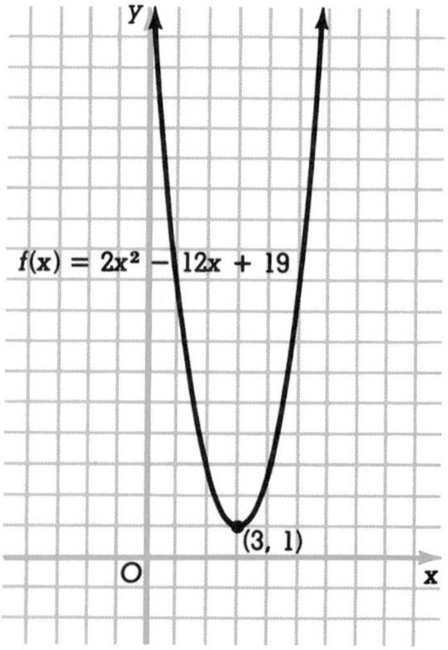

x	$2(x - 3)^2 + 1$	$f(x)$
2	$2(2 - 3)^2 + 1$	3
4	$2(4 - 3)^2 + 1$	3
1	$2(1 - 3)^2 + 1$	9
5	$2(5 - 3)^2 + 1$	9

example 3

Graph $f(x) = {}^-2x^2 - 12x - 22$.

First, write the equation in the form $f(x) = a(x - h)^2 + k$.
To do this, you must complete the square.

$$\begin{aligned} f(x) &= {}^-2x^2 - 12x - 22 \\ &= {}^-2(x^2 + 6x) - 22 \\ &= {}^-2(x^2 + 6x + 9) - 22 + 2(9) \\ &= {}^-2(x + 3)^2 - 4 \end{aligned}$$

Therefore, a is $^-2$, h is $^-3$, and k is $^-4$.
The vertex is $(^-3, {}^-4)$.
The axis of symmetry is $x = {}^-3$.
The graph opens downward and is narrower than the graph of $f(x) = x^2$.

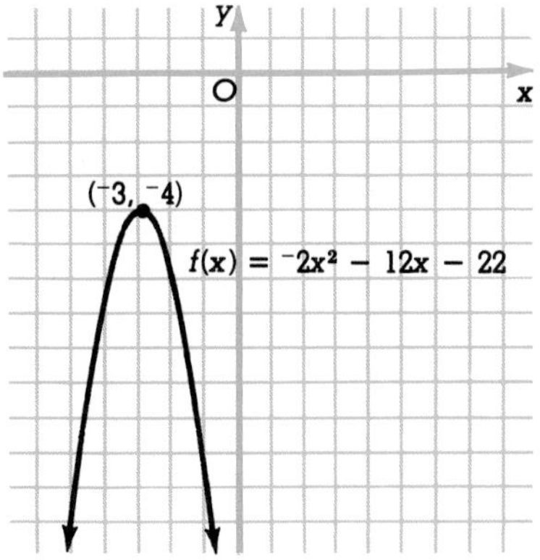

exercises

Max: 1–10, 1–14; Avg: 1–10, 1–13 odds; Min: 1–13 odds

Exploratory **Name the vertex, axis of symmetry, and direction of opening for each of the following.**

1. $f(x) = 3(x - 2)^2 + 5$ $(2, 5)$; $x = 2$; up
2. $f(x) = 4(x - 8)^2$ $(8, 0)$; $x = 8$; up
3. $y = 2x^2$ $(0, 0)$; $x = 0$; up
4. $y = {}^-1(x + 2)^2 - 6$ $(^-2, {}^-6)$; $x = {}^-2$; down
5. $f(x) = {}^-3x^2 + 6$ $(0, 6)$; $x = 0$; down
6. $g(x) = 5x^2 - 6$ $(0, {}^-6)$; $x = 0$; up
7. $f(x) = 2(x - 1)^2 + \frac{1}{3}$ $(1, \frac{1}{3})$; $x = 1$; up
8. $f(x) = 4(x + 2)^2 - \frac{3}{2}$ $(^-2, -\frac{3}{2})$; $x = {}^-2$; up
9. $f(x) = -\frac{1}{3}(x + 2)^2 - \frac{4}{3}$ $(^-2, -\frac{4}{3})$; $x = {}^-2$; down
10. $g(x) = 3\left(x - \frac{1}{2}\right)^2 + \frac{1}{4}$ $(\frac{1}{2}, \frac{1}{4})$; $x = \frac{1}{2}$; up

For answers to problems **1–14**, see Teacher's Guide.

Written **Draw the graph for each of the following.**

1. $f(x) = (x + 2)^2 - 3$
2. $f(x) = (x - 3)^2 + 4$
3. $f(x) = x^2 - 4$
4. $f(x) = 2x^2 + 3$
5. $f(x) = 2(x + 3)^2 - 5$
6. $f(x) = 3(x - 1)^2 + 2$
7. $f(x) = \frac{1}{2}(x + 3)^2 - 5$
8. $f(x) = \frac{1}{3}(x - 1)^2 + 2$
9. $f(x) = {}^-2x^2 + 16x - 31$
10. $f(x) = {}^-x^2 - 4x - 10$
11. $f(x) = {}^-0.25x^2 - 2.5x - 0.25$
12. $f(x) = -\frac{2}{3}x^2 + 4x - 9$
13. Given $f(x) = ax^2 + bx + c$ with $a \neq 0$, complete the square to rewrite the equation in the form $f(x) = a(x - h)^2 + k$. State an expression for h and k in terms of a, b and c.
14. Using the results of problem **13**, write a computer program that takes the values of a, b, and c of any quadratic equation in standard form and prints the axis of symmetry, vertex, and direction of opening.

CAREERS

Optics

Carol Shearer designs lenses to meet the needs of people with visual problems. Two types of lenses are shown below.

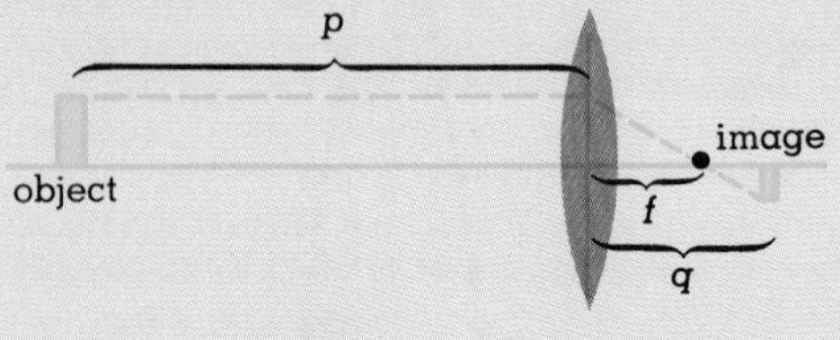

converging lens

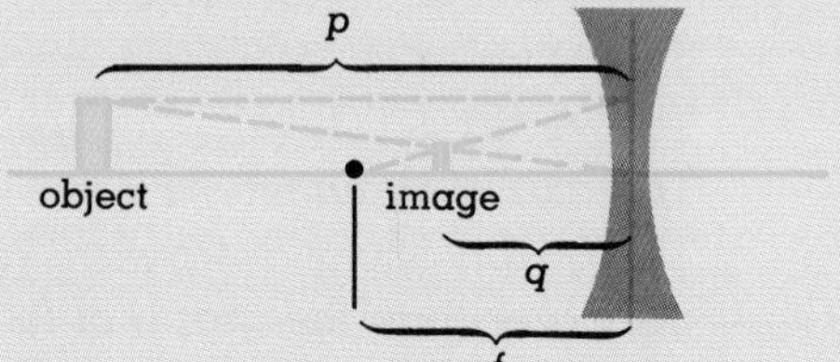

diverging lens

The following formula can be used for determining object and image relations for these lenses.

$$\frac{1}{p} + \frac{1}{q} = \frac{1}{f}$$

p is the object distance from lens
q is the image distance from lens
f is the focal length of lens

For real objects and images, p and q are positive. They are negative for virtual objects and images. For a converging lens, f is positive. It is negative for diverging lenses.

A certain nearsighted person cannot see distinctly objects beyond 80 centimeters. Find the type of lens needed.

$$\frac{1}{p} + \frac{1}{q} = \frac{1}{f}$$

$$0 - \frac{1}{80} = \frac{1}{f}$$

$$f = {}^{-}80$$

The image must be on the same side of the focus as the object, so the image is virtual and $q = {}^{-}80$. For an object at a great distance, p is very large and $\frac{1}{p}$ is 0.

A diverging lens is needed since f is negative.

The power of the lens is calculated as follows.

$$\text{power in diopters} = \frac{1}{f(\text{in meters})}$$

$$= \frac{1}{{}^{-}0.80} \text{ or } {}^{-}1.25 \text{ diopters}$$

Exercises Find the type of lens and the power needed for people who cannot see objects clearly beyond the following distances. all divergent

1. 100 cm $^{-}1$ **2.** 60 cm $^{-}1.67$ **3.** 50 cm $^{-}2$ **4.** 125 cm $^{-}0.8$

7–5 Using Parabolas

Objective: To use quadratic equations to solve problems.

A ball is thrown vertically upward at a starting speed of 80 feet per second. The height it will reach after t seconds is given by the following equation.

$$h(t) = {}^{-}16t^2 + 80t$$

This equation represents height in feet.

At what time does the ball reach its maximum height?

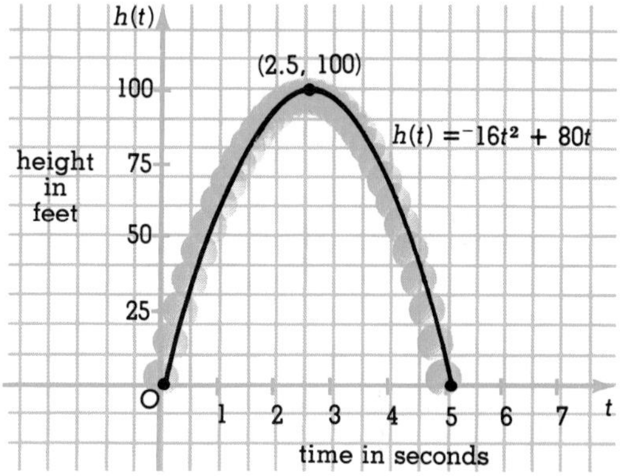

Compare the time-lapse photograph to the graph of $h(t) = {}^{-}16t^2 + 80t$. They both give a visual description of how the ball moves during a certain time period.

The graph is a parabola. Its highest point is the vertex (2.5, 100). This shows that the ball reaches a maximum height of 100 feet in 2.5 seconds.

Many problem situations involve finding **maximum** or **minimum values.** If such a problem can be described by a quadratic equation, it often can be solved by finding the vertex of its graph.

example 1

Find two numbers whose difference is 64 and whose product is a minimum.

Define a variable. Let x stand for the lesser number. Then $64 + x$ stands for the other number.

Write an equation.

$$\begin{aligned}\text{product} &= (x) \cdot (64 + x)\\ &= 64x + x^2\end{aligned}$$

Solve the problem. The equation above is quadratic. So find the vertex by writing the equation in the form $y = a(x - h)^2 + k$. Then the vertex is (h, k). Let y stand for the product.

$$\begin{aligned}y &= 64x + x^2\\ &= x^2 + 64x + \left(\frac{64}{2}\right)^2 - \left(\frac{64}{2}\right)^2\\ &= (x + 32)^2 - 1024\end{aligned}$$

The vertex is $({}^{-}32, {}^{-}1024)$.

The product is minimized when x is $^{-}32$.

So $64 + x$ is $64 + {}^{-}32$ or 32.

Answer the problem. The two numbers are $^{-}32$ and 32.

example 2

A theater has seats for 500 people. It is filled to capacity for each show and tickets cost \$3.00 per show. The owner wants to increase ticket prices. She estimates that for each \$0.20 increase in price, 25 fewer people will attend. What ticket price will maximize her income?

Define a variable. Let p = number of \$0.20 price increases.
Then $3.00 + 0.20p$ stands for ticket price.
And $500 - 25p$ stands for number of tickets sold.

Write an equation.

$$\begin{aligned}\text{Income} &= (\text{number tickets sold}) \cdot (\text{ticket price})\\ &= (500 - 25p) \cdot (3.00 + 0.20p)\\ &= 1500 + 100p - 75p - 5p^2\\ &= 1500 + 25p - 5p^2\end{aligned}$$

Solve the problem. The equation is quadratic. So find the vertex by writing the equation in the form $y = a(x - h)^2 + k$. Let y stand for income.

$$\begin{aligned}y &= 1500 + 25p - 5p^2\\ &= {}^-5(p^2 - 5p) + 1500\\ &= {}^-5\left[p^2 - 5p + \left(-\frac{5}{2}\right)^2\right] + 1500 + 5\left(-\frac{5}{2}\right)^2\\ &= {}^-5\left(p - \frac{5}{2}\right)^2 + \frac{6125}{4}\end{aligned}$$

The vertex is $\left(\frac{5}{2}, \frac{6125}{4}\right)$.

The maximum profit is $\frac{6125}{4}$ dollars or \$1531.25.

The income is maximized when the owner makes $\frac{5}{2}$ or $2\frac{1}{2}$ price increases. That's an increase of \$0.50.

Answer the problem. A ticket price of \$3.50 will maximize the owner's income.

exercises

Max: 1–4, 1–18; **Avg:** 1–4, 1–17 odds; **Min:** 1–17 odds

Exploratory **Define a variable and write an equation for each of the following.**

1. Find two numbers whose sum is 36 and whose product is a maximum. x = one of the numbers, product = $36x - x^2$
2. Find two numbers whose difference is 48 and whose product is a minimum. x = lesser number, product = $48x + x^2$
3. George Polo has 120 meters of fence to make a rectangular pen for ducks. If a shed is used as one side of the pen, what would be the length and width for maximum area? x = width, area = $120x - 2x^2$
4. A taxi service operates between two airports transporting 300 passengers a day. The charge is \$8.00. The owner estimates that 20 passengers will be lost for each \$1 increase in the fare. What charge would be most profitable for the service? x = number of \$1 increases income = $2400 + 140x - 20x^2$

Written Solve each problem.

1-4. Solve problems 1-4 of the Exploratory Exercises. 1. 18 and 18 2. $^-24$ and 24
3. 30 m wide and 60 m long 4. \$11.50

5. An object is fired vertically from the top of a tower at a velocity of 80 feet per second. The tower is 200 feet high. The height of the object above the ground t seconds after firing is given by the formula $h(t) = {}^-16t^2 + 80t + 200$. What is the maximum height reached by the object? How long after firing does it reach maximum height? 300 ft, 2.5 sec

6. A ball is thrown vertically into the air with an initial velocity of 64 feet per second. The formula $h(t) = 64t - 16t^2$ gives its height above the ground after t seconds. What is its height after 1.5 seconds? What is its maximum height? How many seconds will pass before it returns to the ground? 60 ft, 64 ft, 4 sec

7. Find the dimensions and maximum area of a rectangle if its perimeter is 40 centimeters. 10 cm by 10 cm, 100 cm²

8. A wire 36 cm long is cut into 2 pieces and each piece is bent to form a square. How long should each piece be to minimize the sum of the areas of the two squares? 18 cm

A newsletter has a circulation of 50,000 and sells for 40¢ a copy. Due to increased labor and production costs the publishers will raise the price of the newsletter. A publisher's survey indicates that for each 10¢ increase in price, the circulation decreases by 5000.

9. Let x stand for the number of 10¢ price increases. Write an algebraic expression to describe the increased price per copy. $40 + 10x$

10. Write an algebraic expression to describe the reduced circulation after the price increase. $50{,}000 - 5000x$

11. The publisher's income on the newsletter is the product of the price per copy and the circulation. It is also a function of the number of price increases. Write an equation to describe this function.

12. Draw a graph relating the publisher's income to the number of price increases. Use number of price increases for the x-axis and income in dollars for the y-axis. See Teacher's Guide.

13. What price per copy will maximize the publisher's income on the newsletter? 70¢

11. income $= (40 + 10x)(50{,}000 - 5000x)$

A manufacturer can sell x items per month at a price of (300 − 2x) dollars. It costs the manufacturer (20x + 1000) dollars to produce x items.

14. One item sells for $300 - 2x$ dollars. Write an algebraic expression to describe the price of x items. $x(300 - 2x)$ or $300 - 2x^2$

15. The manufacturer's profit is the selling price minus the cost of producing the items. Write an algebraic expression to describe the manufacturer's profit on x items in one month.

15. $[x(300 - 2x)] - (20x + 1000)$ or $^-2x^2 + 280x - 1000$

16. The manufacturer's profit is a function of the number of items sold. Write an equation to describe this function.
profit $= {}^-2x^2 + 280x - 1000$

17. Draw a graph relating the manufacturer's profit to the number of items produced. Use number of items for the x-axis and profit in dollars for the y-axis.
See Teacher's Guide.

18. How many items should the manufacturer produce in one month to maximize profit? 70

7-6 Graphing Quadratic Inequalities

Objective: To graph quadratic inequalities.

The graph of $y = x^2 - 6x + 5$ is a parabola which separates the coordinate plane into two regions. The graph of $y > x^2 - 6x + 5$ is the region *above* the parabola. The graph of $y < x^2 - 6x + 5$ is the region *below* the parabola.

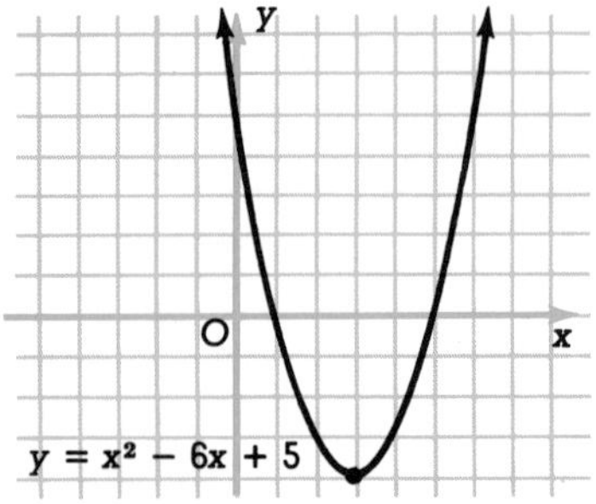

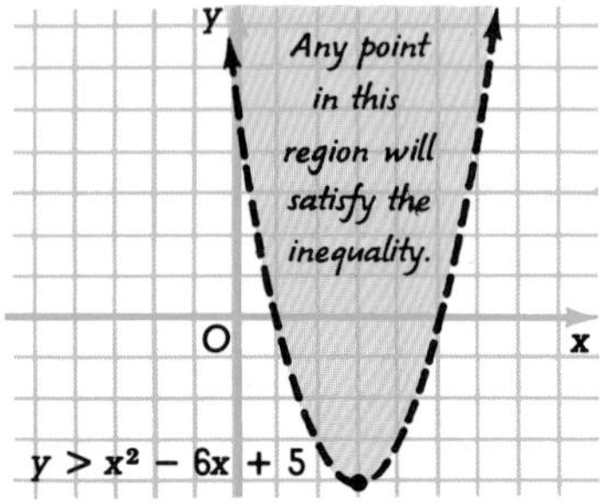

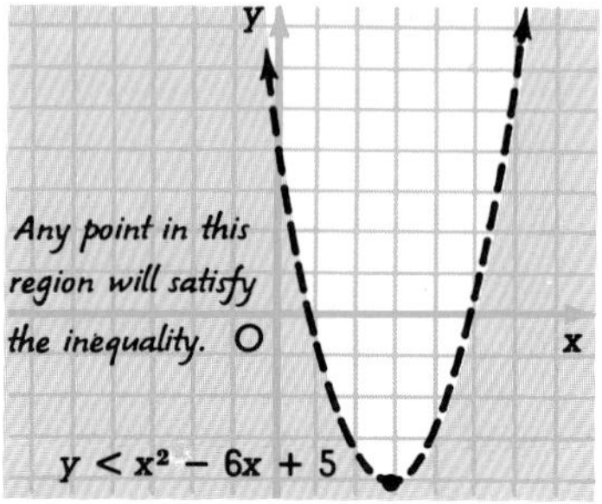

The parabola described by $y = x^2 - 6x + 5$ is called the **boundary** of each region. If it is broken, it is not part of the graph. If it is solid, it is part of the graph.

Note that > tells you the boundary is not included.

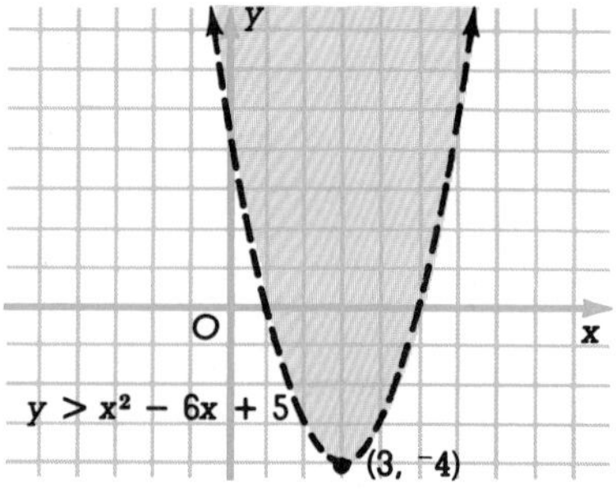

Note that ≥ tells you the boundary is included.

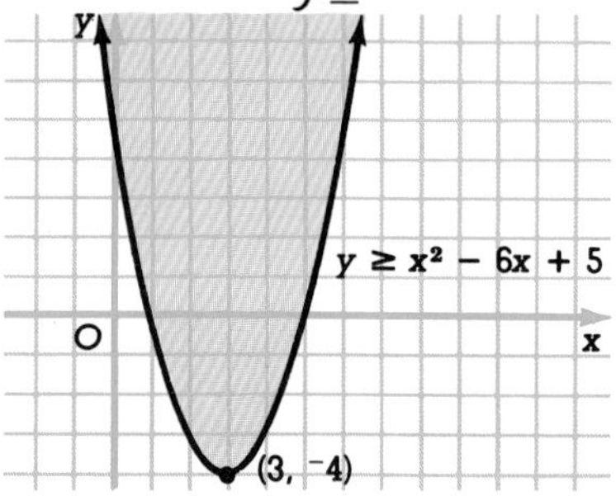

example 1

Graph $y \leq {}^-2x^2 + 8x - 4$.

$y \leq {}^-2x^2 + 8x - 4$

$y \leq {}^-2(x^2 - 4x) - 4$

$y \leq {}^-2\left[x^2 - 4x + \left(-\frac{4}{2}\right)^2\right] - 4 + 2\left(-\frac{4}{2}\right)^2$

$y \leq {}^-2(x - 2)^2 + 4$

The boundary is a parabola with vertex (2, 4), axis of symmetry $x = 2$, and it opens downward.

Test several ordered pairs to determine if the region inside the parabola or the region outside the parabola belongs to the graph.

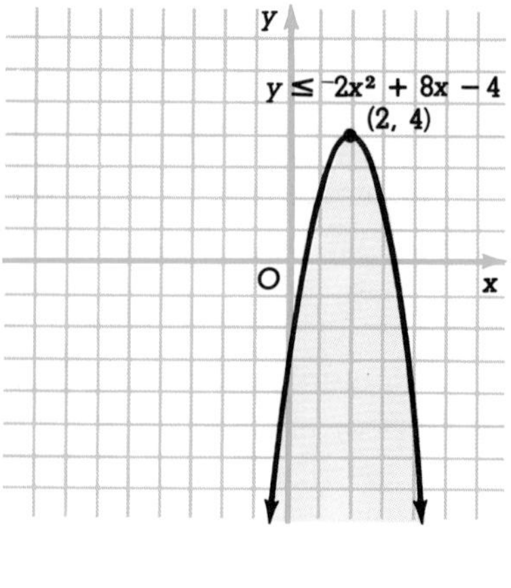

region	(x, y)	$^{-}2x^2 + 8x - 4$	belongs?
inside	(2, 0)	$^{-}2(2)^2 + 8(2) - 4$ or 8	yes
inside	(2, $^{-}3$)	$^{-}2(2)^2 + 8(2) - 4$ or 8	yes
outside	(0, 3)	$^{-}2(0)^2 + 8(0) - 4$ or $^{-}4$	no
outside	($^{-}1$, 0)	$^{-}2(^{-}1)^2 + 8(^{-}1) - 4$ or $^{-}10$	no

2 Graph $y > x^2 - 7x + 10$.

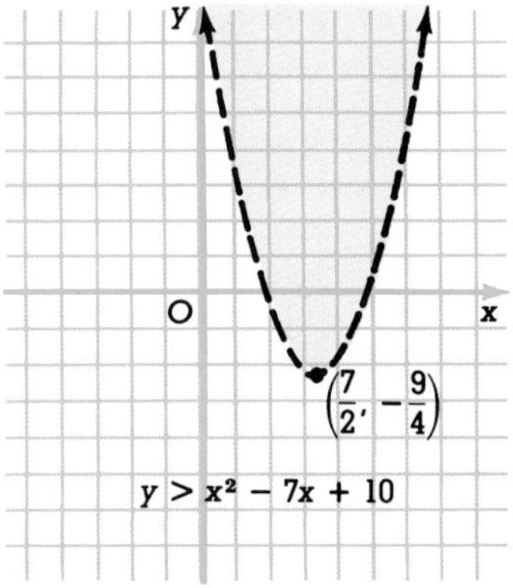

$y > x^2 - 7x + 10$

$y > \left(x - \frac{7}{2}\right)^2 - \frac{9}{4}$

The boundary is a parabola with vertex $\left(\frac{7}{2}, -\frac{9}{4}\right)$, axis of symmetry $x = \frac{7}{2}$, and it opens upward.

Test several ordered pairs to determine if the region inside the parabola or the region outside the parabola belongs to the graph.

region	(x, y)	$x^2 - 7x + 10$	belongs?
inside	(3, 0)	$(3)^2 - 7(3) + 10$ or $^{-}2$	yes
inside	(4, 3)	$(4)^2 - 7(4) + 10$ or $^{-}2$	yes
outside	(0, 0)	$(0)^2 - 7(0) + 10$ or 10	no
outside	($^{-}1$, 2)	$(^{-}1)^2 - 7(^{-}1) + 10$ or 18	no

exercises

Max: 1–10, 1–15; Avg: 1–10, 1–15 odds; Min: 1–15 odds

Exploratory Express each equation in the form $y = a(x - h)^2 + k$.

1. $y = x^2 + 4x + 4$ $\quad y = (x + 2)^2$
2. $y = x^2 + 3x - 1$ $\quad y = (x + \frac{3}{2})^2 - \frac{13}{4}$
3. $y = x^2 - 6x + 9$ $\quad y = (x - 3)^2$
4. $y = 2x^2 + 6x - 5$ $\quad y = 2(x + \frac{3}{2})^2 - \frac{19}{2}$
5. $y = x^2 + 8x + 16$ $\quad y = (x + 4)^2$
6. $y = {}^{-}2x^2 - 8x + 4$ $\quad y = {}^{-}2(x + 2)^2 + 12$
7. $y = x^2 + 10x + 40$ $\quad y = (x + 5)^2 + 15$
8. $y = {}^{-}x^2 + 5x + 10$ $\quad y = {}^{-}(x - \frac{5}{2})^2 + \frac{65}{4}$
9. $y = x^2 - 8x + 4$ $\quad y = (x - 4)^2 - 12$
10. $y = {}^{-}3x^2 + 7x - 8$ $\quad y = {}^{-}3(x - \frac{7}{6}) - \frac{47}{12}$

Written Sketch the graph of each inequality.

1. $y \le x^2 - 13x + 36$
2. $y > x^2 + x - 30$
3. $y \ge x^2 + 3x - 18$
4. $y < x^2 - x - 20$
5. $y \le x^2 - 16$
6. $y > x^2 + 3x - 4$
7. $y < x^2 + 4x + 3$
8. $y > 4x^2 - 8x + 3$
9. $y \le 2x^2 + x - 3$
10. $y > x^2 + 2x + 1$
11. $y \le x^2 + 6x + 9$
12. $y \ge x^2 + 8x + 16$
13. $y > x^2 - 6x + 8$
14. $y \le x^2 - 7x + 10$
15. $y < 3x^2 + 5x + 2$

For answers to problems **1–15**, see Teacher's Guide.

7-7 Solving Quadratic Inequalities

Objective: To solve quadratic inequalities.

Use the graph of $y \geq x^2 + 5x - 6$ to help solve $0 \geq x^2 + 5x - 6$.

All points on the x-axis have y-values of 0. The graph shows that all values of x between ⁻6 and 1 will satisfy the inequality.

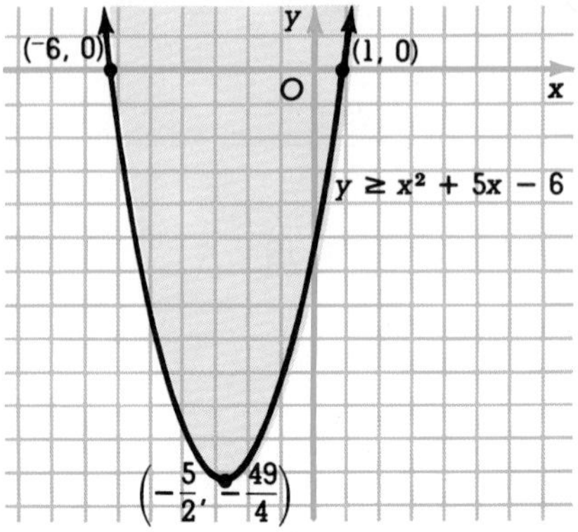

You can also solve the inequality algebraically.

$$x^2 + 5x - 6 \leq 0$$
$$(x - 1)(x + 6) \leq 0 \quad \textit{factor}$$

Recall that the product of two factors is negative only if one factor is positive and one factor is negative.

$x - 1 \leq 0$ and $x + 6 \geq 0$ or $x - 1 \geq 0$ and $x + 6 \leq 0$

$x \leq 1$ $\quad x \geq {}^-6$ $\qquad x \geq 1$ $\quad x \leq {}^-6$

${}^-6 \leq x \leq 1$ $\qquad$ **never true**

Using either the graphic or the algebraic method produces the same solution, $\{x | {}^-6 \leq x \leq 1\}$.

example

Solve $4 + 6x - x^2 \geq 0$.

First, graph $y \leq 4 + 6x - x^2$.

Use the quadratic formula to find the x-intercepts of the parabola.

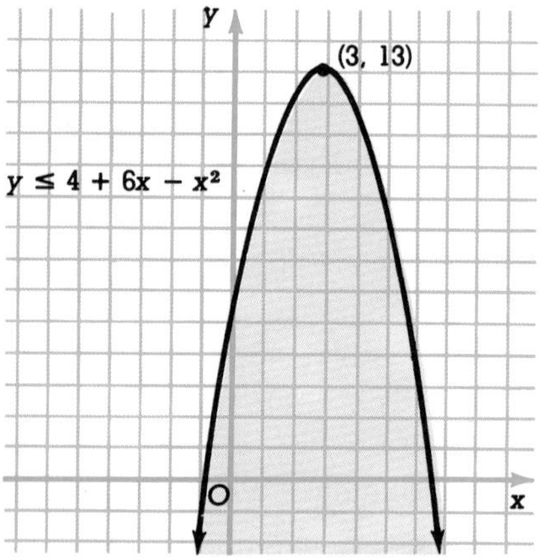

$$x = \frac{{}^-6 \pm \sqrt{6^2 - 4({}^-1)(4)}}{2({}^-1)}$$
$$= \frac{{}^-6 \pm \sqrt{52}}{{}^-2}$$
$$= \frac{{}^-6 \pm 2\sqrt{13}}{{}^-2}$$
$$= 3 \pm \sqrt{13}$$

The solution set is $\{x | 3 - \sqrt{13} \leq x \leq 3 + \sqrt{13}\}$.

exercises

Max: 1–10, 1–12; **Challenge:** 1–5; **Avg:** 1–10, 1–11 odds; **Min:** 1–11 odds

Exploratory Indicate if the factors must be positive or negative in each quadratic inequality.

1. $(x - 8)(x + 2) < 0$ one + and one −
2. $(x + 4)(x - 3) > 0$ both > 0 or both < 0
3. $(x + 6)(x + 2) > 0$ both + or both −
4. $(x - 8)(x - 7) < 0$ one < 0 and one > 0
5. $(x + 2)(x - 3) \geq 0$ both ≥ 0 or both ≤ 0
6. $(x + 7)(x - 11) \leq 0$ one ≤ 0 and one ≥ 0
7. $x^2 + 10x + 25 \leq 0$ one ≤ 0 and one ≥ 0
8. $x^2 - 11x - 26 > 0$ both > 0 or both < 0
9. $x^2 - 8x + 16 \leq 0$ one ≤ 0 and one ≥ 0
10. $x^2 + 3x - 18 > 0$ both > 0 or both < 0

Written Solve each inequality.

1. $x^2 + x - 6 > 0$ $\{x \mid x > 2 \text{ or } x < {}^{-}3\}$
2. $y^2 + 4y - 21 < 0$ $\{y \mid {}^{-}7 < y < 3\}$
3. $p^2 + 2p \geq 24$ $\{p \mid p \geq 4 \text{ or } p \leq {}^{-}6\}$
4. $m^2 - 4m \leq 5$ $\{m \mid {}^{-}1 \leq m \leq 5\}$
5. $2b^2 - b < 6$ $\{b \mid -\frac{3}{2} < b < 2\}$
6. $6r^2 + 5r > 4$ $\{r \mid r < -\frac{4}{3} \text{ or } r > \frac{1}{2}\}$
7. $x^2 - 4x \leq 0$ $\{x \mid 0 \leq x \leq 4\}$
8. $z^2 \geq 2z$ $\{z \mid z \leq 0 \text{ or } z \geq 2\}$
9. $t^2 \leq 36$ $\{t \mid {}^{-}6 \leq t \leq 6\}$
10. $b^2 \geq 3b + 28$ $\{b \mid b \leq {}^{-}4 \text{ or } b \geq 7\}$
11. $r^2 + 12r \leq {}^{-}27$ $\{r \mid {}^{-}9 \leq r \leq {}^{-}3\}$
12. $a^2 - 10a + 25 \geq 0$ all reals

Challenge Solve each inequality.

1. $(x - 3)(x + 4)(x - 1) > 0$ $\{x \mid {}^{-}4 < x < 1 \text{ or } x > 3\}$
2. $(x + 2)(x - 3)(x + 6) < 0$ $\{x \mid x < {}^{-}6 \text{ or } {}^{-}2 < x < 3\}$
3. $(x - 8)(x + 4)(x + 2) \leq 0$ $\{x \mid x \leq {}^{-}4 \text{ or } {}^{-}2 \leq x \leq 8\}$
4. $(x + 5)(x + 6)(x + 7) \geq 0$ $\{x \mid {}^{-}7 \leq x \leq {}^{-}6 \text{ or } x \geq {}^{-}5\}$
5. $(x + 2)(x + 3)(x - 1)(x - 2) > 0$ $\{x \mid x < {}^{-}3 \text{ or } {}^{-}2 < x < 1 \text{ or } x > 2\}$

Baseball

Using Computers

If you hit a baseball up in the air with a velocity of v meters per second, what is its height after t seconds?

The height, h, in meters, of any object thrown upward can be calculated using the computer program on the right.

```
10 INPUT V, T
20 LET H=V*T−4.9*T↑2
30 PRINT "THE HEIGHT IS" H "AFTER" T "SECONDS."
40 PRINT "IF YOU WANT TO SOLVE ANOTHER
45 PRINT "PROBLEM, INPUT 1; OTHERWISE INPUT 0."
50 INPUT Q
60 IF Q=1, THEN 10
70 END
```

Exercises Solve each problem.

1. What is the formula for the height? $h = vt - 4.9t^2$
2. Find h for $t = 0.1$ and $v = 40$. 3.951
3. Find h for $t = 2.1$ and $v = 12.5$. 4.641
4. Find h for $t = 18.5$ and $v = 295$. 3780.475
5. Find h for $t = 12.4$ and $v = 145.6$. 1052.016

Vocabulary

quadratic function (190)
quadratic term (190)
linear term (190)
constant term (190)
parabola (192)
vertex (192)
axis of symmetry (192)
maximum value (203)
minimum value (203)
boundary (206)

Chapter Summary

1. A quadratic function is a function described by an equation of the form $f(x) = ax^2 + bx + c$ where $a \neq 0$.

   The term ax^2 is called the quadratic term.
   The term bx is called the linear term.
   The term c is called the constant term. (190)
2. Graphs of quadratic functions have a general shape called a parabola. (192)
3. If the sketches of parabolas are folded along their axes of symmetry, the two halves of the parabolas coincide. (192)
4. In general, the graph of $f(x) = a(x - h)^2$ has the same shape and direction of opening as the graph of $f(x) = ax^2$. But its position is shifted h units to the right or left. (196)
5. In general, as the value of k changes, the graph of $f(x) = a(x - h)^2 + k$ is shifted vertically. (199)
6.

$y = a(x - h)^2 + k$	a is positive	a is negative
Vertex	(h, k)	(h, k)
Axis of symmetry	$x = h$	$x = h$
Direction of opening	upward	downward
As the value of $\lvert a \rvert$ increases, the graphs of $y = a(x - h)^2 + k$ narrow.		

(199)

7. If a maximum or minimum problem can be described by a quadratic equation, it often can be solved by finding the vertex of the corresponding graph. (203)
8. The graph of a quadratic inequality will include either the region inside the boundary or outside the boundary. The boundary itself may or may not be included. (206)
9. Quadratic inequalities can be solved using either graphic or algebraic methods. (208)

Chapter Review

For answers to problems **7–8**, **11–18**, and **21–22**, see Teacher's Guide.

7-1 **For each equation, identify the quadratic term, the linear term, and the constant term.**

1. $y = x^2 + 2x + 5$ $x^2, 2x, 5$
2. $y = x - 7$ $0, x, ^-7$
3. $y = 16$ $0, 0, 16$
4. $y = {}^-3x^2 + 2$ $^-3x^2, 0, 2$

Write each equation in quadratic form.

5. $y = 3(x + 2)^2 - 7$ $y = 3x^2 + 12x + 5$
6. $y = {}^-3(x - 7)^2 - 6$ $y = {}^-3x^2 + 42x - 153$

7-2 **Draw the graph of each equation.**

7. $y = 2x^2$
8. $y = -\frac{1}{3}x^2$

Determine the value of a so that each point is on the graph of $y = ax^2$.

9. $(6, 3)$ $\frac{1}{12}$
10. $(2, 2)$ $\frac{1}{2}$

7-3 **Draw the graph of each equation. Name the vertex, axis of symmetry, and direction of opening.**

11. $y = (x - 3)^2$ $(3, 0)$; $x = 3$; up
12. $y = x^2 + 4x + 4$ $(^-2, 0)$; $x = {}^-2$; up
13. $y = \frac{1}{2}(x - 4)^2$ $(4, 0)$; $x = 4$; up
14. $y = {}^-3(x + 2)^2$ $(^-2, 0)$; $x = {}^-2$; down

7-4 **Draw the graph of each quadratic equation. Name the vertex, axis of symmetry, and direction of opening.**

15. $y = (x - 2)^2 - 3$ $(2, ^-3)$; $x = 2$; up
16. $y = 2x^2 - 4$ $(0, ^-4)$; $x = 0$; up
17. $y = 2(x + 1)^2 - 2$ $(^-1, ^-2)$; $x = {}^-1$; up
18. $y = \frac{1}{2}(x + 2)^2 - 1$ $(^-2, ^-1)$; $x = {}^-2$; up

7-5

19. Find two numbers whose sum is 64 and whose product is a maximum. 32 and 32
20. Find two numbers whose difference is 5 and whose product is a minimum. $2\frac{1}{2}$ and $^-2\frac{1}{2}$

7-6 **Graph each quadratic inequality.**

21. $y > x^2 + 3x - 4$
22. $y < x^2 + 4x + 3$

7-7 **Solve each quadratic inequality.**

23. $(x - 4)(x + 2) < 0$
    $\{x \mid {}^-2 < x < 4\}$
24. $x^2 + 8x - 9 > 0$
    $\{x \mid x < {}^-9 \text{ or } x > 1\}$

Chapter Test

Write each equation in quadratic form.

1. $y = (x + 2)^2 + 8$ $y = x^2 + 4x + 12$
2. $y = 2(x - 3)^2 + 5$ $y = 2x^2 - 12x + 23$
3. $y = \frac{1}{2}(x + 4)^2 - 7$ $y = \frac{1}{2}x^2 + 4x + 1$
4. $y = {}^-(x + 2)^2$ $y = {}^-x^2 - 4x - 4$

Graph each equation. Name the vertex, axis of symmetry, and direction of opening.
See Teacher's Guide for answers.

5. $y = (x + 2)^2 + 1$ $({}^-2, 1)$; $x = {}^-2$; up
6. $y = (x - 3)^2$ $(3, 0)$; $x = 3$; up
7. $y = \frac{1}{2}(x + 8)^2 - 3$ $({}^-8, {}^-3)$; $x = {}^-8$; up
8. $y = {}^-2(x + 4)^2 - 6$ $({}^-4, {}^-6)$; $x = {}^-4$; down
9. $y = x^2 + 3x + 6$ $({}^-1\frac{1}{2}, 3\frac{3}{4})$; $x = {}^-1\frac{1}{2}$; up
10. $y = x^2 - 8x - 9$ $(4, {}^-25)$; $x = 4$; up

Solve each problem.

11. Find two numbers whose sum is 18 and whose product is a maximum. 9 and 9
12. A rocket is shot vertically with an initial velocity of 40 feet per second. Its height above the ground after t seconds is given by $h(t) = 40t - 16t^2$. What is its maximum height? When will it return to earth? 25 ft, 2.5 seconds

Graph each quadratic inequality. See Teacher's Guide for answers.

13. $y \leq x^2 + 6x - 7$
14. $y < {}^-x^2 + 4x - 4$

Solve each inequality.

15. $(x + 5)(x + 3) < 0$ $\{x | {}^-5 < x < {}^-3\}$
16. $2x^2 + 3x - 2 > 0$ $\{x | x < {}^-2 \text{ or } x > \frac{1}{2}\}$

Chapter

8

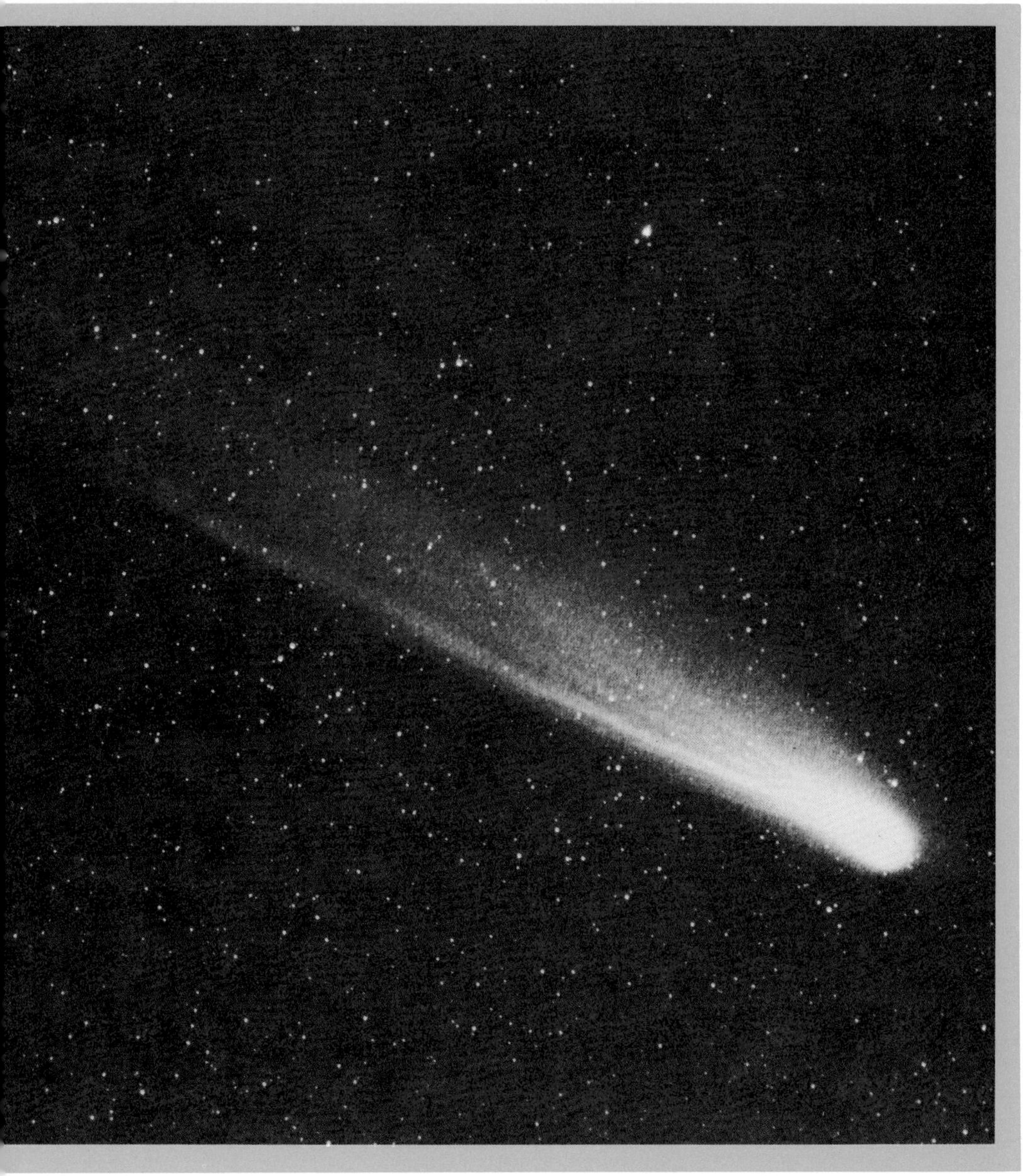

Conics

The orbits of certain comets, satellites, and planets can be described by mathematical curves.

8-1 Distance

Objective: To develop and use the distance formula.

The distance between two points on a number line can be found using absolute value.

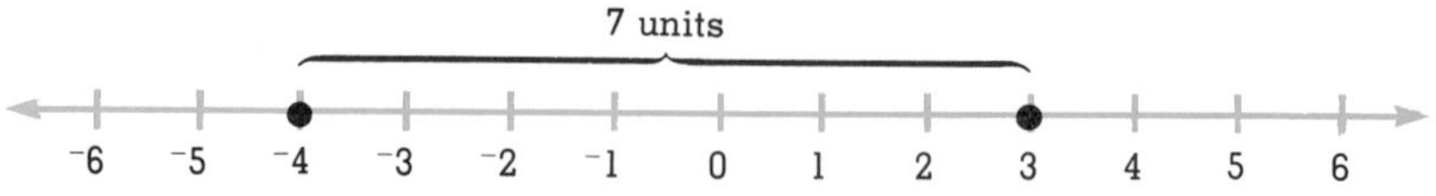

$|^-4 - 3| = |^-7|$ or 7 $\qquad |3 - {}^-4| = |7|$ or 7

Distance Between Points on a Number Line

> **On a number line, the distance between two points whose coordinates are a and b is $|a - b|$ or $|b - a|$.**

Consider two points in a plane with coordinates $(^-2, {}^-6)$ and $(3, {}^-6)$. These points lie on a horizontal line. You can use absolute value to find the distance between the points.

$|^-2 - 3| = |^-5|$ or 5 *Find the difference between the x-coordinates.*

The points with coordinates $(^-2, 3)$ and $(^-2, {}^-6)$ lie on a vertical line. The distance between these two points is 9 units.

$|3 - {}^-6| = |9|$ or 9 *Find the difference between the y-coordinates.*

To find the distance between points with coordinates $(^-2, 3)$ and $(3, {}^-6)$, use the Pythagorean Theorem.

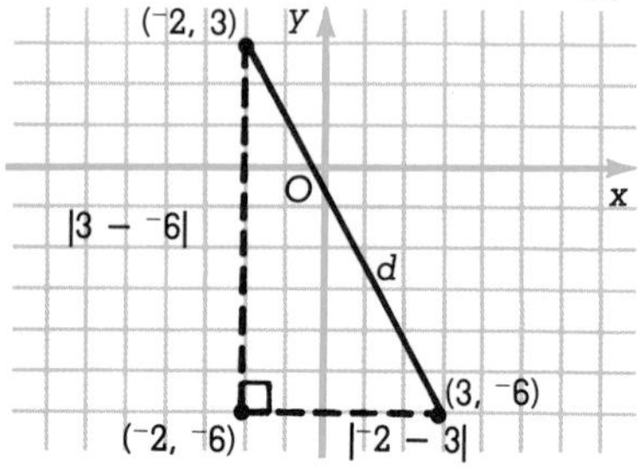

The square of the hypotenuse equals the sum of the squares of the other two sides.

$d^2 = |3 - {}^-6|^2 + |^-2 - 3|^2$

$d^2 = 9^2 + 5^2$

$d^2 = 106$

$d = \sqrt{106}$ *Distance is positive.*

$d \approx 10.2956$

example 1

Find the distance between points with coordinates (1, 2) and $(^-3, {}^-1)$.

$d^2 = |2 - {}^-1|^2 + |1 - {}^-3|^2$

$d^2 = 3^2 + 4^2$

$d^2 = 9 + 16$

$d^2 = 25$

$d = 5$

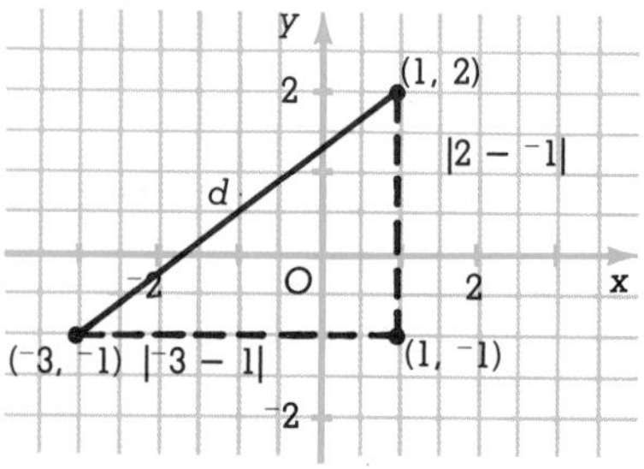

The Pythagorean Theorem can be used to develop a general formula for finding the distance between two points in the plane.

Suppose (x_1, y_1) and (x_2, y_2) are two points in the plane. Form a triangle by drawing a vertical line through (x_1, y_1) and drawing a horizontal line through (x_2, y_2). These lines intersect at the point (x_1, y_2). *Why?*

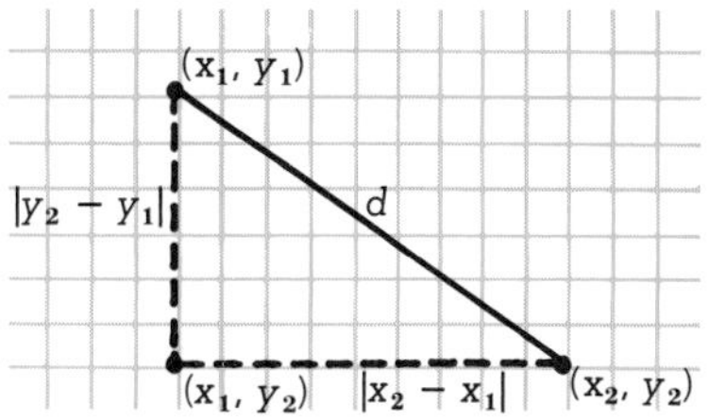

$$d^2 = |x_2 - x_1|^2 + |y_2 - y_1|^2$$
$$d^2 = (x_2 - x_1)^2 + (y_2 - y_1)^2$$
$$d = \sqrt{(x_2 - x_1)^2 + (y_2 - y_1)^2}$$

x_1 is read "x sub one." y_1 is read "y sub one."

Why can $(x_2 - x_1)^2$ be substituted for $|x_2 - x_1|^2$?

The distance between two points with coordinates (x_1, y_1) and (x_2, y_2) is given by the following formula.

$$d = \sqrt{(x_2 - x_1)^2 + (y_2 - y_1)^2}$$

Distance Formula for Two Points in the Plane

example 2

Use the distance formula to find the distance between $(^-1, 6)$ and $(5, ^-4)$.

$$\begin{aligned} d &= \sqrt{(x_2 - x_1)^2 + (y_2 - y_1)^2} \\ &= \sqrt{(5 - {^-1})^2 + (^-4 - 6)^2} \\ &= \sqrt{(6)^2 + (^-10)^2} \\ &= \sqrt{36 + 100} \\ &= \sqrt{136} \\ &= 2\sqrt{34} \end{aligned}$$

The distance is $2\sqrt{34}$ units.

The distance formula can be used to show that a given point on a line segment is the midpoint of that line segment.

example 3

Show that (3, 1) is the midpoint of a line segment having endpoints whose coordinates are $(6, ^-1)$ and (0, 3). This problem assumes that (3, 1) is *on* the line segment.

distance between (3, 1) and $(6, ^-1)$

$$\begin{aligned} d &= \sqrt{(6 - 3)^2 + (^-1 - 1)^2} \\ &= \sqrt{(3)^2 + (^-2)^2} \\ &= \sqrt{9 + 4} \\ &= \sqrt{13} \end{aligned}$$

distance between (3, 1) and (0, 3)

$$\begin{aligned} d &= \sqrt{(0 - 3)^2 + (3 - 1)^2} \\ &= \sqrt{(^-3)^2 + (2)^2} \\ &= \sqrt{9 + 4} \\ &= \sqrt{13} \end{aligned}$$

exercises

Max: 1–12, 1–35; Avg: 1–12, 1–35 odds; Min: 1–35 odds

Exploratory In each of the following, the coordinates of two points are given. Find the distance between these points on a line.

1. 3, 5 2
2. $^-4$, $^-8$ 4
3. $^-3$, 6 9
4. $^-6$, 9 15
5. $^-11$, 0 11
6. 16.2, $^-14.9$ 31.1
7. $^-32$, $^-16$ 16
8. $^-19$, 14 33
9. $^-16$, 0 16
10. $14\frac{2}{5}$, $^-8\frac{3}{10}$ $22\frac{7}{10}$
11. 7.5, $^-7.5$ 15
12. $3\frac{1}{2}$, $^-6\frac{1}{3}$ $9\frac{5}{6}$

Written Use the distance formula to find the distance between each pair of points in the plane whose coordinates are given below.

1. (3, 6), (7, $^-8$) $2\sqrt{53}$
2. (4, 2), ($^-3$, $^-6$) $\sqrt{113}$
3. ($^-3$, 1), (4, $^-2$) $\sqrt{58}$
4. ($^-8$, $^-7$), ($^-2$, $^-1$) $6\sqrt{2}$
5. (6, 7), (8, 0) $\sqrt{53}$
6. (9, 3), ($^-6$, $^-8$) $\sqrt{346}$
7. $\left(\frac{1}{3}, \frac{1}{5}\right)$, (2, $^-4$) $\frac{\sqrt{4594}}{15}$
8. $\left(1, \frac{1}{2}\right)$, $\left(\frac{1}{3}, ^-2\right)$ $\frac{\sqrt{241}}{6}$
9. (0.2, 0.6), (0.3, 0.4) $\sqrt{5}/10$
10. ($^-0.2$, 0.4), ($^-0.5$, $^-0.6$) $\sqrt{1.09}$
11. ($^-2.4$, 0.6), (1.7, 0.8)
12. (3, 3), ($\sqrt{3}$, $\sqrt{3}$) $2\sqrt{6} - 3\sqrt{3}$
13. (3, $\sqrt{3}$), (4, $\sqrt{3}$) 1
14. ($^-2\sqrt{7}$, 10), ($4\sqrt{7}$, 8) 16
15. ($2\sqrt{3}$, $4\sqrt{3}$), ($2\sqrt{3}$, $^-\sqrt{3}$) $5\sqrt{3}$

11. $\sqrt{16.85}$

Each pair of points in the plane represented by the following coordinates is 5 units apart. Find c in each case.

16. (3, 5), (c, 2) 7 or $^-1$
17. ($^-4$, c), ($^-7$, 7) 3 or 11
18. (c, 1.9), (1.2, 5.9) 4.2 or $^-1.8$
19. (13, 10.1), (9, c) 7.1 or 13.1

Suppose a line segment has endpoints with coordinates (x_1, y_1) and (x_2, y_2). Then the midpoint of the line segment has coordinates $\left(\frac{x_1 + x_2}{2}, \frac{y_1 + y_2}{2}\right)$. Find the midpoint of line segments having endpoints with the following coordinates.

20. (6, 7), (8, 0) $(7, \frac{7}{2})$
21. (9, 3), ($^-6$, $^-8$) $(\frac{3}{2}, -\frac{5}{2})$
22. $\left(\frac{1}{3}, \frac{1}{5}\right)$, (2, $^-4$) $(\frac{7}{6}, -\frac{19}{10})$
23. $\left(1, \frac{1}{2}\right)$, $\left(\frac{1}{3}, ^-2\right)$ $(\frac{2}{3}, -\frac{3}{4})$
24. ($^-2.4$, 0.6), (1.7, 0.8) ($^-0.35$, 0.7)
25. (3, 3), ($\sqrt{2}$, $^-\sqrt{2}$) $((3 + \sqrt{2})/2, (3 - \sqrt{2})/2)$

26–31. Use the distance formula to show that each of your answers in problems **20–25** actually represents the midpoint. See student work.

32. Show that $\left(\frac{x_1 + x_2}{2}, \frac{y_1 + y_2}{2}\right)$ is the midpoint of a line segment having endpoints with coordinates (x_1, y_1) and (x_2, y_2). See student work.

33. Find the perimeter of a quadrilateral with vertices at (6, 3), (4, 5), ($^-4$, 6), and ($^-5$, $^-8$). $13\sqrt{2} + \sqrt{65} + \sqrt{197}$

34. Find the lengths of the diagonals of a parallelogram with vertices at (6, 8), ($^-14$, 8), (8, $^-2$) and ($^-12$, $^-2$). $2\sqrt{106}$ and $2\sqrt{146}$

35. Write a computer program to find the distance between any two points in the coordinate plane. Use the points in problems **1–6** as data.

35.
```
10 DATA 3,6,7,-8
20 READ A,B,C,D
30 LET D=SQR((A-C)↑2+(B-D)↑2)
40 PRINT D
50 END
```

8-2 Parabolas

Objective: To graph parabolas using the focus and directrix.

The shape of the reflectors in automobile headlights is based on the **parabola.** The diagram at the right shows a cross section of a reflector. The light source is placed at a special point so the light is reflected in parallel rays. In this way, a straight beam of light is formed.

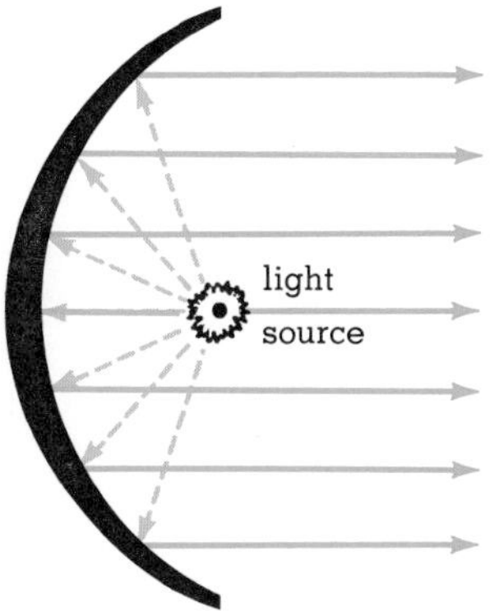

The point where the light source is placed is called the **focus** of the parabola. Parabolas can be defined in terms of the focus.

A parabola is the set of all points which are the same distance from a given point and a given line. The point is called the focus. The line is called the directrix.

Definition of Parabola

The parabola at the right has focus (3, 4) and directrix $y = {}^-2$. You can use the distance formula and the definition of a parabola to find the equation of this parabola. Let (x, y) be a point on the parabola. This point must be the same distance from the focus, (3, 4), as it is from the directrix, $y = {}^-2$.

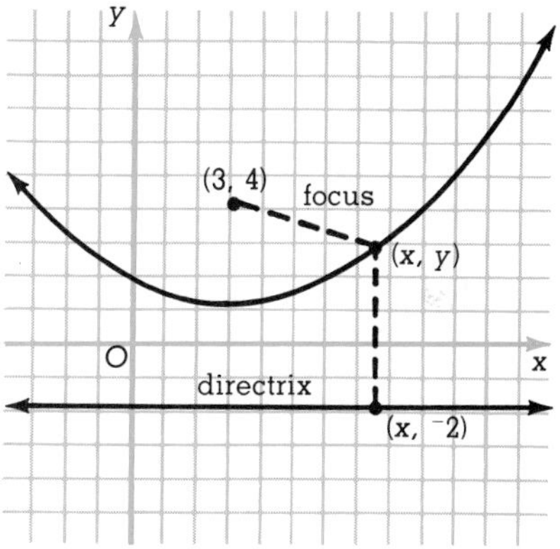

focus *directrix is y = ⁻2*

distance between (x, y) and (3, 4) = distance between (x, y) and (x, ⁻2)

$$\sqrt{(x-3)^2 + (y-4)^2} = \sqrt{(x-x)^2 + (y - {}^-2)^2}$$
$$(x-3)^2 + (y-4)^2 = (x-x)^2 + (y+2)^2$$
$$(x-3)^2 + y^2 - 8y + 16 = y^2 + 4y + 4$$
$$(x-3)^2 = 12y - 12$$
$$\frac{1}{12}(x-3)^2 + 1 = y$$

The equation of a parabola with focus (3, 4) and directrix $y = {}^-2$ is $y = \frac{1}{12}(x-3)^2 + 1$. The vertex is (3, 1) and the axis of symmetry is $x = 3$.

The equation for a parabola can be written in the form $y = a(x - h)^2 + k$ or in the form $x = a(y - k)^2 + h$. Either form provides valuable information about the graph.

Information About Parabolas		
form of equation	$y = a(x - h)^2 + k$	$x = a(y - k)^2 + h$
axis of symmetry	$x = h$	$y = k$
vertex	(h, k)	(h, k)
focus	$\left(h, k + \frac{1}{4a}\right)$	$\left(h + \frac{1}{4a}, k\right)$
directrix	$y = k - \frac{1}{4a}$	$x = h - \frac{1}{4a}$
direction of opening	upward if $a > 0$, downward if $a < 0$	right if $a > 0$, left if $a < 0$

examples

1 **Draw the graph of a parabola with equation $y = 5(x - 2)^2 - 4$.**

vertex: $(2, ^-4)$

axis of symmetry: $x = 2$

focus: $\left(2, ^-4 + \frac{1}{20}\right)$ or $(2, ^-3\frac{19}{20})$

directrix: $y = ^-4 - \frac{1}{20}$ or $^-4\frac{1}{20}$

direction of opening: upward since $a = 5$

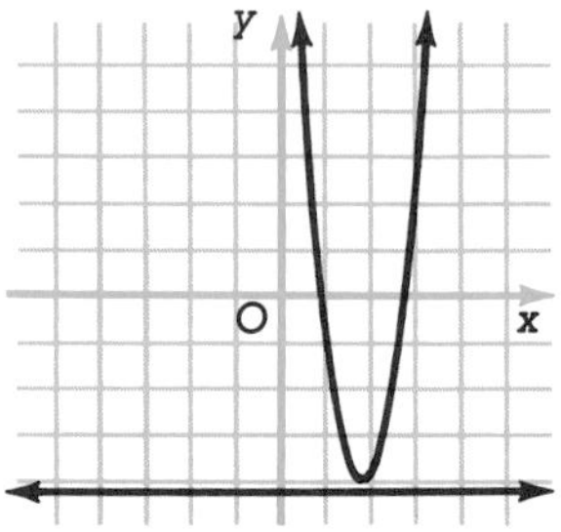

2 **Draw the graph of a parabola with equation $\frac{1}{8}(y + 2)^2 + 3 = x$.**

vertex: $(3, ^-2)$

axis of symmetry: $y = ^-2$

focus: $(3 + 2, ^-2)$ or $(5, ^-2)$

directrix: $x = 3 - 2$ or 1

direction of opening: right since $a = \frac{1}{8}$

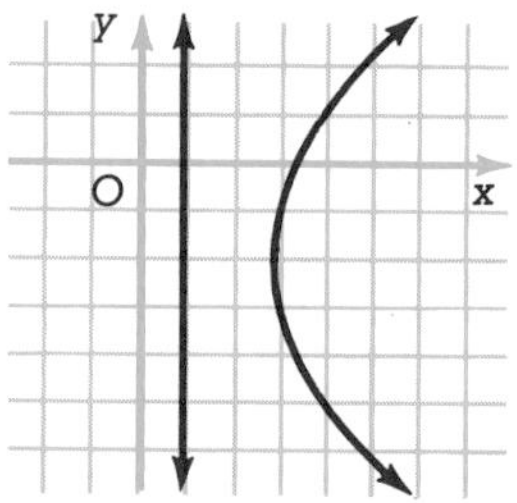

The graph of $y = x^2 - 6x + 6$ is a parabola. This equation can be written in the form $y = a(x - h)^2 + k$ by completing the square.

$$y = x^2 - 6x + 6$$
$$y = x^2 - 6x + \blacksquare - \blacksquare + 6$$
$$y = x^2 - 6x + \left(\frac{-6}{2}\right)^2 - \left(\frac{-6}{2}\right)^2 + 6$$
$$y = (x - 3)^2 - 3$$

exercises

Max: 1–22, 1–38; Avg: 1–22, 1–37 odds; Min: 1–37 odds

Exploratory Complete the square to find the value of c for each expression.

1. $x^2 + 4x + c$ 4
2. $x^2 + 6x + c$ 9
3. $y^2 - 8x + c$ 16
4. $p^2 - 10p + c$ 25
5. $r^2 + 3r + c$ $\frac{9}{4}$
6. $m^2 - 3m + c$ $\frac{9}{4}$
7. $x^2 - 7x + c$ $\frac{49}{4}$
8. $t^2 + 15x + c$ $\frac{225}{4}$
9. $m^2 - 4.1m + c$ 4.2025
10. $n^2 + 0.3n + c$ 0.0225

Change each equation to the form $y = a(x - h)^2 + k$.

11. $x^2 = 10y$ $y = \frac{1}{10}x^2$
12. $x^2 = {}^-2y$ $y = -\frac{1}{2}x^2$
13. $y = x^2 - 6x + 33$ $y = (x - 3)^2 + 24$
14. $y = x^2 + 4x + 1$ $y = (x + 2)^2 - 3$
15. $y = 3x^2 - 24x + 50$ $y = 3(x - 4)^2 + 2$
16. $y = \frac{1}{2}x^2 - 3x + \frac{19}{2}$ $y = \frac{1}{2}(x - 3)^2 + 5$

Change each equation to the form $x = a(y - k)^2 + h$.

17. $6x = y^2$ $x = \frac{1}{6}y^2$
18. $y^2 = {}^-12x$ $x = -\frac{1}{12}y^2$
19. $x = y^2 + 8x + 20$ $x = (y + 4)^2 + 4$
20. $x = y^2 - 14x + 25$ $x = (y - 7)^2 - 24$
21. $x = \frac{1}{4}y^2 - \frac{1}{2}y - 3$ $x = \frac{1}{4}(y - 1)^2 - \frac{13}{4}$
22. $x = 5y^2 - 25y + 60$ $x = 5(y - \frac{5}{2})^2 + \frac{115}{4}$

Written Draw graphs for each of the following equations. Name the vertex, axis of symmetry, focus, directrix, and direction of opening. For problems **1–18** and **29–38**, see the Teacher's Guide.

1. $x^2 = 6y$
2. $y^2 = {}^-8x$
3. $(x + 2)^2 = y - 3$
4. $(x - 4)^2 = 4(y + 2)$
5. $(x - 8)^2 = \frac{1}{2}(y + 1)$
6. $(x + 3)^2 = \frac{1}{4}(y - 2)$
7. $x^2 = (y - 1)$
8. $(x + 2)^2 = 6y$
9. $(y + 3)^2 = 4(x - 2)$
10. $(y - 8)^2 = {}^-4(x - 4)$
11. $y = x^2 - 6x + 33$
12. $x = y^2 + 8y + 20$
13. $x = y^2 - 14y + 25$
14. $y = x^2 + 4x + 1$
15. $x = \frac{1}{4}y^2 - \frac{1}{2}y - 3$
16. $y = \frac{1}{2}x^2 - 3x + \frac{19}{2}$
17. $y = 3x^2 - 24x + 50$
18. $x = 5y^2 - 25y + 60$

Write an equation for each of the following. The focus and directrix of a parabola are given.

19. (2, 4), $y = 6$ $y = -\frac{1}{4}(x - 2)^2 + 5$
20. (3, 5), $y = 1$ $y = \frac{1}{8}(x - 3)^2 + 3$
21. (8, 0), $y = 4$ $y = -\frac{1}{8}(x - 8)^2 + 2$
22. (0, 3), $y = {}^-1$ $y = \frac{1}{8}x^2 + 1$
23. (5, 5), $y = {}^-3$ $y = \frac{1}{16}(x - 5)^2 + 1$
24. (6, 2), $x = 4$ $x = \frac{1}{4}(y - 2)^2 + 5$
25. (3, ⁻1), $x = {}^-2$ $x = \frac{1}{10}(y + 1)^2 + \frac{1}{2}$
26. (4, ⁻3), $y = 6$ $y = -\frac{1}{18}(x - 4)^2 + \frac{3}{2}$
27. (0, 4), $x = 1$ $x = -\frac{1}{2}(y - 4)^2 + \frac{1}{2}$
28. (3, 3), $x = {}^-4$ $x = \frac{1}{14}(y - 3)^2 - \frac{1}{2}$

29–38. Draw graphs for the equations for problems **19–28**.

8–3 Circles

Objective: To graph circles using its equation to find the center and radius.

The shape of record turntables is based on **circles.** All points along the edge of the turntable are the same distance from the spindle.

Definition of Circle

A circle is the set of points in the plane each of which is the same distance from a given point. The given distance is the radius of the circle, and the given point is the center of the circle.

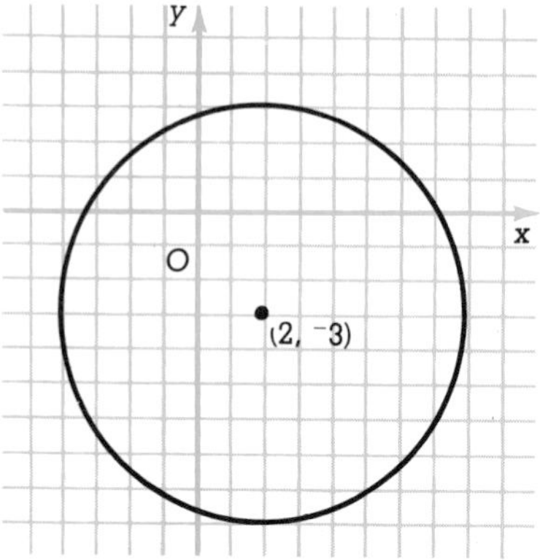

The circle at the left has center $(2, {}^{-}3)$ and radius 6 units. You can use the distance formula and the definition of a circle to find the equation of this circle.

Let (x, y) be a point of the circle. This point must be 6 units from the center of the circle, $(2, {}^{-}3)$.

distance between (x, y) and (2, ⁻3) = 6

$$\sqrt{(x-2)^2 + (y - {}^{-}3)^2} = 6$$
$$(x-2)^2 + (y - {}^{-}3)^2 = 6^2$$
$$(x-2)^2 + (y+3)^2 = 36$$

The equation of a circle with center $(2, {}^{-}3)$ and radius 6 units is $(x-2)^2 + (y+3)^2 = 36$.

Equation of Circle

The equation of a circle with center (h, k) and radius r units is $(x-h)^2 + (y-k)^2 = r^2$.

example 1

Draw the graph of a circle with equation $(x - 10)^2 + (y - 10)^2 = 100$.

Center: (10, 10)
Radius: 10 units

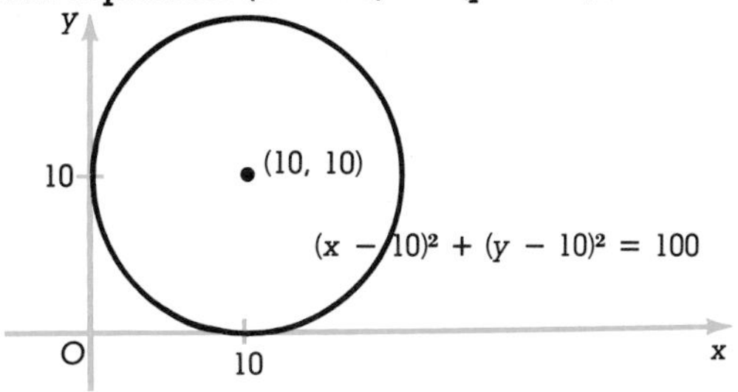

The graph of $x^2 + y^2 - 4x + 10y = 9$ is a circle. To write the equation in the form $(x - h)^2 + (y - k)^2 = r^2$, complete the square.

$$x^2 + y^2 - 4x + 10y = 9$$
$$x^2 - 4x + \blacksquare + y^2 + 10y + \blacksquare = 9 + \blacksquare + \blacksquare$$
$$x^2 - 4x + \left(\frac{^-4}{2}\right)^2 + y^2 + 10y + \left(\frac{10}{2}\right)^2 = 9 + \left(\frac{^-4}{2}\right)^2 + \left(\frac{10}{2}\right)^2$$
$$(x - 2)^2 + (y + 5)^2 = 38$$

The circle has center $(2, {}^-5)$ and radius $\sqrt{38}$ units.

example 2

A circle has equation $y^2 + 3 + x^2 + 9x - 10y = 2$. Find the center and radius of the circle. Draw the graph.

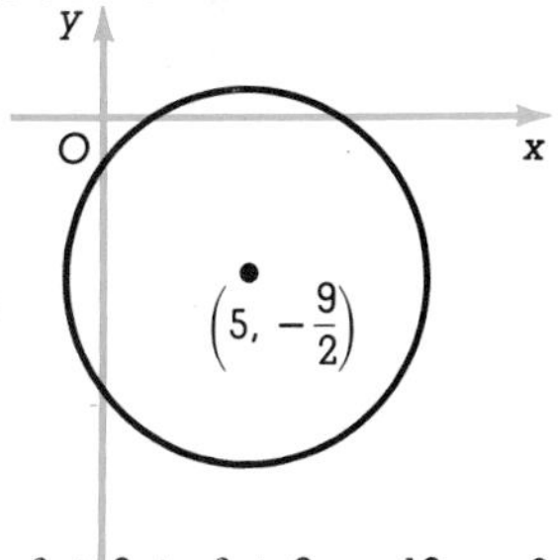

$y^2 + 3 + x^2 + 9x - 10y = 2$

$$y^2 + 3 + x^2 + 9x - 10y = 2$$
$$y^2 - 10y + \blacksquare + x^2 + 9x + \blacksquare = 2 - 3 + \blacksquare + \blacksquare$$
$$y^2 - 10y + \left(\frac{^-10}{2}\right)^2 + x^2 + 9x + \left(\frac{9}{2}\right)^2 = {}^-1 + \left(\frac{^-10}{2}\right)^2 + \left(\frac{9}{2}\right)^2$$
$$(y - 5)^2 + \left(x + \frac{9}{2}\right)^2 = \frac{177}{4}$$

The circle has center $\left(5, -\frac{9}{2}\right)$ and radius $\frac{\sqrt{177}}{2}$ or about 6.7.

exercises

Max: 1–20, 1–32; **Avg:** 1–20, 1–31 odds; **Min:** 1–31 odds

Exploratory State whether the graphs for each of the following equations is a circle or a parabola.

1. $x^2 + y^2 + 7x - 5 = 0$ circle

2. $x^2 + 4x + 4 = 9y + 27$ parabola

3. $y^2 = 6x - 4$ parabola

4. $y = x^2 + 8x + y^2$ circle

5. $x^2 + y + y^2 = 12 - 3x$ circle
6. $x^2 = 5y$ parabola
7. $x^2 + 14x + y^2 + 6y = 23$ circle
8. $y^2 + 8y = 14x$ parabola
9. $y^2 + 6y + 9 = x$ parabola
10. $x^2 = 6y - y^2$ circle

State the center and radius of each circle whose equation is given below.

11. $x^2 + y^2 = 16$ (0, 0), 4
12. $x^2 + (y - 2)^2 = 25$ (0, 2), 5
13. $(x - 2)^2 + y^2 = 9$ (2, 0), 3
14. $x^2 + y^2 = 40$ (0, 0), $2\sqrt{10}$
15. $(x - 10)^2 + (y - 10)^2 = 100$ (10, 10), 10
16. $(x + 2)^2 + (y - 3)^2 = 81$ ($^-2$, 3), 9
17. $(x + 4)^2 + \left(y - \frac{1}{2}\right)^2 = 6$ ($^-4$, $\frac{1}{2}$), $\sqrt{6}$
18. $(x - 4)^2 + y^2 = \frac{16}{25}$ (4, 0), $\frac{4}{5}$
19. $(x + 5)^2 + (y - 2)^2 = \frac{3}{4}$ ($^-5$, 2), $\frac{\sqrt{3}}{2}$
20. $x^2 + (y + 5)^2 = \frac{81}{64}$ (0, $^-5$), $\frac{9}{8}$

Written State the center and radius of each circle whose equation is given below. Then draw the graph.

1. $(x - 2)^2 + y^2 = 9$ (2, 0), 3
2. $(x + 4)^2 + y^2 = 49$ ($^-4$, 0), 7
3. $x^2 + (y - 8)^2 = 64$ (0, 8), 8
4. $x^2 + (y + 2)^2 = 4$ (0, $^-2$), 2
5. $x^2 + y^2 = 64$ (0, 0), 8
6. $x^2 + y^2 = 121$ (0, 0), 11
7. $(x - 2)^2 + (y - 5)^2 = 16$ (2, 5), 4
8. $(x + 2)^2 + (y - 1)^2 = 81$ ($^-2$, 1), 9
9. $(x + 8)^2 + (y - 3)^2 = 25$ ($^-8$, 3), 5
10. $(x - 3)^2 + (y + 2)^2 = 169$ (3, $^-2$), 13
11. $(x + 1)^2 + (y + 9)^2 = 36$ ($^-1$, $^-9$), 6
12. $(x - 5)^2 + (y - 7)^2 = 49$ (5, 7), 7
13. $x^2 + y^2 - 12x - 16y + 84 = 0$ (6, 8), 4
14. $x^2 + y^2 - 18x - 18y + 53 = 0$ (9, 9), $\sqrt{109}$
15. $x^2 + y^2 + 8x - 6y = 0$ ($^-4$, 3), 5
16. $x^2 + y^2 + 14x + 6y = 23$ ($^-7$, $^-3$), 9
17. $x^2 + y^2 - 4x = 9$ (2, 0), $\sqrt{13}$
18. $x^2 + y^2 - 6y = 16$ (0, 3), 5
19. $3x^2 + 3y^2 + 6y + 9x = 2$ ($-\frac{3}{2}$, $^-1$), $\sqrt{141}/6$
20. $x^2 + y^2 + 9x - 8y = {}^-4$ ($-\frac{9}{2}$, 4), $\sqrt{129}/2$
21. $y^2 + 3 + x^2 + 9x - 10y = 6.75$ ($-\frac{9}{2}$, 5), 7
22. $4x^2 + 4y^2 + 36y = {}^-5$ (0, $-\frac{9}{2}$), $\sqrt{19}$
23. $x^2 + 2x + y^2 + 4y = 9$ ($^-1$, $^-2$), $\sqrt{14}$
24. $x^2 + y^2 + 4x = 8$ ($^-2$, 0), $2\sqrt{3}$
25. $x^2 + 2x + y^2 = 10$ ($^-1$, 0), $\sqrt{11}$
26. $x^2 + y^2 + 14x + 6y = {}^-50$ ($^-7$, $^-3$), $2\sqrt{2}$

Write an equation for each of the following. The center and radius of a circle are given.

27. (6, 2), 5 $(x - 6)^2 + (y - 2)^2 = 25$
28. (6, 0), 6 $(x - 6)^2 + y^2 = 36$
29. (0, 3), 2 $x^2 + (y - 3)^2 = 4$
30. ($^-3$, $^-5$), 5 $(x + 3)^2 + (y + 5)^2 = 25$
31. ($^-6$, 2), $\frac{1}{4}$ $(x + 6)^2 + (y - 2)^2 = \frac{1}{16}$
32. ($^-1$, $^-3$), $\frac{2}{3}$ $(x + 1)^2 + (y + 3)^2 = \frac{4}{9}$

Excursions in Algebra

Contest Problem

The following problem appeared in a high school mathematics contest sponsored by the Mathematical Association of America.

In a group of cows and chickens, the number of legs was 14 more than twice the number of heads. How many cows are in the group?

7, the number of chickens can vary.

Investments

Ralph and June Myers have saved \$1000. They want to invest the money so that it is relatively safe and will earn some additional money. They are considering two possibilities.

They can buy a certificate of deposit at the bank and earn $6\frac{1}{2}\%$ interest if they hold the certificate of deposit for two years. How much interest will they earn?

$$\begin{aligned} i &= p \cdot r \cdot t \\ &= 1000 \cdot 0.065 \cdot 2 \\ &= 130 \end{aligned}$$

They will earn \$130 interest.

They will have to pay about 20% income tax on the interest.

20% of \$130 is \$26 $\qquad$ \$130 − \$26 is \$104

They will have \$1000 + \$104 or \$1104 after two years.

They can purchase some preferred stock which pays 7% annual dividends. How much is the dividend for two years?

$$\begin{aligned} i &= p \cdot r \cdot t \\ &= 1000 \cdot 0.07 \cdot 2 \\ &= \$140 \end{aligned}$$

Since there is a \$100 tax exclusion per person per year, they will not be taxed on the dividends. However, they must pay a brokerage fee of about \$20 for buying the stock and about the same for selling it.

\$140 − \$20 − \$20 is \$100

Assuming the value of the stock does not go up or down, they will have \$1100 after two years. The certificate of deposit is the better investment.

Exercises Determine whether stocks or a certificate of deposit would be the better investment if the stock value (\$1000) varies as follows.

1. The stock value (\$1000) goes down 5% over the 2 years. CD
2. The stock value goes up 5% over the 2 years. stock
3. The stock does not pay a dividend but goes up 10% over a 2-year period. The year the stock is sold, income tax of 20% is charged on one-half the amount the stock went up. CD
4. The dividends are 7% per year. The stock goes up 10% in 2 years. The year the stock is sold, income tax of 20% is charged on one-half the amount the stock went up. stock

8–4 Ellipses

Objective: To define and draw the graphs of ellipses.

A circle seen from an angle appears to be another shape, called an **ellipse.** A circle is a special kind of ellipse.

Artists often use ellipses in their work. The instructions below show one way an artist can draw an ellipse.

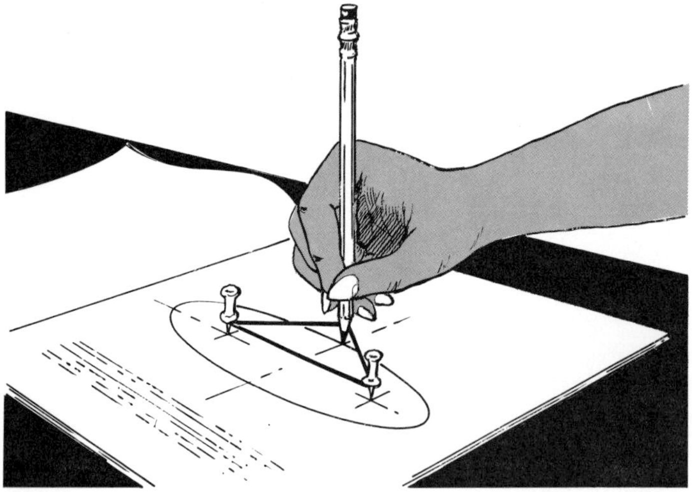

Use a piece of string about 25 cm long. Put two thumbtacks through a piece of paper from the back, about 15 cm apart. Loop the string around the tacks. Place the pencil in the loop. Keep the string tight and draw around the tacks.

The points where the tacks are placed are called the **foci** of the ellipse. Ellipses can be defined in terms of their foci.

Definition of Ellipse

An ellipse is the set of all points in the plane such that the sum of the distances from two given points, called the foci, is constant.

For an ellipse centered at the origin, the portion of the axes that are on or within the ellipse are called the **major** (or longer) **axis** and the **minor** (or shorter) **axis** of the ellipse.

The ellipse at the right has foci $(0, {}^-3)$ and $(0, 3)$. The sum of the distances from the two foci is 8 units. You can use the distance formula and the definition of an ellipse to find the equation of this ellipse.

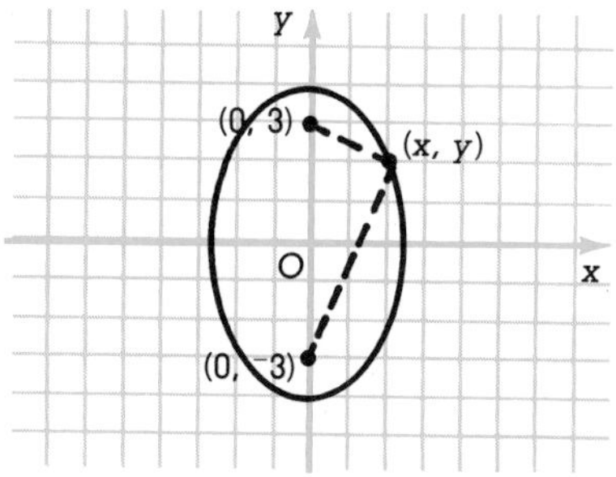

Let (x, y) be a point on the ellipse. The distance between this point and $(0, {}^-3)$ *plus* the distance between the point and $(0, 3)$ is 8 units.

$$\underset{(x, y) \text{ and } (0, {}^-3)}{\text{distance between}} + \underset{(x, y) \text{ and } (0, 3)}{\text{distance between}} = 8$$

$$\sqrt{(x-0)^2 + (y - {}^-3)^2} + \sqrt{(x-0)^2 + (y-3)^2} = 8$$

$$\sqrt{x^2 + (y+3)^2} = 8 - \sqrt{x^2 + (y-3)^2}$$

$$x^2 + (y+3)^2 = 64 - 16\sqrt{x^2 + (y-3)^2} + x^2 + (y-3)^2$$

$$3y - 16 = {}^-4\sqrt{x^2 + (y-3)^2} \quad \textit{Simplify.}$$

$$9y^2 - 96y + 256 = 16[x^2 + (y-3)^2] \quad \textit{Square both sides.}$$

$$112 = 16x^2 + 7y^2 \quad \textit{Simplify.}$$

$$1 = \frac{x^2}{7} + \frac{y^2}{16}$$

The equation of an ellipse with foci $(0, {}^-3)$ and $(0, 3)$, and with 8 units as the sum of the distances from the two foci is $\frac{x^2}{7} + \frac{y^2}{16} = 1$.

The general equation of an ellipse whose foci are $({}^-c, 0)$ and $(c, 0)$, and the sum of the distances from the two foci is $2a$ units, is the following.

$$\frac{x^2}{a^2} + \frac{y^2}{b^2} = 1 \quad \text{when } b^2 = a^2 - c^2$$

Equation of Ellipse

The general equation of an ellipse whose foci are $(0, {}^-c)$ and $(0, c)$, and the sum of the distances from the two foci is $2a$ units, is the following.

$$\frac{x^2}{b^2} + \frac{y^2}{a^2} = 1 \quad \text{when } b^2 = a^2 - c^2$$

Note that $a^2 > b^2$ and $a^2 > c^2$.

The length of the major axis is $2a$ units. The length of the minor axis is $2b$ units.

example 1

Write the equation of an ellipse with foci (6, 0) and (⁻6, 0), and with intercepts (0, 8), (0, ⁻8), (⁻10, 0), and (10, 0). These intercepts are the *vertices* of the ellipse.

To write the equation for this ellipse, you must know the sum of the distances from the two foci. The distance between (⁻10, 0) and (⁻6, 0) is 4 units. The distance between (⁻10, 0) and (6, 0) is 16 units.

$$2a = 4 + 16$$
$$2a = 20$$
$$a = 10$$

Since the foci are (6, 0) and (⁻6, 0), the value of c is 6.

$$b^2 = a^2 - c^2$$
$$b^2 = 10^2 - 6^2$$
$$b^2 = 64$$
$$b = 8$$

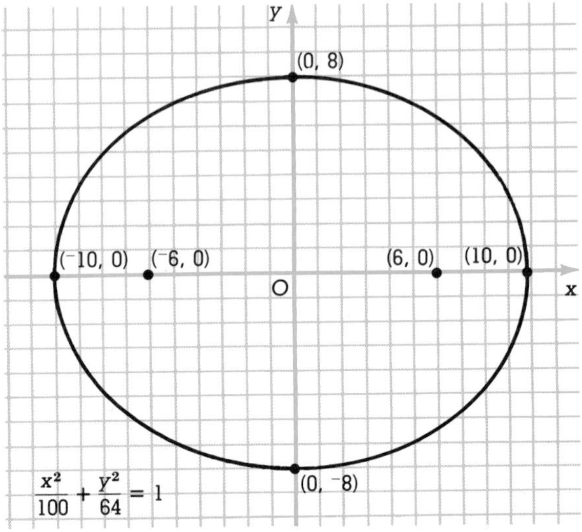

The equation is $\frac{x^2}{100} + \frac{y^2}{64} = 1$.

A circle is a special kind of ellipse. In a circle, the two foci are the same point. This point is the center of the circle. If a circle has center (0, 0), then $b^2 = a^2 - 0$ or a^2. So the equation of the circle can be written in the following form.

$$\frac{x^2}{a^2} + \frac{y^2}{a^2} = 1 \quad \text{or } x^2 + y^2 = a^2$$

Do you see that a represents the radius?

An equation of the form $\frac{x^2}{a^2} + \frac{y^2}{b^2} = 1$ represents an ellipse with center (0, 0). An ellipse with the same shape but center at (h, k) has an equation of the form $\frac{(x - h)^2}{a^2} + \frac{(y - k)^2}{b^2} = 1$.

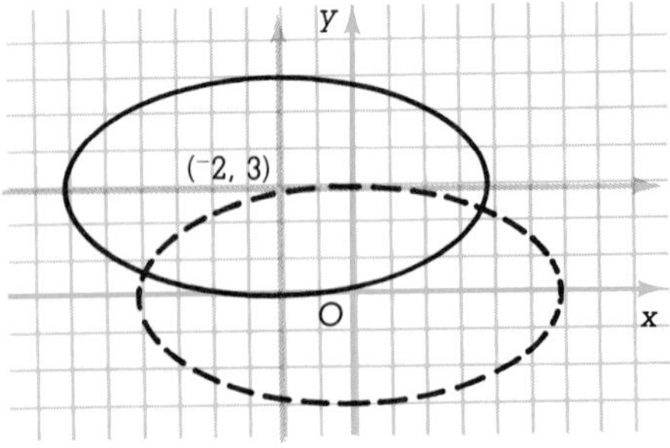

Draw the graph of $\frac{(x + 2)^2}{36} + \frac{(y - 3)^2}{9} = 1$.

The graph has the same shape as the graph of $\frac{x^2}{36} + \frac{y^2}{9} = 1$, but has center at (⁻2, 3) rather than the origin.

exercises

Max: 1–14, 1–24; **Avg:** 1–14, 1–23 odds; **Min:** 1–23 odds

Exploratory State the center of each ellipse with each of the following equations.

1. $\frac{x^2}{9} + \frac{y^2}{4} = 1$ (0, 0)
2. $\frac{x^2}{16} + \frac{y^2}{1} = 1$ (0, 0)
3. $\frac{x^2}{9} + \frac{y^2}{25} = 1$ (0, 0)
4. $\frac{x^2}{10} + \frac{y^2}{36} = 1$ (0, 0)
5. $\frac{x^2}{81} + \frac{(y-5)^2}{49} = 1$ (0, 5)
6. $\frac{(x+3)^2}{25} + \frac{y^2}{9} = 1$ $(^-3, 0)$
7. $\frac{(x-2)^2}{36} + \frac{(y+5)^2}{16} = 1$ $(2, ^-5)$
8. $\frac{(x-4)^2}{16} + \frac{(y-4)^2}{121} = 1$ (4, 4)
9. $\frac{(x+2)^2}{81} + \frac{(y-3)^2}{144} = 1$ $(^-2, 3)$
10. $\frac{(x-2)^2}{16} + \frac{(y+4)^2}{36} = 1$ $(2, ^-4)$

11–14. State the foci of each ellipse given by the equations in problems **1–4**.
11. $(\pm\sqrt{5}, 0)$ **12.** $(\pm\sqrt{15}, 0)$ **13.** $(0, ^\pm4)$ **14.** $(0, \pm\sqrt{26})$

Written State the center, foci, and intercepts for each ellipse given by the following equations. Then draw the graph.

1. $\frac{x^2}{4} + \frac{y^2}{25} = 1$ $(0, 0); (0, \pm\sqrt{21}); (^\pm2, 0), (0, ^\pm5)$
2. $\frac{x^2}{36} + \frac{y^2}{16} = 1$ $(0, 0); (^\pm2\sqrt{5}, 0); (^\pm6, 0), (0, ^\pm4)$
3. $\frac{x^2}{25} + \frac{y^2}{9} = 1$ $(0, 0); (^\pm4, 0); (^\pm5, 0), (0, ^\pm3)$
4. $\frac{x^2}{10} + \frac{y^2}{5} = 1$ $(0, 0); (\pm\sqrt{5}, 0); (\pm\sqrt{10}, 0), (0, \pm\sqrt{5})$
5. $9x^2 + 16y^2 = 144$ $(0, 0); (\pm\sqrt{7}, 0); (^\pm4, 0), (0, ^\pm3)$
6. $3x^2 + 9y^2 = 27$
7. $4x^2 + 9y^2 = 36$ $(0, 0); (\pm\sqrt{5}, 0); (^\pm3, 0), (0, ^\pm2)$
8. $4x^2 + y^2 = 4$ $(0, 0); (0, \pm\sqrt{3}); (0, ^\pm2), (^\pm1, 0)$
9. $36x^2 + 81y^2 = 2916$
10. $x^2 + 16y^2 = 16$ $(0, 0); (\pm\sqrt{15}, 0); (^\pm4, 0), (0, ^\pm1)$

9. $(0, 0); (^\pm3\sqrt{5}, 0); (^\pm9, 0), (0, ^\pm6)$ **6.** $(0, 0); (\pm\sqrt{6}, 0); (^\pm3, 0), (0, \pm\sqrt{3})$

11. Write the equation of an ellipse with foci (0, 8) and $(0, ^-8)$, and with intercepts (0, 10), $(0, ^-10)$, (6, 0), and $(^-6, 0)$. $(x^2/36) + (y^2/100) = 1$
12. Write the equation of an ellipse with foci (0, 12) and $(0, ^-12)$, and with intercepts (5, 0), $(^-5, 0)$, (0, 13), and $(0, ^-13)$. $(x^2/25) + (y^2/169) = 1$

State the center and vertices for each ellipse given by the following equations. Then draw the graph.

13. $\frac{(x-2)^2}{16} + \frac{(y-3)^2}{9} = 1$ $(2, 3); (6, 3), (^-2, 3), (2, 6), (2, 0)$
14. $\frac{(x+3)^2}{36} + \frac{(y-4)^2}{9} = 1$ $(^-3, 4); (^-9, 4), (3, 4), (^-3, 7), (^-3, 1)$
15. $\frac{(x+2)^2}{20} + \frac{(y+3)^2}{40} = 1$ $(^-2, ^-3); (^-2, ^-3 \pm 2\sqrt{10}), (^-2 \pm 2\sqrt{5}, ^-3)$
16. $\frac{(x-8)^2}{4} + \frac{(y+8)^2}{1} = 1$ $(8, ^-8); (10, ^-8), (6, ^-8), (8, ^-9), (8, ^-7)$
17. $\frac{(x+2)^2}{5} + \frac{(y-3)^2}{2} = 1$ $(^-2, 3); (^-2 \pm \sqrt{5}, 3), (^-2, 3 \pm \sqrt{2})$
18. $\frac{(x-4)^2}{121} + \frac{(y+5)^2}{64} = 1$ $(4, ^-5); (15, ^-5), (^-7, ^-5), (4, 3), (4, ^-13)$
19. $9x^2 + 4y^2 - 18x + 16y = 11$
20. $3x^2 + 7y^2 - 12x - 28y = ^-19$
21. $9x^2 + 16y^2 - 18x + 64y = 71$
22. $16x^2 + 25y^2 + 32x - 150y = 159$

19. $(1, ^-2); (1, 1), (1, ^-5), (^-1, ^-2), (3, ^-2)$ **20.** $(2, 2); (2 \pm \sqrt{3}), (2 \pm \sqrt{7}, 2)$
21. $(1, ^-2); (1, 1), (1, ^-5), (5, ^-2), (^-3, ^-2)$ **22.** $(^-1, 3); (^-1, 7), (^-1, ^-1), (4, 3), (^-6, 3)$

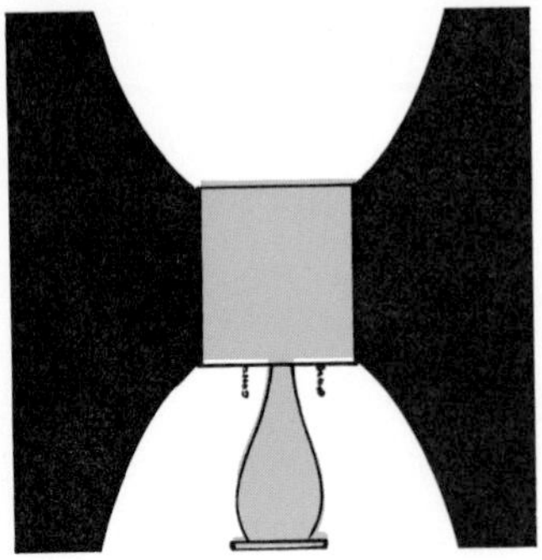

8–5 Hyperbolas

Objective: To define and draw the graphs of hyperbolas.

When the light from a table lamp hits the wall, curves called **hyperbolas** are formed.

Definition of Hyperbola

A hyperbola is the set of all points in the plane such that the absolute value of the difference of the distances from two given points, called the foci, is constant.

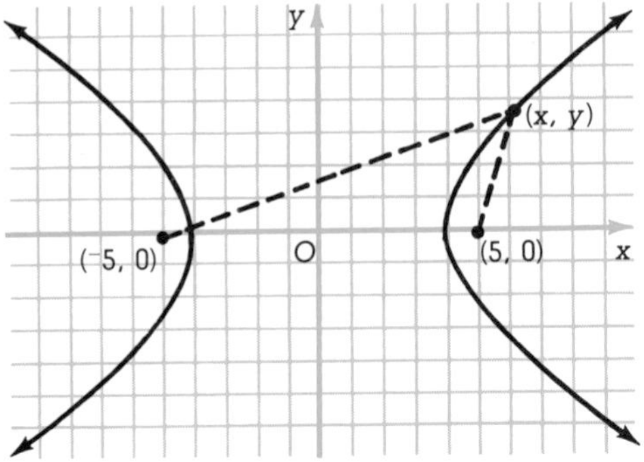

The hyperbola at the left has foci $(^-5, 0)$ and $(5, 0)$. The difference of the distances from the two foci is 8. You can use the distance formula and the definition of a hyperbola to find the equation of this hyperbola.

Let (x, y) be a point on the hyperbola. The distance between (x, y) and $(^-5, 0)$ *minus* the distance between (x, y) and $(5, 0)$ is $^\pm 8$.

distance between (x, y) and $(^-5, 0)$ $-$ *distance between (x, y) and $(5, 0)$* $= {}^\pm 8$

$$\sqrt{(x - {}^-5)^2 + (y - 0)^2} - \sqrt{(x - 5)^2 + (y - 0)^2} = {}^\pm 8$$

$$\sqrt{(x + 5)^2 + y^2} = {}^\pm 8 + \sqrt{(x - 5)^2 + y^2}$$

$$(x + 5)^2 + y^2 = 64 \pm 16\sqrt{(x - 5)^2 + y^2} + (x - 5)^2 + y^2$$

$$5x - 16 = {}^\pm 4\sqrt{(x - 5)^2 + y^2}$$

$$25x^2 - 160x + 256 = 16[(x - 5)^2 + y^2]$$

$$9x^2 - 16y^2 = 144$$

$$\frac{x^2}{16} - \frac{y^2}{9} = 1$$

The equation of a hyperbola with foci $(^-5, 0)$ and $(5, 0)$, and with 8 as the absolute value of the difference between the distances from the two foci is $\frac{x^2}{16} - \frac{y^2}{9} = 1$.

The graph of $\frac{x^2}{36} - \frac{y^2}{64} = 1$ is a hyperbola. Use the following procedure to draw the graph.

1. Find the intercepts.

x-intercepts

$$\frac{x^2}{36} - \frac{0^2}{64} = 1$$
$$\frac{x^2}{36} = 1$$
$$x^2 = 36$$
$$x = {}^{\pm}6$$

The x-intercepts are 6 and $^-6$.

y-intercepts

$$\frac{0^2}{36} - \frac{y^2}{64} = 1$$
$$-\frac{y^2}{64} = 1$$
$$y^2 = {}^-64$$
$$y = {}^{\pm}8i$$

There are no y-intercepts.

2. Find the domain and range.

domain

$$\frac{x^2}{36} - \frac{y^2}{64} = 1$$
$$y^2 = 64\left(\frac{x^2}{36} - 1\right)$$
$$y = {}^{\pm}8\sqrt{\frac{x^2}{36} - 1}$$

Therefore, $\frac{x^2}{36} - 1 \geq 0$. *Why?*

$$x^2 \geq 36$$
$$x \geq 6 \text{ or } x \leq {}^-6$$

The domain is $\{x|x \geq 6 \text{ or } x \leq {}^-6\}$.

range

$$\frac{x^2}{36} - \frac{y^2}{64} = 1$$
$$x^2 = 36\left(\frac{y^2}{64} + 1\right)$$
$$x = {}^{\pm}6\sqrt{\frac{y^2}{64} + 1}$$

Therefore, $\frac{y^2}{64} + 1 \geq 0$. *Why?*

$$y^2 \geq {}^-64$$

Always true.

The range is $\{y|y \text{ is real}\}$.

An asymptote of a curve is a line that the curve approaches but never intersects.

3. Find the asymptotes.

Hyperbolas always have two **asymptotes.** The square roots of the denominators of the equation determine four points. In this case, they are (6, 8), (6, $^-8$), ($^-6$, 8), and ($^-6$, $^-8$). The diagonals of a rectangle with these points as vertices are the asymptotes of the hyperbola.

This statement holds only when the hyperbolas are centered at the origin.

The asymptotes are $y = -\frac{4}{3}x$ *and* $y = \frac{4}{3}x$.

4. Choose several points on the graph.

Substitute values for x and approximate the corresponding values for y.

x	6	8	10	$^-6$	$^-8$	$^-10$
y	0	$^{\pm}7.2$	$^{\pm}10.7$	0	$^{\pm}7.2$	$^{\pm}10.7$

5. Using the asymptotes as a guide, draw a smooth curve through the known points of the graph.

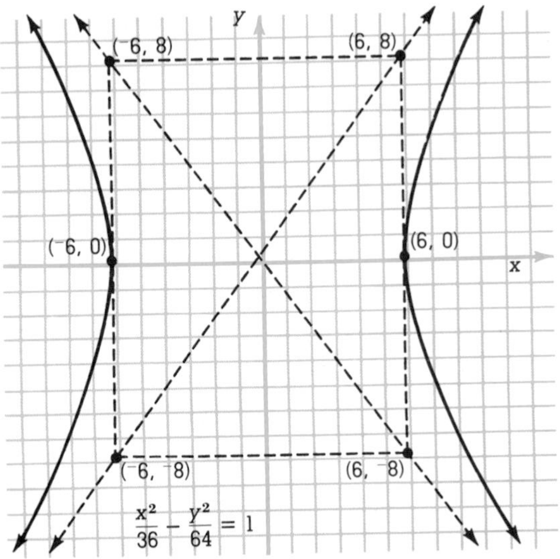

This hyperbola has asymptotes $y = \frac{b}{a}x$ and $y = -\frac{b}{a}x$.

Equation of Hyperbola

The general equation of a hyperbola with foci $(^-c, 0)$ and $(c, 0)$, and with the absolute value of the difference between distances from the two foci $2a$ units, can be written in the following form.

$$\frac{x^2}{a^2} - \frac{y^2}{b^2} = 1 \qquad \text{when } c^2 = a^2 + b^2$$

The general equation of a hyperbola with foci $(0, {}^-c)$ and $(0, c)$, and with the absolute value of the difference between distances from the two foci $2a$ units, can be written in the following form.

$$\frac{y^2}{a^2} - \frac{x^2}{b^2} = 1 \qquad \text{when } c^2 = a^2 + b^2$$

This hyperbola has asymptotes $y = \frac{a}{b}x$ and $y = -\frac{a}{b}x$.

exercises

Max: 1–9, 1–35; **Avg:** 1–9, 1–35 odds; **Min:** 1–35 odds

Exploratory State whether the graph of each of the following equations is an ellipse or a hyperbola.

1. $\frac{x^2}{9} + \frac{y^2}{4} = 1$ ellipse
2. $\frac{x^2}{16} - \frac{y^2}{4} = 1$ hyperbola
3. $\frac{y^2}{18} - \frac{x^2}{20} = 1$ hyperbola
4. $\frac{x^2}{5} + \frac{y^2}{5} = 1$ ellipse
5. $\frac{x^2}{36} - \frac{y^2}{1} = 1$ hyperbola
6. $\frac{x^2}{10} + \frac{y^2}{36} = 1$ ellipse
7. $\frac{y^2}{25} + \frac{x^2}{9} = 1$ ellipse
8. $\frac{x^2}{81} - \frac{y^2}{36} = 1$ hyperbola
9. $\frac{y^2}{100} - \frac{x^2}{144} = 1$ hyperbola

Written State the intercepts and foci of each hyperbola.

1. $\frac{x^2}{9} - \frac{y^2}{25} = 1$ $(^-3, 0); (\pm\sqrt{34}, 0)$
2. $\frac{x^2}{16} - \frac{y^2}{4} = 1$ $(^-4, 0); (\pm 2\sqrt{5}, 0)$
3. $\frac{x^2}{36} - \frac{y^2}{1} = 1$ $(^-6, 0); (\pm\sqrt{37}, 0)$
4. $\frac{y^2}{6} - \frac{x^2}{2} = 1$ $(0, \pm\sqrt{6}); (0, ^-2\sqrt{2})$
5. $\frac{y^2}{81} - \frac{x^2}{25} = 1$ $(0, ^-9); (0, \pm\sqrt{106})$
6. $\frac{y^2}{18} - \frac{x^2}{20} = 1$ $(0, ^-3\sqrt{2}); (0, \pm\sqrt{38})$

State the equations of the asymptotes of each hyperbola.

7. $\frac{x^2}{4} - \frac{y^2}{9} = 1$ $y = \pm\frac{3}{2}x$
8. $\frac{y^2}{16} - \frac{x^2}{25} = 1$ $y = \pm\frac{4}{5}x$
9. $\frac{x^2}{81} - \frac{y^2}{36} = 1$ $y = \pm\frac{2}{3}x$
10. $\frac{y^2}{100} - \frac{x^2}{144} = 1$ $y = \pm\frac{5}{6}x$
11. $\frac{x^2}{9} - \frac{y^2}{16} = 1$ $y = \pm\frac{4}{3}x$
12. $\frac{x^2}{9} - \frac{y^2}{4} = 1$ $y = \pm\frac{2}{3}x$
13. $25x^2 - 4y^2 = 100$ $y = \pm\frac{5}{2}x$
14. $x^2 - y^2 = 4$ $y = ^\pm x$
15. $x^2 - 2y^2 = 2$ $y = \pm(\sqrt{2}/2)x$
16. $y^2 - 4x^2 = 4$ $y = ^\pm 2x$
17. $y^2 = 36 + 4x^2$ $y = ^\pm 2x$
18. $36y^2 - 81x^2 = 2916$ $y = \pm\frac{3}{2}x$

19–24. Graph each equation in problems 1–6. For answers to problems 19–24, see Teacher's Guide.

An equation of the form $xy = k$ when $k \neq 0$ represents a hyperbola having the x-axis and y-axis as asymptotes.

25. Complete the following table of values for $xy = 2$.

x	1	2	4	8	$^-1$	$^-4$	$^-8$
y	2	1	$\frac{1}{2}$	$\frac{1}{4}$	$^-2$	$-\frac{1}{2}$	$-\frac{1}{4}$

26. Find the domain for $xy = 2$.
27. Find the range for $xy = 2$. $\{y|y \text{ is real}, y \neq 0\}$
28. Sketch the graph of $xy = 2$. See Teacher's Guide.
26. $\{x|x \text{ is real}, x \neq 0\}$

The equation $\frac{y^2}{a^2} - \frac{x^2}{b^2} = 1$ represents a hyperbola with center (0, 0). An equation of the form $\frac{(y-k)^2}{a^2} - \frac{(x-h)^2}{b^2} = 1$ represents a hyperbola with center (h, k). Complete the following exercises for a hyperbola with equation $\frac{(y-3)^2}{16} - \frac{(x+2)^2}{9} = 1$.

29. Complete the following table of values. Round to the nearest tenth.

x	$^-5$	$^-4$	$^-3$	$^-2$	$^-1$	0	1	2
y	3 ± 5.7	3 ± 4.8	3 ± 4.2	3 ± 4	3 ± 4.2	3 ± 4.8	3 ± 5.7	3 ± 6.7

30. Find the vertices. $(^-2, 7), (^-2, ^-1)$
31. Find the domain. $\{x|x \text{ is real}\}$
32. Find the range. $\{y|y \geq 7 \text{ or } y \leq ^-1\}$
33. Find the asymptotes. $3y = 4x + 17$, $3y = ^-4x + 1$
34. Sketch the graph. See Teacher's Guide.
35. Compare the graph to the graph of $\frac{y^2}{16} - \frac{x^2}{9} = 1$. The graph is shifted two units to the left and three units upward.

8–6 Conic Sections

Objective: To learn the standard form of the equation for conic sections.

Parabolas, circles, ellipses, and hyperbolas can be formed by slicing a hollow double cone in different directions. The curves, therefore, are called **conic sections.**

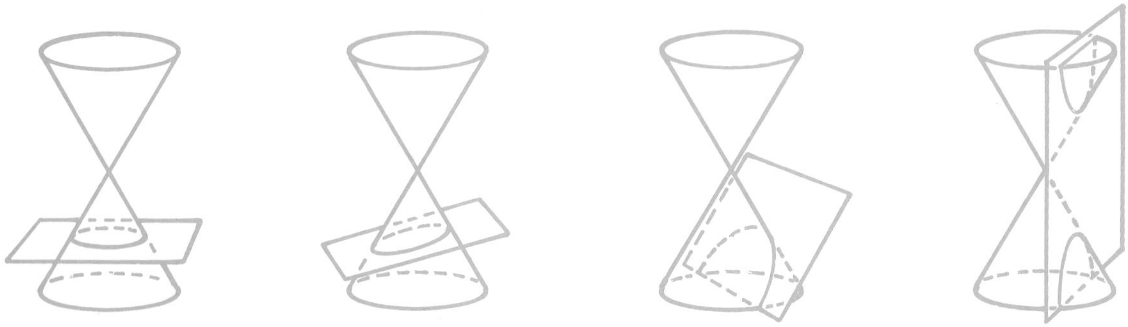

circle ellipse parabola hyperbola

The conic sections are related in another way, too. Each conic section can be described by a quadratic equation in two variables.

Equation for Conic Sections

The equation of a conic section can be written in the form $Ax^2 + Bxy + Cy^2 + Dx + Ey + F = 0$ where A, B, and C are not all zero.

Most of the conic sections you have studied have equations with $B = 0$.

To identify the conic section a quadratic equation in two variables represents, rewrite the equation in the forms you have learned. The following table summarizes these forms. *Often this involves completing the square.*

If $A = C$, the equation represents a circle. If A and C have the same sign, the equation represents an ellipse. If A and C have opposite signs, the equation represents a hyperbola. If either A or C is zero, the equation represents a parabola.

Conic Section	Standard Form of Equation
parabola	$y = a(x - h)^2 + k$ or $x = a(y - k)^2 + h$
circle	$(x - h)^2 + (y - k)^2 = r^2$
ellipse	$\frac{(x - h)^2}{a^2} + \frac{(y - k)^2}{b^2} = 1$ or $\frac{(x - h)^2}{b^2} + \frac{(y - k)^2}{a^2} = 1$
hyperbola	$\frac{(x - h)^2}{a^2} - \frac{(y - k)^2}{b^2} = 1$ or $\frac{(y - k)^2}{a^2} - \frac{(x - h)^2}{b^2} = 1$ or $xy = k$

examples

1 **Is the graph of $(y-4)^2 = 9(x-4)$ a parabola, circle, ellipse, or hyperbola?**

$$(y-4)^2 = 9(x-4)$$

$$\frac{1}{9}(y-4)^2 = x-4$$

$$\frac{1}{9}(y-4)^2 + 4 = x \qquad \textit{a is } \frac{1}{9}\textit{, k is 4, h is 4}$$

The graph is a parabola.

2 **Is the graph of $x^2 + y^2 = x + 2$ a parabola, circle, ellipse, or hyperbola?**

$$x^2 + y^2 = x + 2$$

$$x^2 - x + \blacksquare + y^2 = 2 + \blacksquare$$

$$x^2 - x + \left(-\frac{1}{2}\right)^2 + y^2 = 2 + \left(-\frac{1}{2}\right)^2 \qquad \textit{Complete the square.}$$

$$x^2 - x + \frac{1}{4} + y^2 = 2 + \frac{1}{4}$$

$$\left(x - \frac{1}{2}\right)^2 + y^2 = \frac{9}{4}$$

$$\left(x - \frac{1}{2}\right)^2 + (y-0)^2 = \left(\frac{3}{2}\right)^2 \qquad \textit{h is } \frac{1}{2}\textit{, k is 0, r is } \frac{3}{2}$$

The graph is a circle. The graph is also an ellipse with a and b both 1.
A circle is a special kind of ellipse.

3 **Is the graph of $x^2 - 4x - 1 = \frac{5}{6}(y-1)^2$ a parabola, circle, ellipse, or hyperbola?**

$$x^2 - 4x - 1 = \frac{5}{6}(y-1)^2$$

$$x^2 - 4x + \quad = \frac{5}{6}(y-1)^2 + 1 + \quad$$

$$x^2 - 4x + \left(\frac{-4}{2}\right)^2 = \frac{5}{6}(y-1)^2 + 1 + \left(\frac{-4}{2}\right)^2 \qquad \textit{Complete the square.}$$

$$(x-2)^2 = \frac{5}{6}(y-1)^2 + 5$$

$$\frac{(x-2)^2}{5} = \frac{(y-1)^2}{6} + 1 \qquad \textit{Divide both sides by 5.}$$

$$\frac{(x-2)^2}{5} - \frac{(y-1)^2}{6} = 1 \qquad \textit{h is 2, k is 1, a is } \sqrt{5}\textit{, b is } \sqrt{6}$$

The graph is a hyperbola.

exercises

Max: 1–60; Avg: 1–59 odds; Min: 1–59 odds

Written State whether each graph of the following equations is a parabola, a circle, an ellipse, or a hyperbola. *Remember, a circle is a special kind of ellipse.*

1. $x^2 = 8y$ parabola
2. $x^2 + y^2 = 9$ circle
3. $4x^2 + 2y^2 = 8$ ellipse
4. $3x^2 + 3y^2 = 81$ circle
5. $xy = 6$ hyperbola
6. $y = x^2 + 3x + 1$ parabola
7. $\frac{x^2}{8} - \frac{y^2}{10} = 1$ hyperbola
8. $\frac{x^2}{4} + \frac{y^2}{6} = 1$ ellipse
9. $x^2 + y = x + 2$ parabola
10. $xy = {}^-3$ hyperbola
11. $\frac{x^2}{9} - \frac{y^2}{4} = 1$ hyperbola
12. $\frac{x^2}{4} + \frac{y^2}{4} = 1$ circle
13. $3x^2 + 4y^2 + 8y = 8$ ellipse
14. $9x^2 - 4y^2 = 4$ hyperbola
15. $3xy = 7$ hyperbola
16. $(y - 4)^2 = 9(x - 4)$ parabola
17. $\frac{(x - 3)^2}{9} + \frac{(y + 2)^2}{25} = 1$ ellipse
18. $\frac{y^2}{16} - \frac{x^2}{8} = 1$ hyperbola
19. $13x^2 - 49 = {}^-13y^2$ circle
20. $x = \frac{13}{y}$ hyperbola

21–40. Write each equation in problems **1–20** in standard form.
41–60. Graph each equation in problems **1–20**.

For answers to problems **41–60**, see Teacher's Guide.

22, 25, 27, 28, 30–32, 37, 38 are in standard form. For other answers, see below.

21. $y = \frac{1}{8}x^2$
23. $\frac{x^2}{2} + \frac{y^2}{4} = 1$
24. $x^2 + y^2 = 27$
26. $y = (x + \frac{3}{2})^2 - \frac{5}{4}$
29. $y = {}^-(x - \frac{1}{2})^2 + \frac{9}{4}$
33. $\frac{x^2}{4} + \frac{(y + 1)^2}{3} = 1$
34. $(x^2/\frac{4}{9}) - y^2 = 1$
35. $xy = \frac{7}{3}$
36. $x = \frac{1}{9}(y - 4)^2 - 4$
39. $x^2 + y^2 = \frac{49}{13}$
40. $xy = 13$

Excursions in Algebra

The Capitol

If rays of light or sound are emitted from one focus of an elliptical reflector, these rays are concentrated at the other focus.

The elliptical chamber of the United States Capitol Building in Washington, D.C. has this property. A person standing at one focus and whispering is easily heard by a person standing at the other focus.

8-7 Graphing Quadratic Systems

Objective: To graph quadratic systems.

Consider the following system of equations.

$$y = x^2 - 4$$
$$y = {}^-2x - 1$$

To solve this system you must find the ordered pairs that satisfy *both* equations. One way is to graph each equation and find the intersection of the two graphs.

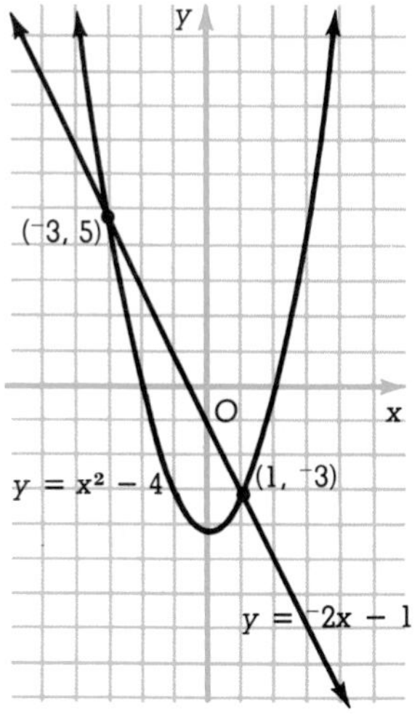

The graph of $y = x^2 - 4$ is a parabola. The graph of $y = {}^-2x - 1$ is a line. The parabola and the line intersect in two points, $({}^-3, 5)$ and $(1, {}^-3)$. The solutions of the system are $({}^-3, 5)$ and $(1, {}^-3)$.

If the graphs of a system of equations are a conic and a straight line, the system will have zero, one, or two solutions.

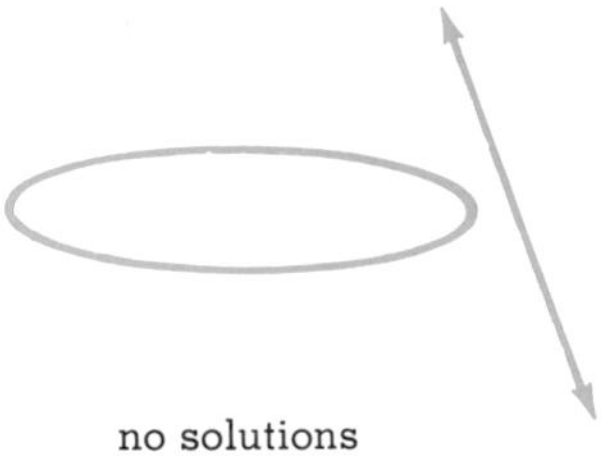

no solutions

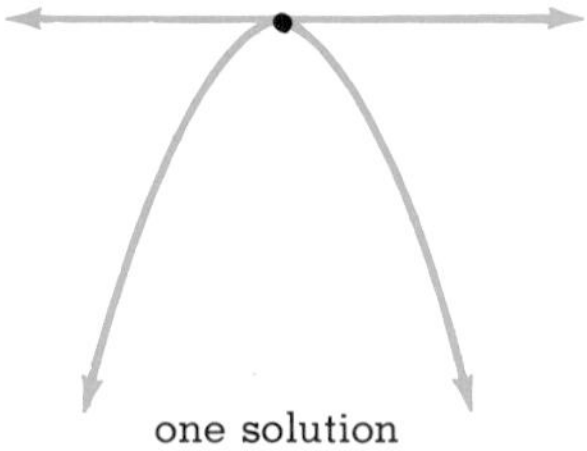

one solution

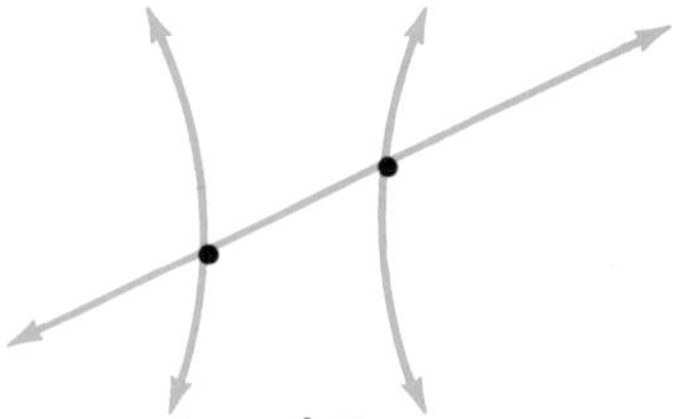

two solutions

example 1

Graph the following system. Then state the solution of the system of equations.

$$\mathbf{x^2 + y^2 = 25}$$
$$\mathbf{y - x = 1}$$

The graph of $x^2 + y^2 = 25$ is a circle centered at the origin with radius 5 units.

The graph of $y - x = 1$ is a line with slope 1 and y-intercept 1.

The solutions of the system are $(3, 4)$ and $({}^-4, {}^-3)$.

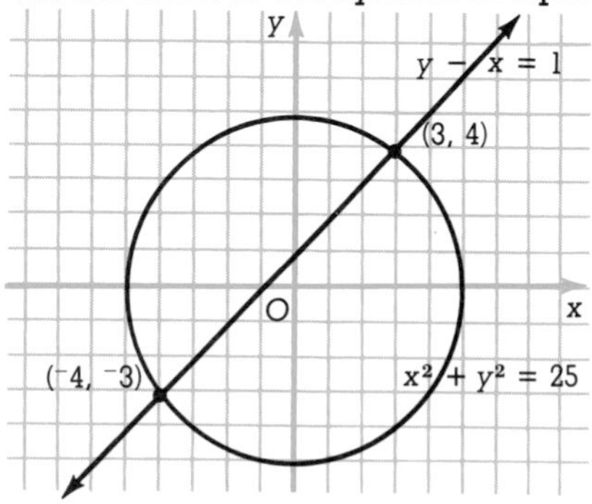

If the graphs of a system of equations are two conics, the system will have zero, one, two, three, or four solutions.

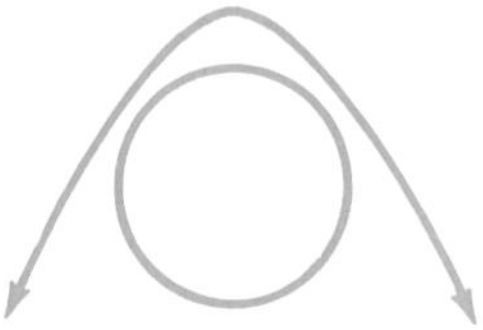

no solutions

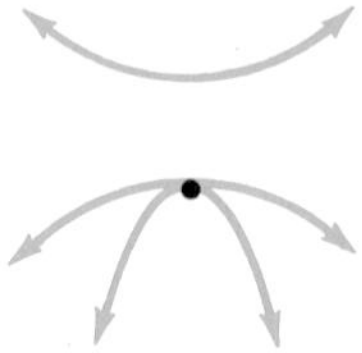

one solution

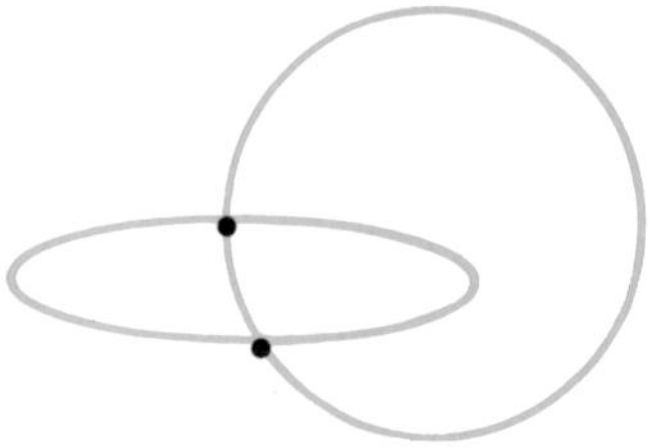

two solutions

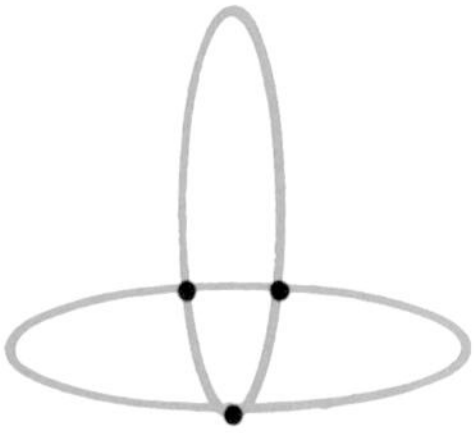

three solutions

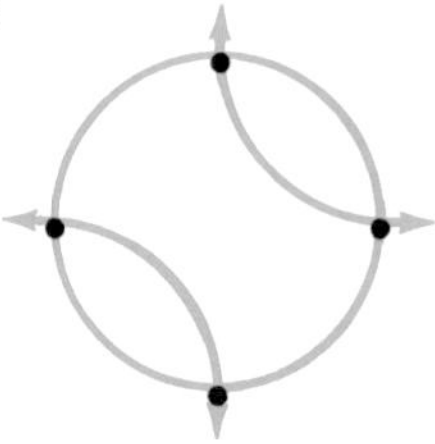

four solutions

examples

2 **Graph the following system. Then state the solution of the system of equations.**

$$x^2 + y^2 = 25$$
$$4y + x^2 = 25$$

The graph of $x^2 + y^2 = 25$ is a circle centered at the origin with radius 5 units. The graph of $4y + x^2 = 25$ is a parabola which opens downward, has vertex $(0, 6\frac{1}{4})$, and x-intercepts 5 and $^{-}5$. The solutions of the system are (5, 0), ($^{-}5$, 0), (3, 4), and ($^{-}3$, 4).

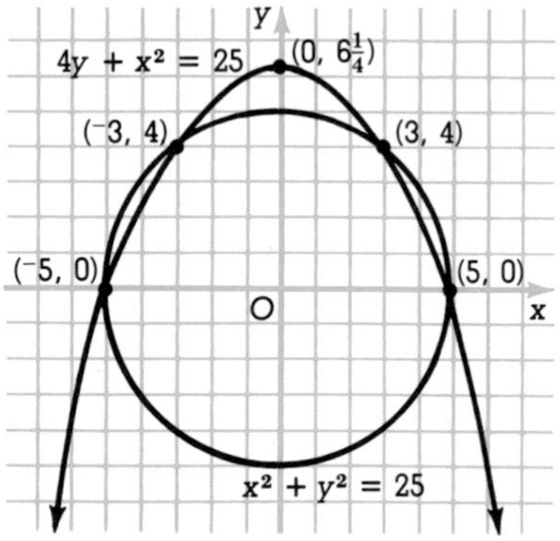

3 **Graph the following system. Then state the solution of the system of equations.**

$$y^2 - x^2 = 16$$
$$x^2 - y^2 = 16$$

The graph of $y^2 - x^2 = 16$ is a hyperbola with y-intercepts 4 and $^{-}4$. The graph of $x^2 - y^2 = 16$ is a hyperbola with x-intercepts 4 and $^{-}4$. The system has *no* solutions.

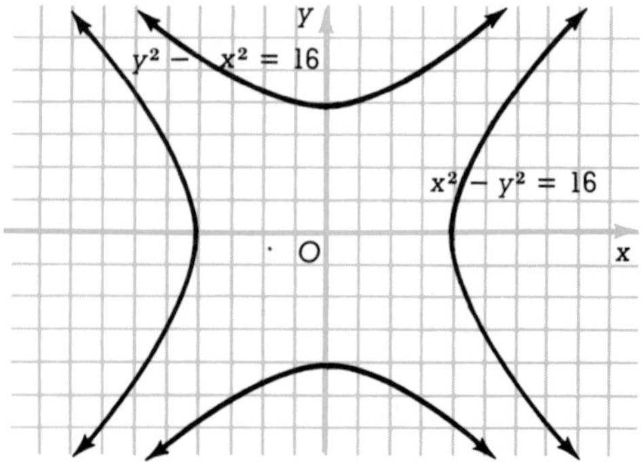

exercises

Max: 1–30; Avg: 1–29 odds; Min: 1–29 odds

Written Graph the following systems of equations. Then state the solutions of the systems.

1. $x^2 + y^2 = 16$ $(^\pm 2\sqrt{3}, 2)$
   $y = 2$
2. $y = x^2$ $(^-1, 1)$
   $y - 2 = x$ $(2, 4)$
3. $x = y$ $(2, 2)$
   $\frac{x^2}{20} + \frac{y^2}{5} = 1$ $(^-2, ^-2)$
4. $xy = 3$ $(1, 3)$
   $y = 3x$ $(^-1, ^-3)$
5. $\frac{x^2}{9} - \frac{y^2}{9} = 1$ $(3, 0)$
   $\frac{2}{3}y = \frac{1}{3}x - 1$ $(^-5, ^-4)$
6. $x^2 + y^2 = 25$ $(^-4, ^-3)$
   $x + y = {^-7}$ $(^-3, ^-4)$
7. $(y - 1)^2 = x + 4$ $(0, ^-1)$
   $y + x = {^-1}$ $(^-3, 2)$
8. $\frac{x^2}{16} + \frac{y^2}{4} = 1$ $(0, 2)$
   $3y + 5x = 6$ $(2.2, -\frac{5}{3})$
9. $y^2 - x^2 = 9$ $(^\pm 5.2, 6)$
   $y = 6$
10. $xy = 1$ $(\frac{1}{4}, 4)$
    $y = 4$
11. $x^2 + y^2 = 9$ no solutions
    $x + y = 7$
12. $\frac{x^2}{4} + \frac{y^2}{1} = 1$ no solutions
    $x - y = 6$
13. $\frac{x^2}{16} - \frac{y^2}{4} = 1$ no solutions
    $y = 3x - 3$
14. $xy = {^-2}$ no solutions
    $y = x$
15. $\frac{(x - 2)^2}{16} + \frac{y^2}{16} = 1$ $(^-2, 0)$
    $y - x = 2$ $(2, 4)$
16. $y = {^-x^2}$ $(^-1, ^-1)$
    $y = {^-x} - 2$ $(2, ^-4)$
17. $x = {^-y^2} + 2$ $(0, \sqrt{2})$
    $2y - 2\sqrt{2} = x(\sqrt{2} + 2)$ $(^-2, ^-2)$
18. $\frac{x^2}{36} - \frac{y^2}{4} = 1$ no solutions
    $y = x$
19. $\frac{(x - 3)^2}{25} + \frac{(y - 4)^2}{9} = 1$ $(3, 7)$
    $5y + 3x = 44$ $(8, 4)$
20. $(x - 3)^2 + (y + 6)^2 = 36$ $(3, 0)$
    $y + 3 = x$ $(^-3, ^-6)$
21. $5x^2 + y^2 = 30$ $(^\pm 1, 5)$
    $y^2 - 16 = 9x^2$ $(^\pm 1, ^-5)$
22. $x^2 - y^2 = 15$ $(^-4, ^-1)$
    $xy = 4$ $(4, 1)$
23. $2y^2 = 10 - x^2$ $(^\pm 2, \sqrt{3})$
    $3x^2 - 9 = y^2$ $(^\pm 2, ^-\sqrt{3})$
24. $4x^2 + 9y^2 = 36$ $(^\pm 3, 0)$
    $4x^2 - 9y^2 = 36$
25. $x^2 + 4y^2 = 4$ no solutions
    $(x - 10)^2 + (y - 11)^2 = 1$
26. $x^2 + 4y^2 = 36$ $(0, 3)$
    $y = {^-x^2} + 3$ $(^\pm 2.4, -\frac{11}{4})$
27. $x^2 - y^2 = 25$ no solutions
    $x^2 - y^2 = 7$
28. $x^2 + y^2 = 16$ no solutions
    $x^2 + y^2 = 9$
29. $x^2 + y^2 = 64$ $(^\pm 8, 0)$
    $x^2 + 64y^2 = 64$
30. $x^2 - y^2 = 16$ no solutions
    $y^2 - x^2 = 16$

8–8 Solving Quadratic Systems

Objective: To solve quadratic systems.

You can use graphs to help find the solutions of a quadratic system. Often you must use algebra to find the exact solutions.

examples

1 **State the solutions of the following system of equations.**

$$x^2 + y^2 = 25$$
$$y - x = 1$$

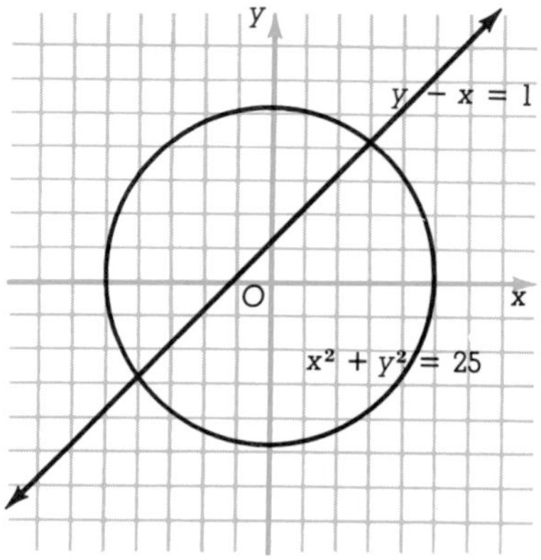

The graphs of the equations are a circle and a straight line. The graphs show that there are two solutions to the system. Also, the values of x are between $^-5$ and 5. And the values of y are between $^-5$ and 5.

Use the substitution method to find the exact solutions. First rewrite $y - x = 1$ as $y = x + 1$.

$$x^2 + y^2 = 25$$
$$x^2 + (x + 1)^2 = 25 \quad \textit{Substitute } x + 1 \textit{ for } y.$$
$$x^2 + x^2 + 2x^2 + 1 = 25$$
$$2x^2 + 2x - 24 = 0$$
$$2(x + 4)(x - 3) = 0$$
$$x + 4 = 0 \quad \text{or} \quad x - 3 = 0$$
$$x = {}^-4 \qquad\qquad x = 3$$
$$y = x + 1 \qquad\qquad y = x + 1$$
$$= {}^-4 + 1 \qquad\qquad = 3 + 1$$
$$= {}^-3 \qquad\qquad = 4$$

The solutions are $(^-4, {}^-3)$ and $(3, 4)$.

2 **State the solutions of the following system of equations.**

$$x^2 + 2y^2 = 10$$
$$3x^2 - y^2 = 9$$

The graphs of the equations are an ellipse and a hyperbola. The graphs show that there are four solutions to the system.

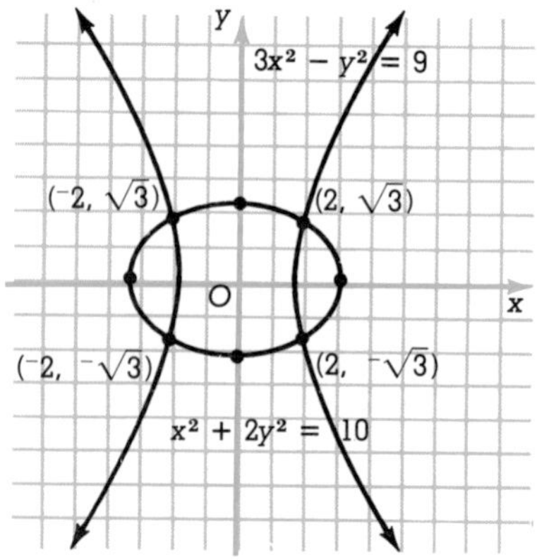

Use the substitution method to find the exact solutions.
First rewrite $x^2 + 2y^2 = 10$ as $x^2 = 10 - 2y^2$.

$$3x^2 - y^2 = 9$$
$$3(10 - 2y^2) - y^2 = 9 \qquad \textit{Substitute } 10 - 2y^2 \textit{ for } x^2.$$
$$30 - 7y^2 = 9$$
$$21 = 7y^2$$
$$3 = y^2$$
$$\pm\sqrt{3} = y$$
$$x^2 = 10 - 2y^2$$

$$x^2 = 10 - 2(\sqrt{3})^2 \quad \text{or} \quad x^2 = 10 - 2(^-\sqrt{3})^2$$
$$x^2 = 4 \qquad\qquad\qquad x^2 = 4$$
$$x = {}^\pm 2 \qquad\qquad\qquad x = {}^\pm 2$$

The solutions are $(2, \sqrt{3})$, $(^-2, \sqrt{3})$, $(2, {}^-\sqrt{3})$, and $(^-2, {}^-\sqrt{3})$.

exercises

Max: 1–29; Avg: 1–29 odds; Min: 1–29 odds

Written State the solutions of the following systems of equations.

1. $x^2 + y^2 = 16$ $(^\pm 2\sqrt{3}, 2)$
   $y = 2$

2. $y = x^2$ $(2, 4)$, $(^-1, 1)$
   $y - 2 = x$

3. $x = y$ $(2, 2)$, $(^-2, ^-2)$
   $\dfrac{x^2}{20} + \dfrac{y^2}{5} = 1$

4. $xy = 3$ $(1, 3)$, $(^-1, ^-3)$
   $y = 3x$

5. $x^2 - y^2 = 9$ $(3, 0)$, $(^-5, ^-4)$
   $8y = 4x - 12$

6. $x^2 + y^2 = 25$ $(^-4, ^-3)$,
   $x + y = ^-7$ $(^-3, ^-4)$

7. $(y - 1)^2 = x + 4$ $(^-3, 2)$,
   $y + x = ^-1$ $(0, ^-1)$

8. $\dfrac{x^2}{16} + \dfrac{y^2}{4} = 1$ $(0, 2)$, $(\frac{240}{109}, -\frac{182}{109})$
   $3y + 5x = 6$

9. $y^2 - x^2 = 9$ $(^\pm 3\sqrt{3}, 6)$
   $y = 6$

10. $xy = 1$ $(\frac{1}{4}, 4)$
    $y = 4$

11. $x^2 + y^2 = 9$ no solutions
    $x + y = 7$

12. $x^2 + 4y^2 = 4$ no solutions
    $x - y = 6$

13. $x^2 - 4y^2 = 16$ no solutions
    $y = 3x - 3$

14. $xy = ^-2$ no solutions
    $y = x$

15. $(x - 2)^2 + y^2 = 16$ $(^-2, 0)$,
    $y - x = 2$ $(2, 4)$

16. $y = ^-x^2$ $(^-1, ^-1)$, $(2, ^-4)$
    $y = ^-x - 2$

17. $x = ^-y^2 + 2$ $(^-2, ^-2)$, $(0, \sqrt{2})$
    $2y - 2\sqrt{2} = x(\sqrt{2} + 2)$

18. $x^2 - 9y^2 = 36$ no
    $y = x$ solutions

19. $\dfrac{(x - 3)^2}{25} + \dfrac{(y - 4)^2}{9} = 1$ $(3, 7)$, $(8, 4)$
    $5y + 3x = 44$

20. $(x - 3)^2 + (y + 6)^2 = 36$ $(3, 0)$, $(^-3, ^-6)$
    $y + 3 = x$

21. $5x^2 + y^2 = 30$ $(1, ^\pm 5)$
    $y^2 - 16 = 9x^2$ $(^-1, ^\pm 5)$

22. $x^2 - y^2 = 15$ $(4, 1)$, $(^-4, ^-1)$
    $xy = 4$

23. $2y^2 = 10 - x^2$ $(2, ^\pm\sqrt{3})$
    $3x^2 - 9 = y^2$ $(^-2, ^\pm\sqrt{3})$

24. $4x^2 + 9y^2 = 36$ $(^\pm 3, 0)$
    $4x^2 - 9y^2 = 36$

25. $x^2 + 4y^2 = 4$ no solutions
    $(x - 10)^2 + (y - 11)^2 = 1$

26. $x^2 + 4y^2 = 36$ $(0, 3)$, $(^\pm\sqrt{23}/2, -\frac{11}{4})$
    $y = ^-x^2 + 3$

27. $x^2 - y^2 = 25$ no solutions
    $x^2 - y^2 = 7$

28. $x^2 + y^2 = 16$ no solutions
    $x^2 + y^2 = 9$

29. $x^2 + y^2 = 64$ $(^\pm 8, 0)$
    $x^2 + 64y^2 = 64$

8-9 Systems with Quadratic Inequalities

Objective: To graph and solve systems with quadratic inequalities.

To graph the solutions of a system of inequalities, you graph each inequality and find the intersection of the two graphs. Consider the following system.

$$x^2 + y^2 \geq 16$$
$$x + y = 2$$

The graph of $x^2 + y^2 \geq 16$ consists of all points on or outside the circle $x^2 + y^2 = 16$. This region is shaded.

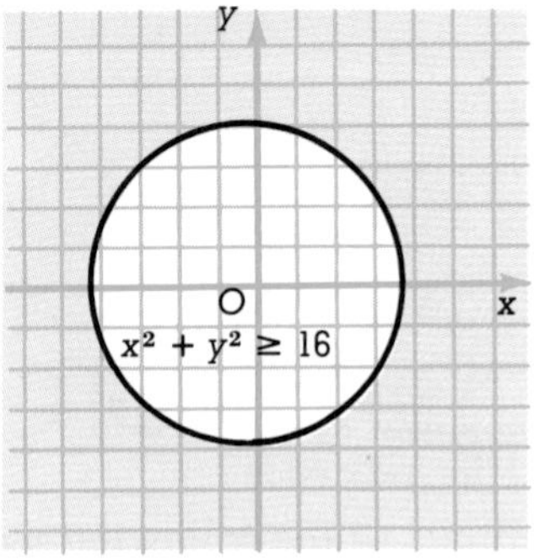

The graph of $x + y = 2$ is a straight line with slope $^{-}1$ and y-intercept 2.

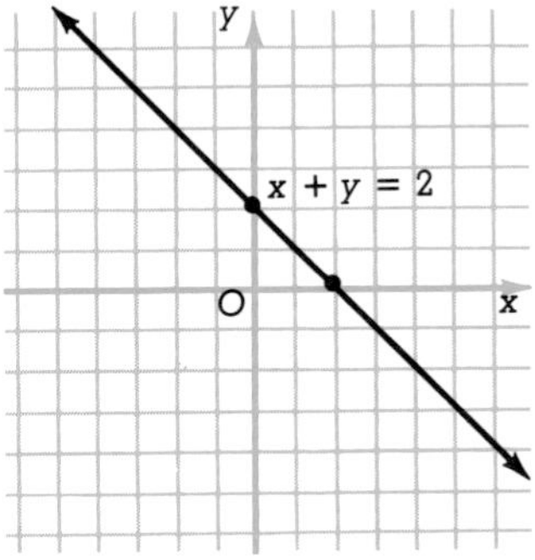

The intersection of the shaded region and the straight line is the graph of the solutions. The graph of the solution is indicated by the thick rays.

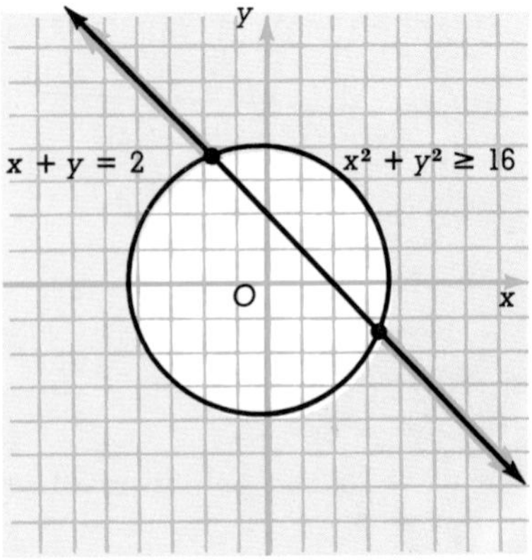

example

Graph the solutions for the following system of inequalities.

$$x^2 + y^2 \le 25$$
$$4y + x^2 \le 25$$

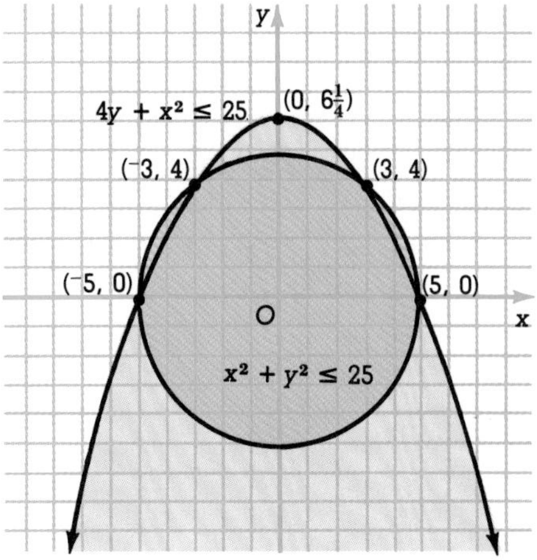

The graph of $x^2 + y^2 \le 25$ consists of all points on or within the circle $x^2 + y^2 = 25$. This region is shaded with gray. The graph of $4y + x^2 \le 25$ consists of all points on or within the parabola $4y + x^2 = 25$. This region is shaded with green.

The intersection of these two graphs represents the solutions for the system of inequalities.

exercises

Max: 1–18; **Avg:** 1–17 odds; **Min:** 1–17 odds

Written **Graph the solutions for the following systems of inequalities.**

1. $x^2 + y^2 < 9$
   $y < {}^{-}x^2$
2. $\frac{x^2}{9} - \frac{y^2}{4} < 1$
   $x^2 + y^2 < 25$
3. $\frac{x^2}{16} - \frac{y^2}{1} \ge 1$
   $x^2 + y^2 \ge 49$
4. $\frac{x^2}{25} - \frac{y^2}{16} \ge 1$
   $xy \ge 2$
5. $x^2 + y^2 > 16$
   $81x^2 + 9y^2 < 729$
6. $x^2 - 4y^2 < 16$
   $x > y^2$
7. $9x^2 + 4y^2 \le 36$
   $4x^2 + 9y^2 \ge 36$
8. $xy < {}^{-}3$
   $x^2 + y^2 < 25$
9. $x^2 + y^2 \ge 4$
   $x^2 + y^2 \le 36$
10. $y \ge x^2 - 4$
    $(y - 3)^2 \ge x + 2$
11. $x + 3 = y$
    $x^2 + y^2 < 25$
12. $4x^2 + 9y^2 \le 36$
    $x = 2$
13. $9x^2 - 4y^2 \ge 36$
    $x + y = 4$
14. $xy \ge 2$
    $2x - 3y = 5$
15. $4x^2 + (y - 3)^2 \le 16$
    $2y = x + 1$
16. $y = {}^{-}x$
    $(x + 2)^2 + 16(y + 3)^2 \ge 16$
17. $x^2 + y^2 \ge 16$
    $x = 4$
18. $x^2 + y^2 \le 36$
    $y = 6$

For answers to problems 1–18, see the Teacher's Guide.

Using Algebra

Parabolic Reflectors

The parabola is a very practical curve. Recall that if a light source is placed at the focus of a parabolic reflector, the light emitted is reflected off the parabola and straight ahead.

Conversely, with sunlight directed at a reflector, temperatures at the focal point can reach over one thousand degrees Fahrenheit, hot enough to melt steel.

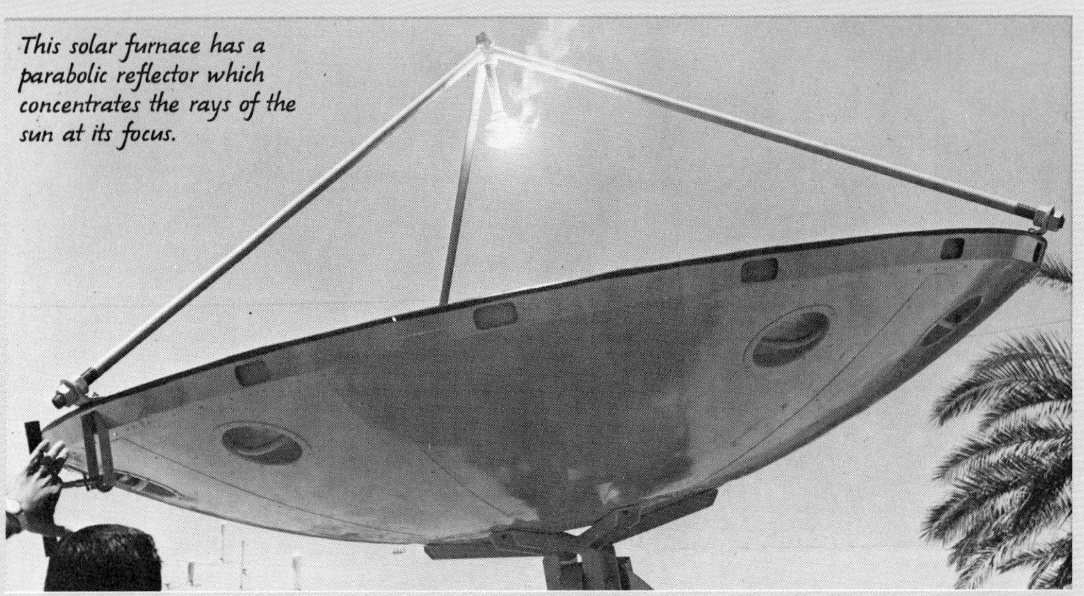

This solar furnace has a parabolic reflector which concentrates the rays of the sun at its focus.

Sound can be reflected in a similar way. If a microphone is placed at the focus of a parabolic reflector, it can pick up very faint noises. You may have seen such a reflector being used at a televised football game. It will pick up the signal calls all the way from the sidelines.

Radar antennas also use parabolic reflectors. Radio signals are focused on a receiver placed at the focus.

The focus for a parabola with equation $y = ax^2 + bx + c$ has the following coordinates.

$$\left(-\frac{b}{2a}, \frac{4ac - b^2 + 1}{4a}\right)$$

Exercises Find the focus for parabolas with each of the following equations.

1. $y = x^2 + 6x + 9$ $({}^-3, \frac{1}{4})$

2. $y = 2x^2 + 4x + 7$ $(1, \frac{41}{8})$

3. $y = \frac{1}{2}x^2 - 2x - \frac{5}{2}$ $(2, {}^-4)$

4. $y = \frac{1}{4}x^2 - 2x + 3$ $(4, 0)$

Vocabulary

parabola (217)
focus (217)
directrix (217)
circle (220)
radius (220)
center (220)
ellipse (224)
foci of ellipse (224)
hyperbola (228)
foci of hyperbola (228)
asymptote (229)
conic section (232)

Chapter Summary

1. Distance Between Points on a Number Line: On a number line, the distance between two points whose coordinates are a and b is $|a - b|$ or $|b - a|$. (214)
2. Distance Formula for Two Points in the Plane: The distance between two points with coordinates (x_1, y_1) and (x_2, y_2) is given by the following formula.

$$d = \sqrt{(x_2 - x_1)^2 + (y_2 - y_1)^2} \quad (215)$$

3. Definition of Parabola: A parabola is the set of all points which are the same distance from a given point and a given line. The point is called the focus. The line is called the directrix. (217)
4. Information about Parabolas

Information about Parabolas		
form of equation	$y = a(x - h)^2 + k$	$x = a(y - k)^2 + h$
vertex	(h, k)	(h, k)
axis of symmetry	$x = h$	$y = k$
focus	$\left(h, k + \frac{1}{4a}\right)$	$\left(h + \frac{1}{4a}, k\right)$
directrix	$y = k - \frac{1}{4a}$	$x = h - \frac{1}{4a}$
direction of opening	upward if $a > 0$ downward if $a < 0$	right if $a > 0$ left if $a < 0$

(218)

5. Definition of Circle: A circle is the set of all points in the plane each of which is the same distance from a given point. The given distance is the radius of the circle, and the given point is the center of the circle. (220)
6. Equation of Circle: The equation of a circle with center (h, k) and radius r units is $(x - h)^2 + (y - k)^2 = r^2$. (220)

7. Definition of Ellipse: An ellipse is the set of all points in the plane such that the sum of the distances from two given points, called the foci, is constant. (224)

8. Equation of Ellipse: The equation of an ellipse whose foci are $(^-c, 0)$ and $(c, 0)$, and the sum of the distances from the two foci is $2a$ units, is $\frac{x^2}{a^2} + \frac{y^2}{b^2} = 1$ when $b^2 = a^2 - c^2$. (225)

9. Equation of Ellipse: The equation of an ellipse whose foci are $(0, ^-c)$ and $(0, c)$, and the sum of the distances from the two foci is $2a$ units, is $\frac{x^2}{b^2} + \frac{y^2}{a^2} = 1$ when $b^2 = a^2 - c^2$. (225)

10. A circle is a special kind of ellipse. In a circle, the two foci are the same point. This point is the center of the circle. (226)

11. Definition of Hyperbola: A hyperbola is the set of all points in the plane such that the absolute value of the difference of the distances from two given points, called the foci, is constant. (228)

12. Equation of Hyperbola: The equation of a hyperbola with foci $(^-c, 0)$ and $(c, 0)$ and with the absolute value of the difference between distances from the two foci $2a$ units, can be written as $\frac{x^2}{a^2} - \frac{y^2}{b^2} = 1$ when $c^2 = a^2 + b^2$. (230)

13. Equation of Hyperbola: The equation of a hyperbola with foci $(0, ^-c)$ and $(0, c)$, and with the absolute value of the difference between distances from the two foci $2a$ units, can be written as $\frac{y^2}{a^2} - \frac{x^2}{b^2} = 1$ when $c^2 = a^2 + b^2$. (230)

14. Equation of Conic Sections: The equation of a conic section can be written in the form $Ax^2 + Bxy + Cy^2 + Dx + Ey + F = 0$ where A, B, and C are not all zero. (232)

15. If the graph of a system of equations is a conic and a straight line, the system will have zero, one, or two solutions. (235)

16. If the graph of a system of equations is two conics, the system will have zero, one, two, three, or four solutions. (236)

17. You can use graphs to help find the solutions of a quadratic system. Often you must use algebra to find exact solutions. (238)

18. To graph the solutions of a system of inequalities, you graph each inequality and find the intersection of the two graphs. (240)

Chapter Review

8-1 Use the distance formula to find the distance between each pair of points whose coordinates are listed below.

1. $(3, 6), (7, {}^-8)$ $2\sqrt{53}$
2. $({}^-8, {}^-7), ({}^-2, {}^-1)$ $6\sqrt{2}$
3. $(0.2, 0.6), (0.3, 0.4)$ $\sqrt{5}/10$
4. $(2, 2), (\sqrt{2}, \sqrt{2})$ $2\sqrt{3 - 2\sqrt{2}}$
5. $({}^-2.4, 0.6), (1.7, 0.8)$ $\sqrt{16.85}$
6. $(2\sqrt{3}, 4\sqrt{3}), (2\sqrt{3}, {}^-\sqrt{3})$ $5\sqrt{3}$

8-2 State the vertex, axis of symmetry, focus, directrix, and direction of opening of each parabola whose equation is given below. Then draw the graph.

7. $4y = x^2$ $(0, 0); x = 0; (0, 1); y = {}^-1$; up
8. $y^2 = {}^-8x$ $(0, 0); y = 0; ({}^-2, 0); x = 2$; left
9. $x^2 = y - 1$ $(0, 1); x = 0; (0, \frac{5}{4}); y = \frac{3}{4}$; up
10. $(y - 8)^2 = {}^-4(x - 4)$ $(4, 8); y = 8; (3, 8); x = 5$; left

8-3 State the center and radius of each circle whose equation is given below. Then draw the graph.

11. $x^2 + y^2 + 6y + 9 = 25$ $(0, {}^-3), 5$
12. $x^2 + y^2 - 8x + 10y = 1$ $(4, {}^-5), \sqrt{42}$

8-4 State the center, foci, and intercepts or vertices for each ellipse whose equation is given below. Then draw the graph.

13. $\frac{x^2}{8} + \frac{y^2}{16} = 1$ $(0, 0); (0, {}^\pm 2\sqrt{2}); ({}^\pm 2\sqrt{2}, 0), (0, {}^\pm 4)$
14. $\frac{(x - 3)^2}{25} + \frac{(y + 1)^2}{4} = 1$ $(3, {}^-1); (3 \pm \sqrt{21}, {}^-1); (8, {}^-1), ({}^-2, {}^-1), (3, 1), (3, {}^-3)$
15. $16x^2 + 49y^2 = 784$ $(0, 0); (\pm\sqrt{33}, 0); ({}^\pm 7, 0), (0, {}^\pm 4)$
16. $9x^2 + 16y^2 = 144$ $(0, 0); ({}^\pm\sqrt{7}, 0); ({}^\pm 4, 0), (0, {}^\pm 3)$

8-5 State the intercepts, foci, and asymptotes for each hyperbola whose equation is given below. Then draw the graph.

17. $\frac{x^2}{16} - \frac{y^2}{81} = 1$ $({}^\pm 4, 0); ({}^\pm\sqrt{97}, 0); y = \pm\frac{9}{4}x$
18. $x = -\frac{2}{y}$ none; $(2, {}^-2), ({}^-2, 2); x = 0, y = 0$
19. $xy = 3$ none; $(\sqrt{6}, \sqrt{6}), ({}^-\sqrt{6}, {}^-\sqrt{6}); x = 0, y = 0$
20. $49x^2 - 16y^2 = 784$ $({}^\pm 4, 0); ({}^\pm\sqrt{65}, 0); y = \pm\frac{7}{4}x$

8-6 State whether each graph of the following equations is a parabola, a circle, an ellipse, or a hyperbola.

21. $(x - 3)^2 = 4y - 4$ parabola
22. $3x^2 - 16 = {}^-3y^2$ circle
23. $4x^2 + 5y^2 = 20$ ellipse
24. $3y^2 - 7x^2 = 21$ hyperbola

8-7 Graph each system of equations. Then state the solutions of the systems. Answers are approximate.

25. $x + y = 1$ $({}^-1.6, 2.6)$
$x^2 + y^2 = 9$ $(2.6, {}^-1.6)$
26. $x + y = 4$ $(1.6, 2.4)$
$y = x^2$ $({}^-2.6, 6.6)$

8-8 State the solutions of the following systems of equations.

27. $(x - 2)^2 + y^2 = 16$ $({}^-2, 0), (2, 4)$
$y - x = 2$
28. $x^2 - y^2 = 16$ no solutions
$y^2 - x^2 = 16$

8-9 Graph the solutions for the following systems of inequalities.

29. $x^2 + y^2 < 25$
$x + y > 5$
30. $y \geq x^2 + 4$
$x^2 + y^2 < 49$

Chapter Test

Find the distance between each pair of points whose coordinates are listed below.

1. $(2, 6), (^-7, ^-2)$ $\sqrt{145}$
2. $(^-3, 5), (^-11, ^-16)$ $\sqrt{505}$

State whether each graph of the following equations is a parabola, a circle, an ellipse, or a hyperbola. Then draw the graph.

3. $2y = x^2$ parabola
4. $x^2 + y^2 + 4x = 6$ circle
5. $9x^2 + 49y^2 = 441$ ellipse
6. $x^2 - 4y^2 = 4$ hyperbola
7. $xy = 2$ hyperbola
8. $x^2 + 4x + y^2 - 8y = 2$ circle
9. $(x - 3)^2 = 4(y + 1)$ parabola
10. $\frac{(x - 3)^2}{81} + \frac{(y + 4)^2}{16} = 1$ ellipse
11. $6x^2 + 6y^2 = 6$ circle
12. $xy = {}^-4$ hyperbola
13. $13y^2 - 2x^2 = 5$ hyperbola
14. $y - x^2 = x + 3$ parabola
15. $x^2 + 5y^2 - 16 = 0$ ellipse
16. $16x^2 - 4y^2 = 64$ hyperbola

Graph each system of equations. Then state the solutions of the systems. Answers are approximate.

17. $x^2 + 16y^2 = 16$
    $x - y = 3$ (3.5, 0.5), (2.2, ⁻0.8)
18. $x^2 + y^2 = 25$ (4.1, ±2.8)
    $x^2 - y^2 = 9$ (⁻4.1, ±2.8)

Graph the solutions for the following systems of inequalities.

19. $x^2 + y^2 < 49$
    $y < {}^-x^2 + 2$
20. $x + y = 5$
    $x^2 + y^2 \geq 49$

Chapter 9

Polynomial Functions

A composer knows the effect of combining different sounds. A mathematician knows the results of combining functions.

9-1 Polynomial Functions

Objective: To recognize and find values of polynomial functions.

The following expressions are examples of polynomials in one variable.

$$3x + 2$$
$$4x^2 + 8x - 7$$
$$19x^3 - 7x^2 + x - 75$$
$$6x^5 + 62x^3 - 12x + 13$$

Definition of Polynomial in One Variable

A polynomial in one variable, x, is an expression of the form

$$a_nx^n + a_{n-1}x^{n-1} + \cdots + a_2x^2 + a_1x + a_0.$$

The coefficients $a_0, a_1, a_2, \ldots, a_n$ are real numbers, and n is a nonnegative integer.

example 1

Which of the following expressions are polynomials in one variable?

$$7x^4 - 9x^2 + 2x + 1$$
$$6x^2y^3 - 8xy + 7z + 2$$
$$x + \frac{1}{x} - 2$$
$$y^2 + 2y + 3$$

$7x^4 - 9x^2 + 2x + 1$ is a polynomial in one variable, x.

$6x^2y^3 - 8xy + 7z + 2$ is *not* a polynomial in one variable. *There are three variables.*

$x + \frac{1}{x} - 2$ is *not* a polynomial in one variable. *$\frac{1}{x}$ cannot be written in the form x^n where n is a nonnegative integer.*

$y^2 + 2y + 3$ is a polynomial in one variable, y. *$a_2 = 1$, $a_1 = 2$, $a_0 = 3$*

The degree of a polynomial in one variable is the greatest exponent of its variable.

5	has degree 0
$3x + 2$	has degree 1
$4x^2 + 8x + 7$	has degree 2
$6x^5 + 62x^3 - 12x + 13$	has degree 5
$a_nx^n + a_{n-1}x^{n-1} + \ldots + a_1x + a_0$	has degree n

A polynomial of degree 0 is called a **constant.**
A polynomial of degree 1 is called a **linear expression.**
A polynomial of degree 2 is called a **quadratic expression.**

Polynomial equations can be used to represent functions. In general, a **polynomial function** is in the form

$$p(x) = a_n x^n + a_{n-1}x^{n-1} + \cdots + a_1 x + a_0.$$

The coefficients $a_0, a_1, a_2, \ldots, a_{n-1}, a_n$ are real numbers, and n is a nonnegative integer.

The equation $p(x) = 3x^2 - 8x + 7$ represents a polynomial function. If 2 is an element of the domain of the function, then $p(2)$ is the corresponding element of the range. To show that the value of $p(2)$ is 3, you write $p(2) = 3$.

examples

2 **Find $p(2) + p(^-2)$ if $p(x) = 3x^2 - 8x + 7$.**

$$\begin{aligned} p(2) + p(^-2) &= [3(2)^2 - 8(2) + 7] + [3(^-2)^2 - 8(^-2) + 7] \\ &= 3 + 35 \\ &= 38 \end{aligned}$$

3 **Find $p(m + 2)$ if $p(x) = 3x - 8x^2 + x^3$.**

$$\begin{aligned} p(m + 2) &= 3(m + 2) - 8(m + 2)^2 + (m + 2)^3 \\ &= 3m + 6 - 8m^2 - 32m - 32 + m^3 + 6m^2 + 12m + 8 \\ &= m^3 - 2m^2 - 17m - 18 \end{aligned}$$

4 **Find $3p(x) + 5p(x - 1)$ if $p(x) = x^3 - 3x^2 + 3x + 1$.**

$$\begin{aligned} 3p(x) + 5p(x - 1) &= 3[x^3 - 3x^2 + 3x + 1] + \\ &\quad 5[(x - 1)^3 - 3(x - 1)^2 + 3(x - 1) + 1] \\ &= [3x^3 - 9x^2 + 9x + 3] + \\ &\quad [5x^3 - 15x^2 + 15x - 5 - 15x^2 + 30x - 15 + 15x - 15 + 5] \\ &= 8x^3 - 39x^2 + 69x - 27 \end{aligned}$$

exercises

Max: 1–14, 1–51; **Avg:** 1–14, 1–51 odds; **Min:** 1–51 odds

Exploratory Which of the following expressions are polynomials in one variable?

1. $8x + y + 1$ no
2. $3x - 2$ yes
3. $xy\sqrt{2} + 3$ no
4. $x^2 + 8x + 7$ yes
5. $\frac{9}{x} + x + 3$ no
6. $5 + \sqrt{x} + 8y$ no
7. $x^3 + 5x^2 + x\sqrt{3} + 2$ yes
8. $x^3 + 9x^2 + 8x + 1$ yes

9. $9x^2 + ix^2 + 8x + 3i$ no

10. $(6 + 2i)x^2 + 3ix + 7i^2$ no

11. $5x^4 - 2$ yes

12. $9m^2 + \frac{3i}{m} + 7$ no

13. $9x^3 + 6x^3 - 5x^3$ yes

14. $6y^2 + 7y - 3$ yes

Written Find $p(1)$ for each of the following.

1. $p(x) = 3x + 1$ 4
2. $p(x) = 4x^2 + 3x - 3$ 4
3. $p(x) = \frac{x^2}{3} + x\sqrt{2} + 4$ $\frac{13}{3} + \sqrt{2}$
4. $p(x) = {}^-3x^3 + 2$ $^-1$
5. $p(x) = {}^-2x^3 + 4x - 1$ 1
6. $p(x) = 5x^4 - 8x^3$ $^-3$
7. $p(x) = 3x - 8x^2 + x^3$ $^-4$
8. $p(x) = 2x^4 - 3x^3 + 8$ 7
9. $p(x) = \frac{5}{2}x^3 - 8$ $\frac{^-11}{2}$
10. $p(x) = 7x^3 + \frac{7}{3}x + 1$ $\frac{31}{3}$

11–20. Find $p(2)$ for the polynomial functions in problems **1–10.**
21–30. Find $p(^-3)$ for the polynomial functions in problems **1–10.**
31–40. Find $p(x + h)$ for the polynomial functions in problems **1–10.**
41–50. Find $2p(x) - 3p(x + 1)$ for the polynomial functions in problems **1–10.**
51. Write a computer program that will evaluate $p(x) = x^4 - x^3 + x^2 - x + 1$ for integer values of x between $^-6$ and 6.

For answers to problems **11–51**, see the Teacher's Guide.

Excursions in Algebra

Area of an Ellipse

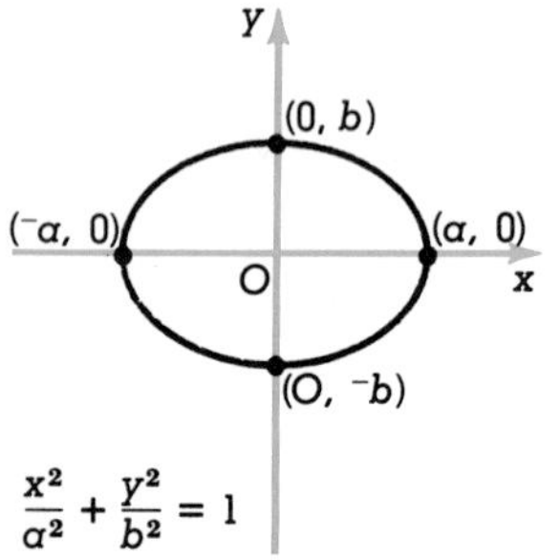

The graph of the ellipse shown below has the equation $\frac{x^2}{a^2} + \frac{y^2}{b^2} = 1$. This ellipse has intercepts at $(a, 0)$, $(^-a, 0)$, $(0, b)$, and $(0, ^-b)$.

The **major axis** of the ellipse is the segment joining $(a, 0)$ and $(^-a, 0)$. Its length is $2a$.

The **minor axis** of the ellipse is the segment joining $(0, b)$ and $(0, ^-b)$. Its length is $2b$.

Do you see a relationship between the major and minor axes of an ellipse, and the diameter of a circle?

The area of this ellipse is given by the formula $A = \pi ab$.

Exercises Find the area of each of the following.

1. $\frac{x^2}{25} + \frac{y^2}{16} = 1$ 20π
2. $\frac{x^2}{9} + \frac{y^2}{49} = 1$ 21π
3. $\frac{x^2}{10} + \frac{y^2}{6} = 1$ $2\sqrt{15}\pi$
4. $25x^2 + 16y^2 = 400$ 20π
5. $32x^2 + 72y^2 = 1152$ 24π
6. The ellipse with intercepts $(0, 8)$, $(0, ^-8)$, $(2, 0)$, and $(^-2, 0)$ 16π
7. The ellipse with intercepts $(6, 0)$ and $(^-6, 0)$ and foci $(2\sqrt{5}, 0)$ and $(^-2\sqrt{5}, 0)$ 24π
8. A circle with a diameter of 7 12.25π

9–2 The Remainder and Factor Theorems

Objective: To make use of the remainder and factor theorems.

You can divide polynomials using long division or synthetic division.

example 1

Divide $x^3 + 4x^2 + 3x - 2$ by $x - 3$.

Long Division

$$\begin{array}{r} x^2 + 7x + 24 \\ x - 3 \overline{) x^3 + 4x^2 + 3x - 2} \\ \underline{x^3 - 3x^2} \qquad\qquad \\ 7x^2 + 3x \qquad \\ \underline{7x^2 - 21x} \qquad \\ 24x - 2 \\ \underline{24x - 72} \\ 70 \end{array}$$

The numbers 1, 7, and 24 are the coefficients of the quotient $x^2 + 7x + 24$. The remainder is 70.

Synthetic Division

$$\begin{array}{r|rrrr} 3 & 1 & 4 & 3 & -2 \\ & & 3 & 21 & 72 \\ \hline & 1 & 7 & 24 & 70 \end{array}$$

The quotient is $x^2 + 7x + 24$ with a remainder of 70.

Check: Multiply $x^2 + 7x + 24$ by $x - 3$ and then add 70.

dividend = *quotient · divisor* + *remainder*

$$x^3 + 4x^2 + 3x - 2 = (x^2 + 7x + 24)(x - 3) + 70$$

Consider $f(x) = x^3 + 4x^2 + 3x - 2$. The value of $f(3)$ is 70. When $f(x)$ is divided by $x - 3$, the remainder is 70.

The Remainder Theorem

If a polynomial $f(x)$ is divided by $x - a$, the remainder is a constant, $f(a)$, and

dividend *quotient* *divisor* *remainder*

$$f(x) = q(x) \cdot (x - a) + f(a)$$

where $q(x)$ is a polynomial with degree one less than the degree of $f(x)$.

example 2

Let $f(x) = x^4 + 3x^2 + 4x - 1$. Show that $f(1)$ is the remainder when $f(x)$ is divided by $x - 1$.

$$\begin{array}{r|rrrrr} 1 & 1 & 0 & 3 & 4 & -1 \\ & & 1 & 1 & 4 & 8 \\ \hline & 1 & 1 & 4 & 8 & 7 \end{array}$$

Use synthetic division.

The remainder is 7.

$f(1) = (1)^4 + 3(1)^2 + 4(1) - 1$ *Evaluate f(1).*

$= 7$ *The result is the same as the remainder.*

Consider the polynomial defined by $f(x) = x^3 + 7x^2 + 2x - 40$. If $f(x)$ is divided by $x - 2$, the remainder is zero.

$$\begin{array}{r|rrrr} 2 & 1 & 7 & 2 & ^-40 \\ & & 2 & 18 & 40 \\ \hline & 1 & 9 & 20 & 0 \end{array} \qquad f(2) = (2)^3 + 7(2)^2 + 2(2) - 40 \text{ or } 0$$

$$x^3 + 7x^2 + 2x - 40 = (x^2 + 9x + 20)(x - 2) + 0$$
$$f(x) = g(x) \cdot (x - 2) + f(2)$$

If the divisor is a factor of a polynomial, then the remainder upon division is zero.

In other words, $x - 2$ is a factor of $x^3 + 7x^2 + 2x - 40$. This example illustrates the factor theorem, a special case of the remainder theorem.

The Factor Theorem

The binomial $x - a$ is a factor of the polynomial $f(x)$ if and only if $f(a) = 0$.

example 3

Show that $x - 4$ is a factor of $x^4 + x^3 - 13x^2 - 25x - 12$.

Let $f(x) = x^4 + x^3 - 13x^2 - 25x - 12$.

$f(4) = (4)^4 + (4)^3 - 13(4)^2 - 25(4) - 12$ *a is 4.*

$= 256 + 64 - 208 - 100 - 12$

$= 0$

Since $f(4) = 0$, the binomial $x - 4$ is a factor of $f(x)$.

The factor theorem is useful for factoring polynomials. For example, suppose you want all the factors of $x^4 + x^3 - 13x^2 - 25x - 12$. First let $f(x) = x^4 + x^3 - 13x^2 - 25x - 12$. Then find $f(a)$ for several values of a.

a	$x^4 + x^3 - 13x^2 - 25x - 12$	$f(a)$	
$^-4$	$(^-4)^4 + (^-4)^3 - 13(^-4)^2 - 25(^-4) - 12$	72	
$^-3$	$(^-3)^4 + (^-3)^3 - 13(^-3)^2 - 25(^-3) - 12$	0	*$x + 3$ is a factor.*
$^-2$	$(^-2)^4 + (^-2)^3 - 13(^-2)^2 - 25(^-2) - 12$	$^-6$	
$^-1$	$(^-1)^4 + (^-1)^3 - 13(^-1)^2 - 25(^-1) - 12$	0	*$x + 1$ is a factor.*
0	$(0)^4 + (0)^3 - 13(0)^2 - 25(0) - 12$	$^-12$	
1	$(1)^4 + (1)^3 - 13(1)^2 - 25(1) - 12$	$^-48$	
2	$(2)^4 + (2)^3 - 13(2)^2 - 25(2) - 12$	$^-90$	
3	$(3)^4 + (3)^3 - 13(3)^2 - 25(3) - 12$	$^-96$	
4	$(4)^4 + (4)^3 - 13(4)^2 - 25(4) - 12$	0	*$x - 4$ is a factor.*

From the chart you know that $x + 3$, $x + 1$, and $x - 4$ are factors of $x^4 + x^3 - 13x^2 - 25x - 12$. Use division to find the last factor.

for $x + 3$

$$\begin{array}{r|rrrrr} -3 & 1 & 1 & -13 & -25 & -12 \\ & & -3 & 6 & 21 & 12 \\ \hline & 1 & -2 & -7 & -4 & \vert\ 0 \end{array}$$

$x^3 - 2x^2 - 7x - 4$

for $x + 1$

$$\begin{array}{r|rrrr} -1 & 1 & -2 & -7 & -4 \\ & & -1 & 3 & 4 \\ \hline & 1 & -3 & -4 & \vert\ 0 \end{array}$$

$x^2 - 3x - 4$

for $x - 4$

$$\begin{array}{r|rrr} 4 & 1 & -3 & -4 \\ & & 4 & 4 \\ \hline & 1 & 1 & \vert\ 0 \end{array}$$

$x + 1$

$$x^4 + x^3 - 13x^2 - 25x - 12 = (x + 3)(x + 1)(x - 4)(x + 1) \text{ or } = (x + 3)(x - 4)(x + 1)^2$$

exercises

Max: 1–8, 1–31; Avg: 1–8, 1–31 odds; Min: 1–31 odds

Exploratory **Divide using synthetic division.** For answers to problems 1–8, see the Teacher's Guide.

1. $(x^2 - 3x + 1) \div (x - 2)$
2. $(x^3 - 4x^2 + 2x - 6) \div (x - 4)$
3. $(x^3 - 8x^2 + 2x - 1) \div (x + 1)$
4. $(x^2 + 8x - 1) \div (x + 3)$
5. $(x^5 + x^4 + 2x - 1) \div (x - 2)$
6. $(2x^4 - x^2 + 1) \div (x + 1)$
7. $(x^5 + 32) \div (x + 2)$
8. $(x^5 - 3x^2 - 20) \div (x - 2)$

For answers to problems 1–10, see the Teacher's Guide.

Written **Divide. Write your answer in the form dividend = quotient · divisor + remainder.**

1. $(2x^3 + 8x^2 - 3x - 1) \div (x - 2)$
2. $(x^3 - 64) \div (x - 4)$
3. $(x^4 - 16) \div (x - 2)$
4. $(x^3 + 27) \div (x + 3)$
5. $(4x^4 + 3x^3 - 2x^2 + x + 1) \div (x - 1)$
6. $(6x^3 + 9x^2 - 6x + 2) \div (x + 2)$
7. $(3x^5 - 2x^3 + 2x + 2) \div (x + 1)$
8. $(^-2x^2 - 3x - 1) \div (x + 2)$
9. $(3x^3 + 2x^2 - 4x - 1) \div \left(x + \frac{1}{2}\right)$
10. $(x^4 - 2x^3 + 4x^2 + 6x - 8) \div \left(x - \frac{1}{2}\right)$

Find the remainder for each of the following.

11. $(x^3 + 2x^2 - 3x + 1) \div (x - 4)$ 85
12. $(2x^2 - 8x + 6) \div (x + 3)$ 48
13. $(x^3 - 8x^2 + 2x + 5) \div (x + 2)$ $^-39$
14. $(x^3 + 8x + 1) \div (x - 2)$ 25
15. $(3x^4 + 8x^2 - 1) \div (x + 1)$ 10
16. $(x^4 + x^3 + x^2 + x + 1) \div (x - 1)$ 5
17. $(x^5 + 8x^3 + 2) \div (x + 2)$ $^-94$
18. $(2x^3 + 2x^2 - 2x - 2) \div (x - 2)$ 18

Factor each polynomial.

19. $x^3 + x^2 - 4x - 4$ $(x + 1)(x + 2)(x - 2)$
20. $x^3 - 6x^2 + 11x - 6$ $(x - 2)(x - 3)(x - 1)$
21. $x^3 + 2x^2 - x - 2$ $(x + 1)(x - 1)(x + 2)$
22. $x^4 - 5x^2 + 4$ $(x - 1)(x + 1)(x - 2)(x + 2)$
23. $x^3 - 3x + 2$ $(x + 2)(x - 1)^2$
24. $x^3 - x^2 - 5x - 3$ $(x - 3)(x + 1)^2$
25. $x^4 - 5x^3 + 9x^2 - 7x + 2$ $(x - 2)(x - 1)^3$
26. $x^4 + 8x^3 + 22x^2 + 24x + 9$ $(x + 3)^2(x + 1)^2$

Find values for k so that each remainder is 3.

27. $(x^2 + 8x + k) \div (x - 2)$ $^-17$
28. $(x^2 + kx + 3) \div (x - 1)$ $^-1$
29. $(x^3 + 8x^2 + kx + 4) \div (x + 2)$ $\frac{25}{2}$
30. $(x^3 + 4x^2 - kx + 1) \div (x + 1)$ $^-1$
31. Write a computer program that uses synthetic division to divide a polynomial by a linear polynomial. See Teacher's Guide.

9-3 Zeros

Objective: To find the zeros of polynomial functions.

Suppose $f(x) = x^3 - 4x^2 + x + 6$ represents a polynomial function and $f(a) = 0$. Then a is called a **zero** of the function. For example, $f(x)$ has three zeros, namely 3, 2, and $^-1$. These zeros also are solutions of the equation $x^3 - 4x^2 + x + 6 = 0$. In general, the zeros of a function defined by $y = f(x)$ are solutions to the equation $f(x) = 0$.

examples

1 **Find the zeros of the function defined by $f(x) = (x - 3)(x + 8)(3x - 7)(2x + 5)$.**

Solve $(x - 3)(x + 8)(3x - 7)(2x + 5) = 0$.

$x - 3 = 0$ or $x + 8 = 0$ or $3x - 7 = 0$ or $2x + 5 = 0$ *Why?*

$x = 3$ $\quad x = {}^-8$ $\quad 3x = 7$ $\quad 2x = {}^-5$

$x = \frac{7}{3}$ $\quad x = -\frac{5}{2}$

The zeros of the function are 3, $^-8$, $\frac{7}{3}$, and $-\frac{5}{2}$. *How can you check the solutions?*

2 **Find the zeros of the function defined by $f(x) = x^2 + 2x - 3$.**

Solve $x^2 + 2x - 3 = 0$.

$(x + 3)(x - 1) = 0$ *Factor $x^2 + 2x - 3 = 0$.*

$x + 3 = 0$ or $x - 1 = 0$

$x = {}^-3$ $\quad x = 1$

The zeros of the function are $^-3$ and 1.

To solve a polynomial equation, you often factor the polynomial. You can find factors by evaluating the polynomial for specific values. The rational zero theorem helps you choose possible values.

Rational Zero Theorem

Let $f(x) = a_nx^n + a_{n-1}x^{n-1} + \cdots + a_1x + a_0$ represent a polynomial with integer coefficients and n be a nonnegative integer. If $\frac{p}{q}$ is a rational number in simplest form and is a zero of $y = f(x)$, then p is a factor of a_0 and q is a factor of a_n.

example 3

Find all zeros of $f(x) = 2x^3 - 5x^2 - 28x + 15$.

According to the Rational Zero Theorem, if $\frac{p}{q}$ is a zero of the function, then p is a factor of 15 and q is a factor of 2.

p is $^{\pm}1$, $^{\pm}3$, $^{\pm}5$, or $^{\pm}15$
q is $^{\pm}1$ or $^{\pm}2$

$\frac{p}{q}$	$2x^3$	−	$5x^2$	−	$28x$	+ 15	$f\left(\frac{p}{q}\right)$	
1	$2(1)^3$	−	$5(1)^2$	−	$28(1)$	+ 15	$^-16$	
$^-1$	$2(^-1)^3$	−	$5(^-1)^2$	−	$28(^-1)$	+ 15	36	
3	$2(3)^3$	−	$5(3)^2$	−	$28(3)$	+ 15	$^-60$	
$^-3$	$2(^-3)^3$	−	$5(^-3)^2$	−	$28(^-3)$	+ 15	0	*$^-3$ is a zero.*
5	$2(5)^3$	−	$5(5)^2$	−	$28(5)$	+ 15	0	*5 is a zero.*
$^-5$	$2(^-5)^3$	−	$5(^-5)^2$	−	$28(^-5)$	+ 15	$^-220$	
15	$2(15)^3$	−	$5(15)^2$	−	$28(15)$	+ 15	5220	
$^-15$	$2(^-15)^3$	−	$5(^-15)^2$	−	$28(^-15)$	+ 15	$^-7440$	
$\frac{1}{2}$	$2\left(\frac{1}{2}\right)^3$	−	$5\left(\frac{1}{2}\right)^2$	−	$28\left(\frac{1}{2}\right)$	+ 15	0	*$\frac{1}{2}$ is a zero.*
$-\frac{1}{2}$	$2\left(-\frac{1}{2}\right)^3$	−	$5\left(-\frac{1}{2}\right)^2$	−	$28\left(-\frac{1}{2}\right)$	+ 15	$\frac{55}{2}$	
$\frac{3}{2}$	$2\left(\frac{3}{2}\right)^3$	−	$5\left(\frac{3}{2}\right)^2$	−	$28\left(\frac{3}{2}\right)$	+ 15	$-\frac{63}{2}$	
$-\frac{3}{2}$	$2\left(-\frac{3}{2}\right)^3$	−	$5\left(-\frac{3}{2}\right)^2$	−	$28\left(-\frac{3}{2}\right)$	+ 15	39	
$\frac{5}{2}$	$2\left(\frac{5}{2}\right)^3$	−	$5\left(\frac{5}{2}\right)^2$	−	$28\left(\frac{5}{2}\right)$	+ 15	$^-55$	
$-\frac{5}{2}$	$2\left(-\frac{5}{2}\right)^3$	−	$5\left(-\frac{5}{2}\right)^2$	−	$28\left(-\frac{5}{2}\right)$	+ 15	$\frac{45}{2}$	
$\frac{15}{2}$	$2\left(\frac{15}{2}\right)^3$	−	$5\left(\frac{15}{2}\right)^2$	−	$28\left(\frac{15}{2}\right)$	+ 15	$\frac{735}{2}$	
$-\frac{15}{2}$	$2\left(-\frac{15}{2}\right)^3$	−	$5\left(-\frac{15}{2}\right)^2$	−	$28\left(-\frac{15}{2}\right)$	+ 15	$^-900$	

The zeros of $f(x) = 2x^3 - 5x^2 - 28x + 15$ are $^-3$, 5, and $\frac{1}{2}$.

It is not always necessary to complete the entire chart. Once a zero is found, the polynomial may be factored.

example 4

Find all zeros of $f(x) = 6x^3 + 4x^2 - 14x + 4$.

According to the Rational Zero Theorem, if $\frac{p}{q}$ is a zero of the function, then p is a factor of 4 and q is a factor of 6.

p is $^{\pm}1$, $^{\pm}2$, or $^{\pm}4$ $\quad$ q is $^{\pm}1$, $^{\pm}2$, $^{\pm}3$, or $^{\pm}6$

$\frac{p}{q}$	$6x^3 + 4x^2 - 14x + 4$	$f\left(\frac{p}{q}\right)$
1	$6(1)^3 + 4(1)^2 - 14(1) + 4$	0

1 is a zero.

Since 1 is a zero of the function, $x - 1$ is a factor of $6x^3 + 4x^2 - 14x + 4$.

$f(x) = (6x^2 + 10x - 4)(x - 1)$ — *Find the other factor by synthetic division.*

$= 2(3x^2 + 5x - 2)(x - 1)$ — *$6x^2 + 10x - 4 = 2(3x^2 + 5x - 2)$*

$= 2(3x - 1)(x + 2)(x - 1)$ — *$3x^2 + 5x - 2 = (3x - 1)(x + 2)$*

Solve $2(3x - 1)(x + 2)(x - 1) = 0$.

$3x - 1 = 0$ or $x + 2 = 0$ or $x - 1 = 0$

$x = \frac{1}{3}$ or $x = {}^{-}2$ or $x = 1$ $\quad$ The zeros are $\frac{1}{3}$, $^{-}2$, and 1.

exercises

Max: 1–17, 1–17; Avg: 1–17, 1–17 odds; Min: 1–17 odds

Exploratory Find all *possible* rational zeros for each function.

1. $f(x) = x^4 + x^2 - 2$
2. $f(x) = x^3 + 2x^2 - 3x + 5$
3. $f(x) = x^2 - 8x + 6$
4. $f(x) = x^2 + 5x^2 - 3$
5. $f(x) = x^3 - 2x^2 + 3x - 8$
6. $f(x) = x^3 - 4x + 10$
7. $f(x) = x^3 + 8x^2 - 3x + 1$
8. $f(x) = x^3 - 2x^2 - 5x - 9$
9. $f(x) = x^3 - 8x^2 - 11x + 20$
10. $f(x) = x^4 + 2x + 15$
11. $f(x) = 6x^4 + 35x^3 - x^2 - 7x - 1$
12. $f(x) = 6x^3 + 4x^2 - 14x - 2$
13. $f(x) = 3x^4 - 5x^2 + 4$
14. $f(x) = 2x^3 + x^2 + 5x - 3$
15. $f(x) = 2x^3 - 5x^2 - 28x + 15$
16. $f(x) = 3x^4 - 2x^2 + 18$
17. $f(x) = 6x^3 - 41x^2 + 58x - 15$

For answers to problems 1-17, see the Teacher's Guide.

Written Find all rational zeros for each function.

1. $f(x) = (x - 3)(x + 5)(2x + 5)$ $\quad 3, {}^{-}5, -\frac{5}{2}$
2. $f(x) = (x - 8)(7x - 5)(x + 3)$ $\quad 8, \frac{5}{7}, {}^{-}3$
3. $f(x) = (x - 3)^2(x + 2)(2x - 1)(3x - 2)$
4. $f(x) = (x + 5)^3(4x - 1)^2(5x + 3)$
5. $f(x) = 2(3x - 2)(x - 5)(x + 1)$ $\quad \frac{2}{3}, 5, {}^{-}1$
6. $f(x) = (x + 1)(2x + 3)(x - 5)$ $\quad {}^{-}1, -\frac{3}{2}, 5$
7. $f(x) = x^3 - x^2 - 34x - 56$ $\quad {}^{-}2, {}^{-}4, 7$
8. $f(x) = x^3 + x^2 - 80x - 300$ $\quad {}^{-}5, {}^{-}6, 10$
9. $f(x) = 2x^3 - 11x^2 + 12x + 9$ $\quad 3, 3, -\frac{1}{2}$
10. $f(x) = x^3 - 3x^2 + x - 3$ $\quad 3$
11. $f(x) = x^3 - 3x^2 - 53x - 9$ $\quad 9$
12. $f(x) = x^3 - x^2 - 40x + 12$ $\quad {}^{-}6$
13. $f(x) = x^4 + 10x^3 + 33x^2 + 38x + 8$ $\quad {}^{-}2, {}^{-}4$
14. $f(x) = x^4 + x^3 - 9x^2 - 17x - 8$ $\quad {}^{-}1, {}^{-}1$

3. $3, 3, {}^{-}2, \frac{1}{2}, \frac{2}{3}$ $\quad$ 4. ${}^{-}5, {}^{-}5, {}^{-}5, \frac{1}{4}, \frac{1}{4}, -\frac{3}{5}$

9-4 Nature of Solutions

Objective: To determine the nature of the solutions to polynomial equations.

Some polynomial equations like $4x^2 - 1 = 0$ have no integer solutions. Some like $x^2 - 2 = 0$ have no rational solutions. Some like $x^2 + 1 = 0$ have no real solutions. All polynomial equations have *at least one solution* in the set of complex numbers.

The Fundamental Theorem of Algebra

> **Every polynomial equation with degree greater than zero has at least one solution in the set of complex numbers.**

Another interesting theorem comes from The Fundamental Theorem of Algebra. It states that a polynomial equation has n complex solutions if its polynomial has degree n.

In the eighteenth century, the Fundamental Theorem of Algebra was not obvious. Karl Friedrich Gauss (1777–1855) is credited with the first proof.

For example, $x^3 + 5x^2 + 4x + 20 = 0$ has three solutions in the set of complex numbers, $2i$, ^-2i, and $^-5$. The equation $x^3 + 7x^2 + 15x + 9 = 0$ has three solutions if $^-3$ is counted twice.

$$x^3 + 5x^2 + 4x + 20 = 0$$
$$(x - 2i)(x + 2i)(x + 5) = 0$$
$$x - 2i = 0 \quad \text{or} \quad x + 2i = 0 \quad \text{or} \quad x + 5 = 0$$
$$x = 2i \qquad\qquad x = {}^-2i \qquad\qquad x = {}^-5$$

$$x^3 + 7x^2 + 15x + 9 = 0$$
$$(x + 1)(x + 3)^2 = 0$$
$$x + 1 = 0 \quad \text{or} \quad (x + 3)^2 = 0$$
$$x = {}^-1 \qquad\qquad x = {}^-3$$

You may have noticed that imaginary solutions to quadratic equations come in pairs. In general, if an imaginary number is a solution, then its conjugate is also a solution.

Complex Conjugates Theorem

> **Suppose a and b are real numbers with $b \neq 0$. Then, if $a + bi$ is a solution to a polynomial equation, $a - bi$ is also a solution to the equation.**

example 1

Find all zeros of $f(x) = x^3 - 7x^2 + 17x - 15$ if $2 - i$ is one solution to $f(x) = 0$.

Since $2 - i$ is a solution, $2 + i$ also is a solution. Thus, both $x - (2 - i)$ and $x - (2 + i)$ are factors of the polynomial.

$$f(x) = [x - (2 - i)][x - (2 + i)][\ ?\ ]$$
$$= (x^2 - 4x + 5)(\ ?\ )$$

$$\begin{array}{r} x - 3 \\ x^2 - 4x + 5 \overline{) x^3 - 7x^2 + 17x - 15} \\ \underline{x^3 - 4x^2 + 5x} \\ {}^-3x^2 + 12x - 15 \\ \underline{{}^-3x^2 + 12x - 15} \\ 0 \end{array}$$

Use division to find the other factor.

$$f(x) = (x^2 - 4x + 5)(x - 3)$$

Since $x - 3$ is a factor, 3 is a solution. The zeros are $2 - i$, $2 + i$, and 3.

The polynomial has degree 3, so it has 3 zeros.

More information about the zeros of a polynomial function was developed by Rene Descartes (1596–1650), a French mathematician.

Descartes Rule of Signs

Suppose $p(x)$ is a polynomial whose terms are arranged in descending powers of the variable. The number of positive real zeros of $y = p(x)$ is the same as the number of changes in sign of the coefficients of the terms, or is less than this number by an even multiple. The number of negative real zeros is the same as the number of changes in sign of $p(^-x)$, or is less than this number by an even multiple.

example 2

State the number of positive and negative real zeros for $p(x) = 2x^4 - x^3 + 5x^2 + 3x - 9$.

The signs, in order, are as follows.

$$\begin{array}{ccccccccc} + & & - & & + & & + & & - \\ & \uparrow & & \uparrow & & & & \uparrow & \end{array}$$

There are three sign changes, so there are three or one positive real zeros.

Next, evaluate the polynomial for ^-x.

$$\begin{aligned} p(^-x) &= 2(^-x)^4 - (^-x)^3 + 5(^-x)^2 + 3(^-x) - 9 \\ &= 2x^4 + x^3 + 5x^2 - 3x - 9 \end{aligned}$$

The signs, in order, are as follows.

$$\begin{array}{ccccccccc} + & & + & & + & & - & & - \\ & & & & & \uparrow & & & \end{array}$$

There is one sign change, so there is one negative real zero.

exercises

Max: 1–20, 1–16; **Avg:** 1–20, 1–15 odds; **Min:** 1–15 odds

Exploratory State the number of positive real zeros.

1. $f(x) = x^4 - 2x^3 + x^2 - 1$ 3 or 1; 1
2. $f(x) = 3x^5 + 7x^2 - 8x + 1$ 2 or 0; 1
3. $f(x) = 4x^4 - 3x^3 + 2x^2 - x + 1$ 4, 2, or 0; 0
4. $f(x) = x^7 - x^3 + 2x - 1$ 3 or 1; 2 or 0
5. $f(x) = x^4 - x^3 + x^2 + x + 1$ 2 or 0; 2 or 0
6. $f(x) = {}^-x^4 - x^2 - x - 1$ 0; 2 or 0
7. $f(x) = x^6 - 2x^5 + 3x^4 - 8x^3 + 7x^2 - 1$ 5, 3, or 1; 1
8. $f(x) = x^3 + x^2 + x + 1$ 0; 3 or 1
9. $f(x) = x^4 + x^3 - 7x - 1$ 1; 3 or 1
10. $f(x) = x^{10} - 1$ 1; 1

11–20. State the number of negative real zeros for each function in problems **1–10**. See second part of answers **1–10** above.

Written 1-10. Complete the chart for each function.

Function	No. Positive Real Zeros	No. Negative Real Zeros	No. Imaginary Zeros
$f(x) = {}^-x^3 + x^2 - x + 1$	3 or 1	0	0 or 2
$f(x) = 3x^4 + 2x^3 - 3x^2 - 4x + 1$	2 or 0	2 or 0	4, 2, or 0
$f(x) = 3x^4 - 8x + 1$	2 or 0	0	4 or 2
$f(x) = {}^-7x^3 - 6x + 1$	1	0	2
$f(x) = x^{10} - x^8 + x^6 - x^4 + x^2 - 1$	5, 3, or 1	5, 3, or 1	0, 2, 4, 6, or 8
$f(x) = x^5 - x^3 - x + 1$	2 or 0	1	4 or 2
$f(x) = 3x^4 - x^2 + x - 1$	3 or 1	1	2 or 0
$f(x) = 4x^5 - x^2 + 1$	2 or 0	1	4 or 2
$f(x) = x^3 + 1$	0	1	2
$f(x) = x^{14} + x^{10} - x^9 + x - 1$	3 or 1	1	12 or 10
$f(x) = x^4 + x^3 + 2x^2 - 3x - 1$	1	3 or 1	2 or 0

11. Let $f(x) = x^3 - 10x^2 + 34x - 40$. Find all zeros if $3 + i$ is one solution to $x^3 - 10x^2 + 34x - 40 = 0$. $3 + i, 3 - i, 4$

12. Let $f(x) = x^3 - 3x^2 + 9x + 13$. Find all zeros if $2 - 3i$ is one solution to $x^3 - 3x^2 + 9x + 13 = 0$. $2 - 3i, 2 + 3i, {}^-1$

13. Let $f(x) = x^3 + 2x^2 - 3x + 20$. Find all zeros if $1 + 2i$ is one solution to $x^3 + 2x^2 - 3x + 20 = 0$. $1 + 2i, 1 - 2i, {}^-4$

14. Let $f(x) = x^4 - 6x^3 + 12x^2 + 6x - 13$. Find all zeros if $3 - 2i$ is one solution to $x^4 - 6x^3 + 12x^2 + 6x - 13 = 0$. $3 - 2i, 3 + 2i, {}^-1, 1$

15. Explain why $4x^3 + 2x^2 + 1 = 0$ must have two complex roots.
It has no positive real roots and only one negative real root. Therefore, there must be two complex roots.

Upper and Lower Bounds

Excursions in Algebra

The function $f(x) = x^3 - 7x + 6$ has real zeros 1, 2, and $^-3$. An **upper bound** for the zeros of a function is a number for which no real zero *greater* than that number exists. For example 2, 3, and 10.9 are upper bounds for the zeros of f. A **lower bound** for the zeros of a function is a number for which no real zero *less* than that number exists. Some lower bounds for the zeros of f are $^-3$, $^-17$, and $^-125.4$.

Example Find lower and upper bounds for the real zeros of $f(x) = x^4 - 2x^3 - 3$.

By Descartes Rule of Signs, there is one positive and one negative real zero. Also, by the Rational Zero Theorem, possible rational zeros are $^-3$, $^-1$, 1, and 3.

Look at f for the values of x between $^-3$ and 3, inclusive. The zeros are $^-1$, and a number between 2 and 3. Thus, a lower bound for the real zeros is $^-1$ and an upper bound is 3.

x	f(x)
$^-3$	132
$^-2$	29
$^-1$	0 ←
0	$^-3$
1	$^-4$
2	$^-3$ ←
3	24

Exercises Find upper and lower bounds for the zeros of the functions in Written Exercises **1-4**. Answers will vary.

9-5 Approximating Zeros

Objective: To approximate the zeros of polynomial functions.

The graph of a continuous curve drawn from a lower point to a higher point must *cross* every horizontal line in between. Thus, if the graph of a polynomial function is in part below the x-axis and in part above the x-axis, it must also cross the x-axis.

The Location Principle

Suppose $y = f(x)$ represents a polynomial function. And suppose a and b are two numbers with $f(a)$ negative and $f(b)$ positive. Then the function has at least one real zero between a and b.

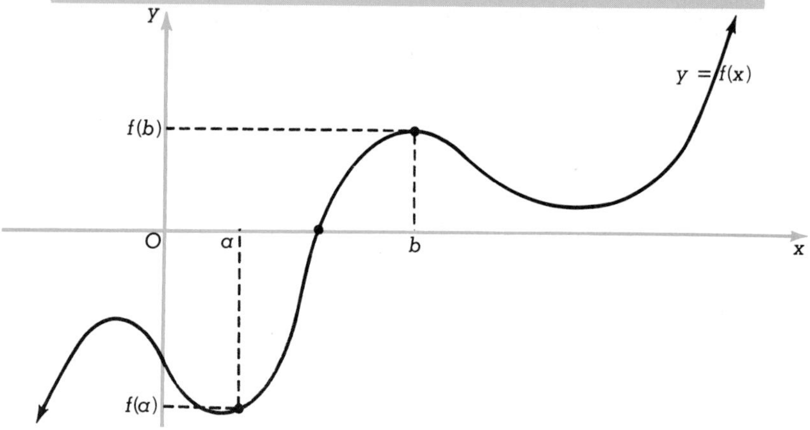

You can use the location principle to find zeros of a polynomial function.

example 1

Approximate to the nearest tenth the real zeros of the function with equation $f(x) = x^4 + x^2 - 6$.

By Descartes Rule of Signs, there is one positive real zero and one negative real zero. The other zeros are imaginary. By the Rational Zero Theorem, the possible rational zeros are $^-6$, $^-3$, $^-2$, $^-1$, 1, 2, 3, or 6.

x	$x^4 + x^2 - 6$	$f(x)$
$^-6$	$1296 + 36 - 6$	1326
$^-3$	$81 + 9 - 6$	84
$^-2$	$16 + 4 - 6$	14
$^-1$	$1 + 1 - 6$	$^-4$
1	$1 + 1 - 6$	$^-4$
2	$16 + 4 - 6$	14
3	$81 + 9 - 6$	84
6	$1296 + 36 - 6$	1326

By the Location Principle there is a zero between $^-1$ and $^-2$, and a zero between 1 and 2.

Locate the negative zero.

x	$f(x)$
$^-1.5$	1.3125
$^-1.4$	$^-0.1984$
$^-1.3$	$^-1.4539$
$^-1.2$	$^-2.4864$
$^-1.1$	$^-3.3259$
$^-1.0$	$^-4$

$f(^-1.45] \approx 0.5$

The zero is "closer" to $^-1.4$.

Why aren't values less than $^-1.5$ tested?

Locate the positive zero.

x	$f(x)$
1.0	$^-4$
1.1	$^-3.3259$
1.2	$^-2.4864$
1.3	$^-1.4539$
1.4	$^-0.1984$
1.5	1.3125

The zero is "closer" to 1.4.

$f(1.45) \approx 0.5$

Why aren't values greater than 1.5 tested?

The real zeros are approximately $^-1.4$ and 1.4. The zeros are actually $\pm\sqrt{2}$.

2 **Approximate to the nearest tenth the real zeros of the function with equation $f(x) = x^4 - x^3 - 4x^2 + 8x - 4$.**

By Descartes Rule of Signs, there are three or one positive real zeros and one negative real zero. By the Rational Zero Theorem, the possible rational zeros are $^-4$, $^-2$, $^-1$, 1, 2, or 4.

x	$x^4 - x^3 - 4x^2 + 8x - 4$	$f(x)$
$^-4$	$256 + 64 - 64 - 32 - 4$	220
$^-2$	$16 + 8 - 16 - 16 - 4$	$^-12$
$^-1$	$1 + 1 - 4 - 8 - 4$	$^-14$
1	$1 - 1 - 4 + 8 - 4$	0
2	$16 - 8 - 16 + 16 - 4$	4
4	$256 - 64 - 64 + 32 - 4$	156

By the Location Principle there is a zero between $^-4$ and $^-2$.

1 is a zero.

Locate the zero between $^-4$ and $^-2$.

First, find $f(^-3)$.

$$f(^-3) = 81 + 27 - 36 - 24 - 4 \text{ or } 44$$
$$= 44$$

By the Location Principle, the zero is between $^-3$ and $^-2$.

x	$f(x)$
$^-2.5$	5.6875
$^-2.4$	0.7616
$^-2.3$	$^-3.4089$

$f(^-2.35) \approx {}^-1.414$

The zero is "closer" to $^-2.4$.

The real zeros are 1 and approximately $^-2.4$.
The other two zeros are imaginary.

exercises

Max: 1–18; Avg: 1–17; Min: 1–17 odds

Written Approximate to the nearest tenth the real zeros of functions with the following equations.

1. $f(x) = x^3 - 2x^2 + 6$ ⁻1.3
2. $f(x) = x^4 - 4x^2 + 3$ 1, ⁻1, 1.7, ⁻1.7
3. $f(x) = 2x^5 + 3x - 2$ 0.6
4. $f(x) = x^4 - x^2 + 6$
5. $f(x) = x^3 + 2x^2 - 3x - 5$
6. $f(x) = x^3 - 5$ 1.7
7. $f(x) = x^5 - 6$ 1.4
8. $f(x) = 3x^3 - 16x^2 + 12x + 6$
9. $f(x) = x^3 - x^2 + 1$ ⁻0.7
10. $f(x) = x^4 - 4x^2 + 6$
11. $f(x) = 3x^2 - 8x + 1$ 0.1, 2.5
12. $f(x) = {}^{-}7x^3 - 6x + 1$ 0.2
13. $f(x) = x^5 - x^3 - x + 1$
14. $f(x) = 3x^4 - x^2 + x - 1$ ⁻1, 0.7
15. $f(x) = x^3 + 1$ ⁻1
16. $f(x) = x^4 - x^2 - 6$ 1.7, ⁻1.7
17. $f(x) = x^3 - 4x + 4$ ⁻2.4
18. $f(x) = x^3 - 3$ 1.4

4. No real solutions 5. 1.6, ⁻1.3, ⁻2.4 8. ⁻0.3, 4.3, 1.4 10. No real solutions 13. 1, 0.8, ⁻1.4

Using Computers

Bisection Method

You can approximate real zeros of a function like $f(x) = x^4 + x^2 - 6$ on a computer by using the **bisection method.** The function has a real zero between ⁻2 and ⁻1, and a real zero between 1 and 2.

Suppose you wish to approximate the zero between ⁻2 and ⁻1.

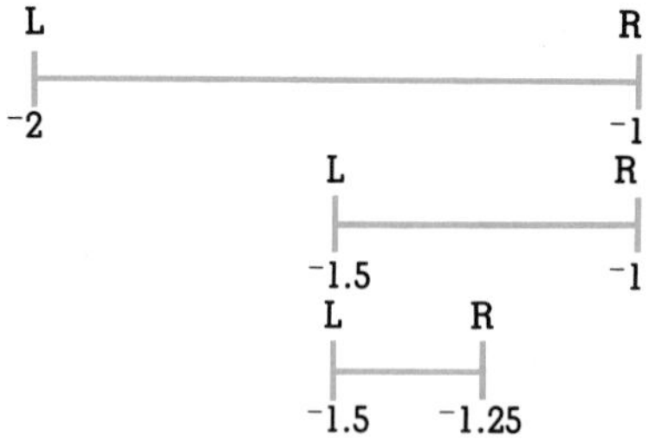

By the location principle, there is a zero between ⁻2 and ⁻1.

Average ⁻2 and ⁻1 $\dfrac{^{-}2 + {}^{-}1}{2} = {}^{-}1.5$

By the location principle, there is a zero between ⁻1.5 and ⁻1.

Average ⁻1.5 and ⁻1 $\dfrac{^{-}1.5 + {}^{-}1}{2} = {}^{-}1.25$

By the location principle, there is a zero between ⁻1.5 and ⁻1.25.

Average ⁻1.5 and ⁻1.25 $\dfrac{^{-}1.5 + {}^{-}1.25}{2} = {}^{-}1.375$

The computer program below continues this process to find ten averages. The tenth average will be printed as the approximate zero.

`10 INPUT L, R`	*The zero is located between two consecutive integers, L and R.*
`20 FOR I=1 TO 10`	*L means left and R means right.*
`30 Y=(L+R)/2`	*Y is the average of L and R.*
`40 LET A=L↑4+L↑2−6`	*A is f(L).*
`50 LET B=Y↑4+Y↑2−6`	*B is f(Y).*
`60 IF A*B<0 THEN 90`	*If A · B is negative, then the zero is between L and Y. Therefore, in Step 90, Y is substituted for R.*
`70 LET L=Y`	
`80 GO TO 100`	*If A · B is positive or zero, the zero is between Y and R. Therefore, in Step 70, Y is substituted for L.*
`90 LET R=Y`	
`100 NEXT I`	
`110 PRINT "THE ZERO IS APPROXIMATELY "Y"."`	
`120 END`	

Exercises Use the computer program to approximate the real zeros of functions in problems **1–6.**
See student's work.

Credit Cards

Credit cards can be used to make purchases and to pay for services at many businesses. They enable you to buy now, but pay later.

If you pay your bill *in full* within the allotted time, usually 25 days, there are no additional charges. However, if you do not, you are assessed an additional charge called credit or *finance charges*. Generally, these charges are at the rate of 1.5% per month or 18% per year.

Example Cecilia used a credit card to purchase a coat for \$60. She decided to pay \$20 a month plus the finance charge for that month. Find the total finance charges and the total amount paid.

First Monthly Bill: The bill is for \$60. Cecilia makes a \$20 payment. There is no finance charge on the first monthly bill.

Second Monthly Bill:

$$\begin{array}{ccccc} \textit{balance} & - & \textit{payment} & = & \textit{new balance} \\ 60 & - & 20 & = & 40 \end{array}$$

Multiply the new balance by 1.5%.

$$\begin{aligned} 40 \cdot 1.5\% &= 40 \cdot 0.015 \\ &= 0.60 \end{aligned}$$

Her second payment is \$20.60.

The finance charge is \$0.60 the second month.

Third Monthly Bill:

$$\begin{array}{ccccccc} \textit{balance} & + & \textit{finance charge} & - & \textit{payment} & = & \textit{new balance} \\ 40 & + & 0.60 & - & 20.60 & = & 20 \end{array}$$

Multiply the new balance by 1.5%.

$$\begin{aligned} 20 \cdot 1.5\% &= 20 \cdot 0.015 \\ &= 0.30 \end{aligned}$$

Her third, and last payment, is \$20.30.

The finance charge is \$0.30 the third month.

The total finance charges are \$0.60 + \$0.30 or \$0.90.
The total amount paid is \$60.90.

Exercises Find the total finance charges and total amount paid for each of the following credit card purchases.

1. Suit: \$90 to pay, \$30 per month. \$1.35, \$91.35
2. Tune-up: \$60 to pay, \$15 per month. \$1.36, \$61.36
3. Luggage: \$50 to pay, \$25 per month. \$0.38, \$50.38
4. Glasses: \$75 to pay, \$15 per month. \$2.26, \$77.26

9–6 Graphing Polynomials

Objective: To graph polynomial functions.

The simplest polynomial graphs are those with equations of the form $f(x) = x^n$ where n is a positive integer.

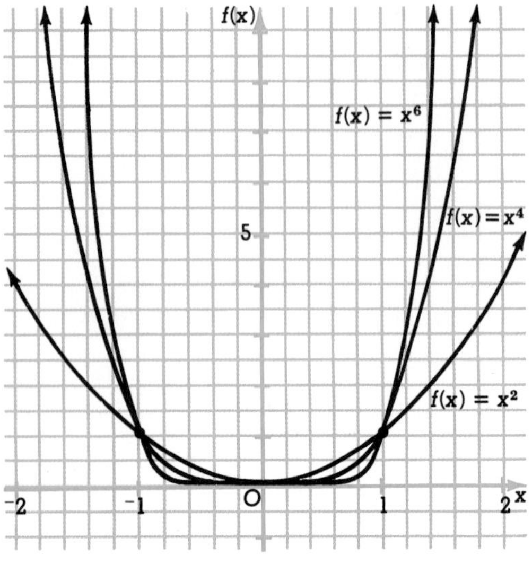

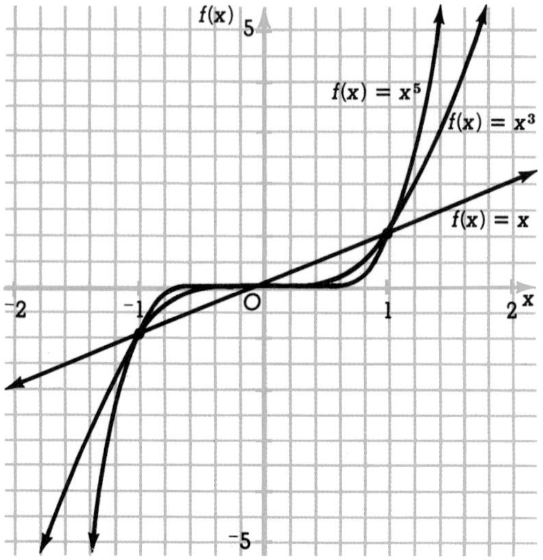

Notice that the horizontal scales on both grids have been exaggerated.

Notice that each graph has only one x-intercept, the origin. The graphs are completed by finding points on the graphs and connecting them with smooth continuous curves.

If a polynomial $f(x)$ can be factored into linear factors, much information about the graph of $y = f(x)$ is available. For example, consider $y = (x - 2)(x - 3)(x + 5)$.

1. The function has three zeros, 2, 3, and $^-5$.
2. The function has negative values when x is less than $^-5$ and when x is between 2 and 3.
3. The function has positive values when x is between $^-5$ and 2 and when x is greater than 3.

The graph crosses the x-axis at $^-5$, 2, and 3. The shaded regions contain no points of the graph.

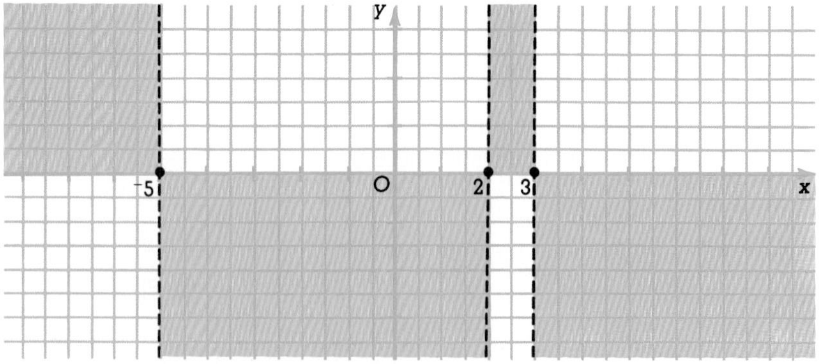

To complete the graph, find and plot points on the graph. Connect them with a smooth continuous curve.

x	y
−6	−72
−5	0
−4	42
−3	60
−2.5	61.875
−2	60
−1	48
0	30
1	12
2	0
2.3	−1.533
2.5	−1.875
2.7	−1.617
3	0
4	18
5	60

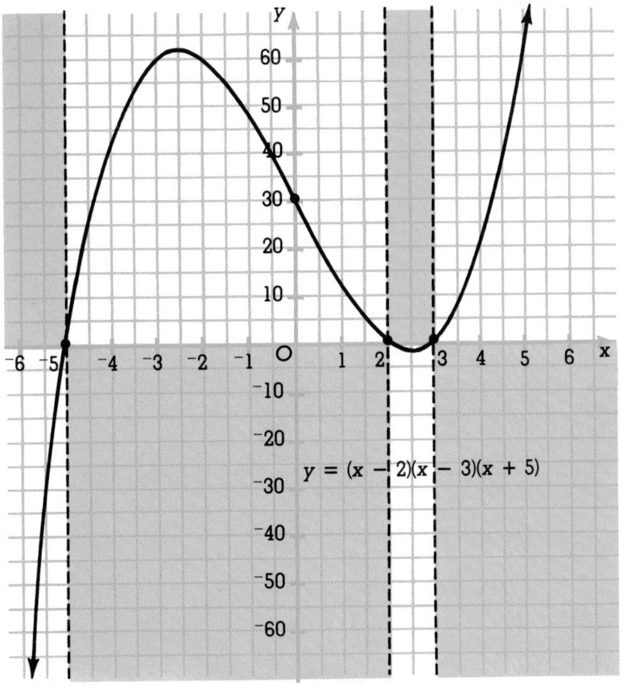

Notice how the vertical scale has been "condensed" so the graph will fit the space provided.

example 1

Graph $f(x) = {}^{-}x^3 + 2x^2 + 4x - 8$.

First, factor the polynomial.

$f(x) = {}^{-}(x - 2)^2(x + 2)$

1. The function has two zeros, 2 and −2.
2. The function has positive values when x is less than −2.
3. The function has negative values when x is greater than −2.

x	−4	−3	−2	−1	0	1	2	3	4
f(x)	72	25	0	−9	−8	−3	0	−5	−24

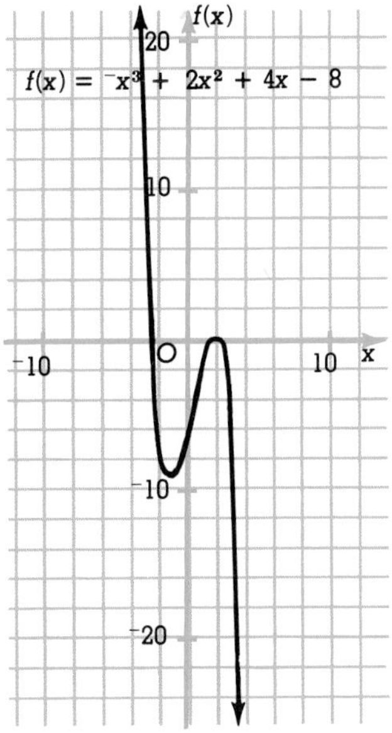

In general, the graph of a cubic polynomial function has a *sideways S* shape. You can use this information to help graph functions that have imaginary zeros.

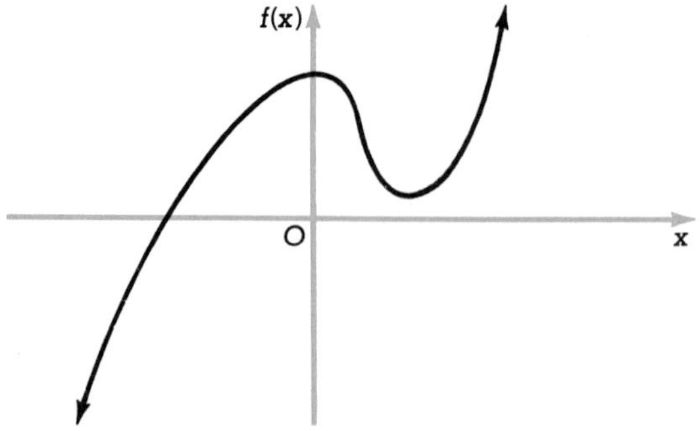

$f(x) = ax^3 + bx^2 + cx + d$, a positive

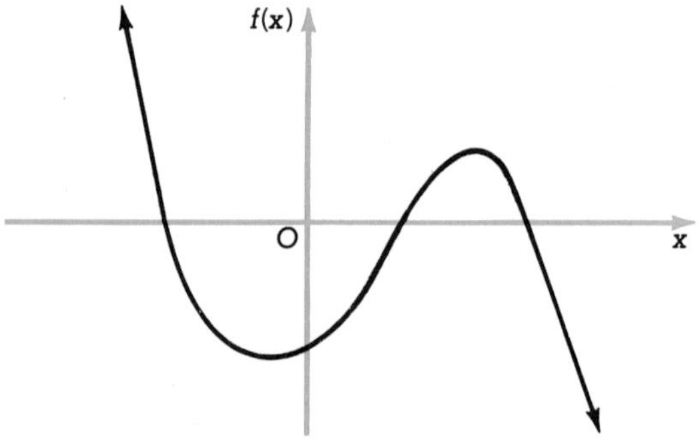

$f(x) = ax^3 + bx^2 + cx + d$, a negative

example 2

Graph $f(x) = x^3 - 6x - 9$.

First, factor the polynomial.
$f(x) = (x - 3)(x^2 + 3x + 3)$

The function has one real zero, 3.

The graph of a cubic polynomial function has a *sideways S* shape. Thus it has one *hill* and one *valley*. Find points of the graph that indicate where the *hill* and *valley* are located.

x	f(x)
$^{-}3$	$^{-}18$
$^{-}2$	$^{-}5$
$^{-}1.5$	$^{-}3.375$
$^{-}1$	$^{-}4$
$^{-}0.5$	$^{-}6.166$
0	$^{-}9$
1	$^{-}14$
1.5	$^{-}14.625$
2	$^{-}13$
3	0
4	31

indicates a hill ($x = {}^{-}2$ to $^{-}1$)

indicates a valley ($x = 1$ to 2)

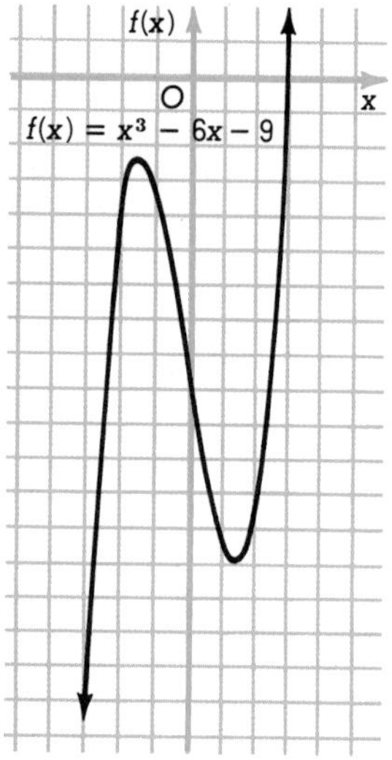

Encourage the use of calculators to facilitate graphing.

exercises

Max: 1–18; **Avg:** 1–18; **Min:** 1–17 odds

Written **Graph each of the following.**

1. $f(x) = x^3$
2. $f(x) = x^6$
3. $f(x) = 4x^6$
4. $f(x) = 3x^5$
5. $f(x) = (x - 1)(x - 2)(x + 2)$
6. $f(x) = (x + 4)(x - 1)(x + 1)$
7. $f(x) = (x - 2)^2(x + 3)$
8. $f(x) = (x - 3)^2(x + 1)$
9. $f(x) = x^3 - x$
10. $f(x) = {}^{-}x^3 - x$
11. $f(x) = x^3 - x^2 - 8x + 12$
12. $f(x) = x^4 - 81$
13. $f(x) = x^4 - 10x^2 + 9$
14. $f(x) = x^3 + 5$
15. $f(x) = 15x^3 - 16x^2 - x + 2$
16. $f(x) = x^3 - 3x - 4$
17. $f(x) = {}^{-}x^3 - 13x - 12$
18. $f(x) = {}^{-}x^3 - 4x^2 - 8x - 8$

For graphs to problems **1–18**, see the Teacher's Guide.

9–7 Composition of Functions

Objective: To find the composition of functions.

Scientists often use the Kelvin temperature scale. Kelvin temperature readings and Celsius temperature readings are related in the following way.

$$K = C + 273$$

Celsius readings and Fahrenheit readings are related in the following way.

$$C = \frac{5}{9}(F + 32)$$

Using these equations, you can write a new equation which shows how Kelvin readings and Fahrenheit readings are related.

$K = C + 273$

$= \frac{5}{9}(F - 32) + 273$ *Substitute $\frac{5}{9}(F - 32)$ for C.*

$= \frac{5}{9}F + \frac{2617}{9}$

The above example illustrates **composition of functions.**

Given functions f and g, the composite function $f \circ g$ can be described by the following equation.

$$[f \circ g](x) = f[g(x)]$$

The range of g is a subset of the domain of f.

Composition of Functions

examples

1 **If $f(x) = x + 273$ and $g(x) = \frac{5}{9}(x - 32)$, find $[f \circ g](x)$.**

$[f \circ g](x) = f[g(x)]$

$= f\left[\frac{5}{9}(x - 32)\right]$ *Substitute $\frac{5}{9}(x - 32)$ for $g(x)$.*

$= \left[\frac{5}{9}(x - 32)\right] + 273$ *Evaluate f when x is $\frac{5}{9}(x - 32)$.*

$= \frac{5}{9}x + \frac{2617}{9}$ *Simplify.*

2 **If $f(x) = x^2 + 3$ and $h(x) = 2x - 1$, find $[f \circ h](2)$.**

$[f \circ h](2) = f[h(2)]$

$= f[2(2) - 1]$ *Substitute $2(2) - 1$ for $h(2)$.*

$= f[3]$ *Substitute 3 for $2(2) - 1$.*

$= 12$ *Evaluate f when x is 3.*

Mappings can be used to show composition of functions. Suppose $f = \{(1, 2), (2, 3), (3, 4)\}$ and $g = \{(2, 3), (3, 1), (4, 2)\}$.

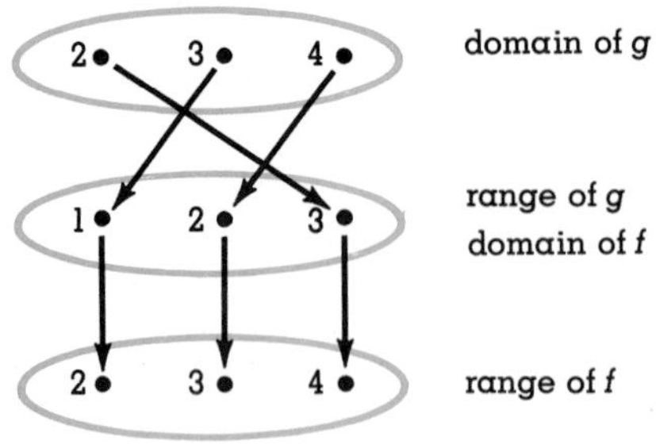

$f \circ g = \{(2, 4), (3, 2), (4, 3)\}$

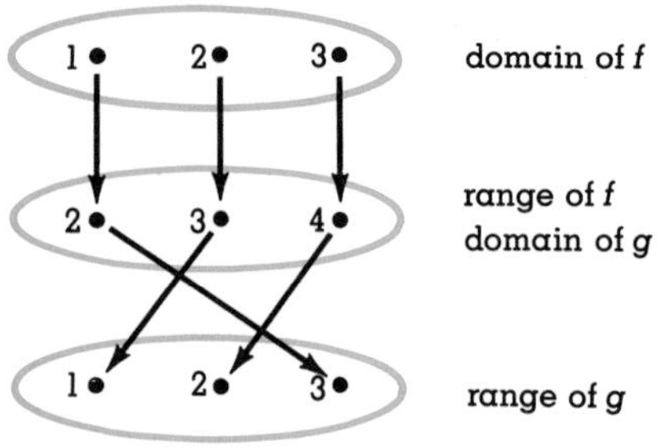

$g \circ f = \{(1, 3), (2, 1), (3, 2)\}$

Notice that in the example above, $f \circ g \neq g \circ f$. In general, composition of functions is not a commutative operation.

example 3

If $f(x) = x + 7$ and $g(x) = 3 + 2x$, find $[f \circ g](x)$ and $[g \circ f](x)$.

$$
\begin{aligned}
[f \circ g](x) &= f[g(x)] \\
&= f[3 + 2x] \\
&= (3 + 2x) + 7 \\
&= 2x + 10
\end{aligned}
\qquad
\begin{aligned}
[g \circ f](x) &= g[f(x)] \\
&= g[x + 7] \\
&= 3 + 2(x + 7) \\
&= 2x + 17
\end{aligned}
$$

Given two functions f and g, the domain of $f \circ g$ may *not* be the same as the domain of g. It may be only a subset.

In some cases, given two functions h and k, the composite functions $h \circ k$ or $k \circ h$ may *not* even exist. For example, let $h = \{(2, 4), (4, 6), (6, 8), (8, 10)\}$ and $k = \{(4, 5), (6, 5), (8, 12), (10, 12)\}$. The range of k is *not* a subset of the domain of h. So, $h \circ k$ *does not exist.* The range of h is a subset of the domain of k. So, $k \circ h$ *does exist.*

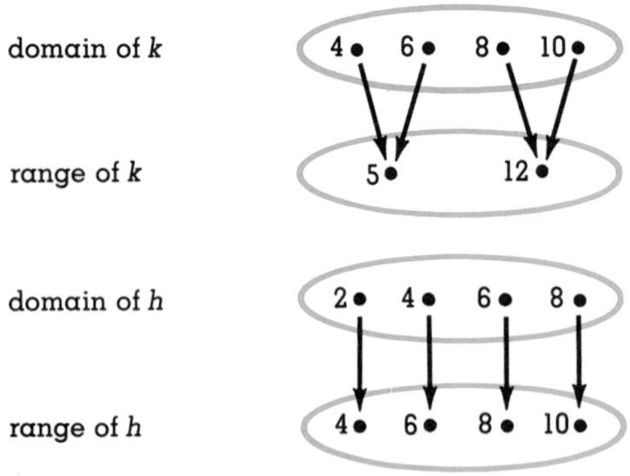

$h \circ k$ does not exist

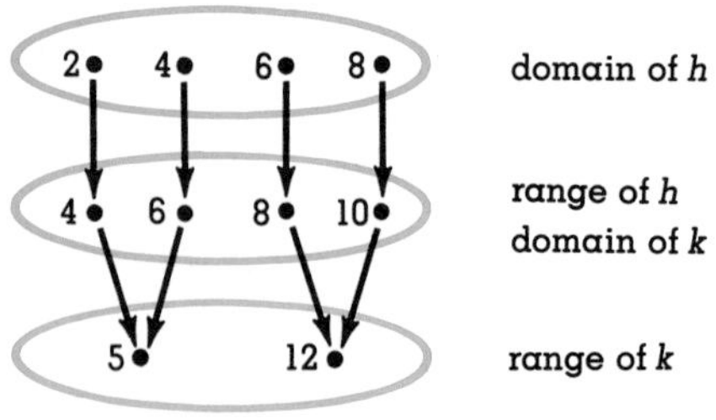

$k \circ h = \{(2, 5), (4, 5), (6, 12), (8, 12)\}$

exercises

Max: 1–10, 1–21; Avg: 1–10, 1–21 odds; Min: 1–21 odds

Exploratory In each exercise find $f(2)$, $f(^-2)$, and $f(0)$.

1. $f(x) = x - 3$ $^-1, ^-5, ^-3$
2. $f(x) = x^2 + 4$ 8, 8, 4
3. $f(x) = x^2 - 2x + 1$ 1, 9, 1
4. $f(x) = |x + 2|$ 4, 0, 2
5. $f(x) = |x| + 2$ 4, 4, 2
6. $f(x) = x^3 - x^2 + x - 1$ $5, ^-15, ^-1$
7. $f(x) = x^4 - 6$ $10, 10, ^-6$
8. $f(x) = x^2 - 8x + 4$ $^-8, 24, 4$
9. $f(x) = x^5 - x^2 + 2$ $30, ^-34, 2$
10. $f(x) = x^2 - x^3$ $^-4, 12, 0$

Written In each exercise, find $[f \circ g](3)$.

1. $f(x) = x + 2$ 4
   $g(x) = x - 1$
2. $f(x) = x^2 + 8$ 8
   $g(x) = x - 3$
3. $f(x) = x^3 - 1$ 63
   $g(x) = x + 1$
4. $f(x) = x$ 3
   $g(x) = x$
5. $f(x) = x^2 + 1$ 65
   $g(x) = x^2 - 1$
6. $f(x) = x^2$ 729
   $g(x) = x^3$

In each exercise, find $f[g(x)]$.

7. $f(x) = 2x + 1$ $2x - 5$
   $g(x) = x - 3$
8. $f(x) = 3x - 4$ $6x + 11$
   $g(x) = 2x + 5$
9. $f(x) = x^2 + 3$ $4x^2 - 4x + 4$
   $g(x) = 2x - 1$
10. $f(x) = x + 2$ $x^2 + 1$
    $g(x) = x^2 - 1$
11. $f(x) = x^2 - 8$ $x^4 - 2x^2 - 7$
    $g(x) = x^2 - 1$
12. $f(x) = x + 2$ x
    $g(x) = x - 2$

In each exercise, find $f[g(^-1)]$ and $g[f(^-1)]$.

13. $f(x) = x - 1$ $^-1, ^-1$
    $g(x) = x + 1$
14. $f(x) = x^2 + 2x + 1$ $1, ^-1$
    $g(x) = x^2 - 1$
15. $f(x) = x^2 + 2$ 18, 0
    $g(x) = x - 3$
16. $f(x) = x^2 + x^3 + 1$ 13, 2
    $g(x) = x^2 + 1$
17. $f(x) = x - 8$ $^-7, 9$
    $g(x) = |x|$
18. $f(x) = |x + 1|$ 1, 1
    $g(x) = |x + 1|$

Express $g \circ f$ as a set of ordered pairs.

19. $f = \{(2, 1), (3, 4), (6, ^-2)\}$ $\{(2, 5), (3, ^-7), (6, ^-3)\}$
    $g = \{(1, 5), (4, ^-7), (^-2, ^-3)\}$
20. $f = \{(3, 8), (4, 0), (6, 3), (7, ^-1)\}$ $\{(3, 6), (4, 4), (6, 6), (7, ^-8)\}$
    $g = \{(8, 6), (0, 4), (3, 6), (^-1, ^-8)\}$

21. Write a computer program that will find $f[g(x)]$ for values of x from $^-6$ to 6 for each of the functions $f(x) = x^2 + 8x - 1$ and $g(x) = x^2 + 2$. See Teacher's Guide.

9–8 Inverse Functions

Objective: To find and recognize inverse functions.

You have learned that two numbers are additive inverses if their sum is 0, the additive identity. Two numbers are multiplicative inverses if their product is 1, the multiplicative identity. Two functions are **inverse functions** if both their compositions are the identity function.

For example, suppose $f(x) = 3x - 2$ and $g(x) = \frac{x + 2}{3}$. Then f and g are inverse functions.

$$\begin{aligned}[f \circ g](x) &= f[g(x)] \\ &= f\left[\frac{x+2}{3}\right] \\ &= 3\left(\frac{x+2}{3}\right) - 2 \\ &= x\end{aligned} \qquad \begin{aligned}[g \circ f](x) &= g[f(x)] \\ &= g[3x - 2] \\ &= \frac{(3x - 2) + 2}{3} \\ &= x\end{aligned}$$

Definition of Inverse Functions

Two polynomial functions f and g are inverse functions if and only if both their compositions are the identity function. That is,

$$[f \circ g](x) = [g \circ f](x) = x$$

The notation f^{-1} is read "f inverse," or "the inverse of f." The $^{-1}$ is not an exponent.

A special notation often is used to show that two functions f and g are inverse functions.

$$g = f^{-1} \quad \text{and} \quad f = g^{-1}$$

The ordered pairs of a function and its inverse are related in a special way. Consider $f(x) = 3x - 2$ and its inverse $f^{-1}(x) = \frac{x + 2}{3}$.

$$\begin{aligned}f(5) &= 3 \cdot 5 - 2 \\ &= 13\end{aligned} \qquad \begin{aligned}f^{-1}(13) &= \frac{13 + 2}{3} \\ &= 5\end{aligned}$$

The ordered pair (5, 13) belongs to f.

The ordered pair (13, 5) belongs to f^{-1}.

Property of Inverse Functions

Suppose f and f^{-1} are inverse functions. Then $f(a) = b$ if and only if $f^{-1}(b) = a$.

The inverse of a function can be found by reversing the order of each pair in the given function.

You can use this idea to define inverse relations.

example 1

Suppose $f(x) = 3x - 5$. Find $f^{-1}(x)$. Also, show that f and f^{-1} are inverse functions.

Recall that $f(a) = b$ if and only if $f^{-1}(b) = a$. Since $f(x) = 3x - 5$, you know $f(a) = 3a - 5$. Use $3a - 5 = b$ to find $f^{-1}(b)$.

Solve the equation for a.

$$3a = b + 5$$
$$a = \frac{b + 5}{3}$$
$$f^{-1}(b) = \frac{b + 5}{3}$$
$$f^{-1}(x) = \frac{x + 5}{3}$$ *Replace b by x.*

Now show that the compositions of f and f^{-1} are identity functions.

$$[f \circ f^{-1}](x) = f[f^{-1}(x)] = f\left[\frac{x + 5}{3}\right] = 3\left(\frac{x + 5}{3}\right) - 5 = x$$

$$[f^{-1} \circ f](x) = f^{-1}[f(x)] = f^{-1}[3x - 5] = \frac{(3x - 5) + 5}{3} = x$$

So, $[f \circ f^{-1}](x) = [f^{-1} \circ f](x) = x$.

Not all functions have inverses which are functions.

example 2

Given $f(x) = x^2 + 3$, find $f^{-1}(x)$.

Since $f(x) = x^2 + 3$, you know $f(a) = a^2 + 3$. Use $a^2 + 3 = b$ to find $f^{-1}(b)$. *Why?*
$f(a) = b$ if and only if $f^{-1}(b) = a$

Solve the equation for a.

$$a^2 + 3 = b$$
$$a^2 = b - 3$$
$$a = \pm\sqrt{b - 3}$$
$$f^{-1}(b) = \pm\sqrt{b - 3}$$ *Substitute a with $f^{-1}(b)$.*
$$f^{-1}(x) = \pm\sqrt{x - 3}$$ *Substitute b with x.*

This equation does *not* define a function. For a given value of x, there is more than one value of $f^{-1}(x)$. For example, $f^{-1}(7) = 2$ or $^{-}2$.

exercises

Max: 1–6, 1–38; **Avg:** 1–6, 1–37 odds; **Min:** 1–37 odds

Exploratory Write the inverse of each function and determine if its inverse is a function.

1. $f = \{(3, 1), (2, 4), (1, 5)\}$ $\{(1, 3), (4, 2), (5, 1)\}$, yes
2. $f = \{(3, 2), (4, 2)\}$ $\{(2, 3), (2, 4)\}$, no
3. $g = \{(3, 8), (4, ^-2), (5, ^-3)\}$ $\{(8, 3), (^-2, 4), (^-3, 5)\}$, yes
4. $g = \{(^-1, ^-2), (^-3, ^-2), (^-1, ^-4), (0, 6)\}$
5. $h = \{(^-3, 1), (2, 4), (7, 8)\}$ $\{(1, ^-3), (4, 2), (8, 7)\}$, yes
6. $h = \{(4, ^-2), (3, 7), (5, 7), (3, 8)\}$

4. $\{(^-2, ^-1), (^-2, ^-3), (^-4, ^-1), (6, 0)\}$, no 6. $\{(^-2, 4), (7, 3), (7, 5), (8, 3)\}$, no

Written Write the equation for the inverse of each function.

1. $y = 2x$ $y = \frac{1}{2}x$
2. $f(x) = x + 2$ $f^{-1}(x) = x - 2$
3. $f(x) = {}^-6x - 5$ $f^{-1}(x) = -\frac{1}{6}x - \frac{5}{6}$
4. $y = 3x - 7$ $y = \frac{1}{3}x + \frac{7}{3}$
5. $y = 3$ $x = 3$
6. $f(x) = \dfrac{1}{2}x + 4$ $f^{-1}(x) = 2x - 8$
7. $f(x) = 0$ $f^{-1}(x) = 0$
8. $f(x) = {}^-3x - 1$ $f^{-1}(x) = -\frac{1}{3}x - \frac{1}{3}$
9. $y = x^2$ $y = \pm\sqrt{x}$
10. $y = x^2 - 4$ $y = \pm\sqrt{x^2 + 4}$

Graph each function and its inverse. For graphs of problems **11–20**, see the Teacher's Guide.

11. $f = \{(2, 1), (3, ^-4), (0, 1)\}$
12. $f = \left\{\left(\dfrac{1}{2}, 3\right), (0, ^-2), (7, 6)\right\}$
13. $y = x$
14. $y = {}^-2x - 1$
15. $y = 3x$
16. $f(x) = x + 2$
17. $f(x) = \dfrac{3x + 1}{2}$
18. $y = \dfrac{x - 3}{5}$
19. $y = x^2 + 1$
20. $f(x) = (x - 4)^2$

Determine if the inverse of each relation graphed below is a function.

21.
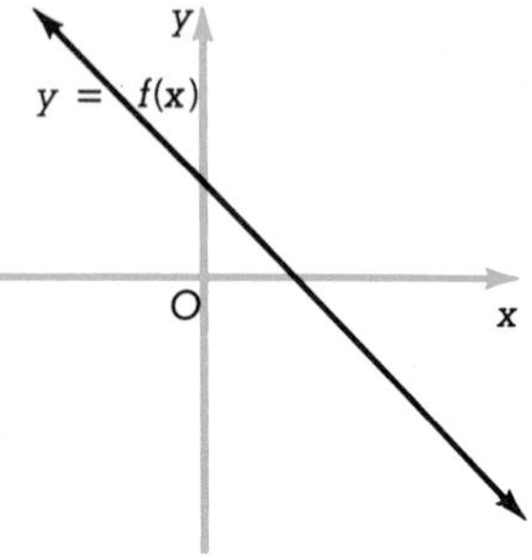

yes

22.
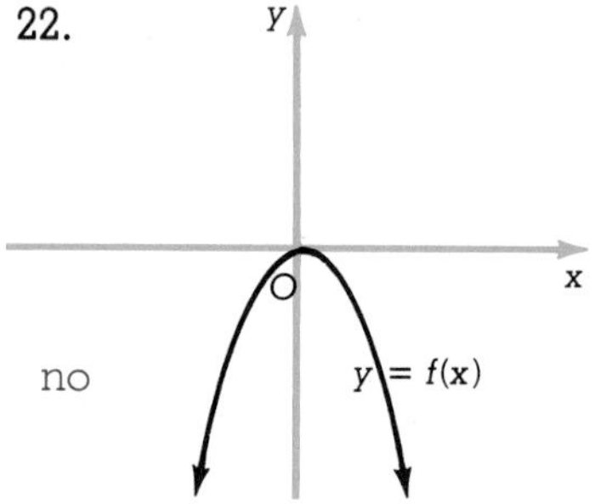

no

23.
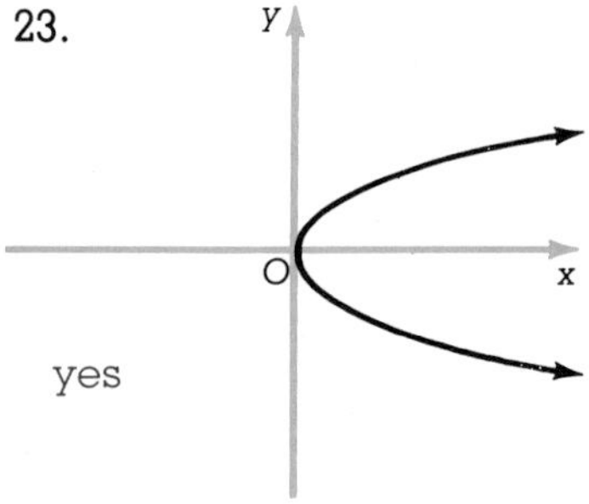

yes

24.
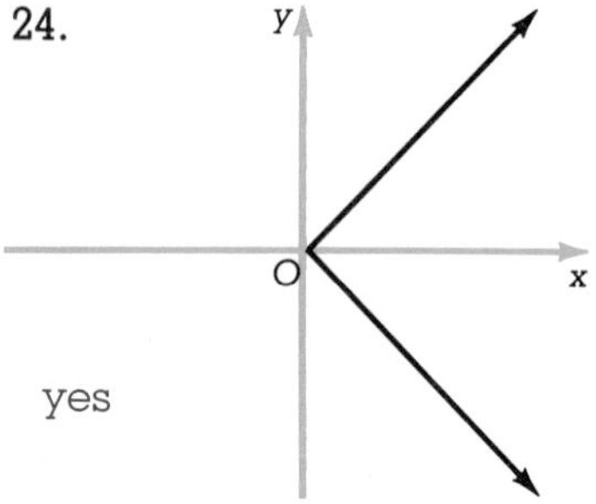

yes

25.
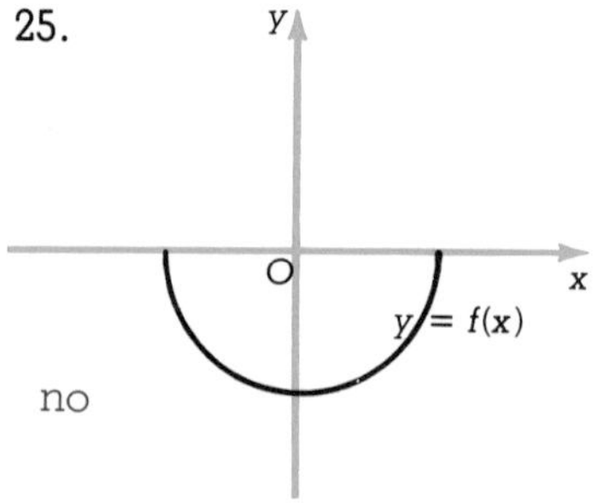

no

26.
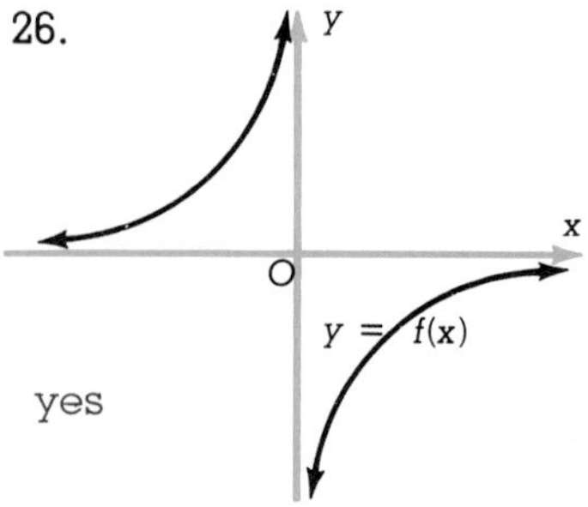

yes

In each of the following, determine whether the given functions are inverses of one another.

27. $y = 2x + 1$ yes
$y = \frac{x - 1}{2}$

28. $y = {}^{-}2x + 3$ no
$y = 2x - 3$

29. $y = x + 4$ yes
$y = x - 4$

30. $f(x) = x + 1$ yes
$f(x) = x - 1$

31. $f(x) = 4x - 5$ yes
$f(x) = \frac{x + 5}{4}$

32. $f(x) = x$ no
$f(x) = {}^{-}x$

Solve each problem. In each case, assume f is a function.

33. If $f(3) = 4$, find $f^{-1}(4)$. 3

34. If $f\left(\frac{1}{2}\right) = 6$, find $f^{-1}(6)$. $\frac{1}{2}$

35. If $f(a) = b$, find $f^{-1}(b)$. a

36. If $f(r) = s$, find $f^{-1}(s)$. r

37. If $f(a + 1) = 2$, find $f^{-1}(2)$. $a + 1$

38. If $f(m + n) = p$, find $f^{-1}(p)$. $m + n$

Excursions in Algebra

History

The Marquise du Châtelet (1706–1749) was born into nobility in Paris, France. She was an extremely brilliant mathematician who concentrated her studies on the works of Euclid and Isaac Newton. One of her major accomplishments was the first translation of Newton's *Principia Mathematica* from English to French. She completed the translation just a few days before her death. In addition to being a mathematician, she was a philosopher of considerable merit. Several of her philosophy papers were published posthumously.

Vocabulary

polynomial in one variable (248)
constant (248)
linear expression (248)
quadratic expression (248)
polynomial function (249)
zero (254)
composition of functions (267)
inverse functions (270)

Chapter Summary

1. A polynomial in one variable, x, is an expression of the form $a_nx^n + a_{n-1}x^{n-1} + \cdots + a_2x^2 + a_1x + a_0$. The coefficients a_0, a_1, a_2, . . . , a_n are real numbers, and n is a nonnegative integer. (248)
2. The Remainder Theorem: If a polynomial $f(x)$ is divided by $x - a$, the remainder is a constant, $f(a)$, and $f(x) = q(x) \cdot (x - a) + f(a)$ where $q(x)$ is a polynomial with degree one less than the degree of $f(x)$. (251)
3. The Factor Theorem: The binomial $x - a$ is a factor of the polynomial $f(x)$ if and only if $f(a) = 0$. (252)
4. The Rational Zero Theorem: Let $f(x) = a_nx^n + a_{n-1}x^{n-1} + \cdots + a_1x + a_0$ represent a polynomial with integer coefficients and n be a nonnegative integer. If $\frac{p}{q}$ is a rational number in simplest form and a zero of $y = f(x)$, then p is a factor of a_0 and q is a factor of a_n. (254)
5. The Fundamental Theorem of Algebra: Every polynomial equation with degree greater than zero has at least one solution in the set of complex numbers. (257)
6. Complex Conjugates Theorem: Suppose a and b are real numbers with $b \neq 0$. Then, if $a + bi$ is a solution to a polynomial equation, $a - bi$ is also a solution to the equation. (257)
7. Descartes Rule of Signs: Suppose $p(x)$ is a polynomial whose terms are arranged in descending powers of the variable. The number of positive real zeros of $y = p(x)$ is the same as the number of changes in sign of the coefficients of the terms, or is less than this number by an even multiple. The number of negative real zeros is the same as the number of changes in sign of $p(^-x)$ or is less than this number by an even multiple. (258)
8. The Location Principle: Suppose $y = f(x)$ represents a polynomial function. And suppose a and b are two numbers with $f(a)$ negative and $f(b)$ positive. Then the function has at least one real zero between a and b. (260)
9. Composition of Functions: Given functions f and g, the composite function $f \circ g$ can be described $[f \circ g](x) = f[g(x)]$. (267)

10. Definition of Inverse Functions: Two polynomial functions f and g are inverse functions if and only if both their compositions are the identity function. That is, $[f \circ g](x) = [g \circ f](x) = x$. (270)
11. Property of Inverse Functions: Suppose f and f^{-1} are inverse functions. Then $f(a) = b$ if and only if $f^{-1}(b) = a$. (270)

Chapter Review

9-1 Find $p(^-2)$ for each of the following.

1. $p(x) = 2x^3 + x^2 - 1$ $^-13$
2. $p(x) = 2x^4 - 3x^3 + 8$ 64
3. $p(x) = x^2 + x\sqrt{2}$ $4 - 2\sqrt{2}$
4. $p(x) = {}^-4x^3 - 5$ 27

9-2 Find the remainder for each of the following.

5. $(x^2 + 5x + 6) \div (x + 1)$ 2
6. $(x^3 + 8x + 1) \div (x - 2)$ 25
7. $(x^5 + 8x^3 + 2) \div (x + 2)$ $^-94$
8. $(x^4 + 3x^2 - 1) \div (x - 4)$ 303

Factor each polynomial.

9. $x^3 + 2x^2 - x - 2$ $(x + 2)(x - 1)(x + 1)$
10. $x^3 + 5x^2 + 8x + 4$ $(x + 1)(x + 2)^2$
11. $x^3 - 3x + 2$ $(x + 2)(x - 1)^2$
12. $x^3 - 6x^2 + 11x - 6$ $(x - 1)(x - 2)(x - 3)$

9-3 Find all rational zeros for each function.

13. $f(x) = (x - 1)^2(2x - 3)^2$ $1, 1, \frac{3}{2}, \frac{3}{2}$
14. $f(x) = (x + 2)(x - 2)(x + 5)^3$ $^-2, 2, {}^-5, {}^-5, {}^-5$
15. $f(x) = 6x^3 - 41x^2 + 58x - 15$ $5, \frac{1}{3}, \frac{3}{2}$
16. $f(x) = 16x^4 - 0.0081$ ± 0.15

9-4 For each function, state the number of positive real zeros, negative real zeros, and imaginary zeros. 17. 3 or 1; 1; 2 or 0

17. $f(x) = 2x^4 - x^3 + 5x^2 + 3x - 9$
18. $f(x) = {}^-x^4 - x^2 - x - 1$ 0; 2 or 0; 4 or 2
19. $f(x) = 7x^3 + 6x - 1$ 1; 0; 2
20. $f(x) = x^4 + x^3 - 7x + 1$ 2 or 0; 2 or 0; 4, 2, or 0
21. Find all zeros of $f(x) = x^3 - 7x^2 + 17x - 15$ if $2 + i$ is one solution to $f(x) = 0$. $2 + i, 2 - i, 3$

9-5 Approximate to the nearest tenth the real zeros of functions with the following equations.

22. $f(x) = x^3 - x^2 + 1$ $^-0.8$
23. $f(x) = 3x^4 - x^2 + x - 1$ $^-1, 0.7$

9-6 Graph each of the following. See Teacher's Guide.

24. $f(x) = (x - 3)^2(x + 2)$
25. $f(x) = x^3 - 3x - 4$

9-7 In each exercise, find $[f \circ g](x)$ and $[g \circ f](x)$.

26. $f(x) = x^2 + 2$ $x^2 - 6x + 1$
    $g(x) = x - 3$ $x^2 - 1$
27. $f(x) = x^2 + 2x + 1$ x^4
    $g(x) = x^2 - 1$ $x^4 + 4x^3 + 6x^2 + 4x$
28. $f(x) = |x|$ $|x - 8|$
    $g(x) = x - 8$ $|x| - 8$
29. $f(x) = |x + 1|$ $2|x - 3| + 1$
    $g(x) = 2|x - 3|$ $2||x + 1| - 3|$

9-8 Graph each function and its inverse. See Teacher's Guide.

30. $f(x) = \dfrac{3x + 2}{2}$
31. $f(x) = (x - 6)^2$

Chapter Test

Find $p(3)$ for each of the following.

1. $p(x) = x^4 - x^3 + x - 1$ 56
2. $p(x) = x^3 - 27$ 0
3. $p(x) = x^2\sqrt{3} - \sqrt{2}$ $9\sqrt{3} - \sqrt{2}$
4. $p(x) = {}^-2x^4 + x - 5$ $^-164$

Find the remainder for each of the following.

5. $(x^2 + 4x + 4) \div (x + 2)$ 0
6. $(x^3 + 8x + 1) \div (x + 2)$ $^-23$
7. $(x^5 + 8x^3 + 2) \div (x - 2)$ 98
8. $(x^4 + x^3 + x^2 + x + 1) \div (x + 1)$ 1

Factor each polynomial.

9. $x^4 - 5x^2 + 4$ $(x + 1)(x - 1)(x + 2)(x - 2)$
10. $x^3 - 3x - 2$ $(x - 2)(x + 1)^2$
11. $x^3 - x^2 - 5x - 3$ $(x - 3)(x + 1)^2$
12. $x^4 - 3x^3 - 7x^2 - 27x - 24$
    $(x + 1)(x^3 - 4x^2 - 3x - 24)$

Find all rational zeros for each function.

13. $f(x) = x^4 + x^3 - 9x^2 - 17x - 8$ $^-1$
14. $f(x) = x^3 - 3x^2 - 53x - 9$ 9
15. $f(x) = 2x^3 - 5x^2 - 28x + 15$ $^-3, 5, \frac{1}{2}$
16. $f(x) = 6x^3 + 4x^2 - 14x + 4$ $^-2, \frac{1}{3}, 1$

17. Find all zeros of $f(x) = x^3 - 10x^2 + 34x - 40$ if $3 + i$ is one solution to $f(x) = 0$.
18. Find all zeros of $f(x) = x^4 - 6x^3 + 12x^2 + 6x - 13$ if $3 - 2i$ is one solution to $f(x) = 0$.
19. Approximate to the nearest tenth the real zeros of $f(x) = x^3 - 3x - 4$. Then draw the graph. 2.2; see Teacher's Guide for graph.
20. Determine whether $f(x) = 2x - 3$ and $g(x) = \dfrac{x + 3}{2}$ are inverses of one another. Show your work.

17. $3 + i, 3 - i, 4$ 18. $3 - 2i, 3 + 2i, 1, {}^-1$

$$f(g(x)) = 2\left(\frac{x + 3}{2}\right) - 3 = x + 3 - 3 = x$$

$$g(f(x)) = \frac{(2x - 3) + 3}{2} = \frac{2x}{2} = x$$

Both $f(g(x))$ and $g(f(x))$ yield the identity function, x. Therefore, they are inverses.

Chapter 10

Rational Polynomial Expressions

Business executives often are concerned with how one quantity, such as profit, varies with respect to another quantity, such as sales. Mathematics often can be used to help them understand how the quantities are related and help them plan their business strategy.

10-1 Multiplying Rational Expressions

Objective: To multiply rational polynomial expressions.

All polynomials, including constants are rational expressions. But not all rational expressions are polynomials.

Rational numbers and **rational algebraic expressions** are similar.

A rational number can be expressed as the quotient of two integers.

$$\frac{2}{3} \qquad \frac{415}{100}$$

There are often values of the variable for which a rational algebraic expression is not defined. The first expression is not defined for $x = 5$. The second expression is not defined for $^{-}2 \pm \sqrt{3}$.

A rational algebraic expression can be expressed as the quotient of two polynomials.

$$\frac{2x}{x-5} \qquad \frac{p^2-25}{p^2+4p+1}$$

To simplify a rational algebraic expression, divide both numerator and denominator by their greatest common factor (GCF).

examples

1 **Simplify** $\frac{2x(x-5)}{(x-5)(x^2-1)}$.

$$\frac{2x(x-5)}{(x-5)(x^2-1)} = \frac{2x}{x^2-1}$$ *The GCF is $(x - 5)$.*

2 **Simplify** $\frac{x^2-x^2y}{x^3-x^3y}$.

$$\frac{x^2-x^2y}{x^3-x^3y} = \frac{x^2(1-y)}{x^3(1-y)}$$
$$= \frac{1 \cdot x^2(1-y)}{x \cdot x^2(1-y)}$$
$$= \frac{1}{x}$$ *The GCF is $x^2(1 - y)$.*

Both rational numbers and rational expressions are multiplied the same way. Multiply numerators and multiply denominators.

$$\frac{2}{3} \cdot \frac{4}{5} = \frac{2 \cdot 4}{3 \cdot 5} \text{ or } \frac{8}{15}$$

$$\frac{(x+1)}{(x-4)} \cdot \frac{(2x+3)}{(3x-1)} = \frac{(x+1)(2x+3)}{(x-4)(3x-1)} \text{ or } \frac{2x^2+5x+3}{3x^2-13x+4}$$

examples

3 Find $\frac{4a}{5b} \cdot \frac{15b}{16a}$.

$$\frac{4a}{5b} \cdot \frac{15b}{16a} = \frac{60ab}{80ab}$$
$$= \frac{3 \cdot 20ab}{4 \cdot 20ab}$$
$$= \frac{3}{4}$$ *The GCF is 20ab.*

4 Find $\frac{x^2 - 9}{x^2 + x - 12} \cdot \frac{x + 2}{x + 3}$.

$$\frac{x^2 - 9}{x^2 + x - 12} \cdot \frac{x + 2}{x + 3} = \frac{(x^2 - 9)(x + 2)}{(x^2 + x - 12)(x + 3)}$$
$$= \frac{(x - 3)(x + 3)(x + 2)}{(x - 3)(x + 4)(x + 3)}$$ *Factor.*
$$= \frac{x + 2}{x + 4}$$ *The GCF is (x − 3)(x + 3).*

exercises

Max: 1–28, 1–42; Avg: 1–28, 1–41 odds; Min: 1–41 odds

Exploratory For each expression, find the greatest common factor (GCF) of the numerator and denominator.

1. $\frac{24}{72}$ 24; $\frac{1}{3}$
2. $\frac{99}{132}$ 33; $\frac{3}{4}$
3. $\frac{13x}{39x^2}$ $13x$; $\frac{1}{3x}$
4. $\frac{42y}{18xy}$ $6y$; $\frac{7}{3x}$
5. $\frac{38a^2}{42ab}$ $2a$; $\frac{19a}{21b}$
6. $\frac{79a^2b}{158a^3bc}$ $79a^2b$; $\frac{1}{2ac}$
7. $\frac{42y^2}{56y}$ $14y$; $\frac{3y}{4}$
8. $\frac{8x^2 - x^3}{16 - 2x}$ $(8 - x)$; $\frac{x^2}{2}$
9. $\frac{y^2 - 9}{y^2 + 6y + 9}$ $y + 3$; $\frac{y - 3}{y + 3}$
10. $\frac{y^2 + 8y - 20}{y^2 - 4}$ $(y - 2)$; $\frac{y + 10}{y + 2}$
11. $\frac{x^2 - x - 20}{x^2 + 7x + 12}$ $(x + 4)$; $\frac{x - 5}{x + 3}$
12. $\frac{y^2 + 4y + 4}{3y^2 + 5y - 2}$ $(y + 2)$; $\frac{y + 2}{3y - 1}$
13. $\frac{a^2 + 2a + 1}{2a^2 + 3a + 1}$ $(a + 1)$; $\frac{a + 1}{2a + 1}$
14. $\frac{2b^2 - 9b + 9}{b^2 - 6b + 9}$ $(b - 3)$; $\frac{2b - 3}{b - 3}$

15–28. Simplify each expression in problems **1–14**. See second part of answers above.

Written Find each product. Write your answers in simplest form.

1. $\frac{3}{8} \cdot \frac{16}{7}$ $\frac{6}{7}$

2. $\frac{21}{35} \cdot \frac{56}{42}$ $\frac{4}{5}$

3. $\frac{18x}{8y} \cdot \frac{3x}{27z}$ $\frac{x^2}{4y}$

4. $\frac{3ab}{4ac} \cdot \frac{6a^2}{3b^2}$ $\frac{3a^2}{2bc}$

5. $\frac{(y-2)^2}{(x-4)^2} \cdot \frac{x-4}{y-2}$ $\frac{y-2}{x-4}$

6. $-\frac{x^2-y^2}{x+y} \cdot \frac{1}{x-y}$ $^-1$

7. $\frac{3a^2b^3c}{4ab^2} \cdot \frac{6c}{1}$ $\frac{9}{2}abc^2$

8. $\frac{4a^2xy}{12bc} \cdot \frac{24bc^2}{6xy}$ $\frac{4a^2c}{3}$

9. $\frac{^-3abc}{9abd} \cdot \frac{7d}{18c^2}$ $-\frac{7}{54c}$

10. $\frac{11xy}{5xz} \cdot \frac{^-15z}{^-66y^2}$ $\frac{1}{2y}$

11. $\frac{12}{5} \cdot \frac{10}{3}$ 8

12. $\frac{1}{3} \cdot -\frac{9}{11}$ $-\frac{3}{11}$

13. $\frac{5}{4} \cdot \frac{16}{20}$ 1

14. $-\frac{68}{34} \cdot \frac{17}{51}$ $-\frac{2}{3}$

15. $\frac{^-200}{700} \cdot \frac{50}{40}$ $-\frac{5}{14}$

16. $\frac{5}{7} \cdot \frac{3}{^-5} \cdot \frac{14}{18}$ $-\frac{1}{3}$

17. $\frac{^-35}{20} \cdot \frac{60}{70} \cdot \frac{^-4}{5}$ $\frac{6}{5}$

18. $\frac{^-49}{147} \cdot \frac{18}{54} \cdot \frac{9}{20}$ $-\frac{1}{20}$

19. $\frac{96}{81} \cdot \frac{27}{16} \cdot \frac{^-49}{^-42}$ $\frac{7}{3}$

20. $\frac{5280}{10{,}560} \cdot \frac{4}{3} \cdot \frac{51}{70}$ $\frac{17}{35}$

21. $\frac{7a}{14b} \cdot \frac{6b^2}{a}$ $3b$

22. $\frac{^-4ab}{21c} \cdot \frac{14c^2}{18a^2}$ $-\frac{4bc}{27a}$

23. $\frac{7xy}{16z} \cdot \frac{^-4z^2}{21x^2}$ $-\frac{yz}{12x}$

24. $\frac{(cd)^3}{a} \cdot \frac{ax^2}{xc^2d}$ cd^2x

25. $\frac{x}{3y} \cdot \frac{9y^4}{3x^5}$ $\frac{y^3}{x^4}$

26. $\frac{y+2}{x} \cdot \frac{x^2}{(y+2)^2}$ $\frac{x}{y+2}$

27. $\frac{3(y+4)^2}{x^2} \cdot \frac{2x^3}{9(y+4)}$ $\frac{2x(y+4)}{3}$

28. $\frac{x-3}{x+4} \cdot \frac{x+4}{2}$ $\frac{x-3}{2}$

29. $\frac{a^3-b^3}{a^2-b^2} \cdot \frac{a+b}{a^2+ab+b^2}$ 1

30. $\frac{x^2-3x-10}{x+2} \cdot \frac{y^3}{x-5}$ y^3

31. $\frac{a^2-b^2}{14} \cdot \frac{35}{a+b}$ $\frac{5(a-b)}{2}$

32. $\frac{x^2-y^2}{70} \cdot \frac{56}{4x-4y}$ $\frac{x+y}{5}$

33. $\frac{3m^2-m}{5m+10} \cdot \frac{4-m^2}{6m}$ $\frac{(3m-1)(2-m)}{30}$

34. $\frac{x^2-8x-48}{2(12-x)} \cdot \frac{4x+4y}{x+y}$ $^-2(x+4)$

35. $\frac{x^2+7x+12}{x^2-9} \cdot \frac{8x}{16y}$ $\frac{x(x+4)}{2y(x-3)}$

36. $\frac{c^2-4cd}{3a} \cdot \frac{18a^2b}{c-4d}$ $6abc$

37. $\frac{x^2+3x-10}{x^2+8x+15} \cdot \frac{x^2+5x+6}{x^2+4x+4}$ $\frac{(x-2)}{(x+2)}$

38. $\frac{x^3+y^3}{x^2-y^2} \cdot \frac{3a}{9ab} \cdot \frac{6xb}{7x}$ $\frac{2(x^2-xy+y^2)}{7(x-y)}$

39. $\frac{x^3+3x^2+3x+1}{x+5} \cdot \frac{x^2-25}{x+1}$ $(x+1)^2(x-5)$

40. $\frac{x^4-1}{x+2} \cdot \frac{x^2-4}{x-1}$ $(x+1)(x^2+1)(x-2)$

41. $\frac{a^3-b^3}{a+b} \cdot \frac{a^2-b^2}{a^2+ab+b^2}$ $(a-b)^2$

42. $\frac{y^2-y-12}{y+12} \cdot \frac{y^2-4y-12}{y-4}$

42. $\frac{(y+2)(y+3)(y-6)}{y+12}$

CAREERS

Electrical Engineer

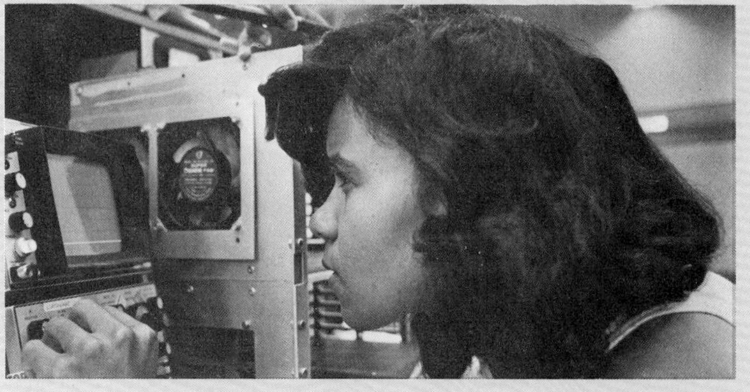

Virginia Boyd is an electrical engineer. Often she needs to find the amount of current or resistance in a circuit.

The resistors in a circuit can be placed in series, or parallel, or in some combination of these circuit designs.

Series

Parallel

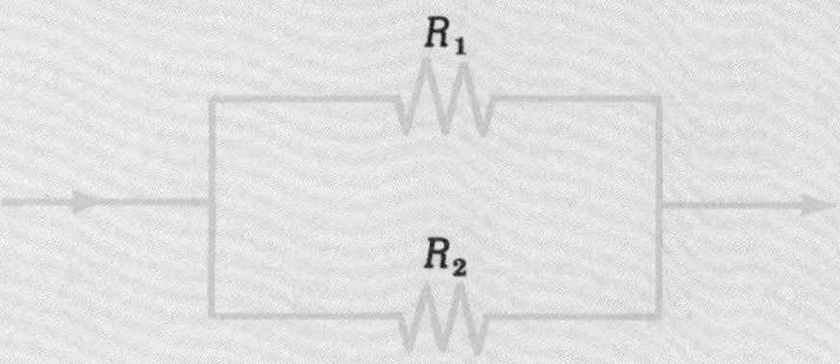

The total resistance R is found for these circuits as follows.

Series

$$R = R_1 + R_2$$

Parallel

$$\frac{1}{R} = \frac{1}{R_1} + \frac{1}{R_2}$$

Find the total resistance in the circuit shown below.

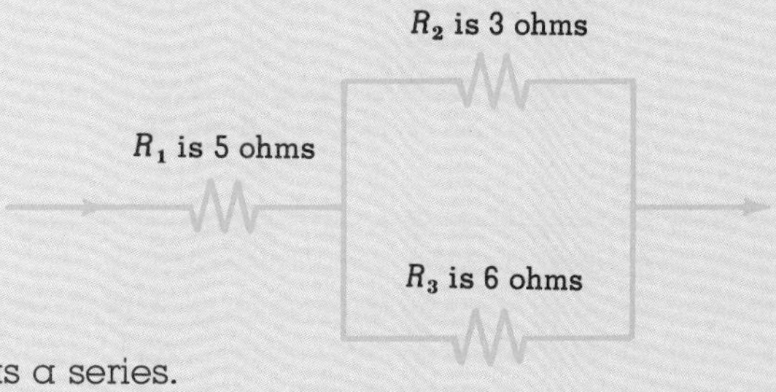

Think of the parallel circuit as being one resistance R_p.

$$\frac{1}{R_p} = \frac{1}{6} + \frac{1}{3} \qquad \frac{1}{R_p} = \frac{1}{R_3} + \frac{1}{R_2}$$

$$= \frac{1}{2} \qquad \text{Therefore, } R_p = 2.$$

The total resistance R_s can be thought of as a series.

$$R_s = R_1 + R_p$$
$$= 5 + 2 \text{ or } 7$$

The total resistance of the circuit is 7 ohms.

Exercises Find the total resistance in the circuit above for the following values.

1. $R_1 = 4$ ohms, $R_2 = 5$ ohms, $R_3 = 6$ ohms
2. $R_1 = 5$ ohms, $R_2 = 8$ ohms, $R_3 = 12$ ohms

1. 6.7 **2.** 9.8

10-2 Dividing Rational Expressions

Objective: To divide rational polynomial expressions.

Recall that dividing by a fraction is the same as multiplying by its inverse.

$$\frac{3}{8} \div \frac{3}{4} = \frac{3}{8} \cdot \frac{4}{3} \qquad \textit{The inverse of } \frac{3}{4} \textit{ is } \frac{4}{3}.$$
$$= \frac{12}{24}$$
$$= \frac{1}{2} \qquad \textit{The GCF is 12.}$$

Recall that a fraction is a rational number.

Similarly, dividing by a rational algebraic expression is the same as multiplying by its inverse.

examples

1 **Find $\frac{4x^2y}{15a^3b^3} \div \frac{2xy^2}{5ab^3}$.**

$$\frac{4x^2y}{15a^3b^3} \div \frac{2xy^2}{5ab^3} = \frac{4x^2y}{15a^3b^3} \cdot \frac{5ab^3}{2xy^2} \qquad \textit{The inverse of } \frac{2xy^2}{5ab^3} \textit{ is } \frac{5ab^3}{2xy^2}.$$
$$= \frac{20x^2yab^3}{30xy^2a^3b^3}$$
$$= \frac{2x}{3ya^2} \qquad \textit{The GCF is } 10xyab^3.$$

The solution is $\frac{2x}{3ya^2}$.

2 **Find $\frac{x^2}{x^2 - 25y^2} \div \frac{x}{x + 5y}$.**

$$\frac{x^2}{x^2 - 25y^2} \div \frac{x}{x + 5y} = \frac{x^2}{x^2 - 25y^2} \cdot \frac{x + 5y}{x} \qquad \textit{The inverse of } \frac{x}{x + 5y} \textit{ is } \frac{x + 5y}{x}.$$
$$= \frac{x^2(x + 5y)}{x(x^2 - 25y^2)}$$
$$= \frac{x^2(x + 5y)}{x(x + 5y)(x - 5y)} \qquad \textit{Factor } x^2 - 25y^2.$$
$$= \frac{x}{x - 5y} \qquad \textit{The GCF is } x(x + 5y).$$

The solution is $\frac{x}{x - 5y}$.

A complex rational expression, also called a **complex fraction,** is an expression whose numerator or denominator, or both, contain rational expressions.

$$\frac{\frac{1}{x} + 3}{\frac{2}{x} + 5} \qquad \frac{\frac{x^2 + y^2}{x - y} + y}{\frac{x^2 - y^2}{x + y} + y}$$

To simplify a complex fraction, treat it as a division problem.

example 3

Simplify $\dfrac{\frac{4 - x^2}{2}}{\frac{2 - x}{5}}$.

$$\frac{\frac{4 - x^2}{2}}{\frac{2 - x}{5}} = \frac{4 - x^2}{2} \div \frac{2 - x}{5}$$

$$= \frac{4 - x^2}{2} \cdot \frac{5}{2 - x}$$ *The inverse of* $\frac{2 - x}{5}$ *is* $\frac{5}{2 - x}$.

$$= \frac{5(4 - x^2)}{2(2 - x)}$$

$$= \frac{5(2 + x)(2 - x)}{2(2 - x)}$$ *Factor.*

$$= \frac{5(2 + x)}{2}$$ *The GCF is* $2 - x$.

exercises

Max: 1–10, 1–33; **Avg:** 1–10, 1–33 odds; **Min:** 1–33 odds

Exploratory **Find the inverse of each expression.**

1. $\frac{3}{8}$ $\frac{8}{3}$
2. $-\frac{7}{43}$ $-\frac{43}{7}$
3. $\frac{7x}{9y}$ $\frac{9y}{7x}$
4. $\frac{18x}{7}$ $\frac{7}{18x}$
5. 16 $\frac{1}{16}$
6. $-\frac{3}{22}$ $-\frac{22}{3}$
7. $\frac{x + y}{2}$ $\frac{2}{x + y}$
8. $\frac{x^2 - 8}{x - 1}$ $\frac{x - 1}{x^2 - 8}$
9. $\frac{(x + 4)^2}{(x - 3)^2}$ $\frac{(x - 3)^2}{(x + 4)^2}$
10. $x + a$ $\frac{1}{x + a}$

Written Find the inverse of each expression.

1. $\frac{14}{a^2}$ $\frac{a^2}{14}$

2. $-\frac{9}{15ab}$ $-\frac{5}{3}ab$

3. $\frac{x + y}{ab}$ $\frac{ab}{x + y}$

4. $\frac{3x}{x^2 + 7x}$ $\frac{x + 7}{3}$

5. $\frac{a^2 + ab + b^2}{a^2 - b^2}$ $\frac{a^2 - b^2}{a^2 + ab + b^2}$

6. $\frac{y - 4}{y^2 - 4y - 12}$ $\frac{y^2 - 4y - 12}{y - 4}$

7. $\frac{3x + 3}{x^2 + 2x - 3}$ $\frac{x^2 + 2x - 3}{3x + 3}$

8. $\frac{3x - 21}{x^2 - 49}$ $\frac{x + 7}{3}$

Find each quotient. Write your answers in simplest form.

9. $-\frac{46}{90} \div \frac{23}{10}$ $-\frac{2}{9}$

10. $-\frac{16.8}{7} \div \frac{8.4}{35}$ $^-10$

11. $\frac{7}{a} \div \frac{14}{a^2}$ $\frac{a}{2}$

12. $-\frac{3}{5a} \div -\frac{9}{15ab}$ b

13. $\frac{1}{x} \div -\frac{3}{x^2}$ $-\frac{x}{3}$

14. $-\frac{b^3c}{d} \div \frac{bc}{d^2}$ $^-b^2d$

15. $\frac{a^2b}{2c} \div \frac{a^2b^2}{c^2}$ $\frac{c}{2b}$

16. $\frac{3d^3c}{a^4} \div -\frac{6dc}{a^5}$ $-\frac{ad^2}{2}$

17. $\frac{(ab)^3}{d^3} \div \frac{a^2b^4}{(cd)^4}$ $\frac{ac^4d}{b}$

18. $\frac{13a^2}{14c} \div \frac{26a^3}{70c^2}$ $\frac{5c}{2a}$

19. $\frac{(x + y)^2}{a} \div \frac{x + y}{ab}$ $b(x + y)$

20. $\frac{x + y}{a} \div \frac{x + y}{a^2}$ a

21. $\frac{5}{m - 3} \div \frac{10}{m - 3}$ $\frac{1}{2}$

22. $\frac{11}{m + 6} \div \frac{22}{(m + 6)^2}$ $\frac{m + 6}{2}$

23. $\frac{a^2 - b^2}{2a} \div \frac{a - b}{6a}$ $3(a + b)$

24. $\frac{y - 5}{6} \div \frac{y - 5}{18}$ 3

25. $\frac{2x + 2}{x^2 + 5x + 6} \div \frac{3x + 3}{x^2 + 2x - 3}$ $\frac{2(x - 1)}{3(x + 2)}$

26. $\frac{3x - 21}{x^2 - 49} \div \frac{3x}{x^2 + 7x}$ 1

27. $\frac{a^2 + 2a - 15}{a - 3} \div \frac{a^2 - 4}{2}$ $\frac{2(a + 5)}{(a + 2)(a - 2)}$

28. $\frac{y^2 - y}{w^2 - y^2} \div \frac{y^2 - 2y + 1}{1 - y}$ $\frac{^-y}{w^2 - y^2}$

Simplify each expression.

29. $\dfrac{\frac{x^2 - y^2}{2}}{\frac{x - y}{4}}$ $2(x + y)$

30. $\dfrac{w^2 + 2w + 1}{\frac{w + 1}{3}}$ $3(w + 1)$

31. $\dfrac{\frac{5a^2 - 20}{2a + 2}}{\frac{10a - 20}{4a}}$ $\frac{a(a + 2)}{a + 1}$

32. $\dfrac{\frac{x^2 - 1}{x^2 - 3x - 10}}{\frac{x^2 - 12x + 35}{x^2 + 3x + 2}}$ $\frac{(x - 1)(x + 1)^2}{(x - 7)(x - 5)^2}$

33. Write a computer program to find the inverse of any nonzero rational number. Print out the results in fraction form and in decimal form. See Teacher's Guide.

Universal Product Code

You have probably seen the striped symbol that now appears on most grocery store items. This symbol is called the Universal Product Code (UPC). It is part of a new computer-equipped check-out system that is appearing in supermarkets across the country.

0 41150 47046 6

Each code identifies the particular product, its brand name, and other important information. At the checkout counter, each item is passed over an electronic eye that *reads* the code. The computer then prints out the name of the item and its price on the receipt.

If an item must be weighed, the computer *reads* the code, but delays charging until the item is weighed on a scale connected to the computer. Then the computer calculates and prints the price.

The computer signals the checkout clerk if an item is unmarked or incorrectly positioned on the eye. The charge in such cases is added to the bill manually.

The Universal Product Code is useful to stores for several reasons.

1. Price changes for specials or daily fluctuations can be programmed into the computer. It will be easier for stores to have specials.
2. The computer checks each item against the store or warehouse inventory. It issues a warning when it is time to reorder an item. Stores will be able to keep the items in stock.

Exercises Solve each problem. Answers vary.

1. List several ways the Universal Product Code is an advantage to consumers.
2. List several ways the Universal Product Code is a disadvantage to consumers.
3. Find out how the numerical code on the Universal Product Code is used.
4. List several ways the Universal Product Code is a disadvantage to stores.

10-3 Adding and Subtracting Rational Expressions

Objective: To add and subtract rational polynomial expressions.

The sum of two rational numbers with common denominators is the sum of the numerators over the common denominator.

You add rational numbers like $\frac{7}{13}$ and $\frac{4}{13}$ in the following way.

$$\frac{7}{13} + \frac{4}{13} = \frac{7 + 4}{13} \quad \text{or} \quad \frac{11}{13}$$

The sum of two rational expressions with common denominators is the sum of the numerators over the common denominator.

If two rational expressions have common denominators, add them in a similar fashion.

$$\frac{7x}{13y^2} + \frac{4x}{13y^2} = \frac{7x + 4x}{13y^2} \quad \text{or} \quad \frac{11x}{13y^2}$$

To add two rational numbers with different denominators, first find two equivalent rational numbers with common denominators. Then add the equivalent fractions.

$$\frac{3}{8} + \frac{2}{3} = \frac{3 \cdot 3}{8 \cdot 3} + \frac{2 \cdot 8}{3 \cdot 8}$$

The least common denominator is 8 · 3.

$$= \frac{9}{24} + \frac{16}{24}$$

$$= \frac{9 + 16}{24} \quad \text{or} \quad \frac{25}{24}$$

One way to find the least common denominator (LCD) is first to factor each denominator into its prime factors. For example, suppose you wish to add $\frac{9}{36}$ and $\frac{7}{24}$.

The prime factors of 36 and 24 are shown below.

$$36 = 2 \cdot 2 \cdot 3 \cdot 3$$
$$24 = 2 \cdot 2 \cdot 2 \cdot 3$$

The least common denominator of 36 and 24 contains each prime factor the greatest number of times it appears.

$$\text{LCD} = 2 \cdot 2 \cdot 2 \cdot 3 \cdot 3 \text{ or } 72$$

Now, add the fractions.

$$\frac{9}{36} + \frac{7}{24} = \frac{18}{72} + \frac{21}{72}$$

$$= \frac{39}{72} \quad \text{or} \quad \frac{13}{24}$$

$$\frac{9}{36} = \frac{9 \cdot 2}{36 \cdot 2} \quad \text{or} \quad \frac{18}{72}$$

$$\frac{7}{24} = \frac{7 \cdot 3}{24 \cdot 3} \quad \text{or} \quad \frac{21}{72}$$

To add rational expressions with different denominators, first find two equivalent expressions with common denominators. Then add the equivalent expressions.

examples

1

Find $\frac{7x}{15y^2} + \frac{y}{18xy}$.

$$\frac{7x}{15y^2} + \frac{y}{18xy} = \frac{7x}{3 \cdot 5 \cdot y \cdot y} + \frac{y}{2 \cdot 3 \cdot 3 \cdot x \cdot y}$$

$$= \frac{7x \cdot 2 \cdot 3 \cdot x}{2 \cdot 3 \cdot 3 \cdot 5 \cdot x \cdot y \cdot y} + \frac{y \cdot 5 \cdot y}{2 \cdot 3 \cdot 3 \cdot 5 \cdot x \cdot y \cdot y}$$

The LCD is $2 \cdot 3 \cdot 3 \cdot 5 \cdot x \cdot y \cdot y$.

$$= \frac{42x^2}{90xy^2} + \frac{5y^2}{90xy^2}$$

$$= \frac{42x^2 + 5y^2}{90xy^2}$$

Remind students to check numerator and denominator for common factors.

2

Find $\frac{1}{x^2 - 2x - 15} + \frac{3x + 1}{2x - 10}$.

$$\frac{1}{x^2 - 2x - 15} + \frac{3x + 1}{2x - 10} = \frac{1}{(x - 5)(x + 3)} + \frac{3x + 1}{2(x - 5)}$$

$$= \frac{2}{2(x - 5)(x + 3)} + \frac{(3x + 1)(x + 3)}{2(x - 5)(x + 3)}$$

The LCD is $2(x - 5)(x + 3)$.

$$= \frac{2 + (3x + 1)(x + 3)}{2(x - 5)(x + 3)}$$

$$= \frac{2 + 3x^2 + 9x + x + 3}{2(x - 5)(x + 3)}$$

$$= \frac{3x^2 + 10x + 5}{2(x - 5)(x + 3)}$$

Simplify the numerator.

Students should check to be sure that $3x^2 + 10x + 5$ cannot be factored.

Use a similar method to subtract rational expressions.

example

3

Find $\frac{x + 4}{2x - 8} - \frac{x + 12}{4x - 16}$.

$$\frac{x + 4}{2x - 8} - \frac{x + 12}{4x - 16} = \frac{x + 4}{2(x - 4)} - \frac{x + 12}{4(x - 4)}$$

Factor each denominator.

$$= \frac{2(x + 4)}{4(x - 4)} - \frac{x + 12}{4(x - 4)}$$

The LCD is $4(x - 4)$.

$$= \frac{(2x + 8) - (x + 12)}{4(x - 4)}$$

$$= \frac{x - 4}{4(x - 4)} \text{ or } \frac{1}{4}$$

Simplify.

exercises

Max: 1–12, 1–38; Avg: 1–12, 1–37 odds; Min: 1–37 odds

Exploratory Find the least common denominator (LCD) for each pair of denominators.

1. 54, $28z$ $756z$
2. 78, 39 78
3. 80, 125 2000
4. 12, 27 108
5. $7a^2$, $14ab$ $14a^2b$
6. $36x^2y$, $20xyz$ $180x^2yz$
7. $x(x-2)$, x^2-4 $x(x-2)(x+2)$
8. $(x+2)(x+1)$, x^2-1 $(x+2)(x+1)(x-1)$
9. x^2+2x+1, x^2-9 $(x+1)^2(x-3)(x+3)$
10. $3x+15$, $x^2+3x-15$ $3(x+5)(x^2+3x-15)$
11. x^2-8x, y^2-8y $x(x-8)y(y-8)$
12. $96x^2$, $16(x+9)$ $96x^2(x+9)$

Written Find each sum. Write your answers in simplest form.

1. $\frac{5}{6a}+\frac{7}{4a}$ $\frac{31}{12a}$
2. $\frac{7}{ab}+\frac{9}{b}$ $\frac{7+9a}{ab}$
3. $\frac{5}{a}+7$ $\frac{5+7a}{a}$
4. $\frac{2x}{3y}+5$ $\frac{2x+15y}{3y}$
5. $\frac{3x}{x-y}+\frac{4x}{y-x}$ $\frac{^-x}{x-y}$
6. $\frac{3a+2}{a+b}+\frac{4}{2a+2b}$ $\frac{3a+4}{a+b}$
7. $-\frac{18}{9xy}+\frac{21}{6x}$ $\frac{7y-4}{2xy}$
8. $-\frac{37a}{42b}+\frac{17b}{6a}$ $\frac{119b^2-37a^2}{42ab}$
9. $\frac{x}{x^2-9}+\frac{1}{2x+6}$ $\frac{3(x-1)}{2(x+3)(x-3)}$
10. $y-1+\frac{1}{y-1}$ $\frac{y^2-2y+2}{y-1}$
11. $\frac{3}{a-2}+\frac{2}{a-3}$ $\frac{5a-13}{(a-2)(a-3)}$
12. $\frac{6}{x^2+4x+4}+\frac{5}{x+2}$ $\frac{5x+16}{x^2+4x+4}$
13. $\frac{3}{x^2-25}+\frac{6}{x-5}$ $\frac{3(2x+11)}{(x-5)(x+5)}$
14. $\frac{5}{x^2-3x-28}+\frac{7}{2x-14}$ $\frac{7x+38}{2(x-7)(x+4)}$
15. $\frac{x-1}{x^2-1}+\frac{3}{5x+5}$ $\frac{8}{5(x+1)}$
16. $\frac{a}{a+4}+\frac{2}{a^2+8a+16}$ $\frac{a^2+4a+2}{(a+4)^2}$
17. $\frac{2}{y^2-4y-5}+\frac{5}{y^2-2y-15}$
18. $\frac{2a}{3a-15}+\frac{^-16a+20}{3a^2-12a-15}$ $\frac{2(a-2)}{3(a+1)}$
19. $\frac{m^2+n^2}{m^2-n^2}+\frac{m}{m-n}+\frac{n}{m+n}$ $\frac{2m}{m-n}$
20. $\frac{x}{x-y}+\frac{y}{y^2-x^2}+\frac{2x}{x+y}$ $\frac{3x^2-xy-y}{x^2-y^2}$

17. $\frac{7y+11}{(y+3)(y-5)(y+1)}$

Find each difference. Write your answers in simplest form.

21. $\frac{3}{4a}-\frac{2}{5a}-\frac{1}{2a}$ $-\frac{3}{20a}$
22. $\frac{11}{9}-\frac{7}{2a}-\frac{6}{5a}$ $\frac{110a-423}{90a}$
23. $\frac{9}{y-2}-\frac{2}{1-y}$ $\frac{11y-13}{(y-2)(y-1)}$
24. $\frac{7}{y-8}-\frac{6}{8-y}$ $\frac{13}{y-8}$
25. $\frac{y}{y-9}-\frac{^-9}{9-y}$ 1
26. $\frac{8}{2y-16}-\frac{y}{8-y}$ $\frac{y+4}{y-8}$
27. $\frac{^-4y}{y^2-4}-\frac{y}{y+2}$ $-\frac{y}{y-2}$
28. $\frac{x}{x+3}-\frac{6x}{x^2-9}$ $\frac{x(x-9)}{(x-3)(x+3)}$
29. $3m+1-\frac{2m}{3m+1}$ $\frac{9m^2+4m+1}{3m+1}$
30. $\frac{y-2}{y-4}-\frac{y-8}{y-4}$ $\frac{6}{y-4}$

31. $\frac{6 - y}{y - 2} - \frac{3 + y}{2 - y}$ $\frac{9}{y - 2}$

32.

33. $\frac{x - 4}{2x - 8} - \frac{x + 5}{4x - 16}$ $\frac{x - 13}{4(x - 4)}$

34.

35. $\frac{x}{x + y} - \frac{x}{x^2 - y^2} - \frac{x}{x - y}$ $-\frac{x(1 + 2y)}{(x + y)(x - y)}$

3

37. $\frac{\frac{x}{2}}{\frac{x}{3}} - \frac{\frac{x}{5}}{\frac{x}{6}}$ $\frac{3}{10}$

Euclidean Algorithm

The Greek mathematician Euclid (300 B.C.) is credited with developing a method for finding the greatest common factor (GCF) of two integers. This method is called the *Euclidean Algorithm.* This algorithm is excellent for computer programming.

Example Find the GCF of 232 and 136.

First, divide the greater number by the lesser and express the division in the form dividend = quotient · divisor + remainder.

dividend = *quotient* · *divisor* + *remainder*

$232 = 1 \cdot 136 + 96$

Then, divide the divisor by the remainder.

$136 = 1 \cdot 96 + 40$

Continue this process until a zero remainder is obtained.

$96 = 2 \cdot 40 + 16$

$40 = 2 \cdot 16 + 8$ *Last nonzero remainder is 8.*

$16 = 2 \cdot 8 + 0$

The last nonzero remainder is the GCF.
The GCF of 232 and 136 is 8.

Exercises Find the GCF for each pair of integers.

1. 187, 221 17
2. 182, 1690 26
3. 4807, 5083 23
4. 1078, 1547 7
5. 714, 2030 14
6. 2205, 516 3

10–4 Solving Rational Equations

Objective: To solve equations involving rational polynomial expressions.

An equation containing one or more rational expressions is a **rational equation.** One way to solve a rational equation is to multiply both sides of the equation by the least common denominator (LCD).

Solve $\frac{x}{9} + \frac{x}{7} = 1$.

$$\frac{x}{9} + \frac{x}{7} = 1$$

$$63\left(\frac{x}{9} + \frac{x}{7}\right) = 63(1)$$ *The LCD is 3 · 3 · 7 or 63.*

$$63 \cdot \frac{x}{9} + 63 \cdot \frac{x}{7} = 63$$ *Use the distributive property.*

$$16x = 63$$

$$x = \frac{63}{16} \text{ or } 3\tfrac{15}{16}$$ The solution is $3\frac{15}{16}$.

2 **Solve $\frac{3}{4} - \frac{3}{y + 2} = \frac{9}{28}$.**

$$\frac{3}{4} - \frac{3}{y + 2} = \frac{9}{28}$$

$$28(y + 2)\left[\frac{3}{4} - \frac{3}{y + 2}\right] = 28(y + 2)\left[\frac{9}{28}\right]$$ *The LCD is 28(y + 2).*

$$28(y + 2)\left(\frac{3}{4}\right) - 28(y + 2)\left(\frac{3}{y + 2}\right) = 9(y + 2)$$

$$21y + 42 - 84 = 9y + 18$$

$$12y = 60$$

$$y = 5$$

Check: $$\frac{3}{4} - \frac{3}{y + 2} = \frac{9}{28}$$

$$\frac{3}{4} - \frac{3}{5 + 2} \stackrel{?}{=} \frac{9}{28}$$ *Substitute 5 for y.*

$$\frac{3}{4} - \frac{3}{7} \stackrel{?}{=} \frac{9}{28}$$

$$\frac{21}{28} - \frac{12}{28} \stackrel{?}{=} \frac{9}{28}$$

$$\frac{9}{28} = \frac{9}{28}$$ The solution is 5.

Always notice the values of the variables for which a rational equation is *not* defined. After multiplying both sides of the equation by the LCD, some of these values may appear as results.

examples

3 **Solve $\frac{7}{x - 3} = \frac{x + 4}{x - 3}$.**

$$\frac{7}{x - 3} = \frac{x + 4}{x - 3}$$

$$(x - 3)\left[\frac{7}{x - 3}\right] = (x - 3)\left[\frac{x + 4}{x - 3}\right] \quad \textit{The LCD is } x - 3.$$

$$7 = x + 4$$

$$3 = x$$

The original equation is *not* defined for 3. So the equation has *no* solution.

4 **Solve $w + \frac{w}{w - 1} = \frac{4w - 3}{w - 1}$.**

$$w + \frac{w}{w - 1} = \frac{4w - 3}{w - 1}$$

$$(w - 1)\left[w + \frac{w}{w - 1}\right] = (w - 1)\left[\frac{4w - 3}{w - 1}\right] \quad \textit{The LCD is } w - 1.$$

$$(w - 1)w + w = 4w - 3$$

$$w^2 - w + w = 4w - 3$$

$$w^2 - 4w + 3 = 0$$

$$(w - 3)(w - 1) = 0$$

$$w = 3 \quad \text{or} \quad w = 1$$

The only solution is 3 because the original equation is not defined for 1.

exercises

Max: 1–9, 1–26; **Avg:** 1–9, 1–25 odds; **Min:** 1–25 odds

Exploratory **Find the least common denominator (LCD) for the expressions in each equation.**

1. $\frac{1}{x} + \frac{1}{2} = \frac{2}{x}$ $2x$
2. $\frac{3}{x + 2} = \frac{4}{x - 1}$ $(x + 2)(x - 1)$
3. $\frac{1}{5} = \frac{2}{10y}$ $10y$
4. $\frac{1}{4} = \frac{s - 3}{8s}$ $8s$
5. $\frac{6}{x} = \frac{9}{x^2}$ x^2
6. $\frac{7}{3a} + \frac{6}{5a^2} = 1$
7. $\frac{4}{x - 3} = \frac{7}{x - 2}$ $(x - 3)(x - 2)$
8. $\frac{9}{x + 5} = \frac{6}{x - 3}$ $(x + 5)(x - 3)$
9. $\frac{3}{m - 5} = \frac{1}{6}$

6. $15a^2$ 9. $6(m - 5)$

Written Solve and check each equation.

1. $\frac{1}{x} + \frac{1}{2} = \frac{2}{x}$ 2

2. $\frac{3}{x + 2} = \frac{4}{x - 1}$ $^-11$

3. $\frac{1}{5} = \frac{2}{10y}$ 1

4. $\frac{1}{4} = \frac{s - 3}{8s}$ $^-3$

5. $\frac{6}{x} = \frac{9}{x^2}$ $\frac{3}{2}$

6. $\frac{1}{9} + \frac{1}{2a} = \frac{1}{a^2}$ $\frac{3}{2}$, $^-6$

7. $\frac{4}{x - 3} = \frac{7}{x - 2}$ $\frac{13}{3}$

8. $\frac{9}{x + 5} = \frac{6}{x - 3}$ 19

9. $\frac{3}{m - 5} = \frac{1}{6}$ 23

10. $\frac{9}{x - 3} = \frac{x - 4}{x - 3}$ 13

11. $\frac{x - 3}{2x} = \frac{x - 2}{2x + 1}$ $^-3$

12. $\frac{2}{x} + \frac{1}{4} = \frac{11}{12}$ 3

13. $1 + \frac{3}{y - 1} = \frac{4}{3}$ 10

14. $\frac{1}{x - 1} + \frac{2}{x} = 0$ $\frac{2}{3}$

15. $x + \frac{12}{x} - 8 = 0$ 2, 6

16. $\frac{y + 1}{3} + \frac{y - 1}{3} = \frac{4}{3}$ 2

17. $\frac{x - 4}{x - 2} = \frac{x - 2}{x + 2}$ 6

18. $\frac{1}{y^2 - 1} = \frac{2}{y^2 + y - 2}$ 0

19. $\frac{1}{1 - x} = 1 - \frac{x}{x - 1}$ all reals except 1

20. $\frac{5}{x + 2} = \frac{5}{x}$ no solution

21. $x + 5 = \frac{6}{x}$ $^-6$, 1

22. $\frac{3x - 3}{4x} = \frac{6x - 9}{6x}$ 3

23. $a + 1 = \frac{6}{a}$ $^-3$, 2

24. $\frac{5}{2x} - \frac{3}{10} = \frac{1}{x}$ 5

25. $\frac{8}{a - 7} = \frac{a - 49}{a^2 - 7a}$ $^-7$

26. $\frac{^-2}{x - 1} = \frac{2}{x + 2} - \frac{4}{x - 3}$ $\frac{1}{7}$

Challenge Solve and check each equation.

1. $\frac{x - 3}{x - 2} + \frac{x^2 - 8x + 20}{x^2 - 5x + 6} = \frac{x - 2}{x - 3}$ 5

2. $\frac{x}{x^2 - 1} + \frac{2}{x + 1} = \frac{1}{2x - 2}$ no solutions

Excursions in Algebra

Contest Problem

This problem appeared in a high school mathematics contest sponsored by the Mathematical Association of America.

The fraction $\frac{5x - 11}{2x^2 + x - 6}$ was obtained by adding the two fractions $\frac{A}{x + 2}$ and $\frac{B}{2x - 3}$. Find the values of A and B.

$A = 3$, $B = {}^-1$

Reading Algebra

Position of Symbols

The position of symbols is very important in algebra. Study the list of expressions below.

$$2x \qquad 2 - x \qquad x - 2 \qquad \frac{x}{2} \qquad \frac{2}{x} \qquad x^2 \qquad \frac{x^2}{x + 2}$$

Each expression contains the symbols 2 and x. However, each expression says something different. The same expressions are listed below. The arrows indicate the order in which the symbols usually are read, and the words on the right are English translations of the expressions.

$2x$	two times x
$2 - x$	two minus x
$x - 2$	x minus two
$\frac{x}{2}$	x divided by two
$\frac{2}{x}$	two divided by x
x^2	x squared
$\frac{x^2}{x + 2}$	x squared divided by the quantity x plus two

Exercises As quickly as possible, look at each list of expressions. Which expressions are the same as the first expression?

1. $\frac{x^3}{3}$ b a. $\frac{x}{3}$ b. $\frac{x^3}{3}$ c. $\frac{x}{3^3}$ d. $\frac{3x}{3}$
2. $\frac{(cd)^3}{a}$ a, d a. $\frac{(cd)^3}{a}$ b. $\frac{cd^3}{a}$ c. $\frac{3(cd)}{a}$ d. $\frac{(cd)^3}{a}$
3. $\frac{1}{x - y}$ d a. $\frac{1}{y - x}$ b. $\frac{1}{x + y}$ c. $\frac{x}{1 - y}$ d. $\frac{1}{x - y}$
4. $\frac{x^2 - 4}{x - 1}$ b a. $\frac{x - 4}{x - 1}$ b. $\frac{x^2 - 4}{x - 1}$ c. $\frac{x^2 - 4}{x^2 - 1}$ d. $\frac{4 - x^2}{x^2 - 1}$
5. $\frac{8x^2 - x^3}{16 - 2x}$ c a. $\frac{8x^2 - x^3}{2x - 16}$ b. $\frac{8x^3 - x^2}{16 - 2x}$ c. $\frac{8x^2 - x^3}{16 - 2x}$ d. $\frac{8x^3 - x^2}{2x - 16}$

6–10. In problems **1–5**, which expressions are different than the first expression? How are they different?

11. Turn to page 284 in this textbook. Copy each expression in the Exploratory Exercises. Draw an arrow to indicate the order you would read the symbols in each expression.

12. Write an English translation for each expression in problem **11**.

Answers vary.

10–5 Using Rational Equations

Objective: To use rational polynomial expressions in problem solving.

Jake Qualls owns two tractors. With his older tractor, his front field can be plowed in 10 hours. With his newer tractor, the same field can be plowed in 6 hours. How long will it take to plow the field using both tractors at once? This question can be answered by solving a rational equation.

Let h stand for the number of hours it will take to plow the field.

What fraction of the field can the older tractor plow in 1 hour?	$\frac{1}{10}$
What fraction of the field can the newer tractor plow in 1 hour?	$\frac{1}{6}$
What fraction of the field can the older tractor plow in h hours?	$\frac{h}{10}$
What fraction of the field can the newer tractor plow in h hours?	$\frac{h}{6}$

fraction older tractor plows in h hours + *fraction newer tractor plows in h hours* = *fraction both tractors plow in h hours*

$$\frac{h}{10} + \frac{h}{6} = 1$$

Now, solve the equation.

$$\frac{h}{10} + \frac{h}{6} = 1$$

$$30\left(\frac{h}{10} + \frac{h}{6}\right) = 30(1) \qquad \textit{The LCD is } 2 \cdot 3 \cdot 5 \textit{ or } 30.$$

$$30 \cdot \frac{h}{10} + 30 \cdot \frac{h}{6} = 30 \qquad \textit{Use the distributive property.}$$

$$3h + 5h = 30$$

$$8h = 30$$

$$h = \frac{30}{8} \text{ or } 3\tfrac{3}{4}$$

It will take $3\frac{3}{4}$ hours to plow the field with both tractors.

The following is another example of how rational expressions can be used to solve verbal problems.

example 1

A car travels 300 kilometers in the same time that a train travels 200 kilometers. The speed of the car is 20 kilometers per hour more than the speed of the train. Find the speed of the car and the speed of the train.

Define a variable. Let r stand for the speed of the car.

Write an equation.

$$\textit{time car travels} = \textit{time train travels}$$

$$\frac{\textit{distance car travels}}{\textit{rate car travels}} = \frac{\textit{distance train travels}}{\textit{rate train travels}}$$

$$\frac{300}{r} = \frac{200}{r - 20}$$

Solve the equation.

$$\frac{300}{r} = \frac{200}{r - 20}$$

$$r(r - 20)\frac{300}{r} = r(r - 20)\frac{200}{r - 20} \qquad \textit{The LCD is } r(r - 20).$$

$$300(r - 20) = 200(r)$$

$$300r - 6000 = 200r$$

$$^{-}6000 = {}^{-}100r$$

$$60 = r$$

$$40 = r - 20$$

Answer the problem. The car's speed is 60 kilometers per hour, and the train's speed is 40 kilometers per hour.

exercises

Max: 1–15; Avg: 1–15 odds; Min: 1–15 odds

Written **Solve each problem.**

1. One computer can schedule classes for the students at John F. Kennedy High School in 5 hours. Another computer can do the job in 4 hours. If the computers work together, how long will it take to do the job? $2\frac{2}{9}$ hours

2. One hose can fill the Sunshine's small swimming pool in 6 hours. A second, newer hose can fill the pool in 4 hours. If both hoses are used, how long will it take to fill the pool? 2 hours 24 minutes

3. Jan Zeiss can tile a floor in 14 hours. Together Jan and her helper Bill can tile the same size floor in 9 hours. How long would it take Bill to do the job alone? 25 hours 12 minutes

4. Elena Dias can paint a 9 by 12 room in $1\frac{1}{2}$ hours. If Luisa Alicea helps, they can paint the same size room in 1 hour. How long would it take Luisa to paint such a room by herself? 3 hours

5. A painter works on a job for 10 days and is then joined by her helper. Together they finish the job in 6 more days. Her helper could have done the job alone in 30 days. How long would it have taken the painter to do the job alone? 20 days

6. A tank can be filled by a hose in 10 hours. The tank can be emptied by a drain pipe in 20 hours. If the drain pipe is open while the tank is filling, how long will it take to fill? 20 hours

7. The denominator of a fraction is 1 less than twice the numerator. If 7 is added to both numerator and denominator, the resulting fraction has a value of $\frac{7}{10}$. Find the original fraction. $\frac{7}{13}$

8. Five times the multiplicative inverse of a number is added to the number and the result is $10\frac{1}{2}$. What is the number? $\frac{1}{2}$ or 10

10. 8 miles per hour 12. \$1800 at 6%

9. The ratio of 4 less than a number to 26 more than a number is 1 to 3. What is the number? 19

10. The speed of the current in the Mississippi River is 5 miles per hour. A boat travels downstream 26 miles and returns in $10\frac{2}{3}$ hours. What is its speed in still water?

11. A boat travels at a rate of 15 kilometers per hour in still water. It travels 60 kilometers upstream in the same time that it travels 90 kilometers downstream. What is the rate of the current? 3 kilometers per hour

12. The simple interest for one year on a sum of money is \$108. Suppose the interest rate is increased by 2%. Then \$450 less than the original sum could be invested and yield the same annual interest. How much is the original sum of money, and what is the original rate of interest?

13. At what time between 5 o'clock and 6 o'clock do the hands of a clock coincide? 5:27 plus 18 seconds

14. Write a computer program to find all the times in a day that the hands of a clock coincide. See Teacher's Guide.

15. The load capacities of two trucks are in the ratio of 5 to 2. The smaller truck has a capacity 3 tons less than that of the larger truck. What is the capacity of the larger truck? 5 tons

10-6 Direct and Inverse Variation

Objective: To solve problems involving direct and indirect variation.

Recall that direct variation is a linear function described by $y = mx$ or $f(x) = mx$ where m is *not* zero. For example, gravity on earth is about six times as great as the gravity on the moon. Thus, weight on earth varies directly with weight on the moon. This relationship can be described by the following equation.

$y = 6x$	y stands for weight on earth x stands for weight on moon 6 is the constant of variation

example 1

If an astronaut weighs 29 pounds on the moon, find the astronaut's weight on earth.

$$\begin{aligned} y &= 6x \\ &= 6(29) \\ &= 174 \end{aligned}$$

The astronaut weighs 174 pounds on earth.

Many quantities are said to be **inversely proportional** or to **vary inversely with** each other. For example, the amount of current in a circuit is inversely proportional to the amount of resistance in the circuit. The following chart shows several corresponding values.

Current (amps)	0.5	1.0	1.5	2.0	2.5	3.0	4.0	5.0
Resistance (ohms)	12	6.0	4.0	3.0	2.4	2.0	1.5	1.2

Let c stand for the amount of current.
Let r stand for the amount of resistance.

The relationship between these quantities can be described by the following equation.

$$c = \frac{6}{r}$$

A rational equation in two variables of the form $y = \frac{k}{x}$, where k is a constant, is called an inverse variation. The constant k is called the constant of variation, and y is said to vary inversely as x.

Definition of Inverse Variation

example 2

The volume of any gas varies inversely with its pressure as long as the temperature remains constant. The volume of a particular gas is 1600 milliliters when the pressure is 25 centimeters of mercury. What is the volume of the gas at the same temperature when the pressure is 40 centimeters of mercury?

Let V stand for volume of gas in milliliters.
Let p stand for pressure of gas in centimeters of mercury.
Let k stand for the constant of variation.

$$V = \frac{k}{p}$$ *Volume varies inversely with pressure.*

Next, find the value of k.

$$1600 = \frac{k}{25}$$ *When volume is 1600 ml, pressure is 25 cm of mercury.*

$$25 \cdot 1600 = k$$ *Solve for k.*

$$40{,}000 = k$$

The relationship between volume and pressure can be described by the following equation.

$$V = \frac{40{,}000}{p}$$

Use the equation to find the volume when the pressure is 40 centimeters of mercury.

$$V = \frac{40{,}000}{(40)} = 1000$$

The volume is 1000 milliliters.

exercises

Max: 1–24, 1–20; **Avg:** 1–24, 1–19 odds; **Min:** 1–19 odds

Exploratory State whether each equation represents direct variation or inverse variation.

1. $x = 4y$ D; $\frac{1}{4}$

2. $xy = {}^{-}3$ I; $^{-}3$

3. $y = {}^{-}4x$ D; $^{-}4$

4. $y = \frac{7}{x}$ I; 7

5. $5 = \frac{y}{x}$ D; 5

6. $\frac{x}{y} = {}^{-}6$ D; $-\frac{1}{6}$

7. $\frac{3}{4}y = x$ D; $\frac{4}{3}$

8. $\frac{x}{2} = y$ D; $\frac{1}{2}$

9. $x = \frac{9}{y}$ I; 9

10. $y = \frac{3}{x}$ I; 3

11. $a = 4b$ D; 4

12. $\frac{3}{5}a = -\frac{5}{4}b$ D; $-\frac{25}{12}$

13-24. Name the constant of variation for each equation in problems **1-12.**
See second part of answers above.

Written **In each of the following, y varies directly as x.**

1. If $y = 8$, then $x = 2$. Find y when $x = 9$. 36
2. If $y = 10$, then $k = {}^{-}3$. Find x when $y = 4$. $-\frac{4}{3}$
3. If $x = 4$, then $y = 0.5$. Find y when $x = 9$. $\frac{9}{8}$
4. If $y = 11$, then $x = \frac{1}{5}$. Find y when $x = \frac{2}{5}$. 22

In each of the following, y varies inversely as x.

5. If $x = 14$, then $y = {}^{-}6$. Find x when $y = {}^{-}11$. $\frac{84}{11}$
6. If $y = \frac{1}{5}$, then $x = 9$. Find y when $x = {}^{-}3$. $-\frac{3}{5}$
7. If $y = 11$, then $x = 44$. Find x when $y = 40$. $\frac{121}{10}$
8. If $x = 20$, then $y = 10$. Find x when $y = 14$. $\frac{100}{7}$
9. If $y = {}^{-}2$, then $x = {}^{-}8$. Find x when $y = \frac{2}{3}$. 24
10. If $y = 7$, then $x = {}^{-}3$. Find y when $x = 4$. $-\frac{21}{4}$

Solve each problem. 11. 118.5 kilograms

11. A map is scaled so that 1 cm represents 15 km. How far apart are two towns if they are 7.9 cm apart on the map?
13. Six feet of steel wire weighs 0.7 kilograms. How much does 100 feet of steel wire weigh? $11\frac{2}{3}$ kilograms
15. Alan Tokashira invested \$5000 at 7% interest. How much must he invest at $6\frac{1}{2}$% interest to obtain the same income? \$5384.62
16. about 3.42 hours
17. A volume of gas is 120 cubic feet under 6 pounds of pressure. What is the volume at the same temperature when the pressure is 8 pounds? 90 cubic feet
19. If y^2 varies inversely as x and $y = 4$ when $x = 2$, find y when $x = 11$. $(\pm 4\sqrt{22})/11$

12. A 75 foot tree casts a 40 foot shadow. How tall is a tree that casts a 10 foot shadow at the same time of day? 18.75 feet
14. Eight pounds of potatoes cost \$1.39. How much do 50 pounds of potatoes cost? \$8.69
16. The time to drive a certain distance varies inversely according to the rate of speed. Mary Bronson drives 47 mph for 4 hours. How long would it take her to make the same trip at 55 mph?
18. If y varies directly as x^2 and $y = 7$ when $x = 9$, then find y when $x = 7$. $\frac{343}{81}$
20. If $ab = k$ and a is tripled while k remains constant, how is b changed? divided by 3

Vocabulary

rational algebraic expression (278)
complex fraction (283)
rational equation (290)
inverse variation (297)
inversely proportional (297)
constant of variation (297)

Chapter Summary

1. To simplify a rational algebraic expression, divide both numerator and denominator by their greatest common factor (GCF). (278)
2. To multiply rational algebraic expressions, multiply numerators and multiply denominators. (278)
3. Dividing by a rational algebraic expression is the same as multiplying by its inverse. (282)
4. A complex rational expression, usually called a complex fraction, is an expression whose numerator or denominator, or both, contain rational expressions. (283)
5. The sum of rational expressions with common denominators is the sum of the numerators over the common denominator. (286)
6. To add or subtract two rational expressions with different denominators, first find two equivalent rational expressions with common denominators. Then add or subtract the equivalent fractions. (286)
7. An equation containing one or more rational expressions is a rational equation. (290)
8. Always notice the values of the variables for which a rational equation is *not* defined. (291)
9. Direct variation is a linear function described by $y = mx$ or $f(x) = mx$ where m is *not* zero. (297)
10. Definition of Inverse Variation: A rational equation in two variables of the form $y = \frac{k}{x}$ where k is a constant is called an inverse variation. The constant k is called the constant of variation, and y is said to vary inversely as x. (297)

Chapter Review

10-1 Simplify each expression.

1. $\frac{25}{80}$ $\frac{5}{16}$
2. $\frac{27}{81}$ $\frac{1}{3}$
3. $\frac{18x^2}{54xy}$ $\frac{x}{3y}$
4. $\frac{29a^2b}{30ab^2c}$ $\frac{29a}{30bc}$

Find each product. Write your answers in simplest form.

5. $\frac{4}{7} \cdot \frac{21}{50}$ $\frac{6}{25}$
6. $\frac{^-4ab}{21c} \cdot \frac{14c^2}{22a^2}$ $\frac{^-4bc}{33a}$

7. $\frac{y-2}{a-x}(a-3)$ $\frac{(y-2)(a-3)}{a-x}$

8. $\frac{c^2-4cd}{3a}\cdot\frac{18a^2b}{c-4d}$ $6abc$

10-2 Find each quotient. Write your answers in simplest form.

9. $\frac{3}{10}\div\frac{3}{8}$ $\frac{4}{5}$

10. $\frac{x+y}{a}\div\frac{x+y}{a^3}$ a^2

11. $\frac{a^2-b^2}{6b}\div\frac{a+b}{36b^2}$ $6b(a-b)$

12. $\frac{y^2-y-12}{y+2}\div\frac{y-4}{y^2-4y-12}$ $(y+3)(y-6)$

Simplify each expression.

13. $\dfrac{\frac{1}{n^2-6n+9}}{\frac{n+3}{2n^2-18}}$ $\frac{2}{n-3}$

14. $\dfrac{\frac{x^2+7x+10}{x+2}}{\frac{x^2+2x-15}{x+2}}$ $\frac{(x+2)}{(x-3)}$

10-3 Find each sum. Write your answers in simplest form.

15. $-\frac{9}{4a}+\frac{7}{3b}$ $\frac{^-27b+28a}{12ab}$

16. $\frac{x-1}{x^2-1}+\frac{2}{5x+5}$ $\frac{7}{5(x+1)}$

17. $\frac{x+2}{x-5}+6$ $\frac{7(x-4)}{x-5}$

18. $\dfrac{\frac{x}{2}}{\frac{3}{x}}+\dfrac{\frac{x}{6}}{\frac{x}{4}}$ $\frac{x^2+4}{6}$

19. $\dfrac{\frac{5x}{4}}{\frac{6x}{5}}+\dfrac{\frac{2x}{ab}}{\frac{3x}{a}}$ $\frac{25b+16}{24b}$

Find each difference. Write your answers in simplest form.

20. $\frac{7}{y}-\frac{2}{3y}$ $\frac{19}{3y}$

21. $\frac{7}{y-2}-\frac{11}{2-y}$ $\frac{18}{y-2}$

22. $\frac{14}{x+y}-\frac{9}{y^2-x^2}$ $\frac{14y-14x-9}{y^2-x^2}$

10-4 Solve each equation.

23. $\frac{3}{y}+\frac{7}{y}=9$ $\frac{10}{9}$

24. $1+\frac{5}{y-1}=\frac{7}{6}$ 31

25. $y+\frac{5}{y}=6$ 5 or 1

26. $\frac{3}{4x}=\frac{6}{x^2}$ 8

10-5 Solve each problem.

27. Bob Lopatka can paint his house in 15 hours. His friend, Jack, can paint the house in 20 hours. If they work together, how long will it take them to paint the house? $8\frac{4}{7}$ hours

28. The ratio of two numbers is 5 to 13. If the lesser number is increased by 6 and the greater number is decreased by 10, the ratio of the new numbers is 11 to 3. Find the original numbers. 5 and 13

10-6 Solve each problem.

29. Suppose y varies inversely as x, and $y = 9$ when $x = 2\frac{1}{2}$. Find y when x is $-\frac{3}{5}$. $-\frac{75}{2}$

30. Suppose y varies directly as x, and $x = 7$ when $y = 21$. Find x when y is $^-5$. $-\frac{5}{3}$

Chapter Test

Perform the indicated operation for each of the following. Write your answers in simplest form.

1. $\frac{7ab}{9c} \cdot \frac{81c^2}{91a^2b}$ $\quad \frac{9c}{13a}$

2. $\frac{7a}{x-y} \cdot \frac{y-x}{77ba^2}$ $\quad -\frac{1}{11}ba$

3. $\frac{x^2-y^2}{a^2-b^2} \cdot \frac{a+b}{x-y}$ $\quad \frac{x+y}{a-b}$

4. $\frac{6a^2}{9} \div \frac{33a^3}{21b}$ $\quad \frac{14b}{33a}$

5. $\frac{a^2-ab}{3a} \div \frac{a-b}{15b^2}$ $\quad 5b^2$

6. $\frac{x^2-2x+1}{y-5} \div \frac{x-1}{y^2-25}$ $\quad (x-1)(y+5)$

7. $\frac{7a}{5} + \frac{6b}{3a}$ $\quad \frac{7a^2+10b}{5a}$

8. $\frac{7}{5a} - \frac{10}{3ab}$ $\quad \frac{21b-50}{15ab}$

9. $\frac{6}{x-5} + 7a$ $\quad \frac{6+7ax-35a}{x-5}$

10. $\frac{9}{a-b} - \frac{10}{b-a}$ $\quad \frac{19}{a-b}$

11. $\frac{x-y}{a-b} - \frac{x+y}{a+b}$ $\quad \frac{2(bx-ay)}{a^2-b^2}$

12. $\frac{x+2}{x-1} + \frac{6}{7x-7}$ $\quad \frac{7x+20}{7(x-1)}$

Simplify each expression.

13. $\frac{\frac{2}{x-4} + \frac{5}{x+1}}{\frac{3x}{x^2-3x-4}}$ $\quad \frac{7x-18}{3x}$

14. $\frac{\frac{1}{x} - \frac{1}{2x}}{\frac{2}{x} + \frac{4}{3x}}$ $\quad \frac{3}{20}$

Solve each equation.

15. $\frac{3}{x} - \frac{7}{x} = 9$ $\quad -\frac{4}{9}$

16. $a - \frac{5}{a} = 4$ $\quad {}^-1$ or 5

Solve each problem.

17. Joni Mills can type 75 pages of manuscript in 8 hours. Ted Szatro can type the same number of pages in 13 hours. If Joni and Ted work together, how long will it take them to type 75 pages?
$4\frac{20}{21}$ hours

18. One integer is 3 greater than another integer. Three times the inverse of the lesser integer, minus 2 times the inverse of the greater integer, is $\frac{19}{130}$. Find both integers. 10 and 13

19. Suppose y varies directly as x. If $y = 10$, then $x = {}^-3$. Find y when x is 20. $\quad -\frac{200}{3}$

20. Suppose y varies inversely as x. If $y = 9$, then $x = -\frac{2}{3}$. Find x when y is ${}^-7$. $\quad \frac{6}{7}$

Chapter

11

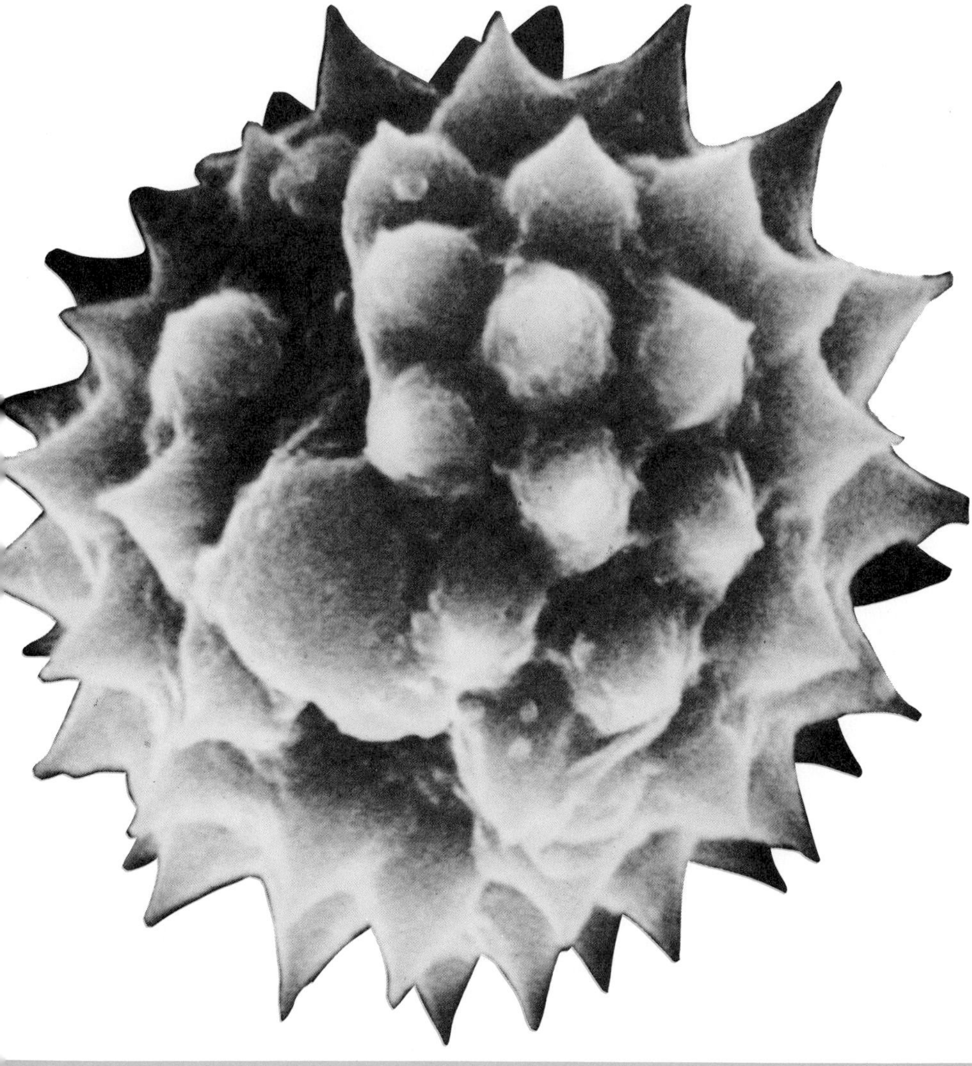

Exponents

Sometimes it is necessary to work with very small or very large numbers. Exponents can be very helpful in expressing such quantities concisely. This photograph shows a pollen grain, 6×10^3 times its actual size.

11-1 Integers as Exponents

Objective: To use zero and negative integers as exponents.

Many patterns have led to mathematical discoveries. Patterns can be used as follows to extend the properties of exponents to include zero and negative integers as exponents.

$$\frac{3^5}{3^1} = 3^{5-1} \text{ or } 3^4$$

$$\frac{3^4}{3^1} = 3^{4-1} \text{ or } 3^3$$

$$\frac{3^3}{3^1} = 3^{3-1} \text{ or } 3^2$$

$$\frac{3^2}{3^1} = 3^{2-1} \text{ or } 3^1$$

Recall that for any numbers a, m and n, $a^m \cdot a^n = a^{m+n}$ *and* $\frac{a^m}{a^n} = a^{m-n}$ *if* $a \neq 0$

Notice that the exponent decreases by one in each step.

What about $\frac{3^1}{3^1}$?

The pattern suggests the following.

$$\frac{3^1}{3^1} = 3^{1-1} \text{ or } 3^0$$

But, you know that 3 divided by 3 is 1.

$$\frac{3^1}{3^1} = \frac{3}{3} \text{ or } 1$$

Thus, the value of 3^0 must be 1.

Other similar examples lead to the following definition.

Zero Exponent

For any number a, except $a = 0$, $a^0 = 1$.

0^0 is not defined because $0^0 = 0^{m-m}$ and $0^{m-m} = \frac{0^m}{0^m}$. Then $\frac{0^m}{0^m}$ implies division by zero since $0^m = 0$. Division by zero is never allowed.

example 1

Simplify $\frac{3^4x^3}{3^4}$.

$$\frac{3^4x^3}{3^4} = (3^{4-4})x^3$$
$$= 3^0x^3$$
$$= 1 \cdot x^3 \text{ or } x^3$$

Patterns also show how negative integers are used as exponents.

$$\frac{4^2}{4^1} = 4^{2-1} \text{ or } 4^1$$

Notice that the exponent decreases by one in each step.

$$\frac{4^1}{4^1} = 4^{1-1} \text{ or } 4^0$$

What about $\frac{4^0}{4^1}$?

The pattern suggests the following.

$$\frac{4^0}{4^1} = 4^{0-1} \text{ or } 4^{-1}$$

But, you know that 1 divided by 4 is $\frac{1}{4}$.

$$\frac{4^0}{4^1} = \frac{1}{4^1} \text{ or } \frac{1}{4}$$

Thus, the value of 4^{-1} must be $\frac{1}{4}$.

Continue the pattern.

$$\frac{4^{-1}}{4^1} = 4^{-1-1} \text{ or } 4^{-2}$$

But, the following also holds.

$$\frac{4^{-1}}{4^1} = \frac{\frac{1}{4}}{4}$$

$$= \frac{1}{4} \cdot \frac{1}{4} \text{ or } \frac{1}{4^2}$$

Recall that 4 can be written $\frac{4}{1}$. To divide, invert the $\frac{4}{1}$ to $\frac{1}{4}$ and multiply.

Thus, the value of 4^{-2} is $\frac{1}{4^2}$.

Other similar examples lead to the following definition.

For any number a, except $a = 0$, and for any positive integer n,

$$a^{-n} = \frac{1}{a^n}.$$

Negative Integer Exponents

examples

2 **Simplify $(3 \cdot 4)^{-2}$.**

$$(3 \cdot 4)^{-2} = \frac{1}{(3 \cdot 4)^2} \text{ or } \frac{1}{3^2 4^2}$$

To simplify this expression, find an equivalent form which uses only positive exponents.

Recall that for any numbers a, b, and m, $(ab)^m = a^m b^m$.

3 **Simplify $\frac{5^{2k}}{5^{2k-3}}$.**

$$\frac{5^{2k}}{5^{2k-3}} = 5^{2k-(2k-3)} \text{ or } 5^3$$

exercises

Max: 1–30, 1–31; Avg: 1–20, 1–31 odds; Min: 1–15 odds, 1–31 odds

Exploratory Simplify.

1. 4^{-3} $\frac{1}{4^3}$
2. m^{-1} $\frac{1}{m}$
3. $\frac{r^4}{r}$ r^3
4. $\left(\frac{3}{r}\right)^{-4}$ $\frac{r^4}{3^4}$
5. 8^{-9} $\frac{1}{8^9}$
6. y^{-3} $\frac{1}{y^3}$
7. $\frac{1}{y^{-3}}$ y^3
8. $\frac{m^{10}}{m^7}$ m^3
9. $\left(\frac{7}{x}\right)^{-5}$ $\frac{x^5}{7^5}$
10. $\left(\frac{1}{4}\right)^{-4}$ 4^4
11. $\frac{1}{m^{-2}}$ m^2
12. $\frac{x^6}{x^8}$ $\frac{1}{x^2}$
13. $\left(\frac{1}{r}\right)^{-6}$ r^6
14. $\frac{z^5}{y^{-2}}$ z^5y^2
15. $\frac{1}{y^{-4}}$ y^4
16. $\frac{y^{10}}{y^{13}}$ $\frac{1}{y^3}$
17. $\frac{x^4}{x^{y-1}}$ x^{5-y}
18. $\frac{w^3}{w^7}$ $\frac{1}{w^4}$
19. $\frac{q^8}{q^3}$ q^5
20. $\frac{1}{q^{-2}}$ q^2

Evaluate.

21. 2^0 1
22. $\left(\frac{10}{9}\right)^0$ 1
23. 6^{-2} $\frac{1}{36}$
24. $\left(\frac{1}{3}\right)^{-3}$ 27
25. 4^{-1} $\frac{1}{4}$
26. $\left(\frac{1}{5}\right)^{-2}$ 25
27. $\frac{8^7}{8^9}$ $\frac{1}{64}$
28. $\left(\frac{2}{3}\right)^{-1}$ $\frac{3}{2}$
29. $3^{-2} \cdot 3^{-1}$ $\frac{1}{27}$
30. $\left(\frac{3}{4}\right)^0$ 1
31. $\frac{2^6}{4^2}$ 4
32. $\left(\frac{3}{5}\right)^{-2}$ $\frac{25}{9}$

Written Simplify.

1. 4^{-6} $\frac{1}{4^6}$
2. 121^{-5} $\frac{1}{121^5}$
3. $\left(\frac{1}{y}\right)^{-5}$ y^5
4. $\left(\frac{1}{m}\right)^{-4}$ m^4
5. $\frac{1}{r^{-3}}$ r^3
6. $\frac{1}{y^{-8}}$ y^8
7. $\left(\frac{2}{b}\right)^{-7}$ $\frac{b^7}{2^7}$
8. $\left(\frac{3}{m}\right)^{-5}$ $\frac{m^5}{3^5}$
9. $\left(\frac{m}{4}\right)^{-2}$ $\frac{4^2}{m^2}$
10. $\left(\frac{y}{x}\right)^{-3}$ $\frac{x^3}{y^3}$
11. $\frac{x^6}{x^{10}}$ $\frac{1}{x^4}$
12. $\frac{r^7}{r^{12}}$ $\frac{1}{r^5}$
13. $\frac{(x+4)^3}{(x+4)^7}$ $\frac{1}{(x+4)^4}$
14. $\frac{s^7}{2s^5}$ $\frac{s^2}{2}$
15. $\frac{6r}{r^3}$ $\frac{6}{r^2}$
16. $\frac{(r+3)^5}{(r+3)^2}$ $(r+3)^3$
17. $\frac{3(x-7)^6}{(x-7)^{10}}$ $\frac{3}{(x-7)^4}$
18. $\frac{3(a+7)^4}{12(a+7)^2}$ $\frac{(a+7)^2}{4}$
19. $(x^3y^2)^{-1}$ $\frac{1}{x^3y^2}$
20. $\frac{2(y^2-5)^3}{8(y^2-5)^5}$ $\frac{1}{4(y^2-5)^2}$
21. $\frac{(b^3+5)^7}{(b^3+5)^6}$ (b^3+5)
22. $\frac{2(x+3y)^5}{8(x+3y)^2}$ $\frac{(x+3y)^3}{4}$
23. $(m^4n^5)^{-2}$ $\frac{1}{m^8n^{10}}$
24. $\frac{1}{m^0+n^0}$ $\frac{1}{2}$
25. $\frac{5}{x^0+y^0}$ $\frac{5}{2}$
26. $\frac{2m}{n^{-1}}$ $2mn$
27. $\frac{5x}{y^{-1}}$ $5xy$
28. $\frac{5^{2x}}{5^{2x+2}}$ $\frac{1}{25}$
29. $\frac{3^{xy+5}}{3^{xy}}$ 3^5 or 243
30. $\frac{r^{2a}}{r^{2a-3}}$ r^3
31. $\frac{x^{3a}}{x^{3a-2}}$ x^2

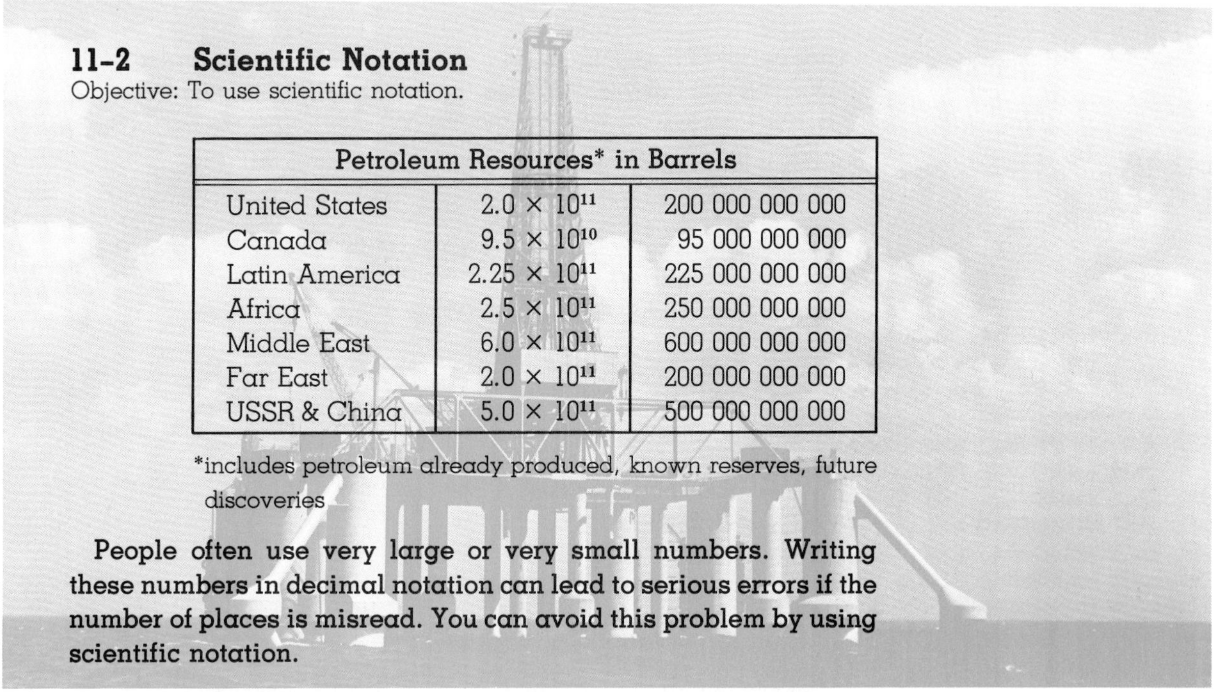

11-2 Scientific Notation

Objective: To use scientific notation.

Petroleum Resources* in Barrels

United States	2.0×10^{11}	200 000 000 000
Canada	9.5×10^{10}	95 000 000 000
Latin America	2.25×10^{11}	225 000 000 000
Africa	2.5×10^{11}	250 000 000 000
Middle East	6.0×10^{11}	600 000 000 000
Far East	2.0×10^{11}	200 000 000 000
USSR & China	5.0×10^{11}	500 000 000 000

*includes petroleum already produced, known reserves, future discoveries

People often use very large or very small numbers. Writing these numbers in decimal notation can lead to serious errors if the number of places is misread. You can avoid this problem by using scientific notation.

Definition of Scientific Notation

A number is expressed in scientific notation when it is in the following form.

$$a \times 10^n$$

Here $1 \leq a < 10$ and n is an integer.

Scientific notation is based on the powers of ten.

$10^6 = 1,000,000$	$10^{-1} = \frac{1}{10}$ or 0.1
$10^5 = 100,000$	$10^{-2} = \frac{1}{100}$ or 0.01
$10^4 = 10,000$	$10^{-3} = \frac{1}{1,000}$ or 0.001
$10^3 = 1,000$	$10^{-4} = \frac{1}{10,000}$ or 0.0001
$10^2 = 100$	
$10^1 = 10$	
$10^0 = 1$	

The exponent in each power of ten shown above is a positive integer or zero. Compare the exponent and the number of places between the decimal point and the one.

The exponent in each power of ten shown above is a negative integer. Compare the absolute value of the exponent and the number of places to the right of the decimal point.

The absolute value of $^-4$ is 4.

The petroleum resources of Latin America are approximately 225,000,000,000 barrels. To write this number in scientific notation, find an expression so that $225{,}000{,}000{,}000 = a \times 10^n$. Move the decimal point left to get a number between one and ten.

2.25 000 000 000
$a = 2.25$ *Do you see how to find a?*
$n = 11$ *How about n?*

In scientific notation, $225{,}000{,}000{,}000 = 2.25 \times 10^{11}$.

examples

1 **Express 72,500 in scientific notation.**

$72{,}500 = 7.25 \cdot 10 \cdot 10 \cdot 10 \cdot 10$
$a = 7.25$ *Do you see how to find n?*
$n = 4$ The solution is 7.25×10^4.

2 **Express 0.001325 in scientific notation.**

Place the decimal point to the right of the first nonzero digit as shown.
001.325
$a = 1.325$ *Do you see how to find n? How about a?*
$n = ^-3$ The solution is 1.325×10^{-3}.

3 **Write 3.102×10^5 in decimal notation.**

$3.102 \times 10^5 = 3.102 \times 100{,}000$ *Here the decimal*
$= 310{,}200$ *point is moved*
$a = 3.102$ *5 places to the right.*
$n = 5$ The solution is 310,200.

4 **Write 4.37×10^{-3} in decimal notation.**

$4.37 \times 10^{-3} = 4.37 \times 0.001$ *Here the decimal*
$= 0.004\,37$ *point is moved*
$a = 4.37$ *3 places to the left.*
$n = ^-3$ The solution is 0.00437.

Scientific notation is useful in computation. For example, find $0.543 \times 617{,}000$.

$0.543 \times 617{,}000 = (5.43 \times 10^{-1})(6.17 \times 10^5)$ *Express each in*
$= 5.43 \times 6.17 \times 10^4$ or 335,031 *scientific notation.*

Divide 0.00086 by 0.031 using scientific notation.

$$\frac{0.00086}{0.031} = \frac{8.6 \times 10^{-4}}{3.1 \times 10^{-2}}$$ *Express each in scientific notation.*

$$= \frac{8.6}{3.1} \times 10^{-2} \text{ or } 0.027$$

exercises

Max: 1–20, 1–32; Avg: 1–20, 1–15 odds, 17–32; Min: 1–11 odds, 1–15 odds

Exploratory Find the value of n in each equation.

1. $40000 = 4 \times 10^n$ 4
2. $600 = 6 \times 10^n$ 2
3. $0.00004 = 4 \times 10^n$ $^-5$
4. $0.0057 = 5.7 \times 10^n$

4. $^-3$

Express each of the following in scientific notation.

5. 67530 6.753×10^4
6. 146000 1.46×10^5
7. 0.000075 7.5×10^{-5}
8. 0.0014 1.4×10^{-3}

Express each of the following in decimal notation.

9. 5.8×10^4 58,000
10. 6.7×10^6
11. 5.4×10^{-3} 0.0054
12. 1.82×10^{-4} 0.000182

10. 6,700,000

Evaluate. Express each answer in scientific notation. Then express it in decimal notation.

13–14. $(6 \times 10^3)^2$ 3.6×10^7; 36,000,000

15–16. $(7 \times 10^4)(8 \times 10^{-6})$ 5.6×10^{-1}; 0.56

17–18. $\dfrac{3 \times 10^{-2}}{5 \times 10^2}$ 6.0×10^{-5} 0.00006

19–20. $\dfrac{6 \times 10^3}{4 \times 10^{-2}}$ 1.5×10^5 150,000

Written Express in scientific notation.

1. 618 6.18×10^2
2. 723 7.23×10^2
3. 0.0021 2.1×10^{-3}
4. 0.0692 6.92×10^{-2}
5. 810.4 8.104×10^2
6. 0.00528 5.28×10^{-3}
7. 9,000,000,000 9×10^9
8. 786,500,000 7.865×10^8
9. 0.000003 3×10^{-6}
10. 0.000000721 7.21×10^{-7}

Express in decimal notation.

11. 6×10^3 6000
12. 9.8×10^4 98,000
13. 5.7×10^{-4} 0.00057
14. 3.21×10^6 3,210,000
15. 7.2×10^{-5} 0.000072
16. 4.27×10^{-2} 0.0427

Evaluate. Express each answer in scientific notation. Then express it in decimal notation.

17–18. $(4.3 \times 10^3)(2.0 \times 10^2)$

19–20. $(3.4 \times 10^4)(5.6 \times 10^4)$

21–22. $\dfrac{3.6 \times 10^{-8}}{1.2 \times 10^{-4}}$ 3.0×10^{-4} 0.0003

23–24. $\dfrac{5.6 \times 10^9}{8.0 \times 10^4}$ 7.0×10^4 70,000

25–26. $\dfrac{(5 \times 10^{-3})(6 \times 10^3)}{1.5 \times 10^{-4}}$ 2.0×10^5 200,000

27–28. $\dfrac{(4 \times 10^2)(8 \times 10^{-2})}{6.4 \times 10^{-3}}$ 5.0×10^3 5000

29–30. $\dfrac{93{,}000{,}000 \times 0.0005}{0.0015}$ 3.1×10^7 31,000,000

31–32. $\dfrac{84{,}000{,}000 \times 0.00004}{0.0016}$ 2.1×10^6 2,100,000

17–18. 8.6×10^5; 860,000

19–20. 1.904×10^9; 1,904,000,000

CAREERS

Energy Analyst

William Sheppard works as an energy analyst at a large research institute. He uses scientific notation regularly in his work. He is involved in energy research planning and in the analysis of economic and environmental impacts of possible approaches to providing more energy. This energy may come from fossil fuels, solar energy, and agricultural residues.

The rates of energy and fuel production and consumption can be reported in a number of different ways. For example, they can be expressed in quadrillion Btu per year, millions of barrels of oil per day, and thousands of cubic feet of natural gas per hour.

1 barrel of oil = 5.8×10^6 Btu
1 cubic foot of natural gas = 1.0×10^3 Btu
1 ton of coal = 2.4×10^7 Btu

One Btu is the energy required to raise the temperature of 1 pound of water 1 degree Fahrenheit.

How many tons of coal per year are equivalent to the rate of production of 1 barrel of oil per day?

$$\frac{(5.8 \times 10^6)(3.65 \times 10^2)}{(2.4 \times 10^7)} = 8.8 \times 10^1 \text{ tons of coal per year.}$$

How many Btu per year are equivalent to the U.S. 1976 coal production rate of 1.8 million tons per day?

$$(1.8 \times 10^6)(3.65 \times 10^2)(2.4 \times 10^7) = 1.6 \times 10^{16} \text{ Btu per year.}$$

Exercises Solve each problem.

1. How many barrels of oil per day are equivalent to the rate of the U.S. total consumption in 1976 (leap year) of 74 quadrillion Btu per year?
$\frac{(7.4 \times 10^{16})}{(3.66 \times 10^2)(5.8 \times 10^6)}$ or 3.5×10^7 barrels of oil per day

2. How many cubic feet of natural gas per hour are equivalent to the U.S. 1977 rate of oil production of 8.4 million barrels per day?
$\frac{(8.4 \times 10^6)(5.8 \times 10^6)}{(2.4 \times 10^1)(1.0 \times 10^3)}$ or 2.0×10^9 cubic feet of natural gas per hour

11-3 Rational Exponents

Objective: To use rational numbers as exponents.

The properties of exponents can also be extended to include rational number exponents. To satisfy these properties, the following must be true.

$$5^{\frac{1}{2}} \cdot 5^{\frac{1}{2}} = 5^{\frac{1}{2}+\frac{1}{2}} = 5$$

$$\text{But } \sqrt{5} \cdot \sqrt{5} = 5 \text{ also.}$$

Thus, the values of $5^{\frac{1}{2}}$ and $\sqrt{5}$ must be equal.

$$4^{\frac{1}{3}} \cdot 4^{\frac{1}{3}} \cdot 4^{\frac{1}{3}} = 4^{\frac{1}{3}+\frac{1}{3}+\frac{1}{3}} = 4$$

$$\text{But } \sqrt[3]{4} \cdot \sqrt[3]{4} \cdot \sqrt[3]{4} = 4 \text{ also.}$$

Thus, the values of $4^{\frac{1}{3}}$ and $\sqrt[3]{4}$ must be equal.

Other similar examples lead to the following definition.

Rational Numbers as Exponents

For any number b and for any integer n, with n greater than one, $b^{\frac{1}{n}} = \sqrt[n]{b}$, except when $b < 0$ and n is even.

examples

1 **Evaluate $27^{\frac{1}{3}}$.**

$27^{\frac{1}{3}} = \sqrt[3]{27}$ or 3 *Recall that $3^3 = 3 \cdot 3 \cdot 3$ or 27.*

2 **Evaluate $32^{\frac{1}{5}}$.**

$32^{\frac{1}{5}} = \sqrt[5]{32}$ or 2 *Recall that $2^5 = 2 \cdot 2 \cdot 2 \cdot 2 \cdot 2$ or 32.*

3 **Evaluate $1000^{\frac{1}{3}}$.**

$1000^{\frac{1}{3}} = \sqrt[3]{1000}$ or 10 *Recall that $10^3 = 10 \cdot 10 \cdot 10$ or 1000.*

4 **Evaluate $16^{\frac{1}{4}}$.**

$16^{\frac{1}{4}} = (2^4)^{\frac{1}{4}}$ or 2 *Note the rational exponent. Recall that $(a^m)^n = a^{mn}$.*

example 5

Evaluate $1{,}000{,}000^{\frac{1}{2}}$.

$$\begin{aligned}(1{,}000{,}000)^{\frac{1}{2}} &= (10^6)^{\frac{1}{2}}\\ &= 10^{6\cdot\frac{1}{2}}\\ &= 10^3\\ &= 1000\end{aligned}$$

The solution is 1000.

The following results show how the properties of exponents can be extended even further.

$$5^{\frac{3}{2}} = (5^{\frac{1}{2}})^3 \text{ or } (\sqrt{5})^3$$
$$5^{\frac{3}{2}} = (5^3)^{\frac{1}{2}} \text{ or } \sqrt{5^3}$$

Thus, the values of $(\sqrt{5})^3$ and $\sqrt{5^3}$ must be equal.

$$7^{\frac{2}{3}} = (7^{\frac{1}{3}})^2 \text{ or } (\sqrt[3]{7})^2$$
$$7^{\frac{2}{3}} = (7^2)^{\frac{1}{3}} \text{ or } \sqrt[3]{7^2}$$

Thus, the values of $(\sqrt[3]{7})^2$ and $\sqrt[3]{7^2}$ must be equal.

Definition of Rational Exponents

For any nonzero number b, and any integers m and n, with $n > 1$

$$b^{\frac{m}{n}} = \sqrt[n]{b^m} = (\sqrt[n]{b})^m$$

except when $\sqrt[n]{b}$ is *not* a real number.

Study the following examples to see how to use the rule above.

examples 6

Evaluate $27^{\frac{2}{3}}$.

$$\begin{aligned}27^{\frac{2}{3}} &= (\sqrt[3]{27})^2\\ &= (3)^2 \text{ or } 9\end{aligned}$$

7

Evaluate $8^{\frac{1}{3}} \cdot 8^{\frac{4}{3}}$.

$$8^{\frac{1}{3}} \cdot 8^{\frac{4}{3}} = 8^{\frac{5}{3}}$$
$$\begin{aligned}8^{\frac{5}{3}} &= (\sqrt[3]{8})^5\\ &= (2)^5 \text{ or } 32\end{aligned}$$

examples

8 Use radicals to express $8^{\frac{1}{3}}x^{\frac{4}{3}}y^{\frac{2}{3}}$.

$$8^{\frac{1}{3}}x^{\frac{4}{3}}y^{\frac{2}{3}} = (8x^4y^2)^{\frac{1}{3}}$$
$$= \sqrt[3]{8x^4y^2}$$
$$= 2x\sqrt[3]{xy^2}$$

Recall that for any numbers a, b, m, and n, $(ab)^n = a^n b^n$.

9 Use rational exponents to express $\sqrt[5]{(32x)^2}$.

$$\sqrt[5]{(32x)^2} = (32x)^{\frac{2}{5}}$$
$$= 32^{\frac{2}{5}} \cdot x^{\frac{2}{5}}$$
$$= (32^{\frac{1}{5}})^2 \cdot x^{\frac{2}{5}}$$
$$= 2^2x^{\frac{2}{5}} \text{ or } 4x^{\frac{2}{5}}$$

exercises

Max: 1–24, 1–32; Avg: 1–24, 1–31 odds; Min: 1–23 odds, 1–31 odds

Exploratory Evaluate.

1. $4^{\frac{3}{2}}$ 8
2. $9^{\frac{3}{2}}$ 27
3. $8^{-\frac{1}{3}}$ $\frac{1}{2}$
4. $16^{-\frac{3}{4}}$ $\frac{1}{8}$
5. $(16^{\frac{1}{2}})^{-\frac{1}{2}}$ $\frac{1}{2}$
6. $27^{-\frac{2}{3}}$ $\frac{1}{9}$
7. $64^{\frac{5}{6}}$ 32
8. $64^{-\frac{1}{3}}$ $\frac{1}{4}$
9. $\sqrt[3]{8^2}$ 4
10. $16^{-\frac{1}{4}}$ $\frac{1}{2}$
11. $\sqrt[4]{81}$ 3
12. $\sqrt[3]{216}$ 6
13. $(6^{\frac{2}{3}})^3$ 36
14. $9^{\frac{1}{3}} \cdot 9^{\frac{5}{3}}$ 81
15. $\dfrac{36^{\frac{3}{4}}}{36^{\frac{1}{4}}}$ 6
16. $16^{-\frac{3}{2}}$ $\frac{1}{64}$
17. $5^{\frac{1}{2}} \cdot 5^{\frac{3}{2}}$ 25
18. $49^{\frac{1}{2}}$ 7
19. $125^{\frac{1}{3}}$ 5
20. $81^{-\frac{1}{4}}$ $\frac{1}{3}$

Written Express each of the following using exponents.

1. $\sqrt{21}$ $21^{\frac{1}{2}}$
2. $\sqrt[3]{30}$ $30^{\frac{1}{3}}$
3. $\sqrt[6]{32}$ $32^{\frac{1}{6}}$
4. $\sqrt[4]{x}$ $x^{\frac{1}{4}}$
5. $\sqrt[3]{y}$ $y^{\frac{1}{3}}$
6. $\sqrt[4]{x^8y^{12}}$ x^2y^3
7. $\sqrt[3]{8m^3r^6}$ $2mr^2$
8. $\sqrt[3]{64x^9y^{15}}$ $4x^3y^5$
9. $\sqrt[4]{27}$ $27^{\frac{1}{4}}$
10. $\sqrt{36x^{12}y^8}$ $6x^6y^4$
11. $\sqrt[3]{n^2}$ $n^{\frac{2}{3}}$
12. $\sqrt[6]{b^3}$ $b^{\frac{1}{2}}$

Express each of the following using radicals.

13. $64^{\frac{1}{6}}$ $\sqrt[6]{64}$
14. $5^{\frac{1}{2}}$ $\sqrt{5}$
15. $6^{\frac{1}{3}}$ $\sqrt[3]{6}$
16. $x^{\frac{3}{4}}$ $\sqrt[4]{x^3}$
17. $a^{\frac{3}{2}}b^{\frac{5}{2}}$ $ab^2\sqrt{ab}$
18. $4^{\frac{1}{3}}x^{\frac{2}{3}}y^{\frac{4}{3}}$ $y\sqrt[3]{4x^2y}$
19. $2^{\frac{5}{3}}x^{\frac{7}{3}}$ $2x^2\sqrt[3]{4x}$
20. $(2x)^{\frac{1}{2}}x^{\frac{1}{2}}$ $|x|\sqrt{2}$
21. $5^{\frac{1}{3}}p^{\frac{2}{3}}q^{\frac{1}{3}}$ $\sqrt[3]{5p^2q}$
22. $(3m)^{\frac{2}{5}}n^{\frac{3}{5}}$ $\sqrt[5]{3^2m^2n^3}$
23. $r^{\frac{5}{2}}q^{\frac{3}{4}}$ $r^2\sqrt[4]{r^2q^3}$
24. $w^{\frac{4}{7}}y^{\frac{3}{7}}$ $\sqrt[7]{w^4y^3}$

Evaluate.

25. $\sqrt{121}$ 11
26. $\sqrt[3]{x^3}$ x
27. $\left(\dfrac{625}{16}\right)^{\frac{1}{4}}$ $\frac{5}{2}$
28. $\left(\dfrac{343}{64}\right)^{\frac{1}{3}}$ $\frac{7}{4}$
29. $\sqrt[5]{\dfrac{1}{32}}$ $\frac{1}{2}$
30. $\sqrt[4]{256}$ 4
31. $\left(\dfrac{256}{10{,}000}\right)^{\frac{1}{4}}$ $\frac{2}{5}$
32. $\left(\dfrac{216}{729}\right)^{\frac{2}{3}}$ $\frac{4}{9}$

11–4 Simplifying Expressions

Objective: To simplify various types of expressions.

The process of changing the form of a rational expression to one without radicals in the denominator is called **rationalizing the denominator.**

examples

1 **Simplify $\frac{1}{\sqrt{2}}$.**

$$\frac{1}{\sqrt{2}} = \frac{1}{\sqrt{2}} \cdot 1$$

$$= \frac{1}{\sqrt{2}} \cdot \frac{\sqrt{2}}{\sqrt{2}} \text{ or } \frac{\sqrt{2}}{2}$$

Notice that 1 is renamed as $\frac{\sqrt{2}}{\sqrt{2}}$. Why was $\frac{\sqrt{2}}{\sqrt{2}}$ chosen?

2 **Simplify $\frac{^-3}{\sqrt{y} + 1}$.**

$$\frac{^-3}{\sqrt{y} + 1} = \frac{^-3}{\sqrt{y} + 1} \cdot 1$$

$$= \frac{^-3}{\sqrt{y} + 1} \cdot \frac{\sqrt{y} - 1}{\sqrt{y} - 1}$$

What is the conjugate of $(\sqrt{y} + 1)$?

Conjugates were first explained on page 141.

$$= \frac{^-3\sqrt{y} + 3}{y - 1}$$

What happens when conjugates appear in a product?

A rational expression which contains a fractional exponent in the denominator must also be rationalized.

example

3 **Simplify $\frac{1}{3^{\frac{1}{2}}}$.**

$$\frac{1}{3^{\frac{1}{2}}} = \frac{1}{3^{\frac{1}{2}}} \cdot 1$$

$$= \frac{1}{3^{\frac{1}{2}}} \cdot \frac{3^{\frac{1}{2}}}{3^{\frac{1}{2}}}$$

Why is $\frac{3^{\frac{1}{2}}}{3^{\frac{1}{2}}}$ chosen?

$$= \frac{3^{\frac{1}{2}}}{3^{\frac{1}{2}+\frac{1}{2}}} \text{ or } \frac{3^{\frac{1}{2}}}{3}$$

It is important to choose a form of one for a multiplier carefully.

Simplify $\frac{1}{5^{\frac{3}{2}}}$. See which form of one you prefer.

$$\frac{1}{5^{\frac{3}{2}}} = \frac{1}{5^{\frac{3}{2}}}\left(\frac{5^{\frac{1}{2}}}{5^{\frac{1}{2}}}\right) = \frac{5^{\frac{1}{2}}}{5^2} \text{ or } \frac{5^{\frac{1}{2}}}{25}$$

$$\frac{1}{5^{\frac{3}{2}}} = \frac{1}{5^{\frac{3}{2}}}\left(\frac{5^{\frac{3}{2}}}{5^{\frac{3}{2}}}\right) = \frac{5^{\frac{3}{2}}}{5^3} = \frac{5 \cdot 5^{\frac{1}{2}}}{5 \cdot 5^2} \text{ or } \frac{5^{\frac{1}{2}}}{5^2}$$

Note that $5^{\frac{3}{2}} \div 5^3 = 5^{\frac{3}{2}-3}$ *or* $\frac{1}{5^{\frac{3}{2}}}$.

An expression is simplified when it meets these conditions.
1. It has no negative exponents.
2. It has no fractional exponents in the denominator.
3. It is not a complex fraction.

Conditions For Simplified Expressions

When you simplify an expression, be sure your answer meets all three of the above rules. In some problems, the simplest form may not always be the most convenient to use. Sometimes the content of a problem determines the most appropriate form for the answer.

examples

4 **Simplify $\frac{a^{\frac{1}{2}} - b^{\frac{1}{2}}}{a^{\frac{1}{2}} + b^{\frac{1}{2}}}$.**

This expression contains fractional exponents in the denominator. It does *not* meet the second condition.

$$\frac{a^{\frac{1}{2}} - b^{\frac{1}{2}}}{a^{\frac{1}{2}} + b^{\frac{1}{2}}} = \frac{a^{\frac{1}{2}} - b^{\frac{1}{2}}}{a^{\frac{1}{2}} + b^{\frac{1}{2}}}\left(\frac{a^{\frac{1}{2}} - b^{\frac{1}{2}}}{a^{\frac{1}{2}} - b^{\frac{1}{2}}}\right) = \frac{a - 2a^{\frac{1}{2}}b^{\frac{1}{2}} + b}{a - b}$$

Why choose to multiply by $\frac{a^{\frac{1}{2}} - b^{\frac{1}{2}}}{a^{\frac{1}{2}} - b^{\frac{1}{2}}}$?

5 **Simplify $r^{-\frac{1}{9}}$.**

This expression contains a negative exponent.
It does *not* meet the first condition.

$$r^{-\frac{1}{9}} = \frac{1}{r^{\frac{1}{9}}} = \frac{1}{r^{\frac{1}{9}}}\left(\frac{r^{\frac{8}{9}}}{r^{\frac{8}{9}}}\right) = \frac{r^{\frac{8}{9}}}{r}$$

Why choose to multiply by $\frac{r^{\frac{8}{9}}}{r^{\frac{8}{9}}}$?

example 6

Simplify $(m^{\frac{1}{4}})^{-\frac{1}{2}}$.

This expression contains a negative exponent.
It does *not* meet the first condition.

$$
\begin{aligned}
(m^{\frac{1}{4}})^{-\frac{1}{2}} &= m^{\frac{1}{4}(-\frac{1}{2})} \\
&= m^{-\frac{1}{8}} \\
&= \frac{1}{m^{\frac{1}{8}}} \\
&= \frac{1}{m^{\frac{1}{8}}}\left(\frac{m^{\frac{7}{8}}}{m^{\frac{7}{8}}}\right) \\
&= \frac{m^{\frac{7}{8}}}{m}
\end{aligned}
$$

Why choose to multiply by $\frac{m^{\frac{7}{8}}}{m^{\frac{7}{8}}}$?

exercises

Max: 1–30, 1–14; **Avg:** 1–30, 1–13 odds; **Min:** 1–15, 16–25, 1–11 odds

Exploratory For each expression, find a factor which can be used to rationalize the expression.

1. $\frac{6}{3^{\frac{1}{2}}}$ $\frac{3^{\frac{1}{2}}}{3^{\frac{1}{2}}}$
2. $\frac{10}{5^{\frac{2}{3}}}$ $\frac{5^{\frac{1}{3}}}{5^{\frac{1}{3}}}$
3. $\frac{16}{4^{\frac{3}{2}}}$ $\frac{4^{\frac{1}{2}}}{4^{\frac{1}{2}}}$
4. $\frac{18}{3^{\frac{3}{2}}}$ $\frac{3^{\frac{1}{2}}}{3^{\frac{1}{2}}}$
5. $\frac{1}{x^{\frac{1}{3}}}$ $\frac{x^{\frac{2}{3}}}{x^{\frac{2}{3}}}$
6. $\frac{1}{y^{\frac{2}{3}}}$ $\frac{y^{\frac{1}{3}}}{y^{\frac{1}{3}}}$
7. $\frac{2}{m^{\frac{3}{4}}}$ $\frac{m^{\frac{1}{4}}}{m^{\frac{1}{4}}}$
8. $\frac{5a}{a^{\frac{5}{6}}}$ $\frac{a^{\frac{1}{6}}}{a^{\frac{1}{6}}}$
9. $a^{-\frac{1}{5}}$ $\frac{a^{\frac{4}{5}}}{a^{\frac{4}{5}}}$
10. $p^{-\frac{3}{2}}$ $\frac{p^{\frac{1}{2}}}{p^{\frac{1}{2}}}$
11. $\frac{1}{x^{\frac{1}{2}} + 1}$ $\frac{x^{\frac{1}{2}} - 1}{x^{\frac{1}{2}} - 1}$
12. $\frac{m + p}{m^{\frac{1}{2}} + p}$ $\frac{m^{\frac{1}{2}} - p}{m^{\frac{1}{2}} - p}$
13. $\frac{r}{r^{\frac{1}{2}} - s^{\frac{1}{2}}}$ $\frac{r^{\frac{1}{2}} + s^{\frac{1}{2}}}{r^{\frac{1}{2}} + s^{\frac{1}{2}}}$
14. $\frac{2}{t^{\frac{3}{2}} + s^{\frac{1}{2}}}$ $\frac{t^{\frac{3}{2}} - s^{\frac{1}{2}}}{t^{\frac{3}{2}} - s^{\frac{1}{2}}}$
15. $\frac{1}{b^{\frac{3}{2}} + 2}$ $\frac{b^{\frac{3}{2}} - 2}{b^{\frac{3}{2}} - 2}$

16–30. Simplify each expression in problems **1–15**. See answers below.

Written Simplify each expression.

1. $\frac{1}{y^{\frac{2}{5}}}$ $\frac{y^{\frac{3}{5}}}{y}$
2. $\frac{3}{r^{\frac{4}{3}}}$ $\frac{3r^{\frac{2}{3}}}{r^2}$
3. $b^{-\frac{1}{4}}$ $\frac{b^{\frac{3}{4}}}{b}$
4. $\frac{15}{5^{\frac{2}{3}}}$ $3 \cdot 5^{\frac{1}{3}}$
5. $\frac{x^{\frac{1}{2}} + 5x^{\frac{3}{2}}}{x^{\frac{1}{2}}}$ $1 + 5x$
6. $\frac{b^{\frac{1}{2}}}{b^{\frac{3}{2}} - b^{\frac{1}{2}}}$ $\frac{1}{b - 1}$
7. $\frac{r^{\frac{3}{2}}}{r^{\frac{1}{2}} + 2}$ $\frac{r^2 - 2r^{\frac{3}{2}}}{r - 4}$
8. $\frac{x^{\frac{1}{3}}}{x^{\frac{2}{3}} - x^{-\frac{1}{3}}}$ $\frac{x^{\frac{2}{3}}}{x - 1}$
9. $\frac{x^{\frac{1}{2}} + y^{\frac{1}{2}}}{x^{\frac{1}{2}} - y^{\frac{1}{2}}}$ $\frac{x + 2x^{\frac{1}{2}}y^{\frac{1}{2}} + y}{x - y}$
10. $(y^{\frac{1}{3}})^{-\frac{3}{4}}$ $\frac{y^{\frac{3}{4}}}{y}$
11. $\left(\frac{x^{-2}y^6}{9}\right)^{-\frac{1}{2}}$ $\frac{3x}{y^3}$
12. $\frac{a^{-\frac{2}{3}}b^{\frac{1}{2}}}{b^{-\frac{3}{2}}\sqrt[3]{a}}$ $\frac{b^2}{a}$

Evaluate the following expressions.

13. $-\frac{4}{9}x^9\left(\frac{3}{x^2} - \frac{1}{\sqrt[3]{2}}\right)$ when $x = \sqrt[6]{2}$ $-\frac{16}{9} \cdot 2^{\frac{1}{6}}$
14. $\frac{3^0y + 4y^{-1}}{y^{-\frac{2}{3}}}$ when $y = 8$ 34

16. $2 \cdot 3^{\frac{1}{2}}$ 17. $2 \cdot 5^{\frac{1}{3}}$ 18. 2 19. $2 \cdot 3^{\frac{1}{2}}$ 20. $\frac{x^{\frac{2}{3}}}{x}$ 21. $\frac{y^{\frac{1}{3}}}{y}$ 22. $\frac{2m^{\frac{1}{4}}}{m}$ 23. $5 \cdot a^{\frac{1}{6}}$ 24. $\frac{a^{\frac{4}{5}}}{a}$ 25. $\frac{p^{\frac{1}{2}}}{p^2}$ 26. $\frac{x^{\frac{1}{2}} - 1}{x - 1}$ 27. $\frac{m^{\frac{3}{2}} - mp + m^{\frac{1}{2}}p - p^2}{m - p^2}$ 28. $\frac{r^{\frac{3}{2}} + rs^{\frac{1}{2}}}{r - s}$ 29. $\frac{2(t^{\frac{3}{2}} - s^{\frac{1}{2}})}{t^3 - s}$ 30. $\frac{b^{\frac{3}{2}} - 2}{b^3 - 4}$

11-5 Solving Equations in Quadratic Form

Objective: To solve equations in quadratic form.

Many equations can be solved using the following property of exponents. For any number a, and any rational numbers m and n,

$$(a^m)^n = a^{mn}$$

examples

1 **Solve $x^{\frac{3}{2}} = 8$.**

$x^{\frac{3}{2}} = 8$

$(x^{\frac{3}{2}})^{\frac{2}{3}} = 8^{\frac{2}{3}}$ — *Raise each side of the equation to the $\frac{2}{3}$ power. Why $\frac{2}{3}$?*

$x = 8^{\frac{2}{3}}$

$x = (8^{\frac{1}{3}})^2$ — *How is the property of exponents listed above used here?*

$x = 2^2$ or 4

2 **Solve $y^{-2} - 64 = 0$.**

$y^{-2} - 64 = 0$

$y^{-2} = 64$

$(y^{-2})^{-\frac{1}{2}} = 64^{-\frac{1}{2}}$ — *Raise each side of the equation to $-\frac{1}{2}$ power. Why $-\frac{1}{2}$?*

$y = 64^{-\frac{1}{2}}$

$y = \frac{1}{8}$

Some equations are written in quadratic form as described below.

For any numbers a, b, and c, except $a = 0$, an equation written as $a[f(x)]^2 + b[f(x)] + c = 0$ is in quadratic form.

Definition of Quadratic Form

In an equation such as $x^2 + 2x + 1 = 0$, the expression $f(x)$ is just x.

example

3 **Find $f(x)$ in the equation $x^{\frac{1}{2}} - 6x^{\frac{1}{4}} + 8 = 0$.**

$x^{\frac{1}{2}} - 6x^{\frac{1}{4}} + 8 = 0$

$x^{\frac{1}{4}\cdot 2} - 6x^{\frac{1}{4}} + 8 = 0$

$(x^{\frac{1}{4}})^2 - 6(x^{\frac{1}{4}}) + 8 = 0$

Then $f(x)$ is $x^{\frac{1}{4}}$.

Equations in quadratic form can be solved by the same methods used for solving quadratic equations.

examples

4 **Solve $x^{\frac{1}{2}} - 6x^{\frac{1}{4}} + 8 = 0$.**

$$x^{\frac{1}{2}} - 6x^{\frac{1}{4}} + 8 = 0$$

$(x^{\frac{1}{4}})^2 - 6(x^{\frac{1}{4}}) + 8 = 0$ *So $f(x)$ is $x^{\frac{1}{4}}$.*

$(x^{\frac{1}{4}} - 2)(x^{\frac{1}{4}} - 4) = 0$ *Factor to solve for $f(x)$.*

$x^{\frac{1}{4}} - 2 = 0$ or $x^{\frac{1}{4}} - 4 = 0$

$x^{\frac{1}{4}} = 2$ $\qquad$ $x^{\frac{1}{4}} = 4$

To solve for x, continue as shown.

$x^{\frac{1}{4}} = 2$ or $x^{\frac{1}{4}} = 4$

$(x^{\frac{1}{4}})^4 = (2)^4$ $\qquad$ $(x^{\frac{1}{4}})^4 = 4^4$

$x = 2^4$ or 16 $\qquad$ $x = 4^4$ or 256

Check: $x^{\frac{1}{2}} - 6x^{\frac{1}{4}} + 8 = 0$

$16^{\frac{1}{2}} - 6(16^{\frac{1}{4}}) + 8 \stackrel{?}{=} 0$ $\qquad$ $256^{\frac{1}{2}} - 6(256^{\frac{1}{4}}) + 8 \stackrel{?}{=} 0$

$4 - 6(2) + 8 \stackrel{?}{=} 0$ $\qquad$ $16 - 6(4) + 8 \stackrel{?}{=} 0$

$12 - 12 \stackrel{?}{=} 0$ $\qquad$ $24 - 24 \stackrel{?}{=} 0$

$0 = 0$ $\qquad$ $0 = 0$

The solutions are 16 and 256.

5 **Solve $4z^{\frac{4}{3}} - 25z^{\frac{2}{3}} + 36 = 0$.**

$$4z^{\frac{4}{3}} - 25z^{\frac{2}{3}} + 36 = 0$$

$4(z^{\frac{2}{3}})^2 - 25z^{\frac{2}{3}} + 36 = 0$ *So $f(z)$ is $z^{\frac{2}{3}}$.*

$(4z^{\frac{2}{3}} - 9)(z^{\frac{2}{3}} - 4) = 0$ *Factor to solve for $f(z)$.*

$4z^{\frac{2}{3}} = 9$ or $z^{\frac{2}{3}} = 4$

$z^{\frac{2}{3}} = \frac{9}{4}$ $\qquad$ $z^{\frac{2}{3}} = 4$

$(z^{\frac{2}{3}})^{\frac{3}{2}} = \left(\frac{9}{4}\right)^{\frac{3}{2}}$ $\qquad$ $(z^{\frac{2}{3}})^{\frac{3}{2}} = 4^{\frac{3}{2}}$

$z = \left(\frac{9}{4}\right)^{\frac{3}{2}}$ $\qquad$ $z = 4^{\frac{3}{2}}$

$z = \frac{27}{8}$ $\qquad$ $z = 8$

Check: $4z^{\frac{4}{3}} - 25z^{\frac{2}{3}} + 36 = 0$

$4\left(\frac{27}{8}\right)^{\frac{4}{3}} - 25\left(\frac{27}{8}\right)^{\frac{2}{3}} + 36 \stackrel{?}{=} 0$

$4\left(\frac{81}{16}\right) - 25\left(\frac{9}{4}\right) + 36 \stackrel{?}{=} 0$

$\frac{81}{4} - \frac{225}{4} + \frac{144}{4} \stackrel{?}{=} 0$

$0 = 0$

$4(8)^{\frac{4}{3}} - 25(8)^{\frac{2}{3}} + 36 \stackrel{?}{=} 0$

$4(16) - 25(4) + 36 \stackrel{?}{=} 0$

$64 - 100 + 36 \stackrel{?}{=} 0$

$0 = 0$

The solutions are $\frac{27}{8}$ and 8.

exercises

Max: 1–22, 1–50; **Avg:** 1–22, 1–36, 37–49 odds; **Min:** 1–22, 1–49 odds

Exploratory Solve each equation.

1. $r^{\frac{1}{3}} = 2$ 8
2. $x^{-\frac{1}{2}} = 4$ $\frac{1}{16}$
3. $y^{\frac{3}{2}} - 8 = 0$ 4
4. $z^{-\frac{1}{3}} - 2 = 0$ $\frac{1}{8}$
5. $y^{\frac{1}{2}} = 5$ 25
6. $x^{\frac{1}{3}} = 3$ 27
7. $z^{-2} = 25$ $\frac{1}{5}$
8. $r^{-3} = 27$ $\frac{1}{3}$
9. $p^{-2} = 169$ $\frac{1}{13}$
10. $y^{\frac{1}{3}} - 4 = 0$ 64
11. $x^{-\frac{1}{2}} + 1 = 2$ 1
12. $a^{\frac{2}{3}} = \frac{4}{9}$ $\frac{8}{27}$

Factor each expression. Use rational exponents with the variable.

13. $x^{\frac{1}{2}} - 8x^{\frac{1}{4}} + 15$ $(x^{\frac{1}{4}} - 3)(x^{\frac{1}{4}} - 5)$
14. $y^{\frac{1}{2}} - 10y^{\frac{1}{4}} + 16$ $(y^{\frac{1}{4}} - 2)(y^{\frac{1}{4}} - 8)$
15. $r^{\frac{2}{3}} - 5r^{\frac{1}{3}} + 6$ $(r^{\frac{1}{3}} - 3)(r^{\frac{1}{3}} - 2)$
16. $s^{\frac{2}{3}} - 9s^{\frac{1}{3}} + 20$ $(s^{\frac{1}{3}} - 4)(s^{\frac{1}{3}} - 5)$
17. $m - 7m^{\frac{1}{2}} + 10$ $(m^{\frac{1}{2}} - 2)(m^{\frac{1}{2}} - 5)$
18. $b - 11b^{\frac{1}{2}} + 30$ $(b^{\frac{1}{2}} - 5)(b^{\frac{1}{2}} - 6)$
19. $a^{-\frac{2}{3}} - 11a^{-\frac{1}{3}} + 28$ $(a^{-\frac{1}{3}} - 7)(a^{-\frac{1}{3}} - 4)$
20. $k^{-\frac{4}{3}} - 10k^{-\frac{2}{3}} + 21$ $(k^{-\frac{2}{3}} - 7)(k^{-\frac{2}{3}} - 3)$
21. $x^{-\frac{3}{2}} - 8x^{-\frac{3}{4}} + 16$ $(x^{-\frac{3}{4}} - 4)^2$
22. $y^{-\frac{1}{3}} - 4y^{-\frac{1}{6}} + 4$ $(y^{-\frac{1}{6}} - 2)(y^{-\frac{1}{6}} - 2)$

Written Write each equation in the form $a[f(x)]^2 + b[f(x)] + c = 0$.

1. $x^{\frac{1}{2}} - 10x^{\frac{1}{4}} + 16 = 0$ $1[x^{\frac{1}{4}}]^2 - 10[x^{\frac{1}{4}}] + 16 = 0$
2. $x^{\frac{2}{3}} - 8x^{\frac{1}{3}} + 15 = 0$ $1[x^{\frac{1}{3}}]^2 - 8[x^{\frac{1}{3}}] + 15 = 0$
3. $x^{\frac{2}{3}} - 9x^{\frac{1}{3}} + 20 = 0$ $1[x^{\frac{1}{3}}]^2 - 9[x^{\frac{1}{3}}] + 20 = 0$
4. $x^{\frac{2}{3}} - 7x^{\frac{1}{3}} + 10 = 0$ $1[x^{\frac{1}{3}}]^2 - 7[x^{\frac{1}{3}}] + 10 = 0$

Factor the left side of each equation.

5. $m - 11m^{\frac{1}{2}} + 30 = 0$ $(m^{\frac{1}{2}} - 5)(m^{\frac{1}{2}} - 6)$
6. $s - 5s^{\frac{1}{2}} + 6 = 0$ $(s^{\frac{1}{2}} - 3)(s^{\frac{1}{2}} - 2)$
7. $k^{-\frac{2}{3}} - 11k^{-\frac{1}{3}} + 28 = 0$ $(k^{-\frac{1}{3}} - 7)(k^{-\frac{1}{3}} - 4)$
8. $a^{-\frac{2}{3}} - 10a^{-\frac{1}{3}} + 21 = 0$ $(a^{-\frac{1}{3}} - 7)(a^{-\frac{1}{3}} - 3)$
9. $x^{\frac{4}{3}} - 8x^{\frac{2}{3}} + 16 = 0$ $(x^{\frac{2}{3}} - 4)^2$
10. $y^{-\frac{2}{5}} - 4y^{-\frac{1}{5}} + 4 = 0$ $(y^{-\frac{1}{5}} - 2)^2$
11. $y^{-1} - 5y^{-\frac{1}{2}} + 6 = 0$ $(y^{-\frac{1}{2}} - 3)(y^{-\frac{1}{2}} - 2)$
12. $k^{\frac{4}{3}} - 6k^{\frac{2}{3}} + 9 = 0$ $(k^{\frac{2}{3}} - 3)^2$
13. $y^3 - 16y^{\frac{3}{2}} + 64 = 0$ $(y^{\frac{3}{2}} - 8)^2$
14. $y^{\frac{4}{3}} - 13y^{\frac{2}{3}} + 36 = 0$ $(y^{\frac{2}{3}} - 4)(y^{\frac{2}{3}} - 9)$

15–28. Solve each equation in problems **1–14.** **15.** 4096, 16 **16.** 27, 125 **17.** 64, 125 **18.** 125, 8 **19.** 25, 36 **20.** 9, 4 **21.** $\frac{1}{343}$, $\frac{1}{64}$ **22.** $\frac{1}{343}$, $\frac{1}{27}$ **23.** 8 **24.** $\frac{1}{32}$ **25.** $\frac{1}{9}$, $\frac{1}{4}$ **26.** $3\sqrt{3}$ **27.** 4 **28.** 8, 27

Special Products

Excursions in Algebra

You know that $x^2 - y^2 = (x - y)(x + y)$. This fact can be used to multiply numbers in your head. Suppose you want to find $36 \cdot 44$. Notice that $36 = 40 - 4$ and $44 = 40 + 4$.

$$\begin{aligned} 36 \cdot 44 &= (40 - 4)(40 + 4) \\ &= 40^2 - 4^2 \\ &= 1600 - 16 \\ &= 1584 \end{aligned}$$

Let $x = 40$ and $y = 4$ in $(x - y)(x + y) = x^2 - y^2$

Try this method to calculate $27 \cdot 33$, $19 \cdot 21$, and $53 \cdot 67$ mentally.

Using Money

Saving for College

Tom and Ann Howard want to set up a savings fund for the education of their first child, who will enter college in ten years. They find they can put \$300 each year in a special account for this purpose. The account earns 6% interest, compounded annually.

They calculate how much will be in the account in a certain number of years by using this formula.

$$S = P \cdot \left(\frac{x}{1 - x}\right)(1 - x^k)$$

S is the amount in the account.
P is the amount deposited each year.
x is [1 + (rate of interest)].
k is the number of years.

Exercises Solve each problem.

1. In the Howard's case, what is the value P? \$300
2. What is the rate of interest, expressed as a decimal? 0.06
3. What is the value of x? 1.06
4. Suppose $k = 1$. Find the value of S at the end of the first year. 300(1.06) or 318

   Hint: $S = 300\left(\frac{1.06}{1 - 1.06}\right)[1 - (1.06)^1]$ *Compute* $\frac{1.06}{1 - 1.06}$.
5. Compute $(1.06)^2$. 1.1236
6. Compute $(1.06)^5$. about 1.34
7. Compute $[(1.06)^5]^2$ or $(1.06)^{10}$. about 1.79

Use the formula to find the following.

8. Find the amount in the account at the end of the second year. $300(^-17.66)(^-0.124)$ or 656.95
9. Find the amount in the account at the end of the fifth year. $300(^-17.66)(^-0.338)$ or 1790.72
10. Find the amount in the account at the end of the tenth year. $300(^-17.66)(^-0.79)$ or 4185.42

11-6 Solving Radical Equations

Objective: To solve equations involving radicals.

Some equations can be written using either rational exponents or radicals. The methods of solving such equations are similar.

Rational Exponents		Radicals
Solve $x^{\frac{1}{3}} = 2$	*Solve each equation by raising both sides to the same power.*	Solve $\sqrt[3]{x} = 2$
$x^{\frac{1}{3}} = 2$		$\sqrt[3]{x} = 2$
$(x^{\frac{1}{3}})^3 = 2^3$		$(\sqrt[3]{x})^3 = 2^3$
$x = 2^3$ or 8		$x = 2^3$ or 8
$8^{\frac{1}{3}} \stackrel{?}{=} 2$	*Check the solution.*	$\sqrt[3]{8} \stackrel{?}{=} 2$
$2 = 2$		$2 = 2$

The following examples solve some radical equations.

examples

1 **Solve $\sqrt[3]{x + 4} = {}^-5$.**

$$\sqrt[3]{x + 4} = {}^-5$$
$$(\sqrt[3]{x + 4})^3 = ({}^-5)^3$$
$$x + 4 = {}^-125$$
$$x = {}^-129$$

How do you know to raise both sides of the equation to the third power?

Check: $\sqrt[3]{x + 4} = {}^-5$

$$\sqrt[3]{{}^-129 + 4} \stackrel{?}{=} {}^-5$$
$$\sqrt[3]{{}^-125} \stackrel{?}{=} {}^-5$$
$${}^-5 = {}^-5$$

The solution is ${}^-129$.

2 **Solve $x + \sqrt{3x - 2} = 4$.**

$$x + \sqrt{3x - 2} = 4$$
$$\sqrt{3x - 2} = 4 - x$$
$$(\sqrt{3x - 2})^2 = (4 - x)^2$$
$$3x - 2 = x^2 - 8x + 16$$

Isolate the radical so that when each side is squared there are no extra terms. Square each side.

$$0 = x^2 - 11x + 18$$

Combine terms.

$$0 = (x - 2)(x - 9)$$

Factor to solve for x.

$x - 2 = 0$ or $x - 9 = 0$

$x = 2$ $\qquad$ $x = 9$

Check: $x + \sqrt{3x - 2} = 4$

$$2 + \sqrt{3(2) - 2} \stackrel{?}{=} 4 \qquad 9 + \sqrt{3(9) - 2} \stackrel{?}{=} 4$$
$$2 + \sqrt{4} \stackrel{?}{=} 4 \qquad 9 + \sqrt{25} \stackrel{?}{=} 4$$
$$4 = 4 \qquad 14 \neq 4$$

The solution is 4. *Does not check.*

You must check all possible solutions in the original equation. Squaring both sides of an equation may produce results that do not satisfy the equation.

examples

3 **Solve $\sqrt{2y-3} - \sqrt{y-2} = 1$.**

$$\sqrt{2y-3} - \sqrt{y-2} = 1$$

$$\sqrt{2y-3} = \sqrt{y-2} + 1 \quad \textit{Isolate one radical.}$$

$$(\sqrt{2y-3})^2 = (\sqrt{y-2} + 1)^2 \quad \textit{Square each side.}$$

$$2y - 3 = y - 2 + \mathbf{2\sqrt{y-2}} + 1 \quad \textit{Note middle term from expansion.}$$

$$y - 2 = 2\sqrt{y-2} \quad \textit{Isolate the other radical.}$$

$$(y-2)^2 = (2\sqrt{y-2})^2$$

$$y^2 - 4y + 4 = 4(y-2)$$

$$y^2 - 8y + 12 = 0$$

$$(y-2)(y-6) = 0$$

$$y - 2 = 0 \quad \text{or} \quad y - 6 = 0$$

$$y = 2 \qquad\qquad y = 6$$

Check: $\sqrt{2y-3} - \sqrt{y-2} = 1$

$$\sqrt{2(2)-3} - \sqrt{2-2} \stackrel{?}{=} 1 \qquad \sqrt{2(6)-3} - \sqrt{6-2} \stackrel{?}{=} 1$$

$$1 - \sqrt{0} \stackrel{?}{=} 1 \qquad \sqrt{9} - \sqrt{4} \stackrel{?}{=} 1$$

$$1 = 1 \qquad 3 - 2 \stackrel{?}{=} 1$$

$$1 = 1$$

The solutions are 2 and 6.

4 **Solve $\sqrt{2y^2 + 5y} = {}^-y - 10$.**

$$\sqrt{2y^2 + 5y} = {}^-y - 10$$

$$2y^2 + 5y = y^2 + 20y + 100 \quad \textit{Square each side.}$$

$$y^2 - 15y - 100 = 0$$

$$(y+5)(y-20) = 0$$

$$y + 5 = 0 \quad \text{or} \quad y - 20 = 0$$

$$y = {}^-5 \qquad\qquad y = 20$$

Check: $\sqrt{2y^2 + 5y} = {}^-y - 10$

$$\sqrt{2({}^-5)^2 + 5({}^-5)} \stackrel{?}{=} {}^-({}^-5) - 10 \qquad \sqrt{2(20)^2 + 5(20)} \stackrel{?}{=} {}^-(20) - 10$$

$$\sqrt{2(25) - 25} \stackrel{?}{=} 5 - 10 \qquad \sqrt{2(400) + 100} \stackrel{?}{=} {}^-30$$

$$\sqrt{25} \stackrel{?}{=} {}^-5 \qquad \sqrt{900} \stackrel{?}{=} {}^-30$$

$$5 \neq {}^-5 \quad \textit{Does not check.} \qquad 30 \neq {}^-30 \quad \textit{Does not check.}$$

There are no solutions.

exercises

Max: 1–14, 1–20; Avg: 1–14, 1–19 odds; Min: 1–13 odds, 1–19 odds

Exploratory Solve each equation. Check each solution.

1. $\sqrt{x-2} - 7 = 0$ 51
2. $\sqrt{y-3} - 5 = 0$ 28
3. $\sqrt[3]{a+2} = 3$ 25
4. $\sqrt[3]{m-3} = 1$ 4
5. $x - \sqrt{7x} = 0$ 0, 7
6. $k - \sqrt{10k} = 0$ 0, 10
7. $\sqrt{4x} + 3 = x$ 9
8. $\sqrt{2m} + 4 = m$ 8
9. $\sqrt{b+1} - b = 1$ 0, −1
10. $\sqrt{2r+1} = r + 1$ 0
11. $\sqrt[3]{5-a} = 2$ −3
12. $\sqrt[3]{x-2} - 1 = 0$ 3
13. $\sqrt{2y+3} + y = 0$ −1
14. $\sqrt{x+2} - x = 0$ 2

Written Solve each equation. Check each solution.

1. $\sqrt{3x+10} = x + 4$ −2, −3
2. $2\sqrt{k-1} = k - 1$ 5, 1
3. $\sqrt[3]{x+1} = 2$ 7
4. $\sqrt[3]{r-2} = 1$ 3
5. $\sqrt{2x+11} = x - 2$ 7
6. $2m - 3 = \sqrt{7m-3}$ 4
7. $\sqrt[3]{x-1} = 2$ 9
8. $\sqrt[3]{5-y} = 2$ −3
9. $\sqrt{y+3} + 3 = y$ 6
10. $\sqrt{a+2} + 4 = a$ 7
11. $\sqrt{x-5} - \sqrt{x} = 1$ no solution
12. $\sqrt{m+12} - \sqrt{m} = 2$ 4
13. $\sqrt{b+4} = \sqrt{b+20} - 2$ 5
14. $\sqrt{2k+1} = 2 - \sqrt{k-3}$ no solution
15. $\sqrt{2t-1} + \sqrt{t-1} = 1$ 1
16. $\sqrt{2a+1} = 1 + \sqrt{a}$ 0, 4
17. $\sqrt{2y+3} - \sqrt{y+1} = 1$ −1, 3
18. $\sqrt[3]{4x+5} - \sqrt[3]{x^2} = 0$ −1, 5
19. $\sqrt{y+4} + \sqrt{y-1} = \sqrt{y-4}$ no solution
20. $\sqrt{m} + \sqrt{m-3} = \dfrac{3}{\sqrt{m-3}}$ 4

Special Products

Excursions in Algebra

Here is another method to find some products mentally. You know the following.

$$(x+1)^2 = x^2 + 2x + 1$$

Suppose you want to find $(101)^2$.

$$(101)^2 = (100)^2 + 2(100) + 1$$
$$= 10000 + 200 + 1$$
$$= 10{,}201$$

Let $x = 100$ in the expression $(x+1)^2 = x^2 + 2x + 1$. Here $2x + 1 = 201$ and $100^2 = 10000$ can be calculated mentally.

Use this method to find the square of a number $(x + 1)$ when you already know the square of x. Can you find 31^2, 13^2, and 201^2 mentally?

Vocabulary

zero exponent (304)
negative integer exponents (305)
scientific notation (307)
rational exponents (311)
rationalize (314)
conjugate (314)
simplified expression (315)
quadratic form (317)
radical equation (321)

Chapter Summary

1. Properties of Exponents: For any numbers a, b, m, and n,

1. $a^m \cdot a^n = a^{m+n}$ (304)
2. $(a^m)^n = a^{m \cdot n}$ (311)
3. $(ab)^n = a^n \cdot b^n$ (313)
4. $\frac{a^m}{a^n} = a^{m-n}$ if $a \neq 0$ (304)

2. Zero Exponent: For any number a, except $a = 0$, $a^0 = 1$. (304)

3. Negative Integer Exponents: For any number a, except $a = 0$, and for any positive integer n, $a^{-n} = \frac{1}{a^n}$. (305)

4. Definition of Scientific Notation: A number is expressed in scientific notation when it is in the form $a \times 10^n$. Here $1 \leq a < 10$ and n is an integer. (307)

5. Rational Numbers as Exponents: For any number b and for any integer n, with n greater than one, $b^{\frac{1}{n}} = \sqrt[n]{b}$ except for $b < 0$ and n even. (311)

6. Definition of Rational Exponents: For any nonzero number b, and any integers m and n, with $n > 1$,
$b^{\frac{m}{n}} = \sqrt[n]{b^m} = (\sqrt[n]{b})^m$ except when $\sqrt[n]{b}$ is not real. (312)

7. The conjugate of $\sqrt{a} + \sqrt{b}$ is $\sqrt{a} - \sqrt{b}$. (314)

8. Conditions for Simplified Expressions: An expression is simplified when it meets these conditions.

1. It has no negative exponents.
2. It has no fractional exponents in the denominator.
3. It is not a complex fraction. (315)

9. Definition of Quadratic Form: For any numbers a, b, and c, except $a = 0$, an equation written as $a[f(x)]^2 + b[f(x)] + c = 0$, where $f(x)$ is some expression in x, is in quadratic form. (317)

10. These steps are usually used to solve a radical equation. Some of them may need to be used more than once.

1. Isolate the radical.
2. Raise both sides to a power.
3. Combine terms.
4. Solve for the variable.
5. Check each solution. (318)

Chapter Review

11-1 Simplify each expression.

1. $\frac{x^6}{x^6}$ 1
2. $y^3 \cdot y^{-4}$ $\frac{1}{y}$
3. $\frac{m^{-3}}{m^2}$ $\frac{1}{m^5}$
4. $r^{-3} \cdot r^{-2}$ $\frac{1}{r^5}$
5. $\frac{3x^2y}{xy^2}$ $\frac{3x}{y}$
6. $2m^3n^{-4}$ $\frac{2m^3}{n^4}$
7. $18v^2 \div 3v$ $6v$
8. $\frac{18v^2}{9v^2}$ 2

Evaluate.

9. 3^{-2} $\frac{1}{9}$
10. 11^0 1
11. $\left(\frac{4}{3}\right)^{-2}$ $\frac{9}{16}$
12. $3^{-3}4^2$ $\frac{16}{27}$
13. $\left(\frac{7}{5}\right)^{-3}$ $\frac{125}{343}$
14. $\left(\frac{2}{3}\right)^0$ 1
15. $(4^2)^{-2}$ $\frac{1}{256}$
16. $\left(\frac{12}{15}\right)^2$ $\frac{16}{25}$

11-2 Copy and complete the chart.

	Decimal notation	Scientific notation
17.	1215	1.215×10^3
18.	3,176,000,000	3.176×10^9
19.	0.0001592	1.592×10^{-4}
20.	0.00078231	7.8231×10^{-4}

Evaluate. Express each answer in scientific notation.

21. $(4.731 \times 10^6)(2.8 \times 10^{-2})$ 1.32468×10^5
22. $\frac{6.921 \times 10^{11}}{8.317 \times 10^3}$ 8.3215×10^7

11-3 For each of the following evaluate or express using exponents.

23. $6^{\frac{1}{2}} \cdot 6^{\frac{3}{2}}$ 36
24. $125^{\frac{1}{3}}$ 5
25. $\sqrt[4]{2401}$ 7
26. $\sqrt[3]{1331}$ 11
27. $\sqrt[4]{x^4y^3}$ $xy^{\frac{3}{4}}$
28. $\sqrt[3]{27m^3n^2}$ $3mn^{\frac{2}{3}}$
29. $\sqrt[5]{32w^{10}r^5}$ $2w^2r$

11-4 Simplify each expression.

30. $\frac{1}{z^{\frac{3}{5}}}$ $\frac{z^{\frac{2}{5}}}{z}$
31. $\frac{w^{-\frac{2}{3}}r^{\frac{1}{2}}}{wr^2}$ $\frac{w^{\frac{1}{3}}r^{\frac{1}{2}}}{w^2r^2}$
32. $\frac{z^{\frac{1}{3}}}{z^{\frac{2}{3}} - z^{\frac{1}{3}}}$ $\frac{z^{\frac{2}{3}} + z^{\frac{1}{3}} + 1}{z - 1}$
33. $\frac{x^{\frac{1}{2}} - y^{\frac{1}{2}}}{x^{\frac{1}{2}} + y^{\frac{1}{2}}}$

Evaluate each expression.

34. $\frac{2}{3}x^3\left(\frac{3}{x^2} - \frac{1}{x^{\frac{1}{3}}}\right)$ when $x = 8$ $-\frac{464}{3}$
35. $\frac{3r^2 + 2r^{-1}}{r^{-\frac{2}{3}}}$ when $r = 3$ $\frac{83}{3} \cdot \sqrt[3]{9}$

11-5 Solve each equation.

36. $m^{-\frac{2}{5}} - 4m^{-\frac{1}{5}} + 4 = 0$ $\frac{1}{32}$
37. $w^3 - 16w^{\frac{3}{2}} + 64 = 0$ 4
38. $z^{-\frac{2}{3}} - 11z^{-\frac{1}{3}} + 28 = 0$

11-6 Solve each equation.

39. $\sqrt[3]{w - 3} = 1$ 4
40. $\sqrt{b + 2} + 4 = b$ 7
41. $\sqrt{r + 12} - \sqrt{r} = 2$ 4

33. $(x - 2x^{\frac{1}{2}}y^{\frac{1}{2}} + y)/(x - y)$ 38. $\frac{1}{343}, \frac{1}{64}$

Chapter Test

Simplify each expression.

1. $\left(\frac{m}{4}\right)^{-2}$ $\frac{16}{m^2}$

2. $\frac{x^6}{x^{10}}$ $\frac{1}{x^4}$

3. $\left(\frac{3n^3}{6n^2}\right)^{-2}$ $\frac{4}{n^2}$

4. $\frac{(x + y)^3}{(x + y)^{-1}}$ $(x + y)^4$

5. $\frac{1}{y^{\frac{2}{3}}}$ $\frac{y^{\frac{1}{3}}}{y}$

6. $\frac{15}{5^{\frac{2}{3}}}$ $3 \cdot 5^{\frac{1}{3}}$

7. $\frac{p^2}{p^{-1}q^0}$ p^3

8. $\left(\frac{2y^{-2}}{3z}\right)^{-1}\left(\frac{m^2n}{y}\right)^0$ $\frac{3zy^2}{2}$

9. $\frac{r + s}{r^{\frac{1}{2}} + s^{\frac{1}{2}}}$

10. $\frac{7m}{m^{-3}} + \frac{3m^3}{m^{-1}}$ $10m^4$

11. $\frac{^-18t^3s^2}{6t^4s}$ $\frac{^-3s}{t}$

12. $\frac{x^{\frac{5}{3}}y + 3x^{-\frac{1}{3}}}{x^{\frac{2}{3}}}$ $\frac{x^2y + 3}{x}$

Evaluate each expression.

13. $\left(\frac{3}{2}\right)^{-4}\left(\frac{3}{2}\right)^2$ $\frac{4}{9}$

14. $27^{-\frac{4}{3}}$ $\frac{1}{81}$

15. $(\sqrt[3]{27})^2$ 9

16. $\frac{16}{4^{\frac{3}{2}}}$ 2 9. $\frac{r + s}{r - s}(r^{\frac{1}{2}} - s^{\frac{1}{2}})$

17. $\left(\frac{3^3}{4^8}\right)\left(\frac{4^2}{3}\right)$ $\frac{9}{4^6}$

18. $25^{\frac{3}{2}}$ 125

19. $\left(\frac{1}{64}\right)^{-\frac{2}{3}}$ 16

20. $243^{\frac{3}{5}}$ 27

Evaluate. Express each answer in scientific notation.

21. $(2.7 \times 10^{11})(3 \times 10^4)$ 8.1×10^{15}

22. $\frac{6.3 \times 10^{-4}}{1.7 \times 10^{-7}}$ 3.7×10^3

23. $\frac{72{,}000{,}000 \times 0.005}{0.0015}$ 2.4×10^8

24. $\frac{84{,}000{,}000 \times 0.0013}{0.021}$ 5.2×10^6

Express each of the following using exponents.

25. $\sqrt[3]{n^2}$ $n^{\frac{2}{3}}$

26. $\sqrt{a^6}$ a^3

27. $\sqrt[3]{8m^2r^7}$ $2m^{\frac{2}{3}}r^{\frac{7}{3}}$

28. $\sqrt[6]{49}$ $49^{\frac{1}{6}}$ or $7^{\frac{1}{3}}$

29. $\sqrt[3]{32} \cdot \sqrt[3]{2}$ 2^2

30. $\sqrt[4]{x^4y^6b^2}$ $xy^{\frac{3}{2}}b^{\frac{1}{2}}$

Solve each equation.

31. $y^{\frac{3}{2}} - 8 = 0$ 4

32. $b^{-\frac{2}{3}} = 9$ $\frac{1}{27}$

33. $t^{-\frac{3}{4}} = \frac{1}{8}$ 16

34. $w^{\frac{4}{3}} - 7w^{\frac{2}{3}} + 12 = 0$ 8, $\sqrt[3]{3}$

35. $x^{\frac{1}{2}} - 10x^{\frac{1}{4}} + 16 = 0$ 16, 4096

36. $m + \sqrt{3m - 2} = 4$ 2

Chapter

12

Exponential and Logarithmic Functions

Often, the best method to determine the age of very old objects is a process called carbon dating. This is done by measuring the amount of carbon and applying an exponential equation.

12-1　An Inverse Relation

Objective: To show that logarithms and exponentials are inverse relations.

In the table on the left, x is the exponent. Compute the power of 2 to find y.

x	$2^x = y$	y
$^-1$	$2^{-1} = y$	?
2	$2^2 = y$	?
3	$2^3 = y$	?
6	$2^6 = y$	?

Exponent to Power

y	$2^y = x$	x
?	$2^y = \dfrac{1}{2}$	$\dfrac{1}{2}$
?	$2^y = 4$	4
?	$2^y = 8$	8
?	$2^y = 64$	64

Exponent from Power

In the table on the right, the emphasis is shifted. You are given x as the value of the power. Work toward finding the exponent, y. In the relation $2^y = x$, y is called the **logarithm** of x. It is more conveniently written as $\log_2 x = y$. The equation $\log_2 x = y$ is read *the log of x to the base 2 equals* y. The logarithm is the exponent.

Exponential Equation　　　　　　　　　　　　　Logarithmic Equation

$$n = b^p \qquad\qquad p = \log_b n$$

exponent or logarithm
base
number

Definition of Logarithm

> Suppose b is a positive number other than 1 and n is a positive number. Then there is a number p such that $\log_b n = p$ if and only if $b^p = n$.

Study the table of corresponding equations.

Exponential Equation	Logarithmic Equation
$6^2 = 36$	$\log_6 36 = 2$
$10^4 = 10{,}000$	$\log_{10} 10{,}000 = 4$
$3^0 = 1$	$\log_3 1 = 0$
$2^{-3} = \dfrac{1}{8}$	$\log_2 \dfrac{1}{8} = {}^-3$
$4^{\frac{1}{2}} = 2$	$\log_4 2 = \dfrac{1}{2}$

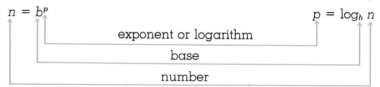

examples

1 **Solve the equation $\log_2 64 = y$.**

$\log_2 64 = y$ implies that $2^y = 64$.
Since $2^6 = 64$, $y = 6$.

The solution is 6.

2 **Solve the equation $\log_9 x = \frac{1}{2}$.**

$\log_9 x = \frac{1}{2}$ implies that $9^{\frac{1}{2}} = x$.

Since $9^{\frac{1}{2}}$ or $\sqrt{9}$ is 3, $x = 3$.

The solution is 3.

3 **Solve the equation $\log_b 16 = 2$.**

$\log_b 16 = 2$ implies that $b^2 = 16$.
Since $4^2 = 16$, $b = 4$.

The solution is 4.

exercises

Max: 1–18, 1–54; **Avg:** 1–18, 1–53 odds; **Min:** 1–53 odds

Exploratory Change each equation to logarithmic form.

1. $3^3 = 27$ $\log_3 27 = 3$
2. $4^2 = 16$ $\log_4 16 = 2$
3. $2^{-3} = \frac{1}{8}$ $\log_2 (\frac{1}{8}) = -3$
4. $5^{-2} = \frac{1}{25}$ $\log_5 (\frac{1}{25}) = -2$
5. $10^3 = 1000$ $\log_{10} 1000 = 3$
6. $10^{-2} = 0.01$ $\log_{10} 0.01 = -2$

Change each equation to exponential form.

7. $\log_4 64 = 3$ $4^3 = 64$
8. $\log_3 9 = 2$ $3^2 = 9$
9. $\log_9 27 = \frac{3}{2}$ $9^{\frac{3}{2}} = 27$
10. $\log_3 \frac{1}{81} = -4$ $3^{-4} = \frac{1}{81}$
11. $\log_{10} 0.1 = -1$ $10^{-1} = 0.1$
12. $\log_{10} 0.0001 = -4$ $10^{-4} = 0.0001$

Evaluate each expression.

13. $\log_{10} 100$ 2
14. $\log_3 81$ 4
15. $\log_5 625$ 4
16. $\log_{11} 121$ 2
17. $\log_2 \frac{1}{8}$ −3
18. $\log_3 \frac{1}{9}$ −2

Written Rewrite each equation in logarithmic form.

1. $3^4 = 81$ $\log_3 81 = 4$
2. $2^6 = 64$ $\log_2 64 = 6$
3. $5^3 = 125$ $\log_5 125 = 3$
4. $8^0 = 1$ $\log_8 1 = 0$
5. $4^{-2} = \frac{1}{16}$ $\log_4 (\frac{1}{16}) = ^-2$
6. $3^{-1} = \frac{1}{3}$ $\log_3 \frac{1}{3} = ^-1$
7. $2^{-4} = \frac{1}{16}$ $\log_2 \frac{1}{16} = ^-4$
8. $7^{-2} = \frac{1}{49}$ $\log_7 \frac{1}{49} = ^-2$
9. $3^{\frac{1}{2}} = \sqrt{3}$ $\log_3 \sqrt{3} = \frac{1}{2}$
10. $9^{\frac{3}{2}} = 27$ $\log_9 27 = \frac{3}{2}$
11. $36^{\frac{3}{2}} = 216$ $\log_{36} 216 = \frac{3}{2}$
12. $\left(\frac{1}{9}\right)^{-2} = 81$ $\log_{\frac{1}{9}} 81 = ^-2$

Rewrite each equation in exponential form.

13. $\log_2 32 = 5$ $2^5 = 32$
14. $\log_8 64 = 2$ $8^2 = 64$
15. $\log_{11} 121 = 2$ $11^2 = 121$
16. $\log_{13} 13 = 1$ $13^1 = 13$
17. $\log_5 1 = 0$ $5^0 = 1$
18. $\log_3 243 = 5$ $3^5 = 243$
19. $\log_{\frac{1}{2}} 16 = ^-4$ $(\frac{1}{2})^{-4} = 16$
20. $\log_8 4 = \frac{2}{3}$ $8^{\frac{2}{3}} = 4$
21. $\log_{10} \frac{1}{10} = ^-1$ $10^{-1} = \frac{1}{10}$
22. $\log_5 \frac{1}{25} = ^-2$ $5^{-2} = \frac{1}{25}$
23. $\log_{\frac{1}{3}} 81 = ^-4$ $(\frac{1}{3})^{-4} = 81$
24. $\log_{27} 3 = \frac{1}{3}$ $27^{\frac{1}{3}} = 3$

Find the value of each expression.

25. $\log_{10} 1000$ 3
26. $\log_6 36$ 2
27. $\log_{12} 144$ 2
28. $\log_{10} 0.01$ $^-2$
29. $\log_{\frac{1}{4}} 64$ $^-3$
30. $\log_4 2$ $\frac{1}{2}$
31. $\log_9 27$ $\frac{3}{2}$
32. $\log_8 16$ $\frac{4}{3}$
33. $\log_{\frac{1}{2}} 8$ $^-3$

Solve each equation.

34. $\log_b 49 = 2$ 7
35. $\log_b 64 = 3$ 4
36. $\log_6 x = 2$ 36
37. $\log_9 x = ^-1$ $\frac{1}{9}$
38. $\log_{\frac{1}{2}} 16 = x$ $^-4$
39. $\log_3 27 = x$ 3
40. $\log_b 81 = 4$ 3
41. $\log_b 18 = 1$ 18
42. $\log_5 x = ^-2$ $\frac{1}{25}$
43. $\log_3 x = ^-3$ $\frac{1}{27}$
44. $\log_{10} \sqrt{10} = x$ $\frac{1}{2}$
45. $\log_5 \sqrt{5} = x$ $\frac{1}{2}$
46. $\log_a \frac{1}{27} = ^-3$ 3
47. $\log_b 36 = ^-2$ $\frac{1}{6}$
48. $\log_{\frac{1}{2}} x = ^-6$ 64
49. $\log_4 x = -\frac{1}{2}$ $\frac{1}{2}$
50. $\log_2 x = ^-4$ $\frac{1}{16}$
51. $\log_{\sqrt{3}} x = 6$ 27
52. $\log_{\sqrt{3}} 27 = x$ 6
53. $\log_x \sqrt{5} = \frac{1}{4}$ 25
54. $\log_x \sqrt[3]{7} = \frac{1}{3}$ 7

Challenge

1. $\log_{\sqrt{x}} 6 = 2$ 6
2. $\log_{\frac{1}{2}} \frac{1}{16} = x^2$ ± 2
3. $\log_{\frac{3}{2}} \left(\frac{9}{4}\right)^2 = x$ $^-4$

12-2 Logarithmic Functions

Objective: To solve equations and evaluate expressions involving logarithms.

Study the graphs of $y = 2^x$ and $2^y = x$.

$y = 2^x$

x	y
$^-4$	$\frac{1}{16}$
$^-3$	$\frac{1}{8}$
$^-2$	$\frac{1}{4}$
$^-1$	$\frac{1}{2}$
0	1
1	2
2	4
3	8

$2^y = x$ or $y = \log_2 x$

x	y
$\frac{1}{16}$	$^-4$
$\frac{1}{8}$	$^-3$
$\frac{1}{4}$	$^-2$
$\frac{1}{2}$	$^-1$
1	0
2	1
4	2
8	3

The x and y values are reversed.

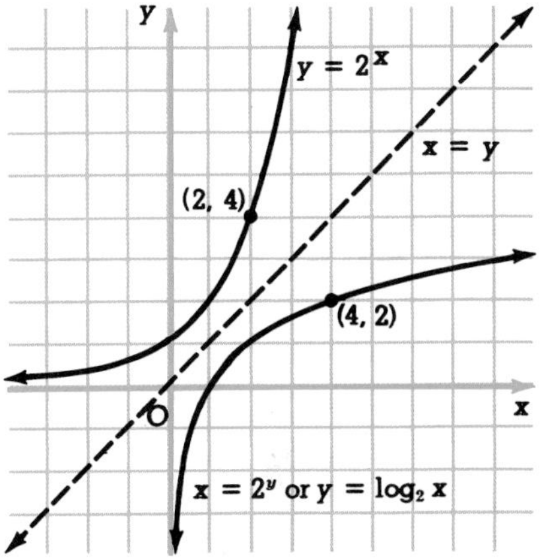

The domain of the logarithmic function is the set of all positive numbers. The range is all real numbers.

From the graph, $y = \log_2 x$ appears to be a function. A vertical line will not intersect the graph in more than one point. Both graphs are symmetrical with respect to the diagonal line $y = x$. For $y = 2^x$, y cannot be negative. For $y = \log_2 x$, x cannot be negative. Both graphs are smooth, unbroken, and continually increasing. By comparing points, such as (2, 4) and (4, 2), you can see that the functions are inverses of each other.

Thus, both $y = b^x$ and its inverse $y = \log_b x$ are functions. Also, the property of equality holds for both exponential and logarithmic functions.

Suppose b is a positive number other than 1. Then $b^{x_1} = b^{x_2}$ if and only if $x_1 = x_2$. Also, $\log_b x_1 = \log_b x_2$ if and only if $x_1 = x_2$.

Property of Equality for Exponential and Logarithmic Functions

example 1

Solve the equation $\log_2 (x^2 - 1) = \log_2 8$.

$\log_2 (x^2 - 1) = \log_2 8$

$x^2 - 1 = 8$ *Property of equality of logarithms*

$x^2 - 9 = 0$

$(x - 3)(x + 3) = 0$

$x - 3 = 0$ or $x + 3 = 0$

$x = 3$ or $x = {}^-3$

The solutions are 3 and $^-3$.

You know that $y = b^x$ and $y = \log_b x$ are inverse functions. Two applications of the property of inverse functions, $f(f^{-1}(x)) = x$, are given below.

same *same*

$3^{\log_3 9} = 3^2$ or 9 and $\log_4 4^2 = \log_4 16$ or 2

Emphasize these statements. $b^{\log_b x} = x$ and $\log_b b^x = x$

examples 2

Evaluate the expression $\log_7 7^4$.

$\log_7 7^4 = 4$

The value of the expression is 4.

3

Solve the equation $3^{\log_3 x} = 3x - 4$.

$3^{\log_3 x} = 3x - 4$

$x = 3x - 4$

$x = 2$ The solution is 2.

exercises

Max: 1–12, 1–38; Avg: 1–12, 1–37 odds; Min: 1–37 odds

Exploratory **Evaluate each expression.**

1. $\log_5 5^2$ 2
2. $\log_9 9^4$ 4
3. $9^{\log_9 2}$ 2
4. $7^{\log_7 3}$ 3

5. $\log_b b^4$ 4
6. $\log_m m^x$ x
7. $b^{\log_b 5}$ 5
8. $8^{\log_8 x}$ x

Solve each equation.

9. $\log_2 x = \log_2 4$ 4
10. $\log_4 10 = \log_4 2x$ 5
11. $\log_3 (x + 1) = \log_3 (2x)$ 1
12. $\log_7 (x^2 - 1) = \log_7 3$ $^-2$ → ± 2

Written **Evaluate each expression.**

1. $\log_4 4^3$ 3
2. $\log_r r^4$ 4
3. $6^{\log_6 7}$ 7
4. $9^{\log_9 5}$ 5
5. $\log_n n^5$ 5
6. $3^{\log_3 21}$ 21

Solve each equation.

7. $\log_3 (2x + 1) = \log_3 (3x - 6)$ 7
8. $\log_{10} (4 + y) = \log_{10} (2y)$ 4
9. $\log_{10} (3n) = \log_{10} (n + 2)$ 1
10. $\log_4 (2x - 3) = \log_4 (x + 2)$ 5
11. $\log_3 (3y - 1) = \log_3 (y + 4)$ 2.5
12. $\log_7 (5x - 1) = \log_7 (3x + 7)$ 4
13. $\log_{10} (x^2 + 36) = \log_{10} 100$ ± 8
14. $\log_{10} (x - 1)^2 = \log_{10} 0.01$ 1.1 or 0.9
15. $\log_9 (x^2 + 9x) = \log_9 10$ 1 or $^-10$
16. $\log_5 (4x - 4) = \log_5 100$ 26

Graph each pair of equations on the same set of axes.

17. $y = 3^x$ and $y = \log_3 x$
18. $y = \left(\frac{1}{2}\right)^x$ and $y = \log_{\frac{1}{2}} x$
19. $y = 4^x$ and $y = \log_4 x$
20. $y = 10^x$ and $y = \log_{10} x$

For graphs of problems 17–20, see the Teacher's Guide.

Show that each statement is true. For answers to problems 21–38, see the Teacher's Guide.

21. $\log_4 4 + \log_4 16 = \log_4 64$
22. $\log_3 27 + \log_3 3 = \log_3 81$
23. $\log_2 32 - \log_2 4 = \log_2 8$
24. $\log_6 36 - \log_6 6 = \log_6 6$
25. $\log_3 27 = 3 \log_3 3$
26. $\log_4 16 = 2 \log_4 4$
27. $\frac{1}{2} \log_3 81 = \log_3 9$
28. $\frac{1}{3} \log_5 25 = 2 \log_5 \sqrt[3]{5}$
29. $\log_2 8 \cdot \log_8 2 = 1$
30. $\log_5 25 \cdot \log_{25} 5 = 1$
31. $\log_{10} [\log_3(\log_4 64)] = 0$
32. $\log_2 64 = 3 \log_8 64$
33. $\log_3 81 = \frac{4}{3} \log_2 8$
34. $\log_4 [\log_2 (\log_3 81)] = \frac{1}{2}$

Solve each equation.

35. $6^{\log_6 x^2} = x + 30$
36. $3^{\log_3 x^3} = \frac{1}{27}$
37. $\log_2 [\log_4 (\log_3 x)] = {}^-1$
38. $\log_{10} [\log_2 (\log_7 x)] = 0$

Using Algebra

Earthquakes

A logarithmic scale called the **Richter scale** is used to measure the strength of an earthquake. Each increase of one on the Richter scale corresponds to a ten-times increase in intensity. In other words, an earthquake that registers 8 on the Richter scale is ten times as intense as an earthquake that registers 7. An earthquake that registers 9 is ten times as intense as the one registering 8, and one hundred times as intense as the one registering 7.

The table below explains the effects of earthquakes of various intensities.

Richter Number	Effect
1	only detectable by seismograph
2	hanging lamps sway
3	can be felt
4	glass breaks, buildings shiver
5	furniture falls
6	wooden houses damaged
7	buildings fall
8	catastrophic damage

On April 18, 1906, in San Francisco, California, was one of the worst California earthquakes in recent history. It caused a fire that burned more than 4 square miles in area. Hundreds of people died. There was from 250 to 300 million dollars worth of property damage. This earthquake measured 8.3 on the Richter scale.

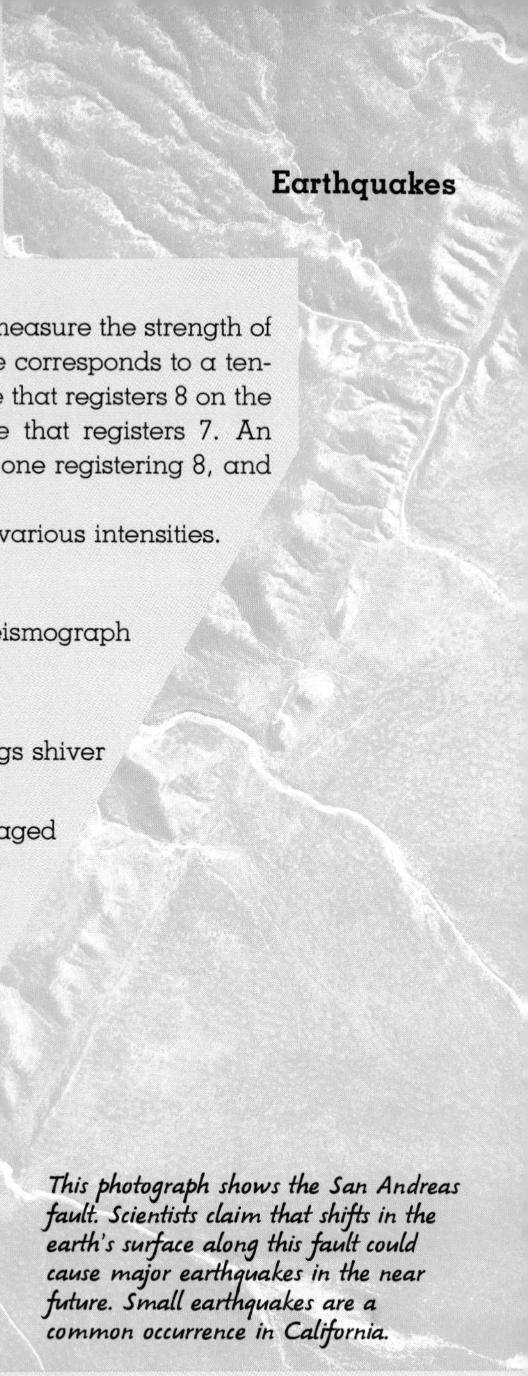

This photograph shows the San Andreas fault. Scientists claim that shifts in the earth's surface along this fault could cause major earthquakes in the near future. Small earthquakes are a common occurrence in California.

Exercises Solve each problem.

1. An earthquake with a rating of 7 is how much stronger than one with a rating of 6?
2. An earthquake with a rating of 7 is how much stronger than one with a rating of 4?
3. Which was stronger, the San Francisco earthquake or the Alaska earthquake which rated 8.4?
4. Which was stronger, the Ecuador earthquake which rated 8.9 or the Alaska earthquake?
5. The San Francisco earthquake was how much weaker than the Ecuador earthquake?

1. 10 times **2.** 1000 times **3.** Alaska **4.** Ecuador **5.** 0.5

12-3 Properties of Logarithms

Objective: To learn and apply the properties of logarithms.

Logarithms are exponents. Thus, the properties of logarithms can be derived from the properties of exponents.

For example, to find the product of powers, add exponents. Thus, to find the logarithm of a product, add logarithms.

$$\begin{aligned}\log_2 (8 \cdot 32) &= \log_2 (2^3 \cdot 2^5)\\ &= \log_2 (2^{3+5})\\ &= 3 + 5\\ &= \log_2 2^3 + \log_2 2^5\\ &= \log_2 8 + \log_2 32\end{aligned}$$

Similarly, to find the quotient of powers, subtract exponents. And, to find the logarithm of a quotient, subtract logarithms.

$$\begin{aligned}\log_2 (32 \div 8) &= \log_2 (2^5 \div 2^3)\\ &= \log_2 (2^{5-3})\\ &= 5 - 3\\ &= \log_2 2^5 - \log_2 2^3\\ &= \log_2 32 - \log_2 8\end{aligned}$$

Finally, to find the power of a power, multiply exponents. Thus, to find the logarithm of a power, multiply by the exponent.

$$\begin{aligned}\log_2 8^4 &= \log_2 (2^3)^4\\ &= \log_2 2^{3 \cdot 4}\\ &= 3 \cdot 4\\ &= (\log_2 2^3) \cdot 4\\ &= (\log_2 8) \cdot 4\\ &= 4 \log_2 8\end{aligned}$$

These properties can be summarized in the following way.

Suppose m and n are positive numbers, b is a positive number other than 1, and p is any number. Then the following properties hold.

Product Property: $\log_b m \cdot n = \log_b m + \log_b n$

Quotient Property: $\log_b \frac{m}{n} = \log_b m - \log_b n$

Power Property: $\log_b m^p = p \cdot \log_b m$

Properties of Logarithms

examples

1 **Given $\log_3 5 = 1.465$, estimate $\log_3 45$ and $\log_3 25$.**

$$\log_3 45 = \log_3 (3^2 \cdot 5)$$
$$= \log_3 3^2 + \log_3 5$$
$$= 2 + 1.465 \quad \text{or} \quad 3.465$$

$$\log_3 25 = \log_3 5^2$$
$$= 2 \cdot \log_3 5$$
$$= 2(1.465) \quad \text{or} \quad 2.930$$

2 **Solve the equation $\log_{12} 72 - \log_{12} 9 = \log_{12} 4m$.**

$$\log_{12} 72 - \log_{12} 9 = \log_{12} 4m$$

$$\log_{12} \frac{72}{9} = \log_{12} 4m$$ *Quotient property of logarithms*

$$8 = 4m$$ *Property of equality of logarithms*

$$2 = m$$

Check: $\log_{12} 72 - \log_{12} 9 = \log_{12} 4m$

$$\log_{12} 72 - \log_{12} 9 \stackrel{?}{=} \log_{12} 4 \cdot 2$$

$$\log_{12} 8 = \log_{12} 8$$ The solution is 2.

3 **Solve the equation $\log_3 (y + 4) + \log_3 (y - 4) = 2$.**

$$\log_3 (y + 4) + \log_3 (y - 4) = 2$$

$$\log_3 (y + 4)(y - 4) = 2$$ *Product property of logarithms*

$$(y + 4)(y - 4) = 3^2$$ *Definition of logarithm*

$$y^2 - 16 = 9$$
$$y^2 - 25 = 0$$
$$(y - 5)(y + 5) = 0$$
$$y - 5 = 0 \quad \text{or} \quad y + 5 = 0$$
$$y = 5 \quad \text{or} \quad y = {}^-5$$

Check: $\log_3 (y + 4) + \log_3 (y - 4) = 2$

$$\log_3 (5 + 4) + \log_3 (5 - 4) \stackrel{?}{=} 2$$
$$\log_3 9 + \log_3 1 \stackrel{?}{=} 2$$
$$2 + 0 = 2$$

$$\log_3 (y + 4) + \log_3 (y - 4) = 2$$
$$\log_3 ({}^-5 + 4) + \log_3 ({}^-5 - 4) \stackrel{?}{=} 2$$
$$\log_3 ({}^-1) + \log_3 ({}^-9) \stackrel{?}{=} 2$$

log is not defined for negative numbers

The only solution is 5.

4 **Show that $\log_b m \cdot n = \log_b m + \log_b n$ for m, n, and b positive and $b \neq 1$.**

$$b^{\log_b m} = m, \quad b^{\log_b n} = n, \quad b^{\log_b m \cdot n} = m \cdot n$$ *Property of inverse function*

$$b^{\log_b m \cdot n} = m \cdot n$$

$$= b^{\log_b m} \cdot b^{\log_b n}$$ *Substitute $b^{\log_b m}$ for m and $b^{\log_b n}$ for n.*

$$= b^{\log_b m + \log_b n}$$ *Add the exponents.*

$$\log_b m \cdot n = \log_b m + \log_b n$$ *Property of equality of exponents*

exercises

Max: 1–18, 1–30; Avg: 1–18, 1–29 odds; Min: 1–29 odds

Exploratory Solve each equation.

1. $\log_2 3 + \log_2 7 = \log_2 x$ 21
2. $\log_5 4 + \log_5 x = \log_5 36$ 9
3. $\log_4 18 - \log_4 x = \log_4 6$ 3
4. $\log_3 56 - \log_3 8 = \log_3 x$ 7
5. $2 \log_7 3 + 3 \log_7 2 = \log_7 x$ 72
6. $2 \log_6 4 - \frac{1}{3} \log_6 8 = \log_6 x$ 8

Express each logarithm as the sum or difference of simpler logarithmic expressions.

7. $\log_3 (xy)$ $\log_3 x + \log_3 y$
8. $\log_4 (rst)$ $\log_4 r + \log_4 s + \log_4 t$
9. $\log_2 (m^4 y)$
10. $\log_2 \left(\frac{y}{r}\right)$ $\log_2 y - \log_2 r$
11. $\log_b \left(\frac{\sqrt{x}}{p}\right)$ $\frac{1}{2} \log_b x - \log_b p$
12. $\log_4 \left(\frac{xy}{z}\right)$
13. $\log_3 (5\sqrt[3]{a})$ $\log_3 5 + \frac{1}{3} \log_3 a$
14. $\log_{10} (ac)^2$ $2 \log_{10} a + 2 \log_{10} c$
15. $\log_2 (ax^{\frac{1}{2}})$

9. $4 \log_2 m + \log_2 y$ 12. $\log_4 x + \log_4 y - \log_4 z$ 15. $\log_2 a + \frac{1}{2} \log_2 x$

Evaluate each expression.

16. $5^{\log_5 3 + \log_5 2}$ 6
17. $7^{\log_7 8 - \log_7 4}$ 2
18. $6^{3 \log_6 2}$ 8

Written **Use $\log_{10} 3 = 0.4771$ and $\log_{10} 7 = 0.8451$ to estimate each expression.**

1. $\log_{10} 21$ 1.3222
2. $\log_{10} \frac{7}{3}$ 0.3680
3. $\log_{10} 27$ 1.4313
4. $\log_{10} 63$ 1.7993
5. $\log_{10} 30$ 1.4771
6. $\log_{10} 0.03$ $^{-}1.5229$
7. $\log_{10} (70 \cdot 3)$ 2.3222
8. $\log_{10} 4.9$ 0.6902

Solve each equation.

9. $\log_3 7 + \log_3 x = \log_3 14$ 2
10. $\log_2 10 - \log_2 t = \log_2 2$ 5
11. $\log_3 y - \log_3 2 = \log_3 12$ 24
12. $\log_3 14 + \log_3 m = \log_3 42$ 3
13. $\log_5 x = 3 \log_5 7$ 343
14. $\log_2 p = \frac{1}{2} \log_2 81$ 9
15. $\log_9 x = \frac{1}{2} \log_9 144 - \frac{1}{3} \log_9 8$ 6
16. $\log_7 m = \frac{1}{3} \log_7 64 + \frac{1}{2} \log_7 121$ 44
17. $\log_{10} 7 + \log_{10} (n - 2) = \log_{10} 6n$ 14
18. $\log_{10} (m + 3) - \log_{10} m = \log_{10} 4$ 1
19. $\log_{10} x + \log_{10} x + \log_{10} x = \log_{10} 27$ 3
20. $4 \log_5 x - \log_5 4 = \log_5 4$ 2
21. $\log_4 (x + 2) + \log_4 (x - 4) = 2$ 6
22. $\log_4 (y - 1) + \log_4 (y - 1) = 2$ 5
23. $\log_{10} (y - 1) + \log_{10} (y + 2) = \log_7 7$ 3
24. $\log_{10} y + \log_{10} (y + 21) = 2$ 4
25. $\log_4 (x + 3) + \log_4 (x - 3) = 2$ 5
26. $\log_2 (9x + 5) - \log_2 (x^2 - 1) = 2$ 3
27. $\log_8 (m + 1) - \log_8 m = \log_8 4$ $\frac{1}{3}$
28. $\log_2 (y + 2) - 1 = \log_2 (y - 2)$ 6

Show that each of the following is true. See student work.

29. the quotient property on page **335**
30. the power property on page **335**

Reading Algebra

Cloze Test

A **cloze test** is one method to test your comprehension of reading material. In a cloze test, a section of text is chosen. The entire first sentence is given. One of the first five words in the second sentence is replaced by a blank. Then every fifth word is replaced by a blank. You must decide which words are missing. You may have to guess at some of the words, but you can find many clues in the material that remains. The following section is taken from this chapter.

Every logarithm has two parts, the characteristic and the mantissa. The ___(a)___ is the logarithm of ___(b)___ number between 1 and ___(c)___. The characteristic is the ___(d)___ of 10 by which ___(e)___ number is multiplied when ___(f)___ number is expressed in ___(g)___ notation.

The table of ___(h)___ is really a table ___(i)___ mantissas. You must supply the characteristic.

From the first sentence, you learn that this section is about logarithms and the two parts of logarithms. The third sentence is talking about the characteristic. Perhaps the blank marked **a** should be *mantissa*. Then the second sentence would read, *The mantissa is the logarithm of* ___(b)___ *number between 1 and* ___(c)___. The blank marked ***b*** could be *a* and the blank marked **c** must be *10*. The characteristic is the power of 10, so the blank marked **d** must be *power*.

Try to fill in the remaining blanks. *Your answers should be (e) that, (f) the, (g) scientific, (h) logarithms, and (i) of.*

You may check your comprehension of any lesson by asking a friend to copy a section of that lesson, leaving a blank for every fifth word.

Exercises Copy the following sentences and fill in each blank.

Logarithms were invented to make computation easier. With logarithms, ________ converts to addition; division ________ to subtraction. What is ________ is a table of ________ for some convenient base. ________ 10 is most useful ________ our numbers are in ________ 10. Logarithms to base ________ are called common logarithms. ________ is written as log x. ________ table of common logarithms ________ numbers between 1 and ________ may be found on ________ 540. To find log 1.23, ________ across the row labeled ________ and down the column ________ 3.

For numbers greater ________ 10 or less than ________, scientific notation and the ________ of logarithms are used ________ find the ________.

multiplication, converts, needed, logarithms, Base, because, base, 10, $\text{Log}_{10}\, x$, A, for, 10, page, read, 12, labeled, than, 1, properties, to, logarithms

12-4 Common Logarithms

Objective: To find logarithms and antilogarithms using tables.

Logarithms were invented to make computation easier. With logarithms, multiplication converts to addition and division converts to subtraction. What is needed is a table of logarithms for some convenient base. Base 10 is most useful because our number system is based on 10. Logarithms to base 10 are called **common logarithms.** $\log_{10} x$ is written as $\log x$.

The values in the table are rounded to the nearest ten-thousandth.

A table of common logarithms for numbers between 1 and 10 may be found on pages 540 and 541. To find log 1.23, read across the row labeled 12 and down the column labeled 3.

Common Logarithms of Numbers

n	0	1	2	3	4
10	0000	0043	0086	0128	0170
11	0414	0453	0492	0531	0569
12	0792	0828	0864	0899	0934

$\log 1.23 = 0.0899$

For numbers greater than 10 or less than 1, scientific notation and the properties of logarithms are used to find the logarithm.

example 1

Find log 745,000 to the nearest ten-thousandth.

$$745{,}000 = 7.45 \times 10^5 \quad \textit{Scientific notation}$$
$$\log 745{,}000 = \log (7.45 \times 10^5) \quad \textit{Property of equality of logarithms}$$
$$= \log 7.45 + \log 10^5 \quad \textit{Product property of logarithms}$$
$$= \log 7.45 + 5$$
$$= 0.8722 + 5 \text{ or } 5.8722 \quad \log 7.45 = 0.8722$$

The log of 745,000 is 5.8722.

Every logarithm has two parts, the **characteristic** and the **mantissa.** The mantissa is the logarithm of a number between 1 and 10. The characteristic is the power of 10 by which that number is multiplied when the number is expressed in scientific notation.

Mantissas range from 0 to 1.

$$\log 745{,}000 = 5.\underline{8722}$$

characteristic (5) — *mantissa* (8722)

$745{,}000 = 7.45 \times 10^5$ — *characteristic* (5)

The table of logarithms is really a table of mantissas. You must supply the characteristic.

example 2

Find log 0.000524.

$\log 0.000524 = \log(5.24 \times 10^{-4})$ *Substitution*

$= \log 5.24 + \log 10^{-4}$ *Product property*

$= 0.7193 + (^-4)$

$= 0.7193 - 4$

The logarithm is approximately $0.7193 - 4$.

To avoid a negative mantissa, do *not* add the $^-4$ and 0.7193. The negative characteristic may be written in many ways.

A third way is $\underline{4}.7193$.

$\log 0.000524 = 0.7193 - 4$

$\log 0.000524 = 6.7193 - 10$ *Note $6 - 10 = {}^-4$.*

We usually use $6 - 10$ for $^-4$. But, in some cases it may be more convenient to use another difference such as $26 - 30$.

Sometimes a logarithm is given and you must find the number. To find the number, use the table of mantissas in reverse. The number is called the **antilogarithm**. *If $\log x = a$, then $x = \text{antilog } a$.*

example 3

If log x = 3.5821, find x.

$\log x = 3.5821$

$x = \text{antilog } 3.5821$ *3 is the characteristic and 0.5821 is the mantissa.*

$= (\text{antilog } 0.5821) \times 10^3$

Find antilog 0.5821 in the table of mantissas. It is in the row labeled 38 and the column labeled 2.

n	0	1	2	3	4
10	0000	0043	0086	0128	0170
37	5682	5694	5705	5717	5729
38	5798	5809	5821	5832	5843
39	5911	5922	5933	5944	5955

$x = (\text{antilog } 0.5821) \times 10^3$

$= 3.82 \times 10^3$

$= 3820$ The solution is 3820.

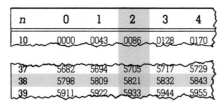

exercises

Max: 1–24, 1–24, Excursion; **Avg:** 1–24, 1–23 odds; **Min:** 1–23 odds

Exploratory **If log 483 = 2.6839, find each number.**

1. characteristic of log 483 2
2. mantissa of log 483 0.6839
3. log 48.3 1.6839
4. log 4830 3.6839
5. log 0.004830 0.6839 − 3
6. antilog 0.6839 4.83
7. antilog 5.6839 483,000
8. antilog 0.6839 − 4 0.000483

State the characteristic of the logarithm of each number. Then use the table on pages 540 and 541 to find the logarithm.

9. 47.5 1; 1.6767
10. 370 2; 2.5682
11. 4.61 0; 0.6637
12. 0.076 $^{-}2$; 0.8808 − 2
13. 0.209 $^{-}1$; 0.3201 − 1
14. 6870 3; 3.8370
15. 55 1; 1.7404
16. 0.00213 $^{-}3$; 0.3284 − 3

State the characteristic of each logarithm and use the table to find the antilogarithm.

17. 1.5527 1; 35.70
18. 3.8096 3; 6450
19. 0.8376 − 2 $^{-}2$; 0.0688
20. 0.6263 − 3 $^{-}3$; 0.00423
21. 4.5955 4; 39,400
22. 0.9513 − 5 $^{-}5$; 0.0000894
23. 0.7910 − 1 $^{-}1$; 0.618
24. 2.1106 2; 129

Written **Use the table of logarithms to find the logarithm of each number.**

1. 58.2 1.7649
2. 715 2.8543
3. 9.58 0.9814
4. 0.000741 0.8698 − 4
5. 7420 3.8704
6. 0.3 0.4771 − 1
7. 0.00211 0.3243 − 3
8. 841,000 5.9248
9. 0.0385 0.5855 − 2
10. 0.671 0.8267 − 1
11. 62,700 4.7973
12. 0.113 0.0531 − 1

Find the antilog of each logarithm.

13. 1.0899 12.3
14. 0.8727 − 2 0.0746
15. 3.9581 9080
16. 0.7846 − 1 0.609
17. 0.9542 − 2 0.09
18. 5.7451 556,000
19. 9.2014 − 10 0.159
20. 0.1673 1.47
21. 5.7168 521,000
22. 1.3075 20.3
23. 3.6656 4630
24. 0.6304 4.27

Logarithms

Excursions in Algebra

Many handheld calculators have logarithmic and exponential functions. If you have such a calculator, use it to find the logarithms in problems **1-12.** Check your answers against the table of mantissas on pages 540 and 541. Explain why the calculator logarithms for numbers less than 1 are different than the logarithms (mantissas) in the table.

To find the antilogarithm, use the exponential key y^x for base 10. To find the antilog of 1.0899 use the keys in the following order.

[1] [0] [y^x] [1] [.] [0] [8] [9] [9]

Use the calculator to find the antilogarithms in problems **13-24.** Check your answers with the table. For logarithms with a negative characteristic, find the antilog of the mantissa only. Why?

12-5 Interpolation

Objective: To approximate logarithms and antilogarithms using interpolation.

The table of logarithms in this text includes mantissas of numbers with 3 significant digits. You can approximate logarithms of numbers with 4 significant digits by a method known as **interpolation.**

examples

1

Approximate the value of log 1.327.

n	0	1	2	3	4
10	0000	0043	0086	0128	0170
11	0414	0453	0492	0531	0569
12	0792	0828	0864	0899	0934
13	1139	1173	1206	1239	1271

The logarithm of 1.327 must be between log 1.32 and log 1.33.

Form a proportion of differences.

	number	mantissa	
	1.320	0.1206	
0.007 = 1.327 − 1.320 → 0.007	1.327	unknown	d ← *d = unknown − 0.1206*
0.0100 = 1.330 − 1.320 → 0.0100	1.330	0.1239	0.0033 ← *0.0033 = 0.1239 − 0.1206*

$$\frac{0.007}{0.0100} = \frac{d}{0.0033}$$

$0.00231 = d$

$0.0023 = d$ *The log tables are given in 4-place decimals. Round to 4 places.*

Since the table is increasing, add 0.0023 to the mantissa of 1.320.

$\log 1.327 = \log 1.320 + d$

$= 0.1206 + 0.0023$

$= 0.1229$ The logarithm of 1.327 is approximately 0.1229.

2

Approximate the value of log 0.001327.

$\log 0.001327 = \log (1.327 \times 10^{-3})$

$= \log 1.327 + \log 10^{-3}$

$= 0.1229 - 3$ *The value of log 1.327 was found in Example 1.*

The logarithm of 0.001327 is about $0.1229 - 3$.

Interpolation can also be used to find an antilogarithm that cannot be obtained directly from the table.

example 3

Find antilog 2.4356.

antilog 2.4356 = (antilog 0.4356) × 10^2

n	0	1	2	3	4
10	0000	0043	0086	0128	0170
26	4150	4166	4183	4200	4216
27	4314	4330	4346	4362	4378
28	4472	4487	4502	4518	4533

In the table of mantissas 4356 lies between 4346 and 4362.

Again, form a proportion of differences.

	mantissa	antilog	
0.0016 (0.0010)	0.4346	2.72	0.01 (d)
	0.4356	unknown	
	0.4362	2.73	

$$\frac{0.0010}{0.0016} = \frac{d}{0.01}$$

$0.00625 = d$

$0.006 = d$

In finding antilogs, interpolation is accurate for one more digit than given in the table.

Since the table is increasing, add 0.006 to 2.72.

antilog 2.4356 = (antilog 0.4356) × 10^2
= (2.72 + 0.006) × 10^2
= 2.726 × 10^2
= 272.6 The antilog of 2.4356 is about 272.6.

exercises

Max: 1–8, 1–40, Excursion; **Avg:** 1–8, 1–39 odds; **Min:** 1–39 odds

Exploratory The logarithms of what two numbers would you use to find the logarithm of each number?

1. 7.413 7.41, 7.42
2. 32,520 32,500, 32,600
3. 0.0007463 0.000746, 0.000747
4. 0.01234 0.0123, 0.0124

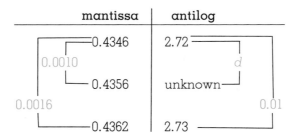

The antilog of each logarithm lies between what two numbers?

5. 0.6209 4.17, 4.18	**6.** 2.7295 536, 537	**7.** 3.9788 9,520, 9,530	**8.** 0.7885 − 2 0.0614, 0.0615

Written Interpolate to find the logarithm of each number.

1. 5.273 0.7221	**2.** 7.184 0.8564	**3.** 27.53 1.4398	**4.** 604.7 2.7815
5. 0.1952 0.2905 − 1	**6.** 0.07635 0.8828 − 2	**7.** 0.003148 0.4980 − 3	**8.** 7.003 0.8453
9. 4167 3.6198	**10.** 60.06 1.7786	**11.** 329.4 2.5177	**12.** 19.79 1.2964
13. 0.04729 0.6748 − 2	**14.** 8.871 0.9480	**15.** 5.008 0.6997	**16.** 0.005364 0.7295 − 3
17. 80.08 1.9035	**18.** 0.7214 0.8582 − 1	**19.** 2148×10^3 6.3320	**20.** 305.4×10^{-4} 0.4849 −

Interpolate to find the antilog of each logarithm.

21. 0.4861 3.063	**22.** 0.5506 3.553	**23.** 3.5748 3757	**24.** 2.7792 601.4
25. 0.3353 − 2 0.02164	**23.** 0.6173 − 3 0.004143	**27.** 0.6409 − 2 0.04374	**28.** 0.4399 − 3 0.002754
29. 3.4193 2,626	**30.** 4.2173 16,490	**31.** 0.5915 − 2 0.03904	**32.** 0.6778 − 3 0.004762
33. 0.1177 − 3 0.001311	**34.** 0.8787 − 2 0.07563	**35.** 2.5082 322.3	**36.** 5.5958 394,300
37. 4.6279 42,450	**38.** 3.4170 2,612	**39.** 0.9172 − 3 0.008264	**40.** 0.5688 − 4 0.0003705

These answers were computed by calculator.
Interpolation answers may differ by ±0.0001.

Excursions in Algebra

Computation Using Logarithms

Before the invention of handheld calculators, logarithms were often used to do computation.

Example Evaluate $\dfrac{(673)(549)(13.82)}{147{,}900}$.

Let $A = \dfrac{(673)(549)(13.82)}{147{,}900}$.

$$\begin{aligned}
\text{Then, } \log A &= \log \left[\frac{(673)(549)(13.82)}{147{,}900}\right] \\
&= \log 673 + \log 549 + \log 13.82 - \log 147{,}900 \\
&= 2.8280 + 2.7396 + 1.1405 - 5.1700 \\
&= 1.5381 \\
\text{And, } A &= \text{antilog } (1.5381) \\
&= 34.52
\end{aligned}$$

The value is about 34.52.

Exercises Use logarithms to evaluate each expression.

1. $\dfrac{(812)(41.5)}{431}$ 78.19
2. $\dfrac{(71.63)(313.4)}{(489.2)}$ 45.89
3. $\dfrac{(665)(899)(0.000172)}{(0.00035)(491)}$ 598.4

12–6 Calculation of Powers and Roots

Objective: To use logarithms to compute powers and roots.

The development of calculators has greatly reduced the need for logarithmic tables. However, finding powers and roots on some calculators is often complicated or impossible. You may find that some problems are easier to solve if logarithms are used.

examples

1 **Use logarithms to estimate the value of $(67.1)^5$.**

$$\begin{aligned}
\text{Let } A &= (67.1)^5 \\
\text{Then, } \log A &= \log (67.1)^5 \\
&= 5 \log 67.1 \\
&= 5(1.8267) \\
&= 9.1335 \\
A &= \text{antilog } 9.1335 \\
&= \text{antilog } (0.1335 + 9) \\
&= (\text{antilog } 0.1335) \times 10^9 \\
&= 1.360 \times 10^9 \text{ or } 1{,}360{,}000{,}000
\end{aligned}$$

The value of $(67.1)^5$ is about 1,360,000,000.

2 **Use logarithms to estimate the value of $\sqrt[4]{0.0815}$.**

$$\begin{aligned}
\text{Let } A &= \sqrt[4]{0.0815} \\
\text{Then, } \log A &= \log \sqrt[4]{0.0815} \\
&= \frac{1}{4} \log 0.0815 \\
&= \frac{1}{4}(0.9112 - 2)
\end{aligned}$$

Since the multiplying factor is $\frac{1}{4}$, the negative characteristic should be a multiple of 4.

$$= \frac{1}{4}(2.9112 - 4)$$

$0.9112 - 2 = 2.9112 - 4$

$$\begin{aligned}
&= 0.7278 - 1 \\
A &= \text{antilog } (0.7278 - 1) \\
&= (\text{antilog } 0.7278) \times 10^{-1} \\
&= 5.343 \times 10^{-1} \\
&= 0.5343
\end{aligned}$$

The value of $\sqrt[4]{0.0815}$ is about 0.5343.

example 3

Estimate the value of $\sqrt[3]{\frac{(86.2)(9.1)^2}{43.71}}$.

The Excursion on page 344 shows how to calculate such expressions using logarithms.

$$\text{Let } A = \sqrt[3]{\frac{(86.2)(9.1)^2}{43.71}}$$

$$\begin{aligned}
\text{Then, } \log A &= \frac{1}{3} \log \left[\frac{(86.2)(9.1)^2}{43.71}\right] \\
&= \frac{1}{3} \log 163.3 \qquad \textit{Use calculator or logarithms to find the radicand.} \\
&= \frac{1}{3}(2.2129) \\
&= 0.7376 \\
A &= \text{antilog } 0.7376 \\
&= 5.465 \qquad \text{The value is about 5.465.}
\end{aligned}$$

Compound Interest Formula

Logarithms may be used to solve compound interest problems. In the compound interest formula, P is the investment, r is the interest rate, n is the number of times the interest is compounded yearly, t is the number of years of the investment, and A is the amount of money accumulated.

$$A = P\left(1 + \frac{r}{n}\right)^{nt}$$

example 4

Native Americans were paid \$24 for Manhattan Island in 1626. If this money had been invested at 6% compounded yearly, what would have been the value of this investment at the bicentennial in 1976 (350 years later)?

$$\begin{aligned}
A &= 24\left(1 + \frac{0.06}{1}\right)^{1 \cdot 350} \qquad \textit{Substitute 24 for P, 0.06 for r, 1 for n and 350 for t.} \\
&= 24(1.06)^{350} \\
\log A &= \log [24(1.06)^{350}] \\
&= \log 24 + 350 \log 1.06 \\
&= 1.3802 + 350(0.0253) \text{ or } 10.2352 \\
A &= \text{antilog } (10.2352) \\
&= (\text{antilog } 0.2352) \times 10^{10} \\
&= 1.719 \times 10^{10} \\
&= 17{,}190{,}000{,}000 \qquad \text{The value would be about \$17,190,000,000.}
\end{aligned}$$

exercises

Max: 1–20, 1–34, Excursion; **Avg:** 1–20, 1–33 odds; **Min:** 1–33 odds

Exploratory **State the logarithm of each power or root in the form $p \log m$.**

1. $(63.9)^3$ $3 \log 63.9$
2. $(49.2)^4$ $4 \log 49.2$
3. $(0.7425)^4$ $4 \log 0.7425$
4. $(0.1783)^5$ $5 \log 0.1783$
5. $(4173)^3$ $3 \log 4173$
6. $(1792)^5$ $5 \log 1792$
7. $\sqrt[4]{594}$ $\frac{1}{4} \log 594$
8. $\sqrt[3]{2079}$ $\frac{1}{3} \log 2079$
9. $(9.813)^{\frac{1}{4}}$ $\frac{1}{4} \log 9.813$
10. $(2.317)^{\frac{1}{2}}$ $\frac{1}{2} \log 2.317$
11. $\sqrt[3]{46^2}$ $\frac{2}{3} \log 46$
12. $\sqrt[5]{82^3}$ $\frac{3}{5} \log 82$

Assume each expression is to be evaluated using logarithms. What would be a convenient form for the characteristic?

13. $(0.0017)^{\frac{1}{3}}$ $0 - 3$
14. $(0.0912)^{\frac{1}{4}}$ $2 - 4$
15. $(0.00721)^{\frac{3}{5}}$ $2 - 5$
16. $(0.00219)^{\frac{2}{3}}$ $0 - 3$
17. $\sqrt[4]{0.0005}$ $0 - 4$
18. $\sqrt[5]{0.0007}$ $1 - 5$
19. $\sqrt[3]{-0.294}$ $2 - 3$
20. $\sqrt[3]{-0.391}$ $2 - 3$

For answers to problems **1-20**, see the Teacher's Guide.

Written **1-20.** Use logarithms to evaluate each expression in the Exploratory Exercises.

Evaluate each expression.

21. $\dfrac{\sqrt[3]{4923}}{462.7}$ 0.03677
22. $\dfrac{\sqrt[4]{84.37}}{321.5}$ 0.009427
23. $\sqrt[3]{(82.7)(4.93)}$ 7.415
24. $\sqrt{(408)(39.6)}$ 127.1
25. $\sqrt[3]{\dfrac{(82.7)(4.93)}{632}}$ 0.8641
26. $\sqrt[3]{\dfrac{(3.29)(63)^2}{5236}}$ 1.356

Solve each problem using logarithms.

27. Compute the value of \$100 invested for 10 years at 6% annual interest compounded semi-annually. \$180.30
28. Compute the value of \$100 invested for 10 years at 8% annual interest compounded quarterly. \$220.80
29. If \$2500 is invested in a bank paying 6% interest compounded quarterly, how much will be in the account at the end of 5 years? \$3,367
30. A pendulum of length l feet makes a single swing back and forth in t seconds where $t = \pi\sqrt{\dfrac{l}{32.16}}$. Find t when $l = 4.135$. 1.126 second

Natural Logarithms

Excursions in Algebra

Frequently, mathematicians and scientists need to solve problems involving a power of e ($e \approx 2.718$). For this reason logarithms to the base e are sometimes more convenient to use than common logarithms. Logarithms to the base e are called *natural logarithms* and are abbreviated ln. Therefore, $\log_e 5$ is written ln 5.

Let $e = 2.718$. Solve each equation using logarithms.

1. $x = e^{0.05}$ 1.051
2. $x = e^{0.06}$ 1.062
3. $x = e^{0.08}$ 1.083
4. $x = e^{0.09}$ 1.094

Talking with Computers

Artificial languages are languages that are used for particular kinds of communication. For example, musical notation and BASIC are both artificial languages. Natural languages are languages that people use in everyday communication. For example, English and Swahili are natural languages.

Some computer scientists are attempting to teach natural languages to computers. During the 1950's, people tried to program computers to translate material from one natural language to another. Many of these attempts were hopeless failures. For example, one program translated the following sentence into Russian and then back into English.

The spirit is willing, but the flesh is weak.

The peculiar result was as follows.

The wine is agreeable, but the meat has spoiled.

At present, many computer scientists are working on question-answering systems. They are attempting to program computers to *understand* the information given, and demonstrate their understanding by answering questions about the information. One experimental system, called the ELIZA program, is an example of how a computer can carry on an *apparently* meaningful conversation. In fact, with this program the computer understands nothing. Notice the problems that the computer has in the following conversation with ELIZA. Lines in capitals are the computer's.

*

```
Hello.
HOW DO YOU DO. PLEASE STATE YOUR PROBLEM.
I want a good example for my book.
YOUR BOOK.
Yes, my book about computers. Can you help me?
YOU'RE BEING SOMEWHAT SHORT WITH ME.
I didn't mean to be.
YOU SAY YOU DIDN'T MEAN TO BE.
That's right. What do you know about computers?
DO COMPUTERS WORRY YOU?
Not at all. I think they can be very useful.
CAN YOU ELABORATE ON THAT?
Computers play a vital role in the operation of
  our society.
WHY DO YOU MENTION COMPUTERS?
Because that is what the book is all about.
IS THAT THE REAL REASON?
Of course. Sometimes you are difficult to talk to.
WHAT MAKES YOU THINK I AM DIFFICULT TO TALK TO?
You answer in such short, stylized phrases.
WE WERE DISCUSSING YOU - NOT ME.
I thought we were discussing computers.
WHAT DO YOU THINK MACHINES HAVE TO DO WITH YOUR
  PROBLEM?
My only problem is to get you to carry on a
  reasonable conversation.
WHY DO YOU SAY YOUR ONLY PROBLEM IS TO GET I TO
  CARRY ON A RESONABLE CONVERSATION?
You don't use very good grammar.
OH, I DON'T USE VERY GOOD GRAMMAR.
That's right. Don't you know the difference
  between nominative and accusative?
YOU'RE NOT REALLY TALKING ABOUT ME - ARE YOU?
I really was, but I'm willing to change
  the subject.
DO YOU SAY YOU REALLY WAS FOR SOME SPECIAL REASON?
The reason is that I would like an interesting
  conversation in the book.
IN WHAT WAY?
So that the readers will not get bored with it.
I AM NOT SURE I UNDERSTAND YOU FULLY.
You don't understand very much, do you!
WHAT ARE YOUR FEELINGS NOW?
I feel that I'm about ready to give up.
TELL ME MORE ABOUT SUCH FEELINGS.
The page is almost full now, so I can end this
  interview.
SUPPOSE THE PAGE WERE NOT ALMOST FULL NOW?
Then we would have to continue this silliness a
  while longer.
PLEASE GO ON.
That's all there is to say. Don't you ever get
  tired?
PERHAPS THAT'S ALL THERE REALLY IS TO SAY.
Yes. Goodbye
YOU SEEM QUITE POSITIVE.
```

Since the invention of ELIZA in 1966, other systems which do have some understanding of what is going on have been invented. ARTIFICIAL PARANOID and WINOGRAD are two examples.

*from THE THINKING COMPUTER: MIND INSIDE MATTER by Bertram Raphael. W. H. Freeman and Company. Copyright © 1976.

12–7 Exponential Equations

Objective: To solve exponential and logarithmic equations.

Equations in which the variables appear as exponents are called **exponential equations.** Such equations can be solved by using logarithms.

examples

1 **Solve the equation $2^x = 27$.**

$$\begin{aligned} 2^x &= 27 \\ \log 2^x &= \log 27 \\ x \log 2 &= \log 27 \quad \textit{Power property} \\ x &= \frac{\log 27}{\log 2} \\ &= \frac{1.4314}{0.3010} \text{ or } 4.7555 \end{aligned}$$

Check: $2^4 = 16$, $2^{4.7555} = 27$, and $2^5 = 32$. *The check helps you determine if the solution is reasonable.*

Since $16 < 27 < 32$ and $4 < 4.7555 < 5$, the answer is within proper limits.

The solution is approximately 4.7555.

2 **Express $\log_3 35$ in terms of common logarithms. Then find its value.**

Let $x = \log_3 35$

Then, $3^x = 35$

$$\begin{aligned} \log 3^x &= \log 35 \\ x \log 3 &= \log 35 \quad \textit{Power property} \\ x &= \frac{\log 35}{\log 3} \end{aligned}$$

The logarithm may be expressed as $\frac{\log 35}{\log 3}$.

$$\begin{aligned} \log_3 35 &= \frac{\log 35}{\log 3} \\ &= \frac{1.5441}{0.4771} \text{ or } 3.2364 \end{aligned}$$

Check: $3^3 = 27$, $3^{3.2364} = 35$, and $3^4 = 81$.

Since $27 < 35 < 81$ and $3 < 3.2364 < 4$, the answer is within proper limits.

The value of $\log_3 35$ is approximately 3.2364.

Change of Bases

Suppose a, b, and n are positive numbers, and neither a nor b is 1. Then the following equation is true.

$$\log_a n = \frac{\log_b n}{\log_b a}$$

examples

3 **Find the value of $\log_4 8$ using the formula above.**

$$\log_4 8 = \frac{\log_2 8}{\log_2 4} \qquad \textit{log}_2 \textit{ was chosen because 8 and 4 are powers of 2.}$$

$$= \frac{3}{2}$$

Check: $\log_4 8 \stackrel{?}{=} \frac{3}{2}$

$$4^{\frac{3}{2}} \stackrel{?}{=} 8$$

$$\sqrt{4^3} \stackrel{?}{=} 8$$

$$\sqrt{64} \stackrel{?}{=} 8$$

$$8 = 8$$

The value of $\log_4 8$ is $\frac{3}{2}$.

4 **Solve the equation $2^{3y} = 3^{y+1}$.**

$$2^{3y} = 3^{y+1}$$

$$\log 2^{3y} = \log 3^{y+1}$$

$$3y \log 2 = (y + 1) \log 3 \qquad \textit{Power property}$$

$$3y \log 2 = y \log 3 + \log 3 \qquad \textit{Distributive property}$$

$$3y \log 2 - y \log 3 = \log 3$$

$$y(3 \log 2 - \log 3) = \log 3 \qquad \textit{Distributive property}$$

$$y = \frac{\log 3}{3 \log 2 - \log 3}$$

$$= \frac{0.4771}{3(0.3010) - 0.4771}$$

$$= 1.1202$$

Check: $2^3 = 8$, $2^{3y} = 2^{3.3}$, and $2^4 = 16$ *Use $y = 1.1$ in check.*

$3^2 = 9$, $3^{y+1} = 3^{2.1}$, and $3^3 = 27$

Since $8 < 2^{3.3} < 16$ and $9 < 3^{2.1} < 27$, the answer is within proper limits.

The solution is approximately 1.1202.

example 5

Solve the equation $m^{\frac{2}{3}} = 17$.

$$m^{\frac{2}{3}} = 17$$

$$(m^{\frac{2}{3}})^{\frac{3}{2}} = 17^{\frac{3}{2}}$$ *Raise both sides of the equation to the $\frac{3}{2}$ power.*

$$m = 17^{\frac{3}{2}}$$

$$\log m = \log 17^{\frac{3}{2}}$$

$$= \frac{3}{2}\log 17$$

$$= 1.8456$$

$$m = \text{antilog } 1.8456$$

$$= \text{antilog } 0.8456 \times 10^1$$

$$= 7.008 \times 10$$

$$= 70.08$$ The solution is about 70.08.

exercises

Max: 1–12, 1–36; **Avg:** 1–12, 1–35 odds; **Min:** 1–35 odds

Exploratory **State x in terms of common logarithms.** 8. log 30/log 5 12. (log 3/log 2) + $\frac{1}{2}$

1. $3^x = 55$ log 55/log 3
2. $5^x = 61$ log 61/log 5
3. $7^{2x} = 74$
4. $10^{3x} = 191$ $\frac{1}{3}$ log 191
5. $x = \log_6 144$
6. $x = \log_5 81$
7. $x = \log_3 12$
8. $x = \log_5 30$
9. $2^{-x} = 10$ $^-$1/log 2
10. $3^{-x} = 15$
11. $3^x = \sqrt{13}$
12. $2^x = 3\sqrt{2}$

3. log 74/2 log 7 5. log 144/log 6 6. log 81/log 5 7. log 12/log 3 10. $^-$log 15/log 3 11. $\frac{1}{2}$log 13/log 3

Written 1–12. Solve each equation in the Exploratory Exercises. For answers to problems 1–12, see the Teacher's Guide.

Approximate each logarithm to three decimal places.

13. $\log_3 7$ 1.771
14. $\log_7 12$ 1.277
15. $\log_4 22$ 2.230
16. $\log_{3.21} 10$ 1.974
17. $\log_6 11$ 1.338
18. $\log_4 24$ 2.292
19. $\log_6 72$ 2.387
20. $\log_5 104$ 2.885

Solve each equation using logarithms. These answers were computed by calculator.

21. $2.7^x = 52.3$ 3.9839
22. $4.3^x = 78.5$ 2.9913
23. $7.6^{n-2} = 41.7$ 3.8393
24. $2.1^{x-5} = 9.32$ 8.0086
25. $9^{x-4} = 6.28$ 4.8362
26. $5^{y+2} = 15.3$ $^-$0.3051
27. $x = \log_4 51.6$ 2.8446
28. $x = \log_3 19.8$ 2.7177
29. $x^{\frac{2}{3}} = 17.7$ 74.47
30. $x^{\frac{3}{4}} = 93.7$ 425.58
31. $5^{x-1} = 3^x$ 3.1507
32. $7^{x-2} = 5^x$ 11.5665
33. $5^{2x} = 9^{x-1}$ $^-$2.1507
34. $12^{x-4} = 4^{2-x}$ 3.2838
35. $7^{x-2} = 5^{3-x}$ 2.4527
36. Let x be any real number and n, a, and b be positive real numbers where a and b do not equal 1. Show that if $x = \log_a n$, then $x = \dfrac{\log_b n}{\log_b a}$. See Teacher's Guide.

12-8 Solving Problems

Objective: To solve problems using logarithms.

The formula for compound interest given on page **346** is one special example of a formula for growth. The general formula for growth and decay in nature has many applications.

$$y = ne^{kt}$$

In the formula, y is the final amount, n is the initial amount, k is a constant, and t is time. The constant k is greater than 0 for growth and less than 0 for decay. The value of e is approximately 2.718 and log e is approximately 0.4343.

example 1

For a certain strain of bacteria, $k = 0.775$ when t is measured in hours. How long will 2 bacteria take to increase to 1000 bacteria?

$y = ne^{kt}$

$1000 = 2e^{0.775t}$ *Substitute 1000 for y, 2 for n, and 0.775 for k.*

$500 = e^{0.775t}$

$\log 500 = \log e^{0.775t}$

$\log 500 = 0.775t \log e$

$\frac{\log 500}{0.775 \log e} = t$ *Solve using calculator or logarithms.*

$8.019 = t$ The solution is approximately 8.019 hours.

Radioactive substances decay with time. Starting with N grams, the number y grams present t years later is given by the equation

$$y = Ne^{kt}$$

example 2

In 10 years, the mass of a 200-gram sample of an element is reduced to 100 grams. This period is called the half-life. Find the constant k for this element.

$y = Ne^{kt}$

$100 = 200\ e^{k \cdot 10}$ *Substitute 100 for y, 200 for N, and 10 for t.*

$0.5 = e^{k \cdot 10}$

$\log 0.5 = \log e^{k \cdot 10}$

$\frac{\log 0.5}{10 \log e} = k$ *Solve using a calculator or logarithms.*

$^{-}0.06931 = k$ The solution is approximately $^{-}0.06931$.

When interest is compounded continuously, the formula becomes

$$A = Pe^{rt}$$

The final amount is A, the beginning investment is P, the annual interest rate is r, and the time in years is t.

example 3

Assume \$100 is deposited in a savings account. The interest rate is 6% compounded continuously. When will the money be double the original amount? If the money is to be doubled, the final amount will be \$200.

$$A = Pe^{rt}$$

$$200 = 100\, e^{0.06t}$$ *Substitute 200 for A, 100 for P, and 0.06 for r.*

$$2 = e^{0.06t}$$

$$\log 2 = \log e^{0.06t}$$

$$= 0.06t \log e$$

$$\frac{\log 2}{0.06 \log e} = t$$

$$\frac{0.3010}{(0.06)(0.4343)} = t$$

$$11.55 = t$$ The solution is approximately 11.55 years.

In business, another formula is used for a fixed rate of growth (appreciation) or decay (depreciation).

example 4

A piece of machinery valued at \$25,000 depreciates at a steady rate of 10% yearly. The value at the end of n years is $V(n) = 25{,}000 \times 0.9^n$. When will the value be \$5000?

$$V(n) = 25{,}000 \times 0.9^n$$

$$5000 = 25{,}000 \times 0.9^n$$ *Substitute 5000 for V(n).*

$$0.2 = 0.9^n$$

$$\log 0.2 = \log 0.9^n$$

$$= n \log 0.9$$

$$\frac{\log 0.2}{\log 0.9} = n$$

$$\frac{^-0.6990}{^-0.0458} = n$$

$$15.26 = n$$ The solution is approximately 15.26 years.

exercises

Max: 1–3, 1–12; **Avg:** 1–3, 1–11 odds; **Min:** 1–11 odds

Exploratory Solve each problem.

1. A certain culture of bacteria will grow from 500 to 4000 bacteria in 1.5 hours. Find the constant k for the growth formula. 1.3863
2. For a radioactive substance, $k = {}^{-}0.08042$. How long will 250 grams of the substance take to reduce to 50 grams? 20.013 years
3. If \$500 is invested at 6% annual interest compounded continuously, when will the investment be tripled? 18.31 years

Written Solve each problem.

1. Find k for a radioactive element for which half of a 20 milligram sample remains after 9 years. $^{-}0.0770$
2. For a certain strain of bacteria, $k = 0.782$ when t is measured in hours. How long will 10 bacteria take to increase to 500 bacteria? 5.0025 hours
3. For a certain strain of bacteria $k = 0.783$ when t is measured in hours. How long will 10 bacteria take to increase to 100 bacteria? 2.94 hours
4. Bacteria of a certain type can grow from 80 to 164 bacteria in 3 hours. Find the constant k for the growth formula. 0.2393
5. Rachel has saved \$2000 to buy a car which will cost about \$2500. If her money is in a savings account paying 7.25% interest compounded continuously, when will she be able to buy the car? 3.078 years
6. Mr. Sterwin wishes to have \$8000 in a savings account in the year 2000. How much should he deposit in 1980 to have this amount, if the account pays 5% interest compounded continuously? \$2943.04
7. Radium-226 decomposes radioactively. Its half-life (the time half the sample takes to decompose) is 1800 years. Find the constant k for the decay formula. Use 100 grams as the original amount. $^{-}0.000385$
8. A piece of machinery valued at \$50,000 depreciates 10% per year by the fixed rate method. The value at the end of n years is $V(n) = 50{,}000 \times 0.9^n$. After how many years will the value have depreciated to \$25,000? 6.579 years
9. Suppose \$1 is invested at 7% interest compounded continuously. When will the investment be worth \$10? Worth \$100? 32.89 years; 65.79 years
10. A radioactive substance decays according to the equation $A = A_0 \times 10^{-0.024t}$ where t is in hours. Find the half-life of the substance (when $A = 0.5A_0$). 12.54 hours
11. Mike has \$500 in his savings account. He is spending 10% of the balance each week. After how many weeks of this spending will the balance be under \$1? Use $B(n) = 500 \times 0.9^n$, where n is the number of weeks. 58.98 or 6 weeks
12. A satellite has a power supply whose output in watts is given by $w(t) = 50e^{-0.004t}$ where t is the time in days. How much power will there be at the end of 500 days? 6.768 watts

Vocabulary

logarithm (328)
common logarithm (339)
characteristic (339)
mantissa (339)
antilogarithm (340)
interpolation (342)

Chapter Summary

1. A logarithm is an exponent. (328)
2. Definition of Logarithm: Suppose b is a positive number other than 1 and n is a positive number. Then there is a number p such that $\log_b n = p$ if and only if $b^p = n$. (328)
3. Both $y = b^x$ and its inverse $y = \log_b x$ are functions. (331)
4. Property of Equality for Logarithmic and Exponential Functions: Suppose b is a positive number other than 1. Then $b^{x_1} = b^{x_2}$ and $\log_b x_1 = \log_b x_2$ if and only if $x_1 = x_2$. (331)
5. Because the logarithmic and exponential functions are inverses, $b^{\log_b x} = x$ and $\log_b b^x = x$. (332)
6. Properties of Logarithms: Suppose m and n are positive numbers, b is a positive number other than 1, and p is any number. Then the following properties hold.

   Product Property: $\log_b m \cdot n = \log_b m + \log_b n$

   Quotient Property: $\log_b \left(\frac{m}{n}\right) = \log_b m - \log_b n$

   Power Property: $\log_b m^p = p \log_b m$ (335)
7. Common logarithms are logarithms to base 10. (339)
8. To find the common logarithm of any number, first write the number in scientific notation. If r is the positive number, $r = a \times 10^n$, where $1 \le a < 10$ and n is an integer. Then, $\log r = \log a + \log 10^n$ and $\log r = \log a + n$. Log a is found in the table of logarithms. It is called the mantissa of log r. The integer n is the characteristic of log r. (339)
9. To find an antilogarithm, use the table to find the antilog of the mantissa. Multiply by a power of ten corresponding to the characteristic. (340)
10. Interpolation is a procedure whereby logarithms and antilogarithms *not* directly found in the table may be calculated. (342)
11. Exponential equations have variables as exponents. They can be solved by using logarithms. (349)
12. Change of Bases: Suppose a, b, and n are positive numbers, and neither a nor b is 1. Then $\log_a n = \dfrac{\log_b n}{\log_b a}$. (350)

Chapter Review

12-1 **Rewrite each equation in logarithmic form.**

1. $7^3 = 343$ $\log_7 343 = 3$
2. $81^{\frac{1}{2}} = 9$ $\log_{81} 9 = \frac{1}{2}$
3. $5^{-2} = \frac{1}{25}$ $\log_5 \frac{1}{25} = {}^-2$
4. $4^0 = 1$ $\log_4 1 = 0$
5. $4^{\frac{3}{2}} = 8$ $\log_4 8 = \frac{3}{2}$
6. $\left(\frac{1}{3}\right)^3 = \frac{1}{27}$ $\log_{\frac{1}{3}} \frac{1}{27} = 3$

Rewrite each equation in exponential form.

7. $\log_4 64 = 3$ $4^3 = 64$
8. $\log_{10} 1000 = 3$ $10^3 = 1000$
9. $\log_8 2 = \frac{1}{3}$ $8^{\frac{1}{3}} = 2$
10. $\log_6 \frac{1}{36} = {}^-2$ $6^{-2} = \frac{1}{36}$
11. $\log_{81} 3 = \frac{1}{4}$ $81^{\frac{1}{4}} = 3$
12. $\log_6 1 = 0$ $6^0 = 1$

Solve each equation.

13. $\log_b 9 = 2$ 3
14. $\log_b 9 = \frac{1}{2}$ 81
15. $\log_5 125 = x$ 3
16. $\log_{16} 2 = x$ $\frac{1}{4}$
17. $\log_3 x = {}^-3$ $\frac{1}{27}$
18. $\log_4 x = -\frac{1}{2}$ $\frac{1}{2}$

12-2 **Evaluate each expression.**

19. $\log_5 5^7$ 7
20. $\log_3 3^{10}$ 10
21. $9^{\log_9 18}$ 18
22. $6^{\log_6 7}$ 7
23. $\log_n n^3$ 3
24. $n^{\log_n 3}$ 3

Solve each equation.

25. $\log_6 12 = \log_6 (5x - 3)$ 3
26. $\log_3 3y = \log_3 (2y + 5)$ 5
27. $\log_5 y = \log_5 (14 - y)$ 7
28. $\log_3 3x = \log_3 (x + 7)$ 3.5
29. $\log_2 (3x - 2) = \log_2 (2x + 6)$ 8
30. $\log_4 (1 - 2x) = \log_4 (x + 10)$ $^-3$
31. $\log_7 (x^2 + x) = \log_7 12$ $^-4$, 3
32. $\log_2 (x - 1)^2 = \log_2 7$ $1 \pm \sqrt{7}$

12-3 **Use $\log_{10} 7 = 0.8451$ and $\log_{10} 4 = 0.6021$ to evaluate each expression.**

33. $\log_{10} 28$ 1.4472
34. $\log_{10} \frac{7}{4}$ 0.243
35. $\log_{10} 49$ 1.6902
36. $\log_{10} 700$ 2.8451
37. $\log_{10} 0.004$ $0.6021 - 3$
38. $\log_{10} \frac{49}{4}$ 1.0881

Solve each equation.

39. $\log_3 x - \log_3 4 = \log_3 12$ 48
40. $\log_5 x + \log_5 3 = \log_5 15$ 5

41. $\log_2 x = \frac{1}{3} \log_2 27$ 3

42. $\log_4 y = 4 \log_4 3$ 81

43. $\log_5 7 + \frac{1}{2} \log_5 4 = \log_5 x$ 14

44. $\frac{1}{2}(2 \log_{10} 4 + 2 \log_{10} 2) = \log_{10} x$ 8

45. $\log_6 (r - 3) + \log_6 (r + 2) = 1$ 4

46. $\log_7 (m + 1) + \log_7 (m - 5) = 1$ 6

12-4 Find the logarithm of each number.

47. 2.65 0.4232

48. 4.5 0.6532

49. 632 2.8007

50. 0.0777 0.8904 − 2

51. 51.2 1.7093

52. 700 2.8451

Find the antilog of each logarithm.

53. 0.7364 5.45

54. 0.0453 1.11

55. 3.8299 6760

56. 0.4409 − 2 0.0276

57. 0.7782 − 4 0.0006

58. 1.5587 36.2

12-5 Interpolate to find the logarithm of each number.

59. 3.415 0.5334

60. 1.123 0.0504

61. 463.2 2.6658

62. 0.04111 0.6139 − 2

63. 2004 3.3019

64. 0.001466 0.1661 − 3

Interpolate to find the antilog of each logarithm.

65. 0.3355 2.165

66. 0.3880 2.443

67. 0.7963 − 2 0.06256

68. 1.0725 11.82

69. 2.9575 906.8

70. 0.8736 − 3 0.007475

12-6 Use logarithms to evaluate each expression.

71. $\sqrt[4]{36}$ 2.45

72. 1972^7 1.16×10^{23}

73. $\sqrt[3]{\frac{321.5}{84.3}}$ 1.56

74. $\sqrt[5]{(0.43)(0.22)}$ 0.62

75. $\sqrt{\frac{(82)(14.4)}{36}}$ 5.72

76. $\sqrt[3]{\frac{(33.2)(1.64)^2}{(131)}}$ 0.880

12-7 Solve each equation.

77. $2^x = 53$ 5.728

78. $4.5^x = 36.2$ 2.386

79. $\log_4 11.2 = x$ 1.743

80. $\log_3 45.2 = x$ 3.469

81. $3.4^{x-2} = 15.6$ 4.245

82. $2.3^{x+1} = 66.6$ 4.041

83. $x^{\frac{2}{3}} = 24$ 117.6

84. $8^{x-2} = 5^x$ 8.849

12-8 Solve each problem.

85. Assume \$200 is deposited in a savings account at 6% annual interest rate compounded continuously. When will the value of the account be \$300? Use $A = Pe^{rt}$. 6.76 years

86. A bacterial culture will grow from 400 to 5000 bacteria in $1\frac{1}{4}$ hours. Find the constant k for the growth formula $y = ne^{kt}$ where t is in hours. 2.02

Chapter Test

Solve problems 1–13 without using a table of logarithms.

1. Rewrite $6^4 = 1296$ in logarithmic form. $\log_6 1296 = 4$
2. Rewrite $\log_3 81 = 4$ in exponential form. $3^4 = 81$

Evaluate each expression.

3. $\log_{12} 12^2$ 2

4. $4^{\log_4 3}$ 3

Solve each equation.

5. $\log_m 144 = 2$ 12

6. $\log_7 x = 2$ 49

7. $\log_2 64 = y$ 6

8. $\log_5 (8r - 7) = \log_5 (r^2 + 5)$ 2, 6

9. $\log_9 (x + 4) + \log_9 (x - 4) = 1$ 5

Use $\log_7 5 = 0.8271$ and $\log_7 3 = 0.5645$ to evaluate each expression.

10. $\log_7 15$ 1.3916

11. $\log_7 9$ 1.129

12. $\log_7 45$ 1.9561

13. $\log_7 \frac{5}{3}$ 0.2626

Solve problems 14–24 using a table of logarithms. Find the logarithm of each number.

14. log 769,000 5.8859

15. log 0.01473 0.1682 − 2

Find the antilog of each logarithm.

16. antilog 3.2754 1.885

17. antilog (0.8351 − 4) 0.000684

Use logarithms to evaluate each expression.

18. $\sqrt[5]{1792}$ 4.474

19. 9.813^4 9,273

20. $\sqrt[3]{36(1.06)^{15}}$ 4.419

Solve each equation.

21. $3^x = 35$ 3.236

22. $\log_4 37$ 2.605

23. $3^x = 5^{x-1}$ 3.151

24. A Pilgrim ancestor of Agnes Stapleton left $10 in a savings account in the Provident Savings Bank. Interest was compounded continuously at 4%. The account is now worth $75,000. How long ago was the account started? ($A = Pe^{rt}$, $e = 2.718$, and $\log e = 0.4343$) 223.1 years

Chapter 13

Sequences and Series

The following sequence of numbers has been discovered in the pattern of beehive construction, in pine cones, and seeds in flowers.

1, 1, 2, 3, 5, 8, 13, 21, 34, . . .

Can you tell what the next number will be? 55

13-1 Arithmetic Sequences

Objective: To define arithmetic sequences and to find the nth term and arithmetic mean.

John Dalton is a race car driver. He increases his speed by 36.3 miles per hour on the straightaway. He enters the straightaway at 91 miles per hour. After eleven seconds, his speed is 127.3 miles per hour.

The speed at each second is shown below.

begin	1	2	3	4	5	6	7	8	9	10	11
91	94.3	97.6	100.9	104.2	107.5	110.8	114.1	117.4	120.7	124.0	127.3

These numbers which represent speeds are an example of a **sequence.** A set of numbers in a specific order is called a sequence. Each number in a sequence is called a term. The first term is denoted a_1, the second term a_2, and so on up to the nth term, a_n.

symbol	a_1	a_2	a_3	a_4	a_5	a_6	a_7	a_8	a_9	a_{10}	a_{11}	a_{12}
term	91	94.3	97.6	100.9	104.2	107.5	110.8	114.1	117.4	120.7	124.0	127.3

Can you see how to get a_{13}?
This sequence is an **arithmetic sequence.**

Definition of Arithmetic Sequence

An arithmetic sequence is a sequence in which the difference between any two consecutive terms is the same.

What is the common difference, d, for the sequence of speeds listed above? Find d for each of the following sequences.

$3, 7, 11, 15, \ldots \qquad d = 4$

$2, \frac{3}{2}, 1, \frac{1}{2}, 0, -\frac{1}{2}, -1, \ldots \qquad d = -\frac{1}{2}$

The three dots mean that the sequence continues infinitely in the same pattern.

example 1

Find the next three terms of the sequence 21, 27, 33.

Find the common difference.

$33 - 27 = 6 \qquad 27 - 21 = 6 \qquad d = 6$

Add 6 to the third term to get the fourth, and so on.

$33 + 6 = 39 \qquad 39 + 6 = 45 \qquad 45 + 6 = 51$

The required terms are 39, 45, 51.

There is a pattern in the way the terms of an arithmetic sequence are formed. Suppose the sequence has $a_1 = 35$ and $d = 7$.

$a_1 = 35$		35
$a_2 = 35 + 7$	add 7 to a_1	$35 + 7$
$a_3 = 35 + 7 + 7$	add $2 \cdot 7$ to a_1	$35 + 2 \cdot 7$
$a_4 = 35 + 7 + 7 + 7$	add $3 \cdot 7$ to a_1	$35 + 3 \cdot 7$
$a_n = 35 + 7 + \cdots + 7 + 7$	add $(n - 1)7$ to a_1	$35 + (n - 1)7$

How many 7's appear here? $(n - 1)$

The nth term of an arithmetic sequence with first term a_1 and common difference d is given by the following equation.

$$a_n = a_1 + (n - 1)d$$

Definition of the nth Term of an Arithmetic Sequence

example 2

Suppose the race car driver continues to increase his speed at the same rate. What will be his speed after 15 seconds?

$a_1 = 91$ $\quad d = 3.3$ $\quad a_{12} = 127.3$ $\quad$ *a_{12} is the speed after 11 seconds.*

Find a_{16} using $a_n = a_1 + (n - 1)d$.

$a_{16} = 91 + 15(3.3)$

$= 91 + 49.5$

$= 140.5$ $\quad$ His speed will be 140.5 mph.

The terms between any two nonconsecutive terms of an arithmetic sequence are called **arithmetic means.**

12, 21, 30, 39, 48, 57, 66, 75, . . .

Thus, 30, 39, and 48 are the arithmetic means between 21 and 57.

example 3

Find the four arithmetic means between 12 and 47. Use $a_n = a_1 + (n - 1)d$.

$a_1 = 12$ $\quad$ *12, ____, ____, ____, ____, 47* $\quad$ *$a_6 = 47$*

$a_6 = a_1 + (5)d$

$47 = 12 + 5d$

$7 = d$ $\quad$ *The common difference is 7.*

$12 + 7 = 19$ $\quad 19 + 7 = 26$ $\quad 26 + 7 = 33$ $\quad 33 + 7 = 40$

The arithmetic means are 19, 26, 33, and 40.

example 4

Find the number of multiples of 13 between 29 and 258.

The least and greatest multiples of 13 between 29 and 258 are 39 and 247. A sequence where $a_1 = 39$, $d = 13$, and $a_n = 247$ will have the required number of terms. Use $a_n = a_1 + (n - 1)d$.

$247 = 39 + (n - 1)13$ ***Here*** $a_n = 247, a_1 = 39, d = 13.$
$208 = (n - 1)13$
$17 = n$ There are 17 such multiples of 13.

exercises

Max: 1–14, 1–19; **Avg:** 1–14, 1–19 odds; **Min:** 1–19 odds

Exploratory **Name the first five terms of each of the following.**

1. $a_1 = 4, d = 3$
2. $a_1 = 7, d = 5$
3. $a_1 = 16, d = {}^-2$
4. $a_1 = 38, d = {}^-4$
5. $a_1 = \frac{3}{4}, d = -\frac{1}{4}$
6. $a_1 = \frac{3}{8}, d = \frac{5}{8}$
7. $a_1 = 2.3, d = 1.6$
8. $a_1 = 0.88, d = 0$

1. 4, 7, 10, 13, 16 **2.** 7, 12, 17, 22, 27 **3.** 16, 14, 12, 10, 8 **4.** 38, 34, 30, 26, 22

Name the next four terms of each of the following. **11.** $^-13, {}^-18, {}^-23, {}^-28$ **14.** 6.6, 10.6, 14.6, 18.6

9. 5, 9, 13, . . . 17, 21, 25, 29
10. 11, 14, 17, . . . 20, 23, 26, 29
11. $2, {}^-3, {}^-8, \ldots$
12. $21, 15, 9, \ldots$ $3, {}^-3, {}^-9, {}^-15$
13. $\frac{1}{2}, \frac{3}{2}, \frac{5}{2}, \ldots$ $\frac{7}{2}, \frac{9}{2}, \frac{11}{2}, \frac{13}{2}$
14. $^-5.4, {}^-1.4, 2.6, \ldots$

5. $\frac{3}{4}, \frac{1}{2}, \frac{1}{4}, 0, -\frac{1}{4}$ **6.** $\frac{3}{8}, 1, \frac{13}{8}, \frac{9}{4}, \frac{23}{8}$ **7.** 2.3, 3.9, 5.5, 7.1, 8.7 **8.** 0.88, 0.88, 0.88, 0.88, 0.88

Written **Use $a_n = a_1 + (n - 1)d$ to find the nth term of each of the following.**

a_1	7	$^-3$	2	$^-7$	$\frac{3}{4}$	20	13	27	15
d	3	$^-9$	$\frac{1}{2}$	3	$-\frac{5}{4}$	4	3	16	80
n	14	11	8	17	13	100	101	23	10
nth term	1. 46	2. $^-93$	3. $\frac{11}{2}$	4. 41	5. $^-14\frac{1}{4}$	6. 416	7. 313	8. 379	9. 735

Find the indicated term in each sequence.

10. a_{12} for $^-17, {}^-13, {}^-9, \ldots$ 27
11. a_{10} for $\frac{5}{6}, \frac{7}{6}, \frac{3}{2}, \ldots$ $\frac{23}{6}$

Find the missing terms.

12. 55, 70, 85, 100, 115
13. $^-8$, $-\frac{13}{3}$, $-\frac{2}{3}$, 3
14. $^-10$, $-\frac{38}{5}$, $-\frac{26}{5}$, $-\frac{14}{5}$, $-\frac{2}{5}$, 2
15. 2, 5, 8, 11, 14, 17, 20
16. $^-13$, $^-6$, 1, 8, 15, 22
17. 56, 49, 42, 35, 28
18. Mark's salary is \$12,500. His raises will be \$700 per year. What will be his salary after 8 years? \$18,100
19. How many multiples of 7 are there between 11 and 391? 54

Rule of 78

Suppose you borrow some money from the local bank. As a general rule, the amount of interest is not the same for each month. You owe more interest the first month than you do the last month. For a one-year loan, the following series is used in figuring the amount of interest for each month.

$$12 + 11 + 10 + 9 + 8 + 7 + 6 + 5 + 4 + 3 + 2 + 1 \text{ or } 78$$

How many months are there in a year? How many addends are there in the series above? 12; 12

The example below shows how the series is used to figure amounts of interest.

Example What part of the interest is paid during the first month of a one-year loan? What part of the interest is paid during the first three months of a one-year loan? What part of the interest is paid during the first six months of a one-year loan?

$\frac{12}{78}$ of the total interest is paid in the first month.

$\frac{12 + 11 + 10}{78}$ or $\frac{33}{78}$ is paid in the first three months.

$\frac{12 + 11 + 10 + 9 + 8 + 7}{78}$ or $\frac{57}{78}$ is paid in the first six months.

The above method is called the **rule of 78.** Do you see why?

For a two-year loan, find the number of months in 2 years. The interest series has how many addends? What are the addends? 24; 24; 24, 23, 22, . . . , 1

Exercises Find the part of the interest owed for each of the following using the rule of 78.

1. first two months of a one-year loan $\frac{23}{78}$
2. first four months of a one-year loan $\frac{7}{13}$
3. last month of a one-year loan $\frac{1}{78}$
4. first month of a two-year loan $\frac{2}{25}$
5. first three months of a two-year loan $\frac{23}{100}$
6. first six months of a two-year loan $\frac{43}{100}$
7. first month of a three-year loan $\frac{6}{111}$
8. last month of a three-year loan $\frac{1}{666}$

13-2 Σ Notation

Objective: To use summation notation.

Dana Thompson plans to start a savings program. She will save five cents the first day, ten cents the second day, fifteen cents the third day, and so on. How much will she save in the first two weeks using this plan?

This is what will be saved, in cents.

$$5 + 10 + 15 + 20 + 25 + 30 + 35 + 40 + 45 + 50 + 55 + 60 + 65 + 70 \text{ or}$$

$$1 \cdot 5 + 2 \cdot 5 + 3 \cdot 5 + 4 \cdot 5 + 5 \cdot 5 + 6 \cdot 5 + 7 \cdot 5 + 8 \cdot 5 + 9 \cdot 5 + 10 \cdot 5 + 11 \cdot 5 + 12 \cdot 5 + 13 \cdot 5 + 14 \cdot 5$$

In mathematics, Σ, the Greek letter sigma, is used to write such a sum in a much shorter way. The symbol is used to indicate a sum. It is used with a variable which is called the index of summation.

$$\sum_{k=1}^{14} 5 \cdot k$$

This is read the summation from k equals 1 to 14 of 5 times k. The index of summation is k.

The terms in the sum can be written in expanded form.

$$\sum_{k=1}^{14} 5 \cdot k = \underset{k=1}{5 \cdot 1} + \underset{k=2}{5 \cdot 2} + \underset{k=3}{5 \cdot 3} + \underset{k=4}{5 \cdot 4} + \underset{k=5}{5 \cdot 5} + \cdots + \underset{k=14}{5 \cdot 14}$$

examples

1 **Write $\sum_{n=3}^{7} (3n - 2)$ in expanded form, and find the sum.**

$$\sum_{n=3}^{7} (3n-2) = \underset{n=3}{(3 \cdot 3 - 2)} + \underset{n=4}{(3 \cdot 4 - 2)} + \underset{n=5}{(3 \cdot 5 - 2)} + \underset{n=6}{(3 \cdot 6 - 2)} + \underset{n=7}{(3 \cdot 7 - 2)}$$
$$= (9-2) + (12-2) + (15-2) + (18-2) + (21-2)$$
$$= (7 + 10 + 13 + 16 + 19) \text{ or } 65$$

The sum is 65.

2 **Write $\sum_{j=1}^{5} 2(4)^{j-1}$ in expanded form and find the sum.**

$$\sum_{j=1}^{5} 2(4)^{j-1} = \underset{j=1}{2 \cdot 4^{1-1}} + \underset{j=2}{2 \cdot 4^{2-1}} + \underset{j=3}{2 \cdot 4^{3-1}} + \underset{j=4}{2 \cdot 4^{4-1}} + \underset{j=5}{2 \cdot 4^{5-1}}$$
$$= 2 \cdot 4^0 + 2 \cdot 4^1 + 2 \cdot 4^2 + 2 \cdot 4^3 + 2 \cdot 4^4$$
$$= 2 \cdot 1 + 2 \cdot 4 + 2 \cdot 16 + 2 \cdot 64 + 2 \cdot 256$$
$$= (2 + 8 + 32 + 128 + 512) \text{ or } 682$$

The sum is 682.

exercises

Max: 1–8, 1–15; **Avg:** 1–8, 1–15 odds; **Min:** 1–15 odds

Exploratory Write each expression in expanded form to find the sum.

1. $\sum_{j=1}^{4} j + 2$ 18
2. $\sum_{k=3}^{5} 4k$ 48
3. $\sum_{r=1}^{3} (r - 1)$ 3
4. $\sum_{k=2}^{6} (3 - k)$ $^-5$
5. $\sum_{i=0}^{4} 2i$ 20
6. $\sum_{m=6}^{8} (^-m)$ $^-21$
7. $\sum_{p=4}^{7} (p + 2)$ 30
8. $\sum_{i=2}^{5} (i + 9)$ 50

Written Write each expression in expanded form and find the sum.

1. $\sum_{t=0}^{4} (13 + 7t)$ 135
2. $\sum_{i=1}^{5} (1 + 7i)$ 110
3. $\sum_{p=3}^{7} (2p - 1)$ 45
4. $\sum_{j=0}^{6} (24 - 9j)$ $^-21$
5. $\sum_{b=2}^{6} (2b + 1)$ 45
6. $\sum_{y=5}^{11} (3y - 5)$ 133
7. $\sum_{i=1}^{7} 2i$ 56
8. $\sum_{r=3}^{6} (r + 2)$ 26
9. $\sum_{z=1}^{9} (10 - z)$ 45
10. $\sum_{s=3}^{8} (2s - 1)$ 60
11. $\sum_{x=6}^{10} (x + 4)$ 60
12. $\sum_{j=^-3}^{3} (2j + 2)$ 14
13. $\sum_{n=4}^{8} 4^n$ 87,296
14. $\sum_{k=1}^{7} 2^{k-2}$ $63\frac{1}{2}$
15. $\sum_{s=1}^{4} 24(-\frac{1}{2})^s$ $^-7\frac{1}{2}$

13-3 Arithmetic Series

Objective: To define and find the sum of arithmetic series.

The amounts that Dana Thompson saved each day form the following arithmetic sequence.

5, 10, 15, 20, 25, 30, . . . 70 where $a_1 = 5$ and $d = 5$

Since Dana wants to know the amount saved in two weeks' time, the sum is written as follows.

$$5 + 10 + 15 + 20 + 25 + 30 + \cdots + 70$$

This sum is an example of an **arithmetic series.**

Definition of an Arithmetic Series

The sum of the terms of an arithmetic sequence is called an arithmetic series.

The symbol S_n is used to represent the sum of the first n terms of an arithmetic series.

Sequence: 3, 10, 17, 24, 31, 38

$S_1 = 3$ $S_2 = 3 + 10$ or 13 $S_3 = 3 + 10 + 17$ or 30

$S_4 = 3 + 10 + 17 + 24$ or 54 $S_5 = 3 + 10 + 17 + 24 + 31$ or 85

$S_6 = 3 + 10 + 17 + 24 + 31 + 38$ or 123

Each sum, S_1, S_2, S_3, S_4, S_5, and S_6 is called a partial sum.

Suppose this sequence continued infinitely. How can the nth term of the sequence 3, 10, 17, 24, . . . be written?

$a_1 = 3$ $d = 7$ $a_n = a_1 + (n - 1)d$

$a_n = 3 + (n - 1)7$

Sigma notation also can be used to express partial sums.

$S_4 = 3 + 10 + 17 + 24$ and $S_4 = \sum_{n=1}^{4} [3 + (n - 1)7]$

Notice that $3 + (n - 1)7$ is the nth term of the sequence.

To see this, write $\sum_{n=1}^{4} [3 + (n - 1)7]$ in expanded form.

$$\begin{aligned} \sum_{n=1}^{4} [3 + (n-1)7] &= [3 + (1 - 1)7] + [3 + (2 - 1)7] + [3 + (3 - 1)7] + [3 + (4 - 1)7] \\ &= 3 + 0 \cdot 7 + 3 + 1 \cdot 7 + 3 + 2 \cdot 7 + 3 + 3 \cdot 7 \\ &= (3 + 10 + 17 + 24) \text{ or } 54 \end{aligned}$$

The sum of the first n terms is written $S_n = \sum_{k=1}^{n} 3 + (k - 1)7$.

For a greater number of terms in a partial sum, the following method can be used to evaluate the partial sums.

$$S_6 = \sum_{k=1}^{6} [3 + (k - 1)7]$$
$$= 3 + 10 + 17 + 24 + 31 + 38$$

Write S_6 twice as follows.

$$S_6 = 3 + 10 + 17 + 24 + 31 + 38$$ *Add each column. All the sums are the same.*

$$S_6 = 38 + 31 + 24 + 17 + 10 + 3$$ *What numbers are added to get the first 41? The last 41?*

$$2 \cdot S_6 = 41 + 41 + 41 + 41 + 41 + 41$$ *Now you have $2 \cdot S_6$.*

$$2 \cdot S_6 = 6 \cdot 41$$

$$S_6 = \frac{6 \cdot 41}{2}$$ Notice the pattern $S_6 = \dfrac{6 \cdot (a_1 + a_6)}{2}$.

From many other examples, we are led to the following definition.

The nth partial sum of a series is found by using the following formula.

$$S_n = \frac{n}{2}(a_1 + a_n)$$

Definition of S_n

example 1

Find the sum of the first 50 positive integers.

$a_1 = 1,\ a_n = 50,\ n = 50$

$$S_n = \frac{n}{2}(a_1 + a_n)$$

$$S_{50} = \frac{50}{2}(1 + 50)$$ *Here $a_1 = 1$, $a_n = 50$, $n = 50$.*

$$= 25(51)$$
$$= 1275$$ The sum of the first 50 positive integers is 1275.

You know that $a_n = a_1 + (n - 1)d$. Using substitution gives another formula for S_n.

$$S_n = \frac{n}{2}(a_1 + a_n)$$

$$S_n = \frac{n}{2}\{a_1 + [a_1 + (n - 1)d]\}$$ *Use $a_n = a_1 + (n - 1)d$.*

$$S_n = \frac{n}{2}[2 \cdot a_1 + (n - 1)d]$$

example 2

Find the sum of the first 60 terms of an arithmetic series where $a_1 = 15$, $n = 60$, and $d = 80$.

$$S_n = \frac{n}{2}[2 \cdot a_1 + (n - 1)d]$$

$$S_{60} = \frac{60}{2}[2 \cdot 15 + (59)80]$$

$$S_{60} = 30(30 + 59 \cdot 80) \quad \text{or} \quad 142{,}500$$

exercises

Max: 1–10, 1–20; **Avg:** 1–9, 1–19 odds; **Min:** 1–9, 1–19 odds

Exploratory Evaluate each of the following series.

1. $4 + 7 + 10 + 13 + 16 + 19 + 22 + 25$ 116
2. $1 + 5 + 9 + 13 + 17 + 21 + 25 + 29$ 120

Find S_n for each series.

3. $a_1 = 2$, $a_n = 200$, $n = 100$ 10,100
4. $a_1 = 5$, $a_n = 100$, $n = 20$ 1050
5. $a_1 = 4$, $n = 15$, $d = 3$ 375
6. $a_1 = 50$, $n = 20$, $d = {}^-4$ 240
7. $9 + 11 + 13 + 15 + \cdots + n = 12$ 240
8. ${}^-3 + {}^-7 + {}^-11 + {}^-15 + \cdots + n = 10$ ${}^-210$
9. Find the sum of the first 100 positive integers. 5050
10. An arithmetic series has a sum of 77. The first term is 2 and the last term is 12. How many terms are there? 11

Written Find the first four terms of each series described below.

1. The first term is 6. The common difference is 30. 6, 36, 66, 96
2. The first term is 7. The common difference is 12. 7, 19, 31, 43
3. The first term is 1. The common difference is 4. 1, 5, 9, 13
4. The first term is 18. The common difference is 17. 18, 35, 52, 69

Find the sum of each series.

5. $7 + 14 + 21 + 28 + \cdots + 98$ 735
6. $6 + 12 + 18 + \cdots + 96$ 816
7. $10 + 4 + ({}^-2) + ({}^-8) + \cdots + ({}^-50)$ ${}^-220$
8. $34 + 30 + 26 + \cdots + 2$ 162

Find S_n for each series described below.

9. $a_1 = 11$, $a_n = 44$, $n = 23$
10. $a_1 = 3$, $a_n = {}^-38$, $n = 8$
11. $a_1 = 5$, $n = 18$, $a_n = 73$
12. $a_1 = 85$, $n = 21$, $a_n = 25$
13. $a_1 = 3$, $n = 9$, $a_n = 27$ 135
14. $a_1 = 34$, $n = 9$, $a_n = 2$ 162
15. $a_1 = 9$, $n = 22$, $a_n = 101$
16. $a_1 = 76$, $n = 16$, $a_n = 31$ 856
17. $a_1 = 5$, $d = 12$, $n = 7$ 287
18. $a_1 = 4$, $d = {}^-1$, $n = 7$ 7
19. $a_1 = 9$, $d = {}^-6$, $n = 14$ ${}^-420$
20. $a_1 = 5$, $d = 3\frac{1}{2}$, $n = 13$ 338

9. 632.5 **10.** ${}^-140$ **11.** 702 **12.** 1155 **15.** 1210

13-4 Geometric Sequences

Objective: To define geometric sequences and to find the nth term and geometric means.

Ann Woodruff read about a *foolproof way to make a million dollars*. The plan is simple. Save a penny the first day. Then each day save double the amount saved on the previous day. How much should Anne save on the fifteenth day? On the twenty-eighth day? How much can be saved in 30 days using this plan? $163.84 $1,342,177.28 $5,368,709.12

Day 1 **1¢**

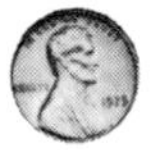

Day 2 **2¢**

Day 3 **4¢**

Day 4 **8¢**

Day 5 **16¢**

Day 6 **32¢**

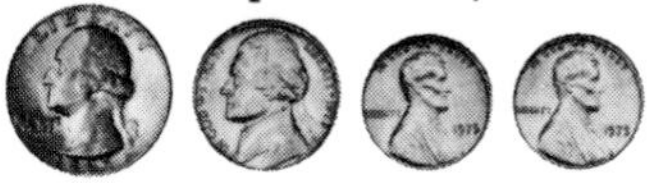

Day 7 **64¢**

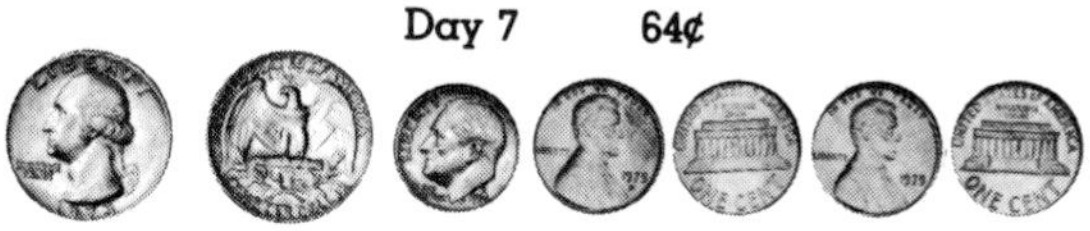

The amounts in the savings program form a geometric sequence.

1, 2, 4, 8, 16, 32, 64, . . . *What is the next term?* 128 *How is it found?* $64 \cdot 2$

In a geometric sequence, each term after the first is found by multiplying the previous term by a constant.

Definition of Geometric Sequence

In any geometric sequence, the constant or common ratio is found by dividing any term by the previous term.

example 1

Find the common ratio and the next two terms of the geometric sequence 4, 12, 36, ...

36 divided by 12 is 3. 12 divided by 4 is 3. The common ratio is 3.
The next two terms are

$36 \cdot 3$ or 108 and $108 \cdot 3$ or 324.

A geometric sequence containing n terms and having common ratio r can be written as follows. The second term, a_2, is found by multiplying the first term, a_1, by the common ratio, r.

a_1	a_2	a_3	a_4	$\cdots$	a_n
a_1	a_1r	a_2r	a_3r	$\cdots$	$a_{n-1}r$
a_1	$a_1 \cdot r$	$a_1 \cdot r^2$	$a_1 \cdot r^3$	$\cdots$	$a_1 \cdot r^{n-1}$

The nth term of a geometric sequence is given by either of the following formulas.

$$a_n = a_1r^{n-1} \qquad a_n = a_{n-1}r$$

Definition of a_n

examples

2 **Write the first seven terms of a geometric sequence in which $a_1 = 4$ and $r = 3$.**

Write each term using the formula $a_n = a_1 r^{n-1}$.

a_1	a_2	a_3	a_4	a_5	a_6	a_7
4	$4 \cdot 3$	$4 \cdot 3^2$	$4 \cdot 3^3$	$4 \cdot 3^4$	$4 \cdot 3^5$	$4 \cdot 3^6$
4	12	36	108	324	972	2916

The seven terms are 4, 12, 36, 108, 324, 972, 2916.

3 **Find the fifth term of a geometric sequence in which $a_1 = 7$ and $r = 2$.**

Use $a_n = a_1 r^{n-1}$.

$a_5 = a_1 \cdot 2^{5-1}$ *Substitute 2 for r and 5 for n.*

$= 7 \cdot 2^4$ *Substitute 7 for a_1.*

$= 7 \cdot 16$

$= 112$

The fifth term is 112.

The terms between any two nonconsecutive terms of a geometric sequence are called the geometric means. In the sequence 3, 12, 48, 192, 768, 3072, . . . , the geometric means between 3 and 768 are 12, 48, and 192.

example

4 **Find the missing geometric means in the sequence 81, ____, ____, 3.**

$a_n = a_1 r^{n-1}$

$a_4 = a_1 \cdot r^3$ *Substitute 4 for n.*

$3 = 81 \cdot r^3$ *Substitute 81 for a_1 and 3 for a_4.*

$\frac{1}{27} = r^3$

$\frac{1}{3} = r$

$a_2 = 81\left(\frac{1}{3}\right)$ $\quad$ $a_3 = 81\left(\frac{1}{3}\right)^2$

$= 27$ $\quad$ $= 9$

The missing terms are 27 and 9.

example 5

A vacuum pump removes $\frac{1}{5}$ of the air from a sealed container on each stroke of its piston. Thus, $\frac{4}{5}$ of the air remains after the first stroke. How much of the air remains after five strokes of the piston? Let the amount of air originally be 1.

The sequence can be indicated as follows.

0	*1*	*2*	*3*	*4*	*5*	*Number of each stroke.*
1,	$\frac{4}{5}$,	___,	___,	___,	___,	
a_1	a_2	a_3	a_4	a_5	a_6	*Number of each term.*

Use $a_n = a_1 \cdot r^{n-1}$

$a_6 = 1 \cdot \left(\frac{4}{5}\right)^5$ or $\frac{4^5}{5^5}$ *Substitute 1 for a_1, 6 for n, and $\frac{4}{5}$ for r.*

$= \frac{1024}{3125}$ or about 0.328 Thus, about 32.8% of the air remains.

exercises

Max: 1–9, 1–12; Avg: 1–9, 1–11 odds; Min: 1–9 odds, 1–11 odds

Exploratory **Tell whether each sequence is geometric. If so, find the common ratio.**

1. 4, 20, 100, 500 yes, 5
2. 9, 6, 4, $\frac{8}{3}$ yes, $\frac{2}{3}$
3. $\frac{3}{2}, \frac{9}{4}, \frac{27}{8}, \frac{81}{16}$ yes, $\frac{3}{2}$
4. 2, 4, 6, 8 no
5. 7, 14, 21, 28 no
6. 1, 4, 9, 16, 25 no

Find the missing terms for each sequence.

7. 5, 15, 45, ~~135~~, ~~405~~
8. 2, 10, 50, ~~250~~, ~~1250~~
9. ~~$\frac{1}{3}$~~, ~~1~~, 3, 9, 27

Written **Find the first four terms of each geometric sequence described below.**

1. $a_1 = \frac{3}{2}, r = 2$ $\frac{3}{2}$, 3, 6, 12
2. $a_1 = 3, r = {}^-2$ 3, ⁻6, 12, ⁻24
3. $a_1 = 12, r = \frac{1}{2}$ 12, 6, 3, $\frac{3}{2}$
4. $a_1 = 27, r = -\frac{1}{3}$ 27, ⁻9, 3, ⁻1

Find the nth term of each sequence described below. Use $a_n = a_1 \cdot r^{n-1}$.

5. $a_1 = 7, n = 4, r = 2$
6. $a_1 = 4, n = 3, r = 5$
7. $a_1 = 2, n = 5, r = 2$
8. $a_1 = 243, n = 5, r = -\frac{1}{3}$
9. $a_1 = 32, n = 4, r = -\frac{1}{2}$
10. $a_1 = 16, n = 5, r = \frac{1}{2}$

5. $a_4 = 56$ 6. $a_3 = 100$ 7. $a_5 = 32$ 8. $a_5 = 3$ 9. $a_4 = {}^-4$ 10. $a_5 = 1$

Solve each problem.

11. A vacuum pump removes $\frac{1}{10}$ of the air from a space capsule on each stroke of the pump. What percent of the air remains after four strokes of the pump? ≈ 65.6%

Remind students to let the original amount of air be 1.

12. The population of Sunville increases by 10% each year. It is now 20,000. What will be the expected population after five years (to the nearest 100 people)? 32,200

13-5 Geometric Series

Objective: To define and to find the sum of a geometric series.

Anne began her savings plan by saving a penny the first day, two cents the second day, and so on. On the seventh day, she saved 64 cents. How much had she saved altogether? The amounts saved on each day form a geometric sequence in which $a_1 = 1$ and $r = 2$.

For the sequence and series, the first term is a_1, the second term is a_2, and so on.

The geometric sequence 1, 2, 4, 8, 16, 32, 64 is determined by Anne's plan. The corresponding **geometric series** is shown below.

$$1 + 2 + 4 + 8 + 16 + 32 + 64$$

Let S_7 be the sum of the first seven terms indicated above. The following method can be used to calculate the sum.

$$S_7 = 1 + 2 + 4 + 8 + 16 + 32 + 64$$
$$2 \cdot S_7 = \quad 2 + 4 + 8 + 16 + 32 + 64 + 128$$

Subtract $2 \cdot S_7$ from S_7.

$$S_7 - 2S_7 = 1 + 0 + 0 + 0 + 0 + 0 + 0 + {}^{-}128$$
$$(1 - 2)S_7 = 1 - 128$$

Factor $S_7 - 2S_7$ to get $(1 - 2)S_7$.

$$S_7 = 127$$ Anne saved 127 cents, or \$1.27.

In this case, $S_7 = \dfrac{1 - 128}{1 - 2}$. *Substitute names of terms of sequence, and r for 2.*

$$S_7 = \frac{a_1 - a_8}{1 - r}$$ *$a_8 = a_1 r^7$*

$$= \frac{a_1 - a_1 r^7}{1 - r}$$ *Can r be one? Why or why not?*

Many similar examples lead to the following definition.

Definition of the Sum of a Geometric Series

The sum of the first n terms of a geometric series is given by the following formula.

$$S_n = \frac{a_1 - a_1 r^n}{1 - r} \quad \text{where } r \neq 1$$

example 1

Find the sum of the first six terms of a geometric series for which $a_1 = 3$ and $r = {}^{-}2$. Use the formula $S_n = \dfrac{a_1 - a_1 r^n}{1 - r}$.

$$S_n = \frac{a_1 - a_1 r^6}{1 - r}$$

$$S_6 = \frac{3 - 3({}^{-}2)^6}{1 - ({}^{-}2)}$$ *Substitute 3 for a_1, $^{-}2$ for r, and 6 for n.*

$$= {}^{-}63$$ The sum of the first six terms is $^{-}63$.

You know that $a_n = a_1r^{n-1}$. Then $a_n \cdot r = a_1r^{n-1} \cdot r$ or a_1r^n. Replacing a_1r^n by a_nr gives another formula for finding the value of S_n.

$$S_n = \frac{a_1 - a_1r^n}{1 - r}$$

$$= \frac{a_1 - a_nr}{1 - r} \qquad \textit{Substitute } a_nr \textit{ for } a_1r^n.$$

examples

2 **Find the sum of a geometric series for which $a_1 = 48$, $a_n = 3$, and $r = -\frac{1}{2}$. Use the formula $S_n = \frac{a_1 - a_nr}{1 - r}$.**

$$S_n = \frac{a_1 - a_nr}{1 - r}$$

$$= \frac{48 - 3\left(-\frac{1}{2}\right)}{1 - \left(-\frac{1}{2}\right)} \qquad \textit{Substitute 48 for } a_1\textit{, 3 for } a_n\textit{, and } -\tfrac{1}{2} \textit{ for } r.$$

$$= \frac{\frac{99}{2}}{\frac{3}{2}} \text{ or } 33 \qquad \text{The sum } S_n = 33.$$

3 **Write $\sum_{k=1}^{6} \left(\frac{1}{2}\right)^{k+1}$ in expanded form and evaluate.**

$$\sum_{k=1}^{6} \left(\frac{1}{2}\right)^{k+1} = \left(\frac{1}{2}\right)^{1+1} + \left(\frac{1}{2}\right)^{2+1} + \left(\frac{1}{2}\right)^{3+1} + \left(\frac{1}{2}\right)^{4+1} + \left(\frac{1}{2}\right)^{5+1} + \left(\frac{1}{2}\right)^{6+1}$$

$$= \frac{1}{4} + \frac{1}{8} + \frac{1}{16} + \frac{1}{32} + \frac{1}{64} + \frac{1}{128}$$

$$S_n = \frac{a_1 - a_nr}{1 - r}$$

$$S_6 = \frac{\frac{1}{4} - \left(\frac{1}{128}\right)\left(\frac{1}{2}\right)}{1 - \frac{1}{2}} \qquad \textit{Substitute 6 for } n\textit{, } \tfrac{1}{4} \textit{ for } a_1\textit{, } \tfrac{1}{128} \textit{ for } a_n\textit{, and } \tfrac{1}{2} \textit{ for } r.$$

$$= \frac{63}{128} \qquad \text{The sum } S_6 = \frac{63}{128}.$$

When $r = 1$, S_n is found by the formula $S_n = n \cdot a_1$. For example, the sum of the series $3 + 3 + 3 + 3 + 3 + 3$ is given by $S_n = 6 \cdot 3$ or 18.

exercises

Max: 1–30, 1–24; **Avg:** 1–29 odds, 1–23 odds; **Min:** 1–23 odds

Exploratory Complete the chart.

Series	First Term	Common Ratio	Last Term	Number of Terms	Sum
$9 - 18 + 36 - 72 + 144$	**1.** 9	**2.** $^-2$	**3.** 144	**4.** 5	**5.** 99
$3 + 1.5 + 0.75 + 0.375 + 0.1875$	**6.** 3	**7.** 0.5	**8.** 0.1875	**9.** 5	**10.** 5.8125
$\sum_{i=1}^{4} 2(4)^{i-1}$	**11.** 2	**12.** 4	**13.** 128	**14.** 4	**15.** 170
$\sum_{s=0}^{3} 20\left(-\frac{1}{4}\right)^{s}$	**16.** 20	**17.** $-\frac{1}{4}$	**18.** $-\frac{5}{16}$	**19.** 4	**20.** $\frac{255}{16}$
$\sum_{k=2}^{5} (^-8)\left(\frac{1}{2}\right)^{(k-1)}$	**21.** $^-4$	**22.** $\frac{1}{2}$	**23.** $-\frac{1}{2}$	**24.** 4	**25.** $-\frac{15}{2}$
$\sum_{b=0}^{4} 7\left(\frac{1}{3}\right)^{b}$	**26.** 7	**27.** $\frac{1}{3}$	**28.** $\frac{7}{81}$	**29.** 5	**30.** $\frac{847}{81}$

Written Find the sum of each geometric series.

1. $2 + (^-6) + 18 + \cdots$ to 6 terms. $^-364$

2. $3 + 6 + 12 + \cdots$ to 6 terms. 189

3. $8 + 4 + 2 + \cdots$ to 6 terms. $15\frac{3}{4}$

4. $\frac{1}{9} - \frac{1}{3} + 1 - \cdots$ to 5 terms. $\frac{61}{9}$

5. $1296 - 216 + 36 - \cdots$ to 5 terms. 1111

6. $7 + 7 + 7 + \cdots$ to 9 terms. 63

7. $75 + 15 + 3 + \cdots$ to 5 terms. $93\frac{18}{25}$

8. $16 + 16 + 16 + \cdots$ to 11 terms. 176

Find the sum of each geometric series described below.

9. $a_1 = 7, r = 2, n = 4$ 105

10. $a_1 = 5, r = 3, n = 5$ 605

11. $a_1 = 12, a_5 = 972, r = {}^-3$ 732

12. $a_1 = 256, r = \frac{3}{4}, n = 5$

13. $a_1 = 243, r = -\frac{2}{3}, n = 5$

14. $a_1 = 16, r = -\frac{1}{2}, n = 6$ $\frac{21}{2}$

15. $a_1 = 625, a_5 = 81, r = \frac{3}{5}$

16. $a_1 = 625, r = \frac{2}{5}, n = 5$

17. $a_1 = 4, a_6 = \frac{1}{8}, r = \frac{1}{2}$ $\frac{63}{8}$

18. $a_1 = 1, a_5 = \frac{1}{16}, r = -\frac{1}{2}$

19. $a_1 = 125, a_5 = \frac{1}{5}, r = \frac{1}{5}$

20. $a_1 = 343, a_4 = {}^-1, r = -\frac{1}{7}$ 300

21. $\sum_{j=1}^{5} (^-2)^j$ $^-22$

22. $\sum_{k=1}^{8} 2^{k-4}$ $\frac{255}{8}$ or 31.875

23. $\sum_{s=1}^{5} \left(\frac{3}{10}\right)^{s}$ $\frac{45}{10}$ or 4.5

24. $\sum_{t=1}^{6} \left(\frac{8}{10}\right)^{t}$ $\frac{84}{5}$ or 16.

12. 781 13. 165 15. 1441 16. 1031 18. $\frac{11}{16}$ 19. $\frac{781}{5}$ or 156.2

Challenge Solve this problem.

The teaching staff of Fairmeadow High School informs its members of school cancellation by telephone. The principal calls 2 teachers, each of whom in turn calls 2 other members, and so on. This process must be repeated 6 times counting the principal's calls as the first time. How many teachers, including the principal, work at Fairmeadow High? 127

13-6 Infinite Geometric Series

Objective: To find the sum of infinite geometric series.

The first swing of a pendulum measures 25 centimeters. The lengths of the successive swings form the geometric sequence 25, 20, 16, 12.8, ...

Suppose this pendulum continues to swing back and forth infinitely. Then the sequence shown above is called an *infinite geometric sequence.*

The distances traveled by the pendulum can be added.

$$25 + 20 + 16 + 12.8 + \cdots$$

The sum of these distances is an infinite geometric series with $a_1 = 25$ and $r = \frac{20}{25}$ or 0.8.

The series can be written as follows.

$$25 + 25(0.8)^1 + 25(0.8)^2 + 25(0.8)^3 + 25(0.8)^4 + 25(0.8)^5 + 25(0.8)^6 + \cdots$$

What happens as 0.8 is raised to various powers?

$(0.8)^1 = 0.8$	$(0.8)^2 = 0.64$	$(0.8)^3 = 0.512$	$(0.8)^4 = 0.4096$
$(0.8)^5 \approx 0.3277$	$(0.8)^6 \approx 0.2621$	$(0.8)^7 \approx 0.2097$	$(0.8)^8 \approx 0.1678$
$(0.8)^{10} \approx 0.1074$	$(0.8)^{20} \approx 0.0115$	$(0.8)^{40} \approx 0.00013$	$(0.8)^{50} \approx 0.00001$

These computations were done using a calculator.

As the values of n become greater, what happens to $(0.8)^n$?

What happens to the terms of the series as the exponents increase?

$a_1 = 25$	$a_2 = 25(0.8)$ or 20	$a_3 = 16$	$a_4 = 12.8$
$a_5 = 10.24$	$a_6 = 8.192$	$a_7 = 6.5536$	$a_8 \approx 5.2429$
$a_{10} \approx 3.3554$	$a_{20} \approx 0.3603$	$a_{40} \approx 0.0042$	$a_{50} \approx 0.0004$

What happens to the sums S_n as n becomes greater?

$$S_1 = 25 \qquad S_2 = \frac{25 - 25(0.64)}{1 - 0.8} \text{ or } 45 \qquad S_3 = \frac{25 - 25(0.512)}{1 - 0.8} \text{ or } 61$$

$$S_4 = \frac{25 - 25(0.4096)}{0.2} = \frac{25 - 10.24}{0.2} = 73.8$$

$$S_5 \approx \frac{25 - 25(0.3277)}{0.2} \approx \frac{25 - 8.1925}{0.2} \approx 84.0375$$

$$S_{10} \approx \frac{25 - 25(0.1074)}{0.2} \approx \frac{25 - 2.685}{0.2} \approx 111.575$$

$$S_{50} = \frac{25 - 25(0.00001)}{0.2} \approx \frac{25 - 0.00025}{0.2} \approx 124.9988$$

$$S_{100} \approx \frac{25 - 25(0.0000000002)}{0.2} \approx \frac{24.999999995}{0.2} \approx 124.99999998$$

Do you think a partial sum of this geometric series is ever greater than 125?

In any geometric series, the sum of the first n terms can be found using the formula at the top of page **376**.

$$S_n = \frac{a_1 - a_1 r^n}{1 - r} \quad \text{or} \quad S_n = \frac{a_1(1 - r^n)}{1 - r}, r \neq 1$$

Suppose r^n is very close to zero. Then S_n is very close to the following expression, called the sum of an infinite series.

$$\frac{a_1(1 - 0)}{1 - r} \quad \text{or} \quad \frac{a_1}{1 - r}$$

Definition of the Sum of an Infinite Geometric Series

The sum, S, of an infinite geometric series is given by the following formula.

$$S = \frac{a_1}{1 - r}, \text{ when } {}^-1 < r < 1$$

Find the sum of the series 25, 20, 16, 12.8, ...

$S = \frac{a_1}{1 - r}$ *Since $^-1 < 0.8 < 1$, you can use the formula.*

$S = \frac{25}{1 - 0.8}$ *Substitute 25 for a_1 and 0.8 for r.*

$= 125$ The sum of the series is 125.

example 1

Find the sum of the infinite geometric series $\frac{4}{3} - \frac{2}{3} + \frac{1}{3} - \frac{1}{6} + \cdots$.

$a_2 = a_1 r$

$-\frac{2}{3} = \left(\frac{4}{3}\right)r$ *Substitute $-\frac{2}{3}$ for a_2 and $\frac{4}{3}$ for a_1.*

$-\frac{1}{2} = r$

Next, find the sum using $S = \frac{a_1}{1 - r}$.

$$S = \frac{\frac{4}{3}}{1 - \left(-\frac{1}{2}\right)}$$

$$= \frac{\frac{4}{3}}{\frac{3}{2}}$$

$= \frac{8}{9}$ The sum is $\frac{8}{9}$.

examples

2 **Express the repeating decimal 0.11111 . . . or $0.\overline{1}$ as a fraction.**

Write $0.\overline{1}$ as an infinite geometric series.

$$0.\overline{1} = \frac{1}{10} + \frac{1}{100} + \frac{1}{1000} + \cdots$$

Then, $a_1 = \frac{1}{10}$ and $r = \frac{1}{10}$ since $\frac{1}{100} = \frac{1}{10}(r)$.

$$S = \frac{a_1}{1 - r}$$

$$S = \frac{\frac{1}{10}}{1 - \frac{1}{10}}$$ *Substitute $\frac{1}{10}$ for a_1 and $\frac{1}{10}$ for r.*

$= \frac{1}{9}$ The repeating decimal $0.\overline{1}$ is equal to $\frac{1}{9}$.

3 **A rubber ball dropped 30 feet bounces $\frac{2}{5}$ of the height from which it fell on each bounce. How far will it travel before coming to rest?**

downward distance

$$S = \frac{30}{1 - 0.4}$$ *a_1 is 30 and r is 0.4.*

$= \frac{30}{0.6}$ or 50

upward distance

$$S = \frac{12}{1 - 0.4}$$ *a_1 is 12 and r is 0.4.*

$= \frac{12}{0.6}$ or 20

total distance = 50 + 20 or 70

exercises

Max: 1–14, 1–32; Avg: 1–14, 5–31 odds; Min: 5–31 odds

Exploratory Find a_1 and r for each series. Then find the sum, if it exists.

1. $\frac{1}{2} + \frac{1}{3} + \frac{2}{9} + \frac{4}{27} + \cdots$ $\frac{1}{2}, \frac{2}{3}, \frac{3}{2}$
2. $12 + 3 + \frac{3}{4} + \frac{3}{16} + \cdots$ $12, \frac{1}{4}, 16$
3. $1 - \frac{1}{3} + \frac{1}{9} - \frac{1}{27} + \cdots$ $1, -\frac{1}{3}, \frac{3}{4}$
4. $1 - 3 + 9 - 27 + \cdots$ 1, $^-3$, no sum
5. $1 + \frac{3}{2} + \frac{9}{4} + \frac{27}{8} + \cdots$ $1, \frac{3}{2}$, no sum
6. $48 + 16 + \frac{16}{3} + \frac{16}{9} + \cdots$ $48, \frac{1}{3}, 72$

Express each repeating decimal as an infinite geometric series. State the ratio for each.

For answers to problems **7–14**, see the Teacher's Guide.

7. $0.\overline{7}$ **8.** $0.\overline{3}$ **9.** $0.\overline{73}$ **10.** $0.\overline{8}$
11. $0.\overline{152}$ **12.** $0.\overline{746}$ **13.** $0.\overline{93}$ **14.** $0.\overline{75}$

Written **Find the first three terms of the infinite geometric series described below.**

1. $S = 9, r = \frac{1}{3}$ **2.** $S = 16, r = \frac{3}{4}$ **3.** $S = 28, r = -\frac{2}{7}$ **4.** $S = \frac{27}{4}, r = -\frac{1}{3}$

1. $6 + 2 + \frac{2}{3}$ 2. $4 + 3 + \frac{9}{4}$ 3. $36 + -\frac{72}{7} + \frac{144}{49}$ 4. $9 + {}^-3 + 1$

Find the sum of the infinite geometric series described below.

5. $a_1 = 6, r = \frac{11}{12}$ 72

6. $a_1 = 18, r = -\frac{2}{7}$ 14

7. $a_1 = 7, r = -\frac{3}{4}$ 4

8. $a_1 = 27, r = -\frac{4}{5}$ 15

9. $9 + 6 + 4 + \cdots$ 27

10. $\frac{1}{3} + \frac{1}{9} + \frac{1}{27} + \cdots$ $\frac{1}{2}$

11. $3 - 2 + \frac{4}{3} - \cdots$ $\frac{9}{5}$

12. $\frac{3}{4} + \frac{1}{2} + \frac{1}{3} + \cdots$ $\frac{9}{4}$

13. $12 - 4 + \frac{4}{3} - \frac{4}{9} + \cdots$ 9

14. $1 - \frac{1}{4} + \frac{1}{16} - \cdots$ $\frac{4}{5}$

15. $10 - \frac{5}{2} + \frac{5}{8} - \cdots$ 8

16. $2 + 6 + 18 + 54 + \cdots$ sum doesn't exist

17. $3 - 9 + 27 - \cdots$ sum doesn't exist

18. $12 + 6 + 3 + \cdots$ 24

19. $10 - 1 + 0.1 - \cdots$ $\frac{100}{11}$

20. $100 + 10 + 1 + \cdots$ $\frac{1000}{9}$ or $111.\overline{1}$

Find a common fraction equivalent to the repeating decimal.

21. $0.\overline{3}$ $\frac{1}{3}$ **22.** $0.\overline{9}$ 1 **23.** $0.\overline{15}$ $\frac{5}{33}$ **24.** $0.\overline{31}$ $\frac{31}{99}$
25. $0.\overline{075}$ $\frac{25}{333}$ **26.** $0.\overline{410}$ $\frac{410}{999}$ **27.** $0.3\overline{7}$ $\frac{17}{45}$ **28.** $0.4\overline{5}$ $\frac{41}{90}$

Solve each problem.

29. The end of a swinging pendulum 90 cm long moves through 50 cm on its first swing. Each succeeding swing is $\frac{9}{10}$ of the preceding one. How far will the pendulum travel before coming to rest? 500 cm

30. The end of a swinging pendulum 30 cm long moves through 20 cm on its first swing. Each succeeding swing is $\frac{10}{11}$ of the preceding one. How far will it travel before coming to rest? 220 cm

31. A silicon ball dropped 12 feet rebounds $\frac{7}{10}$ of the height from which it fell. How far will it travel before coming to rest? 68 feet

32. A hot-air balloon rises 80 feet in the first minute after the balloon is released. If in each succeeding minute the balloon rises only 90 percent as far as in the previous minute, what is the maximum height (altitude) the balloon will reach? 800 feet

13-7 Special Sequences and Series

Objective: To learn about the Fibonacci sequence and special series.

The base of this pine cone shows an example of a pattern which is often found in nature. Count the number of strips which spiral to the left. (8) Count the number of strips which spiral to the right. (13) These two numbers shown in color below belong to a very special sequence.

This sequence is named after its discoverer, Leonardo Fibonacci.

1, 1, 2, 3, 5, 8, 13, 21, 34, 55, 89, 144, . . .

Can you see what the next term will be? What do you think is the pattern used in the Fibonacci sequence?

Let F_i be a term of the sequence.

$F_1 = 1$ $F_2 = 1$ $F_3 = 2$ or $1 + 1$

$F_4 = 3$ or $2 + 1$ $F_5 = 5$ or $3 + 2$

Then $F_5 = 3 + 2$. Thus, $F_5 = F_4 + F_3$.

How do you find the next term from the two previous terms?

In general, if F_n is the nth term of the Fibonacci sequence, then

$$F_n = F_{n-1} + F_{n-2}.$$

The Fibonacci sequence is the basis of other sequences as well. One of these is the sequence of ratios found by dividing each term of the Fibonacci sequence by the preceding term.

$$\frac{1}{1}, \frac{2}{1}, \frac{3}{2}, \frac{5}{3}, \frac{8}{5}, \frac{13}{8}, \frac{21}{13}, \frac{34}{21}, \frac{55}{34}, \frac{89}{55}, \frac{144}{89}$$

Notice that the spirals of the pine cone have the ratio $\frac{13}{8}$. Some other pine cones have the ratio $\frac{8}{5}$. Some daisies have the ratio $\frac{34}{21}$. Sunflower heads have spirals of seeds which may have ratios of $\frac{21}{13}$, $\frac{34}{21}$, or $\frac{55}{34}$.

The Fibonacci sequence first appeared as the answer to a problem about rabbits posed by Leonardo Fibonacci. Begin with a pair of rabbits. Suppose these rabbits produce their first pair of young in the second month, and every month thereafter. Also, the offspring begin producing young in their second month. If none of the rabbits die, how many pairs will there be each month?

	Begin	1st month	2nd month	3rd month	4th month	5th month
Pairs	1	1	2	3	5	8

Some special series often are used in more advanced mathematics. One of these is the Leibniz series for calculating π.

Multiply both sides by 4 to obtain a value for π.

$$\frac{\pi}{4} = 1 + \left(-\frac{1}{3}\right) + \frac{1}{5} + \left(-\frac{1}{7}\right) + \frac{1}{9} + \cdots + \frac{(-1)^{n-1}}{2n - 1} + \cdots$$

An approximation for π can be found by taking a finite number of terms in the sum. However, this is not an efficient way to calculate π. If the last term used is $-\frac{1}{39}$, the partial sum, multiplied by four, is 3.0916248. If the last term used is $\frac{1}{41}$, the partial sum, multiplied by four, is 3.1891856. The average of these two is 3.1404052. To seven decimal places, π is 3.1415926.

Another special series can be used to find natural logarithms (to the base e).

$$\log_e x = \left(\frac{x-1}{x}\right) + \frac{1}{2}\left(\frac{x-1}{x}\right)^2 + \frac{1}{3}\left(\frac{x-1}{x}\right)^3 + \cdots \text{ for } x > \frac{1}{2}$$

What happens to the series if x equals $\frac{1}{2}$? If x is less than $\frac{1}{2}$? Why must x be greater than $\frac{1}{2}$?

Many intelligence and aptitude tests include problems of finding patterns. The following examples illustrate some patterns.

example 1

Find the missing terms of the following sequence.

6, 10, 15, 21, 28, ____, ____, ____, . . .

6, 10, 15, 21, 28, ____, ____, ____

+4 +5 +6 +7 +8 +9 +10

Find the difference of consecutive terms.

The difference increases by one for each term.

The missing terms are 36, 45, and 55.

examples

2

Find the missing terms of the sequence 1, 2, 6, 24, 120, ____, ____, ...

1, 2, 6, 24, 120, ____, ____

$\times 2$ $\times 3$ $\times 4$ $\times 5$ $\times ?$ $120 \times 6 = 720$ $720 \times 7 = 5040$

Note that each term is multiplied by an integer. The integers increase by one each time.

The next two terms are 720 and 5040.

3

Complete the sequence 4, 9, 16, 25, ____, ____, ____, ...

4, 9, 16, 25, ____, ____, ____

2^2 3^2 4^2 5^2

Notice that each term is a perfect square.

The next terms are $6^2 = 36$, $7^2 = 49$, and $8^2 = 64$.

4

Complete the sequence 1, 1, 4, 10, 28, 76, ____, ____, ...

1, 1, 4, 10, 28, 76, ____, ____

$2(1 + 1)$, $2(4 + 1)$, $2(4 + 10)$, $2(28 + 10)$

Notice that each term seems to be double the sum of the two previous terms.

The next two terms are 208 and 568.

exercises

Max: 1–10, 1–4; **Avg:** 1–10, 1, 3; **Min:** 1–9 odds, 1, 3

Exploratory **Find the missing terms of each sequence.**

1. 52, 156, 468, 1404, 4212
2. 1, 2, 4, 7, 11, 16, 22
3. 2, 2.5, 2.75, 2.875, 2.9375
4. 2, 6, 30, 210, 1890
5. 1, 3, 7, 13, 21, 31, 43
6. 64, 32, 8, 1, $\frac{1}{16}$, $\frac{1}{512}$
7. 1, 5, 14, 30, 55, 91, 140
8. 1, 8, 27, 64, 125, 216
9. 1, 3, 4, 7, 11, 18, 29, 47
10. 1, 1, 3, 7, 17, 41, 99, 239

Written **Solve each problem.** For answers to problems **1–4**, see the Teacher's Guide.

1. Find the first twenty terms of the Fibonacci sequence.
2. Find the sum of the first 8 terms of the series $\log_e 2$.
3. Find the first 15 terms of the ratios of the Fibonacci sequence $\frac{1}{1}, \frac{2}{1}, \frac{3}{2}, \frac{5}{3}, \ldots$. Express each as a decimal.
4. The Lucas sequence is 1, 3, 4, 7, 11, 18, 29, 47. How is it related to the Fibonacci sequence? Let L_n be a term of the Lucas sequence. Describe L_n in terms of the Fibonacci sequence.

13-8 The General Term

Objective: To find the general term of sequences and series.

Sequences and series often are described by giving a formula for their general term. This formula may show how to find the nth term.

Sequence type	Formula for the nth term
Arithmetic	$a_n = 7 + (n - 1) \cdot 3$
Geometric	$a_n = 5 \cdot 4^{n-1}$

Sometimes a sequence or series may be described recursively. A **recursive formula** depends on knowing one or more previous terms.

Sequence type	Recursive formula
Arithmetic	$a_{n+1} = a_n + 3,\ a_1 = 7$
Geometric	$a_{n+1} = a_n \cdot 4,\ a_1 = 5$

When a sequence or series is described by a formula for its nth term, any term can be computed directly.

example 1

Find the 99th term of the sequence in which $a_n = 7 + (n - 1)3$.

$a_n = 7 + (n - 1)3$

$a_{99} = 7 + (99 - 1)3$ *Substitute 99 for n.*

$= 7 + 98 \cdot 3$

$= 7 + 294$

$= 301$

When a sequence or series is described by a recursive formula, you may need to compute several terms to find the terms desired.

example 2

Find the first six terms of the sequence in which $a_1 = 1$, $a_2 = 1$ and $a_{n+2} = a_n + 2 \cdot a_{n+1}$.

$a_3 = a_{1+2}$

$= a_1 + 2 \cdot a_2$

$= 1 + 2(1)$ or 3

$a_4 = a_{2+2}$

$= a_2 + 2 \cdot a_3$

$= 1 + 2(3)$ or 7

$a_5 = a_{3+2}$

$= a_3 + 2 \cdot a_4$

$= 3 + 2(7)$ or 17

$a_6 = a_{4+2}$

$= a_4 + 2 \cdot a_5$

$= 7 + 2(17)$ or 41

The first six terms are 1, 1, 3, 7, 17, and 41.

examples

3 **Find the 51st through the 54th terms of the sequence for which $a_n = 2n + 1$.**

These can be written in a chart as follows.

n	$a_n = 2n + 1$
51	$a_{51} = 2(51) + 1$ or 103
52	$a_{52} = 2(52) + 1$ or 105
53	$a_{53} = 2(53) + 1$ or 107
54	$a_{54} = 2(54) + 1$ or 109

4 **Find both a recursive formula and a formula for the nth term of the sequence $3, ^-6, 12, ^-24, 48, \ldots$.**

3	$^-6$	12	$^-24$	48
	$3 \cdot (^-2)$	$^-6 \cdot (^-2)$	$12 \cdot (^-2)$	$^-24 \cdot (^-2)$

Consider the ratio of two consecutive terms.

A recursive formula is $a_{n+1} = a_n(^-2)$ and $a_1 = 3$.
A formula for the nth term is $a_n = 3(^-2)^{n-1}$. *Recall $a_n = a_1 r^{n-1}$.*

5 **Find a formula for the nth term of the following series and express the series in sigma notation.**

$7 + 9 + 11 + 13 + 15 + 17$
$^+2 \quad ^+2 \quad ^+2 \quad ^+2 \quad ^+2$

What is the difference between any two terms?

$a_n = a_1 + (n - 1)d$
$a_n = 7 + (n - 1)2$ *Substitute 7 for a_1 and 2 for d.*
$a_n = 5 + 2n$

$$7 + 9 + 11 + 13 + 15 + 17 = \sum_{n=1}^{6} (5 + 2n)$$

exercises

Max: 1–20, 1–29; **Avg:** 1–20, 1–29 odds; **Min:** 1–19 odds, 1–29 odds

Exploratory Find the ninth and tenth terms of each sequence.

1. $a_n = n(n + 2)$ 99, 120
2. $a_n = 3n - 4$ 23, 26
3. $a_n = n^2 - 1$ 80, 99
4. $a_n = (^-1)^n$ $^-1$, 1

Find the first four terms of each sequence.

5. $a_1 = 8$, $a_{n+1} = a_n - 1$ 8, 7, 6, 5
6. $a_1 = 13$, $a_{n+1} = a_n + 2$ 13, 15, 17, 19
7. $a_1 = {}^-2$, $a_{n+1} = 3a_n$
8. $a_1 = 7$, $a_{n+1} = 2a_n$
9. $a_1 = {}^-4$, $a_{n+1} = (^-1)^{n+1}a_n$
10. $a_1 = 3$, $a_{n+1} = (^-1)^n a_n$

7. $^-2, ^-6, ^-18, ^-54$ **8.** 7, 14, 28, 56 **9.** $^-4, ^-4, 4, 4$ **10.** $3, ^-3, ^-3, 3$

11. $a_1 = 3,\ a_2 = 1,\ a_{n+2} = a_n + a_{n+1}$ 3, 1, 4, 5

12. $a_1 = 0,\ a_2 = 1,\ a_{n+2} = a_n + a_{n+1}$ 0, 1, 1, 2

Find a formula for the *n*th term of each sequence. 13. $a_n = 2n$

13. 2, 4, 6, 8, 10, 12, 14, . . .

14. 3, 5, 7, 9, 11, 13, . . . $a_n = 2n + 1$

15. $\frac{2}{1}, \frac{3}{2}, \frac{4}{3}, \frac{5}{4}, \frac{6}{5}, \ldots$ $a_n = \frac{n+1}{n}$

16. $\frac{1}{3}, \frac{1}{5}, \frac{1}{7}, \frac{1}{9}, \frac{1}{11}, \frac{1}{13}, \ldots$ $a_n = \frac{1}{2n+1}$

Find a recursive formula for each sequence.

17. $1, \frac{1}{3}, \frac{1}{9}, \frac{1}{27}, \ldots$

18. 1, 2, 4, 8, . . .

19. $1, {}^-1, 1, {}^-1, \ldots$

20. $1, -\frac{1}{2}, \frac{1}{4}, -\frac{1}{8}, \ldots$

17. $a_{n+1} = a_n \times \frac{1}{3},\ a_1 = 1$ 18. $a_{n+1} = a_n \times 2,\ a_1 = 1$ 19. $a_{n+1} = ({}^-1)a_n,\ a_1 = 1$
20. $a_{n+1} = (-\frac{1}{2})a_n,\ a_1 = 1$

Written **Find the eighth, ninth, and tenth terms of each sequence.**

1. $a_n = 4n - 3$ 29, 33, 37

2. $a_n = \frac{n}{n+1}$ $\frac{8}{9}, \frac{9}{10}, \frac{10}{11}$

3. $a_n = \frac{2n+1}{n+2}$ $\frac{17}{10}, \frac{19}{11}, \frac{21}{12}$

4. $a_n = \frac{n(n-1)}{3}$ $\frac{56}{3}, \frac{72}{3}, \frac{90}{3}$

5. $a_n = \frac{2}{n}$ $\frac{1}{4}, \frac{2}{9}, \frac{1}{5}$

6. $a_n = 4n^2$ 256, 324, 400

7. $a_n = ({}^-1)^{n+1}2n$ ${}^-16, 18, {}^-20$

8. $a_n = n^2 + 2n + 1$ 81, 100, 121

9. $a_n = \frac{1}{2}(n^2 + n + 4)$ 38, 47, 57

Find the first six terms of each sequence. For answers to problems **10–29**, see the Teacher's Guide.

10. $a_1 = 2,\ a_{n+1} = 3a_n$

11. $a_1 = 7,\ a_{n+1} = a_n + 5$

12. $a_1 = 3,\ a_2 = 5,\ a_{n+2} = a_n + a_{n+1}$

13. $a_1 = 1,\ a_2 = 2,\ a_{n+2} = a_n \times a_{n+1}$

14. $a_1 = 2,\ a_2 = 3,\ a_{n+2} = 2a_n + a_{n+1}$

15. $a_1 = 5,\ a_2 = 11,\ a_{n+2} = a_{n+1} - a_n$

Find both a recursive formula and a formula for the *n*th term of each of the following series.

16. 3, 7, 11, 15, 19, . . .

17. 4, 9, 14, 19, 24, . . .

18. 3, 15, 75, 375, 2375, . . .

19. $\frac{3}{2}, \frac{3}{4}, \frac{3}{8}, \frac{3}{16}, \frac{3}{32}, \ldots$

20. 5, 10, 15, 20, 25, . . .

21. $\frac{7}{2}, \frac{7}{10}, \frac{7}{50}, \frac{7}{250}, \ldots$

Write each series below in sigma notation.

22. $3 + 10 + 17 + 24 + 31$

23. $\frac{4}{5} + \frac{7}{5} + 2 + \frac{13}{5} + \frac{16}{5}$

24. $\frac{3}{3} + \frac{6}{4} + \frac{9}{5} + 2 + \frac{15}{7}$

25. $6 - 2 + \frac{2}{3} - \frac{2}{9} + \frac{1}{27}$

26. $\frac{3}{4} + \frac{3}{2} + \frac{9}{4} + 3 + \frac{15}{4} + \frac{9}{2}$

27. $2 + 2\frac{1}{2} + 3\frac{1}{3} + 4\frac{1}{4} + 5\frac{1}{5} + 6\frac{1}{6}$

28. $2 \cdot 5 + 4 \cdot 7 + 6 \cdot 9 + 8 \cdot 11 + 10 \cdot 13$

29. $1 + \left(-\frac{1}{3}\right) + \frac{1}{5} + \left(-\frac{1}{7}\right) + \frac{1}{9} + \left(-\frac{1}{27}\right)$

13-9 The Binomial Theorem

Objective: To use the binomial theorem to expand binomials.

The binomial expression $(a + b)$ can be raised to various powers. There are patterns to be found in the powers of $(a + b)$ listed below.

$$(a + b)^0 = 1$$

$$(a + b)^1 = 1a + 1b$$ *Note the coefficients of one.*

$$(a + b)^2 = 1a^2b^0 + 2ab + 1a^0b^2$$ *Why can b^0 and a^0 be written here?*

$$(a + b)^3 = 1a^3b^0 + 3a^2b^1 + 3a^1b^2 + 1a^0b^3$$ *What happened to the powers of a?*

$$(a + b)^4 = 1a^4b^0 + 4a^3b^1 + 6a^2b^2 + 4a^1b^3 + 1a^0b^4$$ *What about powers of b?*

Note the sum of the exponents in any term of $(a + b)^4$.
How many terms are in the expansion of $(a + b)^4$?

The following patterns are seen in the expansion of $(a + b)^n$.

1. The exponent of $(a + b)^n$ is the power of a in the first term and the power of b in the last term.
2. In successive terms, the exponent of a decreases by one. It is n in the first term and zero in the last term.
3. In successive terms, the exponent of b increases by one. It is zero in the first term and n in the last term.
4. The degree of each term is n.
5. Suppose you know one term. The coefficient of the next one is found as follows. Multiply the coefficient of the known term by the exponent of a in that term. Divide by the number of the known term. For example, $5a^4b^1$ is the second term of $(a + b)^5$. The coefficient of the third term is $(4 \cdot 5) \div 2$ or 10.
6. The coefficients are symmetric. They increase at the beginning and decrease at the end of the expansion.

example 1

Use the patterns to write $(a + b)^6$ in expanded form.

Indicate expansion with 4 of 7 terms.

$$(a + b)^6 = 1 \cdot a^6b^0 + \frac{6 \cdot 1}{1}a^{6-1}b^{0+1} + \cdots + \frac{6 \cdot 1}{1}a^{0+1}b^{6-1} + 1 \cdot a^0b^6$$

Construct third term and third from last term.

$$= a^6 + 6a^5b^1 + \frac{5 \cdot 6}{2}a^{5-1}b^{1+1} + \cdots + \frac{5 \cdot 6}{2}a^{1+1}b^{5-1} + 6a^1b^5 + 1a^0b^6$$

$$= a^6 + 6a^5b^1 + 15a^4b^2 + \frac{4 \cdot 15}{3}a^{4-1}b^{2+1} + 15a^2b^4 + 6a^1b^5 + 1a^0b^6$$

$$= a^6 + 6a^5b^1 + 15a^4b^2 + 20a^3b^3 + 15a^2b^4 + 6a^1b^5 + b^6$$

The Binomial Theorm includes the patterns found earlier.

The Binomial Theorem

If n is a positive integer, then the following is true.

$$(a + b)^n = 1a^nb^0 + \frac{n}{1}a^{n-1}b^1 + \frac{n(n-1)}{1 \cdot 2}a^{n-2}b^2 + \cdots + \frac{n}{1}a^1b^{n-1} + 1a^0b^n$$

example 2

Use the Binomial Theorem to find the first 5 terms in the expansion of $(x + y)^8$.

Find the first 5 terms. Then, use symmetry to find the remaining terms.

$$(x + y)^8 = 1 \cdot x^8y^0 + \frac{8}{1}x^7y^1 + \frac{8 \cdot 7}{1 \cdot 2}x^6y^2 + \frac{8 \cdot 7 \cdot 6}{1 \cdot 2 \cdot 3}x^5y^3 + \frac{8 \cdot 7 \cdot 6 \cdot 5}{1 \cdot 2 \cdot 3 \cdot 4}x^4y^4 + \cdots$$
$$= x^8 + 8x^7y + 28x^6y^2 + 56x^5y^3 + 70x^4y^4 + \cdots$$
$$= x^8 + 8x^7y + 28x^6y^2 + 56x^5y^3 + 70x^4y^4 + 56x^3y^5 + 28x^2y^6 + 8xy^7 + y^8$$

Note that in terms having the same coefficients the exponents are reversed, as in $28x^6y^2$ and $28x^2y^6$.

In Example 2, some of the denominators are written as shown.

$$1 \cdot 2 \cdot 3 \cdot 4 = 4 \cdot 3 \cdot 2 \cdot 1$$
$$1 \cdot 2 \cdot 3 = 3 \cdot 2 \cdot 1$$

This product of all the numbers from 1 to 4 is called 4 factorial. It is written 4!. Thus $4! = 4 \cdot 3 \cdot 2 \cdot 1$.

Definition of n Factorial

The expression $n!$ (n factorial) is defined as follows if n is an integer greater than zero.

$$n! = n(n-1)(n-2) \cdots (1)$$

By definition, $0! = 1$.

example 3

Evaluate $\frac{7!}{6!}$.

$$\frac{7!}{6!} = \frac{7 \cdot 6 \cdot 5 \cdot 4 \cdot 3 \cdot 2 \cdot 1}{6 \cdot 5 \cdot 4 \cdot 3 \cdot 2 \cdot 1}$$

Write each in expanded form.

$$= \frac{7}{1} \text{ or } 7$$

An equivalent form of the Binomial Theorem uses both sigma notation and factorial notation. It is written as follows.

$$(a + b)^n = \sum_{k=0}^{n} \frac{n!}{k!(n-k)!}a^{n-k}b^k$$

Here n is a positive integer, k is a positive integer or zero.

examples

4 Use the equivalent form of the Binomial Theorem to write $(s + t)^4$ in expanded form.

$$(s + t)^4 = \sum_{k=0}^{4} \frac{4!}{k!(4 - k)!} s^{4-k}t^k \qquad \textit{Now construct each term.}$$

$$= \frac{4!}{0!(4 - 0)!}s^{4-0}t^0 + \frac{4!}{1!(4 - 1)!}s^{4-1}t^1 + \frac{4!}{2!(4 - 2)!}s^{4-2}t^2 + \frac{4!}{3!(4 - 3)!}s^{4-3}t^3 + \frac{4!}{4!(4 - 4)!}s^{4-4}t^4$$

$$= \frac{4 \cdot 3 \cdot 2 \cdot 1}{1 \cdot 4 \cdot 3 \cdot 2 \cdot 1}s^4 + \frac{4 \cdot 3 \cdot 2 \cdot 1}{1 \cdot 3 \cdot 2 \cdot 1}s^3t + \frac{4 \cdot 3 \cdot 2 \cdot 1}{2 \cdot 1 \cdot 2 \cdot 1}s^2t^2 + \frac{4 \cdot 3 \cdot 2 \cdot 1}{3 \cdot 2 \cdot 1 \cdot 1}st^3 + \frac{4 \cdot 3 \cdot 2 \cdot 1}{4 \cdot 3 \cdot 2 \cdot 1 \cdot 1}t^4$$

$$= s^4 + 4s^3t + 6s^2t^2 + 4st^3 + t^4$$

5 Find the fifth term of $(p + q)^9$.

$$(p + q)^9 = \sum_{k=0}^{9} \frac{9!}{k!(9 - k)!} p^{9-k}q^k$$

In the fifth term, k will be 4, since k starts at zero.

The fifth term, $\frac{9!}{4!(9 - 4)!}p^{9-4}q^4$, is $\frac{9 \cdot 8 \cdot 7 \cdot 6}{1 \cdot 2 \cdot 3 \cdot 4}p^5q^4$ or $126p^5q^4$.

exercises

Max: 1–8, 1–14; Avg: 1–7, 1–13 odds; Min: 1–7 odds, 1–13 odds

Exploratory Evaluate each of the following.

1. $7!$ 5040
2. $9!$ 362,880
3. $10!$ 3,628,800
4. $12!$ 479,001,600
5. $\frac{10!}{8!}$ 90
6. $\frac{31!}{28!}$ 26,970
7. $\frac{6!}{3!}$ 120
8. $\frac{10!}{4!6!}$ 210

Written Write each of the following in expanded form. Simplify.

1. $\frac{k!}{(k - 1)!}$ k
2. $\frac{(k + 3)!}{(k + 2)!}$ $k + 3$
3. $(k + 1)!(k + 2)$ $(k + 2)!$
4. $\frac{3!4(k - 3)!}{(k - 2)!}$ $\frac{24}{k - 2}$

Write each of the following in expanded form. Simplify. See Teacher's Guide for answers.

5. $(a + b)^7$
6. $(2x + y)^5$
7. $(x - y)^6$
8. $\left(x - \frac{1}{2}y\right)^7$

Find the requested term of each of the following.

9. Fifth term of $(x + y)^7$ $35x^3y^4$
10. Fourth term of $(2x + 3y)^9$ $145,152x^6y^3$
11. Seventh term of $(x - y)^{15}$ $5005x^9y^6$
12. Fifth term of $(x - 2)^{10}$ $3360x^6$
13. Sixth term of $(2m + 3n)^{12}$ $24,634,368m^7n^5$
14. Eighth term of $(3a + 5b)^{11}$ $2,088,281,250a^4b^7$

Vocabulary

arithmetic sequence (360)
nth term (360)
common difference, d (360)
arithmetic means (361)
sigma notation (364)
index of summation (364)
arithmetic series (366)
sum of first n terms, S_n (366)
partial sums (367)
geometric sequence (369)
common ratio, r (369)
geometric means (370)
sum of geometric series (372)
infinite geometric series (375)
Fibonacci sequence (379)
recursive formula (382)
n factorial (386)
Binomial Theorem (386)

Chapter Summary

1. Definition of Arithmetic Sequence: An arithmetic sequence is a sequence in which the difference between any two consecutive terms is the same. (360)
2. Definition of the nth Term of an Arithmetic Sequence: The nth term of an arithmetic sequence with first term a_1 and common difference d is given by the following. $a_n = a_1 + (n - 1)d$. (361)
3. Definition of an Arithmetic Series: The sum of the terms of an arithmetic sequence is called an arithmetic series. (366)
4. Definition of S_n: The nth partial sum of a series is found by using the formula $S_n = \frac{n}{2}(a_1 + a_n)$. (367)
5. Definition of Geometric Sequence: In a geometric sequence, each term after the first is found by multiplying the previous term by a constant. (369)
6. Definition of a_n: The nth term of a geometric sequence is given by either of the formulas $a_n = a_1 r^{n-1}$ or $a_n = a_{n-1}r$. (369)
7. Definition of the Sum of a Geometric Series: The sum of the first n terms of a geometric series is given by the formula $S_n = \frac{a_1 - a_1 r^n}{1 - r}$ where $r \neq 1$. (372)
8. Definition of the Sum of an Infinite Geometric Series: The sum, S, of an infinite geometric series is given by the following formula: $S = \frac{a_1}{1 - r}$ when $^-1 < r < 1$. (376)
9. The Fibonacci sequence is 1, 1, 2, 3, 5, 8, 13, ... If F_n is the nth term of the Fibonacci sequence, then $F_n = F_{n-2} + F_{n-1}$. (379)
10. Definition of n Factorial: $n! = n(n - 1)(n - 2) \cdots (1)$. (386)
11. The Binomial Theorem: If n is a positive integer, then $(a + b)^n =$
$1 \cdot a^n b^0 + \frac{n}{1}a^{n-1}b^1 + \frac{n(n-1)}{1 \cdot 2}a^{n-2}b^2 + \cdots + \frac{n}{1}a^1 b^{n-1} + 1 \cdot a^0 b^n$. (386)

Chapter Review

13-1 1. Find the first 5 terms of the arithmetic sequence when $a_1 = 6$, $d = 8$. 6, 14, 22, 30, 38

2. Find the next 4 terms of the arithmetic sequence 9, 12, 15, ... 18, 21, 24, 27

Find the nth term of the following arithmetic sequences.

3. $a_1 = 3$, $d = 7$, $n = 34$ 234

4. $a_1 = {}^-9$, $d = {}^-2$, $n = 21$ $^-49$

5. Which term of $^-5$, 2, 9, . . . is 142? 22

6. Find the missing terms for the arithmetic sequence $^-7$, <u>$^-3$</u>, <u>1</u>, <u>5</u>, 9.

13-2 7. Write the sum $\sum_{k=8}^{11} (3k - 4)$ in expanded form. 20 + 23 + 26 + 29

8. Evaluate $\sum_{r=0}^{10} (5 + 8r)$. 495

13-3 **Find the sum of n terms of each of the following arithmetic series.**

9. $a_1 = 12$, $a_n = 117$, $n = 36$

10. $a_1 = 4$, $d = 6$, $n = 18$

11. $d = 4$, $n = 16$, $a_n = 75$

9. 2322 10. 990 11. 720

12. Find the sum of the series 7 + 10 + 13 + · · · + 97. 1612

13-4 13. Find the common ratio of the sequence $\frac{2}{3}, \frac{4}{3}, \frac{8}{3}, \frac{16}{3}, \ldots$. 2

14. Find the next 2 terms for the geometric sequence $\frac{15}{2}$, 15, 30, <u>60</u>, <u>120</u>.

15. Find the 5th term of the geometric sequence in which $a_1 = 7$ and $r = 3$. 567

16. Find the geometric means of 4, <u>12</u>, <u>36</u>, <u>108</u>, 324.

13-5 **Find the sum of the following geometric series.**

17. $a_1 = 6$, $r = 3$, $n = 5$ 726

18. $a_1 = 625$, $a_n = 16$, $r = \frac{2}{5}$ 1031

19. $\sum_{k=1}^{6} 3(2^{k-1})$ 189

20. A ball dropped from a height of 21 feet rebounds $\frac{2}{3}$ of the distance from which it was dropped on each bounce. How far has the ball traveled after 6 bounces (rebounds)? 104.9 feet

21. For the geometric series, find a_1 given that $S_n = 1441$, $r = \frac{3}{5}$, and $n = 5$. 625

13-6 22. Find the sum of the series $\frac{1}{2} + \frac{1}{3} + \frac{2}{9} + \frac{4}{27} + \cdots$. $\frac{3}{2}$

Find a common fraction equivalent to the repeating decimals.

23. $0.\overline{4}$ $\frac{4}{9}$

24. $0.1\overline{7}$ $\frac{8}{45}$

13-7 25. Find the pattern and complete the sequence for 3, 7, 12, 18, 25, <u>33</u>, <u>42</u>, <u>52</u>, <u>63</u>.

$a_n = a_{n-1} + (a_{n-1} - a_{n-2} + 1)$

13-8 26. Find the first 5 terms of this sequence: $a_1 = 1$, $a_2 = 3$, $a_{n+2} = a_{n+1} + 2 \cdot a_n$. 1, 3, 5, 11, 21

27. Write the following series in summation notation 2 + 6 + 12 + 20 + 30 + 42.

$\sum_{k=1}^{6} (k + 1)k$

Chapter Test

Solve each problem.

1. Find the next 4 terms of the arithmetic sequence 42, 37, 32, ... 27, 22, 17, 12

2. Find the 27th term of an arithmetic sequence when $a_1 = 2$, $d = 6$. 158

3. Find the next 2 terms of the geometric sequence $\frac{1}{81}, \frac{1}{27}, \frac{1}{9}, \underline{\frac{1}{3}}, \underline{1}$.

4. Find the sixth term of a geometric sequence if $a_1 = 5$ and $r = {}^-2$. $^-160$

5. Which term of the sequence 7, 13, 19, . . . is 193? 32

6. Find the missing terms for the arithmetic sequence $^-5$, $\underline{1}$, $\underline{7}$, $\underline{13}$, 19.

7. Find the geometric means of 7, $\underline{21}$, $\underline{63}$, 189.

8. A vacuum pump removes $\frac{1}{7}$ of the air from a jar on each stroke of its piston. What percent of the air remains after 4 strokes of the piston? $\approx 53.97\%$

Find the sum of n integers of each of the following arithmetic series.

9. $a_1 = 7$, $n = 31$, $a_n = 127$ 2077

10. $a_1 = 13$, $d = {}^-2$, $n = 17$ $^-51$

Find the sum of the following geometric series.

11. $a_1 = 125$, $r = \frac{2}{5}$, $n = 4$ 203

12. $a_1 = 16$, $a_n = -\frac{1}{2}$, $r = -\frac{1}{2}$ $10\frac{1}{2}$

Solve each problem.

13. How many integers between 26 and 415 are multiples of 9? 44

14. A free-falling body falls distances of 16, 48, 80, 112, . . . in successive seconds. How far will it fall in 10 seconds? 1600

15. Write $\sum_{k=2}^{6} (3k^2 - 1)$ in expanded form.
    $11 + 26 + 47 + 74 + 107$

16. Find the sum of the series $12 - 6 + 3 - \frac{3}{2} + \cdots$. 8

17. Find the sum of the series $91 + 85 + 79 + \cdots + ({}^-29)$. 651

18. Find the pattern and complete the sequence 3, 3, 6, 18, 72, $\underline{360}$, $\underline{2160}$, $\underline{15{,}120}$.
    18. $a_n = (n - 1)(a_{n-1})$

19. Find the first 5 terms of this sequence: $a_1 = 3$, $a_2 = 1$, $a_{n+2} = a_{n+1} + 2 \cdot a_n$.
    3, 1, 7, 9, 23

20. Find the first 3 terms of this arithmetic series: $a_1 = 7$, $n = 13$, $S_n = 1027$.
    7, 19, 31

21. Evaluate $\sum_{k=3}^{15} (14 - 2k)$. $^-52$

22. Find a common fraction equivalent to the repeating decimals $0.\overline{7}$ and $0.3\overline{2}$. $\frac{7}{9}, \frac{29}{90}$

23. Describe the sequence 2, 6, 18, 54, 162, . . . recursively. $a_{n+1} = 3a_n$, $a_1 = 2$

24. Describe the sequence 2, 6, 18, 54, 162, . . . in terms of n. $a_n = 2 \cdot 3^{n-1}$

Chapter

14

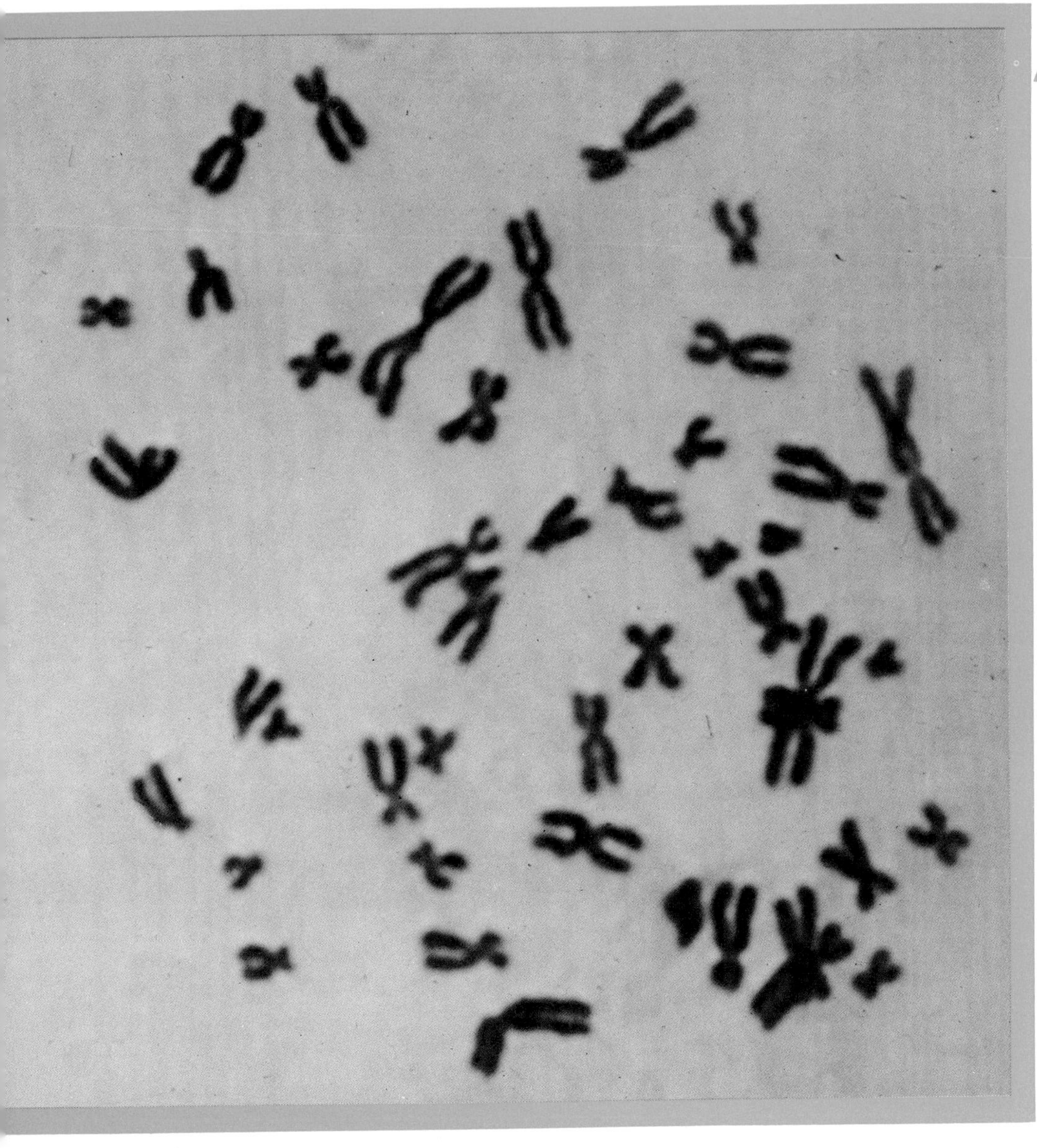

Probability

In studying plants and animals, biologists often gather extensive data. Sometimes they can discover genetic patterns and use probability to predict characteristics of future generations.

14–1 Counting

Objective: To use the Basic Counting Principle.

Jana Lee is ordering a new automobile. She still has three choices to make.

1. V-6 or V-8 engine?
2. Standard or automatic transmission?
3. Blue, white, or orange?

These three choices are called **independent events.** That is, the choice of one of them does not affect the others. Jana's possible choices can be shown in a diagram.

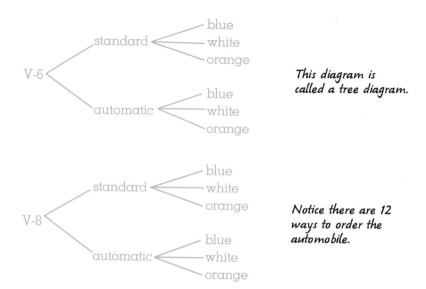

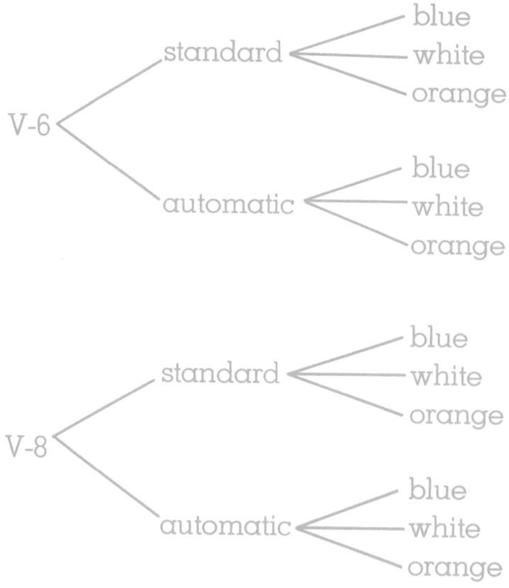

This diagram is called a tree diagram.

Notice there are 12 ways to order the automobile.

You can find the total number of choices that Jana has without drawing a diagram.

Choices:	V-6 or V-8	standard or automatic	blue or white or orange
Number of choices:	2	2	3

If each choice, or event, is indicated by a blank, ____, and then the number of ways each can be chosen is written in the corresponding blank, we have $\underline{2} \cdot \underline{2} \cdot \underline{3} = 12$.

Suppose an event can be chosen in *p* different ways. Another independent event can be chosen in *q* different ways. Then the two events can be chosen successively in $p \cdot q$ ways.

Basic Counting Principle

This principle can be extended to any number of independent events.

examples

1 **How many different three-letter patterns can be formed using the letters *a*, *b*, and *c*?**

Letters:	1st	2nd	3rd
Ways to choose:	$\underline{3}$	$\underline{3}$	$\underline{3}$

A pattern is a selection of three letters. Each one must be a or b or c.

There are $\underline{3} \cdot \underline{3} \cdot \underline{3}$ or 27 possible patterns.

2 **How many different three-letter patterns can be formed using the letters *a*, *b*, and *c* if each letter is used exactly once?**

Letters:	1st	2nd	3rd
Ways to choose:	$\underline{3}$	$\underline{2}$	$\underline{1}$

Note that after the first letter is chosen, it may not be chosen again. That leaves only 2 ways.

There are $\underline{3} \cdot \underline{2} \cdot \underline{1} = 3!$ or 6 patterns.

3 **How many seven-digit phone numbers can begin with the prefix 457?**

Digit in phone number:	4th	5th	6th	7th
Ways to choose:	$\underline{10}$	$\underline{10}$	$\underline{10}$	$\underline{10}$

There are $\underline{10} \cdot \underline{10} \cdot \underline{10} \cdot \underline{10} = 10^4$ or 10,000 numbers.

2. If same person can only hold one position then choice is *not* independent.

exercises

Max: 1–4, 1–14; Avg: 1–4, 1–13 odds; Min: 1–4 odds, 1–13 odds

Exploratory **Tell whether each choice is independent or not.**

1. Choose color and size to order an item of clothing. independent
2. Choose a president, secretary, and treasurer for a club. see above
3. Choose five numbers in a bingo game. not independent
4. Each of five people guess the total number of runs in a baseball game. They write down the guess, without telling what it is. independent

Written **Solve each of the following.**

1. The letters *g, h, j, k,* and *l* are to be used to form five-letter patterns. How many patterns can be formed? Repetitions are allowed. $5^5 = 3125$
2. A license plate must have two letters (not I or O) followed by three digits. The last digit cannot be zero. How many possible plates are there? $24^2 \times 10^2 \times 9 = 518{,}400$
3. There are five roads from Albany to Briscoe, six from Briscoe to Chadwick, three from Chadwick to Dover. How many different routes are there from Albany to Dover? $5 \times 6 \times 3 = 90$
4. A store has 15 sofas, 12 lamps, and 10 tables at half-price. How many different ways could a sofa, a lamp, and a table be bought on sale? $15 \times 12 \times 10 = 1800$
5. How many ways can six different books be placed on a shelf? $6! = 720$
6. How many ways can six books be placed on a shelf if the only dictionary must be on an end? $2 \times 5 \times 4 \times 3 \times 2 \times 1 = 240$
7. How many different 4-letter patterns can be formed from the letters, *a, e, i, o, r, s, t* in which no letter occurs more than once? 840
8. How many of the patterns in problem 7 begin with a vowel and end with a consonant? 240
9. How many 4-digit patterns are there in which all the digits are different? 5040
10. Using the letters from the word *equation*, how many 5-letter patterns can be formed in which *q* is followed immediately by *u*? 480

10. Hint: Count the positions *q* can occupy and the choices available for the others.

11. In how many ways can 3 dice of different colors be thrown at the same time? 216
12. How many five-digit numbers between and including 65,000 and 69,999 can be made if no digit is repeated? 1344
13. A restaurant serves 5 main dishes, 3 salads, and 4 desserts. How many different meals could be ordered if each has a main dish, a salad, and a dessert? 60
14. A bookstore has 9 different gardening books and 15 different cookbooks. How many ways can a person buy a gardening book and then a cookbook? 135

14-2 Linear Permutations

Objective: To use linear permutations to count possible orders of objects.

Suppose a group of objects are placed in an arrangement. The arrangement of things in a certain order is called a **permutation.** In a permutation, the *order* of the objects is very important.

Suppose you are going to make a pattern of beads on a hanging. A pattern of 5 beads is to be repeated. There are eight colors available. The pattern will have only one each of the colors chosen. How many patterns are possible?

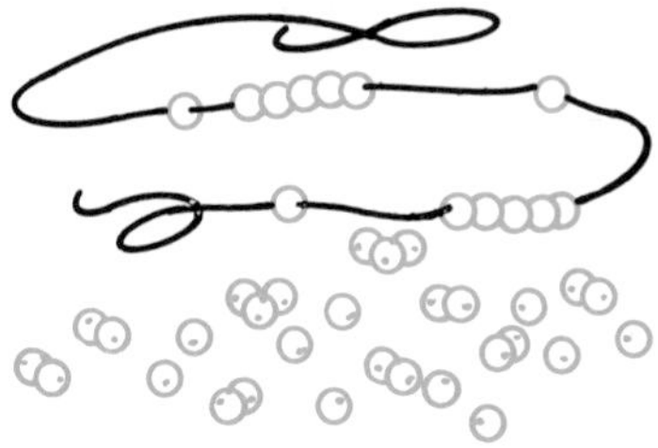

Beads:	1st	2nd	3rd	4th	5th
Ways:	8	7	6	5	4

There are $\underline{8} \cdot \underline{7} \cdot \underline{6} \cdot \underline{5} \cdot \underline{4} = \frac{8!}{3!}$ or 6720 possible patterns.

Factorial notation was introduced in Chapter 13.

In mathematics, this number of ways to arrange 8 things, taking them 5 at a time, is written $P(8, 5)$. Mathematicians speak of taking n objects, r at a time.

Be careful to use only "single-viewable" examples.

The number of permutations of n objects, taken r at a time, is defined as follows.

$$P(n, r) = \frac{n!}{(n-r)!}$$

Definition of $P(n, r)$

Notations equivalent to $P(n, r)$ are $P_{n,r}$ and ${}_nP_r$.

If all the objects are taken at once, you write $P(n, n)$.

$$P(n, n) = \frac{n!}{(n-n)!} \text{ or } \frac{n!}{1}$$

example 1

How many ways can 3 of 7 different candles be arranged on a mantel?

Find the number of permutations of 7 objects, taken 3 at a time.

$$P(n, r) = \frac{n!}{(n-r)!}$$

$$P(7, 3) = \frac{7!}{(7-3)!}$$ *Substitute 7 for n and 3 for r.*

$$= \frac{7 \cdot 6 \cdot 5 \cdot 4 \cdot 3 \cdot 2 \cdot 1}{4 \cdot 3 \cdot 2 \cdot 1} \text{ or } 210$$

There are 210 ways to arrange 3 of 7 different candles.

example 2

How many ways can 3 students be seated in a row of 5 chairs?

$$P(5, 3) = \frac{5!}{(5-3)!}$$

Substitute 5 for n and 3 for r in $P(n, r) = \frac{n!}{(n-r)!}$.

$$= \frac{5 \cdot 4 \cdot 3 \cdot 2 \cdot 1}{2 \cdot 1} \text{ or } 60$$

There are 60 ways the students can be seated.

How many ways can the letters of the word *free* be arranged? The four letters can be arranged in $P(4, 4)$ ways. $P(4, 4) = 4!$ or $4 \cdot 3 \cdot 2 \cdot 1$ or 24. There are 24 ways. However, some of these arrangements look the same. The two e's are not distinguishable. If we call them e_1 and e_2, then e_1fre_2 and e_2fre_1 are different. Drop the subscripts and the two appear the same: *efre*. The two e's can be arranged in $P(2, 2)$ ways. $P(2, 2) = 2!$ or 2.

$$\frac{P(4, 4)}{P(2, 2)} = \frac{4!}{2!}$$

To find the number of arrangements, divide by 2!.

$$= \frac{4 \cdot 3 \cdot 2 \cdot 1}{2 \cdot 1} \text{ or } 12$$

There are 12 ways to arrange the letters.

When some objects are alike, use the following rule to find the number of permutations of those objects.

Permutations with Repetitions

The number of permutations of *n* objects of which *p* are alike and *q* are alike is found by evaluating the following expression. $\frac{n!}{p!q!}$

example 3

How many 7-letter patterns can be formed from the letters of *benzene*?

Find the number of permutations of 7 objects of which 3 are e's and 2 are *n*'s.

$$\frac{7!}{3!2!} = \frac{7 \cdot 6 \cdot 5 \cdot 4 \cdot 3 \cdot 2 \cdot 1}{3 \cdot 2 \cdot 1 \cdot 2 \cdot 1}$$

$$= 420$$

There are 420 7-letter patterns.

exercises

Max: 1–10, 1–22; **Avg:** 1–10, 1–21 odds; **Min:** 1–9 odds, 1–21 odds

Exploratory Tell whether each statement below is true or false.

1. $5! - 3! = 2!$ F
2. $6 \cdot 5! = 6!$ T
3. $\frac{6!}{3!} = 2!$ F
4. $(6 - 3)! = 6! - 3!$ F
5. $\frac{6!}{30} = 4!$ T
6. $\frac{6!}{8!} \cdot \frac{8!}{6!} = 1$ T
7. $3! + 4! = 5 \cdot 3!$ T
8. $1!2!3!2! = 4!$ T
9. $\frac{P(9, 9)}{9!} = 1$ T
10. $\frac{3!}{3} = \frac{2!}{2}$ F

Written How many ways can the letters of the following words be arranged?

1. FLOWER $6! = 720$
2. STUDY $5! = 120$
3. POP $3!/2! = 3$
4. SEE $3!/2! = 3$
5. PEGGY $5!/2! = 60$
6. LEVEL $5!/(2!2!) = 30$
7. MISSISSIPPI $11!/(4!4!2!) = 34{,}650$
8. ALASKA $6!/3! = 120$
9. ALGEBRA $7!/2! = 2520$
10. PARALLEL $8!/(2!3!) = 3360$

Find the value of each of the following.

11. $\frac{P(6, 4)}{P(5, 3)}$ 6
12. $\frac{P(6, 3) \cdot P(4, 2)}{P(5, 2)}$ 72

Find n in each of the following equations.

13. $n[P(5, 3)] = P(7, 5)$ 42
14. $P(n, 4) = 3[P(n, 3)]$ 6
15. $P(n, 4) = 40[P(n - 1, 2)]$ 8
16. $7[P(n, 5)] = P(n, 3) \cdot P(9, 3)$ 12

Solve each problem.

17. Don has 5 pennies, 3 nickels, and 4 dimes. The coins of each denomination are indistinguishable. How many ways can he arrange the coins in a row? 27,720
18. Estelle has 8 quarters, 5 dimes, 3 nickels, and a penny. The coins of each denomination are indistinguishable. How many ways can she place the coins in a straight line? 12,252,240
19. Ten scores received on a test were 82, 91, 75, 83, 91, 64, 83, 77, 91, and 75. In how many different orders might they be recorded? 151,200
20. How many 6-digit numbers can be made using the digits from 833,284? 180
21. There are 3 identical red flags and 5 identical white flags that are used to send signals. All 8 flags must be used. How many signals can be given? 56
22. Five algebra and 4 geometry books are to be placed on a shelf. How many ways can they be arranged if all the algebra books are together? 14,400

14-3 Circular Permutations

Objective: To count arrangements of objects in a circle.

A food vending machine has 6 items on each of the revolving trays. One such tray has an orange, an apple, a can of juice, a salad, a cup of yogurt, and a boiled egg. How many ways can these items be arranged on the tray?

Think of each tray as a circle. Let the letters, o, a, j, s, y, and e stand for the various items on the tray. Three possible arrangements are shown below.

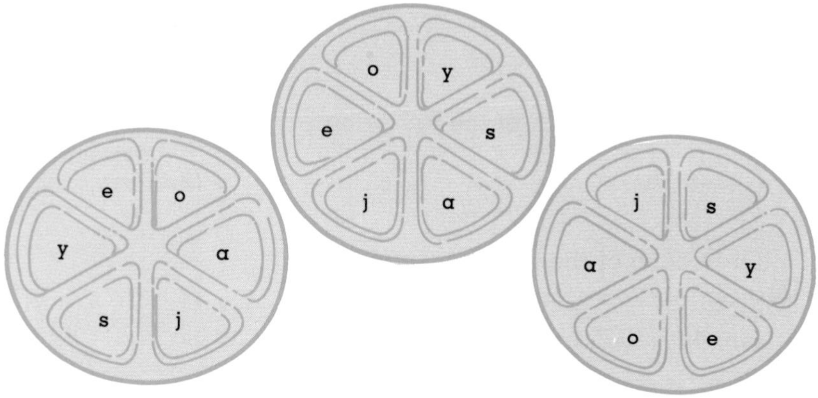

It becomes the third; second.

How does the first arrangement change as the tray is turned? Which arrangement is *really* different from the other two?

When 6 objects are placed in a line, there are 6! or 120 arrangements of the 6 objects taken 6 at a time. However, when they are arranged in a circle, some of the arrangements are alike. These arrangements fall into groups of six, each of which can be found from one another by turning the circle. Thus, the number of really different arrangements around a circle is $\frac{1}{6}$ of the total number of arrangements in a line.

$$\frac{1}{6} \cdot 6! = \frac{6 \cdot 5 \cdot 4 \cdot 3 \cdot 2 \cdot 1}{6}$$
$$= 5 \cdot 4 \cdot 3 \cdot 2 \cdot 1$$
$$= 5! \text{ or } (6 - 1)!$$

There are (6 − 1)! arrangements of 6 objects around a circle.

Suppose n objects are arranged in a circle. Then there are $\frac{n!}{n}$ or $(n - 1)!$ permutations of the n objects around the circle.

Circular Permutations

example 1

Five people are to be seated at a round table. How many seating arrangements are possible?

$(5 - 1)! = 4!$

$= 4 \cdot 3 \cdot 2 \cdot 1$ or 24

Suppose the people are seated around the table. Everyone moves one chair to the left. Each person is now still sitting next to the same two people as before.

If n objects on a circle are arranged in relation to a fixed point, then there are $n!$ permutations.

Suppose now that five people are to be seated at a round table. One of them is seated close to the door as shown. How many arrangements are possible? 120

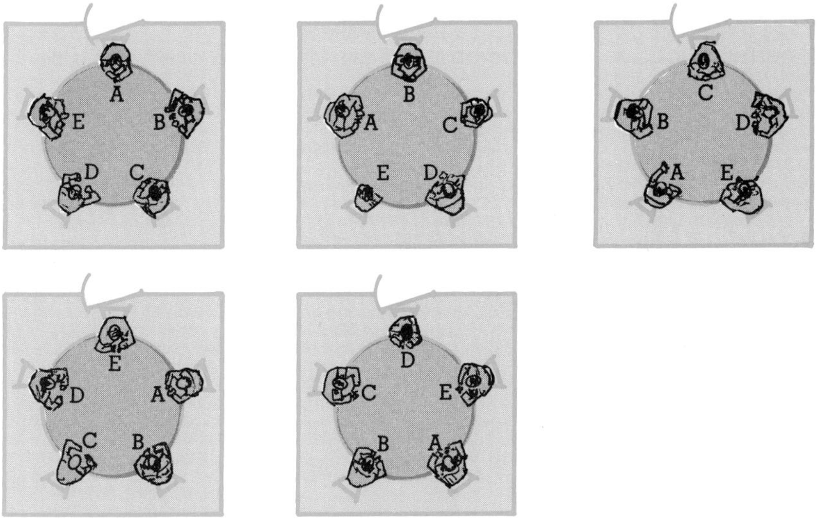

These arrangements are different. In each one, a different person sits closest to the door. Thus, there are $P(5, 5)$ or $5!$ arrangements relative to a fixed point which is the door.

$$5! = 5 \cdot 4 \cdot 3 \cdot 2 \cdot 1 \text{ or } 120$$

Suppose three keys are placed on a key ring. Then it appears that there are at most $(3 - 1)!$ or 2 different arrangements of keys on the ring.

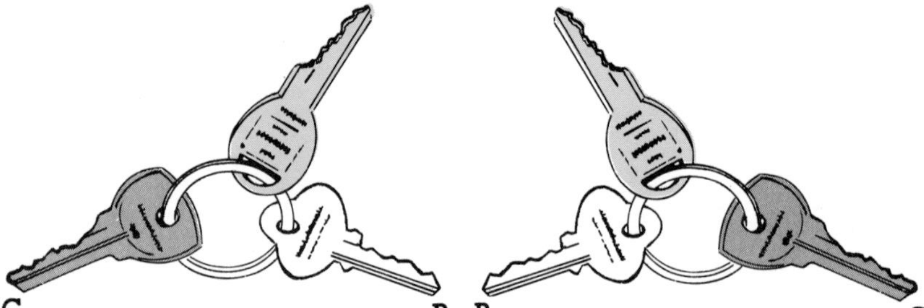

But what happens if the key ring with the first arrangement is turned over? The second arrangement appears. Then there is really only one arrangement of the three keys. These two arrangements are **reflections** of one another. There are only half as many arrangements when reflections are possible.

$$\frac{(3-1)!}{2} = \frac{2}{2} \text{ or } 1$$

examples

2 **How many ways can 5 charms be placed on a bracelet which has no clasp?**

This is a circular permutation. Because the bracelet can be turned over, it is also reflective.

$$\frac{(5-1)!}{2} = \frac{4!}{2}$$
$$= \frac{4 \cdot 3 \cdot 2 \cdot 1}{2} \text{ or } 12$$

There are 12 ways to arrange the charms.

3 **Suppose the bracelet has a clasp.**

This is no longer a circular permutation since objects are arranged with respect to a fixed point, the clasp. However, it is still reflective.

$$\frac{5!}{2} = \frac{5 \cdot 4 \cdot 3 \cdot 2 \cdot 1}{2}$$
$$= \frac{5 \cdot 4 \cdot 3 \cdot 2 \cdot 1}{2} \text{ or } 60$$

There are 60 ways to arrange the charms.

1., 4. reflective; 2., 3., 5., 6., 7., 8., 9., 10., 11. nonreflective

exercises

Max: 1–22, 1–22; **Avg:** 1–22, 1–21 odds; **Min:** 1–21 odds, 1–21 odds

Exploratory **State whether arrangements of the following objects are reflective or not reflective.** See above.

1. charms on a charm bracelet, having no clasp
2. a football huddle of 11 players
3. chairs arranged in a circle
4. beads on a necklace with no clasp
5. chairs in a row
6. a pearl necklace that is open
7. people seated around a square table relative to each other
8. people seated around a square table relative to one chair
9. a baseball team's batting order
10. a list of students in a given class
11. placing 6 coins in a circular pattern on a table

12–22. State whether the arrangements of the objects in problems **1–11** are circular or linear. **12., 13., 14., 15., 18., 22.** circular; **16., 17., 19., 20., 21.** linear

Written **Evaluate each of the following.**

1. $8! - 6!$ 39,600
2. $5!3!$ 720
3. $\frac{6!}{4!}$ 30
4. $3 \cdot 5!$ 360
5. $6! + 5!$ 840
6. $\frac{8! + 6!}{8! - 6!}$ 1.0364
7. $P(8, 5)$ 6720
8. $P(10, 4)$ 5040
9. $3!P(6, 5) \cdot P(9, 2)$ 311, 040
10. $4!3!P(7, 3)$ 30,240
11. $\frac{P(6, 4) \cdot P(5, 2)}{5!}$ 60
12. $\frac{P(8, 3) \cdot P(5, 4)}{P(6, 6)}$ 56
13. $\frac{P(12, 6)}{P(12, 3) \cdot P(8, 2)}$ 9
14. $\frac{P(10, 8)}{5!P(8, 5)}$ 2.25

Solve each of the following.

15. How many ways can 6 keys be arranged on a key ring? 60
16. How many ways can 6 people be seated around a campfire? 120
17. How many ways can 8 charms be arranged on a charm bracelet? 2520
18. How many ways can 4 men and 4 women be seated alternately at a round table? 72
19. How many ways can 5 people be seated at a round table relative to each other? 24
20. How many ways can 5 people be seated at a round table relative to the door in the room? 120
21. How many ways can 5 people be seated around a circular table if 2 of the people must be seated next to each other? 12
22. Twenty beads are strung in a circle. Fourteen are natural wood and 6 are red. How many ways can the red beads be strung in the circle? 969

14-4 Combinations

Objective: To find the number of combinations of n things, taken r at a time.

Nine people have applied for the 5 remaining available jobs in a new grocery store. How many different groups of 5 people can be hired? In this situation, the order in which the people are hired is not a consideration. The selection above is called a **combination** of 9 things taken 5 at a time. It is denoted C(9, 5).

$$C(9, 5) = \frac{9!}{4!5!}$$

9! is the number of arrangements of all 9 people.
5! is the number of arrangements of the 5 people hired.
4! is the number of arrangements of the 4 people not hired.

$$= \frac{9 \cdot 8 \cdot 7 \cdot 6 \cdot 5 \cdot 4 \cdot 3 \cdot 2 \cdot 1}{4 \cdot 3 \cdot 2 \cdot 1 \cdot 5 \cdot 4 \cdot 3 \cdot 2 \cdot 1}$$

$$= \frac{9 \cdot 8 \cdot 7 \cdot 6}{1 \cdot 2 \cdot 3 \cdot 4} \text{ or } 126$$

Note 4 = (9 − 5).

Definition of C(n, r)

> **The number of combinations of n objects, taken r at a time, is written C(n, r).**
>
> $$C(n, r) = \frac{n!}{(n-r)!r!}$$

The main difference between a permutation and a combination is whether order is considered (permutation) or not (combination).

example 1

How many diagonals does a decagon have?

Each diagonal has two endpoints. Suppose one has endpoints A and B. Then segment AB and segment BA are the same. Thus, order is not considered, and the combination of 10 points, taken two at a time, is desired. This gives the total number of line segments. But 10 of them are sides, so the number of diagonals is as follows.

$$C(10, 2) - 10 = \frac{10!}{(10-2)!2!} - 10$$

$$= \frac{10!}{8!2!} - 10$$

Note $10! = 10 \cdot 9 \cdot 8 \cdot 7 \cdot 6 \cdot 5 \cdot 4 \cdot 3 \cdot 2 \cdot 1 = 10 \cdot 9 \cdot 8!$

$$= \frac{10 \cdot 9 \cdot 8!}{8!2!} - 10$$

$$= \frac{10 \cdot 9}{2 \cdot 1} - 10 \text{ or } 35$$

There are 35 diagonals.

examples

2

From a group of 6 men and 4 women, how many committees of 2 men and 3 women can be formed?

Again, order is not considered. The questions are: How many ways can 2 men be chosen from 6? How many ways can 3 women be chosen from 4?

$$
\begin{aligned}
C(6, 2) \cdot C(4, 3) &= \frac{6!}{(6-2)!2!} \cdot \frac{4!}{(4-3)!3!} \\
&= \frac{6!}{4!2!} \cdot \frac{4!}{(1)!3!} \\
&= \frac{6 \cdot 5}{2 \cdot 1} \cdot \frac{4}{1} \\
&= 15 \cdot 4 \text{ or } 60
\end{aligned}
$$

Write out the factorials to see how to get the next line.

There are 60 possible committees.

3

From a deck of 52 cards, how many ways can 5 cards be drawn so that 3 are of 1 suit and 2 are of another?

C(4, 2)	Two of the 4 suits will be chosen.
C(13, 3)	Three from 1 suit will be chosen.
C(13, 2)	Two from the second suit will be chosen.

Thus, the number of ways is as follows.

$$
\begin{aligned}
C(4, 2) \cdot C(13, 3) \cdot C(13, 2) &= \frac{4!}{2!2!} \cdot \frac{13!}{10!3!} \cdot \frac{13!}{11!2!} \\
&= \frac{4 \cdot 3}{2 \cdot 1} \cdot \frac{13 \cdot 12 \cdot 11}{3 \cdot 2 \cdot 1} \cdot \frac{13 \cdot 12}{2 \cdot 1} \\
&= 6 \cdot 286 \cdot 78 \text{ or } 133{,}848
\end{aligned}
$$

There are 133,848 ways.

4

In an urn, there are 17 numbered discs. Eight are red, 5 are white, and 4 are blue. How many ways can 2 red, 1 white, and 2 blue discs be chosen?

C(8, 2)	Two of 8 red ones will be chosen.
C(5, 1)	One of 5 white ones will be chosen.
C(4, 2)	Two of 4 blue ones will be chosen.

$$C(8, 2) \cdot C(5, 1) \cdot C(4, 2) = \frac{8 \cdot 7}{2 \cdot 1} \cdot 5 \cdot \frac{4 \cdot 3}{2 \cdot 1} \text{ or } 840$$

There are 840 ways.

exercises

Max: 1–8, 1–26; Avg: 1–8, 1–25 odds; Min: 1–25 odds

Exploratory State whether arrangements of the following represent a combination or a permutation.

1. a team of 5 people chosen from a group of 12 people
2. three-letter patterns chosen from the letters of the word *algebra*
3. a hand of 5 cards
4. a batting order in baseball
5. seating students in a row
6. the answers on a true-false test
7. a committee of 4 men and 5 women chosen from 8 men and 7 women
8. people seated around a table

1., 3., 7. combination; **2., 4., 5., 6., 8.** permutation

Written Evaluate.

1. $C(8, 3)$ 56
2. $C(8, 5) \cdot C(7, 3)$ 1,960
3. $C(7, 2)$ 21
4. $C(24, 21)$ 2024

Find the value of n in each of the following.

5. $C(n, 3) = C(n, 8)$ 11 Hint: Solve $n - 3 = 8$.
6. $C(n, 5) = C(n, 7)$ 12
7. $C(n, 12) = C(30, 18)$ 30
8. $C(14, 3) = C(n, 11)$ 14

Solve each of the following.

9. From a list of 12 books, how many groups of 5 books can be selected? 792
10. How many baseball teams of 9 members can be formed from 14 players? 2002
11. Suppose there are 9 points on a circle. How many different 4-sided closed figures can be formed by joining any 4 of these points? 126
12. There are 85 telephones at Kennedy High School. How many connections can be made among the school telephones? 3570
13. How many different groups of 25 people can be formed from 27 people? 351
14. Suppose there are 8 points in a plane, no 3 of which are collinear. How many distinct triangles could be formed with these points as vertices? 56
15. From a deck of 52 playing cards, how many different hands can have 5 cards of the same suit? 5148
16. From a deck of 52 playing cards, how many different 4-card hands can have each card from a different suit? 28,561

A bag contains 4 red, 6 white, and 9 blue marbles. How many ways can 5 marbles be selected to meet the following conditions?

17. All the marbles are white. 6
18. All the marbles are blue. 126
19. All the marbles are red. 0
20. Two are red, 2 are white, and 1 is blue. 810
21. Two must be blue. 4320
22. Two are 1 color and 3 are another color. 2808

From a group of 8 men and 10 women, a committee of 5 is to be formed. How many committees can be formed if the committee is to be comprised as follows?

23. All are men. 56
24. There are 3 men and 2 women. 2520
25. There is 1 man and 4 women. 1680
26. All are women. 252

14-5 Probability

Objective: To evaluate the probability that a certain event will occur.

When a coin is tossed, only two outcomes are possible. Either the coin will show a *head* or a *tail*. The desired outcome is called a **success.** Any other outcome is called a **failure.**

Probability of Success and of Failure

If an event can succeed in s ways and fail in f ways, then the probabilities of success $P(s)$ and of failure $P(f)$ are as follows.

$$P(s) = \frac{s}{s + f} \qquad P(f) = \frac{f}{s + f}$$

If the event cannot succeed, $P(s) = 0$. If the event cannot fail, $P(s) = 1$.

$$P(s) + P(f) = \frac{s}{s+f} + \frac{f}{s+f}$$

$$= \frac{s+f}{s+f} \text{ or } 1$$

This is an important property of probabilities.

Because their sum is one, $P(s)$ and $P(f)$ are called complements.

If $P(s)$ is $\frac{1}{3}$, then $P(f)$ is $1 - \frac{1}{3}$ or $\frac{2}{3}$.

examples

1 **A bag contains 5 blue marbles and 4 white marbles. What is the probability that a marble selected will be blue?**

$$P(\text{blue marble}) = \frac{s}{s+f}$$

P(blue marble) is read the probability of selecting a blue marble.

$$= \frac{5}{5+4} \text{ or } \frac{5}{9}$$

A blue marble is a success.
A white marble is a failure.

The probability of selecting a blue marble is $\frac{5}{9}$.

2 **A committee of 2 is to be selected from a group of 6 men and 3 women. What is the probability that the 2 selected are women?**

$$P(\text{two women}) = \frac{C(3, 2)}{C(9, 2)}$$

There are C(3, 2) ways to select 2 of 3 women.
There are C(9, 2) ways to select 2 of 9 people.

$$= \frac{\frac{3!}{1!2!}}{\frac{9!}{7!2!}} \text{ or } \frac{1}{12}$$

The probability of 2 women committee members is $\frac{1}{12}$.

Definition of Odds

> The odds of the successful outcome of an event is expressed as the ratio of the number of ways it can succeed to the number of ways it can fail.
>
> $$\text{Odds} = \text{the ratio of } s \text{ to } f \quad \text{or} \quad \frac{s}{f}$$

examples

3

What are the odds of tossing a die and getting a 3?

The number 3 is on only one face of the die. All 5 of the rest of the faces have a number other than 3.

$\text{Odds} = \frac{1}{5}$ *A 3 can appear only 1 way. Other numbers can appear 5 ways.*

The odds of getting a 3 are 1 to 5.

4

What are the odds that a child will have blue eyes in the following situation?

The father and mother each have brown eyes. In each pair of their parents, one has brown eyes and the other blue eyes. Thus, the father and mother each have the capability to pass on either the brown-eye or the blue-eye characteristic. Let B stand for the brown-eye characteristic, which is dominant over the blue-eye characteristic, b.
The possibilities are shown below.

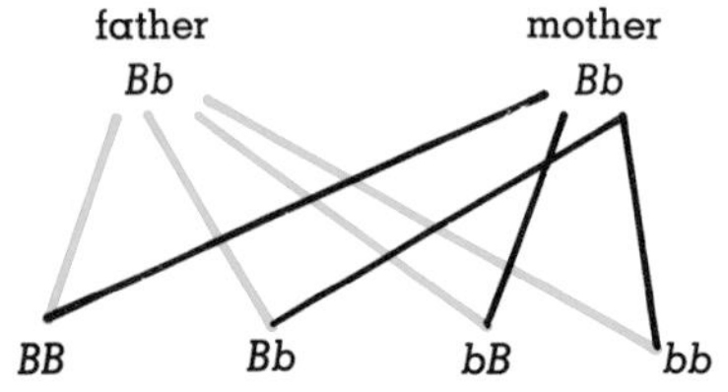

Both parents possible characteristics can be listed Bb.

Whenever B appears, the individual will have brown eyes, since the brown-eye characteristic is dominant.

The odds are 1 to 3 since there is 1 way to be blue-eyed and 3 ways to be brown-eyed (fail to be blue-eyed).

exercises

Max: 1–18, 1–23; **Avg:** 1–18, 1–23 odds; **Min:** 1–17 odds, 1–23 odds

Exploratory State the odds of an event occurring given the probability that it occurs as follows.

1. $\frac{1}{2}$ $\frac{1}{1}$
2. $\frac{3}{4}$ $\frac{3}{1}$
3. $\frac{1}{7}$ $\frac{1}{6}$
4. $\frac{5}{8}$ $\frac{5}{3}$
5. $\frac{7}{15}$ $\frac{7}{8}$
6. $\frac{8}{9}$ $\frac{8}{1}$
7. $\frac{4}{9}$ $\frac{4}{5}$
8. $\frac{3}{20}$ $\frac{3}{17}$

State the probability of an event occurring given the following odds.

9. $\frac{3}{4}$ $\frac{3}{7}$

10. $\frac{5}{1}$ $\frac{5}{6}$

11. $\frac{6}{5}$ $\frac{6}{11}$

12. $\frac{3}{7}$ $\frac{3}{10}$

13. $\frac{7}{3}$ $\frac{7}{10}$

14. $\frac{4}{9}$ $\frac{4}{13}$

15. $\frac{5}{11}$ $\frac{5}{16}$

16. $\frac{1}{1}$ $\frac{1}{2}$

Solve each of the following.

17. The odds are 6-to-1 *against* an event occurring. What is the probability that it will occur? $\frac{1}{7}$

18. The probability of an event occurring is $\frac{3}{4}$. What are the odds that it will not occur? $\frac{1}{3}$

Written Solve each of the following problems.

In a bag are 7 pennies, 4 nickels, and 5 dimes. Three coins are selected at random. Find the probability of each of the following selections.

1. all 3 pennies $\frac{1}{16}$
2. all 3 nickels $\frac{1}{140}$
3. all 3 dimes $\frac{1}{56}$
4. 2 pennies, 1 dime $\frac{3}{16}$
5. 1 penny, 1 dime, 1 nickel $\frac{1}{4}$

In a bag are 5 red, 9 blue, and 6 white marbles. Two are selected at random. Find the probability of each of the following selections.

6. 2 red $\frac{1}{19}$
7. 2 blue $\frac{18}{95}$
8. 2 white $\frac{3}{38}$
9. 1 red and 1 white $\frac{3}{19}$
10. 1 red and 1 blue $\frac{9}{38}$

There are 5 fudgesicles and 8 popsicles in the freezer. If 2 are selected at random, find the probability that the following occurs.

11. 2 fudgesicles $\frac{5}{39}$
12. 2 popsicles $\frac{14}{39}$

Suppose you select 2 letters from the word *algebra*. What is the probability of selecting 2 letters and having the following occur?

13. 1 vowel and 1 consonant $\frac{4}{7}$
14. 2 vowels $\frac{1}{7}$
15. 2 consonants $\frac{2}{7}$

Sharon has 8 mystery books and 9 science-fiction books. Four are selected. Find the probability that the following occurs.

16. 4 mystery books $\frac{1}{34}$
17. 4 science-fiction books $\frac{9}{170}$
18. 2 mysteries and 2 science-fiction $\frac{36}{85}$
19. 3 mysteries and 1 science-fiction $\frac{18}{85}$

From a deck of cards, 5 cards are dealt. What is the probability of the following?

20. 5 aces 0
21. 5 face cards 33/108,290
22. 5 from one suit 33/16,660
23. 2 of one suit and 3 of another 429/41,650

14-6 Multiplying Probabilities

Objective: To evaluate probabilities of independent or dependent events.

Suppose you toss a white die and then toss a green die. The probability that each one will show a 2 is $\frac{1}{6} \cdot \frac{1}{6}$ or $\frac{1}{36}$. Since the outcome of tossing the red die does not affect the outcome of tossing the green die, the events are independent.

Probability of Two Independent Events

If two events, A and B, are independent, then the probability of both events occurring is found as follows

$$P(A \text{ and } B) = P(A) \cdot P(B)$$

example 1

A bag contains 5 red marbles and 4 white marbles. A marble is to be selected, and replaced in the bag. A second selection is then made. What is the probability of selecting 2 red marbles?

These events are independent because the first marble selected is replaced. The outcome of the second selection is not affected.

$$\begin{aligned} P(\text{both red}) &= P(\text{red}) \cdot P(\text{red}) \\ &= \frac{5}{9} \cdot \frac{5}{9} \text{ or } \frac{25}{81} \end{aligned}$$

What is the probability of selecting 2 red marbles from 5 red ones and 4 white ones if the first selection is *not* replaced? These events are dependent because the outcome of the first selection affects the outcome of the second selection. Suppose the first selection is red.

First Selection	Second Selection
$P(\text{red}) = \frac{5}{9}$	$P(\text{red}) = \frac{4}{8}$

$$\begin{aligned} \text{Now } P(\text{both red}) &= P(\text{red}) \cdot P(\text{red following red}) \\ &= \frac{5}{9} \cdot \frac{4}{8} \text{ or } \frac{5}{18} \end{aligned}$$

Probability of Two Dependent Events

Suppose two events, A and B, are dependent. Then the probability of both occurring is found as follows.

$$P(A \text{ and } B) = P(A) \cdot P(B \text{ following } A)$$

example 2

There are 5 nickels, 7 dimes and 9 pennies in a coin purse. Suppose two coins are to be selected, without replacing the first one. What is the probability of selecting a penny and then a dime?

P(*penny and dime*) = *P*(*penny*) · *P*(*dime following penny*)

$$= \frac{9}{21} \cdot \frac{7}{20} \qquad P(A \text{ and } B) = P(A) \cdot P(B \text{ following } A \text{ occurs})$$

$$= \frac{3}{20}$$

The probability is $\frac{3}{20}$.

exercises

Max: 1–4, 1–18; Avg: 1–4, 1–19 odds; Min: 1–3 odds, 1–15 odds

Exploratory Identify the events in each of the following problems as *independent* or *dependent*. Then solve each one.

1. In a bag are 5 red, 3 green, and 8 blue marbles. Three are selected in sequence without replacement. What is the probability of selecting a red, green, and blue in that order? dependent, $\frac{1}{28}$
2. There are 4 glasses of root beer and 3 glasses of ice tea on the counter. Bill drinks two of them. What is the probability that he drank 2 root beers? dependent, $\frac{2}{7}$
3. In a bag are 5 apricots and 4 plums. Marie selects one, replaces it and selects another. What is the probability that both selections were apricots? independent, $\frac{25}{81}$
4. When James plays Ted in cribbage, the odds are 3 to 2 that he will win. What is the probability that he will win the next 4 games? independent, $\frac{81}{625}$

In Problems 3 and 4 order is not important.

Written **A bag contains 5 red, 3 white, and 7 blue marbles. If 3 marbles are selected in succession, what is the probability that they are red, white, and blue in that order?**

1. Suppose no marbles are replaced. $\frac{1}{26}$
2. Suppose each marble is replaced. $\frac{7}{225}$

In a bag are 5 red, 3 blue, and 7 black marbles. Three marbles are chosen, one after the other. What is the probability that there is one of each under the following conditions?

3. No replacement occurs dependent $\frac{3}{13}$
4. Replacement occurs each time independent $\frac{7}{225}$

One hundred tickets, numbered consecutively 1 to 100, are placed in a box. What is the probability that in 5 separate drawings, the following selections occur?

5. 5 odd numbers, if replacement occurs $\frac{1}{32}$
6. 5 odd numbers, if no replacement occurs 1081/38,412
7. 5 consecutive numbers if no replacement occurs 1/94,109,400

The letters *A, B, E, I, J, K,* and *M* are written on cards which are placed in a box. Two letters are selected. What is the probability that the following occurs?

8. both vowels, if no replacement occurs $\frac{1}{7}$
9. both vowels, if replacement occurs $\frac{9}{49}$
10. both the same letter, if no replacement occurs 0

There are 6 plates, 5 saucers, and 5 cups on the counter. Charlie accidentally knocks off two and breaks them. What is the probability that he broke the following?

11. 2 plates $\frac{1}{8}$
12. 2 cups $\frac{1}{12}$
13. a cup and a saucer, in that order $\frac{5}{48}$
14. a cup and a saucer, in any order $\frac{5}{24}$

A red and a green die are tossed. What is the probability that the following occurs?

15. both show 3 $\frac{1}{36}$
16. neither show 3 $\frac{25}{36}$
17. the red shows a 3 and the green shows a 4 $\frac{1}{36}$
18. the red shows a 3 and the green shows any other number $\frac{5}{36}$
19. both show the same number $\frac{1}{6}$
20. both show different numbers $\frac{5}{6}$

Excursions in Algebra

History

Maria Agnesi (ahn *ya* ze) was an Italian mathematician who lived from 1718 to 1799. At one time, she was a professor of mathematics at Bologna, Italy. In 1748, she wrote about a special set of curves which she called *versiera*. The general equation for those curves is shown below.

$$yx^2 = a^2(a - y)$$

The popular name for this type of curve is the *Witch of Agnesi*, because the curve resembles the outline of a witch's hat.

Exercises **Graph each of the following *versiera*. State the value of *a*.**

1. $yx^2 = 4(2 - y)$ $a = 2$
2. $yx^2 = {}^-64 - 16y$ $a = {}^-4$

For the graphs of problems **1-2**, see the Teacher's Guide.

14-7 Adding Probabilities

Objective: To find probabilities for mutually exclusive or inclusive events.

Suppose a card is to be drawn from a standard deck of 52 cards. What is the probability of drawing an ace or a king? Since no card is both an ace and a king, the events are said to be **mutually exclusive.** That is, the two events cannot occur simultaneously.

ways to draw an ace		**ways to draw a king**	
There are 4 aces in a deck.	$\frac{4}{52}$ or $\frac{1}{13}$	$\frac{4}{52}$ or $\frac{1}{13}$	*There are 4 kings in a deck.*

ways to draw an ace or a king

ace		*king*		*ace or king*
$\frac{1}{13}$	$+$	$\frac{1}{13}$	$=$	$\frac{2}{13}$

The probability of one of two mutually exclusive events occurring is the sum of their probabilities.

$$P(A \text{ or } B) = P(A) + P(B)$$

Probability of Mutually Exclusive Events

This rule can be extended to any number of mutually exclusive events. **Inclusive events** are not mutually exclusive.

What is the probability of drawing an ace or a red card? Since there are two red aces, the events are inclusive.

ways to select an ace		**ways to select a red card**	
There is an ace in each suit, hearts, diamonds, spades, and clubs.	$\frac{4}{52}$	$\frac{26}{52}$	*Hearts and diamonds are red.*

ways to select a red ace

$\frac{2}{52}$ *There are two red aces.*

Now the ways to select a red ace already are counted twice, once in the ways to select an ace and once in the ways to select a red card.

ways to select an ace or a red card

ace		*red*		*red ace*				*ace or red*
$\frac{4}{52}$	$+$	$\frac{26}{52}$	$-$	$\frac{2}{52}$	$=$	$\frac{28}{52}$	or	$\frac{7}{13}$

Probability of Inclusive Events

The probability of one of two inclusive events, A and B, occurring is the sum of the individual probabilities decreased by the probability of both occurring.

$$P(A \text{ or } B) = P(A) + P(B) - P(A \text{ and } B)$$

examples

1

Vivian has 6 nickels, 4 pennies, and 3 dimes in her purse. She selects one. What is the probability it is a penny or a nickel?

$$P(\text{penny or nickel}) = P(\text{penny}) + P(\text{nickel}) = \frac{4}{13} + \frac{6}{13} \text{ or } \frac{10}{13}$$

There is no coin which is both a penny and a nickel. These events are mutually exclusive.

The probability of selecting a penny or a nickel is $\frac{10}{13}$.

2

A card is to be selected from a deck of 52 cards. What is the probability that it is a red card or a face card?

$$\begin{aligned} P(\text{red or face card}) &= P(\text{red}) + P(\text{face card}) - P(\text{red face card}) \\ &= \frac{26}{52} + \frac{12}{52} - \frac{6}{52} \\ &= \frac{32}{52} \text{ or } \frac{8}{13} \end{aligned}$$

A deck of cards has 13 hearts and 13 diamonds. The face cards include 4 kings, 4 queens and 4 jacks. The events are inclusive.

The probability of selecting a red card or a face card is $\frac{8}{13}$.

3

A committee of 5 people is to be formed from a group of 7 men and 6 women. What is the probability that the committee will have at least 3 women?

At least 3 *women* means that the committee may have 3, or 4, or 5 women. It is not possible to select a group of 3, a group of 4, and a group of 5 women all to be on the same 5-member committee. The events are mutually exclusive.

$$\begin{aligned} P(\text{at least } 3 \text{ women}) &= P(3 \text{ women}) + P(4 \text{ women}) + P(5 \text{ women}) \\ &= \frac{C(6, 3) \cdot C(7, 2)}{C(13, 5)} + \frac{C(6, 4) \cdot C(7, 1)}{C(13, 5)} + \frac{C(6, 5) \cdot C(7, 0)}{C(13, 5)} \\ &= \frac{140}{429} + \frac{35}{429} + \frac{2}{429} \text{ or } \frac{177}{429} \end{aligned}$$

The probability of at least 3 women on the committee is $\frac{177}{429}$.

exercises

Max: 1–8, 1–16; Avg: 1–8, 1–15 odds; Min: 1–7 odds, 1–15 odds

Exploratory Identify each of the following events as inclusive or exclusive. Then solve the problem. 1. exclusive, $\frac{4}{15}$

1. In a box are slips of paper numbered from 1 to 10. A slip of paper is drawn and a die is tossed. What is the probability of getting a 2 on one of them?
2. Two cards are drawn from a standard deck of playing cards. What is the probability that the 2 cards are both kings or both queens? exclusive, $\frac{2}{221}$
3. In her pocket, Linda has 5 nickels, 3 dimes, and 7 pennies. She selects 3 coins. What is the probability that she has selected 3 nickels or 3 pennies? exclusive, $\frac{9}{91}$
4. From a standard deck of playing cards, 2 cards are drawn. What is the probability of having drawn a black card or an ace? inclusive, $\frac{64}{221}$
5. The Dodger pitching staff has 5 left-handers and 8 right-handers. If 2 are selected, what is the probability that at least one of them is a left-hander?
6. Five coins are dropped. What is the probability of having at least 3 heads? exclusive, $\frac{5}{16}$
   5. exclusive, $\frac{25}{39}$
7. In one class, 3 of the 12 girls are redheads and 2 of the 15 boys are redheads. What is the probability of selecting a boy or a redhead? inclusive, $\frac{2}{3}$
8. There are 8 red, 3 blue, and 12 black marbles in a bag. If 3 are selected, what is the probability that all are red or all are blue? exclusive, $\frac{57}{1771}$

Written In a bag are 6 red and 5 white marbles. Three are selected. What is the probability that the following occurs?

1. all 3 red or all 3 white $\frac{2}{11}$
2. at least 2 red $\frac{19}{33}$
3. at least 2 white $\frac{14}{33}$
4. exactly 2 white $\frac{4}{11}$

Two cards are drawn from a standard deck of cards. What is the probability that the following occurs?

5. both aces or both face cards $\frac{12}{221}$
6. both black or both face cards $\frac{188}{663}$
7. both aces or both red $\frac{55}{221}$
8. both either red or an ace $\frac{63}{221}$

Seven coins are tossed. What is the probability that the following occurs?

9. 3 heads or 2 tails $\frac{7}{16}$
10. at least 5 heads $\frac{29}{128}$
11. 3 heads or 3 tails $\frac{35}{64}$
12. all tails or all heads $\frac{1}{64}$

From a group of 6 men and 8 women, a committee of 6 is to be selected. What is the probability of the following?

13. all men or all women $\frac{29}{3003}$
14. 5 men or 5 women $\frac{128}{1001}$
15. 3 men and 3 women $\frac{160}{429}$
16. 4 men or 4 women $\frac{70}{143}$

Using Algebra

Binomial Expansions

The binomial expansion of $(a + b)^n$ can be written as follows, if n is a positive integer.

$$(a + b)^n = 1 \cdot a^n + \left(\frac{n}{1}\right)a^{n-1}b + \left(\frac{n}{1}\right)\left(\frac{n-1}{2}\right)a^{n-2}b^2 + \left(\frac{n}{1}\right)\left(\frac{n-2}{3}\right)a^{n-3}b^3 + \cdots + 1 \cdot b^n$$

The coefficients and some equivalent expressions are listed below.

Term	Coefficient	Equivalent expressions
1st	1	$C(n, 0)$
2nd	$\frac{n}{1}$	$C(n, 1)$
3rd	$\frac{n}{1} \cdot \frac{n-1}{2}$	$C(n, 2)$

Recall that $C(n, r)$ also is written $\frac{n!}{(n-r)!r!}$ *or* $\frac{n(n-1)\cdots(n-r+1)}{1 \cdot 2 \cdots r}$

Notice, for example, that the coefficient of the 3rd term is $C(n, 2)$. Also, the power of b in the 3rd term is 2. Thus, the coefficient of the rth term is $C(n,(r-1))$. The power of b in the rth term is $(r-1)$ and that of a is $[n-(r-1)]$ or $n-r+1$.

Finding the rth Term in the Binomial Expansion

In the binomial expansion of $(a + b)^n$, the rth term is as follows.

$$C[n,(r-1)]a^{n-(r-1)}b^{r-1} \text{ or } \frac{n!}{(n-(r-1))!(r-1)!}a^{n-r+1}b^{r-1}$$

$$n - (r - 1) = n - r + 1$$

Example Find the fifth term of $(2x - 3y)^6$.

$$\frac{n!}{(n-r+1)!(r-1)!}a^{n-r+1}b^{r-1} = \frac{6!}{(6-5+1)!(4!)}a^{6-5+1}b^{5-1}$$

Substitute 6 for n and 5 for r.

$$= \frac{6 \cdot 5}{1 \cdot 2}(2x)^2(^-3y)^4$$

Substitute 2x for a and ^-3y for b.

$$= 15(4x^2)(81y^4) \text{ or } 4860x^2y^4$$

The fifth term is $4860x^2y^4$.

Exercises Find the indicated term of the given binomial expansion.

1. 4th, $(a + b)^9$ $84a^6b^3$
2. 3rd, $(2x + y)^5$ $80x^3y^2$
3. 5th, $(x - y)^8$ $70x^4y^4$
4. 2nd, $(4x + 3y)^6$ $18{,}432x^5y$
5. $(n + 1)$st, $(5x - 2y)^9$ $\frac{9!}{(9-n)!n!}(5x)^{9-n}(^-2y)^n$
6. 4th, $(x + 2y)^6$ $160x^3y^3$

14-8 Binomial Trials

Objective: To use binomial trials to evaluate probabilities.

Arthur normally wins 1 out of every 3 checker games he plays. In other words, the probability that Arthur wins when he plays checkers is $\frac{1}{3}$.

Suppose Arthur plays 4 games. What is the probability that he will win 3 and lose only one?

The possible ways of winning 3 games and losing one are shown at the right. The illustration shows the combinations of four things, namely games, taken three at a time, namely wins. That is, C(4, 3).

$W\ W\ W\ L$ $\qquad$ $W\ W\ L\ W$

$W\ L\ W\ W$ $\qquad$ $L\ W\ W\ W$

The terms of the binomial expansion of $(W + L)^4$ can be used to express the probabilities.

$$(W + L)^4 = W^4 + 4W^3L + 6W^2L^2 + 4WL^3 + L^4$$

term	meaning	
W^4	1 way to win all 4 games	$C(4, 4)W^4$
$4W^3L$	4 ways to win 3 games and lose 1 game	$C(4, 3)W^3L$
$6W^2L^2$	6 ways to win 2 games and lose 2 games	$C(4, 2)W^2L^2$
$4WL^3$	4 ways to win 1 game and lose 3 games	$C(4, 1)WL^3$
L^4	1 way to lose all 4 games	$C(4, 0)L^4$

The probability that Arthur wins when he plays is $\frac{1}{3}$. And, thus, the probability that he loses is $\frac{2}{3}$. Substitute $\frac{1}{3}$ for W and $\frac{2}{3}$ for L in the term $4W^3L$.

The probability of winning 3 out of 4 games is $4\left(\frac{1}{3}\right)^3\left(\frac{2}{3}\right)$ or $\frac{8}{81}$.

What is the probability of winning 2 games and losing 2 games? $\frac{8}{27}$

Problems which can be solved using a binomial expansion are called **binomial trials**.

Definition of Binomial Trials

A binomial trial exists if and only if the following conditions occur.

1. There are only two possible outcomes.
2. The events are independent.

examples

1

What is the probability that 3 coins show heads and 2 show tails when 5 coins are tossed?

There are only 2 possible outcomes: heads (H) or tails (T). The tosses of 5 coins are independent events. When $(H + T)^5$ is expanded, the term containing H^3T^2 will give the desired probability.

$$C(5, 3)H^3T^2 = \frac{5 \cdot 4}{2 \cdot 1}\left(\frac{1}{2}\right)^3\left(\frac{1}{2}\right)^2 \text{ or } \frac{5}{16}$$

Replace H by P(H) which is $\frac{1}{2}$ and T by P(T) or $\frac{1}{2}$.

The probability of 3 heads and 2 tails is $\frac{5}{16}$.

2

The probability that Amy wins a game with Marla is $\frac{1}{5}$; that Marla wins is $\frac{4}{5}$. Suppose they play 7 games. What is the probability that Amy will win at least 3 of the games?

There are only two outcomes of each game: Amy wins (A) or Marla wins (M). The binomial expansion of $(A + M)^7$ follows.

$$(A + M)^7 = A^7 + 7A^6M + 21A^5M^2 + 35A^4M^3 + 35A^3M^4 + 21A^2M^5 + 7AM^6 + M^7$$

Amy must win 7, 6, 5, 4, or 3 games.

$$A^7 + 7A^6M + 21A^5M^2 + 35A^4M^3 + 35A^3M^4$$

$$= \left(\frac{1}{5}\right)^7 + 7 \cdot \left(\frac{1}{5}\right)^6\left(\frac{4}{5}\right) + 21\left(\frac{1}{5}\right)^5\left(\frac{4}{5}\right)^2 + 35\left(\frac{1}{5}\right)^4\left(\frac{4}{5}\right)^3 + 35\left(\frac{1}{5}\right)^3\left(\frac{4}{5}\right)^4$$

Substitute $\frac{1}{5}$ for A and $\frac{4}{5}$ for M.

$$= \frac{1}{78125} + 7\left(\frac{1}{15625}\right)\left(\frac{4}{5}\right) + 21\left(\frac{1}{3125}\right)\left(\frac{16}{25}\right) + 35\left(\frac{1}{625}\right)\left(\frac{64}{125}\right) + 35\left(\frac{1}{125}\right)\left(\frac{256}{625}\right)$$

$$= \frac{1 + 28 + 336 + 2240 + 8960}{78,125} \text{ or } \frac{2313}{15,625}$$

The probability that Amy will win at least 3 games is $\frac{2313}{15,625}$.

exercises

Max: 1–6, 1–30; Avg: 1–6, 1–29 odds; Min: 1–29 odds

Exploratory **Tell whether each of the following represents a binomial trial or not. Solve those that represent a binomial trial.**

1. Ann tosses a coin 3 times. What is the probability of 2 heads and 1 tail?

Jess draws 4 cards from a deck of playing cards. What is the probability of drawing 4 aces if the following occurs?

2. He replaces the card.
3. He does not replace the card.

1. binomial, $\frac{3}{8}$ 2. binomial, 1/28,561 3. not binomial

There are 8 algebra books and 4 geometry books on a shelf. If 2 are selected, and each is replaced, what is the probability of the following?

4. both algebra **5.** both geometry **6.** one of each

4. binomial, $\frac{4}{9}$ **5.** binomial, $\frac{1}{9}$ **6.** binomial, $\frac{2}{9}$

Written Solve the following.

A coin is tossed 4 times. What is the probability of the following?

1. exactly 1 head $\frac{1}{4}$
2. no heads $\frac{1}{16}$
3. 2 heads and 2 tails $\frac{3}{8}$
4. 3 or more tails $\frac{5}{16}$

A die is tossed 5 times. What is the probability of the following?

5. only one 4 $\frac{3125}{7776}$
6. at least three 4's $\frac{276}{7776}$
7. no more than two 4's $\frac{7500}{7776}$
8. exactly five 4's $\frac{1}{7776}$

Cathy Black has a bent coin. The probability of heads is $\dfrac{2}{3}$ with this coin. She flips the coin 4 times. What is the probability of the following?

9. no heads $\frac{1}{81}$
10. 4 heads $\frac{16}{81}$
11. at least 3 heads $\frac{48}{81}$

Joey Ward guesses on all 10 questions on a true-false test. What is the probability of the following?

12. 7 correct $\frac{15}{128}$
13. at least 6 correct $\frac{193}{512}$
14. all incorrect $\frac{1}{1024}$
15. at least half incorrect $\frac{369}{512}$

A batter is now batting 0.200 (meaning 200 hits in 1000 times at bat). In the next 5 at-bats, what is the probability of having the following?

16. exactly 1 hit $\frac{1280}{3125}$ or $\frac{256}{625}$
17. exactly 3 hits $\frac{160}{3125}$ or $\frac{32}{625}$
18. at least 4 hits $\frac{21}{3125}$

Three coins are tossed. What is the probability of the following?

19. 3 heads $\frac{1}{8}$
20. 3 tails $\frac{1}{8}$
21. at least 2 heads $\frac{1}{2}$
22. exactly 2 tails $\frac{3}{8}$

If a tack is dropped, the probability that it will land point up is $\dfrac{2}{5}$. Ten tacks are dropped. What is the probability of the following?

23. all point up 512/4,882,810
24. exactly 3 point up 419,904/1,953,125
25. exactly 5 point up 1,959,552/9,765,625
26. at least 6 point up 1,623,424/9,765,625

Harold is an excellent skeet shooter. He will hit the clay pigeon 9 of 10 times. If he shoots 12 times, what is the probability of the following?

27. all misses $\left(\frac{1}{10}\right)^{12}$
28. exactly 7 hits ≈ 0.0037881
29. all hits $\left(\frac{9}{10}\right)^{12}$
30. at least 10 hits ≈ 0.8891293

Vocabulary

independent events (392)
event (393)
linear permutation (395)
permutation (395)
circular permutation (398)
reflection (400)
probability (405)
odds (406)
dependent events (408)
mutually exclusive events (411)
inclusive events (412)
binomial trial (415)

Chapter Summary

1. Two events are independent if the result of the first event has no affect on the second. (392)
2. Definition of Basic Counting Principle: Suppose an event can be chosen in p different ways. Another independent event can be chosen in q different ways. Then the two events can be chosen successively in $p \cdot q$ ways. (393)
3. Definition of $P(n, r)$: The number of permutations of n objects, taken r at a time is defined as follows. $P(n, r) = \frac{n!}{(n - r)!}$ (395)
4. Definition of Permutations with Repetition: The number of permutations of n objects of which p are alike and q are alike is found by evaluating the following expression. $\frac{n!}{p!q!}$ (396)
5. Definition of Circular Permutations: Suppose n objects are arranged in a circle. Then there are $\frac{n!}{n}$ or $(n - 1)!$ arrangements. (399)
6. Definition of $C(n, r)$: The number of combinations of n objects, taken r at a time, is written $C(n, r)$. $C(n, r) = \frac{n!}{(n - r)!r!}$ (402)
7. Definition of Probability of Success and of Failure: If an event can succeed in s ways and fail in f ways, then the probabilities of success $P(s)$ and of failure $P(f)$ are as follows.

   $P(s) = \frac{s}{s + f}$ $\quad P(f) = \frac{f}{s + f}$ (405)
8. Definition of Odds: The odds of the successful outcome of an event is expressed as the ratio of the number of ways it can succeed to the number of ways it can fail.

   Odds = the ratio of s to f or $\frac{s}{f}$ (406)

9. Definition of Probability of Two Independent Events: If two events, A and B, are independent, then the probability of both events occurring is found as follows.
$P(A \text{ and } B) = P(A) \cdot P(B)$. (408)
10. Definition of Probability of Two Dependent Events: Suppose two events, A and B, are dependent. Then the probability of both occurring is found as follows.
$P(A \text{ and } B) = P(A) \cdot P(B \text{ following } A)$. (408)
11. Definition of Probability of Mutually Exclusive Events: The probability of one of two mutually exclusive events occurring is the sum of their probabilities. $P(A \text{ or } B) = P(A) + P(B)$ (411)
12. Definition of Probability of Inclusive Events: The probability of one of two inclusive events, A and B, is the sum of the individual probabilities decreased by the probability of both occurring.
$P(A \text{ or } B) = P(A) + P(B) - P(A \text{ and } B)$ (412)
13. Definition of Finding the rth Term in the Binomial Expansion: In the binomial expansion of $(a + b)^n$, the rth term is as follows.
$C[n, (r-1)]a^{n-(r-1)}b^{r-1}$ or $\dfrac{n!}{(n-(r-1))!(r-1)!}a^{n-r+1}b^{r-1}$ (414)
14. Definition of Binomial Trials: A binomial trial problem exists if the following conditions hold. Only two outcomes exist. The trials are independent. (415)

Chapter Review

14-1 **Using only the digits 0, 1, 2, 3, and 4, how many 3-digit patterns can be formed under the following conditions?**

1. Repetitions are allowed. 125
2. No repetitions are allowed. 60

14-2 **On a shelf are 8 mystery and 7 romance novels. How many ways can they be arranged as follows?**

3. all mysteries together 1,625,702,400
4. all mysteries together, romances together 406,425,600
5. Evaluate $\dfrac{C(8, 5)}{C(5, 3)}$ 5.6
6. Evaluate $\dfrac{P(7, 3)}{P(5, 2)}$ 10.5

14-3
7. How many ways can 8 people be seated at a round table? 5040
8. How many ways can 10 charms be placed on a bracelet which has a clasp? 1,814,400

14-4
9. How many baseball teams can be formed from 15 players if only 3 pitch and the others play the remaining 8 positions? 1485
10. From a deck of playing cards, how many different 4-card hands exist? 270,725

14–5 11. In a bag are 6 red and 2 white marbles. If two marbles are selected, what is the probability that one is red and the other is white? $\frac{3}{7}$

14–6 12. In his pocket, Jose has 5 dimes, 7 nickels, and 4 pennies. He selects 4 coins. What is the probability that he has 2 dimes and 2 pennies? $\frac{3}{91}$

14–7 13. From a deck of cards, one card is selected. What is the probability that it is an ace or a face card? $\frac{4}{13}$

14–8 14. Four coins are tossed. What is the probability that they show 3 heads and 1 tail? $\frac{1}{4}$

Chapter Test

Solve each of the following.

1. From 8 shirts, 6 pair of slacks, and 4 jackets, how many different outfits can be made? 192
2. In a row are 8 chairs. How many ways can 5 people be seated? 6720
3. How many ways can 11 books be arranged on a shelf? 39,916,800
4. How many ways can the letters from the word *television* be arranged? 907,200
5. How many ways can 6 keys be placed on a key ring? 60
6. How many different basketball teams could be formed from a group of 12 girls? 792
7. Nine points are placed on a circle. How many triangles can be formed using these points as vertices? 84
8. From a group of 4 men and 5 women, a committee of 3 is to be formed. What is the probability that it will have 2 men and 1 woman? $\frac{5}{14}$
9. A red die and a green die are tossed. What is the probability that the red will show even and the green will show a number greater than four? $\frac{1}{6}$
10. From a deck of cards, what is the probability of selecting a 4 followed by a 7 if no replacement occurs? $\frac{4}{663}$
11. While shooting arrows, William Tell can hit an apple 9 out of 10 times. What is the probability that he will hit it exactly 4 out of the next 7 times? 229,635/10,000,000
12. Five bent coins are tossed. The probability of heads is $\frac{2}{3}$ for each of them. What is the probability that no more than 2 will show heads? $\frac{51}{243}$

4. 3,628,800 **6.** 792

Find the value of each of the following.

13. $P(8, 3)$ 336 **14.** $P(6, 4)$ 360 **15.** $C(8, 3)$ 56 **16.** $C(6, 4)$ 15

Solve the following expression for *n*.

17. $7C(6, 4) = 5C(n, 2)$ $n = 7$

Chapter 15

Statistics

Insurance companies use statistics extensively in calculating rates. For example, an automobile insurance company compiles data such as number of accidents, amount of damages, road conditions, age of drivers, and so on.

15-1 Organizing Data

Objective: To use tables to organize and interpret data.

Statistics provide techniques for collecting, organizing, analyzing, and interpreting numerical information called **data.** Organized data is easier to read and interpret. One way to organize data is by using tables. The following table shows the normal monthly precipitation for selected cities in the United States.

Normal Monthly Precipitation in Inches

City	Jan.	Feb.	Mar.	Apr.	May	Jun.	July	Aug.	Sep.	Oct.	Nov.	Dec.
Albuquerque, NM	0.30	0.39	0.47	0.48	0.53	0.50	1.39	1.34	0.77	0.79	0.29	0.52
Boston, MA	3.69	3.54	4.01	3.49	3.47	3.19	2.74	3.46	3.16	3.02	4.51	4.24
Columbus, OH	2.87	2.32	3.44	3.71	4.10	4.13	4.21	2.86	2.41	1.89	2.68	2.39
Chicago, IL	1.85	1.59	2.73	3.75	3.41	3.95	4.09	3.14	3.00	2.62	2.20	2.11
Houston, TX	3.57	3.54	2.68	3.54	5.10	4.52	4.12	4.35	4.65	4.05	4.03	4.04
Mobile, AL	4.71	4.76	7.07	5.59	4.52	6.09	8.86	6.93	6.59	2.55	3.39	5.92
San Francisco, CA	4.37	3.04	2.54	1.59	0.41	0.13	0.01	0.03	0.16	0.98	2.29	3.98
Seattle, WA	5.79	4.19	3.61	2.46	1.70	1.53	0.71	1.08	1.99	3.91	5.88	5.94

The table organizes the data so that you can answer quickly questions like the following.

What city had the most precipitation in January? Seattle

What is the wettest month in Seattle? Dec.

What city had the least precipitation in August? San Francisco

What is the driest month in Houston? March

example 1

Use the table to answer the following questions.

1. How many master's degrees were earned in 1960?
2. How many degrees were earned in 1940?
3. Did the total number of degrees earned increase from 1940 to 1970?

Earned Degrees (in thousands)

Year	Bachelor's		Master's		Doctorate		Total
	M	F	M	F	M	F	
1940	110	77	17	10	2.9	0.5	217.4
1950	330	104	41	17	6.0	0.6	498.6
1960	256	139	51	24	8.8	1.0	479.8
1970	487	346	126	83	25.9	4.0	1071.9

1. There were (51 + 24) or 75 thousand master's degrees earned in 1960.
2. There were a total of 217.4 thousand degrees earned in 1940.
3. There were a total of 1071.9 thousand degrees earned in 1970 and 217.4 thousand degrees earned in 1940. So, yes, the total number of degrees earned did increase from 1940 to 1970.

By combining data in tables, you can provide more information.

Normal Monthly Precipitation in Inches

City	Jan.	Feb.	Mar.	Apr.	May	Jun.	July	Aug.	Sep.	Oct.	Nov.	Dec.	Total
Albuquerque, NM	0.30	0.39	0.47	0.48	0.53	0.50	1.39	1.34	0.77	0.79	0.29	0.52	7.77
Boston, MA	3.69	3.54	4.01	3.49	3.47	3.19	2.74	3.46	3.16	3.02	4.51	4.24	42.52
Columbus, OH	2.87	2.32	3.44	3.71	4.10	4.13	4.21	2.86	2.41	1.89	2.68	2.39	37.01
Chicago, IL	1.85	1.59	2.73	3.75	3.41	3.95	4.09	3.14	3.00	2.62	2.20	2.11	34.44
Houston, TX	3.57	3.54	2.68	3.54	5.10	4.52	4.12	4.35	4.65	4.05	4.03	4.04	48.19
Mobile, AL	4.71	4.76	7.07	5.59	4.52	6.09	8.86	6.93	6.59	2.55	3.39	5.92	66.98
San Francisco, CA	4.37	3.04	2.54	1.59	0.41	0.13	0.01	0.03	0.16	0.98	2.29	3.98	19.53
Seattle, WA	5.79	4.19	3.61	2.46	1.70	1.53	0.71	1.08	1.99	3.91	5.88	5.94	38.79

The totals provided help you answer questions like the following.

Which city has the most precipitation in one year? Mobile, AL

Which city has the least precipitation in one year? Albuquerque, NM

How many of the cities have more than 30 inches of precipitation in one year? 6

Some tables group data together. For example, you could make a table which provides the normal precipitation in selected cities by seasons.

example 2

Make a table which provides the normal precipitation in selected cities, by seasons. Use the data from the table on page 422.

City	Winter Jan.-Mar.	Spring Apr.-Jun.	Summer Jul.-Sep.	Fall Oct.-Dec.
Albuquerque	1.16	1.51	3.50	1.60
Boston	11.24	10.15	9.36	11.77
Columbus	8.63	11.94	9.48	6.96
Chicago	6.17	11.11	10.23	6.93
Houston	9.79	13.16	13.12	12.12
Mobile	16.54	16.20	22.38	11.86
San Francisco	9.95	2.13	0.20	7.25
Seattle	13.59	5.69	3.78	15.73

Notice that once data has been grouped, individual measurements lose their identities.

exercises

Max: 1–16, 1–15; Avg: 1–16, 1–15 odds; Min: 1–15 odds, 1–15 odds

Exploratory **Use the table below to solve each of the following problems.**

Students learn the technical meaning of *median* in Lesson **15-3.**

Median Income Comparisons of Full-Time Workers
by Educational Attainment, 1975
(persons 25 yr. and over)
Source: Bureau of the Census

Years of School Completed	Median Income	
	Women	Men
Elementary School:		
less than 8 years	5109	8647
8 years	5691	10600
High School:		
1 to 3 years	6355	11511
4 years	7777	13542
College:		
1 to 3 years	9126	14989
4 years or more	11359	18450

1. In 1975, what was the median income of all men who completed 2 years of college? $14,989

2. In 1975, what was the median income of all women who completed 4 or more years of college? $11,359

3. In 1975, what was the median income of all women who completed 3 years of high school? $6,355

4. In 1975, what was the median income of all men who completed 1 year of high school? $11,511

5–10. Find each entry for a new column on the table with the heading, **Difference.**

11–16. Find each entry for a new column on the table with the heading, **Women's Income as a Percent of Men's.**

5. $3,538 **6.** $4,909 **7.** $5,156 **8.** $5,765 **9.** $5,863 **10.** $7,091
11. 59% **12.** 54% **13.** 55% **14.** 57% **15.** 61% **16.** 62%

Written **Two dice were tossed 64 times with the following results.**

5	8	11	10	8	8	7	10	3	9	10	8	2	9	12	3
11	5	2	3	5	7	11	7	11	10	11	10	6	7	8	7
9	5	6	4	4	5	10	8	6	7	4	8	5	10	5	5
8	5	11	9	12	4	7	2	7	4	3	9	2	11	7	6

1. Organize the data into a table with the headings **Number of Dots,** and **Frequency of Occurrences.** See Teacher's Guide.

2. Which number or numbers of dots occurred most frequently? 5 and 7

3. Which number or numbers of dots occurred least frequently? 12

The following represent the total precipitation in inches for cities in 1970.

31	26	35	20	38	30	41	21	23	25
24	27	30	19	27	38	30	31	33	20
22	30	33	27	25	33	25	27	31	27
17	38	46	33	22	27	22	19	25	33
36	30	45	31	45	35	23	25	40	36
20	30	22	26	41	35	25	30	30	27
33	25	28	27	24	45	26	21	41	26
22	31	37	38	26	20	22	26	25	20
27	25	23	27	31	35	27	25	40	24
41	30	17	22	26	19	33	36	30	28

4. Organize the data into a table with the headings **Precipitation** and **Number of Cities.** Under **Precipitation** include 18, 29, 32, 34, 39, 42, 43, and 44. See Teacher's Guide.
5. Which number of numbers of inches occurred most frequently? 27 inches
6. How many cities had 38 inches of precipitation? 4 cities
7. What is the greatest number of inches of precipitation for any of the cities? 46 inches
8. What is the least number of inches of precipitation for any of the cities? 17 inches
9. Organize the data into a table with the headings **Precipitation** and **Number of Cities.** Under **Precipitation** group the data by threes. For example, the first entry under **Precipitation** is 17–19. See Teacher's Guide.
10. How many cities had from 32–34 inches of precipitation? 7 cities
11. How many cities had from 23–25 inches of precipitation? 16 cities

Percent of Households Owning Motor Vehicles, by Income, 1974

Source: U.S. Bureau of Census

Annual Income	One Vehicle	Two or More Vehicles
Under $3000	35.2	11.0
$3000–$4999	48.2	16.1
$5000–$7499	53.3	26.2
$7500–$9999	52.1	36.2
$10,000–$14,999	40.4	53.5
$15,000–$19,999	28.8	67.9
$20,000–$24,999	24.3	73.1
$25,000 and over	19.6	77.6

12. What percent of households with an annual income from $10,000–$14,999 had one vehicle in 1974? 40.4%
13. What percent of households with an annual income from $10,000–$14,999 had two or more vehicles in 1974? 53.5%
14. What percent of households with an annual income under $3000 had one vehicle in 1974? 35.2%
15. What percent of households with an annual income of $25,000 or over had one vehicle in 1974? 19.6%

15-2 Graphs

Objective: To use various types of graphs to compare data.

Graphs often are used to present data and show relationships. There are several ways of presenting the data in the following table.

Average Motor Fuel Consumption in U.S.

gallons per vehicle

Year	1950	1955	1960	1965	1970	1975
Consumption	603	644	661	656	722	676

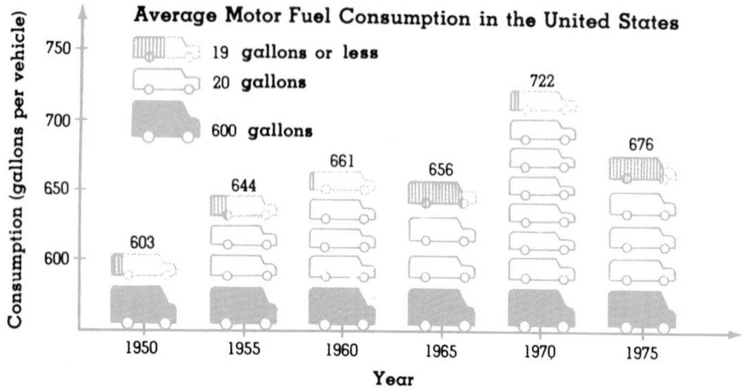

This graph is called a **pictograph.** Like a bar graph, it shows how specific quantities compare.

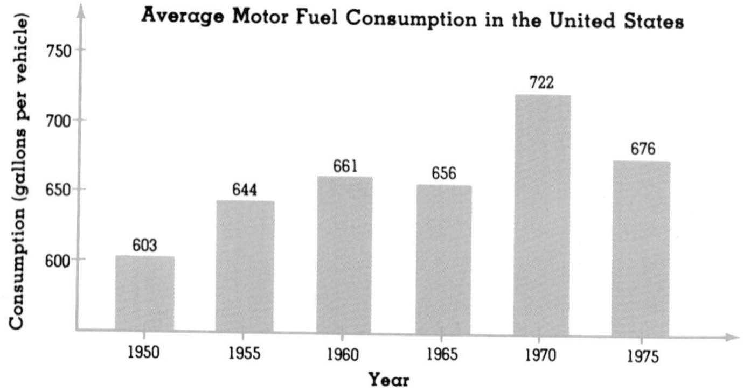

This graph is called a **bar graph.** It shows how specific quantities compare. *Which is easier to draw, a bar graph or a pictograph?*

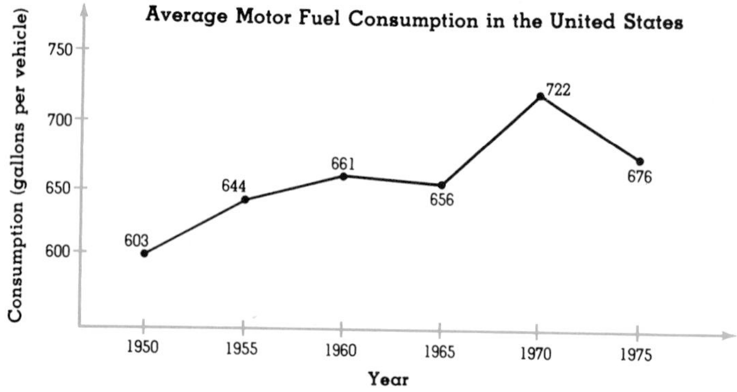

This graph is called a **line graph.** It is helpful for showing trends or changes.

example 1

Draw a bar graph and a line graph to present the following data.

Percent of 18 Year Olds with High School Diplomas

Year	1940	1950	1955	1960	1965	1970	1975
Percent	49.3	60.0	62.5	70.0	73.9	75.6	74.3

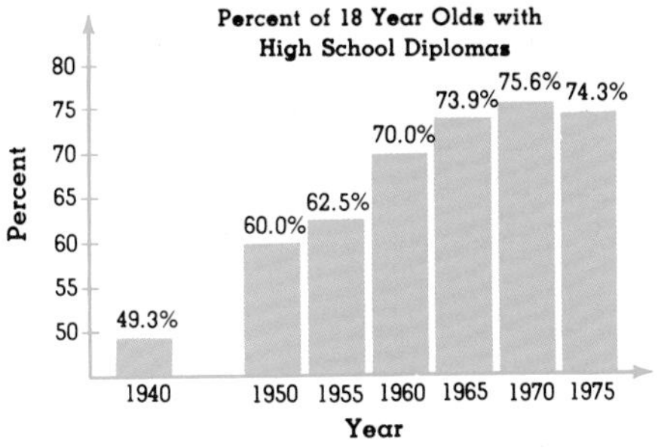

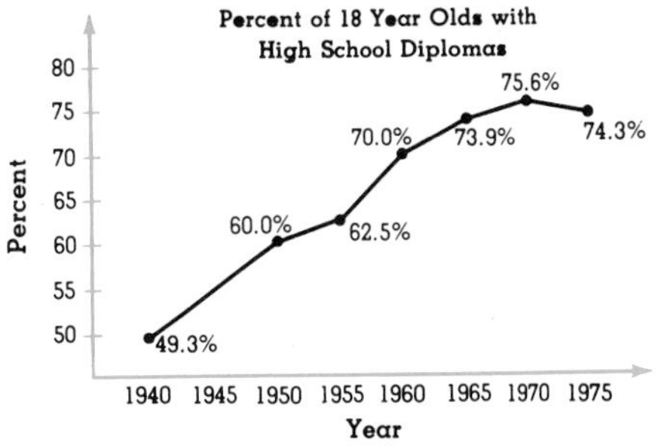

Circle graphs show how parts are related to the whole. For example, the following graph shows the cost of a $4 book.

The circle is separated into proportional parts. For example, 25% of a book's cost goes to royalties and profit. Thus, 25% of the circle, 90°, is used to show this part of a book's cost.

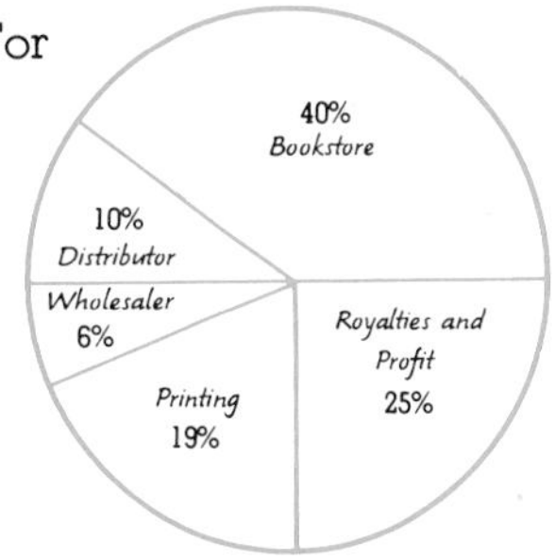

example 2

Draw a circle graph to show how the cost of a $5.98 record is broken down. The manufacturer's cost is $1.83. The manufacturer's income is $0.68. The distributor's income is $0.41. And the retailer's income is $3.06.

First, find the percent of a circle represented by each cost. Then, figure the number of degrees represented by each cost and draw the graph.

Cost	Percent of Circle	Approximate Degrees
Manufacturer's cost	$\frac{1.83}{5.98}$ or 31%	360 × 31% or 111.6
Manufacturer's income	$\frac{0.68}{5.98}$ or 11%	360 × 11% or 39.6
Distributor's income	$\frac{0.41}{5.98}$ or 7%	360 × 7% or 25.2
Retailer's income	$\frac{3.06}{5.98}$ or 51%	360 × 51% or 183.6

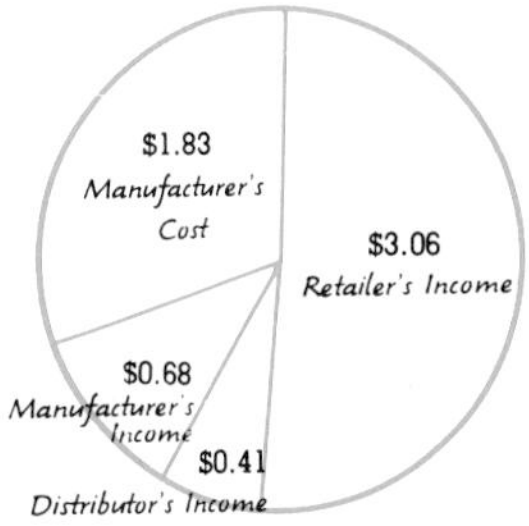

exercises

Max: 1–8, 1–25; Avg: 1–8, 1–25 odds; Min: 1–21 odds

Exploratory Use the bar graph below to solve each of the following.

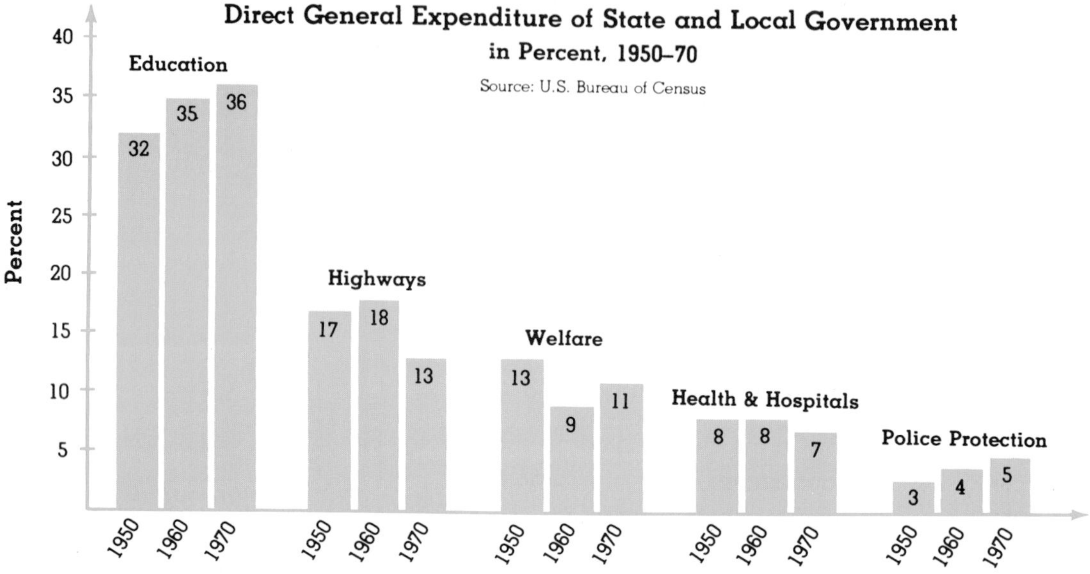

1. In 1950, what percent of expenditures was for highways? 17%
2. In 1950, what percent of expenditures was for police protection? 3%
3. In 1960, what percent of expenditures was for health and hospitals? 8%
4. In 1970, what percent of expenditures was for education? 36%
5. In which year, 1950, 1960, or 1970, was the percent of expenditures for education greatest? 1970
6. In which year, 1950, 1960, or 1970, was the percent of expenditures for welfare least? 1960
7. In 1960, was a greater percent spent on health and hospitals or on police protection? health and hospitals
8. In 1950, was a greater percent spent on highways or on welfare? highways

For graphs of problems 1–25, see the Teacher's Guide.

Written Draw bar graphs for the data in each of the following tables.

1. Fire Loss in Millions of Dollars

Year	1940	1950	1960	1970
Loss	286	649	1108	2328

2. Average Price of Hardcover Books

Year	1970	1973	1974	1975
Price	\$11.66	\$12.20	\$14.09	\$16.19

3. Postal Rates for First Class Mail

Year	1952	1958	1963	1968	1971	1974	1975
Cost/Ounce	3¢	4¢	5¢	6¢	8¢	10¢	13¢

4. Average Motor Fuel Consumption in the U.S.

Year	1950	1955	1960	1965	1970	1974
Gallons/Vehicle	600	640	660	660	720	680

5. Life Expectancies of Males in the U.S.

Year	1930	1940	1950	1960	1970
Age	58.1	60.8	65.6	66.6	67.1

6. Life Expectancies of Females in the U.S.

Year	1930	1940	1950	1960	1970
Age	61.6	65.2	71.1	73.1	74.8

7. World Population by Continents

Continent	Africa	N. America	S. America	Asia	Europe	Oceania
Population (millions)	391	338	212	2677	470	21

8. School Days Missed Due to Illness or Injury, Ages 6–16

Year	1960	1965	1970	1972	1973	1974
Days in Millions	196	214	222	236	221	242

9. Consumption of Fuel in the U.S.

Year	Coal	Crude Petroleum	Natural Gas	Electricity
1940	52.4%	31.4%	12.4%	3.8%
1950	38.0%	37.4%	20.4%	4.2%
1960	22.8%	41.8%	31.7%	3.7%
1965	22.3%	40.1%	33.7%	3.9%
1970	18.9%	40.3%	36.5%	4.3%
1975	18.8%	42.6%	31.8%	6.8%

10–18. Draw line graphs for the data in problems **1–9**.

The following table gives the population distribution by age in the U.S. for 1870 and 1970.

Year	Under 5	5–19	20–44	45–64	65 and over
1870	14.3%	35.4%	35.4%	11.9%	3.0%
1970	8.4%	29.4%	31.7%	20.6%	9.9%

19. Draw a circle graph to show the population distribution by age in 1870.

20. Draw a circle graph to show the population distribution by age in 1970.

The data in the following table gives a breakdown of the civilian labor force in the United States from 1966 to 1970, in millions of persons.

Employment Status	1966	1967	1968	1969	1970
Employed in nonagricultural industries	68.9	70.5	72.1	74.3	75.6
Employed in agriculture	4.0	3.8	3.8	3.6	3.6
Unemployed	2.9	3.0	2.8	2.8	3.7
Total civilian labor force	75.8	77.3	78.7	80.7	82.9

21–25. For each year 1966–1970, draw a circle graph to show the breakdown of the civilian labor force.

15-3 Central Tendency

Objective: To find the median, mean, and mode of sets of data.

During a cold spell lasting 43 days, the following high temperatures (in degrees Fahrenheit) were recorded in Chicago. What temperature is most representative of the high temperatures for that period?

26	17	12	5	4	25	17	23	13
6	25	19	27	22	26	20	31	15
12	27	16	27	16	30	7	31	24
5	29	18	16	22	29	8	31	
13	24	5	$^-7$	20	29	18	12	

The most representative temperature, the average temperature, is neither the greatest nor the least temperature. It is a value somewhere in the middle of the group.

The most commonly used averages are the **median, mode,** and **mean.** They are defined in the following way.

Definition of Median, Mode, and Mean

The median of a set of data is the middle value. If there are two middle values, it is the value halfway between.
The mode of a set of data is the most frequent value. Some sets of data have multiple modes.
The mean of a set of data is the sum of all the values divided by the number of values.

temperatures

31	24	16
31	24	15
31	23	13
30	22	13
29	22	12
29	20	12
29	20	12
27	19	8
27	18	7
27	18	6
26	17	5
26	17	5
25	16	5
25	16	4
		$^-7$

To find the median of the Chicago temperatures, arrange the values in descending order, as shown in the margin. Then, find the middle value. In this case, the median temperature is 19.

To find the mode, determine how many times each particular high temperature occurred. Then find the most frequently occurring value. In this case, there are many modes, 31, 21, 16, 12, and 15.

To find the mean, add all the values. Then divide by 43, the number of values. In this case, the mean temperature to the nearest tenth is 18.5.

This example shows that median, mode, and mean are not always the same value.

The value of every item in a set of data affects the value of the mean. Thus, when extreme values are included, the mean may become less representative of the set. The values of the median and the mode are *not* affected by extreme values.

examples

1

Find the mean of {1, 2, 4, 93} and {24, 25, 25, 26}.

{1, 2, 4, 93}

$$\text{mean} = \frac{1 + 2 + 4 + 93}{4} = \frac{100}{4} = 25$$

The mean is not close to any one of the four values in this set. In this case, it is *not* a particularly representative value.

{24, 25, 25, 26}

$$\text{mean} = \frac{24 + 25 + 25 + 26}{4} = \frac{100}{4} = 25$$

There are *no* extreme values in this set. In this case, the mean is a representative value.

The mean for both sets is 25.

2

Find the median, mean, and mode of the hourly wages of 80 workers. Five workers make \$3.60 per hour, fifteen make \$3.40 per hour, thirty make \$4.70 per hour, ten make \$5.60 per hour, and twenty make \$3.50 per hour.

Arrange the wages in descending order. Then find the middle value.

\$5.60	10 workers
\$4.70	30 workers
\$3.60	5 workers
\$3.50	20 workers
\$3.40	15 workers

There are two middle values, the 40th value 4.70, and the 41st value 3.60. The median is the value halfway between, $\frac{4.70 + 3.60}{2}$ or 4.15.

More workers make \$4.70 per hour than any other wage. So it is the most frequently occurring value. The mode is 4.70.

Add all 80 values. There are 10 values of \$5.60, 30 values of \$4.70, and so on. You can use multiplication to shorten the additions.

$$\text{mean} = \frac{10(5.60) + 30(4.70) + 5(3.60) + 20(3.50) + 15(3.40)}{80}$$
$$= \frac{56.0 + 141.0 + 18.0 + 70.0 + 51.0}{80}$$
$$= \frac{336.0}{80}$$
$$= 4.20$$

The median is 4.15, the mode is 4.70, and the mean is 4.20.

9. none **10.** none **11.** 1 **12.** 7 **13.** none **14.** none **15.** 2.1 **16.** 7

exercises

Max: 1–24, 1–24; **Avg:** 1–24, 1–23 odds; **Min:** 1–23 odds

Exploratory **Find the median for each set of data.**

1. {1, 2, 3, 4, 5} 3

2. {2, 4, 6, 8, 10} 6

3. {1, 1, 2, 4, 1} 1

4. {7, 7, 7, 7, 7, 7, 7} 7

5. {8, 43, 2, 56, 44} 43

6. {7.1, 5.0, 2.7, 9.1, 8.1, 6.3, 8.5} 7.1

7. {2.1, 4.8, 2.1, 5.7, 2.1, 4.8, 2.1} 2.1

8. {1, 7, 7, 0, 2, 0, 4, 1, 3, 7, 7, 5, 4, 1, 8} 4

9–16. Find the mode for each set of data in problems **1-8.** See above.

17–24. Find the mean for each set of data in problems **1-8.**

17. 3 **18.** 6 **19.** 1.8 **20.** 7 **21.** 30.6 **22.** about 6.7 **23.** about 3.4 **24.** 3.8

Written **A die was tossed 25 times with the following results.**

5	3	1	6	5	2	1	5	4	1	6	6	4
6	5	6	3	6	4	4	4	1	1	2	2	

1–3. Find the median, mode, and mean for the tosses. 4, 6, 3.7

4–6. Two dice were tossed 64 times. Find the median, mode and mean for the following results. 7, none, 7.1

5	8	11	10	8	8	7	10	3	9	10	8	2	9	12	3
11	5	2	3	5	7	11	7	11	10	11	10	6	7	8	7
9	5	6	4	4	5	10	8	6	7	4	8	5	10	5	5
8	5	11	9	12	4	7	2	7	4	3	9	2	11	7	6

7–9. The heights in feet of the 20 highest mountains in the world are given below. Find the median, mode, and mean for the heights. 18,590.5; none; about 18,939

29,002	14,255	18,700	28,146	22,835
13,653	14,431	28,250	13,202	14,408
25,263	19,344	19,565	19,887	14,701
15,781	18,481	14,495	14,110	20,270

10–12. Find the median, mode, and mean of the hourly wages of 200 workers. One hundred workers make \$4.00 per hour, ten make \$5.50 per hour, ten make \$6.75 per hour, twenty make \$3.80 per hour, and sixty make \$5.25 per hour. \$4.00, \$4.00, \$4.57

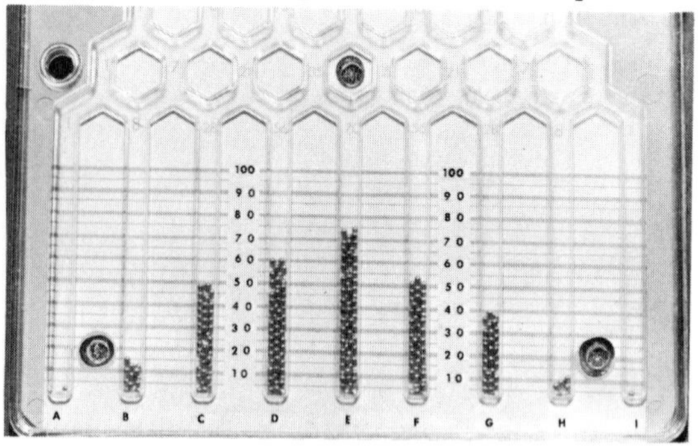

The picture on the left shows a device filled with small steel marbles. The marbles roll past a series of hexagonal obstacles, collecting at the bottom in each of nine columns. The horizontal lines help you estimate the number of marbles in each column.

13–21. Estimate the number of marbles in each column.

22–24. Find the median, mode, and mean for the number of marbles in a column.

For answers to problems **13–24**, see the Teacher's Guide.

15–4 Dispersion

Objective: To use measures of dispersion.

If 10,000 family incomes in a city were all the same, you would know all there is to know about the incomes. However, values in a set of data usually vary. The variation is called **dispersion.**

There are several kinds of measures of dispersion. The simplest measure is called the **range.**

The range of a set of data is the difference between the greatest and least values in the set.

Definition of Range

example 1

The heights of a group of young pine trees in a reforestation plot are 58 cm, 56 cm, 51 cm, 54 cm, 49 cm, 61 cm, 54 cm, and 49 cm. Find the range.

The greatest value is 61 centimeters.
The least value is 49 centimeters.

range = 61 − 49 *The range is the difference between the greatest and least values.*
= 12

Because the range is the difference between the greatest and least values in a set of data, it is affected by unusually extreme values. In such cases, it is not a good measure of dispersion.

The most commonly used measure of dispersion is called the **standard deviation.** The standard deviation for a set of data is an average measure of how much each value differs from the mean.

From a set of data, the standard deviation is calculated by following these steps.

Calculations may be tedious. Calculators will be helpful.

1. Find the mean.
2. Find the difference between each measurement and the mean.
3. Square each difference.
4. Find the mean of the squares.
5. Take the positive square root of this mean.

From a set of data with n values, x_i represents a value such that $1 \le i \le n$, and $\bar{x}$ represents the mean, then the standard deviation can be found as follows.

$$\text{standard deviation} = \sqrt{\frac{\sum_{i=1}^{n} (x_i - \bar{x})^2}{n}}$$

Definition of Standard Deviation

example 2

The heights of a group of young pine trees in a reforestation plot are 58 cm, 56 cm, 51 cm, 54 cm, 49 cm, 61 cm, 54 cm, and 49 cm. Find the standard deviation.

The mean height is $\frac{58 + 56 + 51 + 54 + 49 + 61 + 54 + 49}{8}$ or 54.

$$\text{standard deviation} = \sqrt{\frac{\sum_{i=1}^{n} (x_i - \overline{x})^2}{n}}$$

n is 8
$x_1 - \overline{x}$ is 58 − 54 or 4
$x_2 - \overline{x}$ is 56 − 54 or 2
and so on

$$= \sqrt{\frac{(4)^2 + (2)^2 + (^-3)^2 + (0)^2 + (^-5)^2 + (7)^2 + (0)^2 + (^-5)^2}{8}}$$

$$= \sqrt{\frac{16 + 4 + 9 + 0 + 25 + 49 + 0 + 25}{8}}$$

$$= \sqrt{\frac{128}{8}}$$

$$= \sqrt{16}$$

$$= 4$$

The standard deviation is 4.

To make this point more strongly, compare a standard deviation of $50 with a mean of $100 to a standard deviation of $50 with a mean of $100,000.

When studying standard deviation of a set of data, it is important to keep the mean in mind. For example, suppose a firm manufactures televisions and the standard deviation of the average monthly prices for televisions sold in the last 2 years is $50.

If the mean price over the last 2 years was $200, the standard deviation indicates a great deal of variation. If the mean price over the last two years was $600, the standard deviation indicates very little variation.

exercises

Max: 1–8, 1–19; **Avg:** 1–8, 1–11 odds, 13–19; **Min:** 1–7 odds, 1–12

Exploratory **Find the range for each set of data.**

1. {39, 47, 51, 38, 45, 29, 37, 40, 36, 48} 22
2. {70, 86, 81, 86, 81, 84, 89, 77, 80, 87, 83, 87, 90, 92, 87} 22
3. {50, 92, 79, 61, 76, 83, 65, 98, 82, 64, 76, 63, 57, 96, 75, 53, 66, 88, 59, 85, 95, 65, 81, 71} 48
4. {14.1, 15.8, 15.2, 14.0, 14.8, 14.1, 12.9, 14.4, 16.8, 16.2, 13.2, 15.9, 13.9, 15.4, 13.6, 15.1, 14.7, 13.2} 3.9

5-8. Find the standard deviation for each set of data in problems **1-4**.
5. 6.3 **6.** 5.4 **7.** 13.7 **8.** 1.1

Written The weights in pounds of the 11 players in each of two college football teams is as follows.

How College: 160, 180, 190, 200, 210, 170, 250, 220, 180, 200, 240

Now College: 160, 190, 210, 230, 240, 220, 150, 190, 210, 160, 240

1. Find the range in weights for the How College team. 90
2. Find the range in weights for the Now College team. 90
3. Find the mean weight for the How College team. 200
4. Find the mean weight for the Now College team. 200
5. Find the standard deviation in weights for the How College team. 27
6. Find the standard deviation in weights for the Now College team. 31

The mileage in miles per gallon obtained by the Electric Company and Gas Company cars is as follows.

Electric Company: 15, 13, 14, 18, 19, 12, 20, 16, 15, 21, 18, 25, 23, 11, 12, 12, 20, 16, 28, 13

Gas Company: 12, 16, 22, 24, 13, 13, 23, 21, 15, 11, 24, 27, 20, 11, 12, 24

7. Find the range in mileage for the Electric Company cars. 17
8. Find the range in mileage for the Gas Company cars. 16
9. Find the mean mileage in miles per gallon for the Electric Company cars. 17
10. Find the mean mileage in miles per gallon for the Gas Company cars. 18
11. Find the standard deviation in mileage for the Electric Company cars. 4.6
12. Find the standard deviation in mileage for the Gas Company cars. 5.5

The following tables give two frequency distributions for items. Bar graphs for these distributions are shown.

Item	1	2	3	4	5	6	7	8	9
Frequency	1	0	1	7	9	4	1	1	1

Item	1	2	3	4	5	6	7	8	9
Frequency	4	2	2	3	4	1	2	4	3

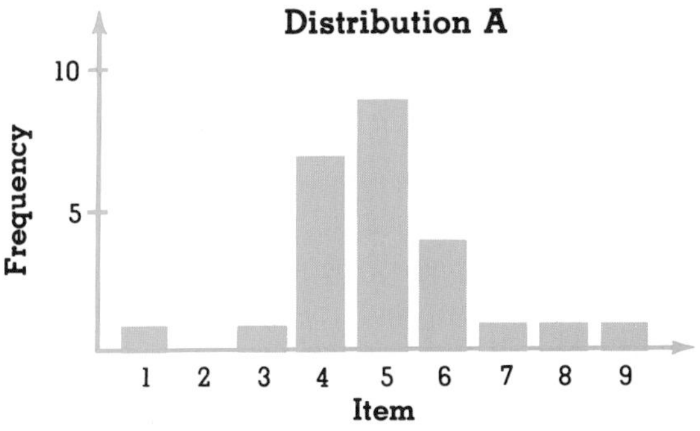

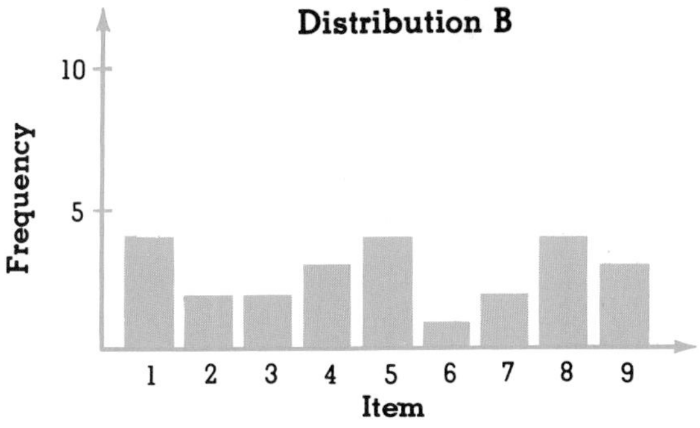

13. Find the range for distribution A. 9
14. Find the range for distribution B. 3
15. Find the mean for distribution A. about 2.8
16. Find the mean for distribution B. about 2.8
17. Find the standard deviation for distribution A. about 3
18. Find the standard deviation for distribution B. about 1
19. Look at the two graphs. Which distribution has its values clustered more around its mean? B
20. Write a computer program to find the standard deviation for n data items. See Teacher's Guide.

Score	Number of People
40–49	5
50–59	0
60–69	0
70–79	2
80–89	8
90–99	35
100–109	50
110–119	40
120–129	15
130–139	5
140–149	9
150–159	1
160–169	0
170–179	3
180–189	0
190–199	2

15–5 The Normal Distribution

Objective: To use the normal distribution to analyze data.

One way of analyzing data is to consider the frequency with which each value occurs. The table on the left gives the frequencies of certain scores on a mechanical aptitude test taken by 175 people.

The following bar graph shows the frequencies of the scores in the table.

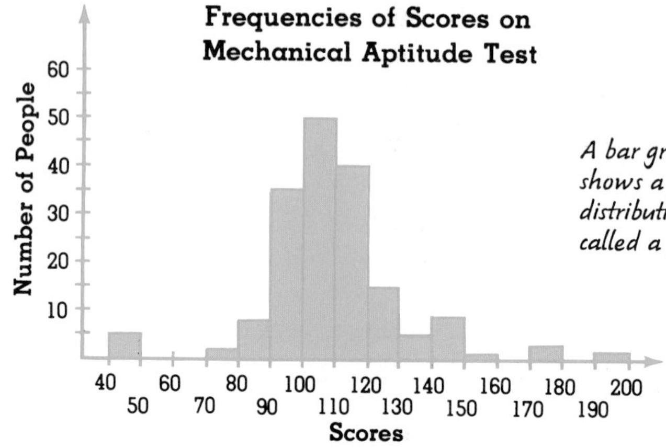

A bar graph which shows a frequency distribution is called a histogram.

The bar graph shows the **frequency distribution** of the scores. In other words, they show how the scores are spread out.

Frequency distributions are often shown by curves rather than histograms, especially when the distribution contains a great number of values. These curves may be of many different shapes. Many distributions have graphs like the following. Distributions with such a graph are called **normal distributions.**

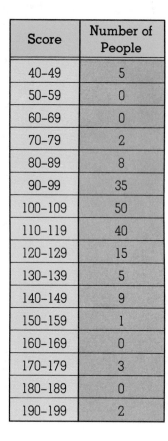

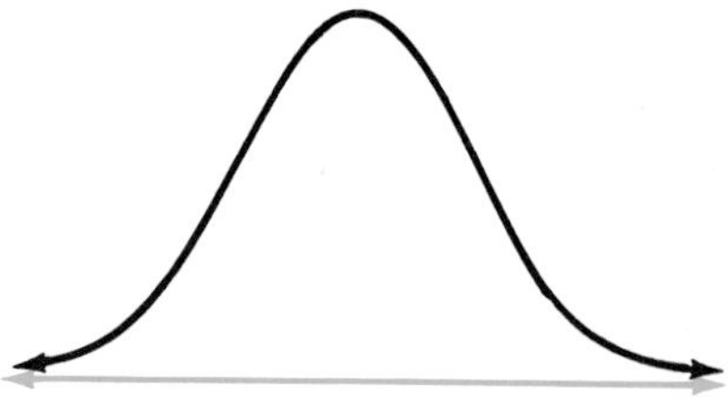

The curve is bell-shaped and symmetric. The shape of the curve indicates that frequencies in a normal distribution are concentrated in the center portion of the distribution. What does this tell you about the mean?

Normal distributions occur very frequently. For example, the diameter of a hole made by a drill press, the number of errors made by a typist, the tosses in a dart game if the player aims at the bull's-eye, the scores on tests, the grain yield on a farm, and the length of a newborn child can all be approximated by a normal distribution provided the number of data is sufficiently great.

Suppose a set of data consists of weights for 600 young people. Also, suppose the mean weight is 100 pounds and the standard deviation is 20 pounds. If the frequency distribution of these weights is a normal distribution, then the graph approximates the curve on the right.

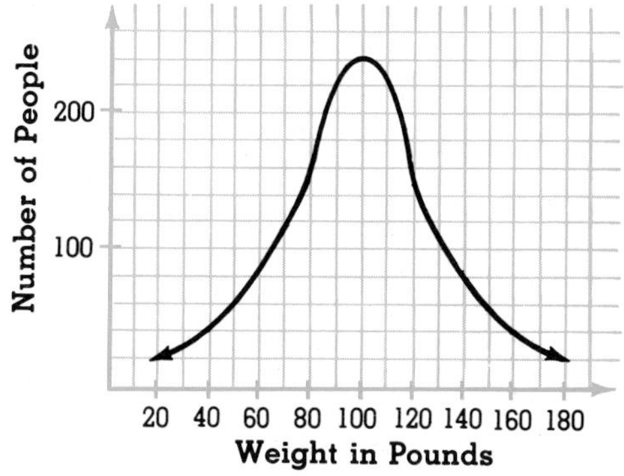

Normal distributions have these properties.

1. The graph is maximized at the mean.
2. About 68% of the items are within one standard deviation from the mean.

   By symmetry, 34% are greater than the mean, and 34% are less than the mean.
3. About 95% of the items are within two standard deviations from the mean.

   By symmetry 47.5% are greater than the mean, and 47.5% are less than the mean.
4. About 99% of the items are within three standard deviations from the mean.

   By symmetry, 49.5% are greater than the mean, and 49.5% are less than the mean.

These percentages are approximate. They may vary slightly in the literature.

As the graph of the distribution above shows, the mean, 100 pounds, is the most frequent weight. Out of 600 young people, about 408 have weights between 80 pounds and 120 pounds. About 570 have weights between 60 pounds and 140 pounds. And about 594 have weights between 40 pounds and 160 pounds.

example 1

The approximate number of hours worked per week for 100 people is normally distributed. The mean is 40 hours per week and the standard deviation is 2 hours per week. About how many people work more than 42 hours per week?

This frequency distribution is shown by the following curve. The percentages represent the percentage of 100 people working the number of hours within the given interval.

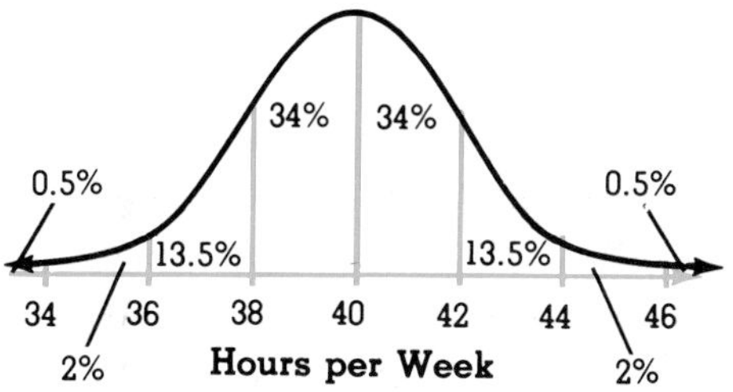

The percentage of people working more than 42 hours per week is 13.5% + 2% + 0.5% or 16%.

$$100 \times 16\% = 16$$

Thus, 16 people work more than 42 hours per week.

exercises

Max: 1–18, 1–16; Avg: 1–18, 1–15 odds; Min: 1–6, 1–15 odds

Exploratory **Suppose 500 items are normally distributed. Solve each problem.**

1. How many items are within one standard deviation from the mean? 340
2. How many items are within two standard deviations from the mean? 475
3. How many items are within three standard deviations from the mean? 495
4. How many items are within one standard deviation less than the mean? 170
5. How many items are within one standard deviation greater than the mean? 170
6. How many items are within two standard deviations greater than the mean? 237.5

7–12. Answer problems **1–6** for a normal distribution of 2000 items.

13–18. Answer problems **1–6** for a normal distribution of 16,000 items.

7. 1,360 **8.** 1,900 **9.** 1,980 **10.** 680 **11.** 680 **12.** 950
13. 10,880 **14.** 15,200 **15.** 15,840 **16.** 5,440 **17.** 5,440 **18.** 7,600

Written Solve each problem.

The lifetimes of 10,000 light bulbs is normally distributed. The mean lifetime is 300 days and the standard deviation is 40 days.

1. How many light bulbs will last between 260 and 340 days? 6800
2. How many light bulbs will last between 220 and 380 days? 9500
3. How many light bulbs will last less than 300 days? 5,000
4. How many light bulbs will last more than 300 days? 5,000
5. How many light bulbs will last more than 380 days? 250
6. How many light bulbs will last less than 180 days? 50

The diameters of metal fittings produced by a machine is distributed normally. The mean diameter is 7.5 centimeters and the standard deviation is 0.5 centimeters.

7. What percentage of the fittings have diameters between 7.0 centimeters and 8.0 centimeters? 68%
8. What percentage of the fittings have diameters between 6.5 centimeters and 8.5 centimeters? 95%
9. What percentage of the fittings have diameters between 6.5 centimeters and 7.5 centimeters? 47.5%
10. What percentage of the fittings have diameters between 7.5 centimeters and 8.0 centimeters? 34%
11. What percentage of the fittings have diameters between 7.0 centimeters and 8.5 centimeters? 81.5%
12. What percentage of the fittings have diameters between 6.5 centimeters and 8.0 centimeters? 81.5%

If you toss a fair coin 100 times, the least number of heads possible is 0, and the most is 100. If this experiment is repeated many times, the number of heads obtained for every 100 tosses is distributed about normally. There would be a mean of 50 and a standard deviation of 5.

13. What percentage of the experiments will show less than 50 heads? 50%
14. What percentage of the experiments will show more than 50 heads? 50%
15. What percentage of the experiments will show more than 65 heads? 0.5%
16. What percentage of the experiments will show between 40 and 60 heads? 95%

15-6 Predictions

Objective: To make predictions using scatter diagrams and prediction equations.

The first step in determining how quantities are related often is making a **scatter diagram.** Such a diagram shows visually the nature of a relationship, both shape and closeness.

Suppose, for example you wish to predict the quantity of a food product sold based on its weekly selling price. The following table shows the quantity sold for each of the last ten weeks, and its selling price.

Quantity Sold (dozens)	30	47	38	28	49	23	47	46	39	42
Price (cents per dozen)	28	22	29	32	20	35	21	20	24	29

The graph on the right is a scatter diagram for the data. The scatter of dots suggests a straight line which slopes downward from the upper left corner to the lower right corner.

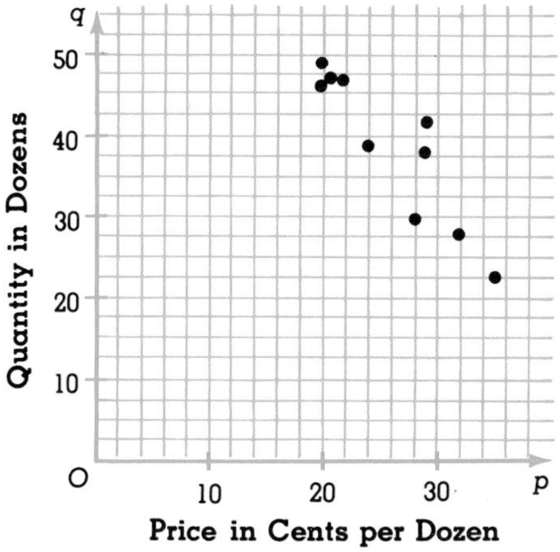

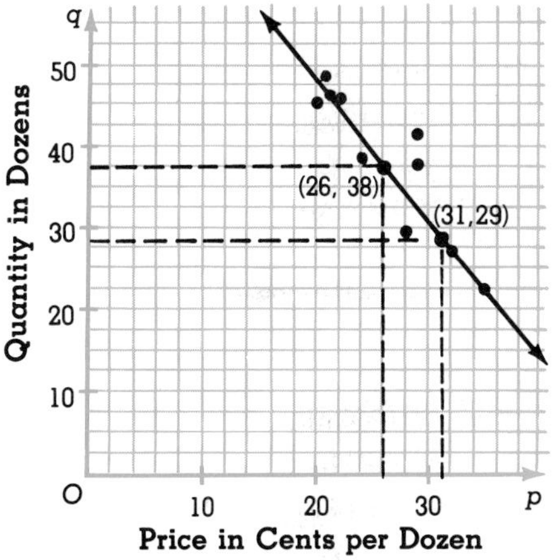

You can draw the line that is suggested by the dots. It represents the relationship between quantity and price. By choosing several points on the line, you can find the equation of the line. This equation is called the **prediction equation** for the relationship.

slope $= \frac{38 - 29}{26 - 31}$ or $^{-}1.8$

$q = {}^{-}1.8p + b$ *q stands for quantity and p stands for price*

$38 = {}^{-}1.8(26) + b$

$84.8 = b$ The equation is $q = {}^{-}1.8p + 84.8$

Now, suppose that next week, the price of the food product will be 30 cents. Using the *prediction equation*, you can estimate that 30.8 dozen items will be sold.

$$q = {}^{-}1.8p + 84.8$$
$$= {}^{-}1.8(30) + 84.8 \quad \text{or} \quad 30.8$$

example 1

Draw a scatter diagram and find a prediction equation to show how typing speed and experience are related. Use the data in the following table.

Typing speed (wpm)	33	45	46	20	40	30	38	22	52	44	42	55
Experience (years)	4	7	8	1	6	3	5	2	9	6	7	10

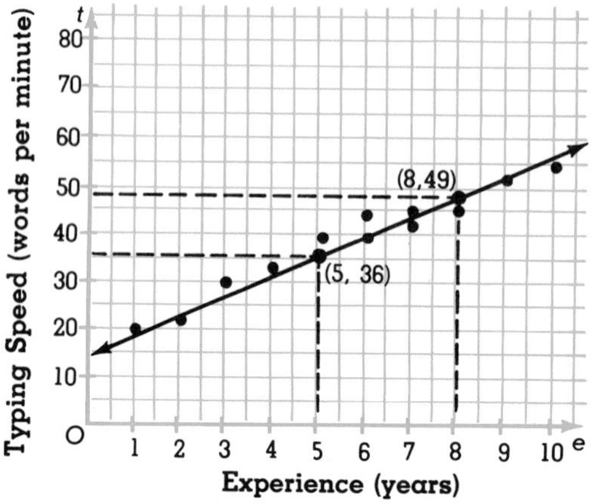

The black line is suggested by the pattern of dots. Two points with coordinates (5, 36) and (8, 49) lie on the line.

$$\text{slope} = \frac{49 - 36}{8 - 5}$$

$$= \frac{13}{3} \quad \text{or about } 4.3$$

Let e stand for experience.
Let t stand for typing speed.

$$t = 4.3e + b \qquad y = mx + b$$
$$36 = 4.3(5) + b$$
$$36 = 21.5 + b$$
$$14.5 = b$$

The prediction equation is $t = 4.3e + 14.5$.

The procedure for determining a prediction equation is dependent on your judgment. Such an equation is satisfactory only when rough prediction is desired. Statisticians normally use other, more precise procedures to determine prediction equations.

exercises

Max: 1–16, 1–20; **Avg:** 1–16, 1–16; **Min:** 1–15 odds, 1–16

Exploratory The prediction equation in a study of the relationship between plant height in centimeters, h, and number of times watered per month, t, is $h = 0.5t + 0.5$. Predict the plant height for each of the following numbers of waterings.

1. 1 1.0 **2.** 3 2.0 **3.** 5 3.0 **4.** 8 4.5
5. 9 5.0 **6.** 10 5.5 **7.** 12 6.5 **8.** 15 8.0

A study of the relationship between cost for a unit of living space, c, and the number of square feet per unit, a, of living space resulted in the prediction equation $c = {}^{-}0.2a + 200$. Predict the cost of units of living space for each of the following areas.

9. 200 160 **10.** 300 140 **11.** 350 130 **12.** 400 120
13. 450 110 **14.** 550 90 **15.** 600 80 **16.** 800 40

Written According to a certain prediction equation, if Acme Soap spends $20,000 on advertising, sales will be $10,000,000. If Acme Soap spends $50,000 on advertising, sales will be $22,000,000. Let x stand for advertising expenditure and y stand for sales revenue.

1. Find the slope of the prediction equation. 400
2. Find the y-intercept of the prediction equation. 2,000,000
3. Find the prediction equation. $y = 400x + 2{,}000{,}000$
4. Predict sales revenue if $10,000 is spent on advertising. $6,000,000
5. Predict sales revenue if $15,000 is spent on advertising. $8,000,000
6. Predict sales revenue if $35,000 is spent on advertising. $16,000,000

A certain study claims that the number of yearly visits to a public health clinic is related to a family's weekly income. According to the study's prediction equation, a family that earns $120 a week will visit the clinic 11 times a year. And a family that earns $170 a week will visit the clinic 6 times a year. Let x stand for family income and y stand for number of visits.

7. Find the slope of the prediction equation. $^-0.1$
8. Find the y-intercept of the prediction equation. 23
9. Find the prediction equation. $y = {}^-0.1x + 23$
10. Predict the number of yearly visits if a family earns $90 a week. 14
11. Predict the number of yearly visits if a family earns $150 a week. 8
12. Predict the number of yearly visits if a family earns $200 a week. 3

The following table shows the amount of sales for each of 8 sales representatives during a given period, and the years of sales experience for each representative.

Amount of Sales	$9,000	$6,000	$4,000	$3,000	$3,000	$5,000	$8,000	$2,000
Years of Experience	6	5	3	1	4	3	6	2

13. Draw a scatter diagram to show how amount of sales and years of experience are related. See Teacher's Guide.
14. Find a prediction equation to show how amount of sales and years of experience are related. $y = 1333x + 2$
15. Predict the amount of sales for a representative with 8 years of experience. $10,666
16. Predict the amount of sales for a representative with no experience. $2

The following table shows the statistics grades and the economics grades for a group of college students at the end of a given semester.

Statistics Grades	95	51	49	27	42	52	67	48	46
Economics Grades	88	70	65	50	60	80	68	49	40

17. Draw a scatter diagram to show how statistics grades and economics grades are related. See Teacher's Guide.
18. Find a prediction equation to show how statistics grades and economics grades are related. $y = \frac{4}{7}x + 32\frac{1}{7}$
19. Predict the economics grade of a student who receives a 75 in statistics. 75
20. Predict the statistics grade of a student who receives an 85 in economics. $92\frac{1}{2}$

Using Algebra

Misuses of Statistics

Statistics can be misleading. Graphs for a set of data can look very different from one another. Compare the following graphs for the data below.

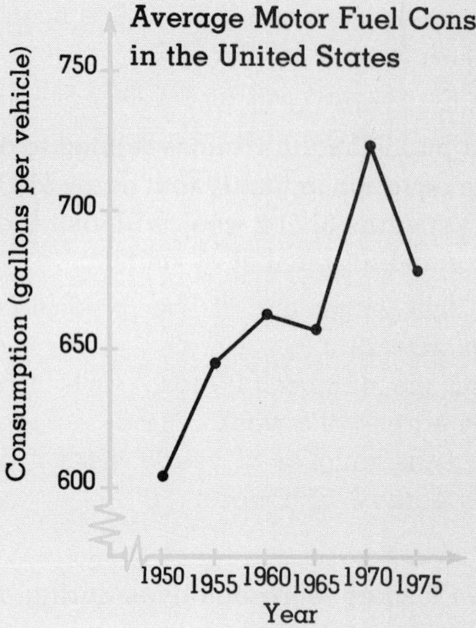

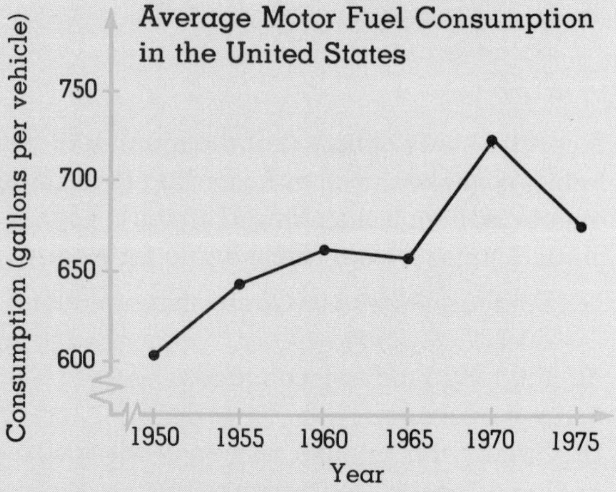

Notice how the vertical and horizontal scales of the two graphs differ. Scales can be "cramped" or "spread out" to make a graph that gives a certain impression. Which graph would you use to give the impression that motor fuel consumption increased a great deal from 1950 to 1970? the first graph

Advertisements often use graphs that have no scales, or only one scale. These graphs *seem* to show statistics, but actually give no information.

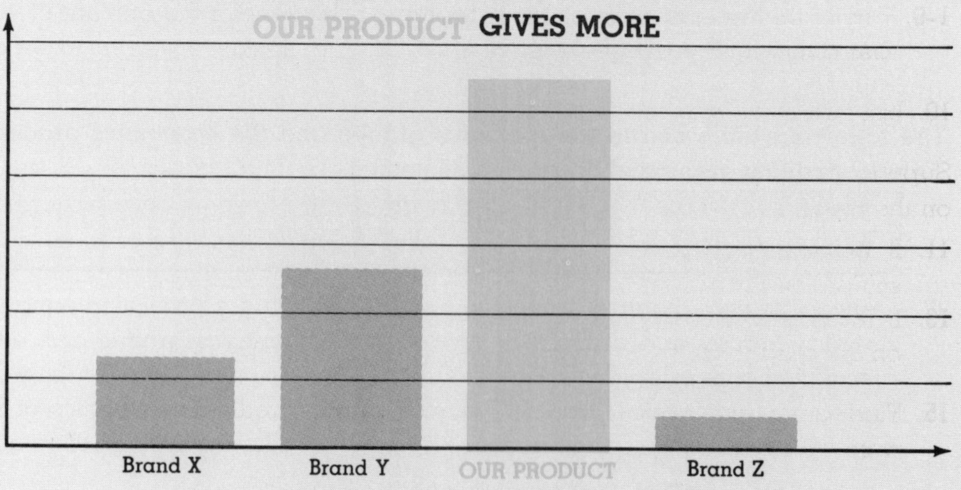

If a sample is small, conclusions drawn from the set of data are *not* always reliable. How many cars should be tested before an advertiser can make the following claim? Answers vary.

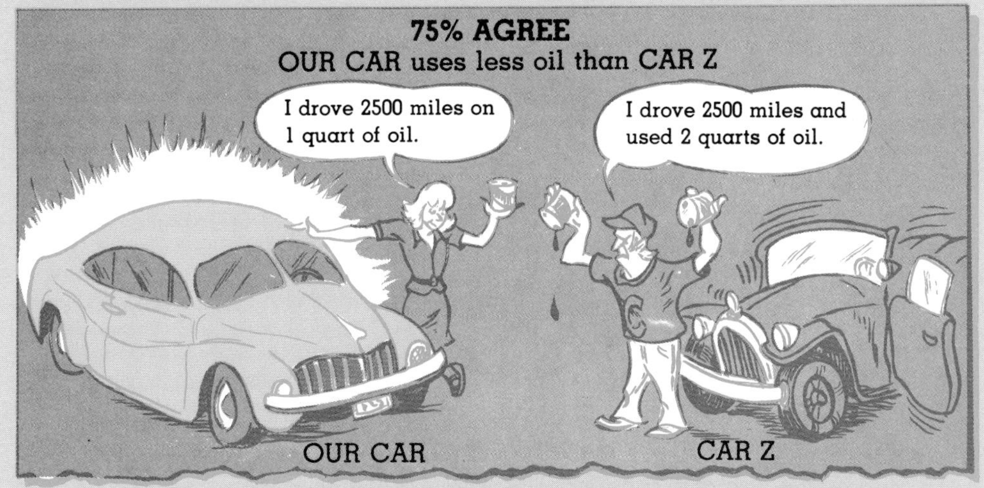

Suppose four people were asked which car used less oil. If 75% agreed, how many people thought that *Our Car* used less oil? Only 3 people

The advertisement above is misleading in other ways. For example, what was the condition of the cars tested? Suppose *Car Z* was old and out of tune, and used more oil than *Our Car*, which was brand new. Is it reasonable to assume that a brand new *Car Z* would use more oil than a brand new *Our Car*? No

Exercises Solve each problem.

1–9. Draw two line graphs for each set of data in problems **1–9** on pages 428 and 429. Use different scales. Answers vary.

10. List additional ways the advertisement about *Our Car* is misleading. Answers vary.

Suppose an advertiser claims that 90% of all of one brand of cars sold in the last 10 years are still on the road.

11. If 10,000 cars were sold, how many are still on the road? 9000

12. If 1000 cars were sold, how many are still on the road? 900

13. If 100 cars were sold, how many are still on the road? 90

14. If 10 cars were sold, how many are still on the road? 9

15. Find an example to show how you think averages could be used in a misleading way. Answers vary.

Vocabulary

data (422)
pictograph (426)
bar graph (426)
line graph (426)
circle graph (427)
median (430)
mode (430)
mean (430)
dispersion (433)
range (433)
standard deviation (433)
histogram (436)
frequency distribution (436)
normal distribution (436)
scatter diagram (439)
prediction equation (439)

Chapter Summary

1. Graphs are used to show relationships among data. Bar graphs and pictographs compare specific quantities. Line graphs show trends. Circle graphs compare parts to the whole. (427)
2. The median of a set of data is the middle value. If there are two middle values, it is the value halfway between. (430)
3. The mode of a set of data is the most frequent value. (430)
4. The mean of a set of data is the sum of all the values divided by the number of values. (430)
5. Definition of Range: The range of a set of data is the difference between the greatest and least values in the set. (433)
6. Definition of Standard Deviation: From a set of data with n values, x_i represents a value such that $1 \leq i \leq n$, and $\overline{x}$ represents the mean, then the standard deviation is $\sqrt{\dfrac{\sum_{i=1}^{n} (x_i - \overline{x})^2}{n}}$. (433)
7. Frequency distributions show how data are spread out. A histogram is a bar graph which shows a frequency distribution. The normal distribution commonly occurs. (436)
8. Normal distributions have the following properties.
   The graph is maximized at the mean.
   About 68% of the items are within one standard deviation from the mean.
   About 95% of the items are within two standard deviations from the mean.
   About 99% of the items are within three standard deviations from the mean. (437)
9. Scatter diagrams picture how quantities are related. Prediction equations give an approximate description of the relationship. (439)

3. no entry 4. $^{-}$\$8 5. $^{+}$\$669 6. $^{+}$\$311 7. $^{-}$\$546 8. $^{+}$\$448

Chapter Review

15-1 **The following table gives the median family income for the years 1970 to 1976.**

Year	1970	1971	1972	1973	1974	1975	1976
Median Income	\$14,465	\$14,457	\$15,126	\$15,437	\$14,891	\$14,510	\$14,958

1. What was the median family income in 1972? \$15,126
2. Did the median family's income increase or decrease from 1974 to 1975?

3–8. Find all the entries for a new row to the table with the heading, *Amount of Gain or Loss.* See above.

2. decrease

15-2 **The following table gives the frequency of the number of diseased plants in garden plots from a certain nursery.**

Number of Diseased Plants per Plot	8	9	10	11	12	13	14	15	16	17	18	19	20	21	22	23	24	25
Number of Plots	1	0	3	5	0	8	0	7	13	16	15	10	9	12	10	18	17	19

15-2 9. Draw a line graph to present the data in the table above. See Teacher's Guide.

15-3 10. Find the median for the distribution in the table above. 20 plants per plot

11. Find the mode for the distribution in the table above. 25 plants per plot
12. Find the mean for the distribution in the table above. about 19.6 plants per plot

15-4 13. Find the range for the distribution in the table above. 17 plants per plot

14. Find the standard deviation for the distribution in the table above. about 4.1

Unless calculators are available, problem 14 is time-consuming.

15-5 **The monthly incomes of 10,000 workers in King City are distributed normally. Suppose the mean monthly income is \$600 and the standard deviation is \$100.**

15. How many workers earn more than \$700 a month? 1600 workers
16. How many workers earn less than \$400 a month? 250 workers

15-6 **According to a certain prediction equation, if a person is 180 centimeters tall, that person weighs about 76 kilograms. A person 160 centimeters tall weighs about 57 kilograms. Let x stand for height in centimeters, and y stand for weight in kilograms.**

17. Find the slope of the prediction equation. 0.95
18. Find the y-intercept of the prediction equation. $^{-}95$
19. Find the prediction equation. $y = 0.95x - 95$
20. Predict the weight of a person who is 174 centimeters tall. 70.3 kilograms

Chapter Test

The following high temperatures in degrees Fahrenheit were recorded during a cold spell in Chicago lasting 43 days.

26	17	12	5	4	25	17	23	13
6	25	19	27	22	26	30	31	15
12	27	16	27	16	30	7	31	24
5	29	18	16	22	29	8	31	
13	24	5	$^-7$	20	29	18	12	

1. Use the data to make a table with headings *Temperature in Degrees Fahrenheit,* and *Frequency.* See Teacher's Guide.
2. How many days was the high temperature 13 degrees? 2 days
3. How many days was the high temperature less than 20 degrees? 22 days
4. Draw a line graph to show the frequency distribution of the temperature. See student work.
5. Find the median of the distribution. 19°F
6. Find the mode of the distribution. 5, 12, 16, 27, 29, 31
7. Find the mean of the distribution. about 18.7°F
8. Find the range of the distribution. 38°
9. Find the standard deviation of the distribution. about 9.2°

Unless calculators are available, problem **9** is time-consuming.

The frequencies of the scores on a college entrance examination are normally distributed. Suppose the mean score is 510 and the standard deviation is 80. And suppose 50,000 people took the examination.

10. What percentage of the scores is above 750? 0.5%
11. How many people scored between 430 and 590? 34,000 people

According to a certain prediction equation, if a person is 50 years old, that person's systolic blood pressure is 135 millimeters. The blood pressure of a person 35 years old is 127.5 millimeters. Let x stand for age in years, and y stand for blood pressure in millimeters.

12. Find the slope of the prediction equation. 0.5
13. Find the y-intercept of the prediction equation. 110
14. Find the prediction equation. $y = 0.5x + 110$
15. Predict the systolic blood pressure of a person who is 45 years old. 132.5 millimeters

Measurements of blood pressure usually include two numbers, such as 120/80. The first number refers to *systolic blood pressure,* pressure when the heart is contracting. The second number refers to *diastolic blood pressure,* pressure when the heart is relaxing.

Chapter

16

Trigonometric Functions and Identities

It has been found that musical sounds are made of precise patterns of waves. These vibrational waves can be described by trigonometric functions.

16-1 Angles and the Unit Circle

Objective: To express angle measure in terms of degrees and radians.

Whether applying trigonometry to circles or triangles, angles are involved. Consider a circle, centered at the origin, with two rays extending from the center. One ray is fixed along the positive x-axis. The other ray can rotate about the center.

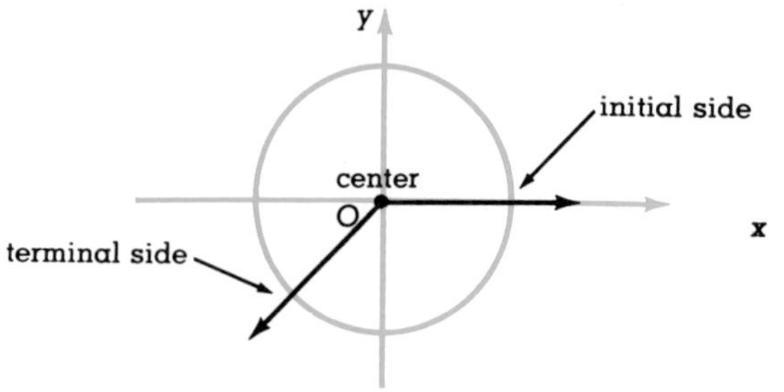

These rays form an angle. The fixed ray is called the initial side and the other is called the terminal side of the angle.

An angle with its vertex at the origin and its initial side along the positive x-axis is in standard position.

Start with both sides along the positive x-axis. As the terminal side is rotated counterclockwise, the measure of the angle formed increases.

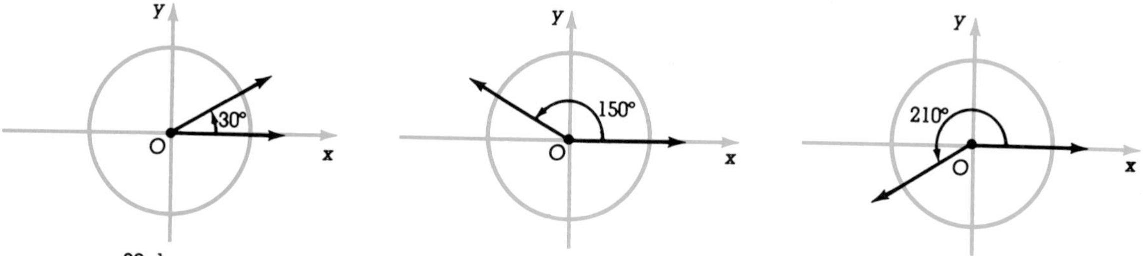

30 degrees 150 degrees 210 degrees

The most widely used unit for measuring angles is the degree.

The rotation of the terminal side of the angle may include one or more complete revolutions about the center. The measurement of an angle representing one complete revolution of the circle is 360 degrees, usually written 360°.

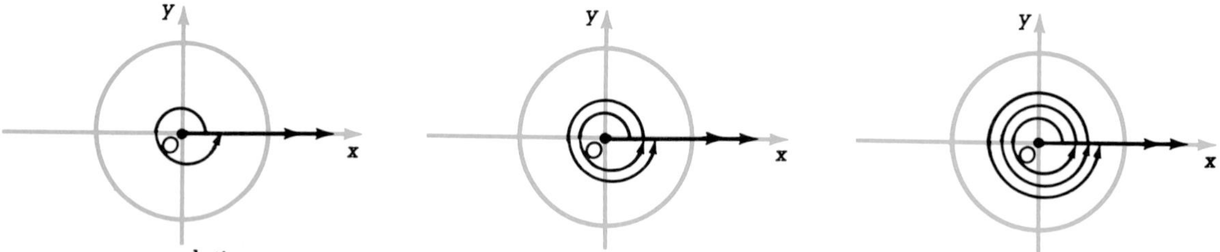

one revolution 360°

two revolutions 360° × 2 or 720°

three revolutions 360° × 3 or 1080°

Angles that differ by complete rotation of the circle are called **coterminal angles.** For example, 74°, 434°, and 794° are coterminal angles.

The terminal side of an angle also can rotate in a clockwise direction. An angle formed in such a way is given a negative measurement.

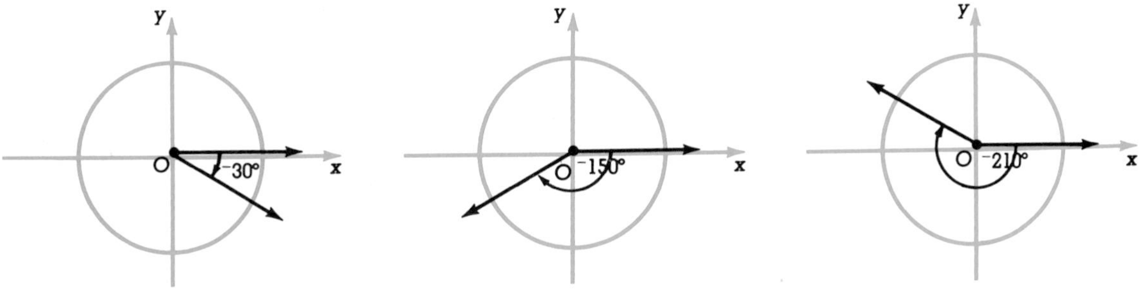

There are units other than degrees that are used in angle measurements.

Suppose a circle with radius 1 unit is centered at the origin. This circle is called a **unit circle.** Form an angle in standard position so that it intercepts an arc whose length is 1 unit. This angle is given the measurement 1 **radian.**

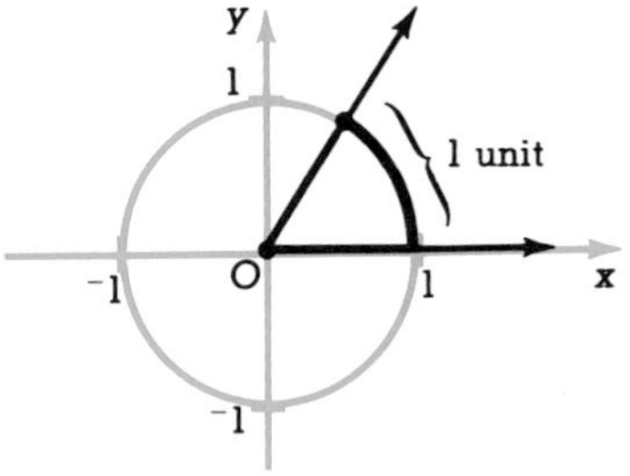

The circumference of a circle with radius 1 unit is $2\pi(1)$ or 2π units. Thus, an angle representing one complete revolution of the circle is 2π radians or 360 degrees. To convert radian measure to degree measure, or vice versa, use the following information.

$$1 \text{ radian is } \frac{360}{2\pi} \text{ or } \frac{180}{\pi} \text{ degrees}$$

$$1 \text{ degree is } \frac{2\pi}{360} \text{ or } \frac{\pi}{180} \text{ radians}$$

When no unit of measure is written, it is assumed the unit is radians. For example, 2π means 2π radians.

example 1

Convert 45°, 240°, and $^-150°$ to radians.

$$45 \cdot \frac{\pi}{180} = \frac{45\pi}{180} \text{ or } \frac{\pi}{4}$$

$$240 \cdot \frac{\pi}{180} = \frac{240\pi}{180} \text{ or } \frac{4\pi}{3}$$

$$^-150 \cdot \frac{\pi}{180} = -\frac{150\pi}{180} \text{ or } -\frac{5\pi}{6}$$

example 2

Convert $\frac{5\pi}{3}$, $-\frac{4\pi}{3}$, and $\frac{5\pi}{8}$ to degrees.

$$\frac{5\pi}{3} \cdot \frac{180}{\pi} = \left(\frac{900\pi}{3\pi}\right)^{\circ} \text{ or } 300^{\circ}$$

$$-\frac{4\pi}{3} \cdot \frac{180}{\pi} = \left(-\frac{720\pi}{3\pi}\right)^{\circ} \text{ or } {}^{-}240^{\circ}$$

$$\frac{5\pi}{8} \cdot \frac{180}{\pi} = \left(\frac{900\pi}{8\pi}\right)^{\circ} \text{ or } 112\frac{1}{2}^{\circ}$$

exercises

Max: 1–24, 1–36; Avg: 1–24, 1–35 odds; Min: 1–35 odds

Exploratory Suppose angles with each of the following measurements are in standard position. For each angle, name the quadrant which contains the terminal sides.

1. 245° III
2. 397° I
3. 800° I
4. 275° IV
5. $\frac{\pi}{3}$ I
6. $\frac{3}{5}\pi$ II
7. $\frac{11}{3}\pi$ IV
8. $2\frac{1}{3}\pi$ I
9. $^{-}240^{\circ}$ II
10. $^{-}32^{\circ}$ IV
11. 440° I
12. 300° IV
13. $\frac{5}{3}\pi$ IV
14. $-\frac{12}{5}\pi$ IV
15. $-\frac{4}{7}\pi$ III
16. $\frac{5}{9}\pi$ II
17. 945° III
18. $^{-}210^{\circ}$ II
19. 198° III
20. $^{-}94^{\circ}$ III
21. $-\frac{9}{4}\pi$ IV
22. 4 III
23. $\frac{2}{3}\pi$ II
24. 7 I

Written Convert each of the following to radians.

1. 90° $\pi/2$
2. 120° $2\pi/3$
3. $^{-}45^{\circ}$ $-\pi/4$
4. 60° $\pi/3$
5. 450° $5\pi/2$
6. $^{-}300^{\circ}$ $^{-}5\pi/3$
7. 150° $5\pi/6$
8. $^{-}600^{\circ}$ $^{-}10\pi/3$
9. 45° $\pi/4$
10. $^{-}120^{\circ}$ $^{-}2\pi/3$
11. 330° $11\pi/6$
12. $^{-}240^{\circ}$ $^{-}4\pi/3$
13. 270° $3\pi/2$
14. $^{-}135^{\circ}$ $^{-}3\pi/4$
15. 180° π
16. $^{-}210^{\circ}$ $^{-}7\pi/6$
17. 405° $9\pi/4$
18. 810° $9\pi/2$
19. $^{-}315^{\circ}$ $^{-}7\pi/4$
20. $^{-}270^{\circ}$ $^{-}3\pi/2$

Convert each of the following to degrees.

21. π 180°
22. $-\frac{\pi}{2}$ $^{-}90^{\circ}$
23. $\frac{\pi}{4}$ 45°
24. $-\frac{\pi}{6}$ $^{-}30^{\circ}$
25. 3π 540°
26. $-\frac{5}{4}\pi$ $^{-}225^{\circ}$
27. $-\frac{8}{3}\pi$ $^{-}480^{\circ}$
28. $-\frac{7}{4}\pi$ $^{-}315^{\circ}$
29. $\frac{\pi}{6}$ 30°
30. $\frac{5}{6}\pi$ 150°
31. $-\frac{\pi}{4}$ $^{-}45^{\circ}$
32. $\frac{3}{4}\pi$ 135°
33. $\frac{11\pi}{6}$ 330°
34. $\frac{7\pi}{4}$ 315°
35. $\frac{7}{6}\pi$ 210°
36. 2 $(360/\pi)^{\circ}$

Reading Algebra

Figures and Drawings

No algebra book would be complete without its share of figures and drawings. These figures and drawings are important aids in understanding the text material. Consider the following portion of this chapter.

Whether applying trigonometry to circles or triangles, angles are involved. Consider a circle, centered at the origin, with two rays extending from the center. One ray is fixed along the positive x-axis. The other ray can rotate about the center.

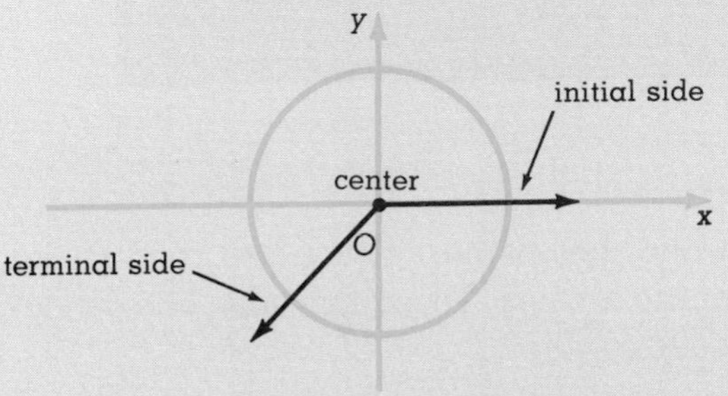

These rays form an angle. The fixed ray is called the initial side, and the other is called the terminal side of the angle.

An angle with its vertex at the origin and its initial side along the positive x-axis is in standard position.

As you read the text material, you should continuously refer to the drawing. The first sentence is a sentence of introduction. The second sentence begins to describe in words what is illustrated in the drawing. You should read the first part of the second sentence, *Consider a circle, centered at the origin,* and then refer to the drawing. Notice the circle in the drawing has its center at the origin. Now, continue the second sentence, *with two rays extending from the center.* Notice the two rays in the drawing are extending from the center. You should continue reading the text in this manner. After each phrase or sentence, study the drawing. By reading the material in this manner, you will receive a better understanding of the ideas presented.

Exercises Study the figures on pages 448, 449, 452, and 453. What ideas are illustrated in each figure? Answers vary.

16-2 Sine and Cosine

Objective: To find values for the sine and cosine.

The photograph below is an oscilloscope display. The curve represents a single pure musical tone without harmonics.

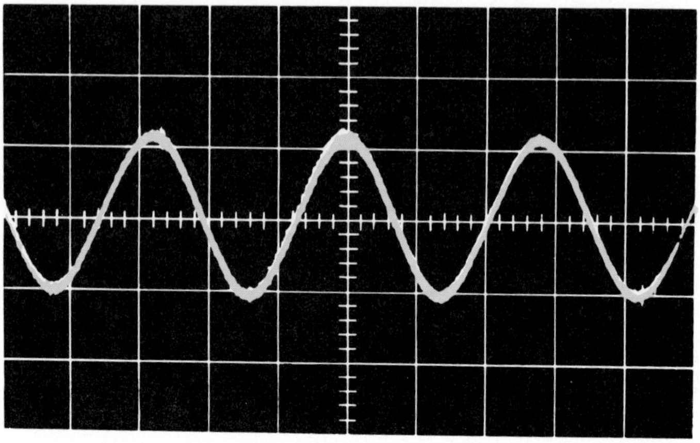

Both the **sine** function and the **cosine** function are used to describe phenomena like musical tones. These functions can be defined in terms of the unit circle.

Consider an angle in standard position on the unit circle. Let θ stand for the measurement of the angle. The terminal side of this angle intersects the circle at a particular point. The x-coordinate of the point is called cosine θ. The y-coordinate of the point is called sine θ.

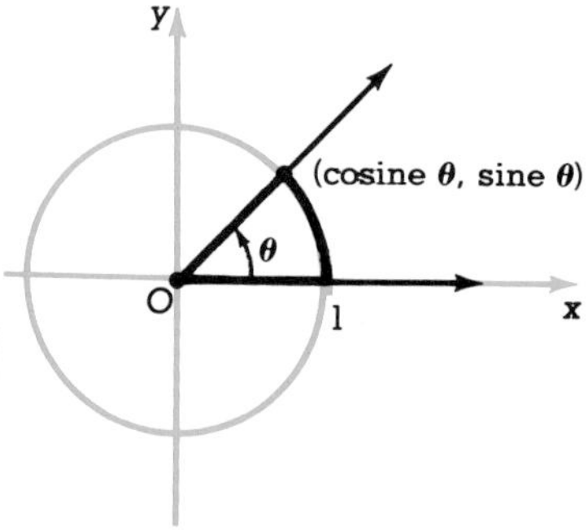

Definition of Sine and Cosine

Let θ stand for the measurement of an angle in standard position on the unit circle. Let (x, y) represent the point where the terminal side intersects the unit circle. Then the following equations hold.

$$\text{sine } \theta = y \text{ and cosine } \theta = x$$

Sine is usually abbreviated *sin*. Cosine is usually abbreviated *cos*.

You can use geometry to find values of sine and cosine for certain angles.

examples

1 **Find sin 45°.**

The initial and terminal sides of a 45° angle are part of a right triangle formed by two sides and the diagonal of a square.

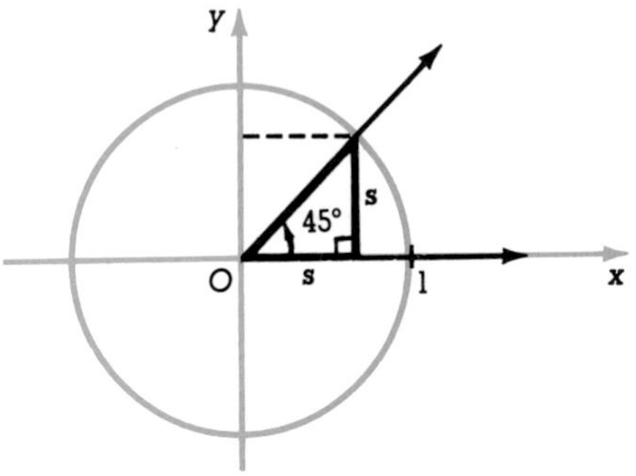

The length of the diagonal is 1 unit. To find the length of each side, s, use the Pythagorean Theorem.

$$s^2 + s^2 = 1^2$$
$$2s^2 = 1$$
$$s^2 = \frac{1}{2}$$
$$s = \sqrt{\frac{1}{2}} \text{ or } \frac{\sqrt{2}}{2}$$

The length of each side is $\frac{\sqrt{2}}{2}$ units.

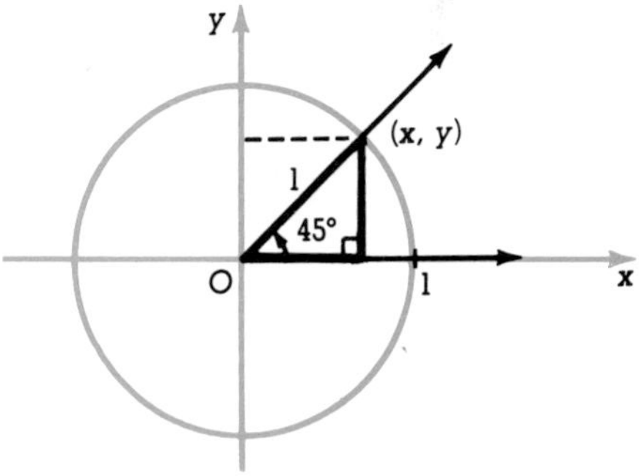

Thus, the coordinates of the point labeled (x, y) are $\left(\frac{\sqrt{2}}{2}, \frac{\sqrt{2}}{2}\right)$.

$$\sin 45° = y$$
$$= \frac{\sqrt{2}}{2}$$

2 **Find cos 60°.**

Look at the graph on the right. The broken line forms a 30°–60° right triangle with the x-axis and the terminal side of the angle. The lengths of the sides of the triangle are 1 unit, $\frac{1}{2}$ unit, and $\frac{\sqrt{3}}{2}$ units. Thus, the x-coordinate of the point labeled (x, y) is $\frac{1}{2}$.

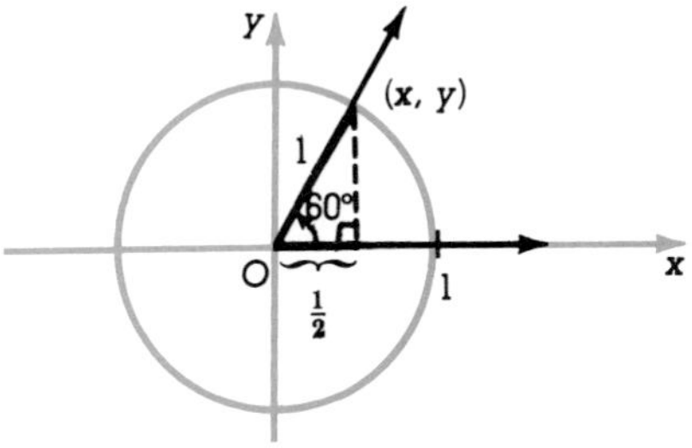

$$\cos 60° = x$$
$$= \frac{1}{2}$$

Using the technique shown in the examples, you should be able to complete a chart like the following.

θ																		
θ	**degrees**	0	30	45	60	90	120	135	150	180	210	225	240	270	300	315	330	360
	radians	0	$\frac{\pi}{6}$	$\frac{\pi}{4}$	$\frac{\pi}{3}$	$\frac{\pi}{2}$	$\frac{2\pi}{3}$	$\frac{3\pi}{4}$	$\frac{5\pi}{6}$	π	$\frac{7\pi}{6}$	$\frac{5\pi}{4}$	$\frac{4\pi}{3}$	$\frac{3\pi}{2}$	$\frac{5\pi}{3}$	$\frac{7\pi}{4}$	$\frac{11\pi}{6}$	2π
sin θ		0	$\frac{1}{2}$	$\frac{\sqrt{2}}{2}$	$\frac{\sqrt{3}}{2}$	1	$\frac{\sqrt{3}}{2}$	$\frac{\sqrt{2}}{2}$	$\frac{1}{2}$	0	$-\frac{1}{2}$	$-\frac{\sqrt{2}}{2}$	$-\frac{\sqrt{3}}{2}$	-1	$-\frac{\sqrt{3}}{2}$	$-\frac{\sqrt{2}}{2}$	$-\frac{1}{2}$	0
cos θ		1	$\frac{\sqrt{3}}{2}$	$\frac{\sqrt{2}}{2}$	$\frac{1}{2}$	0	$-\frac{1}{2}$	$-\frac{\sqrt{2}}{2}$	$-\frac{\sqrt{3}}{2}$	-1	$-\frac{\sqrt{3}}{2}$	$-\frac{\sqrt{2}}{2}$	$-\frac{1}{2}$	0	$\frac{1}{2}$	$\frac{\sqrt{2}}{2}$	$\frac{\sqrt{3}}{2}$	1

Suppose you made a similar chart for angles from 360° to 720°. Are the values for sin θ and cos θ identical to those in the first chart?

θ	**degrees**	360	390	405	420	450	480	495	510	540	570	585	600	630	660	675	690	720
	radians	2π	$\frac{13\pi}{6}$	$\frac{9\pi}{4}$	$\frac{7\pi}{3}$	$\frac{5\pi}{2}$	$\frac{8\pi}{3}$	$\frac{11\pi}{4}$	$\frac{17\pi}{6}$	3π	$\frac{19\pi}{6}$	$\frac{13\pi}{4}$	$\frac{10\pi}{3}$	$\frac{7\pi}{2}$	$\frac{11\pi}{3}$	$\frac{15\pi}{4}$	$\frac{23\pi}{6}$	4π
sin θ		0	$\frac{1}{2}$	$\frac{\sqrt{2}}{2}$	$\frac{\sqrt{3}}{2}$	1	$\frac{\sqrt{3}}{2}$	$\frac{\sqrt{2}}{2}$	$\frac{1}{2}$	0	$-\frac{1}{2}$	$-\frac{\sqrt{2}}{2}$	$-\frac{\sqrt{3}}{2}$	-1	$-\frac{\sqrt{3}}{2}$	$-\frac{\sqrt{2}}{2}$	$-\frac{1}{2}$	0
cos θ		1	$\frac{\sqrt{3}}{2}$	$\frac{\sqrt{2}}{2}$	$\frac{1}{2}$	0	$-\frac{1}{2}$	$-\frac{\sqrt{2}}{2}$	$-\frac{\sqrt{3}}{2}$	-1	$-\frac{\sqrt{3}}{2}$	$-\frac{\sqrt{2}}{2}$	$-\frac{1}{2}$	0	$\frac{1}{2}$	$\frac{\sqrt{2}}{2}$	$\frac{\sqrt{3}}{2}$	1

Every 360°, or 2π radians, represents one complete revolution of a circle. Every 360°, or 2π radians, the sine and cosine functions repeat their values.

We say that the sine and cosine functions are **periodic** and have a **period** of 360°, or 2π radians.

Definition of Periodic Function

A function f is called periodic if there is a number α such that $f(x) = f(x + \alpha)$. The least positive value of α for which $f(x) = f(x + \alpha)$ is the period of the function.

example 3

Find sin 930°.

$$\begin{aligned} \sin 930^\circ &= \sin (570 + 360)^\circ \\ &= \sin 570^\circ \\ &= \sin (210 + 360)^\circ \\ &= \sin 210^\circ \\ &= -\frac{1}{2} \end{aligned}$$

930° = 570° + 360°
Sine has a period of 360°.
570° = 210° + 360°

Caution students that, in general, $\sin (A + B) \neq \sin A + \sin B$.

exercises

Max: 1–12, 1–56; Avg: 1–12, 1–55 odds; Min: 1–55 odds

Exploratory State whether the value of each is positive or negative.

1. $\sin 300°$ $-$
2. $\sin 240°$ $-$
3. $\cos(^-210°)$ $-$
4. $\cos(^-45°)$ $+$
5. $\sin 225°$ $-$
6. $\cos(^-135°)$ $-$
7. $\sin(^-270°)$ $+$
8. $\sin 315°$ $-$
9. $\sin \frac{\pi}{3}$ $+$
10. $\cos \frac{7\pi}{3}$ $+$
11. $\cos \frac{5}{3}\pi$ $+$
12. $\sin\left(-\frac{3}{4}\pi\right)$ $-$

Written For each of the following, find the smallest positive angle that is coterminal.

1. $420°$ $60°$
2. $^-40°$ $320°$
3. $1020°$ $300°$
4. $^-450°$ $270°$
5. 3π π
6. $^-120°$ $240°$
7. $\frac{9}{2}\pi$ $\frac{\pi}{2}$
8. $\frac{11}{5}\pi$ $\frac{\pi}{5}$
9. $-\frac{\pi}{4}$ $\frac{7\pi}{4}$
10. $600°$ $240°$
11. $1200°$ $120°$
12. $1400°$ $320°$
13. $\frac{13}{3}\pi$ $\frac{\pi}{3}$
14. $\frac{27}{4}\pi$ $\frac{3\pi}{4}$
15. $\frac{11}{4}\pi$ $\frac{3\pi}{4}$
16. $680°$ $320°$
17. $^-600°$ $120°$
18. $1240°$ $160°$
19. $-\frac{8}{9}\pi$ $\frac{10}{9}\pi$
20. $^-240°$ $120°$
21. $-\frac{7}{4}\pi$ $\frac{\pi}{4}$
22. $\frac{31}{6}\pi$ $\frac{7\pi}{6}$
23. $-\frac{2}{3}\pi$ $\frac{4\pi}{3}$
24. $\frac{21}{4}\pi$ $\frac{5\pi}{4}$
25. $960°$ $240°$
26. $^-300°$ $60°$
27. $^-760°$ $320°$

Find each value.

28. $\sin 240°$ $-\sqrt{3}/2$
29. $\cos 150°$ $-\sqrt{3}/2$
30. $\cos {}^-150°$ $-\sqrt{3}/2$
31. $\cos \frac{11}{3}\pi$ $\frac{1}{2}$
32. $\sin \frac{17}{4}\pi$ $\frac{\sqrt{2}}{2}$
33. $\cos\left(-\frac{3}{4}\pi\right)$ $-\frac{\sqrt{2}}{2}$
34. $\sin\left(-\frac{5}{3}\pi\right)$ $\frac{\sqrt{3}}{2}$
35. $\sin \frac{3\pi}{2}$ $^-1$
36. $\cos \frac{7}{4}\pi$ $\frac{\sqrt{2}}{2}$
37. $\cos 390°$ $\sqrt{3}/2$
38. $\sin {}^-240°$ $\sqrt{3}/2$
39. $\cos\left(-\frac{7}{4}\pi\right)$ $\frac{\sqrt{2}}{2}$
40. $\sin 660°$ $-\sqrt{3}/2$
41. $\sin 300°$ $-\sqrt{3}/2$
42. $\cos 900°$ $^-1$
43. $\cos 330°$ $\sqrt{3}/2$
44. $\sin {}^-180°$ 0
45. $\cos {}^-60°$ $\frac{1}{2}$
46. $\sin\left(-\frac{\pi}{6}\right)$ $-\frac{1}{2}$
47. $\sin \frac{4}{3}\pi$ $-\frac{\sqrt{3}}{2}$
48. $\cos 1560°$ $-\frac{1}{2}$

Evaluate each expression.

49. $\frac{\sin 30° + \cos 60°}{2}$ $\frac{1}{2}$
50. $\frac{4 \sin 300° + 2 \cos 30°}{3}$ $-\frac{\sqrt{3}}{3}$
51. $4(\sin 30°)(\cos 60°)$ 1
52. $\sin 30° + \sin 60°$ $(1 + \sqrt{3})/2$
53. $(\sin 60°)^2 + (\cos 60°)^2$ 1
54. $8(\sin 120°)(\cos 120°)$ $^-2\sqrt{3}$
55. $\sin 240° + \cos 240°$ $(-\sqrt{3} - 1)/2$
56. $(\sin 240°)(\cos 120°)$ $\sqrt{3}/4$

16–3 Graphing Sine and Cosine

Objective: To graph the sine and cosine functions.

To graph the sine function, use the horizontal axis for θ in either degrees or radians. Use the vertical axis for values of $\sin\theta$. The following charts provide the information necessary for plotting points.

θ		0°	30°	45°	60°	90°	120°	135°	150°	180°
$\sin\theta$	exact	0	$\frac{1}{2}$	$\frac{\sqrt{2}}{2}$	$\frac{\sqrt{3}}{2}$	1	$\frac{\sqrt{3}}{2}$	$\frac{\sqrt{2}}{2}$	$\frac{1}{2}$	0
	nearest tenth	0.0	0.5	0.7	0.9	1.0	0.9	0.7	0.5	0.0

θ		210°	225°	240°	270°	300°	315°	330°	360°
$\sin\theta$	exact	$-\frac{1}{2}$	$-\frac{\sqrt{2}}{2}$	$-\frac{\sqrt{3}}{2}$	$^-1$	$-\frac{\sqrt{3}}{2}$	$-\frac{\sqrt{2}}{2}$	$-\frac{1}{2}$	0
	nearest tenth	$^-0.5$	$^-0.7$	$^-0.9$	$^-1.0$	$^-0.9$	$^-0.7$	$^-0.5$	0.0

Be careful students do not confuse use of y on these graphs with that in the previous section.

After plotting points, complete the graph by connecting the plotted points with a smooth continuous curve.

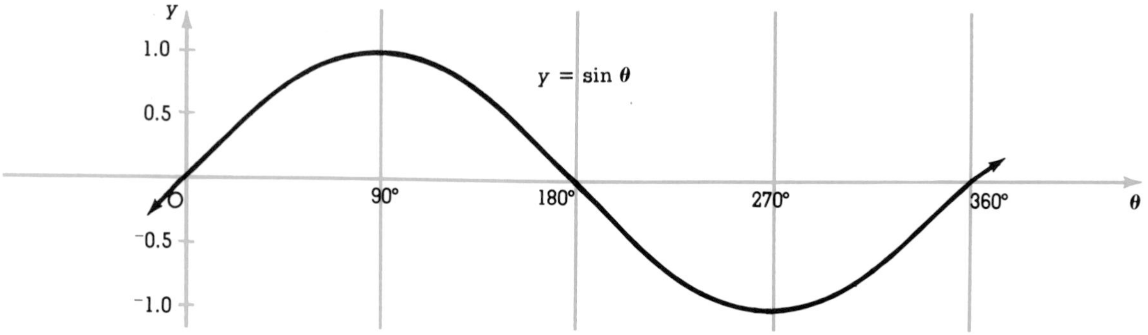

The graph of the cosine function is done in a similar manner.

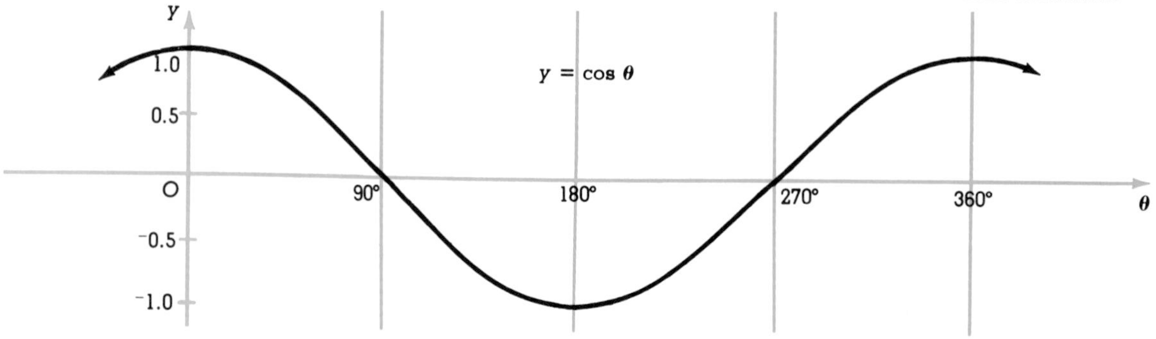

Recall that both the sine and cosine functions have a period of 360° or 2π radians. The following examples are variations of the sine function and have periods other than 360°.

examples

1 **Graph $y = \sin 2\theta$. State the period.**

First, complete a table of values.

θ	0°	15°	30°	45°	60°	75°	90°	105°	120°	135°	150°	165°	180°
2θ	0°	30°	60°	90°	120°	150°	180°	210°	240°	270°	300°	330°	360°
$\sin 2\theta$	0	$\frac{1}{2}$	$\frac{\sqrt{3}}{2}$	1	$\frac{\sqrt{3}}{2}$	$\frac{1}{2}$	0	$-\frac{1}{2}$	$-\frac{\sqrt{3}}{2}$	-1	$-\frac{\sqrt{3}}{2}$	$-\frac{1}{2}$	0

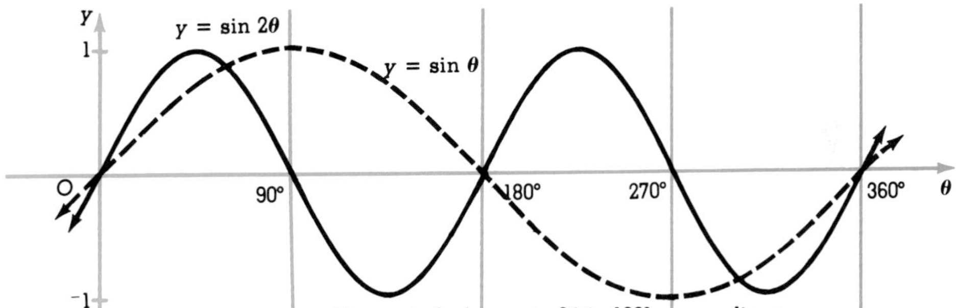

The period of $y = \sin 2\theta$ is 180° or π radians.

2 **Graph $y = \sin \frac{1}{2}\theta$. State the period.**

θ	0°	60°	90°	120°	180°	240°	270°	300°	360°
$\frac{1}{2}\theta$	0°	30°	45°	60°	90°	120°	135°	150°	180°
$\sin \frac{1}{2}\theta$	0	$\frac{1}{2}$	$\frac{\sqrt{2}}{2}$	$\frac{\sqrt{3}}{2}$	1	$\frac{\sqrt{3}}{2}$	$\frac{\sqrt{2}}{2}$	$\frac{1}{2}$	0

Students should complete a table for 360° through 720°.

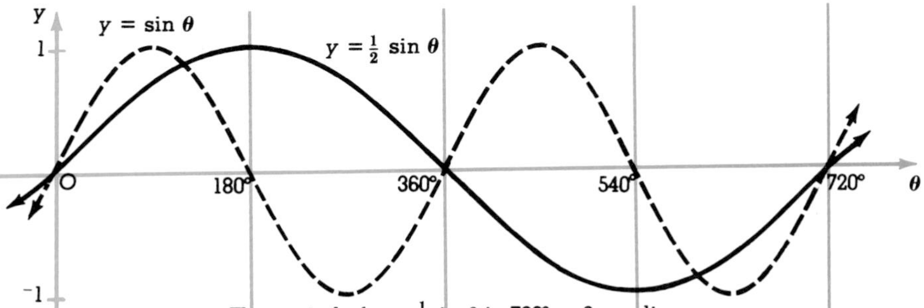

The period of $y = \frac{1}{2}\sin \theta$ is 720° or 2π radians.

All the trigonometric functions you have graphed so far have a maximum value of 1 and a minimum value of $^{-}1$. The **amplitude** of these graphs is 1. In the following examples, the graphs have amplitudes other than 1.

examples

3 **Graph $y = 2 \cos \theta$. State the amplitude.**

θ	0°	30°	60°	90°	120°	150°	180°	210°	240°	270°	300°	330°	360°
$\cos \theta$	1	$\frac{\sqrt{3}}{2}$	$\frac{1}{2}$	0	$-\frac{1}{2}$	$-\frac{\sqrt{3}}{2}$	-1	$-\frac{\sqrt{3}}{2}$	$-\frac{1}{2}$	0	$\frac{1}{2}$	$\frac{\sqrt{3}}{2}$	1
$2 \cos \theta$	2	$\sqrt{3}$	1	0	$^{-}1$	$^{-}\sqrt{3}$	$^{-}2$	$^{-}\sqrt{3}$	$^{-}1$	0	1	$\sqrt{3}$	2

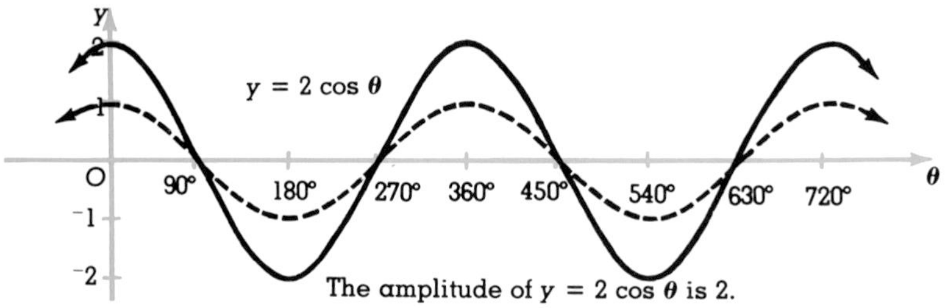

The amplitude of $y = 2 \cos \theta$ is 2.

4 **Graph $y = \frac{1}{2} \cos \theta$. State the amplitude.**

θ	0°	30°	60°	90°	120°	150°	180°	210°	240°	270°	300°	330°	360°
$\cos \theta$	1	$\frac{\sqrt{3}}{2}$	$\frac{1}{2}$	0	$-\frac{1}{2}$	$-\frac{\sqrt{3}}{2}$	-1	$-\frac{\sqrt{3}}{2}$	$-\frac{1}{2}$	0	$\frac{1}{2}$	$\frac{\sqrt{3}}{2}$	1
$\frac{1}{2} \cos \theta$	$\frac{1}{2}$	$\frac{\sqrt{3}}{4}$	$\frac{1}{4}$	0	$-\frac{1}{4}$	$-\frac{\sqrt{3}}{4}$	$-\frac{1}{2}$	$-\frac{\sqrt{3}}{4}$	$-\frac{1}{4}$	0	$\frac{1}{4}$	$\frac{\sqrt{3}}{4}$	$\frac{1}{2}$

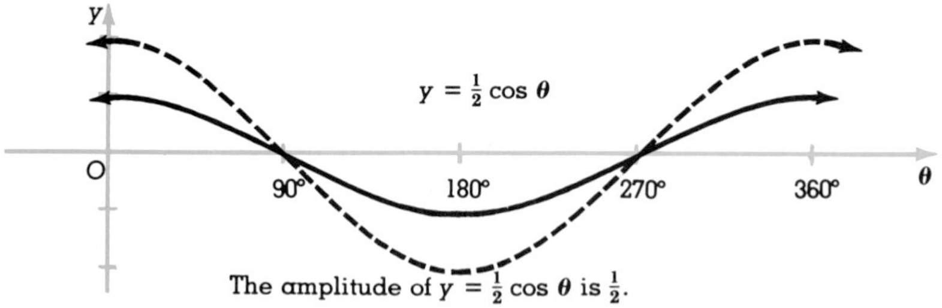

The amplitude of $y = \frac{1}{2} \cos \theta$ is $\frac{1}{2}$.

From these examples, the following generalizations can be made.

Amplitudes and Periods

For functions of the form $y = a \sin b\theta$ and $y = a \cos b\theta$, the amplitude is $|a|$ and the period is $\frac{2\pi}{|b|}$.

example 5

Graph $y = \frac{3}{2} \cos \frac{1}{2}\theta$.

The amplitude is $\left|\frac{3}{2}\right|$ or $\frac{3}{2}$. The period is $\frac{2\pi}{\left|\frac{1}{2}\right|}$ or 4π.

The graph has a shape like $y = \cos \theta$.

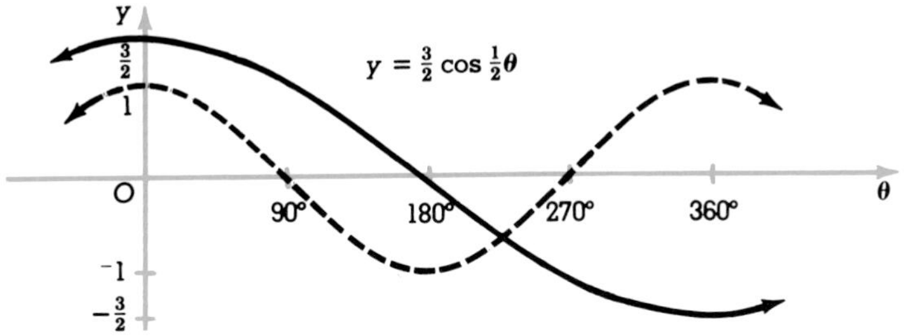

exercises

Max: 1–20, 1–20; **Avg:** 1–20, 1–19 odds; **Min:** 1–19 odds, 1–19 odds

Exploratory State the amplitude and period for each of the following.

1. $y = \sin \theta$ 1, 2π
2. $y = \frac{1}{2} \cos \theta$ $\frac{1}{2}$, 2π
3. $y = \frac{2}{3} \cos \theta$ $\frac{2}{3}$, 2π
4. $y = 3 \sin \theta$ 3, 2π
5. $y = 6 \sin \frac{2}{3}\theta$ 6, 3π
6. $y = 3 \cos \frac{1}{2}\theta$ 3, 4π
7. $y = 4 \cos \frac{3}{4}\theta$ 4, $8\pi/3$
8. $y = 2 \sin \frac{1}{5}\theta$ 2, 10π
9. $y = 5 \sin \theta$ 5, 2π
10. $y = \sin 4\theta$ 1, $\pi/2$
11. $y = \cos 3\theta$ 1, $2\pi/3$
12. $y = \cos 2\theta$ 1, π
13. $y = 4 \sin \frac{1}{2}\theta$ 4, 4π
14. $y = {}^{-}2 \sin \theta$ 2, 2π
15. $y = {}^{-}3 \sin \frac{2}{3}\theta$ 3, 3π
16. $y = {}^{-}6 \sin 2\theta$ 6, π
17. $y = -\frac{1}{2} \cos \frac{3}{4}\theta$ $\frac{1}{2}$, $8\pi/3$
18. $3y = 2 \sin \frac{1}{2}\theta$ $\frac{2}{3}$, 4π
19. $\frac{1}{2}y = 3 \sin 2\theta$ 6, π
20. $\frac{3}{4}y = \frac{2}{3} \sin \frac{3}{5}\theta$ $\frac{8}{9}$, $10\pi/3$

Written Graph each of the following. For graphs of problems 1-20, see the Teacher's Guide.

1. $y = \sin \theta$
2. $y = \frac{1}{2} \cos \theta$
3. $y = \frac{2}{3} \cos \theta$
4. $y = 3 \sin \theta$
5. $y = 6 \sin \frac{2}{3}\theta$
6. $y = 3 \cos \frac{1}{2}\theta$
7. $y = 4 \cos \frac{3}{4}\theta$
8. $y = 2 \sin \frac{1}{5}\theta$
9. $y = 5 \sin \theta$
10. $y = \sin 4\theta$
11. $y = \cos 3\theta$
12. $y = \cos 2\theta$
13. $y = 4 \sin \frac{1}{2}\theta$
14. $y = {}^{-}2 \sin \theta$
15. $y = {}^{-}3 \sin \frac{2}{3}\theta$
16. $y = {}^{-}6 \sin 2\theta$
17. $y = -\frac{1}{2} \cos \frac{3}{4}\theta$
18. $3y = 2 \sin \frac{1}{2}\theta$
19. $\frac{1}{2}y = 3 \sin 2\theta$
20. $\frac{3}{4}y = \frac{2}{3} \sin \frac{3}{5}\theta$

In the Exploratory Exercises, students find values for which these equations are not defined. In the Written Exercises they are asked to find the domains and ranges.

16-4 Other Trigonometric Functions

Objective: To find values of and graph other trigonometric functions.

Other trigonometric functions are defined using sine and cosine.

Definition of Tangent, Cotangent, Secant, and Cosecant

Let θ stand for the measurement of an angle in standard position on the unit circle. Then the following equations hold whenever they are defined.

$$\tan \theta = \frac{\sin \theta}{\cos \theta} \qquad \cot \theta = \frac{\cos \theta}{\sin \theta}$$

$$\sec \theta = \frac{1}{\cos \theta} \qquad \csc \theta = \frac{1}{\sin \theta}$$

example 1

Find the value of tan 150°.

$$\tan 150° = \frac{\sin 150°}{\cos 150°}$$

$$= \frac{\frac{1}{2}}{-\frac{\sqrt{3}}{2}}$$

$$= -\frac{1}{\sqrt{3}} \text{ or } -\frac{\sqrt{3}}{3}$$

After completing a table of values, you can graph $y = \tan \theta$.

θ	0°	30°	45°	60°	90°	120°	135°	150°	180°	210°	225°	240°	270°	300°	315°	330°	360°
$\tan \theta$	0	$\frac{\sqrt{3}}{3}$	1	$\sqrt{3}$	not defined	$^{-}\sqrt{3}$	$^{-}1$	$-\frac{\sqrt{3}}{3}$	0	$\frac{\sqrt{3}}{3}$	1	$\sqrt{3}$	not defined	$^{-}\sqrt{3}$	$^{-}1$	$-\frac{\sqrt{3}}{3}$	0

The tangent function is not defined for 90° or 270°. The graph is separated by vertical asymptotes, indicated by broken lines.

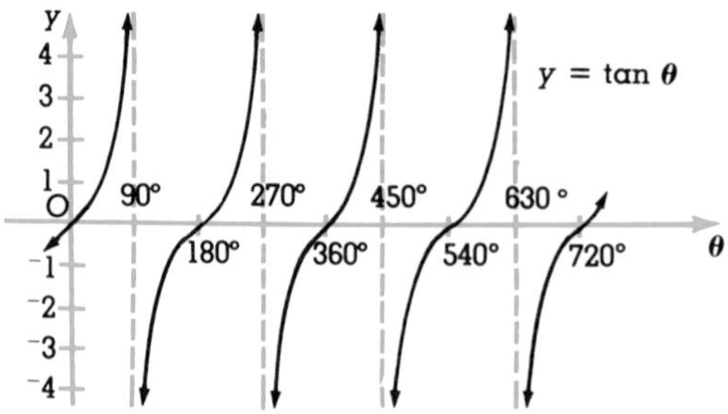

The period of the tangent function is 180°, or π radians. What is the amplitude? The amplitude is *not* defined.

The following are graphs of the secant and cotangent functions. Notice how they compare to the graphs of the cosine and tangent functions, the broken curves.

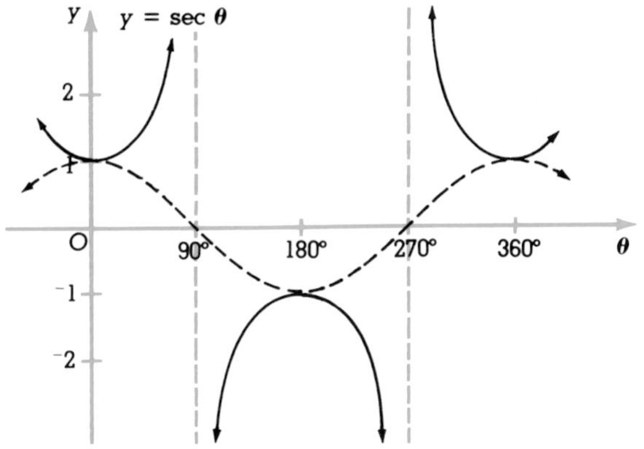

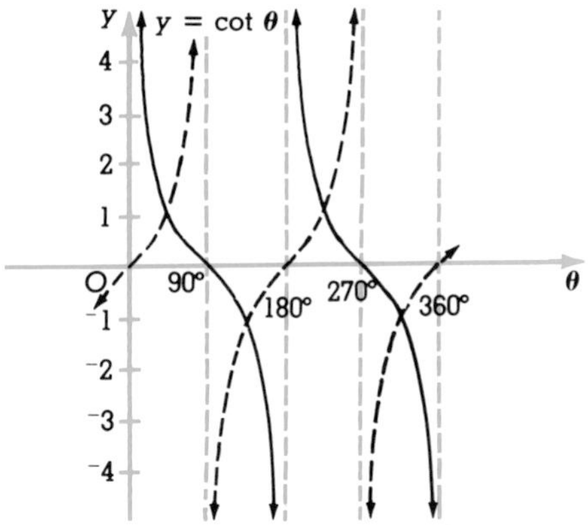

You can draw graphs like those of tangent, cotangent, secant, and cosecant.

example 1

Draw the graph of $y = -\frac{1}{2}\csc 2\theta$.

θ	0°	15°	30°	45°	60°	75°	90°	105°	120°	135°	150°	165°	180°
2θ	0°	30°	60°	90°	120°	150°	180°	210°	240°	270°	300°	330°	360°
$-\frac{1}{2}\csc 2\theta$	not defined	$^-1$	$-\frac{\sqrt{3}}{3}$	$-\frac{1}{2}$	$-\frac{\sqrt{3}}{3}$	$^-1$	not defined	1	$\frac{\sqrt{3}}{3}$	$\frac{1}{2}$	$\frac{\sqrt{3}}{3}$	1	not defined

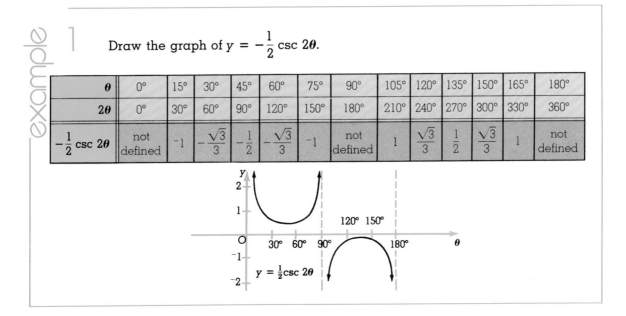

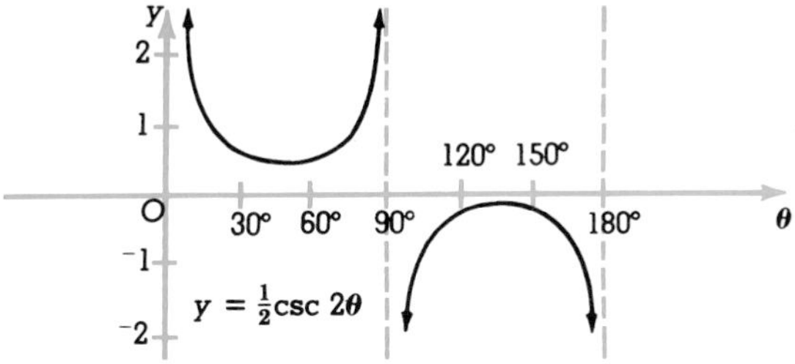

exercises

Max: 1–24, 1–64; **Avg:** 1–24, 1–63 odds; **Min:** 1–63 odds

Exploratory State the values of θ between and including 0° and 360° for which each expression is not defined.

1. $\sin \theta$ none
2. $\cos \theta$ none
3. $\tan \theta$ 90°, 270°
4. $\cot \theta$ 0°, 180°, 360°
5. $\sec \theta$ 90°, 270°
6. $\csc \theta$ 0°, 180°, 360°

State the domain for each of the following. 9. $(2k + 1)\pi/2$, k is an integer 12. $k\pi$, k is an integer

7. $y = \sin\theta$
8. $y = \cos\theta$
9. $y = \tan\theta$
10. $y = \cot\theta$ $k\pi$, k is an integer
11. $y = \sec\theta$ $(2k + 1)\pi/2$, k is an integer
12. $y = \csc\theta$

7-12. All angle measurements with exceptions noted.

13-18. State the range of each equation in problems **7-12**. See Teacher's Guide.

19-24. State the period of each equation in problems **7-12**. 19. 2π 20. 2π 21. π 22. π 23. 2π 24. 2π

Written State whether values of the following functions are increasing or decreasing as values of θ increase from 0° to 90°.

1. $y = \sin\theta$ increasing
2. $y = \cos\theta$ decreasing
3. $y = \tan\theta$ increasing
4. $y = \cot\theta$ decreasing
5. $y = \sec\theta$ increasing
6. $y = \csc\theta$ decreasing

For answers to problems **7-24**, see the Teacher's Guide.

7-12. State whether values of the functions in problems **1-6** are increasing or decreasing as values of θ increase from 90° to 180°.

13-18. State whether values of the functions in problems **1-6** are increasing or decreasing as values of θ increase from 180° to 270°.

19-24. State whether values of the functions in problems **1-6** are increasing or decreasing as values of θ increase from 270° to 360°.

Evaluate each of the following.

25. $\sec 60°$ 2
26. $\tan 120°$ $^-\sqrt{3}$
27. $\cot 135°$ $^-1$
28. $\csc 45°$ $\sqrt{2}$
29. $\tan\left(-\frac{\pi}{3}\right)$ $^-\sqrt{3}$
30. $\csc(^-210°)$ 2
31. $\sec 300°$ 2
32. $\cot(^-60°)$ $^-\sqrt{3}/3$
33. $\cot\left(-\frac{\pi}{6}\right)$ $^-\sqrt{3}$
34. $\sec(^-120°)$ $^-2$
35. $\csc\left(-\frac{\pi}{6}\right)$ $^-2$
36. $\tan\frac{7}{6}\pi$ $\sqrt{3}/3$
37. $\cot\frac{7}{4}\pi$ $^-1$
38. $\tan(^-300°)$ $\sqrt{3}$
39. $\sec 240°$ $^-2$
40. $\csc\frac{\pi}{2}$ 1
41. $\sec 600°$ $^-2$
42. $\tan\frac{9}{4}\pi$ 1
43. $\csc 180°$ undefined
44. $\cot 210°$ $\sqrt{3}$
45. $\tan\left(-\frac{5}{6}\pi\right)$ $\sqrt{3}/3$
46. $\csc\frac{4}{3}\pi$ $^-2\sqrt{3}/3$
47. $\cot 270°$ 0
48. $\sec\frac{4}{3}\pi$ $^-2$
49. $\cot(^-600°)$ $^-\sqrt{3}/3$
50. $\sec\left(-\frac{\pi}{2}\right)$ undefined
51. $\tan 315°$ $^-1$
52. $\csc\left(-\frac{7}{6}\pi\right)$ 2

Graph each of the following. For graphs of problems **53-64**, see the Teacher's Guide.

53. $y = 3\sec\theta$
54. $y = \csc\frac{1}{3}\theta$
55. $y = \frac{1}{3}\sec\theta$
56. $y = \sec 3\theta$
57. $y = \csc 2\theta$
58. $y = 2\sec\theta$
59. $y = \cot\theta$
60. $y = 2\tan\theta$
61. $y = {}^-\cot\theta$
62. $y = \frac{1}{2}\tan\theta$
63. $y = -\frac{1}{2}\cot 2\theta$
64. $y = 3\csc\frac{1}{2}\theta$

16-5 Trigonometric Identities

Objective: To use trigonometric identities to simplify and evaluate expressions.

The unit circle shows that sine and cosine are related in a special way.

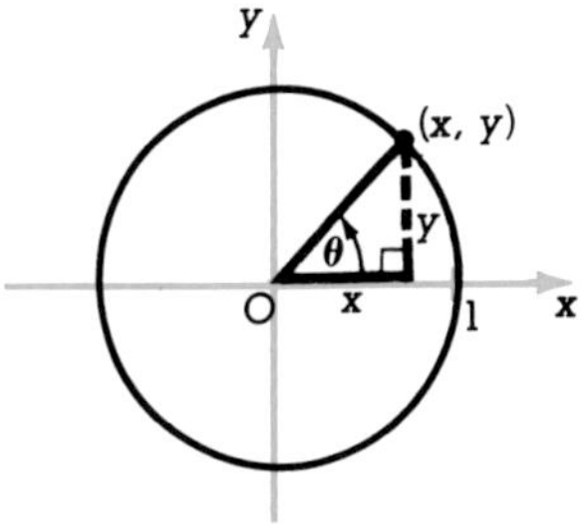

Let θ be the measurement of an angle in standard position on the unit circle. Let (x, y) be the coordinates of the point of intersection of the terminal side and the circle. Then the following equations hold.

$$\cos \theta = x \text{ and } \sin \theta = y$$

The equation for the unit circle is $x^2 + y^2 = 1$. By substituting $\cos \theta$ for x and $\sin \theta$ for y, you obtain the following equation.

Note that the equation for the unit circle can be derived from the Pythagorean Theorem.

$$(\cos \theta)^2 + (\sin \theta)^2 = 1$$

Normally, this equation is written in the following way.

$$\cos^2 \theta + \sin^2 \theta = 1$$

An equation like $\sin^2 \theta + \cos^2 \theta = 1$ is called an **identity** because it is true for *all* values of θ. There are eight basic identities.

Basic Trigonometric Identities

The following trigonometric identities hold for all values of θ except those for which either side of the equation is undefined.

$$\tan \theta = \frac{\sin \theta}{\cos \theta} \qquad \sec \theta = \frac{1}{\cos \theta} \qquad \sin^2 \theta + \cos^2 \theta = 1$$

$$\cot \theta = \frac{\cos \theta}{\sin \theta} \qquad \csc \theta = \frac{1}{\sin \theta} \qquad 1 + \tan^2 \theta = \sec^2 \theta$$

$$\cot \theta = \frac{1}{\tan \theta} \qquad 1 + \cot^2 \theta = \csc^2 \theta$$

example 1

Show that $\cot \theta = \dfrac{1}{\tan \theta}$.

$$\cot \theta = \frac{\cos \theta}{\sin \theta} \quad \textit{Definition of } \cot \theta.$$

$$= \frac{1}{\frac{\sin \theta}{\cos \theta}} \quad \frac{\cos \theta}{\sin \theta} \cdot \frac{\frac{1}{\cos \theta}}{\frac{1}{\cos \theta}} = \frac{1}{\frac{\sin \theta}{\cos \theta}}$$

$$= \frac{1}{\tan \theta} \quad \textit{Definition of } \tan \theta.$$

example 2

Show that $1 + \tan^2 \theta = \sec^2 \theta$.

$$1 + \tan^2 \theta = 1 + \left(\frac{\sin \theta}{\cos \theta}\right)^2 \qquad \textit{Definition of } \tan \theta.$$

$$= 1 + \frac{\sin^2 \theta}{\cos^2 \theta}$$

$$= \frac{\cos^2 \theta}{\cos^2 \theta} + \frac{\sin^2 \theta}{\cos^2 \theta} \qquad 1 = \frac{\cos^2 \theta}{\cos^2 \theta}$$

$$= \frac{\cos^2 \theta + \sin^2 \theta}{\cos^2 \theta}$$

$$= \frac{1}{\cos^2 \theta} \qquad \sin^2 \theta + \cos^2 \theta = 1$$

$$= \sec^2 \theta$$

You can use the trigonometric identities to evaluate or simplify expressions.

examples 3

Suppose $\cot \theta = \frac{3}{5}$. Find $\csc \theta$.

$$\csc^2 \theta = 1 + \cot^2 \theta$$

$$= 1 + \left(\frac{3}{5}\right)^2$$

$$= \frac{34}{25}$$

$$\csc \theta = \pm\sqrt{\frac{34}{25}} \text{ or } \pm\frac{\sqrt{34}}{5}$$

4

Simplify $\frac{1}{1 + \sin x} + \frac{1}{1 - \sin x}$.

$$\frac{1}{1 + \sin x} + \frac{1}{1 - \sin x} = \frac{(1 - \sin x) + (1 + \sin x)}{(1 + \sin x)(1 - \sin x)}$$

$$= \frac{2}{1 - \sin^2 x}$$

$$= \frac{2}{\cos^2 x} \qquad \sin^2 x + \cos^2 x = 1$$

$$= 2 \sec^2 x \qquad \sec x = \frac{1}{\cos x}$$

exercises

Max: 1–8, 1–30; Avg: 1–8, 1–29 odds; Min: 1–29 odds

Exploratory Which of the following are identities?

1. $\sin(^-\theta) = {}^-\sin\theta$ yes
2. $\cos\theta \sec\theta = 1$ yes
3. $\csc^2\theta = \cot^2\theta + 1$ yes
4. $\sin^2\theta - \cos^2\theta = 1$ no
5. $\cot\theta \sin\theta = \cos\theta$ yes
6. $\cos(^-\theta) = \cos\theta$ yes
7. $\cot\theta \sin\theta = 1$ no
8. $\tan\theta \sin\theta = \cos\theta$ no

Written Solve each of the following for values of θ between 0° and 90°.

1. If $\sin\theta = \frac{1}{2}$, find $\cos\theta$. $\sqrt{3}/2$
2. If $\cos\theta = \frac{2}{3}$, find $\sin\theta$. $\sqrt{5}/3$
3. If $\sin\theta = \frac{4}{5}$, find $\cos\theta$. $\frac{3}{5}$
4. If $\sin\theta = \frac{3}{4}$, find $\sec\theta$. $4\sqrt{7}/7$
5. If $\cos\theta = \frac{2}{3}$, find $\csc\theta$. $3\sqrt{5}/5$
6. If $\cos\theta = \frac{4}{5}$, find $\tan\theta$. $\frac{3}{4}$
7. If $\tan\theta = 4$, find $\sin\theta$. $4\sqrt{17}/17$
8. If $\cot\theta = 2$, find $\tan\theta$. $\frac{1}{2}$

Solve each of the following for values of θ between 90° and 180°.

9. If $\sin\theta = \frac{3}{5}$, find $\cos\theta$. $-\frac{4}{5}$
10. If $\sin\theta = \frac{1}{2}$, find $\tan\theta$. $^-\sqrt{3}/3$
11. If $\cos\theta = -\frac{3}{5}$, find $\csc\theta$. $\frac{5}{4}$
12. If $\tan\theta = {}^-2$, find $\sec\theta$. $^-\sqrt{5}$

Solve each of the following for values of θ between 180° and 270°.

13. If $\cot\theta = \frac{1}{4}$, find $\csc\theta$. $^-\sqrt{17}/4$
14. If $\sec\theta = {}^-3$, find $\tan\theta$. $2\sqrt{2}$
15. If $\sin\theta = -\frac{1}{2}$, find $\cos\theta$. $^-\sqrt{3}/2$
16. If $\cos\theta = -\frac{3}{5}$, find $\csc\theta$. $-\frac{5}{4}$

Solve each of the following for values of θ between 270° and 360°.

17. If $\cos\theta = \frac{5}{13}$, find $\sin\theta$. $-\frac{12}{13}$
18. If $\tan\theta = {}^-1$, find $\sec\theta$. $\sqrt{2}$
19. If $\sec\theta = \frac{5}{3}$, find $\cos\theta$. $\frac{3}{5}$
20. If $\csc\theta = -\frac{5}{3}$, find $\cos\theta$. $\frac{4}{5}$

Simplify each of the following.

21. $\tan\theta \cot\theta$ 1
22. $\sec^2\theta - 1$ $\tan^2\theta$
23. $\sin x + \cos x \tan x$ $2\sin x$
24. $\csc\theta \cos\theta \tan\theta$ 1
25. $2(\csc^2\theta - \cot^2\theta)$ 2
26. $\dfrac{\tan^2\theta - \sin^2\theta}{\tan^2\theta \sin^2\theta}$ 1

Show that each of the following is an identity.

For answers to problems 27–30, see the Teacher's Guide.

27. $1 + \cot^2\theta = \csc^2\theta$
28. $\dfrac{\sec\theta}{\csc\theta} = \tan\theta$
29. $\sin x \sec x = \tan x$
30. $\sec\alpha - \cos\alpha = \sin\alpha \tan\alpha$

16-6 Verifying Trigonometric Identities

Objective: To verify trigonometric identities.

Remind students that identities hold for all values of the variable *except* those for which either side of the equation is undefined.

You can use the basic trigonometric identities to verify other identities. For example, suppose you wish to know if the equation $\sin\theta \sec\theta \cot\theta = 1$ is an identity. To find out, you simplify the expression on the left side of the equation by substituting basic identities.

$$\sin\theta \sec\theta \cot\theta \stackrel{?}{=} 1$$

$$\sin\theta \cdot \frac{1}{\cos\theta} \cdot \frac{1}{\tan\theta} \stackrel{?}{=} 1 \qquad \sec\theta = \frac{1}{\cos\theta} \text{ and } \cot\theta = \frac{1}{\tan\theta}$$

$$\frac{\sin\theta}{\cos\theta} \cdot \frac{1}{\tan\theta} \stackrel{?}{=} 1 \qquad \text{Multiply } \sin\theta \text{ and } \frac{1}{\cos\theta}.$$

$$\tan\theta \cdot \frac{1}{\tan\theta} \stackrel{?}{=} 1 \qquad \tan\theta = \frac{\sin\theta}{\cos\theta}$$

$$1 = 1$$

The equation $\sin\theta \sec\theta \cot\theta = 1$ is an identity.

Often it is easiest to work with only one side of the sentence. You may choose either side.

In a way, verifying an identity is like checking the solution to an equation. You do not know if the expressions on each side are equal. That is what you are trying to verify. So, you must simplify one or both sides of the sentence *separately* until they are the same.

examples

1 **Verify $\tan^2 x - \sin^2 x = \tan^2 x \sin^2 x$.**

$$\tan^2 x - \sin^2 x \stackrel{?}{=} \tan^2 x \sin^2 x$$

$$\left(\frac{\sin x}{\cos x}\right)^2 - \sin^2 x \stackrel{?}{=} \tan^2 x \sin^2 x$$

$$\sin^2 x\left(\frac{1}{\cos^2 x} - 1\right) \stackrel{?}{=} \tan^2 x \sin^2 x$$

$$\sin^2 x(\sec^2 x - 1) \stackrel{?}{=} \tan^2 x \sin^2 x$$

$$\tan^2 x \sin^2 x = \tan^2 x \sin^2 x$$

2 **Verify $\cot^2 x \sec^2 x = 1 + \cot^2 x$.**

$$\cot^2 x \sec^2 x \stackrel{?}{=} 1 + \cot^2 x$$

$$\cot x = \frac{\cos x}{\sin x} \qquad \left(\frac{\cos x}{\sin x}\right)^2\left(\frac{1}{\cos x}\right)^2 \stackrel{?}{=} \csc^2 x \qquad 1 + \cot^2 x = \csc^2 x$$

$$\sec x = \frac{1}{\cos x} \qquad \frac{\cos^2 x}{\sin^2 x} \cdot \frac{1}{\cos^2 x} \stackrel{?}{=} \left(\frac{1}{\sin x}\right)^2 \qquad \csc x = \frac{1}{\sin x}$$

$$\frac{1}{\sin^2 x} = \frac{1}{\sin^2 x}$$

The sentence is an identity.

The following suggestions are helpful in verifying trigonometric identities. Study the examples to see how these suggestions can be used.

Suggestions for Verifying Identities

1. **Start with the more complicated side of the equation. Transform the expression into the form of the simpler side.**
2. **Substitute one or more basic trigonometric identities to simplify the expression.**
3. **Try factoring or multiplying to simplify the expression.**
4. **Multiply both numerator and denominator by the same trigonometric expression.**

There is often more than one way to verify an identity.

examples

3 **Verify that $1 - \cot^4 x = 2\csc^2 x - \csc^4 x$.**

$$1 - \cot^4 x \stackrel{?}{=} 2\csc^2 x - \csc^4 x$$

$$(1 - \cot^2 x)(1 + \cot^2 x) \stackrel{?}{=} 2\csc^2 x - \csc^4 x \quad \textit{Factor.}$$

$$[1 - (\csc^2 x - 1)][\csc^2 x] \stackrel{?}{=} 2\csc^2 x - \csc^4 x \quad 1 + \cot^2 x = \csc^2 x$$

$$[2 - \csc^2 x][\csc^2 x] \stackrel{?}{=} 2\csc^2 x - \csc^4 x \quad \textit{Simplify.}$$

$$2\csc^2 x - \csc^4 x = 2\csc^2 x - \csc^4 x$$

4 **Verify that $\dfrac{1 - \cos x}{\sin x} = \dfrac{\sin x}{1 + \cos x}$.**

$$\frac{1 - \cos x}{\sin x} \stackrel{?}{=} \frac{\sin x}{1 + \cos x}$$

$$\frac{1 - \cos x}{\sin x} \stackrel{?}{=} \frac{\sin x(1 - \cos x)}{(1 + \cos x)(1 - \cos x)}$$

Multiply numerator and denominator by $1 - \cos x$.

This procedure is analogous to multiplying by conjugates.

$$\frac{1 - \cos x}{\sin x} \stackrel{?}{=} \frac{\sin x(1 - \cos x)}{1 - \cos^2 x}$$

Simplify the denominator.

$$\frac{1 - \cos x}{\sin x} \stackrel{?}{=} \frac{\sin x(1 - \cos x)}{\sin^2 x}$$

Substitute $\sin^2 x$ for $1 - \cos^2 x$.

$$\frac{1 - \cos x}{\sin x} = \frac{1 - \cos x}{\sin x}$$

Simplify.

exercises

Max: 1–8, 1–20; Avg: 1–8, 1–19 odds; Min: 1–19 odds

Exploratory Verify each identity. For answers to problems 1–8 and 1–20, see the Teacher's Guide.

1. $\csc^2 \theta - \cot^2 \theta = 1$
2. $\tan \theta \cot \theta = 1$
3. $\dfrac{\sin^2 \theta + \cos^2 \theta}{\sin^2 \theta} = \csc^2 \theta$
4. $\dfrac{\tan x}{\sin x} = \sec x$
5. $\csc^2 \gamma - \cot^2 \gamma = 1$
6. $\cos \alpha \csc \alpha = \cot \alpha$
7. $\sin \theta \cot \theta = \cos \theta$
8. $\tan x \csc x = \sec x$

Written Verify each identity.

1. $\tan \beta(\cot \beta + \tan \beta) = \sec^2 \beta$
2. $\cos^2 \theta + \tan^2 \theta \cos^2 \theta = 1$
3. $\csc x \sec x = \cot x + \tan x$
4. $\sec^2 x - \tan^2 x = \tan x \cot x$
5. $\dfrac{\sec \theta}{\sin \theta} - \dfrac{\sin \theta}{\cos \theta} + \cot \theta$
6. $\dfrac{1}{\sec^2 \theta} + \dfrac{1}{\csc^2 \theta} = 1$
7. $\dfrac{\sin \alpha}{1 - \cos \alpha} + \dfrac{1 - \cos \alpha}{\sin \alpha} = 2 \csc \alpha$
8. $\dfrac{\sec \alpha + \csc \alpha}{1 + \tan \alpha} = \csc \alpha$
9. $\dfrac{\cos^2 x}{1 - \sin x} = 1 + \sin x$
10. $\dfrac{1 - \cos \theta}{1 + \cos \theta} = (\csc \theta - \cot \theta)^2$
11. $\dfrac{\sin \theta}{\sec \theta} = \dfrac{1}{\tan \theta + \cot \theta}$
12. $\dfrac{\sec \theta + 1}{\tan \theta} = \dfrac{\tan \theta}{\sec \theta - 1}$
13. $\dfrac{\cot x + \csc x}{\sin x + \tan x} = \cot x \csc x$
14. $\dfrac{1 - 2\cos^2 \theta}{\sin \theta \cos \theta} = \tan \theta - \cot \theta$
15. $\cos^2 x + \tan^2 x \cos^2 x = 1$
16. $\dfrac{\cos x}{1 + \sin x} + \dfrac{\cos x}{1 - \sin x} = 2 \sec x$
17. $\dfrac{1 + \tan^2 \theta}{\csc^2 \theta} = \tan^2 \theta$
18. $\tan x(\cot x + \tan x) = \sec^2 x$
19. $\dfrac{\sec x}{\sin x} - \dfrac{\sin x}{\cos x} = \cot x$
20. $\dfrac{1 + \tan \gamma}{1 + \cot \gamma} = \dfrac{\sin \gamma}{\cos \gamma}$

Excursions in Algebra

Contest Problem

The following problem appeared in a high school mathematics contest sponsored by the Mathematical Association of America.

A tire on a car has an outside diameter of 25 inches. When the radius has been decreased a quarter of an inch, the number of revolutions per mile will be increased by about what percent? about 2%

16–7 Differences and Sums

Objective: To develop and use formulas for the difference and sum of angles.

It is often helpful to use formulas for the trigonometric values of the difference or sum of two angles. For example, you could find sin 15° by evaluating sin(45 − 30)°. The distance formula is used to derive such formulas.

The following diagrams show two different angles in standard position on the unit circle. Both angles have measurements $(\alpha - \beta)$.

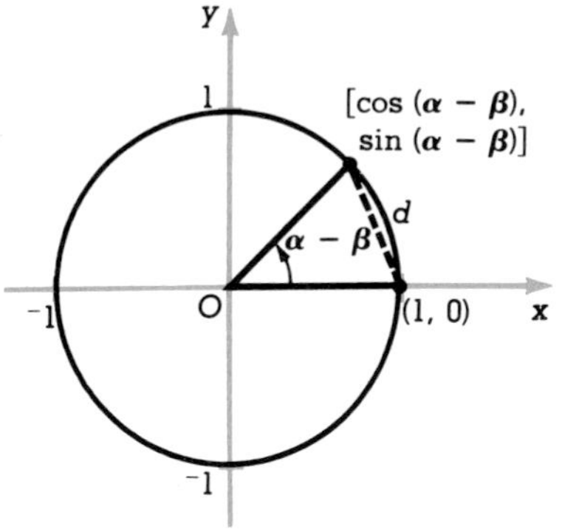

Use the distance formula to find d.

$$d = \sqrt{[\cos(\alpha - \beta) - 1]^2 + [\sin(\alpha - \beta) - 0]^2}$$

$$\begin{aligned} d^2 &= [\cos(\alpha - \beta) - 1]^2 + [\sin(\alpha - \beta) - 0]^2 \\ &= [\cos^2(\alpha - \beta) - 2\cos(\alpha - \beta) + 1] + [\sin^2(\alpha - \beta)] \\ &= \cos^2(\alpha - \beta) + \sin^2(\alpha - \beta) - 2\cos(\alpha - \beta) + 1 \\ &= \qquad 1 \qquad - 2\cos(\alpha - \beta) + 1 \\ &= 2 - 2\cos(\alpha - \beta) \end{aligned}$$

$$d = \sqrt{(\cos\alpha - \cos\beta)^2 + (\sin\alpha - \sin\beta)^2}$$

$$\begin{aligned} d^2 &= (\cos\alpha - \cos\beta)^2 + (\sin\alpha - \sin\beta)^2 \\ &= (\cos^2\alpha - 2\cos\alpha\cos\beta + \cos^2\beta) \\ &\quad + (\sin^2\alpha - 2\sin\alpha\sin\beta + \sin^2\beta) \\ &= \cos^2\alpha + \sin^2\alpha + \cos^2\beta + \sin^2\beta \\ &\quad - 2\cos\alpha\cos\beta - 2\sin\alpha\sin\beta \\ &= 1 + 1 - 2\cos\alpha\cos\beta - 2\sin\alpha\sin\beta \\ &= 2 - 2\cos\alpha\cos\beta - 2\sin\alpha\sin\beta \end{aligned}$$

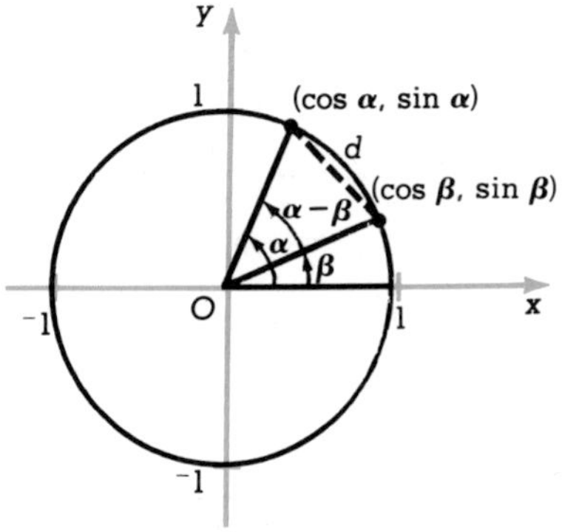

You can equate the expressions obtained, since they describe the same quantity. Then, solve for $\cos(\alpha - \beta)$.

$$2 - 2\cos(\alpha - \beta) = 2 - 2\cos\alpha\cos\beta - 2\sin\alpha\sin\beta$$

$$^{-}1 + \cos(\alpha - \beta) = {^{-}1} + \cos\alpha\cos\beta + \sin\alpha\sin\beta \qquad \textit{Divide both sides by } {^{-}2}.$$

$$\cos(\alpha - \beta) = \cos\alpha\cos\beta + \sin\alpha\sin\beta \qquad \textit{Add 1 to both sides.}$$

Using the formula for $\cos(\alpha - \beta)$, you can find a formula for the expression $\cos(\alpha + \beta)$.

$$\begin{aligned} \cos(\alpha + \beta) &= \cos(\alpha - {^{-}\beta}) \\ &= \cos\alpha\cos({^{-}\beta}) + \sin\alpha\sin({^{-}\beta}) \\ &= \cos\alpha\cos\beta - \sin\alpha\sin\beta \end{aligned}$$

You can use these formulas to find other helpful formulas.

examples

1 **Use the formula for $\cos(\alpha - \beta)$ to find $\cos(90° - \theta)$.**

$$\begin{aligned}\cos(90° - \theta) &= \cos 90° \cos\theta + \sin 90° \sin\theta \\ &= 0 \cdot \cos\theta + 1 \cdot \sin\theta \\ &= \sin\theta\end{aligned}$$

2 **Use the formula $\cos(90° - \theta) = \sin\theta$ to find $\sin(90° - \gamma)$.**

$$\begin{aligned}\sin(90° - \gamma) &= \cos[90° - (90° - \gamma)] \\ &= \cos(90° - 90° + \gamma) \\ &= \cos\gamma\end{aligned}$$

3 **Find $\sin(\alpha - \beta)$.**

$$\begin{aligned}\sin(\alpha - \beta) &= \cos[90° - (\alpha - \beta)] \\ &= \cos[(90° - \alpha) + \beta] \\ &= \cos(90° - \alpha)\cos\beta - \sin(90° - \alpha)\sin\beta \\ &= \sin\alpha\cos\beta - \cos\alpha\sin\beta\end{aligned}$$

In a similar manner, you can derive 2 formulas for $\sin(\alpha + \beta)$.

Explain the use of ∓ to students.

Difference and Sum Formulas

The following identities hold for all values of α and β.

$$\cos(\alpha \pm \beta) = \cos\alpha\cos\beta \mp \sin\alpha\sin\beta$$
$$\sin(\alpha \pm \beta) = \sin\alpha\cos\beta \pm \cos\alpha\sin\beta$$

The examples below show how to evaluate expressions using the formulas in this lesson.

example

4 **Find $\sin 15°$.**

$$\begin{aligned}\sin 15° &= \sin(45° - 30°) \\ &= \sin 45° \cos 30° - \cos 45° \sin 30° \\ &= \frac{\sqrt{2}}{2} \cdot \frac{\sqrt{3}}{2} - \frac{\sqrt{2}}{2} \cdot \frac{1}{2} \\ &= \frac{\sqrt{6} - \sqrt{2}}{4}\end{aligned}$$

exercises

Max: 1–8, 1–40, Challenge; **Avg:** 1–8, 1–39 odds; **Min:** 1–39 odds

Exploratory Write each value in terms of sums or differences of 30°, 45°, 60°, and 90° or their multiples.

1. 105° $60° + 45°$
2. $^-15°$ $30° - 45°$
3. $^-165°$ $^-135° - 30°$
4. 165° $135° + 30°$
5. 75° $30° + 45°$
6. $^-75°$ $^-45° - 30°$
7. 285° $225° + 60°$
8. 255° $225° + 30°$

Written Evaluate each expression.

1. $\sin 75°$ $(\sqrt{6} + \sqrt{2})/4$
2. $\sin 165°$ $(\sqrt{6} - \sqrt{2})/4$
3. $\sin 285°$ $(^-\sqrt{2} - \sqrt{6})/4$
4. $\cos 75°$ $(\sqrt{6} - \sqrt{2})/4$
5. $\cos 195°$ $(^-\sqrt{2} - \sqrt{6})/4$
6. $\cos 255°$ $(^-\sqrt{6} + \sqrt{2})/4$
7. $\cos 15°$ $(\sqrt{6} + \sqrt{2})/4$
8. $\sin 105°$ $(\sqrt{2} + \sqrt{6})/4$
9. $\cos 165°$ $(^-\sqrt{6} - \sqrt{2})/4$
10. $\cos 345°$ $(\sqrt{6} + \sqrt{2})/4$

Verify each of the following. For answers to problems **11–16** and **21–28**, see the Teacher's Guide.

11. $\sin(270° - \theta) = {}^-\cos\theta$
12. $\cos(270° - \theta) = {}^-\sin\theta$
13. $\sin(180° + \theta) = {}^-\sin\theta$
14. $\cos(180° + \theta) = {}^-\cos\theta$
15. $\sin(90° + \theta) = \cos\theta$
16. $\cos(90° + \theta) = {}^-\sin\theta$

Evaluate each expression.

17. $\cos 25° \cos 5° - \sin 25° \sin 5°$ $\sqrt{3}/2$
18. $\sin 40° \cos 20° + \cos 40° \sin 20°$ $\sqrt{3}/2$
19. $\cos 80° \cos 20° + \sin 80° \sin 20°$ $\frac{1}{2}$
20. $\sin 65° \cos 35° - \cos 65° \sin 35°$ $\frac{1}{2}$

Verify each of the following identities.

21. $\sin(x + y)\sin(x - y) = \sin^2 x - \sin^2 y$
22. $\sin\left(\theta + \frac{\pi}{3}\right) - \cos\left(\theta + \frac{\pi}{6}\right) = \sin\theta$
23. $\sin(60° + \theta) + \sin(60° - \theta) = \sqrt{3}\cos\theta$
24. $(\sin x + \cos y)^2 + (\sin y + \cos x)^2 = 2 + 2\sin(x + y)$
25. $\cos(x + y)\cos(x - y) = \cos^2 y - \sin^2 x$
26. $\sin(x + 30°) + \cos(x + 60°) = \cos x$
27. $\cos(30° + x) - \cos(30° - x) = {}^-\sin x$
28. $\sin\left(x + \frac{\pi}{4}\right) + \cos\left(x + \frac{\pi}{4}\right) = \sqrt{2}\cos x$

Use the identity $\tan(\alpha - \beta) = \dfrac{\tan\alpha - \tan\beta}{1 + \tan\alpha\tan\beta}$ **to find the following.**

29. $\tan(30° + 30°)$ $\sqrt{3}$
30. $\tan(315° - 120°)$ $2 - \sqrt{3}$
31. $\tan(225° - 240°)$ $^-2 + \sqrt{3}$
32. $\tan(315° + 60°)$ $2 - \sqrt{3}$
33. $\tan(225° - 120°)$ $^-2 - \sqrt{3}$
34. $\tan(210° + 120°)$ $^-\sqrt{3}/3$
35. $\tan 285°$ $^-2 - \sqrt{3}$
36. $\tan 195°$ $2 - \sqrt{3}$
37. $\tan 165°$ $^-2 + \sqrt{3}$
38. $\tan 75°$ $2 + \sqrt{3}$
39. $\tan(180° - \theta)$ $^-\tan\theta$
40. $\tan(\alpha + \beta)$ $\dfrac{\tan\alpha + \tan\beta}{1 - \tan\alpha\tan\beta}$

Challenge Use the formulas for $\sin(\alpha - \beta)$ and $\cos(\alpha - \beta)$ to derive the formula for $\tan(\alpha - \beta)$. Hint: You will need to divide all terms of an expression by $\cos\alpha\cos\beta$.
See Teacher's Guide for answer.

16-8 Double Angles and Half Angles

Objective: To derive and use double and half angle formulas.

You can use the formula for $\sin(\alpha + \beta)$ to find $\sin 2\theta$.

$$\begin{aligned}\sin 2\theta &= \sin(\theta + \theta)\\ &= \sin\theta\cos\theta + \cos\theta\sin\theta\\ &= 2\sin\theta\cos\theta\end{aligned}$$

Similarly, a formula for $\cos 2\theta$ can be found.

$$\begin{aligned}\cos 2\theta &= \cos(\theta + \theta)\\ &= \cos\theta\cos\theta - \sin\theta\sin\theta\\ &= \cos^2\theta - \sin^2\theta\end{aligned}$$

Alternate forms can also be found by making substitutions.

$\cos^2\theta - \sin^2\theta = (1 - \sin^2\theta) - \sin^2\theta$ or $1 - 2\sin^2\theta$ *Substitute $1 - \sin^2\theta$ for $\cos^2\theta$.*

$\cos^2\theta - \sin^2\theta = \cos^2\theta - (1 - \cos^2\theta)$ or $2\cos^2\theta - 1$ *Substitute $1 - \cos^2\theta$ for $\sin^2\theta$.*

Double Angle Formulas

The following identities hold for all values of θ.

$$\sin 2\theta = 2\sin\theta\cos\theta \qquad \begin{aligned}\cos 2\theta &= \cos^2\theta - \sin^2\theta\\ &= 1 - 2\sin^2\theta\\ &= 2\cos^2\theta - 1\end{aligned}$$

example 1

Suppose x is between 0° and 90° and $\sin x = \frac{3}{5}$. Find sin 2x.

Since $\sin 2x = 2\sin x\cos x$, find $\cos x$ first. Use $\cos^2 x + \sin^2 x = 1$.

$$\cos^2 x + \sin^2 x = 1$$

$$\cos^2 x + \left(\frac{3}{5}\right)^2 = 1 \qquad \textit{Substitute } \tfrac{3}{5} \textit{ for } \sin x.$$

$$\begin{aligned}\cos^2 x &= 1 - \left(\frac{3}{5}\right)^2\\ &= \frac{16}{25}\\ \cos x &= \pm\sqrt{\frac{16}{25}} \text{ or } \pm\frac{4}{5}\end{aligned}$$

But x is between 0° and 90°, so $\cos x$ must be positive.

$$\begin{aligned}\sin 2x &= 2\sin x\cos x\\ &= 2\left(\frac{3}{5}\right)\left(\frac{4}{5}\right)\\ &= \frac{24}{25}\end{aligned}$$

There also are formulas for $\cos \frac{\alpha}{2}$ and $\sin \frac{\alpha}{2}$.

$2\cos^2\theta - 1 = \cos 2\theta$	*Use double angle formulas.*	$1 - 2\sin^2\theta = \cos 2\theta$
$2\cos^2\frac{\alpha}{2} - 1 = \cos\alpha$	*Substitute α for 2θ and $\frac{\alpha}{2}$ for θ.*	$1 - 2\sin^2\frac{\alpha}{2} = \cos\alpha$
$\cos^2\frac{\alpha}{2} = \frac{1+\cos\alpha}{2}$	*Solve for the squared term.*	$\sin^2\frac{\alpha}{2} = \frac{1-\cos\alpha}{2}$
$\cos\frac{\alpha}{2} = \pm\sqrt{\frac{1+\cos\alpha}{2}}$	*Take the square root of both sides.*	$\sin\frac{\alpha}{2} = \pm\sqrt{\frac{1-\cos\alpha}{2}}$

The following identities hold for all values of α.

$$\cos\frac{\alpha}{2} = \pm\sqrt{\frac{1+\cos\alpha}{2}} \text{ and } \sin\frac{\alpha}{2} = \pm\sqrt{\frac{1-\cos\alpha}{2}}$$

Half Angle Formulas

examples

2 **Find cos 105°.**

$$\cos 105° = \cos\frac{210°}{2}$$

$$= \pm\sqrt{\frac{1+\cos 210°}{2}} \qquad \cos 210° = -\frac{\sqrt{3}}{2}$$

$$= \pm\sqrt{\frac{1+\left(-\frac{\sqrt{3}}{2}\right)}{2}} \text{ or } \pm\frac{\sqrt{2-\sqrt{3}}}{2}$$

Since 105° is between 90° and 180°, the value of cos 105° is negative.

The solution is $-\frac{\sqrt{2-\sqrt{3}}}{2}$.

3 **Find sin $67\frac{1}{2}°$.**

$$\sin 67\tfrac{1}{2}° = \sin\frac{135°}{2}$$

$$= \pm\sqrt{\frac{1-\cos 135°}{2}} \qquad \cos 135° = -\frac{\sqrt{2}}{2}$$

$$= \pm\sqrt{\frac{1+\frac{\sqrt{2}}{2}}{2}} \text{ or } \pm\frac{\sqrt{2+\sqrt{2}}}{2}$$

Since $67\frac{1}{2}°$ is between 0° and 90° the value of sin $67\frac{1}{2}°$ is positive.

The solution is $\frac{\sqrt{2+\sqrt{2}}}{2}$.

1. I or II 2. III or IV 3. I or II 4. III or IV 5. I 6. I 7. II 8. II

exercises

Max: 1–16, 1–38; **Avg:** 1–16, 1–37 odds; **Min:** 1–37 odds

Exploratory **Solve each problem.** Assume that the measure of the first angle is between 0° and 360° inclusive.

1. x is a first quadrant angle. In which quadrant does the terminal side for $2x$ lie?
2. x is a second quadrant angle. In which quadrant does the terminal side for $2x$ lie?
3. x is a third quadrant angle. In which quadrant does the terminal side for $2x$ lie?
4. x is a fourth quadrant angle. In which quadrant does the terminal side for $2x$ lie?
5. $2x$ is a first quadrant angle. In which quadrant does the terminal side for x lie?
6. $2x$ is a second quadrant angle. In which quadrant does the terminal side for x lie?
7. $2x$ is a third quadrant angle. In which quadrant does the terminal side for x lie?
8. $2x$ is a fourth quadrant angle. In which quadrant does the terminal side for x lie?
9. $\frac{x}{2}$ is a first quadrant angle. In which quadrant does the terminal side for x lie?
10. $\frac{x}{2}$ is a second quadrant angle. In which quadrant does the terminal side for x lie?
11. $\frac{x}{2}$ is a third quadrant angle. In which quadrant does the terminal side for x lie?
12. $\frac{x}{2}$ is a fourth quadrant angle. In which quadrant does the terminal side for x lie?
13. x is a first quadrant angle. In which quadrant does the terminal side for $\frac{x}{2}$ lie?
14. x is a second quadrant angle. In which quadrant does the terminal side for $\frac{x}{2}$ lie?
15. x is a third quadrant angle. In which quadrant does the terminal side for $\frac{x}{2}$ lie?
16. x is a fourth quadrant angle. In which quadrant does the terminal side for $\frac{x}{2}$ lie?

9. I or II 10. III or IV 11. I or II 12. III or IV 13. I 14. I 15. II 16. II

Written **Find sin 2x for each of the following.**

1. $\sin x = \frac{1}{2}$, x is in the first quadrant $\sqrt{3}/2$
2. $\cos x = \frac{3}{5}$, x is in the first quadrant $\frac{24}{25}$
3. $\cos x = -\frac{2}{3}$, x is in the third quadrant $4\sqrt{5}/9$
4. $\sin x = \frac{4}{5}$, x is in the second quadrant $-\frac{24}{25}$
5. $\sin x = \frac{5}{13}$, x is in the second quadrant $-\frac{120}{169}$
6. $\cos x = \frac{1}{5}$, x is in the fourth quadrant $-4\sqrt{6}/25$
7. $\sin x = -\frac{3}{4}$, x is in the fourth quadrant $-3\sqrt{7}/8$
8. $\cos x = -\frac{1}{3}$, x is in the third quadrant $4\sqrt{2}/9$

9–16. Find $\cos \frac{x}{2}$ for problems **1–8**.

17–24. Find $\sin \frac{x}{2}$ for problems **1–8**.

25–32. Find cos $2x$ for problems **1–8**. For answers to problems **9–38**, see the Teacher's Guide.

Verify each identity.

33. $\cos^2 2x + 4 \sin^2 x \cos^2 x = 1$
34. $(\sin x + \cos x)^2 = 1 + \sin 2x$
35. $\sin^4 x - \cos^4 x = 2 \sin^2 x - 1$
36. $\sin 2x = 2 \cot x \sin^2 x$
37. $\sin^2 \theta = \frac{1}{2}(1 - \cos 2\theta)$
38. $\frac{1}{\sin x \cos x} - \frac{\cos x}{\sin x} = \tan x$

16-9 Solving Trigonometric Equations

Objective: To solve trigonometric equations.

Trigonometric identities are true for *all* values of the variable involved. Most trigonometric equations are true for *some* but *not all* values of the variable.

example 1

Solve $\sin 2\theta + \sin \theta = 0$ if $0° \leq \theta < 360°$.

$$\sin 2\theta + \sin \theta = 0$$

$$2 \sin \theta \cos \theta + \sin \theta = 0 \qquad \textit{sin } 2\theta = 2 \textit{ sin } \theta \textit{ cos } \theta$$

$$\sin \theta (2 \cos \theta + 1) = 0 \qquad \textit{Factor.}$$

$\sin \theta = 0$ or $2 \cos \theta + 1 = 0$

$\theta = 0°, 180°$

$$\cos \theta = -\frac{1}{2}$$

$$\theta = 120°, 240°$$

The graphs often help you find the values of θ.

The solutions are 0°, 120°, 180°, and 240°.

Usually trigonometric equations are solved for values of the variable between 0° and 360° or 0 radians and 2π radians. There are solutions outside that interval. These other solutions differ by integral multiples of the period of the function.

example 2

Solve $\cos \theta + 1 = 0$ for all values of θ.

The equation can be written in the form $\cos \theta = {}^{-}1$. By looking at the graph, the solutions are π, 3π, 5π, and so on and $^{-}\pi$, $^{-}3\pi$, $^{-}5\pi$, and so on.

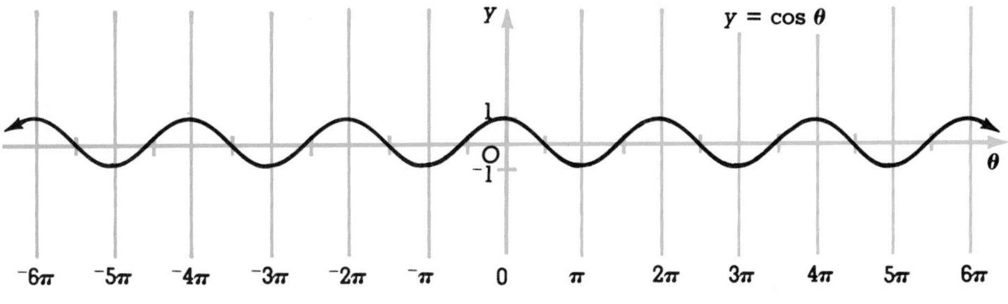

The only solution in the interval 0 radians to 2π radians is π. The period of cosine is 2π radians. So the solutions can be written as $\pi + 2n\pi$ where n is an integer. This is normally written in the form $(2n + 1)\pi$, where n is an integer.

If an equation cannot be easily solved by factoring, try writing the expressions in terms of only one trigonometric function.

example 3

Solve $4 \sin x \cos x = {}^{-}\sqrt{3}$.

$$4 \sin x \cos x = {}^{-}\sqrt{3}$$
$$2(2 \sin x \cos x) = {}^{-}\sqrt{3}$$
$$2 \sin x \cos x = -\frac{\sqrt{3}}{2}$$
$$\sin 2x = -\frac{\sqrt{3}}{2} \qquad \textit{2 sin x cos x = sin 2x}$$
$$2x = \frac{4\pi}{3} + 2n\pi,\ \frac{5\pi}{3} + 2n\pi, \qquad \textit{for n an integer}$$
$$2x = 2\pi\left(\frac{2}{3} + n\right),\ 2\pi\left(\frac{5}{6} + n\right), \qquad \textit{for n an integer}$$
$$x = \pi\left(\frac{2}{3} + n\right),\ \pi\left(\frac{5}{6} + n\right), \qquad \textit{for n an integer}$$

The solutions are $\pi\left(\frac{2}{3} + n\right)$ and $\pi\left(\frac{5}{6} + n\right)$ for n an integer.

Some trigonometric equations have *no solutions*. In other words, there is no replacement for the variable that will make the sentence true. For example, the equation $\cos x = 2$ has no solution. The solution set is $\emptyset$.

example 4

Solve $2 \cos^2 \theta - 3 \cos \theta - 2 = 0$ if $0 \leq \theta < 2\pi$.

$$2 \cos^2 \theta - 3 \cos \theta - 2 = 0$$
$$(\cos \theta - 2)(2 \cos \theta + 1) = 0$$
$$\cos \theta - 2 = 0 \quad \text{or} \quad 2 \cos \theta + 1 = 0$$
$$\cos \theta = 2 \qquad 2 \cos \theta = {}^{-}1$$
$$\cos \theta = -\frac{1}{2}$$
$$\theta = \frac{2\pi}{3} \text{ or } \frac{4\pi}{3}$$

There is no solution to $\cos \theta = 2$ because all values of $\cos \theta$ are less than or equal to 1.

The solutions are $\frac{2\pi}{3}$ and $\frac{4\pi}{3}$.

It is important to check your solutions. Some algebraic operations may introduce answers that are *not* solutions to the original equation.

example 5

Solve $\sin x = 1 - \cos x$ if $0° \leq x < 360°$.

$$\sin x = 1 - \cos x$$
$$\sin^2 x = 1 - 2\cos x + \cos^2 x \quad \textit{Square both sides.}$$
$$1 - \cos^2 x = 1 - 2\cos x + \cos^2 x \quad \textit{$\sin^2 x = 1 - \cos^2 x$}$$
$$0 = 2\cos^2 x - 2\cos x$$
$$0 = 2\cos x(\cos x - 1)$$

$2\cos x = 0$ or $\cos x - 1 = 0$

$\cos x = 0$ $\quad$ $\cos x = 1$

$x = 90°, 270°$ $\quad$ $x = 0°$

The solutions appear to be 90°, 270°, 0°. But, 270° does *not* satisfy the original equation. Thus, the solutions are 0° and 90°.

exercises

Max: 1–18, 1–16; Avg: 1–18, 1–15 odds; Min: 1–15 odds

Exploratory Each equation has how many solutions if $0° \leq \theta < 360°$?

1. $\sin\theta = 1$ 1
2. $\sin\theta = \frac{1}{2}$ 2
3. $\cos\theta = -\frac{\sqrt{3}}{2}$. 2
4. $\tan\theta = 1$ 2
5. $\tan\theta = {}^-3$ 2
6. $\tan^2\theta = 1$ 4
7. $\sin 2\theta = \frac{1}{2}$ 2
8. $\cos 2\theta = \frac{3}{2}$ 0
9. $\sin 2\theta = -\frac{\sqrt{3}}{2}$ 2
10. $\cos^2\theta = 1$ 2
11. $\sin 3\theta = {}^-2$ 0
12. $\cos 8\theta = 1$ 1
13. $\sin^2 2\theta = \frac{1}{2}$ 4
14. $\cos^2 3\theta = \frac{1}{2}$ 4
15. $\tan^2 2\theta = 3$ 4
16. $\sin\frac{1}{2}\theta = \frac{1}{2}$ 2
17. $\sin\frac{1}{2}\theta = -\frac{\sqrt{3}}{2}$ 0
18. $\tan\frac{1}{3}\theta = 1$ 2

Written Find all solutions if $0° \leq x < 360°$.

1. $2\sin^2 x - 1 = 0$ 45°, 135°, 225°, 315°
2. $4\cos^2 x = 1$ 60°, 120°, 240°, 300°
3. $2\sin^2 x + \sin x = 0$ 0°, 180°, 210°, 330°
4. $2\cos^2 x = \sin x + 1$ 30°, 150°, 270°
5. $\sin^2 x + \cos 2x - \cos x = 0$ 0°, 90°, 270°
6. $\cos x = 3\cos x - 2$ 0°
7. $\sin 2x = \cos x$ 30°, 90°, 150°, 270°
8. $\sin 2x = 2\cos x$ 90°, 270°
9. $4\sin^2 x - 4\sin x + 1 = 0$ 30°, 150°
10. $\sin^2 x = \cos^2 x - 1$ 0°, 180°
11. $\cos 2x = \cos x$ 0°, 120°, 240°
12. $\sin^2 x - 2\sin x - 3 = 0$ 270°
13. $\sin x = \cos x$ 45°, 225°
14. $\tan x = \sin x$ 0°, 180°
15. $3\cos 2x - 5\cos x = 1$ 120°, 240°
16. $\tan^2 x - \sqrt{3}\tan x = 0$ 0°, 60°, 180°, 240°

16–10 Inverse Trigonometric Functions

Objective: To define and use inverse trigonometric functions.

The inverse of a function can be found by reversing the order of each ordered pair in the given function.

> Since (0, 1) is on the graph of the cosine function, (1, 0) is on the graph of its inverse function.
> Since $(2\pi, 1)$ is on the graph of the cosine function, $(1, 2\pi)$ is on the graph of its inverse function.

For a given value of x there is more than one value of y.

The inverse of the cosine function is *not* a function. Why?

Consider only a part of the domain of the cosine function, namely any x so that $0 \leq x \leq \pi$. It is possible to define a new function, called Cosine, whose inverse is a function.

$y = \text{Cos } x$ if and only if $y = \cos x$ and $0 \leq x \leq \pi$

Capital letters are used to distinguish the functions with restricted domains from the usual trigonometric functions.

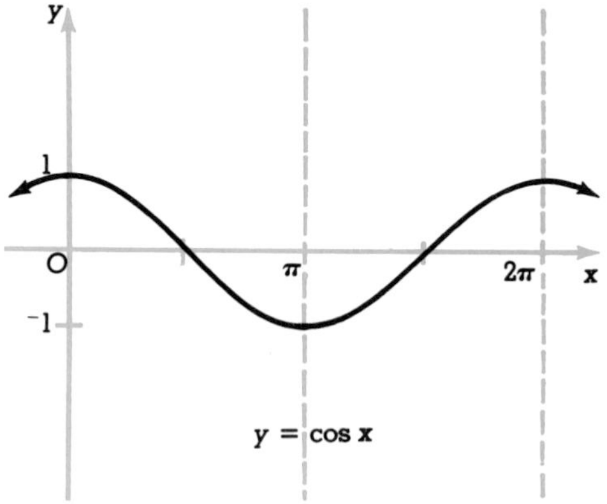

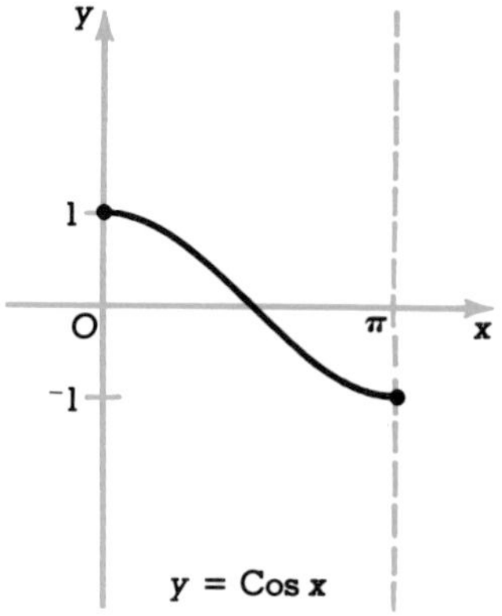

The domain is $\{x | x \text{ is an angle measurement}\}$.
The range is $\{y | {}^{-}1 \leq y \leq 1\}$.
The inverse is *not* a function.

The domain is $\{x | 0 \leq x \leq \pi\}$.
The range is $\{y | {}^{-}1 \leq y \leq 1\}$.
The inverse is a function.

The values in the domain of Cosine are called **principal values.** Other new functions that have inverses can be defined.

$y = \text{Sin } x$ if and only if $y = \sin x$ and $-\frac{\pi}{2} \leq x \leq \frac{\pi}{2}$.

$y = \text{Tan } x$ if and only if $y = \tan x$ and $-\frac{\pi}{2} < x < \frac{\pi}{2}$.

The principal values of x in $y = \text{Sin } x$ are $\left\{x | -\frac{\pi}{2} \leq x \leq \frac{\pi}{2}\right\}$.

The principal values of x in $y = \text{Tan } x$ are $\left\{x | -\frac{\pi}{2} < x < \frac{\pi}{2}\right\}$.

The inverse cosine function is also called the Arccosine function and is symbolized by **Cos⁻¹** or **Arccos.**

> **Given $y = \text{Cos}\, x$, the inverse cosine function is defined by the following equation.**
>
> $$x = \text{Cos}^{-1}\, y$$

Definition of Inverse Cosine

The Arccosine function has the following characteristics.

1. Its domain is the set of real numbers from $^{-}1$ to 1.
2. Its range is the set of angle measurements from 0 to π.
3. $\text{Cos}\, x = y$ if and only if $\text{Cos}^{-1}\, y = x$.
4. $(\text{Cos}^{-1} \circ \text{Cos})(x) = (\text{Cos} \circ \text{Cos}^{-1})(x) = x$
5. Its graph is as follows.

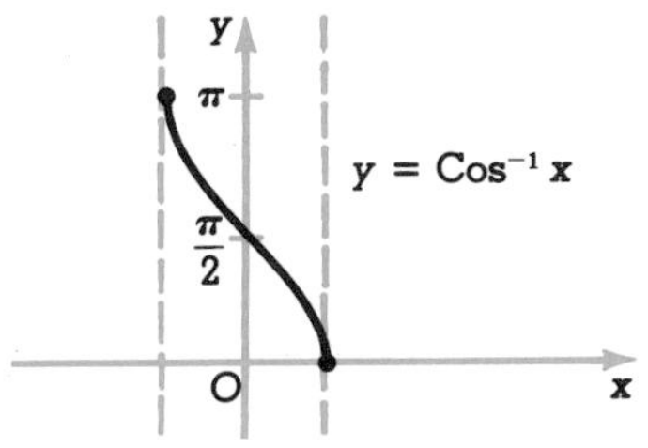

example 1

Find $\text{Cos}^{-1}\left(-\frac{\sqrt{3}}{2}\right)$.

$$\theta = \text{Cos}^{-1}\left(-\frac{\sqrt{3}}{2}\right)$$

$$\text{Cos}\, \theta = -\frac{\sqrt{3}}{2}$$

$$\theta = 150°$$ *Why is θ not 210°?*

The **Arcsine** and **Arctangent** functions are defined similarly.

> **Given $y = \text{Sin}\, x$, the inverse sine function is defined by the following equation.**
>
> $$x = \text{Sin}^{-1}\, y$$
>
> **Given $y = \text{Tan}\, x$, the inverse tangent function is defined by the following equation.**
>
> $$x = \text{Tan}^{-1}\, y$$

Definition of Inverse Sine

Definition of Inverse Tangent

The graphs of the inverse sine and inverse tangent functions are as follows.

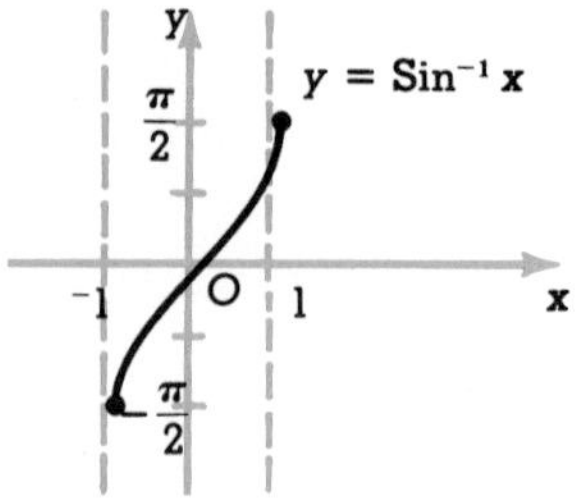

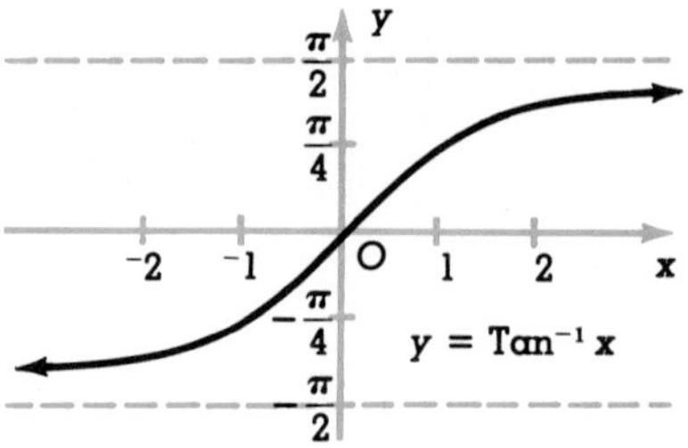

examples

2 **Find $\cos\left(\text{Sin}^{-1}\frac{1}{2}\right)$.**

$$\text{Let } \theta = \text{Sin}^{-1}\frac{1}{2}$$

$$\text{then } \text{Sin}\,\theta = \frac{1}{2}$$

$$\text{so } \theta = 30°$$

$$\text{Cos}\left(\text{Sin}^{-1}\frac{1}{2}\right) = \text{Cos}\,30° = \frac{\sqrt{3}}{2}$$

3 **Find $\sin\left[\text{Cos}^{-1}\left(-\frac{1}{2}\right) + \text{Tan}^{-1}1\right]$.**

Let $\alpha = \text{Cos}^{-1}\left(-\frac{1}{2}\right)$ and let $\beta = \text{Tan}^{-1}1$

$\text{Cos}\,\alpha = -\frac{1}{2}$ $\quad$ $\text{Tan}\,\beta = 1$

$\alpha = 120°$ $\quad$ $\beta = 45°$

$$\sin\left[\text{Cos}^{-1}\left(-\frac{1}{2}\right) + \text{Tan}^{-1}1\right] = \sin(\alpha + \beta)$$

$$= \sin(120° + 45°)$$

$$= \sin 120° \cos 45° + \cos 120° \sin 45°$$

$$= \frac{\sqrt{3}}{2}\cdot\frac{\sqrt{2}}{2} + \left(-\frac{1}{2}\right)\cdot\frac{\sqrt{2}}{2}$$

$$= \frac{\sqrt{6} - \sqrt{2}}{4}$$

exercises

Max: 1–21, 1–30; **Avg:** 1–21, 1–29 odds; **Min:** 1–29 odds

Exploratory Evaluate each of the following.

1. $\text{Sin}\,\frac{\pi}{6}$ $\frac{1}{2}$
2. $\text{Cos}^{-1}\,\frac{1}{2}$ $60°$
3. $\text{Sin}^{-1}\left(-\frac{\sqrt{3}}{2}\right)$ $^-60°$
4. $\text{Cos}\ 300°$ undefined
5. $\text{Tan}\ \pi$ undefined
6. Arctan 1 $\pi/4$
7. $\text{Tan}\,\frac{\pi}{4}$ 1
8. $\text{Sin}^{-1}\left(-\frac{1}{2}\right)$ $^-30°$
9. $\text{Cos}^{-1}\left(-\frac{\sqrt{3}}{2}\right)$ $150°$
10. $\text{Sin}\ 270°$ undefined
11. $\text{Tan}^{-1}\,(1)$ $45°$
12. $\text{Sin}^{-1}\,0$ $0°$
13. $\text{Cos}\left(-\frac{3}{4}\pi\right)$ $-\frac{\sqrt{2}}{2}$
14. $\text{Arcsin}\,\frac{\sqrt{3}}{2}$ $60°$
15. $\text{Sin}^{-1}\frac{\sqrt{3}}{2}$ $60°$
16. $\text{Tan}^{-1}\left(\frac{\sqrt{3}}{3}\right)$ $30°$
17. $\text{Cos}\ 45°$ $\frac{\sqrt{2}}{2}$
18. $\text{Sin}^{-1}\,1$ $90°$
19. $\text{Sin}^{-1}\,(^-1)$ $^-90°$
20. $\text{Sin}\,\frac{5}{6}\pi$ undefined
21. $\text{Cos}^{-1}\,0$ $90°$

Written Evaluate each of the following.

1. $\text{Sin}\ 30°$ $\frac{1}{2}$
2. $\text{Tan}^{-1}\,(^-1)$ $^-45°$
3. $\text{Arccos}\,\frac{\sqrt{3}}{2}$ $30°$
4. $\text{Sin}^{-1}\,1$ $90°$
5. $\text{Cos}^{-1}\left(-\frac{1}{2}\right)$ $120°$
6. $\text{Arctan}\,\sqrt{3}$ $60°$
7. $\sin\left(\text{Sin}^{-1}\frac{1}{2}\right)$ $\frac{1}{2}$
8. $\text{Sin}^{-1}\left(\cos\frac{\pi}{2}\right)$ $0°$
9. $\text{Sin}^{-1}\left(\tan\frac{\pi}{4}\right)$ $90°$
10. $\cos\left(\text{Cos}^{-1}\frac{1}{2}\right)$ $\frac{1}{2}$
11. $\cos\left(\text{Cos}^{-1}\frac{4}{5}\right)$ $\frac{4}{5}$
12. $\sin\left(\text{Sin}^{-1}\frac{\sqrt{3}}{2}\right)$ $\frac{\sqrt{3}}{2}$
13. $\tan\left(\text{Sin}^{-1}\frac{5}{13}\right)$ $\frac{5}{12}$
14. $\tan\left[\text{Cos}^{-1}\left(-\frac{3}{5}\right)\right]$ $-\frac{4}{3}$
15. $\sin\,[\text{Arctan}\,(^-\sqrt{3})]$ $-\frac{\sqrt{3}}{2}$
16. $\sin\left(2\ \text{Cos}^{-1}\frac{3}{5}\right)$ $\frac{24}{25}$
17. $\cos\,(\text{Tan}^{-1}\,\sqrt{3})$ $\frac{1}{2}$
18. $\cos\left[\text{Arcsin}\left(-\frac{1}{2}\right)\right]$ $\frac{\sqrt{3}}{2}$
19. $\sin\left(2\ \text{Sin}^{-1}\frac{1}{2}\right)$ $\frac{\sqrt{3}}{2}$
20. $\cos\,(\text{Tan}^{-1}\,1)$ $\frac{\sqrt{2}}{2}$
21. $\sin\left[\frac{\pi}{2} - \text{Tan}^{-1}\,(1)\right]$ $\frac{\sqrt{2}}{2}$
22. $\cos\left[\text{Cos}^{-1}\left(-\frac{\sqrt{2}}{2}\right) - \frac{\pi}{2}\right]$ $\frac{\sqrt{2}}{2}$
23. $\cos\left[\frac{4}{3}\pi - \text{Cos}^{-1}\left(-\frac{1}{2}\right)\right]$ $-\frac{1}{2}$
24. $\sin\left[\frac{\pi}{2} - \text{Cos}^{-1}\left(\frac{1}{2}\right)\right]$ $\frac{1}{2}$
25. $\sin\left(\text{Sin}^{-1}\,1 - \text{Cos}^{-1}\frac{1}{2}\right)$ $\frac{1}{2}$
26. $\cos\left(\text{Cos}^{-1}\,0 + \text{Sin}^{-1}\frac{1}{2}\right)$ $-\frac{1}{2}$
27. $\cos\left(\text{Tan}^{-1}\,\sqrt{3} - \text{Sin}^{-1}\frac{1}{2}\right)$ $\frac{\sqrt{3}}{2}$
28. $\sin\left(2\ \text{Sin}^{-1}\,\frac{\sqrt{3}}{2}\right)$ $\frac{\sqrt{3}}{2}$
29. $\sin\,(\text{Tan}^{-1}\,1 + \text{Sin}^{-1}\,1)$ $\frac{\sqrt{2}}{2}$
30. $\cos\left[\text{Cos}^{-1}\left(-\frac{1}{2}\right) - \text{Sin}^{-1}\,1\right]$ $\frac{\sqrt{3}}{2}$

Using Algebra

Basketball

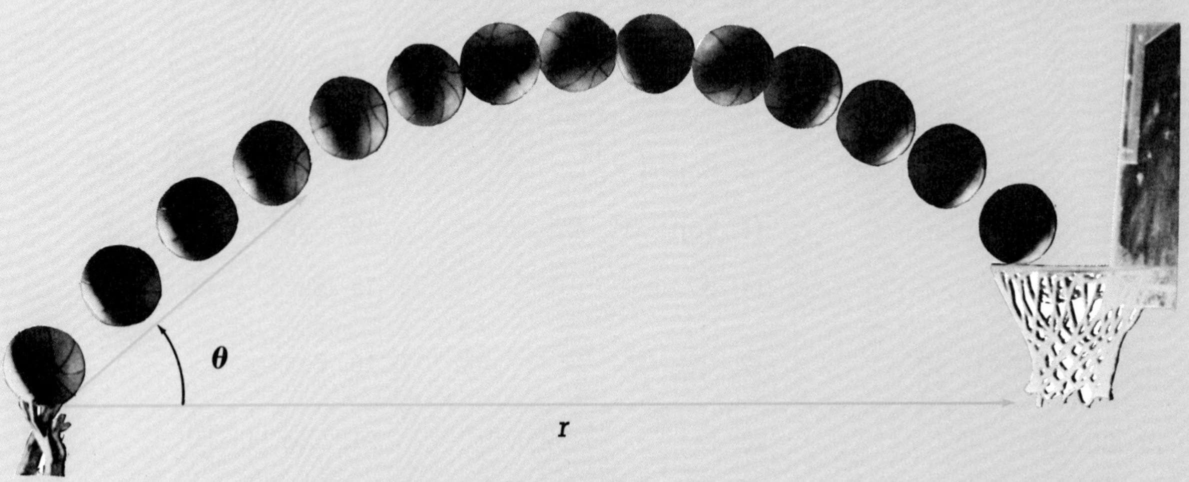

Is there a best way to shoot a basketball based on physics? "Yes!" says Enoch J. Durbin, a professor of aerospace and mechanical sciences at Princeton University. "If you study angles of launch at a basketball game, you will notice that the most accurate shooters are those who shoot at an angle slightly higher than 45 degrees."

Durbin has analyzed basketball shooting using the following equation.

$$r = \frac{v^2 \sin 2\theta}{g}$$

r stands for the range, the horizontal distance the ball travels from shooter to basket

v stands for the launch velocity, the speed of the ball at the moment of release

g stands for the acceleration of the ball due to gravity

θ stands for the angle from which the ball is shot, measured from the horizontal

To arrive at the equation above, Durbin had to make several assumptions. The ball is shot from the same height as the rim of the basketball hoop. The ball is *not* rotating. No opposing players affect the shot. There is no air drag. And the ball is *not* bounced off the rim, *nor* off the backboard.

Exercises Suppose a basketball is shot toward a basket with a launch velocity, v, of 18 feet per second. The acceleration due to gravity, g, is 32 feet per second per second. Estimate the range of the shot for each of the following angles. *Use the Table of Trigonometric Values on pp. 542–546.*

1. 40° 10.0 ft **2.** 43° 10.1 ft **3.** 45° 10.1 ft **4.** 47° 10.1 ft **5.** 50° 10.0 ft **6.** 60° 8.8 ft

Vocabulary

coterminal angles (448)
unit circle (449)
radian (449)
sine (452)
cosine (452)
periodic (454)
period (454)
amplitude (458)
tangent (460)
cotangent (460)
secant (460)
cosecant (460)
principal values (478)
Arccosine (479)
Arcsine (479)
Arctangent (479)

Chapter Summary

1. Definition of Sine and Cosine: Let θ stand for the measurement of an angle in standard position on the unit circle. Let (x, y) represent the point where the terminal side intersects the unit circle. Then sine $\theta = y$ and cosine $\theta = x$. (452)
2. Definition of Periodic Function: A function f is called periodic if there is a number a such that $f(x) = f(x + a)$. The least positive value of a for which $f(x) = f(x + a)$ is the period of the function. (454)
3. Amplitudes and Periods: For functions of the form $y = a \sin b\theta$ and $y = a \cos b\theta$, the amplitude is $|a|$ and the period is $\frac{2\pi}{|b|}$. (458)
4. Definition of Tangent, Cotangent, Secant, and Cosecant: Let θ stand for the measurement of an angle in standard position on the unit circle. Then the following equations hold wherever they are defined. (460)

$$\tan \theta = \frac{\sin \theta}{\cos \theta} \qquad \cot \theta = \frac{\cos \theta}{\sin \theta} \qquad \sec \theta = \frac{1}{\cos \theta} \qquad \csc \theta = \frac{1}{\sin \theta}$$

5. Basic Trigonometric Identities: The following trigonometric identities hold for all values of θ except those for which either side of the equation is undefined. (463)

$$\tan \theta = \frac{\sin \theta}{\cos \theta} \qquad \sec \theta = \frac{1}{\cos \theta} \qquad \sin^2 \theta + \cos^2 \theta = 1$$

$$\cot \theta = \frac{\cos \theta}{\sin \theta} \qquad \csc \theta = \frac{1}{\sin \theta} \qquad 1 + \tan^2 \theta = \sec^2 \theta$$

$$\cot \theta = \frac{1}{\tan \theta} \qquad 1 + \cot^2 \theta = \csc^2 \theta$$

6. Difference and Sum Formulas: The following identities hold for all values of α and β.

$$\cos(\alpha \pm \beta) = \cos\alpha\cos\beta \mp \sin\alpha\sin\beta$$
$$\sin(\alpha \pm \beta) = \sin\alpha\cos\beta \pm \cos\alpha\sin\beta \quad (470)$$

7. Double Angle Formulas: The following identities hold for all values of θ.

$$\sin 2\theta = 2\sin\theta\cos\theta \qquad \cos 2\theta = \cos^2\theta - \sin^2\theta = 1 - 2\sin^2\theta = 2\cos^2\theta - 1 \quad (472)$$

8. Half Angle Formulas: The following identities hold for all values of α.

$$\cos\frac{\alpha}{2} = \pm\sqrt{\frac{1+\cos\alpha}{2}} \text{ and } \sin\frac{\alpha}{2} = \pm\sqrt{\frac{1-\cos\alpha}{2}} \quad (473)$$

9. Definition of Inverse Cosine: Given $y = \text{Cos}\, x$, the inverse cosine function is defined by the following equation. $x = \text{Cos}^{-1} y$. (479)
10. Definition of Inverse Sine: Given $y = \text{Sin}\, x$, the inverse sine function is defined by the following equation. $x = \text{Sin}^{-1} y$. (479)
11. Definition of Inverse Tangent: Given $y = \text{Tan}\, x$, the inverse tangent function is defined by the following equation. $x = \text{Tan}^{-1} y$. (479)

Chapter Review

16-1 Convert each of the following to radian measure.

1. $120°$ $\frac{2}{3}\pi$
2. $^-315°$ $-\frac{7}{4}\pi$
3. $270°$ $\frac{3}{2}\pi$
4. $225°$ $\frac{5}{4}\pi$

Convert each of the following to degree measure.

5. $\frac{\pi}{3}$ $60°$
6. $-\frac{5}{12}\pi$ $^-75°$
7. $\frac{4}{3}$ $\left(\frac{240}{\pi}\right)^{\circ}$
8. $\frac{7}{4}\pi$ $315°$

16-2 For each of the following, find the smallest positive angle that is coterminal.

9. $^-155°$ $205°$
10. $830°$ $110°$
11. $540°$ $180°$
12. $945°$ $225°$
13. $\frac{20}{3}\pi$ $\frac{2}{3}\pi$
14. $-\frac{4}{3}\pi$ $\frac{2}{3}\pi$
15. $-\frac{2}{9}\pi$ $\frac{16}{9}\pi$
16. $-\frac{11}{6}\pi$ $\frac{1}{6}\pi$

Find each value.

17. $\sin 120°$ $\sqrt{3}/2$
18. $\cos 210°$ $^-\sqrt{3}/2$
19. $\cos 3\pi$ $^-1$
20. $\sin(^-150°)$ $-\frac{1}{2}$
21. $\sin {^-30°}$ $-\frac{1}{2}$
22. $\sin\frac{5}{4}\pi$ $^-\sqrt{2}/2$
23. $\cos(^-135°)$ $^-\sqrt{2}/2$
24. $\cos(300°)$ $\frac{1}{2}$
25. $(\sin 30°)^2 + (\cos 30°)^2$ 1
26. $(\sin 45°)(\sin 225°)$ $-\frac{1}{2}$

16-3 Graph each of the following. Then state the amplitude and period for each of the following.

27. $y = \sin x$ $1, 2\pi$
28. $y = -\frac{1}{2}\cos\theta$ $\frac{1}{2}, 2\pi$
29. $y = 4\sin 2\theta$ $4, \pi$

For the graphs in problems **27-29**, see the Teacher's Guide.

16-4 Evaluate each of the following.

30. $\csc \pi$ undefined
31. $\sec (^-30°)$ $2/\sqrt{3}$
32. $\csc 135°$ $\sqrt{2}$
33. $\cos 600°$ $-\frac{1}{2}$
34. $\sin \frac{4}{3}\pi$ $-\frac{\sqrt{3}}{2}$
35. $\cot \frac{7}{6}\pi$ $\sqrt{3}$
36. $\tan 120°$ $^-\sqrt{3}$
37. $\sec (^-60°)$ 2

16-5 Solve each of the following for values of θ between 90° and 180°.

38. If $\sin \theta = \frac{1}{2}$, find $\cos \theta$. $^-\sqrt{3}/2$
39. If $\csc \theta = \frac{5}{3}$, find $\cos \theta$. $-\frac{4}{5}$
40. If $\sec \theta = {^-3}$, find $\tan \theta$. $^-2\sqrt{2}$
41. If $\cot \theta = -\frac{1}{4}$, find $\csc \theta$. $\sqrt{17}/4$

Solve each of the following for values of θ between 270° and 360°.

42. If $\sin \theta = -\frac{4}{5}$, find $\cos \theta$. $\frac{3}{5}$
43. If $\sec \theta = 1$, find $\tan \theta$. 0
44. If $\csc \theta = -\frac{5}{3}$, find $\cot \theta$. $-\frac{4}{3}$
45. If $\sin \theta = -\frac{1}{2}$, find $\sec \theta$. $2\sqrt{3}/3$

16-6 Verify each identity. For answers to problems **46–49** and **54–55**, see the Teacher's Guide.

46. $\sin^4 x - \cos^4 x = \sin^2 x - \cos^2 x$
47. $\dfrac{\sin \theta}{\tan \theta} + \dfrac{\cos \theta}{\cot \theta} = \cos \theta + \sin \theta$
48. $\dfrac{\sin \theta}{1 - \cos \theta} = \csc \theta + \cot \theta$
49. $\tan x + \cot x = \sec x \csc x$

16-7 Evaluate each expression.

50. $\sin 105°$
51. $\cos 240°$ $-\frac{1}{2}$
52. $\cos 15°$
53. $\sin (^-255°)$

50. $(\sqrt{6} + \sqrt{2})/4$ 52. $(\sqrt{6} + \sqrt{2})/4$ 53. $(\sqrt{6} + \sqrt{2})/4$

Verify each of the following identities.

54. $\cos (90° - \theta) = \sin \theta$
55. $\cos (60° + \theta) + \cos (60° - \theta) = \cos \theta$

16-8 56. If $\sin x = -\frac{3}{5}$ and x is in the third quadrant, find $\sin 2x$. $\frac{24}{25}$

57. If $\sin x = \frac{1}{4}$ and x is in the first quadrant, find $\cos 2x$. $\frac{7}{8}$

58. If $\cos 2x = \frac{17}{25}$ and $\cos x = \frac{2}{5}$, find $\sin x$. $\sqrt{21}/5$

16-9 Find all solutions if $0° \le x < 360°$.

59. $2 \cos^2 x + \sin^2 x = 2 \cos x$ 0°
60. $\cos 2x = \cos x$ 0°, 120°, 240°
61. $\cos 2x \sin x = 1$ 270°
62. $\cos x = 1 - \sin x$ 0°, 90°
63. $2 \sin 2x = 1$ 15°, 75°
64. $\tan^2 x + \tan x = 0$ 0°, 135°, 315°

16-10 Evaluate each of the following.

65. $\text{Cos}^{-1}\left(\frac{\sqrt{3}}{2}\right)$ 30°
66. $\text{Sin}^{-1} (^-1)$ $^-90°$
67. $\text{Tan}^{-1} \sqrt{3}$ 60°
68. $\text{Sin}^{-1}\left(\tan \frac{\pi}{4}\right)$ 90°
69. $\cos (\text{Sin}^{-1} 1)$ 0
70. $\sin \left(2\ \text{Sin}^{-1} \frac{1}{2}\right)$ $\frac{\sqrt{3}}{2}$

Chapter Test

For graphs in problems 17 and 18, see the Teacher's Guide.

Convert each of the following to radian measure.

1. $135°$ $\frac{3}{4}\pi$ 2. $275°$ $\frac{55}{36}\pi$ 3. $^-150°$ $-\frac{5}{6}\pi$ 4. $^-4°$ $-\frac{1}{45}\pi$

Convert each of the following to degree measure.

5. $\frac{4}{5}\pi$ $144°$ 6. $\frac{12}{5}\pi$ $432°$ 7. $-\frac{7}{4}\pi$ $^-315°$ 8. 7 $\frac{1260°}{\pi}$

For each of the following, find the smallest positive angle that is coterminal.

9. $620°$ $260°$ 10. $^-260°$ $100°$ 11. $595°$ $235°$ 12. $^-1270°$ $170°$

Find each value.

13. $\sin 225°$ $^-\sqrt{2}/2$ 14. $\cos(^-120°)$ $-\frac{1}{2}$ 15. $\cos\frac{3}{4}\pi$ $-\frac{\sqrt{2}}{2}$ 16. $\sin\frac{7}{4}\pi$ $-\frac{\sqrt{2}}{2}$

Graph each of the following. Then state the amplitude and period.

17. $y = 2\sin 2x$ $2, \pi$ 18. $y = \frac{3}{4}\cos\frac{2}{3}x$ $\frac{3}{4}, 3\pi$

Evaluate each of the following.

19. $\tan 225°$ 1 20. $\csc {}^-120°$ $^-2\sqrt{3}/3$ 21. $\cos\frac{2}{3}\pi$ $-\frac{1}{2}$ 22. $\sec 150°$ $^-2\sqrt{3}/3$

Solve each of the following for values of θ between 180° and 270°.

23. If $\sin\theta = -\frac{1}{2}$, find $\tan\theta$. $\sqrt{3}/3$ 24. If $\cot\theta = \frac{3}{4}$, find $\sec\theta$. $-\frac{5}{3}$

Verify each identity. For answers to problems 25–27, see the Teacher's Guide.

25. $\frac{\cos x}{1 - \sin^2 x} = \sec x$ 26. $\frac{\sec x}{\sin x} - \frac{\sin x}{\cos x} = \cot x$ 27. $\frac{1 + \tan^2\theta}{\cos^2\theta} = \sec^4\theta$

Evaluate each of the following.

28. $\sin 255°$ $(^-\sqrt{6} - \sqrt{2})/4$ 29. $\cos 165°$ $(^-\sqrt{6} - \sqrt{2})/4$

30. If x is in the first quadrant and $\cos x = \frac{3}{4}$, find $\sin\frac{1}{2}x$. $\frac{\sqrt{2}}{4}$

31. If $\cos 2x = \frac{2}{9}$ and $\sin x = \frac{1}{3}$, find $\cos x$. $\frac{\sqrt{3}}{3}$

Find all solutions if $0° \leq x < 360°$.

32. $2\sin x\cos x - \sin x = 0$ $0°, 60°, 180°, 300°$ 33. $\cos 2x + \sin x = 1$ $0°, 30°, 150°, 180°$

34. $\sec x = 1 + \tan x$ $0°$ 35. $2\cos^2 2x + \cos 2x - 1 =$ $30°, 90°, 150°$

Evaluate each of the following.

36. $\text{Tan}^{-1}\frac{\sqrt{3}}{3}$ $30°$ 37. $\text{Sin}^{-1}\left(-\frac{1}{2}\right)$ $^-30°$ 38. $\text{Cos}^{-1}(\sin 30°)$ $60°$ 39. $\sin 2\left(\text{Cos}^{-1}\frac{1}{2}\right)$ $\frac{\sqrt{3}}{2}$

Chapter 17

Right Triangle Trigonometry

For maximum strength, structures must be constructed as designed. Civil engineers often use surveying equipment and trigonometry to check building construction.

17-1 Right Triangles

Objective: To find the missing measures of right triangles.

Trigonometry can be used to find missing measures of triangles. Look at the following right triangle.

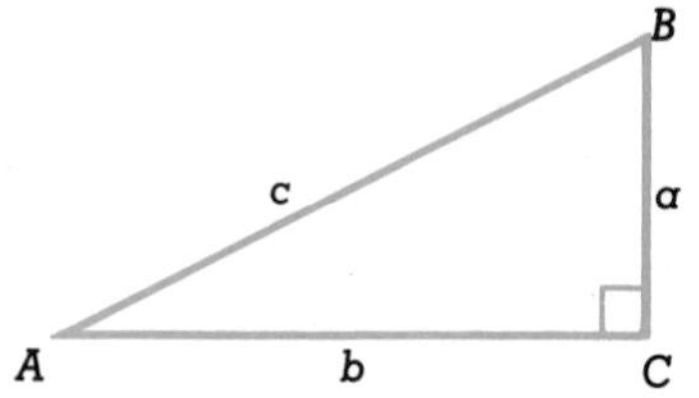

The **hypotenuse** of the triangle is side AB. Its length is c units.

The side opposite angle A is side BC. Its length is a units.

The side adjacent to angle A is side AC. Its length is b units.

For convenience of notation, we refer to the angle with vertex at A as angle A and use A to stand for its measurement. Similarly, we refer to angle B and its measurement, B. And we refer to angle C and its measurement, C.

SOH-CAH-TOA is a helpful mnemonic device for remembering the first 3 equations.

$$\sin = \frac{\text{opposite}}{\text{hypotenuse}}$$

$$\cos = \frac{\text{adjacent}}{\text{hypotenuse}}$$

$$\tan = \frac{\text{opposite}}{\text{adjacent}}$$

Using this right triangle, trigonometric values can be defined in the following way.

$$\sin A = \frac{a}{c} \qquad \csc A = \frac{c}{a}$$

$$\cos A = \frac{b}{c} \qquad \sec A = \frac{c}{b}$$

$$\tan A = \frac{a}{b} \qquad \cot A = \frac{b}{a}$$

example 1

Find the sine, cosine, tangent, cosecant, secant, and cotangent of angle A to the nearest four decimal places.

$\sin A = \frac{6}{10}$ or 0.6000

$\cos A = \frac{8}{10}$ or 0.8000

$\tan A = \frac{6}{8}$ or 0.7500

$\csc A = \frac{10}{6}$ or 1.6667

$\sec A = \frac{10}{8}$ or 1.2500

$\cot A = \frac{8}{6}$ or 1.3333

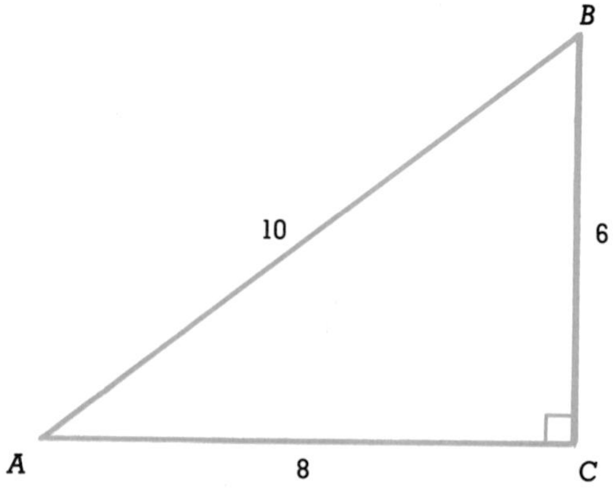

example 2

Find sin A to the nearest four decimal places.

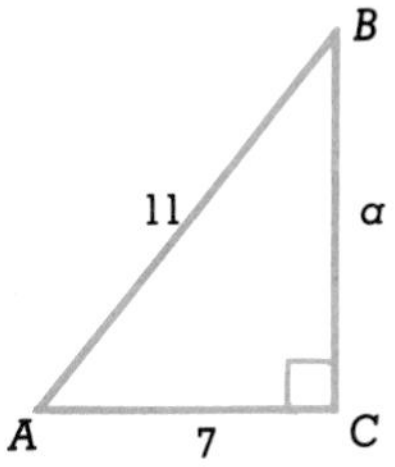

$$a^2 + 7^2 = 11^2$$
$$a^2 = 72$$
$$a = \sqrt{72}$$
$$\sin A = \frac{\sqrt{72}}{11}$$
$\sin A = 0.7714$ The sine of angle A is about 0.7714.

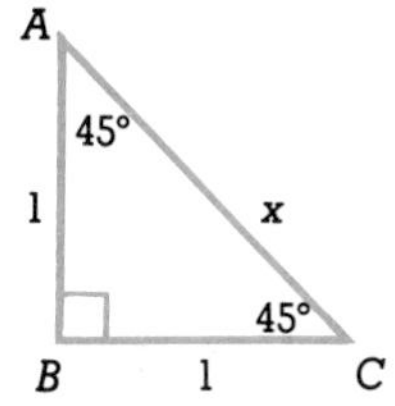

Consider two special right triangles. Triangle ABC is an isosceles right triangle. Assume the congruent sides are each 1 unit long. Use the Pythagorean Theorem to find the length of the hypotenuse.

$$1^2 + 1^2 = x^2$$
$$2 = x^2$$
$\sqrt{2} = x$ The hypotenuse is $\sqrt{2}$ units long.

Now, write the values of the trigonometric functions.

$\sin 45° = \frac{1}{\sqrt{2}}$ or $\frac{\sqrt{2}}{2}$ $\tan 45° = \frac{1}{1}$ or 1 $\sec 45° = \frac{\sqrt{2}}{1}$ or $\sqrt{2}$

$\cos 45° = \frac{1}{\sqrt{2}}$ or $\frac{\sqrt{2}}{2}$ $\csc 45° = \frac{\sqrt{2}}{1}$ or $\sqrt{2}$ $\cot 45° = \frac{1}{1}$ or 1

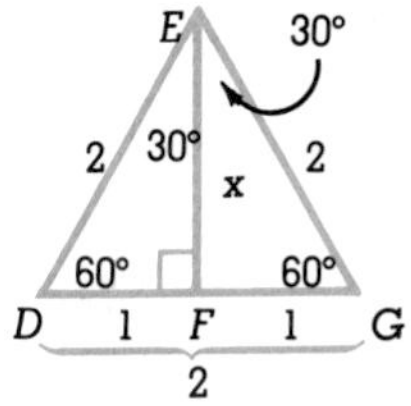

Triangle DEG is an equilateral triangle. Assume each side is 2 units long. The altitude EF forms a triangle whose angle measurements are 30°, 60°, and 90°. Since altitude EF is the perpendicular bisector of side DG, the length of side DF is 1. Find the length of side EF.

$$x^2 + 1^2 = 2^2$$
$$x^2 = 3$$
$x = \sqrt{3}$ Side EF is $\sqrt{3}$ units long.

Now, write the trigonometric values.

$\sin 30° = \frac{1}{2}$ $\sec 30° = \frac{2}{\sqrt{3}}$ or $\frac{2\sqrt{3}}{3}$ $\tan 60° = \frac{\sqrt{3}}{1}$ or $\sqrt{3}$

$\cos 30° = \frac{\sqrt{3}}{2}$ $\cot 30° = \frac{\sqrt{3}}{1}$ or $\sqrt{3}$ $\csc 60° = \frac{2}{\sqrt{3}}$ or $\frac{2\sqrt{3}}{3}$

$\tan 30° = \frac{1}{\sqrt{3}}$ or $\frac{\sqrt{3}}{3}$ $\sin 60° = \frac{\sqrt{3}}{2}$ $\sec 60° = \frac{2}{1}$ or 2

$\csc 30° = \frac{2}{1}$ or 2 $\cos 60° = \frac{1}{2}$ $\cot 60° = \frac{1}{\sqrt{3}}$ or $\frac{\sqrt{3}}{3}$

exercises

Max: 1–9, 1–35; **Avg:** 1–9, 1–35 odds; **Min:** 1–35 odds

Exploratory For each triangle, give the sines of both acute angles. State each answer in fraction form.

1. 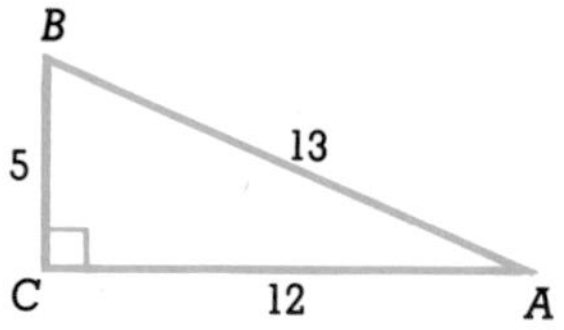

2. 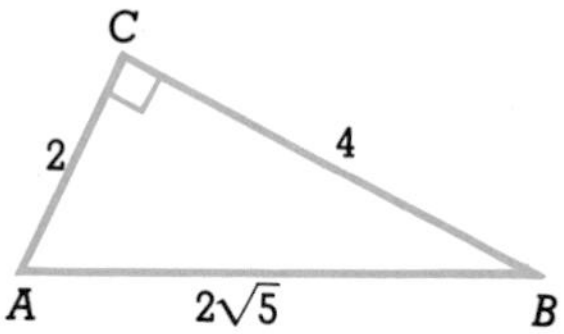

3. 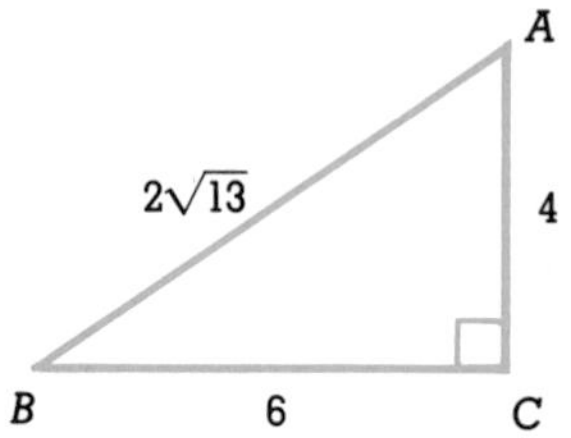

For answers to problems 1–9, see the Teacher's Guide.

4–6. Give the cosines of both acute angles in problems **1–3**.

7–9. Give the tangents of both acute angles in problems **1–3**.

Written Find each value to the nearest four decimal places.

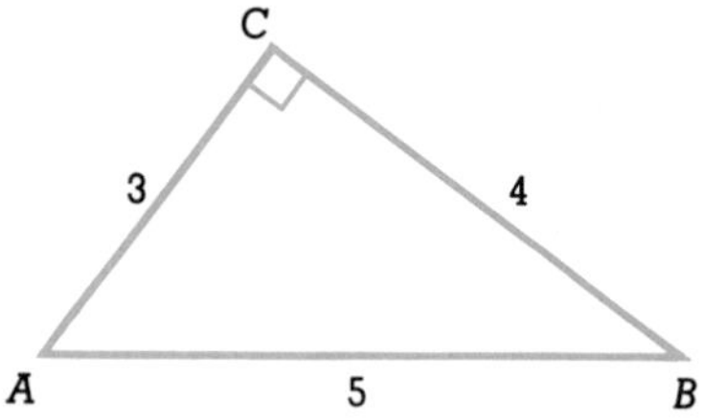

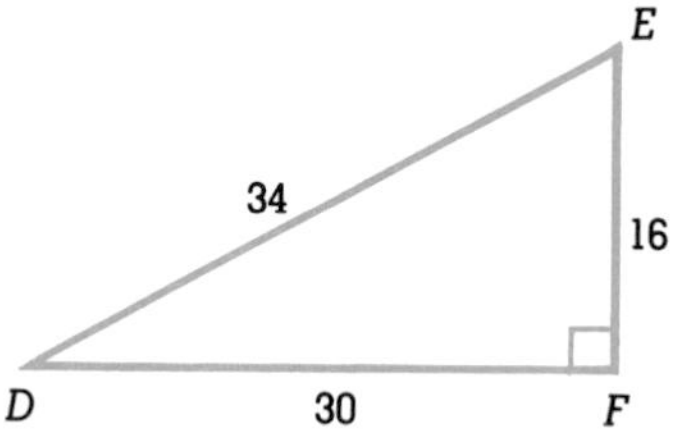

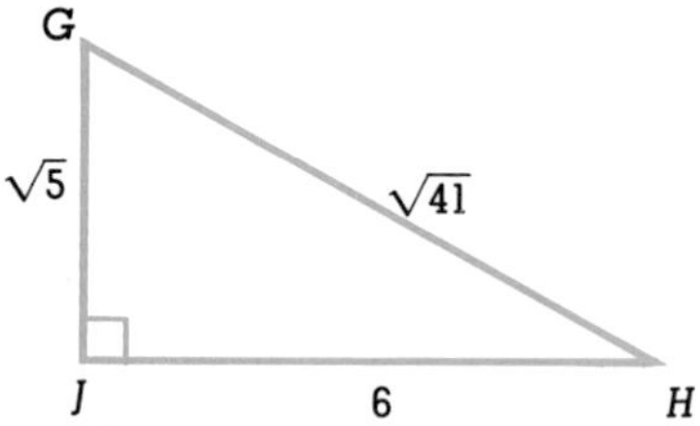

1. sin A 0.8000	**2.** cos A 0.6000	**3.** tan A 1.3333	**4.** sin B 0.6000
5. cos B 0.8000	**6.** tan B 0.7500	**7.** sin D 0.4706	**8.** sin E 0.8824
9. cos D 0.8824	**10.** cos E 0.4706	**11.** tan D 0.5333	**12.** tan E 1.8750
13. cos G 0.3492	**14.** tan G 2.6833	**15.** sin G 0.9370	**16.** cot G 0.3727
17. tan H 0.3727	**18.** sin H 0.3492	**19.** cot B 1.3333	**20.** sec D 1.1333
21. csc H 2.8636	**22.** csc A 1.2500	**23.** sec E 2.1250	**24.** cot A 0.7500

For each triangle, find sin A, cos A, and tan A to the nearest four decimal places. See below.

25. 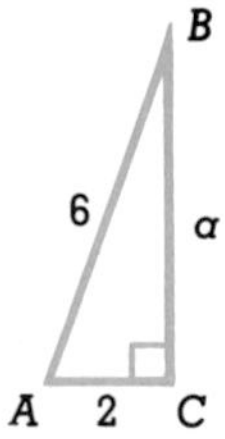

26. 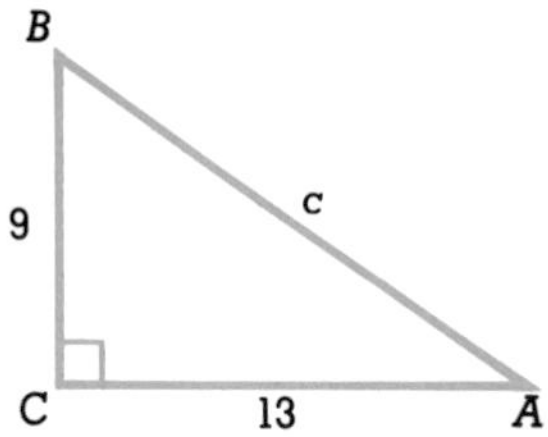

27. 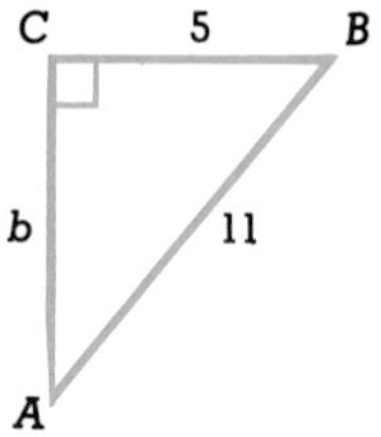

Find the value of each expression. Write each answer in fraction form.

28. $2 \cos 30°$ $\sqrt{3}$

29. $^{-}\sin 60°$ $^{-}\sqrt{3}/2$

30. $\sin^2 45° + \cos^2 45°$ 1

31. $2 \sin 60° \cos 60°$ $\sqrt{3}/2$

32. $\cos^2 30° - \sin^2 30°$ $\frac{1}{2}$

33. $\sin 30° \cos 60° - \sin 60° \cos 30°$ $-\frac{1}{2}$

34. $\csc 45° - \sec 30°$ $(3\sqrt{2} - 2\sqrt{3})/3$

35. $\sec 60° + \cot 30°$ $2 + \sqrt{3}$

25. 0.9428, 0.3333, 2.8284 **26.** 0.5692, 0.8222, 0.6923 **27.** 0.4545, 0.8907, 0.5103

17-2 Trigonometric Tables

Objective: To use trigonometric tables.

Decimal approximations for values of trigonometric functions are given in the back of this book. Angles with measurements from 0° to 90° at intervals of ten minutes are provided. Part of the table of values is shown below.

Degrees are separated into minutes. Sixty minutes are equivalent to one degree. Thus, for example $1\frac{1}{2}$ degrees can be expressed as 1 degree 30 minutes, and is abbreviated 1°30′.

Values of Trigonometric Functions

Angle	Sin	Cos	Tan	Cot	Sec	Csc	
27°00′	0.4540	0.8910	0.5095	1.963	1.122	2.203	63°00′
10′	0.4566	0.8897	0.5132	1.949	1.124	2.190	50′
20′	0.4592	0.8884	0.5169	1.935	1.126	2.178	40′
30′	0.4617	0.8870	0.5206	1.921	1.127	2.166	30′
40′	0.4643	0.8857	0.5243	1.907	1.129	2.154	20′
50′	0.4669	0.8843	0.5280	1.894	1.131	2.142	10′
28°00′	0.4695	0.8829	0.5317	1.881	1.133	2.130	62°00′
10′	0.4720	0.8816	0.5354	1.868	1.134	2.118	50′
20′	0.4746	0.8802	0.5392	1.855	1.136	2.107	40′
30′	0.4772	0.8788	0.5430	1.842	1.138	2.096	30′
40′	[illegible]	[illegible]	[illegible]	[illegible]	[illegible]	[illegible]	[illegible]

Angle measurements from 0°00′ to 45°00′ are listed on the left-hand side of the table. Use the column headings at the top along with angle measurements by reading *down* the left-hand side. For example, cos 27°10′ = 0.8897.

Angle measurements from 45°00′ to 90°00′ are listed on the right-hand side of the table. Use the column headings at the bottom along with angle measurements by reading *up* the right-hand side. For example, cos 54°30′ = 0.5807.

examples

1 **Find tan 31°40′.**

Since 31°40′ is found on the left side of the table, use tan on the top of the table. Look below tan and to the right of 31°40′.

tan 31°40′ = 0.6168   Therefore, tan 31°40′ is about 0.6168.

2 **Round 55°12′ to the nearest 10 minutes. Then find an approximate value for sin 55°12′.**

12 rounded to the nearest tens place is 10. Thus, 55°12′ rounded to the nearest 10 minutes is 55°10′. Since 55°10′ is on the right side of the table, use sin on the bottom of the table. Look above sin and to the left of 55°10′.

sin 55°10′ = 0.8208

Therefore, sin 55°12′ is about 0.8208.

Sometimes you may wish to approximate a trigonometric value for an angle whose measurement is between consecutive entries in the table. In such a case, use **interpolation.** For example, suppose you wish to find sin 28°23′. Use the table to find sin 28°20′ and sin 28°30′.

10′ [3′ [sin 28°20′ = 0.4746] d
sin 28°23′ = unknown]
sin 28°30′ = 0.4772] 0.0026

d stands for the difference between 0.4746 and the unknown value.

Then set up a proportion and solve for *d*.

$$\frac{3}{10} = \frac{d}{0.0026}$$

$$10d = 3(0.0026)$$

$$10d = 0.0078$$

$$d = 0.00078$$

or 0.0008

The table gives the values to the nearest four decimal places. Therefore, round the value for d to four decimal places.

Add 0.0008 to the value of sin 28°20′.

sin 28°23′ = 0.4746 + 0.0008 or 0.4754

The value of sin 28°23′ is about 0.4754.

example 3

Find cot 31°47′.

10′ [7′ [cot 31°40′ = 1.621] d
cot 31°47′ = unknown]
cot 31°50′ = 1.611] $^{-}0.010$

$$\frac{7}{10} = \frac{d}{^{-}0.010}$$

$$10d = 7(^{-}0.010)$$

$$10d = {^{-}0.070}$$

$$d = {^{-}0.007}$$

cot 31°47′ = 1.621 − 0.007 or 1.614

The value of cot 31°47′ is about 1.614.

example 4

Let sin x = 0.7820. Find the value of x to the nearest minute.

$$10' \left[d \left[\begin{array}{l} \sin 51°20' = 0.7808 \\ \sin x \quad\;\; = 0.7820 \end{array} \right. \right. \begin{array}{l} \left. \right] 0.0012 \end{array}$$
$$\sin 51°30' = 0.7826 \qquad 0.0018$$

$$\frac{d}{10} = \frac{0.0012}{0.0018}$$
$$0.0018d = 0.0120$$
$$d = 6.66$$
$$\approx 7 \qquad \textit{Round to the nearest whole number.}$$
$$x \approx 51°21' + 7' \text{ or } 51°27'$$

The value of x is about 51°27′.

exercises

Max: 1–16, 1–35; Avg: 1–16, 1–35 odds; Min: 1–35 odds

Exploratory **Use the table to find each trigonometric value.**

1. sin 42° 0.6691	**2.** cos 81° 0.1564	**3.** sin 68° 0.9272	**4.** tan 5° 0.0875
5. tan 89°50′ 343.7737	**6.** cos 42°20′ 0.7392	**7.** tan 49°30′ 1.1708	**8.** sin 3°10′ 0.0552

Round each angle measurement to the nearest 10 minutes. Then approximate each value.

9. cos 63°18′ 0.4488	**10.** tan 77°14′ 4.3897	**11.** sin 73°46′ 0.9605	**12.** cos 73°58′ 0.2756
13. cos 18°2′ 0.9511	**14.** tan 43°51′ 0.9601	**15.** sin 27°18′ 0.4592	**16.** sin 53°43′ 0.8056

These answers were computed by calculator.
Interpolation answers may differ by ±0.0001.

Written **Approximate each trigonometric value. Use interpolation when necessary.**

1. cos 38° 0.7880	**2.** tan 71°10′ 2.932	**3.** sin 68°13′ 0.9286	**4.** tan 42°51′ 0.9276
5. sin 46°20′ 0.7234	**6.** tan 85°16′ 12.077	**7.** tan 77°19′ 4.443	**8.** sin 38°15′ 0.6191
9. cos 59°10′ 0.5125	**10.** sin 79°42′ 0.9839	**11.** tan 88°52′ 50.55	**12.** sec 47°10′ 1.471
13. csc 33°33′ 1.809	**14.** cot 44°44′ 1.009	**15.** tan 55°55′ 1.478	**16.** sec 11°11′ 1.020
17. csc 32°18′ 1.871	**18.** cot 47°18′ 0.9228	**19.** tan 42°42′ 0.9228	**20.** sin 66°42′ 0.9184

Find x to the nearest minute.

21. cos x = 0.5132 59°7′	**22.** tan x = 1.705 59°36′	**23.** sin x = 0.3291 19°13′
24. tan x = 0.3147 17°28′	**25.** cos x = 0.7193 44°	**26.** sin x = 0.1111 6°22′
27. tan x = 0.2222 12°31′	**28.** cos x = 0.3333 70°32′	**29.** sin x = 0.8081 53°54′
30. tan x = 42.71 88°39′	**31.** csc x = 1.4129 45°3′	**32.** cot x = 0.1234 82°58′
33. sec x = 1.319 40°42′	**34.** csc x = 1.319 49°18′	**35.** cot x = 1.384 35°51′

Finance Charges

Some credit card companies base their finance charges on the beginning or the ending balances. However, many use computers and charge on the *average daily balance*. In this way, finance charges are assessed on the amount owed for the time that it is owed.

Example Find the average daily balance for which finance charges would be assessed for the bill below.

The dates listed go from one transaction to the next.

Transaction No.	Description	Date	Charges	Payment
455487983-1	Previous Balance	6/1	$200.00	
457-06-050302	Go Tane Gas	6/7	$10.00	
471-45-7564-3	payment	6/15	Thanks	$30.00
477 43 7493 4	Rx Drugs	6/20	$15.00	

Closing Date 6/30 Acct. Number 437586 Pay by 7/15

What is the amount owed from 6/1 through 6/6? $200

Multiply this amount by the number of days. $200 \times 6 = 1200$

What is the amount owed from 6/7 through 6/14? $210

Multiply this amount by the number of days. $210 \times 8 = 1680$

What is the amount owed from 6/15 through 6/19? $180

Multiply this amount by the number of days. $180 \times 5 = 900$

What is the amount owed from 6/20 through 6/30? $195

Multiply this amount by the number of days. $195 \times 11 = 2145$

What is the total of the products? $5925

Divide this number by the total number of days. $5925 \div 30 = 197.50$

The finance charge is computed on this amount. The interest rate is 1.5%.

$197.50 \times 1.5\% = 197.50 \times 0.015$ or about $2.96 *finance charge*

Exercise Find the finance charge on the bill above if the payment had been made on 6/10 instead of 6/15. $2.89

17-3 Solving Right Triangles

Objective: To solve problems using right triangle trigonometry.

Trigonometric functions can be used to solve problems involving right triangles.

examples

1 **Find the values of a and b in the right triangle.**

$\frac{a}{14} = \sin 42°$

$\frac{a}{14} = 0.6691$

$a = 9.4$ *Round to the nearest tenth.*

$\frac{b}{14} = \cos 42°$

$\frac{b}{14} = 0.7431$

$b = 10.4$ *Round to the nearest tenth.*

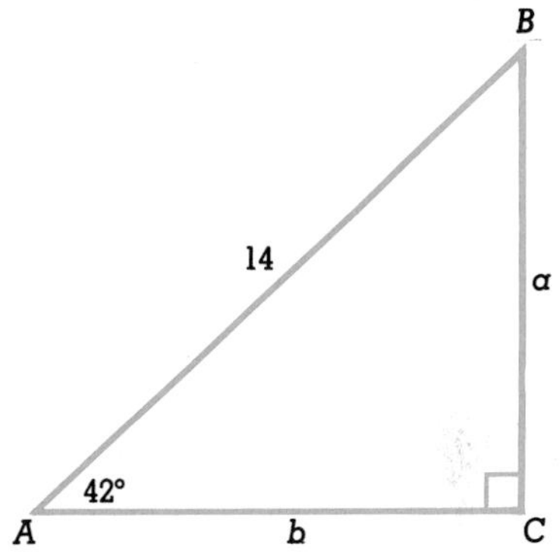

Therefore, $a = 9.4$ and $b = 10.4$.

2 **Solve the right triangle.** *To solve a right triangle means to find all the measures of the sides and angles.*

$49° + B = 90°$ *Angles A and B are complementary.*

$B = 41°$

$\frac{7}{c} = \sin 49°$

$\frac{7}{c} = 0.7547$

$7 = 0.7547c$

$c = 9.3$ *Round to the nearest tenth.*

$\frac{7}{b} = \tan 49°$

$7 = 1.150b$

$b = 6.1$ *Round to the nearest tenth.*

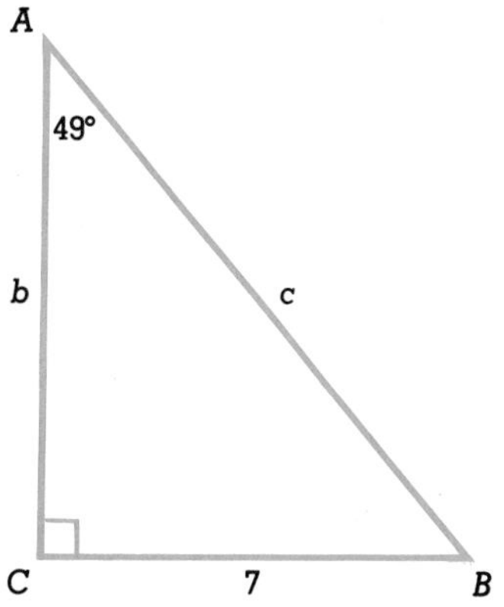

Therefore, $B = 41°$, $c = 9.3$, and $b = 6.1$.

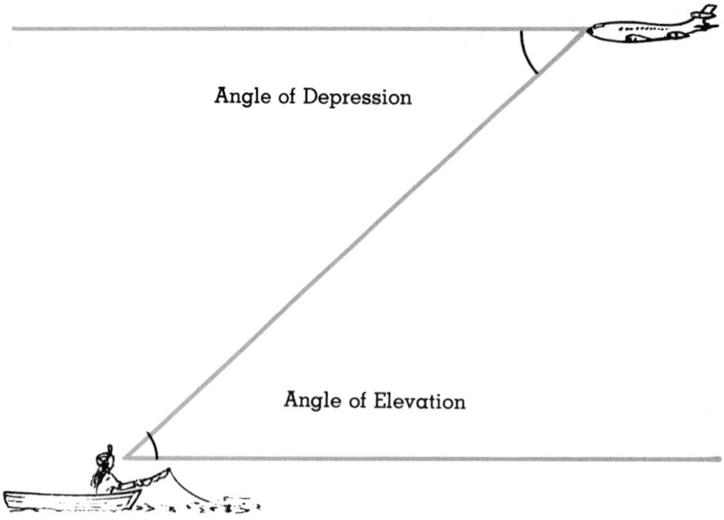

A person fishing on a lake sees a small plane flying overhead. The angle formed by her line of sight to the plane and a horizontal is called the **angle of elevation.** The angle formed by the line of sight from the pilot to the boat and a horizontal is called the **angle of depression.** The line of sight intersects two parallel lines as shown. The angles of elevation and depression are alternate interior angles and have equal measures.

examples

3 **Two hikers are 1500 meters from the base of a radio tower. The measurement of the angle of elevation to the top of the tower is 11°. How high is the tower?**

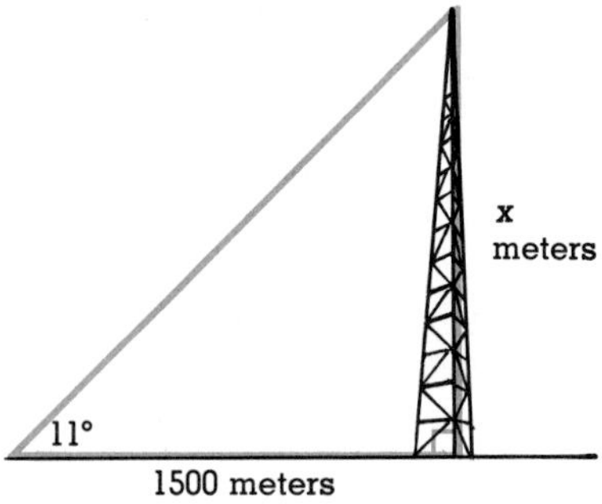

$$\frac{x}{1500} = \tan 11°$$
$$= 0.1944$$
$$x = 0.1944(1500) \text{ or } 291.6$$

The height of the tower is about 292 meters.

4 **Robert is standing on top of a 200 foot cliff above a lake. The measurement of the angle of depression to a boat on the lake is 21°. How far is the boat from the base of the cliff?**

$$\frac{200}{x} = \tan 21°$$
$$= 0.3839$$
$$0.3839x = 200$$
$$x = 521$$

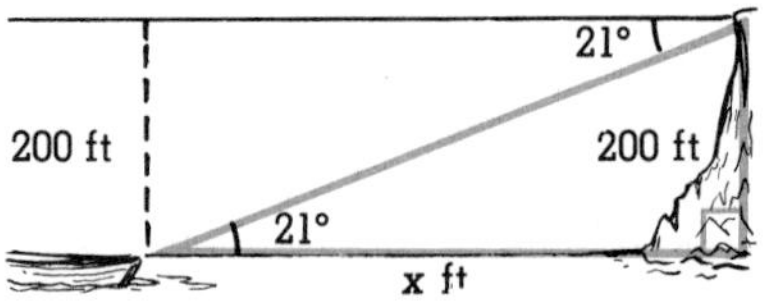

The boat is about 521 feet from the base of the cliff.

Some students may prefer to use cot in Example **4**. It makes the computation a multiplication rather than a division.

exercises

Max: 1–6, 1–23; Avg: 1–6, 1–23 odds; Min: 1–23 odds

Exploratory **State equations that would enable you to solve each problem. Use the triangle below.**

1. If $A = 15°$ and $c = 37$, find a. $\sin 15° = a/37$
2. If $A = 76°$ and $a = 13$, find b. $\tan 76° = 13/b$
3. If $A = 49°13'$ and $a = 10$, find c. $\sin 49°13' = 10/c$
4. If $a = 21.2$ and $A = 71°13'$, find b. $\tan 71°13' = 21.2/b$
5. If $a = 13$ and $B = 16°$, find c. $\cos 16° = 13/c$
6. If $A = 19°07'$ and $b = 11$, find c. $\cos 19°07' = 11/c$

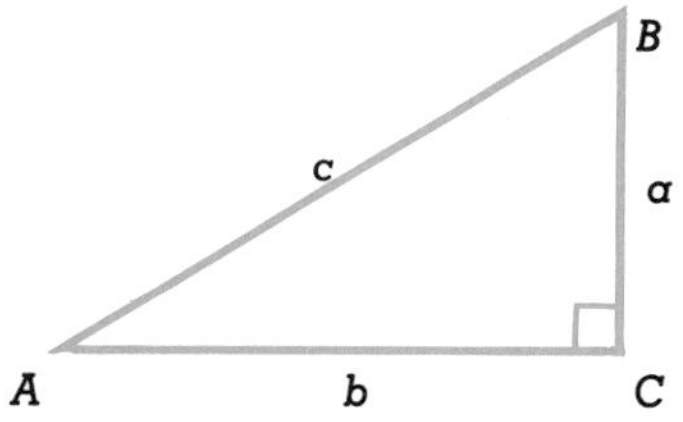

Written **Suppose triangle ABC is a right triangle. Let A and B be the acute angles, and a and b be the measures of the sides opposite these angles. The measure of the hypotenuse is c. Solve each triangle.** Round to two decimal places or the nearest minute.

1. $A = 16°$, $c = 14$
2. $A = 63°$, $a = 9.7$
3. $A = 37°15'$, $b = 11$
4. $B = 64°$, $c = 19.2$
5. $B = 42°10'$, $a = 9$
6. $B = 83°$, $b = \sqrt{31}$
7. $c = 6$, $B = 13°$
8. $a = 9$, $B = 49°$
9. $b = 42$, $A = 77°$
10. $b = 22$, $A = 22°22'$
11. $a = 33$, $B = 33°$
12. $a = 44$, $B = 44°44'$
13. $A = 55°55'$, $c = 16$
14. $B = 18°$, $a = \sqrt{15}$
15. $A = 45°$, $c = 7\sqrt{2}$

See Teacher's Guide for answers to problems 1-15.

Solve each problem. Round all answers to two decimal places.

16. At a point 30 meters from the base of a tree, the measurement of the angle of elevation is 65°. How tall is the tree? 64.34 meters
17. A flagpole casts a shadow 40 feet long when the measurement of the angle of the sun is 31°20′. How tall is the flagpole? 24.35 feet
18. The measurement of the angle of depression of an aircraft carrier from a plane 1000 feet above the water is 63°18′. How far is the plane from the carrier? 1119.36 feet
19. At ground level, the measurement of the angle of elevation of a kite is 70°. It is held by a string 65 meters long. How far is the kite above the ground? 61.08 meters
20. A 24 foot ladder leans against a building. It forms an angle with the building measuring 18°. How far is the foot of the ladder from the base of the building? 7.42 feet
21. The top of a lighthouse is 120 meters above sea level. From the top of the lighthouse, the measurement of the angle of depression of a boat at sea is 43°. Find the distance of the boat from the foot of the lighthouse. 128.68 meters
22. A tree is broken by the wind. The top touches the ground 13 meters from the base. It makes an angle with the ground measuring 29°. How tall was the tree before it was broken? 22.07 meters
23. The pilot of a plane flying 5000 feet above sea level observes two ships in line due east. The measurements of the angles of depression are 30° and 39°. How far apart are the ships? 2485.77 feet

17-4 More on Solving Right Triangles

Objective: To solve problems using right triangle trigonometry.

Trigonometric functions can be used to solve other problems involving right triangles.

examples

1 **Solve the right triangle shown below.**

$7^2 + b^2 = 16^2$ *Use the Pythagorean Theorem.*

$49 + b^2 = 256$

$b^2 = 207$

$b = 14.4$ *Round to the nearest tenth.*

$\sin A = \frac{7}{16}$

$\sin A = 0.4375$

$A = 25°57'$

$\cos B = \frac{7}{16}$

$\cos B = 0.4375$

$B = 64°3'$

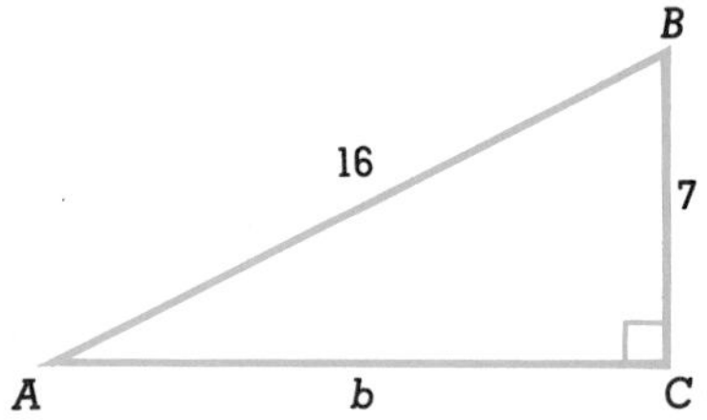

Therefore, $b = 14.4$, $A = 25°57'$, and $B = 64°3'$.

2 **A ladder 14 meters long rests against the wall of a house. The foot of the ladder rests on level ground 2 meters from the wall. What angle does the ladder form with the ground?**

$\cos x = \frac{2}{14}$

$\cos x = 0.1429$

$x = 81°47'$

The measurement of the angle is 81°47′ to the nearest minute.

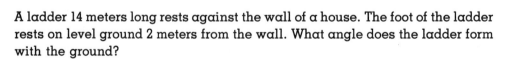

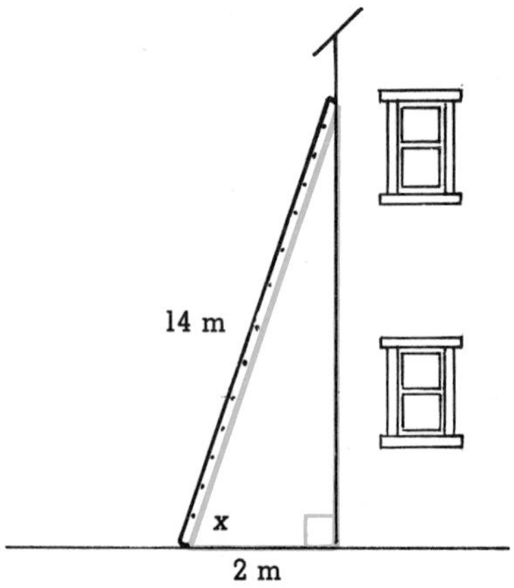

example 3

The base of a television antenna and two points on the ground are in a straight line. The two points are 100 feet apart. From the two points, the measurements of the angles of elevation to the top of the antenna are 30° and 20°. Find the height of the antenna.

$$\tan 30° = \frac{y}{x}$$

$$\tan 20° = \frac{y}{x + 100}$$

$$y = (x + 100) \tan 20°$$

$$x \tan 30° = y$$
$$= (x + 100) \tan 20°$$
$$= x \tan 20° + 100 \tan 20°$$
$$x \tan 30° - x \tan 20° = 100 \tan 20°$$
$$x (\tan 30° - \tan 20°) = 100 \tan 20°$$
$$x = \frac{100 \tan 20°}{\tan 30° - \tan 20°}$$
$$x = \frac{100(0.3640)}{0.5774 - 0.3640}$$
$$= 170.6$$

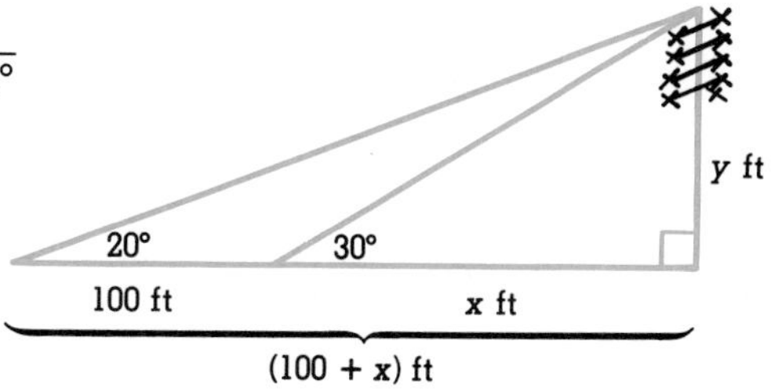

$$y = 170.6 \tan 30°$$
$$y = 170.6(0.5774)$$
$$= 98.5$$

The height is 99 feet to the nearest foot.

exercises

Max: 1–6, 1–18; **Avg:** 1–6, 1–17 odds; **Min:** 1–17 odds

Exploratory State equations you could use to solve each problem. Use the triangle below.

1. If $c = 16$ and $a = 7$, find b. $b = \sqrt{16^2 - 7^2}$
2. If $a = 10$ and $c = 20$, find b. $b = \sqrt{20^2 - 10^2}$
3. If $a = 7$ and $b = 12$, find A. $\tan A = 7/12$
4. If $a = 6$ and $c = 12$, find B. $\cos B = 6/12$
5. If $a = 3$ and $c = 7$, find A. $\sin A = 3/7$
6. If $a = 5$ and $b = 6$, find c. $c = \sqrt{5^2 + 6^2}$

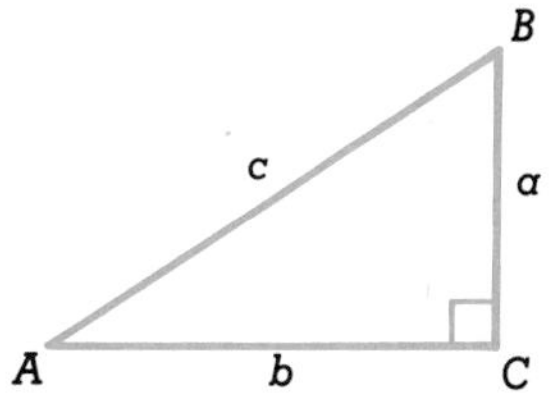

Written Suppose triangle ABC is a right triangle. Let A and B be the acute angles and a and b be the measures of the sides opposite these angles. The measure of the hypotenuse is c. Solve each triangle. Round to two decimal places or the nearest minute.

1. $a = 2$, $b = 7$ $c = 7.28$, $A = 15°56'$, $B = 74°4'$
2. $c = 10$, $a = 8$ $b = 6$, $A = 53°7'$, $B = 36°53'$
3. $c = 13$, $a = 12$ $b = 5$, $A = 67°22'$, $B = 22°38'$
4. $a = 11$, $b = 21$ $c = 23.71$, $A = 27°39'$, $B = 62°21'$
5. $b = 6$, $c = 13$ $a = 11.53$, $A = 62°30'$, $B = 27°30'$
6. $c = 21$, $b = 18$ $a = 10.82$, $A = 31°$, $B = 59°$

Solve each problem. Round all answers to two decimal places or the nearest minute.

7. In a parking garage, each floor is 20 feet apart. The ramp to each floor is 120 feet long. What is the measurement of the angle of elevation of the ramp? 9°35′

8. A railroad track rises 10 feet for every 400 feet along the track. What is the measurement of the angle the track forms with the horizontal? 1°26′

9. The measurement of the angle of elevation to the top of a building from a point on the ground is 38°20′. From a point 50 feet closer to the building, the measurement of the angle of elevation is 45°. What is the height of the building? 188.89 feet

10. Two observers 200 feet apart are in line with the base of a flagpole. The measurement of the angle of elevation of the top from one observer is 30° and from the other 60°. How far is the flagpole from each observer? 100 feet and 300 feet

11. The diagram shows square *ABCD*. The midpoint of side *AD* is *E*. Find the values of x, y, and z to the nearest minute.
$x = 63°26′$, $y = 26°34′$, $z = 63°26′$

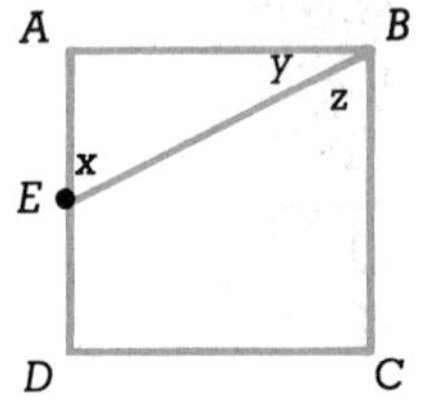

12. Two buildings are separated by an alley. Joe is looking out a window 60 feet above the ground in one building. He observes the measurement of the angle of depression of the base of the second building to be 50°, and that of the angle of elevation of the top to be 40°. How high is the second building? 102.25 feet

13. A television antenna sits atop a building. From a point 200 feet from the base of the building, the measurement of the angle of elevation of the top of the antenna is 80°. That of the angle of elevation of the bottom of the antenna from the same point is 75°. How tall is the antenna? 387.86 feet

14. The Washington Monument is 555 feet high. What is the measurement of the angle of elevation of the top when observed from a point $\frac{1}{4}$ mile from the base? (1 mile = 5280 feet) 22°48′

15. A train travels 5000 meters along a track whose angle of elevation has a measurement of 6°. How much did it rise during this distance? 522.64 meters

16. The isosceles triangle *RST* at the right has base *TS* measuring 10 centimeters and base angles each measuring 39°. Find the length of the altitude *QR*. 4.05 centimeters

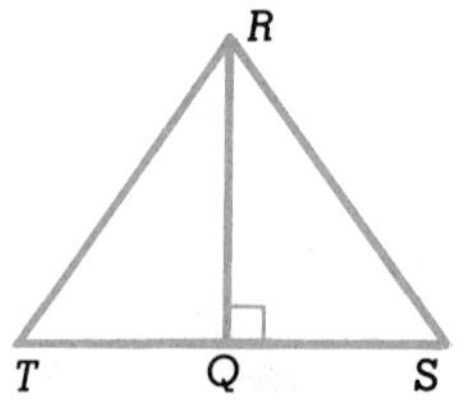

17. A pendulum 50 centimeters long is moved 40° from the vertical. How far did the tip of the pendulum rise? 11.7 centimeters

18. A ship sails due north from port for 90 kilometers, then 40 kilometers east, and then 70 kilometers north. How far is the ship from port? 164.92 kilometers

CAREERS

Civil Engineer

Jon Thomas is a civil engineer. Part of his job is to determine if machinery is being overloaded. Overloading can ruin equipment or make it wear out sooner. Sometimes, it's a potential danger to human safety.

The boom hoist shown below carries a load of 900 pounds. Jon needs to find the tension, t, in the cable and the compression, c, in the boom. To do this, he uses the following method.

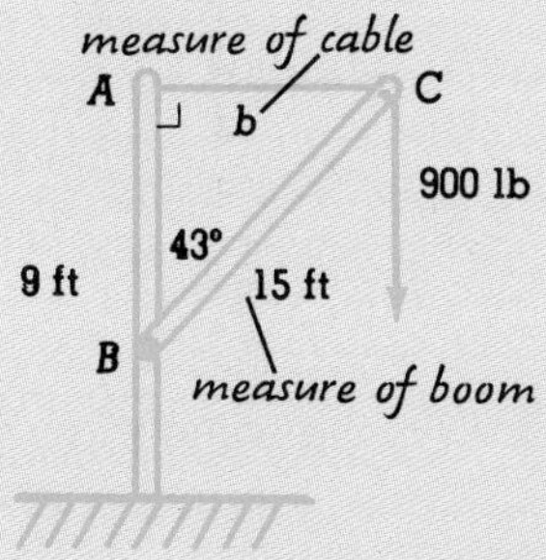

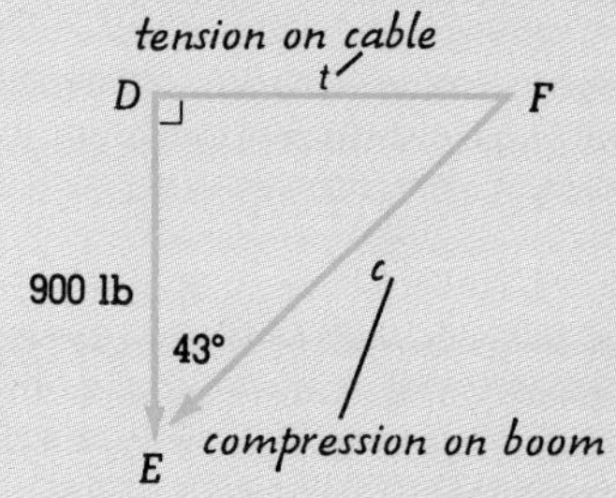

First, assume triangle ABC is a right triangle, and find b.
Use the Pythagorean Theorem.

$$\begin{aligned} b^2 &= 15^2 - 9^2 \\ &= 225 - 81 \\ &= 144 \\ b &= 12 \quad \textit{the measure of the cable} \end{aligned}$$

Since triangle ABC is similar to triangle DEF, the following proportions can be used.

$$\frac{t}{900} = \frac{12}{9} \quad \textit{since } \frac{DF}{DE} = \frac{AC}{AB}$$

$$9t = 10{,}800$$

$$t = 1200$$

The tension is 1200 pounds.

$$\frac{c}{900} = \frac{15}{9} \quad \textit{since } \frac{EF}{DE} = \frac{BC}{AB}$$

$$9c = 13{,}500$$

$$c = 1500$$

The compression is 1500 pounds.

Exercises Find the tension and compression for each of the following weights.

1. 500 pounds 667, 833

2. 1000 pounds 1333, 1667

3. 1200 pounds 1600, 2000

4. 1500 pounds 2000, 2500

Answers are to the nearest pound.

17-5 Law of Sines

Objective: To use the Law of Sines.

The trigonometric functions also can be used to solve problems involving triangles that are *not* right triangles.

Consider triangle ABC with height h units and sides with lengths a units, b units, and c units. The area of this triangle is given by area $= \frac{1}{2}bh$.

Also, $\sin A = \frac{h}{c}$.

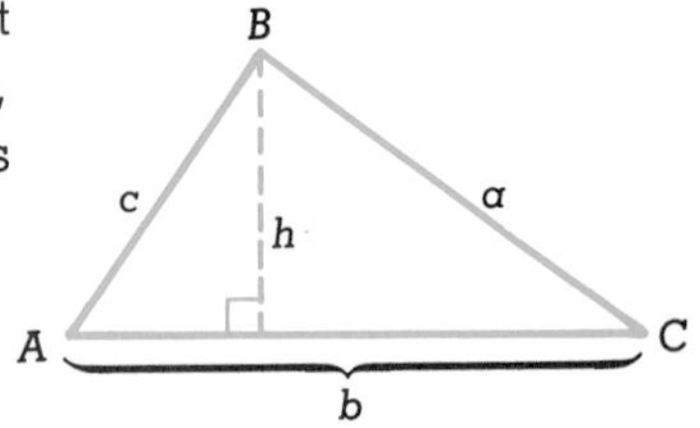

By combining these equations, you can find a new formula for the area of the triangle.

$$\text{area} = \frac{1}{2}bh$$

$$= \frac{1}{2}b(c \sin A) \qquad \sin A = \frac{h}{c}, \text{ so } h = c \sin A$$

In a similar way, you can find two other formulas for the area of a triangle.

$$\text{area} = \frac{1}{2}ac \sin B \qquad\qquad \text{area} = \frac{1}{2}ab \sin C$$

All of these formulas represent the area of the same triangle. Thus, the following must be true.

$$\frac{1}{2}bc \sin A = \frac{1}{2}ac \sin B = \frac{1}{2}ab \sin C$$

If you divide each expression by $\frac{1}{2}abc$, you obtain the **Law of Sines.**

$$\frac{\sin A}{a} = \frac{\sin B}{b} = \frac{\sin C}{c}$$

Law of Sines

Let triangle ABC be any triangle with a, b, and c representing the measures of sides opposite angles with measurements A, B, and C respectively. Then, the following equations are true.

$$\frac{\sin A}{a} = \frac{\sin B}{b} = \frac{\sin C}{c}$$

examples

1 **Find the area of triangle ABC if $a = 6$, $b = 10$, and $C = 40°$.**

$$\text{area} = \frac{1}{2}(6)(10)\sin 40°$$
$$= \frac{1}{2}(6)(10)(0.6428)$$
$$= 19.284$$ To the nearest whole unit, the area is 19 square units.

2 **Solve the triangle on the right.**

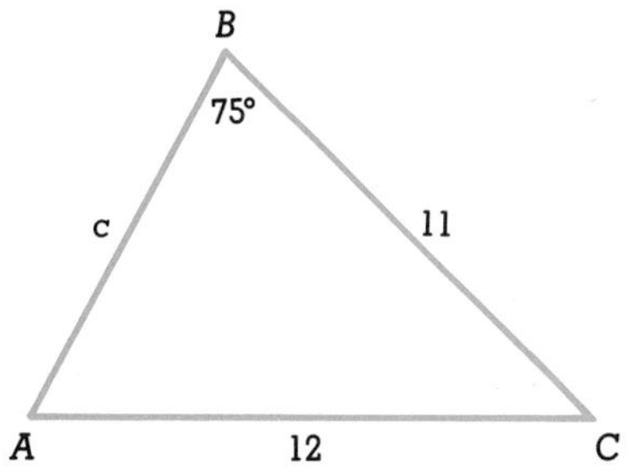

$$\frac{\sin A}{11} = \frac{\sin 75°}{12}$$
$$\sin A = \frac{11 \sin 75°}{12}$$
$$= \frac{11(0.9659)}{12}$$
$$= 0.8854$$
$$A = 62°18'$$

$$62°18' + 75° + C = 180°$$
$$C = 42°42'$$

$$\frac{\sin 42°42'}{c} = \frac{\sin 75°}{12}$$
$$c = \frac{12 \sin 42°42'}{\sin 75°}$$
$$= \frac{12(0.6781)}{(0.9659)}$$
$$= 8.4$$ Therefore, A is $62°18'$, C is $42°42'$, and c is 8.4.

3 **A surveyor measures a benchmark 440 meters long. She takes bearings of a landmark C from A and B and finds that $A = 48°$ and $B = 75°$. Find the distance from A to C.**

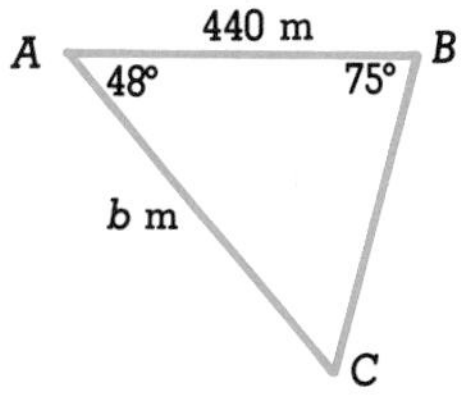

$$48° + 75° + C = 180°$$
$$C = 180° - 48° - 75°$$
$$= 57°$$

$$\frac{\sin 75°}{b} = \frac{\sin 57°}{440}$$
$$b = \frac{440 \sin 75°}{\sin 57°}$$
$$= 506.7$$ To the nearest meter, the distance is 507 meters.

exercises

Max: 1–8, 1–18; Avg: 1–8, 1–17 odds; Min: 1–17 odds

Exploratory State an equation that would enable you to find the area of each triangle.

1. $a = 10$, $b = 17$, $C = 46°$ Area $= \frac{1}{2}ab \sin C$
2. $b = 15$, $c = 20$, $A = 63°$ Area $= \frac{1}{2}bc \sin A$
3. $a = 15$, $b = 30$, $C = 90°$ Area $= \frac{1}{2}ab \sin C$
4. $a = 6$, $c = 4$, $B = 52°$ Area $= \frac{1}{2}ac \sin B$

State an equation that would enable you to solve each triangle described below.

5. If $b = 10$, $a = 14$, and $A = 50°$, find B. $(\sin 50°)/14 = (\sin B)/10$
6. If $A = 40°$, $B = 60°$, and $a = 20$, find b. $(\sin 40°)/20 = (\sin 60°)/b$
7. If $b = 2.8$, $A = 53°$, and $B = 61°$, find a. $(\sin 53°)/a = (\sin 61°)/2.8$
8. If $b = 16$, $c = 12$, and $B = 42°$, find C. $(\sin 42°)/16 = (\sin C)/12$

Written Find the area of each triangle described below.

1. $a = 12$, $b = 12$, $C = 50°$ 55.16
2. $a = 15$, $b = 22$, $C = 90°$ 165
3. $b = 11.5$, $c = 14$, $A = 20°$ 27.53
4. $a = 11$, $c = 5$, $B = 50°6'$ 21.1

5. $C = 74°$, $b = 8.89$, $c = 10.19$ 6. $B = 42°18'$, $C = 92°42'$, $c = 117.25$ 7. $B = 60°19'$, $C = 36°31'$, $c = 47.57$

Solve each triangle described below.

5. $a = 8$, $A = 49°$, $B = 57°$
6. $A = 45°$, $a = 83$, $b = 79$
7. $A = 83°10'$, $a = 80$, $b = 70$
8. $A = 40°$, $B = 60°$, $c = 20$
9. $B = 70°$, $C = 58°$, $a = 84$
10. $A = 30°$, $C = 70°$, $c = 8$

8. $C = 80°$, $a = 13.05$, $b = 17.59$ 9. $A = 52°$, $b = 100.17$, $c = 90.4$ 10. $B = 80°$, $a = 4.26$, $b = 8.38$

Solve each problem. Round all answers to two decimal places.

11. An isosceles triangle has a base of 22 centimeters and a vertex angle measuring 36°. Find its perimeter. 93.19 centimeters
12. A triangular lot faces two streets which meet at an angle measuring 85°. The sides of the lot facing the street are each 160 feet in length. Find the perimeter of the lot. 536.19 feet
13. Two planes leave an airport at the same time. Each flies at a speed of 110 miles per hour. One flies in the direction 60° east of north. The other flies in the direction 40° east of south. How far apart are the planes after 3 hours? 424.24 miles
14. A building 60 feet tall is on top of a hill. A surveyor is at a point on the hill and observes the angle of elevation to the top of the building has measurement 42° and to the bottom of the building has measurement 18°. How far is the surveyor from the bottom of the building? 109.70 feet

For answers to problems **15–18**, see the Teacher's Guide.

Use the Law of Sines to show that each statement is true.

15. $\dfrac{a-c}{c} = \dfrac{\sin A - \sin C}{\sin C}$
16. $\dfrac{b+c}{b-c} = \dfrac{\sin B + \sin C}{\sin B - \sin C}$
17. $\dfrac{a}{b} = \dfrac{\sin A}{\sin B}$
18. $\dfrac{b}{a+b} = \dfrac{\sin B}{\sin A + \sin B}$

17-6 Law of Cosines

Objective: To use the Law of Cosines.

If you are given two sides and the included angle or three sides of a triangle, the Law of Sines will not enable you to solve the triangle. Another formula is needed.

Consider triangle *ABC* with height measuring *h* units and sides with lengths *a* units, *b* units, and *c* units. Suppose segment *AD* is *x* units long. Then segment *DC* is $(b - x)$ units long.

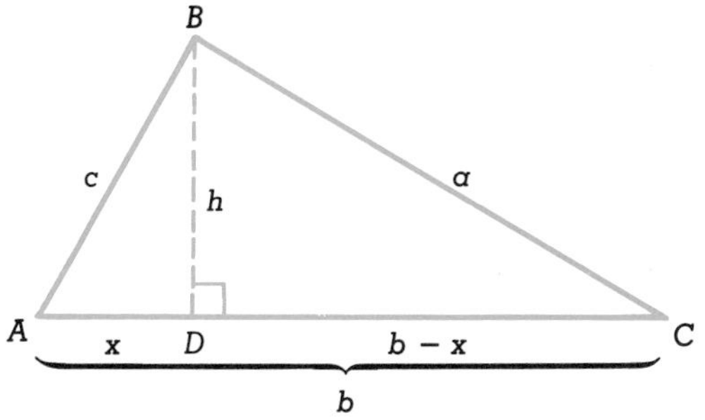

Use the Pythagorean Theorem and the definition of the cosine function to find how *A*, *a*, *b*, and *c* are related.

$a^2 = (b - x)^2 + h^2$	*Use the Pythagorean Theorem.*
$= b^2 - 2bx + x^2 + h^2$	*Expand* $(b - x)^2$.
$= b^2 - 2bx + c^2$	$c^2 = x^2 + h^2$.
$= b^2 - 2b(c \cos A) + c^2$	$\cos A = \frac{x}{c}$ *so* $x = c \cos A$.
$= b^2 + c^2 - 2bc \cos A$	

In a similar way, you can find two other formulas relating the lengths of sides to the cosine of *B* and *C*. All three formulas, the **Law of Cosines,** can be summarized as follows.

Law of Cosines

Let triangle *ABC* be any triangle with *a*, *b*, and *c* representing the measures of sides opposite angles with measurements *A*, *B*, and *C* respectively. Then, the following equations are true.

$$a^2 = b^2 + c^2 - 2bc \cos A$$
$$b^2 = a^2 + c^2 - 2ac \cos B$$
$$c^2 = a^2 + b^2 - 2ab \cos C$$

Use the Law of Cosines to solve a triangle in the following cases.

1. To find the length of the third side of any triangle if the lengths of two sides and the measurement of the included angle are given.
2. To find the measurement of an angle of a triangle if the lengths of three sides are given.

examples

1

Solve the triangle where $A = 35°$, $b = 16$, and $c = 19$.

$$\begin{aligned} a^2 &= 16^2 + 19^2 - 2(16)(19)\cos 35° \quad \text{Use the Law of Cosines.} \\ &= 16^2 + 19^2 - 2(16)(19)(0.8192) \\ &= 118.93 \\ a &= 10.9 \end{aligned}$$

$$\frac{\sin 35°}{10.9} = \frac{\sin B}{16} \quad \text{Use the Law of Sines.}$$

$$\begin{aligned} \sin B &= \frac{16 \sin 35°}{10.9} \\ &= \frac{16(0.5736)}{10.9} \\ &= 0.8420 \\ B &= 57°21' \end{aligned}$$

$$\begin{aligned} 35° + 57°21' + C &= 180° \\ C &= 180° - 35° - 57°21' \\ &= 87°39' \end{aligned}$$

Therefore, $a = 10.9$, $B = 57°21'$, and $C = 87°39'$.

2

Solve the triangle where $a = 11$, $b = 13$, and $c = 15$.

$$\begin{aligned} 11^2 &= 13^2 + 15^2 - 2(13)(15)\cos A \quad \text{Use the Law of Cosines.} \\ 2(13)(15)\cos A &= 13^2 + 15^2 - 11^2 \\ \cos A &= \frac{13^2 + 15^2 - 11^2}{2(13)(15)} \\ &= 0.7000 \\ A &= 45°34' \end{aligned}$$

$$\frac{\sin 45°34'}{11} = \frac{\sin B}{13} \quad \text{Use the Law of Sines.}$$

$$\begin{aligned} \sin B &= \frac{13 \sin 45°34'}{11} \\ &= \frac{13(0.7141)}{11} \\ &= 0.8439 \\ B &= 57°33' \end{aligned}$$

$$\begin{aligned} 45°34' + 57°33' + C &= 180° \\ C &= 180° - 45°34' - 57°33' \\ &= 76°53' \end{aligned}$$

Therefore, $A = 45°34'$, $B = 57°33'$, and $C = 76°53'$.

exercises

Max: 1–10, 1–20; Avg: 1–10, 1–19 odds; Min: 1–19 odds

Exploratory In each of the following, three parts of a triangle are given. Determine whether the Law of Sines or the Law of Cosines would be used first to solve the triangle.

1. $A = 40°, b = 6, c = 7$ cos
2. $a = 10, A = 40°, c = 8$ sin
3. $a = 14, b = 15, c = 16$ cos
4. $A = 40°, C = 70°, c = 14$ sin
5. $C = 35°, a = 11, b = 10.5$ cos
6. $c = 21, a = 14, B = 60°$ cos
7. $c = 10.3, a = 21\frac{1}{2}, b = 16.71$ cos
8. $b = 17, B = 42°58', a = 11$ sin
9. $c = 14.1, A = 29°, b = 7.6$ cos
10. $A = 28°50', b = 5, c = 4.9$ cos

Written Solve each triangle.

1. $a = 140, b = 185, c = 166$
2. $A = 51°, b = 40, c = 45$
3. $a = 5, b = 6, c = 7$
4. $a = 5, b = 12, c = 13$
5. $a = 20, c = 24, B = 47°$
6. $b = 13, a = 21.5, C = 39°20'$
7. $A = 40°, B = 59°, c = 14$
8. $B = 19°, a = 51, c = 61$
9. $a = 345, b = 648, c = 442$
10. $A = 25°26', a = 13.7, B = 78°$

9. $A = 29°59', B = 110°14', C = 39°47'$
10. $a = 2.47, B = 77°50', C = 73°20'$

Solve each problem.

11. A triangular plot of land has two sides which have length 400 feet and 600 feet. The measurement of the angle between those sides is 46°20′. Find its perimeter and area. 1434.26 feet, 86,804.28 square feet

12. The sides of a triangular city lot have length 50 meters, 70 meters, and 85 meters. Find the measurement of the angle opposite the short side. 36°01′

14. 349.7 nautical miles

13. A pilot is flying from Chicago to Columbus, a distance of 300 miles. He starts his flight 15° off course and flies on this course for 75 miles. How far is he from Columbus and by how much must he correct his error to be on course?

14. Two ships leave San Francisco at the same time. One travels 40° west of north at a speed of 20 knots. The other travels 10° west of south at a speed of 15 knots. How far apart are they after 11 hours? (1 knot = 1 nautical mile per hour)

15. A ship at sea is 70 miles from one radio transmitter and 130 miles from another. The measurement of the angle between the signals is 130°. How far apart are the transmitters? 183.03 miles

16. A 40 foot television antenna stands on top of a building. From a point on the ground, the angles of elevation of the top and bottom of the antenna, respectively have measurements of 56° and 42°. How tall is the building? 139.113 feet

13. 228.38 miles, 19°52′

For answers to problems **17–20**, see the Teacher's Guide.

Show that each statement is true.

17. $c^2 = a^2 + b^2 - 2ab \cos C$
18. $b^2 = a^2 + c^2 - 2ac \cos B$
19. $1 - \cos A = \dfrac{(a - b + c)(a + b - c)}{2bc}$
20. $1 + \cos A = \dfrac{(a + b + c)(b + c - a)}{2bc}$

1. $A = 46°37', B = 73°52', C = 59°31'$ 2. $a = 36.87, B = 57°28', C = 71°32'$
3. $A = 44°25', B = 57°7', C = 78°28'$ 4. $A = 22°37', B = 67°23', C = 90°$
5. $A = 54°41', b = 17.92, C = 78°19'$ 6. $B = 35°45', A = 104°55', c = 14.1$
7. $a = 9.11, b = 12.15, C = 81°$ 8. $b = 20.95, A = 52°25', C = 108°35'$

17-7 Examining Solutions

Objective: To solve triangles.

When the lengths of two sides of a triangle and the measurement of the angle opposite one of them is given, one solution does not always exist. In such a case, one of the following will be true.

1. No triangle exists.
2. Exactly one triangle exists.
3. Two triangles exist.

In other words, there may be no solution, one solution, or two solutions.

Suppose you are given a, b, and A. Consider the case where $A < 90°$.

If $a = b \sin A$, the solution is a right triangle.

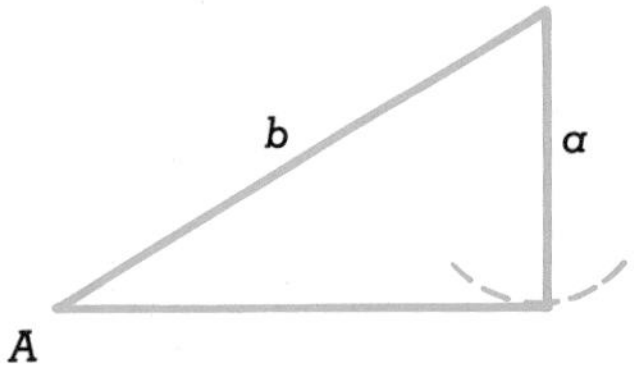

If $a = b \sin A$, one solution exists.

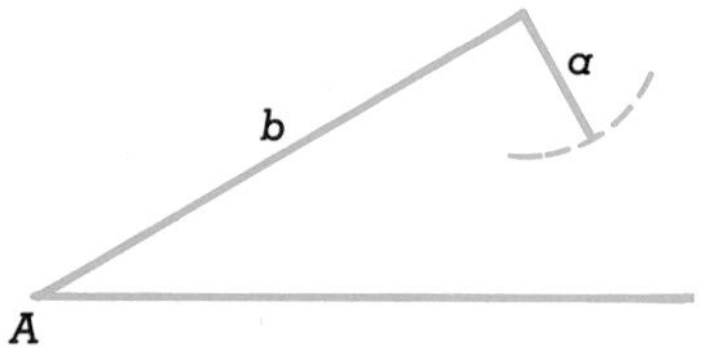

If $a < b \sin A$, no solution exists.

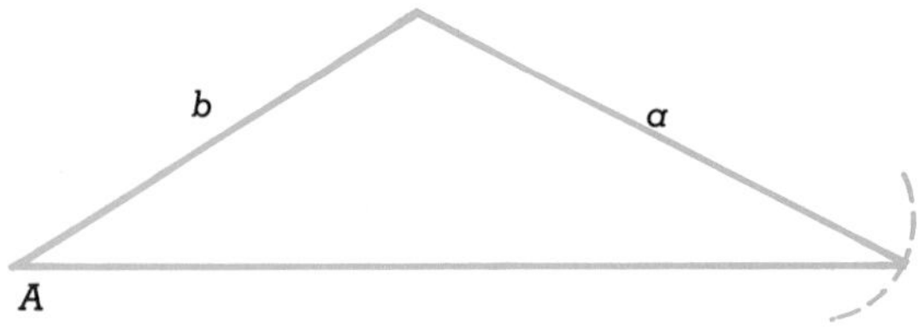

If $a > b \sin A$ and $a > b$, one solution exists

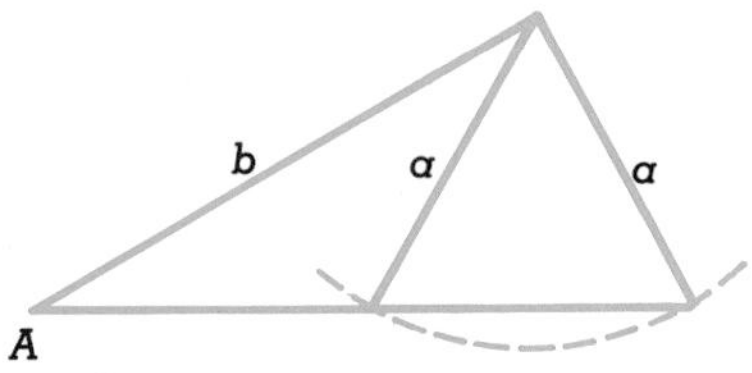

If $b \sin A < a < b$, two solutions exist.

Consider the case where $A \geq 90°$.

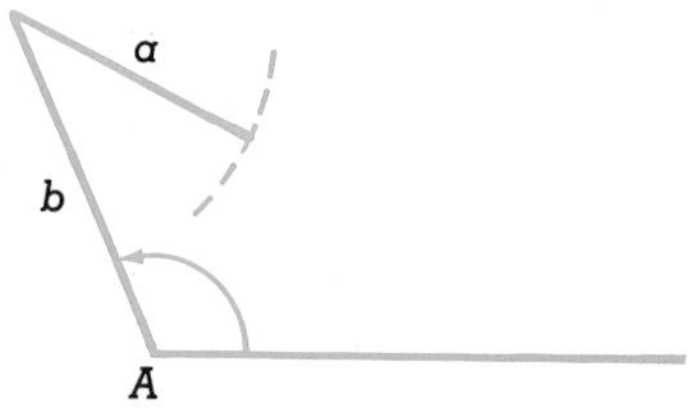

If $a \leq b$, no solution exists.

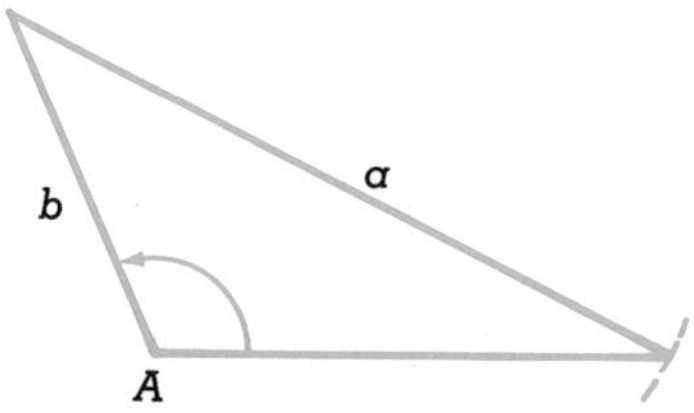

If $a > b$, one solution exists.

examples

1 **Solve the triangle where $A = 50°$, $b = 10$, and $a = 2$.**

$$\begin{aligned} b \sin A &= 10 \sin 50° \\ &= 10(0.7660) \\ &= 7.66 \end{aligned}$$

Since $50° < 90°$ and $2 < 7.66$, no solution exists.

2 **Solve the triangle where $A = 40°$, $b = 10$, and $a = 8$.**

$$\begin{aligned} b \sin A &= 10 \sin 40° \\ &= 10(0.6428) \\ &= 6.428 \end{aligned}$$

Since $40° < 90°$ and $6.428 < 8 < 10$, two solutions exist.

$$\frac{\sin 40°}{8} = \frac{\sin B}{10}$$

$$\begin{aligned} \sin B &= \frac{10 \sin 40°}{8} \\ &= \frac{10(0.6428)}{8} \\ &= 0.8035 \end{aligned}$$

$B = 53°28'$ or $B = 126°32'$

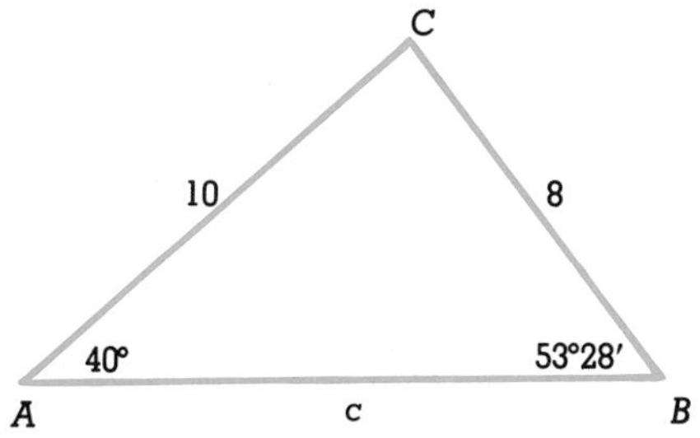

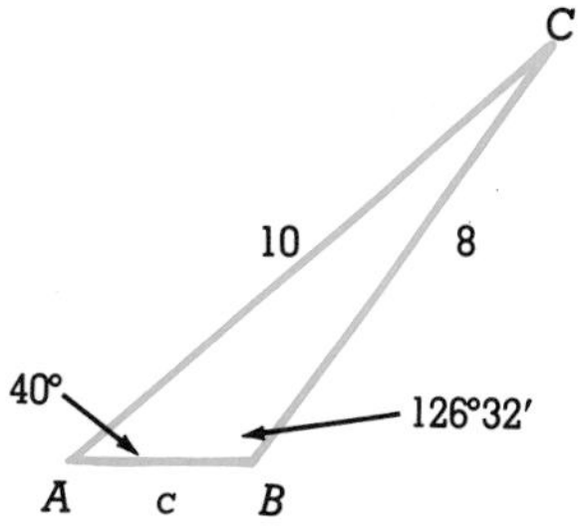

$$\begin{aligned} 40° + 53°28' + C &= 180° \\ C &= 180° - 40° - 53°28' \\ C &= 86°32' \end{aligned}$$

$$\begin{aligned} c &= \frac{8 \sin 86°32'}{\sin 40°} \\ &= \frac{8(0.9981)}{(0.6428)} \text{ or } 12.4 \end{aligned}$$

One solution is $B = 53°28'$, $C = 86°32'$, and $c = 12.4$.

$$\begin{aligned} 40° + 126°32' + C &= 180° \\ C &= 180° - 40 - 126°32' \\ C &= 13°28' \end{aligned}$$

$$\begin{aligned} c &= \frac{8 \sin 13°28'}{\sin 40°} \\ &= \frac{8(0.2328)}{(0.6428)} \text{ or } 2.9 \end{aligned}$$

Another solution is $B = 126°32'$, $C = 13°28'$, and $c = 2.9$.

example 3

Solve the triangle where $A = 40°$, $b = 10$, and $a = 14$.

Since $40° < 90°$ and $14 > 10$, one solution exists.

$$\frac{\sin 40°}{14} = \frac{\sin B}{10}$$

$$\sin B = \frac{10 \sin 40°}{14} = \frac{10(0.6428)}{14} = 0.4591$$

$$B = 27°20'$$

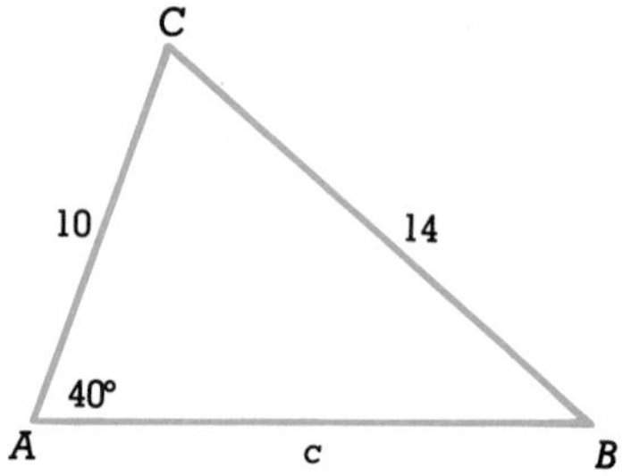

$$40° + 27°20' + C = 180°$$

$$C = 180° - 40° - 27°20'$$

$$C = 112°40'$$

$$\frac{\sin 40°}{14} = \frac{\sin 112°40'}{c}$$

$$c = \frac{14 \sin 112°40'}{\sin 40°} = \frac{14(0.9228)}{0.6428} = 20.1$$

Therefore, $B = 27°20'$, $C = 112°40'$, and $c = 20.1$.

exercises

Max: 1–6, 1–12; Avg: 1–6, 1–11 odds; Min: 1–11 odds

Exploratory State if the given information determines one triangle, two triangles, or no triangle.

1. $A = 140°$, $b = 10$, $a = 3$ 0
2. $A = 118°$, $b = 11$, $a = 17$ 1
3. $A = 30°$, $a = 4$, $b = 8$ 1
4. $A = 43°$, $b = 20$, $a = 11$ 0
5. $A = 58°$, $a = 17$, $b = 13$ 1
6. $A = 38°$, $b = 10$, $a = 8$ 2

Written Determine the number of possible solutions. If a solution exists, solve the triangle.

1. $a = 6$, $b = 10$, $A = 36°52'$ 1
2. $a = 6$, $b = 8$, $A = 150°$ 0
3. $a = 12$, $b = 19$, $A = 57°$ 0
4. $a = 7$, $b = 6$, $A = 30°$ 1
5. $a = 64$, $c = 90$, $C = 98°$ 1
6. $a = 26$, $b = 29$, $A = 58°$ 2
7. $b = 40$, $a = 32$, $A = 125°20'$ 0
8. $a = 9$, $b = 20$, $A = 31°$ 0
9. $a = 12$, $b = 14$, $A = 90°$ 0
10. $A = 25°$, $a = 125$, $b = 150$ 2
11. $A = 40$, $b = 16$, $a = 10$ 0
12. $A = 76°$, $a = 5$, $b = 20$ 0

1. $B = 90°$, $C = 53°8'$, $c = 8$ 4. $B = 25°22'$, $C = 124°38'$, $c = 11.52$ 5. $A = 44°46'$, $B = 37°14'$, $b = 54.9$
6. $B = 71°4'$, $C = 50°56'$, $c = 23.80$; $B = 108°56'$, $C = 13°4'$, $c = 6.93$ 10. $B = 30°28'$, $C = 124°32'$, $c = 24$
$B = 149°32'$, $C = 5°28'$, $c = 28.2$

Vocabulary

hypotenuse (488)
opposite side (488)
adjacent side (488)
sine (488)
cosine (488)
tangent (488)
cosecant (488)
secant (488)
cotangent (488)
interpolation (492)
angle of elevation (496)
angle of depression (496)
Law of Sines (502)
Law of Cosines (505)

Chapter Summary

1. The trigonometric functions relate the side and acute angles of a right triangle as follows. (488)

$$\sin A = \frac{a}{c}$$

$$\cos A = \frac{b}{c}$$

$$\tan A = \frac{a}{b}$$

$$\csc A = \frac{c}{a}$$

$$\sec A = \frac{c}{b}$$

$$\cot A = \frac{b}{a}$$

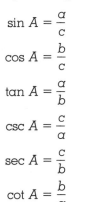

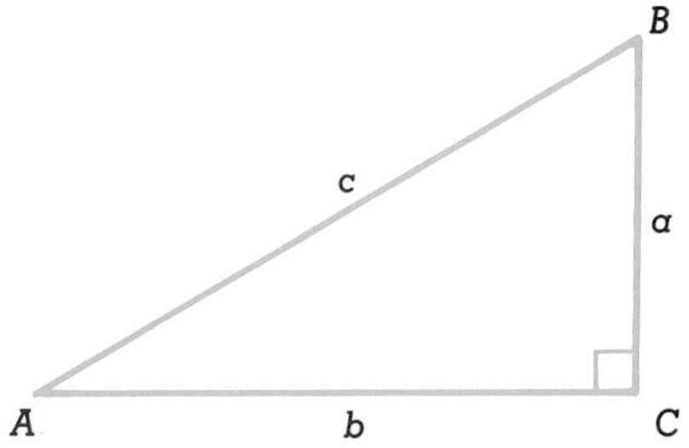

2. The special triangle with angle measurements of 45°, 45°, and 90° has sides whose lengths are in the ratio of 1 to 1 to $\sqrt{2}$. (489)
3. The special triangle with angle measurements of 30°, 60°, and 90° has sides whose lengths are in the ratio of 1 to $\sqrt{3}$ to 2. (489)
4. The value of trigonometric functions may be found in a table. Sometimes interpolation is needed to find a value which is between consecutive entries in the table. (491)
5. Trigonometric functions can be used to solve right triangles. (495)
6. Trigonometric functions may be used to solve many problems including those involving angles of elevation and depression. (496)
7. Law of Sines: Let triangle ABC be any triangle with a, b, and c representing the measures of sides opposite angles with measurements A, B, and C respectively. Then the following equations are true.

$$\frac{\sin A}{a} = \frac{\sin B}{b} = \frac{\sin C}{c} \quad (502)$$

8. Law of Cosines: Let triangle ABC be any triangle with a, b, and c representing the measures of sides opposite angles with measurements A, B, and C respectively. Then, the following equations are true.

$$a^2 = b^2 + c^2 - 2bc \cos A$$
$$b^2 = a^2 + c^2 - 2ac \cos B$$
$$c^2 = a^2 + b^2 - 2ab \cos C \quad (505)$$

9. When the lengths of two sides of a triangle and the measurement of the angle opposite one of them is given, one solution does not always exist. No triangle may exist, one triangle may exist, or two triangles may exist. (508)

Chapter Review

17-1 Find each value to the nearest 4 decimal places.

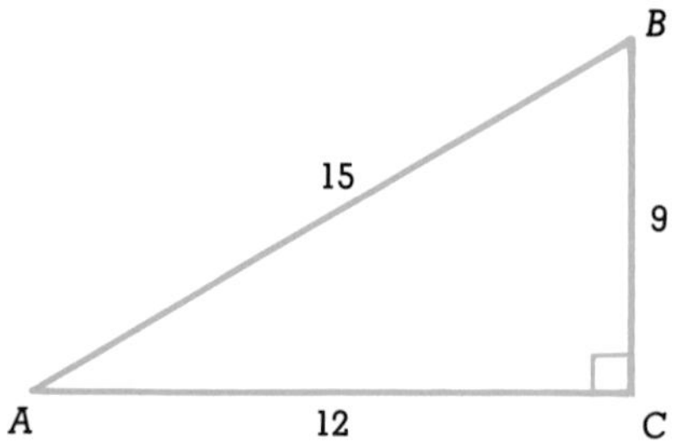

1. sin A 0.6000
2. sin B 0.8000
3. cos A 0.8000
4. cos B 0.6000
5. tan A 0.7500
6. tan B 1.333
7. csc A 1.667
8. sec A 1.250
9. cot B 0.7500

Find the value of each expression. Write each answer in fraction form.

10. cos 30° $\sqrt{3}/2$
11. tan 60° $\sqrt{3}$
12. sin 45° $\sqrt{2}/2$

17-2 Use a table to approximate each trigonometric value. Use interpolation when necessary.

13. sin 70° 0.9397
14. sin 18°20′ 0.3145
15. cos 35° 0.8192
16. cos 81°40′ 0.1449
17. tan 47° 1.072
18. tan 16°30′ 0.2962
19. sin 34°45′ 0.5700
20. tan 13°6′ 0.2327
21. cos 12°12′ 0.9774
22. cos 67°14′ 0.3870
23. tan 88°25′ 36.18
24. sin 81°11′ 0.9882

Find x to the nearest minute.

25. sin x = 0.9272 68°
26. sin x = 0.2164 12°30′
27. cos x = 0.9171 23°30′
28. cos x = 0.5150 59°
29. tan x = 0.3476 19°10′
30. tan x = 1.664 59°
31. tan x = 1.147 48°55′
32. sin x = 0.7284 46°45′
33. cos x = 0.8000 36°52′
34. cos x = 0.5490 56°42′
35. sin x = 0.6621 41°28′
36. tan x = 1.175 49°36′

17-3 Solve each right triangle. See the Teacher's Guide for answers to problems **37-80.**

37. $A = 25°$, $c = 6$
38. $A = 50°$, $a = 11$
39. $B = 85°$, $a = 6.21$
40. $B = 31°$, $c = 12$
41. $A = 16°10'$, $a = 5$
42. $B = 61°20'$, $b = 20$
43. $B = 15°15'$, $c = 32$
44. $A = 47°22'$, $b = 24$

Solve each problem. Round all answers to two decimal places.

45. From a point on the ground 50 meters from the base of a flagpole, the measurement of the angle of elevation of the top is 48°. How tall is the flagpole?

46. A pilot 3000 feet above the ocean notes the measurement of the angle of depression of a ship is 42°. How far is the plane from the ship?

17-4 Solve each right triangle.

47. $a = 1$, $b = 3$
48. $a = 15$, $c = 20$
49. $b = 7$, $c = 10$
50. $a = 10$, $b = 24$
51. $a = 13$, $b = 6.5$
52. $a = 15$, $c = 23$
53. $b = 20$, $c = 30$
54. $b = 2.6$, $c = 5.1$

Solve each problem.

55. A building is 80 feet tall. Find the measurement of the angle of elevation to the top of the building from a point on the ground 100 feet from the base of the building.

56. The base of a monument and two points on the ground are in a straight line. The two points are 50 meters apart. The measurements of the angles of elevation to the top of the monument are 45° and 25°. Find the height of the monument.

17-5 Use the Law of Sines to solve each triangle.

57. $A = 50°$, $b = 12$, $a = 10$
58. $A = 83°10'$, $a = 80$, $b = 70$
59. $B = 46°$, $C = 83°$, $b = 65$
60. $A = 45°$, $B = 30°$, $b = 20$
61. $A = 33°$, $C = 67°$, $b = 16$
62. $A = 42°$, $B = 65°$, $a = 63$
63. $B = 73°$, $a = 9$, $b = 13$
64. $A = 45°$, $B = 70°$, $c = 6.2$

17-6 Use the Law of Cosines to solve each triangle.

65. $A = 60°$, $b = 2$, $c = 5$
66. $C = 65°$, $a = 4$, $b = 7$
67. $C = 40°$, $a = 6$, $b = 7$
68. $B = 24°$, $a = 42$, $c = 6.5$
69. $B = 53°10'$, $a = 14$, $c = 8$
70. $a = 8$, $b = 10$, $c = 8$
71. $a = 11$, $b = 13$, $c = 20$
72. $a = 14$, $b = 14$, $c = 22$

17-7 Determine the number of possible solutions. If a solution exists, solve the triangle.

73. $A = 36°$, $a = 2$, $b = 14$
74. $A = 40°$, $a = 8$, $b = 10$
75. $A = 46°$, $a = 10$, $b = 8$
76. $A = 130°$, $a = 25$, $b = 16$
77. $A = 100°$, $a = 13$, $b = 17$
78. $A = 30°$, $a = 6$, $b = 12$
79. $A = 54°$, $a = 12$, $b = 14$
80. $A = 62°$, $a = 7$, $b = 5.5$

Chapter Test

Find each value to the nearest 4 decimal places.

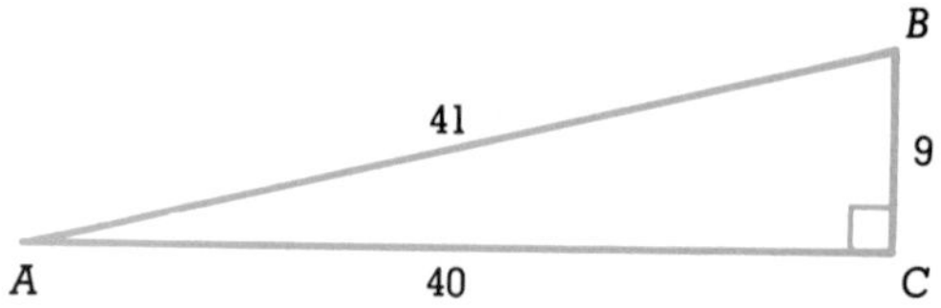

1. $\sin A$ 0.2195
2. $\cos A$ 0.9756
3. $\tan A$ 0.2250
4. $\cos B$ 0.2195

Find the value of each expression. Write each answer in fraction form.

5. $\cos 60°$ $\frac{1}{2}$
6. $\tan 45°$ 1

Use a table to approximate each trigonometric value. Use interpolation when necessary.

7. $\sin 67°$ 0.9205
8. $\cos 38°10'$ 0.7862
9. $\tan 59°38'$ 1.707
10. $\sin 13°3'$ 0.2258

Find x to the nearest minute.

11. $\cos x = 0.4384$ 64°
12. $\tan x = 0.4734$ 25°20′
13. $\sin x = 0.4423$ 26°15′
14. $\tan x = 1.635$ 58°33′

Solve each right triangle.

15. $A = 36°, b = 14$ $a = 10.17, c = 17.3, B = 54°$
16. $B = 75°, b = 6$ $c = 6.21, a = 1.61, A = 15°$
17. $A = 22°, c = 8$ $a = 3, b = 7.42, B = 68°$
18. $a = 7, c = 12$ $A = 35°41', B = 54°19', b = 9.75$

Solve each problem.

19. A 32 foot ladder leans against a building. The top touches the building 26 feet above the ground. What is the measurement of the angle formed by the ladder with the ground? 54°20′
20. From the top of a cliff, a camper sees a deer. The measurement of the angle of depression to the deer is 70°. The cliff is 50 meters high. How far is the deer from the base of the cliff? 18.2 meters

If possible, solve each triangle.

21. $a = 13, b = 11, c = 17$
22. $A = 46°, B = 77°, a = 6$ $b = 8.13, C = 57°, c = 7$
23. $A = 75°, b = 21, a = 30$
24. $A = 65°, b = 21, a = 6$ none
25. $A = 70°, B = 31°, c = 17$
26. $A = 44°, a = 12, b = 14$
27. $A = 140°, b = 10, a = 7$ none
28. $C = 48°, a = 7, b = 9$ $B = 81°41', A = 50°19', c = 6.76$

21. $A = 49°52', B = 40°19', C = 89°47'$ 23. $B = 42°32', C = 62°28', c = 27.54$
25. $C = 79°, b = 8.92, a = 16.27$ 26. $B = 54°8', C = 81°52', c = 17.1; B = 125°52', C = 10°8', c = 3.0$

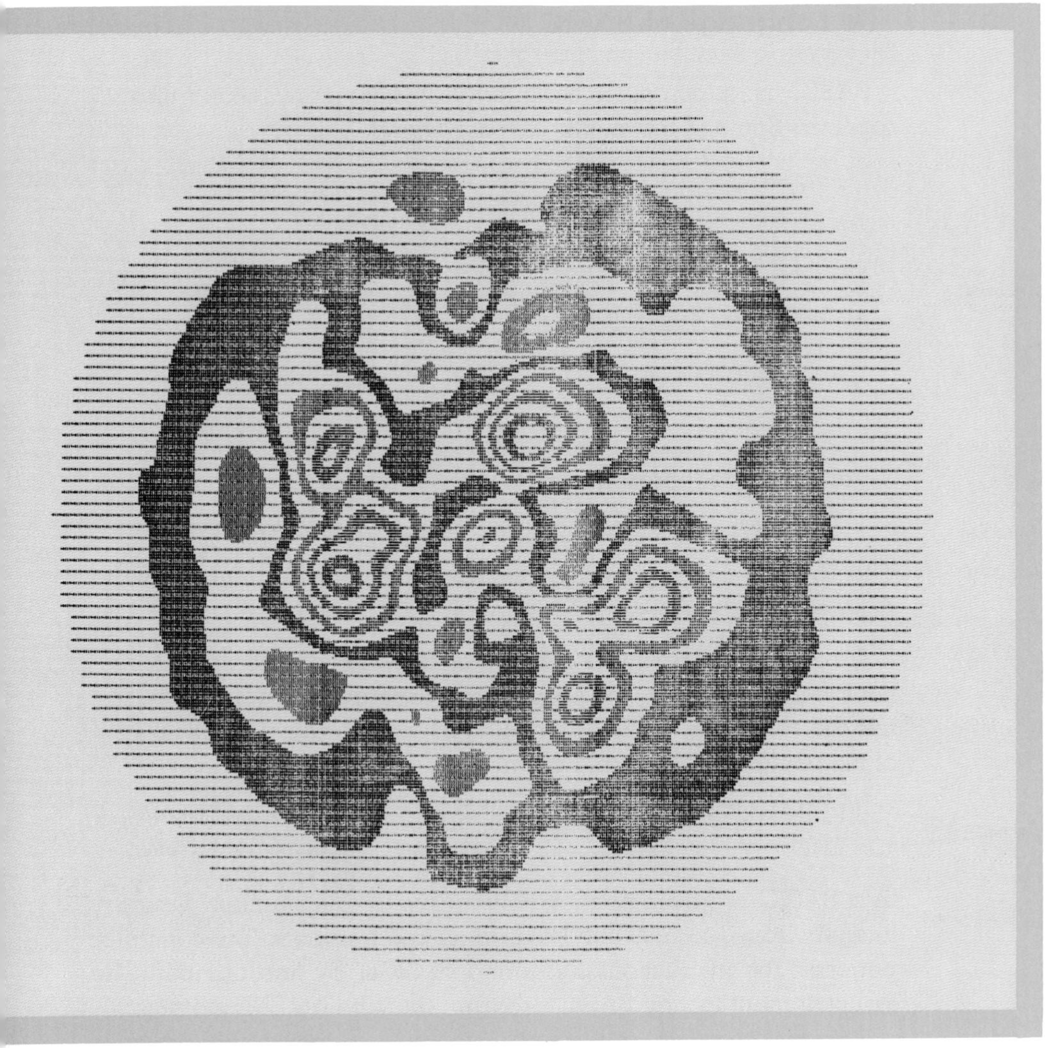

BASIC

A computer can be programmed with equations that attempt to explain atmospheric phenomena. The shaded contours on this map show simulated atmospheric pressure at sea level during one study. This computer pattern is compared with actual conditions over a period of time. The pattern consists of densely packed numbers and letters.

The Language of BASIC

Objective: To learn the language of BASIC.

BASIC is a computer language. It has many similarities to algebra. Some of the similarities are shown below.

In BASIC, raising to a power is indicated by ↑.

Algebra	BASIC	Algebra	BASIC
+	+	>	>
−	−	≥	>=
×	*	≠	<>
÷	/	3^2	3↑2
=	=	a	A
<	<	b	B
≤	<=	x	X

Only single-digit numerals are acceptable.

Variables are represented by a letter or by a letter and a numeral.

A, B, M, Z1, R3, A6 *Notice that a letter precedes a number.*

In BASIC, an operation symbol can never be left out. To write A times B, write A*B, not ab as in algebra.

A computer program is a series of statements which give directions to the computer. The purpose of a program is to get information into the computer, have the calculations done and get the results out of the computer. A sample program follows.

```
5  PRINT 6.731+8.213+3.726
10 END
```

line numbers (5, 10) — *statements* (PRINT 6.731+8.213+3.726, END)

Some computer terminals type only capital letters.

In a BASIC program each statement has a line number. Usually, integers from 1 to 9999 can be used as line numbers. The computer performs the instructions in numerical order by line number. The last statement in any BASIC program must be an END statement.

An INPUT statement can be used instead of the READ and DATA statement combination.

Most programs use only a few statements. In the sample program above the statements each begin with a word. One begins with PRINT, the other with END. Other words which are often used are READ and DATA

Use multiples of ten as line numbers so extra lines can be added.

example 1

Write a program to compute the sum and product of three numbers.

```
10 READ A, B, C
20 PRINT A+B+C
30 PRINT A*B*C
40 DATA 71, 16, 84
50 END
```

The computer assigns the numbers from the DATA statement to the variables A, B, and C in order.

$A = 71 \quad B = 16 \quad C = 84$

The sum and product of any three numbers can be found simply by changing the numbers in the DATA statement on line 40.

Before the computer will do a program it must be given the RUN command. Commands do not have line numbers.

```
10 READ A, B, C        The computer assigns
20 PRINT A+B+C         A = 71, B = 16, C = 84
30 PRINT A*B*C         from the data in line 40.
40 DATA 71, 16, 84
50 END
   RUN                 RUN tells the computer to do the program.
   171                 171 = A+B+C
   95424               95424 = A*B*C
```

There is a specific order of operations used by the computer.

Order of Operations in BASIC

1. **Do all operations in parentheses, from the innermost parentheses outward.**
2. **Evaluate all powers from left to right.**
3. **Do all multiplications and/or divisions from left to right.**
4. **Do all additions and/or subtractions from left to right.**

The use of the order of operations is shown below.

example 2

Evaluate 12/2 − (5 + 3) * 4 ↑ 2 + 3.

12/2 − (5 + 3) * 4 ↑ 2 + 3 = 12/2 − 8 * 4 ↑ 2 + 3 — *Do operations in parentheses.*
= 12/2 − 8 * 16 + 3 — *Evaluate powers.*
= 6 − 128 + 3 — *Do the division and multiplication.*
= ⁻119 — *Do the addition and subtraction.*

The value of the expression is ⁻119.

exercises

Written Write an expression in BASIC for each of the following.

1. $3x + 5y - 7$ 3*X+5*Y−7
2. $a \cdot b \cdot c - 3$ A*B*C−3
3. $5m - 3b + 8$ 5*M−3*B+8
4. $17 \div a$ 17/A

Evaluate each of the following.

5. 6+8*2 22
6. (3+2)↑2 25
7. (2*(5+8))/13 2
8. ((14+10)/4)/2 3
9. 3*(5↑2) 75
10. (6+8)/2+5 12

Evaluate each of the following. Let A = 5, B = 6, C = 15.

11. A*B+3 33
12. A+3*B 23
13. C−B+5 14
14. C/A 3
15. A*(B+3) 45
16. (A+3)*B 48

Write an expression in BASIC for each of the following.

17. $3x^2 + 2x + 5$ 3*X↑2+2*X+5
18. a^{x+2} A↑(X+2)
19. $\frac{x+5}{2y}$ (X+5)/(2*Y)
20. $\frac{5x+3}{2x+4}$ (5*X+3)/(2*X+4)
21. $\frac{a}{b} + n$ A/B+N
22. $\frac{(x^3 + 7x^2 + 5)^3}{x+1}$ ((X↑3+7*X↑2+5)↑3)/(X+1)

Write BASIC programs to compute and print the following. Use only the PRINT and END statements in problems 23–30.

23–24. The sum and product of 31, 14, 62, and 29.

25–26. The difference of 673 and 49 and the quotient of 673 ÷ 49.

27–28. The perimeter and area of a rectangle with length 4.7 cm and width 2.8 cm.

29–30. The circumference and area of a circle with radius 6.37 cm. Use 3.1416 for π.

31–34. Adapt each program in the problems above so it has a READ statement, and a DATA statement. The new program should be able to compute and print the desired information for any appropriate set of numbers. In writing programs such as in problem 23–24, students may write two separate programs or a single program.

23.
```
10 PRINT 31+14+62+29
20 END      output: 136
```

24.
```
10 PRINT 31*14*62*29
20 END      output: 780332
```

25.
```
10 PRINT 673-49
20 END      output: 624
```

26.
```
10 PRINT 673/49
20 END      output: 13.7347
```

27.
```
10 PRINT 2*4.7+2*2.8
20 END      output: 15
```

28.
```
10 PRINT 4.7*2.8
20 END      output: 13.16
```

29.
```
10 PRINT 2*3.1416*6.37
20 END      output: 40.024
```

30.
```
10 PRINT 3.1416*(6.37↑2)
20 END      output: 127.476
```

31.
```
10 READ A,B,C,D
20 PRINT A+B+C+D
30 PRINT A*B*C*D
35 DATA 31,14,62,29
40 END
```

32.
```
10 READ A,B
20 PRINT A-B, A/B
25 DATA 673,49
30 END
```

33.
```
10 READ L,W
20 PRINT 2*L+2*W, L*W
25 DATA 4.7, 2.8
30 END
```

34.
```
10 READ R
20 PRINT 2*3.1416*R, 3.1416*(
25 DATA 6.37
30 END
```

Assignment of Variables

Objective: To assign variables in BASIC.

In BASIC the equals sign, =, is used in a slightly different way than in algebra. In algebra, both sides of an equation may have many terms and variables. In BASIC the left side may only have one variable. The equations shown below illustrate this rule.

Algebra	BASIC
$2x + 15y = 27 + 36y$	X=16*Y+37*Z−5
In this equation, both sides have the same value for some x and y. A sample solution is $x = 24$, $y = 1$	In this statement the value of the expression on the right is computed and *assigned* to the variable on the left.

In BASIC, the equals sign tells the computer to assign the value of the expression on the right to the variable on the left. An equals sign in BASIC is used in a LET statement.

```
10 LET X=6
20 LET Y=3
30 PRINT X↑Y
40 END
   RUN
   216
```

In this program, 6 is assigned to X, and 3 is assigned to Y. The value of X↑Y, or 6^3, is computed and printed. The printout is 216, the value of 6^3.

```
10 READ Y,Z
20 LET X=16*Y+37*Z−5
30 PRINT X
40 DATA 47, 38
50 END
   RUN
   2153
```

*In this program, the data are assigned to the variables as follows: Y = 47, Z = 38. The value of 16*Y+37*Z−5 is then computed and assigned to X in line 20. This value is then printed.*

In doing this program the computation is as follows.

16*Y+37*Z−5
$16 \cdot 47 + 37 \cdot 38 - 5$
$752 + 1406 - 5$
2153

The value 2153 is assigned to the variable X, and then printed.

Many programs increase a number by a certain amount in each step. The LET statement is very useful in doing this. When the LET statement is used in this way, a whole series of values are assigned, one at a time, to a given variable, as in the following example.

```
10  LET M=0
20  PRINT M, M*3.1416
30  LET M=M+1
40  PRINT M, M*3.1416
50  LET M=M+1
60  PRINT M, M*3.1416
70  LET M=M+1
80  PRINT M, M*3.1416
90  LET M=M+1
100 PRINT M, M*3.1416
110 LET M=M+1
120 PRINT M, M*3.1416
130 END
```

M = 0
0   0
Now M = 1
1   3.1416
Now M = 2
2   6.2832
Now M = ___?___
___?___   ___?___
Now M = ___?___
___?___   ___?___
Now M = ___?___
___?___   ___?___

Each time M increases is called a step. Here there is a step of one.

What number belongs in each blank?

Later you will learn how to get the same results with fewer lines by using what is called a loop.

The purpose of a program is to get information into the computer (*input*), have the computer do the calculations (*execution*), and get information out of the computer (*output*). A program has three parts: input, execution, and output. The two programs below show the three parts of a program. Both programs accomplish the same task. Which do you prefer?

```
10  LET A=3                    Input
11  LET B=4
12  LET C=5
13  LET D=6
14  LET X=2
20  LET Y=A*X↑3+B*X−(C*D)      Execution
30  PRINT Y                    Output
40  END
```

```
10  DATA 3, 4, 5, 6, 2         Input
15  READ A, B, C, D, X
20  LET Y=A*X↑3+B*X−(C*D)      Execution
30  PRINT Y                    Output
40  END
```

When the results of computations exceed six significant digits the computer will use **E notation.** This is the computer equivalent of scientific notation. The E means *times 10 to the given power.*

Some systems use .378673E+08.

Result of computation	E Notation	Meaning
37867275	3.78673E+07	3.78673×10^7
0.003629	3.629E−03	3.629×10^{-3}

exercises

Written Write each of the following in scientific notation.

1. 6.17324E+04 6.17324×10^4
2. 7.9E+08 7.9×10^8
3. 2.176E+17 2.176×10^{17}
4. 1.325E−06 1.325×10^{-6}

Write each of the following in E notation.

5. 16,500,000 1.65E+07
6. 0.0000127 1.27E−05

Let A = 3, B = 4, and M1 = 16. What is the value of X in each statement?

7. 190 LET X=6*A 18
8. 30 LET X=M1/B 4
9. 25 LET X=A*B+5 17
10. 170 LET X=A↑4 81
11. 20 LET X=B+M1*3 52
12. 40 LET X=M1−B+3*A 21

Each mathematical expression below is followed by an incorrect BASIC expression. Correct the BASIC expression.

13. $\frac{m+2}{r+4}$ M+2/R+4 (M+2)/(R+4)
14. $\frac{ab}{y+3}$ AB/(Y+3) (A*B)/(Y+3)
15. $\frac{(x+a)^2}{2z}$ (X+A)↑2/2*Z (X+A)↑2)/(2*Z)
16. $\left(\frac{x}{y}\right)^{n-3}$ (X/Y)↑N−3 (X/Y)↑(N−3)

Correct the error in each expression or statement below.

17. 7X+34 7*X+34
18. (7+8/2 (7+8)/2
19. 3*X↑2+4X 3*X↑2+4*X
20. 20 LET Y=3A 3*A
21. 20 LET 2*X=5+13
21. 20 LET X=(5+13)/2
22. 30 LET X+Y=27+12
22. 30 LET X=27+12−Y

For each of the following, write a program which will have input, execution, and output. In each case, the output will be the value of X.

23. A = 3, B = 7, C = 9, X=A+B(C−1)
24. A = 6, B = 18, C = 30, $X=\frac{3}{2}\left(\frac{B}{A}+C\right)$

23.
```
10 READ A,B,C
20 LET X=A+B*(C−1)
30 PRINT X
40 DATA 3, 7, 9
50 END      output: 59
```

24.
```
10 READ A,B,C
20 LET X=(3/2)*(B/A+C)
30 PRINT X
40 DATA 6, 18, 30
50 END      output: 49.5
```

FOR-NEXT Loops

Objective: To use FOR-NEXT loops in BASIC.

Programs which have the computer perform only a few operations for many different sets of data can often be made more efficient by the use of a FOR-NEXT loop. The following programs print multiples of 3.1416. The computer printouts are shown on the right.

```
10  LET M=0
20  PRINT M, M*3.1416
30  LET M=M+1
40  PRINT M, M*3.1416
50  LET M=M+1
60  PRINT M, M*3.1416
70  LET M=M+1
80  PRINT M, M*3.1416
90  LET M=M+1
100 PRINT M, M*3.1416
110 LET M=M+1
120 PRINT M, M*3.1416
130 LET M=M+1
140 PRINT M, M*3.1416
150 END
```

$\pi \approx 3.1416$

```
0     0
1     3.1416
2     6.2832
3     9.4248
4    12.5664
5    15.7080
6    18.8496
```

The same results can be obtained with the program below.

```
10  FOR M=0 to 6 STEP 1
20  PRINT M, M*3.1416
30  NEXT M
40  END
```

The phrase STEP 1 tells the computer to increase M by one each time.

```
0     0
1     3.1416
2     6.2832
3     9.4248
4    12.5664
5    15.7080
6    18.8496
```

If line 10 is changed to read 10 FOR M=0 TO 100 STEP 5, the computer will print multiples of 5 times 3.1416. The FOR-NEXT loop can be used to obtain many results as the following program shows.

```
10  PRINT "N", "2*N", "N↑2", "N↑N"
15  FOR N=1 TO 10 STEP 1
20  PRINT N, 2*N, N↑2, N↑N
30  NEXT N
40  END
```

The printout for this program is shown on the next page.

N	2*N	N↑2	N↑N
1	2	1	1
2	4	4	4
3	6	9	27
4	8	16	256
5	10	25	3125
6	12	36	46656
7	14	49	823543
8	16	64	1.67772E7
9	18	81	3.8742E8
10	20	100	1.0E10

Line 10 of the program helps to organize the results by placing headings at the top of each column. The computer will print exactly what it reads between the quotation marks, including punctuation marks and spaces.

The general form of a FOR statement is shown below.

```
FOR (VARIABLE)=(   ) TO (   ) STEP (   )
FOR N=1 TO 15 STEP 1.5
FOR K=7 TO 21 STEP 2
FOR X=-10 TO 10
```

If the step is not indicated, most computers will automatically use an increment of one. Every time a FOR statement is used, such as FOR N=1 TO 10, there must also be a NEXT statement which says NEXT N.

```
10 LET S=0                    The variable S is assigned a value of zero.
20 FOR X=2 TO 100 STEP 2      What values are assigned to X?
30 LET Y=X↑2                  What values are assigned to Y?
40 LET S=S+Y                  The variable S represents the sum of all
                              values of Y up to this point.
50 NEXT X                     The loop transfers the computer to line 20.
60 PRINT "SUM", S             What would be different about the output if line 60
                              were given the line number 45?
70 END
```

The output of this program is 171700.

It is often useful to have more than one loop. There are only two ways these loops can appear in a program as shown.

Nested Loops	Independent Loops	Not Acceptable
FOR X FOR Y NEXT Y NEXT X	FOR X NEXT X FOR Y NEXT Y	FOR X FOR Y NEXT X NEXT Y
The loops do not cross.	*The loops do not cross. They are not nested.*	*These loops cross.*

exercises

Written

1. Correct the errors in the following programs.

```
10 FOR X=1 TO 5
20 FOR Y=2 TO 4 STEP 2
30 PRINT X*Y
40 NEXT X
50 NEXT Y
60 END   change order
         of lines 40, 50
```

```
10 FOR X=7 TO 15 STEP 3
20 PRINT X, X↑3
30 FOR Y=2 TO 5
40 PRINT Y, Y+2↑Y
50 NEXT X
60 NEXT Y
70 END   change order of 50, 60
```

2. Run your corrected program if possible.

Write programs to do the following.

3. For the integers from 10 to 20, print each integer, its third power, and its fifth power.

```
10 FOR X=10 TO 20
20 PRINT X, X↑3, X↑5
30 NEXT X
40 END
```

4. Use the expression X↑(1/2) to indicate square root and X↑(1/3) to indicate cube root. For the integers from 1 to 15, print the integer, its square root, and its cube root. Check these results with the table on pages 538 and 539.

5. The formula for Celsius to Fahrenheit conversion is C = 5/9 · (F − 32). Write a program to print Fahrenheit temperature, Celsius temperature for F = 0 to 100 in steps of 5.

6. The lengths and widths of 3 rectangles are as follows: 8, 5; 9, 6; and 13, 17. Write a program to compute and print both their perimeters and areas. Arrange these headings at the top: length, width, perimeter, and area. See Teacher's Guide for answer.

7. Compute and print the sum of the cubes of the integers from 1 to 25 inclusive.

4.
```
10 FOR X=1 TO 15
20 PRINT X, X↑(1/2), X↑(1/3)
30 NEXT X
40 END
```

5.
```
10 FOR F=0 TO 100 STEP 5
20 LET C=5/9*(F-32)
30 PRINT F, C
40 NEXT F
50 END
```

7.
```
10 FOR K=1 TO 25
20 LET S=S+K↑3
30 NEXT K
40 PRINT S
50 END
```

IF-THEN Statements

Objective: To use IF-THEN statements in BASIC.

Suppose a program is needed which will print a number N, and the fifth power of N. However, only fifth powers less than one million are desired. A program using a FOR-NEXT loop is started.

```
10  FOR N=1 TO ____ STEP 1
20  LET Y=N↑5
30  PRINT N, Y
40  NEXT N
50  END
```

Can you tell what number belongs in the blank?

What is missing in this program? What work must be done in order to finish the program? Why is this program not an efficient way to solve the problem?

The task can be done in another way. An IF-THEN statement can tell the computer to make a comparison. It also tells the computer what to do next based on the results.

```
10  LET N=0                      Assign a value of zero to N.
20  LET N=N+1                    Change the input to the next integer.
30  LET Y=N↑5                    Assign a value to Y.
40  IF Y>=1000000 THEN 70 ──┐    Do test line.
      │                     │
      │                (Yes)│    Yes: Go to line 70.
    (No)                    │    No: Go to the next
      ↓                     │        line, line 50.
50  PRINT N, Y              │    Compute and print N and Y.
60  GO TO 20                │    Do line 20 next.
70  END ←───────────────────┘
```

Each time through the loop, the computer calculates Y=N↑5. If Y ≥ 1,000,000, the computer goes to line 70 and the program is finished. If it is not, the steps in lines 20, 30, 40, 50, and 60 are repeated.

The IF-THEN statement uses one of the following symbols.

BASIC SYMBOL	EXAMPLE	
=	A=B	
<	A<B	
<=	A<=B	*"A is less than or equal to B"*
>	A>B	
>=	A>=B	*"A is greater than or equal to B"*
<>	A<>B	*"A is not equal to B"*

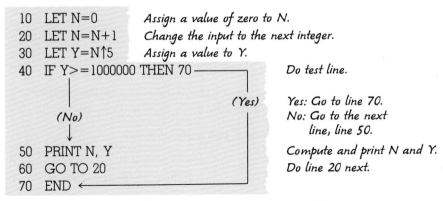

Sometimes a programmer needs to count how many times an operation is performed. In the following program line 30 keeps the count. Each time through the loop the count is increased by one.

example 1

Write a program to count the number of powers of seven between 100 and 1,000,000 and print each one. Express each one both as a number and as a power of seven.

```
10  LET K=0                      Assign a starting value for counter K.
20  LET X=343                    7³ = 343 is the first power of 7 greater than 100.
30  LET K=K+1                    Increase counter K by one.
40  LET X=X*7                    Change to the next power of 7.
50  IF X>=1000000 THEN 80        Check test line.
60  PRINT K, X, "7↑" (K+3)       Why (K + 3) power?
70  GO TO 30
80  END
```

By changing the print statement, the information printed can be organized so it is easier to understand.

```
60  PRINT K "POWERS",X"=7↑"(K+3)" IS GREATEST"
```

The symbols in quotes are printed exactly as they appear. Numerical results are indicated by K, X, (K+3). They do not have quotes.

The PRINT statement has various uses.

```
10  PRINT A                      There is a single output.
20  PRINT X, Y, Z                There are three outputs on the same line.
30  PRINT A+B                    There is one computation, one output.
40  PRINT 7+A, B−9               There are two computations, two outputs.
50  PRINT "EXAMPLE"              Prints text.
60  PRINT "SOLUTION IS", X       Prints text and numerical output.
```

example 2

Write two print statements. The first sets up headings for computing the area of triangles. The second prints the data and the results. Include a READ line for variables B and A.

```
10  READ B, A
20  PRINT "BASE", "ALTITUDE", "AREA OF TRIANGLE"
30  PRINT B, A, (B*A)/2
```

exercises

Written Let A = 5, B = 8, and X = 10. Tell the number of the statement which the computer will do next.

1.
```
10 IF A<20 THEN 75
15 PRINT B
```
75

2.
```
15 IF A>=4 THEN 90
20 PRINT 2*A
```
90

3.
```
10 IF A<>B THEN 50
20 PRINT X
```
50

4.
```
10 IF (A+B)<X THEN 60
20 PRINT 2*X
```
20

5.
```
50 IF (A-B)>X THEN 75
60 PRINT B-A
```
60

6.
```
45 IF (B*X)<A↑3 THEN 10
50 PRINT B*X
```
10

Use the program below to answer problems 7–10. Tell whether A, B, or both A and B will be printed, and give the values of any variables printed.

```
10 IF A>B THEN 40
20 LET A=A+10
25 LET B=B+2
30 IF A>=B THEN 50
40 PRINT A
50 PRINT B
60 END
```

7. Let A = 12, B = 12 B, 14
8. Let A = 14, B = 19 B, 21
9. Let A = 9, B = 21 A, 19; B, 23
10. Let A = 21, B = 5 A, 21; B, 5

Describe what each program below will do.

11.
```
10 LET M=0
20 PRINT M, M↑2
30 LET M=M+3
40 IF M<=30 THEN 20
50 END
```
Prints an integer and its square for multiples of three from 0 to 30.

12.
```
10 LET X=1
20 PRINT 4*X
30 LET X=X+1
40 IF X<21 THEN 20
50 END
```
Prints multiples of 4, from 4 to 80.

Write BASIC programs to do the following. Use an IF-THEN statement.

13. Print the integers from 10 to 1 in descending order.
14. Print the squares of the integers from 21 to 35 inclusive.
15. Print the cubes of the even integers from 10 to 36 inclusive.
16. Count the powers of three less than 900,000. Print the greatest one in decimal notation and as a power of three.

16. See Teacher's Guide for answer.

17. N! is read *N factorial.* N! = N · (N − 1) · (N − 2) · . . . . · (2) · (1). Print N! for N ≤ 10. Organize two columns with headings "N" and "N FACTORIAL." Let P represent the product. Begin the program with P = 1. Use a loop. See Teacher's Guide for answer.

13.
```
10 LET X=10
20 PRINT X
30 LET X=X-1
40 IF X<>0 THEN 20
50 END
```

14.
```
10 LET Q=21
20 PRINT Q↑2
30 LET Q=Q+1
40 IF Q<=35 THEN 20
50 END
```

15.
```
10 LET C=10
20 PRINT C↑3
30 LET C=C+2
40 IF C<=36 THEN 20
50 END
```

Flow Charts

Objective: To use flow charts to help write BASIC programs.

Programmers often use diagrams called flow charts to organize their programs. Some shapes have special meanings in flow charts.

An oval is used to begin or end a program.

A parallelogram shows input or output.
Use it with READ or PRINT statements.

A rectangle shows processing operations.
Use it with a LET statement.

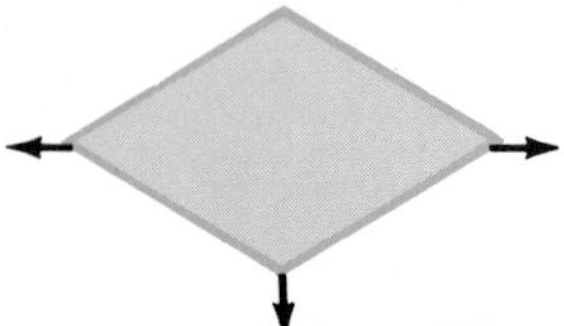

A diamond shows a decision. Arrows show how the flow continues.
Use it with IF-THEN statements.

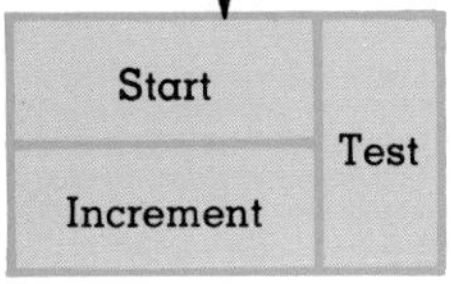

An iteration box shows all parts of a loop.
Iterate means to do over and over.
Use it with FOR-NEXT statements.

Below is a flow chart and a program to print the integers and their squares from 1 to 100.

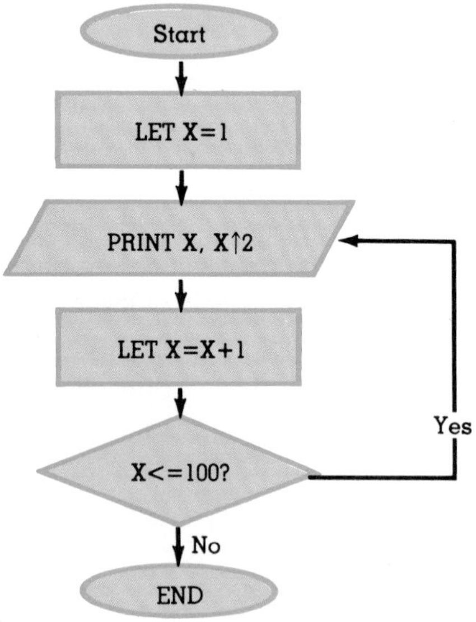


```
10  LET X=1
20  PRINT X, X↑2
30  LET X=X+1
40  IF X<=100 THEN 20
50  END
```

The following example uses an iteration box for a loop.

examples

1 **Make a flow chart and write a program to sum the even integers from 2 to 100.**

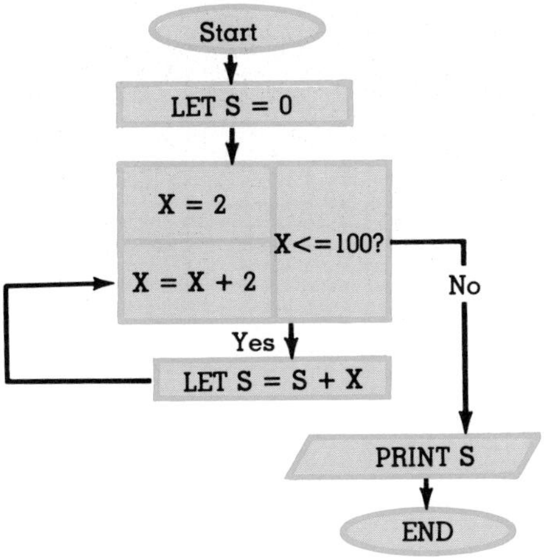


```
10 LET S=0
20 FOR X=2 TO 100 STEP 2
30 LET S=S+X
40 NEXT X
50 PRINT S
60 END
```

2 **Suppose you are given a set of 5 test scores for each of 25 students. Write a flow chart and a program to print the average for each student. Print "FAIL" if the average is less than 60. Print "PASS" if the average is 60 or more. The processing ends after the twenty-fifth average is printed.**

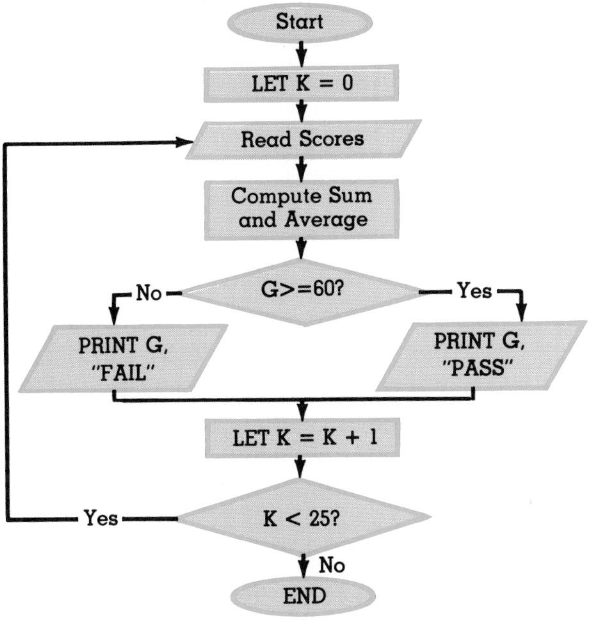


```
10 LET K=0
20 READ A,B,C,D,E
30 LET G=(A+B+C+D+E)/5
40 IF G>=60 THEN 70
50 PRINT G, "FAIL"
60 GO TO 80
70 PRINT G, "PASS"
80 LET K=K+1
90 IF K<25 THEN 20
95 DATA . . .
100 END
```

To use the program, the twenty-five sets of scores listed are in the data line.

exercises

Written **Make a flow chart for each of the following.** See Teacher's Guide for answer.

1.
```
10 LET Y=1
20 PRINT Y, Y↑3
30 LET Y=Y+1
40 IF Y↑3<=1000 THEN 20
50 END
```

2.
```
10 LET S=0
20 FOR M=1 TO 20
30 LET S=S+M
40 NEXT M
50 LET A=S↑(1/2)
60 PRINT A
70 END
```

Write a program from each flow chart below.

3.

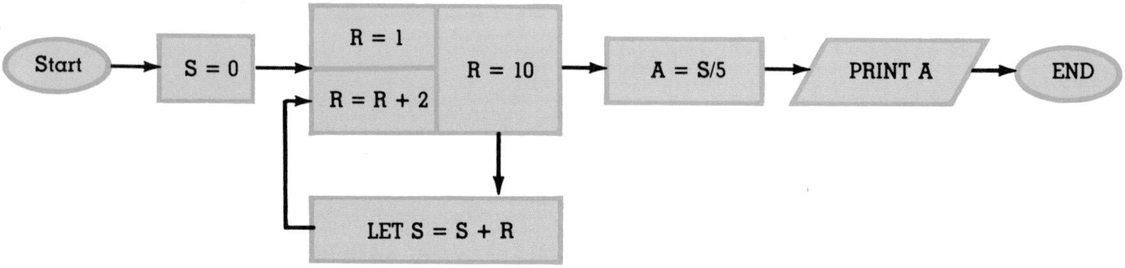

4.

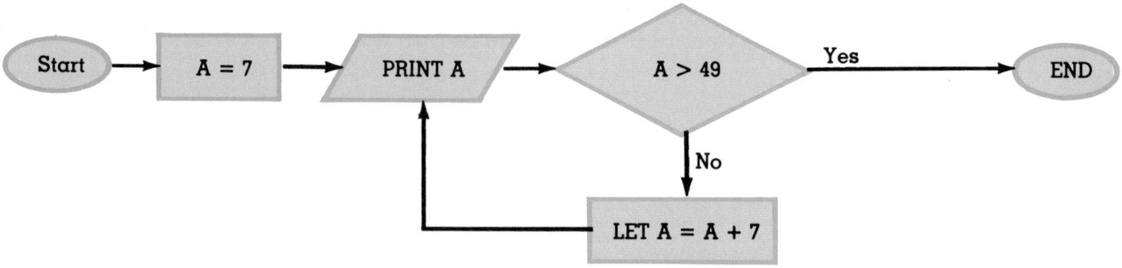

Write a flow chart and a program for each of the following.

5. Find the sum of the first n positive integers, where $n = 50$. 5–7. See Teacher's Guide for answers.

6. You are given three numbers the values of which are unknown to you beforehand. Print the three numbers in increasing order from least to greatest. Make comparisons by pairs and exhaust all possibilities.

7. You are given the coordinates of a point in the xy-plane. Decide in which quadrant the point lies. If the point lies on an axis, decide on which axis the point lies. Include the origin as a possibility.

3.
```
10 FOR R=1 TO 10 STEP 2
20 LET S=S+R
30 NEXT R
40 LET A=S/5
50 PRINT A
60 END
```

4.
```
10 LET A=7
20 PRINT A
30 IF A>49 THEN 60
40 LET A=A+7
50 GO TO 20
60 END
```

Subscripted Variables

Objective: To use subscripted variables in BASIC.

Sometimes it is difficult to provide enough labels for variables in a large amount of data. When this happens, subscripted variables may be used in BASIC.

Algebra	BASIC
$x_1, x_2, x_3, \ldots, x_n$	X(1), X(2), X(3), . . . , X(N)

In BASIC, subscripted variables consist of a single letter and a pair of parentheses. Either a positive integer or an ordered pair of positive integers may appear within the parentheses. These integers may be represented by variables or BASIC expressions.

A(10)
Z(6)
B(3,4) — *This variable refers to an item in the 3rd row, 4th column of an array of data.*

B(A)
Q(M)
N(4+R) — *The computer finds the values of A and M and R from the program.*

Z1(Q) — *This is not allowed. Z1 is a variable which may not be subscripted. Z1(Q) is not a single letter followed by parentheses.*

```
10  DATA 2,3,5,2.2,7,6,9,18,24,11
20  FOR R=1 TO 10
30  READ A(R)
40  PRINT A(R)*3.1416
50  NEXT R
60  END
```

*Data are diameters of circles. This loop yields A(1), A(2), A(3), . . . , A(10). What is the value of A(7)? of A(7)*3.1416? What does this program do?*

If the value of any of the subscripts is greater than 10, the size of the list must be given. A dimension statement, DIM, can do this.

```
10  DIM R(17)
```

The statement above tells the computer to reserve 17 memory spaces for subscripted variables.

The program on the next page shows the use of the DIM statement.

example 1

Write a program to print the square root of the following numbers: 3, 9.2, 7, 11.6, 0, 254, 113, 73.9, 46, 19, 79, 101.

```
10  DIM R(12)               Reserve 12 memory spaces.
20  FOR M=1 TO 12           Set up FOR-NEXT loop.
30  READ R(M)
40  PRINT R(M)↑(1/2)        Compute and print square root.
50  NEXT M
60  DATA 3,9.2,7,11.6,0,254,113,73.9,46,19,79,101
70  END
```

The program below enters into the computer hourly earnings of fifteen workers. It computes and prints the average wage.

```
 10  DIM G(15)              Reserve 15 memory spaces.
 20  LET S=0                S is the sum of wages. It begins at zero.
 30  FOR I=1 TO 15
 40  READ G(I)              Which entry in the data list is G(7)?
 50  LET S=S+G(I)           Add the next wage to the sum of the
 60  NEXT I                 previous wages.
 70  LET A=S/15             Why divide by 15?
 80  PRINT "AVERAGE WAGE IS", A
 90  PRINT "HOURLY WAGES"
100  FOR X=1 TO 15
105  PRINT G(X);
110  NEXT X
120  DATA 4.20,3.15,3.60,4.35,5.10,3.20,3.15,4.05
130  DATA 4.65,3.40,5.50,6.05,4.75,3.80,4.90
140  END
```

Some systems may use semicolons instead of commas in lines 100 and 110.

Suppose the following array is to be read into the computer. The program on the right will do this.

Columns

Rows	1	2	3	4	5
1	13	16	57	86	23
2	41	54	62	27	70
3	5	11	35	81	7

The 62 is in row 2, column 3. It can be represented by B(2, 3).

This loop changes rows. For each row, the inner loop goes through a full cycle.

```
10  DIM M(3,5)
20  FOR R=1 TO 3
30  FOR C=1 TO 5
40  READ M(R,C)
50  NEXT C
60  NEXT R
```

This loop changes columns.

exercises

Written Refer to the array on page 532. Use the letter B and a set of parentheses to write a correct subscripted variable to refer to each of these entries in the array.

1. 13 B(1,1) **2.** 5 B(3,1) **3.** 86 B(1,4) **4.** 7 B(3,5)
5. 35 B(3,3) **6.** 16 B(1,2) **7.** 41 B(2,1) **8.** 70 B(2,5)

Write a BASIC subscripted variable for each of the following.

9. m_3 M(3) **10.** t_4 T(4) **11.** r_y R(Y) **12.** z_{x+1} Z(X+1)
13. q_{24} Q(24) **14.** k_{m+n} K(M+N) **15.** $x_{(1,3)}$ X(1,3) **16.** $y_{(a,r)}$ Y(A,R)

The first four lines of a program are shown below. Use them to evaluate the following.

```
10 DATA 8,−4,16,−12,2,17
20 FOR R=1 TO 6
30 READ A(R)
40 NEXT R
```

17. A(2) $^-4$ **18.** A(5−1) $^-12$
19. A(3)−1 15 **20.** 2*A(4) $^-24$
21. A(1)/2 4 **22.** A(A(5)) $^-4$
23. 6+A(3) 22 **24.** A(6)−A(4) 23

Let K = 3 and J = 2. Evaluate the following. Use the same program lines as in problems 17-24.

25. A(J)*A(K) $^-64$ **26.** A(J*K) 11 **27.** 2*A(J) $^-8$ **28.** A(2*J) $^-12$

Write the necessary DIM statement.

29. $[a_1, a_2, \ldots, a_{40}]$ DIM A(40) **30.** $[m_{41}, m_{42}, \ldots m_{79}]$ DIM M(79)

Write BASIC programs which will do the following 31-32. See Teacher's Guide for answers.

31. Kristy has grades of 67, 72, 74, 63, and 81 in Algebra One. Anne Marie has grades of 91, 87, 81, 83, and 89. Find and print the average of each girl's grades.

32. Print each of the following numbers and its absolute value. Use 5, 3, 7, 0, $^-1$, 15, $^-11$, $^-12$, $^-6$, $^-22$ in the DATA statement.

33. The table below shows the scores for one game in a bowling league. The program computes the average for each team. Copy and complete the program. Use S(M,T) as the variable for entries in the table. Print both the team number and its average.

Teams		1	2	3	4	5	6
Members	1	165	151	130	147	137	132
	2	135	122	146	123	153	114
	3	149	155	101	181	166	127
	4	118	140	135	110	111	175
	5	102	119	179	129	146	159

```
 5 FOR M=1 TO 5
10 FOR T=_1 TO 6_
15 READ S(M,T)
20 NEXT __T__
25 NEXT __M__
30 FOR T=1 TO 6
35 LET S=__O__
40 FOR M=1 TO 5
45 LET S=S+_S(M,T)_
50 NEXT __M__
55 PRINT T,__S/5__
60 NEXT __T__
65 DATA . . .
70 END
```

Fill in data from chart. May need more than one data line.

Internal Functions

Objective: To use internal functions in BASIC.

In BASIC there are several subprograms which are used with problems which occur frequently. Such programs are called functions. Each one has an abbreviation and an argument. The argument is the symbol in parentheses. Some common functions follow.

Abbreviation (argument)

ABS(X)	*This function finds the absolute value of X.*
SQR(X)	*This function finds the square root of X.*
INT(X)	*This function finds the greatest integer less than or equal to X.*
RND(X)	*This function generates a random number between 0 and 1.*

Functions used in trigonometry are also available. X is measured in radians.

SIN(X)	*This function finds the sine of X.*
COS(X)	*This function finds the cosine of X.*
TAN(X)	*This function finds the tangent of X.*

The INT function is called the greatest integer function. Here are some examples. If necessary, refer to page **57**.

INT(2) = 2 INT(3.5) = 3 INT(−2) = $^{-}2$ INT(−2.5) = $^{-}3$

Do you see why the result in the last example is $^{-}3$?

The INT function is useful in finding factors of a number.

examples

1 **Write a test to tell whether 2 is a factor of 5.**

Is it true that INT(5/2) = 5/2?

INT(5/2) = INT(2.5) *What is the greatest integer less than or equal to 2.5?*

= 2 *Thus 2 is not a factor of 5, since 5/2 = 2.5 and INT(5/2) = 2.*

2 **Write a program to find all the factors of a given positive integer.**

```
10  READ N
20  FOR X=1 TO SQR(N)
30  IF INT(N/X)<>N/X THEN 50
40  PRINT X, N/X
50  NEXT X
60  GO TO 10
70  DATA 48,102,235
80  END
```

Why SQR(N)?

RND(X) is a BASIC function which generates random numbers. The X in RND(X) is a placeholder. Each random number generated is a six-digit decimal between 0 and 1. Suppose two such numbers were generated by RND(X).

0.627590 and 0.218802

If integers greater than one are desired, the two functions INT(X) and RND(X) are used together as follows.

PRINT INT(10*RND(X))

The computer would do the following calculations for the two numbers generated above.

INT(10*RND(X)) = INT(10*0.627590)
= INT(6.27590) or 6

INT(10*RND(X)) = INT(10*0.218802)
= INT(2.18802) or 2

Suppose you throw a red die and a green die. Each combination of the dice is equally likely. The combinations occur at random.

Suppose the results of ten throws of a single die are desired. The functions INT(X) and RND(X) can be used to simulate the ten throws of a single die.

example 3

Write a program to simulate the results of ten throws of a single die.

```
10 FOR T=1 TO 10
20 PRINT INT(6*RND(X)+1)
30 NEXT T
40 END
```

Some computers always print the same series of random numbers unless the statement RANDOMIZE is included in the program. The range of the random numbers can be varied.

example 4

Write a statement which will give random integers with values from 1 to 9.

There are 9 integers which can be used. Multiplying a decimal between 0 and 1 by nine gives a number between 0.0 and 8.9999. If 1 is added, the number is between 1.0 and 9.9999. Taking the greatest integer gives a number between 1 and 9. PRINT INT (9*RND(X)+1) is the desired statement. It yields numbers such as 7, 2, 1, 3, 9, 6, 3, and 4.

example 5

Write a statement which will generate random integers with values from 10 to 20 inclusive.

There are 11 integers which could be used. Multiplying by 11 yields results from 0.0 to 10.9999. Since the series is to start with 10, the number 10 is added to each number generated. Then the greatest integer function is used. PRINT INT(11*RND(X)+10) is the desired statement. It yields numbers such as 20, 17, 18, 12, 13, 19, and 15.

In general, when random integers are to be chosen from a set containing A integers, with B the least one, the following can be used:

PRINT INT(A*RND(X)+B)

9.
```
10 RANDOMIZE
20 FOR X=1 TO 5
30 PRINT INT(10000*RND(X)+1);
40 NEXT X
50 END
```

exercises

Written **Describe the result of each of the following PRINT statements.**

1. PRINT INT(3.6)
2. PRINT INT(3.4−3.7)
3. PRINT ABS(−5)
4. PRINT SQR(36)
5. PRINT INT(10*RND(X)+2)
6. PRINT (12*RND(X)+29)

5. Prints random integers from 2 through 11.
6. Prints random integers from 29 through 40

Write a PRINT statement to yield each of the following.

7. The decimal numbers from 0 through 9.9999 PRINT 10*RND(X)
8. The integers from 23 through 38 PRINT INT(16*RND(X)+23)

Write programs using internal functions to do the following.

9. Select five random integers from 1 to 10,000 as winning numbers for a local lottery. See program above.
10. A state lottery commission uses lottery tickets which are printed in random sequence. Write a program to print 5-digit integers (0 through 99,999). Print a sample of ten such numbers. See program above.
11. Simulate the throw of a pair of dice using the random number function. Print the integer appearing on each die for each throw. Keep a count of the number of throws. Print the count the first time two sixes appear.
12. Write a program to find the real roots of any quadratic equations of the form $ax^2 + bx + c = 0$.

10.
```
10 RANDOMIZE
20 FOR X=1 TO 10
30 PRINT INT(100000*RND(X));
40 NEXT X
50 END
```

11.
```
10 LET R=INT(6*RND(X)+1)
20 LET G=INT(6*RND(X)+1)
30 LET K=K+1
40 PRINT R;G
50 IF R+G<>12 THEN 10
60 PRINT K
70 END
```

SYMBOLS

a^n	the nth power of a
$\|a\|$	the absolute value of a
^{-}a	additive inverse of a or the opposite of a
Cos^{-1}	Arccosine
$C(n, r)$	combinations of n elements taken r at a time
$a + bi$	complex number
$^\circ$	degrees
det	determinant
e	base of natural logarithms
$\in$	is an element of
$\emptyset$	empty set
$=$	equals or is equal to
$\neq$	does not equal
$\approx$	approximately equal to
$f(x)$	f of x or the value of f at x
f^{-1}	inverse function of f
!	factorial
$f \circ g$	composition function f of g
$>$	is greater than
$<$	is less than
$\geq$	is greater than or equal to
$\leq$	is less than or equal to
$\log_b x$	the logarithm to the base b of x
$P(n, r)$	permutations of n things taken r at a time
$\pm$	positive or negative
$\{\ \}$	set
$\sqrt{\ }$	the principal square root of
$\sqrt[n]{\ }$	the nth root of
Σ	(sigma) summation symbol

Squares and Square Roots

n	n^2	$\sqrt{n}$	$\sqrt{10n}$
1.0	1.00	1.000	3.162
1.1	1.21	1.049	3.317
1.2	1.44	1.095	3.464
1.3	1.69	1.140	3.606
1.4	1.96	1.183	3.742
1.5	2.25	1.225	3.873
1.6	2.56	1.265	4.000
1.7	2.89	1.304	4.123
1.8	3.24	1.342	4.243
1.9	3.61	1.378	4.359
2.0	4.00	1.414	4.472
2.1	4.41	1.449	4.583
2.2	4.84	1.483	4.690
2.3	5.29	1.517	4.796
2.4	5.76	1.549	4.899
2.5	6.25	1.581	5.000
2.6	6.76	1.612	5.099
2.7	7.29	1.643	5.196
2.8	7.84	1.673	5.292
2.9	8.41	1.703	5.385
3.0	9.00	1.732	5.477
3.1	9.61	1.761	5.568
3.2	10.24	1.789	5.657
3.3	10.89	1.817	5.745
3.4	11.56	1.844	5.831
3.5	12.25	1.871	5.916
3.6	12.96	1.897	6.000
3.7	13.69	1.924	6.083
3.8	14.44	1.949	6.164
3.9	15.21	1.975	6.245
4.0	16.00	2.000	6.325
4.1	16.81	2.025	6.403
4.2	17.64	2.049	6.481
4.3	18.49	2.074	6.557
4.4	19.36	2.098	6.633
4.5	20.25	2.121	6.708
4.6	21.16	2.145	6.782
4.7	22.09	2.168	6.856
4.8	23.04	2.191	6.928
4.9	24.01	2.214	7.000
5.0	25.00	2.236	7.071
5.1	26.01	2.258	7.141
5.2	27.04	2.280	7.211
5.3	28.09	2.302	7.280
5.4	29.16	2.324	7.348

n	n^2	$\sqrt{n}$	$\sqrt{10n}$
5.5	30.25	2.345	7.416
5.6	31.36	2.366	7.483
5.7	32.49	2.387	7.550
5.8	33.64	2.408	7.616
5.9	34.81	2.429	7.681
6.0	36.00	2.449	7.746
6.1	37.21	2.470	7.810
6.2	38.44	2.490	7.874
6.3	39.69	2.510	7.937
6.4	40.96	2.530	8.000
6.5	42.25	2.550	8.062
6.6	43.56	2.569	8.124
6.7	44.89	2.588	8.185
6.8	46.24	2.608	8.246
6.9	47.61	2.627	8.307
7.0	49.00	2.646	8.367
7.1	50.41	2.665	8.426
7.2	51.84	2.683	8.485
7.3	53.29	2.702	8.544
7.4	54.76	2.720	8.602
7.5	56.25	2.739	8.660
7.6	57.76	2.757	8.718
7.7	59.29	2.775	8.775
7.8	60.84	2.793	8.832
7.9	62.41	2.811	8.888
8.0	64.00	2.828	8.944
8.1	65.61	2.846	9.000
8.2	67.24	2.864	9.055
8.3	68.89	2.881	9.110
8.4	70.56	2.898	9.165
8.5	72.25	2.915	9.220
8.6	73.96	2.933	9.274
8.7	75.69	2.950	9.327
8.8	77.44	2.966	9.381
8.9	79.21	2.983	9.434
9.0	81.00	3.000	9.487
9.1	82.81	3.017	9.539
9.2	84.64	3.033	9.592
9.3	86.49	3.050	9.644
9.4	88.36	3.066	9.695
9.5	90.25	3.082	9.747
9.6	92.16	3.098	9.798
9.7	94.09	3.114	9.849
9.8	96.04	3.130	9.899
9.9	98.01	3.146	9.950

Cubes and Cube Roots

n	n^3	$\sqrt[3]{n}$	$\sqrt[3]{10n}$	$\sqrt[3]{100n}$
1.0	1.000	1.000	2.154	4.642
1.1	1.331	1.032	2.224	4.791
1.2	1.728	1.063	2.289	4.932
1.3	2.197	1.091	2.351	5.066
1.4	2.744	1.119	2.410	5.192
1.5	3.375	1.145	2.466	5.313
1.6	4.096	1.170	2.520	5.429
1.7	4.913	1.193	2.571	5.540
1.8	5.832	1.216	2.621	5.646
1.9	6.859	1.239	2.668	5.749
2.0	8.000	1.260	2.714	5.848
2.1	9.261	1.281	2.759	5.944
2.2	10.648	1.301	2.802	6.037
2.3	12.167	1.320	2.844	6.127
2.4	13.824	1.339	2.884	6.214
2.5	15.625	1.357	2.924	6.300
2.6	17.576	1.375	2.962	6.383
2.7	19.683	1.392	3.000	6.463
2.8	21.952	1.409	3.037	6.542
2.9	24.389	1.426	3.072	6.619
3.0	27.000	1.442	3.107	6.694
3.1	29.791	1.458	3.141	6.768
3.2	32.768	1.474	3.175	6.840
3.3	35.937	1.489	3.208	6.910
3.4	39.304	1.504	3.240	6.980
3.5	42.875	1.518	3.271	7.047
3.6	46.656	1.533	3.302	7.114
3.7	50.653	1.547	3.332	7.179
3.8	54.872	1.560	3.362	7.243
3.9	59.319	1.574	3.391	7.306
4.0	64.000	1.587	3.420	7.368
4.1	68.921	1.601	3.448	7.429
4.2	74.088	1.613	3.476	7.489
4.3	79.507	1.626	3.503	7.548
4.4	85.184	1.639	3.530	7.606
4.5	91.125	1.651	3.557	7.663
4.6	97.336	1.663	3.583	7.719
4.7	103.823	1.675	3.609	7.775
4.8	110.592	1.687	3.634	7.830
4.9	117.649	1.698	3.659	7.884
5.0	125.000	1.710	3.684	7.937
5.1	132.651	1.721	3.708	7.990
5.2	140.608	1.732	3.733	8.041
5.3	148.877	1.744	3.756	8.093
5.4	157.464	1.754	3.780	8.143

n	n^3	$\sqrt[3]{n}$	$\sqrt[3]{10n}$	$\sqrt[3]{100n}$
5.5	166.375	1.765	3.803	8.193
5.6	175.616	1.776	3.826	8.243
5.7	185.193	1.786	3.849	8.291
5.8	195.112	1.797	3.871	8.340
5.9	205.379	1.807	3.893	8.387
6.0	216.000	1.817	3.915	8.434
6.1	226.981	1.827	3.936	8.481
6.2	238.328	1.837	3.958	8.527
6.3	250.047	1.847	3.979	8.573
6.4	262.144	1.857	4.000	8.618
6.5	274.625	1.866	4.021	8.662
6.6	287.496	1.876	4.041	8.707
6.7	300.763	1.885	4.062	8.750
6.8	314.432	1.895	4.082	8.794
6.9	328.509	1.904	4.102	8.837
7.0	343.000	1.913	4.121	8.879
7.1	357.911	1.922	4.141	8.921
7.2	373.248	1.931	4.160	8.963
7.3	389.017	1.940	4.179	9.004
7.4	405.224	1.949	4.198	9.045
7.5	421.875	1.957	4.217	9.086
7.6	438.976	1.966	4.236	9.126
7.7	456.533	1.975	4.254	9.166
7.8	474.552	1.983	4.273	9.205
7.9	493.039	1.992	4.291	9.244
8.0	512.000	2.000	4.309	9.283
8.1	531.441	2.008	4.327	9.322
8.2	551.368	2.017	4.344	9.360
8.3	571.787	2.025	4.362	9.398
8.4	592.704	2.033	4.380	9.435
8.5	614.125	2.041	4.397	9.473
8.6	636.056	2.049	4.414	9.510
8.7	658.503	2.057	4.431	9.546
8.8	681.472	2.065	4.448	9.583
8.9	704.969	2.072	4.465	9.619
9.0	729.000	2.080	4.481	9.655
9.1	753.571	2.088	4.498	9.691
9.2	778.688	2.095	4.514	9.726
9.3	804.357	2.103	4.531	9.761
9.4	830.584	2.110	4.547	9.796
9.5	857.375	2.118	4.563	9.830
9.6	884.736	2.125	4.579	9.865
9.7	912.673	2.133	4.595	9.899
9.8	941.192	2.140	4.610	9.933
9.9	970.299	2.147	4.626	9.967

Common Logarithms of Numbers

n	0	1	2	3	4	5	6	7	8	9
10	0000	0043	0086	0128	0170	0212	0253	0294	0334	0374
11	0414	0453	0492	0531	0569	0607	0645	0682	0719	0755
12	0792	0828	0864	0899	0934	0969	1004	1038	1072	1106
13	1139	1173	1206	1239	1271	1303	1335	1367	1399	1430
14	1461	1492	1523	1553	1584	1614	1644	1673	1703	1732
15	1761	1790	1818	1847	1875	1903	1931	1959	1987	2014
16	2041	2068	2095	2122	2148	2175	2201	2227	2253	2279
17	2304	2330	2355	2380	2405	2430	2455	2480	2504	2529
18	2553	2577	2601	2625	2648	2672	2695	2718	2742	2765
19	2788	2810	2833	2856	2878	2900	2923	2945	2967	2989
20	3010	3032	3054	3075	3096	3118	3139	3160	3181	3201
21	3222	3243	3263	3284	3304	3324	3345	3365	3385	3404
22	3424	3444	3464	3483	3502	3522	3541	3560	3579	3598
23	3617	3636	3655	3674	3692	3711	3729	3747	3766	3784
24	3802	3820	3838	3856	3874	3892	3909	3927	3945	3962
25	3979	3997	4014	4031	4048	4065	4082	4099	4116	4133
26	4150	4166	4183	4200	4216	4232	4249	4265	4281	4298
27	4314	4330	4346	4362	4378	4393	4409	4425	4440	4456
28	4472	4487	4502	4518	4533	4548	4564	4579	4594	4609
29	4624	4639	4654	4669	4683	4698	4713	4728	4742	4757
30	4771	4786	4800	4814	4829	4843	4857	4871	4886	4900
31	4914	4928	4942	4955	4969	4983	4997	5011	5024	5038
32	5051	5065	5079	5092	5105	5119	5132	5145	5159	5172
33	5185	5198	5211	5224	5237	5250	5263	5276	5289	5302
34	5315	5328	5340	5353	5366	5378	5391	5403	5416	5428
35	5441	5453	5465	5478	5490	5502	5514	5527	5539	5551
36	5563	5575	5587	5599	5611	5623	5635	5647	5658	5670
37	5682	5694	5705	5717	5729	5740	5752	5763	5775	5786
38	5798	5809	5821	5832	5843	5855	5866	5877	5888	5899
39	5911	5922	5933	5944	5955	5966	5977	5988	5999	6010
40	6021	6031	6042	6053	6064	6075	6085	6096	6107	6117
41	6128	6138	6149	6160	6170	6180	6191	6201	6212	6222
42	6232	6243	6253	6263	6274	6284	6294	6304	6314	6325
43	6335	6345	6355	6365	6375	6385	6395	6405	6415	6425
44	6435	6444	6454	6464	6474	6484	6493	6503	6513	6522
45	6532	6542	6551	6561	6571	6580	6590	6599	6609	6618
46	6628	6637	6646	6656	6665	6675	6684	6693	6702	6712
47	6721	6730	6739	6749	6758	6767	6776	6785	6794	6803
48	6812	6821	6830	6839	6848	6857	6866	6875	6884	6893
49	6902	6911	6920	6928	6937	6946	6955	6964	6972	6981
50	6990	6998	7007	7016	7024	7033	7042	7050	7059	7067
51	7076	7084	7093	7101	7110	7118	7126	7135	7143	7152
52	7160	7168	7177	7185	7193	7202	7210	7218	7226	7235
53	7243	7251	7259	7267	7275	7284	7292	7300	7308	7316
54	7324	7332	7340	7348	7356	7364	7372	7380	7388	7396

The values given are mantissas correct to four decimal places. For example, log 5.42 = 0.7340.

Common Logarithms of Numbers

n	0	1	2	3	4	5	6	7	8	9
55	7404	7412	7419	7427	7435	7443	7451	7459	7466	7474
56	7482	7490	7497	7505	7513	7520	7528	7536	7543	7551
57	7559	7566	7574	7582	7589	7597	7604	7612	7619	7627
58	7634	7642	7649	7657	7664	7672	7679	7686	7694	7701
59	7709	7716	7723	7731	7738	7745	7752	7760	7767	7774
60	7782	7789	7796	7803	7810	7818	7825	7832	7839	7846
61	7853	7860	7868	7875	7882	7889	7896	7903	7910	7917
62	7924	7931	7938	7945	7952	7959	7966	7973	7980	7987
63	7993	8000	8007	8014	8021	8028	8035	8041	8048	8055
64	8062	8069	8075	8082	8089	8096	8102	8109	8116	8122
65	8129	8136	8142	8149	8156	8162	8169	8176	8182	8189
66	8195	8202	8209	8215	8222	8228	8235	8241	8248	8254
67	8261	8267	8274	8280	8287	8293	8299	8306	8312	8319
68	8325	8331	8338	8344	8351	8357	8363	8370	8376	8382
69	8388	8395	8401	8407	8414	8420	8426	8432	8439	8445
70	8451	8457	8463	8470	8476	8482	8488	8494	8500	8506
71	8513	8519	8525	8531	8537	8543	8549	8555	8561	8567
72	8573	8579	8585	8591	8597	8603	8609	8615	8621	8627
73	8633	8639	8645	8651	8657	8663	8669	8675	8681	8686
74	8692	8698	8704	8710	8716	8722	8727	8733	8739	8745
75	8751	8756	8762	8768	8774	8779	8785	8791	8797	8802
76	8808	8814	8820	8825	8831	8837	8842	8848	8854	8859
77	8865	8871	8876	8882	8887	8893	8899	8904	8910	8915
78	8921	8927	8932	8938	8943	8949	8954	8960	8965	8971
79	8976	8982	8987	8993	8998	9004	9009	9015	9020	9025
80	9031	9036	9042	9047	9053	9058	9063	9069	9074	9079
81	9085	9090	9096	9101	9106	9112	9117	9122	9128	9133
82	9138	9143	9149	9154	9159	9165	9170	9175	9180	9186
83	9191	9196	9201	9206	9212	9217	9222	9227	9232	9238
84	9243	9248	9253	9258	9263	9269	9274	9279	9284	9289
85	9294	9299	9304	9309	9315	9320	9325	9330	9335	9340
86	9345	9350	9355	9360	9365	9370	9375	9380	9385	9390
87	9395	9400	9405	9410	9415	9420	9425	9430	9435	9440
88	9445	9450	9455	9460	9465	9469	9474	9479	9484	9489
89	9494	9499	9504	9509	9513	9518	9523	9528	9533	9538
90	9542	9547	9552	9557	9562	9566	9571	9576	9581	9586
91	9590	9595	9600	9605	9609	9614	9619	9624	9628	9633
92	9638	9643	9647	9652	9657	9661	9666	9671	9675	9680
93	9685	9689	9694	9699	9703	9708	9713	9717	9722	9727
94	9731	9736	9741	9745	9750	9754	9759	9763	9768	9773
95	9777	9782	9786	9791	9795	9800	9805	9809	9814	9818
96	9823	9827	9832	9836	9841	9845	9850	9854	9859	9863
97	9868	9872	9877	9881	9886	9890	9894	9899	9903	9908
98	9912	9917	9921	9926	9930	9934	9939	9943	9948	9952
99	9956	9961	9965	9969	9974	9978	9983	9987	9991	9996

Values of Trigonometric Functions

Angle	Sin	Cos	Tan	Cot	Sec	Csc	
0°00′	0.0000	1.0000	0.0000	—	1.000	—	90°00′
10′	0.0029	1.0000	0.0029	343.8	1.000	343.8	50′
20′	0.0058	1.0000	0.0058	171.9	1.000	171.9	40′
30′	0.0087	1.0000	0.0087	114.6	1.000	114.6	30′
40′	0.0116	0.9999	0.0116	85.94	1.000	85.95	20′
50′	0.0145	0.9999	0.0145	68.75	1.000	68.76	10′
1°00′	0.0175	0.9998	0.0175	57.29	1.000	57.30	89°00′
10′	0.0204	0.9998	0.0204	49.10	1.000	49.11	50′
20′	0.0233	0.9997	0.0233	42.96	1.000	42.98	40′
30′	0.0262	0.9997	0.0262	38.19	1.000	38.20	30′
40′	0.0291	0.9996	0.0291	34.37	1.000	34.38	20′
50′	0.0320	0.9995	0.0320	31.24	1.001	31.26	10′
2°00′	0.0349	0.9994	0.0349	28.64	1.001	28.65	88°00′
10′	0.0378	0.9993	0.0378	26.43	1.001	26.45	50′
20′	0.0407	0.9992	0.0407	24.54	1.001	24.56	40′
30′	0.0436	0.9990	0.0437	22.90	1.001	22.93	30′
40′	0.0465	0.9989	0.0466	21.47	1.001	21.49	20′
50′	0.0494	0.9988	0.0495	20.21	1.001	20.23	10′
3°00′	0.0523	0.9986	0.0524	19.08	1.001	19.11	87°00′
10′	0.0552	0.9985	0.0553	18.07	1.002	18.10	50′
20′	0.0581	0.9983	0.0582	17.17	1.002	17.20	40′
30′	0.0610	0.9981	0.0612	16.35	1.002	16.38	30′
40′	0.0640	0.9980	0.0641	15.60	1.002	15.64	20′
50′	0.0669	0.9978	0.0670	14.92	1.002	14.96	10′
4°00′	0.0698	0.9976	0.0699	14.30	1.002	14.34	86°00′
10′	0.0727	0.9974	0.0729	13.73	1.003	13.76	50′
20′	0.0756	0.9971	0.0758	13.20	1.003	13.23	40′
30′	0.0785	0.9969	0.0787	12.71	1.003	12.75	30′
40′	0.0814	0.9967	0.0816	12.25	1.003	12.29	20′
50′	0.0843	0.9964	0.0846	11.83	1.004	11.87	10′
5°00′	0.0872	0.9962	0.0875	11.43	1.004	11.47	85°00′
10′	0.0901	0.9959	0.0904	11.06	1.004	11.10	50′
20′	0.0929	0.9957	0.0934	10.71	1.004	10.76	40′
30′	0.0958	0.9954	0.0963	10.39	1.005	10.43	30′
40′	0.0987	0.9951	0.0992	10.08	1.005	10.13	20′
50′	0.1016	0.9948	0.1022	9.788	1.005	9.839	10′
6°00′	0.1045	0.9945	0.1051	9.514	1.006	9.567	84°00′
10′	0.1074	0.9942	0.1080	9.255	1.006	9.309	50′
20′	0.1103	0.9939	0.1110	9.010	1.006	9.065	40′
30′	0.1132	0.9936	0.1139	8.777	1.006	8.834	30′
40′	0.1161	0.9932	0.1169	8.556	1.007	8.614	20′
50′	0.1190	0.9929	0.1198	8.345	1.007	8.405	10′
7°00′	0.1219	0.9925	0.1228	8.144	1.008	8.206	83°00′
10′	0.1248	0.9922	0.1257	7.953	1.008	8.016	50′
20′	0.1276	0.9918	0.1287	7.770	1.008	7.834	40′
30′	0.1305	0.9914	0.1317	7.596	1.009	7.661	30′
40′	0.1334	0.9911	0.1346	7.429	1.009	7.496	20′
50′	0.1363	0.9907	0.1376	7.269	1.009	7.337	10′
8°00′	0.1392	0.9903	0.1405	7.115	1.010	7.185	82°00′
10′	0.1421	0.9899	0.1435	6.968	1.010	7.040	50′
20′	0.1449	0.9894	0.1465	6.827	1.011	6.900	40′
30′	0.1478	0.9890	0.1495	6.691	1.011	6.765	30′
40′	0.1507	0.9886	0.1524	6.561	1.012	6.636	20′
50′	0.1536	0.9881	0.1554	6.435	1.012	6.512	10′
9°00′	0.1564	0.9877	0.1584	6.314	1.012	6.392	81°00′
	Cos	Sin	Cot	Tan	Csc	Sec	Angle

For the values of cos, sin, tan, and so on for angles greater than 45°, use the angle measures listed on the right and the functions on the bottom. For example, cos 81° = 0.1564.

Values of Trigonometric Functions

Angle	Sin	Cos	Tan	Cot	Sec	Csc	
9°00′	0.1564	0.9877	0.1584	6.314	1.012	6.392	81°00′
10′	0.1593	0.9872	0.1614	6.197	1.013	6.277	50′
20′	0.1622	0.9868	0.1644	6.084	1.013	6.166	40′
30′	0.1650	0.9863	0.1673	5.976	1.014	6.059	30′
40′	0.1679	0.9858	0.1703	5.871	1.014	5.955	20′
50′	0.1708	0.9853	0.1733	5.769	1.015	5.855	10′
10°00′	0.1736	0.9848	0.1763	5.671	1.015	5.759	80°00′
10′	0.1765	0.9843	0.1793	5.576	1.016	5.665	50′
20′	0.1794	0.9838	0.1823	5.485	1.016	5.575	40′
30′	0.1822	0.9833	0.1853	5.396	1.017	5.487	30′
40′	0.1851	0.9827	0.1883	5.309	1.018	5.403	20′
50′	0.1880	0.9822	0.1914	5.226	1.018	5.320	10′
11°00′	0.1908	0.9816	0.1944	5.145	1.019	5.241	79°00′
10′	0.1937	0.9811	0.1974	5.066	1.019	5.164	50′
20′	0.1965	0.9805	0.2004	4.989	1.020	5.089	40′
30′	0.1994	0.9799	0.2035	4.915	1.020	5.016	30′
40′	0.2022	0.9793	0.2065	4.843	1.021	4.945	20′
50′	0.2051	0.9787	0.2095	4.773	1.022	4.876	10′
12°00′	0.2079	0.9781	0.2126	4.705	1.022	4.810	78°00′
10′	0.2108	0.9775	0.2156	4.638	1.023	4.745	50′
20′	0.2136	0.9769	0.2186	4.574	1.024	4.682	40′
30′	0.2164	0.9763	0.2217	4.511	1.024	4.620	30′
40′	0.2193	0.9757	0.2247	4.449	1.025	4.560	20′
50′	0.2221	0.9750	0.2278	4.390	1.026	4.502	10′
13°00′	0.2250	0.9744	0.2309	4.331	1.026	4.445	77°00′
10′	0.2278	0.9737	0.2339	4.275	1.027	4.390	50′
20′	0.2306	0.9730	0.2370	4.219	1.028	4.336	40′
30′	0.2334	0.9724	0.2401	4.165	1.028	4.284	30′
40′	0.2363	0.9717	0.2432	4.113	1.029	4.232	20′
50′	0.2391	0.9710	0.2462	4.061	1.030	4.182	10′
14°00′	0.2419	0.9703	0.2493	4.011	1.031	4.134	76°00′
10′	0.2447	0.9696	0.2524	3.962	1.031	4.086	50′
20′	0.2476	0.9689	0.2555	3.914	1.032	4.039	40′
30′	0.2504	0.9681	0.2586	3.867	1.033	3.994	30′
40′	0.2532	0.9674	0.2617	3.821	1.034	3.950	20′
50′	0.2560	0.9667	0.2648	3.776	1.034	3.906	10′
15°00′	0.2588	0.9659	0.2679	3.732	1.035	3.864	75°00′
10′	0.2616	0.9652	0.2711	3.689	1.036	3.822	50′
20′	0.2644	0.9644	0.2742	3.647	1.037	3.782	40′
30′	0.2672	0.9636	0.2773	3.606	1.038	3.742	30′
40′	0.2700	0.9628	0.2805	3.566	1.039	3.703	20′
50′	0.2728	0.9621	0.2836	3.526	1.039	3.665	10′
16°00′	0.2756	0.9613	0.2867	3.487	1.040	3.628	74°00′
10′	0.2784	0.9605	0.2899	3.450	1.041	3.592	50′
20′	0.2812	0.9596	0.2931	3.412	1.042	3.556	40′
30′	0.2840	0.9588	0.2962	3.376	1.043	3.521	30′
40′	0.2868	0.9580	0.2994	3.340	1.044	3.487	20′
50′	0.2896	0.9572	0.3026	3.305	1.045	3.453	10′
17°00′	0.2924	0.9563	0.3057	3.271	1.046	3.420	73°00′
10′	0.2952	0.9555	0.3089	3.237	1.047	3.388	50′
20′	0.2979	0.9546	0.3121	3.204	1.048	3.356	40′
30′	0.3007	0.9537	0.3153	3.172	1.049	3.326	30′
40′	0.3035	0.9528	0.3185	3.140	1.049	3.295	20′
50′	0.3062	0.9520	0.3217	3.108	1.050	3.265	10′
18°00′	0.3090	0.9511	0.3249	3.078	1.051	3.236	72°00′
	Cos	Sin	Cot	Tan	Csc	Sec	Angle

Values of Trigonometric Functions

Angle	Sin	Cos	Tan	Cot	Sec	Csc	
18°00′	0.3090	0.9511	0.3249	3.078	1.051	3.236	72°00′
10′	0.3118	0.9502	0.3281	3.047	1.052	3.207	50′
20′	0.3145	0.9492	0.3314	3.018	1.053	3.179	40′
30′	0.3173	0.9483	0.3346	2.989	1.054	3.152	30′
40′	0.3201	0.9474	0.3378	2.960	1.056	3.124	20′
50′	0.3228	0.9465	0.3411	2.932	1.057	3.098	10′
19°00′	0.3256	0.9455	0.3443	2.904	1.058	3.072	71°00′
10′	0.3283	0.9446	0.3476	2.877	1.059	3.046	50′
20′	0.3311	0.9436	0.3508	2.850	1.060	3.021	40′
30′	0.3338	0.9426	0.3541	2.824	1.061	2.996	30′
40′	0.3365	0.9417	0.3574	2.798	1.062	2.971	20′
50′	0.3393	0.9407	0.3607	2.773	1.063	2.947	10′
20°00′	0.3420	0.9397	0.3640	2.747	1.064	2.924	70°00′
10′	0.3448	0.9387	0.3673	2.723	1.065	2.901	50′
20′	0.3475	0.9377	0.3706	2.699	1.066	2.878	40′
30′	0.3502	0.9367	0.3739	2.675	1.068	2.855	30′
40′	0.3529	0.9356	0.3772	2.651	1.069	2.833	20′
50′	0.3557	0.9346	0.3805	2.628	1.070	2.812	10′
21°00′	0.3584	0.9336	0.3839	2.605	1.071	2.790	69°00′
10′	0.3611	0.9325	0.3872	2.583	1.072	2.769	50′
20′	0.3638	0.9315	0.3906	2.560	1.074	2.749	40′
30′	0.3665	0.9304	0.3939	2.539	1.075	2.729	30′
40′	0.3692	0.9293	0.3973	2.517	1.076	2.709	20′
50′	0.3719	0.9283	0.4006	2.496	1.077	2.689	10′
22°00′	0.3746	0.9272	0.4040	2.475	1.079	2.669	68°00′
10′	0.3773	0.9261	0.4074	2.455	1.080	2.650	50′
20′	0.3800	0.9250	0.4108	2.434	1.081	2.632	40′
30′	0.3827	0.9239	0.4142	2.414	1.082	2.613	30′
40′	0.3854	0.9228	0.4176	2.394	1.084	2.595	20′
50′	0.3881	0.9216	0.4210	2.375	1.085	2.577	10′
23°00′	0.3907	0.9205	0.4245	2.356	1.086	2.559	67°00′
10′	0.3934	0.9194	0.4279	2.337	1.088	2.542	50′
20′	0.3961	0.9182	0.4314	2.318	1.089	2.525	40′
30′	0.3987	0.9171	0.4348	2.300	1.090	2.508	30′
40′	0.4014	0.9159	0.4383	2.282	1.092	2.491	20′
50′	0.4041	0.9147	0.4417	2.264	1.093	2.475	10′
24°00′	0.4067	0.9135	0.4452	2.246	1.095	2.459	66°00′
10′	0.4094	0.9124	0.4487	2.229	1.096	2.443	50′
20′	0.4120	0.9112	0.4522	2.211	1.097	2.427	40′
30′	0.4147	0.9100	0.4557	2.194	1.099	2.411	30′
40′	0.4173	0.9088	0.4592	2.177	1.100	2.396	20′
50′	0.4200	0.9075	0.4628	2.161	1.102	2.381	10′
25°00′	0.4226	0.9063	0.4663	2.145	1.103	2.366	65°00′
10′	0.4253	0.9051	0.4699	2.128	1.105	2.352	50′
20′	0.4279	0.9038	0.4734	2.112	1.106	2.337	40′
30′	0.4305	0.9026	0.4770	2.097	1.108	2.323	30′
40′	0.4331	0.9013	0.4806	2.081	1.109	2.309	20′
50′	0.4358	0.9001	0.4841	2.066	1.111	2.295	10′
26°00′	0.4384	0.8988	0.4877	2.050	1.113	2.281	64°00′
10′	0.4410	0.8975	0.4913	2.035	1.114	2.268	50′
20′	0.4436	0.8962	0.4950	2.020	1.116	2.254	40′
30′	0.4462	0.8949	0.4986	2.006	1.117	2.241	30′
40′	0.4488	0.8936	0.5022	1.991	1.119	2.228	20′
50′	0.4514	0.8923	0.5059	1.977	1.121	2.215	10′
27°00′	0.4540	0.8910	0.5095	1.963	1.122	2.203	63°00′
	Cos	Sin	Cot	Tan	Csc	Sec	Angle

Values of Trigonometric Functions

Angle	Sin	Cos	Tan	Cot	Sec	Csc	
27°00′	0.4540	0.8910	0.5095	1.963	1.122	2.203	63°00′
10′	0.4566	0.8897	0.5132	1.949	1.124	2.190	50′
20′	0.4592	0.8884	0.5169	1.935	1.126	2.178	40′
30′	0.4617	0.8870	0.5206	1.921	1.127	2.166	30′
40′	0.4643	0.8857	0.5243	1.907	1.129	2.154	20′
50′	0.4669	0.8843	0.5280	1.894	1.131	2.142	10′
28°00′	0.4695	0.8829	0.5317	1.881	1.133	2.130	62°00′
10′	0.4720	0.8816	0.5354	1.868	1.134	2.118	50′
20′	0.4746	0.8802	0.5392	1.855	1.136	2.107	40′
30′	0.4772	0.8788	0.5430	1.842	1.138	2.096	30′
40′	0.4797	0.8774	0.5467	1.829	1.140	2.085	20′
50′	0.4823	0.8760	0.5505	1.816	1.142	2.074	10′
29°00′	0.4848	0.8746	0.5543	1.804	1.143	2.063	61°00′
10′	0.4874	0.8732	0.5581	1.792	1.145	2.052	50′
20′	0.4899	0.8718	0.5619	1.780	1.147	2.041	40′
30′	0.4924	0.8704	0.5658	1.767	1.149	2.031	30′
40′	0.4950	0.8689	0.5696	1.756	1.151	2.020	20′
50′	0.4975	0.8675	0.5735	1.744	1.153	2.010	10′
30°00′	0.5000	0.8660	0.5774	1.732	1.155	2.000	60°00′
10′	0.5025	0.8646	0.5812	1.720	1.157	1.990	50′
20′	0.5050	0.8631	0.5851	1.709	1.159	1.980	40′
30′	0.5075	0.8616	0.5890	1.698	1.161	1.970	30′
40′	0.5100	0.8601	0.5930	1.686	1.163	1.961	20′
50′	0.5125	0.8587	0.5969	1.675	1.165	1.951	10′
31°00′	0.5150	0.8572	0.6009	1.664	1.167	1.942	59°00′
10′	0.5175	0.8557	0.6048	1.653	1.169	1.932	50′
20′	0.5200	0.8542	0.6088	1.643	1.171	1.923	40′
30′	0.5225	0.8526	0.6128	1.632	1.173	1.914	30′
40′	0.5250	0.8511	0.6168	1.621	1.175	1.905	20′
50′	0.5275	0.8496	0.6208	1.611	1.177	1.896	10′
32°00′	0.5299	0.8480	0.6249	1.600	1.179	1.887	58°00′
10′	0.5324	0.8465	0.6289	1.590	1.181	1.878	50′
20′	0.5348	0.8450	0.6330	1.580	1.184	1.870	40′
30′	0.5373	0.8434	0.6371	1.570	1.186	1.861	30′
40′	0.5398	0.8418	0.6412	1.560	1.188	1.853	20′
50′	0.5422	0.8403	0.6453	1.550	1.190	1.844	10′
33°00′	0.5446	0.8387	0.6494	1.540	1.192	1.836	57°00′
10′	0.5471	0.8371	0.6536	1.530	1.195	1.828	50′
20′	0.5495	0.8355	0.6577	1.520	1.197	1.820	40′
30′	0.5519	0.8339	0.6619	1.511	1.199	1.812	30′
40′	0.5544	0.8323	0.6661	1.501	1.202	1.804	20′
50′	0.5568	0.8307	0.6703	1.492	1.204	1.796	10′
34°00′	0.5592	0.8290	0.6745	1.483	1.206	1.788	56°00′
10′	0.5616	0.8274	0.6787	1.473	1.209	1.781	50′
20′	0.5640	0.8258	0.6830	1.464	1.211	1.773	40′
30′	0.5664	0.8241	0.6873	1.455	1.213	1.766	30′
40′	0.5688	0.8225	0.6916	1.446	1.216	1.758	20′
50′	0.5712	0.8208	0.6959	1.437	1.218	1.751	10′
35°00′	0.5736	0.8192	0.7002	1.428	1.221	1.743	55°00′
10′	0.5760	0.8175	0.7046	1.419	1.223	1.736	50′
20′	0.5783	0.8158	0.7089	1.411	1.226	1.729	40′
30′	0.5807	0.8141	0.7133	1.402	1.228	1.722	30′
40′	0.5831	0.8124	0.7177	1.393	1.231	1.715	20′
50′	0.5854	0.8107	0.7221	1.385	1.233	1.708	10′
36°00′	0.5878	0.8090	0.7265	1.376	1.236	1.701	54°00′
	Cos	Sin	Cot	Tan	Csc	Sec	Angle

Values of Trigonometric Functions

Angle	Sin	Cos	Tan	Cot	Sec	Csc	
36°00′	0.5878	0.8090	0.7265	1.376	1.236	1.701	54°00′
10′	0.5901	0.8073	0.7310	1.368	1.239	1.695	50′
20′	0.5925	0.8056	0.7355	1.360	1.241	1.688	40′
30′	0.5948	0.8039	0.7400	1.351	1.244	1.681	30′
40′	0.5972	0.8021	0.7445	1.343	1.247	1.675	20′
50′	0.5995	0.8004	0.7490	1.335	1.249	1.668	10′
37°00′	0.6018	0.7986	0.7536	1.327	1.252	1.662	53°00′
10′	0.6041	0.7969	0.7581	1.319	1.255	1.655	50′
20′	0.6065	0.7951	0.7627	1.311	1.258	1.649	40′
30′	0.6088	0.7934	0.7673	1.303	1.260	1.643	30′
40′	0.6111	0.7916	0.7720	1.295	1.263	1.636	20′
50′	0.6134	0.7898	0.7766	1.288	1.266	1.630	10′
38°00′	0.6157	0.7880	0.7813	1.280	1.269	1.624	52°00′
10′	0.6180	0.7862	0.7860	1.272	1.272	1.618	50′
20′	0.6202	0.7844	0.7907	1.265	1.275	1.612	40′
30′	0.6225	0.7826	0.7954	1.257	1.278	1.606	30′
40′	0.6248	0.7808	0.8002	1.250	1.281	1.601	20′
50′	0.6271	0.7790	0.8050	1.242	1.284	1.595	10′
39°00′	0.6293	0.7771	0.8098	1.235	1.287	1.589	51°00′
10′	0.6316	0.7753	0.8146	1.228	1.290	1.583	50′
20′	0.6338	0.7735	0.8195	1.220	1.293	1.578	40′
30′	0.6361	0.7716	0.8243	1.213	1.296	1.572	30′
40′	0.6383	0.7698	0.8292	1.206	1.299	1.567	20′
50′	0.6406	0.7679	0.8342	1.199	1.302	1.561	10′
40°00′	0.6428	0.7660	0.8391	1.192	1.305	1.556	50°00′
10′	0.6450	0.7642	0.8441	1.185	1.309	1.550	50′
20′	0.6472	0.7623	0.8491	1.178	1.312	1.545	40′
30′	0.6494	0.7604	0.8541	1.171	1.315	1.540	30′
40′	0.6517	0.7585	0.8591	1.164	1.318	1.535	20′
50′	0.6539	0.7566	0.8642	1.157	1.322	1.529	10′
41°00′	0.6561	0.7547	0.8693	1.150	1.325	1.524	49°00′
10′	0.6583	0.7528	0.8744	1.144	1.328	1.519	50′
20′	0.6604	0.7509	0.8796	1.137	1.332	1.514	40′
30′	0.6626	0.7490	0.8847	1.130	1.335	1.509	30′
40′	0.6648	0.7470	0.8899	1.124	1.339	1.504	20′
50′	0.6670	0.7451	0.8952	1.117	1.342	1.499	10′
42°00′	0.6691	0.7431	0.9004	1.111	1.346	1.494	48°00′
10′	0.6713	0.7412	0.9057	1.104	1.349	1.490	50′
20′	0.6734	0.7392	0.9110	1.098	1.353	1.485	40′
30′	0.6756	0.7373	0.9163	1.091	1.356	1.480	30′
40′	0.6777	0.7353	0.9217	1.085	1.360	1.476	20′
50′	0.6799	0.7333	0.9271	1.079	1.364	1.471	10′
43°00′	0.6820	0.7314	0.9325	1.072	1.367	1.466	47°00′
10′	0.6841	0.7294	0.9380	1.066	1.371	1.462	50′
20′	0.6862	0.7274	0.9435	1.060	1.375	1.457	40′
30′	0.6884	0.7254	0.9490	1.054	1.379	1.453	30′
40′	0.6905	0.7234	0.9545	1.048	1.382	1.448	20′
50′	0.6926	0.7214	0.9601	1.042	1.386	1.444	10′
44°00′	0.6947	0.7193	0.9657	1.036	1.390	1.440	46°00′
10′	0.6967	0.7173	0.9713	1.030	1.394	1.435	50′
20′	0.6988	0.7153	0.9770	1.024	1.398	1.431	40′
30′	0.7009	0.7133	0.9827	1.018	1.402	1.427	30′
40′	0.7030	0.7112	0.9884	1.012	1.406	1.423	20′
50′	0.7050	0.7092	0.9942	1.006	1.410	1.418	10′
45°00′	0.7071	0.7071	1.000	1.000	1.414	1.414	45°00′
	Cos	Sin	Cot	Tan	Csc	Sec	Angle

GLOSSARY

absolute value (18) The absolute value of a number is the number of units that it is from zero on the number line.

addition and subtraction properties of equality (11) For any numbers a, b, and c,

$$\text{if } a = b, \text{ then} \quad a + c = b + c \text{ and} \quad a - c = b - c.$$

addition and subtraction properties of inequalities (21) For any numbers a, b, and c,

1. if $a > b$, then $a + c > b + c$ and $a - c > b - c$.
2. if $a < b$, then $a + c < b + c$ and $a - c < b - c$.

algebraic expressions (3) Algebraic expressions are expressions having at least one variable.

amplitude (458) For functions of the form $y = a \sin b\theta$ and $y = a \cos b\theta$, the amplitude is $|a|$.

angle of elevation or depression (496) The angle of elevation or depression is the angle formed by the line of sight to an object and a horizontal line.

antilogarithm (340) If $\log x = a$, then $x = \text{antilog } a$.

arccosine (479) Given $y = \cos x$, the inverse cosine function is defined by $x = \cos^{-1} y$.

arcsine (479) Given $y = \sin x$, the inverse sine function is defined by $x = \sin^{-1} y$.

arctangent (479) Given $y = \tan x$, the inverse tangent function is defined by $x = \tan^{-1} y$.

arithmetic means (361) Terms between any two nonconsecutive terms of an arithmetic sequence.

associative properties (6) For all numbers a, b, and c, $(a + b) + c = a + (b + c)$ and $(a \cdot b) \cdot c = a \cdot (b \cdot c)$.

augmented matrix solution (88) The augmented matrix solution is a method using matrices to solve a system of equations.

bar graphs (426) Bar graphs show how specific quantities compare to one another.

BASIC (516) The word BASIC is the name of a computer language.

basic counting principle (393) Suppose an event can be chosen in p different ways. Another independent event can be chosen in q different ways. Then the two events can be chosen successively in $p \cdot q$ ways.

binomial theorem (386) If n is a positive integer, then the following is true.

$$(a + b)^n = 1a^nb^0 + \frac{n}{1}a^{n-1}b^1 + \frac{n(n-1)}{1 \cdot 2}a^{n-2}b^2 + \cdots + \frac{n}{1}a^1b^{n-1} + 1a^0b^n$$

change of bases (350) Suppose a, b, and n are positive numbers, and neither a nor b is 1. Then the following equation is true.

$$\log a^n = \frac{\log_b n}{\log_b a}$$

characteristic (339) The characteristic is the power of 10 by which that number is multiplied when the number is expressed in scientific notation.

circle (220) The definition of circle is a set of points in a plane each of which is the same distance from a given point. The given distance is the radius of the circle and the given point is the center of the circle.

circle graphs (427) Circle graphs show how parts are related to the whole.

circular permutations (399) Suppose n objects are arranged in a circle. Then there are $\frac{n!}{n}$ or $(n-1)!$ permutations of the n objects around the circle.

common logarithms (339) Common logarithms are logarithms to base 10.

commutative properties (6) For all numbers a and b, $a + b = b + a$ and $a \cdot b = b \cdot a$.

complex conjugates theorem (257) Suppose a and b are real numbers with $b \neq 0$. Then, if $a + bi$ is a solution to a polynomial equation, $a - bi$ is also a solution to the equation.

complex fraction (283) A complex rational expression, also called a complex fraction, is an expression whose numerator and denominator, or both, contain rational expressions.

complex number (154) A complex number is any number that can be written in the form $a + bi$ where a and b are real numbers and i is the imaginary unit.

composition of functions (267) Given functions f and g, the composite function $f \circ g$ can be described by the following equation.

$$[f \circ g](x) = f[g(x)]$$

computer program (516) A computer program is a series of statements which give directions to the computer.

conditions for simplified expressions (315) An expression is simplified when it meets these conditions.

1. It has no negative exponents.
2. It has no fractional exponents in the denominator.
3. It is not a complex fraction.

conditions for simplified radicals (144) A radical expression is simplified when it meets these conditions.

1. The index n is as small as possible.
2. The radicand contains no factor (other than one) which is the nth power of an integer or polynomial.
3. The radicand contains no fractions.
4. No radicals appear in the denominator.

conic sections (232) Conic sections are curves formed by slicing a cone with a plane. The equation of a conic section can be written in the form $Ax^2 + Bxy + Cy^2 + Dx + Ey + F = 0$ where A, B, and C are not all zero.

conjugates (141) Conjugates are binomials of the form $a + b\sqrt{c}$ and $a - b\sqrt{c}$.

constant function (47, 56) A constant function is a function of the form $f(x) = b$ where the slope is zero.

coordinates (38) Coordinates are numbers written as an ordered pair assigned to a point in a coordinate plane.

cosecant (460) Let θ stand for the measurement of an angle in standard position on the unit circle. Then the following equation holds whenever it is defined.

$$\csc \theta = \frac{1}{\sin \theta}$$

cosine (452) Let θ stand for the measurement of an angle in standard position on the unit circle. Let (x, y) represent the point where the terminal side intersects the unit circle. Then the following equation holds.

$$\cos \theta = x$$

cotangent (460) Let θ stand for the measurement of an angle in standard position on the unit circle. Then the following equation holds whenever it is defined.

$$\cot \theta = \frac{\cos \theta}{\sin \theta}$$

coterminal angles (448) Coterminal angles differ by a complete rotation of the circle.

Cramer's Rule (84) Cramer's Rule is a method using determinants to solve a system of equations.

data (422) Numerical observations are called data.

definition of a_n (369) The nth term of a geometric sequence is given by either of the following formulas.

$$a_n = a_1 r^{n-1} \qquad a_n = a_{n-1}r$$

definition of arithmetic sequence (360) An arithmetic sequence is a sequence in which the difference between any two consecutive terms is the same.

definition of arithmetic series (366) The sum of the terms of an arithmetic sequence is called an arithmetic series.

definition of binomial trials (416) A binomial trial exists if and only if the following conditions occur.

1. There are only two possible outcomes.
2. The events are independent.

definition of $C(n, r)$ (402) The number of combinations of n objects, taken r at a time, is written $C(n, r)$.

$$C(n, r) = \frac{n!}{(n - r)!r!}$$

definition of n factorial (386) The expression $n!$ (n factorial) is defined as follows if n is an integer greater than zero.

$$n! = n(n - 1)(n - 2) \cdots (1)$$

definition of geometric sequence (369) In a geometric sequence, each term after the first is found by multiplying the previous term by a constant.

definition of inverse variation (297) A rational equation in two variables of the form $y = \frac{k}{x}$ where k is a constant is called an inverse variation. The constant k is called the constant of variation and y is said to vary inversely as x.

definition of logarithm (328) Suppose b is a positive number other than 1 and n is a positive number. Then there is a number p such that $\log_b n = p$ if and only if $b^p = n$.

definition of nth root (134) For any numbers a and b, and any positive integer n, if $a^n = b$, then a is an nth root of b.

definition of nth term of an arithmetic sequence (361) The nth term of an arithmetic sequence with the first term a_1 and common difference d is given by the following equation.

$$a_n = a_1 + (n - 1)d$$

definition of odds (406) The odds of the successful outcome of an event are expressed as the ratio of the number of ways it can succeed to the number of ways it can fail.

$$\text{Odds} = \text{the ratio of } s \text{ to } f \text{ or } \frac{s}{f}$$

definition of $P(n, r)$ (395) The number of permutations of n objects, taken r at a time, is defined as follows.

$$P(n, r) = \frac{n!}{(n - r)!}$$

definition of quadratic form (317) For any numbers a, b, and c, except $a = 0$, an equation that may be written as $a[f(x)]^2 + b[f(x)] + c = 0$ is in quadratic form.

definition of range (433) The range of a set of data is the difference between the greatest and least values in the set.

definition of rational exponents (312) For any nonzero number b, and any integers m and n, with $n > 1$, $b^{\frac{m}{n}} = \sqrt[n]{b^m} = (\sqrt[n]{b})^m$ except when $\sqrt[n]{b}$ is not a real number.

definition of scientific notation (307) A number is expressed in scientific notation when it is in the form $a \times 10^n$. Here $1 \le a < 10$ and n is an integer.

definition of S_n (367) The nth partial sum of a series is found by using the following formula.

$$S_n = \frac{n}{2}(a_1 + a_n)$$

definition of standard deviation (433) From a set of data with n values, if x_i represents a value such that $1 \le i \le n$, and $\bar{x}$ represents the mean, then the standard deviation is

$$\sqrt{\frac{\sum_{i=1}^{m} (x_i - \bar{x})^2}{n}}.$$

definition of sum of a geometric series (372) The sum of the first n terms of a geometric series is given by the formula $S_n = \dfrac{a_1 - a_1r^n}{1 - r}$ where $r \neq 1$.

definition of sum of an infinite geometric series (376) The sum of an infinite geometric series is given by the formula $S = \dfrac{a_1}{1 - r}$ where $^-1 < r < 1$.

degree of monomial (102) The degree of monomial is the sum of the exponents of its variables.

degree of polynomial (106, 248) The degree of a polynomial in one variable is the greatest exponent of its variable.
Degree 0 is called a constant.
Degree 1 is called a linear expression.
Degree 2 is called a quadratic expression.

Descartes' rule of signs (258) Suppose $p(x)$ is a polynomial whose terms are arranged in descending powers of the variable. The number of positive real zeros of $y - p(x)$ is the same as the number of changes in sign of the coefficients of the terms, or is less than this number by an even number. The number of negative real zeros is the same as the number of changes in sign of $p(^-x)$, or is less than this number by an even number.

determinant (81) A determinant is a square array of numbers having a numerical value.

difference and sum formulas (470) The following identities hold for all values of α and β.

$$\cos(\alpha \pm \beta) = \cos\alpha\cos\beta \mp \sin\alpha\sin\beta$$
$$\sin(\alpha \pm \beta) = \sin\alpha\cos\beta \pm \cos\alpha\sin\beta$$

direct variation (56) A direct variation is a linear function described by $y = mx$ or $f(x) = mx$ where $m \neq 0$.

discriminant (175) The value of $b^2 - 4ac$ from the quadratic formula $ax^2 + bx + c = 0$ is the discriminant.

dispersion (433) Dispersion is the variation of values in a set of data.

distance between points on a number line (214) On a number line, the distance between two points whose coordinates are a and b is $|a - b|$ or $|b - a|$.

distance formula for two points in the plane (215) The distance between two points with coordinates (x_1, y_1) and (x_2, y_2) is $d = \sqrt{(x_2 - x_1)^2 + (y_2 - y_1)^2}$.

distributive property (8) For all numbers a, b, and c, $a(b + c) = ab + ac$ and $(b + c)a = ba + ca$.

dividing powers (104) For all numbers a and integers m and n, $\dfrac{a^m}{a^n} = a^{m-n}$ as long as $a \neq 0$ and $m > n$.

domain (41) The domain is the set of all first coordinates of the ordered pairs of a relation.

double angle formulas (472) The following identities hold for all values of θ.

$$\sin 2\theta = 2\sin\theta\cos\theta$$
$$\cos 2\theta = \cos^2\theta - \sin^2\theta$$
$$= 1 - 2\sin^2\theta$$
$$= 2\cos^2\theta - 1$$

ellipse (224) The ellipse is the set of all points in a plane such that the sum of the distances from two given points, called the foci, is constant. The equation of an ellipse with center at (h, k) is

$$\frac{(x - h)^2}{a^2} + \frac{(y - k)^2}{b^2} = 1 \text{ or}$$
$$\frac{(x - h)^2}{b^2} + \frac{(y - k)^2}{a^2} = 1.$$

END statement (516) An END statement indicates that a program is finished.

exponential equations (349) Equations in which the variables appear as exponents.

exponents (2) An exponent is a numeral written to the right and above a number indicating how many times the number is used as a factor.

factoring difference of two squares (112) For any numbers a and b,

$$a^2 - b^2 = (a - b)(a + b).$$

factoring perfect square trinomial (116) For any numbers a and b,

$$a^2 + 2ab + b^2 = (a + b)^2 \text{ and,}$$
$$a^2 - 2ab + b^2 = (a - b)^2.$$

factoring sum or difference of cubes (113) For any numbers a and b,

$$a^3 + b^3 = (a + b)(a^2 - ab + b^2) \text{ and,}$$
$$a^3 - b^3 = (a - b)(a^2 + ab + b^2).$$

factor theorem (252) The binomial $x - a$ is a factor of the polynomial $f(x)$ if and only if $f(a) = 0$.

Fibonacci sequence (379) A Fibonacci sequence is a special sequence often found in nature named after its discoverer, Leonardo Fibonacci.

field (159) A field is a mathematical system having certain properties.

finding a power of a product (103) For all numbers a, b, and integer m,

$$(ab)^m = a^m b^m.$$

finding the rth term in the binomial expansion (414) In the binomial expansion of $(a + b)^n$, the rth term is

$$\frac{n!}{[n - (r - 1)]!(r - 1)!}a^{n-r+1}b^{r-1}.$$

flow chart (528) A flow chart is a diagram used to organize and plan a program.

FOIL rule for multiplying binomials (108) The product of two binomials is the sum of the products of

F the first terms,
O the outer terms,
I the inner terms, and
L the last terms.

formula (3) A formula is a mathematical sentence about the relationships among certain quantities.

FOR-NEXT loop (522) A FOR-NEXT loop instructs the computer to perform a certain task over and over a prescribed number of times.

frequency distribution (436) A frequency distribution shows how data are spread out.

function (42) A function is a relation in which each element of the domain is paired with exactly one element of the range.

fundamental theorem of algebra (257) Every polynomial equation with a degree greater than zero has at least one solution in the set of complex numbers.

graphs (426) Graphs present data and show relationships.

greatest common factor (GCF) (112) The greatest common factor is the greatest factor that a set of terms has in common.

greatest integer (57) The greatest integer of x is written $[x]$ and means the greatest integer *not* greater than x.

half angle formulas (473) The following identities hold for all values of α.

$$\cos\frac{\alpha}{2} = \sqrt{\frac{1 + \cos\alpha}{2}} \text{ and } \sin\frac{\alpha}{2}\sqrt{\frac{1 - \cos\alpha}{2}}$$

histogram (436) A histogram is a bar graph which shows a frequency distribution.

hyperbola (228) A hyperbola is a set of all points in the plane such that the absolute value of the difference of the distances from two given points, called foci, is constant. The general equation of a hyperbola with center at (h, k) is

$$\frac{(x - h)^2}{a^2} - \frac{(y - k)^2}{b^2} = 1 \text{ or}$$
$$\frac{(y - k)^2}{a^2} - \frac{(x - h)^2}{b^2} = 1.$$

identity elements (7) Zero is the additive identity since $0 + a = a$ and one is the multiplicative identity since $1 \cdot a = a$.

identity function (56) An identity function is a linear function described by $y = x$ or $f(x) = x$.

identity properties (7) For any number a, $a + 0 = a = 0 + a$ and $a \cdot 1 = a = 1 \cdot a$.

IF-THEN statement (525) An IF-THEN statement instructs a computer to make a comparison and tells the computer what to do next, based on the results of the comparison.

imaginary number (150) For any positive real number b, $\sqrt{^-b^2} = bi$, where i is a number whose square is $^-1$. The number i is called the imaginary unit, and bi is called a pure imaginary number.

independent events (393) Independent events mean that the choice of one event does not affect the others.

index of summation (364) An index of summation is a variable used in sigma (Σ) notation.

internal functions in BASIC (534) The internal functions in BASIC perform prescribed tasks. They are ABS(X), SQR(X), INT(X), RND(X), SIN(X), COS(X), and TAN(X).

interpolation (342, 492) Interpolation is a method for approximating values that are between given consecutive entries in a table, such as a table of logarithms or a table of trigonometric values.

inverse functions (270) Two polynomial functions f and g are inverse functions if and only if both their compositions are the identity function. That is,

$$[f \circ g](x) = [g \circ f](x) = x.$$

inversely proportional (297) Quantities that are inversely proportional vary inversely with each other.

inverse properties (7) For any number a, $a + {^-a} = 0 = {^-a} + a$ and if a is *not* 0, $a \cdot \frac{1}{a} = 1 = \frac{1}{a} \cdot a$.

irrational numbers (136) Irrational numbers are real numbers that cannot be written as terminating or repeating decimals.

Law of Cosines (505) Let triangle ABC be any triangle with a, b, and c representing the measures of sides opposite angles with measurements A, B, and C, respectively. Then the following equations are true.

$$a^2 = b^2 + c^2 - 2bc \cos A$$
$$b^2 = a^2 + c^2 - 2ac \cos B$$
$$c^2 = a^2 + b^2 - 2ab \cos C$$

Law of Sines (502) Let triangle ABC be any triangle with a, b, and c representing the measures of sides opposite angles with measurements A, B, and C, respectively. Then the following equations are true.

$$\frac{\sin A}{a} = \frac{\sin B}{b} = \frac{\sin C}{c}$$

LET statement (519) A LET statement assigns a value to a variable.

like radical expressions (140) Two radical expressions with the same indices and the same radicands are called like radical expressions.

linear equation in two variables (46) A linear equation in two variables is an equation that may be written in the form $ax + by = c$, where a, b, and c are real numbers and a and b are *not* both zero.

linear function (47) A linear function is $f(x) = mx + b$ where m and b are real numbers.

linear programming (94) Linear programming is a method used to find maximum or minimum values for a system of inequalities.

linear programming procedure (94) The procedure is as follows.

1. Define variables.
2. Write a system of inequalities.
3. Graph the system. Find vertices of the polygon formed.
4. Write an expression to be maximized or minimized.

5. Substitute values from vertices into the expression.

line graph (427) A line graph shows trends or changes.

location principle (260) Suppose $y = f(x)$ represents a polynomial function. And suppose a and b are two numbers with $f(a)$ negative and $f(b)$ positive. Then the function has at least one real zero between a and b.

mantissa (339) The mantissa is the logarithm of a number between 1 and 10.

matrix (81) A matrix is a rectangular arrangement of numerals.

mean (430) The mean of a set of data is the sum of all the values divided by the number of values.

median (430) The median of a set of data is the middle value. If there are two middle values, it is the value halfway between.

midpoint (321) The midpoint of a line segment with endpoints (x_1, y_1) and (x_2, y_2) has coordinates $\left(\frac{x_1 + x_2}{2}, \frac{y_1 + y_2}{2}\right)$.

minor (83) A minor is the resulting determinant when a row and column are removed. Thus, in $\begin{vmatrix} a & b & c \\ d & e & f \\ g & h & i \end{vmatrix}$ the minor of a is $\begin{vmatrix} e & f \\ h & i \end{vmatrix}$.

mode (430) The mode of a set of data is the most frequent value.

multiplication and division properties of equalities (11) For any numbers a, b, and c, if $a = b$, then $a \cdot c = b \cdot c$, and if c is *not* 0, then $\frac{a}{c} = \frac{b}{c}$.

multiplication and division properties of inequalities (22) For any numbers a, b, and c,

1. if $c > 0$ and $a < b$, then $ac < bc$ and $\frac{a}{c} < \frac{b}{c}$.
2. if $c > 0$ and $a > b$, then $ac > bc$ and $\frac{a}{c} > \frac{b}{c}$.
3. if $c < 0$ and $a < b$, then $ac > bc$ and $\frac{a}{c} > \frac{b}{c}$.
4. if $c < 0$ and $a > b$, then $ac < bc$ and $\frac{a}{c} < \frac{b}{c}$.

multiplying powers (103) For all numbers a and integers m and n, $a^m \cdot a^n = a^{m+n}$.

mutually exclusive (411) Mutually exclusive means that two events cannot occur simultaneously.

negative integer exponents (305) For any number a, except $a = 0$, and for any positive integer n, $a^{-n} = \frac{1}{a^n}$.

normal distribution (436) Normal distributions have bell-shaped, symmetric graphs. About 68% of the items are within one standard deviation from the mean. About 95% of the items are within two standard deviations from the mean. About 99% of the items are within three standard deviations from the mean.

order of operations in BASIC (517) The order of operations in BASIC is as follows.

1. Do all operations in parentheses, from the innermost parentheses outward.
2. Evaluate all powers from left to right.
3. Do all multiplications and/or divisions from left to right.
4. Do all additions and/or subtractions from left to right.

origin (52) The origin is the point on the coordinate plane whose coordinates are (0, 0).

parabola (192, 217) A parabola is the set of all points which are the same distance from a given point and a given line. The point is called the focus. The line is called the directrix. The general equation of a parabola with vertex at (h, k) is $y = a(x - h)^2 + k$ or $x = a(y - k)^2 + h$. All parabolas have a vertex and an axis of symmetry.

parallel lines (70) In a plane, lines with the same slope are called parallel lines. Also, lines having no slope are parallel.

period (454) For a function f, the least positive value of a for which $f(x) = f(x + a)$ is the period of the function. For functions of the form $y = a \sin b\theta$ and $y = a \cos b\theta$, the period is $\frac{2\pi}{|b|}$.

periodic function (454) A function f is called periodic if there is a number a such that $f(x) = f(x + a)$.

permutation (395) A permutation is the arrangement of things in a certain order.

permutations with repetitions (396) The number of permutations of n objects of which p are alike and q are alike is found by evaluating the expression $\frac{n!}{p!q!}$.

perpendicular lines (71) Two nonvertical lines are perpendicular if and only if the product of their slopes is $^-1$. Any vertical line is perpendicular to any horizontal line.

pictograph (426) A pictograph shows how specific quantities compare to one another.

points in the plane (38) Each point in a coordinate plane corresponds to exactly one ordered pair of numbers. Each ordered pair of numbers corresponds to exactly one point in a coordinate plane.

points on the number line (38) Each real number corresponds to exactly one point on a number line. Each point on a number line corresponds to exactly one real number.

polynomial function (249) A polynomial function is in the form $p(x) = a_nx^n + a_{n-1}x^{n-1} + \cdots + a_1x + a_o$. The coefficients $a_0, a_1, a_2, \ldots, a_{n-1}, a_n$ are real numbers and n is a nonnegative integer.

polynomials in one variable (248) A polynomial in one variable, x, is an expression of the form $a_nx^n + a_{n-1}x^{n-1} + \cdots + a_2x^2 + a_1x + a_0$. The coefficients $a_0, a_1, a_2, \ldots, a_n$ are real numbers and n is a nonnegative integer.

prediction equation (439) The equation of the line suggested by the dots on a scatter diagram is a prediction equation.

principal values (478) The values in the domain of the functions like Cosine, Sine, and Tangent are the principal values.

PRINT statement (516) A PRINT statement directs the computer to print out whatever is included in the PRINT statement.

probability of inclusive events (412) The probability of one of two inclusive events, A and B, is the sum of the individual probabilities decreased by the probability of both occurring.

$$P(A \text{ or } B) = P(A) + P(B) - P(A \text{ and } B)$$

probability of mutually exclusive events (411) The probability of one of two mutually exclusive events occurring is the sum of their probabilities.

$$P(A \text{ or } B) = P(A) + P(B)$$

probability of success and of failure (405) If an event can succeed in s ways and fail in f ways, then the probability of success $P(s)$ and of failure $P(f)$ are as follows.

$$P(s) = \frac{s}{s + f} \qquad P(f) = \frac{f}{s + f}$$

probability of two dependent events (408) Suppose two events, A and B, are dependent. Then the probability of both occurring is found as follows.

$$P(A \text{ and } B) = P(A) \cdot P(B \text{ following } A)$$

probability of two independent events (408) If two events, A and B, are independent, then the probability of both events occurring is found as follows.

$$P(A \text{ and } B) = P(A) \cdot P(B)$$

problem solving procedure (14, 26) The problem solving procedure is as follows.
1. Define a variable.
2. Write an equation.
3. Solve the equation.
4. Answer the problem.
5. Check the solution.

product property of radicals (138) For any numbers a and b and any integer n greater than one,
1. if n is even, then $\sqrt[n]{ab} = \sqrt[n]{a} \cdot \sqrt[n]{b}$ as long as a and b are positive.
2. if n is odd, then $\sqrt[n]{ab} = \sqrt[n]{a} \cdot \sqrt[n]{b}$.

properties of logarithms (335) Suppose m and n are positive numbers, b is a positive number other than 1, and p is any number. Then the following properties hold.

Product Property:
$$\log_b m \cdot n = \log_b m + \log_b n$$
Quotient Property:
$$\log_b \frac{m}{n} = \log_b m - \log_b n$$
Power Property:
$$\log_b m^p = p \cdot \log_b m$$

property of equality for exponential and logarithmic functions (331) Suppose b is a positive number other than 1. Then $b^{x_1} = b^{x_2}$ if and only if $x_1 = x_2$. Also, $\log_b x_1 = \log_b x_2$ if and only if $x_1 = x_2$.

property of inverse functions (270) Suppose f and f^{-1} are inverse functions. Then $f(a) = b$ if and only if $f^{-1}(b) = a$.

property of *n*th roots (135) For any number a and any integer n greater than one,
1. if n is even, then $\sqrt[n]{a^n} = |a|$ and
2. if n is odd, then $\sqrt[n]{a^n} = a$.

quadrants (38) The coordinate plane is divided into four areas called quadrants by the coordinate axes. They are labeled as follows.

Quadrant II	Quadrant I
Quadrant III	Quadrant IV

quadratic equation (166) A quadratic equation may be written in the form $ax^2 + bx + c = 0$ where a, b, and c are complex numbers and $a \neq 0$.

quadratic form (184) For any numbers a, b, and c, except $a = 0$, an equation that may be written $a[f(x)]^2 + b[f(x)] + c = 0$, where $f(x)$ is some expression in x is in quadratic form.

quadratic formula (172) The solutions of a quadratic equation of the form $ax^2 + bx + c = 0$ with $a \neq 0$, are given by
$$x = \frac{^-b \pm \sqrt{b^2 - 4ac}}{2a}.$$

quadratic function (190) A quadratic function may be described by an equation of the form $f(x) = ax^2 + bx + c$ where $a \neq 0$.

quotient property of radicals (143) For any numbers a and b, except $b = 0$, and any integer n greater than one, $\sqrt[n]{\frac{a}{b}} = \frac{\sqrt[n]{a}}{\sqrt[n]{b}}$ as long as all roots are defined.

radian (449) A radian is an angle which intercepts an arc whose length is 1 unit.

radical equations (147) Radical equations are equations containing variables in the radicands.

raising a power to a power (103) For all numbers a and integers m and n, $(a^m)^n = a^{m \cdot n}$.

range (41) The range is a set of all second coordinates of the ordered pairs of a relation.

rational algebraic expression (278) A rational algebraic expression can be expressed as the quotient of two polynomials.

rational equation (290) A rational equation contains one or more rational expressions.

rationalizing (143) Rationalizing is the process of eliminating radicals from the denominator of an expression.

rationalizing the denominator (314) Rationalizing the denominator is changing the form of a rational expression to one without radicals in the denominator.

rational numbers as exponents (311) For any number b, with $b \geq 0$, and for any integer n, with $n > 1$, $b^{\frac{1}{n}} = \sqrt[n]{b}$.

rational zero theorem (255) Let $f(x) = a_nx^n + a_{n-1}x^{n-1} + \cdots + a_1x + a_0$ represent a polynomial with integer coefficients and n be a nonnegative integer. If $\frac{p}{q}$ is a rational number in simplest form and a zero of $y = f(x)$, then p is a factor of a_0 and q is a factor of a_n.

READ statement (516) A READ statement instructs the computer to find the indicated data.

recursive formula (382) A recursive formula depends on knowing one or more previous terms.

reflexive property of equality (10) For any number a, $a = a$.

relation (41) A relation is a set of ordered pairs.

remainder theorem (251) When a polynomial in x is divided by $x - a$, the remainder is equal to the value of the polynomial when $x = a$. If a polynomial $f(x)$ is divided by $x - a$, the remainder is a constant, $f(a)$, and $f(x) = q(x) \cdot (x - a) + f(a)$ where $q(x)$ is a polynomial with degree one less than the degree of $f(x)$.

row operations on matrices (89) The row operations on matrices are as follows.

1. Interchange any two rows.
2. Replace any row with a nonzero multiple of that row.
3. Replace any row with the sum of that row and another row.

RUN (517) RUN is a computer command.

scatter diagram (437) A scatter diagram shows visually the nature of a relationship, both shape and closeness.

secant (460) Let θ stand for the measurement of an angle in standard position on the unit circle. Then the following equation holds whenever it is defined.

$$\sec \theta = \frac{1}{\cos \theta}$$

sequence (360) A sequence is a set of numbers in a specific order.

Σ (sigma) (364) The Σ symbol is used to indicate a sum.

sine (452) Let θ stand for the measurement of an angle in standard position on the unit circle. Let (x, y) represent the point where the terminal side intersects the unit circle. Then the following equation holds.

$$\sin \theta = y$$

slope-intercept form (52) The equation $y = mx + b$ is in slope-intercept form. The slope is m and the y-intercept is b.

slope of line (49) The slope of a line described by $f(x) = mx + b$ is m. Slope is also given by the following expression.

$$\frac{\text{change in } y\text{-coordinates}}{\text{change in corresponding } x\text{-coordinates}}$$

solving a right triangle (495) Solving a right triangle means finding all the measures of the sides and angles.

square root (134) For any numbers a and b, if $a^2 = b$, then a is a square root of b.

standard form (47, 53) The standard form is a linear equation in the form of $ax + by = c$ where a, b, and c are real numbers, and a and b are *not both* zero.

statistics (422) Statistics provides methods for collecting, organizing, analyzing, and interpreting data.

subscripted variable (531) Subscripted variables are used when there is a great amount of data. The subscripts provide labels for the different variables.

substitution property of equality (10) For all numbers a and b, if $a = b$, then a may be replaced by b.

sum and product of solutions (178) The solutions to $ax^2 + bx + c = 0$ with $a \neq 0$ are r and s if and only if the following is true.

$$r + s = -\frac{b}{a} \text{ and } rs = \frac{c}{a}$$

symmetric property of equality (10) For all numbers a and b, if $a = b$ then $b = a$.

synthetic division (125) A shortcut method used to divide polynomials by binomials is called synthetic division.

tangent (460) Let θ stand for the measurement of an angle in standard position on the unit circle. Then the following equation holds whenever it is defined.

$$\tan \theta = \frac{\sin \theta}{\cos \theta}$$

term (360) A term is each number in a sequence.

transitive property of equality (10) For all numbers a, b, and c, if $a = b$ and $b = c$, then $a = c$.

trichotomy property (21) For any two numbers a and b, exactly one of the following statements is true.

$$a < b, a = b, a > b$$

unit circle (449) A unit circle has a radius of 1 unit.

vertical line test for a function (42) If any vertical line drawn on the graph of a relation passes through no more than one point of that graph, then the relation is a function.

x-intercept (50) An x-intercept is the value of x when the value of the function is zero.

y-intercept (50) A y-intercept is the value of the function when x is zero.

zero exponent (304) For any number a, except $a = 0$, $a^0 = 1$.

zero of function (379) For any polynomial function $f(x)$, if $f(a) = 0$, then a is a zero of the function.

zero product property (166) For any numbers a and b, if $ab = 0$, then $a = 0$ or $b = 0$.

INDEX

A

B

G

H

I

L

m

n

o

Q

R

S

T

U

V

W

X

Y

Z

SELECTED ANSWERS

CHAPTER 1 EQUATIONS AND INEQUALITIES

Exploratory Exercises Page 4 **1.** 7 **3.** $^{-}44$ **5.** 13 **7.** 21 **9.** 27 **11.** 21 **13.** 0 **15.** 4

Written Exercises Page 4 **1.** 41 **3.** 14 **5.** 6 **7.** 60 **9.** 10 **11.** 22 **13.** 148 **15.** 147 **17.** $\frac{3}{2}$ **19.** 94 **21.** $^{-}72$ **23.** $\frac{3}{7}$ **25.** 180 **27.** 2000 **29.** 128 **31.** 100

Challenge Page 4 $4 + [(8^2 \div 4) \cdot 2] = 36$, $[(4 + 8^2) \div 4] \cdot 2 = 34$, $(4 + 8^2) \div (4 \cdot 2) = 8.5$. Without order of operations agreements $4 + 8^2 \div 4 \cdot 2$ could mean something different to different people. Order of operations prevents ambiguous meanings. Grouping symbols allows us to change the meaning.

Exploratory Exercises Page 9 **1.** associative **3.** distributive **5.** commutative **7.** distributive **9.** commutative **11.** commutative **13.** commutative

Written Exercises Page 9 **1.** commutative **3.** distributive **5.** commutative **7.** commutative **9.** distributive **11.** additive identity **13.** multiplicative inverse **15.** additive identity **17.** commutative **19.** multiplicative inverse **21.** 20 **23.** $31a + 10b$ **25.** $12 + 20a$ **27.** 0, additive identity **29.** 1, multiplicative identity

Challenge Page 9 $\frac{1}{0}$ is *not* defined. Look at the statement of the MULTIPLICATIVE INVERSE PROPERTY. It states that <u>if *a* is *not* zero,</u> then $a\left(\frac{1}{a}\right) = 1$.

Exploratory Exercises Page 12 **1.** reflexive **3.** symmetric **5.** transitive **7.** reflexive **9.** substitution

Written Exercises Page 13 **1.** symmetric **3.** transitive **5.** reflexive **7.** substitution **9.** 208 **11.** 218 **13.** 247 **15.** 11 **17.** 11 **19.** 7.5 **21.** 7 **23.** 12 **25.** 2 **27.** $\frac{4}{9}$ **29.** $^{-}75$ **31.** 33 **33.** $\frac{3}{10}$ **35.** $^{-}4$ **37.** $\frac{2}{25}$ **39.** 11 **41.** 8 **43.** $-\frac{33}{13}$ **45.** 1 **47.** 46 **49.** $^{-}39$ **51.** 210 **53.** $^{-}8.5$ **55.** 23.9

Exploratory Exercises Page 16 **1.** 83 **3.** \$2.75

Written Exercises Page 16 **1.** 87.5% **3.** 120% **5.** 19 cm **7.** length = 36 units, width = 24 units **9.** passenger train 89 mph, express train 99 mph

Exploratory Exercises Page 20 **1.** 5 **3.** 10 **5.** 36 **7.** 5 **9.** 0 **11.** 0 **13.** $^{-}2$ **15.** 11

Written Exercises Page 20 **1.** 31, $^{-}53$ **3.** $^{-}6$, 16 **5.** 5, $^{-}19$ **7.** $^{-}8$, 14 **9.** $^{-}13$, 6 **11.** $8\frac{1}{3}$, $^{-}3\frac{2}{3}$ **13.** $^{-}10.5$, 5.5 **15.** 26, 11 **17.** $^{-}4\frac{1}{3}$, $2\frac{2}{3}$ **19.** $^{-}3.8$, 3 **21.** 3.5, 10.5 **23.** $-\frac{10}{21}$, $-\frac{20}{7}$ **25.** no solutions **27.** $\frac{2}{3}$, $\frac{7}{3}$ **29.** no solutions **31.** 1, 5 **33.** no solutions **35.** no solutions

Exploratory Exercises Page 23 **1.** $>$ **3.** $<$ **5.** $>$ **7.** $>$ **9.** $>$ **11.** $<$ **13.** $=$ **15.** $=$

Written Exercises Page 24 **1.** $\{x|x > 12\}$ **3.** $\{n|n \geq 7\}$ **5.** $\{r|r > 3.2\}$ **7.** $\{x|x > {}^{-}12\}$ **9.** $\{y|y > 17.6\}$ **11.** $\{x|x \geq 6\}$ **13.** $\{x|x > 4.5\}$ **15.** $\{w|w \geq 5\}$ **17.** $\{z|z \leq 3\}$ **19.** $\{t|t < 3.25\}$ **21.** $\{x|x > 2.25\}$ **23.** $\{x|x \geq \frac{3}{7}\}$ **25.** $\{x|x < \frac{2}{3}\}$ **27.** $\{x|x \geq 232\}$ **29.** $\{x|x \leq {}^{-}1.425\}$ **31.** $\{x|x \leq 2.502\}$

Challenge Page 24 **1.** $\{x|{}^{-}1 < x < 3\}$ **3.** $\emptyset$

Exploratory Exercises Page 27 **1.** $88 \leq$ max. oat temp. ≤ 99 **3.** $32 \leq$ min. oat temp. ≤ 41 **5.** $88 \leq b \leq 99$ **7.** $85 \leq x \leq 100$ **9.** $34 \leq n \leq 40$

Written Exercises Pages 27–28 **1.** at least 5.5 points per judge **3.** \$575 **5.** \$60.37 or less **7.** more than 16.4 points **9.** more than 6.3 points **11.** $12.5 \leq g \leq 13.75$ **13.** at least 4 gal

Exploratory Exercises Page 30 **1.** $|x| < 3$ **3.** $|x| > 6$ **5.** $|x| > 3$ **7.** $|x| \leq 4$ **9.** $|x| < 6$ **11.** $|x| < 2$

Written Exercises Pages 30–31 **1.** $\{x|{}^{-}9 < x < 9\}$ **3.** $\{x|x > 2 \text{ or } x < {}^{-}4\}$ **5.** $\{x|{}^{-}4 \leq x \leq 12\}$ **7.** $\{x|x \leq {}^{-}3 \text{ or } x \geq 3\}$ **9.** $\{x|x > 7 \text{ or } x < {}^{-}7\}$ **11.** $\{x|{}^{-}13 \leq x \leq 13\}$ **13.** $\emptyset$ **15.** $\{x|x < {}^{-}20 \text{ or } x > 14\}$ **17.** $\{x|{}^{-}30 < x < 54\}$ **19.** $\{x|{}^{-}9 \leq x \leq 18\}$ **21.** $\{x|x \geq \frac{15}{4} \text{ or } x \leq -\frac{9}{4}\}$ **23.** $\{x|{}^{-}17.6 < x < 14.8\}$ **25.** $\emptyset$ **27.** $\{x|{}^{-}1 \leq x \leq 6\}$ **29.** $\{x|x \geq 0\}$ **31.** all real numbers

Challenge Page 31 **1.** $\{x|{}^{-}1 \leq x \leq 1\}$

Chapter Review   Pages 33–35   1. 92   **3.** 33.5   **5.** 5   **7.** $\frac{13}{12}$ **9.** commutative   **11.** additive identity
13. 402   **15.** $13q - 3p$ **17.** $27 + 9x$ **19.** symmetric   **21.** substitution   **23.** 5   **25.** 21   **27.** $-\frac{33}{13}$ **29.** $\frac{7}{3}$
31. width 11 m, length 21 m   **33.** 12 more days   **35.** 11, 26   **37.** no solutions   **39.** $\{x | x > \frac{39}{5}\}$
41. $\{x | x > -\frac{1}{5}\}$ **43.** 6 tickets   **45.** 15 gal   **47.** all real numbers   **49.** $\{x | -\frac{9}{2} \le x \le -\frac{1}{2}\}$

CHAPTER 2   LINEAR RELATIONS AND FUNCTIONS

Exploratory Exercises   Page 40   1.

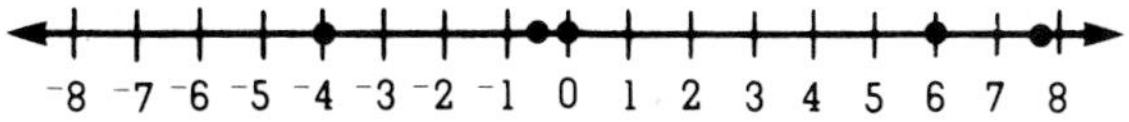

3.   **5.**

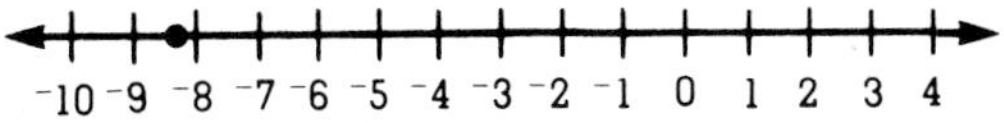

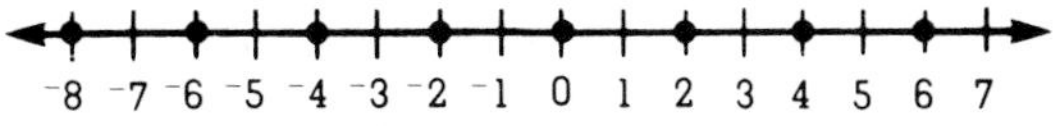

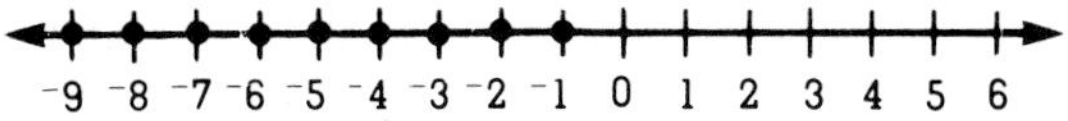

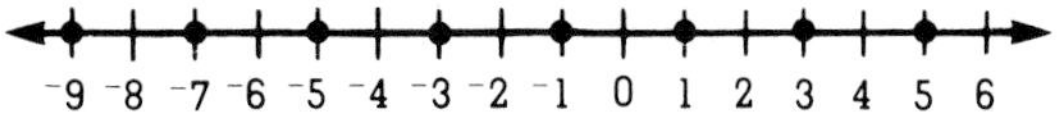

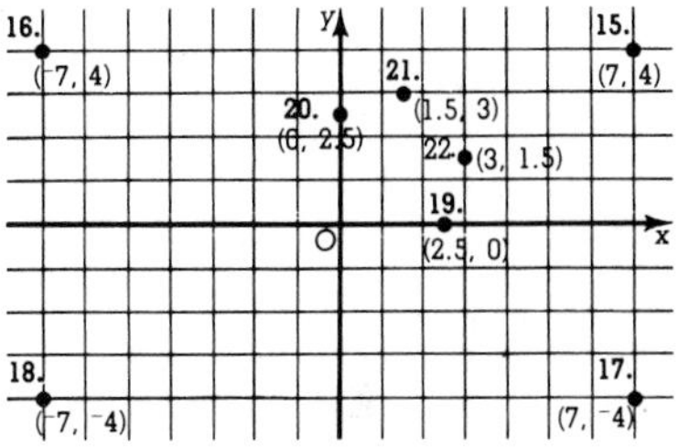

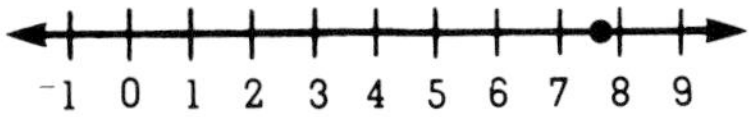

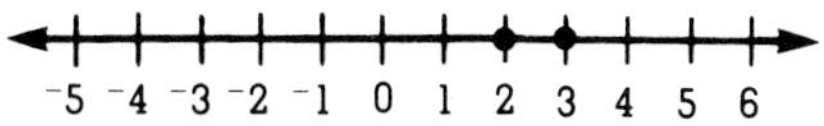

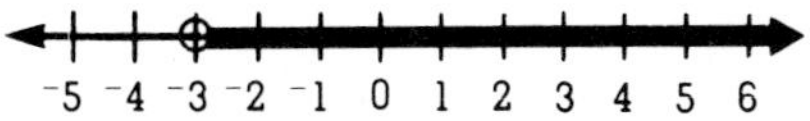

7.   **9.**

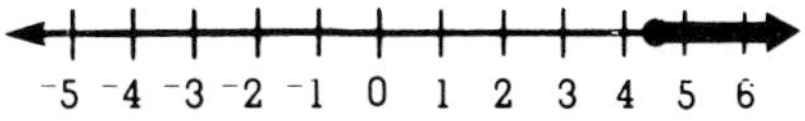

11. quadrant IV   **13.** quadrant II   **15–22.**

Written Exercises   Page 40

1.

3.

5.   **7.**

9.   **11.**

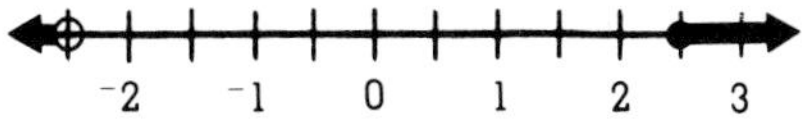

13. 39   **15.** ⁻9

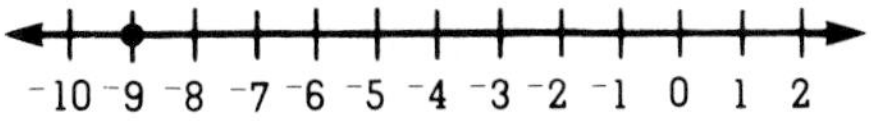

17. 0   **19.** ⁻5

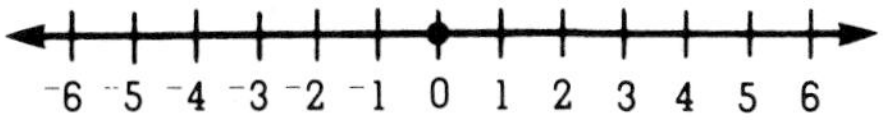

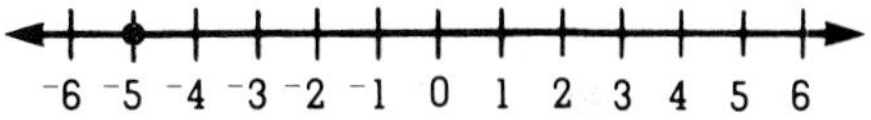

21. 3   **23.** 5

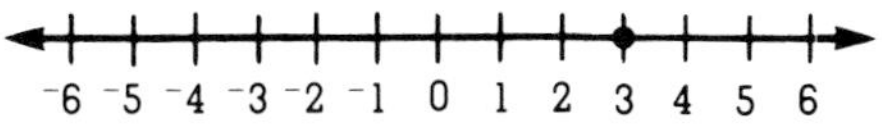

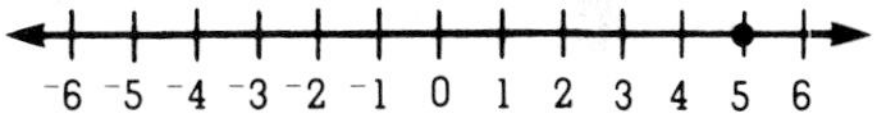

25. 4   **27.** 3, ⁻1

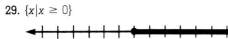

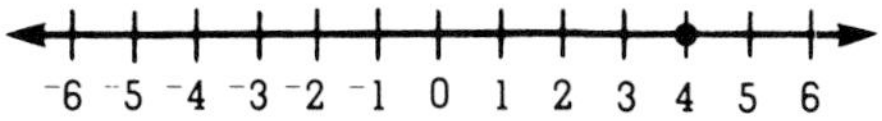

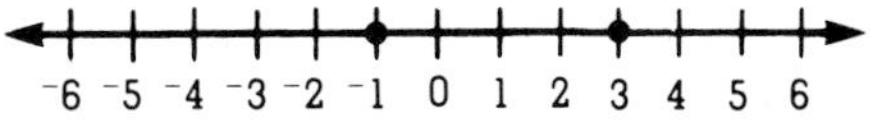

29. $\{x | x \ge 0\}$ **31.** $\{x | x < ^-18\}$

33. $\{r | r \ge 3\}$ **35.** $\{b | b < \frac{5}{3}\}$

37. $\{x | x \ge ^-3\}$ **39.** $\{r | ^-4 \le r \le 1\}$

Exploratory Exercises   Pages 43–44   1. domain = $\{0, 2, 5\}$, range = $\{1, 4\}$ **3.** domain = $\{1, 3, 4\}$,
range = $\{1, 3, 4\}$ **5.** domain = $\{2\}$, range = $\{1, 3, 4, 7\}$ **7.** domain = $\{^-17, 4, 8\}$, range = $\{^-2, 3, 4, 8\}$

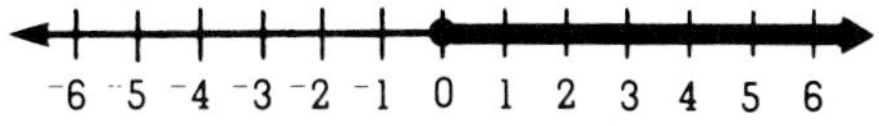

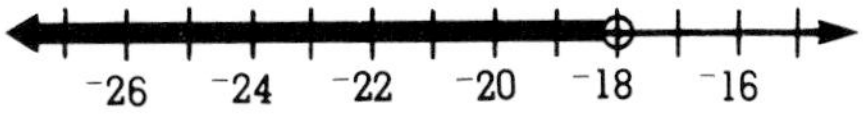

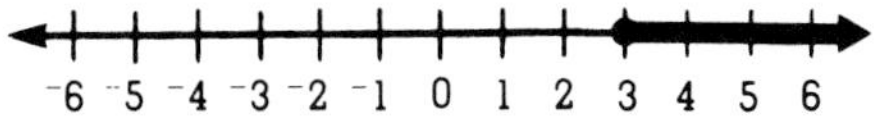

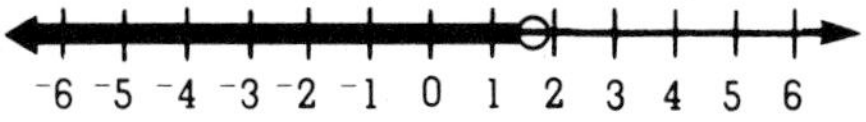

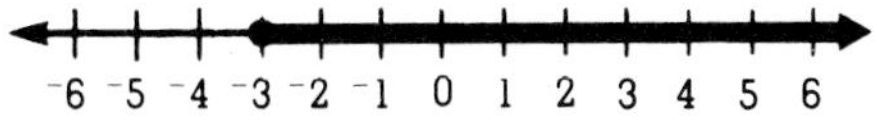

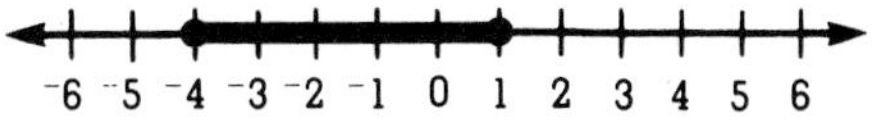

9. domain = {2, 8}, range = {2, 8} 11. domain = {$^-3$, $^-2$, 2, 4}, range = {$^-3$, $^-2$, 2, 4} 13. domain = {8}, range = {6} 15. domain = {$^-3$, 5}, range = {$^-3$, 5} 17. domain = {0}, range = {0} 19. yes 21. yes 23. no 25. no 27. yes 29. yes 31. yes 33. yes 35. yes

Written Exercises Pages 44–45 1. {($^-3$, 3), ($^-2$, 2), ($^-1$, 1), (0, 0), (1, 1), (2, 2), (3, 3)}, domain = {$^-3$, $^-2$, $^-1$, 0, 1, 2, 3}, range = {3, 2, 1, 0} 3. yes 5. yes 7. no 9. no 11. no 13. yes 15. 7 17. 2 19. $-\frac{21}{4}$ 21. $\frac{7}{2}$ 23. $\frac{7}{u}$ 25. 0 27. $^-235$ 29. $^-33$ 31. $^-5\frac{1}{2}$ 33. $4s^3 + 2s^2 + s - 7$

Exploratory Exercises Page 48 1. no 3. yes 5. yes 7. no 9. yes 11. yes

Written Exercises Page 48

1.
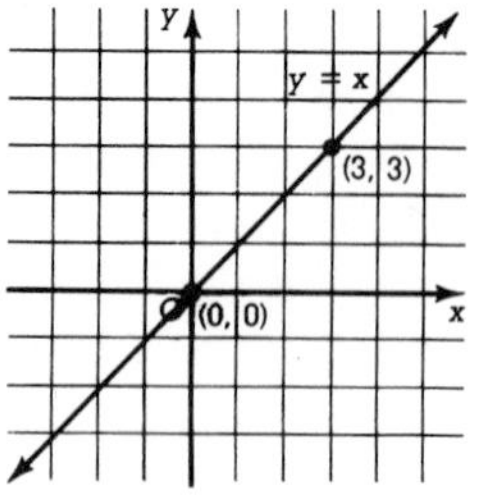

3.
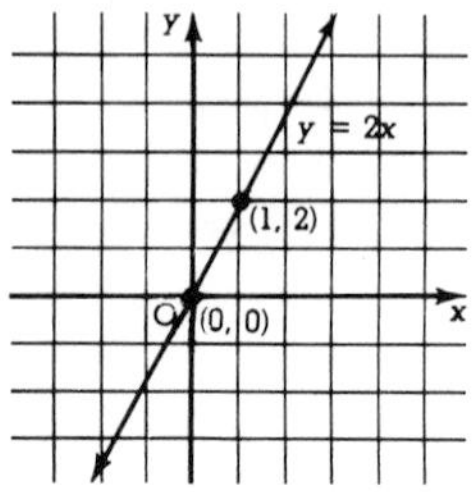

5.
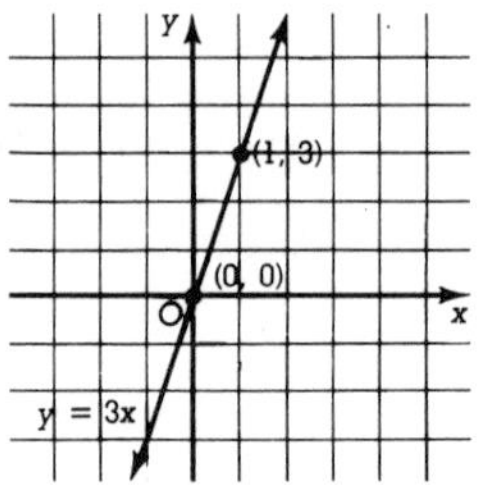

7.
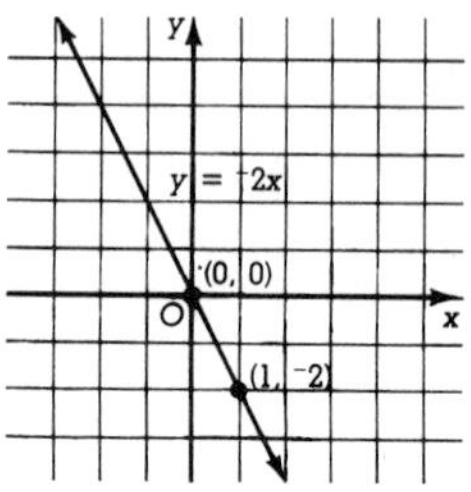

9.
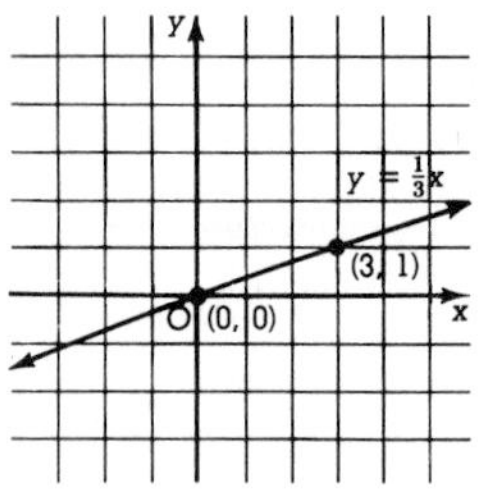

11.
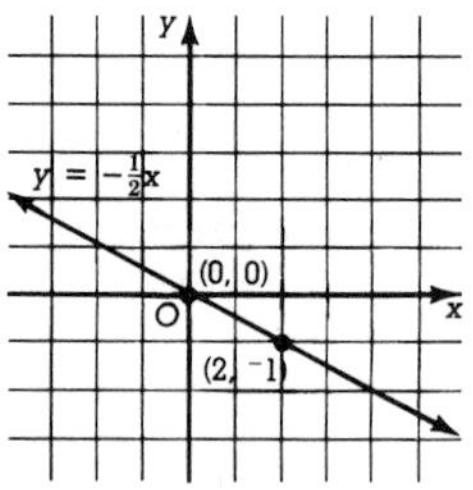

13.
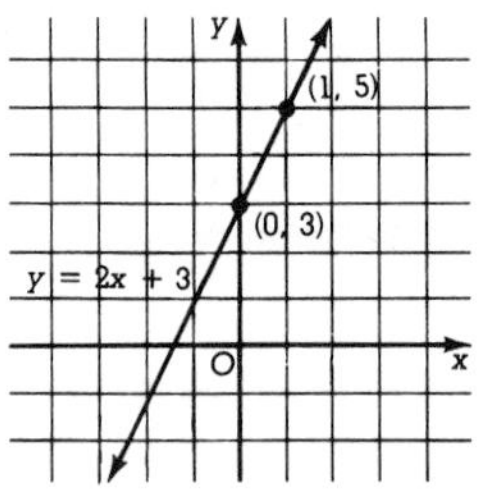

15.
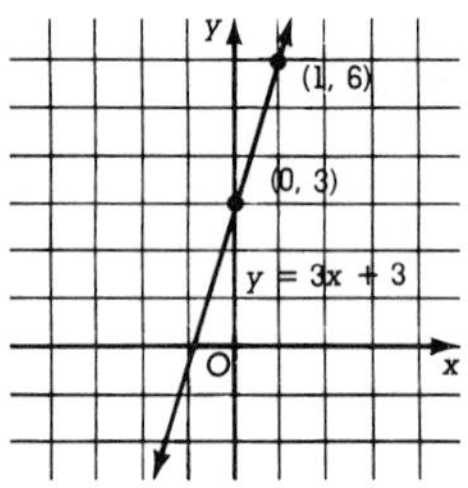

17.
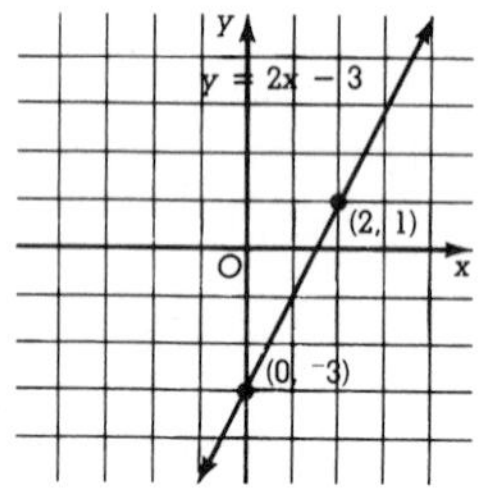

19.
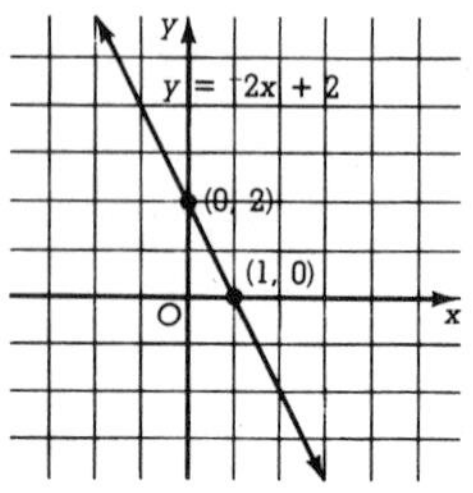

Exploratory Exercises Page 51 1. slope = 1; y-intercept = 2; x-intercept = $^-2$ 3. slope = $^-4$; y-intercept = 4; x-intercept = 1 5. slope = $^-4$; y-intercept = 8 7. slope = 3; y-intercept = 12 9. slope = $\frac{2}{3}$; y-intercept = $-\frac{1}{2}$ 11. slope = $^-1$; y-intercept = 5 13. slope = 1; y-intercept = $^-1$

Written Exercises Page 51 1. slope = 0; y-intercept = 2; x-intercept none 3. slope = 2; y-intercept = $^-4$; x-intercept = 2 5. slope = 3; y-intercept = $^-9$ 7. slope = 7; y-intercept = 1 9. slope = $\frac{1}{3}$; y-intercept = $\frac{4}{3}$ 11. slope = 0.4; y-intercept = 1.2 13. slope = $\frac{3}{4}$; y-intercept = 0 15. slope = 0; y-intercept = $^-2$ 17. $-\frac{5}{2}$ 19. $\frac{2}{11}$ 21. $\frac{5}{2}$ 23. 8 25. 0 27. 15

Exploratory Exercises Page 54 1. $y = -\frac{2}{5}x + 2$ 3. $y = -\frac{2}{3}x + \frac{4}{3}$ 5. $y = 4$ 7. $y = \frac{3}{2}x - 2$ 9. $2x - y = 6$ 11. $x - y = 9$ 13. $5x - 8y = {}^-8$ 15. $3x - y = 0$

Written Exercises Page 54 1. slope = $-\frac{3}{2}$; y-intercept = 3; x-intercept = 2 3. slope = $^-2$; y-intercept = 4; x-intercept = 2 5. slope = 1; y-intercept = $^-3$; x-intercept = 3 7. slope = $\frac{2}{3}$; y-intercept = $-\frac{4}{3}$; x-intercept = 2 9. slope = $-\frac{3}{5}$; y-intercept = $\frac{12}{5}$; x-intercept = 4

11. slope = ⁻11; y-intercept = 4; x-intercept = $\frac{4}{11}$ 13. slope = $-\frac{2}{9}$, y-intercept = 2; x-intercept = 9
15. slope none; y-intercept none; x-intercept = $\frac{11}{4}$ 17. $y = -\frac{2}{3}x + 4$ 19. $y = -\frac{6}{5}x + 6$ 21. $y = \frac{3}{4}x - \frac{1}{4}$
23. $y = -\frac{5}{2}x + 16$ 25. $y = \frac{2}{11}x + \frac{6}{11}$ 27. $y = \frac{5}{2}x + 18$ 29. $y = 3$ 31. $y = \frac{1}{2}x + 1$ 33. $y = \frac{2}{3}x - 6$
35. $y = 4x - 11$ 37. $y = -\frac{3}{2}x + 10$ 39. $2x + 3y = 12$ 41. $6x + 5y = 30$ 43. $3x - 4y = 1$
45. $5x + 2y = 32$ 47. $2x - 11y = {}^-6$ 49. $5x - 2y = {}^-36$ 51. $y = 3$ 53. $x - 2y = {}^-2$ 55. $2x - 3y = 18$
57. $4x - y = 11$ 59. $3x + 2y = 20$

Exploratory Exercises Page 58 1. A 3. D 5. A 7. A 9. G 11. D 13. G 15. A 17. A 19. G 21. C 23. A

Written Exercises Page 58

1.
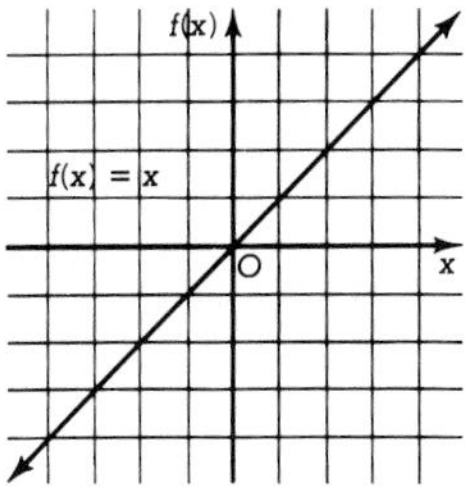

3.
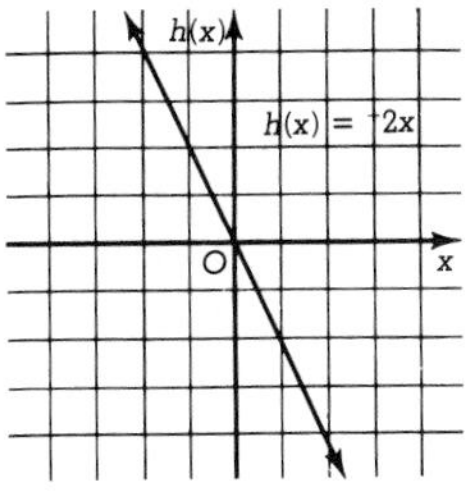

5.
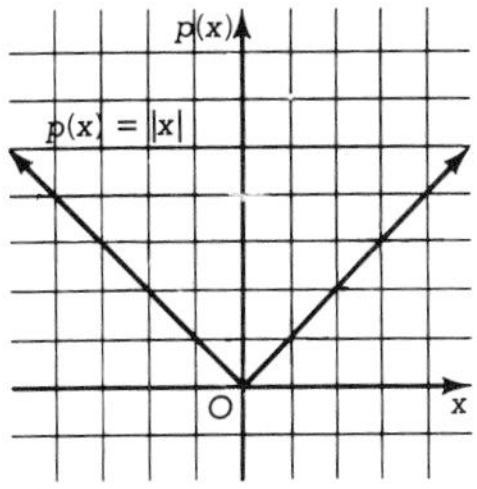

7.
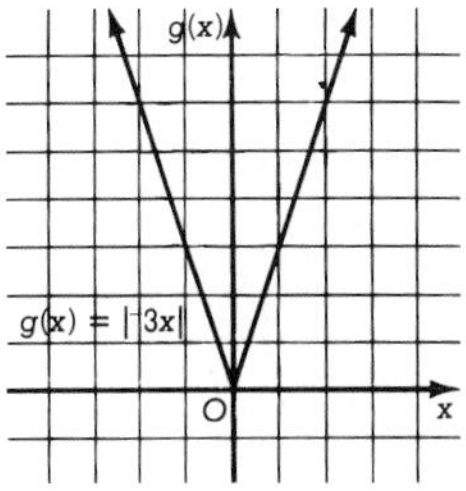

9.
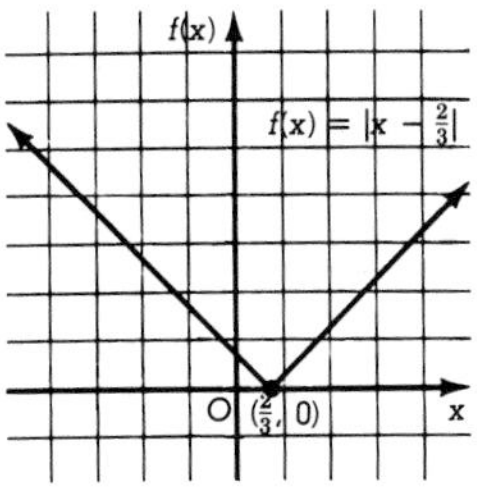

11.
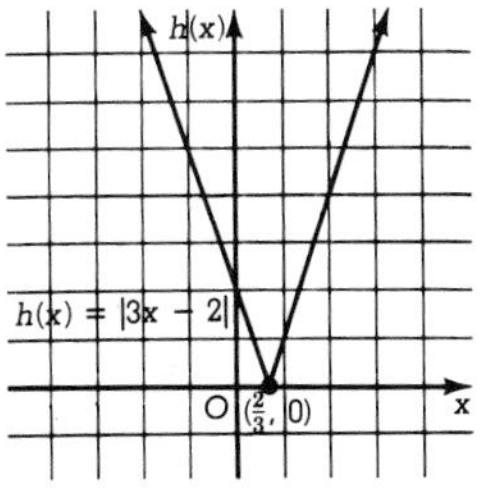

13.
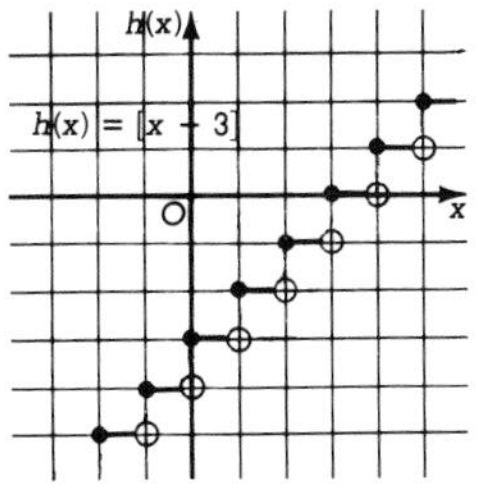

15.
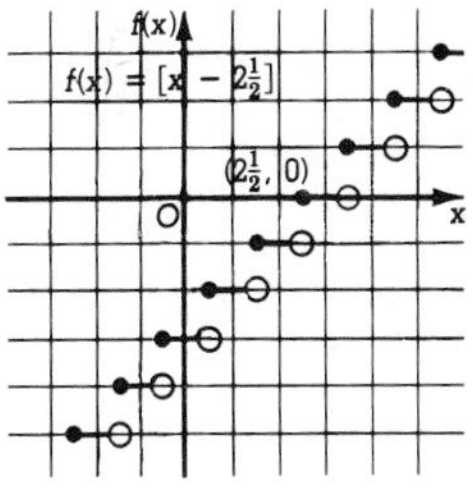

17.
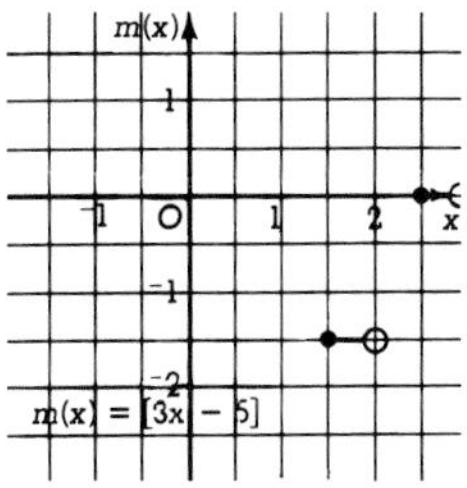

19.
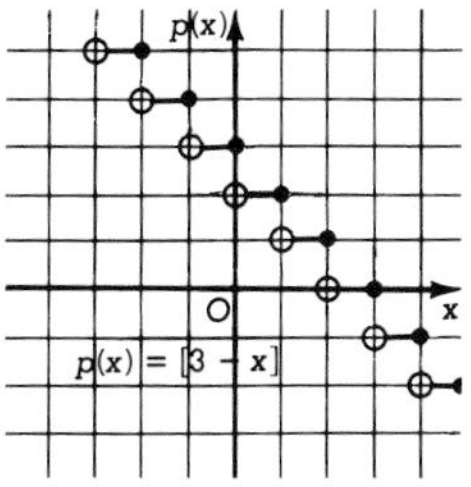

21.
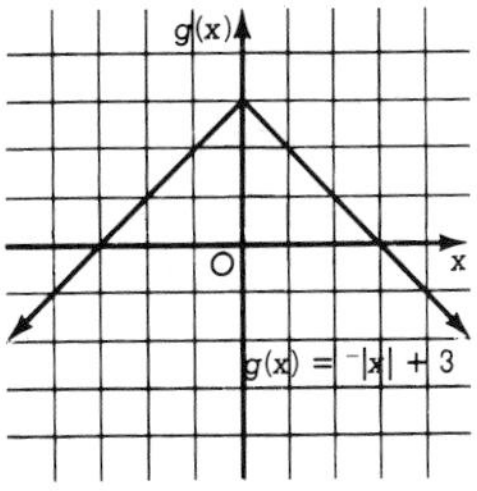

23.
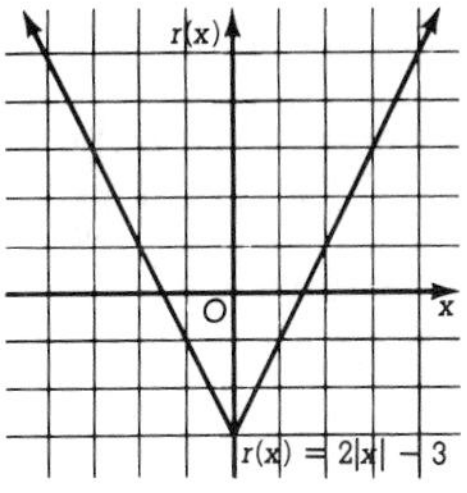

25. The graph of $y = [2x]$ jumps by ones at intervals of $\frac{1}{2}$ unit. The graph of $y = 2[x]$ jumps by twos at intervals of one unit. 27. The graph of $y = |x - 3|$ is like $y = |x|$ moved 3 units *to the right*. The graph of $y = |x| - 3$ is like $y = |x|$ moved 3 units *down*. 29. The graph of $y = |2x + 5|$ is like $y = |2x|$ moved 2.5 units to the *left*. The graph of $y = |2x| + 5$ is like $y = |2x|$ moved 2.5 units *up*. 31. The graphs of $y = |ax|$ and $y = a|x|$ are identical if $a \geq 0$. The graph of $y = a|x|$ opens down if $a < 0$.

Exploratory Exercises Page 61 1. $m = 0.9144y$ 3. ⁻0.08 5. 0.56 7. 1.20 9. 4.40 11. 7.60 13. 12.40 15. 18.80 17. 18.4° 19. 22.4° 21. 26.4° 23. 30.4°

Written Exercises Page 61 1. $c = 12 + 10t$ 3. $37 5. 8.8 hr 7. 1.2 in 9. 110 in

Exploratory Exercises page 63 1. (0, 0), (2, ⁻3), (⁻1, 2) 3. (0, 0), (2, ⁻3) 5. none 7. (2, ⁻3)

Written Exercises Page 63

1.
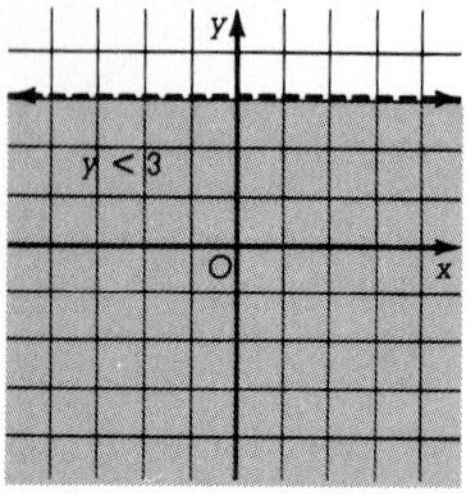

3.
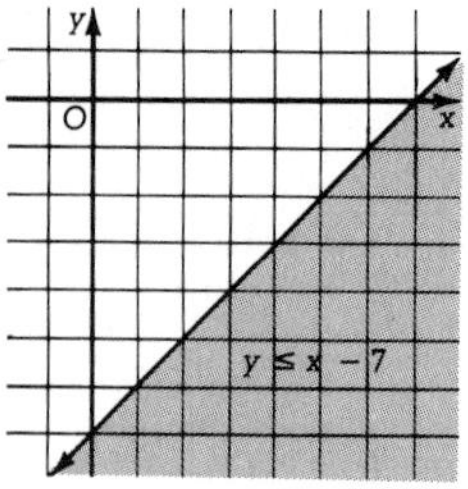

5.
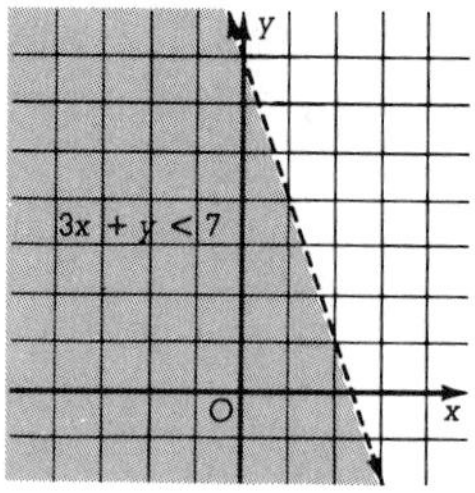

7.
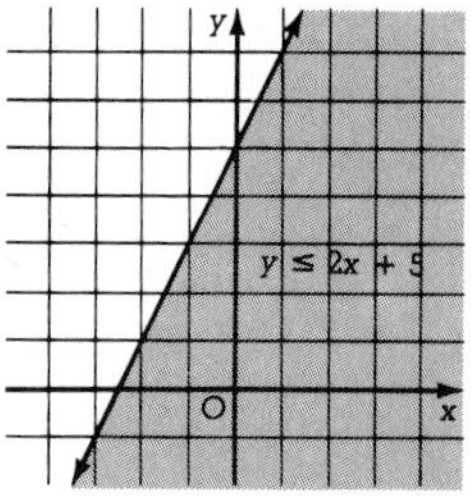

9.
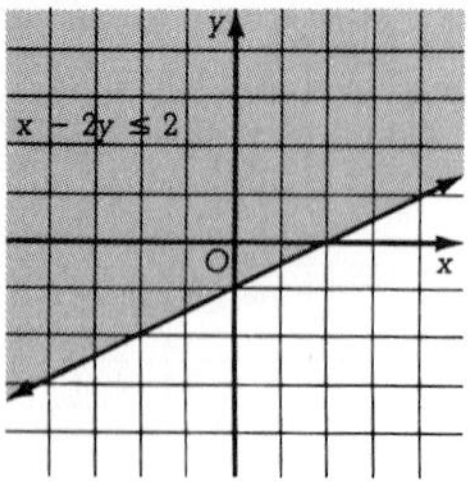

11.
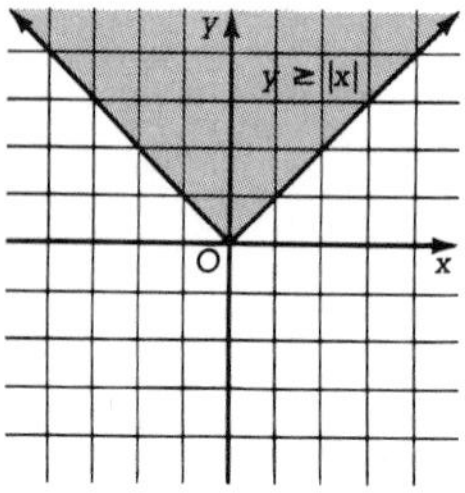

13.
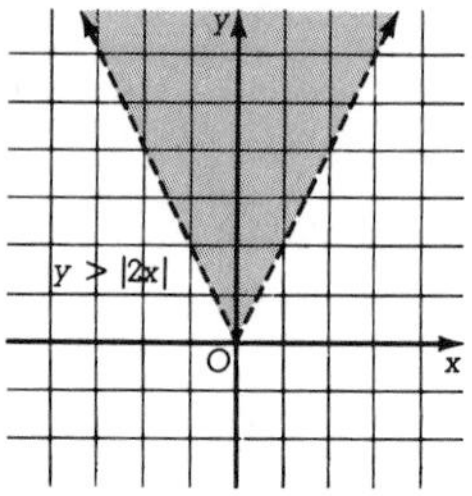

15.
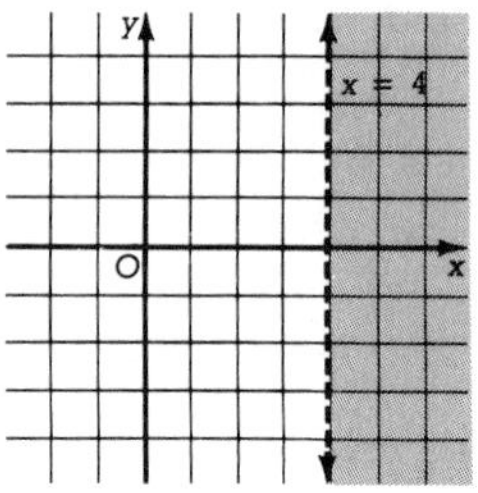

17.
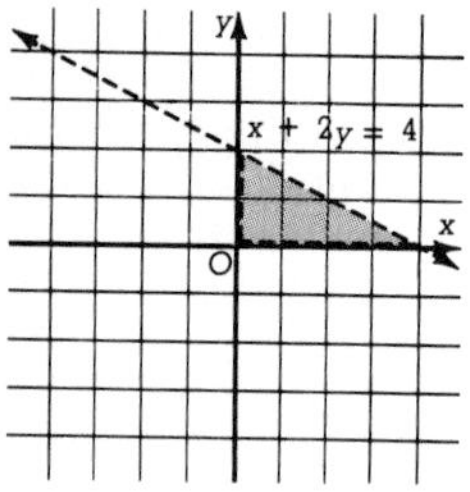

Chapter Review Pages 66–67

1.
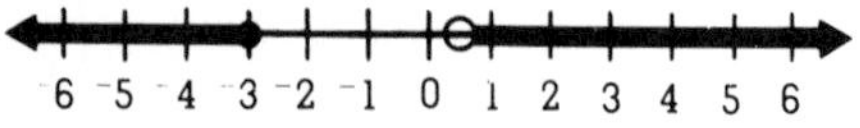

3.
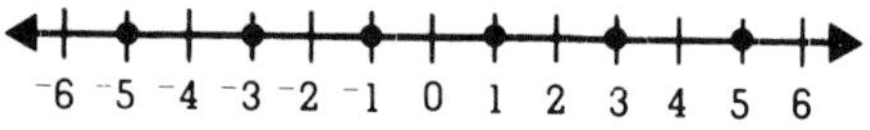

5.
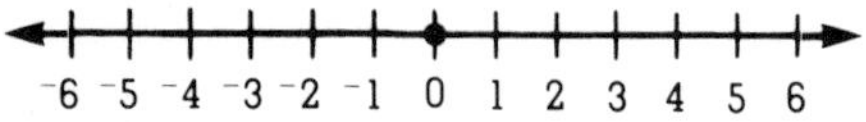

7.
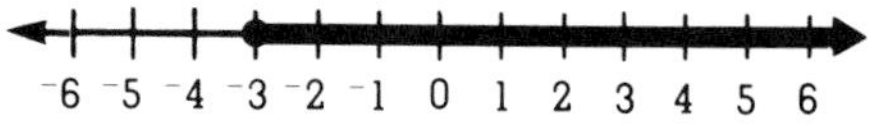

9. domain: $\{^-4.5, ^-3.5, 4.5\}$; range: $\{1, 2, 3, 4\}$ **11.** domain: $\{x|x \text{ is real}\}$; range: $\{4\}$ **13.** no **15.** yes **17.** no **19.** no **21.** $^-29$ **23.** $2(a + b)^3 + 4(a + b)^2 + 4(a + b) + 1$ **25.** no **27.** yes

29.
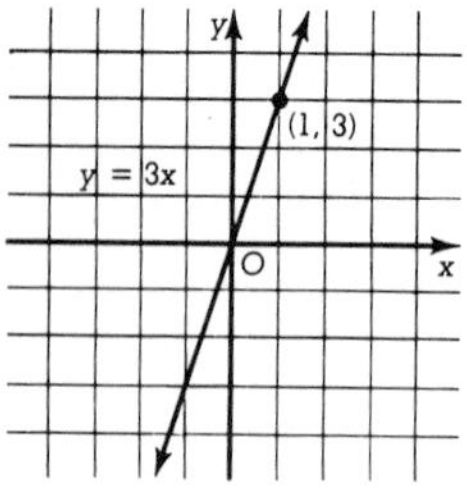

31.
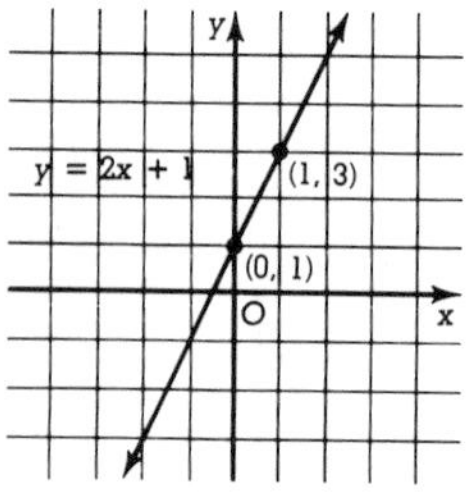

33. slope = 3; y-intercept = 0 **35.** slope = 2; y-intercept = 1 **37.** 6 **39.** $\frac{4}{3}$ **41.** $y = -\frac{6}{7}x - \frac{18}{7}$ **43.** $y = \frac{2}{3}x - \frac{14}{3}$ **45.** $6x + 7y = ^-18$ **47.** $2x - 3y = 14$

53. 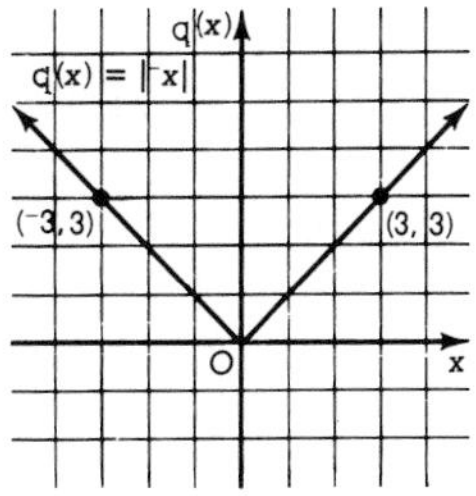

55. 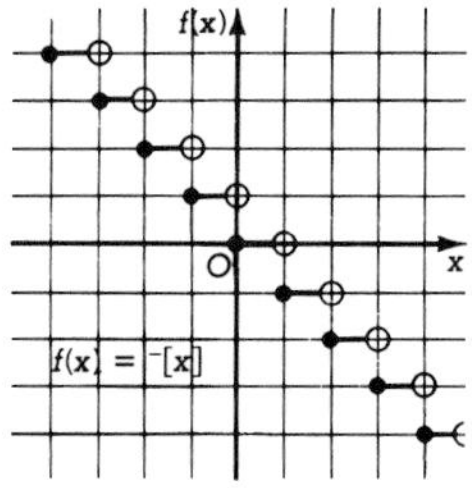

57. 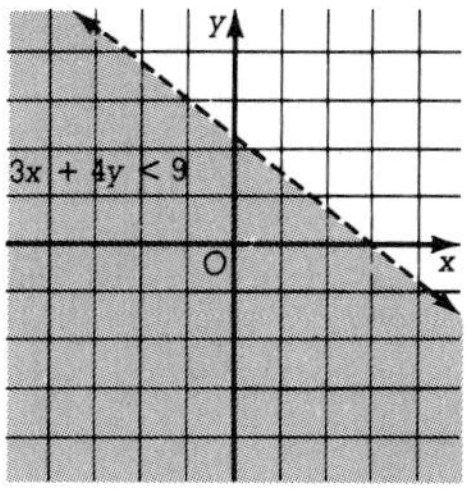

59. 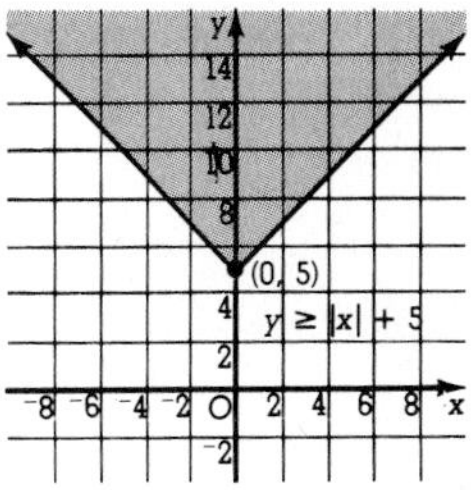

CHAPTER 3 SYSTEMS OF EQUATIONS AND INEQUALITIES

Exploratory Exercises Page 72 **1.** 4 **3.** $-\frac{1}{3}$ **5.** 1 **7.** $-\frac{1}{4}$ **9.** 3 **11.** $^{-}1$

Written Exercises Page 72 **1.** parallel **3.** perpendicular **5.** neither **7.** $y = 2x - 6$ **9.** $y = \frac{1}{3}x$ **11.** $y = {}^{-}x - 4$ **13.** $y = -\frac{1}{2}x + 4$ **15.** $y = {}^{-}3x + 10$ **17.** $y = x + 2$ **19-21.** Note that m is *not* necessarily the slope. **19.** $-\frac{2}{3}$ **21.** $\frac{3}{2}$ **23.** A line connecting (1, 3) and (5, 9) has slope $\frac{3}{2}$. A line connecting (1, 3) and (4, 1) has slope $-\frac{2}{3}$. These two lines are perpendicular since $(-\frac{2}{3})(\frac{3}{2}) = {}^{-}1$.

25.
```
10  INPUT A,B,C,P,Q
20  PRINT "Y="-(A/B)"X+"(Q+(A/B)*P)
30  GO TO 10
40  END
```

Exploratory Exercises Page 76 **1.** $({}^{-}3, 6)$ **3.** (5, 2) **5.** $(2, {}^{-}4)$

Written Exercises Page 76 **1.** (3, 1) **3.** no solutions **5.** $\{(x, y)|x + 2y = 5\}$ **7.** $(2, {}^{-}6)$ **9.** $(-\frac{4}{3}, -\frac{14}{3})$ **11.** no solutions **13.** $(1, {}^{-}2)$ **15.** $\{(x, y)|2x + 3y = 5\}$ **17.** consistent and independent **19.** inconsistent **21.** consistent and dependent **23.** consistent and independent **25.** consistent and independent **27.** inconsistent **29.** consistent and independent **31.** consistent and dependent

Exploratory Exercises Page 78 **1.** Multiply first equation by 3 and second equation by $^{-}2$ to eliminate x. **3.** Multiply second equation by 4 to eliminate y. **5.** Multiply first equation by 2 and second equation by $^{-}3$ to eliminate x. **7.** Multiply first equation by 3 and second equation by 4 to eliminate y.

Written Exercises Page 79 **1.** $(\frac{4}{3}, \frac{2}{3})$ **3.** $({}^{-}3, {}^{-}9)$ **5.** $({}^{-}9, {}^{-}7)$ **7-11.** See answers above. **13.** (12, 2) **15.** $(\frac{10}{3}, \frac{8}{3})$ **17.** $(\frac{1}{3}, 2)$ **19.** (2.8, 0.8) **21.** (5.25, 0.75) **23.** (4, 6) **25.** $({}^{-}3, 6)$ **27.** $\left(\frac{ce - bf}{ae - bd}, \frac{cd - af}{bd - ae}\right)$ **29.** (41, 39)

31.
```
 10  INPUT A,B,C,D,E,F
 20  PRINT A"X+"B"Y="C
 30  PRINT D"X+"E"Y="F
 40  IF A*E-B*D=0 THEN 90
 50  X=(C*E-B*F)/(A*E-B*D)
 60  Y=(A*F-C*D)/(A*E-B*D)
 70  PRINT "THE SOLUTION IS "("X","Y")"
 80  GO TO 10
 90  PRINT "NO UNIQUE SOLUTION"
100  GO TO 10
110  END
```

Exploratory Exercises Page 82 **1.** 14 **3.** 0 **5.** 1 **7.** 14 **9.** 72 **11.** -32

Written Exercises Pages 82–83 **1.** -18 **3.** 343 **5.** -93 **7.** 1 **9.** -12 **11.** 826,353 **13.** 6 **15.** -33 **17.** 29 **19.** -111 **21.** 47 **23.** 0 **25.** 0 **27.** -109 **29.** -676

Exploratory Exercises Page 85 **1.** $\frac{\begin{vmatrix}5 & 2\\ 11 & -6\end{vmatrix}}{\begin{vmatrix}3 & 2\\ 5 & -6\end{vmatrix}}$ $\frac{\begin{vmatrix}3 & 5\\ 5 & 11\end{vmatrix}}{\begin{vmatrix}3 & 2\\ 5 & -6\end{vmatrix}}$ **3.** $\frac{\begin{vmatrix}-11 & -8\\ 3 & -8\end{vmatrix}}{\begin{vmatrix}1 & -8\\ 8 & -8\end{vmatrix}}$ $\frac{\begin{vmatrix}1 & -11\\ 8 & 3\end{vmatrix}}{\begin{vmatrix}1 & -8\\ 8 & -8\end{vmatrix}}$ **5.** $\frac{\begin{vmatrix}11 & 2\\ 5 & -1\end{vmatrix}}{\begin{vmatrix}4 & 2\\ 3 & -1\end{vmatrix}}$ $\frac{\begin{vmatrix}4 & 11\\ 3 & 5\end{vmatrix}}{\begin{vmatrix}4 & 2\\ 3 & -1\end{vmatrix}}$

7. $\frac{\begin{vmatrix}\frac{1}{2} & 6\\ \frac{1}{4} & -8\end{vmatrix}}{\begin{vmatrix}\frac{1}{3} & 6\\ 1 & -8\end{vmatrix}}$ $\frac{\begin{vmatrix}\frac{1}{3} & \frac{1}{2}\\ 1 & \frac{1}{4}\end{vmatrix}}{\begin{vmatrix}\frac{1}{3} & 6\\ 1 & -8\end{vmatrix}}$ **9.** $\frac{\begin{vmatrix}0.56 & 0.41\\ 0.77 & -0.41\end{vmatrix}}{\begin{vmatrix}0.30 & 0.41\\ 0.23 & -0.41\end{vmatrix}}$ $\frac{\begin{vmatrix}0.30 & 0.56\\ 0.23 & 0.77\end{vmatrix}}{\begin{vmatrix}0.30 & 0.41\\ 0.23 & -0.41\end{vmatrix}}$

Written Exercises Page 85 **1.** $(\frac{13}{7}, -\frac{2}{7})$ **3.** $(2, \frac{13}{8})$ **5.** (2.1, 1.3) **7.** $(\frac{33}{52}, -\frac{5}{104})$ **9.** $\left(\frac{0.5453}{0.2173}, \frac{0.1022}{0.2173}\right)$
11. The determinant of the denominator would be zero.

Exploratory Exercises Page 87 **1.** no **3.** no **5.** yes

Written Exercises Page 87 **1.** (1, 2, 3) **3.** (8, -11, 3) **5.** (10, 1, -5) **7.** (1, 2, 1) **9.** (1, -1, 2) **11.** (4, -8, 3) **13.** $(\frac{43}{14}, -\frac{1}{14}, -\frac{33}{14})$

Written Exercises Page 89 **1.** (1, 1) **3.** (-2, 5) **5.** (-1, 2, -3) **7.** $(-\frac{91}{11}, \frac{68}{11}, \frac{98}{11})$ **9.** $(-3, \frac{1}{3}, 1)$

Exploratory Exercises Page 92 **1.** yes **3.** yes **5.** yes **7.** no

Written Exercises Page 92

1.
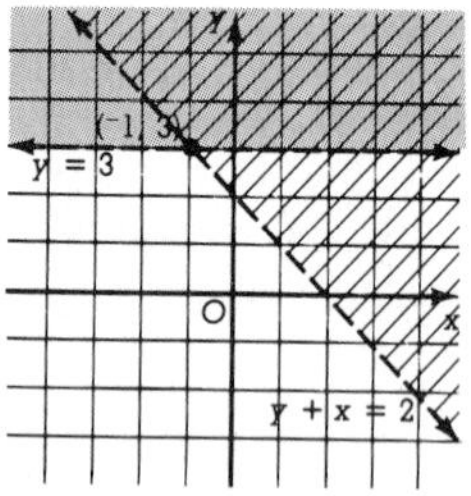

3.
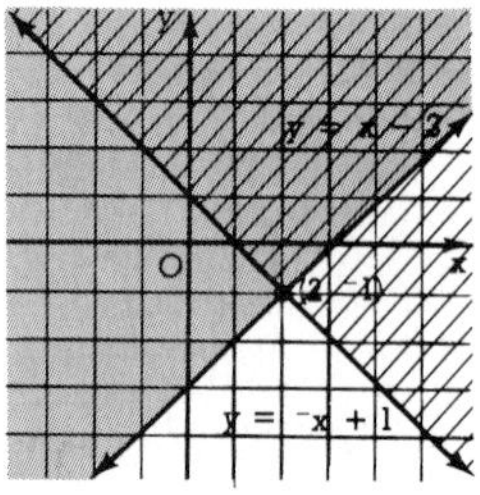

5.
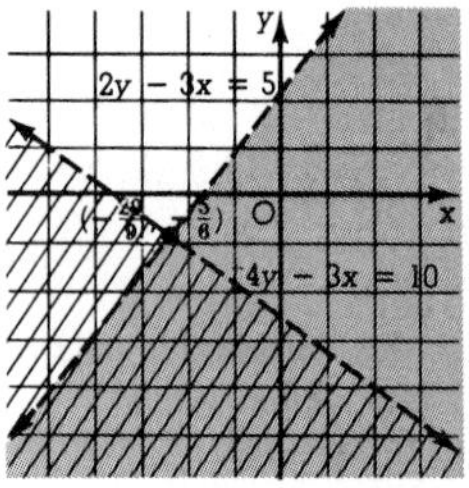

7.
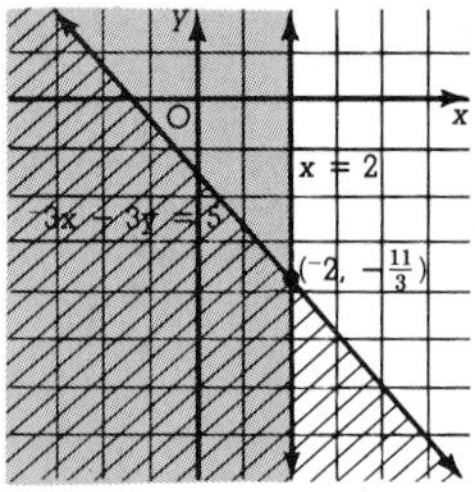

9.
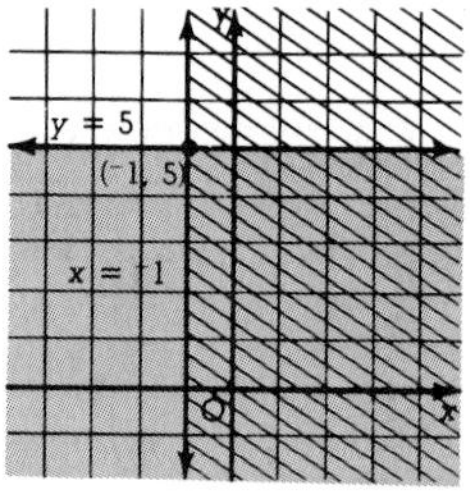

11.
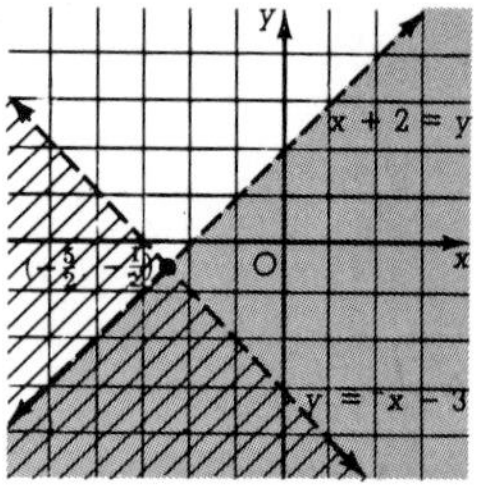

Exploratory Exercises Page 96 **1.** (0, 1), (1, 3), (6, 3), (10, 1) **3.** (0, 1), (6, 13), (6, 1)

Written Exercises Page 96 **1.** vertices: (1, 2), (1, 4), (5, 8), (5, 2); max. 11; min. -5 **3.** vertices: (0, 2), (4, 3), $(\frac{7}{3}, -\frac{1}{3})$; max. 25; min. 6 **5.** vertices: (2, 2), (2, 8), (6, 12), (6, -6); max. 30; min. 8 **7.** vertices: (0, 0), (0, 2), (2, 4), (5, 1), (5, 0); max. 25; min. -6
9. Let r = # rockers built. Let s = # swivels built. $r \geq 0$, $s \geq 0$. $2r + 4s \leq 20$. $3r + s \leq 15$. Profit = $12r + 10s$; vertices: (0, 0), (0, 5), (4, 3), (5, 0); max. 78; $r = 4$, $s = 3$.

Chapter Review Pages 98–99 **1.** $y = 3x - 6$ **3.** $y = 6x + 5$ **5.** $y = -\frac{1}{2}x + \frac{13}{2}$ **7.** $y = \frac{2}{3}x - \frac{1}{3}$ **9.** $(^-2, ^-6)$ **11.** (6, 5) **13.** consistent and independent **15.** consistent and independent **17.** $(5\frac{1}{4}, \frac{3}{4})$ **19.** $(\frac{14}{5}, \frac{4}{5})$ **21.** $^-2$ **23.** 26 **25.** $(\frac{1}{29}, -\frac{39}{29})$ **27.** (1, 1) **29.** (1, 2, 3) **31.** (2, 1)

33.

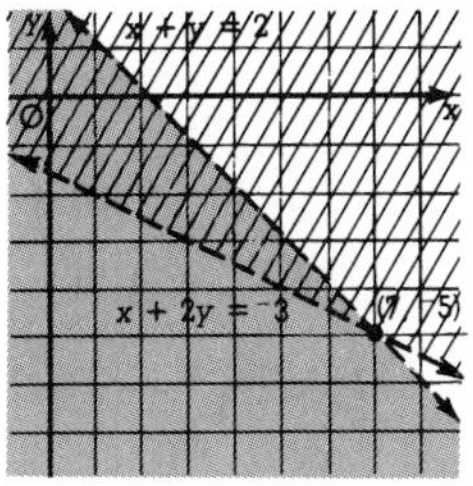

35.

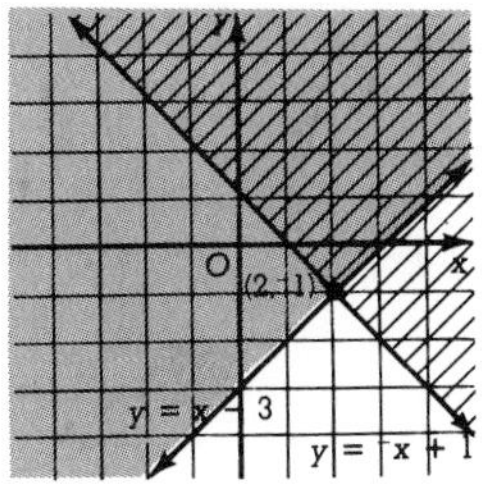

37. vertices: (0, 0), (0, 3), $(\frac{3}{2}, \frac{3}{2})$, (2, 0); max. 12; min. 0

CHAPTER 4 POLYNOMIALS

Exploratory Exercises Page 105 **1.** 3 **3.** 5 **5.** 8 **7.** 2 **9.** 5 **11.** 6 **13.** none **15.** 1

Written Exercises Page 105 **1.** $8m$ **3.** $5d^3$ **5.** $39x^2 - 3y^2$ **7.** y^{12} **9.** m^6 **11.** 2^7 **13.** 8^{14} **15.** y^{10} **17.** 3^4a^4 or $81a^4$ **19.** $2a$ **21.** $20m^3k^5$ **23.** $^-2m^8p^{11}$ **25.** ^-5st **27.** $7a^6$ **29.** $114a^4b^4$ **13.** $32x^3y^6$

Exploratory Exercises Page 108 **1.** 2 **3.** 8 **5.** 5 **7.** 3 **9.** 9

Written Exercises Page 108 **1.** $5x^2 + 1$ **3.** $4p^2 + 10p + 2$ **5.** $r^2 - r + 6$ **7.** $7x^4 - 2x^3 + 7x^2 - 2x + 1$ **9.** $^-r^6 + 4r^4 + r^3 - 2r - 13$ **11.** $p^4 - p^3 + 5p^2 - 6p$ **13.** $6x^2 + 31x + 35$ **15.** $m^4 + m^2 - 20$ **17.** $x^6 + 6x^3 + 9$ **19.** $m^4 - 49$ **21.** $b^4 + 16b^2 + 64$ **23.** $9a^2 - 12ab + 4b^2$ **25.** $a^3 - 3a^2 + a + 1$ **27.** $x^3 + xy^3 - xy^2 - y^4$ **29.** $3m^3 - 7m^2 - 24m + 16$ **31.** $r^3 - 5r^2 + 6r$ **33.** $b^3 + 2b^2 - 5b - 6$ **35.** $2a^3 - 7a^2 + 4a + 4$ **37.** $6y^3 + 16y^2 - 2y$ **39.** $m^2 + 8m + 16$ **41.** $y^2 - 4y + 4$ **43.** $y^2 - 25$ **45.** $4p^2 + 4pq^3 + q^6$ **47.** $a^2 - 36b^2$ **49.** $1 - 14y + 49y^2$ **51.** $16m^2 - 24mn + 9n^2$ **53.** $4 - 12y + 9y^2$ **55.** $1 + 8r + 16r^2$ **57.** $16a^2 - 4b^2$ **59.** $x^6 - y^2$

Exercises Page 109 **1.** 5.0×10^1 **3.** 5.0×10^3 **5.** 2.0691×10^4 **7.** 2.0691×10^2 **9.** 2.34×10^1 **11.** 7.5×10^6 **13.** 9.842×10^4 **15.** 2.006×10^4

Exploratory Exercises Page 111 **1.** 5 **3.** 8 **5.** 7 **7.** 5 **9.** 5 **11.** 4 **13.** $4rs^3$ **15.** $^-35k^4m^3$ **17.** $20z^3a^3$ **19.** ^-108a **21.** $32y$ **23.** 27

Written Exercises Page 111 **1.** $x^4 + 4x^3m + 6x^2m^2 + 4xm^3 + m^4$ **3.** $y^7 + 7y^6p + 21y^5p + 35y^4p^3 + 35y^3p^4 + 21y^2p^5 + 7yp^6 + p^7$ **5.** $b^5 - 5b^4z + 10b^3z^2 - 10b^2z^3 + 5bz^4 - z^5$ **7.** $32m^5 + 80m^4y + 80m^3y^2 + 40m^2y^3 + 10my^4 + y^5$ **9.** $64b^6 + 192b^5x + 240b^4x^2 + 160b^3x^3 + 60b^2x^4 + 12bx^5 + x^6$ **11.** $243x^5 - 810x^4y + 1080x^3y^2 - 720x^2y^3 + 240xy^4 - 32y^5$ **13.** $32y^5 + 80y^4 + 80y^3 + 40y^2 + 10y + 1$ **15.** $\frac{1}{729}y^6 + \frac{2}{27}y^5 + \frac{5}{3}y^4 + 20y^3 + 135y^2 + 486y + 729$ **17.** \$17,715.61

Excursion Page 114 **1.** 1, 4, 6, 4, 1 **3.** 1, 6, 15, 20, 15, 6, 1 **5.** $a^4 + 4a^3b + 6a^2b^2 + 4ab^3 + b^4$ **7.** $a^8 + 8a^7b + 28a^6b^2 + 56a^5b^3 + 70a^4b^4 + 56a^3b^5 + 28a^2b^6 + 8ab^7 + b^8$ **9.** $x^6 + 6x^5y + 15x^4y^2 + 20x^3y^3 + 15x^2y^4 + 6xy^5 + y^6$ **11.** $16a^4 + 32a^3b + 24a^2b^2 + 8ab^3 + b^4$

Exploratory Exercises Page 118 **1.** $(y + 3)^2$ **3.** $(k - 4)^2$ **5.** $(a + 2)(a + 3)$ **7.** $(p - 4)(p - 1)$ **9.** $(m - 5)(m - 2)$

Written Exercises Page 118 **1.** $(a + 7)(a + 5)$ **3.** $(f - 9)^2$ **5.** $(k + 6)^2$ **7.** $(3y + 2)(y + 1)$ **9.** $(2z - 7)(2z - 3)$ **11.** $(a + 2b)^2$ **13.** $(p - 2b)^2$ **15.** $(2r - 5s)^2$ **17.** $2(2k + 3)(k + 5)$ **19.** $4(h + 6)(h - 4)$ **21.** $2y(y - 7)(y + 3)$

Exploratory Exercises Page 121 **1.** $(y + 4k)(3y - 2)$ **3.** $(a - c)(y - b)$ **5.** $(a - 2)(a + b)$ **7.** $(2x^2 + 1)(x - 3)$ **9.** $(x + y - \frac{1}{2})(x + y + \frac{1}{2})$ **11.** $(m - k + 3)(m + k - 3)$ **13.** $(k - 3)(k + 3)(k + 4)$ **15.** $(x + y - 4)(x - y)$

Written Exercises Page 121 **1.** $(y + 4k)(3y - 2)$ **3.** $(a - c)(y - b)$ **5.** $(a - 2)(a + b)$ **7.** $(2x^2 + 1)(x - 3)$ **9.** $(x + y - r)(x + y + r)$ **11.** $(m - k + 3)(m + k - 3)$ **13.** $(k - 3)(k + 3)(k + 4)$ **15.** $(x - y)(x + y - 4)$ **17.** $(a - b + 4)(a + b - 4)$ **19.** $(2a - 1)(b + m)$ **21.** $(x + 3 - a)(x + 3 + a)$ **23.** $(a - \frac{1}{2} - y)(a - \frac{1}{2} + y)$ **25.** $x(x + y)(x - z)$ **27.** $3(2x - 3)(3x + 1)$ **29.** $(b - y - p)(b + y + p)$ **31.** $(2a + b - m)(b + m)$ **33.** $(2a + 3)(4a^2 - 6a + 9)$ **35.** $3r(1 - 3r)(1 + 3r + 9r^2)$ **37.** $(x + y)(x - y)^2$ **39.** $(x - 3)(x + 3)(x - 2)(x + 2)$ **41.** $(r - p)(r + p)^2$

Challenge Page 121 **1.** $a(a - 2b)(a^2 - 10ab + 4b^2)$ **3.** $y(x + 2)(x - 4)(x - 1)$

Exploratory Exercises Page 124 **1.** $\frac{1}{7}$ **3.** g^3 **5.** 1 **7.** $4a^2b^3$ **9.** $3xy^3$ **11.** $^-a^2b + a - \dfrac{2}{b}$

Written Exercises Page 124 **1.** $x - 15$ **3.** $3y - 1$ **5.** $4a + 3 - \dfrac{2}{2a + 7}$ **7.** $4y + 5 + \dfrac{3}{7y - 3}$ **9.** $a - 12$ **11.** $y + 12$ **13.** $2x + 7$ **15.** $a - 2b$ **17.** $2z - \dfrac{16}{3} + \dfrac{28}{3(3z + 7)}$ **19.** $a + 10 + \dfrac{44}{a - 6}$ **21.** $8x - 44 + \dfrac{231}{x + 5}$ **23.** $3a + 7 + \dfrac{4}{2a + 3}$ **25.** $7m - 8 + \dfrac{3}{8m - 7}$ **27.** $2y^2 + 5y + 2$ **29.** $3a^2 - 2a + 3$ **31.** $m^2 + m + 1$ **33.** $y^2 - 6y + 9 - \dfrac{1}{y - 3}$ **35.** $2a^2 + \dfrac{1}{3}a - \dfrac{41}{9} - \dfrac{71}{9(3a + 2)}$ **37.** $m + 3$ **39.** $x^2 - 2x + 8 - \dfrac{20}{x + 2}$ **41.** $x^2 + 2x + 2$ **43.** $a^2 - a - 1$ **45.** yes **47.** $a - 1, a + 1$ **49.** 15 **51.** They are the same.

Exploratory Exercises Page 128 **1.** d **3.** e **5.** a **7.** f

Written Exercises Page 128 **1.** $2x^2 + x + 5 + \dfrac{6}{x - 2}$ **3.** $2a^2 - a - 1 + \dfrac{4}{a + 1}$ **5.** $x^3 + x - 1$ **7.** $6k^2 - k - 2$ **9.** $2b^2 - 5b - 3$ **11.** $y^3 - 11y^2 + 31y - 21$ **13.** $2x^3 + x^2 + 3x - 1 + \dfrac{5}{x - 3}$ **15.** $y^3 + 3y^2 - 16y + 55 - \dfrac{166}{y + 3}$ **17.** $2x^3 + x^2 - 2x + \dfrac{3}{2x - 1}$ **19.** $2x^2 - 8x + 1 + \dfrac{5}{3x - 2}$ **21.** $x^4 - 2x^3 + 4x^2 - 8x + 16$

Chapter Review Page 131 **1.** y^{11} **3.** x^6 **5.** a^4 **7.** $114a^4b^4$ **9.** $b^3 + 15b - 3b - 2$ **11.** $4a^2 + 23a - 35$ **13.** $y^3 + 4y^2 - 16y + 35$ **15.** $2m^3 + 15m^2 + 34m + 21$ **17.** $r^5 + 5r^4s + 10r^3s^2 + 10r^2s^3 + 5rs^4 + s^5$ **19.** $16a^4 + 32a^3m + 24a^3m^2 + 8am^3 + m^4$ **21.** about \$4081.47 **23.** $3s(r^2 - rs + s^2)$ **25.** $q^3(p - 3)(p^2 - 3p + 9)$ **27.** $(2x + y)(x + 3y)$ **29.** $r(r + 4s)(r + 2s)$ **31.** $(3a - 2)(a + 4b)$ **33.** $(3a + b)(a + b)$ **35.** $r^2 + 4r - \dfrac{21}{2} + \dfrac{27}{2(2r + 3)}$ **37.** $2m^2 + 5m + 12 + \dfrac{49}{m - 4}$ **39.** $2x^3 - 11x^2 + 12x + 9 = (2x + 1)(x - 3)^2$. The remainder upon division is zero.

CHAPTER 5 ROOTS

Exploratory Exercises Page 137 **1.** 49 **3.** 27 **5.** 16 **7.** 169 **9.** 11 **11.** 2 **13.** y **15.** y^2 **17.** $^-4$ **19.** $|x + 3|$ **21.** 6.856 **23.** 2.621

Written Exercises Page 137 **1.** $^-9$ **3.** 15 **5.** 3 **7.** $^-1$ **9.** $^-10$ **11.** 0.5 **13.** $9s^2$ **15.** 24 **17.** $^-32$ **19.** $^-11|bg^3|$ **21.** ^-3rs **23.** $|3p + q|$ **25.** $z + a$ **27.** $|y + 3|$ **29.** $|3x + 1|$ **31.** $|m - 4|$

Exploratory Exercises Page 139 **1.** $2\sqrt{2}$ **3.** $5|x|\sqrt{2}$ **5.** $2\sqrt[3]{2}$ **7.** $4\sqrt[3]{2}$ **9.** $2\sqrt[4]{3}$ **11.** $m\sqrt[3]{m}$ **13.** $3\sqrt{5}$ **15.** 6 **17.** $3\sqrt[3]{2}$ **19.** $5 - \sqrt{15}$

Written Exercises Page 139 **1.** $15\sqrt{6}$ **3.** $2\sqrt[3]{3}$ **5.** $9\sqrt{2}$ **7.** $^-5$ **9.** $33\sqrt{2}$ **11.** $4\sqrt[3]{3}$ **13.** $^-60\sqrt{30}$ **15.** $3\sqrt{7} + 7$ **17.** $^-\sqrt{6} - 2$ **19.** 14 **21.** $140\sqrt[3]{5}$ **23.** $^-2$ **25.** $\sqrt[4]{90}$ **27.** $2ab^2\sqrt[3]{ab}$ **29.** $4|xy|\sqrt{x}$ **31.** $2ab^2\sqrt[3]{9b}$ **33.** $3b^2r^2\sqrt[4]{3r}$

Exploratory Exercises Page 141 1. $-\sqrt{7}$ 3. $-7\sqrt[4]{5}$ 5. $3\sqrt[3]{x}$ 7. $5\sqrt[5]{3}$ 9. $5\sqrt[3]{3}$ 11. $12 - 2\sqrt{3}$ 13. $14 + 6\sqrt{5}$ 15. $19 + 8\sqrt{3}$ 17. $6 - 2\sqrt{5}$

Written Exercises Page 142 1. $8\sqrt{2} - 8$ 3. $5\sqrt{5} - 10\sqrt{2}$ 5. $4 - 7\sqrt{3}$ 7. $11\sqrt[3]{5}$ 9. $-\sqrt[3]{2}$ 11. $2\sqrt[3]{2} - 4\sqrt{2}$ 13. $14\sqrt{6} + 2\sqrt[3]{3}$ 15. $2\sqrt{3} + 3$ 17. $3\sqrt[3]{5} - 3\sqrt[3]{3}$ 19. $|x|y^2\sqrt{2}$ 21. $3|yz|\sqrt[4]{z^2}$ 23. $|z| + z^2 + z^4$ 25. $17 + 8\sqrt{2}$ 27. $25 + 5\sqrt{6} - 5\sqrt{2} - 2\sqrt{3}$ 29. $3 - 5\sqrt{11}$ 31. $1 + \sqrt{15}$ 33. $21 + 8\sqrt{5}$ 35. 9×10^4 37. $9\sqrt[3]{2} - 6$ 39. $y^3 + 4$ 41. $(x - \sqrt{5})(x + \sqrt{5})$ 43. $(y - \sqrt{6})(y + \sqrt{6})$ 45. $(b - 5\sqrt{2})^2$

Exploratory Exercises Page 145 1. $\sqrt{2}$ 3. $\sqrt[3]{3y}$ 5. $\frac{\sqrt{5}}{2}$ 7. $\frac{\sqrt[3]{3}}{2}$ 9. $\frac{2\sqrt{3}}{3}$ 11. $\frac{\sqrt{5}}{5}$ 13. $\frac{3\sqrt[3]{2}}{2}$ 15. $\frac{7\sqrt[3]{3}}{3}$ 17. $1 - \sqrt{3}$ 19. $1 + \sqrt{2}$ 21. $3 - \sqrt{5}$ 23. $5 - 3\sqrt{3}$ 25. $-2\sqrt{2} - 3$ 27. $\sqrt{2} + 5\sqrt{3}$

Written Exercises Page 146 1. $\sqrt{5}$ 3. $\sqrt{7}$ 5. $\sqrt[3]{9}$ 7. $\frac{\sqrt{5}}{2}$ 9. $\frac{2\sqrt{2}}{3}$ 11. $\frac{\sqrt[3]{5}}{2}$ 13. $\frac{3\sqrt[3]{2}}{5}$ 15. $\frac{\sqrt[4]{5}}{2}$ 17. $\frac{\sqrt{3}}{3}$ 19. $\frac{\sqrt{6}}{3}$ 21. $\frac{\sqrt{15}}{6}$ 23. $\frac{\sqrt[3]{15}}{3}$ 25. $\frac{\sqrt[4]{54}}{3}$ 27. $\frac{3 - \sqrt{5}}{4}$ 29. $\frac{3 + \sqrt{5}}{2}$ 31. $\frac{5 + 4\sqrt{2}}{7}$ 33. $\frac{19 - 11\sqrt{3}}{-2}$ 35. $-15 - 11\sqrt{2}$ 37. $\frac{16\sqrt{10}}{5}$ 39. $\frac{3}{2}\sqrt[3]{2}$ 41. 1.118 43. 0.943 45 0.855 47. 0.756 49. 2.72 sec 51. 7 in

Exploratory Exercises Page 149 1. 4 3. $7 - 2\sqrt{5}$ 5. 1 7. 29 9. $4\sqrt{3}$ 11. $1 + \sqrt{3}$

Written Exercises Page 149 1. $-\sqrt{3}$ 3. $\frac{12 - 4\sqrt{2}}{7}$ 5. $\frac{-15 - 5\sqrt{3}}{6}$ 7. $\frac{26 + 13\sqrt{11}}{-7}$ 9. 64 11. 54 13. 7 15. 62 17. $40\frac{1}{2}$ 19. 23 21. 3 23. $\pm\sqrt{y^2 - r^2}$ if $y \geq r$ 25. $\frac{u}{4T^2}$ if $T \neq 0$ 27. $\frac{m^6 g^2}{r}$ if $r \neq 0$

Exploratory Exercises Page 152 1. $6i$ 3. $4i\sqrt{2}$ 5. -3 7. $5i$ 9. $6i$ 11. $11i$ 13. $-3i$ 15. -1

Written Exercises Page 152 1. $9i$ 3. $5i\sqrt{2}$ 5. $\frac{2}{3}i$ 7. $\frac{i\sqrt{3}}{3}$ 9. i 11. $-i$ 13. $3i$ 15. $11i$ 17. $5i$ 19. $14i$ 21. -4 23. $-7\sqrt{2}$ 25. -3 27. $-3i\sqrt{3}$ 29. 24 31. $-216i$ 33. $-18i$ 35. $\pm 4i$ 37. $\pm 13i$ 39. $\pm i\sqrt{3}$

Exploratory Exercises Page 156 1. $8 + 11i$ 3. 3 5. 10 7. $20 + 12i$ 9. $7 + (\sqrt{2} + \sqrt{3})i$ 11. $x = 5$, $y = 6$ 13. $x = 7$, $y = 2$ 15. $x = 3$, $y = 0$ 17. $-10 + 10i$ 19. $-10 - 11i$

Written Exercises Page 156 1. $7 + 7i$ 3. $6 + 4i$ 5. $2 + 9i$ 7. $8 - 15i$ 9. $5 - 3i\sqrt{3}$ 11. $-21 - 2i$ 13. $13 - 13i$ 15. $32 - 24i$ 17. $37 + 2i\sqrt{2}$ 19. $5 + 12i$ 21. 3 23. $20 + 15i$ 25. $148 - 222i$ 27. $1 - i$, $-1 + 5i$, $6 + 2i$ 29. 14, $4i$, 53 31. 2, $2i$, 2 33. $x = 2$, $y = 3$ 35. $x = -1$, $y = -3$ 37. $x = 3$, $y = 1$

Exploratory Exercises Page 157 1. $2 - i$ 3. $1 - 3i$ 5. $-4i$ 7. $5i$ 9. 6 11. $5 + 6i$ 13. 5 15. 10 17. 16 19. 25 21. 36 23. 61 25. $2^4 = 16$ 27. $(2i)^4 = 2^4 i^4 = 16 \cdot 1 = 16$

Written Exercises Page 158 1. 58 3. 85 5. 13 7. 4 9. $\frac{5 + i}{2}$ 11. $\frac{5 + i}{13}$ 13. $\frac{5 - 3i}{2}$ 15. $\frac{6 + 5i}{3}$ 17. $\frac{12 + 3i}{17}$ 19. $\frac{4\sqrt{3} - 8i}{7}$ 21. $\frac{1 + 4i\sqrt{3}}{7}$ 23. $\frac{2 - 3i\sqrt{5}}{7}$ 25. $\frac{16 + 63i}{50}$ 27. $\frac{-1 - i}{2}$ 29. $\frac{3 - i}{10}$ 31. $\frac{7 + 3i}{58}$ 33. $1^3 = 1 \cdot 1 \cdot 1 = 1$ 35. $(-\frac{1}{2} - \frac{1}{2}i\sqrt{3})^3 = (-\frac{1}{2} + \frac{1}{2}i\sqrt{3})(-\frac{1}{2} - \frac{1}{2}i\sqrt{3}) = \frac{1}{4} + \frac{3}{4} + \frac{1}{4}i\sqrt{3} - \frac{1}{4}i\sqrt{3} = 1$

Excursions Page 158 R: $2i$; U: 8; L: $9 + 40i$; E: $5 + 10i$; EULER

Exploratory Exercises Page 161 1. no additive identity, no inverses 3. not closed under addition or multiplication, no identities 5. not closed under addition or multiplication, no identities

Written Exercises Page 161 1–5. Answers will vary. 7. $-i\sqrt{3}$ 9. $-11 - i$ 11. $-3 + 4i$ 13. $3 + 2i$ 15. $-5 - 4i$ 17. 3 19. $\frac{-i\sqrt{3}}{3}$ 21. $\frac{11 - i}{122}$ 23. $\frac{3 + 4i}{25}$ 25. $\frac{-3 + 2i}{13}$ 27. $\frac{5 - 4i}{41}$ 29. $-\frac{1}{3}$

31. Let $a + bi$ and $c + di$ be two complex numbers.

$(a + bi)(c + di) = (ac - bd) + (ad + bc)i$	Definition of complex multiplication
a, b, c, and d are real numbers	Definition of complex numbers

ac, bd, ad, and bc are real numbers — Reals are closed under multiplication
$ac - bd$ and $ad + bc$ are real numbers — Reals are closed under addition
$(ac - bd) + (ad + bc)i$ is a complex number — Definition of complex numbers

33. Let $a + bi$, $c + di$, and $e + fi$ be complex numbers.
$[(a + bi)(c + di)](e + fi) = [(ac - bd) + (ad + bc)i](e + fi)$ Definition of complex multiplication
$[(a + bi)(c + di)](e + fi) = [(ac - bd)e - (ad + bc)f] + [(ac - bd)f + (ad + bc)e]i$
Definition of complex multiplication
$[(a + bi)(c + di)](e + fi) = [(ac)e - (bd)e - (ad)f - (bc)f] + [(ac)f - (bd)f + (ad)e + (bc)e]$
Distributivity for reals
$[(a + bi)(c + di)](e + fi) = [a(ce) - b(de) - a(df) - b(cf)] + [a(cf) - b(df) + a(de) + b(ce)]i$
Associativity for multiplication of reals
$[(a + bi)(c + di)](e + fi) = [a(ce) - a(df) - b(cf) - b(de)] + [a(cf) + a(de) + b(ce) - b(df)]i$
Commutativity for addition of reals
$[(a + bi)(c + di)](e + fi) = [a(ce - df) - b(cf + de)] + [a(cf + de) + b(ce - df)]i$ Distributivity for reals
$[(a + bi)(c + di)](e + fi) = (a + bi)[(ce - df) + (cf + de)i]$ Definition of complex multiplication
$[(a + bi)(c + di)](e + fi) = (a + bi)[(c + di)(e + f)]$ Definition of complex multiplication

Chapter Review Page 163 **1.** $7|a|$ **3.** 2 **5.** 3.391 **7.** 941.192 **9.** $2\sqrt[3]{6a^2}$ **11.** $2m\sqrt[4]{2m}$ **13.** $5\sqrt{2} + 2\sqrt{5}$ **15.** $2\sqrt[3]{6} + 3$ **17.** $2xy^2\sqrt[3]{9}$ **19.** $4\sqrt[3]{5}$ **21.** $m^3 + 2$ **23.** $2\sqrt[3]{5}$ **25.** $\sqrt[3]{4}$ **27.** 62 **29.** $2i\sqrt{2}$ **31.** ^-i **33.** $^-3$ **35.** $12 - i$, $2 + 5i$, $41 - 11i$ **37.** $x = 2$, $y = 3$ **39.** $\frac{-3 - 7i}{2}$ **41.** commutative property of addition

CHAPTER 6 QUADRATIC EQUATIONS

Exploratory Exercises Page 167 **1.** yes **3.** yes **5.** no **7.** yes **9.** no **11.** 4, $^-5$ **13.** $^-6$, $^-2$ **15.** 0, 7 **17.** $-\frac{3}{2}$, $\frac{1}{3}$ **19.** $-\frac{7}{3}$, $^-5$

Written Exercises Page 167 **1.** $^-2$, $^-4$ **3.** 4, 5 **5.** $^-5$, 2 **7.** 4, $^-1$ **9.** 0, $^-3$ **11.** $^-6$, 5 **13.** $-\frac{3}{2}$, $^-1$ **15.** $-\frac{3}{2}$, 3 **17.** 0, $\frac{5}{3}$ **19.** $-\frac{3}{2}$, $-\frac{2}{3}$ **21.** $-\frac{4}{3}$, $-\frac{3}{4}$ **23.** $\frac{1}{6}$, $\frac{3}{4}$ **25.** $-\frac{1}{4}$, 3 **27.** 5, $^-8$ **29.** $\frac{2}{3}$, 4 **31.** $-\frac{1}{4}$, $\frac{5}{3}$ **33.** $\frac{5}{6}$, $-\frac{3}{2}$ **35.** $^-2$

Challenge Page 167 **1.** 0, 3, $^-3$ **3.** $\frac{11}{4}$, $-\frac{11}{4}$ **5.** 0, $-\frac{6}{7}$, $\frac{2}{5}$

Exploratory Exercises Page 170 **1.** yes **3.** no **5.** yes **7.** yes **9.** yes **11.** 1 **13.** 400 **15.** 81 **17.** $\frac{81}{4}$ **19.** 2500 **21.** $\frac{225}{4}$

Written Exercises Page 170 **1.** 9 **3.** $\frac{1}{16}$ **5.** $\frac{1}{4}$ **7.** $\frac{9}{4}$ **9.** $\frac{49}{4}$ **11.** 625 **13.** 3, 4 **15.** 3, 5 **17.** $^-10$, 2 **19.** 6, $^-8$ **21.** $^-15$, 12 **23.** 6, $^-14$ **25.** $\frac{3}{2} \pm \frac{\sqrt{37}}{2}$ **27.** 4 **29.** $\frac{7}{2} \pm \frac{\sqrt{29}}{2}$ **31.** $^-2$, $-\frac{1}{3}$ **33.** $^-8$, 5 **35.** 4, $\frac{2}{3}$ **37.** $\frac{5}{3}$, $-\frac{1}{4}$ **39.** no real solutions **41.** no real solutions

Exploratory Exercises Page 173 **1.** 5, $^-3$, 7 **3.** 1, 2, $^-1$ **5.** 5, 0, $^-3$ **7.** 4, 0, $^-7$ **9.** 5, 0, 7 **11.** 4, $^-6$, $^-1$

Written Exercises Page 174 **1.** 6, $^-5$ **3.** $^-5$, 3 **5.** 6, 4 **7.** 4, $-\frac{5}{3}$ **9.** 3, $-\frac{1}{4}$ **11.** $\frac{1}{7}$, $-\frac{5}{2}$ **13.** $\frac{1}{4}$, $-\frac{2}{5}$ **15.** $\frac{5}{6}$, $-\frac{3}{4}$ **17.** 4, 1 **19.** 3, $-\frac{5}{2}$ **21.** $-\frac{2}{3} \pm \frac{i\sqrt{14}}{6}$ **23.** 1, $\frac{3}{2}$ **25.** $\frac{4}{3}$, $-\frac{3}{4}$ **27.** $^-1$, $\frac{1}{21}$ **29.** $\frac{5 \pm i\sqrt{7}}{4}$ **31.** $\frac{3}{2}$, $-\frac{2}{3}$ **33.** $\frac{9 \pm i\sqrt{3}}{2}$ **35.** 0, 13 **37.** $\frac{1 \pm i\sqrt{5}}{6}$ **39.** 1, $-\frac{4}{5}$ **41.** $-\frac{1}{2}$, $-\frac{1}{4}$

Excursion Page 174 **1.** 1 + 2 + 4 + 7 + 14 **3.** 1 + 2 + 4 + 8 + 16 + 32 + 64 + 127 + 254 + 508 + 1016 + 2032 + 4064

Exploratory Exercises Page 177 **1.** +, 2 real **3.** +, 2 real **5.** 0, 1 real **7.** +, 2 real **9.** +, 2 real **11.** −, 2 imaginary **13.** +, 2 real

Written Exercises Page 177 **1.** the discriminant is 144 which means there are two real solutions; 7, $^-5$. **3.** the discriminant is 0 which means there is one real solution; 2 **5.** the discriminant is $^-16$ which means there are two imaginary solutions; $1 \pm 2i$ **7.** the discriminant is 1 which means there are two real solutions; 1, $\frac{1}{2}$ **9.** the discriminant is 81 which means there are two real solutions; $^-5$, $-\frac{1}{2}$

11. the discriminant is 169 which means there are two real solutions; $^-4, \frac{1}{3}$ **13.** the discriminant is $^-144$ which means there are two imaginary solutions; $\frac{2 \pm 3i}{2}$ **15.** the discriminant is 25 which means there are two real solutions; $^-8, ^-3$ **17.** the discriminant is 144 which means there are two real solutions; $\frac{3}{2}, -\frac{3}{2}$ **19.** the discriminant is 196 which means there are two real solutions; $4, -\frac{2}{3}$ **21.** the discriminant is 289 which means there are two real solutions; $6, \frac{1}{3}$ **23.** the discriminant is $^-36$ which means there are two imaginary solutions; $4 \pm 3i$ **25.** the discriminant is 1 which means there are two real solutions; 7, 6 **27.** the discriminant is 81 which means there are two real solutions; $^-4, \frac{1}{2}$ **29.** the discriminant is 0 which means there is one real solution; $-\frac{1}{2}$ **31.** the discriminant is $^-3$ which means there are two imaginary solutions; $\frac{1 \pm i\sqrt{3}}{2}$ **33.** the discriminant is 16 which means there are two real solutions; $-\frac{3}{2}, -\frac{5}{2}$ **35.** the discriminant is 36 which means there are two real solutions; 0, 6 **37.** the discriminant is $\frac{9}{16}$ which means there are two real solutions; $\frac{1}{2}, -\frac{1}{4}$

Exploratory Exercises Page 179 **1.** $^-7, ^-4$ **3.** 3, 5 **5.** $-\frac{7}{3}, ^-3$ **7.** $\frac{3}{5}, 0$ **9.** $0, -\frac{3}{5}$ **11.** $\frac{2}{3}, \frac{11}{3}$ **13.** $\frac{1}{4}, \frac{1}{3}$ **15.** If $b = 0$, they are additive inverses. If $c = 0$, one solution is zero.

Written Exercises Pages 179–180 **1.** $^-6; ^-7; ^-7, 1$ **3.** $^-5; 6, ^-3, ^-2$ **5.** $3; 1; \frac{3 \pm \sqrt{5}}{2}$ **7.** $\frac{8}{3}; -\frac{35}{3}; 5, -\frac{7}{3}$ **9.** $3; \frac{5}{2}; \frac{3 \pm i}{2}$ **11.** $^-1; -\frac{10}{9}; \frac{2}{3}, -\frac{5}{3}$ **13.** $\frac{7}{2}; -\frac{15}{2}; 5, -\frac{3}{2}$ **15.** $\frac{2}{15}; -\frac{8}{15}; \frac{4}{5}, -\frac{2}{3}$ **17.** $^-2; ^-24; ^-6, 4$ **19.** $\frac{2}{5}; \frac{6}{5}; \frac{1 \pm i\sqrt{29}}{5}$ **21.** $-\frac{14}{3}; -\frac{5}{3}; ^-5, \frac{1}{3}$ **23.** $^-25; 156; ^-13, ^-12$ **25.** $-\frac{19}{12}; \frac{1}{3}; -\frac{1}{4}, -\frac{4}{3}$ **27.** $\frac{7}{3}; \frac{5}{3}; \frac{7 \pm i\sqrt{11}}{6}$ **29.** $x^2 - 6x - 16 = 0$ **31.** $x^2 - 10x + 24 = 0$ **33.** $x^2 - 36 = 0$ **35.** $2x^2 - 7x + 3 = 0$ **37.** $4x^2 - 45x - 36 = 0$ **39.** $6x^2 - 5x + 1 = 0$ **41.** $32x^2 - 28x + 5 = 0$ **43.** $64x^2 - 49 = 0$ **45.** $x^2 - 4x + 1 = 0$ **47.** $x^2 - 4x + 29 = 0$ **49.** $x^2 - 10x + 37 = 0$ **51.** $2x^2 - 2x - 3 = 0$

Challenge Page 180 **1.** $k = {}^-6$

Excursion Page 180 $\frac{b^2 - 2ac}{c^2}$

Written Exercises Page 183 **1.** 26, 27 or $^-27, ^-26$ **3.** 37, 39 or $^-39, ^-37$ **5.** 15, 17 **7.** 10, 12 or $^-12, ^-10$ **9.** 10 m **11.** 18 ft by 24 ft

Excursion Page 183 $\frac{n(n-1)}{2} = 28$; 8

Exploratory Page 185 **1.** yes **3.** no **5.** yes **7.** no **9.** no **11.** yes **13.** yes **15.** yes

Written Exercises Page 185 **1.** $^{\pm}2, ^{\pm}1$ **3.** $^{\pm}4, ^{\pm}3$ **5.** $^{\pm}5, ^{\pm}1$ **7.** $^{\pm}i\sqrt{3}, ^{\pm}i\sqrt{6}$ **9.** $^{\pm}\sqrt{3}, ^{\pm}i\sqrt{3}$ **11.** $^{\pm}2, ^{\pm}\sqrt{2}$ **13.** $0, 3, ^-3$ **15.** 64, 1 **17.** 1 **19.** 0, 4096

Chapter Review Page 187 **1.** $-\frac{3}{2}, \frac{1}{3}$ **3.** $-\frac{3}{2}, ^-1$ **5.** $-\frac{6}{5}, \frac{1}{3}$ **7.** 49 **9.** 15, 5 **11.** $-\frac{7}{2}, 3$ **13.** $2, \frac{5}{3}$ **15.** $\frac{9}{2}, ^-1$ **17.** discriminant is 1200 which means there are two real solutions. **19.** the discrimination is zero which means there is one real solution **21.** $12, ^-45$ **23.** $\pm\frac{\sqrt{33}}{3}$ **25.** $x^2 + 2x - 24 = 0$ **27.** $x^2 - 10x + 34 = 0$ **29.** 32 or $^-12$ **31.** 3.5 ft (24.5 is *not* a reasonable answer) **33.** $^{\pm}3, ^{\pm}\sqrt{3}$ **35.** no solutions

CHAPTER 7 QUADRATIC RELATIONS AND FUNCTIONS

Exploratory Exercises Page 191 **1.** yes **3.** no **5.** yes **7.** yes **9.** no **11.** x^2; $3x$; $^-\frac{1}{4}$ **13.** x^2; ^-3x; $-\frac{1}{4}$ **15.** $3a^2$; 0; $^-2$ **17.** x^2; $3x$; 0 **19.** x^2; $6x$; 9

Written Exercises Page 191 **1.** $f(x) = x^2 - 4x + 4$ **3.** $f(x) = {}^-16x^2 + 64x - 64$ **5.** $f(x) = {}^-3x^2 + 24x - 54$ **7.** $A = s^2$ **9.** x = one of the numbers; product = $40x - x^2$ **11.** x = lesser number; product = $64x + x^2$ **13.** x = number of \$1 increases; income = $2400 + 140x - 20x^2$

Exploratory Exercises Page 194 1. 9 3. 4 5. $^-32$ 7. 3 9. $\frac{1}{27}$ 11. $^-18$

Written Exercises Page 194

1. 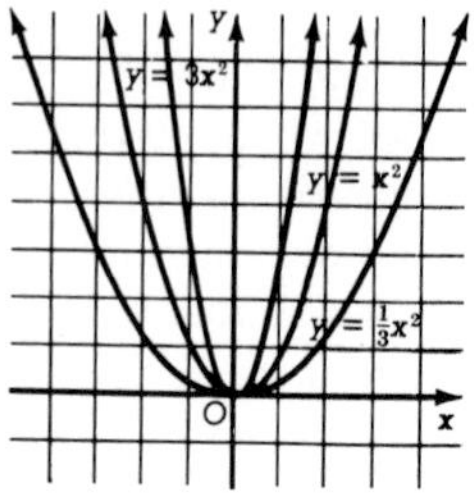

3. 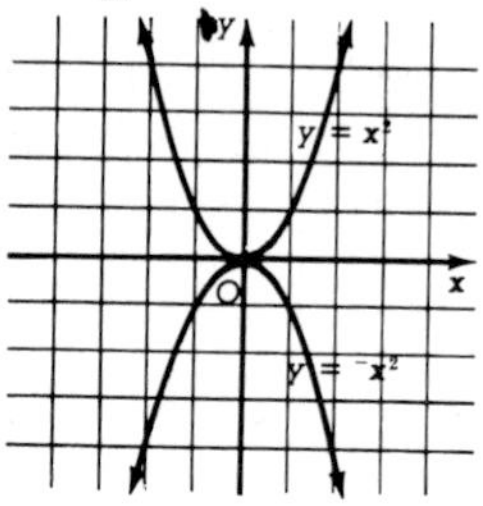

5. 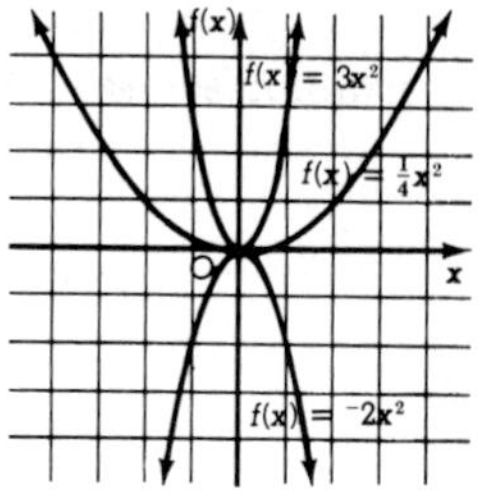

7. (0, 0); $x = 0$; up
9. (0, 0); $x = 0$; down
11. (0, 0); $x = 0$; up
13. (0, 0); $x = 0$; up
15. (0, 0); $x = 0$; down
17. $\frac{1}{2}$ 19. 1 21. $^-2$
23. $^-4$ 25. 3 27. $f(x) = -\frac{1}{4}x^2$

Exploratory Exercises Pages 197-198 1. (0, 0); $x = 0$; up 3. (0, 0); $x = 0$; down 5. (0, 0); $x = 0$; up 7. ($^-2$, 0); $x = {^-2}$; up 9. (2, 0); $x = 2$; up

Written Exercises Page 198 1. $f(x) = (x - 1)^2$ 3. $f(x) = \frac{2}{5}(x + 2)^2$ 5. $f(x) = 6(x + 5)^2$ 7. $f(x) = {^-9}(x - 1)^2$ 9. $f(x) = 4(x - \frac{11}{2})^2$ 11. (1, 0); $x = 1$; up 13. ($^-2$, 0); $x = {^-2}$; up 15. ($^-5$, 0); $x = {^-5}$; up 17. (1, 0); $x = 1$; down 19. ($\frac{11}{2}$, 0); $x = \frac{11}{2}$; up

21. 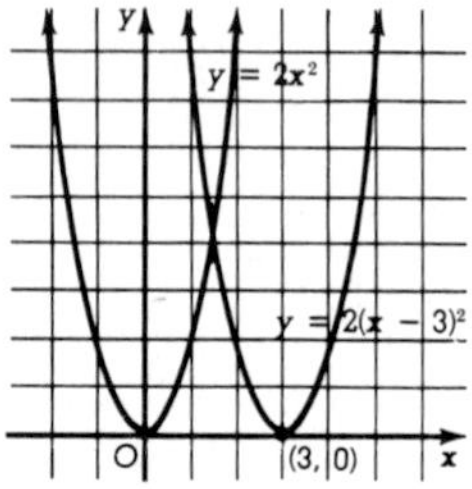

23. 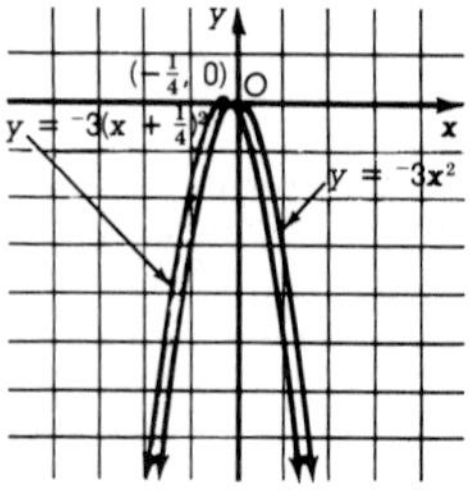

25. 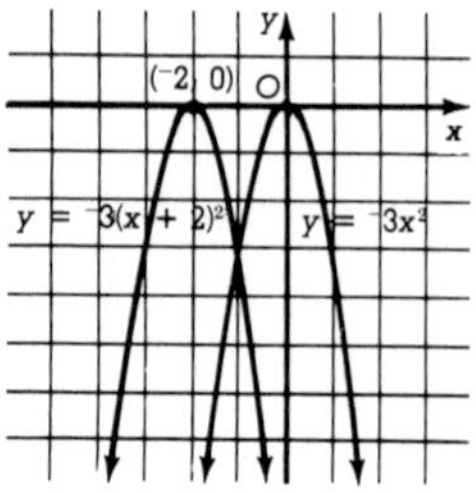

27. $f(x) = (x - 3)^2$
29. $f(x) = -\frac{1}{4}(x + \frac{3}{4})^2$

Excursion Page 198 84

Exploratory Exercises Page 201 1. (2, 5); $x = 2$; up 3. (0, 0); $x = 0$; up 5. (0, 6); $x = 0$; down 7. (1, $\frac{1}{3}$); $x = 1$; up 9. ($^-2$, $-\frac{4}{3}$); $x = 2$; down

Written Exercises Page 201

1. 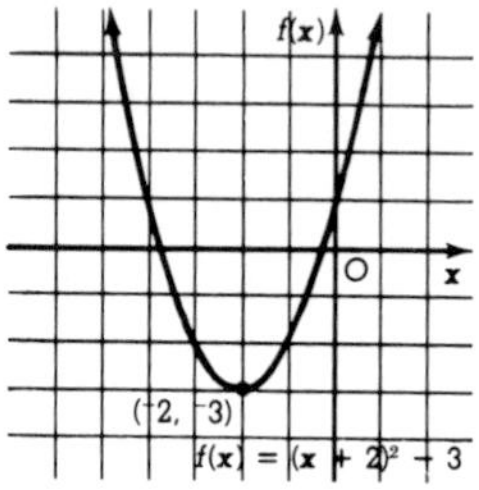

3. 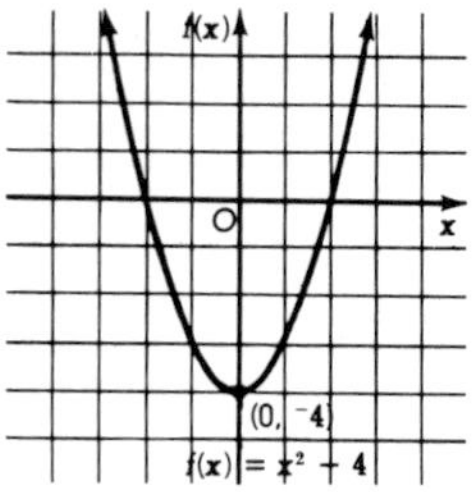

5. 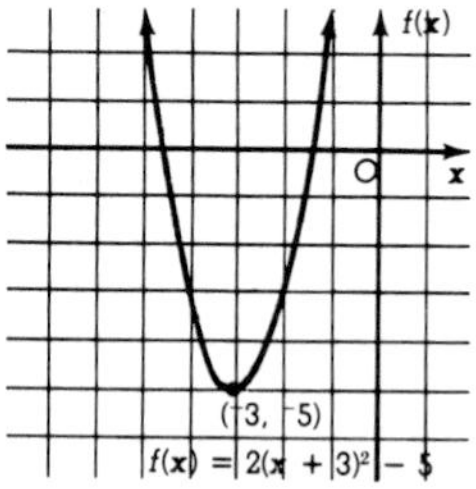

7. 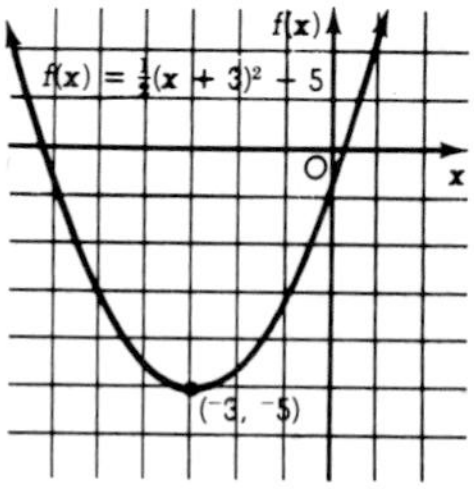

9. 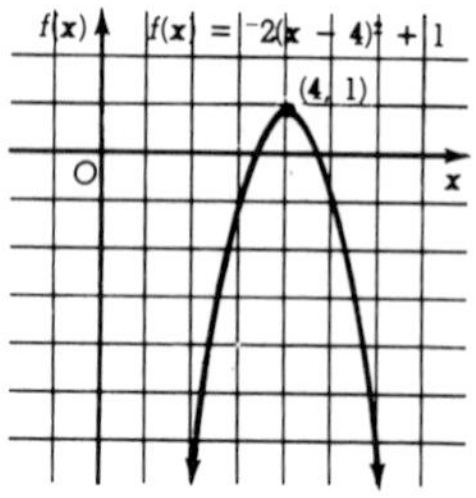

11. 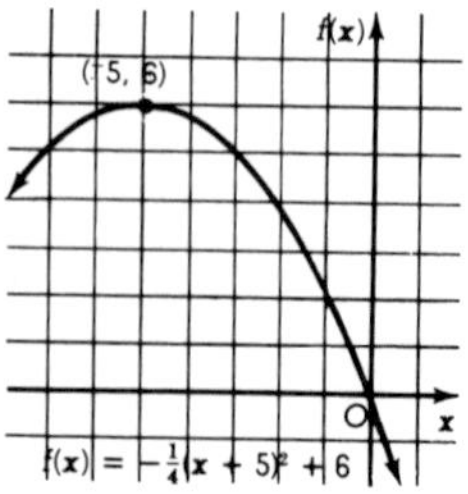

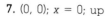

13. $h = -\frac{b}{2a}$; $k = \frac{4ac - b^2}{4a}$

Exploratory Exercises Page 204 1. x = one of the numbers; product = $36x - x^2$ 3. x = width; area = $120x - 2x^2$

Written Exercises Page 205 1. 18 and 18 3. 30 m wide and 60 m long 5. 300 ft, 2.5 sec 7. 10 cm by 10 cm; 100 cm² area 9. $40 + 10x$ 11. income = $(40 + 10x)(50{,}000 - 5000x)$ 13. 70¢ 15. $[x(300 - 2x)] - (20x + 1000)$ or $^-2x^2 + 280x - 1000$ 17.

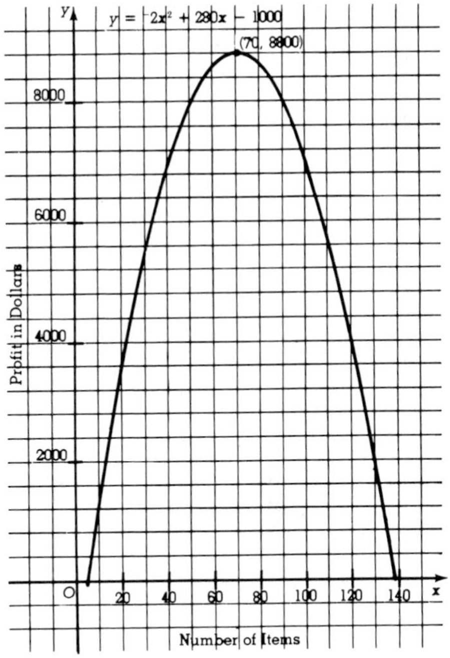

Exploratory Exercises Page 207

1. $y = (x + 2)^2$ 3. $y = (x - 3)^2$ 5. $y = (x + 4)^2$
7. $y = (x + 5)^2 + 15$ 9. $y = (x - 4)^2 - 12$

Written Exercises Page 207

1.

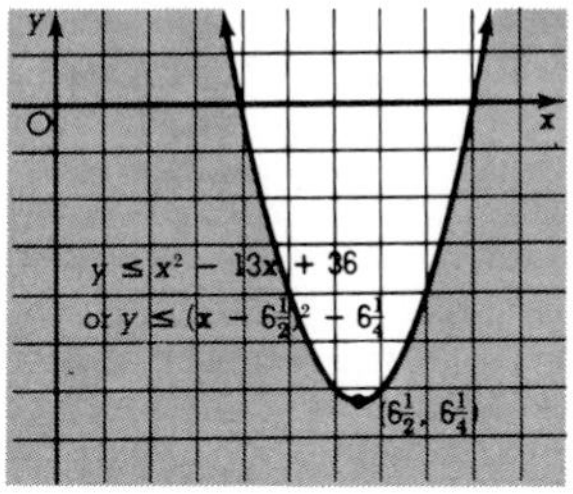

3.

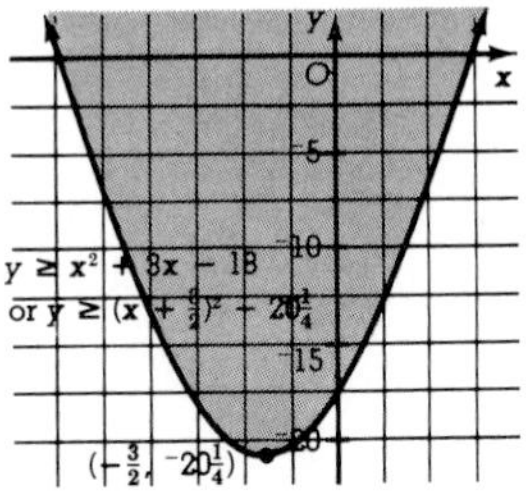

7.

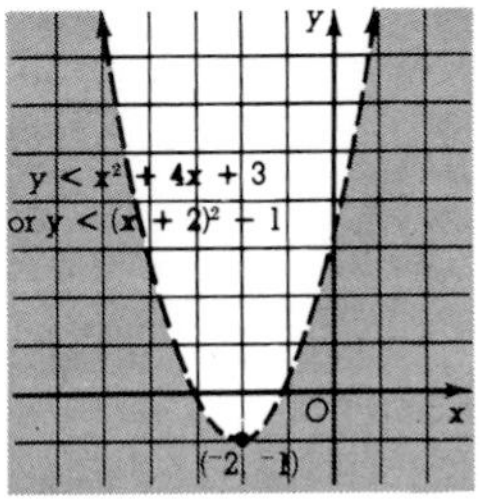

13.

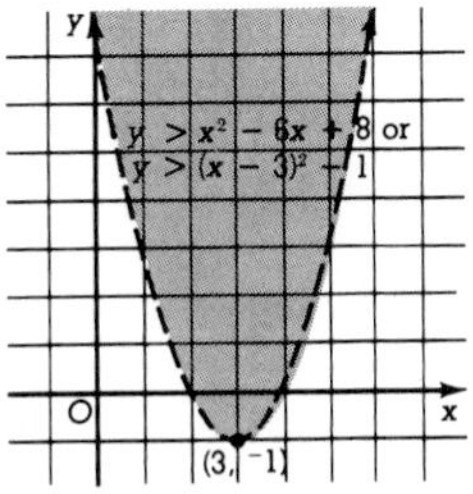

Exploratory Exercises Page 209 1. one + and one − 3. both + or both − 5. both ≥ 0 or both ≤ 0 7. one ≤ 0 and one ≥ 0 9. one ≤ 0 and one ≥ 0

Written Exercises Page 209 1. $\{x \mid x > 2 \text{ or } x < {}^-3\}$ 3. $\{p \mid p \geq 4 \text{ or } p \leq {}^-6\}$ 5. $\{b \mid -\frac{3}{2} < b < 2\}$ 7. $\{x \mid 0 \leq x \leq 4\}$ 9. $\{t \mid {}^-6 \leq t \leq 6\}$ 11. $\{r \mid {}^-9 \leq r \leq {}^-3\}$

Challenge Page 209 1. $\{x \mid {}^-4 < x < 1 \text{ or } x > 3\}$ 3. $\{x \mid x \leq {}^-4 \text{ or } {}^-2 \leq x \leq 8\}$ 5. $\{x \mid x < {}^-3 \text{ or } {}^-2 < x < 1 \text{ or } x > 2\}$

Exercises Page 209 1. $h = vt - 4.9t^2$ 3. 4.641 5. 1052.016

Chapter Review Page 211 1. x^2; $2x$; 5 3. 0; 0; 16 5. $y = 3x^2 + 12x + 5$ 7.

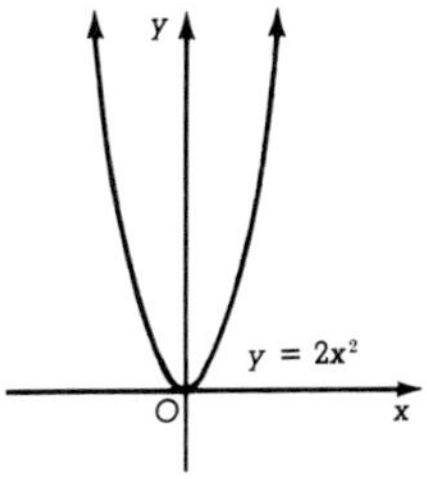

9. $\frac{1}{12}$ 11. (3, 0); $x = 3$; up

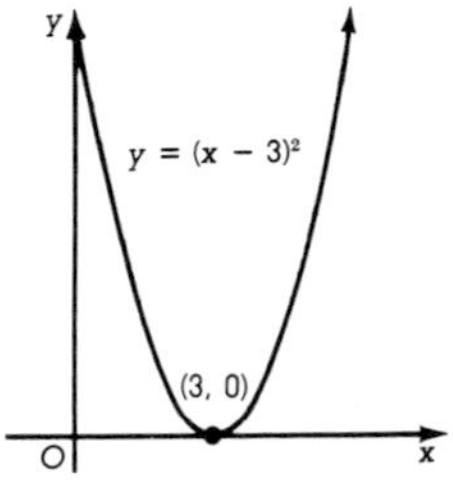

13. (4, 0); $x = 4$; up

15. (2, $^-3$); $x = 2$; up

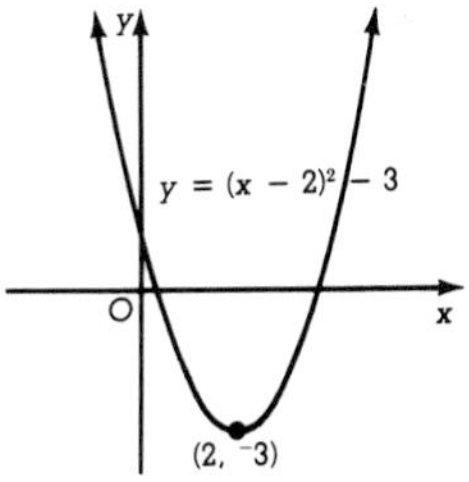

17. ($^-1$, $^-2$); $x = {}^-1$; up

19. 32 and 32

21.

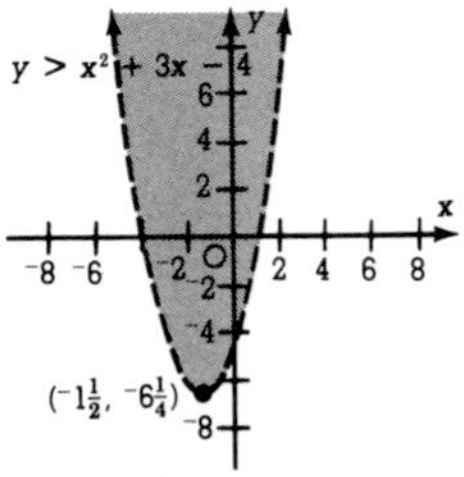

23. $\{x \mid {}^-2 < x < 4\}$

CHAPTER 8 CONICS

Exploratory Exercises Page 216 **1.** 2 **3.** 9 **5.** 11 **7.** 16 **9.** 16 **11.** 15

Written Exercises Page 216 **1.** $2\sqrt{53}$ **3.** $\sqrt{58}$ **5.** $\sqrt{53}$ **7.** $\frac{\sqrt{4594}}{15}$ **9.** $\frac{\sqrt{5}}{10}$ **11.** $\sqrt{16.85}$ **13.** 1 **15.** $5\sqrt{3}$ **17.** 3 or 11 **19.** 7.1 or 13.1 **21.** $(\frac{3}{2}, -\frac{5}{2})$ **23.** $(\frac{2}{3}, -\frac{3}{4})$ **25.** $\left(\frac{3+\sqrt{2}}{2}, \frac{3-\sqrt{2}}{2}\right)$ **33.** $13\sqrt{2} + \sqrt{65} + \sqrt{197}$

35.
```
10 DATA 3,6,7,-8
20 READ A,B,C,D
30 LET D=SQR((A-C)↑2+(B-D)↑2)
40 PRINT D
50 END
```

Exploratory Exercises Page 219 **1.** 4 **3.** 16 **5.** $\frac{9}{4}$ **7.** $\frac{49}{4}$ **9.** 4.2025 **11.** $y = \frac{1}{10}x^2$ **13.** $y = (x-3)^2 + 24$ **15.** $y = 3(x-4)^2 + 2$ **17.** $x = \frac{1}{6}y^2$ **19.** $x = (y+4)^2 + 4$ **21.** $x = \frac{1}{4}(y-1)^2 - \frac{13}{4}$

Written Exercises Page 219 **1.** (0, 0); $x = 0$; $(0, \frac{3}{2})$; $y = -\frac{3}{2}$; up **3.** $(^-2, 3)$; $x = {}^-2$; $(^-2, 3\frac{1}{4})$; $y = 2\frac{3}{4}$; up **5.** $(8, {}^-1)$; $x = 8$; $(8, -\frac{7}{8})$; $y = -\frac{9}{8}$; up **7.** (0, 1); $x = 0$; $(0, \frac{5}{4})$; $y = \frac{3}{4}$; up **9.** $(2, {}^-3)$; $y = {}^-3$; $(3, {}^-3)$; $x = 1$; right **11.** (3, 24); $x = 3$; $(3, 24\frac{1}{4})$; $y = 23\frac{3}{4}$; up **13.** $(^-24, 7)$; $y = 7$; $(^-23\frac{3}{4}, 7)$; $x = {}^-24\frac{1}{4}$; right **15.** $(-\frac{13}{4}, 1)$; $y = 1$; $(-\frac{9}{4}, 1)$; $y = -\frac{17}{4}$; right **17.** (4, 2); $x = 4$; $(4, 2\frac{1}{12})$; $y = 1\frac{11}{12}$; up **19.** $y = -\frac{1}{4}(x-2)^2 + 5$ **21.** $y = -\frac{1}{8}(x-8)^2 + 2$ **23.** $y = \frac{1}{16}(x-5)^2 + 1$ **25.** $x = \frac{1}{10}(y+1)^2 + \frac{1}{2}$ **27.** $x = -\frac{1}{2}(y-4)^2 + \frac{1}{2}$

Exploratory Exercises Pages 221–222 **1.** circle **3.** parabola **5.** circle **7.** circle **9.** parabola **11.** (0, 0); 4 **13.** (2, 0); 3 **15.** (10, 10); 10 **17.** $(^-4, \frac{1}{2})$; $\sqrt{6}$ **19.** $(^-5, 2)$; $\frac{\sqrt{3}}{2}$

Written Exercises Page 222 **1.** (2, 0); 3 **3.** (0, 8); 8 **5.** (0, 0); 8 **7.** (2, 5); 4 **9.** $(^-8, 3)$; 5 **11.** $(^-1, {}^-9)$; 6 **13.** (6, 8); 4 **15.** $(^-4, 3)$; 5 **17.** (2, 0); $\sqrt{13}$ **19.** $(-\frac{3}{2}, {}^-1)$; $\frac{\sqrt{141}}{6}$ **21.** $(-\frac{9}{2}, 5)$; 7 **23.** $(^-1, {}^-2)$; $\sqrt{14}$ **25.** $(^-1, 0)$; $\sqrt{11}$ **27.** $(x-6)^2 + (y-2)^2 = 25$ **29.** $x^2 + (y-3)^2 = 4$ **31.** $(x+6)^2 + (y-2)^2 = \frac{1}{16}$

Excursion Page 222 7 cows; the number of chickens can vary.

Exploratory Exercises Page 227 **1.** (0, 0) **3.** (0, 0) **5.** (0, 5) **7.** $(2, {}^-5)$ **9.** $(^-2, 3)$ **11.** $(\pm\sqrt{5}, 0)$ **13.** $(0, \pm 4)$

Written Exercises Page 227 **1.** (0, 0); $(0 \pm \sqrt{21})$; $(\pm 2, 0)$, $(0, \pm 5)$ **3.** (0, 0); $(\pm 4, 0)$; $(\pm 5, 0)$, $(0, \pm 3)$ **5.** (0, 0); $(\pm\sqrt{7}, 0)$; $(\pm 4, 0)$, $(0, \pm 3)$ **7.** (0, 0); $(\pm\sqrt{5}, 0)$; $(\pm 3, 0)$, $(0, \pm 2)$ **9.** (0, 0); $(\pm 3\sqrt{5}; 0)$; $(\pm 9, 0)$; $(0, \pm 6)$ **11.** $\frac{x^2}{36} + \frac{y^2}{100} = 1$ **13.** (2, 3); (6, 3), $(^-2, 3)$, (2, 6), (2, 0) **15.** $(^-2, {}^-3)$; $(^-2, {}^-3 \pm 2\sqrt{10})$, $(^-2 \pm 2\sqrt{5}, {}^-3)$ **17.** $(^-2, 3)$; $(2 \pm \sqrt{5}, 3)$, $(^-2, 3 \pm \sqrt{2})$ **19.** $(1, {}^-2)$; (1, 1), $(1, {}^-5)$, $(3, {}^-2)$, $(^-1, {}^-2)$ **21.** $(1, {}^-2)$; (1, 1), $(1, {}^-5)$, $(5, {}^-2)$, $(^-3, {}^-2)$

Exploratory Exercises Page 230 **1.** ellipse **3.** hyperbola **5.** hyperbola **7.** ellipse **9.** hyperbola

Written Exercises Page 231 **1.** $(\pm 3, 0)$; $(\pm\sqrt{34}, 0)$ **3.** $(\pm 6, 0)$; $(\pm\sqrt{37}, 0)$ **5.** $(0, \pm 9)$; $(0, \pm\sqrt{106})$ **7.** $y = \pm\frac{3}{2}x$ **9.** $y = \pm\frac{2}{3}x$ **11.** $y = \pm\frac{4}{3}x$ **13.** $y = \pm\frac{5}{2}x$ **15.** $y = \pm\frac{\sqrt{2}}{2}x$ **17.** $y = \pm 2x$ **25.** 2; 1; $\frac{1}{2}$; $\frac{1}{4}$; $^-2$; $-\frac{1}{2}$; $-\frac{1}{4}$ **27.** $\{y \mid y \text{ is real}, y \neq 0\}$ **29.** 3 ± 5.7; 3 ± 4.8; 3 ± 4.2; 3 ± 4; 3 ± 4.2; 3 ± 4.8; 3 ± 5.7; 3 ± 6.7 **31.** $\{x \mid x \text{ is real}\}$ **33.** $3y = 4x + 17$, $3y = {}^-4x + 1$ **35.** The graph is shifted two units left and three units upward.

Written Exercises Page 234 **1.** parabola **3.** ellipse **5.** hyperbola **7.** hyperbola **9.** parabola **11.** hyperbola **13.** ellipse **15.** hyperbola **17.** ellipse **19.** circle **21.** $y = \frac{1}{8}x^2$ **23.** $\frac{x^2}{2} + \frac{y^2}{4} = 1$ **25.** same **27.** same **29.** $y = {}^-(x - \frac{1}{2})^2 + \frac{9}{4}$ **31.** same **33.** $\frac{x^2}{4} + \frac{(y+1)^2}{3} = 1$ **35.** $x \cdot y = \frac{7}{3}$ **37.** same **39.** $x^2 + y^2 = \frac{49}{13}$

Written Exercises Page 238 **1.** $(\pm 2\sqrt{3}, 2)$ **3.** (2, 2), $(^-2, {}^-2)$ **5.** (3, 0), $(^-5, {}^-4)$ **7.** $(0, {}^-1)$, $(^-3, 2)$

9. $(\pm 5.2, 6)$ **11.** no solutions **13.** no solutions **15.** $(-2, 0), (2, 4)$ **17.** $(0, \sqrt{2}), (-2, -2)$ **19.** $(3, 7), (8, 4)$ **21.** $(\pm 1, 5), (\pm 1, -5)$ **23.** $(\pm 2, \sqrt{3}), (\pm 2, -\sqrt{3})$ **25.** no solutions **27.** no solutions **29.** $(\pm 8, 0)$

Written Exercises Page 239 **1.** $(\pm 2\sqrt{3}, 2)$ **3.** $(2, 2), (-2, -2)$ **5.** $(3, 0), (-5, -4)$ **7.** $(-3, 2), (0, -1)$ **9.** $(\pm 3\sqrt{3}, 6)$ **11.** no solutions **13.** no solutions **15.** $(-2, 0), (2, 4)$ **17.** $(-2, -2), (0, \sqrt{2})$ **19.** $(3, 7), (8, 4)$ **21.** $(1, \pm 5), (-1, \pm 5)$ **23.** $(2, \pm\sqrt{3}), (-2, \pm\sqrt{3})$ **25.** no solutions **27.** no solutions **29.** $(\pm 8, 0)$

Chapter Review Page 245 **1.** $2\sqrt{53}$ **3.** $\frac{\sqrt{5}}{10}$ **5.** $\sqrt{16.85}$ **7.** $(0, 0)$; $x = 0$; $(0, 1)$; $y = -1$, up **9.** $(0, 1)$; $x = 0$; $(0, \frac{5}{4})$; $y = \frac{3}{4}$; up **11.** $(0, -3; 5$ **13.** $(0, 0)$; $(0, \pm 2\sqrt{2})$; $(\pm 2\sqrt{2}, 0), (0, \pm 4)$ **15.** $(0, 0)$; $(\pm\sqrt{33}, 0)$; $(\pm 7, 0), (0, \pm 4)$ **17.** $(\pm 4, 0)$; $(\pm\sqrt{97}, 0)$; $y = \pm\frac{9}{4}x$ **19.** none; $(\sqrt{6}, \sqrt{6}), (-\sqrt{6}, -\sqrt{6})$; $x = 0, y = 0$ **21.** parabola **23.** ellipse **25.** $(-1.6, 2.6), (2.6, -1.6)$ **27.** $(-2, 0), (2, 4)$

CHAPTER 9 POLYNOMIAL FUNCTIONS

Exploratory Exercises Pages 249–250 **1.** no **3.** no **5.** no **7.** yes **9.** no **11.** yes **13.** yes

Written Exercises Page 250 **1.** 4 **3.** $\frac{13}{3} + \sqrt{2}$ **5.** 1 **7.** -4 **9.** $-\frac{11}{2}$ **11.** 7 **13.** $\frac{16}{3} + 2\sqrt{2}$ **15.** -9 **17.** -18 **19.** 12 **21.** -8 **23.** $7 - 3\sqrt{2}$ **25.** 41 **27.** -108 **29.** $-\frac{151}{2}$ **31.** $3x + 3h + 1$ **33.** $\frac{(x+h)^2}{3} + (x + h)\sqrt{2} + 4$ **35.** $-2(x + h)^3 + 4(x + h) - 1$ **37.** $3(x + h) - 8(x + h)^2 + (x + h)^3$ **39.** $\frac{5}{2}(x + h)^3 - 8$ **41.** $-3x - 10$ **43.** $-\frac{x^2}{3} - x\sqrt{2} - 2x - 5 - 3\sqrt{2}$ **45.** $2x^3 + 18x^2 + 14x - 5$ **47.** $-x^3 - x^2 + 36x + 12$

51.
```
5  FOR X=-6 OR 6
10 LET Y=X↑4-X↑3+X↑2-X+1
15 PRINT X; Y
20 NEXT X
25 END
```

Exercises Page 250 **1.** 20π **3.** $2\sqrt{15}\pi$ **5.** 24π **7.** 24π

Exploratory Exercises Page 253 **1.** $x - 1$; -1 **3.** $x^2 - 9x + 11$; -12 **5.** $x^4 + 3x^3 + 6x^2 + 12x + 26$; 51 **7.** $x^4 - 2x^3 + 4x^2 - 8x + 16$; 0

Written Exercises Page 253 **1.** $2x^3 + 8x^2 - 3x - 1 = (2x^2 + 12x + 21)(x - 2) + 41$ **3.** $x^4 - 16 = (x^3 + 2x^2 + 4x + 8)(x - 2) + 0$ **5.** $4x^4 + 3x^3 - 2x^2 + x + 1 = (4x^3 + 7x^2 + 5x + 6)(x - 1) + 7$ **7.** $3x^5 - 2x^3 + 2x + 2 = (3x^4 - 3x^3 + x^2 - x + 3)(x + 1) - 1$ **9.** $3x^3 + 2x^2 - 4x - 1 = (3x^2 + \frac{1}{2}x - \frac{17}{4})(x + \frac{1}{2}) + \frac{9}{8}$ **11.** 85 **13.** -39 **15.** 10 **17.** -94 **19.** $(x + 1)(x + 2)(x - 2)$ **21.** $(x + 1)(x - 1)(x + 2)$ **23.** $(x + 2)(x - 1)^2$ **25.** $(x - 2)(x - 1)^3$ **27.** -17 **29.** $\frac{25}{2}$

31.
```
10  DATA . . . (degree, c, coefficients)
20  READ N,C
30  FOR X=0 TO N
40  READ A(X)
50  NEXT X
60  PRINT A(0);
70  FOR X=1 TO N
80  LET A(X)=A(X)-A(X-1)*C
90  PRINT A(X);
100 NEXT X
110 END
```

Exploratory Exercises Page 256 **1.** $\pm 1, 2$ **3.** $\pm 1, 2, 3, 6$ **5.** $\pm 1, 2, 4, 8$ **7.** ± 1 **9.** $\pm 1, 2, 4, 5, 10, 20$ **11.** $\pm 1, \frac{1}{2}, \frac{1}{3}, \frac{1}{6}$ **13.** $\pm 1, 2, 4, \frac{1}{3}, \frac{2}{3}, \frac{4}{3}$ **15.** $\pm 1, 3, 5, 15, \frac{1}{2}, \frac{3}{2}, \frac{5}{2}, \frac{15}{2}$ **17.** $\pm 1, 3, 5, 15, \frac{1}{2}, \frac{3}{2}, \frac{5}{2}, \frac{15}{2}, \frac{1}{3}, \frac{5}{3}, \frac{1}{6}, \frac{5}{6}$

Written Exercises Page 256 **1.** $3, -5, -\frac{5}{2}$ **3.** $3, 3, -2, \frac{1}{2}, \frac{2}{3}$ **5.** $\frac{2}{3}, 5, -1$ **7.** $-2, -4, 7$ **9.** $3, 3, -\frac{1}{2}$ **11.** 9 **13.** $-2, -4$ **15.** $\frac{1}{3}, \frac{3}{2}, 5$ **17.** $-3, \frac{1}{2}, 5$

Exploratory Exercises Page 258 **1.** 3 or 1 **3.** 4, 2, or 0 **5.** 2 or 0 **7.** 5, 3, or 1 **9.** 1 **11.** 1 **13.** 0 **15.** 2 or 0 **17.** 1 **19.** 3 or 1

Written Exercises Page 259 **1.** 2 or 0; 2 or 0, 4, 2, or 0 **3.** 1; 0; 2 **5.** 2 or 0; 1; 4 or 2 **7.** 2 or 0; 1; 4 or 2 **9.** 3 or 1; 1; 12 or 10 **11.** $3 + i$, $3 - i$, 4 **13.** $1 + 2i$, $1 - 2i$, $^{-}4$ **15.** It has no positive real roots and only one negative real root. Therefore, there must be two complex roots.

Written Exercises Page 262 **1.** $^{-}1.3$ **3.** 0.6 **5.** 1.6, $^{-}1.3$, $^{-}2.4$ **7.** 1.4 **9.** $^{-}0.7$ **11.** 0.1, 2.5 **13.** 1, 0.8, $^{-}1.4$ **15.** $^{-}1$ **17.** $^{-}2.4$

Written Exercises Page 266

3.
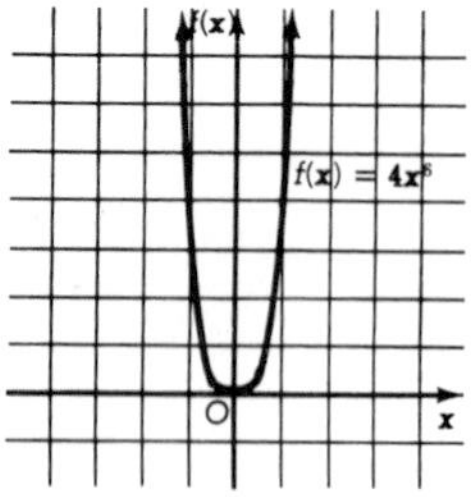

7.
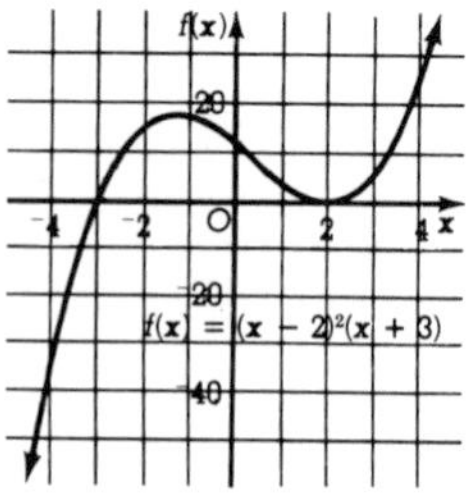

11.
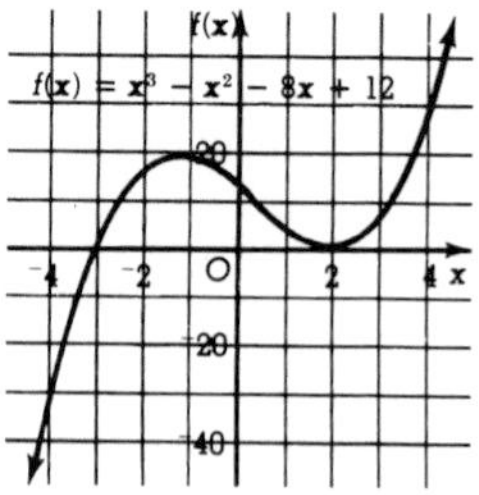

17.
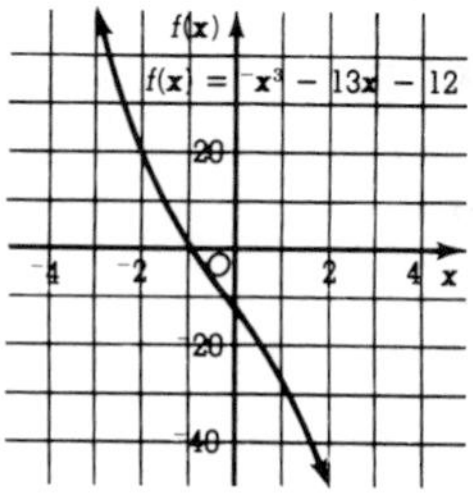

Exploratory Exercises Page 269 **1.** $^{-}1$, $^{-}5$, $^{-}3$ **3.** 1, 9, 1 **5.** 4, 4, 2 **7.** 10, 10, $^{-}6$ **9.** 30, $^{-}34$, 2

Written Exercises Page 269 **1.** 4 **3.** 63 **5.** 65 **7.** $2x - 5$ **9.** $4x^2 - 4x + 4$ **11.** $x^4 - 2x^2 - 7$ **13.** $^{-}1$, $^{-}1$ **15.** 18, 0 **17.** $^{-}7$, 9 **19.** {(2, 5), (3, $^{-}7$), (6, $^{-}3$)}

21.
```
10 FOR X=-6 TO 6
20 LET G=X↑2+2
30 LET F=G↑2+8*G-1
40 PRINT X; F
50 NEXT X
60 END
```

Exploratory Exercises Page 272 **1.** {(1, 3), (4, 2), (5, 1)}, yes **3.** {(8, 3), ($^{-}2$, 4), ($^{-}3$, 5)}, yes **5.** {(1, $^{-}3$), (4, 2), (8, 7)}, yes

Written Exercises Page 272 **1.** $y = \frac{1}{2}x$ **3.** $f^{-1}(x) = -\frac{1}{6}x - \frac{5}{6}$ **5.** $x = 3$ **7.** $f^{-1}(x) = 0$ **9.** $y = \pm\sqrt{x}$

11.
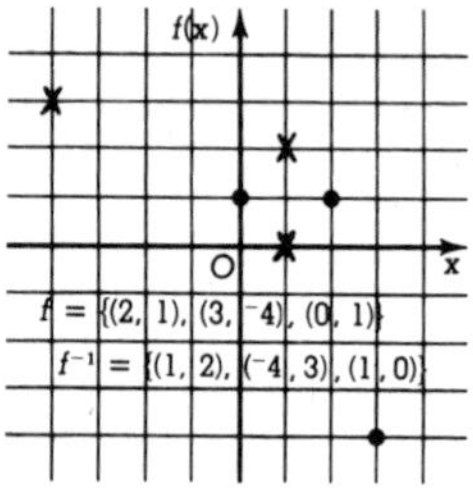

15.
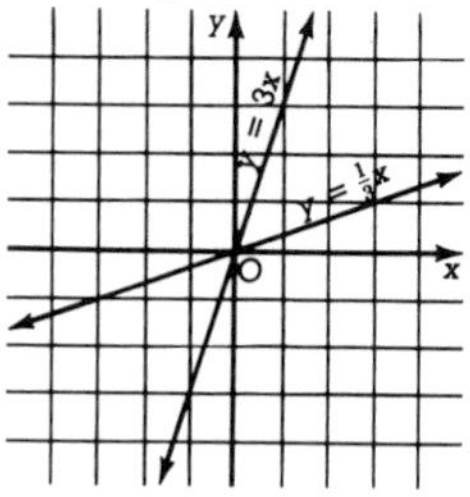

19.
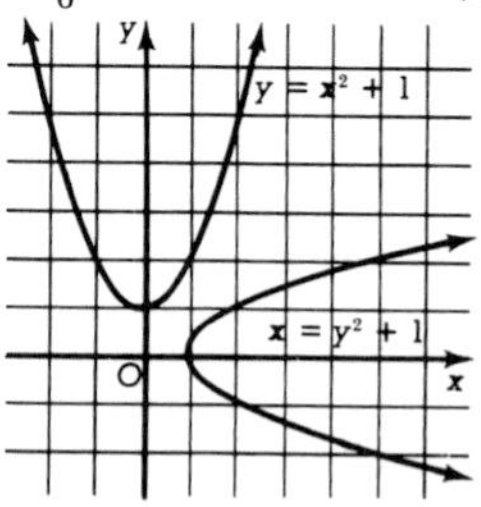

21. yes **23.** yes **25.** no

Chapter Review Page 275 **1.** $^{-}13$ **3.** $4 - 2\sqrt{2}$ **5.** 2 **7.** $^{-}94$ **9.** $(x + 2)(x - 1)(x + 1)$ **11.** $(x + 2)(x - 1)^2$ **13.** 1, 1, $\frac{3}{2}$, $\frac{3}{2}$ **15.** 5, $\frac{1}{3}$, $\frac{3}{2}$ **17.** 3 or 1; 1; 2 or 0 **19.** 1; 0; 2 **21.** $2 + i$, $2 - i$, 3 **23.** $^{-}1$, 0.7 **27.** x^4, $x^4 + 4x^3 + 6x^2 + 4x$ **29.** $2|x - 3| + 1$, $2||x + 1| - 3|$ **31.**

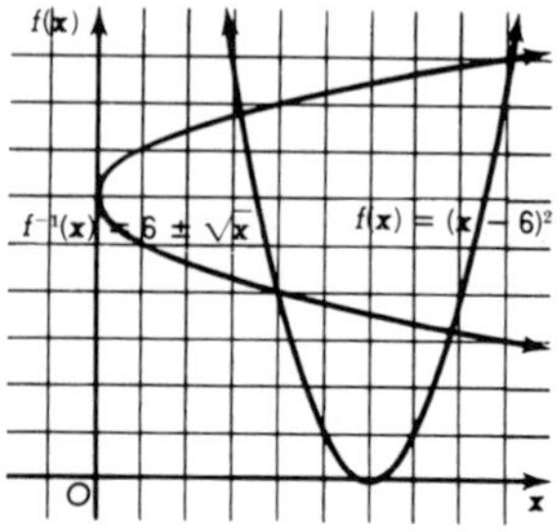

CHAPTER 10 RATIONAL POLYNOMIAL EXPRESSIONS

Exploratory Exercises Page 279 **1.** 24 **3.** $13x$ **5.** $2a$ **7.** $14y$ **9.** $(y + 3)$ **11.** $(x + 4)$ **13.** $(a + 1)$ **15.** $\frac{1}{3}$ **17.** $\frac{1}{3x}$ **19.** $\frac{19a}{21b}$ **21.** $\frac{3y}{4}$ **23.** $\frac{y-3}{y+3}$ **25.** $\frac{x-5}{x+3}$ **27.** $\frac{a+1}{2a+1}$

Written Exercises Page 280 **1.** $\frac{6}{7}$ **3.** $\frac{x^2}{4y}$ **5.** $\frac{y-2}{x-4}$ **7.** $\frac{9}{2}abc^2$ **9.** $-\frac{7}{54c}$ **11.** 8 **13.** 1 **15.** $-\frac{5}{14}$ **17.** $\frac{6}{5}$ **19.** $\frac{7}{3}$ **21.** $3b$ **23.** $-\frac{yz}{12x}$ **25.** $\frac{y^3}{x^4}$ **27.** $\frac{2x(y+4)}{3}$ **29.** 1 **31.** $\frac{5(a-b)}{2}$ **33.** $\frac{(3m-1)(m-2)}{30}$ **35.** $\frac{x(x+4)}{2y(x-3)}$ **37.** $\frac{x-2}{x+2}$ **39.** $(x + 1)^2(x - 5)$ **41.** $(a - b)^2$

Exploratory Exercises Page 283 **1.** $\frac{8}{3}$ **3.** $\frac{9y}{7x}$ **5.** $\frac{1}{16}$ **7.** $\frac{2}{x+y}$ **9.** $\frac{(x-3)^2}{(x+4)^2}$

Written Exercises Page 284 **1.** $\frac{a^2}{14}$ **3.** $\frac{ab}{x+y}$ **5.** $\frac{a^2-b^2}{a^2+ab+b^2}$ **7.** $\frac{x^2+2x-3}{3x+3}$ **9.** $-\frac{2}{9}$ **11.** $\frac{a}{2}$ **13.** $-\frac{x}{3}$ **15.** $\frac{c}{2b}$ **17.** $\frac{ac^4d}{b}$ **19.** $b(x + y)$ **21.** $\frac{1}{2}$ **23.** $3(a + b)$ **25.** $\frac{2(x-1)}{3(x+2)}$ **27.** $\frac{2(a+5)}{(a+2)(a-2)}$ **29.** $2(x + y)$ **31.** $\frac{a(a+2)}{a+1}$

33.
```
10 DATA . . .
20 READ P,Q
30 PRINT Q"/"P
40 PRINT Q/P
50 END
```

Exploratory Exercises Page 288 **1.** 756z **3.** 2000 **5.** $14a^2b$ **7.** $x(x - 2)(x + 2)$ **9.** $(x + 1)^2(x - 3)(x + 3)$ **11.** $x(x - 8)y(y - 8)$

Written Exercises Page 288 **1.** $\frac{31}{12a}$ **3.** $\frac{5+7a}{a}$ **5.** $\frac{^-x}{x-y}$ **7.** $\frac{7y-4}{2xy}$ **9.** $\frac{3(x-1)}{2(x+3)(x-3)}$ **11.** $\frac{5a-13}{(a-2)(a-3)}$ **13.** $\frac{3(2x+11)}{(x-5)(x+5)}$ **15.** $\frac{8}{5(x+1)}$ **17.** $\frac{7y+11}{(y+3)(y-5)(y+1)}$ **19.** $\frac{2m}{m-n}$ **21.** $-\frac{3}{20a}$ **23.** $\frac{11y-13}{(y-2)(y-1)}$ **25.** 1 **27.** $-\frac{y}{y-2}$ **29.** $\frac{9m^2+4m+1}{3m+1}$ **31.** $\frac{9}{y-2}$ **33.** $\frac{x-13}{4(x-4)}$ **35.** $-\frac{x(1+2y)}{(x+y)(x-y)}$ **37.** $\frac{3}{10}$

Exercises Page 289 **1.** 17 **3.** 23 **5.** 14

Exploratory Exercises Page 291 **1.** $2x$ **3.** $10y$ **5.** x^2 **7.** $(x - 3)(x - 2)$ **9.** $6(m - 5)$

Written Exercises Page 292 **1.** 2 **3.** 1 **5.** $\frac{3}{2}$ **7.** $\frac{13}{3}$ **9.** 23 **11.** $^-3$ **13.** 10 **15.** 2, 6 **17.** 6 **19.** all reals except 1 **21.** $^-6$, 1 **23.** $^-3$, 2 **25.** $^-7$

Challenge Page 292 **1.** 5

Excursion Page 292 $A = 3$, $B = {^-1}$

Written Exercises Page 296 **1.** $2\frac{2}{9}$ hr **3.** 25 hr 12 min **5.** 20 days **7.** $\frac{7}{13}$ **9.** 19 **11.** 3 mph **13.** 5:27 plus 18 sec **15.** 5 tons

Exploratory Exercises Page 298–299 **1.** direct **3.** direct **5.** direct **7.** direct **9.** inverse **11.** direct **13.** $\frac{1}{4}$ **15.** $^-4$ **17.** 5 **19.** $\frac{4}{3}$ **21.** 9 **23.** 4

Written Exercises Page 299 **1.** 36 **3.** $\frac{9}{8}$ **5.** $\frac{84}{11}$ **7.** $\frac{121}{10}$ **9.** 24 **11.** 118.5 kg **13.** $11\frac{2}{3}$ kg **15.** $5384.62 **17.** 90 cubic ft **19.** $\frac{\pm 4\sqrt{22}}{11}$

Chapter Review **Pages 300–301** **1.** $\frac{5}{16}$ **3.** $\frac{x}{3y}$ **5.** $\frac{6}{25}$ **7.** $\frac{(y-2)(a-3)}{a-x}$ **9.** $\frac{4}{5}$ **11.** $6b(a-b)$ **13.** $\frac{2}{n-3}$ **15.** $\frac{^-27b+28a}{12ab}$ **17.** $\frac{7(x-4)}{x-5}$ **19.** $\frac{25b+16}{24b}$ **21.** $\frac{18}{y-2}$ **23.** $\frac{10}{9}$ **25.** 5 or 1 **27.** $8\frac{4}{7}$ hr **29.** $-\frac{75}{2}$

CHAPTER 11 INTEGERS AS EXPONENTS

Exploratory Exercises **Page 306** **1.** $\frac{1}{4^3}$ **3.** r^3 **5.** $\frac{1}{8^9}$ **7.** y^3 **9.** $\frac{x^5}{7^5}$ **11.** m^2 **13.** r^6 **15.** y^4 **17.** x^{5-y} **19.** q^5 **21.** 1 **23.** $\frac{1}{36}$ **25.** $\frac{1}{4}$ **27.** $\frac{1}{64}$ **29.** $\frac{1}{27}$ **31.** 4

Written Exercises **Page 306** **1.** $\frac{1}{4^6}$ **3.** y^5 **5.** r^3 **7.** $\frac{b^7}{2^7}$ **9.** $\frac{4^2}{m^2}$ **11.** $\frac{1}{x^4}$ **13.** $\frac{1}{(x+4)^4}$ **15.** $\frac{6}{r^2}$ **17.** $\frac{3}{(x-7)^4}$ **19.** $\frac{1}{x^3y^2}$ **21.** b^3+5 **23.** $\frac{1}{m^8n^{10}}$ **25.** $\frac{5}{2}$ **27.** $5xy$ **29.** 3^5 or 243 **31.** x^2

Exploratory Exercises **Page 309** **1.** 4 **3.** $^-5$ **5.** 6.753×10^4 **7.** 7.5×10^{-5} **9.** 58,000 **11.** 0.0054 **13–14.** 3.6×10^7; 36,000,000 **15–16.** 5.6×10^{-1}; 0.56 **17–18.** 6.0×10^{-5}; 0.00006 **19–20.** 1.5×10^5; 150,000

Written Exercises **Page 309** **1.** 6.18×10^2 **3.** 2.1×10^{-3} **5.** 8.104×10^2 **7.** 9×10^9 **9.** 3×10^{-6} **11.** 6000 **13.** 0.00057 **15.** 0.000072 **17–18.** 8.6×10^5; 860,000 **19–20.** 1.904×10^9; 1,904,000,000 **21–22.** 3.0×10^{-4}; 0.0003 **23–24.** 7.0×10^4; 70,000 **25–26.** 2.0×10^5; 200,000 **27–28.** 5.0×10^3; 5000 **29–30.** 3.1×10^7; 31,000,000 **31–32.** 2.1×10^6; 2,100,000

Exploratory Exercises **Page 313** **1.** 8 **3.** $\frac{1}{2}$ **5.** $\frac{1}{2}$ **7.** 32 **9.** 4 **11.** 3 **13.** 36 **15.** 6 **17.** 25 **19.** 5

Written Exercises **Page 313** **1.** $(21)^{\frac{1}{2}}$ **3.** $(32)^{\frac{1}{6}}$ **5.** $y^{\frac{1}{3}}$ **7.** $2mr^2$ **9.** $(27)^{\frac{1}{4}}$ **11.** $n^{\frac{2}{3}}$ **13.** $\sqrt[6]{64}$ **15.** $\sqrt[3]{6}$ **17.** $ab^2\sqrt{ab}$ **19.** $2x^2\sqrt[3]{4x}$ **21.** $\sqrt[3]{5p^2q}$ **23.** $r^2\sqrt[4]{r^2q^3}$ **25.** 11 **27.** $\frac{5}{2}$ **29.** $\frac{1}{2}$ **31.** $\frac{2}{5}$

Exploratory Exercises **Page 316** **1.** $\frac{3^{\frac{1}{2}}}{3^{\frac{1}{2}}}$ **3.** $\frac{4^{\frac{1}{2}}}{4^{\frac{1}{2}}}$ **5.** $\frac{x^{\frac{2}{3}}}{x^{\frac{2}{3}}}$ **7.** $\frac{m^{\frac{1}{4}}}{m^{\frac{1}{4}}}$ **9.** $\frac{a^{\frac{4}{5}}}{a^{\frac{4}{5}}}$ **11.** $\frac{x^{\frac{1}{2}}-1}{x^{\frac{1}{2}}-1}$ **13.** $\frac{r^{\frac{1}{2}}+s^{\frac{1}{2}}}{r^{\frac{1}{2}}+s^{\frac{1}{2}}}$ **15.** $\frac{b^{\frac{3}{2}}-2}{b^{\frac{3}{2}}-2}$ **17.** $2 \cdot 5^{\frac{1}{3}}$ **19.** $2 \cdot 3^{\frac{1}{2}}$ **21.** $\frac{y^{\frac{1}{3}}}{y}$ **23.** $5 \cdot a^{\frac{1}{6}}$ **25.** $\frac{p^{\frac{1}{2}}}{p^2}$ **27.** $\frac{m^{\frac{3}{2}}-mp+m^{\frac{1}{2}}p-p^2}{m-p^2}$ **29.** $\frac{2(t^{\frac{3}{2}}-s^{\frac{1}{2}})}{t^3-s}$

Written Exercises **Page 316** **1.** $\frac{y^{\frac{3}{5}}}{y}$ **3.** $\frac{b^{\frac{3}{4}}}{b}$ **5.** $1+5x$ **7.** $\frac{r^2-2r^{\frac{3}{2}}}{r-4}$ **9.** $\frac{x+2x^{\frac{1}{2}}y^{\frac{1}{2}}+y}{x-y}$ **11.** $\frac{3x}{y^3}$ **13.** $-\frac{16}{9} \cdot 2^{\frac{1}{6}}$

Exploratory Exercises **Page 319** **1.** 8 **3.** 4 **5.** 25 **7.** $\frac{1}{5}$ **9.** $\frac{1}{13}$ **11.** 1 **13.** $(x^{\frac{1}{4}}-3)(x^{\frac{1}{4}}-5)$ **15.** $(r^{\frac{1}{3}}-3)(r^{\frac{1}{3}}-2)$ **17.** $(m^{\frac{1}{2}}-2)(m^{\frac{1}{2}}-5)$ **19.** $(a^{-\frac{1}{3}}-7)(a^{-\frac{1}{3}}-4)$ **21.** $(x^{-\frac{1}{4}}-4)^2$

Written Exercises **Page 319** **1.** $1[x^{\frac{1}{4}}]^2+10[x^{\frac{1}{4}}]+16=0$ **3.** $1[x^{\frac{1}{3}}]^2-9[x^{\frac{1}{3}}]+20=0$ **5.** $(m^{\frac{1}{2}}-5)(m^{\frac{1}{2}}-6)$ **7.** $(k^{-\frac{1}{3}}-7)(k^{-\frac{1}{3}}-4)$ **9.** $(x^{\frac{2}{3}}-4)^2$ **11.** $(y^{-\frac{1}{2}}-3)(y^{-\frac{1}{2}}-2)$ **13.** $(y^{\frac{3}{2}}-8)^2$ **15.** 4096; 16 **17.** 64; 125 **19.** 25; 36 **21.** $\frac{1}{343}$; $\frac{1}{64}$ **23.** 8 **25.** $\frac{1}{9}$; $\frac{1}{4}$ **27.** 4

Exploratory Exercises **Page 323** **1.** 51 **3.** 25 **5.** 0, 7 **7.** 9 **9.** 0, $^-1$ **11.** $^-3$ **13.** $^-1$

Written Exercises **Page 323** **1.** $^-2$, $^-3$ **3.** 7 **5.** 7 **7.** 9 **9.** 6 **11.** no solution **13.** 5 **15.** 1 **17.** $^-1$, 3 **19.** no solution

Chapter Review **Page 325** **1.** 1 **3.** $\frac{1}{m^5}$ **5.** $\frac{3x}{y}$ **7.** $6v$ **9.** $\frac{1}{9}$ **11.** $\frac{9}{16}$ **13.** $\frac{125}{343}$ **15.** $\frac{1}{256}$ **17.** 1215 **19.** 0.0001592 **21.** 1.32468×10^5 **23.** 36 **25.** 7 **27.** $xy^{\frac{3}{4}}$ **29.** $2w^2r$ **31.** $\frac{w^{\frac{1}{3}}r^{\frac{1}{2}}}{w^2r^2}$ **33.** $\frac{x-2x^{\frac{1}{2}}y^{\frac{1}{2}}+y}{x-y}$ **35.** $\frac{83}{3} \cdot \sqrt[3]{9}$ **37.** 4 **39.** 4 **41.** 4

CHAPTER 12 EXPONENTIAL AND LOGARITHMIC FUNCTIONS

Exploratory Exercises **Page 329** **1.** $\log_3 27 = 3$ **3.** $\log_2 (\frac{1}{8}) = {^-3}$ **5.** $\log_{10} 1000 = 3$ **7.** $4^3 = 64$ **9.** $9^{\frac{3}{2}} = 27$ **11.** $10^{-1} = 0.1$ **13.** 2 **15.** 4 **17.** $^-3$

Written Exercises **Page 330** **1.** $\log_3 81 = 4$ **3.** $\log_5 125 = 3$ **5.** $\log_4 (\frac{1}{16}) = {^-2}$ **7.** $\log \frac{1}{16} = {^-4}$ **9.** $\log_3 \sqrt{3} = \frac{1}{2}$ **11.** $\log_{36} 216 = \frac{3}{2}$ **13.** $2^5 = 32$ **15.** $11^2 = 121$ **17.** $5^0 = 1$ **19.** $(\frac{1}{2})^{-4} = 16$ **21.** $10^{-1} = \frac{1}{10}$

23. $(\frac{1}{3})^{-4} = 81$ 25. 3 27. 2 29. $^-3$ 31. $\frac{3}{2}$ 33. $^-3$ 35. 4 37. $\frac{1}{9}$ 39. 3 41. 18 43. $\frac{1}{27}$ 45. $\frac{1}{2}$ 47. $\frac{1}{6}$ 49. $\frac{1}{2}$ 51. 27 53. 25

Challenge **Page 330** 1. 6 3. $^-4$

Exploratory Exercises **Pages 332-333** 1. 2 3. 2 5. 4 7. 5 9. 4 11. 1

Written Exercises **Page 333** 1. 3 3. 7 5. 5 7. 7 9. 1 11. 2.5 13. 8 15. 1 or $^-10$

21. $\log_4 4 + \log_4 16 \stackrel{?}{=} \log_4 64$
$1 + 2 = 3$

23. $\log_2 32 - \log_2 4 \stackrel{?}{=} \log_2 8$
$5 - 2 = 3$

25. $\log_3 27 \stackrel{?}{=} 3 \log_3 3$
$3 \stackrel{?}{=} 3(1)$
$3 = 3$

27. $\frac{1}{2} \log_3 81 \stackrel{?}{=} \log_3 9$
$\frac{1}{2}(4) \stackrel{?}{=} 2$
$2 = 2$

29. $\log_2 8 \cdot \log_8 2 \stackrel{?}{=} 1$
$3 \cdot \frac{1}{3} \stackrel{?}{=} 1$
$1 = 1$

31. $\log_{10} [\log_3 (\log_4 64)] \stackrel{?}{=} 0$
$\log_{10} [\log_3 3] \stackrel{?}{=} 0$
$\log_{10} 1 = 0$
$0 = 0$

33. $\log_3 81 \stackrel{?}{=} \frac{4}{3} \log_2 8$
$4 \stackrel{?}{=} \frac{4}{3}(3)$
$4 = 4$

35. 6, $^-5$ 37. 9

Exploratory Exercises **Page 337** 1. 21 3. 3 5. 72 7. $\log_3 x + \log_3 y$ 9. $4 \log_2 m + \log_2 y$ 11. $\frac{1}{2} \log_b x - \log_b p$ 13. $\log_3 5 + \frac{1}{3} \log_3 a$ 15. $\log_2 a + \frac{1}{2} \log_2 x$ 17. 2

Written Exercises **Page 337** 1. 1.3222 3. 1.4313 5. 1.4771 7. 2.3222 9. 2 11. 24 13. 343 15. 6 17. 14 19. 3 21. 6 23. 3 25. 5 27. $\frac{1}{3}$

Exploratory Exercises **Page 341** 1. 2 3. 1.6839 5. 0.6839 − 3 7. 483,000 9. 1; 1.6767 11. 0; 0.6637 13. $^-1$; 0.3201 − 1 15. 1; 1.7404 17. 1; 35.70 19. $^-2$; 0.0688 21. 4; 39,400 23. $^-1$; 0.618

Written Exercises **Page 341** 1. 1.7649 3. 0.9814 5. 3.8704 7. 0.3243 − 3 9. 0.5855 − 2 11. 4.7973 13. 12.3 15. 9080 17. 0.09 19. 0.159 21. 521,000 23. 4630

Excursion **Page 341** antilog 1.0899 = 12.2999

Exploratory Exercises **Page 343** 1. 7.41, 7.42 3. 0.000746, 0.000747 5. 4.17, 4.18 7. 9520, 9530

Written Exercises **Page 343** 1. 0.7221 3. 1.4398 5. 0.2905 − 1 7. 0.4980 − 3 9. 3.6198 11. 2.5177 13. 0.6748 − 2 15. 0.6997 17. 1.9035 19. 6.3320 21. 3.063 23. 3757 25. 0.02164 27. 0.04374 29. 2626 31. 0.03904 33. 0.001311 35. 3.223 37. 42,450 39. 0.008264

Exercises **Page 344** 1. 78.18 3. 598.4

Exploratory Exercises **Page 347** 1. 3 log 63.9 3. 4 log 0.7425 5. 3 log 4173 7. $\frac{1}{4}$ log 594 9. $\frac{1}{4}$ log 9.813 11. $\frac{2}{3}$ log 46 13. 0 − 3 15. 2 − 5 17. 0 − 4 19. 2 − 3

Written Exercises **Page 347** 1. 260,900 3. 0.3039 5. 7.267×10^{10} 7. 4.937 9. 1.770 11. 12.84 13. 0.1194 15. 0.0518 17. 0.1495 19. $^-0.6649$ 21. 0.03677 23. 7.415 25. 0.8641 27. \$180.30 29. \$3367

Exploratory Exercises **Page 351** 1. $\frac{\log 55}{\log 3}$ 3. $\frac{\log 74}{2 \log 7}$ 5. $\frac{\log 144}{\log 6}$ 7. $\frac{\log 12}{\log 3}$ 9. $-\frac{1}{\log 2}$ 11. $\frac{\frac{1}{2} \log 13}{\log 3}$

Written Exercises **Page 351** 1. 3.6479 3. 1.1059 5. 2.7737 7. 2.2619 9. $^-3.3219$ 11. 1.1673 13. 1.771 15. 2.23 17. 1.338 19. 2.387 21. 3.9839 23. 3.8393 25. 4.3862 27. 2.8446 29. 74.47 31. 3.1507 33. $^-2.1507$ 35. 2.4527

Exploratory Exercises **Page 354** 1. 1.3863 3. 18.31 years

Written Exercises **Page 354** 1. $^-0.0770$ 3. 2.94 hr 5. 3.078 years 7. $^-0.000385$ 9. 32.89 years, 65.79 years 11. 58.99 or 6 weeks

Chapter Review **Page 356** 1. $\log_7 343 = 3$ 3. $\log_5 \frac{1}{25} = {}^-2$ 5. $\log_4 8 = \frac{3}{2}$ 7. $4^3 = 64$ 9. $8^{\frac{1}{3}} = 2$ 11. $(81)^{\frac{1}{4}} = 3$ 13. 3 15. 3 17. $\frac{1}{27}$ 19. 7 21. 18 23. 3 25. 3 27. 7 29. 8 31. $^-4$, 3 33. 1.4472

35. 1.6902 **37.** 0.6021 − 3 **39.** 48 **41.** 3 **43.** 14 **45.** 4 **47.** 0.4232 **49.** 2.8007 **51.** 1.7093 **53.** 5.45 **55.** 6760 **57.** 0.00060 **59.** 0.5334 **61.** 2.6658 **63.** 3.3019 **65.** 2.165 **67.** 0.06256 **69.** 906.8 **71.** 2.45 **73.** 1.562 **75.** 5.727 **77.** 5.728 **79.** 1.743 **81.** 4.245 **83.** 117.6 **85.** 6.76 years

CHAPTER 13 SEQUENCES AND SERIES

Exploratory Exercises Page 362 **1.** 4, 7, 10, 13, 16 **3.** 16, 14, 12, 10, 8 **5.** $\frac{3}{4}, \frac{1}{2}, \frac{1}{4}, 0, -\frac{1}{4}$ **7.** 2.3, 3.9, 5.5, 7.1, 8.7 **9.** 17. 21, 25, 29 **11.** $^-13, ^-18, ^-23, ^-28$ **13.** $\frac{7}{2}, \frac{9}{2}, \frac{11}{2}, \frac{13}{2}$

Written Exercises Page 362 **1.** 46 **3.** $\frac{11}{2}$ **5.** $^-14\frac{1}{4}$ **7.** 313 **9.** 735 **11.** $\frac{23}{6}$ **13.** $-\frac{13}{3}, -\frac{2}{3}$ **15.** 5, 8, 11, 14, 17 **17.** 56, 42, 35 **19.** 54

Exploratory Exercises Page 365 **1.** 18 **3.** 3 **5.** 20 **7.** 30

Written Exercises Page 365 **1.** 135 **3.** 45 **5.** 45 **7.** 56 **9.** 45 **11.** 60 **13.** 87,296 **15.** $^-7\frac{1}{2}$

Exploratory Exercises Page 368 **1.** 116 **3.** 10,100 **5.** 375 **7.** 240 **9.** 5050

Written Exercises Page 368 **1.** 6, 36, 66, 96 **3.** 1, 5, 9, 13 **5.** 735 **7.** $^-220$ **9.** 632.5 **11.** 702 **13.** 135 **15.** 1210 **17.** 287 **19.** $^-420$

Exploratory Exercises Page 371 **1.** yes, 5 **3.** yes, $\frac{3}{2}$ **5.** no **7.** 135, 405 **9.** $\frac{1}{3}$, 1

Written Exercises Page 371 **1.** $\frac{3}{2}$, 3, 6, 12 **3.** 12, 6, 3, $\frac{3}{2}$ **5.** $a_4 = 56$ **7.** $a_5 = 32$ **9.** $a_4 = {}^-4$ **11.** about 65.6%

Exploratory Exercises Page 374 **1.** 9 **3.** 144 **5.** 99 **7.** 0.5 **9.** 5 **11.** 2 **13.** 128 **15.** 170 **17.** $-\frac{1}{4}$ **19.** 4 **21.** $^-4$ **23.** $-\frac{1}{2}$ **25.** $-\frac{15}{2}$ **27.** $\frac{1}{3}$ **29.** 5

Written Exercises Page 374 **1.** $^-364$ **3.** $15\frac{3}{4}$ **5.** 1111 **7.** $93\frac{18}{25}$ **9.** 105 **11.** 732 **13.** 165 **15.** 1441 **17.** $\frac{63}{8}$ **19.** 156.2 **21.** $^-22$ **23.** 4.5

Challenge Page 374 127

Exploratory Exercises Pages 377–378 **1.** $\frac{1}{2}, \frac{2}{3}, \frac{3}{2}$ **3.** $1, -\frac{1}{3}, \frac{3}{4}$ **5.** 1, $\frac{3}{2}$, no sum **7.** $\frac{7}{10} + \frac{7}{100} + \frac{7}{1000} + \cdots = \frac{7}{9}$
9. $\frac{73}{100} + \frac{73}{10,000} + \frac{73}{10,000,000} + \cdots = \frac{73}{99}$ **11.** $\frac{152}{1000} + \frac{152}{1,000,000} + \cdots = \frac{152}{999}$
13. $\frac{93}{100} + \frac{93}{10,000} + \frac{93}{1,000,000} + \cdots = \frac{31}{33}$

Written Exercises Page 378 **1.** $6 + 2 + \frac{2}{3}$ **3.** $36 - \frac{72}{7} + \frac{144}{49}$ **5.** 72 **7.** 4 **9.** 27 **11.** $\frac{9}{5}$ **13.** 9 **15.** 8 **17.** sum doesn't exist **19.** $\frac{100}{11}$ **21.** $\frac{1}{3}$ **23.** $\frac{5}{33}$ **25.** $\frac{25}{333}$ **27.** $\frac{37}{99}$ **29.** 500 cm **31.** 68 ft

Exploratory Exercises Page 381 **1.** 1404, 4212 **3.** 2.875 **5.** 31, 43 **7.** 91, 140 **9.** 18, 29, 47

Written Exercises Page 381 **1.** 1, 1, 2, 3, 5, 8, 13, 21, 34, 55, 89, 144, 233, 377, 610, 987, 1597, 2584, 4181, 6765 **3.** 1, 2, 1.5, $1.6\overline{6}$, 1.6, 1.625, 1.61538, 1.61905, 1.61765, 1.61818, 1.61798, 1.61806, 1.61803, 1.61804, 1.61803

Exploratory Exercises Pages 383–384 **1.** 99, 120 **3.** 80, 99 **5.** 8, 7, 65 **7.** $^-2, ^-6, ^-18, ^-54$ **9.** $^-4, ^-4, 4, 4$ **11.** 3, 1, 4, 5 **13.** $a_n = 2n$ **15.** $a_n = \dfrac{n+1}{n}$ **17.** $a_{n+1} = a_n \times \frac{1}{3}, a_1 = 1$ **19.** $a_{n+1} = ({}^-1)a_n$, $a_1 = 1$

Written Exercises Page 384 **1.** 29, 33, 37 **3.** $\frac{17}{10}, \frac{19}{11}, \frac{21}{12}$ **5.** $\frac{1}{4}, \frac{2}{9}, \frac{1}{5}$ **7.** $^-16, 18, ^-20$ **9.** 38, 47, 57 **11.** 7, 12, 17, 22, 27, 32 **13.** 1, 2, 2, 4, 8, 32 **15.** 5, 11, 6, $^-5$, $^-11$ **17.** $a_{n+1} = a_n + 5, a_1 = 4; a_n = 5n - 1$ **19.** $a_{n+1} = \frac{1}{2}a_n, a_1 = \frac{3}{2}; a_n = \dfrac{3}{2^n}$ **21.** $a_{n+1} = \frac{1}{5}a_n, a_1 = \frac{7}{2}; a_n = \dfrac{7}{2 \cdot 5^{n-1}}$ **23.** $\sum_{n=1}^{5} \dfrac{3^{n+1}}{5}$ **25.** $\sum_{n=1}^{5} 6(-\frac{1}{3})^{n-1}$ **27.** $\sum_{n=1}^{6} \dfrac{n^2+1}{n}$ **29.** $\sum_{n=1}^{6} \dfrac{({}^-1)^{n+1}}{2n-1}$

Exploratory Exercises Page 387 **1.** 5040 **3.** 3,628,800 **5.** 90 **7.** 120

Written Exercises Page 387 **1.** k **3.** $(k+2)!$ **5.** $a^7 + 7a^6b + 21a^5b^2 + 35a^4b^3 + 35a^3b^4 + 21a^2b^5 + 7ab^6 + b^7$ **7.** $x^6 - 6x^5y + 15x^4y^2 - 20x^3y^3 + 15x^2y^4 - 6xy^5 + y^6$ **9.** $35x^3y^4$ **11.** $5005x^9y^6$ **13.** $24,634,368m^7n^5$

Chapter Review **Page 389** **1.** 6, 14, 22, 30, 38 **3.** 234 **5.** 22 **7.** 20 + 23 + 26 + 29 **9.** 2322 **11.** 720 **13.** 2 **15.** 567 **17.** 726 **19.** 189 **21.** 625 **23.** $\frac{4}{9}$ **25.** $a_n = 2a_{n-1} - a_{n-2} + 1$ **26.** $a_{n+1} = a_n + 4$; $a_n = a_1 + 4(n - 1)$ **27.** $\sum_{k=1}^{6} (k + 1)k$

CHAPTER 14 PROBABILITY

Exploratory Exercises **Page 394** **1.** independent **3.** independent

Written Exercises **Page 394** **1.** $5^5 = 3125$ **3.** $5 \times 6 \times 3 = 90$ **5.** $6! = 720$ **7.** 840 **9.** 4536 **11.** 216 **13.** 60

Exploratory Exercises **Page 397** **1.** F **3.** F **5.** T **7.** T **9.** T

Written Exercises **Page 397** **1.** $6! = 720$ **3.** $\frac{3!}{2!} = 3$ **5.** $\frac{5!}{2!} = 60$ **7.** $\frac{11!}{4!4!2!} = 34{,}650$ **9.** $\frac{7!}{2!} = 2520$ **11.** 6 **13.** 42 **15.** 8 **17.** 27,720 **19.** 151,200 **21.** 56

Exploratory Exercises **Page 401** **1.** reflective **3.** non-reflective **5.** non-reflective **7.** non-reflective **9.** non-reflective **11.** non-reflective **13.** circular **15.** circular **17.** linear **19.** linear **21.** linear

Written Exercises **Page 401** **1.** 39,600 **3.** 30 **5.** 840 **7.** 6720 **9.** 311,040 **11.** 60 **13.** 9 **15.** 60 **17.** 2520 **19.** 24 **21.** 12

Exploratory Exercises **Page 404** **1.** combination **3.** permutation **5.** permutation **7.** combination

Written Exercises **Page 404** **1.** 56 **3.** 21 **5.** 11 **7.** 30 **9.** 126 **11.** 792 **13.** 351 **15.** 1287 **17.** 6 **19.** 0 **21.** 2828 **23.** 56 **25.** 1680

Exploratory Exercises **Page 407** **1.** 1 **3.** $\frac{1}{6}$ **5.** $\frac{7}{8}$ **7.** $\frac{4}{5}$ **9.** $\frac{3}{7}$ **11.** $\frac{6}{11}$ **13.** $\frac{7}{10}$ **15.** $\frac{5}{16}$ **17.** $\frac{1}{7}$

Written Exercises **Page 407** **1.** $\frac{1}{16}$ **3.** $\frac{1}{56}$ **5.** $\frac{1}{4}$ **7.** $\frac{18}{95}$ **9.** $\frac{3}{19}$ **11.** $\frac{5}{39}$ **13.** $\frac{4}{7}$ **15.** $\frac{2}{7}$ **17.** $\frac{9}{170}$ **19.** $\frac{18}{85}$ **21.** $\frac{33}{108{,}290}$ **23.** $\frac{429}{41{,}650}$

Exploratory Exercises **Page 409** **1.** dependent, $\frac{1}{28}$ **3.** independent, $\frac{25}{81}$ **5.** dependent, $\frac{630}{2730}$

Written Exercises **Pages 409–410** **1.** $\frac{105}{2730}$ **3.** $\frac{1}{32}$ **5.** $\frac{1}{7{,}656{,}358}$ **7.** $\frac{6}{49}$ **9.** $\frac{1}{8}$ **11.** $\frac{5}{48}$ **13.** $\frac{1}{36}$ **15.** $\frac{1}{36}$ **17.** $\frac{1}{6}$

Excursion Exercises **Page 410** **1.** $a = 2$

Exploratory Exercises **Page 413** **1.** exclusive, $\frac{4}{15}$ **3.** exclusive, $\frac{9}{91}$ **5.** exclusive, $\frac{25}{39}$ **7.** inclusive, $\frac{2}{3}$ **9.** exclusive, $\frac{1}{3}$

Written Exercises **Page 413** **1.** $\frac{2}{11}$ **3.** $\frac{14}{33}$ **5.** $\frac{12}{221}$ **7.** $\frac{55}{221}$ **9.** $\frac{7}{16}$ **11.** $\frac{35}{64}$ **13.** $\frac{1}{3003}$ **15.** $\frac{160}{429}$

Excursion Exercises **Page 414** **1.** $84a^6b^3$ **3.** $70x^4y^4$ **5.** $\frac{9!}{(9 - n)!n!}(5x)^{9-n}(-2y)^n$

Exploratory Exercises **Pages 416–417** **1.** binomial, $\frac{3}{8}$ **3.** not binomial **5.** binomial, $\frac{1}{9}$

Written Exercises **Page 417** **1.** $\frac{1}{4}$ **3.** $\frac{3}{8}$ **5.** $\frac{3125}{7776}$ **7.** $\frac{7500}{7776}$ **9.** $\frac{1}{81}$ **11.** $\frac{48}{81}$ **13.** $\frac{193}{512}$ **15.** $\frac{319}{512}$ **17.** $\frac{160}{3125}$ **19.** $\frac{1}{8}$ **21.** $\frac{1}{2}$ **23.** $\frac{1024}{9{,}765{,}625}$ **25.** $\frac{1{,}959{,}552}{9{,}765{,}625}$ **27.** $(\frac{1}{10})^{12}$ **29.** $(\frac{9}{10})^{12}$

Chapter Review **Page 419** **1.** 125 **3.** 1,625,702,400 **5.** 5.6 **7.** 5040 **9.** 1485 **11.** $\frac{3}{7}$ **13.** $\frac{4}{13}$

CHAPTER 15 STATISTICS

Exploratory Exercises **Page 424** **1.** \$14,989 **3.** \$6355 **5.** \$3538 **7.** \$5156 **9.** \$5863 **11.** 59% **13.** 55% **15.** 61%

Written Exercises **Pages 424–425** **3.** 12 **5.** 27 inches **7.** 46 inches **11.** 16 cities **13.** 53.5% **15.** 19.6%

Exploratory Exercises **Page 428** **1.** 17% **3.** 8% **5.** 1970 **7.** health and hospitals

Exploratory Exercises **Page 432** **1.** 3 **3.** 1 **5.** 43 **7.** 2.1 **9.** none **11.** 1 **13.** none **15.** 2.1 **17.** 3 **19.** 1.8 **21.** 30.6 **23.** 3.4

Written Exercises **Page 432** **1.** 4 **3.** 3.7 **5.** none **7.** 18,184 **9.** 18,839 **11.** \$4.00

Exploratory Exercises **Page 434** **1.** 22 **3.** 48 **5.** 6.3 **7.** 13.7

Written Exercises **Page 435** **1.** 90 **3.** 200 **5.** 27 **7.** 17 **9.** 17 **11.** 4.6 **13.** 9 **15.** 2.8 **17.** 3 **19.** B

Exploratory Exercises **Page 438** **1.** 340 **3.** 495 **5.** 170 **7.** 1360 **9.** 1980 **11.** 680 **13.** 10,880 **15.** 15,840 **17.** 5440

Written Exercises **Page 438** **1.** 6800 **3.** 5000 **5.** 200 **7.** 68% **9.** 47.5% **11.** 81.5% **13.** 50% **15.** 1%

Exploratory Exercises **Page 440** **1.** 1.0 **3.** 3.0 **5.** 5.0 **7.** 6.5 **9.** 160 **11.** 130 **13.** 110 **15.** 80

Written Exercises **Page 441** **1.** 400 **3.** $s = 400a + 2{,}000{,}000$ **5.** \$8,000,000 **7.** $^-0.1$ **9.** $y = {^-0.1}x + 23$ **11.** 8 **15.** \$10,666 **19.** 75

Chapter Review **Page 445** **1.** \$15,126 **3.** no entry **5.** $^+$\$669 **7.** $^-$\$546 **11.** 25 plants per plot **13.** 17 plants per plot **15.** 1600 workers **17.** 0.95 **19.** $y = 0.95x - 95$

CHAPTER 16 TRIGONOMETRIC FUNCTIONS AND IDENTITIES

Exploratory Exercises **Page 450** **1.** III **3.** I **5.** I **7.** IV **9.** II **11.** I **13.** IV **15.** III **17.** III **19.** III **21.** IV **23.** II

Written Exercises **Page 450** **1.** $\frac{\pi}{2}$ **3.** $-\frac{\pi}{4}$ **5.** $\frac{5\pi}{2}$ **7.** $\frac{5\pi}{6}$ **9.** $\frac{\pi}{4}$ **11.** $\frac{11\pi}{6}$ **13.** $\frac{3\pi}{2}$ **15.** π **17.** $\frac{9\pi}{4}$ **19.** $-\frac{7\pi}{4}$ **21.** 180° **23.** 45° **25.** 540° **27.** $^-$480° **29.** 30° **31.** $^-$45° **33.** 330° **35.** 210°

Exploratory Exercises **Page 455** **1.** − **3.** − **5.** − **7.** + **9.** + **11.** +

Written Exercises **Page 455** **1.** 60° **3.** 300° **5.** π **7.** $\frac{\pi}{2}$ **9.** $\frac{7\pi}{4}$ **11.** 120° **13.** $\frac{\pi}{3}$ **15.** $\frac{3\pi}{4}$ **17.** 120° **19.** $\frac{10\pi}{9}$ **21.** $\frac{\pi}{4}$ **23.** $\frac{4\pi}{3}$ **25.** 240° **27.** 320° **29.** $-\frac{\sqrt{3}}{2}$ **31.** $\frac{1}{2}$ **33.** $-\frac{\sqrt{2}}{2}$ **35.** $^-1$ **37.** $\frac{\sqrt{3}}{2}$ **39.** $\frac{\sqrt{2}}{2}$ **41.** $-\frac{\sqrt{3}}{2}$ **43.** $\frac{\sqrt{3}}{2}$ **45.** $\frac{1}{2}$ **47.** $-\frac{\sqrt{3}}{2}$ **49.** $\frac{1}{2}$ **51.** 1 **53.** 1 **55.** $\frac{^-\sqrt{3} - 1}{2}$

Exploratory Exercises **Page 459** **1.** 1; 2π **3.** $\frac{2}{3}$; 2π **5.** 6; 3π **7.** 4; $\frac{8\pi}{3}$ **9.** 5; 2π **11.** 1; $\frac{2\pi}{3}$ **13.** 4; 4π **15.** 3; 3π **17.** $\frac{1}{2}$; $\frac{8\pi}{3}$ **19.** 6; π

Written Exercises **Page 459**

1.
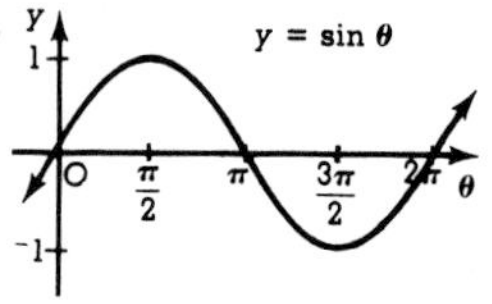

3.
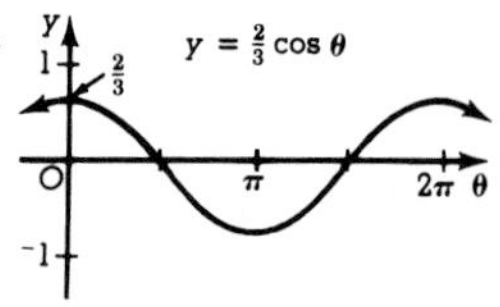

5.
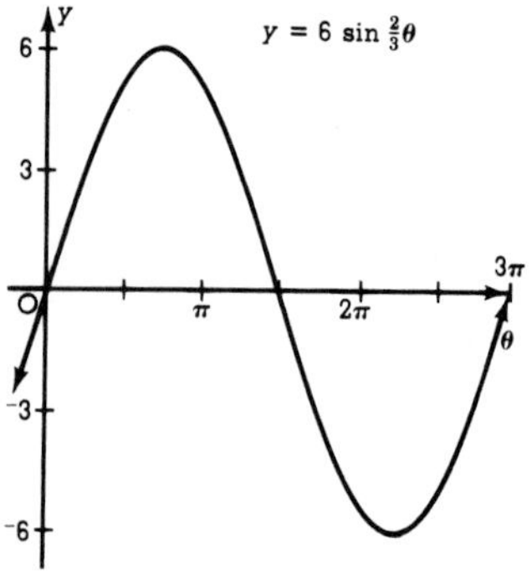

7.
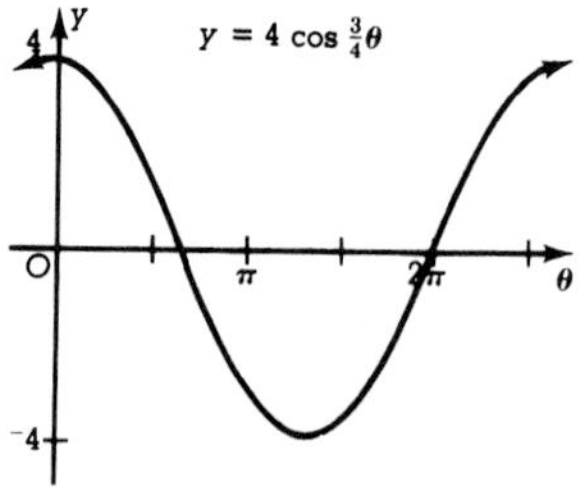

9.
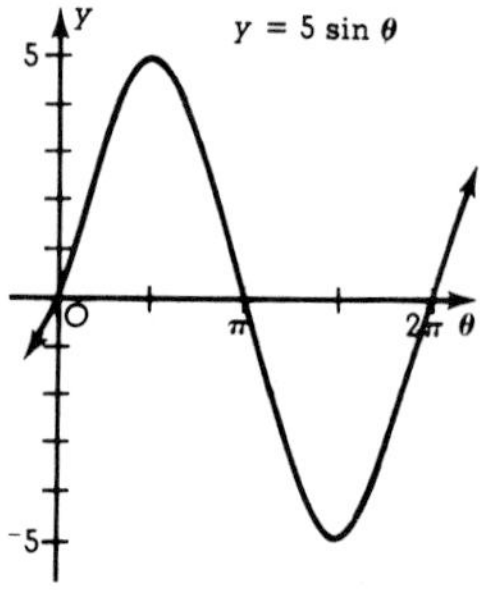

11. 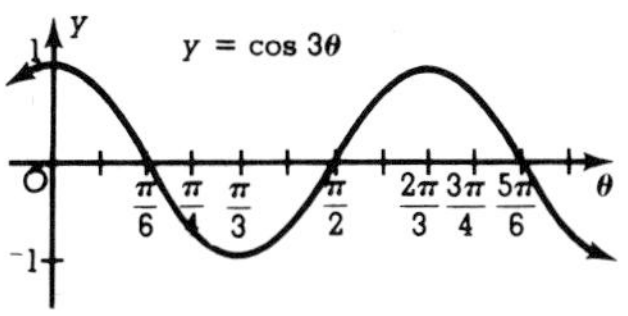

15. 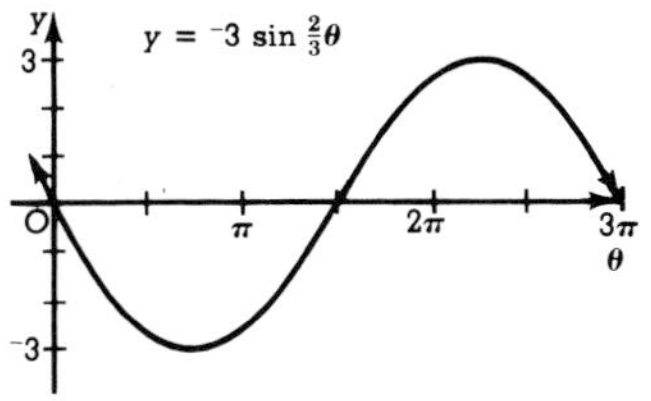

17. 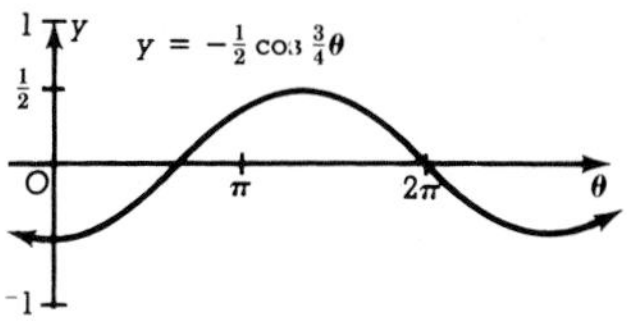

Exploratory Exercises Pages 461–462 **1.** none **3.** 90°, 270° **5.** 90°, 270° **7.** all angle measurements **9 and 11.** all angle measurements except $(2k + 1)\pi/2$, k an integer **13.** $\{y \mid {}^-1 \le y \le 1\}$ **15.** {all real numbers} **17.** $\{y \mid y \ge 1 \text{ or } y \le {}^-1\}$ **19.** 2π **21.** π **23.** 2π

Written Exercises Page 462 **1.** increasing **3.** increasing **5.** increasing **7.** decreasing **9.** increasing **11.** increasing **13.** decreasing **15.** increasing **17.** decreasing **19.** increasing **21.** increasing **23.** decreasing **25.** 2 **27.** $^-1$ **29.** $^-\sqrt{3}$ **31.** 2 **33.** $^-\sqrt{3}$ **35.** $^-2$ **37.** $^-1$ **39.** $^-2$ **41.** $^-2$ **43.** undefined **45.** $\frac{\sqrt{3}}{3}$ **47.** 0 **49.** $-\frac{\sqrt{3}}{3}$ **51.** $^-1$ **55.**

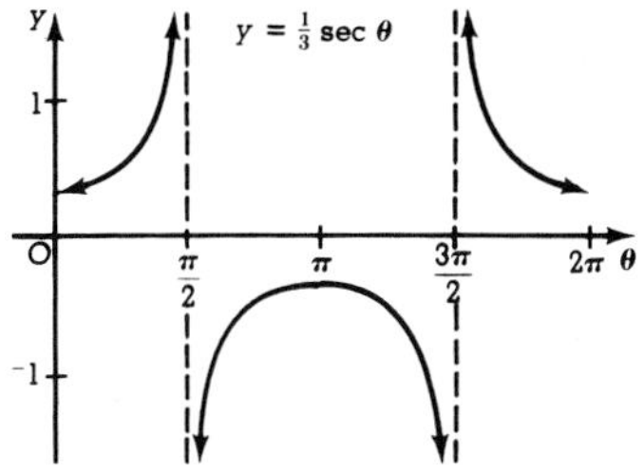

57.

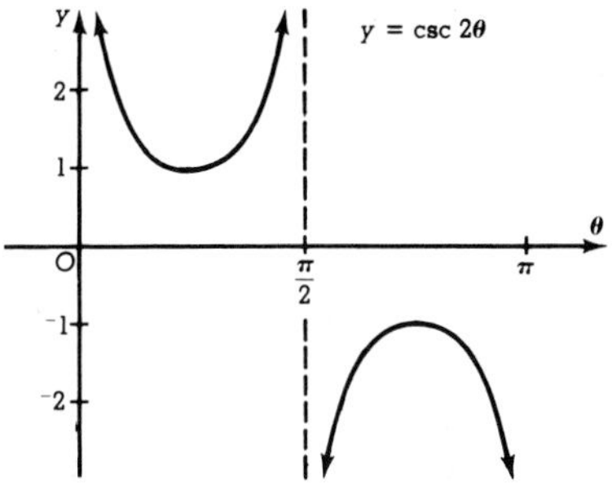

Exploratory Exercises Page 465 **1.** yes **3.** yes **5.** yes **7.** no

Written Exercises Page 465 **1.** $\frac{\sqrt{3}}{2}$ **3.** $\frac{3}{5}$ **5.** $\frac{3\sqrt{5}}{5}$ **7.** $\frac{4\sqrt{17}}{17}$ **9.** $-\frac{4}{5}$ **11.** $\frac{5}{4}$ **13.** $-\frac{\sqrt{17}}{4}$ **15.** $-\frac{\sqrt{3}}{2}$ **17.** $-\frac{12}{13}$ **19.** $\frac{3}{5}$ **21.** 1 **23.** $2 \sin x$ **25.** 2

27.
$$\begin{aligned} 1 + \cot^2\theta &\stackrel{?}{=} \csc^2\theta \\ \frac{\sin^2\theta + \cos^2\theta}{\sin^2\theta} &\stackrel{?}{=} \csc^2\theta \\ \frac{1}{\sin^2\theta} &\stackrel{?}{=} \csc^2\theta \\ \csc^2\theta &= \csc^2\theta \end{aligned}$$

29.
$$\begin{aligned} \sin x \sec x &\stackrel{?}{=} \tan x \\ \sin x \cdot \frac{1}{\cos x} &\stackrel{?}{=} \tan x \\ \frac{\sin x}{\cos x} &\stackrel{?}{=} \tan x \\ \tan x &= \tan x \end{aligned}$$

Exploratory Exercises Page 468

1.
$$\begin{aligned} \csc^2\theta - \cot^2\theta &\stackrel{?}{=} 1 \\ \frac{1}{\sin^2\theta} - \cot^2\theta &\stackrel{?}{=} 1 \\ \frac{1}{\sin^2\theta} - \frac{\cos^2\theta}{\sin^2\theta} &\stackrel{?}{=} 1 \\ \frac{1 - \cos^2\theta}{\sin^2\theta} &\stackrel{?}{=} 1 \\ \frac{\sin^2\theta}{\sin^2\theta} &\stackrel{?}{=} 1 \\ 1 &= 1 \end{aligned}$$

3.
$$\begin{aligned} \frac{\sin^2\theta + \cos^2\theta}{\sin^2\theta} &\stackrel{?}{=} \csc^2\theta \\ \frac{1}{\sin^2\theta} &\stackrel{?}{=} \csc^2\theta \\ \csc^2\theta &= \csc^2\theta \end{aligned}$$

5.
$$\begin{aligned} \csc^2 r - \cot^2 r &\stackrel{?}{=} 1 \\ \csc^2 r - (\csc^2 r - 1) &\stackrel{?}{=} 1 \\ \csc^2 r - \csc^2 r + 1 &\stackrel{?}{=} 1 \\ 1 &= 1 \end{aligned}$$

7.
$$\begin{aligned} \sin\theta \cot\theta &\stackrel{?}{=} \cos\theta \\ \sin\theta \cdot \frac{\cos\theta}{\sin\theta} &\stackrel{?}{=} \cos\theta \\ \cos\theta &= \cos\theta \end{aligned}$$

Written Exercises Page 468

1.
$$\tan \beta (\cot \beta + \tan \beta) \stackrel{?}{=} \sec^2 \beta$$
$$\tan \beta \left(\frac{1}{\tan \beta} + \tan \beta\right) \stackrel{?}{=} \sec^2 \beta$$
$$1 + \tan^2 \beta \stackrel{?}{=} \sec^2 \beta$$
$$\sec^2 \beta = \sec^2 \beta$$

3.
$$\csc x \sec x \stackrel{?}{=} \cot x + \tan x$$
$$\frac{1}{\sin x} \cdot \frac{1}{\cos x} \stackrel{?}{=} \frac{\cos x}{\sin x} + \frac{\sin x}{\cos x}$$
$$\frac{1}{\sin x} \cdot \frac{1}{\cos x} \stackrel{?}{=} \frac{\cos^2 x + \sin^2 x}{\sin x \cos x}$$
$$\frac{1}{\sin x \cos x} = \frac{1}{\sin x \cos x}$$

5.
$$\frac{\sec \theta}{\sin \theta} - \frac{\sin \theta}{\cos \theta} \stackrel{?}{=} \cot \theta$$
$$\frac{1}{\cos \theta \sin \theta} - \frac{\sin \theta}{\cos \theta} \stackrel{?}{=} \cot \theta$$
$$\frac{1 - \sin^2 \theta}{\cos \theta \sin \theta} \stackrel{?}{=} \cot \theta$$
$$\frac{\cos^2 \theta}{\cos \theta \sin \theta} \stackrel{?}{=} \cot \theta$$
$$\frac{\cos \theta}{\sin \theta} \stackrel{?}{=} \cot \theta$$
$$\cot \theta = \cot \theta$$

7.
$$\frac{\sin \alpha}{1 - \cos \alpha} + \frac{1 - \cos \alpha}{\sin \alpha} \stackrel{?}{=} 2 \csc \alpha$$
$$\frac{\sin^2 \alpha + (1 - \cos \alpha)}{(1 - \cos \alpha)(\sin \alpha)} \stackrel{?}{=} \frac{2}{\sin \alpha}$$
$$\frac{\sin^2 \alpha + 1 - 2 \cos \alpha + \cos^2 \alpha}{(1 - \cos \alpha) \sin \alpha} \stackrel{?}{=} \frac{2}{\sin \alpha}$$
$$\frac{2 - 2 \cos \alpha}{(1 - \cos \alpha) \sin \alpha} \stackrel{?}{=} \frac{2}{\sin \alpha}$$
$$\frac{2(1 - \cos \alpha)}{(1 - \cos \alpha) \sin \alpha} \stackrel{?}{=} \frac{2}{\sin \alpha}$$
$$\frac{2}{\sin \alpha} = \frac{2}{\sin \alpha}$$

9.
$$\frac{\cos^2 x}{1 - \sin x} \stackrel{?}{=} 1 + \sin x$$
$$\frac{\cos^2 x}{1 - \sin x} \cdot \frac{1 + \sin x}{1 + \sin x} \stackrel{?}{=} 1 + \sin x$$
$$\frac{\cos^2 x (1 + \sin x)}{1 - \sin^2 x} \stackrel{?}{=} 1 + \sin x$$
$$\frac{\cos^2 x (1 + \sin x)}{\cos^2 x} \stackrel{?}{=} 1 + \sin x$$
$$1 + \sin x = 1 + \sin x$$

11.
$$\frac{\sin \theta}{\sec \theta} \stackrel{?}{=} \frac{1}{\tan \theta + \cot \theta}$$
$$\frac{\sin \theta}{\frac{1}{\cos \theta}} \stackrel{?}{=} \frac{1}{\frac{\sin \theta}{\cos \theta} + \frac{\cos \theta}{\sin \theta}}$$
$$\sin \theta \cdot \cos \theta \stackrel{?}{=} \frac{1}{\frac{\sin^2 \theta + \cos^2 \theta}{\cos \theta \cdot \sin \theta}}$$
$$\sin \theta \cdot \cos \theta \stackrel{?}{=} \frac{1}{\frac{1}{\cos \theta \cdot \sin \theta}}$$
$$\sin \theta \cdot \cos \theta = \cos \theta \cdot \sin \theta$$

13.
$$\frac{\cot x + \csc x}{\sin x + \tan x} \stackrel{?}{=} \cot x \cdot \csc x$$
$$\frac{\frac{\cos x}{\sin x} + \frac{1}{\sin x}}{\sin x + \frac{\sin x}{\cos x}} \stackrel{?}{=} \frac{\cos x}{\sin x} \cdot \frac{1}{\sin x}$$
$$\frac{\frac{\cos x + 1}{\sin x}}{\sin x \left(1 + \frac{1}{\cos x}\right)} \stackrel{?}{=} \frac{\cos x}{\sin x} \cdot \frac{1}{\sin x}$$
$$\frac{\frac{\cos x + 1}{\sin x}}{\sin x \left(\frac{\cos x + 1}{\cos x}\right)} \stackrel{?}{=} \frac{\cos x}{\sin x} \cdot \frac{1}{\sin x}$$
$$\left(\frac{\cos x + 1}{\sin x}\right)\left(\frac{1}{\sin x}\right)\left(\frac{\cos x}{\cos x + 1}\right) \stackrel{?}{=} \frac{\cos x}{\sin^2 x}$$
$$\frac{\cos x}{\sin^2 x} \stackrel{?}{=} \frac{\cos x}{\sin^2 x}$$

15.
$$\cos^2 x + \tan^2 x \cos^2 x \stackrel{?}{=} 1$$
$$\cos^2 x + \frac{\sin^2 x}{\cos^2 x} \cdot \cos^2 x \stackrel{?}{=} 1$$
$$\cos^2 x + \sin^2 x \stackrel{?}{=} 1$$
$$1 = 1$$

17.
$$\frac{1+\tan^2\theta}{\csc^2\theta} \stackrel{?}{=} \tan^2\theta$$
$$\frac{\sec^2\theta}{\csc^2\theta} \stackrel{?}{=} \tan^2\theta$$
$$\frac{\frac{1}{\cos^2\theta}}{\frac{1}{\sin^2\theta}} \stackrel{?}{=} \tan^2\theta$$
$$\frac{1}{\cos^2\theta}\cdot\frac{\sin^2\theta}{1} \stackrel{?}{=} \tan^2\theta$$
$$\frac{\sin^2\theta}{\cos^2\theta} = \tan^2\theta$$
$$\tan^2\theta = \tan^2\theta$$

19.
$$\frac{\sec x}{\sin x} - \frac{\sin x}{\cos x} \stackrel{?}{=} \cot x$$
$$\frac{\frac{1}{\cos x}}{\sin x} - \frac{\sin x}{\cos x} \stackrel{?}{=} \frac{\cos x}{\sin x}$$
$$\frac{1}{\cos x \sin x} - \frac{\sin x}{\cos x} \stackrel{?}{=} \frac{\cos x}{\sin x}$$
$$\frac{1}{\sin x \cos x} - \frac{\sin^2 x}{\sin x \cos x} \stackrel{?}{=} \frac{\cos x}{\sin x}$$
$$\frac{1-\sin^2 x}{\sin x \cos x} \stackrel{?}{=} \frac{\cos x}{\sin x}$$
$$\frac{\cos^2 x}{\sin x \cos x} \stackrel{?}{=} \frac{\cos x}{\sin x}$$
$$\frac{\cos x}{\sin x} = \frac{\cos x}{\sin x}$$

Excursion Exercises Page 468 about 2%

Exploratory Exercises Page 471 **1.** $60° + 45°$ **3.** $^-135° - 30°$ **5.** $30° + 45°$ **7.** $225° + 60°$

Written Exercises Page 471 **1.** $\frac{\sqrt{6}+\sqrt{2}}{4}$ **3.** $\frac{-\sqrt{2}-\sqrt{6}}{4}$ **5.** $\frac{^-\sqrt{2}-\sqrt{6}}{4}$ **7.** $\frac{\sqrt{6}+\sqrt{2}}{4}$ **9.** $\frac{^-\sqrt{6}-\sqrt{2}}{4}$

11. $\sin(270-\theta) = \sin 270 \cos\theta - \cos 270 \sin\theta = {}^-1\cdot\cos\theta - 0\cdot\sin\theta = {}^-\cos\theta$

13. $\sin(180+\theta) = \sin 180 \cos\theta + \cos 180 \sin\theta = 0 - 1\cdot\sin\theta = {}^-\sin\theta$

15. $\sin(90+\theta) = \sin 90 \cos\theta + \cos 90 \sin\theta = 1\cdot\cos\theta + 0 = \cos\theta$

17. $\frac{\sqrt{3}}{2}$ **19.** $\frac{1}{2}$

21.
$$\sin(x+y)\cdot\sin(x-y) \stackrel{?}{=} \sin^2 x - \sin^2 y$$
$$(\sin x\cos y + \cos x \sin y)(\sin x \cos y - \cos x \sin y) \stackrel{?}{=} \sin^2 x - \sin^2 y$$
$$\sin^2 x\cos^2 y - \cos^2 x \sin^2 y \stackrel{?}{=} \sin^2 x - \sin^2 y$$
$$\sin^2 x(1-\sin^2 y) - (1-\sin^2 x)\sin^2 y \stackrel{?}{=} \sin^2 x - \sin^2 y$$
$$\sin^2 x - \sin^2 x\sin^2 y - \sin^2 y + \sin^2 x \sin^2 y \stackrel{?}{=} \sin^2 x - \sin^2 y$$
$$\sin^2 x - \sin^2 y = \sin^2 x \sin^2 y$$

23.
$$\sin(60°+\theta) + \sin(60°-\theta) \stackrel{?}{=} \sqrt{3}\cos\theta$$
$$[\sin 60°\cos\theta + \cos 60°\sin\theta] + [\sin 60°\cos\theta - \cos 60° \sin\theta] \stackrel{?}{=} \sqrt{3}\cos\theta$$
$$\frac{\sqrt{3}\cos\theta}{2} + \frac{\sin\theta}{2} + \frac{\sqrt{3}\cos\theta}{2} - \frac{\sin\theta}{2} \stackrel{?}{=} \sqrt{3}\cos\theta$$
$$\sqrt{3}\cos\theta = \sqrt{3}\cos\theta$$

25.
$$\cos(x+y)\cos(x-y) \stackrel{?}{=} \cos^2 y - \sin^2 x$$
$$(\cos x\cos y - \sin x \sin y)(\cos x\cos y + \sin x \sin y) \stackrel{?}{=} \cos^2 y - \sin^2 x$$
$$\cos^2 x\cos^2 y - \sin^2 x\sin^2 y \stackrel{?}{=} \cos^2 y - \sin^2 x$$
$$(1-\sin^2 x)\cos^2 y - \sin^2 x(1-\cos^2 y) \stackrel{?}{=} \cos^2 y - \sin^2 x$$
$$\cos^2 y - \sin^2 x\cos^2 y - \sin^2 x + \sin^2 x\cos^2 y \stackrel{?}{=} \cos^2 y - \sin^2 x$$
$$\cos^2 y - \sin^2 x = \cos^2 y - \sin^2 x$$

27.
$$\cos(30°+x) - \cos(30°-x) \stackrel{?}{=} {}^-\sin x$$
$$[\cos 30°\cos x - \sin 30° \sin x] - [\cos 30°\cos x + \sin 30°\sin x] \stackrel{?}{=} {}^-\sin x$$
$$\frac{\sqrt{3}\cos x}{2} - \frac{\sin x}{2} - \frac{\sqrt{3}\cos x}{2} - \frac{\sin x}{2} \stackrel{?}{=} {}^-\sin x$$
$${}^-\sin x = {}^-\sin x$$

29. $\sqrt{3}$ **31.** $^-2+\sqrt{3}$ **33.** $^-2-\sqrt{3}$ **35.** $^-2-\sqrt{3}$ **37.** $^-2+\sqrt{3}$ **39.** $^-\tan\theta$

Challenge Page 471

$$\tan(\alpha - \beta) = \frac{\sin(\alpha - \beta)}{\cos(\alpha - \beta)}$$
$$= \frac{\sin\alpha\cos\beta - \cos\alpha\sin\beta}{\cos\alpha\cos\beta + \sin\alpha\sin\beta}$$
$$= \frac{\frac{\sin\alpha\cos\beta}{\cos\alpha\cos\beta} - \frac{\cos\alpha\sin\beta}{\cos\alpha\cos\beta}}{\frac{\cos\alpha\cos\beta}{\cos\alpha\cos\beta} + \frac{\sin\alpha\sin\beta}{\cos\alpha\cos\beta}}$$
$$= \frac{\tan\alpha - \tan\beta}{1 + \tan\alpha\tan\beta}$$

Exploratory Exercises Page 474 **1.** I or II **3.** I or II **5.** I **7.** II **9.** I or II **11.** I or II **13.** I **15.** II

Written Exercises Page 474 **1.** $\frac{\sqrt{3}}{2}$ **3.** $\frac{4\sqrt{5}}{9}$ **5.** $-\frac{120}{169}$ **7.** $\frac{^-3\sqrt{7}}{8}$ **9.** $\frac{\sqrt{2+\sqrt{3}}}{2}$ **11.** $-\frac{\sqrt{6}}{6}$ **13.** $\frac{\sqrt{26}}{26}$ **15.** $-\frac{1}{4}\sqrt{8+2\sqrt{7}}$ **17.** $\frac{\sqrt{2-\sqrt{3}}}{2}$ **19.** $\frac{\sqrt{30}}{6}$ **21.** $\frac{5\sqrt{26}}{26}$ **23.** $\frac{1}{4}\sqrt{8-2\sqrt{7}}$ **25.** $\frac{1}{2}$ **27.** $-\frac{1}{9}$ **29.** $-\frac{119}{169}$ **31.** $-\frac{1}{8}$

33.
$$\begin{aligned} \cos^2 2x + 4\sin^2\cos^2 x &\stackrel{?}{=} 1 \\ \cos^2 2x + \sin^2 2x &\stackrel{?}{=} 1 \\ 1 &= 1 \end{aligned}$$

35.
$$\begin{aligned} \sin^4 x - \cos^4 x &\stackrel{?}{=} 2\sin^2 x - 1 \\ (\sin^2 x - \cos^2 x)(\sin^2 x + \cos^2 x) &\stackrel{?}{=} 2\sin^2 x - 1 \\ (\sin^2 x - \cos^2 x)\cdot 1 &\stackrel{?}{=} 2\sin^2 x - 1 \\ [\sin^2 x \cdot (1 - \sin^2 x)]\cdot 1 &\stackrel{?}{=} 2\sin^2 x - 1 \\ \sin^2 x - 1 + \sin^2 x &\stackrel{?}{=} 2\sin^2 x - 1 \\ 2\sin^2 x - 1 &= 2\sin^2 x - 1 \end{aligned}$$

37.
$$\begin{aligned} \sin^2\theta &\stackrel{?}{=} \tfrac{1}{2}(1 - \cos 2\theta) \\ &\stackrel{?}{=} \tfrac{1}{2}[1 - (1 - 2\sin^2\theta)] \\ &\stackrel{?}{=} \tfrac{1}{2}[2\sin^2\theta)] \\ &= \sin^2\theta \end{aligned}$$

Exploratory Exercises Page 477 **1.** 1 **3.** 2 **5.** 2 **7.** 2 **9.** 2 **11.** 0 **13.** 4 **15.** 4 **17.** 0

Written Exercises Page 477 **1.** 45°, 135°, 225°, 315° **3.** 0°, 180°, 210°, 330° **5.** 0°, 90°, 270° **7.** 30°, 90°, 150°, 270° **9.** 30°, 150° **11.** 0°, 120°, 240° **13.** 45°, 225° **15.** 120°, 240°

Exploratory Exercises Page 481 **1.** $\frac{1}{2}$ **3.** $^-60°$ **5.** undefined **7.** 1 **9.** 150° **11.** 45° **13.** $-\frac{\sqrt{2}}{2}$ **15.** 60° **17.** $\frac{\sqrt{2}}{2}$ **19.** $^-90°$ **21.** 90°

Written Exercises Page 481 **1.** $\frac{1}{2}$ **3.** 30° **5.** 120° **7.** $\frac{1}{2}$ **9.** 90° **11.** $\frac{4}{5}$ **13.** $\frac{5}{12}$ **15.** $-\frac{\sqrt{3}}{2}$ **17.** $\frac{1}{2}$ **19.** $\frac{\sqrt{3}}{2}$ **21.** $\frac{\sqrt{2}}{2}$ **23.** $-\frac{1}{2}$ **25.** $\frac{1}{2}$ **27.** $\frac{\sqrt{3}}{2}$ **29.** $\frac{\sqrt{2}}{2}$

Chapter Review Pages 484–485 **1.** $\frac{2}{3}\pi$ **3.** $\frac{3}{2}\pi$ **5.** 60° **7.** $\frac{240°}{\pi}$ **9.** 205° **11.** 180° **13.** $\frac{2}{3}\pi$ **15.** $\frac{16}{9}\pi$ **17.** $\frac{\sqrt{3}}{2}$ **19.** $^-1$ **21.** $-\frac{1}{2}$ **23.** $-\frac{\sqrt{2}}{2}$ **25.** 1 **31.** $\frac{2\sqrt{3}}{3}$ **33.** $-\frac{1}{2}$ **35.** $\sqrt{3}$ **37.** 2 **39.** $-\frac{4}{5}$ **41.** $\frac{\sqrt{17}}{4}$ **43.** 0 **45.** $\frac{2\sqrt{3}}{3}$